Environmental Viewpoints

Volume 1

Environmental Viewpoints

**Selected Essays and Excerpts
on Issues in Environmental Protection**

Daniel G. Marowski, Editor

**Marie Lazzari, Joseph C. Tardiff,
and Bridget Travers, Associate Editors**

 *Gale Research Inc.* · DETROIT · LONDON

STAFF

Daniel G. Marowski, *Editor*

Marie Lazzari, Joseph C. Tardiff, Bridget Travers, *Associate Editors*

Linda M. Pugliese, *Production Supervisor*
Paul Lewon, Maureen Puhl, Camille Robinson,
Jennifer VanSickle, *Editorial Associates*
Donna Craft, Brandy C. Johnson,
Sheila Walencewicz, *Editorial Assistants*

Sandra C. Davis, *Permissions Supervisor (Text)*
Maria L. Franklin, Josephine M. Keene, Denise M. Singleton,
Kimberly F. Smilay, *Permissions Associates*
Michele Lonoconus, Shelly Rakoczy,
Shalice Shah, *Permissions Assistants*

Maureen Richards, *Research Supervisor*
Mary Beth McElmeel, Tamara C. Nott, *Editorial Associates*
Daniel J. Jankowski, Kathleen Jowziak, Julie K. Karmazin,
Julie Synkonis, *Editorial Assistants*

Mary Beth Trimper, *Production Director*
Mary Winterhalter, *Production Assistant*

Arthur Chartow, *Art Director*

Since this page cannot legibly accommodate all the copyright notices, the acknowledgments constitute an extension of the copyright notices.

∞ ™ This book is printed on acid-free paper that meets the minimum requirements of American National Standard for Information Sciences—Permanence Paper for Printed Library Materials. ANSI Z39.48-1984.

♻ This book is printed on recycled paper that meets Environmental Protection Agency Standards.

ISBN 0-8103-8844-8

Printed in the United States of America

Published simultaneously in the United Kingdom by Gale Research International Limited
(An affiliated company of Gale Research Inc.)

Contents

Preface

Environmental issues are central to our lives. Television, radio, and newspapers worldwide highlight the latest global crises—oil spills, global warming, air pollution, toxic wastes, and many more. Each year new ecological topics add to the complex debate about whether humanity is enhancing or destroying the earth. As environmental concerns multiply, students, teachers, members of special interest groups, and the general public need access to more information—to learn more about the topics, to read of possible solutions that have failed or succeeded, and to reach conclusions about how these issues affect the quality of their lives. *Environmental Viewpoints* has been created in response to just these concerns.

Scope of the Series

Environmental Viewpoints is a convenient source of information about today's most important environmental issues. Part of the Gale Environmental Library, the series is designed to appeal both to the general reader and to the student, reprinting excerpted essays containing general information as well as others of a more technical or issue-specific nature. By presenting several excerpts on each topic, *Environmental Viewpoints* helps foster an awareness of important environmental concerns and offers students the background and varied opinions they need to compose essays and reports for science, geography, or cultural courses.

Each succeeding volume of *Environmental Viewpoints* will include entries on significant new subjects. Updated entries on topics previously included in the series will feature current assessments as well as recent developments in research and legislation. By approaching the material in this manner, *Environmental Viewpoints* will make accessible to readers the most relevant information on both new and ongoing issues.

Highlights of Each Entry

An entry in *Environmental Viewpoints* consists of the following elements: chapter number and title; excerpts of commentary (preceded by descriptive headings and followed by bibliographic citations); quotations from the essay; and a bibliography of sources for further study.

- The *chapter number and title* appears in large print at the top of the first page of the entry. Entries are arranged in alphabetical order based on the first word of the chapter title.

- An entry consists of *several different types of commentary.* The first excerpt included in the entry explains in general terms the topic under consideration, thus allowing the reader to gain a broad understanding of the issues relevant to the topic. Following the introductory essay are excerpted essays devoted to more in-depth analysis of the issues, more technical or specialized pieces, excerpts explaining possible solutions to issue-related problems, and articles explaining future implications of the issues. While commentary has been selected from many sources, *editors have chosen for republication essays that are neither too technical for the general reader nor too sweeping for the student interested in learning about a specific element of the subject.*

- Each excerpt is preceded by a *descriptive heading* that summarizes its content, enabling readers to determine at a glance what the excerpt is about and what kinds of information it contains.

- A brief *bibliographic citation* designed to help the reader locate the original essay follows each piece of criticism. A rule separates each essay in the entry.

- Each page of criticism contains a *block quotation* that highlights the commentary contained in that essay. As with the heading that precedes each essay, users can glean from the quotations the general scope of the criticism and important issues related to the general topic.

- An annotated list of *sources for further study* appears at the end of each chapter, enabling the user to discover even more information about a particular topic.

Cumulative Indexes

Each volume of *Environmental Viewpoints* will include a *cumulative index to topics* listing all topics that have been covered in the series. The *cumulative subject and keyword index* provides easy reference to specific subjects, issues, and key terms discussed in the series.

Special Thanks

Many individuals have contributed to the creation of *Environmental Viewpoints*. In particular, the editors wish to thank the following individuals, who helped refine the list of topics to be included in the series and in large measure defined the scope of the entries:

Katherine Chiang, Computer Files Librarian, Mann Library, Cornell University

Mark Davids, Science Department, Grosse Pointe South High School, Grosse Pointe, Michigan

Julia Gelfand, Applied Sciences Librarian, University of California-Irvine

Matt Hannigan, Reference Librarian, Indianapolis Public Library, Indianapolis, Indiana

Kelly Jons, Library Media Specialist, Shaker Heights High School, Shaker Heights, Ohio

Michael P. Kelly, Educator, National Science Teachers Association

Robert A. Kirsch, Library Director, Lake Forest High School, Lake Forest, Illinois

Mark Scott, Senior Editor, The Taft Group, Washington, D.C.

Ronald J. Smetanick, Science Resource Teacher, Thomas S. Wootton High School, Rockville, Maryland

Thomas Smisek, Head, Technology and Science Department, Minneapolis Public Library, Minneapolis, Minnesota

David A. Tyckoson, Head, Reference Department, State University of New York-Albany

A Note to the Reader

When writing papers, students who quote directly from any volume in the *Environmental Viewpoints* series may use the following general forms to footnote reprinted material. The first example pertains to essays drawn from periodicals, the second to commentary reprinted from books:

[1]Warren T. Brookes, ''The Global Warming Panic,'' *Forbes* 144 (December 25, 1989), 96–100, 102; excerpted and reprinted in *Environmental Viewpoints*, Vol. 1, ed. Daniel G. Marowski (Detroit: Gale Research, 1992), pp. 143–48.

[2]William R. Moomaw, "Near-Term Congressional Options for Responding to Global Climate Change," in *The Challenge of Global Warming*, edited by Dean Edwin Abrahamson (Island Press, 1989); excerpted and reprinted in *Environmental Viewpoints*, Vol. 1, ed. Daniel G. Marowski (Detroit: Gale Research, 1992), pp. 152–58.

Suggestions Are Welcome

Readers who wish to suggest topics to be covered in future volumes, or who have other suggestions, are cordially invited to write the editors.

Acknowledgments

The editors wish to thank the copyright holders of the excerpted criticism included in this volume, the permissions managers of many book and magazine publishing companies for assisting us in securing reprint rights, and Anthony Bogucki for assistance with copyright research. We are also grateful to the staffs of the Detroit Public Library, the Library of Congress, the University of Detroit Library, Wayne State University Purdy/Kresge Library Complex, and the University of Michigan Libraries for making their resources available to us. Following is a list of the copyright holders who have granted us permission to reprint material in this volume of *EV*. Every effort has been made to trace copyright, but if omissions have been made, please let us know.

COPYRIGHTED EXCERPTS IN *EV*, VOLUME 1, WERE REPRINTED FROM THE FOLLOWING PERIODICALS:

American City & County, v. 102, October, 1987; v. 103, August, 1988; v. 103, October, 1988; v. 105, May, 1990; v. 106, April, 1991. © 1987, 1988, 1990 by Communication Channels, Inc. All reprinted by permission of the publisher.—*American Forests,* v. 94, November-December, 1988 for "Is Sustainable Harvest Possible in the Tropics?" by Gerardo Budowski; v. 94, November-December, 1988 for "The Politics of Tropical Deforestation" by T. M. Pasca; v. 95, January-February, 1989 for "IPM: Best Approach to Pest Control" by Zak Mettger and Gary Moll; v. 95, November-December, 1989 for "Federal Forests" by William E. Shands; v. 95, November-December, 1989 for "World Forests" by Barry Walden Walsh; v. 95, November-December, 1989 for "Industrial Forests" by Harold R. Walt. Copyright © 1988, 1989 by The American Forestry Association. All reprinted by permission of the respective authors.—*The Amicus Journal,* v. 11, Summer, 1989; v. 11, Fall, 1989; v. 13, Summer, 1991. Copyright 1989, 1991 by the Natural Resources Defense Council. All rights reserved. All reprinted by permission of the publisher.—*The Atlantic Monthly,* v. 264, December, 1989 for "Rubbish!" by William L. Rathje. Copyright 1989 by The Atlantic Monthly Company, Boston, MA. Reprinted by permission of the author.—*BioCycle,* v. 29, March, 1988. Reprinted by permission of the publisher.—*BioScience,* v. 39, June, 1989 for "Extractive Reserves in Brazilian Amazonia" by Philip M. Fearnside. © 1989 American Institute of Biological Sciences. All rights reserved. Reprinted by permission of the publisher and the author.—*Chemical Engineering Progress,* v. 86, May, 1990 for "Acid Rain and the Clean Air Act" by Dennis A. Leaf. Copyright 1990 by AICHE. Reprinted by permission of the author./ v. 67, March 6, 1989; v. 67, July 24, 1989; v. 67, October 30, 1989. Copyright © 1989 by the American Chemical Society. All reprinted by permission of the publisher.—*Chemical Week,* v. 149, October 19, 1988. Copyright © 1988 by Chemical Week Associates. Reprinted by permission of the publisher.—*CHEMTECH,* v. 19, September, 1989. Copyright © 1989 by the AmericanChemical Society. Reprinted by permission of the publisher.—*The Christian Science Monitor,* August 29, 1991. © 1991 The Christian Science Publishing Society. All rights reserved. Reprinted by permission from *The Christian Science Monitor.*—*Chronicles: A Magazine of American Culture,* v. 15, October, 1991 for "A Nation of Davids: Population Control and the Environment" by Jacqueline R. Kasun. Copyright © 1991 by The Rockford Institute. All rights reserved. Reprinted by permission of the publisher and the author.—*Congressional Digest,* v. 68, February, 1989. Reprinted by permission of the publisher.—*Consumer Reports,* v. 54, May, 1989; v. 55, January, 1990. Copyright © 1989, 1990 by Consumers Union of U.S., Inc., Yonkers, NY 10703. All rights reserved. Both reprinted by permission of the publisher.—*Consumers' Research Magazine,* v. 74, March, 1991. Reprinted by permission of the publisher.—*Design News,* v. 45, February 13, 1989. Reprinted by permission of the publisher.—*Discover,* v. 9, November, 1988; v.11, April, 1990; v. 12, February, 1991; v. 12, May, 1991. Copyright © 1988, 1990, 1991 by Discover Magazine. All reprinted by permission of the publisher.—*The Economist,* v. 307, May 21–27, 1988. © The Economist Newspaper Limited, 1988. Reprinted by permission of the publisher.—*Environment,* v. 32, May, 1990. Copyright © 1990 by the Helen Dwight Reid Educational Foundation. Reprinted by permission of the Helen Dwight Reid Educational Foundation, published by Heldref Publications, 4000 Albemarle Street, N.W., Washington, DC 20016.—*Environmental Policy and Law,* v. 19, December, 1989. © 1989 IOS B.V. Reprinted by permission of the publisher.—*The Environmental Professional,* v. 11, 1989. Copyright © National Association of Environmental Professionals. All rights reserved. Reprinted by permission of the publisher.—*Financial World,* v. 157, December 13, 1988. © copyright 1988 Macro Communications, Inc. Reprinted by permission of the publisher.—*Forbes,* v. 144, December 25, 1989 for "The Global Warming Panic" by Warren T. Brookes; v. 148, September 2, 1991 for "The Strange Case of The Glancing Geese" by Warren Brookes. Copyright © 1989, 1991 Forbes Inc. Both reprinted by permission of the Literary Estate of Warren Brookes./ v. 145, June 11, 1990. Copyright © 1990 Forbes Inc. Reprinted by permission of the publisher.—*Fortune,* v. 120, July 17, 1989; v. 123, June 3, 1991. © 1989, 1991 Time Inc. All rights reserved. Both reprinted by permission of the publisher.—*The Futurist,* v. XXIV, January-February, 1990. Copyright © 1990 World Future Society. All rights reserved. Reprinted by permission of the publisher.—*International Wildlife,* v. 20, March-April, 1990. Copyright 1990 National Wildlife Federation. All rights reserved. Reprinted by permission of the publisher.—*Issues in Science and Technology,* v. VI, Fall, 1989. Copyright © 1989 by the National Academy of Science, Washington, D.C. Reprinted with permission of the

A Word about Gale and the Environment

We at Gale would like to take this opportunity to publicly affirm our commitment to preserving the environment. Our commitment encompasses not only a zeal to publish information helpful to a variety of people pursuing environmental goals, but also a rededication to creating a safe and healthy workplace for our employees.

In our effort to make responsible use of natural resources, we are publishing all books in the Gale Environmental Library on recycled paper. Our Production Department is continually researching ways to use new environmentally safe inks and manufacturing technologies for all Gale books.

In our quest to become better environmental citizens, we've organized a task force representing all operating functions within Gale. With the complete backing of Gale senior management, the task force reviews our current practices and, using the Valdez Principles[*] as a starting point, makes recommendations that will help us to: reduce waste, make wise use of energy and sustainable use of natural resources, reduce health and safety risks to our employees, and finally, should we cause any damage or injury, take full responsibility.

We look forward to becoming the best environmental citizens we can be and hope that you, too, have joined in the cause of caring for our fragile planet.

The Employees of Gale Research, Inc.

---

[*]The Valdez Principles were set forth in 1989 by the Coalition for Environmentally Responsible Economics (CERES). The Principles serve as guidelines for companies concerned with improving their environmental behavior. For a copy of the Valdez Principles, write to CERES at 711 Atlantic Avenue, 5th Floor, Boston, MA 02111.

1: Acid Rain

The Acid Rain Debate

Acid rain has been called 'an unseen plague of the industrial age,' and it is generally regarded as one of the most serious environmental problems of our times. As an issue with both scientific and political dimensions it ranks alongside important contemporary concerns like the global increase of carbon dioxide in the atmosphere, the spread of toxic chemicals in the environment, and the possible environmental consequences of nuclear war. However, it presents a somewhat unique problem in that its consequences are already evident, its adverse effects are already documented, and its impacts are very real to people living in affected areas.

Acid rain is a widespread, serious, and costly problem that will not simply fade away in the public consciousness or cease to create environmental damage. It has been blamed for damage to trees in West Germany, death of fish in Scandinavia, and other unwanted effects (including damage to buildings and human health), and it threatens international relations between the United States and Canada, and between Britain and her European neighbours. The Organization for Economic Co-operation and Development (OECD) has estimated that acid rain costs the countries of the European Community £33–44 billion per annum. (p. 1)

The term 'acid rain' refers to the dilute sulphuric and nitric acids which, many believe, are created when fossil fuels are burned in power stations, smelters, and motor vehicles, and which fall over areas long distances downwind of possible sources of the pollutants. For convenience the term 'acid rain' will be used . . . , although it has been dismissed as 'emotive' and 'inadequately named' (correspondence by Professor B. A. Thrush to *The Times*, 22 September 1984). The term is a misleading short-hand version of 'acid precipitation', which includes the dry fallout of oxides of sulphur and nitrogen (in the form of dry gases and minute aerosols, particles that remain suspended in the atmosphere) as well as wet deposition of acids (in solution or suspension in fog, or on raindrops, snowflakes, or hail). 'Acid rain', as used here, includes both dry and wet deposition.

Acid Rain as a Pollutant

Pollutants can be classified into two groups. First, there are man-made materials (such as persistent synthetic chemicals like DDT), which are not part of natural environmental cycles and therefore do not readily break down when released into the environment. A sub-set of this group would include materials like nuclear waste products that are—strictly speaking—parts of natural cycles, but these cycles operate extremely slowly over long time-spans. The second group comprises materials that already exist naturally in the environment, and that natural environmental processes and cycles can cope with (or neutralize), break down, disperse and recycle, but that appear in much higher concentrations than would normally be the case. Pollutants of this type are not necessarily harmful in themselves—they create problems only when they overload natural biogeochemical cycles.

> As an issue with both scientific and political dimensions acid rain ranks alongside important contemporary concerns like the global increase of carbon dioxide in the atmosphere, the spread of toxic chemicals in the environment, and the possible environmental consequences of nuclear war. However, it presents a somewhat unique problem in that its consequences are already evident, its adverse effects are already documented, and its impacts are very real to people living in affected areas.

Acid rains and the oxides that create them are blown long distances by the wind, often crossing seas and national frontiers to become an invisible export. As a result, the polluted is often far removed downwind from the polluter, who may remain unconvinced that a real problem exists. The polluter may then raise serious and well-intentioned objections to any remedial measures proposed by the polluted that would impose a heavy cost on itself.

Acid rain falls in this second group because its basic ingredients (sulphur dioxide , SO_2, nitrogen oxides, NO_x, and ozone, O_3) do appear naturally in the environment, albeit in smaller concentrations. In fact the natural acidity of rainfall provides free supplies of valuable nutrients for plant growth. Some areas (even parts of Scandinavia) with mineral-deficient soils are happy to receive the sulphur because otherwise costly artificial fertilizers would be required. It is the increased acidity experienced in recent years (which many associate with air pollution) that appears to produce serious environmental problems, and which is the true focus of the acid rain debate.

As a form of pollution, acid rain has some unusual properties. It is invisible, with no discernible taste or smell to humans. It has remained largely undetected even in areas where it has been falling for many years, because its effects on the environment are not readily noticeable in their early stages. It has no rapid, dramatic effects; it is a silent, creeping paralysis form of cumulative pollutant. Only in advanced cases are its effects sufficiently quantifiable to be convincing in any statistical sense.

Neither does acidification normally cause unsightly effects on the landscape, of the sort often associated with nutrient enrichment (eutrophication) with nitrate fertilizers washed from fields, where enriched lakes are draped with dense floating mats of algal blooms. In fact, few who have witnessed Scandinavia's acidic lakes fail to be moved by the air of tranquility offered by the clear lakes, devoid of smell or floating vegetation, with visibility increased considerably (through loss of aquatic life), and lake beds covered by white acid-tolerant mosses. Acidified lakes are reminiscent of Rachel Carson's *Silent Spring* (1962), in which birds and animals died from the effects of toxic pesticides and insecticides like DDT.

The Geography of Acid Rain

Acid rains and the oxides that create them are blown long distances by the wind, often crossing seas and national frontiers to become an invisible export. As a result, the polluted is often far removed downwind from the polluter, who may remain unconvinced that a real problem exists. The polluter may then raise serious and well-intentioned objections to any remedial measures proposed by the polluted that would impose a heavy cost on itself.

Added complexity arises from the fact that, although sulphur and nitrogen oxides are now relatively ubiquitous in industrial nations, not all areas are affected by acid rain, and different locations (even within an area) show different symptoms of acidification. As yet, the areas where acid rain impacts are noticeable have been relatively few and predictable, given the ingredients of the 'acid rain equation'. . . . They tend to have a number of properties in common:

- they are concentrated in the industrialized belt of the northern hemisphere, downwind of dense concentrations of power stations, smelters, and large cities;

- they are often upland or mountainous areas, which are well watered by rain or snow;

- being well watered, they are often dissected by lakes or streams, and often covered by forest; and

- being upland, they often have thin soils and glaciated bedrock.

Many parts of Scandinavia, Canada and the Northeast United States, and northern Europe (particularly West Germany and upland Britain) share these properties, and this is why they figure so prominently in the acid rain debate. Across the Atlantic there are a number of 'acid rain hot spots', including Nova Scotia, the Canadian Shield around southern Ontario and Quebec, and Adirondack Mountains, Great Smoky Mountains, parts of Wisconsin and Minnesota, the Pacific Northwest USA, the Colorado Rockies, and the Pine Barrens of New Jersey.

In contrast, there are two types of 'safe area', where acid rain is not a problem (at present). One comprises those areas that simply do not receive acid rain or the gaseous oxides of sulphur and nitrogen, because of the fortunes of location (away from the not downwind of possible source areas). Almost all of the southern hemisphere, the tropics and parts of the northern hemisphere are so protected (up to now). The second group comprises areas that receive acid precipitation (wet or dry) but can tolerate it. Many areas have a natural resistance (or 'buffering capacity') to acidification, with immunity offered by alkaline soils or limestone bedrock, which neutralize acid inputs. Other forms of buffering are offered in the Midwest United States, where alkaline dust blown from the west neutralizes acid rain before it reaches the ground. Alkaline precipitation has been observed in Sweden in the past (pre-1960) in areas with limestone outcrops and areas where cement was manufactured. (pp. 1–5)

Polarization of Views

There are two main schools of thought in the [acid rain] debate. The majority of scientists, and many Canadian and European politicians, attribute visible damage to lakes, forests, crops, and buildings to man-made emissions of sulphur dioxide (SO_2) and nitrogen oxides (NO_x) from the burning of fossil fuels (mainly in conventional coal-fired power stations). In Britain the scientists and politicians are joined by a range of pressure groups (including Friends of the Earth, Greenpeace, the Ecology Party, the Socialist Environment and Resources Association, and the Young Liberals Ecology Group) who have banded together to forward the 'Stop Acid Rain UK' campaign. This unlikely and at times uncomfortable coalition demands the introduction of remedial measures without delay to significantly reduce emissions from chimneys and thus protect the environment from further damage.

A minority of scientists, and a caucus of influential politicians . . . , are *not* convinced that the case against man-made oxide emissions is proven or that costly emissions reductions imposed on industry would bring about the desired results. These dissenters are therefore resolutely opposed to the adoption of emission control measures, and repeatedly call for more studies on the causes of acid rain.

The relentless exchange of acid rhetoric between these two schools has created a fascinating debate combining science, politics, and diplomacy. . . . The debate has continued for over a decade and by the late 1980s there are still no signs on the horizon of any satisfactory (or even honorable) resolution. The debate ranges far and wide, although there is now little doubt that the acidity of rainfall in many areas has increased in recent years and continues to rise, and no doubt that man-made emissions of SO_2 and NO_x can—if necessary—be reduced (*at a cost*).

However, there remain significant differences of opinion on a number of key areas, including:

- the extent to which man-made emissions of SO_2 and NO_x cause acid rain (i.e. might not natural sources and processes play a significant role?);

- the extent to which observed damage to lakes and rivers, forests, crops, and buildings can be attributed definitely to acid rain (i.e. are the inferred links real and causal, or are other—perhaps as yet hidden or unexplored—factors also involved?);

- the extent to which observed damage is significant (i.e. is the damage serious enough to justify intervention to reduce if not reverse it, and if recovery is possible how long might it take?);

- the extent to which proposed reductions of oxide emissions would be effective (i.e. would there be a proportionate reduction in damage to the environment?); and

- the extent to which proposed reductions of oxide emissions would be cost-effective (i.e. would the value of the benefits—such as improved forestry

The majority of scientists, and many Canadian and European politicians, attribute visible damage to lakes, forests, crops, and buildings to man-made emissions of sulphur dioxide and nitrogen oxides from the burning of fossil fuels (mainly in conventional coal-fired power stations).

A minority of scientists, and a caucus of influential politicians are *not* convinced that the case against man-made oxide emissions is proven or that costly emission reductions imposed on industry would bring about the desired results. These dissenters are therefore resolutely opposed to the adoption of emission control measures, and repeatedly call for more studies on the causes of acid rain.

When Angus Smith coined the term "acid rain" in 1852 to refer to the effect that industrial emissions had on the precipitation of the British midlands, he could scarcely have dreamed that little over a century later the topic would be the subject of research for thousands of environmental scientists that would utilize hundreds of millions of dollars in research funds and would become of international political importance.

and fishing yields and less tangible benefits like improved environmental quality—equal or exceed the costs of installing and running equipment to reduce emissions from chimneys?).

These differences of opinion highlight the complexity of the acid rain debate, because they all relate to relative questions to which there are no black and white answers. Consequently, because each side in the debate starts from different premises and is in pursuit of different goals (protection of environment versus protection of industry and free enterprise). It is extremely difficult for a compromise position to emerge. There is only a winner and a loser in the debate.

In the final analysis, the environment—on which we depend for natural resources (such as food, timber, and materials) and intangibles like quality of life and scenic landscapes—will be the winner or loser. (pp. 7–8)

Chris C. Park, in his Acid Rain: Rhetoric and Reality, *Methuen, 1987, 272 p.*

The Nature and Scope of the Problem

When Angus Smith coined the term "acid rain" to refer to the effect that industrial emissions had on the precipitation of the British midlands, he could scarcely have dreamed that little over a century later the topic would be the subject of research for thousands of environmental scientists that would utilize hundreds of millions of dollars in research funds and would become of international political importance. Although Smith clearly recognized that acid rain caused environmental damage, the continental scale of acid rain effects was not recognized until the mid-20th century. It was not until concern was publicly widespread in the late 1970s that governments sponsored large-scale studies of the problem.

Although much has been learned about the causes, extent, transport, and effects of acid rain, some issues are still debated, which in turn cause polarization among scientists, political parties, states, and countries. These debates are often based on outdated preconceptions. Many statements of opinion or hypothesis have been misrepresented as "proofs" by later investigators. Seldom has such a large proportion of ecological science been published in the unrefereed "gray" literature. Research has solved some problems but has led to the discovery of new ones. (p. 149)

The Origin and Extent of Acid Rain

A decade ago, most scientists believed that natural unpolluted precipitation would have a pH of 5.6, the pH of distilled water saturated with CO_2. Despite evidence to the contrary, this simplistic assumption has persisted until recently. We now know that in remote areas, uncontaminated by either industrial emissions or calcareous dust, precipitation usually has a pH value close to 5.0 because it contains small amounts of both weak and strong acids of natural origin. Unfortunately, in most areas within several hundred kilometers of large centers of human activity, precipitation has much lower pH values. Widespread acid rain has been known in northern Europe and eastern North America for some time. Recent work has led to the discovery of acid rain in western North America, Japan, China, the Soviet Union, and South America. Globally, anthropogenic emissions of sulfur are comparable in magnitude to emissions from natural sources, but regionally, in northern Europe and eastern North America, over 90% of sulfur deposited from the atmosphere is anthropogenic. About 50% of the sulfates falling in eastern Canada are believed to have originated in the United States, and Canadian emissions contribute substantially to the American acid rain problem, particularly in the Northeast. Similarly, much of Scandinavian acid precipitation originates in industrialized areas of central Europe and the United Kingdom. Earlier claims that acids from volcanoes, trees, salt marshes, or other natural sources cause the acid rain problem have largely ceased. Polluted air masses have been convincingly tracked across the Atlantic and over the North Pole from Eurasia to North America, by using the unique trace metal content of polluted air masses. Broad regional to global pollution of the atmosphere with acid rain and many other pollutants is clearly a result of human activities.

The Extent of Acid-Sensitive Areas

The extent of areas that are geologically vulnerable to acid precipitation is much larger than was believed a decade ago. In the United States, large acid-sensitive areas are now known to occur in Minnesota, Wisconsin, upper Michigan, several southeastern states, and many of the mountainous areas of the West, in addition to the well-known northeastern sector of the country. . . . Large acid-sensitive areas are known to exist in all western provinces, the Yukon, the Northwest Territories, and Labrador. In Europe, acid-sensitive areas of the Netherlands, Belgium, Denmark, Switzerland, Italy, West Germany, and Ireland have been added to the better known areas of Scandinavia and the United Kingdom. Vast areas of Precambrian and Cambrian geology in Asia, Africa, and South America are also acid-sensitive.

Rates of Increase in Acid Rain

Precipitation chemistry data from before the mid-1950s are of questionable reliability, causing considerable controversy over the timing of increases in acid rain. As a result, the onset of the ecological effects of acid precipitation can be deduced only from the timing of changes in lake chemistry or acid-sensitive microfossils and metallic pollutants in sediments, as discussed below. The earliest records of lakes acidified by atmospheric emissions come from Scotland, where analyses of diatoms in sediments showed that lakes were becoming acid in the mid-19th century. Widespread damage to ecosystems of Scandinavia and North America did not begin until the 1930s to 1950s. This has puzzled many, because sulfur emissions in North America increased most rapidly before 1920, followed by alternating periods of decline and increase. There are a number of possible reasons for the damage occurring later. The increasing construction of large power plants and smelters with tall smokestacks in the middle of the 20th century was coupled to a decline in the use of coal for home heating, so that a local air pollution problem was transformed into a long-range, transboundary one. Whereas peak fuel combustion once occurred in winter for heating, it now occurs typically in summer, when emissions are directed into a warmer, moister, and thus more reactive atmosphere where oxidation of sulfur compounds is more efficient. Alkaline materials such as fly ash have been removed from emissions to control particulate pollutants. Emissions of nitrogen oxides and of other pollutants that catalyze the oxidation of sulfur and nitrogen oxides has also increased. Finally, it probably took years to decades to deplete the acid-neutralizing capacity of lakes, streams, and their catchments, so that pH depressions were not noticeable for some time after precipitation became acidic. Better recent chemical records have revealed that the acidity of precipitation has recently increased in the southeastern United States. Sulfate concentrations in precipitation are currently from 4 to 16 times as high east of the Mississippi River as they are in regions farther away from anthropogenic sources of sulfur.

The Extent and Rate of Surface Water Acidification

It is now clear that acid rain has already caused widespread acidification of many aquatic ecosystems in the northeastern United States, Canada, Norway, Sweden, and the United Kingdom. Evidence comes from four sources: geochemical theory, analysis of long-term trends, comparison of older with more recent chemical records, and paleoecological analyses. On the other

Although much has been learned about the causes, extent, transport, and effects of acid rain, some issues are still debated, which in turn cause polarization among scientists, political parties, states, and countries. These debates are often based on outdated preconceptions. Many statements of opinion or hypothesis have been misrepresented as "proofs" by later investigators. Seldom has such a large proportion of ecological science been published in the unrefereed "gray" literature. Research has solved some problems but has led to the discovery of new ones.

Clearly, we know enough about the effects of acid rain on aquatic ecosystems to make a strong case for regulating emissions of sulfur oxides.

hand, the rate of change has increased less rapidly in recent years than was feared a decade ago. (pp. 149–50)

Evidence for Biological Change

Most early records of biological damage were confined to adult fishes of species valued for sport. Most of these can tolerate pH values of less than 5.5. Lakes with higher pH values were assumed to be free from biological effects. More recently, juvenile fishes and many organisms lower in the aquatic food web have been shown to be intolerant of much higher pH values. The early disappearance of organisms at lower trophic levels may cause starvation to stress large predatory fishes well before direct toxic action of the hydrogen ion is evident. Several recent studies support this hypothesis.

Because spawning beds are difficult to locate and young fish are usually difficult to catch, populations may have experienced several years of successive recruitment failure before damage is detected. In summary, because assessments of biological effects have focused on adult game fish instead of more sensitive juveniles or organisms lower in the food web, our current estimates of biological damage to aquatic communities caused by acid rain are unquestionably too low.

Among larger game fishes, most autumn-spawning species are usually more sensitive to acidification than spring spawners, because the very sensitive hatchlings are present in shallow nearshore waters in early spring when snowmelt can produce a strong acid and aluminum pulse.

The oligotrophication of acidified lakes, one of the key earlier concerns of ecologists, does not occur in most cases. While there is some evidence for reduced phosphorus inputs or changed forms of phosphorus in acidified lakes, most field investigations have found that significant changes in photosynthetic production, biomass, and nutrient concentrations in acidified lakes did not occur. Indeed, in some cases, phosphorus was mobilized from lake sediments and stream beds during acid pulses. Likewise, although several investigators have observed an increased abundance of coarse organic matter on surface sediments of acidified lakes, this has not always caused decreased microbial decomposition, as had been hypothesized. In contrast to the lack of effect on lake metabolism, changes in species of phytoplankton are dramatic and remarkably similar in most acidified lakes. The formation of mats of benthic algae or bryophytes in littoral regions of acidified lakes is also widespread.

Although the number of zooplankton species is usually lower in acidic lakes, the lower biomass once thought to be caused by acidification has recently been shown to be due to lower availability of nutrients. The few thorough case studies of streams indicate that their biota may be even more sensitive to acidification than that of lakes. The benthic fauna of acidic streams has long been known to be less diverse than in circumneutral ones. Several species of mayflies and stoneflies disappeared from acidified reaches of streams in the Algonquin Highlands of Ontario between 1937–42 and 1984–85. The impoverishment was attributed largely to a decrease in pH of up to 1.5 units during spring snowmelt. Similar conclusions were reached from surveys of stream benthos in Sweden. In Norway, the stream invertebrate fauna has been severely impoverished by acidification. Fish kills that have been observed in streams and rivers during acid pulses and the decline in trout or salmon fisheries in acidified waters are good evidence for ecological damage that results from acid rain.

The Role of Aluminum in Biological Damage

Aluminum is released to lakes and streams from acidified terrestrial soils and lake sediments. Only ionic aluminum and aluminum hydroxide appear to be highly toxic to fishes, and only the former is important at low pH. Other organisms appear to be much less susceptible. The importance of aluminum seems to vary greatly between ecosystems and with the stage of acidification, as a result of differences in watersheds, aquatic chemical complexes, the presence of refugia, and the behavioral responses of fish species. Many of the early effects of acidification mentioned above, at pH values approaching 6, cannot be attributed to aluminum toxicity.

The Resistance of Lakes to Acidification

Until recently, scientists believed that the entire resistance of lakes to acidification was supplied by the weathering of geological substrates or the exchange of hydrogen ions for base cations in terrestrial soils of watersheds. As a result, until recently, published models of acidification have focused exclusively on terrestrial processes.

However, historical studies and whole-lake experiments have revealed that there is an additional resistance to acidification within lakes, and budgets for natural lakes revealed that in some cases terrestrial sources could only account for a part of the observed buffering. These processes are not 100% efficient at neutralizing incoming acids. Therefore, they have not prevented lakes from acidifying. Yet without them, the acidification of lakes would be much more severe. These processes involve first-order reactions at sediment surfaces, so that their efficiency is higher in shallower, more slowly flushing lakes and lower in deeper, rapidly flushing lakes.

Recovery from Acidification

The recovery of lakes and streams after the acidity of precipitation has been reduced is documented in case history studies from areas of eastern Canada where sulfate deposition has decreased substantially in the past 10 to 15 years. In the Sudbury area, a combination of smelter closures and SO_2 controls have reduced emissions to about one-third of their value in the early 1970s. The concomitant decreases in the acidity of local deposition have been accompanied by rapid increases in alkalinity and pH in nearby lakes, and decreased concentrations of SO_4^{2-}, aluminum, and toxic trace metals. The recoveries have occurred at rates more or less predictable from the water renewal rates of the lakes. The acidity of at least some of the lakes decreased enough to prevent the extinction or to allow the reintroduction of lake trout or brook trout. Crustacean zooplankton communities of the lakes have not recovered, but rotifer populations are returning to those typical of less acidic conditions. Decreased acidity of the spring melt pulses in streams was also attributed to the decrease in emissions. Similar increases in pH were observed in 54 lakes of the Algoma region in north-central Ontario. In two of the lakes, white sucker (*Catostomus commersoni*) were able to reinvade and survive.

The reduction of U.S. and Canadian SO_2 emissions has also allowed some recovery of freshwaters in maritime Canada. Sulfate runoff from 12 river watersheds in Nova Scotia and 8 watersheds in Newfoundland has decreased dramatically, accompanied by increases in river pH.

However, it is not clear whether lakes will be able to recover completely. Base cations in soils can be depleted by acidification, and their recovery may take many years. Also, experimental whole-lake studies show that the reversal of acidification allows only some components of the biota to recover rapidly. Acidification of Lake 223 to pH 5.0 eliminated several key species of fishes and invertebrates. Recovery of the lake to a pH of 5.4 to 5.6 by reducing inputs of sulfuric acid allowed two of the remaining species of fishes to resume reproduction. Some species of phytoplankton that had been eliminated by acidification also returned. To date, lake trout have not resumed reproduction. Other species eliminated from the lake have not returned.

Although it is now clear that reducing emissions of SO_2 will allow the rapid chemical recovery of lakes, it is unlikely that original pH values will be reached for many years. Unassisted biological recovery of all original species also appears to be unlikely. Widespread stocking of game fishes and key prey species will be necessary. Even then, the reconstructed food chains may not resemble the original ones. It therefore seems prudent to prevent as much additional ecological damage as we can.

Claims that acids from volcanoes, trees, salt marshes, or other natural sources cause the acid rain problem have largely ceased. Polluted air masses have been convincingly tracked across the Atlantic and over the North Pole from Eurasia to North America, by using the unique trace metal content of polluted air masses. Broad regional to global pollution of the atmosphere with acid rain and many other pollutants is clearly a result of human activities.

It is now clear that acid rain has already caused widespread acidification of many aquatic ecosystems in the northeastern United States, Canada, Norway, Sweden, and the United Kingdom.

Land Use and Acidification

In some circumstances, land-use changes may have a greater acidifying effect on soils than acid deposition. Some investigators have argued that deforestation several decades ago resulted in decreases in the acidity of runoff waters that caused the pH of lakes to increase. They believe that the regrowth of forests has been responsible for the recent increase in acidification of lakes. In heavily populated areas, it has been difficult to separate the two causes of acidification. In individual watersheds, studies have shown that acidification results from land use when large deposits of reduced sulfur are exposed to oxygen in the atmosphere by human disturbance, such as in acid mine drainage and in areas where ancient marine or wetland sediments have been exposed by drainage and cultivation.

However, acidification has occurred in remote parts of the North American Precambrian Shield where land use has not changed. Moreover, where land-use changes have been intensively studied, the evidence does not support the land-management hypothesis. For example, deforestation at Hubbard Brook and the Experimental Lakes Area caused higher losses of H^+ and strong acid anions than under aggrading conditions, as a result of higher nitrification and reoxidation of reduced sulfur compounds. This is the reverse of what was hypothesized by proponents of the land-use hypothesis. Sulfate is usually the predominant anion in runoff from anthropogenically acidified areas, rather than the organic anions expected if forest regrowth were responsible for acidification. In Norway, lakes with pristine watersheds and those where land-use changes had occurred were found to acidify at identical rates. In Scotland and Wales, paleoecological studies have shown that the timing of recent lake acidification is consistent with changes in the strong acid content of precipitation and not with the timing of land-use changes. Similarly, the rapid acidification of Big Moose Lake in the Adirondacks since 1950 correlates to increases in fossil fuel combustion, not watershed changes. In summary, terrestrial processes clearly contribute to the acidity of soils and natural waters, but changes in land use cannot explain the widespread acidification of fresh waters in the 20th century.

How Much Must We Reduce Sulfur Deposition?

Most scientists now agree that reducing deposition of sulfuric acid will benefit aquatic ecosystems. The remaining questions are, what degree of reduction is necessary to protect our aquatic resources, and what is the link to emissions of sulfur oxides? A few aquatic ecosystems are naturally acidic enough to have an impoverished biota, even when the pH of precipitation is 5.0 or greater, implying that any anthropogenic additions to the acidity of deposition would add to the number of acidic lakes. Furthermore, if decades of exposure to high inputs of acid have depleted the base cations in watershed soils, even a return of precipitation to natural levels of acidity would not allow waters to recover fully for many years. Some realistic compromise between ecosystem damage and anthropogenic activity must obviously be struck. (pp. 151–52)

Interaction of Acid Rain with Other Pollutants of Terrestrial Ecosystems

Clearly, we know enough about the effects of acid rain on aquatic ecosystems to make a strong case for regulating emissions of sulfur oxides. However, while the debate about controlling acidifying emissions has focused almost entirely on SO_2, emissions of nitrogen oxides have received little attention and have increased much more rapidly than SO_2 in recent decades. The resulting nitric acid plays an increasing role in the acidification process and is particularly important during the spring, when melting of polluted snow normally causes a strong acid pulse. In addition, nitrogen oxides are known to react in the atmosphere to form ozone, which is highly toxic to terrestrial plants.

Metals are also known to exacerbate the acidification problem. The case of aluminum leached from soils and sediments was discussed earlier. In addition, many toxic trace metals are emitted from the same sources that release oxides of sulfur and nitrogen. These are distributed almost as widely as acid rain. As precipitation becomes more acid, a higher proportion of these will be soluble in rain, mist, and fog. Prior to the industrial revolution, the trace metal inputs to ecosystems were small. In the past 100 to 200 years inputs have increased rapidly, and many of the trace metal biogeochemical cycles are dominated by anthropogenic inputs, even at very remote locations.

At circumneutral pH values, most trace metals are quite insoluble in water, sorbing quickly to particles in lake water, which sink rapidly. Even many fold increases in metal inputs may result in concentrations that are below the limits of detection of standard chemical methods for analyzing lake water. It is therefore much easier to detect increases in lake sediments. However, some of the sedimented trace metals may be remobilized or remain in solution longer as lakes acidify, increasing the exposure to aquatic organisms. The acidification of ground water may also mobilize trace metals, and acidic water supplies are known to dissolve metals from plumbing, possibly constituting a drinking water hazard in some areas. Although there have been few studies, a number of cases have documented ecological effects that result from interactions between acid rain and metals.

Interactions between oxides of sulfur, oxides of nitrogen, ozone, carbon monoxide, hydrocarbons, and methane are known or suspected to contribute to a variety of adverse environmental effects, ranging from acidification of ecosystems to crop damage, depletion of the ozone layer, and climatic change.

In forests, agricultural lands, and wetlands, the causes of observed damage appear to be more complicated than in lakes and streams, with many air pollutants acting in concert, in some cases exacerbating the effects of natural stresses such as cold and drought. Acid rain appears to play some role in the observed damage. It is clearly instrumental in mobilizing the soil aluminum which causes root damage in forests, and in leaching plant nutrients from foliage. Polluted fogs and mists also expose terrestrial plants to concentrations of acid much higher than in rain, causing direct foliar damage in some cases. Long-range transport of sulfur in the atmosphere has caused increased haze in both Arctic and temperate regions. In summary, reducing emissions of sulfur and nitrogen oxides would be beneficial to softwater aquatic ecosystems and probably to terrestrial ecosystems as well. Regional air pollution is much more severe than we believed in the past, and more comprehensive measures to control it are necessary to preserve the integrity of the biosphere. (p. 153)

D.W. Schindler, "Effects of Acid Rain on Freshwater Ecosystems," in Science, *Vol. 239, No. 4836, January 8, 1988, pp. 149–57.*

> **Regional air pollution is much more severe than we believed in the past, and more comprehensive measures to control it are necessary to preserve the integrity of the biosphere.**

Acid Deposition Phenomena

When oil and coal are burned, about one percent of the resulting gaseous effluent consists of oxides of nitrogen and sulfur. Of this percent, part is deposited directly on ground cover, and another part is oxidized in the atmosphere to nitric and sulfuric acids that fall to earth in rain and snow. Some of the acids are deposited close to where the flue gases entered the air, and the rest can be carried over long distances, even to other countries or the oceans. While the distribution patterns and deposition levels of these acids have been studied for some time, there is little definitive information. Acids deposited by precipitation have been most frequently measured, even though the problem stems from both wet and dry acid deposition. Dry deposition refers to the molecular absorption of SO_2 and NO_x as well as the falling out of the atmosphere of particulate nitrates and sulfates.

Acid deposition poses a significant problem because of both the known damaging effects on the environment and other possible but less clearly understood consequences. The corrosive effects of acid deposition, both dry and wet, on man-made structures are amply documented, with accelerated corrosion especially evident in metals exposed to air containing sulfate particulates and sulfur oxides. Acidification of organic systems affects both plants and animals.

Acid deposition poses a significant problem because of both the known damaging effects on the environment and other possible but less clearly understood consequences. The corrosive effects of acid deposition, both dry and wet, on man-made structures are amply documented, with accelerated corrosion especially evident in metals exposed to air containing sulfate particulates and sulfur oxides. Acidification of organic systems affects both plants and animals. Species of sensitive aquatic organisms are no longer found in certain acidified lakes and streams. In Canada, the northeastern United States, the western Sierra Mountains, and Scandinavia, there is increasing evidence of fish mortality and morbidity in water bodies contaminated by strong inorganic acids. The pH of uncontaminated water bodies is controlled by weak natural acids; dissolved aluminum is predominantly organically complexed and essentially nontoxic, so fish survive. In marked contrast, inorganic aluminum complexes occur in certain anthropogenically acidified waters at levels that are lethal to young fish.

While fish kills distress anglers, the economic impact of acid deposition on forests is potentially far greater. Causes of forest dieback in Canada, the eastern United States, and Europe are still much debated; certainly no scientific consensus has been reached. A number of European investigators, but few in the United States, have argued that the observed forest damage is primarily due to oxidants, though acid mist, acid rain, and dry acid deposition enhance the damage. A major oxidant is ozone, a key participant in future surface warming. Oxidants are required to convert sulfur dioxide and oxides of nitrogen into sulfuric and nitric acids. For wet deposition, strong oxidants are required to convert SO_2; uncatalyzed reaction rates with molecular oxygen during the 4–5 day half life of an SO_2 molecule are too low for reactions to take place before rain-out. The principal candidates are ozone and hydrogen peroxide and the hydroxyl and hydroperoxy radicals. In the eastern United States, concentrations of sulfur dioxide and nitrogen oxides in the lower atmosphere are roughly comparable, as are concentrations of the various oxides.

Long-Term Trends in Acid Deposition

Historical trends in the chemistry of acid precipitation differ in the eastern United States and Europe. (p. 17)

The observed spread of highly acid precipitation [in the United States] can be explained by two factors: as air standards became more stringent during the decade 1965–1975, the total amount of SO_2 emitted in the eastern United States did not increase, but the contribution from power plants rose by about 50%. . . . This increasing portion of SO_2 emission came from stacks that grew taller, with a higher effective height of emission. Effective height takes into account the upward momentum of the flue gas as well as the geometric height of the stack. The SO_2 from these stacks could be carried farther and have a longer atmospheric residence time, permitting interaction between the emission and available oxidants. In the same region, total NO_x emissions and NO_x emissions from utilities increased, consistent with the observation that the nitric acid component of acid rain increased.

The history of acid deposition in Europe differs markedly from that in the United States. Between 1955 and 1975, both the nitrate and sulfate loading of acid precipitation increased, as did its geographic distribution. The increase in acidity of Europe's precipitation, as well as the rising sulfuric acid component, can be attributed in part to less stringent controls on sulfur oxide emissions than those imposed in the United States.

Long-Range Transport of Acid Precursors

There is increasing evidence for the long-range transport of both oxidants and SO_2 and NO_x. However, there also exists strong evidence that approximately comparable amounts of sulfate and nitrate, or their precursors, are transported over much greater distances. This conclusion is supported by the following observation: The wet deposition of sulfuric acid in rain and snow varies by only a factor of 2 throughout most of the eastern United States, much less than the variation in emissions. For example, the less industrialized states of Vermont and Arkansas receive about half as much sulfate (and H^+) per unit area than the industrial states of Ohio, Indiana, and Massachusetts, even though the SO_2 emission density of the less industrialized states is almost 50 times lower than the emission density of the industrialized states. This smoothing out of wet sulfate deposition is due mainly to the flow across states of air parcels containing SO_2, sulfate, and oxidants before precipitation occurs. (pp. 18–19)

The long-range transport of pollutants can be understood in terms of the dynamics of the mixing layer of the atmosphere. The mixing layer forms as the result of convective activity set up by the transfer of heat from warmer ground to the atmosphere. In the eastern United States, the mixing layer is thickest about 2 km at midday during the summer when convective activity is greatest. . . . The effective stack height, which is the height to which the flue gas is carried due to buoyancy and upward momentum, also varies with season and time of day. On the average, the effective stack height exceeds that of the mixing layer during winter for most of the day, and during summer for at least half of the day. As long as SO_2, NO_x, and oxidants stay above the mixing layer, they are kept from reaching the ground where they would be absorbed, and the pollutants can be carried at higher levels over long periods of time and long distances. During winter, the time available for oxidation is expected to be greater, since the effective stack height exceeds the mixing layer height. In the United States, the average height of stacks has increased over the last three decades from 200 meters to 600 meters, with some stacks reaching heights of 1200 meters during the later 1960s. This suggests that transport distances and times available for oxidation have been longer during more recent years. These observations are consistent with the geographical spread of acid deposition in the eastern United States.

The climatological regimes in Europe are different, so the behavior of the mixing layer and consequently the distributions of pollutants there are also different. Differences between the European summer and winter are less marked than those in the United States. The mixing layer remains more nearly at a fixed level; consequently, long-range transport of pollutants takes place year-round. Cooler European summers result in lower mixing layer heights, and the average stack height relative to the mixed-layer thickness in Europe is higher. This combination insures that the time available for oxidation of SO_2 and NO_x is longer in Europe than in North America.

Seasonal Variations in Acid Deposition

The relative importance of SO_2, NO_x and oxidants and their seasonal fluctuations can be judged by examining the spatial and temporal patterns of emissions and acid deposition. In the eastern United States, there is no large seasonal variation in the rate at which coal is burned. Coal burned in electrical power plants at an average rate of $30-35 \times 10^6$ tons per month, is the major source of SO_2. In the northeastern United States, where the acidity of precipitation is now the highest, there are very large seasonal variations in certain acid rain components. (pp. 19–23)

As noted earlier, the lower thickness of the mixing layer during winter would enhance the oxidation of SO_2, since oxidants would have more time to interact with SO_2. This effect would tend to increase the deposition of sulfuric acid during winter. While seasonal differences in ground cover may contribute to greater dry deposition of SO_2 (and oxidants) during summer, the principal difference between summer and winter is the well-known seasonal variation in oxidant production. Since oxidants are for the most part photochemical in origin, their concentrations in the mixing layer are greater during the summer.

From these considerations, it appears that $SO_4^=$ and H^+ concentrations in precipitation in the northeastern United States are limited by the amount of oxidants available. The limitation of acid precipitation by the availability of oxidants during winter is consistent with the observation that NO_3^- in wet dep-

While fish kills distress anglers, the economic impact of acid deposition on forests is potentially far greater. Causes of forest dieback in Canada, the eastern United States, and Europe are still much debated; certainly no scientific consensus has been reached. A number of investigators have argued that the observed forest damage is primarily due to oxidants, though acid mist, acid rain, and dry acid deposition enhance the damage. A major oxidant is ozone, a key participant in future surface warming.

**In the public and politi-
cal mind, damages due to
acid deposition are im-
mediate; the long-term
impacts of climate
change, while potentially
far more profound, are
seen as the distant con-
cerns of future genera-
tions. In fact, measures
to control acid deposition
will aid in limiting fu-
ture climatic warming.**

osition is much less seasonally affected than SO_4^- and H^+ deposition. The conversion of NO_2 and HNO_3 occurs much more rapidly than the oxidation of SO_2 to sulfuric acid; this implies that NO_x tends to use the oxidant in an air parcel first, and only the remaining oxidant is available for SO_2 oxidation. In contrast to winter, oxidizers during summer are abundant enough to convert the available SO_2 and NO_x to sulfuric and nitric acids.

The possible role of oxidants in limiting sulfate formation, or conversely, the role of SO_2 in limiting oxidant formation appears to differ in Europe from that in the northeastern United States. The hydrogen ion concentration of European precipitation is greatest during winter, with pH values well below 5, and much lower during summer when the acidity can increase to pH 6 or higher values. This occurs despite the higher concentration of photochemical oxidants during summer. The acidity of European precipitation . . . reflects the large summer-winter variation in SO_2 concentration. Sulfur-containing fuel is burned in greater amounts during winter than summer, primarily due to the lack of air-conditioning requirements. In addition, the mixing layer height is lower in Europe relative to the effective stack height, leading to long-range transport and long times for reaction between oxidants and flue gases. The oxidant concentration is fed by an industrial-urban complex that is geographically more concentrated than that of the United States, and available oxidants appear to be adequate to convert SO_2 to $SO_4^=$, even during winter.

Tropospheric Chemistry

Acid deposition and the trace-gas greenhouse effect basically involve the release into the atmosphere, by man's activities, of reduced compounds (NO_x, SO_2, CO, CH_4), the oxidation of these pollutants by oxidizers (O_3, HO, HO_2, and H_2O_2) formed by photochemical processes, and sequestering of the products as acids or as carbon dioxide. In essence, the atmosphere can be viewed as a dilute, low-temperature combustion chamber, with fuels provided by man and oxidizers provided by the action of sunlight. (pp. 24–6)

Major Acid Rain Questions

In the public and political mind, damages due to acid deposition are immediate; the long-term impacts of climate change, while potentially far more profound, are seen as the distant concerns of future generations. Strategies to limit acid deposition will thus receive priority attention. In fact, measures to control acid deposition will aid in limiting future climatic warming.

Development of appropriate ways to control damage due to acid deposition will depend on answers to the following questions:

1. What is the relative importance of photochemical oxidants and acid deposition in damaging forest?

2. Is the oxidation of SO_2 to sulfuric acid and dry sulfates limited by the amount of oxidant available?

3. Does NO_x, which eventually rains out as nitric acid, consume more oxidant than it produces through catalytic action?

4. What are the relative roles of CO and volatile hydrocarbons in producing oxidants?

5. What is the role of tall stacks in long-range transportation of acid precursors and oxidants?

No definitive answers can at present be given to these questions. The answers may also be different for different regions with varying climatic conditions, as well as for different seasons. (p. 29)

Gordon J. MacDonald, "Acid Deposition," in his Climate Change and Acid Rain, *The MITRE Corporation, 1986, pp. 17–29.*

Causes, Controls, and Effects

Emissions of Acidic Deposition

Power plants located primarily in the middle and northern parts of the United States are currently the primary source of emissions of sulfur dioxide and a major source of nitrogen oxides. However, they have been so only since about 1960.

In earlier years, sources were smaller and less centralized. Transportation and other dispersed activities are a significant source of nitrogen oxides and volatile organic compounds; therefore, those emissions are more evenly distributed over the United States. Man-made emissions of all three major precursors increased substantially between the early part of the century and today because of increased fuel use and industrial activity.

However, over the last decade or so, emissions of sulfur dioxide and volatile organic compounds have declined, and the steady rise in nitrogen oxides appears to have abated in most regions. These recent trends have been influenced primarily by reductions that occurred subsequent to promulgation of the Clean Air Act of 1970 and also from market factors affecting industry.

Additionally, the declining emission trends occurred despite large increases in coal use and motor vehicle registrations over the last decade.

Man-made emissions of sulfur dioxide and volatile organic compounds in the United States, on a per capita and per real dollar of GNP basis, they have decreased by a smaller percentage than sulfur dioxide and volatile organic compounds.

Natural emissions of sulfur compounds appear to contribute only a minor increment to atmospheric acid formation. However, emissions of volatile organic compounds from vegetation may be extremely important, especially in the summer. Natural sources may also contribute a substantial amount of emissions of nitrogen oxides. Emissions of hydrogen chloride, hydrogen fluoride, and primary sulfates probably make only a minor contribution to acidic deposition, but ammonia and alkaline dust seem to be emitted in large quantities and may play a significant role in atmospheric reactions.

Emission Control Technologies

In the utility sector, flue-gas desulfurization is a proven technology for reducing sulfur dioxide emissions by 90–95 percent at high availability. Low-nitrogen oxides burners are commercially available to reduce nitrogen oxides emissions from new and some existing coal-fired power plants by about 50 percent. Physical coal cleaning (10–30 percent sulfur removal) and fuel switching have been traditional ways to reduce sulfur prior to combustion.

A number of innovative electricity-generating technologies are under development with the aim of achieving either higher removal efficiencies at similar cost to conventional technologies or similar removal efficiencies at lower cost. Integrated gasification combined cycle (IGCC) is one promising technology that can potentially achieve 99 plus percent reduction of sulfur dioxide emissions and 95 percent reduction of nitrogen oxides emissions. Atmospheric fluidized-bed combustion (AFBC) can achieve 90–95 percent reduction of sulfur dioxide emissions and 70–80 percent reduction of nitrogen oxides emissions. Both technologies are currently being demonstrated at commercial scale, with costs expected to be competitive with conventional technology.

IGCC and AFBC can be used in new plants or to repower existing plants— where they can extend plan life-times and simultaneously increase generating

A major objective of the National Acid Precipitation Assessment Program is to determine what role, if any, air pollution plays in regional forest health. The primary agents of concern are acidic deposition (wet and dry), its precursors sulfur dioxide, nitrogen oxides, and volatile organic compounds, and their associated oxidants, such as ozone and hydrogen peroxide.

A major objective of NAPAP [the National Acid Precipitation Assessment Program] is to determine what role, if any, air pollution plays in regional forest health. The primary agents of concern are acidic deposition (wet and dry), its precursors sulfur dioxide, nitrogen oxides, and volatile organic compounds, and their associated oxidants, such as ozone and hydrogen peroxide.

capacity. Pressurized fluidized-bed combustion is entering the commercial-scale demonstration phase, with prospects of higher removal and conversion efficiencies but at a higher cost, relative to AFBC.

A variety of other technologies have been or are being developed as retrofit options for existing utility plants and to be used in combination for new plants. Technologies currently being demonstrated are gas reburning and low temperature sorbent injection on utility boilers and a slagging combustor on an industrial boiler. The emerging technologies being developed include advanced flue-gas cleanup and advanced coal cleaning.

Options to reduce automotive nitrogen oxides emissions much below current regulations are limited. Further reductions in volatile organic compounds emissions from automobiles below current standards may have to rely on computer-controlled or ceramic engines, methanol or related new fuels, or electric vehicles. More stringent controls for light-duty trucks and heavy-duty engines are being phased in through 1991.

Effects on Agricultural Crops

Scientific research on the response of crop plants to acidic deposition and associated pollutants, has indicated that there are no measurable and consistent effects on crop yield from the direct effects of simulated acidic rain at ambient levels of acidity. The conclusion is based on yield measurements of grains, forage, vegetable and fruit crops exposed to a range of simulated rain acidity levels in controlled exposure studies, and is supported by results from mechanistic and screening studies. Continued research efforts will examine whether other stress agents (such as drought or insect pests) cause crops to be more sensitive to rainfall acidity.

Effects on Forests

Healthy forests are vital to the nation. A major objective of NAPAP [the National Acid Precipitation Assessment Program] is to determine what role, if any, air pollution plays in regional forest health. The primary agents of concern are acidic deposition (wet and dry), its precursors sulfur dioxide, nitrogen oxides, and volatile organic compounds, and their associated oxidants, such as ozone and hydrogen peroxide.

All forests experience natural stresses caused by plant competition, nutrient limitations, adverse weather, insects, disease, and other factors acting alone or in combination. Man-caused stresses such as incompatible land use, wildfire, and possibly regional air pollution can also contribute to reduced forest health.

On a regional scale, it is useful to consider U.S. forests in four categories: intensive plantations, managed forests, low-elevation natural forests, and above-cloudbase forests. Among the forest lands of the 48 contiguous States, the areal percentages are approximately 8, 22, 69, and 1, respectively.

Intensive plantations have the highest health and most stress resistance. None are reported to have symptoms which point to air pollution impacts. Managed forests are on sites of moderate productivity and are generally managed to avoid serious losses by abiotic or biotic stresses.

Low-elevation natural forests are extensive in geographic distribution, species composition, and environmental variety. However, in the United States, several ongoing declines affecting managed or low-elevation natural forests are suspected of having an air pollution component to their stress.

Effects on Aquatic Systems

Acidifying compounds are deposited on watersheds by wet and dry processes. The acidifying influence of the compounds can be reduced by buffering interactions with vegetation, by mineral weathering, by absorption of the acidifying agents onto soil surfaces, or by buffering processes active within the stream or lake. These mechanisms have been measured in a limited number of field studies, and they can be evaluated using more extensive data.

Surveys were conducted in potentially sensitive regions of the country to determine the chemical status of surface waters. Surveys of lakes larger than four ha [hectare] in the East and one ha in the West sampled during fall turnover show that there are essentially no lakes or reservoirs in the mountainous West, northeastern Minnesota, and the Southern Blue Ridge Province of the Southeast with pH <[less than] 5.0 (at a pH < 5.0 most clear water lakes do not support sports fish) and very few with pH < 5.5. Most other sampled subregions show less than 0.5 percent of the lake area and less than one percent of the number of lakes with pH < 5.0.

The three subregions with the highest percentage of acidic lakes are the Adirondacks and the Upper Peninsula of Michigan where up to two percent of the lake area and 10 percent of lakes have a pH < 5.0, and the Florida subregion where 12 percent of the ales and the lake area are acidic (pH < 5.0). Small lakes (<four ha) particularly in the Adirondacks are an important recreational resource and are more frequently acidic than lakes larger than four ha.

The acidic Florida subregion lakes are found predominantly in two of its five subpopulations. The first is the Okefenokee swamp which is naturally acidic and the second is the Panhandle of Florida where the cause of the acidic of the lakes is uncertain, but many reflect acidic deposition as well as other factors. The stream survey conducted in the Southern Blue Ridge Province found no acidic streams. Episodic pulses of acidic water in streams and lakes occur during snowmelt and during rainstorms. Both anthropogenic and natural sources of acidity contribute to these pulses. (pp. 38–9)

"The Acid Rain Report," in Congressional Digest, *Vol. 68, No. 2, February, 1989, pp. 38–9.*

> **"Our analyses show that acid rain is a significant problem in coastal waters up and down the *entire* eastern seaboard."**
>
> —Diane Fisher,
> Environmental Defense Fund.

The Impact of Acid Rain: Nitrate-Induced Suffocation of Aquatic Species

Acid rain's primary threat to aquatic life has generally been seen as its ability to lower the pH of water. But a study released [in April of 1988] by the New York City-based Environmental Defense Fund (EDF) highlights what its authors contend is an equally deadly but ignored impact of acid rain—nitrate-induced suffocation and light starvation of aquatic species.

Though nitrates are a nutrient, when their levels become excessive they can cause "algal blooms"—essentially an overgrowth of algae and other phytoplankton. These plants quickly consume most of the dissolved oxygen in water, suffocating other aquatic species. Algal overgrowth also clouds the water, preventing necessary light from filtering down to plants on the seafloor.

The EDF study focused on the effects of excess nitrogen on the Chesapeake Bay—the largest U.S. estuary and a major spawning ground for East Coast fisheries from Main to North Carolina. Until now, says Michael Oppenheimer, one of the study's authors, the Environmental Protection Agency (EPA) and others have largely ignored or greatly underestimated acid rain's role in overloading the Chesapeake and other waters with nitrogen. EDF's calculations, based on data from a range of federal and state agencies, including the EPA's Chesapeake Bay Program, indicate that acid deposition contributes at least one quarter of the nitrogen entering the bay as a result of human activity. That makes acid deposition second only to fertilizer runoff as a source of nitrogen pollution.

Acid rain originates from power plants and industries that burn fossil fuels and spew out sulphur dioxide emissions and from internal-combustion vehicles that contribute nitrogen oxide. These substances mix with oxygen and water vapor in the air to form acids. The water vapor, which is now acidic, falls to the ground and is known as acid rain, which can affect everything—soil, water, foliage.

Moreover, says Diane Fisher, who led the EDF study, "Our analyses show that acid rain is a significant problem in coastal waters up and down the *entire* eastern seaboard." Affecting primarily brackish and salt water, it "will continue to grow until nitrogen oxides (NO_x) emissions are controlled," she adds. In fact, efforts already underway to control nitrogen emissions (from sources other than acid rain) into many waterways "could be largely negated if NO_x emissions [from acid deposition] are not further reduced," her study says.

To counter the acid rain nitrate problem, EDF recommends that:

- states in the Chesapeake Bay watershed implement NO_x limits for electric power plants and factories and beef up motor vehicle inspection programs. (Unlike the sulfur dioxide component of acid rain, in which electric power plants contribute 70 percent of the pollution, motor vehicles are the major source of acid rain's nitrates. However, federal law prevents states from setting motor vehicle standards for NO_x.)

- the federal government adopt regulations to reduce industrial and vehicular NO_x emissions by at least 40 percent—a level that matches nitrogen reductions from other sources now being planned for the Chesapeake. (The Clean Air Act reauthorization legislation, pending in the House and Senate, would reduce allowable NO_x emissions from cars by about 60 percent.) EDF particularly endorses energy-efficiency measures to reduce NO_x.

- all governmental bodies acknowledge acid rain's contribution to the deteriorating quality of East Coast waters, and work at reducing nitrogen from sources besides acid rain—especially from sewage treatment plants and fertilizer and manure storage.

The EDF study wins high praise from William C. Baker, president of the Annapolis, Md.-based Chesapeake Bay Foundation. "The Chesapeake Bay is dying," he says, and this new report not only "brings to light an important new source of nitrogen—a major pollutant in the Chesapeake Bay"—but also points to where those involved in saving it must direct their attentions.

Though EPA spokesman Dave Cohen says the EDF scientists "seem to [offer] fairly compelling evidence regarding nitrogen loading" into the Chesapeake from acid rain, he adds that his agency's scientists were "surprised" at the size of the nitrogen contribution being attributed to this source and will therefore being reevaluating the data themselves. If EDF's 25 percent figure is accurate, he says, "then acid rain will be making a greater, more harmful contribution to the bay than we [at EPA] had suspected."

J. Raloff, "New Acid Rain Threat Identified," in Science News, Vol. 133, No. 18, April 30, 1988, p. 276.

National Parks, Forests, and Acid Rain

Scientists and researchers don't know if Shenandoah National Park, which survived past encroachments of people, can survive without major damage from the latest man-made intrusion: air pollution. Nor is it the only national park or forest under siege. According to both the National Park Service and the Forest Service, many units in both public land systems have ozone levels that exceed National Ambient Air Quality Standards (120 ppb [parts per billion] is a danger level) even in remote locations like Acadia National Park in Maine. Monitoring from such outposts as the Shenandoah Station has shown that visibility impairment—a good indicator of air pollution—has been found in varying degrees in all tested parks and that scenic vistas are affected by air pollution more than 90 percent of the time at all monitoring stations in the coterminous United States.

"It's naive for people to think that the parks are encased in a dome," says Jim Watkins, a Park Service Environmental Protection Specialist based in Shenandoah. "This park and the Great Smokies are vulnerable because we're close to cities, but even those out west, away from cities, suffer from the transport of pollution from cities hundreds of miles away." So do national forests: forest managers in the western United States, especially California, report massive damage to trees from air pollution generated in the Los Angeles area several hundred miles to the west.

Watkins witnesses air pollution effects on plants, trees, and lakes every day. "Parks are no more immune to air pollution than the vegetation in your front yard," he says. Getting people to understand the effects, however, is difficult. "We must have years and years of study before people will believe it. There are too many variables. Trying to pinpoint the effects of acid rain, for instance, is a very difficult thing. Milkweed and white pine are good early indicators of ozone, for example, but there are other things that can mimic ozone damage— like some plant diseases." (pp. 19–20)

Nationwide, some kind of leaf damage had been found at forty-one national park units, and the most common cause is ozone, which manifests itself as dark spots on the upper surface of leaves and as yellow mottling on needles of evergreens. Leaf damage has been found on 90 percent of the plants of the most sensitive species, like milkweed, and on about 8 percent of the least sensitive species, like black locust in Shenandoah National Park. (pp. 22–3)

As if ozone were not a serious enough threat there is acid rain—though the dimensions of the danger are harder to measure with this latest entry in the pollution conundrum. Unlike ozone, the effects of acid rain on trees, bodies of water and wildlife are difficult to model. With ozone studies, researchers can fumigate a sequestered greenhouse with ozone and then see the results comparatively quickly. These are the so-called "spray 'em and weigh 'em studies." Acid rain's effects can be much more subtle and harder to document because of the slow deterioration it causes.

First, though, what is this stuff? For the most part, it originates from power plants and industries that burn fossil fuels and spew out sulphur dioxide emissions and from internal-combustion vehicles that contribute nitrogen oxide. These substances mix with oxygen and water vapor in the air to form acids. The water vapor, which is now acidic, falls to the ground and is known as acid rain, which can affect everything—soil, water, foliage.

Some soil that is basic or alkaline (the opposite of acidic) by natural means can counteract the acid rain—but only up to its "buffering" limit. Other soil, which may already be naturally acidic, will become more acidic. The same is true of lakes—which can be rendered all but incapable of supporting fish populations—as have at least two hundred lakes in the Adirondack Mountains of New York. In addition, some lakes seem to be highly sensitive, while others are buffered and apparently immune from its effects. Yet even a highly buffered lake may show no signs of damage for many years and then suddenly exhibit catastrophic problems. "We're definitely seeing a drop in pH in streams," notes Shenandoah's Watkins. "They're losing their buffering capacity, but who knows when it will go or if it will go?"

The so-called pH scale, which measures acidity, ranges from 0, very acid, to 14, very basic. Seven is neutral. Every one drop in pH represents a ten-fold increase in acidity. Normal rain should be about 5.6, yet rainfall in the United States averages 4.2. A pH of 3 is about the acidity of vinegar. (p. 24)

According to park and forest sources [acid rain research] . . . often isn't well organized, lacks funding, and gets little support from higher ups. They complain that when they demonstrate likely acid rain damage, their superiors often tear the evidence apart because of political considerations. "They want the kind of proof that is impossible to obtain," says one researcher. "They'll ask

Unlike ozone, the effects of acid rain on trees, bodies of water and wildlife are difficult to model. With ozone studies, researchers can fumigate a sequestered greenhouse with ozone and then see the results comparatively quickly. These are the so-called "spray 'em and weigh 'em studies." Acid rain's effects can be much more subtle and harder to document because of the slow deterioration it causes.

At Shenandoah National Park, studies showed that the park receives deposits of sulfates and nitrates twelve and fourteen times greater than in remote parts of the world. Surveys showed that about 50 percent of the park's streams have little buffering capacity and that even a slight increase in acidification could injure fish. In addition, if the rate of acid rain deposition stays constant, the soil's buffering capacitycould disappear in twenty to forty years.

you to do a study that you know will take five years, but they want it in two, or they'll say 'Prove beyond a shadow of a doubt that this damage is from acid rain.' You can't do that, and they know it.''

Despite these political hardships, some research studies have emerged from a handful of parks. Most of the research centers on the deposition levels themselves and not the effects on trees, plants, and wildlife, and data is still being collected—the oldest study is only from late 1982—and according to many experts that's not enough time to establish long-term trends. Nevertheless, some individual parks have reported strong evidence of adverse effects based on studies done by individual park service researchers as well as non-service researchers using national park lands as test sites.

Some of the findings have been dramatic, especially in the eastern United States where the problem is older and more severe. Researchers at the New Jersey Bureau of Fresh Water Fisheries, for example, found a sharp drop in rainbow trout and an increase in brook trout populations between 1977 and 1984 in Vancampers Brook in the Delaware Water Gap National Recreation Area. Rainbow trout, being spring spawners, were subjected to highly acidic water as a result of spring runoff from snowmelts. Brook trout spawn in the fall, however, and prefer to spawn in areas where buffered groundwater seeps to the surface, thus protecting the young fish. In addition, studies showed that, in general, brook trout are more acid resistant than rainbows.

At Shenandoah National Park, studies showed that the park receives deposits of sulfates and nitrates twelve and fourteen times greater than in remote parts of the world. Surveys showed that about 50 percent of the park's streams have little buffering capacity and that even a slight increase in acidification could injure fish. In addition, if the rate of acid rain deposition stays constant, the soil's buffering capacity could disappear in twenty to forty years.

Precipitation at Great Smoky Mountains National Park has shown a significant drop in pH levels from 5.3 in 1978 to 3.7 in 1980. ''Most scientists believe that high elevation red spruce are being affected by air pollution,'' notes David Radloff. ''They probably get a greater concentration of pollution than any trees except those near cities. You have to remember that there is a greater concentration of pollution in fog than in regular rain and the higher elevation trees filter out more.'' Radloff adds, however, that the damage to high elevation red spruce attributed to acid rain is contested because there are insects that have been at work on the trees for years. Still, as reported in the November 1988 issue of *Audubon*, after several years of study, plant pathologist Robert I. Bruck is ''ninety percent certain'' that *some* kind of air pollution is killing the red spruce on Mt. Mitchell just north of the park.

Reports in other parks have been less conclusive, but still troubling. In Sequoia and Kings Canyon, which are treated as one unit, researchers are just beginning to establish a baseline from which to measure changes. Preliminary reports, however, show that most of the lakes within the parks are poorly buffered. Emerald Lake, for example, was chosen as a monitoring site and exhibits very low tolerance for acid deposition. Researchers are watching acid sensitive insect populations at the lake for any changes.

The situation at Rocky Mountain National Park is similarly ambiguous. For one thing, the area isn't getting much continuous acid rain deposition, and there is no evidence of negative effects on fish so far. However, the soils in some areas are poorly buffered and may not survive an increase in acid rain. In addition, the park does suffer from severe ''spring acid pulse,'' a condition brought about by acidic snowmelts. It's unclear what effect, if any, these quick pulses of depressed pH will have, though it has been suggested that they could hurt insects born in the spring and ultimately upset the food chain. (pp. 24–5)

Larry Kahaner, ''Something in the Air: 'Creeping Degradation' Joins the List of Threats to the Nation's Parks and Forests,'' in Wilderness, *Vol. 52, No. 183, Winter, 1988, pp. 18–27.*

Acid Rain and the Clean Air Act

Acid Rain

Acid rain starts when oxides of sulfur (SO_x) and nitrogen (NO_x) are oxidized in the atmosphere to form acidic sulfates and acidic nitrates. The oxidation results from compounds formed by the interaction between NO_x and volatile organic compounds (VOCs) emitted to the air. The sulfates and nitrates are then deposited on the earth in either dry (attached to particles) or wet (rain, fog, snow) form.

The focus of acid rain research and control efforts has been on sulfur dioxide because this pollutant is most clearly implicated in the acid rain problem; two-thirds of the hydrogen ions (H^+) are associated with sulfur compounds, and one-third of the H^+ is associated with nitrogen compounds (acidity is a function of the preponderance of hydrogen ions). In a 1983 report, the National Academy of Sciences concluded that sulfur compounds were the primary actors in the acidification process. This led to a sulfur-focused research program.

Sulfate is transformed in the air into sulfuric acid. In surface waters, the continuing acidification leads to a decline in pH, and lower pH translates into an increasing loss of plant and animal life in a lake due to a combination of mechanisms, including an aluminum toxicity that results from the leaching of aluminum from the soils in a watershed by the sulfur and nitrogen compounds. It is generally agreed that few fish species can survive in water with a pH below 5.0. The absence of biological life in a lake can lead to the creation of crystal clear lakes—pleasing to the eye, but lacking life. Another process that occurs is acidic deposition on soils; this causes a cation imbalance in the soil which can lead to problems for tree growth because the trees do not get the minerals they need (many other problems are associated with the decline of some forests, including climate, pests, and tropospheric ozone).

Acid rain is also associated with impaired visibility, human health effects (acidic aerosols leading to pulmonary effects), and impacts on materials (*e.g.*, eroding coating film surfaces and some statues).

Emissions of sulfur dioxide totaled approximately 23 million tons in 1985, while emissions of nitrogen oxides were about 20 million tons. The major sources of sulfur dioxide emissions are electric utility plants (about 70%) and industrial processes and fuel combustion (about 25%). Major sources of emissions of nitrogen oxides are transportation (45%), electrical utilities (35%), and industrial processes and fuel combustion (18%).

Sulfur dioxide is formed during the combustion of fossil fuels, primarily coal. Sulfur in the fuel reacts with oxygen to form SO_2; the SO_2 then goes up the stack and into the atmosphere. Oxides of nitrogen are created during the combustion of fossil fuels at high temperatures when nitrogen combines with oxygen. This occurs both in large emitting sources (such as steam-electric boilers) and in automobile engines.

Emissions of sulfur dioxide can be transported through the atmosphere hundred of miles, leading to acid deposition far from the emitting source. Atmospheric transport models have led to the conclusion that much of the emissions from the U.S. Midwest end up being deposited in the northeastern United States and eastern Canada. Acid deposition has become an international problem on the North American continent because there is a two-way flow of acid rain between the United States and Canada.

The U.S. government invested almost $500 million in acid rain research during the [1980s]. This research is coordinated by the National Acid Precipitation Assessment Program (NAPAP), a 10-year research program on the causes and

Problems associated with acid rain include surface water acidification (leading to an absence of biological life, including fish), potential forest decline through cation depletion, visibility impairment, and human health problems associated with the inhalation of acid aerosols and acid rain precursors.

Although there was earlier clean air legislation, the first piece of legislation embodying a strong federal role was the Clean Air Act of 1970. The 1970 act called for tough standards on criteria air pollutants and gave the newly created Environmental Protection Agency broad powers to enforce the laws. The EPA's primary role, however, was to develop rules, regulations, and guidance documents to help states and localities protect the air in their respective political jurisdictions.

effects of acid deposition. NAPAP is composed of representatives of 12 federal agencies and 4 national laboratories, and its research has included work on atmospheric chemistry and transport and on aquatic, forest, materials, and crop effects. The research conducted on acid rain contributed greatly to our understanding of a number of atmospheric and ecosystem processes, particularly watershed and surface water chemistry. (pp. 25–6)

Scientific research has not yielded all of the answers that some people, particularly in the utility and high-sulfur coal mining industries, believe is needed before we take action on acid rain, especially given the potentially large control costs involved—a 10 million ton (9×10^9 kg) annual reduction in the emission of SO_2 from utility plants is expected to cost $3–4 billion or more on an annual basis. On the other hand, many environmentalists, some members of Congress, and others claim that we knew enough years ago to take action on controlling sulfur dioxide emissions to curb acid rain.

There are many interested parties in the acid rain debate, many with significant direct or indirect financial stakes. These include electric utilities, states that are large emitters of sulfur dioxide (*e.g.*, in the Midwest), states that receive acid deposition and suffer environmental damage (*e.g.*, the Northeast), coal mining interests in both the East (where there is both high and low sulfur) and the West (low sulfur), coal miners, people who transport coal, environmental groups (*e.g.*, the Natural Resources Defense Council, Environmental Defense Fund), and the government of Canada. All have lobbied Congress and the administration on acid rain.

There has been little debate over the potential vehicle for acid rain control. The Clean Air Act is clearly the law that everyone has focused on when considering potential acid rain control. There have been disagreements over whether the Clean Air Act, last amended in 1977, needs to be amended in order to deal with the acid rain problem or if there is enough existing authority to address the problem now. President Bush has made his position clear: the Clean Air Act needs to be amended in order to deal with acid rain. Others have long tried to force the Environmental Protection Agency (EPA) to take action on acid rain either directly or indirectly through various sections of the existing Clean Air Act.

The Clean Air Act

Although there was earlier clean air legislation, the first piece of legislation embodying a strong federal role was the Clean Air Act of 1970. The 1970 act called for tough standards on criteria air pollutants and gave the newly created Environmental Protection Agency broad powers to enforce the laws. The EPA's primary role, however, was to develop rules, regulations, and guidance documents to help states and localities protect the air in their respective political jurisdictions. The existing Clean Air Act recognized that states and localities have the primary responsibility for dealing with air pollution because they are seen by many as being most fit to deal with air pollution, which has traditionally been viewed as a local/state problem.

Sulfur dioxide is defined by the Clean Air Act as a criteria pollutant, *i.e.*, a pollutant that is ubiquitous in the environment and has the potential to cause injury to human health and/or the environment. Other criteria pollutants are nitrogen oxides, lead, ozone, particulates, and carbon monoxide. The act allows for setting both primary and secondary standards for criteria pollutants. Primary standards are developed to protect human health. Secondary standards protect the public welfare, which covers damage to such things as crops, forests, and materials.

Primary and secondary air quality standards are referred to as the National Ambient Air Quality Standards (NAAQS). Ambient air refers to the air all around us. NAAQS are expressed as concentration of pollutant per unit of air for a certain time frame (*e.g.*, 0.3 ppm/m^3, 24 h average). The NAAQS are supposed to be met within air quality control regions, which may include more than one state (*e.g.*, around Philadelphia).

Human health at the local level has traditionally been the focus of the Clean Air Act. Sources that have had to comply could relate their expenditures on controls to the well-being of the community that they were a part of. One unintended consequence of this emphasis on local health was the building of tall stacks, which dilute the concentration of SO_2 in the area around the source but lead to the emissions being placed higher in the atmosphere. When the emissions get up into the atmosphere, they are chemically transformed into species that are not criteria pollutants (*e.g.*, sulfate) and transported far away from the emitting source). Like so many environmental problems, no one set out to create acid rain; it evolved as a consequence of burning coal to produce energy and building tall stacks to protect local health. What is clear in hindsight regarding the transport of these materials in the atmosphere was not so clear at the time it was happening.

In the late 1970s and early 1980s, people became more aware of the acid rain problem, and some demanded action. This resulted in the introduction of many acid rain control bills in congress and demands on the EPA to use the existing Clean Air Act to effect an administrative solution to the problem.

Under Section 115 of the Clean Air Act, if there is reason to believe that pollutants from the United States contribute to air pollution that may endanger the public health or welfare in another country, the administrator is expected to give formal notification of this to the governor of the state in which the emissions originate. This notification is intended to lead to a revision of the state implementation plan (detailed under Section 110 of the act) to prevent or eliminate the danger (*e.g.*, to reduce the allowable amount of pollutant discharged from a certain facility). The actions of the administrator and the affected state are contingent upon a finding, by the administrator, that air pollution laws in the affected country afford the United States essentially the same protection as Section 115 provides to foreign countries.

Based on damage to Canada allegedly attributable to U.S. emissions, the EPA has been both sued and petitioned to take action on acid deposition under Section 115 of the Clean Air Act. The parties demanding that the EPA act include nine northeastern states, four environmental groups, and the province of Ontario. (pp. 26–7)

Section 126 of the Clean Air Act deals with interstate air pollution. States may petition the EPA to determine if sources in other states are emitting pollutants that are preventing the petitioner state from attaining or maintaining National Ambient Air Quality Standards or interfering with their visibility or prevention of significant deterioration (PSD) programs. If the Agency makes the finding, the emitting source can be required to reduce emissions. (p. 27)

Approximately 70 different acid rain control bills were introduced in Congress during the 1980s. Combined with the scientific uncertainties, the potential social and economic impacts of reducing the impacts of acid rain have led to a congressional stalemate over the issue. The acid rain debate can be characterized as often polar, with the Northeast *vs.* the Midwest and high-sulfur coal mining interests in the East *vs.* low-sulfur mining interests in the West. A few states (*e.g.*, Wisconsin and Minnesota) have already enacted their own acid rain control legislation.

The President's Acid Rain Proposal

President Bush's acid rain proposal is part of an overall plan to revise the Clean Air Act in order to deal with the three most pressing air pollution problems: acid rain, ozone nonattainment, and air toxics. It is believed that strong presidential leadership on these issues will help to break the legislative stalemate that has characterized the debate.

The president's decision to propose new legislation dealing with acid rain represents an acknowledgment that the existing Clean Air Act is not suited to dealing with the problem. With its primary emphasis on local air pollution and state implementation plans, the present act is not the proper vehicle for ad-

President Bush's acid rain proposal is part of an overall plan to revise the Clean Air Act in order to deal with the three most pressing air pollution problems: acid rain, ozone nonattainment, and air toxics. It is believed that strong presidential leadership on these issues will help to break the legislative stalemate that has characterized the debate.

The existing Clean Air Act was primarily designed to deal with air pollution at the local and state level, but acid rain is an environmental problem that transcends state and international boundries: emissions contribute to the acid deposition problem in areas hundreds of miles away.

dressing an interregional and international air pollution problem with hundreds of emitting sources and various receptors. (p. 28)

Emissions trading is a key component of the president's acid rain proposal. Under the emission trading provisions, utilities that achieve reductions in excess of their allowed emissions may transfer these excess "allowances" to other plants in their system or sell them to other companies. The marketplace will establish the price for these allowances. The per ton fee for exceeding one's allowed emission level will be $2,000.

Who pays for these emission reductions is, to some, the key question. The president's proposal reflects the proposition that the polluter should pay. In the case of acid rain, this means that the burden of paying for emission reductions should be borne by those utilities (and their customers) who currently have the highest emission levels and would be subject to emission reduction requirements. Many argue that acid rain is a national problem and that everyone should help to pay to control it, perhaps by a fee on electricity consumption, usually expressed as 1/10 of a cent (a mill) per kilowatt hour.

In Conclusion

The existing Clean Air Act was primarily designed to deal with air pollution at the local and state level, but acid rain is an environmental problem that transcends state and international boundaries: emissions contribute to the acid deposition problem in areas hundred of miles away. The problems associated with acid rain include surface water acidification (leading to an absence of biological life, including fish), potential forest decline through cation depletion, visibility impairment, and human health problems associated with the inhalation of acid aerosols and acid rain precursors. . . .

In letters to the president and the EPA, members of Congress have expressed various concerns about the acid rain portion of the president's Clean Air Act proposal, including potential job losses in high-sulfur coal mining and the financing of the pollution control costs. The concerns are about how to make acid rain control work rather than about the need to enact legislation. (p. 29)

Dennis A. Leaf, "Acid Rain and the Clean Air Act," in Chemical Engineering Progress, *Vol. 86, No. 5, May, 1990, pp. 25–9.*

Sources For Further Study

Agren, Christer. "Acid Rain, Aluminum and Senile Dementia." *Acid News*, Nos. 1–2 (August 1987): 18–19.
    Considers the results of a study conducted in Norway that notes a correlation between acidification, aluminum in drinking water, and the incidence of senile dementia.

Burney, Derek. "Canada and the United States in a Global Context: Acid Rain." *Vital Speeches* LVI, No. 2 (1 November 1989): 43–5.
    Text of a speech by the Canadian ambassador to the United States, noting that the two countries share a history of efforts to achieve stability in the economic, military, and environmental sectors and asserts that these efforts must be directed toward solving the problem of acid rain.

Conrad, Jim. "An Acid-Rain Trilogy." *American Forests* 93, Nos. 11–12 (November–December 1987): 21–3, 77–9.
    Explores the role of acid rain in the phenomenon of "forest death" in Germany's Black Forest and on Mount Mitchell in North Carolina and proposes "a philosophy for change" to address the problem.

"A Twist of Lime in a Cocktail of Troubles." *The Economist* 311, No. 7604 (27 May 1989): 85–6.
> Discusses the practice of treating acidified land and water with lime to counteract the effects of acidity.

"Acid Rain Affects Coastal Waters Too." *Environment* 30, No. 5 (June 1988): 22.
> Identifies acid rain as a serious threat to the quality of coastal waters and marine life in the eastern United States.

Howells, Gwyneth. *Acid Rain and Acid Waters.* New York: Ellis Horwood, 1990, 215 p.
> Extensive scholarly and scientific examination of all aspects of the issue of acid rain and acidification of aquatic systems.

Huckabee, John W., et al. "An Assessment of the Ecological Effects of Acidic Deposition." *Archives of Environmental Contamination and Toxicology* 18, No. 1–2 (January–April 1989): 3–27.
> Summarizes research into the ecological effects of acid rain and other acidic precipitation, particularly on plant life, wildlife, and soil and air quality.

Irwin, J. G. "Acid Rain: Emissions and Deposition." *Archives of Environmental Contamination and Toxicology* 18, No. 1–2 (January–April 1989): 95–107.
> Technical account of how models have been developed to map patterns of acidic depositions.

Longhurst, J. W. S., ed. *Acid Deposition: Sources, Effects, and Controls.* Eynsham, Oxford: British Library Technical Communications, 1989, 348 p.
> Includes several chapters under the headings "Acid Deposition: Chemistry and Monitoring," "Freshwater Acidification," "Soils and Forest Systems," "Structural Systems," and "Control Technologies."

Marquardt, W., and Ihle, P. "Acid and Alkaline Precipitation Components in the Mesoscale Range under the Aspect of Meteorological Factors and the Emissions." *Atmospheric Environment* 22, No. 12 (1988): 2707–713.
> Technical discussion of the long-range transmission of contaminants that result in acid rain.

Park, Chris C. *Acid Rain: Rhetoric and Reality.* London: Methuen & Co., 1987, 272 p.
> Extensively researched examination of the acid rain issue. Park includes sections devoted to the acid rain debate in the political, scientific, and business communities; sources of acid rain; its effects water, soil, vegetation, structures, and humans; and explorations of possible solutions. A thorough bibliography of current scholarship on the issue is also included.

Raloff, J. "Acid Rain: Lowdown on Health of Lakes." *Science News* 135, No. 20 (20 May 1989): 311.
> Notes indications that acid rain is contributing to ecosystem decline in many northeastern United States lakes.

Rao, Salem S., ed. *Acid Stress and Aquatic Microbial Interactions.* Boca Raton, Fla.: CRC Press, 1989, 176 p.
> Includes nine reports from some preeminent investigators into microbial acid rain research.

Scott, Wayne. "Acid Rain: What We Know, What We Did, What We Will Do." *Archives of Environmental Contamination and Toxicology* 18, Nos. 1–2 (January–April 1989): 75–82.
> Reviews successful Canadian programs to reduce acid gas emissions, establish strict regulations on such emissions, and work with the United States toward further reductions.

Tan, Barrie. "Extent and Effect of Acid Precipitation in Northeastern United States and Eastern Canada." *Archives of Environmental Contamination and Toxicology* 18, Nos. 1–2 (January–April 1989): 55–63.
> Assesses the range and effect of acid rain on the regions specified.

Tangley, Laura. "Acid Rain Threatens Marine Life." *BioScience* 38, No. 8 (September 1988): 538–39.
  Notes that acid rain, long recognized as a threat to freshwater ecosystems, is increasingly harmful to marine systems as well.

Wellburn, Alan. *Air Pollution and Acid Rain: The Biological Impact.* Harlow, Essex: Longman Scientific & Technical, 1988, 274 p.
  Examines the effect of specific atmospheric pollutants on living organisms, particularly focusing on those pollutants that make up acid rain.

2:   Air Pollution

Clearing the Air

At a time when issues like global warming and ozone depletion dominate the headlines, air pollution and acid rain can sound like yesterday's problems. Unfortunately, evidence to the contrary is widespread. In the West, efforts to combat air pollution since the first outpouring of concern in the early seventies have been only marginally successful. In Eastern Europe, the Soviet Union, and much of the developing world, air pollution is only beginning to be recognized as worthy of serious attention.

Severe health problems related to air pollution span continents and levels of development: In the United States, some 150 million people breathe air considered unhealthy by the Environmental Protection Agency (EPA). In greater Athens, the number of deaths is six times higher on heavily polluted days than on those when the air is relatively clear. In Hungary, a recent report by the National Institute of Public Health concluded that every twenty-fourth disability and every seventeenth death in Hungary is caused by air pollution. In India, breathing the air in Bombay is equivalent to smoking 10 cigarettes a day. And in Mexico, the capital city is considered a hardship post for diplomats because of its unhealthy air, and some governments advise women not to plan on having children while posted there.

The environmental impacts of air pollution are equally grave. Acid rain and air pollution are devastating forests, crops, lakes, and buildings over wide areas of Europe and North America. Indications are that the Third World may be next in line for widespread damage.

The one constant in the air pollution story over the years has been its growing complexity. Just as one problem seems to be coming under control, a new one arises to replace it. In the West, combating smoke and soot emissions from coal-fired factories and heating greatly improved urban air quality, at least until auto-induced pollution emerged as the primary barrier to clean air. Similarly, building tall smokestacks that spew pollutants far away from cities seemed at first an unqualified boon for air quality. But the solution to one problem was the genesis of another: it turned out that sulfur dioxide (SO_2) and nitrogen oxides (NO_x) could be transformed in the atmosphere into acid-forming particles that fall to earth far from their source in what is popularly known as acid rain.

Now industrial nations are waking up to another front in the battle for clean air—airborne toxic chemical emissions. Though the full dimensions of this problem are as yet unknown, recently released data suggest that billions of tons of harmful chemicals are commonly emitted into the air by industries. Once out the stack, these chemicals can be swept by the wind hundreds and even thousands of kilometers from their source before eventually falling to earth.

Acid rain concerns transformed what had once been a national or even a local issue into an international one. Now the need to slow the buildup of heat-trapping greenhouse gases has added a supranational dimension to the air

The one constant in the air pollution story over the years has been its growing complexity. Just as one problem seems to be coming under control, a new one arises to replace it.

Recent U.S. research suggests that ozone causes short-term breathing difficulty and long-term lung damage in lower concentrations than previously believed.

---

debate. Because both air pollution and global warming stem largely from common roots in energy, transportation, and industrial systems, the two problems are properly considered together when examining policy options. It would be particularly foolhardy to adopt air pollution strategies that might undermine efforts to slow global warming.

On this twentieth anniversary of Earth Day, it is useful to look at what has been accomplished around the world in the realm of air pollution control—and what remains to be done. The conclusions apply not only to the West, but also to Eastern Europe and the developing world, which have the enviable opportunity to learn from the mistakes of others.

The Global Health Threat

That air pollution could cause serious health problems first became evident during the industrial revolution, when many cities in Europe and the United States were covered with black shrouds of coal-derived smoke. On days with weather conducive to pollution, sickness and even death were omnipresent. A particularly acute episode of "black fog" in London in 1952 claimed 4,000 lives and left tens of thousands ill.

Incidents such as this prompted many governments to enact legislation to combat the primary pollutants of the day, sulfur dioxide (SO_2) and particulate emissions from stationary sources such as power plants, industries, and home furnaces. Both SO_2 and particulates—either alone or in combination—can raise the incidence of respiratory diseases such as coughs and colds, asthma, bronchitis, and emphysema. Particulate matter (an overall term for a complex and varying measurable mixture of pollutants in minute solid form) can carry heavy metals into the deepest, most sensitive part of the lung.

With the aid of pollution control equipment and improvements in energy efficiency, many industrial countries have made major strides in reducing emissions of these harmful pollutants. The United States, for example, cut sulfur oxide emissions by 28 percent between 1970 and 1987 and that of particulates by 62 percent. In Japan, sulfur dioxide emissions fell by 39 percent from 1973 to 1984. Many West European countries also reduced significantly their emissions in both categories from power plants, industries, and heating of buildings. In certain European cities, however, the widespread introduction of diesel-fueled vehicles, which emit large quantities of particulates and some SO_2, threatens to negate earlier gains.

In Eastern Europe and the Soviet Union, hasty industrialization after World War II powered by the natural endowment of high-sulfur brown coal led to air quality reminiscent of London's "black fog." The lack of a market price signal prevented these countries from realizing the impressive gains in energy efficiency registered in the West after the oil shocks of the seventies, and financial constraints still make investments in pollution control a rarity.

Though emissions data for developing countries are scarce, air quality in many cities is already abysmal. Rapid plans to expand energy and industrial production and the lack of adequate pollution control regulations mean that air quality could get even worse. (p. 98–100)

Nations that built tall stacks to improve local air quality may have simply sent their health problems elsewhere: though acid precipitation is best known as an ecological threat it is also suspected of having grave health repercussions. Sulfur dioxide can be chemically transformed into fine sulfate particles that mix with water in the air, liquefy, and become aerosols that can penetrate the deepest, most delicate tissues of the lungs, bringing toxic metals and gases along with them. Some researchers believe the mix may be responsible for as many as 50,000 deaths in the United States every year—2 percent of total annual mortality. (p. 101)

Pollutants that stem predominantly from cars have been fought around the world even less successfully than sulfur dioxide and particulates. Ozone—a gas formed when hydrocarbons (a product of imperfect combustion in vehicle engines and a by-product of many industrial processes) react with nitrogen oxides (produced by both cars and power plants) in the presence of sunlight—is one of the most worrying pollutants in many areas. Recent U.S. research suggests that ozone causes short-term breathing difficulty and long-term lung damage in lower concentrations than previously believed. Other pollutants of concern emitted in substantial quantity by automobiles include carbon monoxide, nitrogen dioxide by itself, lead, and toxic hydrocarbons such as benzene, toluene, xylene, and ethylene dibromide. (pp. 101–02)

Emissions of carbon monoxide and nitrogen oxides remain a problem even where catalytic converters have been introduced on cars—Australia, Austria, Canada, Japan, Norway, South Korea, Sweden, Switzerland, and the United States—not to mention those where they have not. . . .

By fortuitous coincidence, cars equipped with catalytic converters cannot tolerate leaded gas. Where they are mandatory, the use of lead-free gas has resulted in impressive emissions reductions, with unequivocal benefits to human health. In the United States, lead emissions fell by 96 percent between 1970 and 1987 as a result of this relationship, in conjunction with national legislation requiring steep reductions in the lead content of gas burned in old cars not equipped with converters. As a result, the average lead level in Americans' blood dropped by more than one third between 1976 and 1980. (p. 103)

In the United States, long-overdue attention is finally being paid to the health threat posed by airborne toxic chemicals from industrial sources. Such chemicals—which can cause cancer and birth and genetic defects—have often fallen through the regulatory crack. The current wave of concern has been fueled by EPA's recent announcement that 2.7 billion pounds of hazardous pollutants were released into the air by industries in 1987, including 235 million pounds of known cancer-causing chemicals. Even this number is an underestimate, as it omits sources such as waste dumps, dry cleaners, and cars, and releases into soil or water that enter the air through evaporation. The true number may be in excess of 4.8 billion pounds annually, EPA admits.

In a 1987 study, the agency concluded that air toxic emissions may cause 2,000 cancer deaths a year. Because the study tallied the effects of only a third of the carcinogenic chemicals, it was likely an underestimate. If all the hundreds of chemicals emitted into the air had been included and their synergistic effects considered, the number would probably be far higher. Other studies have found high cancer rates in communities near certain types of factories in West Virginia and Louisiana. (pp. 103–04)

Airborne toxic chemical emissions are likely to rise rapidly in developing countries as polluting industries are built. The Third World's share of world iron and steel production rose from 3.6 percent in 1955 to 17.3 percent in 1984. In India, pesticide production increased from 1,460 tons in 1960 to 40,680 in 1980—nearly thirtyfold. Production of dyes and pigments grew at a comparable pace over the same period, reaching 30,850 tons by 1980. Most of these countries have few pollution controls and little environmental regulation.

Recent evidence suggests that toxic air emissions—like acid deposition—can be carried great distances before falling to the ground. This explains in part why DDT, presumably blown in from Central America or Mexico, is being found in the Great Lakes years after the pesticide was banned in the United States and Canada. And why researchers at McGill University in Montreal have found DDT and polychlorinated biphenyls throughout the Eskimos' food chain, including in bears, fish, berries, and snow.

Putting a dollar value on all these health costs of air pollution is difficult, as it involves judgments about the worth of good health and human life. The few guesses made suggest a very high price. Thomas Crocker of the University of Wyoming, for one, estimates that air pollution costs the United States as much as $40 billion annually in health care and lost productivity. A study conducted

Emissions of carbon monoxide and nitrogen oxides remain a problem even where catalytic converters have been introduced on cars, not to mention those where they have not.

for Los Angeles officials concluded that the proposed air quality management plan for the region would save $9.4 billion a year in health care expenses—more than three times what it is projected to cost.

The Ecological Toll

Though concern for human health was the motivating factor behind the world's first control laws, the last 20 years have demonstrated that air pollution poses an equally grave threat to the natural and built environments. Ecosystems are actually often damaged at lower levels of pollution than humans are, a fact not yet adequately reflected in air pollution standards. Fishless lakes and streams, dying forests, and faceless ancient sculptures all provide sad testament to the destruction that industrialization has wrought.

The first warning came in the late sixties, when scientists in Scandinavia began to suspect that SO_2 emissions from the more urban and industrialized countries of Europe, such as the United Kingdom and West Germany, might be responsible for declining fish stocks in their lakes. American scientists who soon did extensive studies of acidity at the Hubbard Brook Experimental Forest in New Hampshire found similar ominous indications. Extensive investigations in the seventies revealed that acid deposition was indeed acidifying water and killing fish and other aquatic organisms in geologically susceptible areas of Scandinavia and North America.

In recent years, large areas of the world have been found to fall into this worrying category of "geologically susceptible." In the United States, much of the Great Lakes region, several southeastern states, and many of the mountainous areas of the West appear to be at risk, in addition to the Northeast, where damage has been evident for some time. Half the 700,000 lakes in the six eastern provinces of Canada are deemed extremely acid-sensitive, as are large areas in all western provinces, the Yukon, the Northwest Territories, and Labrador. In Europe, similarly vulnerable parts of the Netherlands, Belgium, Denmark, Switzerland, Italy, West Germany, and Ireland have been added to the better known areas of Scandinavia and the United Kingdom. Vast parts of Asia, Africa, and South America are also acid-sensitive. (pp. 104–06)

Recent evidence suggests that the threat to coastal waters may be of similar magnitude. A 1988 study by the Environmental Defense Fund concluded that acid deposition is a major contributor to the degradation of the Chesapeake Bay. By a process known as eutrophication, nitrogen from a variety of sources "fertilizes" algae to the extent that it chokes off the oxygen supply and blocks the sunlight required by other aquatic plants and animals. The study found that airborne nitrates account for fully 25 percent of the total nitrogen load currently entering the Chesapeake. If emissions continue their upward climb, this share will rise to 42 percent by the year 2030. Other research has shown that 27 percent of the Baltic Sea's nitrogen load comes from the air.

In the early eighties, concern about the possible effects of acid deposition spread from lakes and streams to forests. Signs of widespread damage attributed to acid deposition first arose in West Germany. The share of forests there showing signs of damage rose from 8 percent in 1982, the first year a survey was done, to 34 percent in 1983, to 50 percent by the following year. It peaked in 1986, at 54 percent, and has since declined slightly—to 52 percent in 1988. Because dead trees are not included in the surveys, however, slightly lower percentages do not necessarily mean an improving situation.

Wide public debate about the causes and consequences of forest decline followed its discovery. Though the exact mechanisms are still not precisely understood, most scientists believe a complex mixture of pollutants—including acid deposition, ozone, and heavy metals—renders forests susceptible to a range of natural stresses, such as droughts, extremes of heat and cold, and blights, that combine to cause the decline. Though initial fears of massive forest death throughout the continent have not been borne out, a high economic and ecological toll has already been paid. (p. 106)

Though concern for human health was the motivating factor behind the world's first control laws, the last 20 years have demonstrated that air pollution poses an equally grave threat to the natural and built environments. Ecosystems are actually often damaged at lower levels of pollution than humans are, a fact not yet adequately reflected in air pollution standards.

The economic toll to the forestry and tourism industries is potentially enormous. Environmental scientists in Poland predict that forest loss will cost the country $1.5 billion by 1992. Economists Werner Schulz and Lutz Wicke estimate that forest damage will cost West Germany between 5.5 and 8.8 billion deutsche marks ($2.98–4.77 billion) annually over the next 70 years depending upon how strictly emissions are controlled. The losses are not only monetary: Fichtelberg Mountain along the East German and Czechoslovakian border once attracted many visitors who scaled it to marvel at the view. "Now they weep," writes Mike Leary of the *Philadelphia Inquirer*. "What a horrible tragedy," said one woman gazing from the summit at the view below: a huge expanse of dead trees and broad brown patches where forests once stood.

In addition to forests, air pollution also threatens crops. Ozone is the primary concern, although SO_2, nitrogen oxides, and sulfates and nitrates are also thought to be potentially harmful. The most comprehensive studies on this have been conducted in the United States. A 1987 government report by the National Acid Precipitation Assessment Program concluded that current levels of ozone were reducing crop yields by 1 percent or less for sorghum and corn, by about 7 percent for cotton and soybean, and by more than 30 percent for alfalfa. Total crop losses were estimated to be in the range of 5–10 percent of production. According to one estimate, this represents an economic loss of some $5.4 billion.

Reports of similar damage in the Third World are starting to be heard. Damage in China's southwest forests is being increasingly linked by scientists to air pollution and acid rain caused by a heavy reliance on high-sulfur coal. In Sichuan's Maocaoba pine forest, more than 90 percent of the trees have died. On Nanshan hill in Chongqing, the biggest city in southwest China, an 1,800-hectare forest of dense masson pine has been reduced by almost half. Both these regions have highly acidic rain and elevated levels of sulfur dioxide. (pp. 107–09)

Elevated levels of acidity and ozone have been found in tropical rain forests. In Latin America, the pollution is attributed to the enormous fires that rage as cattle ranchers and settlers clear land. In Africa, it stems from fires that burn for months across thousands of kilometers of African savannas. They are set by farmers and herders to clear shrubs and permit the growth of crops and grass. Tropical areas are thought to be especially vulnerable to acidification, because their soils are naturally low in buffering agents.

In contrast to damage to lakes and forests, that to the built environment is most frequently a local problem. Sulfur dioxide and its acidic chemical derivatives are believed to be the chief culprits, though nitrogen oxides, ozone, and other pollutants also contribute.

Corrosion of historical monuments is particularly evident in Europe—from the Acropolis, to the Royal Palace in Amsterdam, to the medieval buildings and monuments of Krakow, Poland. Although some decay is to be expected in structures dating to antiquity, pollution is greatly speeding the process. T. N. Skoulikidis, a Greek specialist on acid corrosion, has estimated that Athenian monuments have deteriorated more in the past 20–25 years from pollution than in the previous 2,400. Damage to historical artifacts and edifices is evident throughout Italy. "Classic marble busts," says *New York Times* correspondent Paul Hofmann, are being "transmogrified into noseless and earless plaster grotesques." . . .

In the United States, air pollution may prevent the nation's historical monuments from ever reaching the ripe old age of Europe's. Already, Independence Hall in Philadelphia, where the Declaration of Independence was signed, is experiencing damage. At the Gettysburg Civil War battlefield, every statue or tablet made of bronze, limestone, or sandstone is being slowly but inexorably eaten away. Both the Statue of Liberty and the Washington Monument are also reportedly threatened.

Again, the Third World is following the example of the First. The Taj Mahal appears to be endangered by emissions from an upwind oil refinery that are

In the western, industrial world, the last 20 years has been a period of intensive political and scientific activity aimed at clearing the air. The approaches to date, however, have tended to be technological Band-Aids rather than efforts to address the roots of the problem: inappropriate energy, transportation, and industrial systems.

Energy efficiency is an essential strategy for reducing emissions from power plants, though it is rarely promoted as such.

eroding its marble and sandstone surfaces. Recent research has found that acid rain falling on the Yucatan Peninsula and much of southern Mexico is destroying the temples, murals, and megaliths of the Mayans. The primary source of the damaging emissions is believed to be uncapped Mexican oil wells andoil-field smokestacks near Coatzacoalcos and Ciudad del Carmen on the Gulf of Mexico. Exhaust from tour buses is also thought to contribute to the decay. (p. 109)

Reduction Strategies

The tremendous damage to health and environment inflicted by air pollution and acid rain has not been lost on the public or on policymakers. In the western, industrial world, the last 20 years has been a period of intensive political and scientific activity aimed at clearing the air. The approaches to date, however, have tended to be technological Band-Aids rather than efforts to address the roots of the problem: inappropriate energy, transportation, and industrial systems. Though they have achieved some success, a more comprehensive strategy will be needed to confront the air quality challenges of the nineties.

The most widespread technological intervention has been the introduction of electrostatic precipitators and baghouse filters for the control of particulate emissions from power plants. Their use is now required in virtually all OECD countries (Western Europe, the United States, Canada, and Japan). Though such technologies can reduce particulate emissions directly from the smokestack by as much as 99.5 percent, they do nothing to prevent acidic particles such as sulfates and nitrates from forming outside the smokestack from gaseous emissions. Such particles can wreak particularly great harm on both human health and the environment.

The predominant technique used to reduce sulfur dioxide has been to put fluegas desulfurization (FGD) technology, popularly known as scrubbers, on coal-burning power plants. Scrubbers can remove as much as 95 percent of a given plant's SO_2 emissions. Among members of OECD, nearly 140,000 megawatts of power plant capacity were either equipped with FGD or had it under construction at the beginning of 1988. The United States led in total "scrubbed" capacity, with 62,000 megawatts. But only 20 percent of the total U.S. coal-fired capacity was equipped with scrubbers as of January 1987, compared with roughly 40 percent in West Germany, 50 percent in Sweden, 60 percent in Austria, and 85 percent in Japan. By the end of the decade, the figures will be 70 percent in Italy, 85 percent in West Germany, 100 percent in the Netherlands, but still only 30 percent in the United States. (p. 110)

Though the technologies just outlined provide necessary immediate reductions, they are not the ultimate solution. For one, they can create environmental problems of their own, such as the need to dispose of scrubber ash, a hazardous waste. Second, they do little if anything to reduce carbon dioxide emissions, so make no significant contribution to solving global warming. For these reasons, they are best viewed as a bridge to the day when energy-efficient societies are the norm and when renewable sources such as solar, wind, and water power provide the bulk of the world's energy.

Energy efficiency is an essential strategy for reducing emissions from power plants, though it is rarely promoted as such. The American Council for an Energy-Efficient Economy (ACEEE) has identified cost-effective, widely available conservation measures that could bring electricity demand 15 percent below utility forecasts in a region of the U.S. Midwest that is responsible for 33 percent of the nation's utility-generated sulfur dioxide emissions. Implementing this amount of conservation would cut SO_2 emissions by 7–11 percent between 1992 and 2002 and NO_x emissions by an undetermined amount.

Equally important, the savings resulting from avoided power plant construction can more than offset the cost of emissions controls at existing plants. Indeed, ACEEE found that consumers in the Midwest could realize a net savings of $4–8 billion if emissions control and accelerated conservation were both pursued as part of a national effort to halve SO_2 emissions, as compared with a scenario in which neither occur. Emissions control in the absence of efficiency investments would run in the billions of dollars.

Around the world, it is essential that governments put economic incentives for energy reform into place as part of their air quality strategies. One way of doing that would be to allow utilities that reduce customers' bills through efficiency investments to earn a slightly higher rate of return than otherwise. Another is by market-based power planning systems that incorporate environmental costs, thereby encouraging both efficiency and renewable energy. The State of New York is already pioneering this approach: fossil-fuel-based generating sources in two utility regions in the state must add nearly a penny per kilowatt-hour to their costs to account for air pollution and an additional half a cent per kilowatt-hour to account for other environmental externalities.

Though materials recycling has caught the public's attention as a way to save on scarce landfill space, its pollution prevention potential is equally important. Each ton of newsprint made from waste rather than wood lowers energy use by one fourth to three fifths and air pollutants by some 75 percent. Aluminum produced from recycled cans rather than virgin ore cuts emissions of nitrogen oxides by 95 percent and of sulfur dioxide by 99 percent.

When it comes to reducing automotive pollution, a similar preventive approach is needed. To date, engine modifications and catalytic converters have been the principal strategies used to lower harmful emissions. However, even in countries that have mandated converters—which reduce a car's hydrocarbon emissions by an average of 87 percent, carbon monoxide emissions by an average of 85 percent, and nitrogen oxides by 62 percent over the life of a vehicle—rising vehicle fleets are overwhelming their efficacy. In addition, converters actually slightly increase carbon dioxide emissions. Again, more fundamental additional measures are required.

Most basically, reducing urban air pollution may require a major shift away from automobiles as the cornerstone of transportation systems. As congestion increases exponentially in most major cities, driving to work is becoming increasingly unattractive anyway. Convenient public transportation, increased car pooling, and facilitated bicycle commuting are for many cities the cheapest, most effective, most sensible way to proceed. (pp. 111–12)

Short of an all-out ban on private cars in downtown areas, city governments can encourage commuters to leave their cars at home by making public transportation inexpensive and convenient. Eradicating or taxing free parking benefits and collecting hefty tolls for road use are other means toward this end. (pp. 112–13)

Probably the most effective incentive for waste reduction is strict regulation of disposal into the land, air, and water. This will force up the price of disposal, making it cost-effective for industries to reduce waste generation. Certain economic incentives could also help. For example, a "deposit-refund" system might be put in place whereby industries would be taxed on the purchase of hazardous inputs, but refunded for wastes produced from them that are recovered or recycled.

Experience in the United States has shown that public access to information about what chemicals a plant is emitting can be instrumental in spurring a response: within weeks of its release of the information on emissions mandated under right-to-know legislation, Monsanto announced its intention to cut back its toxic air emissions by 90 percent by 1992.

Most European countries have yet to provide for the release of information about emissions from industrial plants, although the European Economic Community (EEC) is reported to be considering a draft directive on freedom of information on environmental matters that would improve this somewhat. Glasnost is gradually improving the environmental data flow in some of Eastern Europe and in the Soviet Union, though much progress in this area remains to be made. Grassroots groups in some developing countries are also beginning to break down the secrecy barriers.

Around the world, it is essential that governments put economic incentives for energy reform into place as part of their air quality strategies.

The experience of the past several decades may not indicate as much, but air pollution is an eminently solvable problem. Tinkering with the present system, however, will simply not be adequate. A comprehensive approach will be necessary that focuses on pollution prevention rather than pollution control.

Mobilizing for Cleaner Air

Though the time seems ripe for reform of the current approach to air pollution control, few policymakers are considering implementation of the comprehensive strategies that are necessary. Recent developments at the national and international levels—though steps forward—remain inadequate to the task at hand.

In the United States, Congress is currently debating major amendments to the 1970 Clean Air Act. The long-stalled process was given a boost by the Bush administration, which submitted a plan of its own for Congress to consider. This active presidential leadership, combined with strong public support for strengthened environmental regulations, has raised hopes that legislation will soon be in place that will halve emissions that cause acid rain, tighten emissions standards for automobiles significantly, and require much stricter control of toxic air pollutants.

Though any legislation is an improvement over the status quo, the administration's proposal misses the opportunity to address the problem at a fundamental level through energy efficiency, transportation reform, and waste reduction. From this point of view, the acid rain provisions are probably the most promising, as they would give the utilities their choice of control technique, including energy efficiency. Positive incentives, however, could have helped make this the clear first choice for utilities rather than simply one of many options.

Because air pollution crosses European borders with impunity, international cooperation on reducing emissions is essential. For example, 96 percent of the sulfur deposited in Norway originates in other countries. The Norwegians can thus do little to save their lakes without the help of troublesome neighbors. (pp. 114–15)

Though Europe has been quicker than the United States in addressing acid rain, it has for the most part been much slower to tackle urban air quality problems. Non-EEC countries such as Austria, Norway, Sweden, and Switzerland have had strong auto emissions control legislation in place for several years, but the Community has been unable to agree on stringent standards.

This finally changed in June 1989, when the EEC Council of Environmental Ministers ended a nearly four-year debate and approved new standards for small cars that will be as tough as those now in effect in the United States. To meet them, small cars will have to be equipped with catalytic converters. Though standards for large cars were already on the books, the EEC Environment Commissioner is considering stricter ones for medium and large cars as well. A Community-wide speed limit is also being looked at as an air pollution control measure. Although clearly a step forward, it is somewhat ironic that Europe sees its adoption of U.S. standards as a major victory at the same time that the United States is realizing these regulations do not go far enough.

Los Angeles—with the worst air quality in the United States—is one of the first regions in the world to really understand that lasting change will not come by tinkering with the status quo. Under a bold new air quality plan, automobile use will be discouraged, public transportation boosted, and household and industrial activities that produce emissions tightly controlled. For example, paints and solvents will have to be reformulated, gasoline-powered lawn mowers and barbecues and fuels that require lighter fluid will be banned, and the number of cars per family limited.

In Eastern Europe and the Soviet Union, air pollution has only recently emerged as a potent political issue. Fyodor Morgun, then head of the Soviet Union's State Committee on the Protection of Nature, reported to the Nineteenth Communist Party conference in July 1988 that air pollution levels in 102 Soviet cities, affecting more than 50 million people, were often 10 times higher than the Soviet standard. This official recognition of the problem was an important step forward. Similarly, when Solidarity sat down with the Polish government in March 1989 for the Round Table discussions, environmental issues in general and air pollution in particular figured prominently on the agenda: a fact of enormous significance. More than rhetoric, however, will clearly be necessary to solve the problems. (pp. 116–17)

Air pollution is just beginning to emerge on the political agenda in Third World cities as well. Though the challenge is enormous, at least the issue is starting to be addressed. In Cubatão, Brazil, a notoriously polluted industrial city known as "the Valley of Death," a five-year-old government clean-up campaign is starting to make a dent in the problem. Total emissions of particulates were cut from 236,600 kilograms a day in 1984 to 70,782 in 1989. Mexico City, too, is embarking on an ambitious cleanup. With the support of the World Bank and the German, Japanese, and United States governments, the municipal government hopes to introduce a package of measures to cut automotive pollution dramatically over the next two to three years. (pp. 117–18)

In attempting to help Eastern Europe, the Soviet Union, and the Third World with air pollution problems, western industrial countries should not simply transfer wholesale the pollution control strategies that have not been entirely successful at home. An ill-conceived approach such as this could do more harm than good.

The experience of the past several decades may not indicate as much, but air pollution is an eminently solvable problem. Tinkering with the present system, however, will simply not be adequate. A comprehensive approach will be necessary that focuses on pollution prevention rather than pollution control. Though such a strategy will require some investment, the payback will be great. Faced with ever mounting costs to human health and the environment, the question is not how can society afford to control air pollution. How can we afford not to? (p. 118)

Hilary F. French, "Clearing the Air," in State of the World: A Worldwatch Institute Report on Progress Toward a Sustainable Society, *1990, pp. 98–118.*

> Do the health hazards and the damage to crops, forests, and lakes cry out for legislation that could cost industry and consumers up to $19 billion a year by the mid-1990s?

Air: How Clean Is Clean Enough?

George Bush campaigned as a foursquare environmentalist [in 1988], claiming that he wants to be the most ecology-minded occupant of the White House since Teddy Roosevelt. Congress is more than eager to go along. After eight years of inactivity, it is primed to make the air fresher and the world brighter. But does the evidence justify the expense of the President's new clean-air proposals? Do the health hazards and the damage to crops, forests, and lakes cry out for legislation that could cost industry and consumers up to $19 billion a year by the mid-1990s?

Compared with other threats—drug gangs, slum schools, the budget and trade deficits—a tainted atmosphere seems less urgent. Besides, this is one enemy that is on the run, thanks to the $34 billion a year the U.S. already spends on pollution abatement. But the progress appears to be slowing. *Some* acceleration of the cleanup makes sense, even though the research so far—some of it frightening—is largely inconclusive.

Among the President's goals:

● Drastically reducing airborne toxic chemicals. About half these substances—a grab bag of 320 poisons—emanate from industry. By applying the best abatement techniques or devices available, factories would reduce their wastes so that cancer deaths associated with them—1,500 to 3,000 a year, the Environmental Protection Agency says—would fall 75% to 90% by the mid-1990s.

Bush's offensive against ozone, the most persistent of the main pollutants, is hard to quarrel with. It is also difficult to oppose the President's clampdown on air toxics, which are believed to be linked to respiratory illnesses and birth defects as well as to cancer. But in the proposal to wring out acid rain, the politics have leaped ahead of the science.

- Cutting sulfur dioxide emissions, the main ingredient in acid rain, almost in half by the year 2000. Coal-burning electric utilities in the Midwest and Appalachia would carry out and pay for most of the cleanup. Power companies would also have to reduce nitrogen oxides, another contributor to acid rain escaping from their stacks.

- Breaking an impasse on ozone. A saint in the stratosphere, where it filters radiation from space, ozone is an irredeemable sinner at ground level, where it is the nastiest ingredient in smog. Some 81 urban areas theoretically face federal "sanctions"—bans on new factories, for one—because they have been unable to reduce maximum ozone readings to an EPA health standard that was set in 1979. The President wants stricter controls on auto tailpipe emissions, from which ozone forms, and on fuel vapors that escape from vehicles and gas stations. His plan would also phase in methanol (which is easily made from natural gas) and other clean-burning motor fuels, and would restrict the use of volatile, ozone-creating chemicals at petroleum refineries, paint shops, and dry-cleaning establishments. Under the cleanup plan all but the three most ozone-prone cities would meet the EPA standard by the year 2000. The exceptions—Los Angeles, Houston, and New York City—would get a reprieve until 2010.

Bush's offensive against ozone, the most persistent of the main pollutants, is hard to quarrel with. It is also difficult to oppose the President's clampdown on air toxics, which are believed to be linked to respiratory illnesses and birth defects as well as to cancer. But in the proposal to wring out acid rain, the politics have leaped ahead of the science. Proof that acid rain is murdering trees and fish is still not established. And while Washington worries about mountain lakes, concerns about the *health* effects of sulfur dioxide have been widely overlooked.

For all its ambition, the Administration's plan is not as drastic as clean-air bills already circulating in Congress. Nor does it embrace some of the draconian steps that Los Angeles authorities have called for in a 20-year smog-fighting plan, which may ultimately require electric cars on those ten-lane freeways.

Commendably, the Bush plan allows for flexibility. Power companies, for example, would be allowed to pick their own method for bringing down sulfur dioxide and could even trade pollution permits among themselves. The President also advocates that industry use the cheapest, most cost-effective measures in the early years. Thus, before the big spending must kick in, researchers can learn more about pollution's health risks. And the country can get a clearer idea of how far and how fast it really needs to go.

It has already come a long way. For more than a decade the EPA has set "air-quality criteria" for six major pollutants, mostly expressed as the maximum allowable parts per million. The six are lead, sulfur dioxide, nitrogen dioxide, particulates, carbon monoxide, and ozone. Except for ozone, says Dr. Bernard Goldstein, former EPA research chief and now director of New Jersey's Environmental and Occupational Health Sciences Institute, "we have done a reasonably creditable job of cleaning up."

You sure can't say that about airborne toxics, which were largely ignored when the country went after the six-pack of pollutants. Because of legal hurdles under present law, the EPA has been able to set emissions standards for only seven of the 320 substances. Air toxics include the benzene that leaks from refineries and cars, solvents like acetone, bits of synthetic rubber, and chemicals with names like 1,2-dibromo-3-chloropropane (just call it DBCP). Also on this rogue's roster are metals—cadmium and mercury—suspended as tiny particles in the air.

After the Bhopal disaster in India [in 1984], Congress passed a law requiring factories to disclose how much of these toxics they emitted. In March the EPA announced the total: 2.7 billion pounds in 1987. "The numbers are staggering," says Senator Frank Lautenberg of New Jersey, who together with Representative James Florio, a candidate for governor of the same state, held a press conference in April [of 1989] to dramatize the problem. They stood at what they called "toxic ground zero" amid the refineries and petrochemical plants near Newark Airport, where estimated emissions are 110 times the national average. Lautenberg has introduced one of several bills that would force industry to button up.

The President, too, is indignant, saying at his clean-air announcement: "People who live near industrial factories should not have to fear for their health." The neighbors' increased chances of getting cancer, according to the EPA, may be as high as 1 in 1,000. Still, keep a few facts in mind before making wide detours around Newark. The cancer risks assume day and night exposure over a 70-year lifetime and are based on animal studies open to debate.

An EPA investigation several years ago shows that people may have more to fear from everyday pollutants, such as cigarette smoke and paint thinners, than from the chemical plant next door. For two days some 350 residents of Elizabeth and Bayonne, New Jersey—"ground zero" country for sure—wore monitors so sensitive they registered the effect of a visit to the dry cleaner. The dosage of volatile air toxics from those satanic industrial plants, it turned out, was a fraction of the total inhaled—anywhere from one-half to *one-seventieth*, depending on the pollutant. The total intake of perilous stuff was no greater than in a light industrial city in North Carolina used for comparison, or the farm town of Devil's Lake, North Dakota. Other research suggests that airborne metal dust near factories may be a more serious worry than toxic chemicals.

Even if the health effects of air toxics are hard to nail down, industry lobbyists are not inclined to resist this cleanup. John Holtzman, a vice president of the Chemical Manufacturers Association, says health arguments in the debate over toxic air are "inconsequential if the public thinks there's too much." Cancers caused by air toxics are believed to have fallen 50% since 1970, but the President's further cleanup seems like a good idea. At a cost of roughly $2 billion a year when in full swing, it is the least expensive part of his clean-air plan.

Far more controversial is the proposed assault on acid rain—politically the sexiest item on Bush's checklist. Canada, where much acid rain lands, has pressured Washington to cut way back. President Reagan stalled while awaiting more data. But his successor proudly telephoned Prime Minister Mulroney just before announcing his proposal to halve sulfur dioxide emissions to ten million tons a year.

Why the hurry? Explains economist Paul Portney of Resources for the Future, an environmental research group in Washington: A ten-million-ton-a-year reduction in sulfur dioxide "has become the threshold of credibility" within the beltway. Congress, led by Senate majority leader George Mitchell of Maine, is so determined to battle acid rain that anything below eight digits would have seemed the proverbial drop in the bucket.

Yet sulfur dioxide emissions have already fallen 20% since 1977, to 20 million tons a year, despite a huge increase in coal consumption by utilities. Scrubbers under construction at new power plants promise further, albeit slow, improvement. Nearly all cities are below the EPA health standard for both sulfur dioxide and nitrogen dioxide, each of which can return to earth as acidic fog, rain, or snow.

The science underlying that magic ten million tons is not much firmer than an acid cloud. Last year the agency disclosed that 2.7% of all the miles of streams surveyed in the East were acidic, and blamed industry and the automobile for most of it. Yet an interim report of the National Acid Precipitation Assessment Program, a $500 million, ten-year interagency study that still has a year to go, found no proof that acidity in streams and lakes is getting worse.

Neither did the interim report indict acid rain as a destroyer of forests. Here the evidence is decidedly mixed. Maple syrup production in the province of Quebec, whose decline in recent years had been partly blamed on acid rain, rebounded 69% last year. According to the U.S. Forest Service, the culprit

An EPA investigation several years ago shows that people may have more to fear from everyday pollutants, such as cigarette smoke and paint thinners, than from the chemical plant next door.

Some 100 million Americans live in those 81 urban areas that exceed the federal ozone standard, but the numbers overstate the risks. A city "violates" the standard if only one of several monitoring stations has a reading above 0.12 parts per million (ppm) for one hour on two separate days in an entire year.

killing trees at the summit of North Carolina's Mount Mitchell, the highest mountain in the East, is not pollution but an insect called the balsam woolly adelgid, which feasts on Fraser firs. Even so, a combination of acid fog and ozone may have made trees on this and other Eastern summits more vulnerable to bugs, weather, and drought. Volker Mohnen, an atmospheric chemist at the State University of New York in Albany, who monitors the effects of acid rain in the Northeast, says pollution should be brought down a lot even though its role in forest damage has not been firmly established.

Health concerns, largely overlooked in the crusade to save the trees and fish, may turn out to be one of the best reasons to keep whittling away at the emissions that cause acid rain. About 25,000 of the country's ten million asthmatics are prey to violent bouts of constricted breathing when the sulfur dioxide level is high but still within the EPA's health standard. Because of this the agency has considered—but dropped for now—adopting a stiffer criterion.

The EPA is also looking more closely at so-called acid aerosols (no kin to aerosol sprays in consumer products) that can form from both sulfur dioxide and nitrogen oxides. A Harvard study, which has been following the respiratory health of 18,000 children and 10,000 adults in six cities since 1974, has found that children's bronchitis rates go up when the aerosols rise. Other researchers have noticed higher hospital admissions—even a small but significant number of premature deaths—following an increase in sulfate particulates that are associated with acid aerosols. The EPA may eventually set a separate air-quality standard for acid aerosols. But until more is known, the President's attack on acid rain, which could raise residential electric bills as much as 20% in the Midwest, may be overkill.

"Pound for pound, ozone is by far the most toxic of the usual outdoor pollutants," says environmental physician Goldstein. Sunshine and two parents produce ozone at ground level: nitrogen oxides, which result from any kind of combustion, and volatile organic compounds (VOCs) like gasoline. The destructive offspring is a variant of oxygen composed of three atoms instead of the usual two. It can hardly wait to get rid of the loosely attached extra atom, which oxidizes—or burns—anything from paint to soybean crops to the inside of your lungs.

The tailpipes on today's new cars emit 76% less nitrogen oxides and 96% less VOCs than those of a generation ago. But vehicle traffic has soared, and other ozone outputters—manufacturing companies and utilities—have cut back less or not at all. A typical city's ozone concentrations declined only 9% between 1979 and 1987. With no new legislation, improvement would continue for a while as older cars are scrapped. But with traffic still increasing, total VOC emissions—and ozone—will start to climb around the turn of the century. David Hawkins of the Natural Resources Defense Council, an environmental group, contends that ozone is "a public health emergency."

Anyone coming to the subject cold might wonder what the fuss is about. Some 100 million Americans live in those 81 urban areas that exceed the federal ozone standard, but the numbers overstate the risks. A city "violates" the standard if only one of several monitoring stations has a reading above 0.12 parts per million (ppm) for one hour on two separate days in an entire year. Even in the Los Angeles area, the readings on 35 monitors are below that level 95% of the time. During the 1984 Olympics in Los Angeles, athletes did not complain about smog. So what's the big deal?

To begin with, the Olympians benefited from good weather and strict temporary measures to reduce freeway congestion. Every year thousands of healthy people experience chest pains, coughing, or shortness of breath while playing tennis or golf on summer days in Los Angeles. And the EPA says ozone's damage to crops is costing farmers $2.5 billion a year nationwide.

In 1984 Dr. Henry Gong Jr., associate chief of UCLA's pulmonary disease division, put 17 Olympic and other cyclists through one-hour tests in a smog chamber at various ozone levels. They pedaled vigorously for most of the period, using 80% of their lung capacity, and then made an all-out effort as if approaching a finish line. When Gong revved up the ozone to the federal standard of 0.12 ppm, he says, the cyclists "couldn't tell the difference" over normal air. But a level of 0.20 ppm "significantly compromised them. They couldn't ride as long or as hard." Other research has shown that at that level, the lung capacity of healthy people decreases by about 15%. After repeated one-hour exposures, the effects diminish, suggesting that the body adapts. But what if such exposures go on for years?

They have in Glendora, an affluent suburb of 50,000 at the foot of the haze-obscured San Gabriel Mountains, which trap the smog moving east from Los Angeles. Glendora was America's ozone capital last year, breaching the federal standard of 0.12 ppm on 148 days. But the number of alerts has fallen significantly. The last second-stage alert, which comes when ozone hits 0.35 ppm, was about ten years ago. Fourteen first-stage alerts, called at 0.20 ppm, took place in the 1987-88 academic year. But because of unusually good climatic conditions, only three occurred in the [1988-89 school year]. During the alerts, typically in the late afternoon, a black flag with the letters S-M-O-G goes up at the high school. To the grousing of athletes and coaches, outdoor team practice is delayed for about an hour and a half until readings drop back to a safer level.

More than 1,100 nonsmoking Glendorans age 7 to 59 participated in the only study of the long-term effects of ozone on humans. A team led by Dr. Roger Detels, a UCLA epidemiologist, compared the volunteers' lung functions with those of a similar-size group in Lancaster, a town beyond the hills and far less polluted. The subjects were retested five years later. Everyone's lung capacity increases through the late teens and then goes into a steady decline. But the Glendora group had somewhat lower capacity to begin with. Moreover, children's lung capacity grew more slowly there, and adults' declined more rapidly than in Lancaster. The $2.5 million study had methodological pitfalls, but strongly suggests that ozone is bad stuff. Says Detels: "We've looked at other possible explanations for the differences in the two groups, and haven't been able to find them."

Don't cry just for Glendora. Your own community may have ozone problems too. In most of metropolitan Los Angeles, says Dr. Jack Hackney of the University of Southern California, a longtime pollution researcher, ozone episodes come in short but intense bursts. In the East and Midwest, cities exceed the federal standard fewer days per year—typically 20 or so in the New York City area. Park readings are lower, with New York reaching 0.21 ppm for at least one hour last year to Glendora's 0.34. But the ozone in the Northeast Corridor, particularly during heat waves as the air travels from one city to the next, extends far. Kennebunkport, Maine, was repeatedly above the federal standard [in 1988], as a deputation of environmentalists reminded the President when he was preparing his legislation. Even when the readings are not especially high, Eastern and Midwestern ozone can linger at, or just below, the federal standard for most of the day.

Instruments in Camden, New Jersey, often pick up ozone levels that average more than 0.10 ppm over eight hours. Such readings occurred on 38 days over a three-year period in the mid-1980s. That put the area just over the Occupational Safety and Health Administration's all-day standard for exposure on the job. As recent studies at the EPA's smog chamber in North Carolina show, that's high enough to affect anyone outside, from kids to carpenters. At that level and even lower, the lung capacity of 22 nonsmoking males who exercised moderately but with rest periods over 6.6 hours—walking briskly up a slight incline—dropped by 7% on average, which the researchers found statistically significant. Just as meaningful, the loss of lung power became progressively greater after each hour of exposure.

In normal air the next day, the test subjects regained full breathing capacity. But recovery may take longer after a prolonged ozone spell. That was the experience of children at a New Jersey summer camp who were examined several years ago after four successive days in which readings shot past the federal standard for at least an hour. Their lungs were impaired for up to a week after clear skies returned. Based on what has been learned in animal tests,

"We're talking billions for expenditures to cut ozone, when only pennies are needed for research that might give us the answers."

—Dr. Bernard Goldstein, director of the New Jersey Environmental and Occupational Health Sciences Institute

The World Health Organization estimates that fully 70 percent of the globe's urban population breathes air made unhealthy by high levels of smog, sulfur dioxide, nitrogen oxides and other pollutants.

researchers believe that in long episodes ozone burns away cells that take five to ten days to regenerate. Years of burning and healing can produce stiffened lungs. Hawkins of the Natural Resources Defense Council likens the effect to that of repeated sunburn, which turns the skin leathery.

Eastern and Midwestern ozone may have a partner in crime. Dr. Morton Lippmann, a deputy director of New York University's Institute of Environmental Medicine, who ran the New Jersey summer camp study, suspects that acid aerosols aggravate the lung damage. Is ozone shortening people's lives? Nobody knows, Lippmann says, "but it could be reducing the quality of life at the end of our lives." Fran Du Melle of the American Lung Association adds, "We may be producing a generation of children who will have significantly reduced lung function or chronic lung disease as adults."

Goldstein finds the lack of good statistics deplorable: "We're talking billions for expenditures to cut ozone, when only pennies are needed for research that might give us the answers." For now, jogger Goldstein is putting his running shoes where his mouth is. During heat waves he gets his run in early near his New Jersey home, before the sun sends the ozone climbing.

If his hunches are right, the air cleanup should not just coast along until hundreds more bicyclists have huffed and puffed in smog chambers and thousands of citizens have paraded past epidemiologists. How big a bill should industry and consumers be required to pay? Says Portney of Resources for the Future, who has been working on cost-benefit studies of the Los Angeles 20-year plan and who has felt his own lungs burning there: "We may not want to spend every last dime to get ozone down to the EPA standard everywhere. But we will probably want to spend a lot to lower it."

Whatever the right goal, let's also be looking for ways to achieve it at the lowest cost. James Lents, a tall Tennessean in charge of air pollution control for the Los Angeles area, believes his region's plan will prompt an outpouring of money-saving business innovation. Under the proposal, furniture makers must drastically reduce volatile emissions when applying varnish. Lents asks, "What if we come up with a better method of coating the product? Is that bad?"

A debt-laden nation with such a big agenda has no choice but to pinch pennies, even on something as precious as the planet. Especially when the dimensions of some parts of the problem are still as hazy as New York City on a smoggy summer day. (pp. 54–6, 58, 60)

Edmund Faltermayer, "Air: How Clean Is Clean Enough?" in Fortune, *Vol. 120, No. 2, July 17, 1989, pp. 54–6, 58, 60.*

Last-Gasp Efforts to Reduce Air Pollution

Wedged into a cramped industrial site five minutes from downtown Stockholm, Sweden, is one small victory in the global battle against air pollution. It is a coal-fired electricity-generating plant powerful enough to light nearly 50,000 homes. Yet because it boasts technological innovations such as a "fluidized bed" boiler, it burns half the fuel—and spews out about one-third the pollution—of the cleanest comparably sized North American plant.

With the help of such technology, Sweden has slashed levels of air pollutants like sulfur dioxide by 75 percent between 1965 and 1985.

Sweden isn't the only nation fighting to clean up the air we breathe or to preserve the fragile envelope of beneficial gases that surrounds our planet. West

Germany cut power plan emissions of sulfur dioxide by nearly 90 percent between 1983 and 1989 by forcing companies to install devices that cleanse stack gases. Switzerland and Austria have gone further. With all of Switzerland's high-altitude lakes damaged because of acid rain, and 37 percent of Austria's trees sickened by air pollution, the two countries have adopted the world's toughest regulations. Even motorcycles must have emission controls.

Thanks to the efforts of a few dogged scientists and environmentalists, the world has also recognized threats from other substances that people spew into the atmosphere. Researchers now know that chemicals called chlorofluorocarbons (CFCs), which are used in everything from refrigerators to plastic-foam cups, rise high into the stratosphere. There, about 20 miles above the Earth's surface, they break apart the ozone molecules that shield us from the damaging ultraviolet rays of the sun. In 1988, in response to the threat, more than 40 nations, including Mexico, Egypt, Japan, the United States and Canada, signed the Montreal Protocol, an international treaty that called for a 50 percent reduction in CFCs by 1999.

Then there's the greenhouse effect. Carbon dioxide—released when fossil fuels are burned and forests are cut down—acts in concert with methane, CFCs, smog and other substances to form a huge blanket over the Earth, trapping the heat of the sun. According to scientists' computer models, the planet's temperature may rise 3 to 9 degrees F by 2050, bringing drought to the world's breadbaskets and submerging coastal cities under rising seas. Environmentalists hope that a planned global conference in 1990 will result in a landmark agreement to tackle this tremendous atmospheric problem. "At last, the world seems to be waking," says Irving Mintzer of the Center for Global Change at the University of Maryland. "But now we need real action, not just words."

Powerful leaders . . . are beginning to call for international action. Still, the battle to clean up our fouled atmosphere is just beginning. The World Health Organization estimates that fully 70 percent of the globe's urban population breathes air made unhealthy by high levels of smog, sulfur dioxide, nitrogen oxides and other pollutants. In the United States, nearly every major city exceeds federal standards for maximum smog levels during part of the year— and more than 100 million citizens are exposed to unhealthy smog. While there have been some improvements, notably in industrialized cities, the bulk of the world's population lives in places where pollution levels are rising.

The effects of this polluted air are both damaging and widespread. Ozone, or smog, in the lower atmosphere—formed when unburned gasoline and other chemicals react with sunlight—scars the delicate cells of the lungs. The lungs become less elastic, which dramatically reduces their capability to supply oxygen to the body. Health experts warn that people who exercise vigorously in areas where ozone levels are even moderately high might actually be reducing their overall level of fitness because of this kind of damage to their lungs.

The environmental and financial costs of air pollution are also staggering. Sulfur and nitrogen oxides, which are emitted from power plants and car tail pipes, fall from the sky as tiny acidic particles or acid rain. When they land, they destroy lakes, damage trees and eat through statues, buildings, automobiles and highways. In Germany, air pollution is poisoning not only spruce trees in the Black Forest, but also ornamental shrubs. In Athens, acid from the sky is dissolving the Parthenon and other monuments and buildings that have stood for centuries. The damage done by air pollution to bridges, tombstones, whole cities—in fact, most things built by people—is estimated at more than $20 billion per year in Western Europe. In the United States alone, costs reach an estimated $5 billion annually.

Unless we take action, the prognosis is grim. Air pollution is appearing in new places as Third World countries enter the industrial age. According to the World Resources Institute, monitoring stations in China have recorded a rise of 300 percent in sulfur pollution between 1979 and 1985. Concentrations at some sites were three to five times higher than the most polluted places in Eastern Europe or North America. In the rain forests of Africa, scientists have

Health experts warn that people who exercise vigorously in areas where ozone levels are even moderately high might actually be reducing their overall level of fitness because of [air pollution's] damage to their lungs.

Most of the inexpensive pollution control measures were implemented during the last 20 years, so that future reductions in emissions are likely to be more expensive than earlier ones.

found acid rain and smog levels as high as those of Central Europe. The probable cause: burning of the vast African grasslands.

The emission of CFCs has caused the global ozone shield in the stratosphere to thin by 3 to 5 percent. At certain altitudes over parts of Antarctica, the protective layer all but disappears each spring. Scientists recently reported that the increase in ultraviolet light is already at levels high enough to harm planktonic life in the southern oceans. Researchers also predict an increase in cataracts, skin cancer and other diseases. And they warn that by adding greenhouse gases like carbon dioxide to the atmosphere, humans have started a great global experiment without knowing what the result will be. "The question is not whether humanity is altering the global environment—we already have," says William Moomaw, formerly of the World Resources Institute. "The issue is what the outcome will be."

The problems are indeed serious, and they require drastic solutions. Part of the answer is developing innovative technology, such as Sweden's new power plant, or more fuel-efficient cars, like high-mileage prototypes already built in Sweden, Germany, Japan and the United States. The more daunting challenge is to generate the political will to adopt the new technology and, perhaps, to accept dramatically different life-styles.

Take the case of the Los Angeles Basin in California, where smog alerts are nearly as frequent as sunny days. In order to meet federal standards for "acceptable" levels of air pollution, the South Coast Air Quality Management District has proposed a series of solutions that will transform the way people live. If the plan is carried out, Southern Californians might be prohibited from using gasoline-powered lawn mowers, charcoal lighter fluid—and, eventually, gaspowered automobiles.

Will the people of Southern California make these changes in order to have cleaner air? Perhaps. The plan is already approved at local and state levels, and is awaiting Federal review. "If we fail to adopt a tough clean air plan, no one will want to live here—let alone work and raise their children in such a polluted environment," warns James M. Lents, executive officer of the air quality management district. "We have a moral obligation to get on with the cleanup of our air."

The fate of Southern California's plan will be an important bellwether. Countries like Sweden, Germany and Austria have already managed to reduce their air pollution significantly, showing that progress is possible. The question, however, is whether enough nations have the political will to act—not just against smog and acid rain but global warming. Will the United States, China, Brazil and others cut greenhouse emissions sharply enough to make a difference? It is a tough question, but we need answers fast. "It's crucial to make changes now," says James Hansen of the Goddard Institute for Space Studies. "If we continue business as usual, dramatic climate change will be inevitable—and there will be no turning the clock back."

Curtis A. Moore, "Even the Heavens Gasp with Poisons," in International Wildlife, *Vol. 20, No. 2, March-April, 1990, pp. 14–15.*

Cleaning up Smog: Costs vs. Benefits

Environmental regulation is important to our health and well-being and also is quite expensive. For these reasons, we must look carefully at our environmental laws and regulations to see what they will accomplish and at what cost.

Recently, three major changes were made to the Clean Air Act. First, over the next decade electric power plants must make sharp reductions in emissions of sulfur dioxide (SO_2)—10 million tons per year measured from their 1980 level. Second, most major sources of what are called hazardous air pollutants must install state-of-the-art emissions control equipment and, eventually, further reduce any residual emissions that pose unacceptably high health risks. Third, a number of new measures have been enacted to improve air quality in areas where the national ambient air quality standards (NAAQS) are currently being violated.

This third problem, referred to as nonattainment with regard to the NAAQS, is by far the most difficult to solve. According to the Environmental Protection Agency (EPA), in 1989 more than 66 million people in the United States lived in counties where the ozone standard was being exceeded at one or more monitors.

Most of the inexpensive pollution control measures were implemented during the last 20 years, so that future reductions in emissions are likely to be more expensive than earlier ones.

To help focus debate about the best use of society's resources, it is important to have estimates of the benefits and costs of further improvements in air quality. In this article we develop such estimates, focusing primarily on reductions in ground-level ozone resulting from the control of volatile organic compounds (VOCs). We evaluate proposed efforts at the national level.

Reducing Ozone in Urban Areas

To evaluate the benefits and costs of reducing ambient ozone concentrations, one must first estimate the VOC reductions expected in various areas and the ozone improvements that they imply. Then the costs of the measures to be used to obtain the VOC reductions and the benefits associated with the ozone improvements can be estimated.

In 1989, the Office of Technology Assessment (OTA) released a major study of air quality problems in the United States. The study estimated the changes in emissions of VOCs and, subsequently, reductions in ozone that would result in the years 1994 to 2004 from the application of all currently available VOC control technologies in nonattainment areas and some added control in clean areas.

As estimated by the OTA, by the year 2004 these control measures would reduce total annual emissions of VOCs in nonattainment areas from about 11 million to about 7 million tons, representing a 35% reduction. Depending on the particular urban area in question, the annual VOC reduction would vary from 20% to 50%. Our benefit and cost estimates pertain to this predicted change in air quality.

The VOC controls that the OTA considered were projected to bring 31 of 94 areas in mild violation of the ozone standard in 1985 into attainment by 2004. Areas such as Los Angeles, however, were predicted to remain in violation even after controls were implemented.

Costs. According to the OTA, the annualized cost associated with this ambitious set of measures would be $6.6 billion to $10.0 billion in the nonattainment areas alone, or about $1,800 to $2,700 per ton of VOC reduced there. Adding in the costs that would be borne in attainment areas raises the estimated total to $8.8 billion to $12.8 billion per year.

Of all the control measures examined, reducing the volatility of gasoline accounts for the greatest emission reduction (about 14%) and would also be the most cost-effective control technology, because this reduction would cost between $120 and $740 annually per ton of VOC reduced. At the other extreme, the OTA found that using methanol (an 85% blend) to power fleet vehicles would be an expensive measure: $8,700 to $51,000 per ton of VOC reduction.

In contrast to the removal of lead from gasoline, for which estimated benefits are well in excess of costs, the benefit-cost comparison of national ozone control is unfavorable.

We would all prefer limitless resources so that every pollution control measure physically possible could be pursued. Because resources are scarce, however, the real cost of air pollution control is represented by the government programs or private expenditures that we forgo by putting our resources into reducing volatile organic compound emissions.

A ranking of individual approaches by cost effectiveness shows that marginal costs increase sharply for obtaining any more than a 30% reduction in VOC emissions.

Benefits. How does one ascertain the amount individuals would be willing to pay for the air quality improvements that the OTA projects? We concentrate on acute health benefits because protecting health is the primary justification for setting air quality standards under the Clean Air Act and because only acute health effects have been linked convincingly to ozone concentrations. Other benefits could accrue in the form of reduced damage to exposed materials, crops, and other vegetation, and possibly reductions in the prevalence of chronic illness.

We estimated the reduced incidence of the quantifiable adverse health effects in the year 2004 accompanying a 35% reduction in emissions of VOCs for an estimated 129 million people living in the 94 metropolitan areas (322 counties) predicted to be in nonattainment in 2004. For each metropolitan area, we made separate calculations on the basis of the predicted change in air quality there and then aggregated these estimates to obtain the national estimates.

From the epidemiologic studies, we found that the average asthmatic will experience about 0.2 fewer days per year on which he or she has an asthma attack and that the average non-asthmatic will experience about 0.1 fewer minor restricted activity days per year because of reduced VOC emissions and subsequently improved air quality. In addition, non-asthmatics will experience other minor health benefits in the form of reduced numbers of symptom days.

To convert these predicted changes in physical health into economic benefits, it is necessary to ascertain individuals' willingness to pay for reduced illness and adverse symptoms. To do so, we drew on a number of studies designed to uncover thee values, primarily through questioning of both healthy and infirm respondents with supplemental data on the out-of-pocket medical costs and lost income that may be associated with illness or symptomatic effects. These studies have found a value of $25 for an average asthma attack prevented, $20 for a reduction of one restricted activity day (on which an individual is neither bedridden nor forced to miss work but must alter his or her usual pattern in some way), and $5 for one fewer day of occasional coughing. When reduced incidence is combined with these values, the predicted aggregate dollar benefits across the United States from these improvements in individuals' acute health status amount to $250 million per year.

By using clinical rather than epidemiologic studies to estimate health benefits, we arrive at a somewhat larger value for acute health benefits. For example, we predict that the number of coughing spells of two hours' duration would be reduced by as much as 2.5 episodes per person per year. Also, few episodes of shortness of breath and pain on deep inspiration are predicted to occur. Both are important consequences of air pollution control. We estimate that the annual monetary benefits associated with these improvements in health would be on the order of $800 million annually.

Comparison. To summarize, according to the OTA, the costs associated with a 35% reduction in nationwide emissions of VOCs in nonattainment areas will be at least $8.8 billion annually by the year 2004 and could be as much as $12 billion. Yet the acute health improvements that we predict to result from these changes are valued at no more than $1 billion annually and could be as little as $250 million. The high estimate relies on the most generous of four clinical studies that the EPA sanctioned in its staff paper on the health effects associated with ozone and other photochemical oxidants. We also assumed that exercise rates would be high in the exposed population (which increases health benefits), and we included benefits even for those engaged in light or moderate exercise.

In contrast to, say, the removal of lead from gasoline, for which estimated benefits are well in excess of costs, the benefit-cost comparison of national ozone control is unfavorable. The reasons for this are, in part, the relatively small improvements in ambient ozone levels that the controls effect (which in turn imply fairly small benefits) as well as the high costs of control.

Conclusions and Implications

It is unpleasant to have to weigh in such a calculating manner the pros and cons of further air pollution control efforts. We would all prefer limitless resources so that every pollution control measure physically possible could be pursued. Because resources are scarce, however, the real cost of air pollution control is represented by the government programs or private expenditures that we forgo by putting our resources into reducing VOC emissions. In the health area alone, $10 billion invested in smoking cessation programs, radon control, better prenatal and neonatal health care, or similar measures might contribute much more to public health and well-being.

Because the benefits and costs of air-pollution control are sure to vary considerably among metropolitan areas, it may make economic sense to control a great deal in some places but little in others. Further controls will almost inevitably be justified in the Los Angeles area, where despite concerted efforts over the last 30 years air pollution is quite clearly unacceptable and adverse health effects are the most significant. On the basis of cost estimates made by the South Coast authorities in the Los Angeles area, particularly attractive VOC control possibilities include reformulating coatings used in the manufacture of wood furniture, modifying aircraft engines, and substituting less volatile cleaning solvents. By the same token, one must be especially careful in evaluating the benefits of mandatory van-pooling and other transportation control measures that have possibly larger nonpecuniary costs. Even if such efforts temporarily relieve freeway congestion, new drivers may appear in the commuting brigade and wipe out apparent pollution reductions. The important point to emphasize is that all control measures must be viewed with an eye toward the good that they are likely to do and the costs that they are likely to impose.

Implicit in our discussion is discomfort with the premises on which our national air quality standards are based. If, as seems likely, there are no pollution concentrations at which safety can be assured, the real question in ambient standard setting is the amount of risk that we are willing to accept. This decision must be informed by economics. Although such economic considerations should never be allowed to dominate air pollution control decisions, it is inappropriate and unwise to exclude them.

Alan J. Krupnick and Paul R. Portney, "Cleaning Up Smog: Costs vs. Benefits," in Consumers Research Magazine, *Vol. 74, No. 8, August, 1991, pp. 23–7.*

> **The control of atmospheric pollution, once a local demand, is now a universal necessity. The result has been enactment of new air pollution codes or tightening of existing ordinances.**

Emissions Control Options for Power Plants

Comprehensive clean air legislation continued its progress in Congress during the fall of 1989 and into 1990. Significant provisions in proposed legislation included combating acid rain, toxic air pollution and three pollutants that exceed Clean Air Act health standards in many cities and other areas: Ozone, carbon monoxide and fine particles.

Additional problems addressed by the proposed legislation were chemicals that deplete the stratospheric ozone layer and air pollution from municipal waste combustors as well as indoor air pollution.

The acid rain problem on local, national and global levels continues to be a concern from all environmental perspectives. To reduce acid rain, the House

Fuel substitution is a convenient method for reducing pollution. Gas and distillate oil, although relatively costly, are ideal substitutes. Solid fuel yields layer particles and more nitrogen oxides than residual fuel. Certain coals may be preferred over residual oil in Europe as they release less sulfur dioxide when burned.

bill, for example, required a two-phased, 10-million ton reduction in annual sulfur in nitrogen oxides by the end of the year 2000, with a three-year extension for clean coal repowering technologies.

Many issues remain unresolved and further controversy and discussions are likely. Acid rain control and enforcement are directly related to the power generation industry and this special *Pollution Engineering* report reviews the technical control options within that industry.

The number of power plants that should be required to make sulfur dioxide emission reductions by 1995 is a controversial issue. At stake are incentives for utilities to switch to low-sulfur coal, thereby increasing the loss of high-sulfur coal mining jobs.

The control of atmospheric pollution, once a local demand, is now a universal necessity. The result has been enactment of new air pollution codes or tightening of existing ordinances.

Air pollution means different things to different people. To the factory workers, it may mean in-plant contaminants generated by the manufacturing process. To a motorist, it may mean the lack of visibility and physical discomfort in driving through smog. To a property owner, it may mean the dust falling on household items or damage to an automobile finish.

The American Medical Association has defined air pollution as "the excessive concentration of foreign matter in the air which adversely affects the well-being of the individual or causes damage to property."

The subject of air pollution often conjures thoughts of the products of aircraft, automobiles, buses, locomotives and trucks; products of incinerators and radioactive fallout.

There are pollutants in the air caused by nature and not by man. These include forest fires ignited by lightning, gaseous and dust emissions from volcanoes, decaying vegetation, pollens, sand and dust stirred by storms and bacteria and viruses.

Air Pollution Abatement

Various strategies have been applied to control air pollution from power plants. The strategies include fuel substitution, desulfurization of fuel oil, physical coal cleaning, flue gas scrubbing and desulfurization, hydrogen sulfide removal (H_2S) and nitrogen oxides removal (NO_x). Additional strategies include particulate collection equipment, combustion control, tall stacks, gasification of coal, gas turbines, fluidized bed combustion, nuclear energy, conversion from yellow flame to blue flame oil burners, and conservation of energy.

Fuel substitution is a convenient method for reducing pollution. Gas and distillate oil, although relatively costly, are ideal substitutes. Solid fuel yields layer particles and more nitrogen oxides than residual fuel. Certain coals may be preferred over residual oil in Europe as they release less sulfur dioxide when burned.

This relationship is reversed in the United States, where most coal has a higher sulfur content. In the United States, high-sulfur coal is replaced by low-sulfur coal when availability and price are favorable. Some European countries have followed a guideline of replacing coal with 1 percent sulfur oil in power stations.

Desulfurization of fuel oil is an option chosen by many European countries where residual fuel has been desulfurized to 1 percent sulfur.

Before selecting equipment for pollution control on non-nuclear conventional power plants, whether coal-fired, oil-fired or gas-fired, it is necessary to understand the role sulfur plays in firing fossil fuels.

During combustion, sulfur forms with oxygen to make SO_2 and SO_3. About 95 to 97 percent of the sulfur combines to make SO_2—the remainder is SO_3.

Then SO_2 and SO_3 combine with water to form sulfurous and sulfuric acid. These acids can form directly in the gas stream below the water dew point. These can cause extreme corrosion in a wet scrubber and to a lesser degree, in the other types of equipment.

In recent years, oil-fired power stations have accounted for about one-tenth of the emissions of SO_2 resulting from power generation in the United States.

Many such stations, however, are in urban settings and under pressure to reduce SO_2 emissions. Today, as a result of this pressure, a number of power companies in the U.S. burn oil containing less than 1 percent sulfur.

The lignites and subbituminous coals of the western United States are generally low in sulfur content, yet many cannot meet or may have difficulties in meeting SO_2 emission standards without some SO_2 removal. Flue gas desulfurization (FGD) can be accomplished by a number of processes.

Two important nitrogen oxides which exist in the atmosphere are nitric oxide, (NO), and nitrogen dioxide, (NO_2). There are five more oxides of nitrogen which are also known. These are N_2O, N_2O_3, N_2O_4, NO_3 and N_2. Of those, N_2O_4 and NO_3 are rather unstable under atmospheric conditions.

The oxides of nitrogen are usually represented by the symbol NO_x. In reality the symbol NO_x represents NO_2 and NO, which are the major nitrogen oxide pollutants discussed here.

When gas, coal, or fuel oils are burned with air, the nitrogen in the air combines with some of the oxygen.

Whenever NO is formed, the rate of its decomposition becomes very slow under reaction conditions. It usually is formed at high temperature, and an equilibrium concentration of approximately 2 percent in the air is obtained at 3800°F.

The same process also removes some nitrogen oxides from the polluted air. Of course, the polluted air in general may contain a combination of SO_2 and NO_2 along with a series of other pollutants, depending on the circumstances. A wet-scrubbing process may remove about 20 percent of the nitrogen oxides. The following are some basic processes for removing nitrogen oxides.

Reduction with Natural Gas

Reduction with natural gas is one of the simplest processes, whereby the natural gas combines with the nitrogen oxides and reduces them to harmless nitrogen and water. It is actually a combustion process and a variety of burners have been designed.

The polluted air containing nitrogen oxides in noxious concentrations is fed into a conduit. The reducing gas, such as natural gas, is fed into another conduit. The two streams enter a cylindrical portion and the resulting mixture is passed on to an inverted cone section. This mixture is ignited; the ignition process converts the nitrogen oxides to harmless nitrogen and water which may be discharged safely into the atmosphere. The polluted air must contain sufficient oxygen or another stream of oxygen must be fed in to support the combustion process.

However, since there is no by-product in such a process, it may be useful for small operations. When dealing with power plants, where volumes of stack gas are essentially huge, other processes must be considered for suitability.

Tyco Process

In the Tyco process, the basic chemistry of the chamber sulfuric acid process is applied for the purpose of removing both sulfur oxides and nitrogen oxides

From four carloads of new coal, about one carload of impurities can be removed by physical cleaning. Desulfurization can be accomplished during cleaning by gravity separation, flotation and magnetic separation to remove pyrite sulfur. Organic sulfur can be removed by chemical coal cleaning, but the current cost of various processes under development make such removal prohibitive.

Optimum precipitator efficiency is normally achieved when the highest possible voltage and maximum current is produced. These values are a function of the variable physical and chemical status of the dust laden gas. To ensure a good precipitator operation, an automatic and instantaneous control of voltage and current is desirable.

from a polluted air stream. Polluted air containing sulfur dioxide and nitrogen oxide enters into a reactor. The stream leaving this reactor consists essentially of sulfuric acid mist, NO and NO_2, and it enters a scrubber.

The scrubbing agent is concentrated sulfuric acid which scrubs the entering stream from the acid mist and the nitrogen oxides. The exit gas is clean and harmless. The stream leaving the bottom of a scrubber consists of sulfuric acid and nitrogen thiosulfate, $NOHSO_4$. It enters into a nitrogen oxide stripper whereby the hot stripping gas enters the unit, and NO and NO_2 leave the top of the stripper to enter a nitric acid absorber. Here, the water entering the absorber will react with some of the NO and NO_2 to give a product, HNO_3, leaving the bottom of the absorber.

At the top of the absorber, the stream consists of nitrogen oxides, again NO and NO_2, which enter into an oxidizer. The oxidizer also receives a stream of air or oxygen and transforms NO to NO_2, which enters the original reactor, where it reacts again with the entering polluted stream.

Magnesium Hydroxide Scrubbing

Power plants release large amounts of nitrogen oxides into the atmosphere. Tremendous volumes of flue gas must be dealt with in the cleaning process. For example, a 750 MW gas-fired plant releases almost 5 tons of nitrogen oxides per hour, and the flue gas volume is about 70 million standard cubic feet per hour.

This presents a tremendous engineering problem, and is very expensive because of the necessary equipment and the costly operations. In this process, the effluent from a power plant containing nitrogen oxides and some sulfur dioxide, along with other pollutants and particulate matter, enters into a spray tower where the particulate matter is removed from the bottom and taken to a settling pond. The water is recycled to the spray tower.

The exit gas from this unit enters a scrubber, where the magnesium hydroxide solution enters at the top and the clean air leaves the scrubber at the top. The bottom stream is fed to a settler where the magnesium sulfite is taken from the bottom to a unit for decomposing $MgSO_3$. Sulfur dioxide is given off and taken to a plant to produce sulfuric acid as a by-product.

Magnesium nitrate, $Mg(NO_2)_2$, leaves the settler and moves into the nitrite decomposer, where decomposition takes place, and the magnesium hydroxide enters into a reactor which receives a stream of ammonia and some recyled nitric acid. The product is ammonium nitrate, NH_4NO_3.

A gas stream containing nitrogen oxides exists from the top of the magnesium nitrate decomposer. This stream will combine with an air stream so that both will be fed into an oxidizer, from which some recycled nitric acid is taken to the ammonia reactor, and from the top, recycled nitrogen oxide is taken to be fed into the original scrubber.

Lime water may be used in place of magnesium hydroxide. However, magnesium hydroxide scrubbing provides ease of generating oxides from the sulfites, and nitrites of magnesium.

Another process must be mentioned. The selective reaction with ammonia capable of reducing NO selectively in an oxygen environment is done using a platinum catalyst. The product is harmless nitrogen and water.

Hydrogen Sulfide Removal

The hydrogen sulfide burned is 4.2 percent. The reaction is not completed, so some H_2S remains in the air with its ever-noticed offensive smell. The amount that burns will give SO_2 and water vapor. High humidity of the atmosphere changes SO_2 to acid mist. The health hazard from H_2S is serious whether this substance is burned or not and is present.

Hydrogen sulfide is not as abundant in the air as nitrogen oxide and sulfur dioxide. If a detailed process for its removal were given, it would have to be similar to the processes used for purifying natural gas. Natural gas may contain from 2 to 4 percent hydrogen sulfide which has a very offensive odor, and is an acid which is harmful. Diethanolamine or mono-ethanolamine solutions can be used to react with hydrogen sulfide. The product is stripped in a steam stripping tower.

Finally, pure H_2S is obtained. Pure hydrogen sulfide may be taken through another process for making pure sulfur.

Coal Cleaning Processes

Coal cleaning appears to have been used widely only in the United States. However the Federal Republic of Germany has been steadily increasing the use of the method since 1974.

From four carloads of new coal, about one carload of impurities can be removed by physical cleaning. Desulfurization can be accomplished during cleaning by gravity separation, flotation and magnetic separation to remove pyrite sulfur. Organic sulfur can be removed by chemical coal cleaning, but the current cost of various processes under development make such removal prohibitive.

Particulate Collection Equipment

The primary condition for the selection of the best suited gas cleaning method is a sound knowledge of the different properties of the particulate to be removed entirely, if possible, from the gas. Some of the more important properties are particle size, concentration, distribution and settling velocity in still air.

Particulate size is measured in microns. A micron is 1/1000 of a millimeter, or 1/25400 of an inch. Particles range in size from those larger than 50 microns that can be seen by the naked eye, to those smaller than 0.005 microns that only can be observed through an electron microscope.

Particles are classified according to their mode of formation as dust, fumes, smoke, mist or spray. Dust, fumes and smoke are solid particles. Small solid dust particles are created by breaking up larger particles by crushing, grinding, drilling or explosions. Dust particles are normally larger than 1 micron.

Fumes are fine, solid particles formed by the condensation of vapors of solid materials. The normal size of fumes is less than 1 micron.

Smoke is composed of fine, solid particles resulting from the incomplete combustion of organic materials such as coal and tobacco.

Mists are liquid droplets generated by condensation or by dispersing a liquid as in formation and splashing. They are usually smaller than 10 microns.

Sprays are large liquid droplets created by mechanical disintegration, and range in size between 10 and 400 microns.

An aerosol can be an assembly of small particles, solid or liquid, suspended in a gas. The diameter of the particles may vary from 100 microns down to 0.01 micron or less, such as dust, fog or smoke.

Particulate Concentration

Particulate concentration is a measure of the total mass of all the particles suspended in a given volume of gas. Particulate concentration is usually stated in units of grains per cubic foot or grams per cubic meter. So, 1.0 grain/ft^3 = 2.3 grams/m^3.

Air pollution control systems are classified according to the particulate concentration of the gas to be cleaned. Air filtration concentrations should be

Disposal of sulfur dioxide into the atmosphere by high stacks has been a very controversial subject. It is claimed that emissions can be transported over large distances and can come down in the form of acid rain, damaging buildings and vegetation and causing increases in the acidity of lakes and ground water.

Air pollution means different things to different people. To the factory workers, it may mean in-plant contaminants generated by the manufacturing process. To a motorist, it may mean the lack of visibility and physical discomfort in driving through smog. To a property owner, it may mean the dust falling on household items or damage to an automobile finish.

0.001 to 5 grains/1000 ft³. Industrial air filtration concentrations should be 5 to 100 grains/1000 ft³ and dust control concentrations should run 0.01 to 100 grains/ft³.

In selecting a dust control system (0.1–100 grains/ft³), it is important to know whether the dust concentration is light, medium or heavy.

Particle Size Distribution

Since airborne particulate matter varies considerably in particle size as well as concentration, something must be known about particle size distribution. (pp. 66–71)

Particles are classified as being extremely fine, fine, medium or coarse according to the micron range in which 50 percent or more of the particles appear.

Particle Settling Velocity

Particles suspended in relatively calm atmospheres and regions of low gas velocity surrender to the pull of gravity and proceed to settle out. The force of attraction between the earth and a particle, gravitational force (F_g), causes the particle to move with an increasing downward velocity. A buoyant force (F_b) and a drag force (F_d) resist the downward motion of the particle. As the particle velocity increases, so does the drag force. The particle will fall at a constant velocity when the gravitational force is equalized by the combined effect of the buoyant force and drag force.

Electrostatic precipitators separate dust, fume, or mist from a gas stream by exposing the stream to a high voltage (20 to 80 kV DC) electric field which imparts an electric charge to solid particles in the stream. The particles then migrate to an oppositely charged collecting surface where they cling until removed. The electric field is formed by radiation from electrodes, usually steel wires equidistant from each other and the collecting surface. The collected dust drops into hoppers.

The principal components of an electrostatic precipitator include a collecting system, a high voltage system, a power supply and a gas distribution device.

The collecting system is a series of plates with fins to which the dust will be attached and adhere. Plate rappers are provided to vibrate the plates to remove the collected dust and cause it to fall into the hopper(s).

The high voltage system involves wire electrodes producing an electric field through which the gas must flow to be ionized. Rappers also are provided to vibrate the wire at intervals to dislodge minor dust accumulation.

The high voltage required is produced by the power supply—transformer-rectifiers which increase commercial voltage to approximately 45 kV and convert alternating current to unidirectional current. Automatic voltage controls are required to maintain maximum efficiencies as conditions vary.

Gas Distribution Device—It is imperative that the incoming gas flow be evenly distributed for nearly uniform velocity. The gas distribution device can be a simple perforated plate although certain inlet configurations may require some special gas distribution components.

Optimum precipitator efficiency is normally achieved when the highest possible voltage and maximum current is produced. These values are a function of the variable physical and chemical status of the dust laden gas. To ensure a good precipitator operation, an automatic and instantaneous control of voltage and current is desirable.

Tall Stacks

The development of plume dispersion models for relating tall stacks emissions to ambient SO_2 concentrations has led to the conclusion that tall stacks can be an effective means for controlling ambient SO_2 concentrations in the vicinity of large coal-fired power plants.

An evaluation of potential SO_2 control strategies at a number of coal-fired power plants led historically to the decision to build taller stacks at some plants. The comparative benefits of proposed taller stacks over the existing stacks has been studied.

This technique has been needed in France and the United Kingdom to reduce ground-level sulfur dioxide concentrations by dispersion into the upper atmosphere. To take full advantage of this technique, it is used with fuels with the highest possible sulfur content, to allow low-sulfur fuels to be burned in locations where tall stacks cannot be used.

The practice followed in the United Kingdom since 1958 for large, conventionally fueled power stations has been to discharge flue gases through a single stack exceeding 150 meters in height at an effective velocity of 15 to 23 m/sec and a temperature of 110 to 150°C. Under these conditions, the momentum and buoyancy of flue gases carry them above any temperature inversions of the atmosphere.

Measurements have shown that British power stations have not contributed appreciably to ground-level sulfur dioxide concentrations, even when meteorological conditions are such that pollutants discharged at lower levels tend to accumulate.

In France, the exit velocity is somewhat higher, 20 to 30 m/sec, to ensure that ground-level sulfur dioxide concentrations will not exceed 0.25 mg/m³.

Disposal of sulfur dioxide into the atmosphere by high stacks has been a very controversial subject. It is claimed that emissions can be transported over large distances and can come down in the form of acid rain, damaging buildings and vegetation and causing increases in the acidity of lakes and ground water.

The United States explicitly rejects tall stacks as a satisfactory solution to international pollution problems. (pp. 71–3)

Paul N. Cheremisinoff, "Power Plants Face Stricter Controls for Clean Air," in Pollution Engineering, *Vol. 22, No. 6, June, 1990, pp. 66–73.*

The primary condition for the selection of the best suited gas cleaning method is a sound knowledge of the different properties of the particulate to be removed entirely, if possible, from the gas. Some of the more important properties are particle size, concentration, distribution and setteling velocity in still air.

Sources For Further Study

Begley, Sharon; Hager, Mary; and Hurt, Harry III. "Is Breathing Hazardous to Your Health?" *Newsweek* CXIII, No. 14 (3 April 1989): 25.
    Relates the findings of an EPA report which indicates that air may be much more poisonous than previously believed.

Berger, David A., and Ayers, Karl C. "Advancing Air Pollution Control Technologies for Burning Coal." *Tappi Journal* 72, No. 8 (August 1989): 67–74.
    Surveys the various types and performance characteristics of clean coal technologies currently being developed, with an emphasis on industrial boiler applications.

Boron, David J., and Wan, Edward I. "Controlling Toxic Emissions." *Coal* 96, No. 6 (June 1990): 121–25.
    Argues that coal preparation can significantly reduce the threat of toxic emissions by removing harmful metals from the mineral before it is used for combustion in power stations.

Carey, John. "The Mystery of Arctic Haze." *Weatherwise* 41, No. 2 (April 1988): 97–9.
   Discusses the origin of artic haze, an atmospheric condition resulting from prevailing winds carrying air pollutants primarily from Western Europe and the Soviet Union to the North Pole.

Carver, Philip C. "What Will Be the Fate of Clean-Coal Technologies?" *Environmental Science & Technology* 23, No. 9 (September 1989): 1059–60.
   Maintains that since newly-developed clean coal technologies will not be ready for implementation until the late 1990s, they may be passed over in favor of conventional pollution control methods in order to meet regulatory deadlines.

Cone, Marla. "Blueprint for Cleaner Skies." *Sierra* 74, No. 4 (July–August 1989): 16–17.
   Examines a plan adopted by Los Angeles to control emissions from industries to backyard barbecues in an effort to reduce air pollution by 80% in twenty years.

Consumers' Research Magazine 73, No. 3 (March 1990).
   Provides a series of special reports on various aspects of air pollution, including air purity, air toxins, urban smog, and acid rain.

Cooper, Ken. "Taking Up the Green Issue." *Financial Times* (3 November 1988): 11.
   Discusses methods by which the United Kingdom can comply with the efforts of the rest of the European Economic Community to combat air pollution.

Cortese, Anthony D. "Clearing the Air." *Environmental Science & Technology* 24, No. 4 (April 1990): 442–47.
   Suggests that one approach to combatting air pollution is to view the atmosphere as an integrated resource and to consider local, regional, and global impacts of societal activities in proposed solutions.

Durman, Eugene C. "Air Pollution." *EPA Journal* 15, No. 1 (January–February 1989): 23–4.
   Explores the potential ramifications of global warming caused by the greenhouse effect, focusing on the problem of ground-level ozone.

Easterbrook, Gregg. "Air Pollution: It's All Legal." *Newsweek* CXIV, No. 4 (24 July 1989): 28–9, 32–5.
   Examines reductions in air pollution levels since the passage of the Clean Air Act in 1970. Easterbrook contends that emission reductions have not been substantial and that political infighting impedes the passage of productive new legislation.

French, Hilary F. "Industrial Wasteland." *World Watch* 1, No. 6 (November–December 1988): 21–30.
   Offers a detailed examination of the air, water, and soil pollution problem in Eastern Europe and documents how in the era of *glosnost* environmental groups are being established to address these concerns.

———. "You Are What You Breathe." *World Watch* 3, No. 3 (May–June 1990): 27–34.
   Provides an overview of the air pollution problem, discussing scientific and political efforts to control its harmful emissions.

———. "A Global Agenda for Clean Air." *Energy Policy* 18, No. 6 (July–August 1990): 583–85.
   Contends that air pollution reduction strategies to date have not been effective in controlling harmful emissions and maintains that improved energy efficiency is necessary to reduce pollution.

Graedel, Thomas E., and Crutzen, Paul J. "The Changing Atmosphere." *Scientific American* 261, No. 3 (September 1989): 53–68.
   Assesses the known and unknown ramifications of humankind's alteration of the complex composition of gases in the atmosphere.

Gutfeld, Rose. "EPA to Propose Its New Rules on Air Pollution." *The Wall Street Journal* (24 April 1991): A14.
    Evaluates an EPA proposal to implement an air pollution permit system that would greatly increase the reporting requirements for numerous industrial facilities.

Landsberg, Hans H. "Coal Revisited." *Resources* 94 (Winter 1989): 8–11.
    Examines the future of generating electrical power with coal-fired plants, particularly emphasizing its role in relation to such environmental concerns as air pollution and global warming.

Lovins, Amory B. "Abating Air Pollution at Negative Cost Via Energy Efficiency." *The Environmental Professional* 12, No. 2 (1990): 164–68.
    Argues that reductions in air pollution can be achieved by developing new methods of efficient end-use of energy rather than by investing in costly technology or by assuming inconvenient changes in lifestyle.

Lyons, Carol E. "Environmental Problem Solving: The 1987-88 Metro Denver Brown Cloud Study." *Chemical Engineering Progress* 86, No. 5 (May 1990): 61–71.
    Documents the findings of a 1987-88 study which sought to determine the cause of visible air pollution in Denver, Colorado. The study concludes that coal-fired power plants are not principally responsible for creating Denver's brown cloud; rather, motor vehicles, wood burning, and road dust are the top three contributors to the phenomenon.

Mathy, P., ed. *Air Pollution and Ecosystems: Proceedings of an International Symposium Held in Grenoble, France, 18–22 May 1987*. Dordrecht, Holland: D. Reidel Publishing Company, 1988, 981 p.
    Detailed examination of various aspects of the air pollution problem, including its effect on agriculture, forests, and aquatic ecosystems. The volume also recommends preventive and curative measures to control pollution.

Moore, Curtis, "Atmosphere." *World Resources 1990–91: A Report by The World Resources Institute*, pp. 201–15. New York: Oxford University Press, 1990.
    Surveys recent trends in urban air pollution, especially the rapidly growing role that automobiles play in this dilemma, and outlines various approaches to pollution control.

Nichols, Mark. "Smog over the North Pole." *Maclean's* 101, No. 29 (11 July 1988): 45.
    Briefly discusses the emergence of arctic haze.

Nriagu, Jerome O. "A Global Assessment of Natural Sources of Atmospheric Trace Metals." *Nature* 338, No. 6210 (2 March 1989): 47–9.
    Argues that a proper inventory of natural atmospheric emissions is essential to fully understand the atmospheric cycle of trace metals and to assess the extent of regional and global pollution by toxic metals.

Padmanabhamurty, B. "Impact of Tall Stacks on the Atmospheric Environment." *Energy Environment Monitor* 5, No. 1 (March 1989): 59–63.
    Proposes mathematical processes and models to determine the influence of stack height on local air pollution.

Rittenhouse, R. C. "New SO_2 Limits Will Challenge Particulate Control Systems." *Power Engineering* 94, No. 6 (June 1990): 18–25.
    Surveys evolving particulate control technologies to determine the most plausible methods to deal with potential legislation calling for emissions restrictions.

Romieu, Isabelle; Weitzenfeld, Henyk; and Finkelman, Jacobo. "Urban Air Pollution in Latin America and the Caribbean: Health Perspectives." *WHO World Health Statistics Quarterly* 43, No. 3 (1990): 153–67.
    Reviews the problem of air pollution in Latin America and the Caribbean and the potential for adverse health effects on their populations.

Rose, Bleys W. "Clearing the Air on Air Cleaners." *Home Energy* 6, No. 2 (March–April 1989): 27–31.
    Examines the effectiveness of various products marketed in the U.S. for cleaning indoor household air.

Sastry, C. A. "Environment, Pollution, and Development." *Indian Journal of Environmental Protection* 8, No. 5 (May 1988): 342–48.
    Broad overview of global pollution, chiefly focusing on the social, biological, physical, and chemical dimensions of the problem. Sastry concludes that national policies should be implemented to maintain sustainable economic development combined with a natural resources conservation strategy to better combat environmental pollution.

Seinfeld, John H. "Urban Air Pollution: State of the Science." *Science* 243, No. 4892 (10 February 1989): 745–52.
    Technical analysis of the progress made in reducing airborne levels of sulfur dioxide and carbon monoxide. Seinfeld asserts that ozone "remains the most resistant to efforts at abatement."

Shen, Thomas T. "Air Quality Impact Assessment." In *Encyclopedia of Environmental Control Technology,* edited by Paul N. Cheremisinoff, Vol. II, pp. 1–36. Houston: Gulf Publishing Company, 1989.
    Proposes that air quality impact assessment (AQIA)—a mechanism that can identify, predict, and evaluate critical variables and potential changes in air quality—can be used as a screening device for setting priorities for pollution control.

Smith, Kirk R. "Air Pollution: Assessing Total Exposure in Developing Countries." *Environment* 30, No. 10 (December 1988): 16–18, 28–30, 33–5.
    Posits that scientists should refocus their assessments of human exposure to air pollution from indoor/outdoor evaluations to a more specific assessment of where the people are in relation to affected areas. Such an observation may seem obvious, Smith asserts, but "considering the traditional narrow focus on urban outdoor air quality, [the idea's] acceptance amounts to a revolution in the way air pollution sources, victims, and control measures are evaluated."

Speth, James G. "Energy Policy and Environmental Pollution: A Look to the Future." *International Journal of Global Energy Issues* 1, Nos. 1–2 (1989): 5–17.
    Provides a detailed overview of air pollution, contending that three phenomena exemplify global atmospheric pollution: acid rain, ozone depletion, and the greenhouse effect. Speth asserts that the key to solving these global problems lies in the establishment of a viable energy policy.

Swanson, David L., and Beck, Robert A. "A Lower Cost Approach to Clean Air." *Electric Perspectives* 13, No. 4 (September–October 1989): 8–15.
    Maintains that a greater flexibility on legislative restrictions that make the utilities industry conform to the Clean Air Act would lower operating costs for the affected companies and therefore lessen the general economic impact on consumers.

United Nations Environment Programme and the World Health Organization. "Monitoring the Global Environment: An Assessment of Urban Air Quality." *Environment* 31, No. 8 (October 1989): 6–13, 26–37.
    Evaluates the current status of those aspects of urban air pollution that are considered to have the most direct affects on human health.

Valenti, Michael. "Bringing on Those Emission Controls." *Chemical Business* 12, No. 3 (March 1990): 14–15.
    Asserts that increased emissions controls will create new market opportunities for companies that manufacture catalytic converters.

3:   Alternative Fuels

The Fuels of the Future

Every motor fuel available today pollutes the air, but gasoline is one of the dirtiest. Automobiles that run on gasoline emit unburned hydrocarbons and oxides of nitrogen, which react with sunlight to create smog. Automobiles account for about 30 percent of the nation's total carbon-dioxide emissions and for virtually all carbon-monoxide emissions in urban areas. Carbon dioxide is the main contributor to the greenhouse effect—the slow warming of the earth's atmosphere. Carbon monoxide is a toxic gas.

People who inhale gasoline exhaust may suffer from eye and respiratory-system irritation. Worse than that, the fumes contain a number of other airborne toxics, including benzene, a known carcinogen. The EPA estimates that toxic fumes from automobiles cause as many as 1800 cases of cancer every year.

Gasoline doesn't have to contaminate the air as much as it does. But until recently most oil companies didn't pay much attention to formulating a less-polluting fuel. Now, however, Government interest in alternative fuels has threatened the oil industry's unchallenged domination of the motor-fuels market. So oil companies are hustling to concoct a cleaner gasoline.

Cleaning Up Gasoline

The gasoline used today is a complex combination of as many as 100 different hydrocarbons, plus additives. In the past 10 or 15 years, as lead has been phased out of gasoline, refiners have altered the composition of gasoline to maintain the octane levels that lead used to provide. Unfortunately, these changes also increased emissions of airborne toxics.

To make a gasoline that results in less pollution overall, refiners will probably add oxygenated compounds, which allow more complete combustion. That would reduce the emission of both airborne toxics and carbon monoxide. The most common oxygenates are methanol (wood alcohol), ethanol (grain alcohol made from corn or sugar cane), and ethers made from methanol or ethanol.

But there's a catch. Although oxygenates decrease the release of carbon monoxide, they can increase smog formation. So oxygenated fuels make most sense in areas with carbon-monoxide problems but little smog. Some cities in Arizona, Colorado, and Nevada already require the use of oxygenated fuels during the winter, when carbon-monoxide levels peak, and of regular gasoline in the summer to lessen smog.

The American Petroleum Institute, 14 major oil companies, and all three domestic automakers recently joined forces in a clean-gasoline research project. The group predicts that an early version of the resulting product could be test-marketed as soon as this summer. (Last year, Atlantic Richfield Co. introduced in some California stations a lead-free fuel for older cars that would otherwise need leaded gasoline. The company says it will take more work to produce a cleaner unleaded gasoline.)

Gasoline doesn't have to contaminate the air as much as it does. But until recently most oil companies didn't pay much attention to formulating a less-polluting fuel. Now, however, Government interest in alternative fuels has threatened the oil industry's unchallenged domination of the motor-fuels market. So oil companies are hustling to concoct a cleaner gasoline.

Methanol is far from an ideal fuel from an environmental perspective. Methanol exhaust contains four to eight times more formaldehyde than gasoline exhaust. Formaldehyde contributes to ozone formation in the lower atmosphere. It's also an eye and respiratory-system irritant and a probable carcinogen.

If refiners come up with a viable "clean" gasoline, the fuel would offer one obvious advantage over gasoline substitutes: it could be used in all existing and future cars without costly conversions. Further, any environmental benefits of clean gasoline would be felt immediately, which is not the case with other alternative-fuel programs. However, clean gasoline would do nothing to reduce carbon-dioxide emissions that cause global warming.

Vehicles that run on clean gasoline won't require design changes, but clean gasoline is expected to cost at least two or three cents more per gallon than today's gasoline.

Methanol: Hype and Reality

As the nation moves into the post-petroleum age, the chief rival to gasoline is methanol, an alcohol fuel made from coal, wood, natural gas, or garbage.

Methanol-powered vehicles will pollute less and have more pep, say the fuel's advocates, including the Bush Administration and the U.S. Environmental Protection Agency. Methanol exhaust contains at least 35 percent less smog-producing hydrocarbons and 30 to 40 percent less airborne toxics than gasoline. And the fuel's superior combustion gives cars designed to run on methanol up to 20 percent more horsepower and faster acceleration than gasoline-powered cars.

Critics of the fuel argue that methanol would be a nightmare for consumers. A gallon of methanol goes only half as far as a gallon of gasoline, so drivers would have to fill up more often. They would also have to take special care when refueling, since methanol can damage both metal and rubber. Slopped on the side of a car, the fuel can remove paint or change its color.

Methanol is far from an ideal fuel from an environmental perspective. Methanol exhaust contains four to eight times more formaldehyde than gasoline exhaust. Formaldehyde, the same stuff used to preserve dead frogs in high-school biology classes, contributes to ozone formation in the lower atmosphere. It's also an eye and respiratory-system irritant and a probable carcinogen. Automakers will have to design a catalyst to control formaldehyde emissions. (Methanol advocates counter that gasoline can produce almost as much atmospheric formaldehyde as methanol, although its formaldehyde forms in the air *after* the fumes leave the tailpipe.)

Methanol presents other problems as well. Cars that run on straight methanol can be hard to start at temperatures below 50°F. When the fuel burns, its flame is an almost-invisible blue; if you had an auto accident on a bright day, you might not immediately notice a fire. Methanol is also poisonous; swallowing as little as one ounce can blind or kill you.

Two of these drawbacks are overcome by a fuel blend known as M85—85 percent methanol and 15 percent gasoline. It can start cars at −20°, and it burns with gasoline's typical bright yellow flame. But M85 compromises some of methanol's clean-air benefits. For example, hydrocarbon emissions per mile from straight methanol are 90 percent lower than from gasoline, but M85 cuts hydrocarbon emissions by only 35 percent.

Automakers plan to make it difficult for people to swallow methanol accidentally by installing devices in fuel tanks that prevent the siphoning of fuel. The National Capital Poison Center at Georgetown University Hospital estimates that without such gadgets, nearly 200 people could die each year after accidentally swallowing methanol.

Methanol, the EPA predicts, will cost the same as regular gasoline, mile-for-mile. But oil-industry spokespeople and other researchers contend that methanol may cost as much as 50 percent more per mile than gasoline. Cars that use it may cost $300 to $2000 more to buy.

Some methanol advocates argue that a switch to methanol would help ease U.S. dependence on Middle East oil. But that's a debatable proposition. Most methanol would be produced from natural gas. Although the U.S., Canada, and Mexico have enough natural gas to provide methanol for about 10 percent of America's market, most of the fuel would likely be produced overseas, including the Middle East, near extensive natural-gas reserves. Methanol can also be made from coal, which is abundant in the U.S. But that method is expensive and dirty using current technology.

Methanol's impact on global warming depends on how the methanol is made. All methanol produces the same amount of carbon dioxide when burned. But when both production and combustion are considered, methanol made from natural gas generates about 10 percent less carbon dioxide than gasoline, while methanol made from coal produces up to 100 percent more.

Other Alternatives

Cars could run on fuels other than gasoline or methanol. Here are the most likely candidates:

Ethanol, the alcohol fuel made from corn and sugar cane, offers many of methanol's clean-air benefits. It's also less corrosive than methanol and contains one-third more energy per gallon. Ethanol can help lower carbon-dioxide emissions because the plants it's made from use carbon dioxide from the air as they grow. Much of that benefit is, however, offset by the carbon-dioxide emissions from the tractors used to care for the crops and from the fermentation processes.

Ethanol is too expensive to compete as a straight motor fuel. It costs nearly twice as much as gasoline. Supplies are also limited. If 40 percent of the total U.S. grain harvest were turned into ethanol, it would provide just 10 percent of the fuel consumed in the U.S. each year.

Ethanol has been used as a gasoline extender and octane enhancer since the energy shortages of the 1970s, and it will undoubtedly continue to be important as an ingredient in clean gasoline. Today it's found in about 8 percent of the gasoline sold in the U.S.

Compressed natural gas, already used for cooking and heating, makes sense for fleet vehicles that service a limited geographic area and can return to a central point at night for refueling. It now powers more than 30,000 vehicles in the U.S.—from school buses in Oklahoma to United Parcel Service delivery trucks in Brooklyn, N.Y.

Compressed natural gas emits at least 40 percent less hydrocarbons and 30 percent less carbon dioxide per mile than gasoline. Carbon monoxide, formaldehyde, and airborne toxics are nearly eliminated. It's also cheap—about 70 cents for the energy equivalent of a gallon of gasoline at current prices.

But this gas isn't a practical alternative fuel for passenger cars; you'd either have to load down your car with extra fuel tanks or refuel every 100 miles or so. If compressed-natural-gas cars reach the consumer market, they will cost about $800 more than conventional cars, in part to cover the cost of the heavy cylinders needed to keep the fuel under pressure.

Electricity remains the cleanest alternative to gasoline. Like battery-powered golf carts, electric cars would emit no exhaust, although the power plants that produced the electricity would probably burn the fuel *they* use in a less than pristine way.

At this point, it is impractical to manufacture an electric-powered passenger car. The lead-acid batteries used in today's models weigh as much as 1000 pounds and require six to eight hours of recharging for every 60 to 100 miles. Significant technological breakthroughs will be needed before these vehicles can satisfy consumer needs.

Solar-hydrogen fuel may be the most promising of long-term alternatives. Large solar cells set up in sunny parts of the U.S. would convert the sun's

Solar-hydrogen fuel may be the most promising of long-term alternatives. Large solar cells set up in sunny parts of the U.S. would convert the sun's energy into electricity, which would then be used to split water molecules and form hydrogen. Vehicles that run on hydrogen release only water vapor and oxides of nitrogen; they do not emit carbon dioxide or other gases that contribute to global warming.

"In the Seventies there was virtually no solar industry. Today it's a mature, billion-dollar industry."

—Scott Sklar,
executive director of
Solar Energy Industries
Association

energy into electricity, which would then be used to split water molecules and form hydrogen. Vehicles that run on hydrogen release only water vapor and oxides of nitrogen; they do not emit carbon dioxide or other gases that contribute to global warming. Research on this technology is under way, but hydrogen-powered passenger cars are unlikely to be available for decades. Even farther down the road are cars powered by solar-generated electricity. (pp. 11–15)

"The Fuels of the Future," in Consumer Reports, *Vol. 55, No. 1, January, 1990, pp. 11–15.*

Alternative Fuel Sources: A Status Report

Will coal, even so-called clean coal, be stoking the world's stove in 2025? Will petroleum products propel our cars—and continue to wreak havoc on fragile ecosystems? Never has the cost of energy—the environmental cost, that is—been more profound.

The urgency with which the earth's citizens investigate these questions, in fact, has never been greater. Policymakers and politicians have gotten wind of this build-up of harmful greenhouse gases around the globe, primarily due to the burning of fossil fuels. They must answer to an increasingly concerned public no longer willing to tolerate the polluting energy sources and policies of the past.

Researchers and engineers are also hunkering down, fine-tuning the technologies for clean, renewable energy alternatives. Forward-thinking entrepreneurs are pitching in, too, by finding the means to make them economical.

These efforts are already bearing fruit. Today there is an array of renewable energy sources that hold promise for the future. The status reports that follow highlight some of the energy options facing world leaders and utility companies. As we race toward the twenty-first century, however, we will need to face an even greater issue: Our entire energy infrastructure must be reevaluated. On to the post-fossil era.

Has Solar Eclipsed?

Once upon a time, solar power was the golden child of energy. In the Seventies politicians embraced it, environmentalists hailed it as the answer to the energy crisis, and enterprising businesses took advantage of generous federal incentives to develop solar ventures. President Jimmy Carter even had solar panels installed on the White House.

Within months of President Ronald Reagan's inauguration, however, he ditched the solar collectors, signaling the slashing of solar research budgets for eight consecutive years. From 1981 to 1989, U.S. funding for solar energy and other renewables was cut from $750 million to $150 million, according to Christopher Flavin of the WorldWatch Institute. Hundreds of solar collector manufacturers went out of business or left for other shores.

Despite federal funding barriers, however, the solar industry has flourished. More than 1.2 million U.S. buildings now sport solar water heating systems, and the political climate for developing other uses for solar energy appears, well, sunny. And in 1990 federal research and development budgets increased by 30 percent. "In the Seventies there was virtually no solar industry," says Scott Sklar, executive director of the Solar Energy Industries Association. "Today it's a mature, billion-dollar industry." Nowhere is this more apparent than in California's Mojave Desert, where an array of collectors now produces roughly 350 megawatts of power, almost half the capacity of a nuclear power plant and 92 percent of the world's solar supply. Built by the Luz Corporation, the system uses mirrors mounted on parabolic troughs to focus sunlight onto pipes carrying synthetic oil. Heat from the oil creates steam that drives a turbine generator. Luz's electricity costs about eight cents per kilowatt-hour, close to the residential average.

The drawback: Prime sites for such solar thermal-electric plants are confined to the sunny Southwest. Other solar technologies, however, such as seasonal solar energy storage systems could potentially fill in where sunlight is less abundant. Demonstrated primarily in Europe, these systems gather heat during summer months and store it underground for use in the winter.

Solar photovoltaic cells, however, hold the greatest potential. Semiconductor devices, photovoltaics convert sunlight directly into electricity, producing no pollution or noise, and don't require any moving parts. Today's best cells convert 36 percent of their area's sunlight into electricity, up from about 16 percent in the mid-Seventies. Promising thin-film devices, one fiftieth the thickness of human hair, should let the sun shine even brighter.

Photovoltaic electricity now costs five times more than conventionally produced energy. But photovoltaics should eventually yield electricity cheaper than what we have today because thin-film cells can be easily mass-produced, says Princeton University energy analyst Robert Williams.

The climate for solar development may be improving, but some industry watchers fear that it may be too late for the United States to reclaim its early edge in the world market. "It's a question of whether we're going to do it ourselves or sit back and let the Japanese run our solar energy factories, just like they're doing in the auto industry," Sklar says.—*Steve Nadis*

Biomass for the Masses

In a remote village in central India, a barefoot farmer beams with pride as he shows off the community's power source: an underground tank where cow manure, straw, and other plant residues are converted into methane gas for cooking and lighting.

Bioenergy—burning plants, wood, and agricultural waste for fuel—is nearly as old as man. Today millions of Indians and Chinese use such materials for energy. Biomass, mainly in the form of firewood, already provides 14 percent of the world's energy, equal to the 21 million barrels of oil produced by OPEC every day, according to the Biomass Users Network, a consortium of 46 Third World nations. And with concern over harmful greenhouse gases associated with fossil fuels, researchers are now taking a closer look at the potential of biomass energy. By converting biomass to electricity in numerous small-scale power plants, Third World countries could radically reduce their consumption of oil and coal, says Princeton's Robert Williams.

Indeed, produced at a sustainable rate, biomass has a lot going for it. Carbon dioxide, released when biomass is processed, burned, or fermented, balances the carbon dioxide consumer during photosynthesis. The bottom line: Unlike fossil fuels, biomass does not contribute to global warming.

Williams believes biomass, especially in the form of wood chips and sugarcane waste, could power electric plants that use new technologies borrowed from jet engines, as well as the coal-fired power plants that biomass could ultimately phase out. The plants would rely on gasification, a process of converting the solid fuel into gas by burning it with low oxygen, similar to banking a fire in a wood stove by shutting down the air intake. A by-product of gasification, carbon monoxide would burn in a superefficient turbine generator like those in jets; waste heat would be recycled to power an additional steam-driven electric generator.

Such technologies could easily furnish electricity in the 80 developing nations that grow sugar. Over the next 40 years, the gasification of waste bagasse,

Mexico, New Zealand, and Iceland already produce much of their energy from geothermal, and scientists say the Philippines, Indonesia, and other oil-poor developing nations of the Pacific Rim, rich in volcanic heat, could easily reap this earthly treasure.

"Since 1981 costs have dropped from twenty-five cents per kilowatt-hour to less than ten cents, and reliability has increased from sixty to ninety-five percent."
—Randall Swisher, executive director of the American Wind Energy Association

the part of sugarcane with the juice extracted, could produce 70 percent more electric power than all the countries produced by burning coal and oil in 1987. Biomass power plants could also gasify low-quality wood harvested from forests or grown as an energy crop on hundreds of millions of acres of nonproductive grasslands, pastures, range, and deforested lands.

To succeed, producing energy from biomass will require responsible agricultural and industrial practices, warns Sam Baldwin, a physicist with the Office of Technology Assessment. In Brazil, for example, 44 million cars are currently powered by ethanol, a biomass fuel made from fermented sugar, and the discharge of untreated ethanol by-products has fouled many of the rivers in the country's northwest.

Moreover, if countries fail to use only surplus, waste, or specially grown fuels, biomass power plants could end up consuming trees needed to control erosion, dung needed for fertilizer, straw necessary to replenish soils, and even such food ingredients as cornstarch and sugar. "I'd hate to see a choice being made between food for the poor and fuel for the rich," Baldwin says.

—Ben Barber

Nuclear Winner?

The two words nuclear energy pack as much emotional punch as *A-bomb, cancer,* or *AIDS.* Chernobyl and Three Mile Island have become emblems of great hopes dashed much as the *Challenger* disaster forced NASA to overhaul the U.S. space program. Unlike the space program, however, the nation's nuclear industry—which has contracted no new plants since 1978—appears indefinitely stalled.

But not doomed. Growing concern about global warming may offer the ailing industry a chance for a comeback, says Carl Goldstein, vice president of the U.S. Council for Energy Awareness. According to a 1989 council report, nuclear-generated electricity reduced utility emissions of carbon dioxide by 20 percent. Nuclear plants produce almost no particulate emissions, carbon monoxide, volatile organic compounds, or methane. Nor do they generate noise or visible pollution or require large numbers of vehicles to haul fuel.

That's the good news. The downside of nuclear power—the safety of reactors and the disposal of radioactive waste—continues to challenge researchers. Nuclear's "second coming" will require solutions to both problems.

Most American nuclear power plants, including the one that neared meltdown at Three Mile Island, have light water reactors. For many of them, when problems crop up, plant personnel must activate systems designed to avert potential disasters. The U.S. Nuclear Regulatory Commission (NRC) is currently reviewing plans for an advanced light water reactor (ALWR) that takes human fallibility into account. It sports passive safety features dependent on natural physical processes—gravity, natural circulation, and convection. The ALWR is simpler to build and operate and has lower generating costs than current nuclear plants.

The United States is far from alone in the search for a safe reactor. One promising though untried reactor is the process inherent ultimately safe reactor, a radically passive design from Sweden. The reactor would be completely submerged in a pool of water laced with heat-absorbing boron and would cool by natural convection. The reactor would be virtually invulnerable to a catastrophe caused by operator error, terrorist attack, or conventional war.

Even as scientists come up with safer reactors, they still must solve the problems of storing long-lived radioactive waste and decommissioning worn-out reactors. To date public outcry has halted the establishment of any long-term dump site for nuclear by-products.

Indeed, widespread fear of nuclear power may be the industry's foremost roadblock. In two recent polls, more than 75 percent of Americans reported that they believed nuclear power to be important. The same percentage of respondents, however, rejected or reserved judgment on a nuclear plant in their own neighborhoods.

Thomas Murley, director of the NRC's Office of Nuclear Reactor Regulation, believes time is on nuclear's side. "In the beginning, people were afraid of electricity or of riding in a vehicle that ran on gasoline," he says. "If we don't scare people every five or ten years with an accident, then they might begin to feel that nuclear power really is a viable alternative."—*Steven Scott Smith*

Last Gas

Picture this: The earth's deserts are sown with solar collectors, sprouting vast fields of photovoltaic cells that convert sunlight directly into electricity. An electric current is then passed through pools of water, splitting the H_2O into its component gases (one part oxygen, two parts hydrogen). Hydrogen gas is captured, stored, and piped to urban areas. Boilers burn it to heat homes. Power plants use it to fire the generators that produce electricity. Filling stations pump it into cars, trucks, and buses. Hydrogen, the most abundant element in the universe, is harnessed in the service of humankind. And because it returns to the atmosphere and recombines with oxygen, all you get when you burn it is more water.

Although solar technologies are not the only way to electrolyze water and produce hydrogen gas, solar-based hydrogen systems offer one of the best long-range prospects for hydrogen. Joan Ogden of Princeton University's Center for Energy and Environmental Studies estimates that it would take only 24,000 square miles of solar collectors (about half of one percent of U.S. land area) for hydrogen to replace all of the oil used in the United States.

Hydrogen enjoys widespread use in industry today, most notably to manufacture ammonia and process petroleum products; and photovoltaic technology is familiar to anyone with a solar-powered pocket calculator. But an overhaul like the one Ogden envisions, requiring the erection of a whole new energy infrastructure, is decades away.

Steady advances in solar-cell technology may advance the hydrogen age in more piecemeal fashion. By the mid-Nineties, Solartex, the largest U.S.-owned manufacturer of photovoltaic cells, will be inexpensively mass-producing photovoltaics made of ordinary window glass coated with a thin film of silicon. By the end of this decade, Solarex vice president David Carlson believes, solar-hydrogen systems will begin to appear on a small, independent scale in communities isolated from traditional energy sources. A village in Africa, for example, could set up a small photovoltaic array, hook it up to a modest-size electrolyzer, electrolyze the hydrogen on-site, and then store or use it for heat and car fuel, or run it through fuel cells to generate electricity at night.

Hydrogen-powered cars, of course, require an infrastructure before they become commonplace. (Hydrogen gas stations, for example, must be readily accessible.) In the meantime, engineers face a big challenge: how to store enough hydrogen in a car to give the vehicle a reasonable traveling range. BMW has developed a car that runs on liquid hydrogen and has a range of 190 to 200 miles. But the system still requires two to three times the volume of a normal gasoline tank. Liquid hydrogen must also be kept at $-423°F$, making self-service hydrogen gas pumps impossible, says Christoph Huss, BMW's product information manager in North America. And because some hydrogen may be released when the engine is not running, garages would have to sport sophisticated ventilation systems.

Beyond the technical obstacles to these solar-hydrogen applications there are the inevitable political ones. "Solar energy in the Sahara alone can supply the world's energy needs," Huss says. "But if you use the Sahara or the desert in the Arabian states, many people will still be afraid of depending on these countries for energy."

Carbon dioxide, released when biomass is processed, burned, or fermented, balances the carbon dioxide consumed during photosynthesis. The bottom line: Unlike fossil fuels, biomass does not contribute to global warning.

Mexico, New Zealand, and Iceland already produce much of their energy from geothermal, and scientists say the Philippines, Indonesia, and other oil-poor developing nations of the Pacific Rim, rich in volcanic heat, could easily reap this earthly treasure. But geothermal energy also promises to help meet America's power needs.

Considering the Persian Gulf conflict, Huss's point is well taken. But with fossil fuel supplies dwindling, political discussions of the future of clean, limitless hydrogen may well be academic.—*Mary McDonnell*

Hot Prospects

Deep within the earth, where tectonic plates collide, magma boils and sputters, creating a steamy brew that represents a gold mine of untapped power: geothermal energy.

Mexico, New Zealand, and Iceland already produce much of their energy from geothermal, and scientists say the Philippines, Indonesia, and other oil-poor developing nations of the Pacific Rim, rich in volcanic heat, could easily reap this earthly treasure. But geothermal energy also promises to help meet America's power needs.

Current systems, like those lighting up much of Southern California, tap into steam deposits 6,000 feet to 10,000 feet below the ground to turn turbines and generate electricity. Science, however, is fine-tuning the process. Acting as high-tech divining rods, computers pinpoint geothermal hot spots, and a new crop of sturdy pipes and materials defy the corroding heat of the underground. Scientists at Southeastern Massachusetts University, moreover, are perfecting systems that test the resilience of well gear in the lab, a step up from costly wait-and-see drilling.

Researchers are also finding ways to trick nature into providing an endless supply of steam by making use of hot dry rock. To test the technology, U.S. Department of Energy (DOE) scientists have targeted a site in the mountains near New Mexico's Los Alamos National Laboratory where volcanoes rumbled hundreds of thousands of years ago.

To produce steam, scientists drill two wells 10,000 to 15,000 feet deep into rock and then force water down one well to create fractures in the bottoms of both wells. The goal: to pump water through the latticework of fractures so that it emerges from the second well as superheated steam.

Molten rock, however, represents an even hotter geothermal prospect. In a pilot project in Long Valley, California, DOE researchers will drill down 20,000 feet to just above the chamber of molten rock in a dormant volcano, where temperatures could reach 1200°C—potentially producing enough steam energy to power a city of 1 million.

But you don't have to have a volcano in your backyard to take advantage of the earth's changing temperature, says Paul Lienau, director of the Oregon Institute of Technology's Geo-Heat Center. Some 110,000 homes and businesses nationwide use low-temperature heat pumps that rely on a network of pipes less than ten feet underground. The pipes are warmed in winter and cooled in summer. Water running through the pipes heats or cools the facilities. The cost: about $8,000 per unit.

Within 20 years, says Ted Mock, the DOE's director of geothermal research, geothermal energy should provide the United States with about 5,000 megawatts of electricity (equal to five large nuclear plants) with minimal risk to the environment and public safety. Call it no contest against geothermal's chief competitor, natural gas. "If we are really serious about our future," says Dave Anderson of the National Geothermal Association, "geothermal is ready."
—*Dana Points*

Winds of Change

Hikers along California's Cameron Ridge have a choice of spectacular views: To the east the Mojave stretches under a cloud-cluttered sky. To the west, on every hilltop, rows of giant pinwheels spin like hummingbirds in overdrive. This is wind power in action.

Born out of 1980 tax incentives, wind farms got off to a stormy start. In order to harvest time-limited credits thousands of faulty machines were rushed into action, and millions of dollars were sunk into ill-conceived projects. By 1985 the government had withdrawn incentives and cut research grants by 90 percent. Observers confidently penned obituaries for the industry.

Today wind power, among the cleanest and most competitive of renewable energy sources, is making a brisk comeback. "Since 1981 costs have dropped from twenty-five cents per kilowatt-hour to less than ten cents, and reliability has increased from sixty to ninety-five percent," says Randall Swisher, executive director of the Washington-based American Wind Energy Association. In California, Pacific Gas and Electric, the state's largest utility, will purchase most of the 2.5 billion kilowatt-hours that state wind farms are expected to produce this year.

For the handful of wind entrepreneurs who prevailed, the Eighties proved to be a time of trial and error. For example, once planners learned that the energy output of two machines just 100 feet apart could vary by as much as 20 percent, they began "siting" the placement of every windmill they installed, rather than grouping them. Moreover, farm operators now wash their equipment once or twice a month to clean away grime, which can reduce a turbine's efficiency by 30 percent.

The industry plans greater technological fixes in the future. In one promising cooperative effort, the Electric Power Research Institute, Pacific Gas and Electric, and wind turbine manufacturer U.S. Windpower are testing prototypes of a 300-kilowatt wind turbine that will spin at the speed of the wind, rather than at the fixed speed of standard turbines, increasing wind capture by as much as 10 percent. Other groups aim to improve windmill efficiency through better blade design.

Other things to look for: advanced materials that yield lighter, stronger components, extra tall towers, and rotors that can bob up and down, in addition to moving east and west in pursuit of the wind. These improvements should reduce the costs of wind electricity to about five cents per kilowatt-hour by the mid-Nineties. According to DOE estimates, costs should drop even more in the next 20 years.

Even so, while the technical problems are solvable, wind power could use a little help from Uncle Sam, says Robert Jans, an energy consultant in Byron, California. Government funding for the development of wind turbine technology in Europe is currently estimated to exceed U.S. federal support ten times. "Unlike us," Jans says, "they have decided that the environmental and social costs of not doing this are much too high."—*Beth Livermore* (pp. 50–2, 80–7)

Steve Nadis, Ben Barber, Steven Scott Smith, Mary McDonnell, Dana Points, and Beth Livermore, "Alternative Sources: A Status Report," in Omni, *Vol. 13, No. 8, May, 1991, pp. 50–2, 80–7.*

Any serious discussion of breaking our petroleum addiction has to focus on transportation. Vehicles drink nearly 12 million of the 18 million barrels we use daily, and most of that goes into cars, trucks, and buses.

Kicking the Oil Habit: Alternative Fuels Available Right Now

For years I had been substance-dependent and it was time to get out. The stuff had always made life easier—until the after-effects kicked in. As friends warned me it would, it was starting to ruin my health. Sure, it was relatively cheap, but I could no longer dodge the fact that kids were dying so foreign cartels could feed my habit. I had to do something. Oil was ruining my life.

Natural gas vehicles (NGVs) not only contribute a lot less to local smog than do gasoline or diesel vehicles, they also emit 25 percent less carbon dioxide, which means less risk of global warming.

What I got my hands on was one answer to U.S. petroleum dependence—natural gas, a fuel that's cheap, clean, and domestically abundant. There I was, wind in my hair, tiger in my tank, driving a standard full-size Chrysler and enjoying as smooth a ride as Lee Iacocca ever promised. The only thing missing was the gasoline.

Any serious discussion of breaking our petroleum addiction has to focus on transportation. Vehicles drink nearly 12 million of the 18 million barrels we use daily, and most of that goes into cars, trucks, and buses. Transportation is 97 percent oil-dependent, while electricity generation is only 5 percent. Although oil use for purposes besides transportation has dropped 20 percent since the mid-seventies, vehicles have boosted their demand by about the same amount. As a result, we're back to the oil consumption peak of 1976, with less crude in the ground and little hope for stability in the major oil-rich countries. But we have the tools to get the oil-monkey off our backs—if only we'd choose to use them.

Of the contenders to replace oil, compressed natural gas and electricity are the most immediately promising. Both are cleaner than gasoline. Both are available now, without pie-in-the-sky technological advances. Neither poses the national security problems of petroleum. And when environmental effects are counted, both cost less. The trick is to identify the transportation niche that each can fill and then gradually begin displacing gasoline-powered vehicles. The ideal initial target group for converting to natural gas, for instance, is fleet vehicles—which consume 20 percent of our road transportation energy. That's about as much oil as we import from the Persian Gulf.

It was a bit of a letdown when I finally got to drive an automobile powered by natural gas. Out on the open road, I flipped a switch on the dash to go from gasoline to compressed natural gas (CNG) and . . . nothing happened. An instant's hesitation, and then the Chrysler drove as it had before. Or so it seemed. In fact, from the planet's perspective, the situation had changed radically. After all, the smog-producing components of my exhaust had suddenly dropped 80 percent.

Natural gas vehicles (NGVs) not only contribute a lot less to local smog than do gasoline or diesel vehicles, they also emit 25 percent less carbon dioxide, which means less risk of global warming. Because the fuel is so much cleaner than gasoline, vehicles running on it require less maintenance and fewer oil changes.

And this is no fantasy fuel; some 750,000 NGVs are already on the road, and doing quite nicely. Unfortunately, only 30,000 of them are in the U.S.—about one car in 6,000. Canada, with one-tenth of our population, has an NGV fleet two-thirds as large. Australia and Italy have 50 times as many NGVs per capita; New Zealand's proportion is 320 times as high as the U.S.'s. Those countries haven't wrecked their economies or deprived their citizens of the inalienable right to the thrill of the open road. With the help of NGVs, cleaning up the air and protecting the beaches, reducing the risk of global warming and keeping troops out of the Middle East can be achieved without drastically changing your life.

The fuel itself is 30 to 50 percent cheaper than gasoline, and likely to stay that way for at least a few more automobile lifetimes. Like the Chrysler I drove, nearly all NGVs now on the road have modified ("dual-fuel") gasoline engines. Adding compressed natural gas capability runs about $2,000, in part because it is done on a small custom scale. (The NGV I drove is owned by Washington Gas, which had to send the car to West Virginia for conversion.) In a typical family car, money saved on fuel could take eight years to pay for the retrofit. This isn't likely to be a big hit with the average consumer, although reduced maintenance costs would sweeten the deal. But several technologies now in development will improve the picture for NGVs. A "dedicated CNG engine" will get higher efficiency and performance by taking advantage of the 135 octane rating of natural gas. This higher efficiency will help close the gap in driving range between NGVs and conventional cars—CNG currently requires four times the fuel-storage volume as gasoline. Better fuel tanks should reduce weight and increase range.

You may agree that the warm feeling of doing a little extra for national security and the environment would more than balance any small differences in cost and convenience. But before you rush into anything, let me warn you of a little problem you'll run into 100-odd miles down the road. Have you ever seen a CNG filling station?

I have personally visited one-third of all the supposedly public CNG pumps in America: at the Amoco station at 9th and Pennsylvania in Southeast D.C. (the other two are in Colorado). The pump is a simple white box sporting Amoco's green-leaf CNG logo and two thin hoses. Because of an archaic utility regulation prohibiting resale, this D.C. outlet, which isn't yet operational, won't even be able to sell natural gas to the public. But surely the scarcity problem is fixable. When personal computers came out, there weren't too many stores where you could buy floppy disks, either. That didn't mean we should have given up on PCs.

The ABCs of NGVs

Converting to natural gas vehicles poses a chicken-and-egg dilemma. Detroit would be willing to optimize an NGV if there were a solid market for it, and mass production would eliminate the high cost of retrofits. Buyers would be attracted to its low operating costs—if they could readily refuel it. And gas station owners would install CNG compressors if there were enough demand to make that investment profitable. But no one will make the first move.

The key to breaking this gridlock is to begin with cars that travel local routes and can be centrally fueled. "Fleet vehicle," the catch-all category, includes buses, delivery vans, garbage trucks, taxicabs, even rental cars—in all, about 10 percent of American vehicles. These vehicles consume some 20 percent of road transportation energy, because they log double the annual mileage of the average family car (which means that retrofits will pay off twice as quickly). The conversion sequence could work like this:

1) Start with government-owned or -operated cars, buses, and trucks that run on regular schedules. Put inexpensive overnight-fill compressors at their central parking lots. (Off-hours fueling makes better use of gas pipelines, too, by leveling out demand.) In Texas, one-third of new transit and private fleet purchases in metropolitan areas must be alternative fuel vehicles by 1994; that number will go up to 50 percent in 1996, and 90 percent by 1998. The more cities that follow Texas's model, the cheaper conversion will be for all.

2) Convert private fleets of company cars, delivery vans, and taxis. (Imagine what this could do for New York City's air quality.)

3) Switch longer-range government vehicles to natural gas.

4) Convert most rental cars to natural gas. Customers who rent for local use could get discounts for renting NGVs. After all, the majority of clients at National, Hertz, and Avis are businessmen who tend to use their cars only to get around town (a National employee in D.C. estimated that the average businessman puts only 20 miles on the odometer). And because 85 percent of all rentals are dropped off where they were picked up, many rental sites could be easily converted to centralized compressed gas fueling.

By step four, there'd be enough demand to support some private filling stations in big cities, and automakers would be producing engines to take advantage of CNG's greater efficiency. The cost advantages of NGVs would then become compelling to commuters, especially if air regulations cracked down on traditional fuels at the same time. Once this snowball effect gets big enough, perhaps Americans will be able to drive coast-to-coast in natural gas vehicles . . . which means we'd finally catch up to the Canadians, who already can.

GM has already built a prototype high-performance electric sportscar, regrettably called "Impact." The Impact has a top speed of 110 mph and a range of 120 miles.

Electric vehicles are quiet, rechargeable virtually anywhere, and clean. Even when you take into account the emissions caused by making the electricity they use, EVs contribute less to local smog than gasoline-powered cars. Using coal-fired power, they produce slightly more carbon dioxide, but 90 percent less when they use nuclear, and 100 percent less with renewable energy. Think about it: streets full of softly humming vehicles, not a tailpipe in sight.

Silent Running

While we're waiting for these natural gas filling stations to sprout up, we can begin switching to electric vehicles (EVs). EVs are quiet, rechargeable virtually anywhere, and clean. Even when you take into account the emissions caused by making the electricity they use, EVs contribute less to local smog than gasoline-powered cars. Using coal-fired power, they produce slightly more carbon dioxide, but 90 percent less when they use nuclear, and 100 percent less with renewable energy. Think about it: streets full of softly humming vehicles, not a tailpipe in sight.

An EV drives pretty much like any other car, except that the brakes feel odd. That's because when you step on the brake pedal, the motor becomes a generator, pumping energy back into the batteries instead of dumping it overboard as waste heat. When the motor is not needed to push the car (at a stoplight, for instance), it simply shuts off like a light. For environmental reasons, this feature makes EVs more attractive in traffic-congested areas. They'd be a godsend in Southern California, where some 20 percent of gasoline is burned in cars stuck in traffic, getting zero miles per gallon.

By plugging an on-board charger into a socket at home, you could juice up your EV overnight for about half the cost of the gasoline it would take to drive as far. But although EVs have been around for a century, they are still rare creatures, numbering less than 10,000 worldwide. Why? Probably because their range stinks: I recently drove an electric "G-Van" owned by Southern California Edison—a smooth and quiet ride, but the van could go only 60 miles before it needed to recharge for several hours.

But if you apply a little common sense and consider the statistics, this problem starts to shrink. We all know two-car families—in fact, there are about 40 million U.S. households, and more every year, with two or more cars. Clearly, in many of these households—more common sense—the family tends to rely on one car for trips around town, another for trips on the open road. Now consider this fact: The average commute to work by car—round trip—is only *10 miles*. And it takes place at an average speed of 31 mph. For that trip, you don't exactly need the Batmobile.

EVs can also be used commercially. Although the G-Van is simply a low-tech variant of a vehicle built to run on oil—the gasoline engine, transmission, exhaust system, and radiator have been stripped out and replaced with one ton of batteries and an electric motor—it is ideal for predictable, short-haul urban driving. The electric van would cost about five percent less to own and operate than a gasoline-powered one. That's why the British have used electric delivery vans for years, and why electric trucks are hauling trash in, of all places, Saudi Arabia.

Put one EV in each multi-car family, throw in all those short-range fleet cars and vans, and you're talking about a hefty slice of the market. In fact, General Motors is aiming to have a marketable EV on the road by mid-decade. With the help of Paul MacCready, the American Society of Mechanical Engineers' "Engineer of the Century," GM has already built a prototype high-performance electric sportscar, regrettably called "Impact." The Impact has a top speed of 110 mph and a range of 120 miles. GM is currently touting Impact research in television spots. Through more aerodynamic designs, higher pressure tires, and an improved power train, MacCready thinks we can double auto energy efficiency without loss of safety or performance. Improved efficiency not only cuts oil demand directly, but it also strengthens the case for lower-density alternatives like EVs, by easing the problems of energy storage and range.

Guilt- and Gulf-free

Aside from waging war in the Gulf, the Bush energy strategy should include more than just lobbying for oil pumping in environmentally sensitive areas. That sort of pumping will meet one year of national demand at best, while leaving the U.S. with less in reserve for the next crisis. If, as Bush suggested it would in his State of the Union Address, the administration focuses in the next year on the need for a credible energy policy, here are some more imaginative steps it might consider:

- Consumer Information: as in labeling, for example. If we can require labels on cigarette packs and beer bottles, we can certainly do so on automobiles. Sure, we have EPA mileage ratings, but they run 15 percent higher than reality, and they aren't much use in buying decisions. A smarter system would put a statement on each sticker such as: "This car will cost about $W per year to own and operate." To better inform more conscientious consumers, the label might add, "It will do X, Y, and Z to the environment." A lot of us would discover that driving can be much cheaper than it is now—and guilt-free at the same time.

- Get Fuel Prices Right: Until the price of each commodity reflects the side effects of its use, we won't get the full benefits of a free market. Since our troops are presumably not dying to protect OPEC's right to overcharge us for oil, let's assume that when the war ends, oil will finally trade at its market price. All energy sources should then be taxed in proportion to the costs they impose on society through pollution, resource depletion, and security risks. Estimates of these costs don't have to be perfect to be better than what we use now.

- Reward as well as Penalize Automakers: A sliding scale of tough penalties on dirty gas guzzlers balanced by rebates for the leanest and cleanest would tell Detroit and Japan what to do. We can then let them figure out how to do it.

- Support Efficiency and Renewables Research: Department of Energy efficiency programs of the early eighties are yielding thousands of dollars in direct energy savings for each research dollar spent. In the long run, putting money into efficiency R&D will do as much to protect and improve the American way of life as investing in more Patriot missiles.

"We are doing everything we can to guarantee . . . that there will be an adequate supply of hydrocarbons," declared George Bush during the early days of the Gulf crisis—in retrospect, perhaps the most chilling comment on American preparations for war. Once the dust settles in the desert, maybe Americans will realize that there are better ways to get their hydrocarbons than by fighting for them, and that there are better ways to get to work in the morning than by driing a gas guzzler. Oil may have helped make the United States great, but it's time to start letting go. (pp. 32–5)

Peter Gray, "Kicking the Oil Habit," in The Washington Monthly, *Vol. 23, No. 3, March 1991, pp. 32–5.*

In August [1990], when crude prices soared and so did polite ones, Americans were reminded once again that someday we're going to have to kick our 8-million-barrel-a-day petroleum habit.

Converting Waste into Fuel

"What's that you're burning in the furnace, dear?"

"Mutton, honey."

Exchanges like this could become common if we follow the example set by Fenland Sheepskins. The Bridgewater, England, processing plant expects to save $50,000 over the next five years by powering its boilers with a mixture of fuel oil and mutton fat extracted from sheepskins before they're made into coats.

During the 1981–82 school year two university buses actually ran on peanut oil as efficiently as they had on diesel fuel.

"People thought we were crazy when we started burning the mutton fat back in July," says the plant's managing director, Andrew Tinnion. He didn't feel sheepish for long. "Two days later Iraq invaded Kuwait, fuel became dear, and overnight we doubled our savings—twenty percent of our oil bill."

In August [1990], when crude prices soared and so did polite ones, Americans were reminded once again that someday we're going to have to kick our 8-million-barrel-a-day petroleum habit. President Bush would like us to cut our consumption by 530,000 barrels a day (no oil, just barrels). He hasn't come right out and said we're going to have to change our life-style or anything. He knows people still haven't forgiven Jimmy Carter for suggesting in 1977 that we turn down the heat and, a far more serious offense, *for wearing a sweater on television*. (Bush has made it clear to top aides that he's not to be photographed within 60 feet of a cardigan.)

We might, as the Department of Energy suggests, save oil by inflating our automobile tires more fully, but then we risk a serious air shortage. And such a measure would just postpone the inevitable: the only workable long-term solution is the development of alternative fuels.

Like mutton fat. Or four unusual biomass fuels—those created from renewable, living things—that I've recently run across: peanuts, tumbleweed, and a new Belgian import, called Wonderfuel, made from agricultural trash so densely compressed that its distributor claims a ton of it formed into logs takes up only 40 square inches of floor space. (Of course, the top log can be reached only by a nice young couple on Jupiter, but hey.) Oh yes, and cannabis.

Sure, those aren't the obvious choices. But we should keep an open mind as we map our national energy strategy, and we should not be so quick to say baaaah humbug to sheep. What if Fenland had?

The company was having trouble finding environmentally safe dumping sites for the 100 gallons of mutton fat it produced each week. In fact, Fenland was saddled with a five-year blubber backlog. So engineers decided to find a way to add the fat to the fuel-oil burners that produce the steam needed for tanning and processing sheepskins.

"We start with fuel oil," Tinnion explains. "Then, when the burners are going, we add filtered fat until the mix is fifty-fifty when we're going flat out." Now the company uses one-fifth less oil than it did prefat. "And our boiler chap is confident we'll get into a higher proportion of fat."

Animal by-products are a venerable source of fuel. In India, for example, cow dung has been burned for millennia (not the same piece, of course); beef tallow and whale oil powered nineteenth-century candles and lamps (although animal rights activists may argue that depending for power on the by-products of animal slaughter was never a good idea). At first, however, engineers at Fenland were stumped over how to filter the mutton fat so that it could be clean enough to burn.

"We begin with a hot, foul brew of fat and other muck recovered as waste from the tanning process," Tinnion says. "There's some residual dirt, sand, abrasives, and tanning chemicals." But the biggest problem at first was loose wool—yessir, yessir, three bags full—which clogged every conventional filter they tried.

"Eventually we found a special pressure-sensitive filter that cleans itself when it senses that it's blocked. Recently, though, we've discovered a new problem; some fine particles of an abrasive used for cutting suede nap are going through the filter and wearing out the teeth on the gear pumps. We're now looking at an American pump that's guaranteed to cope."

What else will be run on the lamb? Tinnion sees no reason why other industries should eschew the fat if they find a steady source; home heating is also a distant possibility. If the fuel were suited for transportation, it would give new meaning to the word *ramjet*, but using it in high-power engines is virtually impossible. (Still, users will have to be sure not to overdo. Although there's no reason now to count sheep, if mutton fat is too enthusiastically embraced, there'll never be another ewe.)

A University of Georgia agricultural engineer says we could run diesel engines, at least, for peanuts—if we run them *with* peanuts. For ten years John Goodrum has been researching the use of peanut oil as a substitute for diesel fuel. "It's a renewable resource, and it's inexpensive to refine," he says.

During the 1981–82 school year two university buses actually ran on peanut oil as efficiently as they had on diesel fuel, Goodrum says. He'll repeat that experiment once he's bred peanut plants that are less expensive to grow and that produce less-viscous oil; the fuel thickens in cold weather. (There are those who believe that an additive—perhaps grape jelly, perhaps marshmallow topping—might solve that problem.) Goodrum's gooberoil costs $1.75 a gallon. It's low in cholesterol, and drivers will have the option of filling up with regular or chunky.

From Belgium, birthplace of the french fry—you can look it up—comes a biomass fuel that its American distributor says beats the ash off any other run-of-the-mill pellet, briquette, or pressed fireplace log (my favorite brand of which says on the package, "Takes the heartbreak out of romance").

Wonderfuel burns twice as hot and much longer than any other available pressed log, according to Gary Scott, president of Scott Associates of Salt Lake City, importers of the equipment for making the stuff. The secret, he says, is a patented process invented in 1980 by Belgian engineer Marcel Neumann that involves high temperatures and pressure loads that densify the absolute heck out of sawdust, nutshells, rice hulls, olive pits, flax stems, cotton trash, and other agricultural wastes. "We can use virtually any type of vegetable matter," Scott explains, "as long as it contains fifteen percent or more of lignin, a substance that's a chief constituent of wood."

Melted lignin becomes the natural binder that holds Wonderfuel together. "You can snap other pressed logs in two by hand. Our log can't be broken. Try to crack it across your knee, and you'll break your knee."

As if the prospect of a patella fractured in the name of conscientious consumerhood weren't enough of a selling point, Scott has other good news. He says that while most fireplace logs are consumed in a couple of hours, foot-long Wonderfuel logs four inches in diameter burned from 11 to 17 hours in lab and field tests. Because Wonderfuel is so compressed, it burns very hot, nearly consuming itself and thus producing very little smoke. Wonderfuel burns so hot that in experiments at the University of Ghent, in Belgium, it was used to achieve temperatures over 2500 degrees. "For the first time in the history of man," Scott says (and he's a man, so he should know), "wood was used in the smelting of steel."

Possibly you don't want to smelt steel in your living room. Maybe you just want to toast marshmallows and make a few s'mores. Then you needn't buy the $250,000 machine that processes Wonderfuel; you can wait for the retail product, which will sell for $170 per ton. Wonderfuel's been selling briskly in Belgium, France, and Holland for about five years; Scott's the first to bring Eurotrash engineering to the States.

"We've identified twenty-five hundred companies in the United States that might like to turn their biowaste disposal problem into a source of income," he says. "For example, we're talking to a California manufacturer of church furniture that creates sixteen tons of waste sawdust and scrap wood a day. Depositing it at the local dump costs them thirty-eight thousand dollars a year." Imagine all those church furniture scraps festering in a landfill—pew!—when they could be turned into Wonderfuel.

"That same material run through our machine could solve their waste problem and provide a two-hundred-thousand-dollar net profit. We'd arrange for the retail outlets."

Researchers discovered years ago that, pressed into conventional logs and briquettes, tumbleweed has a cost and energy efficiency equivalent to that of low-grade coal.

A small minority in this country claims that the answer to our energy prayers lies in a plant illegal in the United States since 1937—cannabis hemp, whose leaves and flower tops are used to make marijuana.

In addition, Scott intends to talk to the folks in charge of the 56 million tons of waste corncobs and 600,000 tons of peanut shells produced in this country every year, to some of the sawmills that each produce 50 to 500 tons of sawdust a day, and to a single olive-processing plant that generates 35,000 tons of pits a year. "Think of all the renewable energy resources that can be converted through our process!" Scott crows.

Biochemist Jim Hageman of New Mexico State University has a wonderful Wonderfuel candidate. Tumbleweed, aka Russian Thistle and *Salsola*, its botanical name, could even qualify as fast food, if the wind's blowing hard enough.

Along with agronomist Jim Fowler, Hageman has spent 12 years carefully selecting and breeding the peripatetic plant, which entered this country a century ago as an illegal alien, its seeds hiding in flax shipments from Russia to South Dakota. Designed by nature to dry up and blow away, spreading seeds as it rolls, the bush is despised by farmers because it piles up and knocks down fences, clogs machinery, fuels prairie fires, and, worst of all, squeezes out legitimate crops.

But Hageman thinks the pariah plant may help fight hunger: because it's fast-growing, disease-resistant, protein-rich, sun- and salt-proof, and needs little water, it will make an excellent animal (and perhaps human) feed for arid Third World countries and the American Southwest. I myself make it a practice never to eat anything that's been the subject of a song by the Sons of the Pioneers, so tumbleweed, cool, clear water, and old paint are out. You, however, and you know who you are, may start the day with a big bowl of tumbleweedies. "We've been breeding for large plants, free of spines, with a balance of protein and fiber," he says. "We've been growing tumbleweeds six feet high and wider around, getting a tons-per-acre yield similar to alfalfa, while using considerably less water."

And *Salsola* can be more than a wind-powered snack. Researchers discovered years ago that, pressed into conventional logs and briquettes, tumbleweed has a cost and energy efficiency equivalent to that of low-grade coal.

With an investor, Hageman and Fowler had plans to harvest and liquefy huge amounts of tumbleweed, separating it into various components: protein and other nutrients for food supplements; chemicals that could be used to make vitamins and drugs like vasodilators, which enhance blood flow; and fibrous leftovers to be made into fuel. But the investor pulled out, and they were forced to burn their test acreage before the weeds blew into neighboring fields.

If you're worried that there aren't enough tumbleweeds around to fuel our civilization, talk to Darrell Bender, mayor of Mobridge, South Dakota. In November 1989, literally overnight, 30 tons of tumbleweed buried his prairie town of 4,100 souls and an equal number of bodies. Grown gargantuan on the margins of nearby Lake Oahe and set traveling by 60-mile-per-hour westerly winds, the rambling brambles, some as big as cars, jammed doors, hid houses, blocked streets, and crushed fences. "The largest one I saw was just under twenty-one feet in circumference and stood six feet high," Bender says. "Thousands of them were piled up on homes, up to the roofs."

If life hands us lemons, we are to make lemonade, according to the aphorism favored by the pathologically cheerful. Well, suppose life hands us tumbleweed? What the hell are we supposed to make then? With no vegetation-specific credo to guide him, Bender made bales. The town spent $8,500, its entire snow-removal budget, to have local farmers cart off, for use as windbreaks, 60 half-ton bales of the killer weed.

Speaking of which: a small (but festive) minority in this country claims that the answer to our energy prayers lies in a plant illegal in the United States since 1937—cannabis hemp, whose leaves and flower tops are used to make marijuana. (Perhaps you've seen the American Hemp Council's bumper stickers, which read HEMP, HEMP HOORAY: FUEL, FIBER, FREEDOM.)

Maybe it's not such a dopey idea. No one can deny that for millennia, cannabis hemp fibers have been used throughout the world for cloth, rope, and ship sails (the word *canvas* is thought to be a corruption of *cannabis*). Oil from its seeds has powered lamps and even engines. In the United States hemp was a popular crop from colonial times until its banning. During World War II, when the Japanese blocked Philippine hemp shipments, the prohibition was partially lifted and farmers could apply for a permit to grow the plant. (In fact, the Department of Agriculture made a film called *Hemp for Victory*, urging farmers to pitch in and raise hemp needed for military rope, twine, shoe thread, and parachute webbing: "American hemp will go on duty. . . . Just as in the days when *Old Ironsides* sailed the seas victorious with her hempen shrouds and hempen sails. Hemp for victory!")

Until hemp is legalized, proponents say, the United States is being cheated out of a fabulous source of alternative energy. "Hemp may be the best energy crop on the planet," claims John Dunlap, director of public affairs at the National Organization for the Reform of Marijuana Laws. "Its woody stalks, which contain seventy-seven percent cellulose and four percent lignin, produce ten tons of biomass per acre in four months. The stalks could be fermented into methanol, and the oil from seeds could be used for diesel fuel." This could give new meaning to the words *high octane*. "The seeds could also be turned into a high-protein, tofulike cake or an animal feed requiring no additives. And its fibers can be blended with cotton in clothing, it would made disposable diapers ten times more absorbent than cotton and biodegradable, and it could save our forests by providing paper pulp."

Hemp boosters say it's silly to act as if cars would be running on marijuana. ("This is drugs. This is your Hyundai on drugs. Any questions?") They insist that hemp grown for fuel makes such poor marijuana that there wouldn't be the tiniest temptation to smoke it or sell it for that purpose. During Prohibition, they point out, the government didn't outlaw the corn plant.

The real reason hemp was declared illegal, enthusiasts contend, was not because it produces marijuana but because textile and paper companies, terrified of the competition, lobbied to have hemp suppressed.

Paranoid fantasy or paranoid reality? It's not for us to say. About those biomass claims, though: energy consultant Kerry Sachs, an associate at RCG/Hagler, Bailly (a consulting firm in Washington, D.C.), says that other plants, like corn, sugarcane, coffee, and kenaf, a hemplike plant that's a member of the hibiscus family, may produce cellulose as efficiently as hemp. "I know of no comparative studies showing hemp to be the fastest-growing biomass source," says Sachs. "Hemp doesn't seem as good as locally available wood chips or pelletized sawdust or eucalyptus wood, which has a phenomenal growth rate. And I doubt whether hemp would be economical."

Finally, I've been tracking down a rumor that California winemakers in Napa and Sonoma counties are experimenting with making a methanollike fuel out of grape waste. I talked to vintners and growers all over the country in quest of the fuel that would give new meaning to the words *tank up*. Everyone thought it was a great idea, and thought he knew some guy who was working on it; but alas, each guy thought he knew another guy, and no Uberguy—or Wonderwastewoman—materialized.

"Grape waste's time may come," Sachs consoled me. And I'd rather burn no wine before its time. But I was really disappointed about winohol. I wanted to be able to say my car ran on an audacious little fuel, delicately dry with an ideal balance of fruity undertaste and carbon monoxide tones, with a medium body and lingering finish that make it the perfect accompaniment to grilled poultry and antifreeze. But now I guess I won't be able to. (pp. 37–41)

"Hemp may be the best energy crop on the planet. Its woody stalks, which contain seventy-five percent cellulose and four percent lignin, produce ten tons of biomass per acre in four months. The stalks could be fermented into methanol, and the oil from seeds could be used for diesel fuel."

—John Dunlap, National Organization for the Reform of Marijuana Laws

Judith Stone, "Wonderfuel Life," in Discover, *Vol. 12, No. 2, February, 1991, pp. 37–41.*

The United States could cut its petroleum consumption by 20 percent, replacing fossil fuels with clean-burning oils drawn from tree bark, underbrush, sawdust, paper, and other waste.

A New Petroleum Resource: Extracting Oil from Wood

Renewed interest has been sparked in alternative fuels. One promising option—though one unfamiliar to the general public—is oil distilled from wood. Within just a few years, its proponents say, the United States could cut its petroleum consumption by 20 percent, replacing fossil fuels with clean-burning oils drawn from tree bark, underbrush, sawdust, paper, and other waste.

It's not a new idea. Nearly all trees contain a sometimes gluey mix of polymers that, if properly extracted, can burn like petroleum. In 1973, during the first oil crunch, the Georgia Tech Research Institute developed a method of pyrolysis that, its inventors said, would be able to cook some of the wood into oil.

Chunks of wood were placed on a conveyer belt and heated to 842 degrees. Although wood ordinarily burns at half that temperature, the pyrolytic reactors were kept free of oxygen to prevent a flame from ever getting started. Without burning, the high heat could decompose the wood into three separate compounds: a low-energy gas, a char, and the desired oil.

The process worked, but the reactors were inefficient, able to convert no more than 25 percent of the raw wood to oil. Undaunted, the Georgia Tech engineers went back to the drawing board and came up with their far more efficient "entrained flow" pyrolysis reactor. "In the original pyrolysis systems," explains project director Daniel J. O'Neil, "the wood moved through too slowly. After the initial breakdown the oil would continue to decompose into more char and gas. We needed to reduce the time the wood spent in that hot chamber."

In the new system wood chunks are first ground into a fine powder and kept in a feed bin. A stream of conveying gas—made up of carbon dioxide, carbon monoxide, and water vapor—is then blown over the powder. The gas, once again heated to 842 degrees, sweeps some of the wood powder into a smoke-stacklike reaction chamber, where the heated grains again begin to separate into their components.

The tiny grains need only an instant to break down in the reaction chamber, and that's all they get. Almost immediately the gas blows the decomposed grains into the "cyclone," a spinning chamber in which they start to cool. When the heating and cooling happen so quickly, the oil drawn from the wood does not have time to break down further into char, and thus the oil yield is much higher. The spinning chamber then separates the char that does form. The remaining material—mostly gas—flows into condensers, where much of it is cooled into oil and separated out.

In 1983 the Georgia Tech engineers got a prototype of their reactor up and running and produced some staggering results: up to 60 percent of its raw wood material was converted into useful oil. "If you used a system like this to process all the unused wood we can identify," says O'Neil, "you could produce the equivalent of six hundred million barrels of oil every year."

For now, wood oil is too crude to be used in automobile engines, but it could run power plants and other industrial facilities. O'Neil envisions building multiple-reactor facilities in which wood waste, recyclable paper, and agricultural wastes like corn husks would be fed into a single grinder; the material would then be cooked in as many as five reactors, producing up to 50 tons of oil per day.

Georgia Tech has been peddling its system to a number of industries in the United States, but until recently it had received few nibbles. Now it is getting some attention not only here but abroad; the university has begun negotiations with entrepreneurial firms in Denmark, Italy, Spain, Greece, and other countries where the sky-high price of petroleum makes the oil problem all the more pressing.

Even if nothing comes of these early negotiations, O'Neil is confident that waste-wood pyrolysis will remain the wave of the energy future. "From the beginning," he says, "we had the idea of creating something that could ultimately be refined into gasoline quality. We're not there yet, but even at this intermediate phase the technology has enormous commercial value."

Art Kleiner, "Oily Wastes and Wants," in Discover, *Vol. 12, No. 5, May, 1991, p. 30.*

> **The auto industry is not anxious to build vehicles powered solely by methanol or any other alternative fuel. But seeing the writing on the wall, the industry for years has been developing flexible-fuel cars that can run on gasoline or methanol or blends of the two.**

Reformulated Gasolines of the Future

Three of the nation's largest automakers and 14 of its major oil refiners have joined ranks in an expensive study of alternative fuels and alternative-fueled cars and trucks. The two-phase study, their first ever cooperative venture, is a major effort to influence Congressional debate over how to control the seemingly intractable problem of urban ozone, especially in the nine most smog-laden cities.

President Bush's answer in his clean air proposal is to have the auto industry build and sell 500,000 alternative-fueled cars in those nine cities beginning in 1995, and to increase this to 1 million vehicles to be sold annually from 1997 on. Bush's proposal is not generally accepted as being fuel-neutral—it relies primarily on methanol as the alternative to gasoline.

Methanol, the fuel of choice for Indianapolis 500 drivers, is a cleaner burning fuel, producing less hydrocarbon emissions than gasoline. It is less volatile than gasoline and thus less likely to contribute to smog through fugitive emissions at refueling stations or when a vehicle is idling. Because of more complete combustion and a higher octane rating, engines powered by methanol produce up to 20% more horsepower. But because of its molecular structure methanol yields only 60% as much energy per gallon as gasoline, meaning more refueling stops.

Methanol is also highly corrosive, which means that fuel tanks have to be made of stainless steel and hoses have to be made of Teflon—or something equivalent—wrapped in stainless-steel mesh. Methanol has other major drawbacks. It burns with a colorless flame. Imbibed, it can cause blindness or even death and when burned it produces formaldehyde, a possible human carcinogen.

For economic reasons neither the auto nor the oil industries wholly support the Bush proposal. The auto industry is not anxious to build vehicles powered solely by methanol or any other alternative fuel. But seeing the writing on the wall, the industry for years has been developing flexible-fuel cars that can run on gasoline or methanol or blends of the two. For their part, oil refiners are hoping to devise a cleaner burning gasoline that can be produced in existing refineries.

But until that happens the two industries are employing heavy lobbying to detour the Bush methanol bandwagon. Their wooing of the House Energy & Commerce Subcommittee on Health & the Environment, plus disorganization within the Administration, has paid off.

The auto and oil industries would prefer to use reformulated gasolines because they can be produced in volume in existing refineries and can be used in existing or slightly modified cars and trucks. The methanol/gasoline mixture of 85% methanol to 15% gasoline to be tested can be used in flexible fuel vehicles that can run on methanol mixtures or straight gasoline.

Recently the subcommittee voted to delete the alternative fuels proposal from the Bush package of Clean Air Act amendments. In its place the subcommittee substituted language calling on the automakers to certify that they "have the capacity to produce, distribute, and offer to sell" clean-fueled vehicles.

In an odd alliance, ardent environmentalist and subcommittee chairman Henry A. Waxman (D.-Calif.) for once found himself siding with the Administration. Pitted against them were full committee chairman John D. Dingell (D.-Mich.), who represents the Detroit automakers, and ranking subcommittee Republican Norman F. Lent of New York. Dingell and Lent also just happen to be the House sponsors of President Bush's clean air bill H.R. 3030.

The Senate has yet to address this issue and could vote to retain some language calling for cleaner fuels and clean-fuel cars and trucks. Waxman has already promised to push for a reinstatement of clean fuels and vehicles language on the House floor.

Regrouping its efforts, the Administration has offered a new option to try to resurrect the mainstay of its ozone-fighting proposal. Instead of requiring that automakers sell 1 million alternative-fuel vehicles annually by 1997, the new requirement would have Detroit "offer" such vehicles for sale. Dingell has repeatedly said that there was no way the government could mandate the sale of alternative-fueled vehicles.

Auto and oil industry officials realize that some type of alternative fuels requirement is likely to be part of a final clean air bill. Hence the rationale for their study.

"We hope the results of our joint research will produce sufficient scientific data to enable government and the public to make the best possible decisions on the fuels and technologies needed to make further progress in improving air quality," says Joseph M. Colucci, cochairman of the study and head of fuels and lubricants at General Motors Research Laboratories.

The first phase of the study, which is to be completed by mid-1990, is a fact-finding task to determine the availability and pollution-cutting potential of reformulated gasoline (created by varying aromatics, olefins, oxygenate levels, and the quantity of components with higher boiling points), methanol, and ethanol added to reformulated gasoline. Industry officials estimate the cost of this phase at $11.3 million. Costs for the completed studies are to be shared equally by both industries.

The second phase is scheduled to begin within a month or two and run through 1990. It will delve more closely into advanced, cleaner burning vehicles and fuels. There is no estimated cost for this phase of study.

The goal of the two-part study is to "permit objective assessment of relative reductions in vehicle emissions and improvements in urban air quality, especially ozone, achievable with reformulated gasolines and with methanol fuels," says Keith McHenry, study cochairman and senior vice president of technology at Amoco.

The first phase will test several methanol fuels used in prototype vehicles (some of which will be able to switch from gasoline to methanol), and reformulated gasolines used in 1983 to 1985, and 1989 cars. Using these various fuels, the study will analyze tailpipe, evaporative, and running losses (idling) emissions.

The auto and oil industries would prefer to use reformulated gasolines because they can be produced in volume in existing refineries and can be used in existing or slightly modified cars and trucks. The methanol/gasoline mixture of 85% methanol to 15% gasoline to be tested can be used in flexible fuel vehicles that can run on methanol mixtures or straight gasoline.

Specific chemical constituents of the various emissions will be characterized using gas chromatographic techniques. These data will be cranked into atmospheric-chemistry and air quality models to discern potential cuts in urban ozone. In addition, cost/benefit relationships using the various fuels will be ascertained.

Data from the first phase will be fed into the second phase, which is still being developed. This second tier of studies will test advanced methanol and reformulated gasoline fuels in vehicles of the future. Here the reformulated gasolines will require refinery changes and will be usable only in gasoline-powered prototype cars with sophisticated emission control systems. This second phase also may test compressed natural gas as an alternative fuel.

Fuel blending will be done by Phillips Petroleum Co., a sponsor of the program. Test vehicles are to be purchased by the program.

Some environmentalists have charged that the hidden agenda for these studies is to promote petroleum-based reformulated gasolines over alcohol or other alternative fuels such as compressed natural gas. McHenry vehemently disputes this. "The program has no bias as to which fuels are best for air quality."

To ensure that the studies are bias-free, the industry consortium has set up an advisory panel of researchers from academia who are experts in air quality, combustion/emissions, and statistics. Those who will peer review the program are John B. Heywood, Massachusetts Institute of Technology; John H. Seinfeld, California Institute of Technology; Robert F. Sawyer, University of California-Berkeley; J. Stuart Hunter, emeritus professor, Princeton University; and Jack Calver, National Center for Atmospheric Research.

Appropriate government agencies are also being asked to advise and comment on the program and its findings. These include the Environmental Protection Agency, the Energy Department, California Air Resources Board, and Northeast States for Coordinated Air Use Management, among others.

There are hints that methanol may not prove to be the panacea for cleaner vehicles and cleaner urban air the Bush Administration hoped for. The oil and auto industries are putting big bucks into a project they trust will produce topnotch science proving that reformulated gasolines are the fuels of the future. (pp. 17–18)

Lois R. Ember, "Auto, Oil Industries Join Forces to Study Clean Fuels," in Chemical and Engineering News, *Vol. 67, No. 44, October 30, 1989, pp. 17–18.*

The fundamental importance of energy has often been analyzed. Motor fuels are of particular significance not only because transportation is important to our life style and our overall economy but also because motor fuels play a major role in our 12-digit balance-of-trade deficit that arises from our importation of foreign oil.

Alternative Fuels: Progress and Prospects

Hydrocarbon mixtures manufactured from petroleum—gasoline and, more recently, diesel and jet fuels—have served as transportation fuels for more than 70 years. Manufacture and use of these motor fuels was determined almost solely by economic considerations. But recent fundamental changes reflect new public concerns for social and environmental factors. Indeed, these concerns have become important for both supply and use of fuel. Factors of new importance include:

- sociopolitical issues such as energy security within national borders, balance of trade, and tax policies;

- environmental protection;

- industry-government economics issues, changing roles of petroleum-chemical manufacturers, automobile-fuel industry interface and internationalization;

Of petroleum used in 1988 in the United States, 43% was imported, and this is expected to grow to more than 50% in the next decade.

- new fuel supply technology; and

- new vehicle technology.

These concerns may make it necessary to provide new alternatives for transportation fuels. Changing priorities in national policy already have resulted in new regulations and legislative actions that have altered the pattern of fuel supply and use. An example is the actions that stem from the phase-out of lead in gasoline.

The fundamental importance of energy has often been analyzed. Motor fuels are of particular significance not only because transportation is important to our life style and our overall economy but also because motor fuels play a major role in our 12-digit balance-of-trade deficit that arises from our importation of foreign oil.

An important point is that, of major users of fuels, only the transportation sector is not flexible. Coal, gas, or nuclear energy cannot substitute for petroleum for motor fuel use.

In this context fuel oxygenates—particularly alcohols and ethers—have emerged as an increasingly attractive option to meet the challenge of our motor fuel needs. Favorable factors are their high octane characteristics, their manufacture from our abundant national resources (e.g., coal, gas, petroleum fractions including residua biomass, and agricultural products), and their ability to lessen environmental damage. Oxygenates of fuel interest have the potential to revolutionize the manufacture and use of motor fuels.

Alcohols have long been used as automobile fuels. Methanol is the preferred fuel for racing cars because it can produce more power than a similar gasoline-fueled engine. Additionally, for the past several years alcohol in gasoline blends, particularly 10% ethanol/90% unleaded gasoline blends (gasahol), have been on the market. Also, low-level blends of methanol plus higher alcohols with gasoline have been used in the United States and in Europe. In Brazil more than one-third of the country's 10 million automobiles operate on 96% ethanol/4% water fuel made from sugar cane, and the remainder runs on gasoline blends containing up to 20% ethanol.

However, it is the recent phenomenal growth in the use of methyl-*tert*-butyl ether (MTBE) in gasoline blends that has captured worldwide attention. Introduced to the market in 1973 in Italy, its favorable properties have resulted in its use in 13 countries and its manufacture in about 45 plants in the free world and about 52 plants worldwide.

Sociopolitical Factors

On Oct. 14, 1988, President Reagan signed the Alternative Motor Fuels Act of 1988 (PL 100-494) stating that the bill "gives American automobile companies a real incentive to start building cars powered by alternative fuels by adjusting the federally mandated average fuel economy rating to reflect the gasoline saved by these vehicles. [It] also opens up new markets for natural gas and coal . . . [and] takes advantage of existing government programs and mechanisms to assist alternative fuels. Most important, it's not intended to create massive new bureaucracies or new taxpayer subsidies."

This act provides for a number of actions, including establishment of an Interagency Commission headed by the Secretary of Energy or designee to "develop and implement a national alternative motor fuels policy [and] ensure the development of a long-term plan for the commercialization of alcohols, natural gas, and other potential alternative motor fuels" by 1992.

The basis for this significant law is that 97% of U.S. transportation depends on oil as the fuel resource. The U.S. share of world oil consumption is 36%, and transportation accounts for 63% of this amount. Transportation use has exceeded total U.S. production since 1975. Of petroleum used in 1988 in the United States, 43% was imported, and this is expected to grow to more than

50% in the next decade. In 1987 our oil imports accounted for more than a quarter of our national trade deficit. Although only 18% of the world supply of petroleum comes from the Middle East, that region holds 63% of the proven reserves. Saudi Arabia has been the swing producer of oil (a role it would like to relinquish), currently supplying about 5 million bbl/day out of a capacity of around 10 million bbl/day. Only 2% of the free world's surplus oil production capacity is outside OPEC. Interestingly, Saudi Arabian production comes from about 100 wells, whereas the 180,000 wells in the United States produce less.

Recognizing these facts, the U.S. Department of Energy presented a document in 1987 titled "Energy Security—A Report to the President" which the president, in turn, presented to Congress. That report concluded that if present trends continue, the United States and its principal allies are likely to become far more dependent on the historically unstable Persian Gulf for oil. The report recognized that "the most promising technological opportunities for further reductions in oil consumption rest in the development of alternative fuel systems."

As a consequence, DOE significantly expanded an ongoing assessment of automotive use of methanol to include natural gas and electric vehicles. The goal of the study is to provide detailed cost-benefit information on establishing a transportation system by the year 2000 that permits fuel flexibility in highway vehicles. Currently only the transportation sector cannot switch fuels between petroleum products and alternatives. The study addresses replacement of 1 million bbl/day of oil. It does not include synthetic gasoline and distillate or oxygenated gasoline blends, as these can be used in existing equipment and infrastructure without significant special provisions. The study will not make recommendations, but rather will provide the basis for public debate and consideration by Congress and the president.

Although the DOE study will not be completed until late 1989, results are being published as they are ready, and several reports have already been distributed. These seem to suggest that although natural gas and electric vehicles can serve in some niche applications, methanol offers the opportunity for broad geographical and utilitarian use. However, the use of natural gas as the near-term resource for methanol production is critical. To build a fuel supply structure, it will be necessary in a free market to initially use foreign supply, basically tied to gas that is now either flared or reinjected.

But government involvement is not limited to talk. PL 100-494 has provisions in two other categories that are aimed at stimulating commercialization. The first, and possibly most important, is an incentive to the auto industry to produce alternative-fueled vehicles by use of a more liberal method of calculating fuel economy of such vehicles. Under the Corporate Average Fuel Economy (CAFE) regulation, auto manufacturers must produce vehicles that on a sales-weighted average meet or exceed a specified fuel economy level, currently 26.5 mpg. This represents the third year of respite from the congressionally mandated 27.5 mpg (required for the 1990 model year), reflecting to some degree the desire of motorists to buy less efficient vehicles in this period of relatively inexpensive gasoline. Starting in model year 1993, autos that can use alternative fuels will be included in CAFE calculations based on the amount of gasoline or diesel fuel in M85 (e.g., 85% methanol, 15% gasoline) fuel. For vehicles dedicated to an alternative fuel, only the 15% hydrocarbon component will be charged to the fuel economy. For vehicles that can operate on either hydrocarbons or an alternative fuel, it is assumed for calculations that the vehicle will operate half time on each fuel, so the arithmetic average of fuel economies on each of the two fuels will be used. These benefits can be used up to a maximum of 1.2 mpg effect on the overall results.

Other sections of PL 100-474 require DOE to establish the use of vehicles within the federal government fleet, over-the-road demonstrations of heavy-duty trucks operating on natural gas and on methanol, and assistance to state and local bus operations for collection and analysis of data on methanol- and natural gas-fueled buses.

> **Under the Corporate Average Fuel Economy (CAFE) regulation, auto manufacturers must produce vehicles that on a sales-weighted average meet or exceed a specified fuel economy level, currently 26.5 mpg. This represents the third year of respite from the congressionally mandated 27.5 mpg (required for the 1990 model year), reflecting to some degree the desire of motorists to buy less efficient vehicles in this period of relatively inexpensive gasoline.**

As lead levels began to drop, oxygenates were more seriously considered for their octane value, and this and other fuel-performance properties now play a major role in prices and volume. Prior to that, synthetic fuels, including oxygenates, were thought of in terms of their energy content in relation to the petroleum for which they would substitute.

Environmental Protection

Interest in alternative motor fuels has cycled back and forth between environmental and energy fuel supply concerns. Recently environmental concerns have been the most influential factor, resulting in new laws and regulations that alter the manufacture and use of motor fuels. This shift started more than a decade ago with the widespread introduction of unleaded gasoline. More recently this has escalated by the required phase-out of tetraethyl lead use in gasoline. Because use of lead conveniently and inexpensively boosts the octane (antiknock) rating of gasoline, its removal created a need for enhancing refinery "pool" gasoline by other means. Lead removal signaled that other metallic compounds would be unacceptable, so the burden fell on organics. Addition of oxygenates to gasoline boosts the octane rating of gasoline to the levels needed for today's high compression-ratio automobile engines. Low molecular weight alcohols are readily available and inexpensive. However, the characteristics of ethers are generally closer to those of gasolines than those of the alcohols. Ethers are benign in their effect on fuel system materials and are miscible in gasoline; therefore, they are not subject to phase separation in the presence of water, as is methanol. Ethers are nonpolar. They are of low volatility and thus give low evaporative emissions.

The refining industry produces considerable amounts of aromatics to provide desired octane levels. In particular, this involves the use of benzene, toluene and xylene. The acceptable level of aromatics used is a topic of considerable controversy, and discussions regarding restrictions particularly center on benzene, which is carcinogenic. Although the Environmental Protection Agency is not planning to propose reduced benzene levels, the California Air Resources Board is proposing that in California a 0.8 vol % limit of benzene in gasoline would take effect in January 1993. The scientific data of EPA and the California Air Resources Board have substantial differences that motivate their varied approaches. EPA focuses on levels at the automobile tailpipe, where benzene levels are greatly reduced by the exhaust catalyst, along with other hydrocarbon emissions.

The Role of Oxygenates

The first introduction of oxygenates following limitations on composition of new fuels established by the Clean Air Act of 1970 was that of adding 10 vol % anhydrous ethanol to 90 vol % unleaded gasoline. Industry subsequently received EPA waivers for commercial use of two groups of oxygenates: fuel blends having 2 wt % oxygen and those having about 3.7%. The former results from a ruling that the 2 wt % oxygen level was used in some commercial gasolines prior to the Act, and any monohydric oxygenate used in gasoline will result in a product that is "substantially similar" to earlier gasolines acceptable under the Act. As lead levels began to drop, oxygenates were more seriously considered for their octane value, and this and other fuel-performance properties now play a major role in prices and volume. Prior to that, synthetic fuels, including oxygenates, were thought of in terms of their energy content in relation to the petroleum for which they would substitute.

Oxygenates have taken on a large role in improving air quality. The Clean Air Act of 1970 included requirements for atmospheric air quality by year-end 1987. Considerable emphasis was placed on the automotive market because a few manufacturers can achieve significant results by meeting more stringent requirements. The law included the requirement to reduce automobile exhaust emissions by 90%. Although this goal has been largely attained and great strides have been made in reducing emissions from stationary sources, the air is not as clean as was originally anticipated. At year-end 1987, 68 metropolitan areas had not met the standard for ozone set for that date. Almost 80 million people live in these areas. A high fraction of the noncompliance areas are in California. Where the standard was not met, plans to do so within five years were required. Where states have not complied, EPA is charged with imposing its plan. Such a plan has been proposed for Arizona, and EPA is working on one for Southern California. Amid considerable controversy and subsequent uncertainty as to how to proceed, EPA has published a notice seeking comments on controlling ozone in the California South Coast Basin (the greater Los Angeles area) immediately or in 5 or 20 years. All are based on reducing hydrocarbon emissions from the largest oil-based sources, stationary and mobile, by 80 or 90%. EPA favors a 20-year plan, reflecting the extent of the problem, but is operating under a court ruling that it must adhere to a five-year schedule. Vehicles operated on alcohol or natural gas fuel or on electricity offer potential for reduced or less reactive hydrocarbon emissions and lower NO_x emissions, both of which contribute to photochemical ozone generation in the atmosphere. A 20-year plan for the South Coast Basin proposed by the South Coast Air Quality Management District (SCAQMD) anticipates that achieving the required ozone level would require 40% of passenger vehicles and 70% of trucks to operate on clean fuel or electricity.

About 85 metropolitan areas populated by nearly 30 million people have failed to achieve the carbon monoxide standard. Highway vehicles produce most of the CO. However, CO noncompliance occurs in the winter, heavily affected by excessive CO during starting of balking cold engines. In a homogeneous charge engine, typically used in the automobile, major performance, fuel economy, and exhaust emission characteristics are a function of the air-fuel ratio. Excess air converts CO to CO_2, reduces unburned fuel (called hydrocarbons when the fuel is petroleum), increases thermal efficiency and thereby betters fuel economy, reduces power, and causes variable changes in NO_x. Thus in an engine without electronic mixture feedback control, one means of reducing CO emissions is to use a leaner fuel-air mixture. This happens when an oxygenated fuel is substituted for straight gasoline. Although automobile driveability deteriorates as the mixture is enleaned, this effect is gradual at small oxygen levels, increasing exponentially. In the 1970s automotive and fuel experts almost universally felt that the public would not accept driveability of an engine set up for gasoline operating with fuel having 3.7% oxygen, but the success of gasohol proved that wrong, so this level is now considered by most as the limit for engines without feedback control.

A few areas have mandated the use of oxygenates in the winter. Colorado took the initial action, instituting it in the Frontal Range area, focused on Denver. More than 80% of Colorado's population is located along this eastern edge of the mountains. In the winter of 1987–88, a fuel with at least 1.5% oxygen was required. About 90% of the fuel in this period used a gasoline blend having 8 vol % MTBE, and the other 8-10% was gasohol. Authorities considered the program to be successful, and in winter 1988–89 they required fuel with at least 2% oxygen (11% MTBE). A recent EPA waiver permitting use of 15% MTBE provides the basis for going to a somewhat higher level if that is desired in the future. Some wanted to go to 3.7%, even early on, but that has been resisted by the authorities because all existing vehicles might not operate satisfactorily at that level.

EPA has encouraged this approach based on assessment of potential benefits that show between 10 and 20% CO reduction over the next decade. Although new autos have electronic engine control systems that maintain a stoichiometric air-fuel ratio, such systems do not operate during starting and initial warm-up, so some benefits accrue from the new as well as the older vehicles. Although this CO benefit is not enough to meet air quality requirements, mandating the use of oxygenates has been encouraged as part of an overall plan. Following Colorado's lead and such encouragement, others have moved toward similar requirements. Arizona instituted a voluntary program to use oxygenates for 1989–90 winter in Maricopa county (Phoenix) and will require use next winter. This will be extended to Tucson a year later. Albuquerque is experimenting this winter with a well-publicized voluntary plan for oxygenate use with encouraging early response.

Greater benefits can be obtained if fuel alcohol is used. Neat methanol gives the greatest benefits. This is tempered when some gasoline is added as it is in M85. Steady-state NO_x emissions are perhaps half those with gasoline, all other things being equal. This benefit is not as large under transient conditions. Alcohols will burn much leaner than gasoline, so that operation near the

Oxygenates constitute some of the largest scale synthetic organic chemicals manufactured. For example, 3 million gal/day of methanol is produced in the United States. However, this is only 1% of the 300 million gal/day of gasoline made.

The viewpoints of petroleum companies toward including methanol in gasoline blends has been greatly influenced by concern for customer dissatisfaction. This stems from real or imagined poor performance attributed to methanol that can occur from improper blending and also from alleged damage to fuel systems in vehicles designed for use of neat gasoline.

lean limit will assure low CO, even lower relative NO_x, and probably lower unburned fuel. However, the aldehyde fraction of the unburned fuel is about 10 times as high as for gasoline, although the absolute number is quite low. The matter of aldehydes is often raised, and it is one of the most highly investigated and reported areas in alternative fuels work. Experts feel that the problem is manageable as long as the requirements are reasonable. Aldehydes generated in the engine tend to decompose as they move down the tailpipe and into the air, so have a shorter life and lower effect than those generated photochemically in the atmosphere. The exhaust catalyst also substantially reduces the aldehyde level and is definitely required. The California Air Resources Board plans to regulate the amount of aldehydes emitted. EPA does not at the start. EPA has established requirements for manufacturer certification of vehicle designs wherein only total unburned fuel is regulated, as is the case for gasoline, so that no undue obstacles be put on introduction of new fuels.

The several substantial potential environmental benefits associated with methanol use have resulted in significant effort by the California Energy Commission (CEC), and more recently by the California Air Resources Board and SCAQMD, to promote the use of this motor fuel. Several batches of factory-supplied methanol vehicles have been operated under CEC sponsorship since 1981, and it is in the process of procuring up to 5000 flexible-fuel vehicles that will run on methanol, gasoline, or any combination of these. As part of these activities, the CEC has provided pumps for 15-20 gasoline retail outlets that use the same type of equipment as for gasoline. Selected methanol compatible materials have been used, and special credit cards are used to control fuel access. Arrangements have been made with Chevron and ARCO to each provide about 25 locations. SCAQMD now requires that when a retail underground tank is replaced or constructed at new retail gasoline outlets, at least one underground tank and associated plumbing must be methanol and gasoline compatible.

Another environmental action that has implications regarding oxygenates is that of heavy-duty diesel engine emissions. These impose more stringent requirements on particulate and NO_x emissions. Engine manufacturers appear confident of meeting 1991 truck standards with improved engine technology and no exhaust treatment. However, to meet the more stringent 1991 bus/1994 truck standards, it may be necessary to use either a particulate trap or an alternative fuel. The particulate trap is a filter that collects particles and regenerates the trap effectiveness by burning off the accumulated particulates at selected times. This technology still faces several obstacles to commercialization. There is optimism that this technology can be available by 1994, but it will not be ready for use in 1991. The new particulate standards are so stringent that in many instances the particulate emissions of engines from the engine lubricating oil alone exceeds the amount allowed.

In the presence of the uncertainties associated with environmental requirements, diesel engine manufacturers and refiners have jointly agreed that in late 1993 the refiners will make a new grade diesel fuel having ≤0.05% sulfur. This fuel will be differentiated from current diesel fuels and heating oils. On the other hand, facing the need to meet the earlier deadline, Detroit Diesel Corporation—the manufacturer of most urban bus engines now in use and in production—has committed to manufacturing a methanol-fueled version of its two-cycle bus engine in 1991.

Fuel Supply

Manufacture of most oxygenate fuels consist of a two-step process. First a mixture of hydrogen and carbon oxides (synthesis gas or syngas) is made from natural gas (methane), coal, or petroleum fractions including residua. Then the syngas is catalytically converted to the desired products. The products depend on the nature of the catalyst.

Methanol or mixed alcohols can be synthesized. Alternatively, hydrocarbon fuels can be produced by using Fischer-Tropsch catalysts, as is done by SASOL in South Africa. Or synthetic methanol can be converted to high-octane gasoline using Mobil's MTG (methanol-to-gasoline) process, as is done in New Zealand.

Fuel ethanol is produced by fermentation of corn or sugar cane. Although not of strong current interest, isopropanol and *sec-* butyl alcohol are candidates for use in blended fuels. They are manufactured by hydration of propylene and butylenes, respectively.

tert-Butyl alcohol (TBA) is a byproduct in the manufacture of propylene epoxide. TBA has been used in gasoline blends, alone and with methanol (marketed as Oxinol by ARCO). However, at present TBA is primarily used to manufacture isobutylene, which reacts with methanol to give MTBE. Ethyl-*tert*-butyl ether is made by using ethanol instead of methanol. *tert*-Amylmethyl ether is produced by using isomylenes (isopentenes) instead of isobutylenes. Diisopropyl ether has also been used commercially as an octane-enhancing agent. Interest in diisopropyl ether continues, particularly in developing better methods for its manufacture. Furthermore, there is some interest in dimethyl ether, which is readily manufactured from methanol or indeed directly from syngas. (pp. 549–56)

Oxygenates constitute some of the largest scale synthetic organic chemicals manufactured. For example, 3 million gal/day of methanol is produced in the United States. However, this is only 1% of the 300 million gal/day of gasoline made. Thus we see a potential for an enormous increase in oxygenates for motor fuel, with far-reaching impact on the petrochemical industry, both domestic and in the Mid East. . . .

One factor that has contributed to the adoption of MTBE by petroleum companies is their control of supply of isobutylene, which can be recovered from refinery streams. MTBE is also favored not only because it performs well but also because it seems to reduce customer problems.

The viewpoints of petroleum companies toward including methanol in gasoline blends has been greatly influenced by concern for customer dissatisfaction. This stems from real or imagined poor performance attributed to methanol that can occur from improper blending and also from alleged damage to fuel systems in vehicles designed for use of neat gasoline. Similar views have been expressed about the use of ethanol, which is more benign than methanol. Petroleum companies have been divided in their attitudes. Some, in fact, have advertised that their gasoline does not contain methanol or ethanol. (p. 556)

E. Eugene Ecklund and G. Alex Mills, "Alternative Fuels: Progress and Prospects," in Chemtech, Vol. 19, No. 9, September, 1989, pp. 549–56.

> Interest in alternative motor fuels has cycled back and forth between environmental and energy fuel supply concerns. Recently environmental concerns have been the most influential factor, resulting in new laws and regulations that alter the manufacture and use of motor fuels.

Sources For Further Study

Begley, Sharon. "Running on Swamp Gas." *Newsweek* CXVI, No. 11 (10 September 1990): 41–2.
    Details the major alternative fuels being developed to replace fossil fuels.

Bleviss, Deborah. "Transportation: The Auto." *EPA Journal* 16, No. 2 (March-April 1990): 26–7.
    Argues that the key to decreasing automobile carbon dioxide emissions, which greatly contribute to global warming, lies in improving fuel efficiency, converting to alternative fuels, and switching to more energy-efficient modes of travel.

Bretz, Elizabeth A. "Specifying Powerplant Fuels and Combustion Systems." *Electrical World* 205, No. 2 (February 1991): 40–5.
> Maintains that the recent trend away from fossil fuels to cleaner alternative fuels may have an adverse affect on power-producing facilities that rely on such natural resources as coal. Bretz then proposes various strategies to help power plants cope with possible changes in fuel consumption.

Buchanan, John. "Solar Race Sets the Pace." *Missouri Resource Review* 7, No. 2 (Summer 1990): 22–5.
> Describes a joint effort by the Missouri Department of Natural Resources and Crowder College to build a solar-powered automobile that will travel statewide for two years to demonstrate the viability of using this renewable resource for transportation.

Busby, Rebecca L. "NGVs Now on the Fast Track." *Grid* 13, No. 1 (Spring 1990): 2–11.
> Surveys current and future uses for compressed natural gas vehicles (NGVs), noting that emissions from these automobiles are less reactive than those powered by methanol and that NGVs appear to be safer than other alternative fuel vehicles.

Cannon, James S. "Drive for Clean Air: Natural Gas and Methanol Vehicles." *INFORM Report* (1989): 169 p.
> Surveys the positive and negative effects resulting from the use of natural gas and methanol-powered vehicles.

Chemical & Engineering News 69, No. 24 (17 June 1991).
> Special issue that devotes four feature articles to the discussion of energy policy, coal, nuclear energy, and solar power.

Cook, William J. "The Future of Power." *U.S. News and World Report* (23 April 1990): 65, 69–70.
> Argues that burning hydrogen gas as a fuel is more environmentally sound than burning fossil fuels since its only by-product is water.

Cruver, Philip C. "Greenhouse Response Strategies Affecting Electric Power." *Power Engineering* 94, No. 4 (April 1990): 39–42.
> Focuses on the electric power producers contending that they are responsible for a large volume of carbon dioxide emissions worldwide. Cruver then explores how legislation to curb emissions will likely affect electric utilities in both industrial and developing nations.

DiChristina, Mariette. "How We Can Win the War against Garbage." *Popular Science* (October 1990): 59–63, 95.
> Proposes various methods of efficient garbage disposal, devoting much discussion to incinerating garbage to generate electric power.

"Algae as an Alternative Fuel." *Environment* 30, No. 6 (July-August 1988): 23–4.
> Outlines a system developed by scientists at the Solar Energy Research Institute in which lipids produced by algae during photosynthesis can be converted into diesel oil or gasoline.

"Air Quality Benefits of Alternative Fuels." *EPA Report* (July 1987): 32 p.
> Details the EPA's estimates for potential air quality improvements if various alternative fuel programs are implemented. The figures in this government report are based on the assumption that methanol vehicles will replace gasoline vehicles by 2000; states will integrate methanol vehicles into their gasoline-powered fleets; and reformulated fuels will replace gasoline in all automobiles.

Fisher, Arthur. "Global Warming: Part Three, Saving the Planet." *Popular Science* 235, No. 4 (October 1989): 51–6, 92–8.
> Analyzes how such alternative energy sources as wind, solar, and nuclear power can help reduce the threat of global warming to the planet.

Freund, Ken. "Alternative Fuels: Cleaner Fuels Are on the Horizon, But What Will Be Their Effect?" *Trailer Life* 50, No. 4 (April 1990): 48–51, 106–16.
Asserts that in response to numerous environmental crises, tougher emissions control standards are being developed by the state and federal governments that emphasize the need to develop alternative fuels. Freund then surveys both the availability and viability of the major alternative resources, particularly focusing on reformulated gasoline.

Fumento, Michael. "What Kind of Fuel Am I?" *The American Spectator* 23, No. 11 (November 1990): 25, 28–31.
Offers a skeptical evaluation of various alternative automobile fuels, particularly ethanol. Fumento maintains that ethanol will probably gain congressional acceptance as the "most successful" alternative fuel, not because it is more effective than the others, but because of the massive lobbying efforts by grain processors.

"Air Pollution: Air Quality Implications of Alternative Fuels." *GAO Report RCED-90-143* (July 1990): 21 p.
Contends that while most alternative fuels will reduce the most common air pollutants, there remains some question about the extent of these reductions and how alternative resources may increase other pollutant levels.

Grable, Ron. "Alternative Engine Fuels: What'll We Do When the Tank Runs Dry?" *Motor Trend* 37, No. 2 (February 1985): 116, 120.
Assesses the positive and negative ramifications of several alternative fuels, including compressed natural gas, propane, and reformulated gasoline.

Gromer, Cliff. "New Gas: Hype or Hope?" *Popular Mechanics* 167, No. 11 (November 1990): 48–50.
Examines the major oil companies' efforts to develop cleaner-burning reformulated gasolines.

Gutfeld, Rose. "Fleets Steer toward Alternative Fuels." *The Wall Street Journal* (12 April 1991): B1, B8.
Discusses a proposal by President Bush to convert most of the nation's motor vehicle fleets from gasoline and diesel fuel to such alternative fuels as natural gas, propane, methanol, ethanol, and electricity by 1995.

Hampson, Christopher. "Energy and the Environment." *International Journal of Global Energy Issues* 2, No. 3 (1990): 177–82.
Contends that increasing the efficiency of energy production and utilization is an environmentally and commercially sound concept in that such practices will ultimately reduce both greenhouse emissions and energy costs.

Ivey, Mark. "Fuel Wars: Big Oil Is Running Scared." *Business Week*, No. 3162 (4 June 1990): 132, 136.
Asserts that major oil companies are introducing reformulated gasolines in response to pressure from the federal government to produce cleaner-burning fuels.

Knickerbocker, Brad. "Renewables and Conservation Are Finding a Place in the Sun." *The Christian Science Monitor* (27 August 1991): 6–7.
Maintains that although funding for renewable energy sources was drastically cut during the Reagan presidency, various factors indicate that research for renewable resources will make gains in the future.

Luoma, John R. "Burn Garbage for Electricity? Yes, No, Maybe." *Audubon* (March 1990): 96–7.
Discusses the pros and cons of incinerating garbage to produce electric power, noting that the biggest drawback to this process is the emission of air pollutants.

Neill, D., et. al. "Renewable Transportation Alternatives." *Solar Today* 4, No. 4 (July-August 1990): 21–4.
Summarizes data obtained from the research and development of electric and hybrid vehicles, methanol fuels, and hydrogen-powered vehicles at the Natural Energy Institute in Hawaii.

Neporozhniy, P. S., and Kozlov, V. B. "Environmental Problems Associated with the Soviet Electric Power Industry: A Survey." *Energy Systems & Policy* 14, No. 1 (1990): 1–36.
> Examines the environmental implications of constructing and operating fossil-fuel-fired and other types of power plants in the USSR.

Nerad, Jack R. "The Good News about Alternative Fuels." *Motor Trend* 42, No. 2 (February 1990): 8.
> Argues that alternative fuels provide performance advantages over current gasoline formulations because they have a higher octane rating than gasoline.

Phillips, Vic, and Takahashi, Patrick. "Renewable Energy Development." *Environmental Science & Technology* 23, No. 1 (January 1989): 10–13.
> Asserts that by converting to technologies based on abundant sources of renewable energy, we can protect our health and habitat from further deterioration.

Rodhe, Henning. "A Comparison of the Contribution of Various Gases to the Greenhouse Effect." *Science* 248, No. 4960 (8 June 1990): 1217–219.
> Compares the contributions of fossil fuels and compressed natural gas emissions to the greenhouse effect, asserting that compressed natural gas is preferable to fossil fuel as long as its leakage can be held to between three and six percent.

"A Mild Alternative?" *Scientific American* 257, No. 6 (December 1987): 37, 40.
> Discusses the potential benefits of a coal-gasification process that could provide industries with a more efficient and economical fuel.

Simanaitis, Dennis. "Alternative Fuels: Fill 'er Up, But Whatever With?" *Road and Track* 41, No. 3 (November 1989): 72–6, 85–7.
> Considers advantages and disadvantages of several alternative fuels.

Sperling, Daniel, and DeLuchi, Mark A. "Transportation Energy Strategies and the Greenhouse Effect." *OECD/IEA Energy Technologies for Reducing Emissions of Greenhouse Gases Symposium* 2 (12-14 April 1989): 53–68.
> Estimates the percent change in greenhouse gases that would result from switching automobiles to alternative fuels and emphasizes the urgency of testing and modeling emissions and ozone formation under the same conditions and engine types for all alternative fuels.

Spitzer, J., and Haas, J. "Consequences of an Enhanced Use of Biomass Technologies on CO_2 Concentration in the Atmosphere." *OECD/IEA Energy Technologies for Reducing Emissions of Greenhouse Gases Symposium* 2 (12-14 April 1989): 355–61.
> Argues that introducing bioenergy into a closed carbon circle is an obvious solution for reducing carbon dioxide emissions into the atmosphere, noting that it is unlikely that the current energy system can be maintained too far into the twenty-first century.

Williams, Ronald L., et. al. "Formaldehyde, Methanol, and Hydrocarbon Emissions from Methanol-Fueled Cars." *Air & Waste Management Association Journal* 40, No. 5 (May 1990): 747–56.
> Presents emissions data from experimental methanol vehicles and concludes that although hydrocarbons are lower when the proportion of methanol to gasoline is greater, formaldehyde emissions are significantly higher for methanol fuel than they are for gasoline.

Wright, Thomas L. "An Electric Utility Perspective on CO_2 Emissions from Alternative Transportation Fuels." *Energy Systems & Policy* 13, No. 4 (1989): 241–48.
> Maintains that electric utilities can help reduce carbon dioxide emissions by increasing coal combustion efficiency and by developing alternative transportation fuels such as methanol and effective battery-powered vehicles.

4: Desertification

The Threatening Desert

Desertification is one of the most serious problems facing the world today. Large parts of the dry areas that cover more than one-third of the earth's land surface are being degraded, with serious effects on the environment, food production, and the lives of millions of people. Desertification, characterized by the degradation of soil and vegetative cover, can occur in any dry area, not just on the fringes of natural deserts. It is a global phenomenon, affecting both developed and developing nations, and is a particular problem in Africa, the Middle East, India and Pakistan, China, Australia, the USSR, the USA, Latin American countries such as Brazil and Chile, and European countries such as Greece, Spain and Portugal. (p. 1)

Desertification has been occurring for millennia, but became a matter of worldwide concern in the early 1970s when a major drought in the Sahel region of West Africa, which in the opinion of most experts continues to this day, killed between 50,000 and 250,000 people, about 3.5 million cattle, and countless sheep, goats and camels. This prompted the United Nations to convene a Conference on Desertification (UNCOD) in Nairobi in 1977 to agree on a Plan of Action to combat desertification and bring it under control by the year 2000.

The extensive scientific investigations which preceded UNCOD showed that the Sahel tragedy was not just a natural disaster caused by lack of rainfall, but the result of a chronic process of land degradation in which people had a key role. The four main direct causes of desertification were identified as over-cultivation, overgrazing, deforestation and the mismanagement of irrigated cropland. However, while poor land use can simply be the result of bad management, it is greatly influenced by periods of drought, during which cropping and grazing become more intensive in order to maintain overall food production; by poverty and other aspects of economic underdevelopment, which make it difficult for farmers to manage their lands in a sustainable way; and by misguided government policies, which are often biased against the maintenance or improvement of traditional farming systems. (pp. 1–2)

There is much debate about the relative contributions of human impact and drought to desertification. Annual rainfall totals are highly variable in dry areas and so droughts (periods of below-average rainfall) occur quite frequently. UNCOD considered that human impact was the main cause of desertification, and that the role of drought was rather like a catalyst, merely speeding up the long-term process of degradation that had been occurring before the drought began. Normally, droughts are relatively short-term phenomena, lasting for only a few years at most. Whereas droughts in other dry regions have come and gone since UNCOD, the drought in the Sahel has continued despite several years of relatively good rainfall (such as 1988). It is therefore possible that the region is actually experiencing a long-lasting decline in rainfall. The exact cause of this is not known, although a number of explanations have been proposed. Some experts claim that the drought has been prolonged by a change in

> **Desertification is a problem that will not go away. It transcends the boundaries of nations, scientific disciplines and land uses.**

Controlling desertification will not guarantee an end to famine, but it will make an important contribution towards that end.

the reflective properties of the ground surface caused by desertification in the region, while others see it as a consequence of a much wider change in global climate caused by such mechanisms as the "greenhouse effect".

Soil erosion and the removal of vegetative cover [are] the two main physical characteristics of desertification. They are actually found throughout the tropics, not just in dry areas, and present a major challenge to governments concerned with finding a balance between economic development and the conservation of natural resources. Thus, although there are similarities between land degradation in the Sahel and that occurring in mountain areas like the Himalayas and tropical rain forest areas like the Amazon Basin, desertification in the drylands is distinguished by the involvement of drought, and by the very severe effects which it has on the environment and on human and animal populations.

One way in which desertification affects human beings is by undermining food production and contributing to malnutrition and famine. However, famine need not inevitably follow drought or desertification. We have seen in Ethiopia, Sudan and elsewhere that it can occur even in their absence when poverty, war, misguided government food policies and other factors prevent food shortages in one area from being compensated by supplies from another. UNCOD was certainly prompted by the famine that occurred in the Sahel region in the early 1970s, but it focused on the way in which famine and other forms of human misery were the result of a long-term process of degradation that was exacerbated by drought. UNCOD argued that short-term relief measures during and immediately after the drought were not enough to prevent such tragedies from recurring in the future. Also needed was a long-term commitment to sustainable agricultural development and environmental rehabilitation. That message is as true today as it was in 1977. Controlling desertification will not guarantee an end to famine, but it will make an important contribution towards that end.

The differing views on the role of climate in desertification referred to above are a predictable consequence of our quite limited knowledge of the subject, which allows a high degree of subjectivity to enter into the opinions of experts on dryland issues. Further scientific studies of the causes, effects and scale of desertification are therefore required so that judgements in the future can be based on fact rather than intuition. According to one estimate, the area suffering from at least moderate desertification is at the most 20 million square kilometres (sq km); but another gives an area of 32 million sq km, almost a quarter of the earth's land surface. The only estimate we have of the rate of desertification is 202,460 sq km per annum. All of these estimates are known to be very inaccurate, and lack of good data is a major constraint on the willingness of governments and international agencies to allocate funds for the control of desertification. It is vital to improve the monitoring of desertification by using the many sophisticated remote-sensing techniques, such as satellite imaging, which are at our disposal. Before this can be done, however, desertification needs to be defined much more rigorously in terms of measurable ground characteristics (called desertification indicators). This would have the additional benefit of helping to secure greater agreement on what desertification is and how it is caused.

UNCOD was much more than a forum at which representatives from ninety-five countries, fifty UN agencies and offices, eight intergovernmental organizations and sixty-five non-governmental organizations vowed to bring desertification under control. It agreed on a Plan of Action giving detailed guidelines to countries prone to drought and desertification to help them ensure that their agricultural production would be sustainable in the face of further climatic variations and would not lead to environmental degradation. The Plan also contained a list of priority recommendations for immediate action by governments and international agencies, and a set of ambitious transnational programmes in which governments of countries in a number of regions would work together to halt desertification.

The major contribution of the UNCOD Plan of Action undoubtedly lay in emphasizing that the key to controlling desertification was not to erect physical barriers against desert encroachment but to make land use more sustainable. It suggested various techniques and approaches by which rainfed cropping, irrigated cropping, livestock management and forest resource management could each be improved in order to prevent continued overcultivation, salinization and waterlogging of irrigated lands, overgrazing and deforestation respectively. The general aim was to improve both the productivity and the sustainability of each land use, while at the same time ensuring that it was only practised on the types of land appropriate to it. Thus, it was hoped that making rainfed cropping more productive on the better lands would prevent its expansion on to less fertile lands that were highly prone to soil erosion. (pp. 2–4)

The number of projects which have been successful in controlling desertification is remarkably small, and little has been done to implement the priority recommendations of the UNCOD Plan of Action or the cooperative, transnational programmes which it proposed. Why so little progress? The easiest answer, that the governments of both developed and developing nations have lacked the interest and the will to take action, is nevertheless quite a valid one. UNCOD came about because of a relatively short-term problem—the Sahel drought and its aftermath—but it proposed a long-term solution, attacking causes rather than symptoms. As often happens, when the symptoms appeared to go away, interest in a long-term cure waned. Another reason was that the Plan was very radical, challenging many traditional notions of agricultural development held by officials in governments and international agencies. Implementing certain of its recommendations would therefore require major shifts in policy. Furthermore, parts of the Plan were politically naïve, for while the large-scale international collaborative programmes which it proposed were highly principled and fully appropriate to the magnitude and seriousness of the problem, some of them were impractical because of the poor relations, or even enmity, which existed between countries that were required to work together.

Yet another reason for the lack of progress is that if techniques for improving land use are to be widely adopted they must be economically attractive to people living in the affected areas and compatible with their cultures. The Plan did include recommendations dealing with social needs, but these were not integrated with the techniques recommended for improving land use. When projects do not take into account the needs and wishes of local people they run into tremendous obstacles and are likely to fail. Some experts may claim that we have at our disposal all the techniques necessary to control desertification, but experience has proved otherwise. The social and policy components of projects are not optional extras or even supplementary to basic techniques for resource management. They are absolutely essential, and need to be fully integrated with resource management if projects are to succeed. An element of "social engineering" is therefore required, as well as the introduction of new agricultural technologies. Arousing people's awareness and enthusiasm is a lot more difficult than performing fairly mechanical processes like sowing seeds or planting trees. Therein lies the challenge for controlling desertification and the reason why so many projects have failed. (pp. 5–6)

Desertification is a problem that will not go away. It transcends the boundaries of nations, scientific disciplines and land uses. It challenges us to look afresh at the relationship between environment and development. It exposes the limitations of our ability to manage natural resources for human sustenance in some of the world's harshest climes. It reveals our woeful ignorance of a problem of global proportions. In many instances questions are asked which cannot yet be answered, and obstacles are identified which we do not know how to overcome. If desertification is to be controlled, there is clearly much to be done. (p. 6)

Alan Grainger, in an introduction to his The Threatening Desert: Controlling Desertification, *Earthscan Publications Ltd., 1990, pp. 1–6.*

The United Nations Conference on Desertification (UNCOD) considered that human impact was the main cause of desertification, and that the role of drought was rather like a catalyst, merely speeding up the long-term process of degradation that had been occurring before the drought began.

Desertification is well under way in much of Africa's Sahelian zone, the band of countries just south of the Sahara that stretches from Senegal and Mauritania on the Atlantic coast, to Chad and parts of Sudan in the east. But nowhere is the process so obvious as in the sand invasion of Mauritania, where a combination of natural and human forces is at work.

Mauritania: A Desertification Case Study

In a slow but steady advance, the sands of the Sahara are encroaching upon Mauritania's oases, villages and vital irrigation sources. Parts of the Highway of Hope, the main artery of the country's road system, are buried under dunes six feet high. Rural dwellers have had no choice but to abandon their homes to the advancing sand and migrate southward to urban shantytowns already bursting with refugees from the desert.

Sand dunes have not always been such a menace. They were once a stable feature of the Mauritanian landscape. Vegetation held them so firmly in place that travelers even oriented themselves using dunes as landmarks. Now much of that protective cover is gone.

Denuded sand dunes not only move but can be whipped into a destructive fury by ever more frequent sandstorms. The decade of the sixties saw only 43 storms; the seventies, ten times as many; and in 1983 alone, no fewer than 240 sandstorms were recorded.

Mauritania's shifting sand dunes are but the most visible sign of a more subtle process called desertification—the degeneration of productive land into a barren landscape. At an accelerating rate, people are removing the drylands' precious vegetation to feed their herds, make way for crops and provide fuel. Tragically, the resulting impoverishment of the land assures impoverishment of the people.

Desertification is well under way in much of Africa's Sahelian zone, the band of countries just south of the Sahara that stretches from Senegal and Mauritania on the Atlantic coast, to Chad and parts of Sudan in the east. But nowhere is the process so obvious as in the sand invasion of Mauritania, where a combination of natural and human forces is at work.

Mauritania, desert-like to begin with, is distinguished by sandy soils, forceful winds and wide temperature variations. Of the country's 386,000 square miles of land (half again larger than Texas), only 0.2 percent is arable (compared with an average of 8 percent for its Sahelian neighbors). Much of the remainder is uninhabitable.

A population nearing two million is rapidly and painfully feeling the limits of Mauritania's fragile resources. The Sahel has suffered from below-normal rainfall for most of the past 20 years. This drought has thinned precious vegetative cover, and what greenery remains is overexploited by a growing number of people and livestock struggling to survive. As rangeland becomes wasteland, the country's meager forest cover is cleared to make way for more grazing. Any available woody vegetation is cut to produce charcoal, the main household fuel. As a result, the forest that once covered 3 percent of the country's territory has been reduced by almost a third in less than a decade.

Traditionally, the overwhelming majority of Mauritania's people were pastoralists who, with herds of camels, goats and sheep, followed the seasonal rains to briefly flourishing oases that provided ample grazing. The remainder of the year they spent in settlements. By never staying in one place longer than the land could support them, these nomads lived in balance with the fragile desert ecology.

But the combined effects of failed rains and population growth have upset this equilibrium. As surface water and vegetation have become scarce, herds have died of starvation and thirst. With the animals goes the pastoralists' way of life. This has led to resettlement in a narrow patch of towns in the southeast, where nine-tenths of the population is now concentrated.

This retreat has changed Mauritania into a predominantly urban nation. In 1965, less than half of its citizens were counted as urbanites; in 1986, 85 percent were. Nouakchott, the capital, has grown from fewer than 20,000 people in 1960 to more than 350,000. Half of them are refugees from desertified lands. One can only wonder how well the country's southern extreme will hold up under its population burden.

For now a most obvious and urgent task is to stabilize the sand dunes that threaten roads, dams, irrigation projects and entire villages. The best long-term method is revegetation. Fast-growing tree species and bushes can be planted to anchor the sand with their roots. As the trees grow, they offer the added benefit of providing branches for fuelwood.

Another approach is to establish physical obstacles on the crests of dunes—often in a grid pattern surrounding a town—using discarded materials or homemade panels woven with twigs and leaves.

Several external aid agencies—among them, the Danish Agency for International Development (DANIDA), the United Nations Development Program, and the U.S. Peace Corps—are sponsoring dune-fixing efforts that have met with varying degrees of success. But passivity and cynicism within some of the target communities have precluded the local support on which these projects depend.

A dune-fixing project initiated in 1984 by DANIDA succeeded by mobilizing local people to see the direct personal benefits of participating. A town of 4,000 families has been encircled with a new forest belt planted by people working energetically to protect their homes.

Holding sand dunes at bay brings immediate results and, therefore, encouragement. But the larger problems shifting sands represent—devolution of Mauritania's fragile land into lifeless deserts—are more difficult to combat. Persistent drought intensifies the need for a change in the relationship between people and the land from which they draw life.

Even if natural relief does literally fall from the sky, it will not be enough; if the delicate desert ecology is to support more people and animals, it is up to humans to ensure that more vegetation is replanted than is removed. Unless this happens, the Highway of Hope may become a sand-covered mockery of a land in deepening despair. (pp. 38–9)

Marcia D. Lowe, "The Sahara Swallows Mauritania," in World Watch, *Vol. 1, No. 5, September-October, 1988, pp. 38–9.*

Holding sand dunes at bay brings immediate results and, therefore, encouragement. But the larger problems shifting sands represent—devolution of Mauritania's fragile land into lifeless desert—are more difficult to combat.

Halting Land Degradation

Major droughts in Africa, China, India, and North America over the last four years have spotlighted an immutable reality for much of the world: despite a myriad of sophisticated technologies and scientific advances, humanity's welfare remains tightly linked to the land. Millions in these drought-stricken regions have watched their economic futures—or, in the worst cases, their chances for survival—fade. For the first time in more than a decade, global food security has come into question.

While these headline-making events ignite concern for a few weeks or months, the true tragedy goes unnoticed. Much of the world's food-producing land is being sapped insidiously of its productive potential through overuse, lack of care, or unwise treatment—a process scientists call "desertification." While the term conjures up images of the Sahara speading beyond its bounds to

Each year, irreversible desertification claims an estimated 6 million hectares (14.8 million acres) worldwide—a land area nearly twice the size of Belgium, lost beyond practical hope of reclamation.

engulf new territories, its most worrisome aspects are less dramatic. Desertification refers broadly to the impoverishment of the land by human activities. Perhaps a more appropriate term is land degradation, which we will use interchangeably with desertification.

Each year, irreversible desertification claims an estimated 6 million hectares (14.8 million acres) worldwide—a land area nearly twice the size of Belgium, lost beyond practical hope of reclamation. An additional 20 million hectares (49 million acres) annually become so impoverished that they are unprofitable to farm or graze. Most of the affected land, however, lies on the degradation continuum, somewhere between fully productive and hopelessly degraded. Unfortunately, much of it is sliding down the diminishing productivity side of the scale.

Although the technologies to restore resilience and productivity to stressed lands exist, so far the political will does not. The majority of people affected are poor farmers and pastoralists living at society's margins and lacking a political voice. A lasting victory over land degradation will remain a distant dream without social and economic reforms that give rural people the security of tenure and access to resources they need to improve the land. And with degradation rooted in excessive human pressures, slowing population growth lies at the heart of any effective strategy.

Land degradation may be difficult to rally around and adopt as a cause. Yet its consequences—worsened droughts and floods, famine, declining living standards, and swelling numbers of environmental refugees—could not be more real or engender more emotion. A world of 5.1 billion people, growing by nearly 90 million each year, cannot afford to be losing the productivity of its food base. Without good land, humanity quite literally has nothing to grow on.

Lands and People at Risk

More than a decade has passed since government representatives from around the world gathered at the United Nations Conference on Desertification. Held during the summer of 1977 in Nairobi, Kenya, the meeting followed on the heels of a devastating drought that struck much of western and north-central Africa from 1968 through 1973. It focused the world's attention for the first time on the problems and prospects of fragile lands.

Out of Nairobi came a Plan of Action to Combat Desertification, which recommended 28 measures that national, regional, and international institutions could take to halt land deterioration around the world. Sadly, the action plan never got off the ground, a victim of inadequate funding and lack of sustained commitment by governments. When severe drought and famine repeated themselves in Africa in 1983 and 1984, again bringing tragedy, Canadian meteorologist F. Kenneth Hare remarked grimly: "It is alarming that ten years later . . . the news stories should be so familiar."

Seven years after the Nairobi conference, the United Nations Environment Programme (UNEP) took a more careful look at the overall status and trends of desertification worldwide. This included sending a questionnaire to 91 countries with lands at risk. These data—incomplete, sketchy, and lacking in geographic detail though they are—remain the best available and are more than sufficient to grasp the severity of the problem.

According to the UNEP's 1984 assessment, 4.5 billion hectares (11 billion acres), or 35 percent of the earth's land surface, are threatened by desertification. Of this total—on which a fifth of humanity makes it living—three fourths has already been at least moderately degraded. Fully one third has already lost more than 25 percent of its productive potential.

What lies behind these numbers is a deteriorating relationship between people and the land that supports them, a situation all the more tragic because people themselves are not only degradation's victims but its unwitting agents. The four principal causes of land degradation—overgrazing on rangelands, overcultivation of croplands, waterlogging and salinization of irrigated lands, and deforestation—all stem from excessive human pressures or poor management of the land.

Overgrazing on Rangelands

Rangelands and the animals that graze them play an important role in the global food supply. The 3 billion cattle, sheep, goats, and camels that roam the world's pastures can do something humans cannot: They convert lignocellulose—a main product of photosynthesis that is indigestible to humans—into meat and milk that provide the human population with high-quality protein. Shifts to livestock fed on grain or forage have diminished dependence on grazing animals in some regions. But in much of Africa and the Middle East, and in parts of India and Latin America, roaming ruminants still underpin subsistence economies and support millions of pastoralist families.

Degradation on rangelands mainly takes the form of a deterioration in the quality and, eventually, the quantity of vegetation as a result of overgrazing. As the size of livestock herds surpasses the carrying capacity of perennial grasses on the range, less palatable annual grasses and shrubs move in. If overgrazing and trampling continue, plant cover of all types begins to diminish, leaving the land exposed to the ravages of wind and water. In the severest stages, the soil forms a crust as animal hooves trample nearly bare ground, and erosion accelerates. The formation of large gullies and sand dunes signals that desertification can claim another victory.

Ironically, years of abundant rainfall—seemingly beneficial to pastoral peoples—can often sow the seeds of further degradation and hardship. During wetter periods the area suitable for grazing expands, leading pastoralists to increase the sizes of their herds as insurance against another drought. When the next dry spell hits, the number of livestock exceeds what the reduced area of grass can sustain. The result is overgrazing and accelerated land degradation, a pattern most visible in Africa, where more than half the world's livestock-dependent people live.

Livestock watering holes, a popular feature of international development projects, have contributed to rangeland desertification as well. Cattle cannot go more than three days without water, so digging water holes to sustain herds during dry seasons seems logical. But the concentration of livestock around the watering points leads to severe localized overgrazing, which gradually spreads outward from this central area. When drought strikes again, the animals rarely will die from thirst, but rather from lack of forage.

Overcultivation of Croplands

For more than two decades, farmers in south-central Niger have lamented in Hausa to development workers that *kasar mu, ta gaji,* "the land is tired." Peasants in western parts of the country strike a more ominous chord in Zarma with *Laabu, y bu,* "the land is dead." The phrases aptly depict land suffering from overcultivation, which now affects at least 335 million hectares (827 million acres) of rainfed cropland worldwide (excluding the humid regions), more than a third of the global total.

Agricultural land left without vegetative cover or situated on steeply sloping hillsides is subject to the erosive power of wind and rainwater. An inch of soil takes anywhere from 200 to 1,000 years to form; under the most erosive conditions, that same soil can be swept off the land in just a few seasons. Erosion saps the land's productivity because most of the organic matter and nutrients are in the upper layers of soil. According to one estimate, about half the fertilizer applied to U.S. farmland each year is replacing soil nutrients lost through erosion. In addition, erosion degrades the soil's structure and diminishes its water-holding capacity. As a result, crops have less moisture available to them, which, especially in drier regions, is often erosion's most damaging effect.

For more than two decades, farmers in south-central Niger have lamented in Hausa to development workers that *kassar mu, ta gaji,* "the land is tired." Peasants in western parts of the country strike a more ominous chord in Zarma with *Laabu, y bu,* "the land is dead."

According to one esti-mate, about half the fer-tilizer applied to U.S. farmland each year is re-placing soil nutrients lost through erosion.

Only a handful of countries have attempted to estimate their rates of soil loss in any detail, so the magnitude of the problem worldwide is difficult to gauge in other than broad terms. One useful measure is the load of earth materials carried to the sea by rivers and streams. This figure totals at least 20.3 billion tons per year, which includes 15.3 billion tons of suspended sediment, 4 billion of dissolved material, and 1 billion of coarser bed load. Since this accounts only for material reaching the sea—and excludes, for instance, sediment trapped behind dams—it underestimates the total amount of soil lost from the land.

A look at the geographic distribution of these sediment loads gives a quick sense of where severe erosion is taking place. A 1987 expedition of the inter-nationally sponsored Ocean Drilling Program estimated that the Ganges and Brahmaputra rivers on the Indian subcontinent transport 3 billion tons of sedi-ment to the Bay of Bengal each year, far more than any other river system. The sediment fan on the floor of the bay now spans 3 million square kilometers (1.6 million square miles). Much of that sediment originates in the Himalayas, where deforestation and cultivation of steep slopes in recent decades has added to millions of years of massive erosion from natural geologic activity.

In China, the Huang He (Yellow River), with a drainage area half that of the Ganges-Brahmaputra system, carries more than a billion tons of sediment to the sea each year. About half of it comes from the Loess Plateau, in the Huang He's middle reaches, among the most water-eroded areas on earth. Deeply cut gullies and denuded hillsides span 430,000 square kilometers (165,900 square miles), and erosion rates average some 65 tons per hectare annually.

Waterlogging and Salinization

Today roughly one third of the world's food is grown on the 18 percent of crop-land that is irrigated. Irrigated fields typically yield two to three times more than those watered only by rain, and because crops are protected from the rav-ages of drought, provide a crucial degree of food security.

Unfortunately, poor irrigation practices have degraded much of this valuable cropland. Over time, seepage from canals and overwatering of fields cause the underlying water table to rise. In the absence of adequate drainage, water eventually enters the root zone, damaging crops. Farmers belonging to a large irrigation project in the Indian state of Madhya Pradesh have referred to their once fertile fields as "wet deserts."

In dry regions, salinization usually accompanies waterlogging as moisture near the surface evaporates, leaving behind a layer of salt that is toxic to plants. An air view of severely salinized fields can give the impression they are cov-ered with snow. UNEP's assessment placed the irrigated area damaged by salinization at 40 million hectares (99 million acres).

About half of the affected area is in India and Pakistan, but other regions suf-fering from salinization's effects include the Tigris and Euphrates basins in Syria and Iraq, California's San Joaquin Valley, the Colorado River basin, China's North Plain, and Soviet Central Asia. In the Soviet republic of Turk-menistan, the government blamed salinization for a cotton harvest shortfall of one third in 1985. Meanwhile, another salinity threat has struck Soviet Central Asia: Because so much irrigation water is being siphoned off from the two ma-jor rivers flowing into the Aral Sea, the sea's surface area has shrunk by 40 percent since 1960 and its volume has dropped by two thirds. Winds picking up dried salt from the basin are now annually dumping some 43 million tons of it on more than 15 million hectares (37 million acres) of cropland and pas-ture surrounding the shrinking sea.

Deforestation

The last major cause of land degradation—deforestation—cuts across all land use types. By accelerating soil erosion and reducing the soil's water-absorbing capacity, deforestation often accentuates the effects of overcultivation and overgrazing. Moreover, though forest clearing in humid regions was not included in UNEP's desertification assessment, in many cases it results in a net decline in the productivity of land. Most of the nutrients supporting moist tropical forests are held in the vegetation, so forest clearing removes them as well. Having lost its inherent fertility, the land cannot long support intensive agriculture. Large areas of pasture and cropland in the Brazilian Amazon, for example, have been abandoned.

The U.N. Food and Agriculture Organization (FAO) estimates that each year 11.3 million hectares (28 million acres) of tropical forest are lost through the combined action of land clearing for crop production, fuel-wood gathering, and cattle ranching.

Recent satellite data from Brazil, however, indicate that 8 million hectares (19.7 million acres) of forest were cleared in 1987 in the Brazilian Amazon alone—strongly suggesting that the widely cited FAO figure is far too low. Some portion of deforested land goes into sustainable land uses—such as traditional shifting cultivation, which includes a fallow period that restores the land's fertility—but the bulk of it does not. In the tropics today, deforestation usually translates into land degradation.

Unearthing Degradation's True Causes

Desertification's direct causes—overgrazing, overcultivation, salinization, and deforestation—are easy to enumerate, but only by grappling with the complex web of conditions leading to these excessive pressures is there hope of stopping desertification's spread. Though they vary greatly from place to place, these underlying forces generally are rooted in population densities greater than the land can sustain and, more fundamentally, in social and economic inequities that push people into marginal environments and vulnerable livelihoods.

The number of people a given land area can support—what scientists call its carrying capacity—depends on climatic factors, the land's inherent productivity, the products it yields, and the methods used to increase its productivity. Though carrying capacity is difficult to measure accurately, few pieces of data are moral crucial to wise development planning or tell more about the threat of desertification.

In response to mounting concern about environmental deterioration in West Africa, the World Bank set up a special working group led by Jean Eugene Gorse to study the problem in more detail. Gorse's group focused on a band of seven countries in what are known as the Sahelian and Sudanian zones: Burkina Faso, Chad, Gambia, Mali, Mauritania, Niger, and Senegal. In these countries, annual rainfall increases from north to south—from less than 200 millimeters (mm) (8 inches) in the northernmost zone to more than 800 mm (32 inches) in the southernmost—and so, consequently, does the carrying capacity of traditional farming and livestock practices. The study found that in two out of the five east-west trending zones, the rural population in 1980 had already exceeded that for which the land could sustainably provide sufficient food. Only in the southernmost band could the land withstand a substantial increase in human numbers.

Even more important, wood resources emerged as the limiting factor in the carrying capacity of every zone in the region. Indeed, the 1980 population of all seven countries collectively exceeded the number of people the region's wood resources could support by 10.1 million. This finding is critical to development strategies because it means that efforts to raise the carrying capacity of the cropping and livestock systems will not increase the total population this land can sustain until more trees are planted—or some other means is found of meeting energy needs.

Not surprisingly, this imbalance between what the land can sustainably yield and the numbers of people living on it has led to pervasive desertification. Virtually all the rangeland and an estimated 82 percent of the rainfed cropland in

Over time, seepage from canals and overwatering of fields cause the underlying water table to rise. In the absence of adequate drainage, water eventually enters the root zone, damaging crops. Farmers belonging to a large irrigation project in the Indian state of Madhya Pradesh have referred to their once fertile fields as "wet deserts."

The surface area of the Soviet Union's Aral Sea has shrunk by 40 percent since 1960 and its volume has dropped by two thirds. Winds picking up dried salt from the basin are now annually dumping some 43 million tons of it on more than 15 million hectares (37 million acres) of cropland and pasture surrounding the shrinking sea.

those same seven countries is already at least moderately degraded. Moreover, with a projected population in the year 2000 of 55 million—a 77 percent increase over the 1980 total—pressures on the land will increase markedly, and land productivity is bound to fall even further.

Similarly, in India, growth in the human and animal populations, both of which have doubled since 1950, has outstripped the sustainable production levels of the nation's fuelwood and fodder resources. Estimated fuelwood and fodder demands in the early eighties exceeded available supplies by 70 and 23 percent, respectively. As a result, overgrazing and deforestation have led to extensive degradation. Out of an estimated 266 million hectares (657 million acres) of potentially productive land, 94 million (35 percent) suffer varying degrees of degradation from water erosion, wind erosion, or salinization. Of the 75 million hectares (185 million acres) of forestland, 40 million are degraded—30 million lacking tree cover and 10 million having only shrubs—and satellite data show that the nation continues to lose forests at the rate of 1.3 million hectares (3.2 million acres) per year.

Next to population pressures, perhaps no other factors foster more degradation than the inequitable distribution of land and the absence of secure land tenure. In an agrarian society, keeping a disproportionate share of land in the hands of a few forces the poorer majority to compete for the limited area left, severely compromising their ability to manage sustainably what land they do have. . . .

Striking inequities in land holdings compound population pressures. About 44 percent of South African blacks are forced to live in the "Bantu homelands," which have an average population density of 79 people per square kilometer compared with 15.5 people per square kilometer in the rest of the country. Much of the land set aside for the native people is not even arable, yet the majority of them are subsistence farmers. As John Hanks of the World Wide Fund for Nature says, "it is hardly surprising that these areas have some of the worst cases of overgrazing, deforestation, and soil erosion in the whole of the African continent."

The flip side of the unequal distribution of land is lack of secure land tenure. Since land is often needed as collateral, farmers without land titles have difficulty getting the loans they need to invest in their land's productivity, and as a result often abandon worn-out fields for less-degraded new land. Lack of secure tenure pervades much of the Third World. In Thailand, for example, only about 20 percent of all private land had title deeds as of 1985, and an estimated 500,000 farm families were landless.

In many areas, these problems are aggravated by the denial of social and economic rights to women. In Africa, women grow 80 percent of the food their families eat, and, with their children's help, collect the water and wood their households need for cooking and heating. Yet despite their crucial role in the agrarian economy, women rarely have property rights or even access to their husbands' incomes. Extension services and training programs usually are directed toward men, even though it is the women who till the fields. Because women lack the resources needed to improve their farms' productivity, the land—and the families living on it—suffers.

Unless existing land distribution patterns change, the number of smallholder and landless families in the developing world will grow by nearly 30 percent by the year 2000—to a total of 220 million households. Without access to secure property, credit, and extension services, these rural people will have no choice but to overuse the land and to farm areas that should not be cultivated.

Finally, national land use policies foster degradation as well. For example, the governments of Brazil and Indonesia—supported by World Bank loans—have sponsored resettlement programs that encourage people to clear tropical forest to create new cropland, even though that land will only sustain cropping for a few years. During the mid-seventies, U.S. officials encouraged the plowing up of grassland to expand crop production in response to higher world grain prices, even though much of that land would experience soil erosion reminiscent of the Dust Bowl days. And numerous governments and development institutions have supported irrigation projects without adequate attention to drainage, even though the problem of salinization dates back at least to ancient Mesopotamia. Whether they reflect a profound ignorance of the land or simply a lack of concern for its long-term health, such misguided policies produce the same unfortunate result: more degraded land.

Drought, Desertification, and the Hydrological Cycle

As natural phenomena, droughts come and go with unpredictable regularity. They are the bane of a farmer's existence, for without sufficient water, agricultural land will bear only a meager harvest at best no matter how deep and fertile the topsoil, how high-yielding the variety of seed, or how well-tended the farmer's field. Human activities are now altering the hydrological cycle—on global, regional, and local scales—in ways that have profound implications for future food production and the long-term productivity of the land. . . .

For good reason, climate change now commands higher priority in the halls of governments, in research institutes, and on the international environmental agenda. Far less attention, however, is being devoted to a less dramatic but equally serious change in the earth's physical condition: alterations in the hydrological cycle as a result of land degradation.

The Sahel had just gone through six dry years when Massachusetts Institute of Technology meteorologist J. G. Charney put forth the idea in 1975 that the removal of vegetation in dry regions could cause rainfall to diminish because of an increase in the albedo, the share of sunlight reflected back from the earth. Desert sands and bare rock, for example, have higher albedos than grassland, which in turn reflects more sunlight than a dense forest does. According to Charney's hypothesis, less of the sun's radiation is absorbed at the earth's surface as albedo increases, so surface temperatures drop. This in turn fosters greater subsidence, or sinking motion in the atmosphere. Since subsiding air is dry, rainfall would decline. The degraded area would feed on itself, becoming ever more desert-like.

Tests of Charney's hypothesis using climate models generally confirmed it: large increases in albedo did indeed reduce rainfall. Less clear, however, was how smaller changes in reflectivity would affect rainfall and whether the patchy pattern of desertification could produce albedo changes sufficient to affect rainfall levels.

Another worrisome link surfaced from the modeling studies of J. Shukla and Y. Mintz. They examined the effects on rainfall of changes in evapotranspiration, the transfer of water vapor from the land surface to the atmosphere through evaporation or transpiration by plants. For evapotranspiration to occur, the soil must be sufficiently moist and vegetation must be present to bring that moisture into contact with the air. Presumably if evapotranspiration is an important source of atmospheric water vapor in a given locale, rainfall levels could decline if it diminishes. Shukla and Mintz found just that, although, as with Charney's study, their findings pertained to changes of a large magnitude and wide extent. Once again, land degradation—by diminishing the evapotranspiration—was linked to climatic change.

Meanwhile, meteorologist Sharon Nicholson was analyzing rainfall data from roughly 300 sites in some 20 countries of Africa. She calculated a long-term average from data covering 1901–74, and then calculated the annual percentage departures from that long-term average for 1901–84. Between 1967 and 1984, the region experienced 17 consecutive years of below-normal rainfall, by far the longest series of consecutive sub-par rains in the 84-year record. Annual rainfall in 1983 and 1984 fell more than 40 percent short of the long-term average. Interestingly, Nicholson also analyzed northern sub-Saharan rainfall levels according to three east-west trending zones and found that drought was most persistent in the northernmost, most arid band, where the albedo and low evapotranspiration feedbacks would be greatest.

> **Human activities are now altering the hydrological cycle—on global, regional, and local scales—in ways that have profound implications for future food production and the long-term productivity of the land.**

What appear to be consequences and signs of meteorological drought—withered crops, falling groundwater levels, and dry stream beds—can actually be due to land degradation.

The global circulation models used in climate studies are composed of equations that mathematically describe the laws governing atmospheric motion. Such models allow scientists to examine how changes in certain parameters—such as albedo, soil moisture, or the carbon dioxide concentration—affect large-scale atmospheric circulation. Unfortunately, they are not sufficiently fine-tuned to predict changes for specific locations. Yet as meteorologist F. Kenneth Hare points out, plausible hypotheses exist "that blame the albedo and soil moisture feedbacks for the intensification of drought in Africa." While scientists cannot yet know whether dryness will persist, he says, "there are now many more climatologists who are prepared to say that dessication will continue than there were at UNCOD [the U.N. Conference on Desertification] in 1977."

Research in the Amazon basin of Brazil suggests that land degradation can alter the hydrological cycle in humid regions as well. Eneas Salati has studied the water budget of a 25-square-kilometer (10 square miles) basin located 60 kilometers (37 miles) north of Manaus and found that streams carry away roughly 25 percent of rainfall, while transpiration by trees and plants return to the atmosphere nearly 50 percent and evaporation the remaining 25 percent. Thus, fully three quarters of the rainwater falling in the basin returns as water vapor to the atmosphere.

Salati points out that moisture-laden air from the Atlantic Ocean carried westward by the winds provides about half the water vapor leading to rainfall in the Amazon region. Evapotranspiration from the forest itself supplies the other half. Thus, water recycling by the Amazon vegetation plays a crucial role in sustaining rainfall levels, a role that increases in importance at greater distances from the Atlantic.

Deforestation alters this hydrologic pattern. More rainfall runs off, and less gets recycled back to the atmosphere to generate new rainfall. It remains uncertain what amount of forest clearing might initiate significant rainfall declines, or if the crossing of some deforestation threshold could precipitate a sudden change. An estimated 12 percent of Amazonian rain forest in Brazil already has been cleared. Salati suspects, though he cannot support this, that changes in the water budget may become noticeable when 20–30 percent of the region has been deforested, especially if most of the clearing occurs in the eastern Amazon, where rainfall recycling begins.

Satellite data shows clearly that deforestation in parts of the Amazon is accelerating. In the Brazilian state of Rondonia, for example, the area deforested has grown at an exponential rate between 1975 and 1985; 1 million hectares (2.47 million acres) were cleared just between 1984 and 1985. If the exponential rate continues, half of the state's tropical forests will disappear by the early nineties, and all will be gone sometime around the turn of the century.

As noted earlier, satellite data for the whole Brazilian Amazon show that 8 million hectares (19.8 million acres) were cleared in 1987 alone, 5 to 6 million more than were thought to have been cleared annually in the early eighties. If clearing continues at such a pace, Brazilians may face a multiple tragedy: the replacement of productive rain forest with cropland or grassland that loses its fertility and must be abandoned after several years, and reduced rainfall—not only in the Amazon basin itself, but, because the basin exports water vapor to the south, possibly in the agricultural lands of the central plateau.

Regardless of whether desertification and deforestation cause rainfall to diminish, hydrologic balance hinges on how the land and its vegetative cover are managed. When rainwater hits the land, it either immediately runs off into rivers and streams to head back to the sea, soaks into the subsurface to replenish groundwater supplies, or is evaporated or transpired back into the atmosphere. Land degradation shifts the proportion of rainfall following each of these paths. With less vegetative cover and with soils less able to absorb water, degraded land increases runoff and decreases infiltration into the subsurface. The resulting reduction in soil moisture and groundwater supplies worsens the effects of drought, while the increase in rapid runoff exacerbates flooding.

It's Not Drought, but Land-Use

What appear, then, to be consequences and signs of meteorological drought—withered crops, falling groundwater levels, and dry stream beds—can actually be due to land degradation. Perhaps nowhere has this case been made more convincingly than in India, where a growing number of scientists now blame deforestation and desertification for the worsening of droughts and floods. Writes Jayanta Bandyopadhyay of the Research Foundation for Science, Technology and Natural Resource Policy in Dehra Dun, "With an amazing rapidity acute scarcity of water has grabbed the centre stage of India's national life. . . . State after state is trapped into an irreversible and worsening crisis of drought, desertification and consequent water scarcity, threatening plant, animal and human life." . . .

Michael Mortimore of Bayero University in Nigeria has studied villagers' responses to drought and famine in parts of the northern states of Kano and Borno. He finds that their survival strategies lead inevitably to further degradation of the land, diminishing their chances for complete recovery. When drought claims large portions of their livestock and crops, for example, they may turn to cutting and selling more firewood, construction materials, and other wood products, thereby increasing pressures on local woodlands. To compensate for lower yields, they may also shorten fallow periods and cultivate additional marginal land. Their reduced animal herds supply less manure, leading to a drop in the fertility of their fields.

When drought ends, the villagers thus begin their recovery from a severely compromised position: more highly degraded fields and woodlands, not to mention greater poverty. As Mortimore says, "By a set of actions—rational in themselves—the overall productivity of the system deteriorates in a series of irreversible steps linked with the occurrence of droughts. It is only necessary for us to add population growth—as an independent variable—to complete this scenario of a structurally unstable system."

Drought and degradation reinforce each other by preventing land from recovering from stress. Whereas healthy land will bounce back to its former productivity after a drought, degraded and abused land frequently will not. For much of the Third World, especially parts of Africa and India, a return to "normal" rainfall levels may not mean a return to past levels of productivity. And if land degradation actually causes rainfall to diminish, a cycle could be set in motion that leads to long-term economic and environmental decline—and to even greater hunger and human suffering than witnessed in Africa and India during the eighties.

Sandra Postel, "Halting Land Degradation," in State of the World: A Worldwatch Institute Report on Progress Toward a Sustainable Society, *1989, p. 21.*

Drought and degradation reinforce each other by preventing land from recovering from stress. Whereas healthy land will bounce back to its former productivity after a drought, degraded and abused land frequently will not.

Regaining Land Productivity

A search for solutions to halting desertification's spread turns up no quick fixes. With the causes tied to varied mixes of physical, social, and economic conditions, the remedies inevitably must be diverse and tailored to the problems and needs of particular locales. But here and there—in villages, grassroots organizations, research institutes, experiment stations, development agencies, and government bureaus—technologies and policies geared to restoring the land are being devised, tried, and shown to have promise.

Since much degradation stems from the extension of cropping or grazing onto marginal lands that cannot sustain those activities, changes in the way land is used and managed lie at the heart of rehabilitation efforts. In some cases,

Since much degradation stems from the extension of cropping or grazing onto marginal lands that cannot sustain those activities, changes in the way land is used and managed lie at the heart of rehabilitation efforts.

degrading lands can simply be removed from production and allowed to recover. The U.S. government has done just this in setting up a Conservation Reserve and calling for 16 million hectares (40 million acres) of highly erodible cropland to be planted in grass or trees by 1990. Farmers get compensation from the government for their lost production, and have already placed an estimated 12 million hectares into the reserve under 10-year contracts. Three fourths of the way to its 1990 goal, the program has slashed the national erosion rate by a half-billion tons per year—nearly one fourth of the excessive soil losses from U.S. cropland before the program began.

Hungry Peoples Can't Let the Land Rest

A creative initiative, the Conservation Reserve works in large part because a price-depressing surplus of crops made the removal of land from production attractive to farmers and the government alike. Removing the most erodible, marginal land only makes good sense. But in most Third World regions threatened with desertification, the struggle to keep food production increasing apace with population growth and the swelling numbers of land-hungry peasants make shifting a large portion of cropland out of production almost unthinkable.

In a few pockets of the developing world, however, land is being restored in ways that both conserve the resource base and improve people's living standards. These efforts take various forms, but center around measures that concentrate production on the most fertile, least erodible land, that stabilize soils on sloping and other marginal land, and that reduce rural people's vulnerability to crop failure, often by diversifying income-generating options at the village level.

China's Erosion Control Strategy

One such effort is under way in China's Loess Plateau, a highly eroded area spanning some 60 million hectares around the middle reaches of the Huang He. Because of the constant threat that the silt-laden river will flood, the central government has supported efforts to control erosion on the plateau for several decades. Planting of trees and grass and the construction of terraces on sloping land have helped stabilize soils on some 10 million hectares, nearly one quarter of the area suffering from erosion.

During the past decade, the Chinese government's erosion control strategy has turned to sustainable land use systems that improve the livelihoods of the region's rural inhabitants. In 1979, with support from the United Nations Development Programme, an experiment station was established in Mizhi County in northern Shaanxi Province, a drought-prone, highly gullied area, where more than 60 percent of the land slopes at angles of 25 degrees or greater. Scientists developed a plan aimed at intensifying crop production on a smaller cropland area, planting much of the sloping land in trees or grass, and developing animal husbandry as an added source of income for the villagers.

In 1984, armed with promising results from pilot experiments, the government sought assistance from FAO's World Food Programme (WFP) to replicate the strategy in a portion of Mizhi County encompassing 105,000 people and 241 villages. WFP provides food as an incentive for farmers to do the work of land reclamation and as compensation for the cropland converted to trees or grass.

Quanjiagou, one of the villages in the project, gives a visitor who has traversed hundreds of kilometers of the degraded Loess Plateau an overwhelming sense of a land transformed. Earthen dams built across the deep gullies have captured topsoil eroding off the hillsides, creating flat, fertile fields where farmers have planted corn, potatoes, and vegetables. Terraces allow cropping with minimal erosion on a portion of the slopes, while cash crop trees, such as apple, and a leguminous shrub good for fuel and fodder stabilize the remaining sloping land. Between 1979 and 1986, the area planted in crops was halved, but total crop production increased 17 percent—an amazing 134-percent gain in productivity. With the added value from tree products and animal husbandry, per capita income in the village has more than doubled.

Average costs of these efforts, including the value of grain supplied by WFP, total about $162 per hectare if the villagers' labor is valued monetarily, $54 per hectare if it is not. While this sum is large relative to per capita income, the investment is modest compared with many other development projects, such as establishing fuelwood plantations or expanding irrigation, which often cost upwards of $1,000 per hectare.

In the drought-plagued, degraded highlands of Ethiopia, similar food-for-work projects are under way in some 44 catchments. Like efforts on the Loess Plateau, they are aimed at integrating conservation and development to both rehabilitate the land and boost crop production. A key feature of the Ethiopian efforts are simple structures called bunds, walls of rock or earth constructed across hillsides to catch soil washing down the slope. Soil builds up behind the bund, forming a terrace that both diminishes erosion and enhances water infiltration. Between 1976 and 1985, through projects sponsored by the United Nations and various foreign aid agencies, Ethiopian farmers built 600,000 kilometers of bunds and about 470,000 kilometers of terraces for reforestation of steep slopes. Though impressive, these efforts are only a start: just 6 percent of the threatened highlands are now protected.

Farmers, Scientists and Development Experts Must Work Together

No matter how creative a strategy, land rehabilitation hinges on a set of effective technologies that will be adopted. By working in partnership with villagers, scientists and development workers come to know their needs, priorities, and cultural practices, and can promote appropriate technologies. Soil scientist Rattan Lal makes the basic but crucial observation that "the subsistence farmer who risks famine would consider a successful technology to be the one that produces some yield in the worst year rather than the one that produces a high yield in the best."

Simple techniques of soil and water conservation that add nutrients and moisture to the land form the core of promising rehabilitation efforts. Work at the International Institute of Tropical Agriculture in Ibadan, Nigeria, has shown, for example, that applying a mulch of crop residues at rates of six tons per hectare can provide nearly complete erosion control on slopes of up to 15 percent, allowing sustainable cropping of such land. The mulch protects the soil from the impact of raindrops, increases rainfall infiltration, conserves soil moisture, and improves soil structure, all helping to boost yields. In field trials, a mulch of six tons per hectare has led to yield increases over nonmulched plots of 83 percent for cowpeas, 73 percent for cassava, 33 percent for soybeans, and 23 percent for maize.

Many subsistence farmers are aware of the benefits of mulching, but usually do not have sufficient plant residues to apply to their fields at the needed rates. One strategy that remedies this is alley cropping—an agroforestry design in which food crops are planted in alleys between hedgerows of trees or shrubs. The hedgerow trimmings provide a good mulch for the crop, besides helping meet other needs such as fodder for animals and fuelwood for heating and cooking. Planting for hedges along the contours of sloping land reduces rainfall runoff and soil erosion. Even though the hedgerows take up land, crop yields per hectare suffer little if at all, and sometimes even increase. . . .

Without Incentives, Farmers Won't Get Involved

Land restoration also requires incentives that motivate rural people to build terraces, plant trees, or do whatever needs to be done and—equally important—to maintain what they put in place. Without such incentives, governments

No matter how creative a strategy, land rehabilitation hinges on a set of effective technologies that will be adopted. By working in partnership with villagers, scientists and development workers come to know their needs, priorities, and cultural practices, and can promote appropriate technologies.

Land restoration also requires incentives that motivate rural people to build terraces, plant trees, or do whatever needs to be done and— equally important—to maintain what they put in place.

and aid organizations face the prospect of footing the bill for land rehabilitation efforts everywhere they are needed—clearly, an impossible task.

Recent economic reforms in China, for example, give farmers the security in land tenure and fair prices needed to encourage improvements in the land. Under the "responsibility system," farmers can sell on the free market whatever they produce above their quota to the state. Although the government still owns the land, families can enter into long-term contracts to use the land, and in many cases this right-of-use is inheritable. In Mizhi County, each household's allocation of cropland remains valid for 15 years. Tenure for pasture and wooded land ranges from 30 to 50 years, and can often be passed on to children.

In Ethiopia, on the other hand, the government owns the land and gives Peasant Associations the responsibility of allocating it to farm families for their use. Since the Peasant Associations can redistribute the land, farmers using any given plot have no guarantee that they will benefit from any long-term improvements they make. As in many countries, a long-standing policy of keeping food prices low to appease urban dwellers has further discouraged farmers from investing in land productivity. A promising step was taken in mid-1988, however, when plans were announced to begin raising prices in certain regions for the portion of crops that farmers must sell to the government.

Not Much Success for Range- And Irrigated-Land Rehab

Unfortunately, successes with rangeland rehabilitation form a rather short and unconvincing list. Restoring the naturally fluctuating range resource—given periodic drought, shifting numbers of range animals, and the fact that mobility is central to nomadic pastoralists' survival—presents formidable challenges. Yet a few promising efforts dot the landscape. In northern Nigeria, researchers at the International Livestock Center for Africa (ILCA) are experimenting with "fodder banks," reserves of nitrogen-fixing crops that can provide nutritious feed for livestock during the dry season. Other efforts focus on redistributing livestock to even out pressures on the range. For example, ILCA is helping Ethiopian pastoralists to dig more ponds that retain water for several months into the dry season, thereby hoping to reduce localized overgrazing.

Perhaps the clearest success in rangeland restoration springs from the revival of the ancient "Hema" system of cooperative management in Syria. Cooperatives are established that each have sole right to graze a demarcated area of range. Families in the cooperative are then granted a license to graze a certain number of sheep within that area. By reducing overgrazing, the system has enabled the revegetation of 7 million hectares of rangeland.

Much less irrigated cropland than rainfed land suffers from degradation, but the cost of this degradation is great, both because of irrigated land's high production potential and because of the large investments that have gone into it. An expensive and daunting task, rehabilitation of salinized land has not received the attention it deserves. Pakistan, among the countries most affected, has perhaps tried hardest to tackle it, but has achieved only mixed results.

In 1960 the government committed itself to draining salt-affected lands by installing vertical tube wells. Two decades and over 12,000 tube wells later, the area reclaimed still fell far short of the target. Although the technology had proved effective, the public programs had actually reclaimed less land than the combined effects of private tube wells and an improved water supply. The Sixth Five Year Plan, 1983 to 1988, allocates an astonishing 43 percent of the total water budget to drainage activities, and uses credits and subsidies to further encourage private development of tube wells.

In Egypt, a drainage system covering only a small portion of the Nile Delta Valley has been estimated to cost $1 billion. Such high sums partly explain why governments tend to ignore the problem, and why preventing salinization in the first place—by increasing irrigation efficiency and providing for adequate drainage when irrigation systems are built—is crucial.

Joining the Battle

Why, more than a decade after a global goal was set to stop desertification by the year 2000, are we losing more trees, more topsoil, and more grazing land than ever before? The easy answers are that governments fail to grasp the severity of the threat, lack the political will to give it priority, and devote insufficient financial resources to combat it. But a more fundamental reason may lie in the very nature of "desertification control" itself. It crosses all traditional disciplinary and bureaucratic boundaries, including agriculture, forestry, pastoralism, and water management. Lasting solutions are rooted as much in social and economic reforms as in effective technologies. Telescoping desertification control into a single program or plan of action defies the reality that it is inseparable from the broader notion of sustainable development.

All the elements needed to reverse land degradation exist, but they have not been joined effectively in the battle or given the resources needed to mount an adequate fight. In the United Nations Environment Programme and its Executive Director, Mostafa Tolba, desertification control has a strategic headquarters and a strong, committed leader. But the amount of funding mobilized for desertification control over the last decade has fallen far short of needs. Harold Dregne estimated that an average of $170 million per year had been spent by donor agencies on field-level desertification control between 1978 and 1983, compared with an estimated $1.8 billion of annual expenditures needed to combat desertification adequately. UNEP places investment needs at $4.5 billion per year to bring desertification under control within 20 years. Several countries have developed the national plans of action called for by the 1977 Nairobi conference, but only three—Burkina Faso, Mali, and Tunisia—have apparently drummed up sufficient support to begin successfully implementing them. The United Nations Sudano-Sahelian Office intends to push implementation of four existing plans before the end of 1989 in this northern part of Africa.

Efforts At the Village Level

While this top-down approach proceeds at a glacial pace with few measurable gains, efforts at the village level have produced numerous, albeit small successes. On the island of Cebu in the Philippines, for example, local farmers have been working with U.S.-based World Neighbors since 1982 to develop measures to stem soil erosion on the steep slopes they cultivate. Initially, the World Neighbors project director led the seminars on contouring and other techniques; later, villagers familiar with the methods took over the presentations. Two years into the project, 74 farmers were participating and 25 kilometers of erosion control structures had been built. Three new sites were added by the end of 1987, and project workers now expect 750 farmers to adopt the conservation techniques.

In western Kenya, 540 different local organizations—mostly women's groups and primary schools—are working with the U.S.-based organization CARE to promote reforestation. CARE provides the materials needed to establish nurseries, as well as training and extension services, but local people do the planting. Each group plants between 5,000 and 10,000 seedlings annually, collectively amounting to nearly a third of the plantings the government estimates are needed.

The greatest hope of reversing land degradation lies in marrying stepped-up international support and technical guidance through U.N. agencies, bilateral and multilateral donors, and national governments with the commitment and experience of organizations operating at the local level. Although that presents an onerous set of institutional challenges, there are some promising signs.

Recognizing that community-based initiatives have higher success rates and more lasting impacts than "top down" projects, UNEP is strengthening its cooperation with nongovernmental organization (NGOs). The agency currently

In western Kenya, 540 different local organizations—mostly women's groups and primary schools—are working with the U.S.-based organization CARE to promote reforestation. . . . Each group plants between 5,000 and 10,000 seedlings annually, collectively amounting to nearly a third of the planting the government estimates are needed.

Last solutions to desertification are rooted as much in social and economic reforms as in effective technologies. Telescoping desertification control into a single program or plan of action defies the reality that it is inseparable from the greater notion of sustainable development.

supports several grassroots projects through the Nairobi-based African NGOs Environmental Network, and has also helped launch the Deforestation and Desertification Control NGO Network in the Asia-Pacific region. A similar network is being established for Latin America. In addition, UNEP has provided $35,000 to bolster tree planting efforts in southern India through the Millions of Trees Club, a grassroots group that has set up people's nurseries and training centers for reforestation. During the two years of UNEP's support, the number of nurseries grew from 20 to 45, and from them more than 2 million trees and shrubs were planted.

The Cairo Plan: Ecologically Based Development

Another promising sign emerged in December 1985, when representatives from 41 African governments, regional organizations, and NGOs gathered in Cairo for the first African Ministerial Conference on the Environment. The conference's prime objective was developing a cooperative program aimed at arresting environmental degradation on the continent and helping Africans achieve food and energy self-sufficiency. Toward that end, a Cairo Plan was set forth that called for two sets of pilot projects.

The first involves selecting three villages in different ecological zones in each of 50 African countries and implementing ecologically based development schemes in each. The second focuses on rehabilitating rangelands, and calls for one pilot project in each of 30 countries designed to produce fodder from small plots irrigated by animal-powered water pumps. The goal is to produce enough fodder to carry village herds through the dry season so that degraded rangelands have a chance to recover. It is hoped that through these 180 demonstration projects, which will involve working closely with NGO's and villagers, successful and replicable strategies will emerge.

Funding for the Cairo Plan is to come from African governments themselves as well as from international donor agencies. UNEP, which is helping coordinate the effort, is currently working to round up support. So far, about 5 projects have received funding, and up to 20 others are in the pipeline.

Bilateral donor agencies also have an important role to play in stimulating action at the local level. By funneling more money through NGOs rather than national government agencies, they can often ensure more bang for the development buck. The U.S. Agency for International Development (AID), for example, sponsors a $27-million Agroforestry Outreach Project in Haiti, which is administered through three private voluntary organizations. Operation Double Harvest produces and distributes seedlings and manages demonstration tree farms. CARE provides agroforestry training and extension services to farmers in the severely degraded northwestern region. And the Pan American Development Foundation works with more than 120 Haitian voluntary groups, many of them church-related, by training "promoters" to help farmers plant and care for trees on their farms and to report back on what strategies are proving successful.

So far, some 130,000 farmers have planted more than 35 million trees, not only conserving soils and boosting crop yields, but helping meet their needs for fuel and fodder. While initially the project paid farmers to plant and care for the seedlings, the benefits of agroforestry soon rendered the payments unnecessary. Indeed, farmers' demand for seedlings currently exceeds what the nurseries can provide. Project officials hope that, having tapped into and strengthened existing networks at the local level, the reforestation effort will continue long after the project money is spent.

Building Bridges between Science and Farming

Building institutional bridges between research organizations and farmers' fields is also crucial in the battle against land degradation. Technologies perfected on experimental research plots often need adapting to suit the needs and conditions of small farmers. The Tropical Agricultural Research and Training Center (CATIE, from the Spanish), located in Turrialba, Costa Rica, serves just such a role for its six Central American and Caribbean members: Costa Rica, the Dominican Republic, Guatemala, Honduras, Nicaragua, and Panama.

CATIE's activities focus on developing integrated crop, livestock, and forest production systems suited to subsistence farming in the tropics. David Joslyn of AID, which provides 65 percent of CATIE's $13-million annual budget, knows of no other organization like it: "In both training and research, the organization accomplishes what the small countries of Central America could never accomplish alone."

Without adequate incentives for small farmers to invest in their land, the technologies developed at research institutes and the land use strategies tested through aid projects will not spread widely enough to make more than a dent in desertification. As noted earlier, reforming land ownership and tenure policies and providing access to credit for smallholders is crucial to the reversal of land degradation. Special emphasis needs to be placed on the status of women—especially in Africa, where the disparity between the work women do and the rights they have is greatest.

Of the multilateral development organizations, the International Fund for Agricultural Development (IFAD) is heads above the others in incorporating these needs into its projects more thoroughly. This decade-old U.N. agency has now carried out about 190 projects, and in the words of IFAD president Idriss Jazairy, they are "people-oriented" and built upon the philosophy that development involves the "liberation of (people's) creative potential."

An IFAD project in Kenya, for example, operates through women's savings clubs and other groups to enhance women's access to credit, farm supplies, and extension services. Another, in The Gambia, works to uphold women's traditional cultivation rights under a new land distribution scheme and establishes day-care centers for children of women whose workloads have increased with the introduction of double-cropping. While the provision of child-care services may seem far removed from desertification control, freeing women to do the work of raising land productivity could in fact be a crucial first step.

Expanded research into crop varieties and production systems appropriate for the lands and people at risk from desertification is also crucial. With the high-yielding, Green Revolution package of technologies having captured the research limelight over the last several decades, efforts to improve the productivity of subsistence farming are just beginning to get the attention they deserve. Research on cowpeas, for example, an important leguminous crop in Africa, has led to varieties harvestable in 50–60 days instead of 90–100. That paves the way for double- or even triple-cropping in some regions, which would reduce pressures to extend cultivation to marginal lands. A new drought-tolerant sorghum has yielded double or triple that of traditional varieties in the Sudan. By boosting per-hectare production, its spread among smallholders also would allow some erodible lands that would otherwise be cultivated to be planted in soil-stabilizing tree or fodder crops.

Finally, with much degradation stemming from excessive human pressures on the land, reversing it will require a dramatic slowing of population growth. If current growth rates persist, Africa's worn-out lands will need to support an additional 263 million people by the year 2000, roughly equivalent to adding two more Nigerias. India will grow by nearly 200 million people, or 24 percent, and the Philippines—with the fastest growth rate in Southeast Asia—by more than a third. No matter how much funding comes forth, or how fast effective technologies spread, or how diligently governments implement land reforms, a lasting victory over land degradation will remain out of reach until population pressures ease.

Sandra Postel, "Halting Land Degradation," in State of the World: A Worldwatch Institute Report on Progress Toward a Sustainable Society," 1989, p. 21.

While the provision of child-care services may seem far removed from desertification control, freeing women to do the work of raising land productivity could in fact be a crucial first step.

The term "desertifica-
tion" is deeply flawed,
says Camilla Toulmin of
the International Insti-
tute for Environment and
Development (IIED), a
UN-funded agency based
in London. There is
little agreement among
scientists about what it
means. Some use the
term to imply an irreversible change. Others
do not.

Is the Desert Really Moving?

New deserts are forming from Mexico to Rajasthan and from Mauritania to Botswana. The process is called desertification. The world has an image to go with the word: an emotive picture of inexorable shifting sands encroaching on valuable farmland. The word and the image have sustained a decade-long effort by the United Nations Environment Program (UNEP) to combat the spread of deserts. Now an increasing number of scientists are arguing that the image is a mirage and the efforts have been largely misdirected. Countries such as Mali, on the southern fringes of the Sahara Desert, have used international aid to plant millions of trees as a barrier against the encroaching sands. But is the desert really moving?

Soils around the world are suffering various forms of degradation—that is certain. The damage is worst in the dry lands, which cover roughly a third of the land surface of the planet and support some 850 million people. But the fear is that attempts to encapsulate this problem with the phrase "desertification" have obscured solutions.

UNEP claims that desertification costs $26 billion a year in lost food production. The damage, it says, could be prevented by spending $4.5 billion each year. To date, the program's calls for funds have fallen on deaf ears. But the real argument is about whether what money has been spent has been spent wisely. There has been "too much unfounded assertion and exaggeration," says Ridley Nelson in a paper published recently by the environmental arm of the World Bank. And Jeremy Swift, in a paper from the Institute of Development Studies, claims that existing definitions of the problem of desertification have led to "big public policies based on very little bits of science."

The UN's prime initiative on deserts, which set the current guidelines for halting the degradation of soils in dry lands, was the Conference on Desertification (UNCOD) held in Nairobi, Kenya, in 1977. The conference asserted, among other things, that the Sahara Desert of North Africa had moved south by about 62 miles between 1958 and 1975, an average of 3.5 miles a year. At a major review held by the UN in 1984, Mostafa Tolba, the director of the UNEP, said, "Currently, 35 percent of the world's land is at risk. . . . Each year, 52 million acres is reduced to near or complete uselessness."

These figures have become part of the furniture in the study of desertification, enshrined, as Nelson put it, as "institutional fact." The numbers frequently accompany compelling pictures of forlorn children standing on their dune-covered homes. All of this has focused attention on the edges of existing deserts. This, say the critics, is a major error. "There is extremely little scientific evidence based on field research or remote sensing for the many statements about the extent of desertification," says Nelson. Many of the figures come from the answers to a questionnaire sent out by the UNEP in 1982. "In Africa, governments were completing it in many cases at the height of a drought," he explains. Even experts from sophisticated governments say that they had great difficulty answering the questions. They had little of the data that they were asked for. There were no proper guidelines for how to answer critical questions about the degree of desertification of land.

The UN's figure for the southward march of the Sahara comes from an investigation conducted in 1975 by Hugh Lamprey, an ecologist who is now director of the Worldwide Fund for Nature in East Africa, who concluded: "The desert's boundary has shifted south by 50–60 miles between 1958 and 1975." In a paper published last November, two geographers from University College, London, Clive Agnew and Andrew Warren, dispute this claim. The estimate of the position of the edge of the desert in 1958, they say, was based on very limited data from weather stations. Moreover, in 1975, there was a drought. Lamprey failed to distinguish between the temporary effects of the drought on the boundaries of the desert and any permanent "desertification," they say.

The term "desertification" is deeply flawed, says Camilla Toulmin of the International Institute for Environment and Development (IIED), a UN-funded agency based in London. There is little agreement among scientists about what it means. Some use the term to imply an irreversible change. Others do not. Some want to include changes due solely to a decline in rainfall. Others say this should be excluded.

The UN defines the process as "the diminution or destruction of the biological potential of land that can lead ultimately to desert-like conditions." This definition is so wide that it includes, for instance, waterlogging from irrigation canals. Nelson says that the process must be caused "at least partly by man"— a "radiating out from centers of excessive population pressure." This is a sharply different view, suggesting an entirely different agenda.

Some researchers stress the decline in rainfall across the Sahel since the late 1960s as being at the heart of that region's recurrent crisis. But it is not clear how permanent such changes may prove to be. Swedish researchers say that even after years of drought in the Sahel, there are few real signs of irreversible land degradation in the area of the Sudan that they have studied in detail. When the rainfall returned to normal, as it did last summer, they report, "the productivity recovered." One study concludes: "No ecological zones have shifted southward, and the boundaries between different vegetation associations appear to be the same now as they were 80 years ago."

Satellite studies of the Sahara in the 1980s show not an inexorably advancing desert but "a generally southward retreating vegetation front in the Sahel from 1982 to 1984 and a generally northward advancing vegetation front in 1985, 1986, and 1987," says Nelson. Parts of the Sahara turn green rapidly whenever rain returns. Researchers in the arid lands of Australia also point to a remarkable recovery of some badly degraded soils in New South Wales and claim that improved rainfall is a prime reason.

The only sensible strategy for many places hit by "desertification" could thus be to wait for the rains to return. But that, says Swift, depends on some knowledge of whether a drop in rainfall is part of a short-term trend or a long-term trend. If, as some suggest, the Sahel is drying out because of some consequence of the greenhouse effect, the African farmers could be in for a long wait. The truth is that there is not enough long-term data to predict trends, says Graham Farmer, a climatologist at the University of East Anglia. Even short-term predictions are shaky. Last spring, the Meteorological Office in Britain predicted one of the driest summers for the Sahel "in a hundred years." Because of changes in the ocean currents and temperatures, the region experienced the wettest rainy season for at least 20 years.

An assessment of exactly how much land turns into desert each year hinges largely on definitions. Most researchers are skeptical about the figure of 52 million acres of land lost each year, which is repeatedly quoted by the UN. Satellite images are an obvious source of data. But there are problems. One UNEP report on desertification in Bangladesh mistakenly included all paddy fields as desert, because they were dry when the pictures were taken.

Critics of the orthodox idea of spreading deserts say it is still implanted in the minds of policy makers. The president of the World Bank, Barber Conable, said in one speech: "We know we must stop the advance of the desert. . . . In Mali, the Sahara has been drawn 218 miles south by desertification over the past 20 years." With the wrong problem planted in the minds of decision makers, some of the policies adopted to fight the loss of land have been "futile and even damaging," say the critics.

Correct diagnosis is essential in responding to crises in the dry lands of the world. As Agnew and Warren put it: "If the problem is thought to be drought, lasting no more than two or three years, food aid may be adequate. If it is seen as climatic change, permanent withdrawal is called for. If there has been

> **Swedish researchers say that even after years of drought in the Sahel, there are few real signs of irreversible land degradation in the area of the Sudan that they have studied in detail.**

An assessment of exactly how much land turns into desert each year hinges largely on definitions. Most researchers are skeptical about the figure of 52 million acres of land lost each year, which is repeatedly quoted by the UN.

near-complete devegetation, in the absence of a climatic change, the treatment is reseeding or replanting. If the diagnosis is that the desert is expanding at its margins, then some kind of holding line might be the answer." Many countries, including Mali, Algeria, Iran, Sudan, and Somalia, have planted trees in an effort to halt the desert. Yet, say Agnew and Warren, "active sand dunes seldom threaten valuable land. . . . The cost-benefit [ratio] of planting is low or negative."

Some governments and aid agencies are already changing their views. Consultants from Mali and China, working with the UN Sahelian office, have taken a second look at the 1985 Malian national plan. It proposed building a "green belt" of trees across Mali to halt advancing sand dunes. The consultants say that this was founded on the erroneous idea that it was possible to block the southward march of the Sahara. The new idea is to intervene in the life of individual villages to halt soil degradation.

The redefinition of the problem does not make solutions any easier. "Soil degradation is a problem that won't readily be solved by an annual investment," says Nelson. Basic research, say Agnew and Warren, "must precede the monitoring that is such a popular cause among the desertification organizations. We cannot know what to monitor if we do not understand the basic processes and their impact on people's lives." (pp. 33–5)

Bill Forse, "The Myth of the Marching Desert," in New Scientist *Vol. 121, February 4, 1989, p. 31.*

Sources For Further Study

Cortner, Hanna J. "Desertification and the Political Agenda." *Population and Environment* 11, No. 1 (Fall 1989): 31–41.
    Examines why little progress had been made in implementing the United Nations' Plan of Action to Combat Desertification.

Cribb, Julian. "How to Stop the Desert's March." *World Press Review* 36, No. 4 (April 1989): 32.
    Reports on efforts to stem desertification in Australia.

Dejene, Alemneh. *Environment, Famine, and Politics in Ethiopia: A View from the Village.* Boulder: Lynne Rienner Publishers, 1990, 151 p.
    Identifies "the political and socioeconomic forces that feed the cycle of environmental degradation and famine in Ethiopia."

"Dune." *The Economist* 320, No. 7721 (24 August 1991): 26–7, 30.
    Addresses the possibility that the North American plains are succumbing to desertification.

Long, Bill L. "Desertification . . . in Perspective." *Population and the Environment* 10, No. 4 (Summer 1989): 237–44.
    Focuses on the reasons why desertification remains a threat despite the high level of international attention directed toward it.

Ross, Virginia A. "Desert Restoration: The Role of Woody Legumes." In *Environmental Restoration: Science and Strategies for Restoring the Earth,* edited by John J. Berger, pp. 23–30. Washington D.C.: Island Press.
    Discusses how the study of legume woodland ecosystems in the American southwest can aid in combating desertification.

Schlesinger, William H., et. al. "Biological Feedbacks in Global Desertification." *Science* 247, No. 4946 (2 March 1990): 1043–48.

Presents data from a study of ecosystem processes on the Jornada Experimental Range in New Mexico and their link to desertification.

Sunquist, Fiona. "Vast Green Seas Shrivel to Desert." *International Wildlife* 20, No. 2 (March-April 1990): 10–11.

Reports on the desertification of grasslands due to overgrazing and the efforts of local communities to check this trend through sustainable use agriculture.

5: Forest Management

Forests under Siege

Americans clamor for an end to worldwide deforestation. Yet, while our accusing eyes turn toward the tropical regions of the globe, chainsaws scream virtually unchecked through the Earth's last vestiges of temperate rain forests in our own country. Today, less than five percent of this nation's original, native forests remain unharmed by human intrusion, and they continue to topple at the rate of 240 acres a day. While the waxing wave of environmentalism largely neglects their liquidation by a profit-crazed timber industry, the forest ecologies suffer irreconcilable damage with global ramifications.

These native forests (also known as virgin, ancient, or old-growth) are concentrated most highly in the Federally owned national forests of the Pacific Northwest. Under Congressional mandates, the U.S. Forest Service must dole out the last remnants of majestic firs, pines, spruces, hemlocks, cedars, and redwoods to private timber companies. The government's timber operations add up to an annual loss of more than $1,000,000,000, creating another taxpayer subsidy of an already enormously profitable and subsidized industry.

America's native forests exist as some of the only unaltered low-elevation ecology left in the country—untamed, natural wilderness thriving on millions of years of biological evolution. Timber advocates claim they are simply dead, decadent, and rotting—a fortune of resources just wasting away. Yet, the wealth of decomposing mass provides the very nourishment of a rich, healthy soil that supports more living vegetation per acre than any other place in the world. These self-sustaining ecosystems will continue their indigenous processes if simply left alone.

The strength of native forests lies in their biological diversity—a fundamental principle of durability and prosperity. The trees' variety of ages and species reinforce the over-all health and balance of the system. As many as 1,500 species of invertebrates may inhabit any particular grove of trees, and each individual tree may support up to 100 different species of mosses and other vegetation. The forests create their own climate that is cooler and moister than the surrounding environment. For this reason, they distinctly can be called rain forests—the last of their kind in the temperate regions of the world. Their unscrupulous removal rapidly diminishes the gene pools and threatens to destroy their unique genetic blueprints forever.

Clear cutting—the practice of cutting down every tree on a large tract of land—used widely in the native forests has the single most devastating impact on a forest ecosystem. The canopy of trees that encloses and insulates the unique, self-contained climate and all its distinctive vegetation and wildlife is eliminated instantly and entirely. The land permanently loses rain forest characteristics, the abundance of mosses and vegetation dry up, and the temperature becomes prone to extremes. The exposed soil subsequently suffers permanent degradation. In a native forest, three percent of the rainfall is lost to surface runoff; the rest percolates into the ground. In a clear-cut, 60% of all rainfall runs off the surface, eroding away a proportionate amount of nutrients and topsoil, fouling streams with mud and silt, and spoiling local water supplies.

> While our accusing eyes turn toward the tropical regions of the globe, chainsaws scream virtually unchecked through the Earth's last vestiges of temperate rain forests in our own country. Today, less than five percent of this nation's original, native forests remain unharmed by human intrusion, and they continue to topple at the rate of 240 acres a day.

Clear cutting—the practice of cutting down every tree on a large tract of land—used widely in the native forests has the single most devastating impact on a forest ecosystem.

Man has inflicted the Earth with permanent scars by stripping it of its forests. Trees once surrounded the Mediterranean Sea. By 1000 B.C., northern Africa had lost every forest. In Greece, the soil erosion was so severe that, by 350 B.C., much of the country could no longer sustain trees. The original brown forest soil of the entire region gave way to a limestone bedrock now regarded as a typical Mediterranean soil profile. Rome lost many harbors around the mouth of the Tiber River to siltation after soil from the denuded hillsides washed into the tributaries upstream. No amount of research or innovative forestry can solve erosion caused by clear-cutting. The same destruction that forever altered the Mediterranean landscape occurs every day in American forests.

Focusing on commodity resource values, the Forest Service assists in revegatating the clear-cuts with trees destined to fall again within 50 to 80 years. In place of the lush woodlands with immense age and species diversity, it plants relatively dry, even-aged, single-species crops known not as forests, but as tree farms. To facilitate the growth of only the desired species, it attempts to sterilize the land completely by removing or killing the gene pools of all other "competing vegetation." In the rush to create a monetary resource, it bypasses nature's initial stage of convalescence in which scrappy bushes and thrifty hardwoods first hold and replenish the soil for an ensuing grove of softwoods.

Environmental Repercussions

This process involves burning all remaining sticks and logs (slash burning) and aerial spraying of chemical herbicides. These practices have far-reaching environmental repercussions. Ninety percent of the soil's essential nitrogen is volatilized in slash burning. In the Northwest, it accounts for 40% of all carbon emissions—a primary cause of global warming. Chemical herbicides long have been known to seep into the water table and work their way up the food chain, triggering disease and infertility in animals and humans alike.

Tree farms are physically inferior to natural forests. Aside from resembling a crop with few forest characteristics (each tree is a virtual clone of the others), they have inherent weaknesses that make them far more susceptible to disease, insects, and fire. The trees come from nurseries where every seed is germinated. In a forest, only the fittest eventually sprout. Limited to only one species, the tree farm is vulnerable to any number of diseases or insects. In the Southeast, where tree farms prevail, the budworm wreaks havoc in areas previously unharmed when the original forests existed. Fire usually damages only particular stands of trees in a native forest, while others of different age and species survive. In the dryer climate of a uniform tree farm, fire can raze the entire crop.

Never in the history of the world have humans achieved successful perpetual rotations of clear-cutting and replanting. The cumulative effects of erosion, slash burning, chemicals, and loss of natural fertilizer—the trees never are allowed to decompose and nourish the system—deplete the soil and further diminish its ability to produce with each successive rotation. All over Europe, the forests are dying. In China, they have found the soil can not support the Chinese fir after only two or three rotations. In the southeast U.S., the dosage of chemical fertilizers continually has increased while timber output has decreased sharply.

A severe toll on wildlife closely follows the destruction of native forests. The northern spotted owl, which can survive only in this environment, has stirred a swell of controversy between conservationists and the timber industry. While the industry and pro-timber politicians maintain that the owl has no business obstructing *status quo* economics, others cite existing laws intended to guard against species extinction. Ecologists maintain that the owl population serves as an indicator for a variety of other creatures and plants. Should the owl lose its habitat, so too will the pileated woodpecker, tree vole, Roosevelt elk, Columbian black-tailed deer, and a host of other identified and unidentified species that depend on native forests for survival. Streams, kept distinctively cool in the native forests, support a variety of fish that can not survive in water above a certain critical temperature. Coupled with the suffocating effects of siltation, a rise in temperature has rendered many streams and rivers virtually deserted of fish life. Even wildlife refuges, supposedly set aside for permanent preservation, recently have suffered logging under a concept that clear-cutting enhances wildlife.

The impact outside the regions undergoing excessive logging is felt on many levels. The loss of biological diversity threatens not only the Earth's ecology and biosphere, but may eliminate potential breakthroughs in the medical field. The Pacific yew tree has shown cancer-fighting promise in recent experiments. Fifty percent of all medication comes from organic sources. In eradicating a deep reservoir of unique plant and animal species, we may be destroying the only cure for some of the world's most devastating diseases.

The temperate rain forests help counter global warming. Yet, once they are destroyed, the ensuing tree farms have a finite life span. Historical evidence suggests that harvesting the forest as a crop will exhaust the land to the point of infertility, and one more chunk of the world's carbon dioxide-consuming, oxygen-producing forests will disappear permanently.

The rush to cut this national treasure stems not from our country's lumber needs, but from the timber's cash value on the international market. As the streams of logs flowing from the forests swell, so too do the stockpiles at the ports awaiting shipment to Japan. An existing ban on Federal whole-log exports has little effect on this lucrative overseas market since a number of loopholes render it largely ineffective and all raw-material forms such as pulp, chips, squared logs, slabs, and many others escape the ban. Less than 40% of timber cut in the Northwest is processed domestically into finished products.

Exports and increased automation deprive Washington and Oregon of an estimated 37,000 jobs in wood products processing and manufacturing. The Louisiana-Pacific timber company plans to eliminate some 1,000 potential jobs in northern California by barging rough redwood lumber to a new mill in Mexico that will employ cheap labor.

The boom/bust phenomenon of timber-dependent economies born out of the industry's cut-and-run policies threatens to destroy communities throughout the Northwest. The current unsustainable cut levels pose an inevitable shortage in timber-related employment. Historically, such economies have suffered a sudden, violent collapse, and industry shows few intentions of easing the blow. After a recent leveraged buyout, the Pacific Lumber company doubled its rate of cutting. Once hailed by workers and environmentalists alike for cutting at truly sustainable levels and selectively taking only a few trees from each stand, it now employs wide-scale clear-cutting to pay off the junk bonds used to purchase the company. The workers themselves openly oppose the new policy and hope to capture a controlling share of the company using an employee stock ownership plan.

To obscure the mounting evidence linking unemployment to poor management, automation, and exports and to propagate the image of a clean, conscientious industry, 17 major timber companies, operating as the American Forest Council, have collaborated on a $12,000,000 advertising budget. Full-page spreads in national magazines such as *Smithsonian, Life,* and *National Geographic* and abundant advertising on local television draw heavily on public sympathy for the blue-collar worker, claiming that forest preservation threatens jobs and "a way of life" in many rural communities. Yet, they fail to admit that the rate of employment continues to drop despite a steady rise in the amount of timber cut. In Oregon, the industry has eliminated 20% of the timber jobs while increasing cutting by 18%. Despite the evidence that the industry and its workers each want something entirely different—the former wanting short-term profits; the latter, long-term job security—the industry projects the illusion that it acts in the interest of regional economies and its employees.

A severe toll on wildlife closely follows the destruction of native forests. The northern spotted owl, which can survive only in this environment, has stirred a swell of controversy between conservationists and the timber industry.

In the summer of 1989, Congress approved Section 318 of the Interior Appropriations Bill that mandated the cutting "notwithstanding any provision of law" of more than 5,700,000,000 board feet of timber from Northwest Federal forests in 1990—more than they ever have had to relinquish in any single year. Among the laws that Section 318 countermanded were the Endangered Species, National Environmental Policy, Federal Land Policy and Management, Clean Water, and Migratory Bird Acts.

Pro-Timber Policies

Feeding this insatiable appetite is a government that continually has pursued pro-timber policies. Since 1980, native forests on Federally owned land in Oregon and Washington nearly have doubled their timber yield, reaching unprecedented levels. Pres. Bush's 1991 budget maintains the current Federal quotas.

In the summer of 1989, Congress approved Section 318 of the Interior Appropriations Bill that mandated the cutting "notwithstanding any provision of law" of more than 5,700,000,000 board feet of timber from Northwest Federal forests in 1990—more than they ever have had to relinquish in any single year. Among the laws that Section 318 countermanded were the Endangered Species, National Environmental Policy, Federal Land Policy and Management, Clean Water, and Migratory Bird Acts. It also includes a clause that effectively renders judicial review of timber sales useless, directly contradicting our constitutional concept of separation of powers. The Northwest delegation hailed it as an appropriate and innovatively conceived compromise, while conservationists, left with the prospect of losing an unprecedented acreage of native forest, feel abandoned and betrayed.

The Forest Service claims that it spends 35% of its budget on timber while recreation, fish and wildlife, and soil and water receive only two to three percent each. Conservationists' estimates of the timber budget run as high as 90%, noting that other categories such as road building and brush disposal primarily serve timber functions. In either case, both agree that the budget shortchanges non-consumptive, ecology oriented forest management.

The Forest Service sells the timber to the industry, but its annual operating deficit of over $1,100,000,000 indicates that the trees may not be fetching their true value. In Alaska's Tongass National Forest, the Forest Service grossed less than two cents in receipts for every dollar spent. It sold standing trees worth $700 each on the open market for as low as $1.48—less than the price of a Big Mac.

As one might imagine, not all Forest Service employees agree with current policy. Many rifts within the agency have surfaced and gained substantial publicity. The most notable is a Eugene, Ore.-based organization called the Association of Forest Service Employees for Environmental Ethics (AFSEEE). Formed in 1989 by a timber sale planner on the Willamete National Forest, AFSEEE has created a vehicle of expression and political leverage for employees distressed with the environmental degradation they must witness and foster in executing their jobs. Its primary focus is to promulgate this strong current of dissent and effect a shift in agency priorities from achieving Congressionally mandated, inflated harvest levels to ecologically sound stewardship of the forests. For more than 2,000 current and former Forest Service employees, AFSEEE provides a long overdue unification, and its membership continues to expand.

Possibly even more jolting to the upper echelon of the Forest Service hierarchy was the public disclosure of two November, 1989, letters to the Forest Service Chief, Dale Robertson. One came from the Region One Forest Supervisors, the other from the 63 Supervisors of Regions One, Two, Three, and Four. In them, they intimated a grave resentment over the continuing "focus on commodity resources" and expressed their exasperation with the agency's "conflicting values." In summing up their sentiments, the Region One Supervisors stated, "there is a growing concern that we have become 'an organization out of control.' "

For those who have seen the clear-cut landscapes, soiled rivers, and skylines of billowing smoke from slash fires, it is clear that something is quite amiss. Recently, a farmer from California took his family to Oregon for a vacation. "It doesn't take a scientist to realize what's going on; even my 10-year-old could see that they're cutting trees faster than they're planting them," he remarked. "I went up there to relax for a little while, and I came back madder than ever."

The lumber industry touts its ability to sustain "endless cycles of harvest and renewal." Yet, the Georgia-Pacific, Weyerhaeuser, and James River Corporation timber companies reportedly are seeking forests in the Soviet Far East, presumably because of a dwindling domestic supply.

The need not only to preserve, but to begin rehabilitating the world's forest lands is ripening in the public's mind as an issue of dire importance. We are experiencing noticeable changes in climatic trends—below-average annual snow and rainfall, rising mean temperatures, and expanding deserts—and the threat of global warming looms over the 21st century as a most fearful consequence of the rapid consumption of natural resources.

Now that the world has lost over half of its forests to development and agriculture, the time to stop their careless ruin is abruptly at hand. With nearly all of our nation's woodlands either eradicated, exploited, or converted to tree farms, the environment can not afford our jeopardizing the existence of its original, native forests. They are the last seeds of the natural, fruitful ecosystems needed to help heal and restore this neglected planet. Anything less than total and permanent preservation is environmental insolence.

Moreover, simple measures can be taken to make environmental protection economically feasible. We stringently must prohibit whole-log and raw-material exports, thereby drastically reducing demand and creating more domestic manufacturing jobs; further reduce demand by encouraging alternative, non-forest products; rechannel governmental funds currently allocated for excessive timber sales into restoration employment; and legislatively mandate proper, sustained-yield management.

Native forests remain the Earth's best hope for withstanding and resisting violent climatic change. To continue assaulting them is not only hypocritical of a country pointing fingers at Brazil, but economically illogical and environmentally disastrous. (pp. 17–21)

Jeffrey L. Chapman, "Forests under Seige," in USA Today, *Vol. 119, No. 2550, March, 1991, pp. 17–21.*

Loggers are an endangered species, but the environmental groups, which so righteously protect endangered species in the animal kingdom, have no concern for their fellow human beings under siege. Loggers are a much misunderstood people, pictured as brutal rapists of our planet, out to denude it of trees and, as a result, of our wildlife.

A Logger's Lament

My father was a logger. My husband is a logger. My sons will not be loggers. Loggers are an endangered species, but the environmental groups, which so righteously protect endangered species in the animal kingdom, have no concern for their fellow human beings under siege. Loggers are a much misunderstood people, pictured as brutal rapists of our planet, out to denude it of trees and, as a result, of wildlife.

It is time to set the record straight. Loggers take great pride in the old-growth trees, the dinosaurs of the forests, and would be sorry to see them all cut. There are in the national forests in Washington and Oregon (not to mention other states) approximately 8.5 million acres of forested land, mostly old growth set aside, never to be used for timber production. In order to see it all, a man would have to spend every weekend and holiday for 60 years looking at timber at a rate of more than 1,000 acres per day. This does not include acreage to be set aside for spotted-owl protection.

In addition to this huge amount of forested land never to be logged, the State of Washington Forest Practices Act, established in 1973, specifies that all land that is clear-cut of trees must be replanted unless converted to some other use. As a tree farmer generally plants more trees per acre than he removes, more

Legislation is constantly being introduced to take away the private-property rights of tree farmers. They are beleaguered by the public, who believe that any forest belongs to the public. Who, after all, buys the land and pays the taxes? Who invests money in property that will yield them an income only once every 20 to 30 years? Would John Q. Public picnic in a farmer's wheat field?

trees are being planted than are being cut. In the last 20 years in Clark County, Wash., alone, the Department of Natural Resources has overseen the planting of at least 15,000 acres of previously unforested private lands.

The term logger applies to the person harvesting trees. A tree farmer is the one who owns the land and determines what is to be done with it. To a tree farmer, clear-cutting is no more than the final harvest of that generation of trees. The next spring, he reforests the land. To the public, clear-cutting is a bad word. Does the public cry shame when a wheat farmer harvests his crop and leaves a field of stubble in place of the beautiful wheat?

In the Pacific Northwest, in five years, the newly planted trees will grow taller than the farmer's head; in 10 years, more than 15 fee tall; and in 20 to 30 years, the trees will be ready for the first commercial harvest. The farmer then thins the trees to make room for better growth. In 40 to 50 years, he will be ready to clear-cut his farm and replant again. Contrary to public opinion, it does *not* take 300 to 400 years to grow a Douglas fir tree to harvestable age.

Tree farming keeps us in wood products. We build with wood, write on paper and even use the unmentionable in the bathroom. But in order to keep this flow of wood products available, we need to keep it economically feasible to grow trees. If we restrict the tree-farming practices because we do not like clear-cuts or because some animal might (and probably might not) become extinct, or we restrict markets for the timber by banning log exports or overtax the farmer, we are creating a situation where the farmer will no longer grow trees. If he cannot make money, he will not tree-farm. He will sell his tree farm so that it can grow houses. The *land* that grows trees is the natural resource; the *trees* are just a crop.

Legislation is constantly being introduced to take away the private-property rights of tree farmers. They are beleaguered by the public, who believe that any forest belongs to the public. Who, after all, buys the land and pays the taxes? Who invests money in property that will yield them an income only once every 20 to 30 years? Would John Q. Public picnic in a farmer's wheat field?

The tree farmer must have a diversified market. When there is a building slump in this country, it is vital to the industry to have an export market. Earlier recessions were devastating to tree farmers until markets were developed overseas. Some trees have little market value in the United States. The logs China and Korea bought in the late '80s could not be sold here to cover the cost of delivery.

As to the wildlife becoming extinct, that is a joke that is not very funny. Animals thrive in clear-cuts better than in old-growth timber. Look at the Mount St. Helens blast area. Nature created an immense clearing and now deer, elk and other wildlife are returning in numbers. Why? Because there is more food growing in an open area than under the tall trees. And as for the spotted owl, surely the 8.5 million acres set aside is enough to maintain quite a respectable owl population. Numerous recent observations show that the owl lives in second-growth timber as well as in old growth. In the Wenatchie National Forest there are more than 250 examples of spotted owls living in other than old-growth timber. The owl is a tool of the environmentalist groups to get what they want: the complete eradication of the species *Logger*.

Consider the scenic value of a preserved old-growth forest versus a managed stand of timber. In Glacier National Park, Mont., for example, which is totally untouched, one sees the old trees, the dead and dying trees, the windfalls crisscrossing the forest. In a managed forest, one sees the older stands with the forest floor cleared of the dead windfalls, leaving a more parklike setting. In the younger stands, one sees the beautiful new trees with their brilliant greens thrusting their tops to the sky and, in the clear-cuts, before the new trees obscure the view, one sees the huckleberry bushes with their luscious-tasting berries, the bright pink of fireweed and deer and elk feeding. True environmentalists husband the land; they do not let the crops stagnate and rot. Tree farming regenerates the trees *and* utilizes the product.

A tree farmer from Sweden (where they are fined if they do *not* tree-farm their forests) asked me recently why we do not just explain these facts to the environmental groups so that they will work *with* us instead of *against* us. Well, do you know the difference between a terrorist and an environmentalist? It is easier to reason with the terrorist.

Leila L. Kysar, "A Logger's Lament," in Newsweek, *Vol. CXVI, No. 17, October 22, 1990, p. 10.*

At Logger-heads: The Timber Industry and Endangered Forest Species

Despite the industry rhetoric that "good forest management is good wildlife management," many animal species have difficulty adapting to modern logging practices. Perhaps the most famous of these is the northern spotted owl, a small relative of the better-known barred owl. Dependent on the closed canopies of the Pacific Northwest's ancient rainforests, spotted owl numbers have declined by 60 percent throughout its range, due to logging of old-growth timber. The owls appear unwilling to fly across clearcuts to unlogged forest remnants, so even a deliberate policy of leaving uncut islands of timber will not ensure their future.

Noted biologist Jack Ward Thomas of the United States Forest Service headed up a recent panel of senior scientists charged with finding a way to ensure the continued survival of a species whose population is estimated at fewer than 4000 pairs. Noting that spotted owl habitat in British Columbia has been mostly lost, the panel's report, released earlier this year, called for 3.2 million hectares of valuable old-growth timber to be placed off-limits to logging. This would protect patches of owl habitat in various parts of the northwestern US, but would still allow almost half the world's surviving spotted owls to die.

Nobody was happy with the compromise solution. Loggers argued that entire communities in the states of Oregon and Washington would have to be shut down in the wake of job losses associated with the protection plan. Conservationists maintained that, with 60 percent of spotted owl habitat already lost to overcutting, no further losses are acceptable.

The spotted owl, in some ways, is only a symbol in a bigger debate over the value of old-growth forests. Certainly it is far from being the only wildlife species that depends on them. Old growth is relatively rare in the dry valleys of interior British Columbia, and in many parts of boreal Canada where fire is a widespread, recurring feature of the forest ecosystem. But at high elevations in the Rockies, and in the moist temperate rainforests of the BC coast, many forests have existed for hundreds, or thousands, of years.

Each of Canada's natural regions has species that depend on old growth ecosystems. Caribou rely on lichens that take more than a century to become well-established in northern forests. Roosevelt elk and black-tailed deer depend on ancient forests to intercept heavy snowfalls along the Pacific Coast, allowing the ungulates to forage in the shelter of huge trees. Vaux's swifts nest in the broken tops of old cedars; and many species of fungus, insect, woodpecker, owl, and orchid rely on an abundance of dying and dead trees for food, shelter, and climate control.

Wilderness-dependent species are typically wide-ranging, have low reproductive rates, and occur at low densities. They cannot cope with the loss of key habitat areas, and are highly vulnerable to disturbance by motor vehicles. Forest management that identifies and protects key habitat, while restricting motorized access to logging areas, can help to reduce the impact of development on wilderness species like grizzly, wolf, mountain goat, and trumpeter swan.

Selective logging—removal of a few mature trees at regular intervals while leaving the rest of the forest intact—may offer a solution to the challenge of managing forests for both lumber and wildlife that are dependent on old growth.

Clearcutting replaces old growth with dense young stands of conifers that will never be allowed to reach old age. The single-aged stands also offer far less diversity and a different microclimate. Conventional rhetoric that forests are a renewable resource falls down where old growth is concerned; once mined, ancient forests will never be replaced.

Selective logging—removal of a few mature trees at regular intervals while leaving the rest of the forest intact—may offer a solution to the challenge of managing forests for both lumber and wildlife that are dependent on old growth. In BC, however, root rots and other natural fungi seem to increase with selective logging of old growth. The ecosystem may be too complex to manage for timber; if so, then more large ecological reserves and parks will be necessary to protect the plants and animals that rely on Canada's various old-growth forests.

Following the lead of the US Forest Service, whose traumatizing experience with the spotted owl led it to finally acknowledge the need to preserve old-growth stands as part of its overall forest management strategy, the BC Forest Service has recently begun to look for ways to protect old growth. In a consensus released in late 1989, the BC forest land use liaison committee made the unprecedented statement that: "The conservation and protection of old-growth forests is a legitimate land use."

Only a few species can be considered truly dependent on old-growth forest. Some may be able to thrive in a managed forest where old spars or scattered stands of big trees provide nest sites and food. The BC consensus statement calls for research to determine the extent to which the needs of some species can be met in younger stands.

Another class of animals that have not fared well in the face of forestry development are those that depend on wilderness settings. Some of these, like the caribou, also require old growth. Others, like the grizzly, can adapt to a greater mix of vegetation types but are particularly vulnerable to the side-effects of forestry—things like garbage dumps, harassment, and increased hunting pressure.

Some grizzlies in southeastern British Columbia's Flathead Valley coexist well with logging trucks and chainsaws, often feeding and bedding right next to active logging areas. Nonetheless, remote logging camps expose grizzlies to the temptation to dine on garbage, and trouble bears are either trapped and moved to locations where they must compete with other grizzlies, or are quietly destroyed. In Yoho National Park, at least three of eight radio-collared grizzlies were killed by hunters in logging areas adjacent to the park.

Attempts to protect a naturally re-established wolf pack in the lower Flathead River watershed in Montana nearly failed when wolves wandered into southern BC. Hunters, taking advantage of newly developed logging roads, killed several of the animals before the provincial government closed the hunting season.

Wilderness-dependent species are typically wide-ranging, have low reproductive rates, and occur at low densities. They cannot cope with the loss of key habitat areas, and are highly vulnerable to disturbance by motor vehicles. Forest management that identifies and protects key habitat, while restricting motorized access to logging areas, can help to reduce the impact of development on wilderness species like grizzly, wolf, mountain goat, and trumpeter swan.

Woodland caribou, being both dependent on old-growth forest, and a wilderness-dependent species, face a double whammy from the pulp and lumber industries. If government and industry can ensure the future of Canada's beleaguered caribou, then Canadians may finally have a working definition of sustainable forestry. (pp. 26–7)

Kevin Van Tighem, "At Logger-heads," in Nature Canada, *Vol. 19, No. 4, Fall, 1990, pp. 26–7.*

The Future of Forestry

We in the United States today can boast of the highest-yielding forests in the entire world. Even with the pressures of developing this country over the past three centuries, nearly three-fifths of the forestland that existed when Columbus arrived in 1492 is woodland again. Many people find this hard to believe and are surprised to learn that more than half of New Jersey, our most heavily populated state, is forested and that forests make up two-thirds of the total land area of the Northeast.

Though small in scope as compared with the U.S.S.R. or Canada, American timberlands are by far the most productive. And despite past and present practices of harvesting this renewable resource and the recurring devastation of fires and insects, the volume of wood fiber on these lands is actually increasing each year.

Profile of the Industry

Only about 15 percent of this timber resource—some 71 million acres—is owned and managed by private forest-products companies, a little over half that currently held in the public domain.

Timber is the nation's most valuable agricultural crop, accounting for 24 percent of the total harvest, as compard with 23 percent for corn, 17 percent for soybeans, 16 percent for hay, 12 percent for fruits and nuts, and 9 percent for wheat. It dominates some local economies. In 1986 the total value of the industry's output exceeded $200 billion or about 6 percent of the gross national product.

Individual companies processing timber are typically small. In 1982, for example, 91 percent of the establishments had fewer than 50 employees. But some firms are huge and rank with the nation's leading manufacturers. Among the top five are Weyerhaeuser, Georgia-Pacific, Boise Cascade, Louisiana-Pacific, and Willamette. Total 1988 sales: $74 billion.

A distinct trend is evident in the industry toward larger and fewer companies. This change reflects two major phenomena that affected the industry during the 1980s. First was the application of high technology and the quest for greater efficiency to stay competitive with other countries and alternate products. Computerized lasers and "green chains" (conveyor belts) are now commonplace in sawmills, plywod manufacturers are introducing innovative lathe equipment, and papermills are installing efficient new pollution-reduction equipment.

The second phenomenon was a shift in the source and nature of raw materials from the woods. We saw a significant move from the Pacific Northwest to the South, as reductions in old-growth timber were placed by greater availability of southern pines. By 1986, according to Perry R. Hagenstein of Resource Issues, Inc., the South accounted for just over one-half of the total removals from growing stock in the United States, up from about 45 percent 16 years earlier.

Reforestation

More than a billion tree seedlings are planted each year by the forest-products industry. This represents about 55 percent of the annual reforestation effort in the entire United States and reflects the industry's longtime commitment to maintaining our renewable resource.

Replanting serves the goal of producing more and better timber while at the same time protecting watersheds and wildlife habitat. Since 1980, for example,

More than a billion tree seedlings are planted each year by the forest-products industry. This represents about 55 percent of the annual reforestation effort in the entire United States and reflects the industry's longtime commitment to maintaining our renewable resource.

The stage is set for a resurgence of the timber industry. But it must meet the 21st century head on and not wait to be dragged, kicking and screaming, into the future.

when Mount St. Helens blew its top and leveled miles of the surrounding area, Weyerhaeuser foresters have completely restocked the company's devastated tree farm. This is an incredible accomplishment, which Weyerhaeuser people characterize as the equivalent of planting 800 trees a minute, 400,000 trees a day, each working day for 20 years.

This exemplary sense of stewardship for the land is entirely consistent with a new conservation program—Global ReLeaf—initiated last year by the American Forestry Association. Planting trees, whether in rural or city locations, has a direct and positive impact on environmental quality. Urban trees play an important role in reducing carbon-dioxide levels, a major cause of the dreaded greenhouse effect. According to the AFA, urban afforestation serves also to improve public health, moderate temperatures, reduce noise, improve recreational opportunities, and lower human stress levels.

As for rural areas, officials of the U.S. Forest Service point out that more than 20 million acres in our southern states would be more economically productive and environmentally stable if reforested to native pines rather than being continued in marginal crop production or erodible pasturelands. And current estimates suggest that we are wasting the economic opportunity to produce—through stepped-up reforestation—up to 16 billion cubic feet more wood each year—enough to tie up half a billion tons of atmospheric carbon dioxide annually.

Problems

The forest-products industry has confronted serious problems during the decade of the 1980s—economic slowdowns, supply shortages, trade restrictions, foreign competition, to name a few. Scott Wallinger, senior vice president of Westvaco Corporation, points out that future fiber supplies will depend heavily on industrial forest ownerships that are intensively managed. Local economies must compete with tree plantations in Brazil, Chile, New Zealand, and similar places where intensive forestry is fueling major economic development and export. It is my personal view that many American companies have not yet awakened to this present-day reality.

But of all the problems the industry is facing, none has been as pervasive or as difficult to deal with as those involving people eager to exert their personal property rights to aesthetic views, privacy, clear air, and clean water.

Industry executives, in my opinion, have been slow in recognizing and understanding a major demographic trend that has evolved in recent years: the urbanization of the nation's wildlands. Unfolding before our eyes is a mass movement to the country, as harassed and often frightened city dwellers seek to escape the urban blight of smog, crime, drugs, and transportation gridlock. The explosion of high-technology information and communication systems has often facilitated this shift in demographics by promulgating the notion that people can perhaps work more effectively at home than at the office.

Conversely, with the recent strides toward greater national affluence, mobility, and early retirement, the demand has also increased for outdoor recreation, second homes, and large public forestlands set aside as Wilderness preserves. The 155 National Forests administered by the U.S. Forest Service (and viewed by the forest-products industry since their inception as a major source of timber supply) now accommodate more tourists than does the single-use National Park System. A new strategy initiated by the Forest Service for encouraging and managing recreation in our National Forests raises serious questions about the agency's traditional multiple-use policy and its relationships with the forest-products industry.

This is not to imply that the demographic shifts we are seeing are limited to public lands. The impacts on the future of timber harvesting are every bit as evident on private and state lands. Nor are the shifts occurring just in our faster-growing states. Every part of our country is experiencing the pressure of wildlands urbanization. In New England, for example, 89,000 acres of formerly commercial forest were recently sold in a single block for development into homesites.

Conservation easements and other innovative means are being used to control and minimize damage to environmental quality. Soon after the city dwellers relocate to their sylvan hideaways, it becomes apparent to neighboring forest-products industries that the refugees bring with them a set of urban values that conflict with normal timbering operations. Timber-harvest plans are soon challenged on such grounds as disturbances created by noise and dust, dangers posed to schoolchildren by logging trucks, and destruction of the forest views the urbanites moved for in the first place.

These complaints are then followed by even more persuasive arguments calling attention to the cumulative effects of timbering on watersheds, destruction of wildlife-dependent habitat, and damage to streams and fish—all of which the courts find convincing more often than not. The net effect is to delay, if not to curtail, harvesting operations on both private and public ownerships.

In the case of federal land, it is often fairly easy to halt any forest-management action proposed by federal agencies—usually at the cost of a few postage stamps. In Oregon and Washington, for example, we have witnessed over the past two years a dramatic increase in the number of appeals against timber-harvesting plans proposed by the U.S. Forest Service. The average annual number of appeals filed against the government from 1983 to 1987 was 66. But in 1988 alone, more than 400 such appeals were filed by citizens to stop timber harvesting!

The Future

The momentum for change has only begun gathering. My personal views were summed up in a lecture I gave several years ago at the University of California:

> My objective here is to offer a plausible argument that the future of forestry in California will be whatever the public-at-large *wants* it to be. Not what industry leaders *think* it should be. And not what the profession *hopes* it will be. Whether we have boundary-to-boundary concrete covering tomorrow's California, or extensive common ownership of public parklands, or well-managed open spaces of forest and range shared both pleasurably and profitably by rural owners and urban visitors, depends, I think, on how creditably foresters and industry executives can project a favorable image of their resource stewardship.

What I was suggesting, of course, is an attitudinal change essential for survival of the forest-products industry. The industry's leaders must, in my opinion, face squarely what Peter F. Drucker describes in his most recent book as "the new realities." The world is changing fast, and the forest-products industry must change with it. In this context, the spotted owl and the other old-growth-dependent wildlife must be considered as surrogates for the underlying causes of public concern about the forest-products industry.

The Mead Corporation, an Ohio-based forest-products company, provides an example of the responsible good neighbor. The company's 1.5 million acres of forestlands in the Midwest and South are managed by professional foresters under a straightforward corporate policy that states: "While serving economic purposes in perpetuity—the *primary* reason for Mead's fee ownership of forestland—Mead believes that forests must also serve a broad variety of other important purposes."

According to corporate forester Emmerentia M. Guthrie, these noneconomic uses include hunting, fishing, hiking, skiing, and snowmobiling. Free maps are provided to the public covering 80 to 90 percent of Mead's timberlands, and haul roads are maintained by the company for year-round access.

Soon after the city dwellers relocate to their sylvan hideaways, it becomes apparent to neighboring forest-product industries that the refugees bring with them a set of urban values that conflict with normal timbering operations. Timber-harvest plans are soon challenged on such grounds as disturbances created by noise and dust, dangers posed to schoolchildren by logging trucks, and destruction of the forest views the urbanites moved for in the first place.

The purposes of the National Forests, as set forth in the Organic Act of 1897, are to protect watersheds and ensure a continuing supply of timber. The Multiple-Use Sustained Yield Act of 1960 made it clear, however, that the forests are to be managed for a variety of resources—outdoor recreation, range, timber, watershed, and fish and wildlife.

Interpretive nature trails are also maintained, and ponds and lakes on company lands are stocked with fish.

Wildlife plantings including grass and clover fields are established and maintained to enhance habitat for deer, grouse, and geese. Mature islands of aspen, wildlife dens, mast trees, and vegetated buffer strips are purposely left undisturbed during harvest operations. Finally, areas of company ownership have been set aside to preserve rare or endangered species such as the golden star lily and the flaming azalea in Ohio.

The business world of the past few years is full of examples of first-rate firms that became second-rate firms or even went out of business because they were inflexible and wanted to do things in the same old way. They failed to recognize change. (pp. 27–8, 72–3)

The future will provide ample opportunity for enhanced forest-products business. Some economists envisage the beginning of a strong, new upward business cycle starting in 1991. Housing starts should remain strong. Manufactured lumber exports have their greatest potential ever, as new markets arise in the less-developed countries and global economic interdependence materializes. The stage is set for a resurgence of the timber industry. But it must meet the 21st century head on and not wait to be dragged, kicking and screaming, into the future. (p. 73)

Harold R. Walt, "Industrial Forests," in American Forests, *Vol. 95, Nos. 11 & 12, November–December, 1989, pp. 26–8, 72–3.*

Managing the Great Outdoors: The Role of the U.S. Forest Service in the '90s

As the 1980s dawned, the furor over clearcutting—the issue of the 1970s—was dying out, but murmurings were already starting over what was to become *the* federal forest management issue of the new decade—below-cost timber sales. Now, as the 1980s draw to a close, a small and secretive owl has seized the country's attention.

The controversy over the northern spotted owl and, by implication, the preservation of large areas of old-growth in the Pacific-Northwest suggest the kinds of National Forest issues likely to dominate the 1990s. Environmental organizations are already pressing for management of large areas of federal forests as relatively natural ecosystems. Emphasizing nonconsumptive uses and minimal development, they take the Greater Yellowstone Ecosystem as the prototype. Biodiversity is the new watchword.

Global environmental and economic issues also will exert a much greater influence on federal forest management in the 1990s.

Meanwhile, the nearly 29,000 men and women who manage the National Forests must address the sticky problem of how to satisfy growing demands for virtually everything the National Forests produce.

The National Forest System encompasses 191 million acres of publicly owned forests and grasslands from the Chugach National Forest surrounding Alaska's Prince William Sound to the Caribbean National Forest in Puerto Rico's Luquillo Mountains. Although units of the National Forest System are found in 42 states and Puerto Rico, the bulk of the system—more than 165 million acres—is located in the 11 westernmost contiguous states and Alaska. East of the Rockies, National Forests appear on the map as relatively small flecks of green.

The system includes millions of acres devoted to special uses—32.4 million acres of Wilderness (one National Forest acre in every six, as Forest Service officials point out), 3.3 million acres in National Monuments (including Mount St. Helens), 1.9 million acres in 13 congressionally designated National Recreation Areas, and 3,331 miles of Wild and Scenic Rivers.

The purposes of the National Forests, as set forth in the Organic Act of 1897, are to protect watersheds and ensure a continuing supply of timber. The Multiple-Use Sustained Yield Act of 1960 made it clear, however, that the forests are to be managed for a variety of resources—outdoor recreation, range, timber, watershed, and fish and wildlife (and, through other laws, minerals).

Most of the attention paid to the National Forests is given to them because they provide sources of timber and opportunities for outdoor recreation.

About 13 percent of the timber cut each year in the U.S. comes from the National Forests. Moreover, they contain nearly 50 percent of all the nation's softwood sawtimber, which is primarily used for building homes. In 1988, 20 of the 122 forest-administrative units (which may include two or more National Forests) accounted for approximately half of the 10.5 billion board-feet of timber harvested from the National Forests that year. Most of the big timer producers lie west of the crest of the Cascades in Oregon and Washington, and in the mountains of northern California.

Though most of the land managed by the Interior Department's Bureau of Land Management tends more toward range than timber, BLM does manage about eight million acres of highly valuable multiple-use forestland, most of it in Oregon, northern California, and Idaho. The Oregon and California (O&C) lands—a railroad grant reclaimed by the federal government—are checkerboarded along the Coast Range and Cascade foothills bordering Oregon's Willamette Valley and include some of the most productive forestland in the country.

In 1988 some 1.1 billion board-feet of timber worth $152 million was harvested from BLM lands, with 947 million board-feet valued at $146 million cut from BLM's lands in western Oregon alone. As might be expected, BLM's lands are subject to much the same pressures and issues as the National Forests in the Pacific Northwest.

Less than one-third of the National Forest System—about 56.4 million acres—is classed as economically and environmentally suitable for growing timber. Environmentalists and timber interests usually find no particular reason to squabble over the remaining two-thirds. The real battlegrounds are those potential timber-producing areas that remain without roads—and thus are candidates for Wilderness status so long as they are left in an unroaded state. Many of these pristine acres are in the mature forests of the Cascades and the central and northern Rockies.

The National Forests also are popular with the public as places to play. In 1988, the National Forests accommodated more than 242 million recreational-use visitor days (RVDs)—about twice that of the National Parks. That figure of 242 million RVDs is roughly equal to every person in the United States spending one 12-hour day in a National Forest. After a decline in recreational use in the mid-1980s, the 1988 figure was nearly 10 million RVDs above the 1980 total.

As population centers have grown and expanded (and highways improved), the National Forests have become less and less remote. Few of them are more than a day's drive from a major metropolitan center, and most are within half a day.

Others have become the backyards of the nation's growing metropolises. Several of the urbanized forests—the Tonto (Phoenix), Angeles (Los Angeles), Wasach-Cache (Salt Lake City), and Mount Hood (Portland, Oregon) are among the top 10 recreational-use forests in the nation. But some popular forests are more distant from urban centers—the Inyo, Tahoe, and Shasta Trinity in California, and the White River in Colorado, for example. In most respects,

As population centers have grown and expanded, the National Forests have become less and less remote. Few of them are more than a day's drive from a major metropolitan center, and most are within half a day.

As we enter the 1990s, the major issues are likely to revolve around the role the National Forests are to play in a regional land-use context, global environmental and economic developments, and the changing social context in which the National Forests are managed.

the National Forests are in reasonably good shape. Systemwide, more wood is grown than is being cut, game animals are increasing in numbers, water quality overall is in good condition. But it is difficult and risky to try to generalize. For every good example, someone can point to a bad one. Judgments about the condition of the forests, especially where timber, scenery, and wildlife are concerned, are tinted by the values one considers to be most important.

To many casual visitors, the most apparent problem is overcrowding at some of the more popular recreational areas. On occasion, members of the public may also notice that some recreation facilities are poorly maintained. With many campgrounds, visitor centers, picnic areas, trails, and boat ramps built 20 years ago or more, the need for maintenance is acute.

In recent years, however, money for maintaining facilities has fallen far behind need. The Forest Service estimates that at least $284 million is required to eliminate the maintenance backlog and prevent the loss of valuable capital investment.

The forests did not escape what was arguably the most visible social issue of the 1980s—drugs. Virtually every National Forest has some problem with illegal marijuana growing. In 1988, approximately 500,000 plants were uprooted and 500 persons arrested. At one time, some 960,000 acres (by comparison, the Mount Hood National Forest has 1,061,381 acres, the Monongahela 895,221 acres) were "constrained" to Forest Service management because of the danger posed by growers defending their plots.

Naturally, the National Forests are afflicted by the same problems that affect forests throughout the United States. Visitors now find vast expanses defoliated by pests—the gypsy moth in the eastern hardwoods and the pine bark beetle in the Rocky Mountains' conifers. National Forest users also see the short-term effects of wildfires, including nature's recovery, following two severe fire seasons.

Meanwhile, scientists are concerned about more subtle and long-term threats to the health of all forests—acid rain and global wraming caused by a buildup of greenhouse gases in the atmosphere.

Cutbacks in funding for resources management throughout the 1980s also raised questions about the future of resources in the National Forests. If the trends of the 1980s continue, according to the Forest Service's draft 1990 Resources Planning Act Program, we can expect to see reductions in watershed, recreation, and range quality as well as a decline in the long-term sustained yield of timber.

While below-cost timber sales dominated news space and Congressional hearings during the 1980s, the decade also saw the birth of the Forest Service's recreation initiative, renewed attention to the fate of remaining old-growth on the National Forests in the West, and a deeper public recognition of some pervasive, long-term threats to forest health. And, more than 10 years after enactment of the National Forest Management Act (NFMA), forest plans came to fruition.

Below-Cost Sales

Though the issue of below-cost sales (timber sales in which the Forest Service receives less for the sale than the costs of building access roads and cutting the timber) was raised in the 1970s, environmental organizations hammered the issue home to the press and public in the 1980s. The result is likely to be long-term changes in the way the Forest Service does business.

The Timber Sale Program Information Reporting System (TSPIRS) generated new information on costs and returns from National Forest timber sales. The Forest Service is now looking closely at sales that lose money with little or no benefit to other resources, and the agency is seeking to reduce the overall costs of selling timber. Moreover, the General Accounting Office and Forest

Service are working on a reporting system for *all* resource programs. The cost-effectiveness of recreation, wildlife, range, and other nontimber programs is likely to come under scrutiny in the 1990s.

Old-Growth

Old-growth timber is both an ecological and an economic asset. Virtually all the remaining old-growth in the West is on National Forest land. Undeniably, old-growth forest ecosystems continue to decline in the National Forests of the West, but the Forest Service and Wilderness Society are in sharp disagreement over just how much remains.

Forest Service officials are now working to develop a definition of old-growth that they hope will win broad public acceptance. At the same time, the agency is collecting information on old-growth in the National Forests to help with management of these ecosystems. Since the Forest Service has promised to maintain a base of old-growth, how much exists and where it is located is essential information.

Preservation of old-growth is a key element in the controversy over the northern spotted owl, which seems to prefer old-growth and mature forests. About half of the timber harvested from the National Forests in Washington and Oregon is old-growth. Critics assert that this level of harvest, dependent on the continued cutting of remaining old-growth, is not sustainable over the long term. Indeed, the forest plans in Washington and Oregon (the Forest Service's Region 6) call for a significant decrease in timber sales over the next four decades. This has raised concerns not only about the future of the timber industry in the Pacific Northwest but also about the fate of many small communities that traditionally have depended on timber for their economic base.

Forest Health

The long-term health of all America's forests is a matter of grave concern, and the National Forests are no exception. Some areas of the South have experienced a significant slowing of radial growth in natural pine stands. Among the prime suspects are acid deposition, drought, and loss of soil fertility in old farm fields. Whatever the causes, the situation raises questions about the long-term health of valuable forests in the region.

For some years, scientists have been studying the death of trees at high elevations in the National Forests of the southern Appalachians and in the Green Mountain National Forest in Vermont. Again, acid precipitation is believed to play a part.

For the longer-term, global climate change caused by the accumulation of trace gases in the atmosphere could have severe implications for the National Forests as regional climates and forest environments change.

Recreation Initiative

The current focus on recreation in the National Forests could also have an enduring impact on how the Forest Service perceives its job. Aggressively building on the 1987 report of the President's Commission on Americans Outdoors, the present initiative promotes the National Forests as "America's Great Outdoors."

The strategy is unabashed entrepreneurship. The plan: enlist users of National Forest recreational opportunities as partners in doing the work that needs to be done. The benefits: the strategy saves tax money and expands the National Forest constituency. The most visible accomplishment to date: the designation of 51 National Forest Scenic Byways in 27 states totaling 2,700 miles. The private sector has pledged to pay for signs and improvements to enhance the most popular National Forest recreational activity—driving for pleasure.

Old-growth timber is both an ecological and an economic asset. Virtually all the remaining old-growth in the West is on National Forest land. Undeniably, old-growth forest ecosystems continue to decline in the National Forests of the West, but the Forest Service and Wilderness Society are in sharp disagreement over just how much remains.

> **Wilderness advocates are shifting their focus from the preservation of distinct, well-defined parcels to the coordinated management of large ecosystems with lands held by many owners, public and private. The challenge will be to devise management practices and patterns that blend preservation with different levels of management and development to satisfy environmental, economic, and social objectives.**

Forest Planning

The 1980s were the decade in which forest planning matured, and foresters learned a great deal about the resources in their care—and themselves. Forest plans provided interest groups with effective handles to tug on when trying to change policy direction. The Forest Service found itself besieged by battalions of experts employed by those interest groups. And the plans generated tensions between what some see as democracy gone wild and the trust-us-we-know-what's-best school of management.

Forest plans, with all their alternatives, showed that there are many ways to manage a forest and that the choices are as much political as technical.

As we enter the 1990s, the major issues are likely to revolve around the role the National Forests are to play in a regional land-use context, global environmental and economic developments, and the changing social context in which the National Forests are managed.

Increasingly, the National Forests are being perceived not as self-contained units but as components of a larger land-use mosaic. Typically, in addition to National Forests, the regional mosaic includes private lands in a variety of ownerships, state lands, and other federal lands, all managed for different objectives.

Wilderness advocates are shifting their focus from the preservation of distinct, well-defined parcels to the coordinated management of large ecosystems with lands held by many owners, public and private. The challenge will be to devise management practices and patterns that blend preservation with different levels of management and development to satisfy environmental, economic, and social objectives.

The environmental effects of loss of tropical forests and the prospect of global climate change have captured the public's attention as shown by the response to the American Forestry Association's Global ReLeaf campaign. Just how this might affect management of the National Forests is still a matter for conjecture. One might expect to see the public's growing interest in tree planting reflected in support for accelerated reforestation of National Forest lands, and possibly an interest in deliberate management of highly productive acres to enhance the forests' capacity to sequester carbon dioxide.

The globalization of the economy and concerns about American competitiveness also will influence how National Forests are managed. We see manifestations today, ranging from increased numbers of foreign tourists at National Forest resort and recreation sites to Brazilian eucalyptus logs being unloaded at Great Lakes ports in competition with timber from National Forests (and other forests) in the Northeast. International economic pressures can be expected to complicate tensions between national policy for the forests and local desires.

The National Forests will be called upon to respond to changes in our society—a population growing older; smaller households, with increasing numbers headed by single women; the continuing rise of women in the workforce; increased numbers of immigrants that both enrich and challenge our society; and telecommunications technologies that can only be imagined.

These developments will challenge a Forest Service that itself is changing swiftly. Women are moving into ever higher positions in the agency. The Forest Service has initiated an aggressive program to recruit blacks and other minorities. Forest Service Chief Dale Robertson is determined to change the agency's "corporate culture" and seems to be achieving some success.

One can be sure that the Forest Service of the year 2000 will be considerably different from that of today. Because of retirements and turnover, fully half the people who will be staffing the Forest Service 10 years from now have not yet been hired!

The challenges of anticipating problems, responding to new demands, working with an increasingly complex society and workforce will be formidable. In the 1990s, we will see an even greater premium on managers who can work with diverse publics, build consensus on policy and program direction, motivate people, and otherwise accomplish all that needs to be done to manage these priceless public resources. (pp. 22–4, 50–1)

William E. Shands, "Federal Forests," in American Forests, *Vol. 95, Nos. 11 & 12, November-December, 1989, pp. 22–4, 50–1.*

In the long term, the most serious threat to man is in the loss of the woods' role as a watershed, depriving us of drinking water and the rain needed to grow crops.

Cutting Down Canada's Woodlands

At a spring press conference last year on Parliament Hill, Canada's Future Forests Alliance unveiled evidence of a home-made woodlands assult rivalling that of the Amazon. On an enormous map of Canada, the areas cut and those that will be were etched out in grey and black against a dark green background. It amounted to over half the accessible forested land. "This is the biggest crisis facing our future," said Colleen McCrory, speaking for the alliance, who spent six months collecting the data. "In the next 15 years we're going to take down the whole ecosystem of the nation, and we don't even know the effect of this."

At Forestry Canada, the new federal department's coordinator of forest biology research, Jim Richardson, confirmed that "all the accessible productive forest land except that preserved could be designated for cutting." It's a policy provincial governments, who have jurisdiction over most of the country's forested lands, have illustrated by signing over huge tracts to logging interests in 20- to 25-year leases. In 1990 alone, an area larger than the three prairie provinces combined has been allocated to the industry. Ultimately, Richardson suggests 3 percent of our productive forest lands will be left completely untouched, mostly in parks and reserves scattered across the country.

One month before the alliance's press conference, the Canadian Nature Federation (CNF) presented a brief to the House of Commons standing committee on forestry and fisheries. Quoting statistics showing how little is being done to replace the harvested trees, the CNF's submission stated that only 26 percent of the areas logged are reforested, and only 40 to 50 percent of those trees survive. Richardson puts the successful replanting figure closer to 20 percent, saying the rest is seeded or left to regenerate naturally. It isn't being planted, he says, "because the money isn't being spent to do it." As a result of lower reforestation rates in the past, his department anticipates that demand for merchantable timber will exceed supply in 10 years.

The mandate of Forestry Canada reflects government and industry response to the forestry crisis: a case of too little too late. Richardson says one of the department's first priorities is developing an accurate inventory of the country's forests to determine a responsible course for the future. Meanwhile, the inventory is rapidly disappearing.

Responding to mounting world demand, logging companies are eager to increase their annual harvests. In its 1989 annual report, the Canadian Pulp and Paper Association (CPPA) estimated world consumption of paper and board would grow by 60 million tonnes—over double Canada's current output—by the year 2000. If given access to enough fibre, pulp and paper companies could increase shipments abroad to 35 million tonnes in the next 10 years, a 10-million-tonne increase.

However, the wood the industry needs to maintain its expansion simply won't be there. "We're approaching the limit of the natural forest resource, and in

"The untrained person might walk into a plantation and feel it's a forest. But a perceptual difference is not the same as an ecological difference. If you eliminate all species of no importance to industry, you destroy the resource base on which the forest depends. Eventually the forest won't be able to perpetuate itself."

—Paul Giss, executive director for the Canadian Nature Federation

some parts of Canada, have reached the limit," says Richardson, referring to the Maritimes where production is expected to slow down over the next decade.

Louis Fortier, the CPPA's spokesperson, acknowledges that in the face of greater world demand, the Canadian industry won't be able to sustain its growth. "A number of companies are changing to hardwoods to provide fibre," he says; but, despite a shift away from depleted softwood stock like pine and spruce, "expansion will still have to be delayed, and production reduced."

The cause of the pending shortfall lies in mismanagement of the resource in the past. Historically, the logging industry has seen Canada's forests as an endless supply of timber. In his 1985 book *Heritage Lost*, writer Donald MacKay documented a consistent pattern of missed chances to develop a sustained yield of wood. (pp. 27–8)

So far, widespread cutting has not caused the devastation in Canada that it has inflicted on other nations. But neither have the results been encouraging. In *Heritage Lost*, MacKay stated that many of the stripped territories have come back as "junk forest"—scrubby hardwood regions that won't be productive for industry, and are of little attraction to nature lovers.

Scott Findlay, an assistant professor of biology at the University of Ottawa who has surveyed first-hand huge denuded lands in South America, warns that continued clearcutting of the same land will increasingly hamper its ability to regenerate. "After a clearcut, there's a lot of runoff. This creates erosion and a great loss of nutrients trees need to grow," he says.

For proof, Findlay points to a study in New Hampshire showing that the particular nitrates needed for growth are flushed out when wood is harvested. He adds that in some areas being cut for the first time, there's no evidence the trees or the many life forms they harboured will come back. "In the tropical rainforest, cutting has contributed to species extinction at an unprecedented rate, so they can never bounce back."

One of the most controversial tracts of land earmarked for cutting in Canada is a 221,000-square-kilometre area of the boreal forest in northern Alberta, almost equal in size to the Maritimes. When it leased this territory, the Alberta govenment made no provisions for replanting. Only after a public outcry, and an order from Environment Canada that an environmental impact assessment be performed prior to harvesting, was a reforestation clause considered. Left alone, conservationists are concerned this fragile region, lining the edge of the sparsely wooded grasslands leading into the Northwest Territories, would be incapable of regenerating.

Currently, these wilds are populated by a broad diversity of species. The woodland caribou, already rare, uses these dense forests as protection from weather and predators. Logging would encourage the proliferation of moose and deer populations, which prefer open spaces, thus exposing the caribou to the wolves and hunters that prey on these animals.

Other species that prefer dense, old-growth forests include wood warblers, woodpeckers, and spotted owls. Findlay says the extinction of the spotted owl may not impair human existence directly, "but the aesthetic value of our lives is enriched by seeing other species. You can't put a dollar figure on aesthetics."

In the long term, the most serious threat to man is in the loss of the woods' role as a watershed, depriving us of drinking water and the rain needed to grow crops. Despite this danger, areas at least equal to the size of the one in Alberta are slated for clearcutting in British Columbia, Manitoba, and Quebec, while most of the Maritimes' and half of Ontario's accessible forests have been converted into tree farms.

The logging industry maintains the country is not moving toward killing off its woods, but to an eventual state of intensively managed forests. "Our objective is management on a sustained-yield basis," says Fortier, "but with values other than forestry taken into account." He says these carefully tended forests will be capable of fulfilling all the same functions as the original natural forests.

The first step toward establishing a managed forest is harvesting the wood. The area then undergoes a massive replanting with seedlings in the spring, and is carefully tended for at least the next 10 years. When it reaches the free-to-grow stage, it can continue on its own to maturity, and a second harvest.

Fortier says many provincial governments are shifting the responsibility of reforestation to the companies themselves, asking that all land be renewed within five years. "This makes more sense because we have the most expertise, and if a company doesn't replant it'll lose the right to harvest the land."

Vancouver Island boasts one of the most intensively managed forests in Canada, with Canadian Pacific Forest Products overseeing a complete fertilization program, from seed orchards to active tree tending. The company has 80 unique tree farm licenses (TFLs) under its stewardship, all at various stages of growth, as part of achieving a sustained yield of wood. The example most lauded is TFL 19, where every hectare cut has been replanted—a total of 19 million seedlings. By growing Douglas fir and hemlock at nurseries with genetically improved seeds and tending the budding trees onsite, the company has raised its seedling survival rate here from 65 to 90 percent in the past 10 years.

Bruce Devitt, the company's chief forester, says the replanted forest can "mimic" the original, so that eventually people don't know the difference from natural woods. "People are happy in the second-growth forest, very happy. It's good for fishing and hunting." He says the company also takes precautions for animals and runoff, leaving large areas of timber stands for elk, migration corridors, and eagle nesting sites. They also protect cave openings, and schedule harvests to minimize drainage and flooding.

But in the world of reforestation the Vancouver Island example is a best-case scenario; even at that, it does not escape criticism. As most of the island's logging has taken place since the Second World War, the second crop is less than 40 years old, not yet half-grown. Before these trees mature, the company will cut much of the old growth on the island to support its sawmills, pulp mills, and newsprint plants.

One such area slated for cutting includes the Carmanah Valley, a region that has become a potent symbol for the few remaining old-growth forests in Canada. As part of another group of the island's TFLs, these ones belonging to MacMillan Bloedel, the valley became the centre of a conflict between conservationists and the forestry giant. To solve the issue, the provincial government will turn half the valley into a park. Devitt says this action injures the industry's goal of establishing a sustained yield of wood, and will damage the island's economy. Opponents like McCrory say the parks are the only way the old-growth ecosystems can be preserved, and half a valley is scarcely enough.

Some doubt that tree farms can become sustainable. The goal of industry, as described by the CPPA in its publications, is to develop trees as uniform, fast-growing, straight, tall, and resistant to insects and disease as possible. To achieve this aim, most plantations are monocultures, where only the most merchantable species is planted, and all vegetation that could hinder this species' growth is suppressed. They're also treated with herbicides to help the trees grow faster, and insecticides to protect them from infestation.

Even without this biological doctoring, CNF executive director Paul Griss says a natural forest can never be replicated. "The untrained person might walk into a plantation and feel it's a forest. But a perceptual difference is not the same as an ecological difference. If you eliminate all species of no importance to industry, you destroy the resource base on which the forest depends. Eventually the forest won't be able to perpetuate itself."

To sustain the industry for another 10 years, most of Canada's dense forested land will be shredded, with no one able to confidently predict the chances of sustainable renewal that both conservationists and the forest industry advocate. Ultimately, much of the economy provided for by forestry will still have to be replaced.

[Holistic forestry is] a concept that proposes moving decision-making power from large corporations to the community level, and replacing clearcutting with selective logging. That labour-intensive technique would create jobs while leaving much of the forest intact, allowing non-timber values and environmental concerns to take precedence over industry profits.

Griss says the CNF's vision for the future is not entirely incompatible with industry aims. He supports the transition of much of Canada's wilds to managed forests, but insists that clearcutting be prohibited in areas not likely to regenerate in a reasonable period of time, like the northern boreal forest, and that herbicide use be abolished altogether. Where clearcutting is practised, he adds, the areas stripped should be greatly reduced to soften the imact on the environment.

The CNF also suggests preserving large areas where no harvesting is permitted. These would consist of tracts of land large enough to be perpetually renewable, and would represent all indigenous forest species. Ideally, they'd be left entirely alone to grow, age, decay, and begin anew. To help achieve this goal, the organization favours the establishment of a national network of protected areas.

The World Commission on Environment and Development proposed a figure of 12 percent as the minimum amount of natural areas each country should preserve. The CNF believes the percentage could be even higher, stating it is particularly crucial that old-growth forests be included, both for their aesthetic value and their role as habitat for many species. Under the rotational cutting scheme envisioned by industry, these forests would disappear.

Members of Canada's Future Forests Alliance, such as Greenpeace and BC's Valhalla Wilderness Society, call for more drastic changes in how the country's forestry industry is operated—changes articulated by BC environmentalist Herb Hammond who champions "holistic forestry." It's a concept that proposes moving decision-making power from large corporations to the community level, and replacing clearcutting with selective logging. That labour-intensive technique would create jobs while leaving much of the forest intact, allowing non-timber values and environmental concerns to take precedence over industry profits. The secondary manufacturing of products, or value-added forestry, is also encouraged by holistic forestry advocates to make better economic gain from the resources available.

Given the current state of the industry, it appears that neither the CNF's nor the alliance's alternatives are likely to become government policy. With most of the accessible forested land already earmarked for cutting, and a shortage predicted in 10 yeras, the cutbacks in harvesting that would result from these proposals would only hasten the inevitable economic downturn.

"The government will not do anything that will jeopardize employment in this country," says Richardson, suggesting one reason why the voice of industry has always been stronger than that of conservationists. Instead, governments will likely continue to tenure out the land, and even allow production rates to increase, bearing the economic costs when the shortage occurs. In an economy based on steady growth, alternatives like selective logging are scarcely taken seriously. The idea of preserving areas entirely, a costly venture for governments, is looked on as even worse.

"Right now 15 percent of Vancouver Island is protected," says Devitt of CP. "If you want more than that, it'll have a big impact economically on communities. In 50 more years we'll be ready to cut the next growth. Meanwhile we can go on cutting pure forests or shut down and lose jobs. The question then becomes: how will you replace that part of the economy?"

To sustain the industry for another 10 years, most of Canada's dense forested land will be shredded, with no one able to confidently predict the chances of sustainable renewal that both conservationists and the forest industry advocate. Ultimately, much of the economy provided for by forestry will still have to be replaced.

Speaking before the microphones and cameras of the national media months ago, McCrory stressed the problem's gravity. "We are the very last generation that can set forests aside for the future," she said. The more likely result, the press conference conveyed, was that we'd be the last generation to experience truly natural forests at all. (pp. 29–34)

David Wylynko, "State of the Industry: How Well Are We Managing Our Forests?" in Nature Canada, *Vol. 20, No. 1, Winter, 1991, pp. 26–34.*

Protecting the World's Forests to Combat Global Warming

The earth has adapted to temperature changes before and may again, though at what cost to existing species remains to be seen. If we are not ready to enter a brave new greenhouse world, can we at least slow the carbon-dioxide buildup?

Temperate forests expanded during the past decade, but the reverse was true globally. With deforestation running rampant in the tropics, the global forest contracted by perhaps 100 million hectares (247 million acres).

The "perhaps" is necessary in the absence of complete figures. The Food and Agriculture Organization of the United Nations (FAO) completed the first global inventory of tropical forests in 1981 with data from 76 nations. Advances in satellite imagery are expected to benefit a second FAO inventory of tropical forests now under way. (p. 28)

Global Forests

About half the world's forests are temperate, and half are tropical. Throughout much of history, forestlands have been declining, and that trend continued in the 1980s with a vengeance. In the temperate regions, the hectares of forest are expanding, but these increases were more than offset by decreases in the tropical regions.

The majority of the world's forests are closed, their branches forming a canopy overhead that creates shade and prevents the growth of grasses and shrubs on the forest floor. Open forests and woodlands occupy drier locations and are more resistant to drought and fire. Grasses and shrubs grow between the trees. The FAO figures represent a spectrum of forests, open and closed, from the equator to the frozen higher latitudes, and from coastal mangroves to montane treelines.

The figures only hint at what is actually happening in the forest. A number reflecting the rate of deforestation does not even begin to convey the impact of an eroded field where a rainforest once stood. Temperate forests recorded a modest expansion because of trees growing on abandoned cropland. But at the same time, these forests of the temperate zones showed the effects of a crisis facing the developed nations: extensive forest dieback from a variety of causes ranging from air pollution to not-yet-understood blights. Europe, for example, may have lost 15 percent of its standing volume.

North America

Forests in Canada, the United States, and Mexico were among those that experienced pollution stress. In a joint Canadian-U.S. study of the sugar-maple decline in New England and Canada, scientists are investigating possible causes, including acid rain, ozone, drought, parasites, and poor cultural practices. The ozone being studied is not the beneficial high ozone that shields the earth from ultraviolet rays, but the toxic low ozone that damages trees and people.

Outside Mexico City, a popular park lost so much *Abies religiosa*, a fir held sacred by the Aztecs, that people began calling the park "the graveyard." Foresters attributed the dieback to automobile emissions, and they eventually

The World Wildlife Fund and The Nature Conservancy recently agreed to absorb $9 million of Ecuador's foreign debt. In return, Fundacion Natura, Ecuador's leading conservation group, will receive comparable funds from the government to protect Andean and Amazonian national parks and reserves.

clearcut and planted a more tolerant pine. Upwind of Mexico City, the sacred fir continues to grow well.

Europe

West Germans blame air pollution that crosses their borders for their forest dieback. Acid fogs caused by industrial and automobile emissions are believed to cause damage to trees through an aluminum toxicity that interferes with nutrient absorption. Experiments with forest fertizilers caused some recovery, but at the same time German foresters also began removing all sick trees, thus selecting for more acid-tolerant individuals.

The extent of the thinning was graphically described by a resident of the Black Forest, who said: "In years past, to read the newspaper in my cabin in broad daylight required a lamp. Now I need no lamp."

German forests are largely manmade, with heavy plantings of spruce, and past forest management could be contributing to the present dieback. German foresters are studying natural mixed stands that may be more resistant to stress.

Latin America

In 1985, the FAO published a Tropical Forestry Action Plan, enlisting the nations of the world in a coordinated effort to reverse tropical deforestation. A forest plan for each tropical nation was among the objectives.

Bolivia, ninth in the top-10 forested nations of the world, is losing 117,000 hectares (288,990 acres) to deforestation each year. In a recently completed five-year plan, Bolivia gives priority to agroforestry projects, especially in the hard-hit high Andean region.

Brazil, the second most-forested nation in the world, relies on forest conversions to raise funds needed to pay foreign debts. Brazil is losing 2.3 million hectares (5.7 million acres) of forest each year.

Africa

The FAO figures reveal that Africa, alone among the continents, has twice as many dry, open forests as closed, shaded ones. It also has the Sahara Desert, which continued to extend its southern reaches into the Sahel during the past decade. A prolonged drought contributed to the desertification, but deserts can also form in times of good rain if land is abused.

Coastal deforestation may be feeding the drought cycle, and a major reforestation effort could ease drought conditions. Shelterbelts of trees between fields and other arid-zone agroforestry projects show promise, but the scope of the problem is vast.

U.S.S.R.

The Union of Soviet Socialist Republics has more forests than any other nation, but trees grow slowly in the frozen North. Russia has a long history of forest management, predating the formation of the U.S.S.R., and although the amount of logging was reduced in the past decade, the Soviet Union has the potential to become a major wood exporter.

Asia

India is one of the world's leading wood producers and has an advanced forest research program, yet India is suffering a fuelwood crisis. This Asian nation's deforestation rate has proved higher than FAO estimates, and the cause—as in many developing nations—is a population explosion. India is hard on the heels of China and may replace it as the most populated nation on earth.

In Java, the population has increased from 5 million to 95 million during this century, forcing landless people to clear upland forests for cropland. Indonesia, a leading wood exporter, will run out of trees if the current rate of deforestation continues. Japan, a leading wood products producer, buys logs from Indonesia as well as from the United States, Canada, Russia, and others.

Oceania

Open and closed forests approach a balance in Australia, Fiji, New Zealand, Papua New Guinea, and the Pacific Islands. On many of the islands, water is the most valuable forest product, and island nations that protect their forested watersheds have the best water supplies.

Australia, eighth among the top-10 forested nations, exports eucalyptus seeds for fast-growing tree plantations around the world. The Australian government recently announced a "One Billion Trees" program. The ambitious tree-planting project calls for planting one billion trees by the year 2000. The Australian Prime Minister, Bob Hawke, has committed $4 million for the first year of this regreening effort.

Global Warming

As the you-can-have-it-all decade advanced, so did atmospheric concentrations of carbon dioxide, methane, hydrofluorocarbons, and ozone. These gas molecules trap heat that would otherwise escape into space, creating a greenhouse effect that is expected to warm the global climate, raise sea levels, and bring on drought.

The earth has adapted to temperature changes before and may again, though at what cost to existing species remains to be seen. If we are not ready to enter a brave new greenhouse world, can we at least slow the carbon-dioxide buildup?

Energy conservation and substitutes for fossil fuels would lower carbon emissions, as would reducing tropical deforestation. Most tropical forests are being cut to clear cropland, not for timber. The trees are left on the ground to dry, and then the whole area is burned. The carbon released by these deliberately set fires contributes up to 25 percent of the excess carbon in the atmosphere, but fossil fuels remain the chief culprit.

Carbon Sinks

If we cannot eliminate carbon emissions, can we somehow remove excess carbon from the atmosphere? Roger Sedjo, of Resources for the Future, suggests that young tree plantations could serve as carbon sinks. During the early stages of a tree's growth cycle, it removes large amounts of carbon dioxide from the air. While releasing oxygen, it stores carbon in new leaves, branches, the trunk, and roots.

How many trees would be needed to sink the 2.9 billion tons of free carbon added to the atmosphere each year? Sedjo estimates that it would require 465 million hectares (114.9 billion acres).

Is there enough vacant land for this many new trees? The degraded lands appearing in the tropics are prime candidates, since most tropical forests do not make good cropland. Once the trees are cleared and the site burned, not much is left in the soil in the way of nutrients. After several seasons of crops and pasture, the remaining nutrients are depleted. Continued use produces sites that can hardly support weeds.

These "green deserts" (as they are sometimes called) spreading through the tropics will not be easy to plant to trees. Sedjo puts the cost of establishing and maintaining carbon-sink plantations on degraded lands in the tropics at $250 billion.

The Australian government recently announced a "One Billion Trees" program. The ambitious tree-planting project calls for planting one billion trees by the year 2000. The Australian Prime Minister, Bob Hawke, has committed $4 million for the first year of this regreening effort.

The figures hint at what is actually happening in the forest. A number reflecting the rate of deforestation does not even begin to convey the impact of an eroded field where a rainforest once stood.

Who Will Pay?

A U.S. power company is funding a reforestation project in Guatemala to offset carbon-dioxide emissions from a new coal-burning plant in Connecticut. Far-fetched? Maybe, but some see this as the ultimate think-globally, act-locally stratagem.

The power company, AES Thames, went to World Resources Institute, a non-profit environmental think tank, for ideas on how to mitigate 387,000 tons of carbon anually over the 40-year lifespan of the plant. The Institute recommended the reforestation project in Guatemala.

Cosponsored by the Guatemalan Forestry Service and CARE (Cooperative for American Relief Everywhere), the project entails 40,000 small-holder farmers to plant 50 million trees in woodlots and agroforestry plantations. The U.S. power company is earmarking $2 million for trees in its $275 million budget. The carbon trade-off could work, unless the farmers decide to harvest and burn their wood within the next 40 years.

The World Wildlife Fund and The Nature Conservancy recently agreed to absorb $9 million of Ecuador's foreign debt. In return, Fundacion Natura, Ecuador's leading conservation group, will receive comparable funds from the government to protect Andean and Amazonian national parks and reserves.

This is the largest of the debt-for-nature swaps initiated since the concept was coined in 1987 to encourage developing nations to resist environmentally destructive development. U.S. conservation groups assumed $13 million in foreign debt in earlier swaps—two in Costa Rica and one each in Bolivia, the Philippines, and Ecuador.

Projections

What does the next decade hold for the forests? The following professionals offer some educated guesses.

- Bruce Cabarle, a forester with World Resources Institute, foresees new sources of funding for tropical forestry, such as greenhouse tax on oil and gas. "Whole nations could be taxed for their production of greenhouse gases," he says. "No one wants the World Bank to be in charge of the global environment."

- Roger Sedjo, senior fellow and director of a forest economics and policy program for Resources for the Future, projects a worldwide trend toward forest plantations. "Just as agriculture evolved from hunting and gathering to cropping and livestock raising," he says, "so will forestry move from a foraging stage to the intensive management of wood plantations." He foresees less growth in the demand for solid wood, but increased acceptance of products like waferboard and newsprint that can be made from tree species once considered junk wood.

- Paul Miller, recognized as the dean of ozone research for the U.S. Forest Service, sees an urgent need to "do something about the traffic problems of the world's major cities"—especially the gridlocks—since an idling engine produces more carbon emissions than a moving car.

  Working from a laboratory outside Los Angeles, Miller is confident that despite ozone, acid deposition, and drought, some types of forests will grow. "It's our job," he adds, "to manage around these problems."

- Katharine Hunter, of the U.S. Forest Service's forestry support program, believes that the next decade will reinforce the contention that tropical deforestation cannot be reduced without addressing the problems of the people, including individuals and families in refugee camps. She notes, "Political instability is bad for the environment."

- Richard Smythe, of the U.S. Forest Service's forest and environment research division, predicts a growing "one worldness" as international ties become more and more obvious. He sees a large role for the world's media in increasing public awareness of the interdependence of all life forms.

- Timothy Resch, food and voluntary assistance coordinator with the U.S. Forest Service, predicts that agroforestry will come into its own. Attention will be given to the role of trees in supporting agricultural production, especially in arid and semiarid lands. Resch observes, "Foresters are by nature optimists who think in the long term, but one can see genuine reasons for optimism in the '90s." Even so, Resch concludes that when it comes to the state of the world's forests, "Neither the Cassandra nor the Pollyanna view is accurate."

Presumably, it's up to each of us to ensure that the Pollyannas of the world turn out to be more right than the Cassandras. (pp. 29–31, 65–6)

Barry Walden Walsh, "World Forests," in American Forests, *Vol. 95, Nos. 11 & 12, November-December, 1989, pp. 28–31, 65–6.*

> "Just as agriculture evolved from hunting and gathering to cropping and livestock raising, so will forestry move from a foraging stage to the intensive management of wood plantations."
>
> —Roger Sedjo, Resources for the Future

Sources For Further Study

Bailey, Eric A. "Good Forest Management for the Future." *Environmental Views* 12, No. 2 (September 1989): 11–14.
   Asserts that while the Canadian Forest Service has adhered to a sustainable-yield policy for years, plant species with a longer succession cycle than 30 to 80 years cannot sustain themselves. Bailey contends that increasing awareness of this problem has called into question the viability of this forest management method.

"Government Policies Promote Deforestation." *BioScience* 38, No. 8 (September 1988): 540.
   Cites a World Resources Institute report that states that the poorly-conceived economic policies of some countries is a major cause of deforestation.

Booth, William. "New Thinking on Old Growth." *Science* 244, No. 4901 (14 April 1989): 141–43.
   Examines several conflicting studies from various ecological and governmental agencies to determine what forests are considered old-growth and how many acres of these natural resources remain untouched.

Bouler, David W. K. "Global Economic Wood Supply: The Opportunity." *The Forestry Chronicle* 66, No. 1 (February 1990): 35–40.
   Forecasts that as global demand for increasingly scarce wood supplies rises after the year 2000, Canada will be in a position to provide a significant amount of old-growth timber if the country implements a more dynamic approach to market development of the wood industry now.

Byrnes, Patricia. "Ancient Forests Agreement." *Wilderness* 53, No. 187 (Winter 1989): 3–4.
   Discusses Congress's Hatfield/Adams amendment to the Interior 1990 appropriations bill that will institute a one-year moratorium on logging ancient forests in the Pacific Northwest in 1990 as a "compromise more pragmatic than pleasing" to environmentalists.

Caufield, Catherine. "The Ancient Forest." *The New Yorker* LXVI, No. 13 (14 May 1990): 46–84.
   Provides a detailed account of the history of old-growth forests in the Pacific Northwest as well as the devastating effects that clear-cutting has had on stability of the woodland environment.

Egan, Timothy. "Courts' Role as Land Manager Grows." *The New York Times* (1 May 1991): A16.
  Focuses on the rising importance of courts in determining the fate of endangered forests and wildlife.

Findley, Rowe. "Will We Save Our Own?" *National Geographic* 178, No. 3 (September 1990): 106–15, 122–36.
  A comprehensive examination of the conflict between loggers and environmentalists over endangered species and woodlands in the Pacific Northwest.

"The Role of CIDA in International Forestry Development." *The Forestry Chronicle* 66, No. 3 (June 1990): 219–35.
  Presents the context within which the Canadian International Development Agency supports global forestry development and explains the goals of the Agency's Forestry Sector for the coming decade.

Gillis, Anna Maria. "The New Forestry: An Ecosystem Approach to Land Management." *BioScience* 40, No. 8 (September 1990): 558–62.
  Analyzes the benefits of "new forestry," which emphasizes the "dual goals of commodity production and maintenance of ecological integrity." This concept of forest management, Gillis contends, could potentially satisfy both environmentalists and lumber companies.

Green, Lee. "The U.S. Forest Service's Darkest Secret: They've Been Raping the Giant Sequoias." *Audubon* 92, No. 3 (May 1990): 112–18, 120–24.
  Documents the Forest Service's cutting of sequoias.

Harmon, Mark E.; Ferrell, William K.; and Franklin, Jerry K. "Effects on Carbon Storage of Conversion of Old-Growth Forests to Young Forests." *Science* 247, No. 4943 (9 February 1990): 699–702.
  Contends that simulated carbon storage tests show that the conversion of old-growth forests to young fast-growing forests generally will not decrease atmospheric levels of carbon dioxide, as has been previously argued.

Helgason, Gail. "Getting the Public Involved in Forest Management." *Environmental Views* 12, No. 2 (September 1989): 21-4.
  Examines how the proposed site for a single-line pulp mill in Alberta, Canada galvanized local involvement in the development decisions affecting the project.

Hubbard, James E. "Private Nonindustrial Forests." *American Forests* 95, Nos. 11–12 (November-December 1989): 24–6, 57.
  Focuses on the challenge to devise an appropriate public policy to protect the cutting of private forests that are increasingly being used for other purposes, including recreation, wildlife, water resources, and urban development.

Kimmins, J. P. "Modelling the Sustainability of Forest Production and Yield for a Changing and Uncertain Future." *The Forestry Chronicle* 66, No. 3 (June 1990): 271–80.
  Examines various methods for assessing the probable outcome and sustainability of forest production in a variety of future growing conditions.

Knize, Perri. "The Mismanagement of the National Forests." *The Atlantic Monthly* 268, No. 4 (October 1991): 98–104.
  Asserts that the U.S. Forest Service is devastating America's national forest resources through needless and unprofitable timber sales. Knize further contends that there is a feasible and inexpensive policy alternative to this problem.

Kreutzwiser, R. D. "Factors Influencing Integrated Forest Management of Private Industrial Forest Land." *Journal of Environmental Management* 30, No. 1 (January 1990): 31–46.
  Surveys the forest management practices of ninety-seven timber companies to compile information about non-timber land uses and attitudes toward integrated forest management.

Ledig, F. Thomas. "The Conservation of Diversity in Forest Trees: Why and How Should Genes be Conserved?" *BioScience* 38, No. 7 (July-August 1988): 471–79.
> Proposes a method of gene conservation of forest trees, asserting that such a practice will preserve these natural resources for future use.

Levine, Jonathan B. " 'The Spotted Owl Could Wipe Us Out'." *Business Week,* No. 3124 (18 September 1989): 94, 99.
> Maintains that listing spotted owls as an endangered species and reserving federal forests for them will significantly reduce employment and production levels in the timber industry.

MacKay, Donald. *Heritage Lost: The Crisis in Canada's Forests.* Toronto: Macmillan of Canada, 1985, 272 p.
> Examines the effect of deforestation on Canada's woodlands in an "attempt to present the problem, its causes, its size and ubiquity, and how it affects people's lives, pocketbooks, and well-being, whether they work in the wood products industry or not."

McWilliams, William H., and Rosson, James F., Jr. "Composition and Vulnerability of Bottomland Hardwood Forests of the Coastal Plain Province in the South Central United States." *Forest Ecology and Management* 33–34, Nos. 1–4 (June 1990): 485–501.
> Summarizes the forest composition and related vulnerability to decline of bottomland hardwood forests using data from the many existing resource bulletins and the current inventory data base maintained by the USDA Forest Service.

Mitchell, John G. "War in the Woods: Swan Song." *Audubon* 91, No. 6 (November 1989): 94–131.
> Explores the tensions between conservationists and lumber workers regarding forest issues in the Flathead Country of Montana.

Nielsen, John. "Temperate Forests: Expanses of Trees Fall Sick and Die." *International Wildlife* 20, No. 2 (March-April 1990): 18–19.
> Offers a brief history of how various logging, agricultural, and industrial practices have affected temperate forests throughout the world.

Proulx, E. Annie. "Our Vanishing Forests." *Organic Gardening* 36, No. 3 (March 1989): 60–7.
> Provides a synopsis of various threats to the stability of forest ecosystems, including insect damage, disappearing species, man-made pollutants, and the greenhouse effect.

Raloff, Janet. "Unraveling the Economics of Deforestation." *Science News* 133, No. 22 (4 June 1988): 366–67.
> Argues that although many governments attempt to protect their woodland resources from deforestation, their efforts generally fail due to "misguided and unintentionally costly economic policies."

Robertson, F. Dale. "1990 RPA: New Era for the Nation's Forests?" *American Forests* 95, Nos. 11–12 (November-December 1990): 46–7, 72–3.
> Presents three different viewpoints regarding the future of forest management if the 1990 Resources Planning Act is passed in Congress.

Satchell, Michael. "The Endangered Logger." *U.S. News and World Report* 108, No. 25 (25 June 1990): 27–9.
> Asserts that a variety of factors threaten the livelihoods of loggers in the Pacific Northwest, including the classification of the spotted owl as an endangered species and the fact that large timber companies are driving independent mill operators out of business.

Sedjo, Roger A. "Forests: A Tool to Moderate Global Warming?" *Environment* 31, No. 1 (January-February 1989): 14–20.
> Asserts that a significant buildup of forest stocks would provide humankind with several additional decades to find other methods to combat carbon dioxide accumulation and further global warming.

Siegel, William C., and Haines, Terry K. "State Wetland Protection Legislation Affecting Forestry in the Northeastern United States." *Forest Ecology and Management* 33–34, Nos. 1–4 (June 1990): 239–52.
    Documents a number of significant developments in wetland- and water-resource protection legislation in the U.S. in recent years that affect forestry.

Solomon, Lawrence. "Save the Forests—Sell the Trees." *American Forests* 96, Nos. 1–2 (January-February 1990): 48–9, 74.
    Argues that governments should return state forestlands to private landowners who "don't cut at a loss, they don't cut for employment reasons, and they manage their forests not as an undifferentiated commodity but as multi-purpose properties with timber being but one asset."

Tomkins, J. "Recreation and the Forestry Commission: the Case for Multiple-Use Resource Management within Public Forestry in the U.K." *Journal of Environmental Management* 30, No. 1 (January 1990): 79–89.
    Attempts to determine the optimal timber-recreation product combination in multi-use forests of the U.K. by analyzing product transformation rates and their prices.

Torgersen, Torolf R., and Torgersen, Anna S. "Saving Forests the Natural Way." *American Forests* 96, Nos. 1–2 (January-February 1990): 31–3, 46.
    Discusses the evolving technology of biological control of forests, in which scientists use natural predators to eradicate harmful insects.

Turner, Tom. "Razing the Forest Primeval." *Mother Earth News*, No. 112 (July-August 1988): 110–12.
    Discusses the threat that clear-cutting old-growth forests poses to the existence of the spotted owl and the efforts of various wildlife groups to have the bird listed as an endangered species.

Watkins, T. H. "Blueprints for Ruin." *Wilderness* 52, No. 182 (Fall 1988): 56–60.
    Surveys the findings of a Wilderness Society report that analyzes the implications of the Forest Service's fifty-year management plan for the Pacific Northwest timberlands. Watkins concludes that the plans "tell a tale of institutionalized destruction."

Wellman, J. Douglas. "Public Forestry and Direct Democracy." *Environmental Professional* 12, No. 1 (1990): 77–86.
    Argues that greater public involvement in forestry management decisions would better apprise professionals of ongoing social and political changes and help them increase the appropriateness of management decisions with current needs.

6:   Global Warming

The Greenhouse Effect: Present Facts and Future Possibilities

Imagine a long, hot summer—longer, hotter, and stranger than any earthly season experienced today. In some regions, spring, fall, winter, and summer all merge into the hottest season within memory. Imagine days of searing 100-degree heat, beastly nights, bad air, parched fields, wildcat forest fires.

Human history contains no analog for the climatic conditions into which a "greenhouse effect" could plunge Earth. We must go back to the time when dinosaurs roamed the planet, several million years ago (when temperatures ranged from as much as 9 to 16 degrees higher than today's), or forward to science fiction, to glimpse such "hothouse" worlds.

We can also compare these visions to other planets in our solar system. Twenty-six million miles from Earth, in an orbit much closer to the sun, Venus spins through space with a furnacelike surface temperature of over 800 degrees Fahrenheit—much hotter than its proximity to the sun alone would make it. Scientists agree that the planet fell victim to a runaway "greenhouse effect," as the heat-trapping gas carbon dioxide somehow took over its atmosphere and rendered it lifeless.

Unlike its hellish sister planet, Earth is blessed with an atmosphere rich in nitrogen and oxygen, with only relatively small traces of carbon dioxide (only 0.03 percent, compared to 98 percent for Venus). But Earth's atmosphere has been transformed during the last century, as our society has pumped into it billions of tons of carbon dioxide and large amounts of other gases that absorb the heat energy emitted from the planet's surface. These gases are trapping enough thermal radiation to warm the globe by several degrees; and, if current trends continue, the buildup of these gases will warm the planet further, perhaps by as much as 8 or 9 degrees Fahrenheit by the middle of the twenty-first century. Even if we stopped adding to the buildup now, the increase that has already occurred could warm Earth by 0.9 to 3.2 degrees.

No one suggests that Earth will suffer a fate akin to that of Venus. But scientists do fear that a global warming greater than any known to humankind might occur and that it would do so at an unprecedented speed (within a century), taking a catastrophic toll on human societies and natural ecosystems.

Not since the beginning of written history some 8,000 years ago was Earth even 4 degrees Fahrenheit warmer than it is today. The only change of such magnitude on record in human history was in the other direction—cooling [in the fourteenth century]. (pp.1–2).

Scenarios written by scientists—not science fiction writers—now suggest that even more devastating changes could be in store for the twenty-first century. The warming could seriously disrupt the weather, altering rain and snow patterns, shifting growing seasons, and possibly disturbing air and ocean currents enough to produce more intense and frequent hurricanes and tornadoes than plague us now. The melting of land glaciers and the gradual thermal

If the world heats up as much as some scientists now fear, the change will alter virtually every facet of contemporary life, playing havoc with farming, forestry, transportation, water supplies, and energy.

The melting of land glaciers and the gradual thermal expansion of seawater could raise sea levels enough to inundate coasts and make today's shoreline maps relics by the third quarter of the next century.

expansion of seawater could raise sea levels enough to inundate coasts and make today's shoreline maps relics by the third quarter of the next century.

If the world heats up as much as some scientists now fear, the change will alter virtually every facet of contemporary life, playing havoc with farming, forestry, fishing, transportation, water supplies, and energy. Even military strategy might be affected; certainly, Pentagon officials and other national security experts will have to develop contingency plans to deal with the prospect of millions of new environmental refugees.

In the fierce heat of the world's hottest years on record—1987 and 1988—and the drought of 1988, warnings of a global warming took on a particularly striking significance. After years of routine science reporting on a possible greenhouse problem in the future, newspaper and TV reports were saturated with coverage of scientific predictions. Headlines read: "Feeling the Heat," "The Heat *Is* On," and even "Is the World Coming to an End?" (pp.2–3)

In June 1988, climate change became "official" to most Americans. Atmospheric scientist James Hansen of NASA's Goddard Institute for Space Studies told a U.S. Senate committee that the most searing heat and drought of this century were just a warm-up for what's to come. Shocking the public, he claimed to be "99-percent confident" that the continued rise in global temperatures over the last decade was not a random event, but a real sign of the predicted warming trend. "The greenhouse effect," he proclaimed, "has been detected and it is changing our climate now."

Besides capturing public attention, these events galvanized political will, leading many to conclude that the scientists who warned that we may be changing our climate unalterably were right. By summer's end, a campaigning George Bush called 1988 "the year the Earth spoke back" and promised to combat the greenhouse effect with a "White House effect."

In the cooler months that followed, there were conflicting reports. Some scientists presented evidence suggesting that the drought was not necessarily connected to the much-vaunted global warming. No, they said, the summer's heat was instead a manifestation of natural climatic cycles; specifically, shifts in the oceans and in the jet streams in the upper atmosphere were the cause. Researchers at the National Oceanic and Atmospheric Administration reported that they had found no evidence of a global warming trend in the century-long records of U.S. average annual temperatures. Many then wondered how seriously the warnings of a "greenhouse effect" were to be taken. Was the issue overplayed because of flukishly warm weather? Had the media sounded a false alarm?

The answer, according to many scientists, is no. Whether or not the air feels warmer or cooler from one summer to the next, whether or not one year's drought is part of a warming already under way, most scientists and experts believe that, if current trends in greenhouse gas emissions continue, the planet will undergo a long-term warming. The consequences of an anticipated warming are vividly stated in a 600-page U.S. government report released in 1988. According to the U.S. Environmental Protection Agency (EPA), the warming would degrade most of the spectrum of natural ecosystems and affect "when, where, and how we farm; the availability of water to drink and to run our factories; how we live in our cities; the wetlands that spawn our fish; the beaches we use for recreation; and all levels of government and industry."

Conducted at the request of Congress, the EPA study draws upon 54 research projects by government and academic scientists on coastal resources, water, forests, agriculture, biological diversity, air pollution, electric power demand, and human health. According to EPA, the most immediate impacts would probably be felt in agriculture and forestry, particularly among species sensitive to temperature rise. Greatly decreased forest yields, crop losses, and "moving" grain belts are among the predictions. The EPA findings "collectively suggest a world that is different from the world that exists today." The landscape would change in ways that couldn't be "fully predicted," the agency reports, but the resulting impacts would be "irreversible." Other recent research from around the world confirms this judgment.

Intemperate Zones

Although the *theory* of the "greenhouse effect"—that gases in the atmosphere trap heat close to Earth and redirect some of that heat back to Earth's surface—has been accepted for many years, a number of *facts* now make the global warming much more certain. The total planetary temperature has jumped 1.0 degree Fahrenheit during the last century, leaving the temperature in the 1980s higher than at any time since it was first systematically measured 130 years ago. Levels of carbon dioxide have risen 25 percent since preindustrial times, and they are increasing by an estimated 1.4 to 2.5 parts per million each year (0.4–0.7 percent annually), according to the National Academy of Sciences. Other greenhouse gases are also building up in the atmosphere.

This warming trend shows no sign of letting up. Data gathered around the world indicate a more rapid warming rate in the 1980s than in any earlier period. In 6 out of the last 10 years, average global temperatures were the highest on record during the last century, according to figures released in early 1989 by scientists with the Meteorological Office of the United Kingdom and the University of East Anglia. These temperature increases have been occurring despite natural factors—low levels of solar radiation, high levels of volcanic activity, shading, and increased dust and sulfate particles in the air—that keep the world cooler than it might otherwise have been. (pp. 3–5)

What Causes the Greenhouse Effect?

The greenhouse effect has been an essential part of Earth's history for billions of years. Natural background concentrations of carbon dioxide and water vapor in the air have warmed the planet from about 0 to 59 degrees Fahrenheit. This warming allowed water to exist as a liquid in the oceans, streams, and lakes that cover six-sevenths of Earth's surface. Without liquid water, life as we know it would not have evolved.

Since the Industrial Revolution, this age-old balance has changed. Today, the presence of additional quantities of greenhouse gases threatens to make our simple "greenhouse" look far more ominous than its name implies. In particular, five important trace gases are combining to amplify the natural greenhouse effect:

- *Carbon dioxide* emissions from human activities currently account for about half the anticipated temperature increase. It is produced mostly by burning such fossil fuels as natural gas, coal, and petroleum, and by burning wood. About 80 percent of all global emissions come from fossil fuel combustion; the rest stem from deforestation (as trees and vegetation are burned or cut and allowed to decay). The concentration of carbon dioxide has increased by 10 percent just since 1958, by 25 percent since the early nineteenth century. In 1988, roughly 5.6 billion tons of carbon were released as carbon dioxide from fossil fuel burning. Between 0.5 and 2.5 billion tons were released by deforestation and land-use changes.

- *Methane* (which makes up about 96 percent of "natural gas") is, molecule for molecule, a much more potent greenhouse gas than carbon dioxide. Each molecule of methane has 20 to 30 times the heat-trapping effect of a molecule of carbon dioxide. Each year, about 50 million more tons of methane enter the atmosphere than leave it.

  Methane is produced when wood is burned inefficiently, when grasslands are set afire, and when fossil fuels are extracted and transported. Together, these sources contribute 100 to 200 million tons per year, according to EPA, and they account for recent atmospheric increases of this gas. But its biggest source (250 to 650 million tons per year) is a range of biological processes—among them, the rotting of organic matter in peat bogs, wetlands, rice paddies, landfills, and ocean sediments, as well as bacteria living in the entrails

> Whether or not the air feels warmer or cooler from one summer to the next, whether or not one year's drought is part of a warming already under way, most scientists and experts believe that, if current trends continue, the planet will undergo a long-term warming.

[We] have changed the atmospheric concentration of carbon dioxide almost as much in a century as natural events did in the previous 10,000 years.

of farm animals and termites. Ice cores from Greenland and Antarctica show that the concentration of methane, which remained stable for 10,000 years at about 0.75 parts per million, has more than doubled since 1750. Today, it has reached 1.65 parts per million because sources are increasing and the atmosphere's ability to remove methane is being reduced by other pollutants. Methane's growth rate in the atmosphere is now about 1 percent per year.

• *Nitrous oxide* is produced in coal burning and forest fires, results from bacterial action on chemical fertilizers, and is a natural product of soil microbes' digestion. The concentration of nitrous oxide—also known as laughing gas—has gone up 10 percent since 1880, and by 0.2–0.3 percent annually in recent years. This gas stays in the atmosphere for centuries and eventually floats up into the stratosphere, where it also helps destroy the ozone layer.

• *Chlorofluorocarbons* (CFCs) are used in refrigeration and air conditioning, as blowing agents in packing materials and other plastic foams, and as solvents for cleaning such modern necessities as electronic parts; *halons* (closely related chemicals) are used in fire extinguishers only. Absent from the preindustrial atmosphere, they have both added tremendously to the warming problem in just the last few decades. CFCs are far more effective than carbon dioxide in trapping Earth's thermal radiation. Indeed, one molecule of the most dangerous CFC has about 20,000 times the heat-trapping power of a molecule of carbon dioxide! Theses high-power greenhouse gases also attack the ozone layer, and each CFC molecule can destroy 10,000 or more molecules of ozone. Concentrations of CFCs are now growing by about 5–7 percent annually.

Who first singled these gases out as environmental problems? The term *greenhouse effect* was coined by the nineteenth-century scientist Jean Fourier. His great insight was that the atmosphere possesses special properties that allow sunlight to enter but also allow absorption of radiant heat emitted from Earth's surface. Fourier first likened these qualities to the windows of a greenhouse. (Purists will note that *greenhouse* is a misnomer because such glass walls actually keep warm air from circulating and mixing with cooler air from outside besides absorbing radiant heat themselves. But the term accurately conveys the heat-trapping effect of this gaseous blanket.)

Later, in 1896, Swedish chemist Svante Arrhenius, who was acquainted with Fourier's findings, probed further. As a scientist living during the Industrial Revolution, he was concerned about what could happen if coal plants continued to spew carbon dioxide into Earth's atmosphere. He calculated that, if the concentration of carbon dioxide doubled in the atmosphere, the planet could warm by as much as 9 degrees Fahrenheit. Although this pioneering scientist relied on simpler assumptions than scientists use today, Arrhenius's pencil-and-paper calculations came astonishingly close to the best current estimate of 3–8 degrees Fahrenheit—an estimate reached by contemporary scientists with a far better understanding of weather forces and with access to much better data.

As this nutshell history makes clear, the greenhouse *effect* became the greenhouse *problem* only during the last century. Not until the Industrial Revolution did human activities begin contributing significant portions of carbon dioxide and other gases that trap heat in the atmosphere.

Although some measurements of carbon dioxide in the atmosphere had been made around the time of Arrhenius, not until 1938 was the body of facts great enough to support detailed scientific analysis. In that year, the British engineer G. D. Callendar compared the measured growth of carbon dioxide in the atmosphere and the long-term temperature records from 200 meteorological stations. Updating and confirming Arrhenius's now-famous calculation, he proposed a link between increased atmospheric carbon dioxide and global warming, which the prestigious British Royal Society greeted with skepticism. (pp. 6–11)

Although Callendar's data base was far superior to Arrhenius's, precise daily measurements of carbon dioxide in the atmosphere didn't begin until 1958, when Roger Revelle of California's Scripps Institution of Oceanography persuaded one of his graduate students, chemist Charles David Keeling, to measure carbon dioxide levels at a remote site, the Mauna Loa Observatory in Hawaii, to get an uncontaminated sample. Keeling began the best continuous record of carbon dioxide measurements on the planet, and the data gathered in Hawaii over the past three decades show that carbon dioxide levels have risen each year, from about 315 parts per million by volume of air in 1958 to about 350 today—the highest level in 130,000 years.

Very recently, other important evidence documenting the buildup of carbon dioxide was unearthed. In 1987, a team of French and Soviet scientists drilled an ice core 2,000 meters deep near a research station at Vostok, Antarctica. Analyzing air samples trapped in the ice, researchers estimated the atmospheric composition and local air temperature over the past 160,000 years. During a balmy interglacial period 130,000 years ago, carbon dioxide levels were just under 300 parts per million, dropping to 200 during the last Great Ice Age about 20,000 years ago. During the most recent 10,000 years, these levels climbed back to 280 as the planet entered the current interglacial warm spell. In the last 150 years, the level has reached 350, as recorded in Mauna Loa, and half of that increase occurred in just the last three decades. In short, we have changed the atmospheric concentration of carbon dioxide almost as much in a century as natural events did in the previous 10,000 years.

Ice cores can't tell us whether changes in atmospheric carbon dioxide levels cause temperature changes or follow them, but, as William Moomaw of World Resources Institute reports in *Orion* magazine, "What these measurements suggest is that the rate of change in temperature projected by the greenhouse theory is three to ten times faster than any of which we have knowledge—and that by 2030 we may well have brought about temperatures higher than any in 160 *millennia*."

Although the 25-percent increase in atmospheric carbon dioxide since the beginning of the Industrial Revolution is bound to have transforming effects on our planet and the diverse creatures who call it home, it is important to understand that carbon dioxide is not a poison or even, at historical levels, a menace. Indeed, it is a vital part of Earth's chemistry, and it has shaped the evolution of life on the planet by stabilizing its temperature. Were it not for the atmospheric blanket of carbon dioxide and water vapor enveloping the planet, scientists estimate that Earth's temperature would be much lower, perhaps by as much as 60 degrees Fahrenheit. This natural greenhouse effect, as mentioned, created the conditions that allowed modern life to evolve. (pp. 11–14)

How Big is the Problem?

For billions of years, Earth has moderated temperature swings by releasing back into space as much energy as it receives from the sun.

Read that last sentence again. And then consider that for the first time ever, during the last 100 years, human technology has proven it can alter the fundamental processes that govern the composition and "behavior" of the atmosphere. (p. 14)

As emissions of carbon dioxide and other gases have grown, more and more of Earth's radiant heat has been temporarily trapped and reemitted downward, warming the surface. Historically, carbon dioxide and water vapor increases contributed most to the enhanced greenhouse effect. In fact, since 1880, carbon dioxide has been responsible for two-thirds of the warming above background levels. But, during the last few decades, CFCs, methane, nitrous oxide, and other so-called trace gases have together contributed almost as much to the problem as carbon dioxide. The effect of these additional trace gases on global warming will be dramatic: they have accelerated the onset of the greenhouse

> **Although the 25-percent increase in atmospheric carbon dioxide since the beginning of the Industrial Revolution is bound to have transforming effects on our planet . . . , it is important to understand that carbon dioxide is not a poison or even, at historical levels, a menace.**

[If] scientists don't yet know the full range of the direct effects and side effects of warming, who knows what other feedbacks remain to be discovered?

problem by several decades. If higher carbon dioxide levels were the only problem, the world could be 3 to 9 degrees Fahrenheit warmer by 2075, according to the National Academy of Sciences. But, as if that weren't enough, the presence of the other trace gases pushes up the date by which the planet is committed to such a warming to about 2030.

As a sign of how quickly changes can overtake us, consider that an editorial on climate change in *Science* magazine in September 1977 warned, "By the year 2000 the carbon dioxide concentration will exceed preindustrial levels by about 25 percent." We reached that threshold already—in 1986, 14 years before the millennium!

In decades, the human race could induce changes that have been experienced in the past only over eons. In the last 10,000 years, the average temperature of the planet has increased less than 4 degrees Fahrenheit, but over the past 100 years alone, Earth's average temperature has risen by about 1.0 degree Fahrenheit. What's more, not all the effects of previous emissions have registered yet: no matter what we do from now on, according to Veerabhadran Ramanathan, atmospheric chemist at the University of Chicago, we must live with an additional 1.8 to 4.5 degrees Fahrenheit (1 to 2.5 degrees Celsius) warming *still to come* as a result of these same past emissions.

A warming of just 3.6 degrees Fahrenheit (2 degrees Celsius) will make Earth warmer than at any time in written human history. An increase of as much as 7.2 to 10 degrees Fahrenheit (4 to 5 degrees Celsius) will make our planet warmer than at any time in the last 1 million years.

As numerous studies of the greenhouse effect confirm, a 3.6-degree Fahrenheit (2 degrees Celsius) temperature change would bring with it profound and pervasive changes. Atmospheric scientists meeting in Villach, Austria, in 1985 projected some startling impacts worldwide should temperatures increase by 1.4 degrees Fahrenheit (0.8 degrees Celsius) per decade: extreme shifts in temperature in the high latitudes, more rain in the wet tropics, and a sea-level rise of as much as 1.5 meters by the middle of the next century—enough to erode beaches and coasts, destroy wetlands, and bring on severe flood damage to many low-lying countries.

The calculated temperature rise from greenhouse warming is only a global average, of course. High-latitude areas would experience temperature rises much greater than the global average and would face dramatic climate change if global temperatures rose 3–9 degrees Fahrenheit. Overall, polar regions would warm by two to three times the global average, while warming in the tropics would be limited to 50–75 percent of that average.

By bringing on in a matter of decades profound atmospheric changes that used to take thousands of years, we are also accelerating the rate of climate change. According to Stephen Schneider, the greenhouse problem could change climate many times faster than natural climate changes have occurred in the past. For perspective, the natural rate has been less than 1 degree Fahrenheit per 1,000 years, but an artificially induced warming could amount to as much as 10 degrees Fahrenheit in less than a century.

Why is this matter of degrees so important? The Soviet scientist M. I. Budyko, who has long studied critical epochs in Earth's geological history, notes that rapid climate changes have usually been accompanied by massive biological changes—often mass extinctions. "There exists a simple ecological principle," he writes, "the more rapid the action of an unfavorable factor . . . the greater the damage caused to organisms." Although some types of organisms can stay one step ahead of climate changes by migrating long distances, many cannot. (pp.14–18)

Although such speculations lie well within the bounds of accepted science, no one knows *exactly* what the impacts of a global warming will be. And although scientists are working overtime to try to simulate possible effects and gauge their probability, we could well be in for some big surprises.

No Twin Earth Available

The first computer models used to predict climate pictured a simplistic world with only one continent, one season, and one cloud. Some of today's number-crunching machines complete as many as 500 billion arithmetic computations to try to simulate the weather in dynamic, three-dimensional terms. (For perspective, that involves about as many computations as humanity had collectively made up until 1940 or so.) But the climate's complexity still defies even the most sophisticated models.

The role that clouds play in Earth's weather is particularly mysterious, and it illustrates some of the problems that computer modelers face. Because cloud surfaces are white, they reflect nearly 30 percent of the sun's rays back into space, contributing to the planet's albedo, or reflectivity. But recent research suggests that clouds may also be part of a dimly understood climate-control system that includes the oceans and perhaps living creatures. One research team has proposed that even microscopic marine organisms may play a part in the weather by influencing clouds. U.S. and British scientists together found that in warmer weather oceanic plant plankton increase production of a natural byproduct called dimethylsulfide. This sulfurous gas reacts with oxygen in the atmosphere to form aerosols, tiny particles around which water vapor condenses to form clouds. The group hypothesizes that this plankton-cloud system might act as a global thermostat to help regulate Earth's temperature. When Earth warms—due to the greenhouse effect, for example—more clouds are formed and more of the sun's radiation is reflected away from the surface. The net results: a cooler Earth.

So do clouds warm or cool the atmosphere? Scientists aren't yet in agreement, and research has only begun to unravel the intricacies of Earth's climate. (pp. 18–19)

As Wallace Broecker writes in *National History* magazine, "Scientists struggle to increase our understanding of how the earth's environmental system operates in the hopes that we will be able to predict at least some of the coming consequences." But, as the "cloud problem" makes clear, scientists can't predict everything that could happen. Broecker warns, for instance, that scientific inquiries "have recently revealed a piece of disquieting information. Geological studies suggest that the earth's climate system resists change until pushed beyond some threshold; then it leaps into a new mode of operation." Likening the phenomenon to a radio dial that leaps to the next frequency point, he says that "the effects of greenhouse gas buildup may come in sudden jumps, rather than gradually." Such "nonlinear responses"—that is, responses disproportionately greater than changes in causes would suggest—could shock human societies and damage natural ecosystems even more than the gradual temperature increases and weather anomalies that most scientists predict. (pp. 19–21)

Another wild card in predicting climate change is that there could be a kind of chain reaction of reinforcing effects. For example, as the polar regions warm, permafrost in the tundra could melt, releasing methane from compounds locked in the ground. This greenhouse gas would cause further warming, leading to even larger releases of methane into the atmosphere. Similarly, if the Arctic region warms, the ice covering the ocean there could melt. Thus bared, the uninsulated ocean would absorb more of the sun's direct energy than ice does and transfer heat to the atmosphere.

Responses like these are known as positive feedbacks because they tend to amplify the effect in question. Negative feedbacks, on the other hand, counteract or even wipe out a given effect. In many cases, the *net* effect is difficult for scientists to predict. As mentioned, it's hard to predict the effects of changes in cloud cover, which could tend to create either more solar reflectivity (because clouds are white) or more heat-trapping potential (because they absorb radiant heat). "The net result of the different [feedback] processes is a tripling of the warming caused by the doubled carbon dioxide levels," says David Rind of the Goddard Institute for Space Studies. "Yet, it is only the initial greenhouse

Human history contains no analog for the climatic conditions into which a "greenhouse effect" could plunge Earth. We must go back to the time when dinosaurs roamed the planet, several million years ago . . . , or forward to science fiction, to glimpse such "hothouse" worlds.

The total planetary temperature has jumped 1.0 degree Fahrenheit during the last century, leaving the temperature in the 1980s higher than at any time since it was first systematically measured 130 years ago.

effect due to the increased carbon dioxide increases and other trace gases that we know with great confidence."

With no twin Earth to experiment with, scientists employ "general circulation models" of the atmosphere, which are vast computer simulations of what the atmosphere is likely to do. These strictly numerical models are used for roughly calculating how the climate system responds to increases in gases. Most of the models divide the atmosphere into numerous cells or boxes—a kind of longitude/latitude/altitude grid. In each cell, the calculations take into account such variables as wind, temperature, moisture, incoming radiation, outgoing radiation, and the like. These models solve fundamental equations concerning the conservation of mass, energy, and momentum in each cell and then simulate exchanges among cells. But as complex as they are, the models still vastly oversimplify the workings of our planetary system. In such models, for instance, the oceans behave clumsily. Represented as a thin pond or a series of connected compartments, the oceans seem to behave more like flowing mud or dough than water carrying nutrients and heat in waves.

Penelope Boston, a researcher at the National Center for Atmospheric Research, sums up qualms about such oversimplification this way: "We run huge global climate models, in which we put in basic physical factors, and up to a certain point we can mimic the atmosphere, the latent heat, and movement of air masses. We have theories about certain parts of the behavior of oceans, and we have theories about certain parts of the behavior of the atmosphere. But we have no way of doing a computer model for the interactions *between* oceans and atmosphere. What I suspect is that all these subtle interactions elude our grasp."

Although scientists using these models can fairly accurately predict the degree of initial warming, given the presence of various greenhouse gases, they can't predict exactly how the rest of the system will react to the warming. Small changes in one of the planet's many systems—say oceans, plant life, or atmosphere—can provoke enormous nonlinear responses in another. Scientists just don't know, as renowned environmentalists Barbara Ward and René Dubos put it two decades ago, whether the tiny pebble that gets moved is all that wedges a great boulder securely against the mountain wall.

Scientists also don't know exactly how climate change will affect various regions—a sizable problem because this is the level at which the changes will be felt and the level at which some of the initiatives needed to solve the problem must take place. For instance, even slight changes in the evaporation rate can alter humidity, cloud cover, and regional rainfall patterns, but models cannot reliably track these changes at the regional level.

Many scientists are concerned about relying too heavily upon limited, or even flawed, models. "My feeling is we overestimate our ability to predict," Wallace Broecker told the *New York Times* in January 1989. (pp. 21–3)

Although a major push is under way to understand feedback loops better, the fact is that most climate models today incorporate only a few of the major feedback processes. In 1989, the Environmental Protection Agency released a new study by Daniel A. Lashof and Dennis Tirpak, who assessed a range of feedback processes not now included in the climate models. Here are some of the mechanisms they found that could speed up global warming:

- As the temperature rises, methane from ocean sediments and tundra will be released faster.

- Vegetation that can't adjust rapidly enough to climate warming will die off, decaying and giving off more carbon dioxide. But this increase should be offset in part because carbon dioxide stimulates the growth of plants that absorb carbon from the air.

- The chemistry and circulation of the oceans could change as Earth warms, and oceans may no longer have as much capacity to absorb carbon dioxide.

- Higher temperatures could lead to higher levels of ground-level ozone (smog)—a heat absorber that could, in turn, accelerate global warming.

(One study by Gary Whitten of SAI, Inc., predicts that smog over Nashville will worsen 40 percent with the temperature rise and stratospheric ozone depletion expected over the next 50 years.)

Scientists don't yet—and may never—have enough information and understanding to predict confidently the regional effects of global warming on natural systems, agriculture, and a host of other matters important to human beings. As Wallace Broecker warns, "We will know the results of the buildup of the gases [only] if our learning rate greatly accelerates." And if scientists don't yet know the full range of the direct effects and side effects of warming, who knows what other feedbacks remain to be discovered?

No Exit?

Considering how sensitive to stresses Earth's systems seem to be and how slow human beings have been to figure out how to live with that sensitivity, we might ask whether human experimentation on the planet ought, for ethical reasons, to be stopped—or, at the least, slowed down. Broecker took on this ponderous question in a 1986 article. To a great extent, he said, the greenhouse gas buildup has become "an inescapable by-product of our civilization." How, he asked, does one prevent carbon dioxide from escaping from power plants into the atmosphere? So far, we have no inexpensive and effective technology available to do so, or any program for reducing fossil fuel use. Several technologies have been proposed for "scrubbing" carbon dioxide from the exhaust gas produced by power plants. Unfortunately, all such approaches require considerable quantities of energy and add large amounts to the cost of power production. Even if they could be developed economically, disposing of the carbon dioxide by-product would still be daunting. So, Broecker concluded, "If five or so billion people are be to maintained on our planet, we must continue the greenhouse experiment. We are hooked." (pp. 23–4)

Francesca Lyman and others, "Is Earth Really Getting Warmer?" in their The Greenhouse Trap: What We're Doing to the Atmosphere and How We Can Slow Global Warming, *Beacon Press, 1990, pp. 1–24.*

> **The greenhouse effect has been an essential part of Earth's history for billions of years.**

The Fictional Greenhouse: Is the Globe Really Warming Up?

On Nov. 7 [1989] the U.S. and Japan shocked environmentalists around the world by refusing to sign a draft resolution at a Netherlands international conference on global climate change calling for the "stabilization" of emissions of carbon dioxide (CO_2) and other "greenhouse gases" by the year 2000. Instead, they made the conference drop all reference to a specific year, and to a specific CO_2 reduction target. The Bush Administration view was set forth by D. Allan Bromley, the presidential science adviser, in testimony to Senator Albert Gore's subcommittee on Science, Technology & Space: "My belief is that we should not move forward on major programs until we have a reasonable understanding of the scientific and economic consequences of those programs."

President Bush was immediately savaged by environmentalists, and by politicians like Senator Gore (D-Tenn). The Bush viewpoint does not sit too well with most of the media, either. Last January [1989] *Time* published a cover story on environmental catastrophes, declaring that greenhouse gases could create a climatic calamity. The *New York Times* weighed in [in November 1989] with a story about how melting polar ice would flood the nations that can least afford to defend themselves, Third World countries like Bangladesh and India. Or

Since most of the forecast rise in [greenhouse gases] is a function of simple economic growth in the Third World, there is no realistic economic way to prevent a CO_2 doubling without slashing growth and risking a revolt of the have-not nations against the haves.

perhaps you have seen the ads for Stephen Schneider's *Global Warming*, accompanied by a blurb from Senator Tim Wirth (D-Colo.). In his book this well-known climatologist paints a future of seas surging across the land, famine on an epidemic scale and eco-system collapse.

Is the earth really on the verge of environmental collapse? Should wrenching changes be made in the world's industry to contain CO_2 buildup? Or could we be witnessing the 1990s version of earlier scares: nuclear winter, cancer-causing cranberries and $100 oil? The calamitarians always have something to worry us about. Consider this: In his 1976 book, *The Genesis Strategy*, Schneider lent support to the then popular view that we could be in for another ice age. . . . (p. 97)

At the very moment Bromley was testifying to Gore's subcommittee, MIT'S prestigious *Technology Review* was reporting on the publication of an exhaustive new study of worldwide ocean temperatures since 1850 by MIT climatologists Reginald Newell, Jane Hsiung and Wu Zhongxiang. Its most striking conclusion: "There appears to have been little or no global warming over the past century." In fact, the average ocean temperature in the torrid 1980s was only an eighth of a centigrade degree (a quarter of a Fahrenheit degree) higher than the average of the 1860s. Ocean temperature is now virtually the same as it was in the 1940s. Since two-thirds of the buildup of CO_2 has taken place since 1940, the MIT data blow all of the global warming forecasts into a cocked hat. President Bush wisely told reporters: "You can't take a policy and drive it to the extreme and say to every country around the world, 'You aren't going to grow at all.'"

That is the central issue of the global warming debate, and it explains why the U.S. and Japanese position was supported by some 30 other developing nations which see that just as Marxism is giving way to markets, the political "greens" seem determined to put the world economy back into the red, using the greenhouse effect to stop unfettered market-based economic expansion.

In simplest terms, the earth's atmosphere does operate as a greenhouse. In addition to oxygen, nitrogen and water vapor, the atmosphere contains several gases that trap radiated heat, including methane and CO_2. Carbon dioxide is essential not only to warmth but to vegetation. It is also essential to life in another way: Without its heat-containing effect the planet would freeze, like the atmospherically naked moon.

Throughout most of human history that atmospheric blanket has held global temperatures at an average of about 60 degrees F., plus or minus 5 degrees F. During most of human history, the CO_2 concentration in that blanket has, until this century, hovered around 270 parts per million, although in earlier geologic epochs it reached as high as 20,000.

Over the last 100 years the CO_2 concentration has risen from 270 to today's level of 350. The culprit: man. Most of the greenhouse gas increase is the result of fossil fuel consumption. Add to that the rise in other man-generated trace gases—methane, nitrogen oxides and chlorofluorocarbons—and total greenhouse gases are now at 410 ppm. In other words, because of the combined effect of these gases, we have already gone over half-way to a doubling of CO_2. Even so, there has been less than half a degree of warming in the last 100 years.

What do the environmental pessimists make of all this? The earliest versions of their computer "general circulation models" predicted that the earth would warm up by anywhere from 3 to 5 degrees centigrade, or 5 to 9 degrees Fahrenheit, by the year 2050. The most extreme scenarios warn of coastal flooding (from melting ice caps) and rising inland droughts. However, as the level of sophistication of the models has risen, these forecast effects have been steadily reduced to a new range of 1.5 to 2.5 degrees centigrade.

One major exception to this declining rate of doom is the model run by James Hansen of the National Aeronautics & Space Administration, who shocked a congressional hearing in June 1988 during the middle of a scorching near-nationwide drought, by saying he was "99% confident" the greenhouse effect is now here.

Even though the vast majority of the climatological community was outraged by Hansen's unproven assertions, environmental advocate Stephen Schneider notes in *Global Warming*, "Journalists loved it. Environmentalists were ecstatic. Jim appeared on a dozen or more national television news programs. . . ."

By the end of 1988, with Hansen and Schneider's enthusiastic support, global warming was deeply embedded in the public consciousness. Now over 60% of the public is convinced it will worsen, even as the evidence of that alleged trend is under increasingly sharp and solid scientific attack.

On the contrary, that attack has been used as a premise for even more immediate action. As one TV anchorman argued, "Even if we aren't sure it's true, shouldn't we take precautions and act now as if it were?"

Unfortunately, "taking such precautions" could well spell the end of the American dream for us and the world. Once CO_2 is in the atmosphere, we can't easily remove it. Since most of the forecast rise in the gas is a function of simple economic and population growth in the Third World, there is no realistic economic way to prevent a CO_2 doubling without slashing growth and risking a revolt of the have-not nations against the haves. The Washington, D.C.-based Center for Strategic & International Studies points out that, even though the U.S. is now the largest carbon fuel user, it's the developing countries that will quadruple their energy consumption by 2025. (pp. 97–8)

The Environmental Protection Agency finds that just to stabilize U.S. CO_2 emissions at present levels would force 30% taxes on oil and coal, while to meet environmentalists' demands for a 20% reduction in U.S. CO_2 emissions would require a tax of $25 per barrel on oil, and $200 a ton on coal, effectively doubling U.S. energy costs.

Unfortunately, the popular media don't seem to care. In May the national press erupted in a two-day firestorm when Hansen told Senator Gore's subcommittee that the Office of Management & Budget had censored his florid global warming testimony by adding the modest caveat, "These changes should be viewed as estimates from evolving computer models and not as reliable predictions."

Yet, at the moment of that testimony, 61 of the world's top climatologists, gathered for a five-day workshop in Amherst, Mass., were largely agreeing with OMB. (p. 98)

Conference leader Michael Schlesinger, another top modeler (University of Illinois), agreed: "[Hansen's] statements have given people the feeling the greenhouse effect has been detected with certitude. Our current understanding does not support that. Confidence in its detection is now down near zero."

That conclusion was buttressed by one of the deans of U.S. climatology, Reid Bryson, a founder of the Institute for Environmental Studies at the University of Wisconsin, who said in July: "The very clear statements that have been made [by Hansen] that the greenhouse warming is here already and that the globe will be 4 degrees [centigrade] warmer in 50 years cannot be accepted."

On Dec. 24, 1988, Hansen received an unwelcome Christmas present in the form of a new research paper by one of the world's most universally respected climatologists, Thomas Karl, and two of his colleagues at the National Oceanographic & Atmospheric Administration, Kirby Hanson and George Maul. Their review of the best climate record in the world—that of the 48 contiguous United States—concluded: "There is no statistically significant evidence of an overall increase in annual temperature or change in annual precipitation for the contiguous U.S. 1895–1987." . . . As Karl says in an interview, "If there is a greenhouse warming effect, you can't find it in the U.S. records."

> "If there is a greenhouse warming effect, you can't find it in the U.S. records."
>
> —Thomas Karl,
> National Oceanographic and
> Atmospheric Administration

[In] June 1988,
V. Ramanathan of the
University of Chicago
and a team of scientists
at NASA concluded from
preliminary satellite data
that "clouds appear to
cool earth's climate,"
possibly offsetting the
atmospheric greenhouse
effect.

That news alone should have cooled off the global warming movement. But the environmentalists accepted Hansen's dismissal of the paper as "not significant" because the data covered only 1.5% of the earth's surface, not nearly enough to identify major trends.

But MIT meteorologist Richard Lindzen says that Hansen's rebuttal is out of line. He points out that because of the law of large numbers—the fact that a large enough sample is likely to give an accurate picture of a larger population—"the absence of any trend in the record of the contiguous U.S. leads to the suspicion that all the trends in the global record may be spurious."

The major reason for this is that when you fully subject global temperature records (as Karl did the U.S. records) to adjustment for the effects of urbanization (cities are heat islands that artificially inflate temperature records), the global warming trend since 1880 has been only a third of a degree centigrade, and over the Northern Hemisphere land masses, no trend at all.

Here's another fact, noted by Hugh Ellsaesser of Lawrence Livermore Laboratories, that should trouble the calamity theorists: Most of the past century's warming trend took place by 1938, well before the rise in CO_2 concentration. From 1938 to 1970 temperature plunged so sharply a new ice age was widely forecast. Furthermore, the warming trend since 1976 has been just the opposite of that forecast by the greenhouse model, with *cooling* in both the northern Pacific and North Atlantic.

In fact, the Northern Hemisphere shows no net change over the last 55 years, during which CO_2 concentration rose from approximately 300 to 350 ppm and other thermally active trace gases were in their steepest growth phases.

In spite of this clear lack of correlated warming evidence, one of the leading climate models now predicts that a 1% annual rise in CO_2 should, over 30 years, produce a 0.7-degree centigrade warming. But when Patrick Michaels of the University of Virginia applied that formula to the period from 1950 to 1988, when greenhouse gases rose 1.2% per year, he found a tiny 0.2-degree warming in land temperatures, where the model would have predicted 1.3 degrees. When a model cannot come within 500% of explaining the past, it is useless as a predictor of anything.

As Reid Bryson concludes in a 1988 paper, "A statement of what the climate is going to be in the year A.D. 2050 is a 63-year forecast. Do the models have a demonstrated capability of making a 63-year forecast? No. A 6.3-year forecast? No. Have they successfully simulated the climatic variation of the past century and a half? No. They are marvels of mathematics and computer science, but rather crude imitators of reality."

The major weakness of the models is their assumption that the CO_2 buildup is the significant climate variable, and should *ceteris paribus* (all other things being equal) generate warming. But, at it turns out, the *ceteris* are decidedly not *paribus*.

One of those variables is cloud cover, which is at least 100 times more powerful in affecting temperatures than greenhouse gases and is infinitely variable. Yet, because cloud cover has been documented only for a decade or so (by weather satellites), the models have little to go on. Until recently, the modelers assumed that warmth gave rise to the kind of clouds that trap heat, contributing still further to warming, in a vicious cycle. But in June 1988, V. Ramanathan of the University of Chicago and a team of scientists at NASA concluded from preliminary satellite data that "clouds appear to cool earth's climate," possibly offsetting the atmospheric greenhouse effect.

The supreme irony is that this "cooling effect," most pronounced in the Northern Hemisphere, coincides with the paths of coal-burning emission plumes with their high concentration of sulfur dioxide. That confirms a long-held thesis that sulfur dioxide creates "cool clouds." Of course, it is very upsetting to an environmentalist to discover that a pollutant has a beneficial side effect.

Sulfur dioxide emissions not only acidify rain, they combine with water vapor to form what are known as "aerosols," which have the effect of brightening clouds and making them reflect more heat away from the earth. Wisconsin's Reid Bryson described this effect as early as 20 years ago. Bryson's thesis was scorned at the time. But last June [1989], Thomas Wigley, one of England's top climatologists and a global warming enthusiast, conceded in a paper in *Nature* magazine that sulfur dioxide cooling "is sufficiently large that the effects may have significantly offset the temperature changes that resulted from the greenhouse effect." (pp. 98–100)

"This should make you wonder," says Michaels, "why Hansen [and others] have only perturbed their models with CO_2, and not with SO_2 as well. If you only perturb the model with CO_2, it will predict the greenhouse warming effect. If you only perturb it with SO_2, you get an ice age."

Hugh Ellsaesser says the main reason the models have been so completely wrong in "predicting" the past is that they completely ignore the countervailing, thermostatic effects of the hydrological cycle of evaporation and condensation. Two-thirds of the predicted global warming is due not directly to CO_2's radiative power but to an indirect effect: Carbon dioxide warming supposedly causes a threefold amplification of water vapor surface evaporation into the atmospheric blanket.

But Ellsaesser says in the warmer, tropical latitudes, where the temperature change from sea-level upward is most rapid, evaporation has the opposite effect. There, water vapor rises by deep convection in fast-rising towers. This in turn leads to more rapid condensation and precipitation, which then causes a drying and thinning of the upper atmosphere in a process called subsidence. "In the lower latitudes, a rise in CO_2 emissions will produce a 3-to-1 rise in greenhouse blanket *thinning* due to condensation. That's exactly the opposite of what the models predict," he says.

An eminent British scientist, Sir James Lovelock, says this hydrological process "is comparable in magnitude with that of the carbon dioxide greenhouse, but in opposition to it." National Oceanographic scientist Thomas Karl agrees: "We will eventually discover how naive we have been in not considering CO_2's effects on cloud cover and convection. As CO_2 speeds up the hydrological cycle, more convection creates more clouds and more cooling. So the greenhouse effect could turn out to be minimal, or even benign."

MIT'S Richard Lindzen thinks that correcting for deep convection alone could lower the global warming estimates by a factor of six. As a result, he says, "It is very unlikely that we will see more than a few tenths of a degree centigrade from this cause [CO_2] over the next century."

In the face of such mounting evidence, U.S. businesses may stop worrying about devastating legislative enactments. That could be a mistake. As Nobel economist James Buchanan argues, what drives Washington policymaking is not economic or scientific realities but "public choice," the pursuit of power and funding.

The public choice potential of global warming is immense. Under a global warming scenario, the EPA would become the most powerful government agency on earth, involved in massive levels of economic, social, scientific and political spending and interference, on a par with the old Energy Department. (pp. 100, 102)

Bernard Cohen, physicist at the University of Pittsburgh, warns, in a 1984 book: "Our government's science and technology policy is now guided by uninformed and emotion-driven public opinion rather than by sound scientific advice. Unless solutions can be found to this problem, the U.S. will enter the 21st century declining in wealth, power and influence. . . . The coming debacle is not due to the problems the environmentalists describe, but to the policies they advocate."

"Global warming" may well prove Cohen right. (p. 102)

> The major weakness of the [global climate] models is their assumption that the CO_2 buildup is the significant climate variable, and should *ceteris paribus* (all other things being equal) generate warming. But, as it turns out, the *ceteris* are decidedly not *paribus*.

Warren T. Brookes, "The Global Warming Panic," in Forbes, *Vol. 144, No. 14, December 25, 1989, pp. 96–100, 102.*

Even an increase of 1 °C can produce profound ecological change.

Global Warming and the Threat to Biological Diversity

The greenhouse effect is no longer controversial, although estimates of how hot the world will become vary considerably. Most climatologists believe that the overall rise in temperature will be about 3 °C in the next 50 years—with a small increase in the tropics and a much larger increase towards the poles. An increase of 3 °C will make the world warmer than it has been for 100,000 years—warming at a rate the Earth has probably never experienced before. In the US, Stephen Schneider, of the National Center for Atmospheric Research in Boulder, Colorado, suggests that the rate of change is some 10 to 40 times as fast as that after the last ice age. The climatic changes that took place then totally revamped the face of the planet. Among just the mammals, at least 32 genera became extinct.

The speed of the change could leave many species stranded—left behind in an unsuitable environment as the conditions they have evolved to live in alter faster than they can. Extinctions are inevitable as plants and animals fail to track their shifting habitats, or adapt too slowly to the new conditions.

Unfortunately, no one is certain precisely what will happen as the concentrations of carbon dioxide and other greenhouse gases (notably methane) increase. Climatologists have several models, all dealing with changes on a very broad scale. So far no one can predict what will happen in particular regions or even countries. The lack of detail in climatological models makes life difficult for ecologists who need to predict the effects on habitats, communities and individual species. But from these broad models, their knowledge of how most types of organisms function and an idea of what happened after previous climatic upheavals, biologists and ecologists have outlined the sorts of changes we might expect in the next few decades.

Changes have begun already. Even an increase of 1 °C can produce profound ecological change. Perhaps more important from a biological point of view, the increase will vary from place to place. Estimates range from an increase of 1 °C at the equator to as much as 12 °C at the poles. Other, equally damaging changes will accompany the rise in temperature. Sea level will rise both because water expands as it heats up and because the polar ice will begin to melt. In many parts of the world, storms will be more frequent and more ferocious; heat waves will be longer and hotter and droughts protracted. Elsewhere, rains will be more severe.

Ecologists do not wholly understand what controls the distribution of species. Many factors, including climate, food supply and an ability to compete with other species, are involved—and all these factors affect each other in a complex web of interactions. The change in climate, and all the associated changes, can act on any part of the web and still place stress on the ecosystem and individuals in it. The most direct effect is physiological. Different types of organisms have a variety of mechanisms to help them to cope with a change in temperature or supply of water. Microorganisms generally evolve quickly to adapt to the new environment. Other species are slower to adapt, and a great expansion of microorganisms could lead to an imbalance in the ecosystem. . . .

Indirectly, changes in climate can affect interactions between members of a community, such as predation and competition. A species that is successful in today's climate might be ousted by invaders better suited to the new climate. (p. 38)

Changes in the temperature and moisture in the soil can affect the structure of food webs and the processes of mineralisation and decomposition—and so the supply of nutrients to plants. In the end, these indirect changes will probably defeat species at the limits of their range.

Adult animals and mature plants are much hardier than the younger stages. If the young do not survive, the population will not replace its older generation as it dies. Moreover, stress, such as too hot a temperature or a lack of water, often interferes with reproduction. Some plants will not flower or set seed if it is too hot and dry; some will not flower if it is too wet—both conditions that will occur in some places as the greenhouse effect takes hold. Many animals do not breed at all if their offspring are likely to be born into a hostile world. Many invertebrates, for example, and most of those in the soil, go into some form of suspended animation in bad times. Birds lay smaller and fewer clutches of eggs.

Some animals already have strategies to cope with bad times. The red kangaroo, for example, delays implantation of its embryo when there is drought, waiting until a time when any offspring born would have a supply of food. Even with such a mechanism, if conditions were bad for many years the kangaroo would produce no offspring and the population would begin to decline.

Among some reptiles, the sex of the offspring depends on the temperature at which the eggs are incubated. This is probably related to how fast the embryos develop and which sex would benefit from being bigger. For example, in the alligator, eggs incubated at a temperature lower than 30 °C develop into females; a higher temperature, around 34 °C, produces males. In this species the males are very competitive and bigger males do better. At higher temperatures, embryos develop faster and grow bigger. In contrast, in some turtles, the females need to be bigger than the males because they have to produce so many large eggs. The eggs of sea turtles, such as the loggerhead, develop into females at the higher temperature and males at lower temperatures. If the temperature is permanently higher, it would unbalance the normal sex ratios needed to maintain viable populations.

In the oceans, the survival of a species often depends on the dispersal of larvae to new places. Many invertebrates produce mobile larvae, which settle and continue their development only where the conditions are right. Changing climate and changing patterns of currents in the oceans could condemn many to stay in their larval form, never finding a place to settle and eventually dying without producing offspring.

Migratory species may be some of the first to disappear. Although designed to travel long distances to find the conditions they need at particular times of the year, they time their journeys to fit in with food supplies along the route. . . . If these events get out of phase, the effects on the migrants would be catastrophic.

The loss of synchrony might be one of the more important aspects of the changing climate and how it affects the ecosystem. Another example is the timing of ice melt each year, an event that has important implications for both aquatic and terrestrial organisms. Normally, snow and ice melt over a period of several weeks. The acidic meltwater drains through the soil, which neutralises it before it runs off into lakes and rivers. In a warmer climate the melt would be earlier and faster; the meltwater would run over the soil and into the rivers, introducing a pulse of acid water, at a time when many animals are at their most vulnerable stage—eggs or fish fry, for example. Mortality of many species would be much heavier. Another effect of an early melt is that less water is available in the following months, and with a warmer summer, water is likely to be short. More seedlings will die. The pools and shallow lakes of the taiga and tundra—home to large populations of waterbirds—will become seasonal.

Although the individual species will respond in many different ways, we will begin to see some broad trends. Most evident will be the changes in the belts of vegetation that encircle the world. The most dramatic changes will be in the

Vera Alexander, director of the Institute of Marine Science at the University of Alaska, Fairbanks, suggests that if the calculations of the climatologists are right, many of the most familiar animals of the Arctic—such as polar bears and walruses—will disappear.

To the south of the Arctic Ocean, the great expanses of tundra will shrink, almost to nothing according to some ecologists, pushed to the edge of the ocean by advancing boreal forests.

northern hemisphere, where the greatest mass of land and most continuous belts of vegetation are. Moreover, if the arctic ice melts, the climatic equator will shift north, pushing the vegetation belts towards the North Pole.

Tropical forests will show little overall change. The temperature will rise only a little, perhaps 1 °C. To either side of the equatorial belt, most types of vegetation will begin to move towards the poles. As mixed deciduous forests move north they will squeeze the northern boreal forests up into the far north, in turn squeezing the tundra into remote refuges in the high Arctic. According to Ian Woodward, of the University of Cambridge, this trend has already begun. (pp. 39–40)

In some regions the vegetation will move uphill as well as shifting north and south. As a general rule, moving up 500 metres is equivalent climatically to moving 250 kilometres north. But as the treeline moves upwards, the new forests will drive alpine vegetation and its associated fauna to the highest altitudes, perhaps displacing it altogether.

Biological diversity varies hugely in the different "life zones" of the world. Tropical forests are the richest in species yet the loss of fewer species in other zones may have greater consequences. The Arctic Ocean is more vital to the functioning of the biosphere than a count of species would suggest. It is also the region that will suffer most and soonest.

Vera Alexander, director of the Institute of Marine Science at the University of Alaska, Fairbanks, suggests that if the calculations of the climatologists are right, many of the most familiar animals of the Arctic—such as polar bears and walruses—will disappear. The Arctic Ocean would become less productive and, more significantly, the changes in the Arctic would have repercussions through all the oceans. Changes in the cold waters of the Arctic will alter the pattern of circulation in the world ocean, disrupting currents, food supplies for species that make up some of the world's richest fisheries, and the climate of other parts of the world.

Areas covered by sea ice might be exposed to the greatest increase in temperatures—and more in winter than in summer. If the ice melts in summer, winter temperatures might not be low enough for it to refreeze. An increase of 5 °C in the next 50 years will melt even the permanent Arctic ice. The loss of ice would also speed up the warming of the ocean because it would reduce the albedo—the reflectance—of the water, which would absorb more heat.

Seasonal sea ice is a vital part of the Arctic ecosystem. The algae that grow on its underside form the base of the food chain that ultimately supports vast numbers of seabirds, fish and seals. The ice also serves as a platform from which seals search for food and on which they breed. The spotted seal breeds only at the edge of the ice. Harp seals, ringed seals, ribbon and bearded seals all live in association with the ice.

The first signs of a biological response to global warming in the Arctic might be an invasion of more southerly species. True Arctic species will be pushed farther north, but there is a limit to how far they can go. As the sea ice disappears from the north coast of Alaska, Arctic species will retreat to strongholds in the Canadian high Arctic and Svalbard. If warming continues, however, these refuges may also disappear.

To the south of the Arctic Ocean, the great expanses of tundra will shrink, almost to nothing according to some ecologists, pushed to the edge of the ocean by advancing boreal forests. The tundra is both at risk and a risk. Below the top few centimetres of vegetation lies an enormous depth of permanently frozen peat—a vast store of organic material. If the ice melts, the peat will begin to decompose and release enormous quantities of carbon to the atmosphere, enhancing the greenhouse effect. About 14 per cent of the Earth's organic carbon is tied up in the frozen peat beneath the tundra. If the ice melts, the structure of the tundra will also begin to break up, with severe erosion and collapse of the soil.

What happens to the permafrost depends largely on what happens to the layer of vegetation—mosses, sedges, grasses and small hardy shrubs—that blankets it. This layer protects the frozen ground in the short, hot Arctic summer, preventing it from melting.

The great forested zones of North America and Eurasia will change much more slowly. Trees generally live a long time and most will stick out deteriorating conditions at the southern boundaries of their ranges for several decades. These old surviving forests will differ from today's in one vital element: they will not be renewing themselves. In the new climate, seeds might not germinate or seedlings might fail to establish themselves. Eventually, the old trees will succumb to storms, forest fires or pests—and there will be no young ones to take their place. We may see signs of such changes in 20 to 60 years, depending on the types of trees. (pp. 39–43)

In the tropics, the change in the pattern of rainfall will have more effect than the rise in temperature. The lack of a dry season, or a dry season that is longer than usual, can produce strong responses in plants and animals. In the forest of La Selva in Costa Rica, there is usually no dry season. After a few weeks without rain, young seedlings begin to wilt and die. . . .

Like tropical forests, tropical waters are rich in species. Although the change in temperature in the tropics will be small, other factors will disturb the equilibrium of the ecosystem. Coral reefs grow only in warm tropical and subtropical waters. Two-thirds of the species of fish in these waters live around reefs. The reefs are threatened more by the rise in sea level than the change in temperature. Corals grow actively only near the surface of the water and most do not grow fast enough to keep up with the rising waters. Antler corals do grow quickly, but break easily in storms. Storms are likely to worsen in the area where coral reefs are.

The question for both conservationists and politicians is: is the world bound to become a different place? Even if governments take steps to prevent global warming, some change is still probably inevitable. According to Michael Soule, president of the Society for Conservation Biology, a rise of 2 °C is inevitable in the next 30 to 50 years, so conservationists must plan their strategy now. Plans to preserve wildlife and whole ecosystems will have to be on a totally different scale to anything done before. The traditional way to protect wildlife is to create a reserve. But reserves are "man-locked" refuges, says Thomas Lovejoy of the Smithsonian Institution in Washington DC—islands trapped in a sea of artificial landscape. Reserves will not help in a changing climate, as the species in the reserve will have to move out of it to find the conditions they need. Outside its borders, migrating species will fact a hostile landscape, meeting barriers of farmland, cities and motorways, as well as natural barriers such as mountain ranges.

One way around this problem is to create corridors between reserves. The US already has plans for a network of greenways over the country. In other parts of the world, however, corridors would have to cross national borders to be of any use. In some cases, there will be nowhere for the migrant species to go, especially those that now live along shorelines and in coastal wetlands that will soon lie under water. Even corridors will restrict movement to defined pathways—so that only a small number of migrating species find a route. Some ecologists would like to see the whole landscape managed in an attempt at conservation. . . .

[Jerry Franklin of the U.S. Forestry Service] proposes that if nature cannot act fast enough, then people must work on its behalf—they must become ecological engineers. "We need to collaborate with nature to save diversity in the face of global climatic change," he says. Ecological engineers could attempt, for instance, to recreate natural forests in new locations, says Margaret Davis. . . . [However, recreating] an entire ecosystem is a tall order and many conservationists argue against such interference. Experiments to find appropriate and acceptable ways to maintain natural habitats take many years, perhaps as long as it will take the greenhouse effect to produce its changes.

Plans to preserve wildlife and whole ecosystems will have to be on a totally different scale to anything done before.

The difficult challenge to policy makers is how to respond to such a supreme threat when the only evidence is a theory, the prediction of computer models, data revealing a slight warming over the past century, some tantalizing paleoclimate evidence, and a lot of uncertainty.

In the Arctic, it will be impossible to recreate the ecosystem—unless someone finds a way to refreeze the ocean. If governments do not act now to halt global warming, the future for the walrus and the polar bear looks bleak. (p. 43)

Stephanie Pain "No Escape from the Global Greenhouse," in New Scientist, *Vol. 120, No. 1638, November 12 , 1988, pp. 38–43.*

Responding to Global Climate Change: Legislative Options

Background

Two aspects of global change issues are striking to any observer. The first is the rapidity with which the problem is entering the public and political consciousness, and the second is the dramatic shortening of the projected time before the effects of climate change and sea-level rise begin to be felt. Public awareness is obviously a function of the closeness of the consequences, but what is remarkable is the desire to address what all of us recognize as the most challenging environmental, economic, and political issue we have ever faced. The complexity of human-caused global environmental change arises because of the intrinsic linkages that exist among the major issues considered here, the so-called greenhouse effect in which the emission of carbon dioxide and other gases released by energy production, agriculture, and industrial processes contributes to global warming. The warming and emissions in turn are linked to a host of related critical problems including climate modification, sea level rise, deforestation, acid rain, air pollution, and stratospheric ozone depletion. It would be more than a little presumptuous to assume that one could even identify all of the issues that Congress should address in a paper of this scope, much less describe all of the policy options that should be considered. Despite these reservations, I hope to provide a focus for the discussion of a congressional agenda that addresses near-term global change policy options. (pp. 305–06)

The seriousness of [global warming's] projected consequences and their time frames and degree of irreversibility provide important yardsticks against which we can measure various policy proposals. Despite the irreversible, adverse consequences of our release of greenhouse gases, the focus of concern appears to be more on the irreversible impact of policy changes that might be enacted to solve these problems. What if we are mistaken and there is no global warming? One way to approach this dilemma is to initially phase in those policies that are most easily reversed, that have the lowest negative impact on the current economy, are most effective in reducing greenhouse gas emissions, and which have additional environmental and economic benefits as well. In any case, there exist many problems which we should be addressing that happen to be linked to the greenhouse issue. By a proper choice of action, we can effectively address both a problem like stratospheric ozone depletion and global warming. (p. 309)

Research Initiatives

Our new awareness of the extent and timing of greenhouse effects has occurred as the result of new research tools and new strategies for carrying out "global science." Without the contribution from satellites, a worldwide network of monitoring stations, research laboratories, interdisciplinary institutes, and the array of regular and supercomputers to correlate the data and model the complexities of climate, we would remain blissfully ignorant of the threat we face. The obvious challenge to scientists is to develop more accurate predictive models and to devise a more sensitive test that can identify a greenhouse fingerprint or lack thereof as soon as possible.

To achieve those goals, there must be a sustained, decades-long scientific research effort. . . . (p. 310)

Congress will need to provide significant new funds to ensure that satellites for remote monitoring and experiments are available as are the computers needed to handle the monitoring data and to model the results. In addition to the need for new satellites like the polar platform, Congress should determine whether funding should be provided for equipment like Landsat that is slated for abandonment. Considerable research needs to be supported to understand the continuing increases in methane and nitrous oxide, two important greenhouse gases. The development of strategies to reduce the important air pollutant and greenhouse gas tropospheric (lower atmosphere) ozone should also be a high priority. Much more work needs to be done on climate dynamics, especially nonlinear effects. We also need to increase our understanding of the role of the biosphere in climate change, and the implications for a range of representative ecosystems utilizing both space and ground level observation. All aspects of global change research and monitoring are currently underfunded, even in the short term. Yet they could be expected to provide major insights into the greenhouse and other linked problems. Responsibility for particular programs must continue to evolve among NASA, NOAA [National Oceanic and Atmospheric Administration], NSF [National Science Foundation], EPA, and DOE [Department of Energy]. Enhanced authority to coordinate and shape priorities and ensure cooperation among agencies, universities, the private sector, and international research efforts also needs to be provided to some office within the government.

A second area of needed research is the exploration of policy options. It may seem peculiar in a presentation of policy options to advocate research on the very proposals being advocated, but we need to learn which mechanisms are likely to be the most effective in reducing greenhouse gas emissions most rapidly, most completely, most economically, and with least disruption to society. Because the necessary actions will be so pervasive, it is essential that they have a high degree of support by the public in order to be both politically acceptable and capable of being implemented. The U.S. and other nations now have some experience with several strategies designed to reduce pollution and promote energy efficiency. There also exists a significant body of general research on the relative merits of tax breaks, gasoline or oil import consumption taxes, pollution (in this case carbon) taxes, incentives, trade-offs, penalties, regulations, and negotiations. What is needed is to apply each of these ideas—and any others one can think of such as the imaginative debt for tropical forest swap—to specific greenhouse problems in order to determine which approach is most effective in which circumstances. Carrying out policy research is perhaps the only possible way to resolve the ideological biases that engulf most policy debate.

Organizing Governmental Response

The difficult challenge to policymakers is how to respond to such a supreme threat when the only evidence is a theory, the prediction of computer models, data revealing a slight warming over the past century, some tantalizing paleoclimate evidence, and a lot of uncertainty. If one is to give any credence to the predictions, then it is clear that some action is essential long before we can be certain of the extent of future damage and its timing. Waiting until we are certain that our own emissions are increasing global temperatures could well commit us to ruinous levels of climate change. . . . To respond effectively will require mobilizing government authority and resources in new arrangements. Rather than create a new "Pentagon for global climate change," it is far more realistic to divide the many aspects of this problem among the appropriate departments and agencies and then to develop an effective means for coordinating them. In some ways we have already begun since a number of the scientific aspects are already coordinated by the National Climate Program.

For Congress there is the additional challenge of organizing the task of gathering the necessary information, developing and passing authorizing

> **Improving efficiency is the fastest and least-cost strategy for reducing CO$_2$ emissions for an economy like ours, and is also the most effective option for new energy products in developing countries which will provide a large share of new CO$_2$ emissions in the coming decades.**

While it is neither politically possible nor practically desirable to close down existing coal-powered electric generators, it is not too soon to plan for their orderly replacement.

legislation, and then appropriating the necessary funding to implement the many facets of a complex response to a complex problem. A look at the various dimensions of the problem suggests that at least a dozen different subcommittee jurisdictions and as many federal agencies (not to mention state and local governments and the private sector) might be involved. Simply allocating tasks among the agencies and figuring out coordination mechanisms will be a major task. High-level positions will need to be created at the EPA and the Department of Energy, and coordinating offices will be necessary in the Departments of State, Interior, Agriculture, Housing and Urban Development, and Defense. To be certain that responsibilities are met in a coherent way requires that ultimate responsibility be vested in a single cabinet-level official with sufficient staff to coordinate the research and policy implementation. (pp. 310–13)

International Initiatives

The recent achievement of the Montreal Protocol on Substances That Deplete the Ozone Layer has been hailed as evidence that a similar agreement might be reached with regard to limiting greenhouse gases. The two issues share in common a global dimension and the absolute need for global cooperation. It should be a high priority of the Congress to press for an international meeting within the next two years to develop an agreement for controlling greenhouse gases.

Secondly, we must increase our financial commitment and involvement in international research activities such as those sponsored by UNEP [The United Nations Environment Programme] and the International Geosphere-Biosphere Program. We also need to actively pursue bilateral research and policy options with the Soviet, Chinese, Japanese, and European governments. The recent summit agreement with the Soviets to cooperate on global climate change issues represents an important step forward.

Since much of the future increase of greenhouse gases will come from increased industrialization and agricultural production in developing countries, it is essential that development assistance projects sponsored by U.S. AID, the World Bank, and other development agencies promote technologies that protect global climate. This is particularly true for the energy field, where a recent study has shown the tremendous potential for the cost-effective introduction into developing countries of energy-efficient technology that also reduces both capital expenditures and the debilitating cost of imported fuels that contribute so much to Third World debt.

Slowing Growth of Greenhouse Gases

Energy Efficiency

Using less energy to provide the same end-use services not only reduces global warming through a reduction in carbon dioxide emissions, it also reduces the production of air pollutants that cause acid rain, decreases our dependence on foreign oil, improves our trade balance, and provides an opportunity for entrepreneurs to create new technologies. Improved efficiency also lowers the levels of another important greenhouse gas and smog component, tropospheric ozone. Congress went a long way in this direction by recently passing appliance efficiency standards (twice!), which according to one estimate will eliminate the need for 40 large coal-fired plants. On the other hand, weakening the gas mileage standards for automobiles (CAFE [Corporate Average Fuel Economy] standards) and allowing energy efficiency tax credits to expire has discouraged manufacturers and the public from choosing more efficient cars and homes. More efficient heating, lighting, and air conditioning of new buildings especially in the residential and commercial sector, as well as retrofitting existing structures, can have a dramatic effect on CO_2 emissions. Removing barriers to these innovations, introducing incentives, and considering compulsory national building standards like those in California should be high on the congressional agenda. Improving efficiency is the fastest and lease-cost strategy for reducing CO_2 emissions for an economy like ours, and is also the most effective option for new energy projects in developing countries which will provide a large share of new CO_2 emissions in the coming decades.

Fuel Switching

Among fossil fuels themselves there are enormous differences in the amount of CO_2 emitted for each unit of energy produced. Coal releases about twice as much carbon dioxide as does natural gas, with petroleum approximately half-way in between. Refining and burning shale oil and other synfuels yield from 2.5 to 3.5 times as much CO_2 as does burning natural gas. New gas turbine technology is so efficient that the effective emissions advantage over coal may climb from a factor of 2 to a factor of 3. As the debate over the Clean Air Act and the support for "clean coal" technology indicates, replacing abundant U.S. coal with scarcer natural gas will not be politically easy. Furthermore, we and the Soviet Union have comparable coal reserves together accounting for half of the global total, while China and Europe each account for 10% more. Hence, we face the possibility of intense international disagreement as well as interstate rivalry over the use of coal.

Despite these obstacles, Congress did repeal the provisions of the Fuel Use Act which had prohibited the use of natural gas for electrical utilities and large industrial boilers. The provisions of PURPA [Public Utilities Regulatory Policy Act] also encourage smaller-scale production of electricity and cogeneration which is both more efficient and more readily accomplished using oil and gas rather than coal. Unfortunately, there still exist regulatory barriers to fuel switching including the possibility of co-burning coal with natural gas to achieve significant reductions in CO_2 and sulfur and nitrogen oxides at very low costs. Congress should amend the Clear Air Act to remove barriers to innovation, and ensure that efforts to meet local and national air quality standards do not exacerbate the greenhouse problem. (pp. 313–15)

While it is neither politically possible nor practically desirable to close down existing coal-powered electric generators, it is not too soon to plan for their orderly replacement. . . . A program of incentives to phase out the oldest, least efficient, and most polluting coal plants on an accelerated schedule would help with both the greenhouse problem and acid rain. A strategy similar to this was successfully pursued by the Tennessee Valley Authority during the 1970s. Natural gas can help bridge the energy supply route to the future along with reduced demand through efficiency improvements until renewable technologies such as solar and wind or an acceptable and economical nuclear option can be developed.

Develop Renewable Energy Technologies

Renewable resources are abundant, but often diffuse. In appropriate circumstances, however, they can make a significant contribution to energy supply. Electricity generation by wind power in the U.S. now exceeds 1,500 megawatts and is expanding. The U.S. geothermal capacity of 2,000 megawatts currently exceeds 40% of the world's total, and the immense Geysers geothermal plant in California may soon be joined by an additional 500-megawatt plant in Hawaii. Photovoltaic production of electricity continues to expand for remote sites as the cost of production drops with each new technological development; two companies are constructing photovoltaic power stations in the 10-megawatt range. Steam and electricity production from biomass and combustible solid waste is a growing industry. . . . Solar and wind technologies have the advantage of producing no greenhouse gases, while biomass and trash (principally paper and garbage) produce no more CO_2 than they consumed during growth of the raw materials that produced them.

It is clear that tax incentives offered by some states in combination with progressive utilities and utility commissions have strongly encouraged investment in renewables, whereas the termination of federal tax credits has virtually halted the boom in solar domestic hot water heating. A reconsideration of federal tax policies as they affect renewables is certainly in order at this time as is an examination of those utility policies that have been effective. A redistribution of federal research and development funds into several promising areas

As the debate over the Clean Air Act and the support for "clean coal" technology indicates, replacing abundant U.S. coal with scarcer natural gas will not be politically easy.

The massive deforestation under way in the tropics and elsewhere is believed to contribute about one-fifth of the observed excess in the annual carbon budget.

such as amorphous and crystalline silicon photovoltaics could yield large dividends in the near term.

Reassess the Nuclear Option

Despite its perceived and real problems, nuclear power does have the advantage of not producing any greenhouse gases in the production of electricity. The current leveling off of nuclear plant construction at less than 20% of U.S. electricity generating capacity is a consequence of excessively high capital costs, quality control problems, an inability to resolve the waste problem in a timely fashion, and a loss of public confidence in nuclear power following the accidents at Three Mile Island and Chernobyl. The rate of introduction of nuclear electric generating capacity is slowing in most parts of the world, and this appears to be a propitious time to assess this technology and its future. Congress may wish to address such questions as how much nuclear capacity do we need and how much are we capable of managing and operating safely? Should we begin research on a new generation of inherently safer and more economical designs? Given the significant cost advantage and ease of incremental introduction of energy-efficient technologies and the promise of renewables, how should we allocate our limited R&D funds between these options and nuclear power?

Reforestation

Not all of the carbon dioxide increase in the atmosphere arises from the burning of fossil fuels. The massive deforestation under way in the tropics and elsewhere is believed to contribute about one-fifth of the observed excess in the annual carbon budget. Halting the destruction of forests combined with reforestation will provide a significant sink for CO_2 and create additional benefits such as restoration of local ecosystems, reduce soil erosion, and establish sustainable wood fuel and timber resources especially in developing countries. . . . We also need to examine the international debt situation and initiate debt-for-forest swaps as well as find other strategies for reducing pressures on developing countries to further cut their forests. A Tropical Forest Action Plan has been prepared jointly by the World Resources Institute, the World Bank, the United Nations Development Program, and the Food and Agriculture Organization of the United Nations which describes various policy mechanisms that may be used to protect this resource and the economies of developing countries.

Reduce Chlorofluorocarbon Emissions

Chlorofluorocarbons (CFCs) now contribute 30 to 40% as much as CO_2 to global warming, and their release is increasing at nearly ten times the CO_2 rate. The recently signed Montreal Protocol commits the U.S. and other countries to additional significant reductions in CFC production. Encouraging the development of substitutes through tax incentives and negotiation with producers and by regulation that will hasten the replacement of these substances with environmentally less harmful chemicals would be one of the fastest and most effective ways to reduce future commitment to global warming while simultaneously slowing the rate of destruction of stratospheric ozone. (pp. 315–18)

Pricing Options

While the United States has moved away from subsidies such as oil depletion allowances, which encouraged the inefficient use of petroleum, there still remain areas such as natural gas and electricity pricing and R&D funding that favor some energy options over others. It would be useful to examine all such subsidies to determine their effect on the economy and on environmental problems such as greenhouse gas emissions. Similarly, the cutting of tropical forests has been greatly accelerated by literally billions of dollars in subsidies, while our own U.S. Forest Service is losing at least $85 million annually on timber sales, according to a just-released study.

A second pricing problem occurs when all of the real costs are not included in the price being paid by the user. The current low energy prices we are now enjoying do not include the costs of Persian Gulf security or environmental damage such as acid rain, smog, and the greenhouse effect. These artificially low prices encourage excessive consumption of nonrenewable energy resources along with their additional pollution burden. The simplest method for dealing with this problem is to place a fee on each form of energy that reflects its environmental or other social costs.

One option that would respond to the greenhouse issue is a carbon fee that would be highest for those fuels that emit large amounts of CO_2 for each unit of useful energy produced. . . . [This strategy would include charging] a fee on all petroleum products or perhaps only gasoline. As unpopular as gasoline taxes are, they have an advantage during this time of low fuel prices in more accurately reflecting future oil replacement costs. Not only would such a fee promote energy efficiency and reduce CO_2 and other emissions, it would also make our economy less vulnerable to the inevitable shocks we face in the near future as our domestic reserves continue to decline. Finally, as Federal Reserve Chairman Alan Greenspan has observed, a modest increase in the gasoline tax would make a significant contribution to reducing the federal deficit. (pp. 318–19)

The basic focus of all of these suggestions is to use the market mechanisms in the economy to reduce emissions of greenhouse gases and other pollutants. An advantage of using pricing mechanisms is that the incentives can be adjusted to achieve any desired level of emissions reduction, and the emitter may determine the most cost-effective method. It may be necessary if energy prices are raised in this manner to respond to the needs of low-income citizens with some form of assistance.

Preparing for Adaptation

Since we cannot respond rapidly enough to stop all future contributions to global warming, and because there is already a commitment to a significant global warming from the greenhouse gases that have already been released to the atmosphere, it is essential that we consider adaptation options now. The longer we wait to take action to slow the buildup of these gases, however, the more we will be placed in a reactive mode of coping with the consequences of our actions (or lack thereof). Comparing the cost of adaptive and preventive strategies is also useful in providing us with an informed basis for implementing the policy options that have been described in this paper. In the following paragraphs, several examples of adaptive strategies are described.

To protect future coastal development, *Housing and Urban Development* should revise the national flood insurance program to deny insurance to any dwelling constructed in an area that would be flooded by projected sea-level rise during its lifetime.

The *U.S. Department of Agriculture* should prepare a long-range plan for adapting U.S. agricultural and forestry policies to the potential consequences of climate change. This should include consideration of possible shifts in areas of agricultural and forestry production and major shifts in agricultural productivity and crop type. USDA and the Forest Service should also prepare for a large increase in the number and size of forest fires.

Water resource plans need to be prepared by the *U.S. Department of the Interior* and the *Army Corps of Engineers* to address the implications of potential changes in the timing, distribution, and variability of precipitation. This plan should include the need for water conservation policies, the capacity of urban reservoirs, revised estimates of dependable power from hydroelectric sites, predictability of river levels for barge traffic, and other implications of changes in precipitation for federal water projects and irrigation. DOI should also include climate change issues in its long-range management plans for national parks, wildlife reserves, and other public lands.

Strategies for managing public energy resources in an era constrained by water shortages, limits on coral development, and other potential results of global

The current low energy prices we are now enjoying do not include the cost of Persian Gulf security or environmental damage such as acid rain, smog, and the greenhouse effect. These artificially low prices encourage excessive consumption of nonrenewable energy resources along with their additional pollution burden.

Despite its perceived and real problems, nuclear power does have the advantage of not producing any greenhouse gases in the production of electricity.

climate change should be developed jointly by the *Department of Energy* and the *Department of the Interior*. The implications of fuel switching, use of renewables, and improved efficiency on the demand for conventional fuels from public lands also need to be determined.

The *Federal Emergency Management Agency* should consider climate programs responsive to the potential for an increase in the frequency of severe storms, coastal flooding, and other weather extremes possible from global climate change. FEMA and *Health and Human Services* should study responses to increasing heat waves.

The *Department of State* needs to plan for increased aid requests from nations adversely affected by drought, desertification, and agricultural failures.

The *Department of Labor* should determine the implications for a significantly altered labor market should large-scale shifts in our pattern of energy use occur.

Conclusions

We clearly face a problem of global dimensions that will affect all nations on a scale that has never been encountered in human history. The encouraging fact is that there is something that we can do about it. It is also clear, however, that we must begin acting now to slow the growth in the emission of greenhouse gases. Waiting until a clear greenhouse fingerprint is unequivocally proven will, if current models are correct, commit us to an additional warming. These same studies also show, however, that by taking action of the kind described here, we can reduce future warming significantly.

The Congress is perhaps the most critical forum in which the course of the U.S. response to climate change will be decided. In times of tight budget constraints, priorities must be set for scientific and policy research as well as for programs within the Department of Energy and other agencies. Choices that will be made now will determine not only our own contribution to future warming, but will significantly influence the rapidly evolving international discussion of appropriate responses. A great deal can be accomplished in a cost-effective manner within the next few years by improving the efficiency of our transportation sector and both end-use and production efficiency of electric power. This strategy will have other, multiple benefits for clean air, balance of payments, and energy security as well. We can also move more rapidly to replace chlorofluorocarbons with chemicals that contribute less to both global warming and depletion of the ozone layer. The sooner we can begin reforestation programs both in the U.S. and in the tropics, the greater will be the CO_2 absorptive capacity during the critical first half of the next century. On the other hand, a commitment to a major synfuels program would accelerate the already rapid rise in global warming. By a careful choice of policies that simultaneously slow the release of greenhouse gases and help solve other problems, we can effectively and prudently buy ourselves some insurance against a rapid global warming and its destructive consequences. (pp. 320–22)

William R. Moomaw, "Near-Term Congressional Options for Responding to Global Climate Change," in The Challenge of Global Warming, *edited by Dean Edwin Abrahamson, Island Press, 1989, pp. 305–26.*

Sources For Further Study

Abrahamson, Dean Edwin, ed. *The Challenge of Global Warming.* Washington, D.C.: Island Press, 1989, 358 p.

Collection of studies and essays on global warming by such scientists and policy-makers as James E. Hansen, Rafe Pomerance, and Jill Jaeger.

Abrams, Isabel S. "Gauging the Greenhouse Effect." *Current Health* 17, No. 3 (November 1990): 25–6.
Briefly defines and discusses the greenhouse effect.

Bardach, John E. "Global Warming and the Coastal Zone." *Climate Change* 15, Nos. 1–2 (October 1989): 117–50.
Charts the possible effects of global warming upon various coastal regions of the world and upon related industries, including fishing and tourism.

Committee on Science, Engineering, and Public Policy. *Policy Implications of Greenhouse Warming*. Washington, D.C.: National Academy Press, 1991, 127 p.
Results of a study conducted by the National Academy of Sciences, the National Academy of Engineering, and the Institute of Medicine on U.S. government policy options for mitigating and responding to global climate change.

Crosson, Pierre. "Greenhouse Warming and Climate Change." *Food Policy* 14, No. 2 (May 1989): 107–18.
Investigates potential changes in crop distribution and production as a result of global warming.

Daniel, R. Edrea. "Greenhouse Warming: Searching for the Facts." *Environmental Views* 11, No. 3 (December 1988): 16–21.
Addresses the debate between scientists concerning the actual causes and future implications of the greenhouse effect.

Flavin, Christopher. "Slowing Global Warming." In *State of the World 1990: A World Watch Institute Report on Progress Toward a Sustainable Society*, edited by Lester R. Brown, et. al., pp. 17–38. New York: W. W. Norton, 1990.
Summarizes the factors that contribute to global warming and proposes ways to curtail emissions of greenhouse gases.

Karas, Jacqueline H. W. "Greenhouse Gases in the Atmosphere: Sources and Effects." In *Energy—Environment—Quality of Life (Interscience Enterprises) 13th Annual International Scientific Forum*, 1989.
Outlines the sources of greenhouse gases, the historic variations of their levels, and changes in temperature that have accompanied these variations.

La Brecque, Mort. "Clouds and Climate: A Critical Unknown in the Global Equation." *Mosaic* 21, No. 2 (Summer 1990): 2–12.
Speculates on what role clouds may play in offsetting or intensifying the greenhouse effect.

Lesser, Jonathan A. "Energy Use and Global Warming: What Are the Options?" *Washington State Energy Office Dispatch* 12, No. 6 (November-December 1989): 4–6.
Reviews ways in which improvements in energy efficiency and conservation could mitigate global warming trends.

Lester, R. T., and Meyers, J. P. "Global Warming, Climate Disruption, and Biological Diversity." In *Audubon Wildlife Report 1989/1990*, edited by William J. Chandler, pp. 177–221. San Diego: Academic Press, Inc., 1989.
Discusses how ecosystems may be disturbed or destroyed by the effects of global warming.

Mintzer, Irving. "Weathering the Storms in a Warming World." *Public Power* 46, No. 6 (November-December 1988): 14–16, 18, 20–1.
Outlines the role of utilities in the generation and reduction of greenhouse gases.

Molion, Luiz Carlos. "The Amazonian Forests and Climatic Stability." *Ecologist* 19, No. 6 (November-December 1989): 211–14.
Explains how the carbon released by burning Brazil's rain forests contributes to global warming.

Moore, Curtis A. "Does Your Coffee Cup Cause Forest Fires?" *International Wildlife* 19, No. 2 (March-April 1989): 38–47.
    Illustrates how such simple acts as drinking from a styrofoam cup, using electricity, or driving a car contribute to climate change.

Myers, Norman. "The Greenhouse Effect: A Tropical Forestry Response." *Biomass* 18, No. 1 (1989): 73–9.
    Examines how tropical reforestation projects could curb global warming.

Nierenberg, William A. "Atmospheric CO_2: Causes, Effects, and Options." *Chemical Engineering and Progress* 85, No. 8 (August 1989): 27–36.
    Technical overview of the scientific and political issues surrounding the greenhouse effect.

Pierce, Fred. "Methane: The Hidden Greenhouse Gas." 122, No. 1663 (6 May 1989): 37–42.
    Explores the production and environmental impact of this greenhouse gas.

Rathjens, George W. "Energy and Climate Change." In *Preserving the Global Environment: The Challenge of Shared Leadership,* edited by Jessica Tuchman Mathews, pp. 154–86. New York: W. W. Norton, 1991.
    Argues that the prospects for immediate reductions in greenhouse gas emissions are poor unless more tangible data concerning global warming is uncovered.

Rosenfeld, Arthur H., et. al. "Policies to Improve Energy Efficiency and Reduce Global Warming." *Strategic Planning & Energy Management* 9, No. 2 (Fall 1989): 7–31.
    Proposes that the enactment of certain government policies aimed at reducing energy consumption in the U.S. could curtail the emission of carbon dioxide and other greenhouse gases.

Schneider, Stephen. *Global Warming: Are We Entering the Greenhouse Century?* San Francisco: Sierra Club Books, 1989, 317 p.
    Presents the origins and possible consequences of global warming.

————. "Global Warming: Is It Real?" *Forum for Applied Research and Public Policy* 4, No. 4 (Winter 1989): 24–30.
    Addresses the discrepancies that exist between global climate models and their predictions of future warming.

————. "The Greenhouse Effect: Science and Policy." *Science* 243, No. 4892 (10 February 1989): 771–81.
    Analyses the various factors that may influence future global warming trends, including CO_2 emissions and global climate response.

Stanfield, Rochelle L. "Greenhouse Diplomacy." *National Journal* 21, Vol. 9 (4 March 1989): 510–13.
    Examines the inconsistencies in President Bush's global warming policy based on his appointments to several key administrative positions.

Sylvester, Kathleen. "Global Warming: The Answers Are Not Always Global." *Governing* 3, No. 7 (April 1990): 42–4, 46, 48.
    Focuses on Newark, New Jersey, and other cities to examine how global warming and other environmental issues have increasingly figured in local politics.

Turner, Wayne C., and Moses, Scott A. "Responses to the Global Warming Crisis." *Strategic Planning & Energy Management* 9, No. 2 (Fall 1989): 31–44.
    Asserts that an estimated 50% reduction in carbon dioxide emission would stabilize the atmospheric concentration of the gas and proposes that alternative fuels and energy efficiency improvements would significantly aid in this decrease.

Wheeler, David J. "Scientists Studying 'The Greenhouse Effect' Challenge Fears of Global Warming." *Journal of Forestry* 88, No. 7 (July 1990): 34–6.
    Relates the uncertainties expressed by some climatologists concerning the validity of global warming.

"Climate Change: A Global Concern." *World Resources Institute Report: World Resources 1990–91*, 1990, 11–32.
    Reviews the major issues surrounding global warming.

7:   Nuclear Energy

Nukespeak: Spreading Propaganda about the Viability and Safety of Nuclear Power

"Just as America gave birth to nuclear technology in the 1940s, we can lead the world into a new era of safe, reliable, economical, and environmentally clean nuclear power in the 1990s," President George Bush recently told the Nuclear Power Assembly. "This clean domestic source of power lessens the risk of energy dependence on foreign sources."

This glowing pro-nuclear promise—note the word "clean" in each of the two sentences—plays on some acute public fears. The Persian Gulf crisis has once again highlighted the vulnerability of foreign oil supplies. A decade of grim warnings from scientists points to excessive fossil-fuel burning as a cause of global warming. The options seem painfully clear: Either we revamp our petroleum-based economy or we face ever-spiraling fuel prices and a bloody war in the Middle East.

Against that backdrop, the energy conglomerates have mounted an intense media campaign to persuade the public and policymakers of the need for nuclear power. With prompting from a former nuclear engineer, Presidential aide John Sununu, the Bush Administration is putting its weight behind nuclear power. And despite a popular belief that the nuclear industry entered a terminal tailspin after the 1979 Three Mile Island accident, nuclear power is poised for a major revival.

The device for making this happen is "nukespeak," the use of manipulative messages aimed at achieving public acceptance of nuclear power. Nukespeak involves a calculated distortion and suppression of facts about nuclear power, and corporate control over scientific research and public information.

Spearheading the propaganda effort is the U.S. Council for Energy Awareness (USCEA). The industry's seasoned media-relations arm, known until 1987 as the Atomic Industrial Forum, USCEA sees public acceptance as the key to a nuclear comeback.

"The primary obstacle is not the industry, which has an excellent track record, but public perception," says Scott Peters, USCEA's manager of media services. The Council has called on politicians, utility managers, business executives, and university scientists to "reexamine nuclear's environmental benefits"— and spread "the good news."

The nuclear-power industry is seizing on the Persian Gulf crisis and heightened concern about the environment. "Nothing creates a climate for nuclear better than a perception of need," says Carl Goldstein, vice president of USCEA. "If the public feels that it is needed, then they will overcome their qualms about it. With the [Gulf] crisis and concerns over global warming, the public is waking up to the benefits of nuclear. It is a clean energy form in most respects."

> **Nukespeak involves a calculated distortion and suppression of facts about nuclear power, and corporate control over scientific research and public information.**

As the publicists succeed in refining nukespeak, mainstream coverage of nuclear power tilts toward industry. Editors who buy USCEA's sales pitch routinely indulge in selective quoting, sensationalism, trivialization, or other kinds of misrepresentation of nuclear issues.

USCEA works constantly to determine which images and phrases incline public opinion toward nuclear power. According to the Council's official media brochure, *Mission, Methods, and Benefits,* the primary function of USCEA is to "marshal research, advertising, media, and public relations . . . to draw attention to the issue, generate positive editorial comment, broaden public support, and . . . provide a more favorable business climate at the Federal, state, and local levels now and in the future."

How do Americans feel about nuclear power? Polling data gathered by USCEA this year suggest that people want nuclear plants to be "safer," "new and improved," and to have "advanced" designs. People dislike such terms as "passively safe," "inherently safe," "user friendly," and "standardized designs."

The key stratagem of nukespeak is to turn reality on its head, to make irrational policy seem rational. Thus, energy conglomerates now promote nuclear power as among the cleanest energy sources available. The West's economic engine will be fueled by electric power, we are told, and a new generation of nuclear plants is our only hope of doing this without dirtying the skies. Solar and wind power, nuclear's primary eco-competitors, are branded by nuclear supporters as pie-in-the-sky solutions.

As the publicists succeed in refining nukespeak, mainstream coverage of nuclear power tilts toward industry. Editors who buy USCEA's sales pitch routinely indulge in selective quoting, sensationalism, trivialization, or other kinds of misrepresentation of nuclear issues.

One of the more egregious examples is an article called, "Must We Have Nuclear Power?" by Frederick Seitz, a prominent physicist, in the August 1990 *Reader's Digest.* Seitz lavishes praise on nuclear power—the only way to achieve "cleaner air *and* economic growth." And he glosses over the problems of nuclear energy. For instance, he says of the nuclear-waste problem: "The spent fuel remains radioactive for years." Years? Try *hundreds of thousands* of years.

At USCEA, such terms as "atomic" and "power" are strictly avoided because they remind people of the Bomb and "old-generation" atomic reactors. Instead of energy efficiency, the propagandists speak only of conservation, a term most Americans associate with privation and discomfort. From every angle, the industry paints nuclear power as the bright hope of a high tech; growth-oriented future.

The drive to sell nuclear power, however, is not merely an exercise in linguistic subterfuge. Equally potent is the industry's recruitment of academic scientists whose credibility, in the public eye, far exceeds that of an explicitly corporate team of "experts." Whenever lawsuits or bad press pose a threat, the nuclear industry rolls out an esteemed Ph.D., invariably cited as an "independent" source, to offer opinions consistent with the industry's point of view. Not surprisingly, independent scientists whose positions oppose the industry's are either selectively quoted or never heard from. And when new studies about health risks come out, the industry twists the results to its own advantage.

Last September, for example, the National Cancer Institute released a major study of cancer deaths in 107 counties containing sixty-two nuclear facilities. The report acknowledged high rates of cancer in some counties and low rates in others, and concluded that nuclear power plants posed no significant hazard overall. But the report had serious flaws.

"The NCI study didn't look at other environmental sources of cancer, such as chemical plants, in control counties," says John Gofman, a physician and professor of medical physics at the University of California, Berkeley, and former associate director of the Lawrence Livermore Laboratory. "Since the study did not measure any releases from the facilities, there's no way to know which areas of excess cancer were due to excess radiation. It's exactly the wrong kind of study to do."

Also, "radioactive fallout could have been carried from the nuclear plants to nearby control counties, making them look relatively worse," Gofman notes.

"None of my colleagues take this kind of study very seriously," Gofman adds. "But I believe it will be used very, very opportunistically as proof that nuclear facilities don't hurt anyone."

In its own glossy version of the report, sent out to major news media, the USCEA stated that the conclusions were not surprising to the scientific community, "which believes health risks posed by nuclear energy plants are virtually nil."

The U.S. Government has systematically downplayed the hazards of nuclear power. As early as 1974, *The New York Times* exposed the Atomic Energy Commission's ten-year effort to suppress research findings on safety and health risks associated with nuclear energy. Since then, many critics have accused Federal officials of abusing the science of radiation and health.

This year, Jay Gould, formerly a Westinghouse employee and member of the Environmental Protection Agency's science advisory board, provided evidence that the Government was running a disinformation campaign in which EPA press releases were presented as scientific reports. EPA officials have not only misrepresented the risks, claims Gould, but have frequently falsified radiation measurements taken around nuclear power plants.

Fudging figures and reconstructing data are tantamount to criminal offenses among scientists. But a more intractable problem involves optimistic interpretations of data used to determine risk—a practice less likely to be detected and rebuked. Lack of clear information and consensus on radiation-related risks leads to confusion about human safety. Because risk estimates involving radiation exposure entail a wide range of statistical uncertainty, nuclear proponents tend to focus on the lowest part of the range, which is associated with the lowest risk.

Such optimism is clearly unrealistic and dangerous. "Altogether, the ranges of estimated hazards to public health from . . . nuclear power plants are so wide as to extend from negligible to substantial in comparison with other risks to the population," writes John Holdren in the September 1990 *Scientific American*. "The very size of the uncertainty is itself a significant liability."

Gofman concurs: "The fact that there's a wide range of uncertainty in current risk-estimates does not justify a retreat to wishful thinking." The 1990 report of the National Academy of Sciences committee on the biological effects of ionizing radiation used *animal* research to justify lowering risk estimates by two- to ten-fold for low-level radiation exposure, Gofman notes. But findings from at least nine well-designed studies on *human* populations indicate a five-to-thirty-fold increase in the risk from low-level exposures, which take their toll in a cumulative fashion.

The most extreme instance of unrealistic optimism among the "experts" is the view that *beneficial* health effects may result from low doses of ionizing radiation—a theory known as "hormesis." In a 1989 *Science* article, Leonard Sagan argued that low-dose radiation stimulates the DNA-repair and immune systems, thereby increasing resistance to disease. Gofman devoted an entire chapter of his 1990 book, *Radiation-Induced Cancer from Low-Dose Exposure*, to a careful review of each paper cited by Sagan and other hormesis proponents. Not one of the studies offered unequivocal support for the theory.

Despite the growing popularization of such theories in the mass media, the public's concern about radiation hazards continues to bedevil the nuclear industry. While acknowledging that high-level radiation exposure does pose a threat, the industry insists that low-level radiation is safe because there's a "threshold" of exposure below which no hazard exists. This is based, in part, on the idea that the body "repairs" such damage to its DNA. But such speculative concepts as "safe threshold" and "repair" are, in Gofman's view, "a misuse of science in the service of nuclear politics."

Since the 1970s, the industry has used the term "permissible" for those releases of radiation authorized by the Government and determined by cost/

Because risk estimates involving radiation exposure entail a wide range of statistical uncertainty, nuclear proponents tend to focus on the lowest part of the range, which is associated with the lowest risk.

The most extreme instance of unrealistic optimism among the "experts" is the view that *beneficial* health effects may result from low doses of ionizing radiation—a theory known as "hormesis."

benefit analysis to pose an "acceptable risk" to public health. "Safe threshold" is the underlying rationale for the Nuclear Regulatory Commission's recent move to declare some low-level radwastes "below regulatory concern"—a decision that would allow nuclear facilities to dump radioactive garbage at any municipal landfill or incinerator. Since the NRC has no plans to monitor radiation levels at these disposal sites, the chances for abuse are substantial. Deregulating portions of this waste as "below regulatory concern" will save the industry an estimated $1 billion in waste management costs over the next two decades.

The ultimate costs, however, would be borne by the public. The NRC's assumption of "acceptable risk" is one incidence of cancer for every 100,000 people. Thomas Cochran of the National Resources Defense Council told *The Bulletin of the Atomic Scientists* that, by NRC logic, "it is 'below regulatory concern' to randomly fire a bullet into a crowded Manhattan street on the basis that the individual risk to a person in New York City is less than one in several million."

Having developed a new generation of reactors, the industry hopes to persuade utilities to order new plants—something they haven't done in more than fifteen years. The industry's main strategy is to declare the reactors "inherently safe," based on a generic, modular design that would include "natural" control features.

Though the new breed of reactors seems headed for regulatory acceptance, some seasoned engineers remain skeptical.

"Frankly, I don't believe any of the new generation should be called inherently safe," says Greg Minor, an engineer who worked with General Electric for sixteen years before joining a nuclear consulting firm. "They may be safer in some respects, but it's misleading to say they're safe, period. You can't put enough design detail down in advance to known how well a plant is going to operate. There will be a period of learning by trial and error. Some of the new plants will be built without containment and prototypes; and the first one that goes awry in ways that aren't anticipated is going to erode public confidence immediately."

Depicting reactors as kinder and gentler is a first step toward making nuclear power seem cleaner and greener. Ever since last spring's Earth Day, when the USCEA produced flashy posters and brochures propounding a benign nuclear ecology, the green theme has become increasingly pivotal to the industry's propaganda campaign.

Consider the *Forbes* article of June 11, 1990, called "The Greenest Form of Power," by Fleming Meeks and James Drummond. On the cover, nuclear power is referred to as "the environmentalists' best friend." The article begins by saying that since the 1970s and 1980s, when "antinuclear groups . . . fed the media a steady diet of exaggerated horror stories . . . nuclear has proved that it can coexist peacefully with the environment." The authors have apparently concluded that all is well at Three Mile Island and Chernobyl—and always has been.

Judging by appearances, of course, nuclear power *is* cleaner than fossil fuels. No one has ever seen or smelled radioactivity. Unlike coal- and oil-fired plants, nuclear generators don't produce smoke or other emissions rich in carbon dioxide. A September 10, 1990, news release from USCEA stated, "Nuclear energy is the only major source of electricity—other than hydroelectric dams—that does not emit greenhouse gases or other pollutants." No emissions—that's what two top USCEA officials told us.

But nuclear power plants are by no means a "smokeless" antidote to air pollution. In the real world, such plants routinely produce several hundred varieties of fission products, some of which are gaseous—the kryptons and the xenons. These radioactive gases are released daily from nuclear plants at "permissible" (NRC-sanctioned) levels. When USCEA says "no emissions," it really means "no greenhouse gases," or no emissions worth mentioning.

The nuclear industry has rightly pegged coal as a major source of sooty smoke, smog, greenhouse gases, and acid rain, all of which are absent from nuclear energy production. But then comes the more devious claim: "A coal-fired electric plant spews more radioactive pollution into the air than a nuclear plant," as *Reader's Digest* put it last August.

It's true that coal contains uranium and that coal-fired plants create radioactive emissions. But when one considers the total nuclear fuel cycle, much greater quantities of radon and other radioactive gases are emitted in the mining and milling of uranium, before the fuel even reaches a nuclear reactor. "Figuring in this initial step, the amount of airborne radioactive pollution produced in the overall operation of any one nuclear plant far exceeds that which a coal-fired plant produces," says Gofman.

Accidental radioactive releases further undermine the industry's bold green message. The Nuclear Regulatory Commission documented more than 30,000 "mishaps' at nuclear plants in the United States between 1979 and 1987. By the NRC's own estimates, the chance of "a severe core meltdown" occurring at one of the 112 licensed U.S. nuclear plants in the next fifteen years runs as high as 45 per cent. The global scenario is even more disturbing: West German and Swedish scientists predict a 70 per cent chance of a Chernobyl-scale accident occurring at one of the world's nuclear plants over the next five or six years.

Many U.S. officials say that nothing like Chernobyl exists in the United States. But the Chernobyl explosion produced radioactive clouds that sent fallout as far as Japan and the United States, and Gofman calculates that almost half a million cancer deaths and just as many nonfatal cancers may eventually result from Chernobyl's fallout in Europe and the Soviet Union alone.

And the difficulty of getting rid of radioactive waste renders all talk of "clean" nuclear power irrelevant. No safe method of containing high-level waste has been found, and any attempt to curb global warming with more nuclear power would mean a corresponding increase in such radwaste.

"If 400 nuclear power plant were built (possibly enough to make some impact on global warming)," notes Scott Denman of the Washington-based Safe Energy Communications Council (SECC), "approximately five radwaste dumps the size of the proposed Yucca Mountain (Nevada) site would have to be built—an extremely difficult technical problem and a near political impossibility."

Some nuclear advocates contend that climate changes could ultimately claim far more human casualties and cause far greater environmental damage than any nuclear accident. But posing these stark alternatives assumes that no benign solution exists.

"It only makes sense to choose an energy source that doesn't have a harmful end-product," says Gofman. "We're talking about an absurd trade-off. Compared to fossil fuels, nuclear power produces far more *lethal* pollution and is already moving toward sacrificing a safe food chain for millennia."

When nuclear power supporters apply green rhetoric to battling the greenhouse effect, they ignore the fact that the automobile is the principal source of greenhouse gases. According to SECC, substituting nuclear plants for all existing power facilities would reduce greenhouse gases by only about 5 per cent. Some estimates suggest that curbing worldwide emissions of carbon dioxide even marginally would require building one new power plant every two days for the next thirty-eight years. And at that rate, the energy required for the complete process—mining and processing uranium, constructing facilities,

Depicting reactors as kinder and gentler is a first step toward making nuclear power seem cleaner and greener. Ever since last spring's Earth Day, when the USCEA produced flashy posters and brochures propounding a benign nuclear ecology, the green theme has become increasingly pivotal to the industry's propaganda campaign.

By the NRC's own estimates, the chance of "a severe core meltdown" occurring at one of the 112 licensed U.S. nuclear plants in the next fifteen years runs as high as 45 per cent. The global scenario is even more disturbing: West German and Swedish scientists predict a 70 per cent chance of a Chernobyl-scale accident occurring at one of the world's nuclear plants over the next five or six years.

enriching fuel, and disposing of radwastes—would conceivably result in an increase rather than a decrease in climatic devastation.

Asked whether nuclear power would have any role in fueling automobiles, USCEA's Scott Peters says blithely, "I wouldn't rule it out. There may come a day when we're all driving around in electric cars that get recharged at nuclear power plants."

But that day will be a long way off. Long lead times for reactor construction definitively bar nuclear power from any environmental scenario. Many climatologists say we may have only ten years before the greenhouse effect runs irretrievably out of control. But the construction of nuclear plants in the United States requires at least twelve years, and the "new generation" of nuclear plants is barely onto blueprints—as much a pie-in-the-sky concept as nuclear proponents assign to solar energy.

As Alan Miller and Irving Mintzer wrote in the June 1990 *Bulletin of the Atomic Scientists,* "Nuclear power would not reduce the risks of global warming for many years. And in the meantime, it could make the problem worse."

Economist Amory Lovins of the Rocky Mountain Institute agrees but emphasizes cost-competitiveness in the energy marketplace.

"You have to look at all the ways to get electricity and pick the cheapest," Lovins says. "You can define 'cheapest' in narrow economic terms or add in uncounted environmental costs. Either way, the cheapest way is to use the electricity we already have far more efficiently.

"When you buy efficiency, a dollar's worth saves a great deal of electricity and thus displaces a lot of coal-burning. If you spent a dollar on a nuclear plant instead, you wouldn't buy many kilowatt hours per dollar, so you wouldn't displace much coal-burning for the investment. By spending your dollar on the expensive option instead of the cheap option, you get extra greenhouse emissions that wouldn't have been created if the best buy had been chosen first. That's why nuclear power actually makes global warming worse."

Nuclear power is, in fact, the most capital-intensive of all energy sources. Several studies show that energy efficiency is cheaper by a factor of seven to ten than operating a typical nuclear plant, *even if the plant is built free.* West Germany and Japan, with two of the world's strongest economies, are running at twice the energy efficiency of the United States; they use half the energy to produce the same unit of gross national product.

Though centralized hard-tech energy options have dominated the media, a 1989 poll indicated that almost 80 per cent of American voters ranked funding of renewable sources—solar and wind power—as top budget priorities for the Department of Energy, and preferred by a margin of three-to-one using electricity more efficiently rather than building new power plants.

Recent administrations, however, have taken the opposite route. Ronald Reagan slashed R&D for energy efficiency by 70 per cent, and for renewable energy sources by 85 per cent. The Bush Administration has done little to redress the imbalance and continues to subsidize nuclear power above all other energy sources.

But as oil supplies dwindle and become more costly, the economy and the political system face difficult decisions regarding sustainable energy use. Fortunately, nuclear power is not the only available alternative. When it comes to cleaner and greener energy technologies, efficiency and renewable sources represent the sane energy path—if we can compel our leaders to follow it. (pp. 18–21)

Nathaniel Mead and Ray Lee, "Nukespeak," *in* The Progressive, *Vol. 54, No. 12, December, 1990, pp. 18–21.*

Nuclear Power and the Environment

The difference in the levels of energy consumption between the states with the highest living standards and those with the lowest is staggering. The electricity consumption of Norway is about 23,000 kWh per capita and year, while that of Bangladesh is 50 kWh per capita and year.

I am not going to suggest to you that nuclear power is the solution to the environmental damages and threats which our excessive and careless use of fossil fuels have led to: acid rains, dying lakes and forests and global warming. It is a fact, however, that nuclear power reactors emit no sulphur dioxide (SO_2), no nitrogen oxides (NO_x) and no carbon dioxide (CO_2) and that the wastes which they do give rise to are minuscule in volume compared to the wastes of the fossil fuels and can be isolated almost in their entirety from the biosphere. My aim is more modestly to show that a continued and expanded use of nuclear power must be one among several measures, all of which must be relied on to restrain our use of fossil fuels and thereby to limit the emissions which their burning gives rise to, including those of carbon dioxide.

Energy is the lifeblood of our societies. An enormous increase in the use of hydropower, coal, oil and gas has helped to raise the standards of living in many countries to unprecedented levels. The difference in the levels of energy consumption between the states with the highest living standards and those with the lowest is staggering. The electricity consumption of Norway is about 23,000 kWh per capita and year, while that of Bangladesh is 50 kWh per capita and year. Still, when we are now examining the environmental consequences of the accelerated use of energy by the rich countries with increasing alarm, we must note, sadly, that low per capita energy use has by no means protected developing countries from severe environmental damage. Rapid population growth has led to an ever growing total use of firewood, and to deforestation and desertification. More and more people have to seek their fuel from an ever less plentiful supply. Thus, when we focus on the environmental threats caused by the rich countries' consumption of energy, we must remember that there is another environmental crisis caused by energy use in many parts of the underdeveloped world.

The significant risks posed to future generations by the wastes arising from the civilian nuclear power industry have been the subject of much discussion. It is to be welcomed that attention is now devoted also to the very real and imminent dangers which are posed in particular to the global climate by the burning of fossil fuels at present levels. Are we creating a greenhouse for ourselves, our children and grandchildren? If so, what can we do to avoid it? A conference of twenty-four heads of State and government at the Hague last spring went so far as to call for the creation of a new international authority with power, if need be, to decide on measures even if these were not unanimously supported. In the United Nations General Assembly last autumn, the Soviet Foreign Minister called for a United Nations Council capable of taking effective decisions to ensure ecological security. The United Nations Environment Programme and the World Meteorological Organization have offered a forum for examination of the issue of climate change and recent statements have called for an international convention to combat climate change. The Government of the United Kingdom is among those that address the issue most actively.

The proposals we have seen are evidence of the concern that exists at the highest levels in our various governments. They are welcome as far as they go. However, an international convention must embody some agreement on effective action and an international authority, whatever competence is given to it, must be able to take decisions which result in effective action. What measures can be taken to counter global warming?

Let us note with satisfaction that one of the actions needed is already being taken. Under agreements that have recently been reached the chlorofluorocarbons (CFCs) which have been identified as responsible both for destructive

We cannot plan substantial reductions in the use of coal, oil or gas on the basis of dreams. We need to escape from the greenhouse, yes, but we need also to escape from the dreamhouse!

effects on the world's ozone layer and for about 20% of the greenhouse effect, are likely to be largely phased out in the next decade.

It is when we look beyond this measure that we see, so far, relatively little basis for common action. The methane emissions that are judged to account for another 20% of the greenhouse effect cannot be easily limited, as they are mainly linked to rice cultivation and cattle rearing. With a continued increase in the world population, neither of these activities is likely to stagnate. Methane also gets into the atmosphere as a result of leakage of natural gas. A gradual switch from the use of coal to the use of gas, sometimes advocated because it would result in less CO_2 for the same quantity of energy generated, is thus in practice advantageous in terms of greenhouse response only if leakages of methane can be kept very low—less than one to two percent of the quantity of gas used.

Attention is naturally concentrated on the emissions of carbon dioxide (CO_2). About 50% of the greenhouse effect is attributed to the increasing carbon dioxide levels in the atmosphere. A smaller part of these emissions are the result of deforestation. Forceful programmes for reforestation and a halt to deforestation are desirable measures. We should remember, however, that such programmes may not be easy to implement in poverty stricken countries with rapid population growth. There remains the major emissions for which the industrialized countries carry the greatest responsibility, namely the emission of CO_2 through the burning of fossil fuels, *e.g.*, for heating, transportation and electricity generation. These emissions cannot be prevented by technical means, as can be done with emissions of SO_2 and NO_x, which have been linked to acid rain and dying forests. CO_2 emissions can only be reduced by limiting the burning of coal, oil and gas.

More scientific research is needed to clarify what level of global CO_2 emissions might be tolerable. There seems to be a widely held scientific view, however, that present levels are too high. We may take note of the conclusions of the Conference on the Changing Atmosphere that was held in Toronto last year to the effect that a 20% reduction in present CO_2 levels by the year 2005 should be set as a goal. Others have proposed more severe limitations. Since present CO_2 emissions from the burning of fossil fuels are around 20,000 million tons per year, the reduction under the Toronto proposal would have to be around 4,000 million tons. It is when we raise the question of how a reduction of this magnitude is to be achieved that the answers become unconvincing and certainly not yet adequate as a basis for a convention or an international decision to protect the world's climate.

For more than a decade, most environmentalists have been advocating two main responses to the environmental threats from energy use, whether acid rains, dying forests or the arrival of the greenhouse, and these are energy conservation and an expanded use of renewable energy sources, in particular solar power, wind power and biomass.

At the time when I participated in the Swedish public debate before the referendum on nuclear power in 1980, the opponents proposed an immediate halt to the construction of further nuclear plants and a closure of operating plants by 1990. They denied that any increased fossil fuel use would be required and argued that energy conservation, solar and wind power and biomass could be used instead. Today Sweden uses 35% more electricity than in 1980. About 45% of the total electricity generation comes from nuclear power, and about 50% from hydro power. Solar and wind power provide 0.004%. Biomass in the form of wood chippings and other waste products is used by industry, but mainly for heating purposes. A victory for the anti-nuclear option in 1980 would have been an unmitigated environmental and economic disaster for Sweden.

When we are now faced with the contentions that conservation, solar power, wind power, biomass use and various other energy sources are adequate to enable us both to reduce the burning of fossil fuels and to do away with nuclear power, let us have a full-scale public discussion of these options to determine their real value—and to discard their illusory value. We cannot plan substantial reductions in the use of coal, oil or gas on the basis of dreams. We need to escape from the greenhouse, yes, but we need also to escape from the dreamhouse! Let us respect those who withdraw to the countryside to cultivate biodynamic carrots and get their electricity from a windmill. But don't let us believe that they have the recipes for the rest of us. (pp. 198–99)

Now let me turn to nuclear power. It is recognized that nuclear power plants are capable of producing very large amounts of electric energy without adding CO_2 or SO_2 and NO_x to the atmosphere. Yet, a number of arguments are now mobilized to try to convince the world that nuclear power is totally irrelevant to our needs to generate energy without generating CO_2. Let me discuss some of these arguments.

We hear, for instance, that electricity now only accounts for 29% of the total energy consumption and that fossil-fired power plants today contribute only some 12–15% to the greenhouse effect. It is implied that it is not worthwhile doing anything in this sector, except saving electric energy.

I submit that this is an uncaring attitude. I shall not claim that a continued and expanded use of nuclear power is a panacea for the problem of CO_2 emissions, but I shall try to show that it can make a contribution that, along with others, is most helpful to contain those emissions. Let me point out in the first place that if the electric energy that was generated from nuclear power last year had instead been produced by coal-fired power plants, this would have given rise to additional emissions of about 1600 million tons of CO_2. This figure is not small when you compare it with the 4000 million tons which the Toronto Conference recommended as a target for reductions. Let me point out, in the second place, that electricity is a constantly growing part of energy consumption and that it is helpful in efficiently substituting for the direct use of fossil fuels. Even extreme low energy scenarios assume that we will use about twice as much electricity in the world around 2020 as we use now. That would require an addition of a 1000 MW(e) plant every 4.4 days on the average (2500 GW(e)). There would further be a need for replacements for old and obsolete plants—both nuclear and fossil-fuelled. It is not without interest from the viewpoint of CO_2 emissions whether these new plants and replacement plants will be fuelled by coal, gas, uranium or hydro where available. If all the additional electricity that is assumed in the low energy scenario to be needed by 2020 were to be generated by coal, there would be an annual added emission of some 16,500 million tons of CO_2. If, instead all of this new electricity were to be by nuclear power or hydropower, there would be further CO_2 emissions. Such extreme scenarios are not realistic, of course. Both among additional plants and replacement plants there will be a mix of coal, nuclear, gas and hydro. The figures help to clarify, however, that it is of considerable importance how this mix is made. The more fossil, the more CO_2, the more nuclear and hydro, the less CO_2. A current standard objection to nuclear power's relevance for CO_2 abatement is that it would require a new nuclear power plant to be put into operation every 2.5 days over 35 years to replace coal-fired plants. Such a perspective is evidently meant to deter everybody from devoting a further thought to the possible relevance of nuclear power. As I said a moment ago, however, there will be a mix and it matters how it is constituted. Let me also remind you that in each of the years 1984 and 1985, 33 new nuclear power plants actually came into operation, or one new plant every 11 days on the average. There exists a capacity to build many more nuclear plants than we do today.

A further objection to future increased reliance on nuclear power is that the world's uranium resources should be too limited to permit nuclear power to be anything but a short parenthesis. The reality is that already known low-cost uranium resources are sufficient to sustain a much larger nuclear power sector than we now have. If we include the resources which geologists consider likely to exist, we might well fuel ten times more reactors than we now have over their whole lifetimes, even with the present type of reactors and without plutonium recycling.

> **Even extreme low energy scenarios assume that we will use about twice as much electricity in the world around 2020 as we use now.**

The reality which is becoming increasingly recognized by all who do not choose to close their eyes is that a continued and expanded use of nuclear power will be an indispensable contribution to the efforts to restrain CO_2 emissions.

A perennial argument is that nuclear power plants are unacceptable expensive. There are indeed cases of plants which have become very expensive. The nuclear industry is not the only one in which this happens. Moreover, the statement conveniently overlooks the highly successful and economic nuclear programmes in, for example, Canada, Belgium, France, Japan, Sweden and Switzerland. There have also been studies of the economics of nuclear power by the Nuclear Energy Agency of the OECD in Paris, in cooperation with Union of Producers and Distributors of Electricity (UNIPEDE) and IAEA. The results show that nuclear power remains competitive in most OECD countries. Nuclear plants generally cannot compete economically with coal-fired plants built near coal-mines.

My conclusion is that the arguments which have been advanced against the use of nuclear power in the face of the CO_2 problem and which I have cited are all thin and contrived. The reality which is becoming increasingly recognized by all who do not choose to close their eyes is that a continued and expanded use of nuclear power will be an indispensable contribution to the efforts to restrain CO_2 emissions.

The real objections to nuclear power—present or expanded—are not new. They relate to safety, waste disposal and the risk of proliferation of nuclear weapons. Let me deal with them in the reverse order.

The proliferation risk exists whether we have a nuclear power industry that is of today's size or larger, or none. Even a worldwide closing of nuclear power stations would not eliminate the risk and probably not significantly reduce it. Let me remind you that all nuclear-weapon States had their weapons first and power reactors second. Further disarmament, on the other hand, may well promote a fuller commitment to non-proliferation, verified by the IAEA. It should also be remembered that the current nuclear power use, apart from relieving the world of huge quantities of CO_2, reduces the pressures on oil resources. It would take the peak oil production of Saudi Arabia of 1974 to generate the electricity we obtain from nuclear power today (about 400 Mtoe). This effect is not insignificant in a world where competition for oil resources is a major security issue—like the risk of proliferation.

Let me now turn to the question of wastes. All fuel cycles give rise to wastes, for instance, tailings from uranium mining, slag heaps from coal mining, leakage of methane gas, oil spills in the ocean, ashes, etc.

In the nuclear fuel cycle, the amounts of highly radioactive wastes are small. To be a bit provocative, one might say that the wastes are one of the great assets of nuclear power compared to other energy sources. The limited quantities make it possible for us to manage safely and dispose of practically all the waste that arises, and certainly all that is hazardous, in a controlled manner. The operation of all nuclear power plants in the world last year gave rise to some 7000 tons of spent fuel. If the electricity generated by that fuel had been generated by the combustion of oil, it would have resulted—as I have already mentioned—in the emission of 1600 million tons of CO_2 and tens of millions of tons of SO_2 and NO_x, even with the best flue gas cleaning equipment available. In addition, there would have been some 100,000 tons of poisonous heavy metals, including arsenic, cadmium, chromium, copper, lead and vanadium. These, of course, remain poisonous forever, and are not isolated from the biosphere.

It is often argued by opponents of nuclear power that we do not know how to isolate the nuclear waste safely. That is not correct. Detailed designs for packaging the wastes, whether in the vitrified form after reprocessing, or as compacted spent fuel assemblies, have been worked out and have been approved by safety authorities. When most countries have decided to store such spent fuel for some 30 to 50 years before either disposing of it as waste or reprocessing it, it is for the reason that allowing the radioactivity to decay simplifies the design of both the waste container and the storage and makes it easier to achieve the safe isolation which is required for a very long time period.

It is sometimes suggested that our generation is reaping the benefits of nuclear power, while leaving the financial cost of waste disposal to succeeding generations. However, in several countries there is a legal requirement to add to the price of the nuclear kWh a charge covering the future costs of the management and disposal of the radioactive wastes, and also of future decommissioning of the plants. Here in the UK, the kWh cost includes a charge for these purposes. These costs are not overwhelming. In Sweden, the addition to the kWH price is two hundredths of a Swedish Crown per kWh, or about 10% of the total price. The estimates of the costs are not very different in other countries.

Let me end my comments on nuclear waste by saying that if other industries had as good methods for waste management and disposal as the nuclear power industry does, the world would have far fewer environmental problems.

The concern mostly voiced about nuclear power relates to safety. In the Chernobyl accident large amounts of radioactive substances were released. Some 200–300 persons—operational and firefighting staff—received high doses and suffered radiation sickness. Twenty-nine of them died of their radiation injuries, but most of the others are back in productive work after hospital treatment. Over 100,000 persons have been evacuated from their homes and have been settled in other areas. In the restricted zone that was established within a radius of 30 km around the power plant, comprehensive decontamination has been carried out. Some people have moved back, but no general return has been authorized.

Chernobyl was a grave and extremely costly industrial accident by any standard but it was certainly not unique in the number of deaths or injuries. Other ways of generating energy also take their tolls. The oil platform that exploded last year in the North Sea took 165 lives. An explosion in a coal mine in the Federal Republic of Germany, likewise in 1988, killed 57 miners. A gas explosion in Mexico City in 1984 left some 450 dead and thousands of people injured. A dam that burst in India in 1979 killed 15,000 people. And last month, an explosion caused by a leak from a gas pipeline destroyed two trains in the Soviet Union and caused more than 600 deaths.

Yes, people will say, but what about the cancer cases that may be caused by the radioactive fall-out? We shall probably never know how many additional cases there may be, if any, as a result of the fall-out from Chernobyl, because the number of cancer cases from other causes in the same population is so high that a small addition will hardly be discernible. Even for the most exposed population in White Russia, the average additional dose of radioactivity caused by Chernobyl was less than one year's natural dose. These low average values must not, of course, conceal the fact that a number of people in the vicinity of Chernobyl received much higher doses.

Although the Chernobyl reactor was very different from most power reactors operating in the world, and this kind of release is implausible in reactors which, like the Three Mile Island reactor, have containments designed to stop release into the environment, no one contends that there are no risks in using nuclear power. However, these risks should be compared to the risks and damage connected with the main alternative way of generating the electricity, namely through the use of fossil fuels.

We should, of course, compare the whole fuel cycles. The health and environmental consequences of the mining of uranium must be compared with those of the mining of coal and the extraction of gas and oil; one should also compare the transportation of each, the fission of the uranium with the burning of fossil fuels and the emissions from the burning of these fuels with the disposal of nuclear waste. One should compare the number of casualties and health injuries and the amount of environmental damage per quantity of electricity generated. Such examinations are, in fact, underway and from what we have seen so far, they point to a positive picture for nuclear power.

Whether such rational comparisons will help to overcome anxiety about nuclear power is less certain. We have not accepted and tucked away the risks of nuclear power in our minds as we have done with, say, the risks of coal mine accidents. Perhaps the ambition need not be to eliminate all anxiety. After all,

It is often argued by opponents of nuclear power that we do not know how to isolate the nuclear waste safely. That is not correct. Detailed designs for packaging the wastes, whether in vitrified form after reprocessing, or as compacted spent fuel assemblies, have been worked out and have been approved by safety authorities.

Today nuclear [power] accounts for just 20% of electricity in the U.S. Compare this to Sweden, where the figure is 47%, and Belgium, where it is 65%. In France, 74% of electricity is generated in nuclear plants, up from under 4% in 1970.

lots of people rationally accept flying despite feelings of anxiety. We certainly need to de-mystify nuclear power—but this may take time. Meanwhile, perhaps, we should be content merely to get broad acceptance of the use of nuclear power. The anxiety which continues to exist should continue to spur all those who are connected with nuclear power to reduce even further the risks of significant accidents. There must be an increased awareness, however, that if broad acceptance is not achieved for nuclear power, we shall have to face the risks that are connected with the alternatives—including their environmental consequences.

Let me conclude: Nuclear power can help significantly to meet growing needs of electricity without contributing to global warming, acid rains or dying forests.

A responsible management and disposal of nuclear wastes is entirely feasible.

The safety of nuclear power, like the safety of any other industrial activity, must be continuously strengthened through technological improvements and methods of operation.

There is a dire need for more factual information to narrow the gap between the real and the perceived risks of nuclear power and to demonstrate the risks of the alternatives. (pp. 201–03)

Hans Blix, "Nuclear Power and the Environment," in Environmental Policy and Law, *Vol. 19, No. 6, December, 1989, pp. 198–203.*

The Nuclear Renaissance: Environmentalists Take Another Look at Nuclear Power

In the fight against nuclear power during the 1970s and 1980s, the U.S. antinuclear groups won. They picketed, they lobbied, they fed the media a steady diet of exaggerated horror stories. They so tied up nuclear plants in the courts and in the regulatory agencies that delays lengthened and costs piled higher and higher. Then the antinukes blamed the nuclear plant owners for their cost overruns. They effectively killed nuclear power as an alternative energy source in the U.S.

Over 100 nuclear plants have been canceled since the mid-1970s. Public Service Co. of New Hampshire was forced into bankruptcy after antinukers delayed operation of its Seabrook plant, upping the plant's cost by $2 billion. (Seabrook, issued a construction permit in 1976, was completed in 1986 but did not receive a full power license until earlier this year [1990].) And Long Island's Shoreham plant has been mothballed at a cost of $5.5 billion, nearly half of which will be paid by the area's ratepayers for many years to come. All this while, from the San Onofre nuclear plant in southern California to the Indian Point facility in New York, nuclear has proved that it can coexist peacefully with the environment.

Today nuclear accounts for just 20% of electricity in the U.S. Compare this to Sweden, where the figure is 47%, and Belgium, where it is 65%. In France, 74% of electricity is generated in nuclear plants, up from under 4% in 1970.

Not that the nuclear industry didn't make its share of mistakes. The industry oversold the public on the simplicity of nuclear technology, and embarked on projects without sufficient in-house expertise to monitor them. They refused to standardize reactor designs. When public relations problems multiplied, the industry did a horrendous job of handling them.

Meanwhile, U.S. oil imports to feed conventional power plants climbed higher and higher.

But as the greens, flush from their nuclear victory, move on to new scares—global warming, acid rain, the ozone hole, the whales and dolphins—their old antinuclear rhetoric sounds discordant.

Some of the groups are beginning to concede as much. Testifying before Congress last month, Jan Beyea, National Audubon Society staff scientist, recommended government funding for a new generation of nuclear reactors. Why? "As a sort of global warming insurance policy, in case the transition to renewable energy systems fails to materialize."

There are other signs that, without fanfare, nuclear is in the early stages of a comeback. Nuclear reactor vendors are once again making sales calls on the electric utilities. The U.S. Nuclear Regulatory Commission recently streamlined the licensing process for new plants. Smelling opportunity, the Europeans, their own nuclear markets near saturation, are buying up American reactor makers.

Environmentalists who object to a nuclear renaissance find themselves in a difficult position. If they argue too loudly that economic growth is bad—that everyone must give up cars and disposable diapers and go back to riding bicycles and manning (or womaning) scrub boards—they will antagonize a public that is sympathetic to their calls for clean air and pure water. But if they support fossil-fuel-fired economic growth, they must accept the likelihood of more oil spills, more acid rain, more disruption of such sacrosanct, oil-laden places as the Santa Barbara Channel and Alaska's Arctic National Wildlife Refuge.

Unless the greens are prepared to argue for fewer jobs and a lower standard of living, and thus lose support, they will have to accept some kind of power generation. Solar power and wind power and the like are pie-in-the-sky. Clean, safe nuclear power is a reality. Listen to liberal Senator Timothy Wirth (D-Colo.), who has become increasingly pronuclear in recent years: "We have an obligation to try to look toward the future. One of those future technologies is solar, one is conservation and one is nuclear."

The U.S. is facing a power crunch in the 1990s. Already the power shortages are beginning to crop up. When the big freeze hit Florida last winter, utilities had to resort to rolling black-outs—cutting power to particular neighborhoods intermittently for up to two hours. During the sweltering summer of 1988, residents of New England experienced brownouts. And projections show demand for electricity continuing to grow faster than capacity—over twice as fast in New England over the next decade, and nearly twice as fast in Florida.

Even factoring in plants on the drawing board that, if built, will produce 168,000 megawatts by the year 2010, the U.S. will need another 186,000 megawatts of electrical capacity. Filling the gap will require new generating capacity equivalent to a quarter of the current generating capacity in the U.S.—or almost 200 large coal or nuclear plants. This conservative estimate comes from the U.S. Energy Information Administration, an independent forecasting unit within the Department of Energy.

Will they be coal plants? Fifty-six percent of the country's electricity now comes from plants fired by coal, of which plentiful reserves still exist. But it's hard to be for coal and against acid rain. Each 1,000-megawatt coal plant annually spews out 70,000 tons of sulfur oxides—the chief culprit in acid rain.

What of oil- and gas-fired generators? The more oil is shipped, the more Valdez-type oil spills are possible. Moreover, the U.S. is already setting up the world for another round of OPEC-led financial instability: Oil imports are today near their 1977 high of 46.5%. And while natural gas is inexpensive right now, few experts believe it will remain so.

> **Environmentalists who object to a nuclear renaissance find themselves in a difficult position. If they argue too loudly that economic growth is bad . . . they will antagonize a public that is sympathetic to their calls for clean air and pure water. But if they support fossil-fuel-fired economic growth, they must accept the likelihood of more oil spills, more acid rain, more disruption of such sacrosanct, oil-laden places as the Santa Barbara Channel and Alaska's Arctic National Wildlife Refuge.**

Energy conservation programs have reduced peak U.S. power requirements by 21,000 megawatts, or 3% of total current capacity. That helps, but it is only a beginning.

Solar farms? Windmills? After 20 years of costly experiment, these together contribute 1% of total U.S. electric production.

Energy conservation programs have reduced peak U.S. power requirements by 21,000 megawatts, or 3% of total current capacity. That helps, but it is only a beginning.

Quietly, nuclear is already taking the first steps toward a comeback. One important such step is the Nuclear Regulatory Commission's streamlined licensing procedures for new nuclear facilities. Unlike big nuclear users like Sweden and France, the U.S. has required a two-step licensing process before a nuclear plant can go on-line. This regulatory system has proved an effective weapon in the hands of the antinuclear forces. Under it, utilities must face months of public hearings to get a construction permit, then run the gauntlet again when the plant is finished many years later. The two-step licensing process dramatically increases the chances of costly delays because of the public hearings and last-minute changes in design standards. As a result, in this country it can take 12 years to complete and operate a plant that the French can have up and running in 6.

The simplified procedure, issued by the NRC a year ago, provides for approval of the complete design at the beginning of the process. Under the new rules, which antinuclear groups are now fiercely fighting, the owner of the new reactor would automatically be allowed to fire up the plant on completion, as long as it meets the agreed-upon design standards.

This licensing change is particularly meaningful in light of a new generation of modular 600-megawatt nuclear plants, now on the drawing boards at Westinghouse and General Electric. In theory, once these standardized designs are completed and licensed—perhaps five years down the road—a utility or independent power producer could get site approval in advance and, in effect, buy the generic plans off the shelf, license and all.

Moreover, since the design would be generic, the cost of building nuclear plants could be substantially reduced.

Westinghouse projects the cost of its new modular plant at $1,370 per kilowatt-hour, or about $825 million (not including interest costs) for a 600-megawatt plant. That cost is in line with the cost of comparable coal-fired plants now. But the Clean Air Act [of 1991 has significantly increased] . . . emissions standards for coal-fired plants. That will increase their cost and make the new generation of nuclear plants more competitive.

Why would these plants come in so much cheaper than their predecessors, which cost as much as $2,500 per kilowatt (again excluding interest costs) to build? Unlike in the past, each new reactor would not have to reinvent the nuclear wheel, and many of the new reactors' components could be assembled in factories, where inspection and quality control are easy to maintain, rather than on the plant sites themselves.

Jerome Goldberg is head of nuclear operations at Florida Power & Light, which currently generates 30% of its energy in four nuclear plants. In the past six months, he says, Westinghouse and Combustion Engineering have made several presentations on the new reactors to his engineers and managers. Goldberg says FP&L's immediate plans call for building six new gas-fired generators to ease Florida's power crunch. Just the same, he's listening carefully to what the nuclear vendors are telling him.

''Eventually, there will be the recognition that shutting out the nuclear option was not a good idea,'' he says.

Here's a telling indication of how interest in nuclear is building again: In its 19-year history, Greenpeace, the radical activist environmental group, never bothered to take a position on nuclear power. Greenpeace leaders say they thought the battles had already been fought and won.

But now that reports of nuclear's death appear to be exaggerated, Greenpeace is mounting its own anti-nuclear campaign. Says Eric Fersht, who heads the campaign: "We see a lot of signs that things are at work that need to be responded to in a big way." Judging by past Greenpeace campaigns, its anti-nuclear campaign will be both emotional and confrontational. Nevertheless, sparing dolphins is one thing; turning down the air conditioner on a sweltering day is something else again.

Sensing that the U.S. is becoming a potentially lucrative market for nuclear plants, in January, Asea Brown Boveri, a $25 billion (sales) Zurich-based power and environmental engineering firm, paid $1.6 billion to acquire Combustion Engineering, the nuclear plant maker that built 16 U.S. plants. And in September of last year, Framatome Group, the big French nuclear plant construction firm, paid $50 million for a 50% interest in Babcock & Wilcox Co.'s nuclear services division. Framatome is working in partnership with the German giant Siemens to develop new reactors in the U.S.

Says Nuclear Regulatory Commission Chairman Kenneth Carr, "The foreigners recognize that the market today is in the U.S., and they're focusing on this tremendously."

Among domestic reactor makers, GE and Westinghouse have designs in the works aimed at making reactors that are even safer than today's reactors, in theory as well as in practice. The new GE and Westinghouse reactors are known as advanced passive light-water reactors. They are designed around an almost fail-safe technology, which uses gravity and natural convection to cool the reactor's core if it begins to overheat. The idea is to leave as little room for human error as possible; it was human error that led to the partial meltdown at Three Mile Island.

Meanwhile, the industry has focused on training programs to keep the skills of operators at current plants well honed. At Three Mile Island, for instance, operators spend one week in six in training. What's more, there are currently 73 elaborate control room simulators in use around the country (up from just a handful before the accident at 1979 Three Mile Island). These simulators, built specifically for individual plants, can run operators through dozens of emergency situations from a loss of coolant to loss of power within the plant itself.

With the new passive light-water reactors, if the core begins to overheat, valves automatically open, flooding the core with massive amounts of water stored in tanks above the reactor. This automatic process is designed to protect the reactor from damage for three days before human intervention is necessary.

On another front, a new generation of gas-cooled reactors—preferred by the Audubon Society's Beyea and most other environmentalists who are willing to consider nuclear—is under development. Lawrence Lidsky, professor of nuclear engineering at MIT, notes that in theory, these gas-cooled reactors are so fail-safe that a plant could withstand the simultaneous failure of the reactor's control rods, as well as a complete failure of the cooling systems. Gas-cooled reactors are probably ten years away from commercial use, but they are on the way.

If new nuclear plants are to be built in this country, how will they be financed? Robert Newman, vice president of nuclear operations at ABB Combustion Engineering, envisions the following scenario: A consortium including the reactor maker, the architect/engineering firm, and one or more utilities would all kick in equity for some of the new plant's funding, and turn to the debt markets for the balance. Westinghouse, too, says it would be willing to take an equity stake in future nuclear plants.

Obstacles to nuclear power remain—and they are formidable. While the Nuclear Regulatory Commission has simplified the federal regulatory process, state utility commissions must also sign off on new nuclear projects. Key to getting the new plants built will be the cooperation of state utility commissions in setting up cost parameters, in advance, and guaranteeing utilities that they will be able to recover costs, so long as they stay within those parameters.

"The foreigners recognize that the market today is in the U.S., and they're focusing on this tremendously."

—Kenneth Carr,
Chairman, Nuclear
Regulatory Commission

High-level waste in any of its forms continually generates high-energy ionizing radiation which is extremely destructive to living cells with which it may come in contact. The radiation can be absorbed and rendered harmless by a variety of materials, for example, the water and metal of the fuel-rod basins and the concrete and earth around the tanks holding the reprocessing waste. Thus the waste at present poses no threat to its surroundings but could do great harm if any appreciable quantity should escape.

Nuclear waste, too, remains a problem, though not an insurmountable one.

Severe as these problems are, the need for power is immense if we are to maintain our standard of living and improve it. It may take the balance of this century, but emotion on nuclear power will give way to economic and social necessities. Realities change; perceptions change more slowly.

Last year Three Mile Island, the would-be icon for everything that is wrong with the nuclear power industry, was ranked by respected international trade magazine *Nucleonics Week* as the most efficient nuclear power plant in the world. (pp. 116–20)

Fleming Meeks and James Drummond, "The Greenest Form of Power," in Forbes, *Vol. 145, No. 12, June 11, 1990, pp. 116–20.*

Disposal of High-Level Nuclear Waste: Is It Possible?

Disposing of high-level radioactive waste has become a problem of first magnitude, if dollars and time spent on efforts to solve it are an appropriate measure. For more than 30 years the problem has been recognized as serious, yet this most dangerous kind of nuclear waste still remains without a generally accepted means of disposal. What has gone wrong?

High-level waste (HLW) is a product of the operation of nuclear reactors. It is distinguishable from low-level waste (also a problem, but a less intractable one) by its high concentration of radioactive elements and by the length of time—up to a few million years—that some of them will remain dangerous if released to the biosphere. In the United States, material regarded as HLW has two forms: the spent fuel rods discarded from a reactor after several months of operation and the liquid waste produced when fuel rods are dissolved in acid for the production of plutonium for military purposes. The fuel rods at present are kept in large basins of cold circulating water at reactor sites, and the liquid reprocessing waste is stored in steel tanks sunk just below the ground surface at the two places where plutonium has been produced in large quantity, Hanford in southern Washington and the Savannah River plant in South Carolina. In some other countries the fuel rods are not considered waste, because plutonium obtained from them can be used as a commercial energy source as well as for making weapons. Both in this country and abroad efforts are under way to convert at least some of the liquid waste into a more easily handled solid material, most commonly a kind of glass.

High-level waste in any of its forms continually generates high-energy ionizing radiation which is extremely destructive to living cells with which it may come in contact. The radiation can be absorbed and rendered harmless by a variety of materials, for example, the water and metal of the fuel-rod basins and the concrete and earth around the tanks holding the reprocessing waste. Thus the waste at present poses no threat to its surroundings but could do great harm if any appreciable quantity should escape.

Escape is unlikely as long as surveillance of the waste is maintained, that is, as long as someone is present to check for leaks or corrosion or malfunctioning of equipment and to take action if any of these occur. Can we expect such surveillance to continue for the long time during which the waste will remain dangerous? This hardly seems likely; it would imply a continuity of social order for more than ten millennia, which on the basis of past history seems a dubious assumption. Such thinking has led producers of HLW the world over to the conclusion that a better means of disposal must be developed, that somehow a place must be found to put the waste where it will stay out of human environments for the necessary long times without the need of caretakers.

How can this be accomplished? Many clever schemes have been suggested, but there is now general agreement, here and abroad, that the best method is disposal underground. HLW must be buried deeply enough so that it cannot affect the present living world and in a geologic situation stable enough to prevent any appreciable amount from reaching the surface for at least a hundred centuries. Seemingly this should not be difficult. Let a geologist find an area that is tectonically stable and where the rock a few hundred meters down is strong, dry, and chemically unreactive. Let an engineer sink a shaft and drive tunnels from its base as if he were developing a mine, then enclose the waste in metal containers and put the containers in holes drilled into walls or floors of the tunnels. These are all standard procedures, well within the capability of current technical know-how. A waste repository of this sort could be constructed immediately, and the problem of HLW disposal would be solved.

But of course it is not this simple. A major difficulty is ground water: Rock at depths of a few hundred meters is nearly everywhere saturated with water and the water is slowly moving. The tunnels in a few decades will fill with water, the metal containers will eventually corrode, and water will come in contact with waste. Some of the radioactive elements may dissolve and be carried by the water to points on the surface where it emerges in springs and seepages. All this will take a long time. Are the rates of the different processes—groundwater movement, metal corrosion, waste dissolution—slow enough to keep hazardous amounts of radioactive material from appearing at the surface during the next 10,000 years? If not, can the design of the repository be changed, or can its walls be coated, or can it be filled with sorbent material, to make the rates sufficiently slow?

Questions like these are troublesome for both geologists and engineers because they demand the unaccustomed exercise of attempting predictions for a long future. Many years of research in many laboratories have gone into developing the background for such predictions: research on solubilities of different forms of waste, on rates of metal corrosion, on reactions of the different radioactive elements with the rock through which they would move, and on the different kinds of rock and different kinds of tectonic situation in which a repository might be located. For most in the technical community the predictions give adequate assurance that geologic sites can be found and repositories can be constructed so that any escape of radioactive elements will be minor, well within limits prescribed by current regulations.

But inevitably such predictions have uncertainties, and some scientists are hesitant to accept the majority view until additional research is done. A few reject the majority opinion altogether. In a situation like this—general agreement among supposed experts that repositories will be safe but some lingering doubts and a few loud objections—should repository construction be authorized? Or should it be delayed pending results of further research? These are not technical questions, but questions for the man in the street and his elected representatives. On their shoulders must rest the ultimate decision as to whether and when waste disposal should begin. But the lack of unanimity among experts makes the decision particularly difficult.

A dilemma of this sort is not unique to waste disposal. Differences of technical opinion about details can arise for any large construction project, say the building of a bridge, the excavation of a mine, the siting of a power plant. If voters are called on for approval, they may well have worries about the differences, but normally the worries do not prevent construction from going ahead. By contrast, with regard to HLW disposal the concern about technical disagreement has been sufficient to stop even the preliminary steps of repository construction, both here and in other countries.

To break the impasse, some sort of government action seems called for. The U.S. government has indeed responded to the need, but the result of its

> **A major difficulty [facing HLW disposal] is groundwater: Rock at depths of a few hundred meters is nearly everywhere saturated with water and the water is slowly moving. The tunnels in a few decades will fill with water, the metal containers will eventually corrode, and water will come in contact with waste. Some of the radioactive elements may dissolve and be carried by the water to points on the surface where it emerges in springs and seepages.**

People are afraid of radioactivity and want no installation with even the slightest chance of radioactive release near their homes. Waste should be disposed of, everyone will agree, and as quickly as possible—but always in some other state and someone else's backyard.

attempted guidance has been only a long series of frustrations. Congress tried valiantly to do its part by passing the Nuclear Waste Policy Act of 1982, which set out a detailed schedule of activities by the Department of Energy (DOE) and the Nuclear Regulatory Commission that would lead to the start of HLW disposal into a mined repository not later than 1998. The record of compromises that have pushed this starting date ever further into the future is testimony to the difficulty of HLW disposal and to the apparent inability of government to deal effectively with the problem.

The carefully crafted program spelled out in the act quickly ran afoul of objections from state governments and local groups. Despite generous provisions for consultations with the states, even for financial aid to any state selected as a repository host, all states with any prospect of being selected proved hostile. No state wanted a repository within its borders. After several years of fruitless attempts by DOE to make the detailed studies of sites in a number of states that the act called for, Congress in 1987 felt obliged to amend its legislation by designating a single site, Yucca Mountain, Nevada, as the most promising one for a repository and therefore the one on which exploratory research should be concentrated. At about the same time DOE moved its projected date for opening the first repository to 2003, and in 1989 the date was further postponed to 2010. Meeting even this deadline now seems highly improbable.

Limiting intensive study to a single site in Nevada has brought little progress. The DOE has indeed marshaled its forces for the long investigation. But the state is implacably opposed and has voiced its displeasure by publicizing every possible technical objection to the Yucca Mountain site and by refusing to grant permits even for preliminary surface clearing and drilling. The controversy is now headed for the courts: Nevada claims that it vetoed selection of the site, as permitted by the 1982 legislation, and is suing DOE to stop its activity; DOE is suing the state for its obstructionist tactics. The only moral to be drawn from this story is its demonstration of the inadequacy of government action to assure that repository construction will be accomplished—or will even be shared.

The failure of government is understandable. People are afraid of radioactivity and want no installation with even the slightest chance of radioactive release near their homes. Waste should be disposed of, everyone will agree, and as quickly as possible—but always in some other state and someone else's backyard. One can point out, as DOE's scientists have done repeatedly, that the risk from a well-sited and well-constructed repository is less than other risks that citizens accept as a matter of course in ordinary life. But the risk is not zero: no scientist or engineer can give an absolute guarantee that radioactive waste will not someday leak in dangerous quantities from even the best of repositories. And without such a guarantee people are swayed by their fears, especially when they know that a few of the technical experts are less certain than the majority about the long-term performance of a repository. In the United States this means that ways can always be found to block construction indefinitely, either by state governments defying the federal interlopers or by individuals who, honestly or not, feel that their estimates of radioactive release are better than those accepted by most of their colleagues.

Faced with this seemingly hopeless situation, one is tempted to ask: Why is building a repository so urgent? As long as the waste is not harming its surroundings, why not for a time just leave it where it is? In answer to this query, efforts to dispose of HLW in a hurry are commonly justified on three grounds. First, waste kept in containers near the earth's surface is always subject to massive release by acts of nature—violent storms or earthquakes—or by sabotage, or by carelessness on the part of those supposedly watching over it. Second, if a method of disposal cannot be demonstrated soon the nuclear energy industry is in deep trouble: opponents can claim that waste is an insoluble problem, hence that production of more should be stopped at once. And third, in a more philosophical vein, the waste that we do not dispose of now will remain as an unjustified burden for our children and grandchildren to cope with. These arguments have seemed convincing to the U.S. public but less so abroad. The drive to get repository construction under way soon is stronger in the United States than in most other countries.

The other side of the question, putting off disposal to an indefinite future, can be defended with arguments that seem equally good. For one thing, waste becomes easier to handle on standing because its radioactivity steadily decreases. Also, with the rapid progress of technology, we can expect that a half-century hence we will know more about the optimum design of repositories and about finding the best geologic locations. And finally, leaving waste in storage near the surface keeps it readily accessible, an advantage if sometime later a use is found for some of its constituents. Considerations of this sort have led most European countries to adopt a deliberate policy of postponing final disposal of HLW for at least several decades.

In the United States it looks increasingly as if a choice between these alternatives will be made for us automatically. At present schedules no HLW will be put underground until 2010 and most likely not until much later. By the time actual burial begins, much of the waste will be more than 50 years old, as old as the waste that is planned for later disposal in Europe. Despite pushes by Congress to speed up the program and well-meant efforts by DOE and other federal agencies to play their assigned roles, a combination of public dread of all things radioactive, of technical disagreements about the safety of long-term burial, and of disputes among the many federal and state agencies involved has made it impossible to accomplish waste disposal quickly.

Perhaps this is not to be deplored. If indefinite postponement is accepted as a necessary evil, the pace of the disposal program can be made less frantic, and its continued delays will seem less frustrating. The long and expensive effort to find a suitable site and to ensure compliance with accepted standards of radioactive release, discouragingly unproductive as it now appears, will not have been in vain. The years of research have taught us a great deal about repository construction and about the behavior of radioactive elements in natural environments, perhaps even about handling federal-state opposition. When a decision is finally reached for us or our children to get disposal started, this background of knowledge and experience should make it possible to complete the job in short order. (pp. 1231–32)

Konrad B. Krauskopf, "Disposal of High-Level Nuclear Waste: Is It Possible?" in Science, *Vol. 249, No. 4974, September 14, 1990, pp. 1231–32.*

In 1980 Congress passed a law requiring states— either individually or jointly—to find permanent storage sites for low-level waste by 1986; in 1985, when it was clear that almost all the states would miss the 1986 deadline, legislators moved it back a decade. So far, only seven states have definitely found a long-term site.

Indecent Burial: Obstacles to the Disposal of Nuclear Waste Proliferate

As calls for a resurgence of nuclear power in the U.S. multiply . . . , so do political, legal and practical obstacles to the long-term disposal of nuclear waste. All the major programs for burying waste—from literally hot uranium fuel rods to boots with a few specks of americium on them—face protracted delays. A lack-of-progress report follows.

Plans for a permanent repository for high-level waste have undergone the most serious setbacks. High-level waste includes spent fuel rods from power plants and by-products from the manufacture of nuclear weapons. In 1982 Congress ordered the Department of Energy (DOE) to find a site for an underground repository and to open it by 1998. In 1987 Congress pushed the opening date back to 2003 and told the DOE to consider henceforth only one site—Yucca Mountain, a bone-dry ridge abutting an Air Force base in Nevada.

Radioactive-waste disposal, it would seem, remains an issue too hot to handle.

Recently Secretary of Energy James D. Watkins announced that the repository can open no sooner than 2010. Some observers consider even that date optimistic. Probably the biggest barrier to the repository is opposition by Nevadans, including virtually every politician in the state. The state has refused to grant the permits needed for the DOE to drill exploratory shafts into Yucca Mountain. The DOE has asked the Department of Justice to sue the state and thereby force it to issue the permits. Nevadans, some of whom have compared the DOE to the Kremlin (pre-Gorbachev), have vowed to take the fight to the U.S. Supreme Court, if necessary.

Another legal encumbrance stems from the DOE's attempts to find an "integrating contractor" to help it manage the project. Last year the department selected Bechtel, Inc. Then an unsuccessful bidder, TRW, sued, claiming the DOE had been biased toward Bechtel. As part of its case, TRW pointed out that one of the DOE officials awarding the contract was a former Bechtel employee. Last summer a federal court ruled that the contract should go to TRW. The DOE is appealing; Watkins has also intimated that the DOE might proceed without an integrating contractor. TRW, naturally, has threatened to sue again unless the contract is fulfilled.

When, or if, the political and legal issues are settled, the DOE must still prove that Yucca Mountain can contain its deadly contents for 10,000 years, the standard set by the Environmental Protection Agency. How is the inspection to proceed? Even that is in dispute. The DOE has proposed excavating exploratory shafts with drills and dynamite. Recently the Nuclear Waste Technical Review Board, a group of independent advisers appointed by the President, pointed out that the water needed to lubricate the drill and the fractures caused by the dynamite could themselves threaten the proposed repository's integrity.

When *that* issue is resolved, the DOE must investigate serious questions about the site's natural suitability. Yucca Mountain lies near seismically active faults and a volcano that erupted less than 10,000 years ago; there are signs that the region's water table has been historically unstable and could rise far enough above its present level to invade the repository. If Yucca Mountain proves unsuitable—and the DOE has emphasized recently that it might—the department reports back to Congress for further instructions; there is no backup site or contingency plan.

Delays in the Yucca Mountain project have also blocked progress toward a temporary storehouse where high-level waste could be held until a permanent repository is ready. In the mid-1980's the DOE recommended building such a storehouse, called a monitored retrievable storage facility, at a site in Tennessee. State officials there loudly objected, however, and in 1987 Congress rejected the DOE's recommendation; it also stipulated that the DOE could not even consider new sites for a temporary facility until a site for a permanent repository had been approved. Of course, this approval has been indefinitely postponed—and indeed may never be granted. The DOE has asked Congress to allow work on a temporary facility to proceed regardless of the status of the permanent site. If Congress agrees (which is in doubt), the department still must find a state willing to house the nation's high-level waste "temporarily."

The U.S. has actually built one underground nuclear-waste repository. Called the Waste Isolation Pilot Plant (WIPP), it consists of a vast chamber carved into salt deposits near Carlsbad, N.M., and it is meant to hold so-called transuranic waste generated by DOE nuclear-weapons facilities. Transuranic waste contains radioactive elements heavier than uranium (such as plutonium); although the radioactivity emitted by the waste is less penetrating than that generated by high-level waste, it is long-lasting and still dangerous.

Begun in 1983, the WIPP was scheduled to start accepting deposits two years ago. But before the grand opening a panel of the National Academy of Sciences warned that salty water in the cavern might corrode waste containers and allow radioactive materials to leak into the surrounding aquifer. The panel recommended that the problems be studied further. After much debate the DOE recently agreed that the WIPP would accept only small amounts of waste for at least three years while tests proceed. Yet the department and its outside advisers have not been able to agree on exactly how much waste should be involved or on how the tests should be done. The experiments have yet to begin, and the WIPP remains empty.

Finally, there are the repositories for so-called low-level waste. Such waste includes everything from gloves worn by a nurse handling a short-lived radioactive tracer to reactor piping that will remain radioactive for hundreds of years. In 1980 Congress passed a law requiring states—either individually or jointly—to find permanent storage sites for low-level waste by 1986; in 1985, when it was clear that almost all the states would miss the 1986 deadline, legislators moved it back a decade. So far, only seven states have definitely found a long-term site: Alaska, Hawaii, Oregon, Utah, Idaho, Montana and Washington will all dump their waste in Hanford, Wash., which is already home to a DOE nuclear-weapons facility. At least one state, New York, has announced that it intends to challenge the constitutionality of the law on low-level waste, and several other states are reportedly considering similar action.

Radioactive-waste disposal, it would seem, remains an issue too hot to handle.

John Horgan, "Indecent Burial," in Scientific American, *Vol. 262, No. 2, February, 1990, p. 240.*

The economic fallout from Chernobyl has harmed the commercial prospects of the international nuclear industry, which is now eager to make up the losses as quickly as possible. It wants to reverse the rising tide of public opposition to nuclear power and to reap the profits from its hefty investments in nuclear technology and equipment.

Nuclear Safety after Chernobyl

The cost of the Chernobyl accident to the Soviet Union is put at eight billion roubles. It is a huge sum but one that is difficult for those outside the country to put a value on. For a start, the rouble is not a convertible currency: officially, one rouble is worth about one pound sterling; unofficially, US dollars can buy 10 roubles apiece. More importantly, it is not clear how the Soviet Union arrived at this figure. What is certain is that the economic fallout from Chernobyl has harmed the commercial prospects of the international nuclear industry, which is now eager to make up the losses as quickly as possible. It wants to reverse the rising tide of public opposition to nuclear power and to reap the profits from its hefty investments in nuclear technology and equipment. And its operators appear confident of success.

Last month's inaugural meeting in Moscow of the World Association of Nuclear Operators (WANO) focused on collaboration and the presentation of a new image: East and West agreed to work together to make nuclear power stations safer and more reliable. Nearly all the utilities that produce electricity from nuclear power sent a representative to pledge support for WANO. Those unable to attend are expected to sign the WANO charter soon. Everyone agreed the new spirit of nuclear glasnost could not have happened without the accident.

The estimated cost of the Chernobyl accident came from Nikolai Lukonin, Minister of Atomic Energy. He refused to provide a breakdown of the figure, nor would he say exactly what it covered. He brushed aside a request for some idea of the cost of making safe the network of RBMK (thermal, water-cooled graphite-moderated) nuclear reactors, similar to the one that exploded at Chernobyl just over three years ago. (There are 13 units of 1000 megawatts and two of 1500 megawatts in the country.) All Lukonin would say is that engineers will complete the modifications to the design of the RMBK reactors, all sited in the Soviet Union under his jurisdiction, by the end of this year.

One advantage of specifying a financial toll is that it gives respectability to the notion that the authorities have at last determined the consequences of the

The Soviet estimate of the national damage caused by the Chernobyl accident, using an unofficial exchange rate that values the rouble more realistically than the official one, is the equivalent of $1 billion, equal to a recently published figure for the cost of the cleanup at Three Mile Island.

accident. Such a public relations exercise is not wasted in the Soviet Union where, officially, at least 650,000 people risk developing a cancer induced by Chernobyl's radioactive fallout. The Department of Radiation Medicine of the Ukrainian Academy of Sciences in Kiev lists these people on a national register and invites them for regular checkups, once or twice a year. They are evacuees from territory within 30 kilometres of the Chernobyl power station and from other areas that received high doses of radiation; people involved in the emergency operations to make the rogue reactor safe; and workers now living in the evacuated areas and their newborn children.

Another facet of this PR exercise is that the official death toll has been revised, downwards. The original figure was 31. Two workers at the power station died immediately after the explosions at the site, buried under rubble, and another 28 people died soon after from acute radiation disease. An old man, whose body was found near the site, has now been scratched from the accident's death list: pathologists discovered later that he died of a heart attack. "There have been some further deaths among those with less acute radiation doses," says Anatoli Chumak, head of immunology in the department's Institute of Clinical Radiology, "but they were not due to the accident." Doctors made their diagnoses after thorough autopsies, which are obligatory for potential victims of the accident, he says. "It is difficult to separate what is the consequence of radiation and what is the effect of other factors," adds Chumak.

A further advantage of drawing up the accident's financial toll, and one that appears to be of considerable political importance to the Soviet authorities, is that it allows the scale of the Chernobyl accident to be compared more easily with earlier mishaps with nuclear reactors. The incidents the authorities have in mind are those at Three Mile Island in the US in 1979 and at Windscale, now Sellafield, in England, in 1957. The Soviet estimate of the national damage caused by the Chernobyl accident, using an unofficial exchange rate that values the rouble more realistically than the official one, is the equivalent of $1 billion, equal to a recently published figure for the cost of the cleanup at Three Mile Island. Western nuclear engineers tend to set the Chernobyl accident apart in the hierarchy of the industry's catalogue of disasters; their Eastern counterparts are less selective. Boris Shcherbina, deputy leader of the Soviet Council of Ministers and the person who led the government inquiry into the Chernobyl accident, is no exception. He referred to "Chernobyl and other major accidents" in his welcome to WANO delegates.

Against this background, founder members of the association, from East and West, are justifiably pleased that they have managed to launch the organisation. Now they have only to keep talking to each other to ensure it functions effectively. WANO plans to exchange details of how its members are operating their nuclear power stations, with the aim of refining a set of working practices that should ultimately produce the safest and most reliable procedures ever. But the organisation will ignore other areas of the fuel cycle, notably reprocessing of spent fuel and disposal of radioactive waste.

WANO's role model is the Institute of Nuclear Power Operations (INPO), an American organisation based in Atlanta, Georgia. The American nuclear power industry established INPO in 1979 after the accident at Three Mile Island. It did not take much prompting to set up the organisation once the government's inquiry discovered that the accident might never have happened if people in the industry, a very competitive network of private utilities, had been prepared to discuss individual problems collectively. The investigators quickly uncovered the cause of the accident, a faulty valve for relieving steam pressure in the reactor vessel. In the process, they were shocked to hear operators of other power stations describe similar, unreported problems that could have served as warnings to the industry as a whole.

INPO decided to try to improve the performance of its members by exploiting the industry's natural competitiveness. It identified a set of characteristics reflecting the way nuclear power stations are run; devised a method of measuring these "performance indicators" so that it could calculate average values for the industry every three months; and then encouraged each operator to aim for a target in 1990 by letting them compare their own performance with that of the industry as a whole every six months. The institute started with six indicators, added a seventh in 1985, two more in 1987 and another last year.

Most of these indicators are aimed at improving the reliability of power stations—that is their ability to generate electricity cheaply and efficiently—rather than at enhancing safety. They gauge how much useful work the operator of a power station extracts from its labour force, plant and equipment. Only one indicator, the amount of radioactivity leaking form a reactor, seems to be concerned exclusively with the safe running of a power station. And even this indicator could be interpreted as a factor influencing reliability: big leaks would presumably incur financial penalties eventually. But the industry maintains that safety and reliability mean the same thing. Better returns for the stockholders and fewer risks of radioactive pollution are the combined benefits of operating plants more safely and reliably, says Bill Lee, chief executive of Duke Power, which owns and operates seven reactors in the US. Lee was the founder-chairman of INPO, and delegates in Moscow elected him to be the first president of their new organisation, an honorary post, in recognition of his "contributions towards the mission of WANO."

According to INPO, the indicators record an astonishing turnaround in the industry's operating performance. Of the seven performance indicators for which information is available, the industry achieved the 1990 targets for three of them last year, and is already close to meeting the targets for another three. INPO attributes the success of its programme to "peer pressure", the eagerness of individual American utilities to be seen to be performing better than the others. WANO likes the idea, which it believes can work on an international scale.

Improvements in the industry's operating record since the Three Mile Island accident have not succeeded in reducing the American public's hostility to nuclear power. "Two-thirds of people believe more nuclear power will be necessary," said Lee, "but less than half of them want it." Slower growth in the demand for electricity compounds the industry's problems. Lee says the US has enough power stations to meet the country's continuous demand until the turn of the century; even new units to cover peak demand will not be needed for another six to eight years, he adds, and anyway these will be fossil fuel stations or pumped storage schemes. Energy conservation and reduced economic activity have cut the demand for power, says John Taylor, vice-president, nuclear power, at the Electric Power Research Institute, an organisation funded by American utilities. "Demand is now doubling every 30 years instead of every 10 as it used to."

Widespread Opposition

The American industry is not alone. In Sweden, Italy, Japan and the Soviet Union, public opposition to nuclear power has forced governments to tread warily. Nuclear power meets as much as 50 per cent of Sweden's demand for electricity and yet the government has told the industry to prepare to start decommissioning its nuclear stations from 1995. In Italy, the government has already shut down its nuclear reactors, which were meeting about five per cent of demand, and shelved plans to increase the ratio to 20 percent by the end of the century. The decision was an expensive one, says Paolo Fornaciari, deputy director of ENEL, the state utility that runs the country's electricity system. Construction sites have been abandoned and one half-built nuclear power station is being converted to run on fossil fuel, he says. Japan has one of the most ambitious programmes for expanding the size and diversity of a national network of nuclear power stations. The local industry, however, worries that an anti-nuclear movement, which has mushroomed since the beginning of last year, could make life difficult, says Shoh Nasu, president of Tokyo Electric Power. Soviet authorities, too, are having to heed public opposition to official plans. One of their first responses has been to consider a public relations campaign: a publicity officer with the Ministry of Atomic Energy was quizzing British delegates at the WANO meeting about the methods and arguments

Improvements in the industry's operating record since the Three Mile Island accident have not succeeded in reducing the American public's hostility to nuclear power.

Thousands of tons of highly radioactive spent fuel rods rest temporarily today in pools of water— some dangerously over- crowded—near nuclear power plants around the country.

used to win planning permission for the new generation of pressurised-water reactors (PWRs) in Britain.

Cynics believe these governments are merely paying lip service to public opin- ion. Sweden has still not come up with a viable alternative to nuclear power and few people believe that the government will be in a position to press the industry into fulfilling its commitment. The industry expects to have to close down two of its oldest stations, dating from the mid-1970s, as a token gesture, but that is all, says Lars Gustafsson, executive vice-president of the Swedish State Power Board. In the meantime, the government is turning a blind eye to major contracts for the repair and rehabilitation of its network of PWRs and boiling-water reactors. In Italy, nuclear engineers are trying to come up with a new design for a safer reactor; until they do, the state is importing electricity generated by nuclear power stations in France. Japan, meanwhile, is already drawing up plans to establish a domestic fuel cycle: it wants to be able to en- rich uranium, to reprocess spent fuel and to dispose of radioactive waste lo- cally by the beginning of the 21st century. And in the Soviet Union, revisions to the government's approach to nuclear power appear to be more a result of pressure from the international industry in the wake of Chernobyl than a re- sponse to public appeals.

At this time of mixed fortunes for nuclear power, the industry has snatched the opportunity of Chernobyl to create WANO. And as concern about the greenhouse effect heightens, the industry is delighted to promote nuclear power as the environmentally friendly solution: it ignores the fact that emis- sions from fossil fuel stations are responsible for only about 11 per cent of glo- bal warming. Lord Marshall of Goring, the head of Britain's largest utility, the Central Electricity Generating Board, and the new leader of WANO's govern- ing board, is convinced the association is on the right track. "The greenhouse effect gives added impetus to nuclear power," he said. "I've been defending nuclear power for two decades; now I can afford to sit back and wait for people to come over to my side." In Moscow, he recalled a recent meeting he had with British premier Margaret Thatcher, who has shown an increasing interest in environmental matters. "I believe she will be advocating an expansion of nu- clear power," said Marshall. "There is no alternative." (pp. 59, 62–5)

Bill O'Neill, "Nuclear Safety after Chernobyl," in New Scientist, *Vol. 122, No. 1670, June 24, 1989, pp. 59, 62–5.*

The Yucca Mountain Project: A Nuclear Graveyard

The apocalyptic scenario begins with an earthquake near Yucca Mountain, a barren ridge 90 miles northwest of Las Vegas that is the burial site for the nation's most lethal nuclear waste. The tremblor is minor; it does not even rupture the tunnels and chambers honeycombing the mountain. But fresh movement in the earth's crust causes ground water to well up suddenly, flood- ing the repository. Soon, a lethal brew of nuclear poisons seeps into the water that flows underground to nearby Death Valley. Insects, birds and animals drink at the valley's contaminated springs, and slowly the radioactivity spreads into the biosphere. "It would be a terrible disaster," says Charles Archambeau, a geophysicist at the University of Colorado.

Much has been made of this scary scenario by the state of Nevada, which is fighting the federal government's plan to bury all the nation's high-level nu- clear refuse inside Yucca Mountain. But in fact, the risk to Nevadans may be overstated. Increasingly, experts view this arid, desolate ridge as a good spot for a permanent nuclear graveyard. The threat to Americans posed by the federal government's bungled attempts to find a safe burial site for the waste looms large, however. Thousands of tons of highly radioactive spent fuel rods rest temporarily today in pools of water—some dangerously overcrowded—near nuclear power plants around the country. At the nation's weapons factories, corroding tanks are leaking nuclear poisons into the ground water. This stalemate over nuclear waste is strangling the nuclear power industry, and experts are increasingly troubled by the possibility that nuclear waste could become the weapon of choice for a new breed of terrorist.

The twin virtues of the Yucca Mountain site are its remoteness and aridity. From the summit, the only sign of civilization is the dusty trace of a dirt road cutting across a brown, barren valley. The ridge is located on the southwest corner of the Nevada Test Site, where the government explodes nuclear weapons, so access is tightly restricted. Sagebrush, creosote bushes and other desert plants attest to the locale's remarkable dryness.

Indeed, only 6 inches of rain fall on the mountain each year, and most of the moisture evaporates, leaving as little as one fiftieth of an inch to soak into the ground. The water table is unusually deep, more than one third of a mile below the surface. According to the Department of Energy, which is charged with building the repository, nuclear waste could be buried far beneath the ground yet still rest safely above the ground water.

Geological Turmoil

The landscape also provides stark reminders of why critics are so concerned. To the southeast stands Busted Butte, a peak that was sheared in half long ago by earthquakes; to the west, four smooth-sloped volcanoes rise out of a high valley. The reason for the geological turmoil is that immense forces inside the earth are stretching the earth's crust apart here, much like a sheet of rubber. Earthquakes relieve the strain, but they also disrupt the water table: As the crust snaps back into shape, rocks contract, and water that has seeped into fractures is forced up toward the surface.

The repository site must be capable of isolating atomic waste for 10,000 years. By all accounts, there could be a frightful mess if the poisons escaped the site. By the year 2000, the nation will have produced 48,000 tons of high-level nuclear waste, the most concentrated products of the nuclear era. Every speck of this refuse is intensely poisonous.

Water is the worst enemy of buried nuclear waste. If water did find its way into the repository, it would corrode the storage canisters and hasten the escape of radioactive particles through the rock. Scientists cannot know absolutely whether ground water will well up under Yucca Mountain during the next 10,000 years. The calculation simply has too many unknowns: A new ice age, global climate change, erosion, volcanoes and earthquakes all could affect the water table. To gauge the probabilities, scientists reconstruct the past. If the water table has risen in the past, scientists assume, it is likely to do so again.

Jerry Szymanski, a maverick engineering geologist with DOE, claims that he has rock-hard evidence that ground water was once as much as 500 meters higher than it is today. He has devoted the past seven years to blowing the whistle on what he believes to be a fatally flawed site, and his arguments have received extensive media attention. Szymanski bases his case largely on the presence of thick, cream-colored veins of a crystalline deposit, known as calcite, that plunge through the mottled, grey bedrock of Yucca Mountain. In Szymanski's view, these calcite bands must have been deposited slowly, layer by layer, as mineral-rich ground water welled up into fractures in the rock. "Ground water will rise again in the next 10,000 years," he says flatly. "It is as certain as death."

Other Voices

But according to an increasing number of earth scientists, it is not the site but Szymanski's conclusion that is fatally flawed. Largely as a result of Szymanski's

The twin virtues of the Yucca Mountain site are its remoteness and aridity.

Scientists cannot know absolutely whether ground water will well up under Yucca Mountain during the next 10,000 years. The calculation simply has too many unknowns: A new ice age, global climate change, erosion, volcanoes and earthquakes all could affect the water table.

warnings, the National Academy of Sciences convened a panel of researchers to evaluate the risks associated with ground water. The panel has not yet released its final report, but already many members are convinced that there is no evidence for Szymanski's hypothesis—but there are several good reasons to doubt it. Most believe that rainwater, not upwelling ground water, probably produced the calcite veins. One strong reason to suspect precipitation, says Bob Fournier, a geologist with the United States Geological Survey in Menlo Park, Calif., is that the calcite veins around Yucca Mountain do not exhibit the common structural characteristics of ancient springs. For instance, upwelling water typically leaves snowy-white mounds of calcite on the ground, deposits that are formed when the water evaporates; few such signatures can be found at Yucca Mountain.

Preliminary chemical analyses also suggest that the disputed calcites were deposited by rainwater. Doug Rumble, a geochemist at the Carnegie Institution in Washington, D.C., analyzed several existing studies of the chemical character of the disputed Yucca Mountain veins, the ground water underneath and ancient and modern ground water deposits; he found no evidence that the calcites at Yucca are or ever were caused by ground water.

Somewhat surprisingly, scientists are much more concerned about ground water seepage than they are about more-dramatic geologic events like volcanoes and earthquakes. Fresh eruptions from the small volcanoes along Yucca Mountain's western flank probably wouldn't threaten the repository because the flows would be small and localized, most geologists believe. The possibility of a direct hit, a new upwelling of magna right beneath the repository, is minute, they say.

Earthquakes are not a major concern either, scientists contend. Though Yucca Mountain is ringed with seismic faults, many of them known to be active, most geologists do not worry that shock waves from an earthquake could rupture the repository. Experience with tremblors throughout the world has shown unequivocally that tunnels and mines stand up well to them. For instance, a devastating earthquake killed 250,000 people in a coal-mining city in China in 1976. Reportedly, workers in the mines below did not feel even the slightest tremor. Closer to home, underground nuclear explosions on the nearby test site have shown that tunnels can withstand forces even greater than those produced by earthquakes.

"From what we know now, I would feel quite comfortable with Yucca Mountain," says George Thompson, a geologist at Stanford University and a member of the National Academy of Sciences' panel. Though panel members agree that a lot more study is needed, most do not believe that the geological complexity disqualifies the site. Explains Clarence Allen, a geologist from Caltech in Pasadena, Calif., "If you asked me to find a site with fewer earthquakes or volcanoes, I could. But an overall better site? I'm not so sure."

Indeed, the biggest problem at Yucca Mountain may be local opposition fomented in part by federal mishandling of the site-selection process. Nine years ago, Congress passed the Nuclear Waste Policy Act. In 1983, DOE selected nine sites around the country for consideration as a possible repository. A couple of years later, the list was winnowed to three—Yucca Mountain, Hanford, Wash., and Deaf Smith County, Texas. Then, in 1987, Congress ordered the DOE to focus solely on Yucca Mountain, a move that Nevadans feel was made for political reasons; Nevada has one of the smallest delegations on Capitol Hill. Today, anti-dump sentiment runs deep. Fully 4 out of 5 Nevadans oppose the project.

Nevadans are also unnerved by the DOE's horrible environmental record and long-standing culture of secrecy. Indeed, billions of gallons of radioactive and toxic materials were dumped secretly over the past few decades at weapons factories around the country. According to a recent report by the Congressional Office of Technology Assessment, the DOE's two-year-old effort to clean up the mess left on and under DOE weapons facilities is proceeding abysmally.

Changing Benchmarks

In their own defense, DOE officials argue that it is unfair to judge past practices by today's more stringent environmental standards. Moreover, they say the Yucca Mountain project has many layers of external oversight, unlike the weapons facilities that were cloaked in secrecy from the start. DOE has a point. Every aspect of site evaluation will be scrutinized by the Nuclear Waste Technical Review Board, a panel of experts recommended by the National Academy of Sciences and appointed by the President. Ultimately, the facility will be licensed by the U.S. Nuclear Regulatory Commission.

But Nevadans have a case when they argue that their state has much to lose and little to gain by hosting the site. With its booming economy, Las Vegas doesn't need the 3,000 jobs the facility would provide during construction. Also, a nuclear accident, even a minor one, could harm the Silver State's gaming-based economy by keeping tourists away.

Many critics believe that the very notion of a site that could be "safe" for 10,000 years is ridiculous, and this has intensified local opposition. Science simply cannot prove that a site will be safe for such a long period of time, and citizens know it and feel as if they are being conned, says Frank Parker, chairman of the National Academy of Sciences' Board on Radioactive Waste Management. Parker holds that a more honest—and in the end more reassuring—assessment that the government could have offered Nevadans is that the likelihood of a catastrophic breach is very slim and that the DOE is prepared to act swiftly if problems occur.

Maintaining the pretense of an unassailable site also has had an unfortunate impact on the design of the repository. Currently, the DOE plans to build a complex that would be backfilled and sealed off after it had been loaded to capacity. Experts like Stanford's George Thompson assert that this approach is foolish. Instead, the government should design the facility so that the waste could be easily retrieved if the repository failed.

Congress must have had an inkling in 1987 that forcing the project on Nevada might not work out in the end. In the same bill that designated Yucca Mountain the sole candidate for site evaluation, Congress established the Office of the U.S. Nuclear Waste Negotiator, which is charged with finding a willing state or Indian tribe to host the repository. David Leroy, who took the job last summer, is putting together a package of incentives and assurances that he hopes will lure several state or tribal leaders to the bargaining table. The assurances include promises of local participation in deciding how the facility is operated and the freedom to back out of the evaluation process at any time. When it comes to incentives, the sky's the limit. Highways? Airports? Schools? Harbor clean-ups? "You tell me what the problem is and let's see if we can address it," he says. Who knows, maybe Leroy can find a way to make even cynical Nevadans willing to host the repository. (pp. 72–4)

Betsy Carpenter, "A Nuclear Graveyard," in U.S. News & World Report, *Vol. 110, No. 10, March 18, 1991, pp. 72–4.*

> **With its booming economy, Las Vegas doesn't need the 3,000 jobs the facility would provide during construction. Also, a nuclear accident, even a minor one, could harm the Silver State's gaming-based economy by keeping tourists away.**

Sources For Further Study

Ahlberg, Brian. "A Comeback for Nuclear Power?" *Utne Reader*, No. 30 (November-December 1988): 34–6.
    Argues that interest in nuclear energy is returning due to the industry's effective lobbying before Congress and nuclear power's potential to help curb global warming.

Anspaugh, Lynn R., Catlin, Robert J., and Goldman, Marvin. "The Global Impact of the Chernobyl Reactor Accident." *Science* 242, No. 4885 (16 December 1988): 1513–19.
    Calculates the amount of radioactive material deposited throughout the Northern Hemisphere as a result of the Chernobyl accident and estimates the number of people possibly affected by radiation.

Atkinson, Adrian. "The Environmental Impact of Fusion Power." *Energy Policy* 17, No. 3 (June 1989): 277–84.
    Surveys the potential environmental impact of commercial fusion power systems.

Beauchamp, Marc. "Caution: This Corpse is Radioactive." *Forbes* 141, No. 5 (7 March 1988): 117–19.
    Explores the ramifications of decommissioning some of the U.S.'s older nuclear power plants, noting that the project's cost is staggering and that no way to effectively dispose of radioactive waste yet exists.

Bernero, R. M., and Kalman, K. L. "The U.S. Nuclear Regulatory Commission's Role in the Management of Radioactive Wastes." *Radioactive Waste Management and the Nuclear Fuel Cycle* 12, Nos. 1–4 (1989): 19–25.
    Provides an overview of the Nuclear Regulatory Commission's programs for managing high-level and low-level radioactive wastes and uranium mill tailings.

Blix, Hans. "The Role and Development of Nuclear Power." *Environmental Policy and Law* 18, No. 5 (October 1988): 142–54.
    Evaluates the nuclear industry's increasing role as a provider of electricity for the world and enumerates the various challenges to developing nuclear power as a safe and efficient energy source.

Boiteux, Marcel. "Nuclear Energy, Ecology, and Chernobyl." *Public Utilities Fortnightly* 123, No. 6 (16 March 1989): 28–32.
    Discusses the merits and demerits of commercial nuclear power in Europe, from the highly successful nuclear reactors in France to the Chernobyl disaster in the Soviet Union.

Cramer, Jerome. "They Lied to Us." *Time* 132, No. 18 (31 October 1988): 60–5.
    Documents numerous instances where aging and unsafe nuclear weapons plants have jeopardized the health and well-being of employees and people in nearby communities.

Doll, Richard. "The Effects of Low-Level Radiation: Current Epidemiology." *British Nuclear Energy Society Journal* 29, No. 1 (February 1990): 13–19.
    Suggests that the risk of cancer from acute radiation doses may be higher than previously suspected due to recent re-evaluations of data from survivors of Hiroshima and Nagasaki.

"Whose Rubbish?" *The Economist* 311, No. 7607 (24 June 1989): 23.
    Records numerous instances where health and safety concerns have generally been ignored in favor of increased production in nuclear weapons factories and details efforts underway to address the problem.

Emmerson, B. W. "Intervening for the Protection of the Public Following a Nuclear Accident." *IAEA Bulletin* 30, No. 3 (1988): 12–19.
    Discusses the renewed efforts by international organizations to establish principles of post-accident intervention and criteria for controlling the consumption of potentially contaminated foodstuffs in the wake of the Chernobyl disaster.

"Nuclear Power: A Forum." *EPA Journal* 16, No. 2 (March-April 1990): 17–19.
    Assembles five different perspectives from eminent figures in the field of nuclear power regarding the viability and safety of nuclear energy as well as the energy source's potential for limiting global warming.

Faas, Ronald C. "Nuclear Waste Disposal Policy: Socioeconomic Impact Management Issues." In *Natural Resource and Environmental Policy Analysis: Cases in Applied Economics*, pp. 91–110. Edited by George M. Johnson, David Freshwater, and Philip Favero. Boulder: Westview Press, 1988.
  Examines through statistical theory the various aspects of the risks involved in living near a radioactive waste disposal site and proposes policies to insure safeguards from exposure to radiation.

Faltermayer, Edmund. "Taking Fear out of Nuclear Power." *Fortune* 118, No. 3 (1 August 1988): 105–07, 110, 114, 118.
  Contends that if new nuclear reactor designs can surmount fears about atomic safety, nuclear power could play a leading role in combatting the greenhouse effect.

Flavin, Christopher. "Ten Years of Fallout." *World Watch* 2, No. 2 (March-April 1989): 30–7.
  Examines the aftermath of the 1979 Three Mile Island partial meltdown, describing the various complex obstacles as well as the exorbitant cost involved in the clean-up effort. Flavin concludes that the lessons learned from the Three Mile Island accident should make the U.S. wary of building a new generation of nuclear reactors.

Gittus, John H. "Radiation in Perspective: The Acceptability of Nuclear Energy." *International Journal of Global Energy Issues* 1, Nos. 1–2 (1989): 67–72.
  Discusses the differing perspectives of the nuclear industry and the public regarding large nuclear accidents and radiation.

Gofman, John W. "Radiation-Induced Cancer from Low-Dose Exposure: An Independent Analysis. San Francisco: Committee for Nuclear Responsibility, Inc., 1990.
  Refutes the widely held claim in the scientific community that low doses of radiation are not harmful. Gofman presents human and physical evidence proving that carcinogenesis from ionizing radiation does occur at the lowest conceivable doses and dose-rates.

Green, Patrick. "Radiation: An Environmental Viewpoint." *International Journal of Global Energy Issues* 1, Nos. 1–2 (1989): 72–6.
  Documents the running debate between environmentalists and the nuclear power industry regarding the correlation between leukemia levels and their proximity to nuclear installations.

Grossman, Dan, and Shulman, Seth: "A Nuclear Dump: The Experiment Begins." *Discover* 10, No. 3 (March 1989): 48–56.
  Comprehensive evaluation of the benefits and drawbacks of the proposed Yucca Mountain nuclear dumpsite.

Häfele, Wolf. "Energy from Nuclear Power." *Scientific American* 263, No. 3 (September 1990): 137–42, 144.
  Maintains that nuclear energy's vast potential can be realized only if issues of safety, radioactive waste disposal, and nuclear weapon proliferation are addressed by a globally administered institution.

Katz, Jeffrey L. "Will Nuclear Waste End Up in Landfills?" *Governing* 4, No. 3 (December 1990): 12.
  Assesses a new Nuclear Regulatory Commission proposal that would allow low-level nuclear waste to be buried like household trash.

Kay, C. E. "Public Acceptance and Its Importance to the U.S. Waste-Management Program." *Radioactive Waste Management and the Nuclear Fuel Cycle* 12, Nos. 1–4 (1989): 1–9.
  Discusses the U.S. Department of Energy's efforts to manage and dispose of spent nuclear fuel and high-level radioactive waste in view of the fact that the public has not been persuaded that the waste can be safely isolated. According to Kay, the DOE remains optimistic that a continued exchange of

information with all affected groups will ultimately lead to a greater acceptance of the program.

Lowther, William, and Schug, Deborra. "Nuclear Negligence." *Maclean's* 101, No. 46 (7 November 1988): 54–5.
    Addresses revelations that nuclear weapons plants have cut corners on maintaining safe reactors and have illegally disposed of radioactive waste with governmental approval.

McCollam, William, Jr. "National Energy Policy Act of 1989." *Electric Perspectives* 13, No. 2 (May-June 1989): 40–7.
    Maintains that the electric utility industry is aggressively pursuing numerous ways to meet U.S. energy needs while reducing emissions of greenhouse gases, including the increased use of nuclear power.

Miettinen, Jorma K. "Lessons of Chernobyl: A Commentary." *Environment International* 14, No. 2 (1988): 201–04.
    Asserts that while the Chernobyl accident resulted in a major economic setback for the USSR, it cannot be considered a disaster in terms of human loss. The lack of preparedness by the nations exposed to radioactive fallout, Miettinen continues, was evident in the exaggerated reporting by the media and the confused actions of national governments.

O'Sullivan, R. A. "International Consensus for the Safe Transport of Radioactive Material: An Experience to Imitate." *IAEA Bulletin* 30, No. 3 (1988): 31–5.
    Examines the effectiveness of the International Atomic Energy Agency in regulating the safe transport of radioactive material and how participating nations have not experienced accidents or fatalities since the inauguration of the program.

Rodhe, Henning, and Bjorkstrom, Anders. "How Would Closing Nuclear Power Plants Affect Climate?" *Forum for Applied Research and Public Policy* 3, No. 3 (Fall 1988): 63–6.
    Maintains that a possible shift from nuclear energy to other energy sources would have no discernable impact on global warming.

Saleska, Scott. "Nuclear Legacy: An Overview of the Places, Problems, and Politics of Radioactive Waste in the United States." *Public Citizen Critical Mass Energy Project Report* (September 1989). 17 p.
    Asserts that new strategies are needed to control the increasing production of radioactive waste and to ensure public health and safety in the face of this potential threat.

Scheibla, Shirley Hobbs. "Nuclear Pollution." *Barron's* 68, No. 49 (5 December 1988): 15, 24, 26, 28.
    Comments on the U.S. government's plan to pay contractors as much as $200 billion for cleaning up aging and contaminated nuclear power plants over the next two decades.

Seitz, Frederick. "Must We Have Nuclear Power?" *Reader's Digest* 137, No. 820 (August 1990): 113–20.
    Argues that nuclear power is a viable alternative to fossil fuel energy in that it is less harmful than coal-fired plants and that it has the abundance to meet our increasing demand for electricity.

Stinson, Stephen C. "Nuclear." *Chemical & Engineering News* 69, No. 24 (17 June 1991): 36–40.
    Describes three redesigned nuclear power plants that promise increased generating capacity, easier licensing, and advanced reactor safety.

Tyrell, R. Emmett, Jr. "Nature Fakers." *The American Spectator* 23, No. 10 (October 1990): 10–11.
    Asserts that an increased production of domestic nuclear power will curtail the U.S.'s dependence on foreign countries for fossil fuel.

Walker, J. Samuel. "The Controversy over Radiation Safety: A Historical Overview." *AMA Journal* 262, No. 5 (4 August 1989): 664–69.

Provides an historical account of the controversy surrounding radiation from the discovery of X-rays in 1895 to nuclear power and weapons in the 1980s.

Weinberg, Alvin M. "Nuclear Energy and the Greenhouse Effect." *International Journal of Global Energy Issues* 2, No. 2 (1990): 99–105.
Explores possible future trends in developing expanded nuclear power facilities to combat the greenhouse effect.

8: Nuclear, Biological, and Chemical Weapons

Chemical and Biological Weapons: Research and Deployment

> The noise of fourteen thousand aeroplanes advancing in open order. But in the Kurfurstendamm . . . , the explosion of anthrax bombs is hardly louder than the popping of a paper bag.
>
> Aldous Huxley, *Brave New World*, 1932

In the nuclear age, another type of weapon of mass destruction is often forgotten; yet, the stockpile of nerve gas in the United States alone is said to be "sufficient to kill the entire population of the world 4000 times over," given an efficient delivery system. Chemical and biological weapons may be the ultimate "capitalist weapon," leaving the economic infrastructure intact to an even greater extent than the neutron bomb.

Chemical and biological weapons may be the ultimate "capitalist weapon," leaving the economic infrastructure intact to an even greater extent than the neutron bomb.

History

However unthinkable the use of these horrific weapons, there is ample historical precedent. In 1347, the Tatars, afflicted by bubonic plague during their siege of Caffa, used catapults to hurl their dead into the city, spreading the disease to Genoese defenders, who took the "black death" with them when they fled to Italy. In colonial days, the British gave American Indians "gifts" of smallpox-carrying blankets. In World War I, at least 1.3 million men were wounded by gas (including Adolf Hitler), and 91,000 of them died. In the 1930s, the Italian army repeatedly gassed Ethiopians, and Japan launched more than 800 gas attacks in its conquest of Manchuria, China. The Japanese also may have used biological agents to attack the Chinese and are believed to have conducted experiments with the agents in thousands of Chinese prisoners of war. Many other examples could be cited.

In World War II, the use of chemical and biological weapons could have been far more extensive than it actually was. The Germans had developed tabun and sarin, extremely potent cholinesterase inhibitors, and German factories were capable of producing approximately 11,000 tonnes of poison gas per month. The *Luftwaffe* had a half million gas bombs. Although lagging in research on nerve gas, the British biological warfare project was years ahead of the Nazis'. The British actually produced 5 million cattle cakes filled with anthrax, and the United States had a contingency plan to use the anthrax bomb against Germany.

Existing and Potential Weapons

The United States stockpiled approximately 36,000 tonnes of chemical warfare agents before production ceased around 1969. The agents include phosgene, hydrogen cyanide, and mustard gas. Approximately half the inventory is nerve gas. Because of chemical deterioration, only approximately 10% of the stockpile has immediate military utility, and an additional 10% to 20% has

The persistent ecological consequences of producing and testing chemical (and especially biological) agents are potentially more harmful and certainly less well understood than the radiological effects of nuclear weapons tests. The myxomatosis inoculation of a few rabbits in France in 1952 resulted in the spread of disease over an entire continent.

limited utility, according to the Department of Defense. Currently, the United States is reducing the stockpile of unitary chemical weapons. However, the United States continues to produce binary chemical weapons, which contain two components that form a lethal agent when mixed. The Soviets are believed to have stockpiled 270,000 to 360,000 tonnes of a variety of chemical weapons, including phosgene, nerve agents (tabun, sarin, and soman), hydrogen cyanide, and blistering agents (mustard gas). At The Paris Conference on Chemical Weapons in January 1989, the Soviet Union announced that it would destroy its stockpile, which it declares consists of 45,000 tonnes of toxic substances.

Numerous pathogenic organisms, including bacteria, rickettsiae, viruses, and fungi, have been proposed and probably investigated as agents of biological warfare. Many of the organisms are highly lethal, although others (such as brucellosis, developed as a potential weapon by the United States during World War II) might be used with the intention of simply incapacitating the enemy for long periods. Smallpox virus has been called the most important agent, possibly because there is an effective vaccine as well as a somewhat useful (but generally unavailable) antiviral drug, methisazone. Conceivably, a nation might protect its own population, then unleash the virus against an unvaccinated world. (Although widely believed to be extinct, samples of the virus are still kept in maximum-security reference repositories, under the auspices of the World Health Organization, in Atlanta, Ga, and Moscow.)

Instead of the organisms themselves, their toxins might be used. Although toxins could not start epidemics, they might survive transport better. A number of toxins, including botulinus toxin, have been studied by the US Department of Defense. Trichothecenes, derived from the mold fusaria and allegedly found in a few samples related to "yellow rain" attacks, are believed to be produced at Berdsk Chemical Works near the Soviet city of Novosibirsk, a facility suspected of involvement in chemical and biological warfare. At least 22 articles in the Soviet literature concern the optimum conditions for biosynthesis of this agent in large quantities.

Advancements in biotechnology open prospects for the development of organisms that are resistant to existing drugs and vaccines or that produce more lethal toxins, possibly by modifying normally harmless or relatively benign microorganisms. The Soviets have recognized this possibility for at least two decades. The incorporation of the genetic code for a component of cobra venom into viruses such as influenza virus is one of the ominous possibilities suggested in a series of articles in the *The Wall Street Journal*. Cobra venom is composed of more than 20 protein components, such as cobrotoxin, a potent neurotoxin that binds to the acetylcholine receptor. The role for such weapons was discussed during a Warsaw Pact scientific conference in East Germany in 1971, where it was reported that:

> the rapid development of biological engineering will make it possible in just a few years to produce synthetic or partially synthetic toxins on a large scale. Such toxin agents represent a combination of the hitherto chemical and biological weapons. . . .

> Neurotropic toxins are toxic proteins which are primarily byproducts of the life cycles of microorganisms. The neurotropic toxins are the most toxic chemical substances. . . . Under combat conditions, they can be used as an aerosol or in solid or liquid state in mixed elements of ammunition; they can also be used for sabotage purposes.

Delivery Mechanisms

The effectiveness of aerosols for dispersing biological weapons has been demonstrated in the Soviet literature as well as more than 200 experiments in the United States. In 1950, US Navy vessels released clouds of *Bacillus globigii* and *Serratia marcescens* over San Francisco, Calif. Nearly everyone in the city inhaled 5000 or more particles contaminated with bacteria. In 1966, the Chemical Corps Special Operations Division released aerosols of bacteria (believed to be harmless) in the New York City subway. Because of the turbulence generated by the trains, bacteria were carried to the ends of the tunnels within minutes. These methods could easily be employed by terrorists.

Many types of delivery mechanisms are feasible: missiles, artillery, mines, multiple-rail and tube-launched rockets, fighter-bombers, and attack helicopters. Intercontinental delivery of chemical and biological agents is now possible with ballistic missiles. Some investigation has been carried out in the Soviet Union into the effects of warhead "tumbling" as a means of dissemination of chemical agents from large missiles.

Cruise missiles might be the ideal delivery system for biological weapons because of their ability to place a toxic cloud close to the ground. Flight at subsonic speeds would avoid some of the problems of heating the agent when it is ejected into the wind stream. The combination of the cruise missile and existing lethal organisms would be vastly superior to the blast effect of nuclear weapons and would rival nuclear weapons fallout in terms of area coverage per tonne of payload. The calculations that led to this conclusion are based on atmospheric tests of nuclear weapons, experiments in the dispersal of non-lethal agents from aircraft and the lethal dose of various biological agents, and assumptions about meteorological conditions. In the BRAVO test explosion at Bikini Atoll, Marshall Islands (yield, 12.7 to 13.6 megatonnes), the lethal fall-out contour (3 Gy in 96 hours) covered an area of approximately 26,000 km^2. Given suitable weather conditions and a cruise missile that flies like a crop duster, 100 g of a biological agent (approximately 10^{10} lethal doses of anthrax spores) could cover approximately 2.6 km^2 under light wind conditions at night, and 0.9 tonnes could cover approximately 26,000 km^2—an area the same order of magnitude as the lethal fallout from a ground-burst nuclear warhead that weighs more than 0.9 tonnes (a warhead that weighs 0.9 tonnes has a yield of approximately 0.9 megatonnes).

Proliferation

The recent furor over the Libyan complex near Rabta, which is potentially capable of producing tens of tonnes of toxic substances daily, has called attention to the "poor man's atomic bomb." The US Defense Intelligence Agency believes that approximately 20 other nations (in addition to the United States, the Soviet Union, and France) now possess chemical weapons. Many other Third World nations have chemical warfare capability. Iraq is said to have produced several thousand tonnes of mustard gas, tabun, and sarin since the early 1980s. In addition, 10 nations are believed to be developing biological weapons. The appeal of such weapons to Third World nations is obvious. Sophisticated technology is not required, and the weapons are very cost-effective. For a large-scale operation against a civilian population, casualties might cost $2000 per square kilometer with conventional weapons, $800 per square kilometer with nuclear weapons, $600 per square kilometer with nerve gas, and $1 per square kilometer with biological weapons.

Long-range delivery systems are also proliferating. Aging, "obsolete" ballistic missiles cast off by the superpowers are being acquired by Third World nations. The range of the missiles is extended if they carry a lighter, chemical or biological warhead, and inaccuracy is a lesser problem. The Soviet SCUD missile is believed to be in the hands of Iran, Iraq, North Korea, Libya, Syria, and several other nations. The US Nike-Hercules missile has been modified by South Korea, and Argentina, China, and Brazil are marketing new missiles.

Disadvantages of Chemical and Biological Weapons

While chemical and biological weapons can terrorize their victims with ghastly effectiveness, they also pose problems for the user. Invading troops would have to operate in a contaminated environment. Biological weapons might outwit their creators' precautions for protecting their own population as living organisms can develop resistance to vaccines or antibiotics. Accidents at production facilities could threaten enormous numbers of people.

Numerous pathogenic organisms, including bacteria, rickettsiae, viruses, and fungi, have been proposed and probably investigated as agents of biological warfare.

Chemical and biological weapons exist and are proliferating. There is considerable precedent for their use. It is clearly in the interest of humankind to prevent the future use of such agents of mass destruction, particularly as they become ever more lethal with advances in bioengineering.

The persistent ecological consequences of producing and testing chemical (and especially biological) agents are potentially more harmful and certainly less well understood than the radiological effects of nuclear weapons tests. The myxomatosis inoculation of a few rabbits in France in 1952 resulted in the spread of disease over an entire continent. At the scene of British World War II tests of anthrax bombs on the island of Gruinard, a 1979 survey still detected viable spores, despite an effort at decontamination by burning off the heather. By 1983, the area of significant contamination was small enough to make effective decontamination feasible using sporicides such as potassium permanganate, formaldehyde, glutaraldehyde, and peracetic acid, although such agents might also raise ecological concerns.

Methods for Preventing the Use of Chemical and Biological Weapons

There has always been a particular revulsion against chemical and biological weapons. In 1925, the Geneva Protocol was established to forbid the *first* use of these weapons. As of 1986, the protocol has been signed by 108 nations. While this protocol prohibits the use of these weapons, it does not prohibit production or stockpiling. Despite this protocol, there have been at least 40 allegations (many not verifiable) of chemical and biological weapons use between 1969 and 1986.

Production and research into the use and effects of these weapons continue. Those who argue for expanded US investment in research on these weapons can cite deterrence as the rationale. Since World War I, the victims of chemical agents have been nations that had no capacity to retaliate in kind.

A variety of circumstances may have prevented Hitler from using his secret weapons (tabun and sarin) against the Allies, although nothing prevented him from testing them on inmates of concentration camps. It is possible that Hitler hesitated because of his belief, based on extremely flimsy evidence, that the British also possessed these weapons. Retaliation would not only have killed many German civilians, but might have incapacitated the Wehrmacht's transportation system, which was heavily dependent on horses. (Late in the war, Hitler might have used poison gas despite the risk of retaliation, but by then he lacked an air force to deliver it.)

One might infer that in-kind deterrence is part of Soviet doctrine based on their extensive capacity to engage in chemical—and possibly biological— warfare. At the end of World War II, German attempts to destroy their own chemical warfare plants failed, and the Soviets acquired whole factories along with technical information. The US Defense Intelligence Agency reported that the Soviet production, testing, and storage facilities were continuing to expand as of 1985. At that time, more than 45,000 troops that specialized in chemical warfare served in the ground forces alone. Another report claims that up to 2,000 scientists and technicians are employed by the Institute of Molecular Biology near Novosibirsk, the largest of three research and development institutes believed to be concerned with biological warfare.

The existence of defenses against chemical and biological weapons might also be considered a part of deterrence (by preventing an enemy from achieving his objective) or alternately as evidence of intentions to use such agents. It is possible that the British manufacture of 40 million gas masks in 1939 might have helped discourage Hitler from launching a gas attack. In addition, allied military leaders arranged to inoculate approximately 100,000 soldiers against botulism, hoping to convince the Germans that the Allies were prepared for biological retaliation; the Germans never called the bluff.

Many western scientists argue against deterrence or defenses and in favor of relying solely on international agreements to ban chemical and biological weapons. (Such scientists generally seem to see deterrence or defense and arms control as mutually exclusive, although proponents of the former do not necessarily oppose arms agreements *in addition* to defense.) To date, there has been better success in obtaining agreements to limit chemical and biological agents than to limit nuclear weapons. The US generals were never able to answer a question posed by Matthew Meselson in the 1960s: under what circumstances would they actually order the use of biological weapons? Because the effects of biological weapons are so unpredictable, any available alternative would be used instead. Even for retaliation against a massive and deliberate biological attack, "the alternative of nuclear weapons was available and would be preferred." Convinced by this argument, President Richard Nixon ordered unilateral disarmament of biological weapons in 1969: the abandonment of development programs for biological weapons and the destruction of weapons stockpiles.

In 1972, the Biological and Toxin Weapons Convention was established to supplement the Geneva Protocol and since then has been signed by 103 nations, including the United States and the Soviet Union. Unlike the Geneva Protocol, this convention prohibits the development, production, and stockpiling of biological and toxin weapons. However, the Convention does not outlaw research into defenses against biological weapons. Recent increases in spending for such research ($60 million in 1988) have been opposed by scientists. More than 800 scientists have signed a pledge not to do work that could help develop biological weapons. Many believe this includes the development of vaccines against such weapons because "offensive and defensive research are indistinguishable." It is also argued that there is no feasible defense against biological weapons, given the vast number of possible agents (unless the agent to be used is known), but that attempts to develop a specific defense would make it possible to use that specific agent offensively, thus making the use of the weapons less unthinkable.

A ban on the use of existing vaccines has also been proposed: "negotiating an end to the vaccination of troops [by the United States and the Soviet Union], with its reassuring implications for reduced biological warfare risk, would be a final step in ending the fear of smallpox." In this view, vulnerability to a weapon seems to be a prerequisite for assuring compliance with a ban against its use.

Confidence in the Biological and Toxin Weapons Convention has been shaken by accusations of treaty violations. While there have been many allegations of chemical and biological weapons use, including claims that the United States used biological agents in Cuba and North Korea, the two allegations of greatest threat to US confidence in the convention are (1) the alleged use of mycotoxins in Southeast Asia and (2) an incident in the Soviet city of Sverdlovsk.

The US claims of Soviet use of the chemical toxin trichothecenes, or yellow rain, in Southeast Asia have been criticized by many scientists who have been persuaded by the bee feces explanation for the yellow substance. This hypothesis was formulated by Matthew Meselson, the man who is credited with fathering the treaty that might be destroyed by proof of Soviet use of mycotoxins. Others, citing inadequacies in the investigations, have an equally strong conviction that toxin weapons were used in Southeast Asia. However, incontrovertible evidence was not adduced to support this conviction.

The Sverdlovsk incident continues to be a subject of heated controversy. The report of an anthrax outbreak caused by an explosion at a Soviet biological weapons factory in Sverdlovsk apparently originated in *Posev,* an obscure magazine, based in Frankfurt, East Germany, published by Soviet émigrés. The Soviet news agency Tass admitted that there had been outbreaks of anthrax in Sverdlovsk, but attributed them to contaminated meat. The US intelligence analysts claimed that cases of inhalational anthrax had occurred, that aerial decontamination attempts were consistent with an accident at the military facility, and that the 1000 or more cases exceeded the annual incidence of anthrax throughout the Soviet Union by at least a factor of 100. Soviet officials countered that there had been no cases spread by inhalation, no aerial decontamination, and only 96 cases of illness. (Earlier, a Soviet official had stated that decontamination had been necessary because some "undisciplined workers" had thrown contaminated meat into open garbage containers.) Their

> **Biological weapons are very cost-effective. For a large-scale operation against a civilian population, casualties might cost $2000 per square kilometer with conventional weapons, $800 per square kilometer with nuclear weapons, $600 per square kilometer with nerve gas, and $1 per square kilometer with biological weapons.**

In 1972, the Biological and Toxin Weapons Convention was established to supplement the Geneva Protocol and since then has been signed by 103 nations, including the United States and the Soviet Union.

explanations persuaded a group organized and led by Matthew Meselson, whose requests to meet with Soviet scientists were granted under President Gorbachev's *glasnost*, but the Pentagon remains unconvinced.

While some persons, alarmed by reports of alleged biological warfare activities as well as by the proliferation of the weapons, call for improvements in intelligence and in response capabilities, others consider these recommendations an "irresponsible provocation" that might weaken prospects to "stave off a biological arms race." Proponents of the latter view believe that we must restore confidence in the existing legal regimes of prohibition and that the main burden for doing so resides in Washington, DC, not Moscow. In this view, the best hope for preventing the use of biological weapons is a ban on research into medical defense against biological war, except for investigations of "passive defenses" (clothing and vehicles impervious to chemical and biological agents) that do not involve actual testing with pathogenic organisms or toxic chemicals.

The lack of verification provisions in previous treaties has been noted. Possible verification strategies have been extensively discussed, along with the difficulties that result from the relative ease of production of chemical and biological weapons by using technology that has many legitimate applications such as the manufacture of fertilizer, pesticides, and pharmaceuticals. Beyond verification, assuring compliance may be the key issue.

Civil Defense in Case of Actual Use of Chemical and Biological Agents

Because the 1972 treaty as well as current initiatives to restrict chemical weapons may fail to prevent use of such agents, some nations currently deploy defenses. These nations may still recall the failure of the Geneva Protocol of 1925.

The Soviet corps of chemical warfare specialists has approximately 30,000 vehicles for decontamination and reconnaissance and has developed more than 200 areas for teaching all forces how to protect themselves and how to clean up the area following combat in which chemical weapons have been used. The training includes the use of actual chemical agents. Soviet civil defense textbooks used in institutions of higher education instruct citizens in how to recognize a chemical or biological attack and in protective measures. Gas masks are shown as part of standard equipment for shelters. Filmstrips for required civil defense classes show detailed instructions for the decontamination of areas affected by various agents (including mustard gas and sarin) with solutions of hypochlorite, lime, sodium hydroxide, or ammonia. Specifications for ventilating systems in Soviet blast shelters include provision for operation in "filter-ventilation" or "total isolation" mode to protect against radioactive fallout, chemical agents, or toxic gases from combustion. The exhaust blast valves are designed to maintain a small positive pressure to prevent unfiltered air from entering.

In contrast, specific training in chemical warfare defense is not given to citizens or even to civil defense organizations or fire and police personnel within nations in the North Atlantic Treaty Organization. Apart from Switzerland and Sweden, no nation outside the Warsaw Pact has any detection or alarm provision for the civilian population. (Swiss blast and radiation shelters are also equipped with absolute filters to remove chemical and biological agents.) Currently, detectors of aerosols that might carry biological agents are only in the developmental stage. However, several possible detection methods seem promising.

With regard to biological weapons, Soviet inattention to public health (as illustrated by the fact that anthrax is endemic in the Soviet Union, irrespective of the cause of the Sverdlovsk outbreak) can be said to constitute a "window of vulnerability." An efficient network of disease control centers has been proposed . . . as a "minimal defensive necessity."

In addition to the passive defenses discussed previously, active defenses might also be deployed against the delivery systems. Some argue that strategic defenses such as those designed for use against nuclear-armed intercontinental ballistic missiles would work equally well against missiles armed with other types of warheads. In this view, such defenses would be more effective against a few missiles launched by a Third World power than against a massive attack by a superpower. A substantially less expensive technology—the "Brilliant Pebbles" concept—has recently been proposed with a cost estimate of $10 billion.

While some have argued that strategic defenses would be ineffective against cruise missiles, which are better carriers for biological weapons, these subsonic projectiles are actually targeted more easily than intercontinental ballistic missiles. Soviet SA-10 surface-to-air missiles and Foxhound fighter airplanes with look-down, shoot-down radar can already destroy US cruise missiles.

Comment

Chemical and biological weapons exist and are proliferating. There is considerable precedent for their use. It is clearly in the interest of humankind to prevent the future use of such agents of mass destruction, particularly as they become ever more lethal with advances in bioengineering.

As with nuclear weapons, the argument regarding the best preventive strategy often pits deterrence and defense against disarmament treaties. In actual practice, the Soviet Union has a substantial investment in the former, although it does sign treaties. Western nations (except Switzerland in the realm of defense only) have a much more limited investment in the development and production of weapons or protective measures.

Difficulties in verifying (or enforcing) treaties are illustrated by alleged treaty violations. These same difficulties apply to all nations that possess or aspire to possess these weapons. Irrespective of treaties that concern weapons production, serious discussion is needed regarding improvements in the means of protecting the civilian population, as well as troops, against this growing threat. (pp. 644–47)

Jane M. Orient, "Chemical and Biological Warfare: Should Defenses Be Researched and Deployed?" in The Journal of the American Medical Association, *Vol. 262, No. 5, August 4, 1989, pp. 644–48.*

> **The United States maintains a stockpile of lethal chemical agents and munitions stored in bulk containers and in explosively and non-explosively configured munitions. The agents are of two types—nerve agents, and vesicant (blister) mustard agents. This stockpile is stored in the continental United States at eight Army installations, at Johnston Atoll in the central Pacific Ocean, and in the Federal Republic of Germany.**

The Chemical Weapons Stockpile

The United States maintains a stockpile of lethal chemical agents and munitions stored in bulk containers and in explosively and non-explosively configured munitions. The agents are of two types—nerve agents (GA, GB, and VX) and vesicant (blister) mustard agents (H, HD, HT, and Lewisite). This stockpile is stored in the continental United States at eight Army installations, at Johnston Atoll in the central Pacific Ocean, and in the Federal Republic of Germany.

In December 1985, Congress directed the U.S. Department of Defense (DOD) to destroy the U.S. stockpile by September 30, 1994, in such a manner as to provide:

(1) maximum protection of the environment, the general public, and the personnel involved in the destruction,

(2) adequate and safe facilities designed solely for the destruction of the stockpile, and

(3) cleanup, dismantling, and disposal of the facilities when the disposal program was complete (Title 14, Part B, Section 1412 of Public Law 99-145).

The stockpile of chemical weapons is lethal. It is old and getting older. Although the Army is required to operate at safety levels established by the Department of Health and Human Services and in conformance with applicable environmental protection regulations and permits, there is the very small but finite probability of an accidental release of agent that, depending on its severity, could kill people, contaminate the environment, destroy critical habitat, and otherwise constitute an environmental disaster.

Congress also directed the DOD to consider on-site disposal and regional and national disposal centers.

The Department of the Army, as executive agent for the DOD, established the Program Manager for Chemical Demilitarization (PM Cml Demil) as the agency responsible for implementing the disposal program. PM Cml Demil initiated its compliance with the National Environmental Policy Act (NEPA) for this Congressionally mandated program with a Notice of Intent to prepare a programmatic environmental impact statement and other appropriate site-specific environmental documents for disposal of the stockpile stored in the continental United States. Through an interagency agreement between the Department of the Army and the Department of Energy, Oak Ridge National Laboratory (ORNL) provided NEPA assistance to PM Cml Demil.

After public scoping meetings were held at or near each of the eight storage sites and with state and federal agency personnel in regional locations, a draft programmatic environmental impact statement (DPEIS) was prepared and published on July 1, 1986 (U.S. DA, 1986). Comments on the DPEIS and on the disposal program itself were extensive. In addition to over 300 pages of written correspondence, the Army held public hearings at or near each of the storage sites, with some hearings lasting over six hours. Public and agency comments on the DPEIS led to substantial additional efforts by the PM Cml Demil and contractors to characterize the technologies, risks, and impacts of disposal alternatives. In addition, in response to a comment at one of the hearings, the Army funded community study groups to evaluate the DPEIS and provide independent assessments of disposal program alternatives.

The Army published and released its three-volume final programmatic EIS (FPEIS) in late 1987 and issued its programmatic record of decision (stipulating on-site disposal), signed by Under Secretary of the Army James R. Ambrose. The PM Cml Demil is now preparing site-specific NEPA documentation for each of the proposed disposal sites and implementing programmatic mitigation (i.e., intergovernmental consultation and coordination and enhancements to emergency planning and preparedness) at each of the storage/disposal sites. In a recent report to Congress, the Army indicated that, contrary to the deadline stipulated in Public Law 99-145, it will complete disposal of the stockpile in 1997 so that additional experience from operation of a comparable destruction facility on Johnston Atoll can be factored into the CONUS destruction program. (pp. 279–80)

Background: The Lethal Unitary Chemical Stockpile

The chemical stockpile was produced as part of the nation's retaliatory arsenal until 1969, when President Nixon stopped further production. Mustard agents had been used in World War I by major combatants, resulting in thousands of casualties. Nerve agents were produced in large quantities by Germany prior to and during World War II, with U.S. production following the war. However, with the exception of uses of mustard agent by the Japanese, no lethal chemical agents were used during World War II.

The toxicity of the agents varies substantially. Although both nerve and blister agents are lethal, the nerve agents are substantially more lethal (by dose or concentration value). Mustard agents, although less lethal if exposure is acute (on a dose/concentration basis), are carcinogens, leading to the possibility of latent cancers years after exposure. (pp. 280–81)

Although agents are stored in a variety of explosively and non-explosively configured munitions, most (approximately 60 percent by agent tonnage) are stored in bulk containers—ton containers, spray tanks, and bombs. The explosively configured munitions (e.g., M55 rockets, M23 land mines, mortars, cartridges, and some projectiles) are more problematic since separating the explosives or energetic materials from the agent, the first stage in the disposal process, is itself a hazardous activity. (p. 281)

Explosively configured weapons are stored in earth-bermed bunkers or igloos. Nerve agents, whether explosively or non-explosively configured, are protected from the environment in igloos or in warehouses. The only agents/munitions stored in the open are mustard ton containers.

Stockpile Distribution

Although unofficial estimates of stockpile size have been published . . . , precise details regarding the absolute quantity and composition of the U.S. stockpile are classified for national security reasons. Other than approximately 6 percent (by agent tonnage) stored in the Federal Republic of Germany and on Johnston Atoll in the Pacific Ocean, the stockpile is stored at eight installations. The Johnston Atoll inventory is scheduled for destruction at a facility already under construction covered by separate NEPA documentation.

The largest amount, about 42 percent by agent tonnage, is stored at Tooele Army Depot, south of the City of Tooele and southwest of Salt Lake City, Utah, and the smallest (about 1.6 percent) at Lexington-Blue Grass Army Depot, immediately southeast of Richmond, Kentucky. The Umatilla Depot Activity, near Hermiston, Oregon; Pine Bluff Arsenal, near Pine Bluff, Arkansas; Anniston Army Depot, near Anniston, Alabama; and Tooele Army Depot have the most heterogeneous inventories, both in terms of agent and munition type. The Pueblo Depot Activity, near Pueblo, Colorado, stores only mustard agent, in bulk containers and explosively configured munitions. Together with Lexington-Blue Grass Army Depot, Aberdeen Proving Ground, near Edgewood, Maryland, and the Newport Army Ammunition Plant, near Newport, Indiana, have the smallest quantities of agent. Aberdeen and Newport store agent only in ton containers, with mustard at Aberdeen and VX at Newport.

The Chemical Stockpile Disposal Program

The legislative mandate to destroy the stockpile of lethal unitary chemical munitions and agents was not unexpected. [In a footnote, Carnes explains: "Unitary munitions contain chemical agent that is lethal at the time the agent is loaded in a weapon or munition or stored in a bulk container; binary weapons, which are now in production, contain two chemicals that may each be hazardous, but are not lethal until they are mixed after firing or other intentional use of the munition."] The Department of the Army had been examining such matters for a number of years in anticipation of such a requirement (partly because of previous Congressional debates linking binary weapons production with destruction of the unitary stockpile). The U.S. Army Toxic and Hazardous Materials Agency, a predecessor to PM Cml Demil, had incinerated over 6 million lbs of mustard agent and chemically neutralized more than 8 million lbs of nerve agent GB in the early to mid-1970s at Rocky Mountain Arsenal near Denver, Colorado. It had begun operating a pilot plant, the Chemical Agent Munitions Disposal System at Tooele, in 1979 to further test destruction technologies. The Army was constructing the Johnston Atoll Chemical Agent Disposal System (JACADS), an industrial-scale incineration facility, to destroy chemical agents stored on that largely man-made island several hundreds of miles southwest of Hawaii.

After substantial testing and use of both incineration and neutralization technologies, and after receiving advice from the National Research Council, the Army decided in 1982 to abandon neutralization and adopt incineration for the disposal of chemical agents and munitions. [Carnes adds in a footnote: "Although this selection was to be questioned subsequently by some members of the public, the National Research Council (1984) examined the problem at the request of the Army in 1982 and concluded that incineration was the most effective, economical, and safe means of disposal."] If neutralization were to be used, the much larger (three to four times larger) quantities of hazardous wastes would have to be disposed of, and given hazardous waste disposal options viable today, would probably have to be incinerated or otherwise reduced substantially prior to land disposal. Moreover, the neutralization process was

Unitary munitions contain a chemical agent that is lethal at the time the agent is loaded in a weapon or munition or stored in a bulk container; binary weapons contain two chemicals that may each be hazardous, but are not lethal until they are mixed after firing or other intentional use of the munition.

On-site disposal vs. centralized disposal present a risk distribution problem of significant proportions. Is it better to destroy the stockpile where it sits (in some cases near reasonably densely populated areas) or to put additional resources at risk (i.e., those in a transport corridor) by moving the stockpile to less densely populated areas for incineration?

found to result in extremely slow reaction times (days as opposed to the expected hours), require large quantities of caustic solution (sodium hydroxide), and could under certain conditions be reversible (at least for GB agent). In addition to incineration and neutralization, the Army had also considered "novel" destruction techniques in the late 1970s and early 1980s (e.g., nuclear detonation, biodegradation, etc.), but these were so problematic and/or premature as not to be considered reasonable methods. Historic methods, such as open pit burning and ocean disposal, were legally as well as publicly unacceptable means. Thus, the Army's preferred method of disposal, as identified in both the DPEIS and the FPEIS, was incinerated at the given Army installation(s), with disposal of residuals at permitted commercial hazardous waste disposal facilities. On-site disposal of incinerator residuals was never seriously considered by the Army.

The technology and process designs for JACADS are planned for use as a baseline for the other disposal plants, regardless of the disposal alternative ultimately implemented. Generally, the JACADS designs formed the technical basis for hazard and public safety risk analysis and other technical studies completed for the disposal alternatives under consideration. . . . The JACADS technology involves incineration of the agent, any energetic (i.e., explosive) materials, any transportation dunnage (e.g., packing material), and decontamination of the munition hardware in a specially designed system using four controlled furnaces and subsequent treatment of all process wastes and residues to ensure their safety for appropriate disposal.

The operation of the facility will create agent releases within the process areas. To address this, the Army design provides agent containment through cascade filtration. Where both agent and energetic material are combined in the munition and activities that could cause the munition to explode are encountered, a specially designed room (explosion containment cubicle) is utilized. This agent/explosive cubicle will contain the explosive force, the released agent, and the munition fragmentation for any munition or agent combination in the disposal program. The design also includes a ventilation/filter system. The process facility includes ventilation flows that continuously sweep room air from less agent-contaminated to more agent-contaminated areas and through redundant charcoal filter banks, where any agent is removed from the air prior to discharge up a stack. The movement of air prevents contaminated air from flowing into clean areas and dilutes agent concentrations in the more contaminated process areas. The redundant charcoal systems with agent monitoring between the systems ensure that agent levels (if any) in the ventilation air stack remain below allowable stack concentrations.

The liquid incineration furnace will destroy all liquid agents drained from the munitions. Two separate furnace systems, the deactivation furnace system and the metal parts furnace, will destroy the energetic materials and decontaminate all of the munitions bodies/ton containers, respectively. The fourth furnace system, the dunnage incinerator, will be used to thermally decontaminate other materials that may have been in contact with the agent (e.g., transportation pallets and used protective clothing). The solid wastes will be recycled where feasible (e.g., steel projectile bodies will probably be sold as scrap metal). Ashes will be disposed of in accordance with methods approved under the Resource Conservation and Recovery Act.

Each of the furnace systems has two stages, where the secondary stage destroys any residual agent that might carry over from the first stage. Each two-stage incinerator has its own pollution abatement system, which cools and removes from the exhaust gases the acidic components and particles associated with incineration of these compounds to ensure that the exhaust gases meet applicable federal and state air emissions standards. These incinerator systems are designed and operated to destroy the lethal agent to such an extent that the remaining concentrations in the exhaust gases are below the levels which would be hazardous to human health or the environment. Emissions are monitored continuously to alert operators to any excursions beyond these levels.

If the Army were to transport part of the stockpile off-site to an alternative installation for disposal, a detailed logistics and packaging program would be followed. The Army and its contractors developed and considered air and rail transportation logistics in the course of completing programmatic NEPA documentation. The Under Secretary of the Army determined that marine transport of the Aberdeen inventory to Johnston Atoll was not reasonable, given the risks to the environmentally sensitive Chesapeake Bay, the need for extensive studies to investigate the option's feasibility, and the availability of alternative off-site transportation options. (pp. 281–85)

Summary

The stockpile is lethal. It is old and getting older. It is something that nobody wants, but which some people already have—a variation on the NIMBY ("not in my backyard") phenomenon. Although the Army will be required to operate at safety levels established by the Department of Health and Human Services and in conformance with applicable environmental protection regulations and permits (e.g., Clean Air Act, Resource Conservation and Recovery Act), there is the very small but finite probability of an accidental release of agent that, depending on its severity, could kill people, contaminate the environment, destroy critical habitat, and otherwise constitute an environmental disaster.

The strategic options presented by Congress (i.e., on-site disposal vs. centralized disposal) and analyzed by the Army thus present a risk distribution problem of significant proportions. Is it better to destroy the stockpile where it sits (in some cases near reasonably densely populated areas) or to put additional resources at risk (i.e., those in a transport corridor) by moving the stockpile to less densely populated areas for incineration? What are the tradeoffs, and what information and data were systematically available and useful to the public and decision makers? What approaches and methods could best focus on these issues? (p. 289)

S. A. Carnes, "Disposing of Chemical Weapons: A Desired End in Search of an Acceptable Means," in The Environmental Professional, Vol. 11, No. 4, 1989, pp. 279–90.

> **"The proliferation of chemical and biological weapons, and the ability to deliver them at long ranges will be one of the most important security issues of the 1990s and of the 21st Century."**
>
> —Dan Quayle,
> Vice President of
> the United States,
> *OMNI*, February 1991

A History of Chemical Warfare

Chemical warfare is as old as life itself. It is nature's gift to the weak or vulnerable against threats, real or perceived. Millions of years of evolution have armed legions of plants, insects, fish, reptiles, amphibians, and invertebrates with biochemical means of neutralizing enemies or prey by emitting, squirting, or injecting vile-smelling, paralyzing, or lethal substances. This is survival of the fittest in its most elementary form: It is an imperative that, in the animal world, transcends morality because instinct and reflex—not premeditation—regulate animal behavior.

Nature, however, pales beside our inventiveness. Savage brews concocted by humans can spread disease for military goals, make an enemy's air unbreathable and foul, seed clouds with substances that turn rain into liquid death. Humans trained pigeons and bats to deliver "mini" bombs. They bred mosquitoes contaminated with yellow fever, malaria, and dengue. They cultivated fleas infected with the plague. They spawned ticks carrying tularemia and Colorado spotted fever. They sired houseflies tainted with cholera, anthrax, and dysentery. Even mice and migrating geese have been considered as vehicles for the delivery of death. Venomous snakes may be next. These weapons and their creators transform nature itself into an instrument of war.

"The face of war is about to change in a manner unimagined even ten years ago. The next decade is likely to witness the global use of chemical and biological weapons in conflicts of all sizes."

—H. J. McGeorge,
Public Safety Group

And we've only just begun, says H. J. McGeorge, president of the Public Safety Group, a Virginia-based-international security research organization. "The face of war is about to change in a manner unimagined even ten years ago. The next decade is likely to witness the global use of chemical and biological weapons in conflicts of all sizes." The rationale, says McGeorge, a munitions expert and former Secret Service technical specialist, is that "the use of chemical weapons will not win a war but might prevent the user from losing it."

Equally frightening is the ease with which chemical and, to a certain extent, biological weapons can be acquired. There's now a poison in every caldron. Chemical weapons are now available not only to major powers but to Third World nations as well. A study released by the U.S. Defense Department in 1984 listed 14 countries as possessing a chemical warfare capability, about ten more than had been previously estimated. The number now exceeds 38. There is strong evidence that yet another 15 to 20 nations are seeking to secure chemical weapons.

No wonder. Chemical weapons are easy to make. They call neither for high-tech resources nor much money. In fact, the manufacturing process and necessary ingredients for nerve agents are similar to those for common fertilizers and insecticides. And their power can be devastating. Minute amounts can become militarily significant, especially in hot or tropical regions where protective clothing severely limits the effectiveness of besieged forces.

Now biochemical technology is entering the weapons field. The same technology that has resulted in so many dramatic improvements in care and cure is now capable of producing new horrors easily transformed into weapons of choice. Genetic engineering will further refine the art of killing with the development of "designer diseases" for which there exists no known cure. New poisons may be produced from once innocuous substances. Even the means to alter and manipulate human behavior and thought are at hand.

A report issued late in 1990 by *BioWorld Today* says that Iraq, which has signed but never ratified the 1972 Biological and Toxin Weapons Convention, is developing a biological arsenal. The convention prohibits the possession of biological weapons but not, sadly, research and development. Indeed, the convention permits research into defensive biotechnology, despite the fine line between defensive mechanisms and offensive weapons. Biological agents capable of spreading typhoid, cholera, and anthrax are said to be in the works at laboratories south of Baghdad, near the village of Salman Pak. U.S. Army Medical Corps scientists themselves must now look to genetic engineering for the means to thwart such threats. In recent years, in fact, only the National Institutes of Health has exceeded U.S. Department of Defense in biotechnology research funding.

The subtlety and sophistication of the biochemical weapons threat continues to grow. But the threat itself is not at all new.

The Alchemy of Aggression

No one knows how primitive man waged chemical war. One can safely assume that flinging excrement at one another, a strategy still observed among primates, might have satisfied our ancestors' aggressive drive—not to mention their need for self-expression. *Homo sapiens* has since refined the art of mudslinging but the message is the same. Chemistry and biology provide us with ways of killing each other.

Around 450 B.C., at the height of the Second Peloponnesian War, the Spartans burned pitch and sulfur to release poisonous fumes under the enemy's city walls. Incendiary chemicals, dubbed Greek fire, were used as early as 1200 B.C. Gradually refined for use on dry land, Greek fire, a precursor of napalm, played a leading role in many battles for more than a millennium.

Civil War general Patrick Gilmore used Greek fire, causing Confederate general Pierre Beauregard to claim that Gilmore had shot "the most destructive missiles ever used in war."

Nor is biological warfare a contemporary phenomenon. During the siege of Kaffa in 1347, the Mongols hurled the bodies of plague victims over the walls of the Genoese defenders. Genoese ships then carried the disease back to Europe, where the Black Death promptly erupted.

In North America in the Eighteenth century, British military leaders, such as Jeffrey Amherst, offered a gift of smallpox-infected blankets to Native Americans, who were particularly susceptible to the deadly disease. This act of malevolence cost thousands of Indian lives.

Modern Malevolence

In the Thirties, the Japanese, at war with China, used biological weapons to spread plague and famine. They also tested biological munitions on tethered prisoners.

The first wholesale use of toxic agents took place in World War I when the Germans discharged chlorine gas on French and British troops. French and other forces responded with "blood gases," which prevent the transfer of oxygen from the blood to body tissue. This prompted the Germans to unleash mustard gas, a blistering agent that consumes the flesh. Under attack, U.S. troops retaliated with phosgene, a choking gas. When the carnage ended in 1918, the "war to end all wars" had claimed more than 9 million lives, with more than 100,000 of those deaths officially attributed to gas attacks. The toll is now believed to have been considerably higher.

In 1925, seven years after the end of the Great War, an international agreement known as the Geneva Protocol prohibited the use of bacteriological and chemical weapons—but not production or stockpiling. The Geneva Protocol did not prevent the French from dropping mustard-filled bombs in Morocco, nor did the Italians shy away from deploying mustard gas in the 1935–36 war against Abyssinia (Ethiopia).

In 1939, in search of deadlier, swifter poisons, the Germans also invented two nerve gases, Tabun and sarin, both colorless, almost odorless, both capable of penetrating the skin and causing death in less than two minutes. Deterred because the Allies themselves possessed chemical weapons, the Nazis did not use theirs against Allied forces during World War II. They used them instead to murder millions in death camps.

At war's end in 1945, the Soviets seized large stocks of nerve agents and other raw chemical warfare products, as well as a fully equipped—and staffed—Tabun factory, which they transferred to the USSR lock, stock, and barrel.

During the Fifties and Sixties, military research produced still meaner nerve agents, including the "V" series nerve agent, produced by both the United States and the Soviets, and dreaded because of its supertoxicity, persistence, and environmental stability. The Fifties also witnessed the development of mentally incapacitating but nonlethal chemicals.

Tear gases and herbicides (defoliants) were also extensively released by the United States in Vietnam. Arguably, these were "nonlethal" and authorized under the Geneva Protocol. Of all the chemicals used to strip the tropical forest bare, one that created the greatest bitterness was the dioxin-laced Agent Orange.

The defoliant sent vegetation on a self-destructive binge. Plants literally exploded, leaving a surrealistic landscape where weeds had grown into bushes and where trees, fractured and splintered, bowed down by the weight of their fruit, lay rotting in the foul-smelling jungle. The effect of Agent Orange on humans, especially its alleged carcinogenic effect, remains a matter of controversy today.

Countries possessing chemical or biological weapons: Bulgaria, Burma, China, Egypt, Ethiopia, France, Iran, Iraq, Israel, Libya, Somalia, Syria, Taiwan, USA, USSR, Vietnam

Countries thought to possess chemical or biological weapons: Cuba, Czechoslovakia, Germany, Hungary, Laos, North Korea, Poland, Romania, Sudan, Yugoslavia

Countries seeking chemical or biological weapons: Argentina, Brazil, Chile, India, Indonesia, Jordan, Pakistan, Peru, Saudi Arabia, South Africa, South Korea, Thailand

We are entering an age of "novel weapons." That seemingly innocuous phrase encapsulates the dawning era of bio-chemical weapons un-paralled in their viciousness, tenacity, and ability to penetrate even the most carefully considered defenses.

Toxic War Today

By the end of the Seventies, a growing number of intelligence and press reports hinted that chemicals were being regularly deployed by Soviet-supported forces in a "variety of minor conflicts." A particularly nasty batch of mustard gas had already been used by Egypt during the 1962–67 Yemen war, an occurrence that took several months to surface in the press.

Another report claimed that Laotian troops, aided and abetted by the Soviets and the Vietnamese, had been using agents of biological origin ("Yellow Rain") since 1975 against the H'mongs, a tribal people dwelling in the mountainous regions of Laos.

In Kampuchea (Cambodia), Vietnamese forces were reported to have used chemical agents against the troops of "Democratic Kampuchea."

In Afghanistan, strong circumstantial evidence indicates that Soviet and "loyal" Afghan forces waged periodic chemical war against the mujahedeen, the ragtag band of tough, iron-willed nationalist rebels.

Iran reported that between 1983 and 1984 Iraq had carried out more than 31 chemical attacks against Iran. International protest did not prevent Iraq from repeating the deed until the recent break in hostilities. Nor did it discourage Iran from readying to respond in kind.

Iraq's invasion of Kuwait [in August of 1990] and Saddam Hussein's own military proclivities have rekindled old fears. According to a recent communiqué by the Jaffee Center of Strategic Studies at Tel Aviv University in Israel, Iraq has

> emerged as a crucial country of the 90's, not only for Israel but for the area as a whole.
>
> Iraq emerged from its war with Iran with the region's largest and best equipped armed forces, under a firmly ensconced leader who has proven capable of using them ruthlessly. Of all the Arab states, Iraq appears most likely (as it proved in Iran and against its own people, the Kurds) to move the Middle East firmly into the nonconventional arena. [Chemical weapons] are a virtually indispensable component of a renewed Eastern front.

Seventy-two years after the end of World War I, despite the Geneva Protocol and the 1972 convention, a growing number of nations have steadily developed an appetite for higher forms of killing. That appetite is voracious, with new and ever deadlier weapons being brought to the table.

Tomorrow's Toxins

We are entering an age of "novel weapons." That seemingly innocuous phrase encapsulates the dawning era of biochemical weapons unparalleled in their viciousness, tenacity, and ability to penetrate even the most carefully considered defenses. Careful consideration, in fact, might well lead to the conclusion that there is no effective defense against biochemical attack.

For one thing, effective defense requires that you know what you're defending against. But modern technology is yielding so large and disparate a variety of chemical and biological agents that a uniform defense becomes impossible to achieve.

Gas masks and protective clothing worn to ward off mustard gas, for example, may be useless against new chemical weapons engineered to penetrate even the most tightly woven fabrics, the most impermeable seals and gaskets. Vaccination has long been explored as a possible defense against viral attacks; yet how do we determine which viruses to vaccinate against? How do we develop vaccines to protect us from new viruses developed in weapons laboratories? Suppose a virus is developed that does not respond to vaccines?

As we grow more capable of manipulating genetic and other material, so do the capabilities of biochemical weapons grow more fearsome. Imagine a weapon whose initial symptoms—a rash, perhaps—imply one course of treatment. Upon application of the appropriate treatment, though, the weapon reveals its true nature, unleashing a wholly different variety of systemic attack. How do you defend against such a weapon? You don't, because you can't.

Even detecting the use of biochemical weapons grows problematic. Much effort and research has been applied to the development of "biosensors," materials that use living organisms to detect the presence of chemical agents. In theory, biosensing devices serve as warning beacons, alerting troops in the field to the need to don protective clothing. All of which assumes that the enemy will use weapons the sensors "recognize," and against which protective clothing forms of effective shield.

None of the defenses take into account the sheer impossibility of protecting large civilian populations, susceptible to biochemical attack through water supplies, agricultural products, or food processing plants.

Nor does an escalating biochemical arms race take fully into account the environmental devastation that could be unleashed as a result of the use of biological agents. On a theoretical level, at least, perhaps the most appealing biological weapons are those that can be tailored to reside in common bacterium, especially bacteria that are common to human physiology.

Design and produce, for example, a toxic bacterium that lives quite comfortably in the human stomach. Because the cause for which you fight is "just," tailor the organism so that it can reproduce. Use it against your enemy. As the weapon wreaks its havoc, it also makes more weapons, a vicious cycle necessary to ensure victory for your cause.

But isn't there a flaw in that argument? Isn't there the possibility that the multiplying weapon will wend its way back behind your own lines, attacking your own population?

There may be a way around that. Target your weapon to attack and kill only specific genetic signatures. That way you can eliminate whole ethnic groups, without worrying too much that your attack will backfire.

None of these weapons exist yet, and they may never be produced. Genetic research is costly and complex. It's one thing to imagine a designer weapon, quite another to design and build it. It may in fact be easier to build nuclear weapons than to tailor genetic bombs. Many scientists feel that highly sophisticated genetic weapons will remain theoretical concepts rather than battlefield tools. On the other hand, it might well be easier to build a large arsenal of biochemical agents than a huge nuclear stockpile.

More likely, though, is a scenario in which traditional biochemical weapons—toxic gases or diseases such as anthrax—are enhanced in the laboratory, made more powerful and harder to stop.

Research into the enhancement of known toxins and biological agents is widespread today and will spread farther tomorrow.

Virtually every developed nation is currently funding research in areas that can easily be adapted to produce weapons. Much of that research is justified as necessary for defensive purposes, or even as medical science.

"How do you know what's going on in a biological research center?" says H. J. McGeorge. "Most nations have dozens of them. How do you know if someone is doing biological research on a disease in order to find a cure for that disease, or if they are trying to figure out how to package that disease?" This conundrum has haunted all attempts to arrive at a comprehensive ban on biological and chemical weapons research.

And so a new arms race seems about to burst into full bloom, even as we discuss the abandonment of the nuclear standoff. Pandora's box gapes once more, with chemical and biological weapons pouring out. Because of their nature,

Effective defense requires that you know what you're defending against. But modern technology is yielding so large and disparate a variety of chemical and biological agents that a uniform defense becomes impossible to achieve.

these modern plagues may prove harder to stop and more difficult to ban than any weapons previously employed. (pp. 44–8, 111)

W. E. Gutman, "A Poison in Every Cauldron," in OMNI, Vol. 13, No. 5, February, 1991, pp. 42–6, 48, 111–13.

Far too belatedly, the whistle has been blown on Government complacency, recklessness and secrecy. Under assault from congressional critics, citizen lawsuits and probing reporters, the private contractors and their see-no-evil federal supervisors have admitted to shocking practices and promised to clean up after their predecessors. That effort could cost as much as $100 billion and take 20 to 30 years. Unwilling to spend money to keep their aging equipment in repair or to plan for orderly replacements, they have allowed their network of plants to become so disabled as to threaten the very reason for their creation: the maintenance of a credible nuclear deterrent.

Nuclear Hazards

Across the country, the outrage and sense of disbelief are mounting. The nation's production-obsessed, scandalously shortsighted nuclear weapons industry is virtually under siege by its critics. And no wonder. Operating secretively behind a screen of national security for more than four decades, the bomb-makers have single-mindedly, sometimes recklessly, pursued their goal: to churn out all the warheads the military believes, perhaps prudently, are needed to maintain the U.S. nuclear deterrent. Now they are being charged with ignoring the dangers that their operation of deteriorating facilities may have inflicted on the very citizens they were supposed to protect. Ohio's Senator John Glenn summed up the situation with ironic clarity: "We are poisoning our people in the name of national security."

Whether left unsupervised by lax Government officials or, worse yet, ordered by them to stifle their own concerns, the private contractors who ran the major U.S. weapons plants released huge quantities of radioactive particles into the air and dumped tons of potentially cancer-inducing refuse into flowing creeks and leaking pits, contaminating underground water supplies in a seepage that cannot be stopped. No one knows how many people may have been needlessly afflicted with such ailments as cancer, birth deformities and thyroid deficiencies—and no one in relevant offices seemed to care. Why? Because a legalistic, bureaucratic shuffle left no one responsible for whatever human and environmental damage was inflicted.

Only recently, that attitude has begun to change. The Department of Energy in 1977 took over responsibility for the nuclear weapons network, which had long been overseen by the now defunct Atomic Energy Commission, and finally seems bent on reform. Information about the weapons-production system has emerged that only begins to suggest the past callousness of both Government officials and private contractors. At the sprawling Hanford plutonium-processing complex in Washington State, managers once deliberately released 5,050 curies of radioactive iodine into the air. The reason: to see if they could reduce the amount of time uranium must be cooled before being processed into plutonium, presumably to increase production.

Operating well out of the public eye and, at least for a time, beyond Washington's view as well, technicians running an aging reactor at the Savannah River plant near Aiken, S.C., made errors in 1970 leading to the partial melting of a fuel rod. If the process had not been checked, it could eventually have led to a disaster on the order of the 1979 debacle at Three Mile Island. That frightening episode jolted the entire nation and inspired sharp reforms in the U.S. civilian nuclear power industry.

Despite the claims, there is no undisputed evidence that radioactive materials released into the environment around DOE facilities have harmed anyone. In general, such contamination is believed to fall into a category that, according to Jacob Fabrikant, an expert on the biological effects of radiation, is "far too low to pose a risk to the health of individuals." Yet there is agreement that radiation doses of more than 50 rems, a measure of the effect of radiation on the body, can sicken and even kill. It may do so by changing the chemical makeup of cells. A large enough dose can cause genetic defects and lead to cancer. Massive exposure in a brief period can result in radiation sickness and death within a short time.

As poisonous wastes from the weapons plants pile up alarmingly and no proven solution to their safe disposal is found, yet another dilemma looms. [In October 1988] Idaho Governor Cecil Andrus, a former Secretary of the Interior, . . . ordered state police to stop any shipments of nuclear military wastes from entering the state. Since 1952 some 75% of the defense industry's low-level radioactive brew has been deposited in 120,000 drums and 11,000 boxes on a "temporary" basis at the Idaho National Engineering Laboratory, waiting for a new federal Waste Isolation Pilot Plant near Carlsbad, N.Mex., to open. There, the stuff will be buried in 3,000-ft.-deep salt formations. But no one knows when WIPP, started in 1983, will be ready. "If we can't resolve what we're going to do with the waste, then we have no business generating it," declared Andrus.

Far too belatedly, the whistle has been blown on Government complacency, recklessness and secrecy. Under assault from congressional critics, citizen lawsuits and probing reporters, the private contractors and their see-no-evil federal supervisors have admitted to shocking practices and promised to clean up after their predecessors. That effort could cost as much as $100 billion and take 20 to 30 years. Unwilling to spend money to keep their aging equipment in repair or to plan for orderly replacements, they have allowed their network of plants to become so disabled as to threaten the very reason for their creation: the maintenance of a credible nuclear deterrent. (pp. 61–2)

Even as a newly aroused DOE bureaucracy struggles with the massive task of trying to clean up improperly stored radioactive wastes from 40 years of bomb-making, no solution is in sight for a demonstrably safe permanent disposal system that will last for the required millenniums. At just two facilities, Hanford and Savannah River, nearly 100 million gal. of highly radioactive wastes have been generated. At Hanford alone, some 200 billion gal. of the more benign low-level wastes have been dumped into ponds, pits and basins—enough to create a lake 40 ft. deep and large enough to cover Manhattan.

In the catalog of previously concealed horrors, one of the worst records was compiled by the Hanford facility. Documents secured in the past three years by a Spokane environmental group under the Freedom of Information Act revealed that between 1944 and 1956, a startling 530,000 curies, a measure of emitted radioactivity, of iodine were released into the air by the facility—an amount greater than any ever recorded at a U.S. nuclear plant. In 1953 and 1954 a large quantity of radioactive material was emitted, depositing particles near the ranching town of Mesa, about 15 miles from Hanford's boundary. (pp. 62–3)

The federal Centers for Disease Control in Atlanta plan to study how individuals living near Hanford have been affected physically. In a preliminary estimate, CDC researchers suggested that 20,000 children in eastern Washington may have been exposed to unhealthy levels of radioactive iodine by drinking milk from cows grazing in contaminated grasslands. Other scientists are already attempting to determine the actual doses of radiation received by residents, a study that may take five years and cost up to $10 million. Concedes Hanford manager Michael Lawrence: "There is no question that releases from the plants in the '40s and '50s were far higher than would be allowed today."

At Ohio's Feed Materials Production Center in Fernald, a uranium-processing plant, the innocent-sounding name and the red-and-white checkerboard design on a water tower led some nearby residents to think it produced cattle feed or pet food. They have learned, to their dismay, that not only was the facility fabricating uranium rods for nuclear-reactor fuel cores and components for warheads, but one of its even scarier outputs was radioactive pollution. . . .

The strange happenings at Fernald illustrate the baffling ways officials, private or public, involved in the mismanagement seem able to escape legal and

At Ohio's Feed Materials Production Center in Fernald, a uranium-processing plant, the innocent-sounding name and the red-and-white checkerboard design on a water tower led some nearby residents to think it produced cattle feed or pet food. They have learned, to their dismay, that not only was the facility fabricating uranium rods for nuclear-reactor fuel cores and components for warheads, but one of its even scarier outputs was radioactive pollution.

**Since 1952 some 75%
of the defense industry's
low-level radioactive
brew has been deposited
in 120,000 drums and
11,000 boxes on a "tem-
porary" basis at the
Idaho National Engineer-
ing Laboratory, waiting
for a new federal Waste
Isolation Pilot Plant near
Carlsbad, N. Mex., to
open. There, the stuff
will be buried in 3,000-
ft.-deep salt formations.**

financial liability for their actions. Records released [in September 1988] show that when the operation began in 1953, the Atomic Energy Commission told the contractor, National Lead of Ohio, to dump radioactive refuse into pits dug in the ground, then standard practice. When rainwater caused the pits to over-flow, the AEC stonewalled the contractor's suggestions for fixing the problem. In 1958 National Lead warned that liquid was leaking through concrete storage tanks that had cracked. The commission's expedient solution: don't get new tanks, just keep the liquid below the cracks. The flawed tanks are still in use.

Richard Shank, director of Ohio's environmental protection agency, estimates that the Fernald operation has released 298,000 lbs. of uranium wastes into the air since the plant started. Beyond that, he cites the deliberate discharge of 167,000 lbs. of wastes into the Great Miami River over 37 years. An addi-tional 12.7 million lbs. were placed in pits, all of which may be leaking. Sena-tor Glenn is still awaiting an analysis he requested three years ago from the Energy Department on whether such estimates are correct.

The department has admitted that the Government was aware of these haz-ardous events at Fernald all along. A class-action lawsuit was filed against National Lead in 1985 by some 14,000 Fernald area residents. All too aware that radiation exposure is difficult to link conclusively with specific health problems, the residents are seeking $300 million in damages from lowered property values and the emotional trauma created by living near the plant. Their problem now is that the Federal Government is largely immune from such lawsuits. A recent Supreme Court decision ruled that a contractor meet-ing specifications set by the Government is cloaked with immunity from legal action. No one, it appears, is liable—or accountable. (p. 64)

At the Savannah River layout, where discharges of reactor coolant emerge hot enough to boil a frog, a DOE official admits, "It's not too good for the fish around here either." The agency also concedes that a network of shallow aqui-fers under the vast acreage is contaminated with radioactive compounds. A deeper aquifer contains toxic, nonradioactive materials. The only argument: whether this supply is the source of drinking water for the surrounding area.

It is at Savannah River that some of the weapons industry's most disturbing blunders have been exposed. Congressional investigators have turned up in-ternal memos from the facility's manager, E. I. du Pont de Nemours, citing nu-merous incidents over three decades. On May 10, 1965, operators ignored a loud alarm for 15 minutes. Then they saw water spilling across the reactor-room floor. Fully 2,100 gal. of fluid had leaked out of the reactor, leaving the level of coolant too low. The reactor shut itself down automatically.

Only two fuel meltdowns are known to have occurred in U.S. reactors before the crisis at Three Mile Island. Those were in the pioneering days of nuclear weaponry. Besides the partial melting of a fuel rod in 1970, a more recent near calamity took place in March 1982, when a technician at one of the Savannah River reactors left a water valve open, and for twelve hours the undetected flow flooded a large plutonium-processing room. The contaminated water was 2 ft. deep.

William Lawless, a former engineer at Savannah River, contends that plant managers paid little attention to workers who spotted what they considered unsafe practices. He says he was overruled when he tried to warn officials in 1982 about storing highly radioactive liquid waste in holding tanks whose floors had corrosive pits. "It's just like the shuttle disaster," he says. "Engi-neers weren't allowed to stop something they should have. Management con-trols them."

The disclosures have ignited a public spat between the Energy Department and Du Pont chairman Richard Heckert. He charges that DOE has inflated the Savannah River troubles so that Westinghouse Electric, which is scheduled to take over the plant's operation from Du Pont on April 1, will look better. Heck-ert also contends that DOE is promoting the furor to gain public support and congressional funding for a new tritium-producing reactor at the huge instal-lation. It would cost at least $6 billion and take more than six years to build.

"Despite all the hullabaloo," Heckert says of his company's operation of the plant, "nobody was ever injured or killed."

The gloom at Rocky Flats began on Oct. 8 when the Energy Department ordered work stopped in Building 771, where operations vital to the functioning of the entire facility were conducted, severely curtailing activity for the foreseeable future. The shutdown came after three people walked into a room that contained contaminated equipment. The warning sign that should have alerted them was covered by an electrical panel. Although the workers were not seriously exposed, the sloppy attitude toward safety has a long history at the plant. In its early days of operation, it was prone to fires, culminating in a blaze in May 1969 that caused $21 million in damage. The installation also faces a huge cleanup bill for its careless handling of wastes in the past. The price is placed at $755 million by DOE; critics contend it will be twice that amount.

Inevitably, many hardy souls who work in the nuclear plants or whose communities rely heavily on the income they bring scoff at what they consider the alarmist fears being raised. Charges John Poynor, mayor of Richland, the closest town to the vast Hanford spread: "The types of people who are critical of Hanford and other nuclear reactors don't like anything except whales. I'd ship them all off to Alaska and let them rescue those three whales that are stuck."

Among those who are not especially concerned about the safety of the weapons-production network are residents of Oak Ridge, Tenn., where enriched uranium has been produced since the very beginnings of the atomic age. Radiation is such a humdrum part of their daily lives that they take the red-and-white warning signs posted along Popular Creek in stride. When area hunters bag a deer, they routinely run parts of it past a wildlife agent for radiation tests before serving it for dinner. The sight of coverall-clad workers chopping down "hot" trees growing in contaminated soil causes little concern.

But for many, the invisible nature of radiation does stir emotions and feed paranoiac imaginations. Yet by operating for so long behind veils of secrecy, the weaponsmakers have left a void of perception that is all too easy to fill with worries that may or may not be exaggerated. In certain ill-defined and perhaps unknown quantities, radiation in the air, soil and water can, of course, be deadly. Some of its forms may persist for many centuries. As federal officials and fiercely independent private contractors finally step out of the nuclear closet and seek vast sums to clean up the mess they have created, repair aging facilities or build new ones, they face an unfamiliar challenge. Only candor and a new determination to give public safety priority over arms production can win the support they need. (p. 65)

Ed Magnuson, " 'They Lied to Us'," in Time, *New York, Vol. 132, No. 18, October 31, 1988, pp. 60–5.*

The stockpile inventory includes both organophosphate (nerve) and vesicant (blister) agents. Each of these agents was formulated especially to cause major injuries or death to enemy forces in wartime and is acutely lethal at sufficiently high doses.

Health Concerns

Stockpile Characterization

Although there are unofficial estimates of the size of the lethal unitary chemical weapons stockpile . . . , precise details regarding the absolute quantity and composition are classified for national security reasons. The M55 rocket is the only declassified stockpile element; as of December 31, 1983, there were 404,596 rockets, each containing approximately 5 kg of agent GB (sarin) or agent VX. Other than the approximately 6% (combined total by agent tonnage) stored in the Federal Republic of Germany and on Johnston Atoll, the unitary stockpile is stored at [eight installations: Umatilla Depot, Oregon;

Much interest has been expressed by the public regarding the possibility of chronic disease states or delayed effects developing at some time after exposure to nerve agents. All analyzed data indicate that nerve agents do not cause mutations or cancer and do not damage fetuses or induce reproductive dysfunction.

Tooele Army Depot, Utah; Pueblo Depot, Colorado; Pine Bluff Arsenal, Arkansas; Anniston Army Depot, Alabama; Lexington-Blue Grass Army Depot, Kentucky; Aberdeen Proving Ground, Maryland; and the Newport Army Ammunition Plant, Indiana]. (p. 654)

Agent Characterization

The stockpile inventory includes both organophosphate (nerve) and vesicant (blister) agents. The nerve agents include GA (tabun ["G" for German, identifying this agent as one found among German military stores captured at the close of World War II]), GB (sarin), and VX ("V" for venom). Agents held in research and development quantities, such as the nerve agent GD (soman), are not considered part of the retaliatory stockpile (quantities are too small to be considered militarily significant) and are not included in the Chemical Stockpile Disposal Program. The vesicant agents include H, HD, HT (various formulations of sulfur mustard) as well as lewisite (an organic arsenical). Each of these agents was formulated especially to cause major injuries or death to enemy forces in wartime and is acutely lethal at sufficiently high doses. . . .

Nerve Agents

The fact that nerve agents are acutely lethal at relatively low concentrations (eg, human skin median lethal dose of 0.04 mg/kg for agent VX) was the paramount factor in considering nerve-agent toxicity during the environmental impact statement process. Differences in the volatility of individual agents generate agent-specific considerations in the evaluation of human health effects. For example, an accidental (ie, unintentional) release could disperse toxic concentrations of the highly volatile agent GB (22×10^4 mg/m^3 saturated air concentration at 25°C) over a wide area. With the less-volatile agent VX (10.5 mg/m^3 saturated air concentration at 25°C), toxic concentrations would not disperse as widely but could persist in the environment long after an accidental release.

The toxic effects of nerve agents are due not only to their ability to irreversibly inhibit acetylcholinesterase but also to generate noncholinergic neurotoxic responses. (p. 656)

Much interest has been expressed by the public regarding the possibility of chronic disease states or delayed effects developing at some time after exposure to nerve agents. All analyzed data indicate that nerve agents do not cause mutations or cancer and do not damage fetuses or induce reproductive dysfunction. Agents GA and GB cause delayed neuropathy in susceptible animals (usually chickens; mice and rats are resistant to this condition), but only after short-term exposure to concentrations many times the lethal dose. In fact, chickens must be protected from lethal effects by prophylactic pretreatment with antidotes to perform necessary behavioral effects tests. Agent VX is not known to induce delayed neuropathy.

In the hypothetical event of accidental human exposure to massive doses of GA or GB, the obvious overwhelming concern would be protection from acute lethality. If emergency support measures were successful, then any exposed persons certainly should be monitored for late development of neuropathic symptoms. Our analysis leads us to conclude that delayed neuropathy is not a relevant issue compared with the more immediate concerns to acute lethality.

The possibility of long-term brain dysfunction after exposure to a nerve agent also has been raised. Study of chemical weapons factory workers from Rocky Mountain Arsenal (Denver, Colo) who had experienced one or more unintended acute exposures to GB sufficient to produce clinical signs of organophosphate exposure and an erythrocyte cholinesterase depression of at least 25% below individual preexposure baseline suggests that functional changes in brain activity may be expressed as memory disturbances or electroencephalographic changes for at least 1 year after the last acute exposure. The behavioral significance of these findings is not known. Concentrations of GB responsible for these effects were not reported, although the minimum effective dose for GB-induced miosis or muscle tremors is estimated at 2 to 4 mg-min/m^3 in humans. There were no instances of acute or delayed mortality in this worker population (n = 77 over a period of at least 6 years).

Exposures of comparable magnitude are probable in the event of an energetic release during an inadvertent explosion or fire. The principal medical concern again would be that of acute lethality. There is no evidence to suggest that brain dysfunction could occur on exposure to the maximum atmospheric concentrations of nerve agent that may be expected during normal operation of an incineration plant (occupational 8-hour exposure of 1×10^{-4} mg/m^3 for GA/GB and 1×10^{-5} mg/m^3 for VX; general population 72-hour time-weighted average of 3×10^{-6} mg/m^3 for GA/GB and VX).

Vesicant Agents

While nerve agents produce lethality at low doses, the vesicants as a group are not acutely lethal at similar concentrations under comparable exposure conditions. The vesicant agent HT is a notable exception because of the blended presence of agent T, which increases the stability of the mixture and possesses significant toxic properties of its own. All vesicants are cellular poisons. Mustard is an alkylating agent, while lewisite (an organic arsenical) fatally alters critical cellular enzyme systems (Table 1).

After exposure to any formulation of mustard agent, there is usually a latency period of several hours before signs of toxic exposure, such as eye inflammation and irritation or blistering of the skin and respiratory tract, begin to appear. Lesions are slow to heal, and full recovery from large blisters may require months. Extensive medical and life support often is necessary to prevent subsequent infection or fatal pulmonary edema. As a result, sulfur mustard is considered primarily an incapacitating rather than a lethal agent; hospital records from World War I and the recent Iran-Iraq conflict indicate 1% to 3% acute lethality from battlefield exposures approximating 1500 to 2000 mg-min/m^3 of mustard agent.

Contact with mustard-agent droplets or vapor also can induce delayed effects to the eye (keratitis) and respiratory tract (chronic bronchitis and cancers of the pharynx, larynx, trachea, and lung). Long-term follow-up of World War I veterans and mustard-factory workers in Germany and Japan has led the International Agency for Research on Cancer, in Lyons, France, to conclude that mustard agent is a "group I" human carcinogen. Other respiratory carcinogens in the same category include arsenic, asbestos, and vinyl chloride.

Lewisite is not as well characterized as sulfur mustard but possesses generally similar vesicant properties. It does not exhibit the latency period displayed by mustard agent, and it is noted for causing immediate severe pain on contact with skin or eyes. At sufficiently large doses it is toxic to the liver and kidneys and is known from one case report to induce Bowen's disease, a usually nonfatal intraepidermal squamous cell carcinoma. (pp. 656–57)

[Because] current regulatory thinking considers that there is no threshold for exposure to carcinogens, control limit concentrations pose some degree of calculated risk. An estimate of this risk was developed in a recent assessment that incorporated maximal assumptions of hypothetical exposure to incinerator workers and the general public. The estimated lifetime cancer risk for mustard incinerator workers approximates 3×10^{-4}, while that for the general public approximates 3×10^{-5}. Note for comparison that the present US lifetime cancer incidence from all causes is approximately 2.5×10^{-1}. (p. 657)

There are no specific antidotes for mustard-agent poisoning; chemical reaction with biologic tissue is so rapid as to be irreversible for all practical purposes. Attempts at treatment have been aimed at rapid decontamination and symptomatic therapy to relieve the effects of chemical burns to the skin, eyes, and respiratory tract. Exposure to lewisite can be effectively countered by treatment with British antilewisite after time lapses of as much as 1 hour. Newer, water-soluble British antilewisite analogues (meso-dimercaptosuccinic acid

Nerve agents are acutely lethal at relatively low concentrations (eg, human skin median lethal dose of 0.04 mg/kg for agent VX).

Reducing the regional threat posed by aging chemical weapons will require much work by scientists, concerned citizens, and agencies of local, state, and federal governments. The task is neither easy nor straightforward. Involvement of an informed medical community can provide invaluable insight and leadership to the essential process of community readiness in anticipation of agent disposal.

and the sodium salt of 2,3-dimercapto-1-propanesulfonic acid) can be administered orally or by intravenous drip and are effective in laboratory animals as late as 4 hours after exposure. These analogues have also been successful in treating occupational victims of methylmercury and lead poisoning. However, prolonged oral treatment (>5 days) with some formulations of 2,3-dimercapto-1-propanesulfonic acid has been associated with development of Stevens-Johnson syndrome. Preliminary experiments on swine skin indicate that pretreatment with meso-dimercaptosuccinic acid or 2, 3-dimercapto-1-propanesulfonic acid in a thin collagen film also may be protective against the blistering reaction of lewisite on the skin. Dose and treatment protocols for the British antilewisite analogues have not yet been developed in the United States because these compounds are considered "orphan drugs." Admittedly, treatment with British antilewisite or one of its analogues has limited scope; the sole stockpile of lewisite is reported to be comparatively small and exists at only one site (Tooele Army Depot).

Role of Health and Environmental Impact Analysis in Stockpile Disposal

The programmatic assessment, published in draft form in July 1986 and as a final report in January 1988, evaluated the impacts of three alternatives: disposing of the inventory on site at each of the eight current storage locations; moving the individual site inventories to one national or two regional installations for disposal; or continuing to store the stockpile indefinitely (the "no action" alternative required to be assessed by the National Environmental Policy Act). In accordance with regulations implementing the act, the draft programmatic environmental impact statement assessed the impacts of each alternative but did not compare them or make a recommendation regarding which alternative was preferred from a health and environmental perspective. Following substantial review and comment by government agency personnel, interest group representatives such as the Natural Resources Defense Council and The League of Kentucky Sportsmen and members of the public (through comments made during public hearings held at or near each of the eight sites), the final programmatic environmental impact statement was prepared.

In both the draft and final programmatic statements, the impacts of "normal operations" (ie, with no unintended release of chemical agent) and accident scenarios were examined. Impacts resulting from normal operations were found to be significant with respect to two concerns: (1) confusion and miscommunication about the program and (2) the inadequacy of existing emergency preparedness to mitigate adverse effects of unplanned releases. The former had resulted in apprehension over the program timetable and choice of disposal technology as well as credibility problems between responsible government agencies and the public.

The assessment used a sequence of technical studies and analyses to develop estimates for several health risk measures (ie, the probability of one or more fatalities, maximum fatalities, expected fatalities, and person-years at risk) for all considered alternatives. This sequence included (1) a quantitative risk analysis that identified credible agent-release scenarios for all considered alternatives and estimated their probabilities and the quantities of agent released; (2) an analysis and estimation of the plume geometries of lethal agent for the agent-release scenarios identified in the risk analysis, using an atmospheric dispersion model and computer code developed especially for use with lethal chemical agents; and (3) a computer-assisted estimation of potential fatalities resulting from laying the plume geometries over the 1980 distribution of residential populations that surround each of the eight sites and potential off-site transportation corridors. The estimated numbers of fatalities derived from this assessment ranged from zero or negligible to catastrophic. We define a negligible accident (zero to five fatalities) as involving a small release (eg, 1 to 10 kg of agent) in a sparsely populated area (eg, near Tooele Army Depot). A catastrophic accident (> 1000 fatalities) would involve a large release (eg, 100 to >1000 kg of agent) in a moderately populated area (eg, near Aberdeen Proving

Ground or Lexington-Blue Grass Army Depot). Probabilities of individual accidents ranged from 1×10^{-4} to 1×10^{-10} over the life of the disposal program for the entire stockpile.

A formal procedure for analyzing data was developed to compare options and select the alternative preferred on public health and environmental grounds in the final programmatic environmental impact statement. This procedure had three stages: (1) disposal alternatives were compared on the health risk measures identified above, and those found significantly worse than the others were eliminated from further consideration; (2) alternatives found to pose equivalent public health risks were compared on the basis of potential environmental insult (eg, loss of critical habitat and contamination of public water supplies); and (3) alternatives equivalent on public health and environmental grounds were compared on the basis of the potential for reduced public health risks resulting from improvements to emergency planning and preparedness (a mitigation measure applicable to and intended for all disposal alternatives). On-site incineration/disposal was the resulting preferred alternative from a health and environmental perspective.

Following public hearings on the final programmatic environmental impact statement, Under Secretary of the Army James R. Ambrose decided on February 23, 1988, to proceed with on-site disposal pending completion of site-specific analyses. These analyses currently are under way. The basis of the under secretary's decision was essentially that on-site disposal "(1) is the best choice from a public health and environmental perspective, (2) reflects a realistic appraisal of our ability to mitigate accidents, (3) is less vulnerable to terrorism and sabotage, and (4) is far less complex in terms of logistics, including security and emergency response." His decision also stipulated that the army would seek funds from Congress and initiate enhanced emergency planning and preparedness at each site. In addition, the disposal program's implementation would be subjected to significant oversight by both the National Academy of Sciences and by intergovernmental (ie, federal, state, and local governments) consultation and coordination boards.

Implementation of Emergency Preparedness

The lethal unitary stockpile should be eliminated by 1997 under the assumptions of (1) timely congressional appropriations, (2) reasonable progress in site-specific environmental documentation and permitting, (3) aggressive development, procurement, installation, and maintenance of emergency planning and preparedness improvements at each of the eight sites, and (4) a minimum of litigation by those opposed to on-site disposal. These issues, however, are not resolved easily.

The incipient emergency planning and preparedness program is comprehensive and multifaceted and incorporates the efforts of many parties (eg, various parts of the army, including the installations and their contractors, other federal agencies such as the Federal Emergency Management Agency and the Department of Health and Human Services, and relevant state and local agencies). Although some of the activities are being pursued simultaneously, there is a temporal flow to the program:

- 1987: evaluated baseline emergency planning and preparedness capability at each site and developed a generic emergency response plan.

- 1988: meshed upgraded community emergency preparedness plans with existing installation emergency plans, assuming no increase in capital budgets; enlisted the participation of local health care providers and state/local health agencies.

- 1988 to 1989: prepare site-specific chemical emergency protocols; initiate technical studies on topics that include protective action, public education, technical training, and reentry criteria to support decision making by all pertinent agencies and jurisdictions.

The lethal unitary stockpile should be eliminated by 1997 under the assumption of (1) timely congressional appropriations, (2) reasonable progress in site-specific environmental documentation and permitting, (3) aggressive development, procurement, installation, and maintenance of emergency planning and preparedness improvements at each of the eight sites, and (4) a minimum of litigation by those opposed to on-site disposal.

For all three munition categories, the demilitarization process involves two distinct operations: preparation for thermal treatment, followed by thermal processing.

- 1989 to 1990: installations and affected local/state government agencies will design site-specific emergency response plans, including designation of emergency planning zones and selection of warning systems/protective actions; train civilian emergency workers; implement public education effort.

- 1990 to 1997: install and support designed emergency response systems until the disposal program is completed; periodically test and evaluate systems via exercises.

A multidisciplinary effort by all concerned parties will be necessary to develop the technical bases for informed decision making and implementation of community emergency preparedness plans that provide sensible, maximum protection. Input from the medical community and health protection agencies such as the Department of Health and Human Services is and will continue to be essential throughout the disposal program.

The Center for Environmental Health and Injury Control, one of nine major units of the Centers for Disease Control, was delegated review and oversight responsibility for any DOD plans to dispose and/or transport chemical weapons by Public Law 91-121 (The Armed Forces Appropriation Authorization of 1970) and Public Law 91-441 (The Armed Forces Appropriation Authorization of 1971). In addition to mandatory review, the DOD has since requested that the Center for Environmental Health and Injury Control provide assistance in developing medical aspects of emergency planning for all disposal sites. A recent example is a training program in the medical management of chemical exposures for health care professionals. Instruction in the elements of first response and differential diagnosis of exposure to warfare agents, pesticides, phosgene, chlorine, and atropine are combined with first-hand experience in providing basic medical care (ie, suturing simulated wounds and taking the carotid pulse) and decontamination of simulated victims while clothed in full protective gear. The extensive use of case studies and class discussion is designed to provide participants with an understanding of the resources each host site and community should have available for various levels of medical emergency. The first training session was held at Umatilla in October 1988.

Collaboration among Centers for Disease Control staff and environmental impact statement team members already has resulted in the joint development of guidelines for the use of antidotes and prophylactic drugs in the event of a release likely to produce casualties in the host community. Drugs considered in the guidelines were the antidotes atropine, pralidoxime, and other oximes alone or in combination with benactyzine and diazepam for nerve agents (British antilewisite and its analogues for lewisite) and prophylactic combinations of pralidoxime mesylate, atropine, diazepam, pyridostigmine, physostigmine, and aprophen (for nerve agents). At present, there is no substitute for use of these compounds in treating the adverse effects of agent exposure or protecting emergency personnel such as fire fighters and ambulance attendants from incapacitation or death. Nevertheless, mishandling or use of an improper dose of these compounds can cause serious injury, and strong potential exists for substance abuse or accidental poisoning. The operational protocol is that only trained or emergency and medical personnel have access to and administer antidotes or prophylactic drugs. In addition, treatment with antidotes is performed only when agent exposure is relatively certain. Additional collaboration is under way to develop guidelines for other protective actions.

Reducing the regional threat posed by aging chemical weapons will require much additional work by scientists, concerned citizens, and agencies of local, state, and federal governments. The task is neither easy nor straightforward. Involvement of an informed medical community can provide invaluable insight and leadership to the essential process of community readiness in anticipation of agent disposal. (pp. 657–59)

Sam Abbott Carnes and Annetta Paule Watson, "Disposing of the US Chemical Weapons Stockpile: An Approaching Reality," in The Journal of the American Medical Association, *Vol. 262, No. 5, August 4, 1989, pp. 653–59.*

Sources For Further Study

Anderson, Roger. "Environmental, Safety and Health Issues at U.S. Nuclear Weapons Production Facilities, 1946–1988." *Environmental Review* 13, Nos. 3–4 (Fall-Winter 1989): 69–92.
   Recounts the poor environmental, safety, and health record of United States nuclear weapons plants.

Beardsley, Timothy M. "Easier Said Than Done: Burning Chemical Weapons Is No Simple Process." *Scientific American* 263, No. 3 (September 1990): 48, 50.
   Outlines some technical difficulties of incinerating chemical weapons.

Broad, William J. "For U.S. Arms Complex, Much Work, Then Less." *The New York Times* (1 October 1991): A7.
   Reviews President Bush's call for the destruction of existing tactical short-range nuclear weapons and considers how this will affect the nation's weapons complex.

Campbell, Christy, and Matthews, Robert. "The Dregs of the Cold War: Time for the Cleanup." *World Press Review* 37, No. 9 (September 1990): 16–17.
   Addresses the difficulty and expense of safely disposing of the world's chemical munitions.

Charles, Dan. "Will These Lands Ne'er Be Clean?" *New Scientist* 122, No. 1670 (24 June 1989): 36–7.
   Discusses the enormous cost and difficulty of cleaning up radioactive and toxic contamination at nuclear plants in the United States.

Crawford, Mark. "DOE Calls in the Labs for Defense Waste Cleanup." *Science* 246, No.4926 (6 October 1989): 24–5.
   Examines Department of Energy research into on-site stabilization of radioactive and chemical wastes.

The Environmental Professional: Professional Reports—Integrated Environmental Assessment for a Major Project 11, No. 4 (1989).
   Issue of *The Environmental Professional* devoted to chemical weapons. Articles about the hazards of storing, transporting, and disposing of chemical weapons are included. Several articles from this periodical are excerpted in the entry above.

Hedges, Stephen J. "Bomb Makers' Secrets." *U.S. News and World Report* 107, No. 16 (23 October 1989): 22–3, 27–8.
   Account of thirty-seven years of improperly handled radioactive and toxic waste at the Fernald, Ohio nuclear weapons plant.

Holmes, H. Allen. "Biological Weapons Proliferation." *Department of State Bulletin* 89, No. 2148 (July 1989): 43–5.
   Outlines United States policy on biological weapons.

Lamartine, Roland J. "The United States' Nuclear Defense Industry." *Environmental Conservation* 15, No. 3 (Autumn 1988): 264–66.
   Notes potential environmental and health problems resulting from ordinary operations of the nuclear defense industry, concluding with questions about the need for nuclear weapons.

Lord, Mary. "A World Away." *U.S. News and World Report* 109, No. 19 (12 November 1990): 17.
   Notes that the United States has begun chemical weapons disposal on Johnston Atoll.

Piller, Charles. "Lethal Lies about Fatal Diseases." *The Nation* 247, No. 8 (3 October 1988): 271–72, 274–75.
   Documents "gross omissions and misrepresentations" in U.S. Army records regarding biological warfare testing programs of the 1950s and 1960s.

Pittock, A. Barrie. "The Environmental Impact of Nuclear War: Policy Implications." *Ambio* XVIII, No. 7 (1989): 367–71.
> Examines ways that knowledge of the potential environmental consequences of nuclear war affects political strategies.

Schneider, Keith. "U.S. Plans to Burn Chemical Weapons Stirs Public Fear." *The New York Times* (29 April 1991): Al, A12.
> Notes design and operation flaws that are hindering plans to incinerate the United States' stockpile of chemical weapons and examines safety concerns about the procedures.

Sigal, Lorene L., and Suter, Glenn W. II. "Potential Effects of Chemical Agents on Terrestrial Resources." *The Environmental Professional* 11, No. 4 (1989): 376–84.
> Assesses probable consequences of the impact on natural resources of accidents during the disposal of U.S. Army chemical agent stockpiles.

Stenehjem, Michele A. "Pathways of Radioactive Contamination: Beginning the History, Public Enquiry, and Policy Study of the Hanford Nuclear Reservation." *Environmental Review* 13, Nos. 3–4 (Fall-Winter 1989): 94–119.
> Traces the history of radioactive waste releases from the Hanford nuclear facility and raises questions about United States policy decisions regarding atomic matters.

Tolbert, Virginia R., and Breck, James E. "Effects of Chemical Agent Destruction on Aquatic Resources." *The Environmental Professional* 11, No. 4 (1989): 367–75.
> Predicts the effects of accidental releases of toxic chemical agents into aquatic system through atmospheric releases or spills. The authors suggest that their analysis can be used to facilitate emergency planning in the event of accidents.

United States General Accounting Office. National Security and International Affairs Division. Washington, D.C.: GAO (24 May 1990): 1–31.
> Reviews the Department of Defense's Chemical Stockpile Disposal Program and assesses the status of efforts to destroy obsolete chemical weapons.

Whiteside, Thomas. "Annals of the Cold War: The Yellow-Rain Complex, Parts I and II." *The New Yorker* LXVI, No. 52 (11 February 1991): 38–42, 44–7, 50–2, 54–5, 57–67; No. 53 (18 February 1991): 44–68.
> Offers an extensive examination of private as well as United States government research into alleged Soviet development and use of chemical and biological weapons.

9:   Ocean Dumping

Sending Out an SOS: Oceans Plagued by Pollution

After sweltering through a succession of torrid, hazy and humid days [in 1988], thousands of New Yorkers sought relief . . . by heading for the area's public beaches. What many found, to their horror and dismay, was an assault on the eyes, the nose and the stomach. From northern New Jersey to Long Island, incoming tides washed up a nauseating array of waste, including plastic tampon applicators and balls of sewage 2 in. thick. Even more alarming was the drug paraphernalia and medical debris that began to litter the beaches: crack vials, needles and syringes, prescription bottles, stained bandages and containers of surgical sutures. There were also dozens of vials of blood, three of which tested positive for hepatitis-B virus and at least six positive for antibodies to the AIDS virus.

To bathers driven from the surf by the floating filth, it was as if something precious—*their* beach, *their* ocean—had been wantonly destroyed, like a mindless graffito defacing a Da Vinci painting. Susan Guglielmo, a New York City housewife who had taken her two toddlers to Robert Moses State Park, was practically in shock: "I was in the water when this stuff was floating around. I'm worried for my children. It's really a disgrace." Said Gabriel Liegey, a veteran lifeguard at the park: "It was scary. In the 19 years I've been a lifeguard, I've never seen stuff like this."

Since the crisis began, more than 50 miles of New York City and Long Island beaches have been declared temporarily off limits to the swimming public because of tidal pollution. Some of the beaches were reopened, but had to be closed again as more sickening debris washed in. And the threat is far from over: last week medical waste was washing up on the beaches of Rhode Island and Massachusetts. "The planet is sending us a message," says Dr. Stephen Joseph, New York City's health commissioner. "We cannot continue to pollute the oceans with impunity."

As federal and state officials tried to locate the source of the beach-defiling materials, an even more mysterious—and perhaps more insidious—process was underway miles off the Northeast coast. Since March 1986, about 10 million tons of wet sludge processed by New York and New Jersey municipal sewage-treatment plants has been moved in huge barges out beyond the continental shelf. There, in an area 106 nautical miles from the entrance to New York harbor, the sewage has been released underwater in great, dark clouds.

The dumping, approved by the Environmental Protection Agency, has stirred noisy protests from commercial and sport fishermen from South Carolina to Maine. Dave Krusa, a Montauk, N.Y., fisherman, regularly hauls up hake and tilefish with ugly red lesions on their bellies and fins that are rotting away. Krusa is among those who believe that contaminants from Dump Site 106 may be borne back toward shore by unpredictable ocean currents. "In the past year, we've seen a big increase of fish in this kind of shape," he says. Who will eat them? New Yorkers, says a Montauk dockmaster. "They're going to get their garbage right back in the fish they're eating."

> "The planet is sending us a message. We cannot continue to pollute the oceans with impunity."
>
> —Dr. Stephen Joseph, New York City health commissioner

Today scientists have begun to shift the focus of research away from localized sources of pollution, like oil spills, which they now believe are manageable, short-term problems. Instead, they are concentrating on the less understood dynamics of chronic land-based pollution: the discharge of sewage and industrial waste and—possibly an even greater menace—the runoff from agricultural and urban areas.

[The] pollution of Northeastern beaches and coastal waters is only the latest signal that the planet's life belt, as Cousteau calls the ocean, is rapidly unbuckling. True, there are some farsighted projects here and there to repair the damage, and there was ample evidence in Atlanta last week that the Democrats hope to raise the nation's consciousness about environmental problems. The heightened interest comes not a moment too soon, since marine biologists and environmentalists are convinced that oceanic pollution is reaching epidemic proportions.

The blight is global, from the murky red tides that periodically afflict Japan's Inland Sea to the untreated sewage that befouls the fabled Mediterranean. Pollution threatens the rich, teeming life of the ocean and renders the waters off once famed beaches about as safe to bathe in as an unflushed toilet. By far the greatest, or at least the most visible, damage has been done near land, which means that the savaging of the seas vitally affects human and marine life. Polluted waters and littered beaches can take jobs from fisherfolk as well as food from consumers, recreation from vacationers and business from resorts. In dollars, pollution costs billions; the cost in the quality of life in incalculable.

In broadest terms, the problem for the U.S. stems from rampant development along the Atlantic and Pacific coasts and the Gulf of Mexico. Between 1940 and 1980, the number of Americans who live within 50 miles of a seashore increased from 42 million to 89 million—and the total is still mounting. Coastal waters are getting perilously close to reaching their capacity to absorb civilization's wastes.

Today scientists have begun to shift the focus of research away from localized sources of pollution, like oil spills, which they now believe are manageable, short-term problems. Instead, they are concentrating on the less understood dynamics of chronic land-based pollution: the discharge of sewage and industrial waste and—possibly an even greater menace—the runoff from agricultural and urban areas.

Conveyed to the oceans through rivers, drainage ditches and the water table, such pollutants include fertilizers and herbicides washed from farms and lawns, motor oil from highways and parking lots, animal droppings from city streets and other untreated garbage that backs up in sewer systems and spills into the seas. Says Biologist Albert Manville of Defenders of Wildlife, a Washington-based environmental group: "We're running out of time. We cannot continue to use the oceans as a giant garbage dump."

The oceans are broadcasting an increasingly urgent sos. Since June 1987 at least 750 dolphins have died mysteriously along the Atlantic Coast. In many that washed ashore, the snouts, flippers and tails were pocked with blisters and craters; in others, huge patches of skin had sloughed off. In the Gulf of Maine, harbor seals currently have the highest pesticide level of any U.S. mammals, on land or in water. From Portland to Morehead City, N.C., fishermen have been hauling up lobsters and crabs with gaping holes in their shells and fish with rotted fins and ulcerous lesions. Last year's oyster haul in Chesapeake Bay was the worst ever; the crop was decimated by dermo, a fungal disease, and the baffling syndrome MSX (multinucleate sphere X).

Suffocating and sometimes poisonous blooms of algae—the so-called red and brown tides—regularly blot the nation's coastal bays and gulfs, leaving behind a trail of dying fish and contaminated mollusks and crustaceans. Patches of water that have been almost totally depleted of oxygen, known as dead zones, are proliferating. As many as 1 million fluke and flounder were killed earlier this summer when they became trapped in anoxic water in New Jersey's Raritan Bay. Another huge dead zone, 300 miles long and ten miles wide, is adrift in the Gulf of Mexico.

Shellfish beds in Texas have been closed eleven times in the past 18 months because of pollution. Crab fisheries in Lavaca Bay, south of Galveston, were forced to shut down when dredging work stirred up mercury that had settled in the sediment. In neighboring Louisiana 35% of the state's oyster beds are closed because of sewage contamination. Says Oliver Houck, a professor of environmental law at Tulane: "These waters are nothing more than cocktails of highly toxic substances."

The Pacific coastal waters are generally cleaner than most, but they also contain pockets of dead—and deadly—water. Seattle's Elliott Bay is contaminated with a mix of copper, lead, arsenic, zinc, cadmium and polychlorinated biphenyls (PCBs), chemicals once widely used by the electrical-equipment industry. "The bottom of this bay is a chart of industrial history," says Thomas Hubbard, a water-quality planner for Seattle. "If you took a core sample, you could date the Depression, World War II. You could see when PCBs were first used and when they were banned and when lead was eliminated from gasoline." Commencement Bay, Tacoma's main harbor, is the nation's largest underwater area designated by the Environmental Protection Agency as a Superfund site, meaning that pollution in the bay is so hazardous that the Federal Government will supervise its cleanup.

Washington State fisheries report finding tumors in the livers of English sole, which dwell on sediment. Posted signs warn, BOTTOMFISH, CRAB AND SHELLFISH MAY BE UNSAFE TO EAT DUE TO POLLUTION. Lest anyone fail to get the message, the caution is printed in seven languages: English, Spanish, Vietnamese, Cambodian, Laotian, Chinese and Korean.

San Francisco Bay is also contaminated with copper, nickel, cadmium, mercury, and other heavy metals from industrial discharges. [In 1987] toxic discharges increased 23%. In Los Angeles urban runoff and sewage deposits have had a devastating impact on coastal ecosystems, notably in Santa Monica Bay, which gets occasional floods of partly processed wastes from a nearby sewage-treatment plant during heavy rainstorms. Off San Diego's Point Loma, a popular haunt of skin divers, the waters are so contaminated with sewage that undersea explorers run the risk of bacterial infection.

U.S. shores are also being inundated by waves of plastic debris. On the sands of the Texas Gulf Coast one day last September, volunteers collected 307 tons of litter, two-thirds of which was plastic, including 31,733 bags, 30,295 bottles and 15,631 six-pack yokes. Plastic trash is being found far out to sea. On a four-day trip from Maryland to Florida that ranged 100 miles offshore, John Hardy, an Oregon State University marine biologist, spotted "Styrofoam and other plastic on the surface, most of the whole cruise."

Nonbiodegradable plastic, merely a nuisance to sailors, can kill or maim marine life. As many as 2 million seabirds and 100,000 marine mammals die every year after eating or becoming entangled in the debris. Sea turtles choke on plastic bags they mistake for jellyfish, and sea lions are ensnared when they playfully poke their noses into plastic nets and rings. Unable to open their jaws, some sea lions simply starve to death. Brown pelicans become so enmeshed in fishing line that they can hang themselves. Says Kathy O'Hara of the Center for Environmental Education in Washington: "We have seen them dangling from tree branches in Florida."

Some foreign shores are no better off. Remote beaches on Mexico's Yucatán Peninsula are littered with plastics and tires. Fish and birds are being choked out of Guanabara Bay, the entryway to Rio de Janeiro, by sewage and industrial fallout. Japan's Inland Sea is plagued by 200 red tides annually; one last year killed more than 1 million yellowtail with a potential market value of $15 million. In the North Sea chemical pollutants are believed to have been a factor in the deaths of 1,500 harbor seals this year. Last spring the Scandinavian fish industry was hard hit when millions of salmon and sea trout were suffocated by an algae bloom that clung to their gills and formed a slimy film. Farmers towed their floating fishponds from fjord to fjord in a desperate effort to evade the deadly tide.

For five years, at 200 locations around the U.S., the National Oceanic and Atmospheric Administration has been studying mussels, oysters and bottom-dwelling fish, like flounder, that feed on the pollutant-rich sediment. These creatures, like canaries placed in a coal mine to detect toxic gases, serve as reliable indicators of the presence of some 50 contaminants. The news is not

U.S. shores are also being inundated by waves of plastic debris. On the sands of the Texas Gulf Coast one day, volunteers collected 307 tons of litter, two-thirds of which was plastic, including 31,733 bags, 30,295 bottles and 15,631 six-pack yokes.

Despite the overwhelming evidence of coastal pollution, cleaning up the damage, except in a few scattered communities, has a fairly low political priority. One reason: most people assume that the vast oceans, which cover more than 70% of the world's surface, have an inexhaustible capacity to neutralize contaminants, by either absorbing them or letting them settle harmlessly to the sediment miles below the surface.

good. Coastal areas with dense populations and a long history of industrial discharge show the highest levels of pollution. Among the worst, according to Charles Ehler of NOAA: Boston Harbor, the Hudson River-Raritan estuary on the New Jersey coast, San Diego harbor and Washington's Puget Sound.

[In 1988] the EPA added six major estuaries to the half a dozen already on the list of ecologically sensitive coastal areas targeted for long-term study. Estuaries, where rivers meet the sea, are the spawning grounds and nurseries for at least two-thirds of the nation's commercial fisheries, as well as what the EPA calls sources of "irreplaceable recreation and aesthetic enjoyment."

Although the poisoning of coastal waters strongly affects vacationers, homeowners and resort operators, its first (and often most vocal) victims are fishermen. Commercial fishing in the U.S. is a $3.1 billion industry, and it is increasingly threatened. Fisherman Richard Hambley of Swansboro, N.C., recalls that only a few years ago, tons of sturgeon and mullet were pulled out of the White Oak River. "Now that is nonexistent," he says. "There are no trout schools anymore. Crabs used to be like fleas. I'm lucky to get a few bushels." Ken Seigler, who works Swansboro's Queens Creek, has seen his income from clams and oysters drop 50% in seven years; this year he was forced to apply for food stamps. New Jersey Fisherman Ed Maliszewski has used his small boat for only two weeks this year. He is trying to bail out, and so are others.

In the diet-and-wellness '80s, fish has been widely touted as a healthful food. Not only do smaller catches mean ever higher prices, but also the incidence of illnesses from eating contaminated fish—including gastroenteritis, hepatitis A and cholera—is rising around the U.S. Pesticide residues and other chemicals so taint New York marine waters that state officials have warned women of childbearing age and children under 15 against consuming more than half a pound of bluefish a week; they should never eat striped bass caught off Long Island. Says Mike Deland, New England regional administrator for the EPA: "Anyone who eats the liver from a lobster taken from an urban area is living dangerously."

Fish and shellfish that have absorbed toxins can indirectly pass contaminants to humans. Birds migrating between Central America and the Arctic Circle, for example, make a stopover in San Francisco's wetlands, where they feast on clams and mussels that contain high concentrations of cadmium, mercury and lead. Says Biologist Gregory Karras of Citizens for a Better Environment: "The birds become so polluted, there is a risk from eating ducks shot in the South Bay."

Despite the overwhelming evidence of coastal pollution, cleaning up the damage, except in a few scattered communities, has a fairly low political priority. One reason: most people assume that the vast oceans, which cover more than 70% of the world's surface, have an inexhaustible capacity to neutralize contaminants, by either absorbing them or letting them settle harmlessly to the sediment miles below the surface. "People think 'Out of sight, out of mind,' " says Richard Curry, an oceanographer at Florida's Biscayne National Park. The popular assumption that oceans will in effect heal themselves may carry some truth, but scientists warn that this is simply not known. Says Marine Scientist Herbert Windom of Georgia's Skidaway Institute of Oceanography: "We see things that we don't really understand. And we don't really have the ability yet to identify natural and unnatural phenomena." Notes Sharron Stewart of the Texas Environmental Coalition: "We know more about space than the deep ocean."

Marine scientists are only now beginning to understand the process by which coastal waters are affected by pollution. The problem, they say, may begin hundreds of miles from the ocean, where nutrients, such as nitrogen and phosphorus, as well as contaminants, enter rivers from a variety of sources. Eventually, these pollutants find their way into tidal waters. For the oceans, the first critical line of defense is that point in estuaries, wetlands and marshes where freshwater meets salt water. Marine biologists call this the zone of maximum turbidity—literally, where the water becomes cloudy from mixing.

There, nutrients and contaminants that have dissolved in freshwater encounter the ionized salts of seawater. The resulting chemical reactions create particles that incorporate the pollutants, which then settle to the bottom. As natural sinks for contaminants, these turbidity zones protect the heart of the estuary and the ocean waters beyond.

But the fragile estuarine systems can be overtaxed in any number of ways. Dredging can stir up the bottom, throwing pollutants back into circulation. The U.S. Navy plans to build a port in Puget Sound for the aircraft carrier U.S.S. *Nimitz* and twelve other ships; the project will require displacement of more than 1 million cu. yds. of sediment, with unknown ecological consequences. Similarly, natural events such as hurricanes can bestir pollutants from the sediment. The estuarine environment also changes when the balance of freshwater and salt water is disturbed. Upstream dams, for example, diminish the flow of freshwater into estuaries; so do droughts. On the other hand, rainstorms can cause an excess of freshwater runoff from the land.

Whatever the precise cause, trouble begins when the level of pollutants in the water overwhelms the capacity of estuaries to assimilate them. The overtaxed system, unable to absorb any more nutrients or contaminants, simply passes them along toward bays and open coastal areas. "When the system is working," says Maurice Lynch, a biological oceanographer at the Virginia Institute of Marine Science, "it can take a lot of assault. But when it gets out of whack, it declines rapidly."

It is then that the natural growth of sea grass may be ended, as has happened in Chesapeake Bay, or sudden blooms of algae can occur, particularly in stagnant waters. The exact reasons for these spurts of algal growth are unknown. They can be triggered, for example, by extended periods of sunny weather following heavy rains. Scientists believe algal growth is speeded up by the runoff of agricultural fertilizers. The burgeoning algae form a dense layer of vegetation that displaces other plants. As the algae die and decay, they sap enormous amounts of oxygen from the water, asphyxiating fish and other organisms.

Some kinds of algae contain toxic chemicals that are deadly to marine life. When carcasses of more than a dozen whales washed up on Cape Cod last fall, their deaths were attributed to paralytic shellfish poisoning that probably passed up the food chain through tainted mackerel consumed by the whales. Carpets of algae can turn square miles of water red, brown or yellow. Some scientists speculate that the account in *Exodus 7:20* of the Nile's indefinitely turning red may refer to a red tide.

When such blights occur in coastal areas, the result can be devastating. Last November a red tide off the coast of the Carolinas killed several thousand mullet and all but wiped out the scallop population. Reason: the responsible species, *Ptychodiscus brevis*, contains a poison that causes fish to bleed to death. Brown tides, unknown to Long Island waters before 1985, have occurred every summer since; they pose a constant threat to valuable shellfish beds.

A study of satellite photographs has led scientists to believe that algae can be conveyed around the world on ocean currents. The Carolinas algae, which had previously been confined to the Gulf of Mexico, apparently drifted to Atlantic shores by way of the Gulf Stream. One species that is native to Southern California is thought to have been carried to Spain in the ballast water of freighters.

The effects of man-made pollution on coastal zones can often be easily seen; far less clear is the ultimate impact on open seas. The ocean has essentially two ways of coping with pollutants: it can dilute them or metabolize them. Pollutants can be dispersed over hundreds of square miles of ocean by tides, currents, wave action, huge underwater columns of swirling water called rings, or deep ocean storms caused by earthquakes and volcanoes.

Buried toxins can also be moved around by shrimp and other creatures that dig into the bottom and spread the substances through digestion and excretion. Though ocean sediment generally accumulates at a rate of about one-half inch

The effects of man-made pollution on coastal zones can often be easily seen: far less clear is the ultimate impact on open seas. The ocean has essentially two ways of coping with pollutants: it can dilute them or metabolize them. Pollutants can be dispersed over hundreds of square miles of ocean by tides, currents, wave action, huge underwater columns of swirling water called rings, or deep ocean storms caused by earthquake and volcanoes.

"We can expect to see an increase in the chronic contamination of coastal waters, an increase in health advisories and an increase in the closing of shellfish beds and fisheries."

—Clifton Curtis,
president of
the Oceanic Society

per thousand years. Biogeochemist John Farrington of the University of Massachusetts at Boston cites discoveries of plutonium from thermonuclear test blasts in the 1950s and 1960s located 12 in. to 20 in. deep in ocean sediment. Thus contaminants can conceivably lie undisturbed in the oceans indefinitely—or resurface at any time.

There is little question that the oceans have an enormous ability to absorb pollutants and even regenerate once damaged waters. For example, some experts feared that the vast 1979 oil spill in the Gulf of Mexico would wipe out the area's shrimp industry. That disaster did not occur, apparently because the ocean has a greater capacity to break down hydrocarbons than scientists thought. But there may be a limit to how much damage a sector of ocean can take. Under assault by heavy concentrations of sludge, for example, the self-cleansing system can be overwhelmed. Just like decaying algae, decomposing sludge robs the water of oxygen, suffocating many forms of marine life. What effect chronic contamination from sludge and other wastes will have on the oceans' restorative powers is still unknown.

Rebuckling the planet's life belt may prove formidable. The federal Clean Water Act of 1972 overlooked runoff pollution in setting standards for water quality. Meanwhile, the nation's coasts are subject to the jurisdiction of a bewildering (and often conflicting) array of governmental bodies. One prime example of this confusion, reports *Time* Houston Bureau Chief Richard Woodbury, is found in North Carolina's Albemarle-Pamlico region. There both the federal Food and Drug Administration and a state agency regulate the harvesting of shellfish. A third agency, the state's health department, surveys and samples the water and shellfish. And another state body sets the guidelines for opening or closing shellfish beds. Complains Douglas Rader of the Environmental Defense Fund: "The crazy mix of agencies hurts the prospects for good management."

Lax enforcement of existing clean-water policies is another obstacle. According to Clean Ocean Action, a New Jersey-based watchdog group, 90% of the 1,500 pipelines in the state that are allowed to discharge effluent into the sea do so in violation of regulatory codes. Municipalities flout the rules as well. Even if Massachusetts keeps to a very tight schedule on its plans to upgrade sewage treatment, Boston will not be brought into compliance with the Clean Water Act until 1999—22 years after the law's deadline. Meanwhile, the half a billion gallons of sewage that pour into Boston Harbor every day receive treatment that is rudimentary at best.

Some communities are leading the way in trying to preserve their shores and coastal waters. In March the legislature of Suffolk County on Long Island passed a law forbidding retail food establishments to use plastic grocery bags, food containers and wrappers beginning next year. Sixteen states have laws requiring that the plastic yokes used to hold six-packs of soda or beer together be photo- or biodegradable. Last December the U.S. became the 29th nation to ratify an amendment to the Marpol (for marine pollution) treaty, which prohibits ships and boats from disposing of plastics—from fishing nets to garbage bags—anywhere in the oceans. The pact goes into effect at the end of this year.

Compliance will not be easy. Merchant fleets dump at least 450,000 plastic containers overboard every day. The U.S. Navy, which accounts for four tons of plastic daily, has canceled a contract for 11 million plastic shopping bags, and is testing a shipboard trash compactor. It is also developing a waste processor that can melt plastics and turn them into bricks. The Navy's projected cost of meeting the treaty provision: at least $1 million a ship. Supporters of the Marpol treaty readily acknowledge that it will not totally eliminate plastic pollution. "If a guy goes out on deck late at night and throws a bag of trash overboard," says James Coe of NOAA's National Marine Fisheries Service in Seattle, "there's no way that anyone will catch him."

Stiff fines and even prison sentences may get the attention of landbound polluters. Under Administrator Mike Deland, the EPA's New England office has acquired a reputation for tough pursuit of violators. In November 1986 the agency filed criminal charges against a Providence boatbuilder for dumping PCBs into Narragansett Bay. The company was fined $600,000 and its owner $75,000; he was put on probation for five years.

Washington is one of the few states with a comprehensive cleanup program. Three years ago, the Puget Sound water-quality authority developed a master plan for cleaning up the heavily polluted, 3,200-sq.-mi. body of water. The state legislature has levied an 8¢-a-pack surtax on cigarettes to help pay the bill; this year the tax will contribute an estimated $25 million to the cleanup. The Puget Sound authority and other state agencies closely monitor discharge of industrial waste and are working with companies on ways to reduce effluent.

An aggressive effort is being made to limit runoff as well. Two counties have passed ordinances that regulate the clearing of land and the installation and inspection of septic tanks. Farmers are now required to fence cattle away from streams. Zoning has become more stringent for construction in a critical watershed area: a single-family house requires at least two acres of land. The number of livestock and poultry per acre is also controlled.

The Puget Sound group has an educational program that teaches area residents everything from the history of the sound to what not to put down the kitchen sink. Controlling pollution is promoted as everyone's task. High school students take water samples, and island dwellers have been trained in what to do if they spot an oil spill. Says Seattle Water-Quality Planner Hubbard: "Bridgetenders are great at calling in with violations. They are up high, and when they see a black scum or a little slick, they let us know about it."

Officials hope the cleanup program will have the same result as a decades-long effort mounted by the Federal Government and four states in the Delaware River estuary, an area ringed by heavy industry and home to almost 6 million people. The Delaware's pollution problems began in Benjamin Franklin's day. By World War II, the river had become so foul that airplane pilots could smell it at 5,000 ft. President Franklin Roosevelt even considered it a threat to national security. In 1941 he ordered an investigation to determine whether gases from the water were causing corrosion at a secret radar installation on the estuary.

Although the Delaware will never regain its precolonial purity, the estuary has been vastly improved. Shad, which disappeared 60 years ago, are back, along with 33 other species of fish that had virtually vanished. Estuary Expert Richard Albert calls the Delaware "one of the premier pollution-control success stories in the U.S."

Such triumphs are still rare, and there is all too little in the way of concerted multinational activity to heal the oceans. That means pollution is bound to get worse. Warns Clifton Curtis, president of the Oceanic Society, a Washington-based environmental organization: "We can expect to see an increase in the chronic contamination of coastal waters, an increase in health advisories and an increase in the closing of shellfish beds and fisheries." Those are grim tidings indeed, for both the world's oceans and the people who live by them. (pp.44–50)

Anastasia Toufexis, "The Dirty Seas," in Time, *New York, Vol. 132, No. 5, August 1, 1988, pp.44–50.*

There is little question that the oceans have an enormous ability to absorb pollutants and even regenerate once damaged waters. . . .But there may be a limit to how much damage a sector of ocean can take. Under assault by heavy concentrations of sludge, for example, the self-cleansing system can be overwhelmed. Just like decaying algae, decomposing sludge robs the water of oxygen, suffocating many forms of marine life. What effect chronic contamination from sludge and other wastes will have on the oceans' restorative powers is still unknown.

Hype Tide: Exposing Exaggerations of the Beach Debris Crisis

Little did Manhattanite Herminio Rodrogues suspect that the pill bottle he accidentally dropped into the East River at 92nd Street last June would

Washups of beach debris are nothing new. A wave of New York-area beach closings comparable to the closings of last summer struck in 1976. And as long ago as 1931 the cost of beach cleanup in New York was put at $10,000 per mile.

wash up on a beach in Queens a month later as "medical waste." But wash ashore it did, amid condoms, syringes, six-pack rings, soda containers, garbage bags, tampon applicators, and raw sewage. It thus did its tiny part to put the subject of medical waste on the cover of *Newsweek,* and to treat *New York Daily News* readers to such headlines as "SUMMER BUMMER—BEACH POLLUTION POISONS VACATIONS."

Washups of beach debris are nothing new. A wave of New York-area beach closings comparable to the closings of last summer struck in 1976. And as long ago as 1931 the cost of beach cleanup in New York was put at $10,000 per mile. What caught the public's attention—and imagination—[in 1988] was the seeming novelty of finding syringes and blood vials at the seashore. Fear of AIDS and general squeamishness had the press and public combing the beaches for medical waste, theorizing about legions of "midnight dumpers," and speculating feverishly about the health risks of wading.

The facts about medical waste have their good and bad sides. The good news is that any syringe that washed up on your local beach does not, in fact, present a major public health hazard. By all accounts, there is virtually no possibility of becoming infected with AIDS or hepatitis after being stuck by a needle derived from medical or hospital waste; any such virus that did find its way onto a syringe would never survive the days of exposure to sewage, salt water, and sunlight. More important, there is far less medical waste floating around than [the] press coverage would have led you to believe.

The bad news is that medical waste may well be an uninvited guest at some beach parties in the mid-Atlantic region for some time to come. Those midnight dumpers originally thought responsible for the problem are now considered (by the New York Department of Environmental Conservation [DEC] among others) to be minor culprits. The real source of the trouble is much harder to bring to justice: social and technological trends, weather patterns, and a failure to deal adequately with garbage disposal in general.

Connecticut and Staten Island lifeguards say syringes have been around on beaches for years, and that last summer was the first time anyone noticed. Still, it's true that medical waste has become a more prominent constituent of beach debris in the last decade, thanks largely to the American obsession with a pathogen-free life-style. Disposable plastics now constitute up to 30 percent of all wastes produced by New York hospitals. Disposable means floatable, so items like blood vials are more likely than ever to escape into public waters and be carried ashore. Nonetheless, most estimates place the amount of medical debris at only between one percent and ten percent of all debris that washed ashore last summer, with one DEC report comparing it to one lunch bag's worth for every two five-ton truckloads of debris.

Most beachgoers saw things differently. 1988 was the year of the misidentified floating object. Cigar containers were reported as blood vials, animal fat became human organs, household rubber gloves became surgical gloves, sewer rats became laboratory rats. One *Newsday* article last July bemoaned the sudden closing of Rockaway Beach after the discovery of "nine dead laboratory rats and what appeared to be a human stomach lining were found amid 125 blood vials and syringes." A subsequent study by the New York DEC found the story to be on target, except for the part about the laboratory rats, the stomach lining, and the blood vials; there were 26 *sewer* rats and assorted *animal* intestines, along with tampon inserters, condoms, and other vaguely vial-shaped objects.

Thanks to AIDS hysteria, the most feared of all medical waste is the hypodermic needle. The sighting of one lone syringe was enough to close the entire Smith Point Park Beach in New York. Some 3,000 needles were actually collected on New York City beaches [in 1988], mainly on Staten Island. They were almost exclusively the type used by diabetics to inject insulin, and in fact were a small fraction of the 60,000 to 112,000 that diabetics in New York dispose of *daily,* either in household trash or down the john. (Traces of blood found in some of these small syringes suggest that the city's 250,000 drug users—more likely to discard used syringes into storm drains—may be partly culpable, but these syringes are no more dangerous than any others found on beaches.) New York City's eminently fallible solid waste disposal system guarantees that a sizable number of these syringes will end up in public waters.

In fact, the ever expanding Fresh Kills Landfill on Staten Island is one of the primary culprits for last summer's washups. Rarely does all of the 20,000-plus tons of garbage that New York City daily sends to Fresh Kills reach its destination. Last year spillage from transport barges was observed on four out of five hauls; monitors estimate that three to four tons of debris are lost in the water each month. At the start of last summer, investigators deemed "floatables" on beaches just below Fresh Kills landfill "too numerous to count."

The other significant source of beach debris is the city's combined sewer overflow system. Most of New York's sewage pipes share their space with storm water drains. Any rainfall greater than one-fourth of an inch causes sewage to bypass sewage treatment plants. So millions of gallons of raw sewage, insulin syringes, condoms, tampon inserters, and anything else you might find in your toilet would mingle with mangled umbrella spokes, dead rats, and anything else you might find in the streets and go directly into public waters.

The least controllable factor in [the 1988] washup bonanza was the weather. Currents normally carry the plume of New York's debris past Staten Island and Sandy Hook, New Jersey, on its way out to sea. At the beginning of last summer, however, unusually persistent southwest winds pushed the plume northeast, depositing large quantities of debris along the shores of Brooklyn, Queens, and sections of Long Island. A report by the National Oceanic and Atmospheric Administration concludes that whatever floatables were present in the mouth of Raritan Bay on June 6, when the winds shifted southwest, would have washed up in July on beaches from Atlantic Beach to Fire Island— i.e., the approximately 30 miles of beach that were closed during that period because of medical waste. These wind patterns were almost identical to those in 1976, the year New York beaches last faced significant washups.

The city has launched a couple of medical waste countermeasures, notably a program to scoop floatables out of the water before they have a chance to be blown onto the beaches. Though even critics say this will help, common sense puts the plan at best two steps away from solving the real problem of combined sewer overflows. The DEC has noted that "if no changes occur in the City's handling of its solid waste, it can be expected that given the same weather conditions, washups will occur again."

The Environmental Protection Agency, meanwhile, has decided to go after the elusive "midnight dumper." It has posted rules for dumping in order to "track" medical waste and make each handler more accountable for its step of the disposal process. But if the illegal dumping of waste from hospitals and other big-time operators accounts for only a tiny fraction of the medical waste, this won't help the average beachgoer much. In fact, as one critic of the policy has noted, it may well exacerbate the problem; the legislation could increase the cost of legal disposal, thereby multiplying incentives for large institutions to dispose of waste illegally.

Dirty diapers pose a more serious health risk than any syringe or vial you might encounter in the sand. Fecal coliform bacteria, the invisible companion of raw sewage, can infect seafood and shellfish, and generates symptoms similar to food poisoning. New Yorkers will be cheered to know that there's no evidence of any bacterial plague on their beaches; all of the relatively few beach closings last summer that were due to elevated bacteria levels could be tied to specific breakdowns or power failures at sewage treatment plants. Beach proprietors also test the waters more rigorously than in past years. "In the 1960s they wouldn't test until you saw a turd floating past your head," says Will Berson of New Jersey's Department of Environmental Protection. In that sense, beaches on the East Coast are safer than ever—provided you can find one that's open. (pp. 15–18)

Alan Burdick, "Hype Tide," in The New Republic, *Vol. 202, No. 24, June 12, 1989, pp. 15–18.*

1988 was the year of the misidentified floating object. Cigar containers were reported as blood vials, animal fat became human organs, household rubber gloves became surgical gloves, sewer rats became laboratory rats.

A Brief History of Ocean Disposal

Accurate worldwide records on the amounts of wastes disposed at sea prior to 1976 are virtually impossible to obtain. However, as a result of the international activities leading to conventions or agreements, information is becoming available on the number of ocean dumping permits issued by many countries, dumpsite locations, and the kinds and quantities of wastes dumped.

During the last 20 years, the open ocean has come under increasing pressure from waste disposal. Meanwhile, the coastal ocean continues to receive greater amounts of contaminants from outfalls and land runoff. Because water and marine life have no sense of political boundaries, international organizations play a vital role in providing discussion, regulation, and policy on what society disposes of in the ocean.

Historically, most coastal countries used the sea for waste disposal. It was generally the most economic way to manage the waste, since land usually had, and still has, a high price tag while the sea has no private owner in the normal sense. In addition, dilution processes served the illusion that dumping at sea does not cause any permanent damage. So why risk contaminating land or drinking water with wastes if the sea is close by?

For some countries, the systematic disposal of wastes into the ocean has a long and fairly well-documented history. Until very recently, the New York metropolitan region always considered the ocean as disposal grounds for much of its sewage sludges, dredged material, garbage, demolition material, and street sweepings. For decades, Britain disposed of sewage sludges and coal wastes, including colliery waste-shale and power plant fly ash, at sea.

The most common form of ocean dumping today is disposal from ships or barges, but specially constructed incineration vessels also burn liquid organic wastes such as PCBs and other organohalogens. The list of wastes dumped at sea is very long, and is topped by dredged material, industrial waste (usually acid-iron and alkaline waste, scrap metal, fish by-products, coal ash, and flue-gas desulfurization sludges), and sewage sludge.

Worldwide concern about effects of ocean dumping did not exist prior to 1960. Earlier environmental interest focused on the pollution of streams, rivers, lakes, and estuaries from outfalls and land-based emissions such as industrial waste, agricultural runoff, and, in general, very careless waste management practices.

In 1967, interest in protecting the ocean from chemical pollution, industrial and transportation disasters, and ocean dumping began to climb after the *Torrey Canyon* oil spill off the Cornish coast. According to Douglas M. Johnston, editor of the 1981 book *The Environmental Law of the Sea*, this disaster sparked a number of international meetings dealing with basic issues of ocean pollution, including the need to develop policy, regulation, and an international infrastructure to deal with ocean dumping, exclusive of such manmade disasters as oil spills.

In the United States, the evolution of ocean dumping regulation, policy, and research took a huge jump forward in 1970, when the Council on Environmental Quality published its landmark report. This was the first concerted scientific effort to determine the fate and effects of wastes dumped at sea; and had the report not been published, it was likely that U.S. ocean dumping would have increased. However, in the 20 years since the report, we have seen changes in federal legislation and policy leading to the cessation of several ocean dumpsites, comprehensive scientific research on the fates and effects of waste dumped at sea, and heightened public interest due to well-publicized beach closings.

The U.S. Environmental Protection Agency (EPA) presently has designated about 109 ocean dumpsites that fall into two categories: interim and noninterim. The 46 interim sites received their designations on the basis of historical usage. While EPA reviews of the 63 noninterim sites are yet to be completed, the agency has found that the sites meet ocean-dumpsite regulations and criteria. Ninety-five percent of the sites are used for the disposal of dredged material.

In June, 1971, the Inter-Governmental Working Group on Marine Pollution (IWGMP, established by the UN Conference on the Human Environment) met in London and expressed the need for an international agreement to regulate dumping at sea. The U.S. delegation submitted a draft of a document known as the "Convention for Regulation of Transportation for Ocean Dumping." The IWGMP encouraged member states of the United Nations to give written opinions, and that November held a second meeting in Ottawa, Canada.

Several of the draft articles on ocean dumping were accepted at this second meeting. The draft was subjected to further revisions at an April, 1972, meeting in Reykjavík, Iceland; at two meetings held later in the year in Britain; and at the 1972 Conference on the Human Environment held in Stockholm, Sweden. Through this process, the revised draft became the London Dumping Convention (LDC), which entered into force on 30 August 1975.

As of 25 December 1989, 64 countries, the so-called "contracting states," ratified or acceded to the LDC. Areas under the convention's jurisdiction include both territorial seas and high seas. These areas are further defined to include all marine waters except internal waters of contracting states.

The LDC defines ocean dumping as:

● Any deliberate disposal at sea of wastes or other matter from vessels, aircraft, platforms or other manmade structures at sea.

● Any deliberate disposal at sea of vessels, aircraft, platforms or other manmade structures at sea.

The at-sea discharge of primary, secondary, and tertiary treated sewage effluent (and sewage sludge off the southern California coast) from outfalls is not considered ocean dumping; nor is the disposal of incidental material such as sea- or freshwater used in the operation of vessels, aircraft, and platforms or other structures. At-sea discharge of mining and smelting wastes from exploration, exploitation, and associated offshore processing of seabed minerals is similarly not considered ocean dumping.

The LDC uses the black-list/grey-list format for categorizing substances for permit purposes. Annex I of the LDC defines black-list substances while Annex II defines grey-list substances. Dumping of black-list substances is prohibited. Industries affected by the ban include pesticide, chemical, and rope manufacturing; electroplating; and domestic and military nuclear. The grey-list substances also are produced and/or used by an array of industries, and can be dumped only after obtaining a special permit. Dumping of all other substances requires a general permit from the appropriate federal administrative organization within the contracting state.

Accurate worldwide records on the amounts of wastes disposed at sea prior to 1976 are virtually impossible to obtain. However, as a result of the international activities leading to conventions or agreements, information is becoming available on the number of ocean dumping permits issued by many countries, dumpsite locations, and the kinds and quantities of wastes dumped. Worldwide, the national authorities of the contracting states annually issue a total of about 50 permits for the ocean disposal of sewage sludge, 150 for industrial wastes, 380 for dredged material, and 50 for other materials—such as ships, low-level nuclear wastes, and the incineration of chlorinated hydrocarbons.

LDC policy on ocean dumping is similar to that of such other regional agreements as the Barcelona, Helsinki, and Oslo conventions. The Barcelona and Helsinki conventions prohibit the disposal of all forms of nuclear waste,

Most countries that use the sea for waste disposal are industrialized and enjoy a high standard of living. Developing countries will likely take a more active interest in ocean dumping as they industrialize and improve land-based sanitation and waste management.

If past ocean-dumping practices are any indication, ocean dumping is bound to continue. Countries continue to use the sea for the disposal of wastes, although North Sea countries intend to halt all at-sea dumping except for dredged material. Interest in the health of the sea is now a worldwide issue. . . .

nosilicon compounds, and acid and alkaline compounds that are not rapidly rendered harmless by processes occurring at sea. Other organizations that address this issue include the Bonn Agreement, the Kuwait Final Act, the Paris Commission, UN Environment Program's (UNEP) Regional Seas Program, and the Joint Group of Experts on the Scientific Aspects of Marine Pollution.

The International Maritime Organization (IMO, previously called the Inter-Governmental Maritime Consultative Organization) provides the administrative mechanism for cooperation among the LDC's contracting states. The IMO's Marine Environmental Division, located in London, collects and disseminates information through the Office of the LDC on all aspects of dumping at sea by contracting states. The division also convenes the annual LDC consultative and scientific meetings. (pp. 29–33, 36)

The large number of organizations attending both the consultative and scientific meetings of the LDC demonstrate the strong international interest in issues of ocean dumping. The meetings provide the inter- and nongovernmental organizations with opportunities to present their points of view.

If past ocean-dumping practices are any indication, ocean dumping is bound to continue. Countries continue to use the sea for the disposal of wastes, although North Sea countries intend to halt all at-sea dumping except for dredged material. Interest in the health of the sea is now a worldwide issue and therefore each ocean-dumping proposal should be considered cautiously.

The volume of dredged material for disposal has been steadily increasing and probably will continue to do so. While the disposal of industrial waste seems to be declining, this may be temporary as companies that used the sea for waste disposal make adjustments, such as relocating the regions where public or legal opposition to ocean dumping does not exist. For sewage sludge, only two countries, the United States and Britain, dump large quantities of sludge into the ocean, although the United States plans to end at-sea sludge disposal by the end of 1991 and Britain will phase it out by 1998. Britain also will end at-sea dumping of industrial waste as soon as 1992, but no later than 1993.

As the ocean receives less of the "traditional" forms of waste, new forms appear for consideration. There is the problem of decommissioned offshore platforms and structures: should they be disposed of at sea or not? The 12th consultative meeting of the LDC discussed whether toppling such structures and redesignating them as artificial reefs is really "dumping." The meeting also heard discussions on the possible ocean disposal of decommissioned nuclear submarines, and proposals for restructuring the annexes.

Most countries that use the sea for waste disposal are industrialized and enjoy a high standard of living. Developing countries will likely take a more active interest in ocean dumping as they industrialize and improve land-based sanitation and waste management.

These issues will be best faced by international organizations, such as the LDC, which can provide information on alternatives to dumping, and the expected fate and effects of the wastes in the ocean, through either its own organization or the contracting states. In this regard, the eighth consultative meeting of the LDC received an important report from "Task Team 2000," the LDC's policy-planning group, that identified nine feasible mitigative measures that could protect the marine environment.

The impact of international scientific and political activities on ocean dumping during the 15 to 20 years since publication of the Council on Environmental Quality report and formation of the LDC has been rapid and productive. Some industries are using cleaner technologies and some countries are either taking a precautionary view on ocean dumping, or eliminating it altogether. Such steps could lead to a more optimistic prediction that the oceans will become cleaner. However, ocean outfalls, nonpoint sources, catastrophic oil spills, and, in general, overuse and exploitation of coastal regions are major threats still to be reckoned with. (pp. 36–8)

Iver W. Duedall, "A Brief History of Ocean Disposal," in Oceanus, *Vol. 33, No. 2, Summer, 1990, pp. 29–33, 36–8.*

Throughout the world, important water bodies— especially the oceans— have become virtual wastebins for the tons of plastic products dumped daily by commercial fishermen, military vessels, merchant ships, passenger liners, pleasure boats, offshore oil and gas drilling operations, the plastics industry and sewage treatment plants.

Grim Harvest: Plastic Debris Kills and Maims Marine Life

It is dawn on the Gulf of Mexico, nature's rush hour. Sunbathers and pleasure boaters, sleeping off the arid heat of July, haven't yet descended on the shore. All along the water's edge, seabirds strut and dive for fish, while ghost crabs and ground squirrels scurry for food. But this morning there's a human intrusion. A large, bearded man slowly drives a tan pickup truck down the beach, his right hand gripping the steering wheel, his left continuously punching a portable computer to record what the tide brought in.

As Tony Amos jabs computer keys programmed for the most common discoveries, he rattles off the items in the staccato tone of an inventory clerk:

"Plastic bottle, plastic bottle, plastic bag, Styrofoam, plastic glove, plastic lids, foam packaging, plastic rope, plastic produce sack, Karo syrup jug, six-pack ring, another glove, Styrofoam cup, cup, plastic bag, plastic fishing line, plastic bleach bottle, plastic egg carton, piece of plastic net, 50-pound plastic bag of sea salt, Bic lighter.

"More synthetic gloves—this is going to be a world-record glove day. . . . Here's an interesting plastic bottle, mineral water made in France. There's a Mexican bleach, a green bottle. You see a lot of them. . . . Oh God, more gloves. . . . "

Finally he brakes and gets out to inspect a specimen for which there is a special computer key designated "dead." A three-foot-long redfish, its scales shimmering in the sun, has washed ashore. The fish is ringed tightly by a black plastic gasket, which has caused a deep gash and eroded the gills. Apparently, months earlier, the fish had darted into the gasket, which had lodged behind its gill cover. As the fish grew, the plastic ring became a noose, damaging the gills and thus eventually cutting off the animal's supply of oxygen.

Amos has come to expect such casualties. An oceanographer at the University of Texas Marine Science Institute who has combed the same seven and a half miles of beach every other day for ten years, he is one of a growing number of scientists who are documenting plastic pollution of the ocean and its perils for the creatures that live there.

The thousands of plastic objects that Amos logs in during every sweep of Mustang Island's beach represent a tiny fraction of the debris floating a few miles off the Texas shore. And the problem extends far beyond the Gulf. Throughout the world, important water bodies—especially the oceans—have become virtual wastebins for the tons of plastic products dumped daily by commercial fishermen, military vessels, merchant ships, passenger liners, pleasure boats, offshore oil and gas drilling operations, the plastics industry and sewage treatment plants.

No one knows how much plastic pollutes the seas. In 1975, the National Academy of Sciences estimated that seven million tons of garbage are dumped into the world's oceans every year. There was no overall breakdown for plastics, but the academy itemized trash from several specific sources. Measured in terms of weight, less than 1 percent of that litter was categorized as plastic. But some experts believe such findings greatly understate the problem because plastic is so much lighter than other debris. The production of plastics has

It is one of the sad ironies of modern times that the synthetic developed by Man to outlast and outperform products made from natural materials is ravaging nature in the process.

more than doubled since 1975. Plastic soft drink bottles, for instance, were not introduced until the late '70s. This dramatic increase is reflected in more recent studies of marine debris. A 1985 report estimated that merchant ships dump 450,000 plastic containers each day into international waters.

Another measure of the problem is the vast amount of plastic that is washed ashore. Mustang Island and other tourist beaches along the Gulf of Mexico, a body of water that shelters a busy international port and hosts extensive offshore oil activities, look like cluttered landfills. One three-hour-long cleanup of 157 miles of Texas shoreline in September 1987 reaped 31,773 plastic bags, 30,295 plastic bottles, 15,631 plastic six-pack rings, 28,540 plastic lids, 1,914 disposable diapers, 1,040 tampon applicators and 7,460 plastic milk jugs.

It is one of the sad ironies of modern times that the synthetic developed by Man to outlast and outperform products made from natural materials is ravaging nature in the process. Since the exigencies of World War II spurred large-scale production of plastic as a substitute for scarce resources, it has become the favored American material—more durable than wood and rubber, lighter than metals, safer than glass and less expensive than leather. It is present in virtually every product line from Army helmets to artificial hearts to Styrofoam cups.

Today, the plastics industry occupies a major place in the U.S. economy, employing more than one million workers in almost every state and in 1985 producing $138 billion in finished goods. The 1.2 trillion cubic inches of plastic manufactured in that year was nearly double the combined output of steel, aluminum and copper.

As with all revolutions, however, there is a "trade-off," as Ronald Bruner, of the Society of the Plastics Industry, describes it. The very durability of the synthetic has created a massive disposal problem, especially in the marine environment where seagoers traditionally unload their domestic wastes and gear. Bruner contends that it is not plastics themselves that are the problem, but rather the way people dispose of them. Regardless of where the blame lies, the problem has caught up with us. Whereas other materials degrade relatively quickly or sink to the bottom, plastic persists. Buoyant, it floats on the surface and can be easily mistaken for food. Often transparent, it nets or entwines animals that cannot see it. It is the most common type of sea litter today.

Like Individual Mines Floating Around

A number of scientists believe that plastic is the most far-reaching, man-made threat facing many marine species, annually killing or maiming tens of thousands of seabirds, seals, sea lions and sea otters, and hundreds of whales, dolphins, porpoises and sea turtles. "You can go to an oil spill or a toxic chemical spill and see animals struggling to survive," says David Laist, senior policy and program analyst for the U.S. Marine Mammal Commission. "But those dangers are concentrated in one place. With plastic pollution, it's a different situation. Plastics are like individual mines floating around the ocean just waiting for victims." Until only recently, no laws have specifically prohibited ocean disposal and dumping of plastics. As a result, vessels worldwide have made the ocean their home—and their dumping grounds, disposing of wastes with a wantonness that never would be permitted on land. Joe Cox, of the American Institute of Merchant Shipping, explained the rationale for dumping: "You go weeks without seeing any other people and you begin to think there's an awful lot of water out there. Taking it down to the baseline of human behavior, it's just easier to do it."

Plastic's devastating effect on an entire population of marine animals was first observed in the late 1970s. The victims were the northern fur seals of the Pribilof Islands, which are located in the Bering Sea west of Alaska. Scientists from the National Marine Mammal Laboratory (NMML—a division of the National Marine Fisheries Service) found that, beginning in 1976, the seal population was declining at a rate of 4 to 6 percent annually. They concluded that plastic entanglement was killing up to 40,000 seals a year.

Naturally curious, the seals were playing with fragments of plastic netting or packing straps floating in the water, often catching their necks in the webbing, according to Charles Fowler, an NMML biologist who visits the islands every summer during mating season. The debris can constrict a seal's movements, preventing normal feeding. Unable to extricate itself, the animal eventually drowns, starves to death, or dies of exhaustion or infection from deep wounds caused by the tightening of the material around its back and neck. Many seal pups grow into the plastic collars, which tighten as their necks thicken. In time, says Fowler, the plastic severs the seal's arteries or strangles it.

Fowler says that often more than one seal can become entangled in the same piece of netting. He once came upon a mother and pup whose necks were ringed this way. "Every time the mother moved," the biologist recalls, "she dragged the pup along with her. It was a pathetic sight."

Some of the fur seals are also dying in the large plastic nets used by foreign fishing boats in the North Pacific. Draped like curtains for miles across the ocean, these nets become death traps for many unintended victims, including birds. Unable to see the translucent material, they dive for fish trapped in the nets, get caught and then drown.

Whales are also among the victims. They sometimes lunge for schools of fish and surface with netting caught in their mouths or wrapped around their heads and tails. A whale dragging hundreds of feet of net may be unable to eat. The extra weight impedes the whale's movement and can exhaust it. Beached whales have been found on both the East and West coasts, their bodies emaciated and entangled in plastic net. In the fall of 1982, a humpback whale entangled in 50 to 100 feet of net washed up on a Cape Cod beach. It was starving and so thin that its ribs were showing. "In a couple of hours, the animal was so weak it simply died," said Phil Clapham, cetacean research director at the Center for Coastal Studies in Provincetown. "At that point, it had been digesting its stomach."

Mounting Rescue Efforts for Whales

In the past four years [since 1984], Clapham's center has received reports of entanglement of about 20 humpbacks, an endangered species with not more than 8,000 survivors in the North Atlantic. Twelve were dangerously ensnared; two eventually died. The center mounts rescue efforts to save entangled whales. One success story involves a 25-ton female humpback, which staffers called Ibis because a line under her tail suggested the long, curved bill of that elegant bird. A playful, friendly whale that swam near boats in the early 1980s, she was a favorite of scientists and whale watchers along the New England coast.

In the summer of 1984, Ibis got tangled in 300 feet of net. She was briefly seen in October and then not spotted again. Experts at the center feared she had drowned. But on Thanksgiving Day Ibis, very thin, tired and still badly entangled, appeared just outside Provincetown Harbor. Crews in small, inflatable boats approached her and managed to hook a rope onto the tangled net. The rope was attached to buoyant floats, which were designed to thwart Ibis' attempts to dive.

After trying to submerge a few times, Ibis gave up. She simply lay on the water's surface, allowing the rescuers to pull the net out of her mouth and off her tail. Freed in two hours, she recovered and two weeks later set forth for her winter migration. A healthy whale returned the following May, and by June 1986, Ibis was swimming with a calf. "A lot of champagne was flowing among the whale scientists on the East Coast," recalls Clapham. (pp. 59–62)

Such happy endings are rare for the victims of plastic entanglement. Along Florida's coasts, brown pelicans diving for fish sometimes go for fisherman's

> **A number of scientists believe that plastic is the most far-reaching, man-made threat facing many marine species, annually killing or maiming tens of thousands of seabirds, seals, sea lions and sea otters, and hundreds of whales, dolphins, porpoises and sea turtles.**

Until only recently, no laws have specifically prohibited ocean disposal and dumping of plastics. As a result, vessels worldwide have made the ocean their home— and their dumping grounds, disposing of wastes with a wantonness that never would be permitted on land.

bait and get hooked. Sport fishermen will usually cut the line, thinking the pelican will then be free. But the line is a killer. Sometimes the synthetic wraps so tightly around the bird's feet and wings that these limbs atrophy. More often, the lines snag branches of the squat, gnarled mangrove trees clustered on the islands where the birds traditionally roost.

"Then the birds just hang there until they're skeletons," says Ralph Heath, who runs a seabird rescue mission near St. Petersburg. "They don't last long once they're suspended from the tree limbs. They can't bite the line loose. The can't shake it loose. So, they keep thrashing until they die."

From a distance, the mangrove islands along Florida's west coast dazzle in the sun, ornamented by large pelicans perched on boughs. But inside the tropical grove, skeletons of seabirds dangle from plastic strands, feathers broken in the furious struggle for survival, splintered wings fallen to the swampy island floor. Since Heath founded his Suncoast Seabird Sanctuary in 1972, he has witnessed hundreds of other entangled birds, freeing them from tree limbs or cutting off lines and hooks.

Cruising Boca Ciega Bay in a 24-foot motorboat, Heath anchors near a mangrove island owned by the sanctuary. He is looking for injured birds. An assistant hurls Spanish sardines into the water, luring dozens of pelicans from the rookery. Heath spots a bird with a bloody wing and scoops it up with a net. A piece of fishing line is wound around its flank, deeply etching its humerus and cutting into tissue. Heath carefully disentangled the bird and returns it to the water. "If it wraps any tighter, it acts like a tourniquet and cuts off circulation," he explains. During the next 20 minutes he nets and disentangles five more birds. "Once that happens, it's all over."

Heath has found pelican chicks dead in their nests, strangled by hundreds of feet of fishing line that had probably been dragged there by their parents. He has seen pelicans garroted by plastic six-pack rings—including one with a fish stuck in its throat, held there firmly by the plastic yoke.

In small shapes and sizes, plastic resembles the food supply of some marine creatures. But it is dangerous to consume. Seabirds, mistaking spherical resin pellets (the raw material used to manufacture plastic products) for fish eggs and other natural food, suffer intestinal blockage and ulceration. Whales are also victims of plastic ingestion. On New Year's Day 1984, an infant pigmy sperm whale beached itself alongside its dying mother on Galveston Island in the Gulf of Mexico. Named Lafitte after a French pirate who had once landed there, the calf was taken to an aquarium and nursed. Lafitte seemed to be healthy, eating some squid and diving playfully in the holding tank. Suddenly he stopped eating and on January 11, he died. Dr. Raymond Tarpley, a Texas A&M University veterinarian, participated in the necropsy. The conclusion: Lafitte had died of severe infection of the abdominal cavity lining. In the animal's stomach he found, among other items, a 30-gallon plastic garbage-can liner, a plastic bread wrapper and a corn-chip bag.

Most worrisome is the danger of plastic to indiscriminate eaters such as ocean turtles, especially hatchlings that spend their early lives at sea surviving off surface organisms. To a turtle, says zoologist George Balazs of the National Marine Fisheries Service in Honolulu, a transparent plastic bag or particle can look like a jellyfish, plankton or the larval stage of a crab. Once in the turtle's intestines, he adds, the indigestible material can block fecal matter, prevent assimilation of nutrients and make the turtle too buoyant to dive for food. It is gruesome—but true—that dead turtles with plastic bags and fishing line extending from both ends have been found in the Gulf of Mexico, in the Hawaiian Islands and along the East coast. "When turtles eat that much plastic," says Balazs, "you reach a point of no return. Their ability to swim around is severely impaired. Then they're at the mercy of the ocean."

In a way, the marine plastic pollution problem crept up on American lawmakers. While several international conventions and federal laws have included provisions to limit or prohibit marine dumping of chemicals, oil and other substances, none of them has applied directly to the more recently recognized problem of plastic debris. The 1973 International Convention for the Prevention of Pollution from Ships (MARPOL) contained an annex (Annex V) that would prohibit ocean disposal of plastics, limit other garbage disposal and require ports to provide facilities for receiving trash from incoming ships. But that annex needed separate ratification and it languished, lacking the requisite number of signatory nations to become international law (at least 15 nations representing half of the world's gross commercial shipping tonnage). The holdouts included the United States.

A key turning point occurred in 1984 when a conference on marine debris was held in Honolulu under the auspices of the National Marine Fisheries Service (a division of NOAA, the National Oceanic and Atmospheric Administration). That meeting brought into focus the scope of the problem and led to the founding of NOAA's Marine Entanglement Research Program. It also mobilized governmental agencies and environmental groups to push for ratification of Annex V.

In the wake of that conference, Congress was urged by the U.S. Coast Guard, the Marine Mammal Commission, NOAA and numerous environmental groups to ratify the annex. Finally, in the last week of 1987, the United States completed its ratification process, pushing the percentage of tonnage represented by signatory nations over the level necessary for Annex V to become effective.

Parties to the law now have one year to put their domestic programs in place. Thus, beginning on December 31, 1988, it will be illegal for ships registered in signatory nations, and all other ships within the waters of those countries that prohibit dumping, to discard plastics into the ocean.

"I think that it is a remarkable thing that it happened," says Kathy O'Hara, who is a marine biologist and plastic specialist for the Center for Environmental Education. "It was an incredible public-awareness event. A lot of the environmental community's energy was focused for the last two years on U.S. ratification. It definitely will make a difference."

But O'Hara and other environmentalists also point out that although the annex will help, it will by no means solve the problem. It only deals with ocean disposal, for one thing, ignoring pollution from such land sources as sewage treatment plants and plastics manufacturers. In addition, nations not party to the annex don't have to adhere to its conditions unless their ships are in the waters of party nations.

Moreover, it will be difficult to get compliance. Consider, for instance, the disposal choices facing a captain bringing his ship into U.S. waters from a foreign port. An already existing American law requires that any garbage on this ship that has been in contact with food must be incinerated or sterilized before port disposal. (This law's purpose is to prevent the spread of pests or infectious diseases.) Facing incineration fees as high as $450 per truckload, however, fewer than 3 percent of ships now bring their trash into American ports, often choosing instead to throw it overboard at sea. Much of this trash is plastic. Although Annex V will severely restrict this option, the temptation to cheat is obvious. The U.S. Coast Guard, which will enforce Annex V for the United States, is currently developing regulations for its implementation.

There is the additional problem of military vessels, which are exempt from Annex V. American warships alone discharge four tons of plastic every day, says Larry Koss, environmental program manager for the U.S. Navy's shipboard program. While U.S. military vessels are being required by Congress to comply with Annex V within five years, each signatory nation will be handling this question independently. Koss says the Navy is exploring the idea of a special thermal waste processor for plastics that will compact large loads of the synthetic trash into small bricks that can be more easily stored and carried by ships to port.

"To a turtle a transparent plastic bag or particle can look like a jellyfish, plankton or the larval stage of a crab. Once in the turtle's intestines . . . the indigestible material can block fecal matter, prevent assimilation of nutrients and make the turtle too buoyant to dive for food."

—George Balazs,
a zoologist for
the National Marine
Fisheries Service

In a way, the marine plastic pollution problem crept up on American lawmakers. While several international conventions and federal laws have included provisions to limit or prohibit marine dumping of chemicals, oil and other substances, none of them has applied directly to the more recently recognized problem of plastic debris.

The plastics industry also is addressing the problem of plastics disposal. One spotlight is turned on degradable plastics; the technology for some types is already in place and research continues for wider and appropriate applications.

Several companies now offer degradable resins for sale, a few manufacturers in the United States, Italy and Canada are making degradable plastic bags. A photodegradable agricultural mulch has been available for several years, and to comply with laws in 11 states, manufacturers have developed six-pack rings that also break down in sunlight.

There has been some progress, too, in the area of recycling. Plastics industry sources say that, in this country, 20 percent of all plastic soft drink bottles are being recycled into items like polyfill stuffing, paintbrushes and industrial strapping. Technology is also available for "commingled" recycling—mixing different types of plastics in the recycling process—and that process is now being used to produce a new building material called plastic lumber.

Ronald Bruner, spokesman for the industry's trade association, says his members feel the "black eye" of stories linking their products to wildlife losses. The environmental concerns are warranted, he says, but they should not overshadow the great benefits of the plastics revolution. "Look at how many human lives plastic saves. Take disposable products like syringes that prevent the spread of disease; in medical procedures, the use of plastic in sutures, prosthetic devices."

Meanwhile, back on Mustang Island, Tony Amos drives his truck along the beach every other morning, documenting the plastic debris that the tide has brought in. "I never know what I'm going to find next," says Amos, the professional trashcomber, who estimates that up to 90 percent of the plastic items he finds are dumped off ships. To prove his point, he boasts a personal collection of plastic containers that could have originated only on foreign vessels—Korean shampoo, Cuban bleach, Moroccan mineral oil and toilet bowl cleaners from Hong Kong and Czechoslovakia. He agrees that Annex V is a solid step toward addressing the problem, but he points out, as do many others, that further steps must follow. People in his line of work don't tend to get overly optimistic. "I have pictures of girls in bikinis lying among piles of the stuff on the beach," says Amos. "People have almost got used to this. Maybe it'll become acceptable—part of the environment." It's something to think about. (pp. 63–6)

Michael Weisskopf, *"Plastic Reaps a Grim Harvest in the Oceans of the World," in* Smithsonian, *Vol. 18, No. 12, March, 1988, pp. 58–67.*

The Benefits of At-Sea Incineration

There is only one place in the world where chemical waste is regularly burnt at sea: about 100 miles off the north-eastern coast of England. The sea is sacred to environmentalists—more so, if possible, than mother earth herself. So even that isolated waste-burning will probably have to stop by 1994, thanks to an agreement signed by European ministers last year. The victorious environmentalists say that science is clearly on their side. A gathering of experts in London last month disagreed. Science does not grant its favours so lightly.

According to Dr John Parker of Ocean Combustion Services (a subsidiary of an American company, Waste Management), some 110,000–120,000 tonnes of waste are incinerated at sea each year, most of it from West Germany. Ocean Combustion Services operates from Rotterdam and owns the good ship

Vulcanus II, which does most of the dirty deed. The best sorts of waste to burn—on land or sea—are complex organic molecules made from elements such as carbon, hydrogen and chlorine. Such molecules can be burned in oxygen to form simple, safer ones like carbon dioxide, water and an acidic gas, hydrogen chloride.

There are two good reasons for burning at sea. Nobody wants hazardous wastes moved around and burnt anywhere near his own backyard. And some wastes are cheaper to burn at sea: Dr Parker estimates that it costs £100–300 ($190–570) per tonne. Wastes which produce extreme amounts of hydrogen chloride could cost up to £5,000 per tonne to burn on land. This gas cannot be allowed to escape on land because it would wipe out neighbouring animals and vegetation as it settled. So land-based incinerators use expensive scrubbers in their chimneys to collect the gas and neutralise it with sodium hydroxide. The beauty of the sea is that it is naturally alkaline. So long as no ships are nearby, it can absorb the hydrogen chloride for nothing.

The sea incinerators claim that only around 0.005% of their toxic waste escapes. An environmental group, Greenpeace, say that this figure is wrong, partly because it fails to take the effects of hydrogen chloride into account; and partly because of something that is true for all incinerators, whether on land or sea.

Take the point about hydrogen chloride first. According to research at the Studsvik Institute in Sweden, fragments of waste molecules could, in theory, react with hydrogen chloride in the plume of gases that emerge from a ship's funnels. The products of these reactions would be as deadly as the waste itself. Nobody knows how much of these chemicals get in to the plume because they are too tricky to measure. The incinerators say this proves that they are too diluted to matter. Greenpeace replies that they are absorbed into the microscopic film or organisms which live on the sea's surface and are gobbled into the food chain. The only evidence for this comes from rather tricky laboratory mock-ups.

Greenpeace's other complaint concerns how the efficiency of a burn-up is measured. One of the ways to calculate this figure compares the concentration of a particular waste going into the furnace with the concentration in the emerging gases. Greenpeace says that this method ignores some new compounds that may have been formed inside the furnace. It says that an analysis of the ash left in furnaces reveals traces of them. Those who favour incineration retort that these traces are even fainter than those in ordinary soil.

The proponents of incineration at sea claim that they are the innocent victims of green politics. The British government may well have sacrificed sea-burning in order to be able to keep on dumping waste in other ways. The trouble with Greenpeace's scientific objections—apart from the point that they are largely speculative—is that most of them would also apply to burning on land. Its own answer, storing everything until some other means of disposal turns up, fails to appreciate how nasty some chemical wastes are to have around.

"Stinks Ahoy," in The Economist, *Vol. 307, No. 7551, May 21–27, 1988, p. 100.*

> **There are two good reasons for burning at sea. Nobody wants hazardous waste moved around and burnt anywhere near his own backyard. And some wastes are cheaper to burn at sea.**

Managing Dredged Materials

Navigable waterways and their role in transportation and defense are vital components of the economic growth and stability of coastal nations. However, most near-shore and estuarine areas are naturally shallow. Depths

Uncontaminated, or "clean" dredged material may be placed at the broadest range of locations with environmental concern limited only to physical impacts, the most significant of which is habitat modification in the aquatic environment.

that support modern shipping are maintained only by dredging, which removes sediment and aquatic soil that naturally accumulate in navigation channels.

Annually, hundreds of millions of cubic meters of dredged material are brought up from the world's harbors, and it must be placed and managed in an economically and ecologically sound manner. Since the annual cost of port and waterway maintenance worldwide ranges in the hundreds of millions of dollars, officials seek the least costly, environmentally sound methods of dredged-material transport and placement—either on land, at sea, or at another estuarine location.

Dredged material is a mixture of sand, silt, and clay. It can include rock, gravel, organic matter, and contaminants from a wide range of agricultural, urban, and industrial sources. If it were not for those contaminants, dredged sediments would consist only of natural components of the Earth's crust deposited by natural erosional and mineralization processes. Contaminated or otherwise unacceptable dredged material accounts for only a small fraction of the total—less than 10 percent in the U.S. and globally.

Uncontaminated, or "clean" dredged material may be placed at the broadest range of locations with environmental concern limited only to physical impacts, the most significant of which is habitat modification in the aquatic environment. Clean material has many positive uses. These include the development and enhancement of wetlands, and aquatic and wildlife habitat; beach nourishment; land development; offshore mound and island construction; agriculture; mariculture; and construction aggregate. The benefits of such positive uses are significant and should receive highest priority in a dredged-material management policy. An increase in the positive use of dredged material would signal a decrease in the use of disposal sites.

In industrialized harbors, typical contaminants are toxic metals, organohalogens like PCBs, petrochemical by-products, excess nutrients, and harmful microbes. As many waterways are located in industrialized areas, the disposal of contaminated sediments generates serious environmental concerns.

Regulatory controls in the United States are developed by the U.S. Environmental Protection Agency (EPA) through the authority of the Marine Protection Research and Sanctuaries Act of 1972. This act authorizes the U.S. Army Corps of Engineers to issue permits for the ocean placement of dredged material, and apply the EPA's controls. Internationally, the 1972 Convention on the Prevention of Marine Pollution by Dumping of Wastes and Other Matter, often called the London Dumping Convention (LDC) regulates ocean placement of dredged material. In 1986, the convention agreed on special guidelines for the management of such placement.

The LDC guidelines separate the regulation and assessment of dredged material from that of other wastes, and require alternatives to ocean placement to be reviewed. The alternatives are assessed on the basis of such human-health and environmental concerns as safety, economics, and the possible exclusion of future uses for disposal areas. Furthermore, the guidelines recognize that "Sea disposal [of dredged material] is often an acceptable disposal option," and encourage positive uses. The LDC's approach and the EPA's regulations are fully compatible.

Procedures for assessing dredged material include:

- analyzing toxicological characteristics,

- analyzing proposed placement site characteristics,

- reviewing placement methods, and

- considering alternate placement sites.

The EPA and Corps of Engineers classify dredged material using the results of tests that determine the presence of specific contaminants, their bulk toxicity, leachability, and biological availability. Sediments that have toxic and biologically available contaminants are banned from ocean placement. The tests range from simple water leaches to multiorganism benthic bioassays.

Placement-site characteristics include topography, and proximity to recreation areas, fisheries, waterways, and sensitive marine-resource areas. Proposed sites also must be amenable to monitoring and management.

When dredged material is deposited at a placement site, the release of contaminants from it may be drastically enhanced or retarded, depending on how the water-sediment geochemical environment is changed. For example, a significant release of such metals as zinc can occur under acidic oxidizing conditions, which do not normally occur in aquatic placement. Laboratory studies simulating upland placement where drying and oxidation can occur show that dredged material so placed can become acidic. Upland placement of marine sediments with a high level of sulfide led, after several months of drying and oxidation, to acid conditions and subsequent metal leaching.

Laboratory research also indicates, however, that there is minor release of most manmade chemicals from dredged material because they bind so tightly to clay and organic matter.

Sediment-bound contaminants emphasize the need for determining the biological effects of the solid fraction. The solid phase of dredged material rapidly settles to the bottom and has intimate association with the benthic, or bottom-dwelling, organisms. Sediment-bound contaminants may be made available to aquatic biota through ingestion or direct contact by the organism or, on the other hand, buried at the placement site with clean sediment effectively isolating them from marine organisms. Regardless of the chemical nature of the solid phase, the physical effects on various organisms also must be thoroughly evaluated.

Investigations have been carried out to determine the effects of suspended dredged material on aquatic organisms, the ability of organisms to migrate vertically through deposits of settled material, and the bioaccumulation of sediment-bound contaminants. The ecological effects of sediments contaminated with a wide range of pollutants continue to be investigated by various organizations in countries around the world. Results of these investigations form the basis for the management of dredged material placement.

The short-term and long-term chemical, physical, and biological impacts of open-water placement have been determined by large investigations in numerous locations. The locations were largely regarded as nondispersive or low-energy environments with regard to sediment resuspension or transport. Chemical effects in the water column duplicated the laboratory test results previously reported.

When material was placed in a nondispersive aquatic site, movement or release of the chemical constituents in relation to reference sites was not apparent. Suspended particulate concentrations were less than concentrations that have been established to have an impact on a broad range of aquatic organisms. These low concentrations persisted only for a few hours.

A significant impact is the formation of mounds of dredged material at aquatic placement sites. Biological recolonization of these mounds demonstrates that conditions eventually return to the original state. Biological recolonization is rapid on fine-grained sediment, while sandy substrates exhibited slower recovery. Sites that receive multiple placements continue to reflect physical impacts and must be carefully chosen to minimize damage to important amenities of the marine environment.

The sediment characteristics that most affect the mobility and biological availability of dredged materials are particle size, organic matter content, amount and type of ions, amount of iron and manganese, oxidation/reduction potential, pH, and salinity.

In industrialized harbors, typical contaminants are toxic metals, organohalogens like PCBs, petrochemical by-products, excess nutrients, and harmful microbes. As many waterways are located in industrialized areas, the disposal of contaminated sediments generates serious environmental concerns.

For sediments that have been determined to represent a high environmental risk, placement methods favoring containment of potentially toxic substances should be considered.

When the physical-chemical environment of a contaminated sediment is altered by removal and placement, the chemical and biological processes important to mobilization or immobilization of potentially toxic materials may be affected. Frequently, an altered physical-chemical environment that results in the release of contaminants from one chemical form will favor other immobilizing reactions. As an example, aquatic placement under reducing, neutral pH conditions will favor immobilization of toxic metals while having little effect on mobility of organohalogens. The placement methods on the release of contaminants must be identified.

In addition to the chemical properties of the contaminant, the chemical and physical properties of the dredged material will influence the mobility of contaminants at relocation sites. A number of readily identified properties of dredged material affect the mobility and biological availability of various contaminants. Some of these properties can change when the material is moved from one type of disposal environment to another; whereas other properties are not affected by changes in water content, aeration, or salinity.

Much of the dredged material removed during harbor and channel maintenance dredging contains a high proportion of organic matter and clay and is biologically and chemically active. It is usually devoid of oxygen and may contain an appreciable amount of sulfide.

These conditions favor effective immobilization of many contaminants provided the dredged material is not subject to mixing, resuspension, and transport induced by waves or currents. Coarse-textured sediments that have a low organic matter content are much less effective in immobilizing metal and organic contaminants. These materials do not tend to accumulate contaminants unless a contamination source is nearby. Should sediment contamination exist, then potentially toxic substances may be released to the water column or leaching and uptake of contaminants by plants may occur under intertidal or land placement conditions.

Many contaminated sediments are initially anoxic and have a near-neutral pH. Subaqueous disposal into quiescent waters will generally maintain these conditions and favor immobilization of contaminants. By contrast, certain noncalcareous sediments contain appreciable reactive iron and particularly reduced sulfur compounds. These sediments may become moderately to strongly acid upon gradual drainage and subsequent oxidation, as may occur when upland disposal takes place. This offers a high potential for mobilizing potentially toxic metals.

For sediments that have been determined to represent a high environmental risk, placement methods favoring containment of potentially toxic substances should be considered.

Many examples demonstrate that highly contaminated dredged material can be managed in ocean locations if sufficient care is exercised with site selection to ensure that the material is isolated from the biotic zone of the marine system. This approach can involve site management techniques such as covering with clean sediment, or locating sites in abiotic areas. The available scientific and engineering data indicate that, for the greater part, dredged material should be regarded as a highly manageable resource for productive use in the marine environment.

No simple solution to the placement of contaminated dredged material exists, but with proper management, the aquatic environment can offer a logical and environmentally sound alternative to land-based sites. The approach of carefully managing open-water sites should be considered a primary management solution to a perplexing problem. The same degree of waste management should also be strictly applied to land containment or inland disposal of dredged material. The majority of sediments dredged from the coastal zone can be used for a wide range of productive and beneficial uses that should be a high priority in the selection of placement alternatives. (pp. 63–9)

Robert M. Engler, "Managing Dredged Materials," in Oceanus, Vol. 33, No. 2, Summer, 1990, pp. 63–9.

U.S. Legislative Policy and Waste Disposal at Sea

Since the early 1970s, Congress has played a major role in developing and implementing U.S. policy on waste disposal at sea. Although Congress has occasionally reacted to initiatives from the Executive Branch, more often than not policy has been molded by strong pressures from coastal residents. Legislation often has been passed despite substantial scientific uncertainty.

In our democratic system of government, when the public demands environmental protection and the scientific community fails to speak with one voice, Congress generally reacts by passing legislation to afford that protection. This has been the case with disposal of wastes at sea.

Congress turned its full attention to the issue of waste disposal at sea in 1972, after decades of ocean dumping. Congress first regulated ocean disposal of wastes when it passed the Marine Protection, Research, and Sanctuaries Act (commonly called the Ocean Dumping Act). That legislation regulated the dumping of all types of materials into ocean waters and prevented or strictly limited the dumping of any material that would adversely affect human health, welfare, the marine environment, ecosystems, or economic potentialities.

Under the Ocean Dumping Act, disposal was prohibited unless the dumper obtained a permit from the Environmental Protection Agency (EPA) and could demonstrate that the materials to be dumped would not "unreasonably degrade or endanger human health or the marine environment." Certain materials, such as radiological, chemical, and biological warfare agents and high-level radioactive wastes were fully banned. The dumping of dredged materials from navigable waters was put under the regulation of the Army Corps of Engineers.

The Ocean Dumping Act had its origins in a 1970 report issued by the Council on Environmental Quality (CEQ), which Congress had recently established. The report, entitled Ocean Dumping—A National Policy, called for the development of a national and international policy on ocean dumping. The CEQ report also called for ocean dumping of undigested sewage sludge to be stopped immediately and the dumping of treated sewage sludge to be phased out.

The law was enacted during a time when the nation was undergoing a significant rise in environmental consciousness. There was an explosion of environmental legislation and "dead sea" stories began to appear in some newspapers in the Northeast.

The most controversial question facing Congress was the dumping of sewage sludge at sea. Sewage sludge is a by-product of the municipal wastewater treatment process and is permitted to be dumped under the 1972 Act, provided it meets environmental standards.

According to a 1987 report by the U.S. Congress Office of Technology Assessment (OTA) entitled Wastes in Marine Environments, the amount of sludge dumped in marine waters has increased steadily, from more than 2.5 million

Under the Ocean Dumping Act, disposal was prohibited unless the dumper obtained a permit from the Environmental Protection Agency (EPA) and could demonstrate that the materials to be dumped would not "unreasonably degrade or endanger human health or the marine environment."

According to a 1987 report by the U.S. Congress Office of Technology Assessment entitled *Wastes in Marine Environments*, the amount of sludge dumped in marine waters has increased steadily, from more than 2.5 million wet tonnes in 1959 to about 7.5 million wet tonnes in 1983. The amount of sludge dumped today in the ocean is close to 9 million wet tonnes.

wet tonnes in 1959 to about 7.5 million wet tonnes in 1983. The amount of sludge dumped today in the ocean is close to 9 million wet tonnes.

A series of pollution incidents in 1976 forced Congress to take another look at the ocean dumping of municipal sludge and industrial waste. That summer, large quantities of foul materials washed up on the beaches of Long Island, New York, causing many of the area's largest public beaches to be closed to swimmers. There also was a major fish kill off the East Coast from Long Island to Delaware.

In 1977, as a result of beach closures and fish kills, Congress passed new amendments to the Ocean Dumping Act specifically addressing sludge and industrial waste. The amendments called for an end to ocean dumping of sewage sludge and industrial waste as soon as possible, with no permits to be granted after December 31, 1981. The type of sludge and industrial waste prohibited after 1981 was that which would "unreasonably degrade" or endanger human health or the marine environment. In January of 1977, the EPA issued final regulations stating its intention to stop issuing permits by the end of 1981.

Following the enactment of the 1977 amendments, more than 150 municipalities, including the City of Philadelphia, ended their practice of ocean dumping of municipal sludge, turned to landfilling, and met the 1981 deadline. But New York City, a major user of the ocean for sludge disposal, and several New Jersey municipalities believed they had no economically viable alternative.

In 1980, New York City challenged EPA's decision not to renew the city's ocean dumping permit on the grounds that the decision was inconsistent with the intent of the 1977 amendments. New York City argued that the 1977 amendments did not prohibit all dumping of sewage sludge, but only that which would, in the language of the amendments, "unreasonably degrade" the marine environment.

The Federal Court for the Southern District of New York agreed with the city. In a 1981 opinion, the court ruled that EPA had been arbitrary in presuming that the city's sludge did not meet the act's environmental standards. New York City, Nassau County, Westchester County, New York, and six New Jersey municipalities were allowed to continue dumping their sludge in the ocean pursuant to court order.

Although ocean dumping of sewage sludge continued after the 1977 amendments, EPA moved the site for the dumping from the New York Bight Apex, called the 12-mile site, to a new location some 115 nautical miles east of Atlantic City, New Jersey. This site, on the edge of the continental shelf, is called the 106-Mile Dump Site.

Congress codified EPA's administrative decision to move the dump site to deeper waters in the Water Resources Development Act of 1986. This act required all dumpers to move their operations to the 106 site by December 31, 1987. It also prohibited any new dumpers from using the site. All dumpers met the deadline for moving their operations, although it meant, in New York City's case, the acquisition of larger barges for transporting the sludge to the new site.

The summer of 1987 was another bad summer for U.S. coastal communities. Public beaches in numerous New Jersey townships were closed as a result of medical debris washing ashore, high bacteria counts in the water, and sewage plant overflows. The public was particularly aghast at the sight of needles on public beaches, and naturally concerned about the risk of contracting contagious diseases. The effect on the New Jersey tourist economy was disastrous, the lost business estimated to be in the billions of dollars. The public also witnessed and mourned an unusually high number of dolphins dying and washing up along the Atlantic coast.

Although the dolphin deaths were subsequently attributed to a naturally occurring toxin, the possibility that the incidents were exacerbated by high levels of contaminants in the animals could not be ruled out. In addition, fishermen near the 106 site reported shell diseases in fish, which they attributed to the dumping of sludge at the site. The clamor for Congress to do something was deafening.

As a result, Congress again re-examined the Ocean Dumping Act. This time, in the Ocean Dumping Ban Act of 1988, Congress made clear what had not been clear in the 1977 amendments—all ocean dumping of sewage sludge and industrial waste, whether or not it unreasonably degraded the marine environment, would cease after December 31, 1991.

Moreover, all dumpers would have to enter into enforceable agreements with EPA in which they had to commit to specific schedules to phase out ocean dumping of sewage sludge or face stiff penalties. By the time of the enactment of the 1988 amendments, the remaining industrial waste dumpers had agreed to stop using the ocean.

The penalties start at $600 a ton for any sludge dumped after the 1991 deadline, and escalate incrementally in each subsequent year. The penalties are not strictly punitive; dumpers will be allowed to retain a certain percentage of the penalties if they dedicate the money to developing land-based alternatives.

New Jersey plans to landfill its sludge to meet the deadline and, in the long term, to construct incinerators to burn dewatered sludge. New York City, which dumps close to 5.3 million wet tonnes of sludge a year at the 106 site, has agreed to phase out ocean dumping of 20 percent of its sludge by the 1991 deadline, with the remainder by June 30, 1992 (subject to the payment of civil penalties). The city is studying all possible options for long-term management of the sludge. The design of eight dewatering facilities is now under way.

Although it will soon be illegal to dump sludge and industrial waste in the ocean, we are continuing to use the ocean as a disposal medium for dredged materials. According to the OTA report, an annual average of about 180 million wet tonnes of dredged material is disposed of in the marine environment: about two-thirds in estuaries, one-sixth in coastal waters, and one-sixth in the open ocean.

There is growing public concern about the presence of contaminated sediments in the materials dredged from ports and harbors. The sediments are contaminated by metals and organic chemicals that settle as a result of industrial discharges and runoff of pollutants. Congress is beginning to examine the issue of contaminated sediments to determine if additional controls on their ocean disposal are required.

In the area of environmental protection, there has been no clear consensus among marine scientists about what caused past pollution incidents or, if there is, it has not been effectively communicated to Congress. What is clear is that the capacity of the oceans to absorb waste materials is a matter of continuing debate among oceanographers, with no apparent resolution in sight.

Given this debate, a cautious and responsible legislative response is to ban the activity until sufficient information becomes available. We have seen this approach in recent congressional reactions to offshore oil and gas development, ocean incineration, and the dumping of sludge and industrial waste at sea.

For now, Congress has established a clear policy prohibiting the ocean disposal of sewage sludge, industrial waste, high-level radioactive waste, chemical and biological warfare agents, and the ocean incineration of toxic materials. Opening up the debate about changing this policy will not be easy.

Yet, Congress is a dynamic institution, affected by new technological developments, advances in science, and hard data about risks and benefits. No policy debate is closed forever. Increased restrictions on landfills will create its own environmental cost-benefit calculations that could, someday, require a revisiting of this established policy. (pp. 23–8)

Thomas R. Kitsos and Joan M. Bondareff, "Congress and Waste Disposal at Sea," in Oceanus, *Vol. 33, No. 2, Summer, 1990, pp. 23–8.*

Although it will soon be illegal to dump sludge and industrial waste in the ocean, we are continuing to use the ocean as a disposal medium for dredged materials. According to the OTA report, an annual average of about 180 million wet tonnes of dredged material is disposed of in the marine environment: about two-thirds in estuaries, one-sixth in coastal waters, and one-sixth in the open ocean.

Sources for Further Study

Calmet, Dominique P. "Ocean Disposal of Radioactive Waste: Status Report." *IAEA Bulletin* 31, No. 4 (1989): 47–51.
  Examines the International Atomic Energy Agency recommendations to protect humankind and the marine environment from the ocean dumping of hazardous nuclear waste.

Campbell, Lee Anne. "Plastics are Forever." *Nor'easter* 1, No. 2 (Fall 1989): 10–16.
  Addresses the disposal of plastics in the ocean, asserting that commercial, fishing, and shipping industries are believed to be the largest polluters. Campbell also explores various ways to prevent at-sea dumping of plastics in the future.

Cotter, John. "Sea Disposal—Licensing and Monitoring." *Chemistry and Industry*, No. 9 (2 May 1988): 290–93.
  Surveys the reasons for licensing and the procedures for monitoring waste disposal and at-sea incineration in the coastal waters of the United Kingdom.

D'Arcy, Jenish. "Summer's Dark Side." *Maclean's* 103, No. 35 (27 August 1990): 42–3.
  Maintains that the rash of beach closings in many coastal Canadian provinces is due to the discovery of a high concentration of fecal coliform bacteria in surrounding waters.

Deland, Michael R. "Boston Harbor: No Party After the Tea Party." *EPA Journal* 14, No. 5 (June 1988): 24–7.
  Discusses the efforts underway to clean up the heavily-polluted Boston Harbor, a project that will take an estimated eleven years and six billion dollars.

Finlayson, Ann. "Warnings from the Seas." *Maclean's* 101, No. 37 (5 September 1988): 48–9.
  Offers a synopsis of various ocean dumping practices. Finlayson concludes that "the troubles of the world's oceans will only worsen without swift corrective action."

Fretheim, Alte. "Dumping at Sea." *Marine Policy* 14, No. 3 (May 1990): 247–51.
  Maintains that many countries consider ocean dumping an unacceptable means of waste disposal. Fretheim asserts that The World Commission on Environment and Development stresses three imperatives in dealing with this problem: the oceans need effective global management, regional management is compulsory, and international action regarding land-based threats to the oceans is necessary.

Goodavage, Maria. "Murky Waters." *Modern Maturity* 32, No. 4 (August–September 1989): 44–50.
  Observes that while humankind is just beginning to unlock the secrets of the ocean, ocean dumping jeopardizes the potential for increased knowledge through its the reckless destruction of marine ecosystems.

Juda, Lawrence, and Burroughs, R. H. "The Prospects of Comprehensive Ocean Management." *Marine Policy* 14, No. 1 (January 1990): 23–36.
  Argues that oil drilling, ocean dumping, and fishing rights are three significant issues that must be addressed to provide better ocean management. Juda and Burroughs then outline various obstacles that threaten the realization of this goal.

MacQuitty, Miranda. "Pollution beneath the Golden Gate." *New Scientist* 118, No. 1619 (30 June 1988): 62–7.

Explores the methods of various campaigns to clean up San Francisco Bay, noting that the estuary is still severely polluted. MacQuitty also discusses how the EPA has proposed using funds from the National Estuary Program to help clean up the bay.

Manville, Albert M., II. "Tracking Plastic in the Pacific." *Defenders* 63, No. 6 (November–December 1988): 10–16.
    Analyzes the effect that discarded plastic trash has had on the marine environment around the Aleutian Islands in the Pacific Ocean. Manville attributes the deaths of some seabirds and seals to plastics pollution.

"Big Fines for At-Sea Trash Dumpers." *Marine Log* 93, No. 11 (December 1988): 34–7.
    Surveys the possible implications of handling plastic waste at sea once Annex V of the International Convention for the Prevention of Pollution by Garbage from Ships takes effect on December 31, 1988, prohibiting the dumping of this waste from ships.

Marshall, Eliot. "The Sludge Factor." *Science* 242, No. 4878 (28 October 1988): 507–08.
    Focuses on the destructive effect that dumping contaminated sludge has on the coastal waters around New York and New Jersey. Marshall also discusses legislation being considered by the U.S. Congress that will outlaw sludge disposal in the ocean by January 1992.

Marx, Wesley. "Cry of the American Coast." *Reader's Digest* 133, No. 800 (December 1988): 110–15.
    Provides a general discussion of waste disposal in the oceans off U.S. coasts and measures currently underway to address the problem.

Merriman, Kristin. "Coast Watch." *Outdoor America* 54, No. 2 (Spring 1989): 7–12.
    Assess the threat that overpopulation in U.S. coastal zones has had on the marine ecosystems of those areas.

Millman, Beth. "Wretched Refuse Off Our Shores." *Sierra* 74, No. 1 (January–February 1989): 26–8.
    Examines current practices and possible legislation regarding sludge dumping in the ocean and at-sea incineration of garbage.

Morganthau, Tom. "Don't Go Near the Water." *Newsweek* CXII, No. 5 (1 August 1988): 42–7.
    Discusses the disastrous effects of waste disposal in the ocean on beaches, harbors, and marine life.

"Medical Waste Just One Threat to Beaches." *National Parks* 63, Nos. 1–2 (January–February 1989): 9–10.
    Argues that toxins such as polychlorinated biphenyls (PCBs), petroleum, and chlorinated hydrocarbons pose more of a threat to the ocean and its marine life than the much-publicized medical waste washing up on east coast beaches.

Nelson, Lori. "The Dolphins of Monkey Mia." *Sea Frontiers* 36, No. 4 (July–August 1990): 16–23.
    Contends that the rising level of pollutants in the waters around Monkey Mia, Australia, may have contributed to the deaths and disappearances of dolphins that frequented the area.

"The Dredge Spoil Disposal Dilemma." *Oceans* 21, No. 6 (November–December 1988): 69–70.
    Discusses dredge disposal in the ocean and legislative measures that have been initiated to combat the problem.

O'Hara, Kathryn J. "Plastic Debris and Its Effects on Marine Wildlife." In *Audubon Wildlife Report 1988/1989*, edited by William J. Chandler, pp. 395–434. New York: Academic Press, Inc., 1988.

Addresses the issue of dumping plastic debris in the ocean and its effect on various marine species. O'Hara particularly focuses on the problems that entanglement and ingestion of plastic poses for marine life.

Reynolds, Clarence V. "Beachless Summer." *Discover* 10, No. 1 (January 1989): 38.

Surveys the medical waste disposal crisis in New York and New Jersey, asserting that there are no short-term solutions to preventing the reoccurrence of the problem.

Srivastava, Chandrika Prasad. "The Role of the International Maritime Organisation." *Marine Policy* 14, No. 3 (May 1990): 243–47.

Outlines the ways in which the International Maritime Organization regulates marine transport and at-sea dumping of hazardous substances.

Stegeman, John J. "Detecting the Biological Effects of Deep-Sea Waste Disposal." *Oceanus* 33, No. 2 (Summer 1990): 54–60.

Asserts that through the use of biomarkers—tools that can detect biochemical changes in marine species due to chemical pollution—scientists have determined that "some chemicals may already be causing biological change in the deep ocean, a region far removed from the known point-sources of those chemicals."

Stutz, Bruce. "Last Summer at the Jersey Shore." *Oceans* 21, No. 4 (July–August 1988): 8–15.

Analyzes the effect that waters contaminated by medical waste in New Jersey have had on swimmers there. Stutz asserts that several medical studies indicate that there was not an increase in reported illnesses; however, environmental organizations and citizens' groups maintain that more incidents of infection did occur.

Taylor, Gary. "Water, Water Everywhere—No Place Else to Dump?" *The National Law Journal* 11, No. 12 (28 November 1988): 8.

Reviews the first attempted ocean dumping prosecution under the Marine Protection, Research, and Sanctuaries Act of 1972. Taylor maintains that in the 1988 case *U.S. v. Odfjell Westfal-Larsen (USA) Inc.*, U.S. District Judge Lynn N. Hughes thwarted prosecutors' attempts to impose stiff fines and jail terms on company officers, claiming that the suit was primarily based on circumstantial evidence.

"Why a Flood of Filth Laps the Beaches." *U.S. News and World Report* 105, No. 8 (22 August 1988): 7–8.

Recounts the incident of medical waste washing up on New York and New Jersey beaches, and explores possible reasons for the occurrence.

Van Dyke, Jon M. "Ocean Disposal of Nuclear Wastes." *Marine Policy* 12, No. 2 (April 1988): 82–96.

Reviews four recent scientific studies that evaluate the viability of dumping low-level radioactive waste in the ocean.

"Oceans and Coasts." In *World Resources Institution Report: World Resources 1990–91*, pp. 179–201.

Contends that coastal areas provide habitats for most of the ocean's marine species and that these areas are particularly vulnerable to various forms of waste contamination. This association report then analyzes the effects of pollution on marine environments in the Caribbean Sea and in Antarctica.

10: Ozone Depletion

Protecting The Ozone Layer

When British scientists reported in 1985 that a hole in the ozone layer over Antarctica had been occurring each spring since 1979, the news came as a complete surprise. Although the theory that a group of widely used chemicals called chlorofluorocarbons (CFCs) would someday erode upper atmospheric ozone had been advanced in the mid-seventies, none of the models had predicted that the thinning would first be evident over the South Pole—nor that it would be so severe. Scientists were baffled: What was threatening this key life-support system? And how many other surprises lay in store?

Ozone, the three-atom form of oxygen, is the only gas in the atmosphere that prevents harmful solar ultraviolet radiation from reaching the surface of the earth. Most of it is found at altitudes of between 12 and 25 kilometers, but even there, at its greatest concentration, it is present at only a few parts per million. Sunlight-triggered chemical reactions constantly replenish ozone above the tropics and global air circulation transports some of it to the poles.

By the Antarctic spring of 1987, the average ozone concentration over the South Pole was down 50 percent. In isolated spots it had essentially disappeared. Although the depletion was alarming, many were convinced that the thinning was seasonal and unique to Antarctica, a phenomenon attributable to altered atmospheric chemistry and to perplexing polar air circulation.

A scientific report issued in March 1988 shattered this view: more than 100 international experts reported that the ozone layer around the entire globe was eroding much faster than any model had predicted. Between 1969 and 1986, the average global concentration of ozone in the stratosphere had fallen by approximately 2 percent. The magnitude of the decline varied by latitude and by season, with the most heavily populated regions of Europe, North America, and the Soviet Union suffering a year-round depletion of 3 percent and a winter loss of 4.7 percent.

As ozone diminishes in the upper atmosphere, the earth receives more ultraviolet radiation, which promotes skin cancers and cataracts and depresses human immune systems. Reduced crop yields, depleted marine fisheries, materials damage, and increased smog are also attributable to higher levels of radiation. The phenomenon is global and will affect the well-being of every person in the world.

Compounds containing chlorine and bromine, which are released from industrial processes and products and then move slowly into the upper atmosphere, are considered the primary culprits. Most of the chlorine comes from CFCs; the bromine originates from halons used in fire extinguishers. Spurred to action by the ozone hole over Antarctica, 35 countries have signed an international agreement—the Montreal Protocol—aimed at halving most CFC emissions by 1998 and freezing halon emissions by 1992. Although an impressive diplomatic achievement and an important first step, the agreement is so riddled with loopholes that its objectives will not be met. Furthermore, scientific findings subsequent to the negotiations reveal that even if the treaty's

---

As ozone diminishes in the upper atmosphere, the earth receives more ultraviolet radiation, which promotes skin cancers and cataracts and depresses human immune systems. Reduced crop yields, depleted marine fisheries, materials damage, and increased smog are also attributable to higher levels of radiation. The phenomenon is global and will affect the well-being of every person in the world.

Scientists were alarmed not only by the documented damage to the ozone layer, but by the inadequacy of their models to predict it.

goals were met, significant further deterioration of the ozone layer would still occur. The fact that CFCs and halons are also "greenhouse gases" and that global warming may already be underway strengthens the need to further control and eliminate emissions.

The fundamental links between CFCs, halons, and ozone depletion are no longer in doubt. Currently available control technologies and stricter standards governing equipment operation and maintenance could reduce CFC and halon emissions by some 90 percent. But effective government policies and industry practices to limit and ultimately phase out chlorine and bromine emissions have yet to be formulated. Encouraging steps have been taken by some countries, particularly in Scandinavia, and by some corporations. But just as the effects of ozone depletion will be felt worldwide, a lasting remedy to the problem must also be global.

The Ozone Depletion Puzzle

In 1985, a team led by Joseph Farman, of the British Antarctic Survey, startled the world by reported a 40-percent loss in the springtime ozone layer over Antarctica. (pp. 77–8)

Faced with evidence of a phenomenon that had not been predicted by atmospheric models, scientists scurried to explain the cause and to determine if more widespread depletion, outside of Antarctica, was likely. Numerous theories based on both chemical and natural causes were put forth. A reassessment of satellite and terrestrial data was planned, along with ground- and air-based expeditions to the continent. . . .

[In 1987, the] pieces of the puzzle started to fall into place. During the long, sunless Antarctic winter (from about March to August), air over the continent becomes isolated in a swirling polar vortex that causes temperatures to drop below minus 90 degrees Celsius. This is cold enough for the scarce water vapor in the dry upper atmosphere to freeze, forming polar stratospheric clouds. Chemical reactions on the ice crystals convert chlorine from nonreactive forms such as hydrogen chloride and chlorine nitrate into molecules that are very sensitive to sunlight. In addition, gaseous nitrogen oxides able to inactivate chlorine are transformed into frozen, and therefore nonreactive, nitric acid.

The first spring sunlight releases the chlorine, and the virulent ozone-destroying chain reaction proceeds unimpeded for five or six weeks. The reactions transform two molecules of ozone into three molecules of ordinary oxygen, and the chlorine survives unscathed, ready to attack more ozone. . . .

Diminished ozone in the vortex means that less incoming solar radiation is absorbed, thereby perpetuating lower temperatures and the vortex itself. . . . [Therefore, polar] stratospheric clouds were more pervasive and persistent. In essence, the ozone hole was feeding on itself. (p. 79)

While many of the meteorological and chemical conditions conducive to ozone depletion are unique to Antarctica, ground-based research in Greenland in the winter of 1988 found elevated chlorine concentrations and depressed ozone levels over the Arctic as well. Although a strong vortex does not develop there and temperatures are not as low, polar stratospheric clouds do form. (p. 80)

A greater understanding of and consensus about ozone depletion was made possible by the release of the NASA Ozone Trends Panel report on March 15, 1988. More than 100 scientists from 10 countries spent 16 months reviewing the published literature and performing a critical reanalysis and interpretation of nearly all ground-based and satellite-derived ozone data. Their purpose: to eliminate any errors caused by improperly calibrated instruments.

Ozone losses were documented around the globe, not just at the poles; the blame, particularly for the Antarctic ozone hole, was firmly placed on chlorofluorocarbons. . . .

The report's findings startled policymakers, industry representatives, and researchers around the world. Prior to March 15, the phenomenon of global ozone depletion and the role of CFCs had been hotly contested. Within a matter of weeks the report's conclusions were widely accepted, and public debate on the issue was building to a new fever pitch. Suddenly, ozone depletion was real, no longer just a theory, and people around the globe knew just how bad the problem overhead had become.

Scientists were alarmed not only by the documented damage to the ozone layer, but by the inadequacy of their models to predict it. Ozone depletion is occurring far more rapidly and in a different pattern than had been forecast. Projections of the amount and location of future ozone depletion are still highly uncertain. Although the fundamental mechanisms of ozone depletion are generally understood, the quantitative effect of cloud surface chemistry, the rate of various chemical reactions, and the specific chemical pathways are still in doubt. According to Sherwood Rowland, one of the first to sound a warning, policy decisions now and for at least another decade must be made without good quantitative guidelines of what the future holds. (p. 81)

Chemical Wonders, Atmospheric Villains

Chlorofluorocarbons are remarkable chemicals. They are neither toxic nor flammable at ground level, as demonstrated by their discoverer Thomas Midgley, Jr., in 1930 when he inhaled vapors from a beaker of clear liquid and then exhaled to extinguish a candle. A safe chemical that was inexpensive to produce was exactly what the refrigeration industry was looking for, and CFCs soon became a universal coolant, marketed by E.I. du Pont de Nemours & Company under the trademark Freon. (In chemical shorthand, it is referred to as CFC-12.) International production soared, rising from 545 tons in 1931 to 20,000 tons in 1945.

Another use for the chemical, as a blowing agent in rigid insulation foams, was discovered in the late forties. In this application, liquid CFC-12 is vaporized into a gas that forms lightweight, closed cell bubbles that are poor conductors of both heat and cold. Consumers referred to the product as Styrofoam, the Dow Chemical Company trademark. From 1945 to 1950, total production of CFCs doubled.

Over the ensuing years, new chemical formulations were discovered, and the versatility of the various CFCs seemed almost endless. CFC-11 and CFC-12 were first used as aerosol propellants during World War II in the fight against malaria. In the postwar economy, they were employed in aerosol products ranging from hairspray and deodorant to furniture polish. By the late fifties, a combination of the blowing agents CFC-11 and carbon dioxide was used to make softer furniture cushions, carpet padding, and automobile seats.

Many social and technological developments in recent decades were assisted, at least in part, by the availability of CFCs. Huge chillers made it possible to build and cool shopping malls, sports arenas, and high-rise office buildings. Air conditioning brought comfort, business, and new residents to regions with warm climates. Automobile air conditioners, now installed in 80 percent of the cars sold in the United States, put the nation on wheels for summer vacations. And healthier, more interesting diets are now available because three fourths of the food eaten in the United States is refrigerated at some point in the production and distribution chain. (p. 85)

Around the world, aerosols are still the largest user of CFCs, accounting for 25 percent of the total. Rigid foam and solvent applications, the fastest growing uses for CFCs, are tied for second place. In 1987, global CFC production (excluding China, the Soviet Union, and the Eastern bloc) surpassed the peak set in 1974, and came close to 1 million tons. . . .

Many social and technological developments in recent decades were assisted, at least in part, by the availability of CFCs.

Total per capita use of the three most common CFCs is the highest in the United States. . . . Indeed, Americans use six times the global average.

Total per capita use of the three most common CFCs is highest in the United States—at 1.2 kilograms—but Europe and Japan are not far behind. In most of the rest of the world, consumption rates are far lower. Indeed, Americans use six times the global average. (p. 86)

Unlike most chemicals, CFCs are not broken down in the troposphere, the layer of air surrounding the earth. Instead, they waft slowly upward and after six to eight years reach the upper layer of the atmosphere, the stratosphere. Once there, the chemicals can survive for up to 100 years. When they are broken down, each chlorine atom released is capable of destroying tens of thousands of ozone molecules before it eventually gets washed out of the atmosphere.

Halons are also inert at ground level. They contain bromine, a more effective ozone destroyer than chlorine, and are long-lived in the atmosphere. . . .

Alarming though the latest ozone measurements are, they reflect only the response to gases released through the early eighties; gases now rising through the lower atmosphere will take six to eight years to reach the stratosphere. An additional 2 million tons of substances containing chlorine and bromine are trapped in insulation foams, appliances, and fire-fighting equipment. (p. 87)

CFCs and halons are insidiously and inexorably destroying the planet's protective ozone shield. Biological systems around the globe will soon start to suffer adverse effects, but the real losers will be future generations who inherit an impoverished environment and wonder at the folly of their ancestors.

Reducing Emissions

Determining the largest sources of potential ozone depletion is the first step toward curbing emissions. To do this requires knowing how much of each ozone-depleting chemical is currently used, its emissions profile, and the uses to which it is put. Only then can individual countries assess the technical and economic feasibility of limiting emissions from specific markets.

Immediate reductions in CFC emissions can be achieved by banning CFC propellants in aerosols and by eliminating rapid evaporation of cleaning solvents. Intermediate savings are obtainable by capturing the blowing agents used to inflate flexible foams, by plugging the leaks in refrigeration and air-conditioning systems, and by recovering the refrigerants drained during system recharging. Long-term reductions involve alternative product disposal methods, use of substitute chemicals, and development of new process technologies. (pp. 87–8)

Worldwide, aerosol cans are still the largest source of CFC emissions, contributing 224,000 tons annually, some 33 percent of combined global emissions of CFC-11 and CFC-12. Rising concern about ozone depletion among consumers and governments should soon curtail this use. And because some nations took the lead, economical and often less expensive substitutes are already widely available. (p. 89)

Another area that offers significant savings, at a low cost, is improved design, operating, and maintenance standards for refrigeration and air conditioning equipment. These uses account for 30 percent of combined CFC-11 and CFC-12 consumption. Codes of practice to govern equipment handling are being drawn up by many major trade associations. Key among the recommendations are to require worker training, to limit maintenance and repair work to authorized personnel, to install leak detection systems, and to use smaller refrigerant charges. Another recommendation, to prohibit venting of the refrigerant directly to the atmosphere, requires the use of recovery and recycling technologies.

Careful study of the automobile air-conditioning market in the United States, the largest user of CFC-12 in the country, has found that 34 percent of emissions can be traced to leakage, 48 percent occur during recharge and repair servicing, and the remainder happen through accidents, disposal, and manufacturing, in that order. Equipment with better seals and hoses would curb emissions and result in less need for system maintenance.

When car air conditioners are serviced, it is now standard practice to drain the coolant and let it evaporate. Several companies have seen the folly of this approach and designed recovery systems, known as "vampires." The refrigerant is pumped out of the compressor, purified, and reinjected into the automobile by equipment costing several thousand dollars. Because the coolant contains few contaminants, up to 95 percent of it can be reused. Refrigerant can also be stored and transported to a central recycler, though this option appears to offer less promise. (p. 90)

Over the longer term, phasing out the use and emissions of CFCs will require the development of chemical substitutes that do not harm the ozone layer. The challenge is to find alternatives that perform the same function for a reasonable cost, that do not require major equipment modifications, that are nontoxic to workers and consumers, and that are environmentally benign. . . .

Many of the major chemical manufacturers are placing their bets on HCFC-22, -123, -141b, and -142b. The added hydrogen atom makes the ozone depletion potential of these compounds only 5 percent that of the chemicals they would replace. Their cost, on the other hand, would be three to five times greater.

One major delay associated with the commercialization of new chemical compounds is the need for extensive toxicity testing; tests are run for five to seven years. (p. 91)

In some instances, new product designs can eliminate or reduce the need for CFCs and substitute chemicals while providing additional benefits. In automobiles, for instance, side vent windows, window glazings that slow solar absorption, and new solar ventilation systems can reduce interior heating and curb or eliminate the need for air-conditioning, thereby saving energy. Helium refrigerators, long used for space and military applications, have been adapted for civilian use in trucks and homes. . . .

Rigid foam insulation in refrigerators and freezers may ultimately be replaced by vacuum insulation, the type used in thermos bottles. Work done at the U.S. Solar Energy Research Institute indicates that vacuum panels take up less space than foams and make appliances more energy-efficient.

Halon emissions appear relatively easy to curtail, although there are no promising substitutes on the horizons. Most halons produced are never used, they just need to be available in case of emergency. At present, halon flooding systems are tested when first installed by releasing all the halon in the system. Discharge testing now contributes more emissions than fire fighting does. Using alternative chemicals or testing procedures that are acceptable to the insurance industry and eliminating accidental discharges would cut annual emissions by two thirds. (p. 92)

The approach taken to reducing CFC and halon emissions varies greatly among nations and industries. Companies in Sweden, for example, view the development of alternative products and processes as an economic opportunity. They are poised to seize new international markets in a changing global economy. On the other hand, the major chemical producers in France, Japan, the United Kingdom, the United States, and West Germany have traditionally viewed emissions controls as a threat to their international competitiveness. They have been loath to go along with unilateral control measures for fear of losing their market share.

The time has come to ask if the functions performed by CFCs are really necessary and, if they are, whether they can be performed in new ways. (pp. 92–3)

The Montreal Protocol will not arrest depletion, merely slow its acceleration.

If all known technical control measures were used, total CFC and halon emissions could be reduced by approximately 90 percent. Many of these control strategies are already cost-effective, and more will become so as regulations push up the price of ozone-depleting chemicals. The speech with which controls are introduced will determine the extent of ozone depletion in the years ahead and the date when stratospheric healing will begin.

If all known technical control measures were used, total CFC and halon emissions could be reduced by approximately 90 percent. Many of these control strategies are already cost-effective, and more will become so as regulations push up the price of ozone-depleting chemicals. The speed with which controls are introduced will determine the extent of ozone depletion in the years ahead and the date when stratospheric healing will begin.

Moving Beyond Montreal

On September 16, 1987, after years of arduous and heated negotiation, the Montreal Protocol on Substances that Deplete the Ozone Layer was signed by 24 countries. (As of mid-November 1988, that total had increased to 35 countries.) Provisions of the agreement include a freeze on CFC production (at 1986 levels) by 1989, a 20-percent decrease in production by 1993, and another 30-percent cut by 1998. Halon production is subject to a freeze based on 1986 levels starting in 1992.

An international document calling for a 50-percent reduction in the production of a ubiquitous, invisible chemical feared responsible for destroying an invisible shield is unprecedented. The achievement is a tribute to the United Nations Environment Programme that spearheaded the effort; to government negotiators from all countries, especially those from the so-called Toronto group who kept pushing for tougher regulations; and to the many nongovernmental organizations and scientists who worked to build support among policymakers and the general public. (p. 93)

Unfortunately, even this level of support will not be enough to protect the fragile ozone layer.

Ozone does not differentiate the source of chlorine and bromine emissions. All nations, including those in the Third World, must rapidly step up their reduction efforts. Developing countries are an important part of the control strategy because of their large and growing populations and their rapidly increasing CFC use. Some of the key developing countries are Brazil, China, India, Indonesia, and South Korea. In China, for example, only 1 household out of 10 now owns a refrigerator, but the government hopes that by 2000 every kitchen will have one. South Korea and Brazil are world-class automobile manufacturers.

Some of the provisions that enhance the treaty's appeal to signatories include extended deadlines, allowances to accommodate industry restructuring, and loose definitions of the products that can legitimately be traded internationally. The Soviet Union and Eastern bloc countries, for example, are permitted to carry out the erection or expansion of any production facilities that are part of their current five-year plans before adopting restrictions, provided total consumption will not exceed 0.5 kilograms per capita. Developing countries have been given a 10-year grace period past the industrial-country deadline, during which CFC use can grow to meet "basic domestic needs," up to a limit of 0.3 kilograms per capita (one third the current per capita level in some industrial countries). After that, they too must freeze and then cut their use of controlled chemicals by 50 percent.

The treaty also grants a country that enacts more than the prescribed measures the right to transfer production capacity to low-volume producers. And although imports of chemicals from nonsignatory countries are to cease within a year after the treaty takes effect, trade in products containing or manufactured with CFCs is permitted until at least the mid-nineties. The cumulative effect of these loopholes means that, even with widespread participation, the protocol's goal of halving worldwide CFC use by 1998 will not be met.

Signatories of the Montreal Protocol were operating under the assumption that implementation of the treaty would result in a maximum ozone loss of 2 percent by the year 2075. Furthermore, because negotiations preceded results of the 1987 Antarctic expedition, delegates were effectively told not to consider the hole when adopting their positions. Yet less than one year later, there was widespread agreement that average global ozone concentrations had already fallen by more than 2 percent, and by considerably more close to the poles. A recent EPA report concluded that by 2075, even with 100-percent global participation in the protocol, chlorine concentrations in the atmosphere would triple. The agreement will not arrest depletion, merely slow its acceleraton. In light of these findings, it is obvious that the treaty and other regulatory measures need to be strengthened.

Curtailing chlorine and bromine emissions enough to prevent widespread environmental damage requires a virtual phaseout of CFC and halon emissions by all countries as soon as possible. Releases of other compounds containing chlorine and bromine not currently covered under the treaty also need to be controlled and in some cases halted. (pp. 93–4)

As noted, it is technically feasible to reduce CFC and halon emissions by 90 percent by 1995. The challenge is for governments to muster the political will to phase out CFC and halon emissions as soon as possible.

Timing is crucial. Analysts at EPA examined the effects of a 100-percent CFC phaseout by 1990 versus a 95-percent phaseout by 1998. Peak chlorine concentrations would differ by 0.8 parts per billion, some one third of current levels. Under the slower schedule, atmospheric cleansing would be considerably delayed: chlorine levels would remain higher than the peak associated with the accelerated schedule for at least 50 years. (pp. 94–5)

Priming the research and development pump is a role for governments around the world. Although chemical manufacturers are spending some $100 million annually to develop safe chemical substitutes, they have no interest in alternative product designs that would cut into their markets.

Research on new refrigeration, air-conditioning, and insulation processes is the most worthy of government support. Phasing out the use of CFCs in these applications would protect the ozone layer and delay the greenhouse effect— directly by reducing the emissions of CFCs that absorb infrared radiation, and indirectly by promoting more energy-efficient processes that would trim carbon dioxide emissions. Cooling cars, offices, and factories with equipment dependent on chemicals and powered by fuels that warm the earth is ludicrous. Unfortunately, international funding to develop new approaches is probably less than $5 million.

As mentioned in the text of the Montreal Protocol, results of this research, as well as new technologies and processes, need to be shared with developing countries. Ozone depletion and climate warming are undeniably global in scope. Not sharing information on the most recent developments is like refusing to tell the driver of a car that is about to hit you where the brakes are. And it ensures that environmentally damaging and outdated equipment will continue to be used for years to come, further eroding the technology base in the Third World. Developing countries are also the most vulnerable to the effects of ozone depletion because they rely primarily on fish for their protein and have inadequate health care facilities. (pp. 95–6)

As with so many of the major environmental problems now facing policymakers, the timing and fortitude of their response is crucial. The ultimate goal of negotiators has always been the eventual phaseout of all ozone-depleting chemicals. The question is, How quicky are countries willing to act in order to protect human health, food supplies, and the global climate?

The scientific fundamentals of ozone depletion are known. Although current models of future change vary in their predictions, the evidence is clear enough to warrant an immediate response. Because valuable time was lost when governments and industries relaxed their regulatory and research efforts during the early eighties, a crash program is now essential. Given the relatively high degree of understanding and consensus surrounding ozone depletion, the support that can be garnered for putting an end to chlorine and bromine emissions may be indicative of the political will to protect the earth's habitability. (p. 96)

Ozone does not differentiate the source of chlorine and bromine emissions. All nations, including those in the Third World, must rapidly step up their reduction efforts. Developing countries are an important part of the control strategy because of their large and growing populations and their rapidly increasing CFC use.

Cynthia Pollock Shea, "Protecting the Ozone Layer," in State of the World 1989: A Worldwatch Institute Report on Progress Toward a Sustainable Society, *W. W. Norton, 1989, pp. 77–96.*

Without the protective ozone veil, ultraviolet-b would scrub the earth clean of life.

The Ultraviolet Zone: Health Effects of Ozone Depletion

A biological experiment on a grand scale, started when the first ozone-depleting chlorofluorocarbons (CFCs) were produced in the 1930s, is now unfolding. These chemicals are being phased out, but for the next thirty to fifty years, the earth's surface will be exposed to mounting levels of ultraviolet radiation.

The ozone layer filters out solar rays on the high-energy end of the ultraviolet spectrum, called ultraviolet-B (UVB). Since UVB damages DNA, the protein code every living cell holds, the biological effects of UVB are wide-reaching. Crops, trees, human and animal immune systems, as well as the microscopic phytoplankton at the base of the food chain, are all vulnerable. Without the protective ozone veil, UVB would scrub the earth clean of life.

The recent findings by NASA that ozone depletion is more than twice what had been expected a year ago has scientists worried. A 5 percent loss of ozone, detected over the southern United States this spring could increase UVB by 10 percent. Depletion is no longer focused at the polar extremes but has moved over heavily populated regions.

The numbers of human skin cancers—the biological injury scientists understand best—will leap as a result, to 12 million in the United States alone according to William Reilly, administrator of the Environmental Protection Agency. U.S. skin cancer deaths over the next fifty years will increase twentyfold, to 200,000, from the 9,300 EPA predicted in 1988.

Worldwide, higher doses of UVB are likely to have much more widespread effects on plants, animals, and ecosystems, but these impacts are the least understood. Biological researchers are now trying to answer a host of questions about ultraviolet radiation: What regions of the world will be most affected? Might sea mammals be deprived of their diet and die out? How is radiation linked to tropical diseases such as malaria? How much more susceptible are children?

While some scientists predict catastrophe, others take a less alarmist stance. Henry Lee, who heads EPA's team researching ozone depletion's effects on marine life, puts himself somewhere in between. "I don't think [those effects] will be catastrophic, but a change in UV may have a minor effect on oceans, but those effects will be extremely widespread, because water covers 70 percent of the earth's surface," Lee says.

Except for the plants and animals inhabiting the dark reaches of the oceans where ultraviolet cannot penetrate, all life has had to adapt to natural levels of UVB. Ultraviolet radiation has even become necessary to sustain life, in some instances. Humans, for example, require UV to synthesize vitamin D. But for the most part, UVB is injurious to life. Human skin fends off UVB by thickening and producing melanin, the pigment that blocks UV. By absorbing or blocking UV, sunscreens perform the same role.

Certain animals and plants produce substances that act like sunscreens, according to Deneb Karentz, a researcher at the University of California studying the effects of UVB on Antarctic species. Eighty-six percent of fifty-seven marine species Karentz studied in Antarctica—including algae, sponges, sea anemones, leeches, sea spiders, and krill—all produce such substances. Land animals cloaked in fur or feathers are also shielded. However, these adaptations may prove less effective as exposure to UV is intensified.

Among the members of a species, ability to handle UV varies widely; there is a 100-fold range among Antarctic plankton in susceptibility to UV, Karentz has found. As UV levels grow, populations will shift toward those best able to survive, she predicts. Whether or not these resistant species can satisfy appetites up the food chain is one of the big questions. Herbivores that are very selective about what they eat may find less appealing or less nutritious food. Such changes will trickle up to the upper levels of the food chain, says Karentz, but so far scientists do not have enough data to predict what those changes might be.

Human skin cancer has been the most studied impact of UV exposure. Skin cancer has three manifestations: basal and squamous cell carcinomas are for the most part disfiguring rather than fatal, and are linked to the amount of UV absorbed over a lifetime; melanoma is rarer and often fatal, and is believed to result from a bad sunburn early in life, according to Margaret Kripke, chairman of the department of immunology at M. D. Anderson Hospital and Tumor Institute in Texas.

> **In recent decades, skin cancer has become dramatically more prevalent in the United States and Europe because of the popularity of outdoor recreation and tanned skin. Under the EPA's newly revised ozone data, both melanoma and non-melanoma skin cancers will rise even more dramatically.**

In recent decades, skin cancer has become dramatically more prevalent in the United States and Europe because of the popularity of outdoor recreation and tanned skin. Under EPA's newly revised ozone data, both melanoma and non-melonoma skin cancers will rise even more dramatically.

Children are especially susceptible. By age eighteen, most people incur half of the damaging effects of sunlight that they will incur over the course of their lifetime. "Children born in the last ten years are most vulnerable," says Janice Longstreth, a risk assessment expert at Battelle Laboratories who is updating a report on the health effects of ozone depletion for the United Nations Environment Program (UNEP).

Ultraviolet radiation may induce skin cancer by lessening the skin's ability to fight off invasive organisms—including the body's own cells made malignant by exposure to UVB, says Kripke. UV exposure has also been linked to herpes simplex, leprosy, tuberculosis, lupus, and other genetic and metabolic diseases; exposure to UVB may also make the skin more permeable to parasites carried by insects or that live in water, such as Lyme disease and malaria, Kripke says. UV may even shift the AIDS virus infecting skin cells from an inactive to active state, according to a 1988 report in the journal *Nature*. UV can also cause conjunctivitis, and later in life, cataracts and blindness.

Because the ozone shield will thin unevenly around the globe, some regions will be bathed in more radiation than others. Australia, the most populated land mass near Antarctica, had skin cancer levels that topped those worldwide before ozone depletion began. In the skies above the continent, ozone loss is 17 to 22 percent greater during the summer than at corresponding latitudes in the northern hemisphere. San Francisco and Melbourne, Australia are at about the same latitude north and south, yet the rates of melanoma are 33.8 percent higher for men, and 82.8 percent higher for women in Melbourne.

Because the nation's exposure is so severe, Australia has taken an aggressive stance in public education and public policy. Campaigns now encourage Australians to protect themselves from the sun's rays with sunscreens, hats, and clothing. Aussies have begun planting trees in schoolyards and have regimented outdoor programs for children around the time of day when they will get the least exposure, and the government has even mandated hats as part of the school uniform.

Countries that are not close to the poles may be jeopardized in other ways; increased radiation could endanger global food supplies. Fisheries may be damaged by even small increases in UVB, and fish provides more than half of the diet for many people.

Atmospheric researchers who were conforted by the thought that the warmer Northern Hemisphere is strongly protected from the processes that lead to massive losses of ozone during the spring in Antarctica now see very little standing in the way of an Arctic ozone hole.

Two-thirds of about 300 crops and other plants tested for their tolerance to UVB are also sensitive to it, according to a 1989 report by the UNEP. Among the most vulnerable were peas and beans, melons, mustard, and cabbage; also hurt were tomatoes, potatoes, sugar beets, and soy beans.

Forests appear to be vulnerable too, according to studies carried out by Alan Teramura, a researcher at the University of Maryland. About half of the conifers Teramura has studied were adversely affected by UVB. "Small changes [in UV] can accumulate and ultimately have catastrophic effects," Teramura told *New Scientist* magazine last fall.

UVB damages not only living things but polymers used in buildings, paints, packaging, and countless other substances, which it degrades and turns brittle. Increased radiation could cause damage running into the billions of dollars each year, according to UNEP.

Scientists are working toward a better understanding of the impacts of UV, yet they have scant data about the amount of radiation now hitting the earth. One reason, ironically, is that ground-level ozone pollution due to smog is obscuring information about ground-level UV. Ultraviolet is measured at meterologic stations at airports, which are mostly found in smog-blanketed cities, says Longstreth.

Studies of UVB could light the way as we try to adapt to its growing intensity, yet basic science research is losing funding. "EPA has decided that because we have a [CFC] protocol, we don't need to look at the health effects anymore—we've got a regulatory fix," said Longstreth. EPA's own program, too, is in jeopardy, said Bob Worrest, its director, as its already small budget hangs in the balance for 1992.

Former Secretary of the Interior Donald Hodel was ridiculed in 1987 for his suggestions that U.S. policy be based on "personal protection"—that we rely on hats, sunscreens, and sunglasses rather than a meaningful global accord to protect the ozone layer. Yet in Australia, hats have become public policy, as the reality of life under the ozone hole has hit home. How far away is that scenario for the rest of the world? (pp. 24–6)

Beth Hanson, "The Ultraviolet Zone," in The Amicus Journal, *Vol. 13, No. 3, Summer, 1991, pp. 24–6.*

Northern Hole: Arctic Ozone Loss

Scientists have returned from the first comprehensive probe of the Arctic stratosphere with unexpectedly dire results: The winter atmosphere in the north polar region is loaded with the same destructive chlorine compounds that cause the Antarctic ozone hole. Atmospheric researchers who . . . were comforted by the thought that the warmer Northern Hemisphere is strongly protected from the processes that lead to massive losses of ozone during spring in Antarctica now see very little standing in the way of an Arctic ozone hole.

The inescapable conclusion is that only a complete phaseout of fully halogenated chlorofluorocarbons—CFCs, the ultimate source of man-made chlorine in the stratosphere—can prevent further deterioration of the ozone layer. Even with an immediate ban on CFCs, their long atmospheric lifetimes mean it would take decades to centuries for the atmosphere to recover.

This new bleak outlook stems from data gathered during the first six weeks of [1989] by the Airborne Arctic Stratospheric Expedition. During that international mission, two National Aeronautics & Space Administration research aircraft each flew 14 flights north from Stavanger, Norway.

The goal of the $10 million project was to determine to what extent the heterogeneous chlorine chemistry that is responsible for the Antarctic ozone hole also takes place in the Arctic. The answer—that heterogeneous chemistry has primed the Arctic air for ozone destruction—was a surprise to virtually all of the 150 or so scientists who participated.

Specifically, a key experiment by Harvard chemistry professor James G. Anderson's group found chlorine monoxide (CIO) concentrations as high as 800 ppt [parts per trillion] within the polar vortex—almost as high as the researchers had found within the Antarctic ozone hole. Chlorine monoxide has been dubbed the "smoking gun" of ozone depletion, because the chain reactions believed to destroy ozone depend on chlorine monoxide to carry the chain. ("Normal" amounts of chlorine monoxide would be about 10 to 20 ppt.)

Now the atmospheric science community is anxiously waiting to see what happens next. The only factor that is preventing substantial ozone destruction in the Arctic region is that the air containing active chlorine is still mostly in the darkness of the polar night. Once the air is hit by sunlight, chlorine-catalyzed chain reactions that chew up ozone will take off—unless competing processes can first reconvert the active chlorine compounds to nondestructive inert forms.

"All our observations have shown that the Arctic stratosphere looks a heck of a lot like the Antarctic stratosphere," says chemist Susan Solomon of the National Oceanic & Atmospheric Administration's aeronomy lab in Boulder. "The dangerous chemicals are there. What we don't know is how close to the edge we are."

So far, there is no large ozone hole in the Arctic, says Robert T. Watson, NASA's program manager for upper atmospheric research. . . . Rather, a small, long-term loss of ozone—on the order of 5 to 6% since 1970—has occurred in the high northern latitudes in winter.

However, with the new insight provided by the just-completed Arctic campaign, "We can't rule out the potential for a very rapid onset of a decrease in ozone in the Arctic regions," Watson says.

Before the scientists left for Norway, there was a consensus that the Antarctic ozone hole was a result of Antarctica's unique frigid meteorology. (pp. 29–30)

Now, that conventional wisdom has to be revised. The Arctic results show that the stratosphere does not have to get so cold as it does in Antarctica to set up the conditions that change inert chlorine compounds to destructive ones.

In both the Antarctic and Arctic regions, stable wind patterns in the stratosphere known as polar vortices circle the dark poles in wintertime. Air within the vortices, isolated from the sun and from warmer air from the temperate regions, gets extremely cold.

The Antarctic polar vortex, however, gets much colder than does the Arctic. In winter in Antarctica, stratospheric temperatures drop to −90 °C and the vortex persists for about five months, well into spring. In the Arctic, minimum temperatures tend to be about 10 degrees warmer, and the vortex itself only holds together for a few months, usually breaking up by late February or early March. The climatic differences between the two hemispheres reflect the difference in land distribution. Much more dynamical activity from land masses in the lower latitudes reaches the Arctic polar region than reaches Antarctica, which is surrounded by ocean.

The winter temperatures at both poles are cold enough for two types of clouds to form even within the extremely dry stratosphere. It is these polar stratospheric clouds that are the key to the Antarctic ozone hole—and as it turns out, whatever is happening in the Arctic. One kind of cloud (Type I) is

"We cannot rule out the potential for a very rapid onset of a decrease in ozone in the Arctic regions."

—Robert T. Watson, NASA

"Even if we were to stop producing the fully halogenated CFCs today, the Antarctic ozone hole would be here for centuries to come. Time is of the essence. Every year we continue to put chlorine in adds 10 years to the time it will take to remove it."

—Robert T. Watson, NASA

composed mostly of nitric acid trihydrate and forms at about −77 °C. Type II clouds are mostly water ice and require still lower temperatures to grow—about −85°C.

On the 1987 aircraft expedition to Antarctica to study the ozone hole, wherever researchers found high levels of active chlorine, they also found low levels of nitric acid and water vapor. "From our experience in Antarctica, we had come to correlate high chlorine monoxide with denitrification and dehydration," Watson says.

The scientists reasoned that that correlation could be explained by the occurrence of Type II polar stratospheric clouds. The clouds provide surfaces on which inactive forms of chlorine are converted to destructive forms. The heterogeneous reactions convert chlorine nitrate ($ClONO_2$) and hydrogen chloride—molecules that are relatively inert—to more active molecular chlorine and hypochlorous acid ($HOCl$). . . . (p. 30)

The molecular chlorine and the hypochlorous acid fly off into the gas phase, where both can be easily photolyzed by even small levels of light to radicals that can catalyze ozone destruction. In contrast, the nitric acid (HNO_3) that is produced sticks to the cloud particles, tying up nitrogen species that, if free, could react with the reactive chlorine to reform inert chlorine nitrate.

As the ice crystals of the Type II clouds grow large enough, they precipitate out of the stratosphere, removing both water and nitric acid. When the sun comes up in the Antarctic spring, the active chlorine compounds begin to destroy ozone photochemically. The process stops only when the Antarctic polar vortex breaks down after it has been in the sun for a month or more, allowing air full of nitrogen oxides to rush in.

In the Arctic, however, it is rare for the temperature to get down to −85 °C, the temperature at which Type II clouds form, Watson says. And, indeed, on this year's Arctic expedition, the scientists observed very little of the dehydration that would be expected to accompany Type II clouds. Although they did occasionally observe Type II clouds, the Type I nitric acid trihydrate clouds were much more frequent. Nevertheless, they saw very high levels of chlorine monoxide.

"This means that Type I [clouds] are enough to perturb the chemistry," Watson says. "The surprise is you only have to get down to −77 °C to allow reservoir chlorine to be converted to active chlorine. That happens much more frequently in the Arctic than −85 °C."

That the north polar vortex usually breaks up before the sun comes up is probably what has prevented a full-blown Arctic ozone hole so far. However, in some unusual years the vortex has held together until April or May, notes NOAA's Adrian F. Tuck.

"If the vortex holds together for a few more weeks, we should see an ozone loss," Tuck says. "The degree of Arctic ozone depletion [that will actually appear] depends on the rate at which normal partitioning of chlorine species is re-established. We don't know how much exposure to sunlight the primed air is going to get; we don't know how much the vortex is going to wobble about." (pp. 30–1)

"One way or another there will be some ozone lost," Watson says. "There is now a very large volume of air, roughly reaching from the North Pole to about 70° N, with very high chlorine monoxide levels. When the vortex breaks down and that air gets sent out to lower latitudes, it will indeed destroy ozone. The amount of ozone destruction will be limited by how quickly the chlorine will be converted back into its reservoir forms."

"It's a race between how fast molecular diffusion can bring in nitrogen oxides to react with the active chlorine and how fast the chlorine chain can destroy ozone," says Michael J. Kurylo III, a chemist on assignment to NASA from the National Institute of Standards & Technology.

Unfortunately, the Arctic expedition scientists left Norway with their instruments in mid-February and so will not be able to track any upcoming changes in ozone with the sophisticated array of equipment that was assembled on the NASA research aircraft . . . .

The official statement of preliminary findings from the Arctic expedition asserts that it is too soon to say whether the perturbed chemistry the researchers found in the Arctic can quantitatively explain the decreases in ozone reported [in March 1988] by the International Ozone Trends Panel. That study found that since 1970, ozone between about 40° and 60° N had decreased 5 to 6% in the winter months.

Despite the scientists' reluctance to say so definitely, it is clear that blobs or streamers of air rich in active chlorine from the Arctic vortex drifting into sunlight at lower latitudes could account for that wintertime decrease in ozone in the Northern Hemisphere. Although not nearly so striking as the Antarctic ozone hole, such small changes in ozone over a populated area are still significant. The Environmental Protection Agency has estimated that each 1% depletion of ozone leads to a 2% increase in skin cancer among fair-skinned people.

The latest findings in the Arctic are leading both scientists and policymakers to step up their calls to strengthen the terms of the Montreal Protocol on Substances That Deplete the Ozone Layer. That international treaty, which went into effect Jan. 1, calls for a 50% reduction in output in CFCs by mid-1998. However, the photochemical models that were used as a basis for negotiating the treaty did not include any heterogeneous processes, now known to be so devastating to ozone.

"We're much more concerned than before we went to Norway about protecting atmospheric ozone, especially in the polar regions," Watson says. "It's now absolutely clear that the terms of the Montreal protocol will not lead to adequate protection of ozone in Antarctica and probably not in the Arctic.

"There's about 3 ppb [parts per billion] of chlorine in the atmosphere today," he says. "Under the Montreal protocol, chlorine will continue to increase to about 6 ppb. Even if we were to stop producing the fully halogenated CFCs today, the Antarctic ozone hole would be here for centuries to come. Time is of the essence. Every year we continue to put chlorine in adds 10 years to the time it will take to remove it." (pg. 31)

Pamela S. Zurer, "Arctic Ozone Loss: Fact-Finding Mission Concludes Outlook Is Bleak," in Chemical and Engineering News, *Vol. 67, No. 10, March 6, 1989, pp. 29–31.*

The Montreal Protocol stands as a landmark— a symbol both of fundamental changes in the kinds of problems facing the modern world and of the way the international community can address those problems.

Ozone Diplomacy: The Montreal Protocol

On September 16, 1987, representatives of countries from every region of the world reached an agreement unique in the annals of international diplomacy. In the Montreal Protocol on Substances that Deplete the Ozone Layer, nations agreed to significantly reduce production of chemicals that can destroy the stratospheric ozone layer (which protects life on earth from harmful ultraviolet radiation) and can also change global climate.

The protocol was not a response to an environmental disaster such as Chernobyl, but rather *preventive* action on a global scale. That action, based at the time not on measurable evidence of ozone depletion or increased radiation but rather on scientific hypotheses, required an unprecedented amount of foresight. The links between causes and effects were not obvious: a perfume spray in Paris helps to destroy an invisible gas 6 to 30 miles above the earth, and

The protocol's greatest significance may be its demonstration that the international community is capable of undertaking complicated cooperative actions in the real world of ambiguity and imperfect knowledge.

thereby contributes to deaths from skin cancer and extinction of species half a world and several generations away.

The ozone protocol was only possible through an intimate collaboration between scientists and policymakers. Based as it was on continually evolving theories of atmospheric processes, on state-of-the-art computer models simulating the results of intricate chemical and physical reactions for decades into the future, and on satellite-, land- and rocket-based monitoring of remote gases measured in parts per trillion, the ozone treaty could not have occurred at an earlier point in human history.

Another noteworthy aspect of the Montreal Protocol was the negotiators' decision not to take the timid path of controlling through "best available technology"—the traditional accommodation to economic interests. Instead, the treaty boldly established firm target dates for emissions reductions, even though the technologies for accomplishing these goals did not yet exist.

The ozone protocol sounded a death knell for an important part of the international chemical industry, with implications for billions of dollars in investment and hundreds of thousands of jobs in related industries such as food, transportation, plastics, electronics, cosmetics, and health care. Here, as in many other areas, international economic competition clashed with the need for international environmental cooperation, but in this case concerns about the environment eventually carried the day.

Similar conflicts between economic and environmental imperatives are bound to arise in the future, as more and more environmental problems cross national boundaries and require international solutions. Furthermore, there will be a growing number of threats to the environment that, although not obvious or immediate, pose serious long-term dangers. So it is worth considering what factors contributed to the Montreal Protocol's success, and what lessons the negotiations might hold for future attempts to deal with similar situations. (pp. 43–4)

The Great Atlantic Divide

As scientists analyzed the effects of CFCs on the ozone layer and the resultant implications for human health and the environment, the United States and the European Community (EC)—comprising 12 sovereign nations—emerged as the principal protagonists in the diplomatic process that culminated in the Montreal Protocol. Despite their shared political, economic, and environmental orientations, the United States and the European Community, which together accounted for 84 percent of world CFC output in 1974, differed over almost every issue at every step along the route to Montreal.

The U.S. Congress held formal hearings on the ozone layer soon after the theories were published, which led in 1977 to ozone protection legislation that banned use of CFCs as aerosol propellants in all but essential applications. This affected nearly $3 billion worth of sales in a wide range of household and cosmetic products, and rapidly reduced U.S. production of CFCs for aerosols by 95 percent. The U.S. action was paralleled by Canada (a small producer), and by Sweden, Norway, Denmark and Finland (all nonproducing, importing countries).

In contrast, European parliaments (except for the German Bundestag) showed scant interest in CFCs. The European Community delayed until 1980, and then enacted a 30 percent cutback in CFC aerosol use from 1976 levels and announced a decision not to increase production capacity.

These EC actions, however, were feeble compared to the U.S. regulation. With respect to the 30 percent aerosol reduction, European sales of CFCs for this purpose had, by 1980, already declined by over 28 percent from the 1976 peak year. Moreover, the European Community two years later defined "production capacity" in a manner that would enable current output to increase by over 60 percent. The capacity cap was therefore a painless move, supported by European industry, which gave the appearance of control while in reality permitting undiminished rates of expansion for at least two more decades.

Relative to gross national product, EC production of CFCs was over 50 percent higher than that of the United States. Aerosols, which had virtually disappeared in the U.S., still comprised during the 1980s over half of CFC sales within the European Community. The European Community was also the CFC supplier to the rest of the world, particularly the growing markets in developing countries. EC exports rose by 43 percent from 1976 to 1985 and averaged almost one-third of its production, whereas the United States consumed virtually all it produced.

These developments were reflected in growing differences in attitude between the chemical industries on the two sides of the Atlantic. Shaken by the force of public reaction in the 1970s over the threat to the ozone layer, American producers had quickly developed substitutes for CFCs in spray cans. U.S. chemical companies were also constantly aware of their vulnerability in the environmentally charged domestic atmosphere. In their public pronouncements, industry spokespersons took the ozone problem with growing seriousness, and appeared increasingly concerned about its effect on companies' reputations. The threat of a patchwork of state laws—legislation against CFCs was actually introduced or passed by Oregon, New York, California, Michigan, Minnesota, and others—made U.S. industry not only resigned to but even publicly in favor of federal controls, which would at least be uniform and therefore less disruptive.

There was also resentment among American producers that their European rivals had escaped meaningful controls. A constant theme in the U.S. chemical industry during the 1980s was the need to have a "level playing field"—to avoid recurrence of unilateral U.S. regulatory action that was not followed by the other major producers.

In September 1986, the Alliance for Responsible CFC Policy, a coalition of about 500 U.S. producer and user companies, issued a pivotal statement. Following the obligatory reiteration of industry's position that CFCs posed no immediate threat to human health or the environment, the Alliance spokesman declared that "large future increases in . . . CFCs . . . would be unacceptable to future generations," and that it would be "inconsistent with [industry] goals . . . to ignore the potential for risk to those future generations." Thus, only three months before the protocol negotiations began, U.S. industry announced its support for new international controls on CFCs.

This unexpected policy change, which came after much soul-searching within the U.S. industry, aroused consternation in Europe. The British and French had been suspicious all along that the United States was using an environmental scare to cloak commercial motivations. Now, some Europeans surmised (incorrectly) that the United States wanted CFC controls because they had substitute products on the shelf with which to enter the profitable EC export markets.

For its part, EC industry's primary objective was to preserve its dominance and to avoid the costs of switching to alternative products for as long as possible. Taking advantage of public indifference and political skepticism, European industrial leaders were able to persuade most EC governments that substitutes for CFCs were neither feasible nor necessary—despite the demonstrated U.S. success in marketing alternative spray propellants. Industry statements were echoed in official EC pronouncements that continually stressed the scientific uncertainties, the impossibility of finding effective substitutes, and the adverse effects of regulations on European living standards.

Self-Serving Positions

Although the United States and the European Community were the major CFC producers, the ozone problem threatened the entire world and therefore could be solved only by international agreement. Filling a catalytic role for

Under the dynamic leadership of its executive director, Mostafa Tolba, an Egyptian scientist, the UN Environmental Programme soon made ozone protection a top priority. The agency worked to inform governments and world public opinion about the danger to the ozone layer, it provided a nonpolitisized international forum for the negotiations, and it was a driving force behind the consensus that was eventually reached.

One of the central disputes of the negotiations was whether restrictions would be placed on the production or consumption of the substances covered by the agreement. This issue, though seemingly arcane, was one of the most important and most difficult to resolve.

such an agreement became the mission of a small and hitherto little-publicized United Nations agency, the UN Environment Programme (UNEP). Under the dynamic leadership of its executive director, Mostafa Tolba, an Egyptian scientist, UNEP soon made ozone protection a top priority. The agency worked to inform governments and world public opinion about the danger to the ozone layer, it provided a nonpoliticized international forum for the negotiations, and it was a driving force behind the consensus that was eventually reached.

In January 1982, representatives of 24 countries met in Stockholm under UNEP auspices to decide on a "Global Framework Convention for the Protection of the Ozone Layer." The following year a group of countries, including the United States, Canada, the Nordic nations, and Switzerland, proposed a worldwide ban on "nonessential" uses of CFCs in spray cans, pointing out that the United States and others had already demonstrated that alternatives to CFC sprays were technically and economically feasible. In late 1984, the European Community countered with a proposal for alternative controls that would prohibit new additions to CFC production capacity.

Each side was backing a protocol that would require no new controls for itself, but considerable adjustment for the other. The United States had already imposed a ban on nonessential uses of CFCs, but U.S. chemical companies were operating at close to capacity and thus would suffer under a production cap. Their European counterparts, on the other hand, had substantial underutilized capacity and could expand CFC production at current rates for another 20 years before hitting the cap.

Despite these disagreements, by March 1985 the negotiators had drafted all elements of a protocol for CFC reductions except the crucial control provisions. Meeting in Vienna, all major producers except Japan signed an interim agreement—the Vienna Convention on Protection of the Ozone Layer—which promoted international monitoring, research, and exchange of data and provided the framework for eventual protocols to control ozone-modifying substances. Over strong objections from European industry representatives, the Vienna Conference passed a separate resolution that called upon UNEP to continue work on a CFC protocol with a target for adoption in 1987.

As formal negotiations began in December 1986, governments were divided into three camps. Despite growing internal strains, the European Community followed the European industry line and mirrored the views of the UK, France, and Italy. The European Community continued to advocate the kind of production capacity cap it had favored during the meetings leading up to the Vienna Convention. Because the scientific models showed there would be at least two decades before any significant ozone depletion would occur, EC negotiators felt there was time to delay production cuts and wait for more evidence. This perspective was initially shared by the USSR and Japan.

Opposing this view were the United States, Canada, Norway, Sweden, Finland, Switzerland, and New Zealand, all favoring stronger new controls. They argued that action needed to be taken well before critical levels of chlorine accumulated: The long atmospheric lifetimes of these compounds meant that future ozone depletion stemming from past and current production was inevitable, and the process could not suddenly be turned off like a faucet. These countries were concerned about the health and environmental risks of delay, and maintained that postponing meaningful action could necessitate draconian and thus costlier measures later on.

A third group of active participants, including Austria, Australia, and a number of Third World countries, were initially uncommitted, but as the arguments developed they moved toward favoring more, rather than less, stringent regulations.

Complicating the entire process was the fact that the European Community had to achieve internal consensus among its member countries before (and during) international negotiations, which tended to make it a difficult and inflexible negotiating partner. There were deep divisions within the European Community on the ozone issue. Germany, the Netherlands, Belgium, and

Denmark were increasingly disposed toward strong CFC controls; but of these, only Germany was a major producer. The UK, supported by France and Italy—all large producers—resisted every step of the way. Greece, Spain, Ireland, Portugal, and Luxembourg did not even participate in most of the negotiations.

Another key factor was the EC presidency, which automatically rotates every six months among the member countries. Progress in the protocol negotiations occurred only after Belgium replaced the UK in the presidency in January 1987. Britain remained in the EC "troika" (past, present, and future presidents), which participated in closed meetings of key delegation heads during the negotiations, but only until the presidency rotated again in July 1987. At that point, the troika included Belgium, Denmark, and Germany, all favoring stringent controls, and it may well be that this constellation, in the right place at the right time, influenced ultimate EC acceptance of considerably stronger measures than it had originally endorsed.

Deep Cuts

One of the central disputes of the negotiations was whether restrictions would be placed on the production or consumption of the substances covered by the agreement. This issue, though seemingly arcane, was one of the most important and most difficult to resolve.

The European Community pushed for controls on production, arguing that it was simpler to control output since there were only a small number of producing countries, whereas there were thousands of consuming industries and countless points of consumption. But the United States, Canada, and others who favored a consumption-related formula pointed out that controlling production would confer unusual advantages on the European Community while particularly prejudicing importing nations, including the developing countries. Since about a third of EC output was exported and there were no other exporters in the picture, a production limit essentially locked in the EC export markets. The only way the United States or others could supply those markets would be to decrease their domestic consumption.

The European Community, with no viable competitors, would thus have a virtual monopoly. If European domestic consumption should rise, the European Community could cut back its exports, leaving the current importing countries, with no recourse to other suppliers, to bear the brunt of CFC reductions. Because of this vulnerability, there would be incentives for importing countries to remain outside the treaty and build their own CFC facilities.

To meet the valid EC argument about controlling multiple consumption points, the United States and its allies came up with an ingenious solution: A limit would be placed on production *plus* imports *minus* exports to other Montreal Protocol signatories. This "adjusted production" formula eliminated any monopoly based on current export positions, in that producing countries could raise production for exports to protocol parties without having to cut their own domestic consumption. Only exports to nonparties would have to come out of domestic consumption, and this would be an added incentive for importing countries to join the protocol, lest they lose access to supplies. Additionally, an importing signatory whose traditional supplier raised prices excessively or refused to export could either produce on its own or turn to another producer country.

The single most contentious issue was the timing and extent of reductions. Again, the European Community and the United States were the principal opponents. The United States originally called for a freeze to be followed by three phases of progessively more stringent reductions, all the way up to a possible 95 percent cut. But even late into the negotiations, the European Community was reluctant to consider reductions beyond 10 to 20 percent.

The United States and others rejected this as inadequate. In fact, Germany, which had become increasingly concerned over the ozone problem, was

The international community can no longer pretend that nothing is happening, or that the planet will somehow automatically adjust itself to the billions of tons of man-made pollutants to which it is annually being subjected.

The treaty as signed stipulated an initial 20 percent reduction from the 1986 level of CFCs, followed by 30 percent. Halons were frozen at 1986 levels, pending further research. And one innovative provision— that these reductions were to be made on specific dates regardless of when the treaty should enter into force—removed any temptation to stall enactment of the protocol in the hopes of delaying cuts, and also provided industry with dates upon which to base its planning.

already planning an independent 50 percent reduction and early in 1987 it made urgent appeals to the other EC members also to accept deep reductions. Meanwhile, new scientific research was demonstrating that all of the control strategies under consideration would result in some degree of ozone depletion, the extent of which would depend on the stringency of international regulation. These developments helped garner support for deep cuts.

(An interesting sideshow during the negotiations was the attempt by some antiregulatory ideologues within the Reagan administration to overturn or weaken the U.S. position by reopening basic questions about the science and possible impacts of ozone depletion. These efforts, which did not even have support from most of American industry, were effectively countered by the combined efforts of the Department of State, EPA, and the Council of Economic Advisors, among other agencies. The issue went for decision to the President, who reaffirmed the basic elements of the U.S. drive for strong international regulation of CFCs and halons.)

The turning point in the negotiations came when Mostafa Tolba, head of UNEP, began to play a central role. He personally proposed a freeze by 1990, followed by successive 20 percent reductions every two years down to a complete phaseout, and he pressed for deep cuts during informal consultations with heads of key delegations.

Ultimately, even the most reluctant parties—the European Community, Japan, and the Soviet Union—agreed to a 50 percent decrease. The treaty as signed stipulated an initial 20 percent reduction from the 1986 level of CFCs, followed by 30 percent. Halons were frozen at 1986 levels, pending further research. And one innovative provision—that these reductions were to be made on specific dates regardless of when the treaty should enter into force—removed any temptation to stall enactment of the protocol in the hopes of delaying cuts, and also provided industry with dates upon which to base its planning.

Negotiators at Montreal also faced the difficult task of encouraging developing countries to participate in the treaty. Per capita consumption of CFCs in those countries was tiny in comparison to that of the industrialized world, but their domestic consumption requirements—for refrigeration, for example—were growing, and CFC technology is relatively easy to obtain. The protocol thus had to meet their needs during a transition period while substitutes were being developed, and it had to discourage them from becoming major new sources of CFC emissions.

A formula was developed whereby developing countries would be permitted a 10-year grace period before they had to comply with the control provisions. During this time they could increase their consumption up to an annual level of 0.3 kilogram per capita—approximately one-third of the 1986 level prevailing in industrialized countries. It was felt that the realistic prospects of growth in CFC use to these levels in the developing countries was not great, as they would not want to invest in a technology that was environmentally detrimental and would soon be obsolete.

Basis for Optimism

Science is demonstrating that this planet is more vulnerable than had previously been thought. For example, the Antarctic ozone hole discovered in 1985 made it clear that the atmosphere, upon which all life depends, is capable of surprises: There is a potential for large and unexpected change. The international community can no longer pretend that nothing is happening, or that the planet will somehow automatically adjust itself to the billions of tons of man-made pollutants to which it is annually being subjected.

But now there is some basis for optimism. In September 1987, 24 countries signed the Montreal Protocol on Substances That Deplete the Ozone Layer; many other countries added their signatures over the ensuing months. Six months later, in a rare display of unanimity, the U.S. Senate approved the protocol by a vote of 83-0, and President Reagan promptly signed the ratification instrument, making the United States the second nation to ratify (after Mexico).

The treaty entered into force on January 1, 1989. By the time of the First Meeting of the Parties, held in Helsinki May 2–5, 1989, 36 countries, accounting for about 85 percent of global consumption of CFCs and halons, had ratified it. Even now, under the farsighted process established by the negotiators, governments are actively considering whether to strengthen the protocol's control provisions on the basis of more recent scientific evidence concerning the impact of CFCs and halons on the ozone layer.

The Montreal Protocol stands as a landmark—a symbol both of fundamental changes in the kinds of problems facing the modern world and of the way the international community can address those problems. Mostafa Tolba has described it as "the beginning of a new era of environmental statesmanship." But the protocol may also have relevance for dealing with other common dangers, including national rivalries and war. The ozone treaty reflects a realization that nations must work together in the face of global threats, and that if some major actors do not participate, the efforts of others will be vitiated.

In the realm of international relations, there will always be uncertainties—political, economic, scientific, psychological. The protocol's greatest significance may be its demonstration that the international community is capable of undertaking complicated cooperative actions in the real world of ambiguity and imperfect knowledge. The Montreal Protocol can be a hopeful paradigm of an evolving global diplomacy, one wherein sovereign nations find ways to accept common responsibility for stewardship of the planet and for the security of generations to come. (pp. 45–50)

Richard Elliot Benedick, "Ozone Diplomacy," in Issues in Science and Technology, *Vol. VI, No. 1, Fall, 1989, pp. 43–50.*

The Montreal Protocol was out of date even before it went into effect. Since it was negotiated in 1987, a flood of scientific data has indicated the treaty as currently written will not adequately protect the ozone layer from chlorine-catalyzed destruction.

CFC Phaseout: Industry Realities

For the chlorofluorocarbon (CFC) industry, nothing is certain these days but death and taxes. The business of producing CFCs is doomed—the only question is how quickly the end will come. And the Bush Administration is determined to impose a windfall profits tax on the makers of CFCs as production of the chemicals is cut back.

But surrounding those harsh realities are many uncertainties. The timetable for phasing out the ozone-depleting chemicals is still being debated, both in the international arena and among U.S. policymakers. Within the U.S., state governments are adding their own restrictions to those already imposed by the federal Environmental Protection Agency (EPA).

The chemicals, processes, and technologies that will replace CFCs in their myriad uses are still being identified. One of the industries that uses CFCs, rigid foam insulation, fears for its life. Many others, ranging from the electronics industry to automobile manufacturing, are shaken by the need to forego CFCs. And the most likely chemical substitutes—chlorofluorocarbons that bear hydrogen atoms (HCFCs)—may themselves end up being regulated as potential ozone depleters.

On July 1 [1989], the first restrictions on the manufacture of fully halogenated CFCs went into effect. Producers were required to freeze their output of the chemicals at 1986 levels. That production cap—required under the terms of the Montreal Protocol on Substances That Deplete the Ozone Layer and by

"The government is restricting the supply of CFCs for a good environmental reason. [Yet the] effect is the same as the OPEC cartel's oil restrictions' effect on oil prices. If the price goes up but the production costs don't, that's pure windfall profit."

—David D. Doniger,
National Resources
Defense Council

EPA regulations that implement that international treaty within the U.S.—is turning out to be a production cut of 15% or more, because output of CFCs has grown since 1986.

As they now stand, the Montreal protocol and EPA rules require that CFC production be reduced another 20% by mid-1993, then an additional 30% by mid-1998. Output of halons (fluorocarbons that contain bromine) is to be frozen at 1986 levels in 1992. EPA has set up a quota system that allocates future production of the controlled chemicals based on each U.S. producer's share of the 1986 market for halons.

But the Montreal protocol was out of date even before it went into effect. Since it was negotiated in 1987, a flood of scientific data has indicated the treaty as currently written will not adequately protect the ozone layer from chlorine-catalyzed destruction. (p. 7)

[In the two years since the Montreal protocol, the] accumulation of bad news about the layer of ozone that protects Earth's surface from harmful ultraviolet (UV) radiation has led to a consensus that tighter controls on chemicals that carry halogen atoms into the stratosphere are necessary. If provisions set in the Montreal protocol were to be followed, chlorine concentrations would continue to increase for more than a century. Stricter controls on halogenated compounds are required simply to stabilize the chlorine content of the atmosphere at today's levels of about 3 ppb, much less reduce them below the concentrations—about 2.7 ppb—that existed when the Antarctic ozone hole was first identified in 1985.

Given the reality of the science, over the past 18 months industrial producers and users of CFCs—led by Du Pont, the company that makes about 25% of CFCs produced worldwide and dominates the U.S. market—have joined environmental groups, scientists, and politicians calling for a phaseout of CFCs.

"When the industry decided in 1986 to support an international agreement to limit the use of CFCs, it recognized that the long-term life of the current compounds was going to be limited," says Kevin J. Fay, executive director of the Alliance for Responsible CFC Policy. That industry group is a coalition of all five domestic CFC manufacturers and several hundred businesses that use CFCs.

"Now, based on science and the political climate of today, it's clear they are going to be a lot more limited than we thought the science justified in 1986," Fay says. "Back then it appeared that you only had to cap the growth in use of the compounds. I don't think anybody believes that anymore. Even under the Montreal protocol, you get substantial increases in chlorine concentrations in the atmosphere."

But the Montreal protocol soon will be strengthened. In Helsinki in early May [1989], delegates to the first meeting of the countries that have joined the treaty agreed on their intention to phase out production and consumption of CFCs no later than the year 2000. They also agreed to eliminate halons and control other ozone-depleting substances like carbon tetrachloride (CCl_4) and methyl chloroform (CH_3CCl_3) as soon as feasible.

Four review panels set up by the United Nations Environment Program (UNEP) are now completing scientific, environmental, technical, and economic assessments of the issues surrounding these tighter controls. Once UNEP has received their reports, amendments to the Montreal protocol will be drafted this fall. A CFC phaseout is expected to be formally adopted next spring when the parties meet again to renegotiate the treaty.

However, although an eventual phaseout of CFCs now appears inevitable, the timing of their elimination is still being negotiated. The year 2000 is too late, according to some environmentalists and politicians. The most extreme position is that taken by Greenpeace, an international environmental group, which is calling for an immediate ban on all production and consumption of CFCs and halons. Others, while conceding the need for some transition time, argue the phaseout must be speeded up. A new bill in the Senate, for example, calls for their elimination within five years.

"The 2000 date is not acceptable in our view," says Liz Cook, project director for the Friends of the Earth Foundation's (FOE's) ozone campaign. "That schedule is based on a timetable the chemical industry has set for itself. It doesn't force technological innovation."

Some Scandanavian countries have already committed themselves to phase-outs before 2000, Cook points out. Others, including the European Community, have pledged to cut CFC output 85% as soon as possible.

"The idea is to have an orderly transition over the next decade or so," argues C. Anthony McCain, program manager of Du Pont's Freon products division. "There will be immediate injuries to people if we move too fast, because they will not choose the best solutions. They'll be exposed to toxic, flammable materials."

EPA agrees that 2000 is soon enough. "Although some people have said they would like a phaseout faster than 2000, we don't believe there is much environmental benefit to doing it faster and there is a downside," says Eileen B. Claussen, director of the agency's office of atmospheric and indoor air programs. "You might pick poorer alternatives because they are available first."

The fate of halons is also uncertain. Although output of halons is small compared with CFCs, bromine derived from those compounds is even more destructive to stratospheric ozone than chlorine. The U.S. and some other countries have called for an international phaseout of halons by 2000, but the extent and timing of further controls remains to be negotiated.

Carbon tetrachloride and methyl chloroform are also in limbo. EPA argued forcefully at the Helsinki meeting that both could be significant future sources of chlorine in the stratosphere if their output is allowed to grow unchecked.

Carbon tetrachloride is used primarily as a chemical intermediate in the U.S., but Soviet bloc and developing countries use it in ways that allow emissions to the atmosphere, according to Claussen. As for methyl chloroform, EPA fears that manufacturers will use it as a substitute for other solvents—primarily CFC-113 ($C_2Cl_3F_3$)—that have been restricted.

"I am sure that both carbon tet and methyl chloroform will end up in the re-negotiation" of the Montreal protocol, Claussen says. "But whether they end up at a freeze or some reduction I don't know yet. Technically, if you want to stabilize chlorine in the atmosphere—which is not necessarily a wonderful environmental goal—you probably have to do away with both of them over some period of time."

Meanwhile, prices of CFCs have already begun to rise as the supply shrinks under the current restrictions—from about 60 and 70 cents per lb for CFC-11 (CCl_3F) and CFC-12 (CCl_2F_2) a year ago to approximately 80 and 90 cents per lb today. EPA estimates prices may eventually rise as much as fivefold, bringing producers several billion extra dollars, depending on how fast users switch to substitute products or alternative technologies.

"The government is restricting the supply of CFCs for a good environmental reason," says attorney David D. Doniger, director of the Natural Resources Defense Council's ozone protection project. "The effect is the same as the OPEC cartel's oil restrictions' effect on oil prices. If the price goes up but the production costs don't, that's pure windfall profit."

Almost a year ago, EPA floated the idea of imposing a regulatory fee on CFC producers or an auction system to recoup those additional revenues. Otherwise, the agency suggested, CFC producers might lack the incentive to come up with substitutes.

EPA still has not taken any action. But the Bush Administration has included $400 million in CFC windfall profits revenue in its proposed fiscal 1990 federal

The Bush Administration has included $400 million in CFC windfall profits revenue in its proposed fiscal 1990 federal budget and is projecting another $1.4 billion for the following year—much to the fury of CFC producers.

The EPA has no plans to restrict the use of HCFCs, although some politicians and environmentalists are calling for controls. . . . The hydrogen atoms on HCFCs make them susceptible to oxidation in the lower atmosphere. But some fraction reaches the stratosphere where UV radiation can release chlorine atoms that catalyze ozone depletion.

budget and is projecting another $1.4 billion for the following year—much to the fury of CFC producers.

"This is definitely inappropriate," says Anthony Vogelsberg, environmental manager of Du Pont's Freon products division. "The scheme would extract the very revenues necessary to do the research and development work necessary to replace CFCs."

Such a tax would also place U.S. companies at a competitive disadvantage, argues William Corcoran, director of public affairs for Allied-Signal, the second largest U.S. CFC producer. "The American companies are doing a good job with moving ahead with alternatives," he says. "Now we'll be hit with a big tax—which no other country imposes—that makes it tougher for us to maintain our lead."

However, that view hasn't garnered a lot of sympathy in some quarters. "There are no entities who deserve the windfall less than the CFC producers that stonewalled this issue for so long and got us into this mess," NRDC's Doniger says. "So we are in favor of the windfall profits mechanism to take those profits away. We're encouraged by EPA's discussion and even more encouraged by the Bush Administration's inclusion of the money in the budget."

Congress, not EPA, looks likely to make the final decision on the issue. Although EPA is careful to refer to potential CFC windfall revenues as "fees," they bear a strong resemblance to taxes—which only Congress can impose. (pp. 8–10)

The Senate Environment & Public Works Committee has embraced CFC taxes as a way to come up with most of the $450 million it has orders to slash from the fiscal 1990 budget. The committee is leaning toward a tax on each pound of CFCs and halons produced, with the amount increasing each year until the compounds are phased out.

Although the final budget won't be enacted until fall, CFC producers are facing the likely reality of having to pay a windfall profits tax. "In order to get that money we would have to triple the prices of CFCs next year," Du Pont's McCain says bluntly. "If we have to pay that money we will pass that cost on to the user. He'll pay for it and we'll pass it on to the government for him. Some users will go out of business."

The CFC users that will suffer the most as supplies become short and prices rise are makers of rigid insulating foam. CFC-11 is used to blow the polyurethane and polyisocyanate foam insulation widely used in new construction and remodeling. The CFCs not only mechanically expand the foams, but are trapped within them, contributing to their insulating capacity.

The foams already face stiff competition from other types of insulation, such as glass fiber, notes Stephen O. Anderson, chief of EPA's technology and economics branch in the division of global change. "They face a fragile market because there are so many other good alternatives," he says.

The foam insulation industry is evaluating HCFCs-123 ($CHCl_2CF_3$) and -14lb (CH_3CCl_2F) as substitutes for CFC-11. But these compounds are still undergoing long-term toxicity testing and process development and are not yet available in commercial quantities. (p. 10)

In any case, the HCFCs will cost several times what CFCs now cost—perhaps too expensive for foams to compete with other types of insulation. If a windfall profits tax is imposed on the current CFCs, the industry argues, foam insulation makers will be out of business that much sooner.

The auto industry is fighting additional restrictions on CFCs on a different front—the state level. In May, the Vermont legislature outlawed the registration of cars with air conditioners that use CFCs beginning with 1993 models. California's lawmakers may soon follow suit. A bill just introduced in the U.S. Senate would make it illegal to sell or export cars that use CFCs in their air conditioners after 1993.

U.S. carmakers say they can't make the 1993 deadline. "We may not have any cars that use the substitutes by the '93 auto year," says General Motors' Gerald F. Stofflet, chairman of the Motor Vehicles Manufacturers Association's CFC subcommittee.

About 90% of the new cars sold in the U.S. have air conditioners. All use CFC-12. Automakers in the U.S., Europe, and Japan are testing new systems that use HFC-134a (CH_2FCF_3), which contains no chlorine atoms. Both Du Pont and ICI are working on commercial-scale plants to produce HFC-134a, which also has potential uses in home and commercial refrigeration. But as is the case with the HCFCs, toxicity tests and process development on HFC-134a won't be completed for several years. Furthermore, as Du Pont's McCain points out, HFC-134a is not a "drop-in" replacement for CFC-12.

"Everybody's working, trying to get HFC-134a in, but there are still many uncertainties," Stofflet says. "We release the 1993 models for tooling at the end of this year and trying to put in a different system after that is a disaster. The earliest we can do it is the 1994 model year."

Even then, Stofflet says, the auto companies will be taking a big risk because they will have to finalize their designs before all testing is complete. And the new air-conditioning systems require so many changes throughout the cars that the companies will not be able to put them in all models at once, he says, but will have to phase them in over three or four years.

The headache that the automakers are facing stems from an outpouring of legislation pending at the state and local level that restrict CFCs. "We're running around putting out fires," Stofflet says. "It's a real problem. Each state proposes something a little bit different."

Not all the proposed legislation involves the auto restrictions that Vermont's does. Instead, most proposed bills are more like one recently enacted in Hawaii, which requires recycling of CFC-12 when auto air conditioners are serviced and bans the sale of small cans of the refrigerant for home use. Other pending bills would require labeling of products that contain or are made with CFCs.

All this legislation—some 90 bills in more than 20 states this spring—is a result of EPA's decision that its federal regulations controlling production of CFCs do not preempt the rights of states and municipalities to enact their own restrictions on the chemicals. CFC producers and users are most unhappy with that decision—and environmental groups are taking full advantage of it.

"It would be disingenuous for me to pretend that we are not aware that it can be inconvenient to companies who want uniform national markets," NRDC's Doniger says. "So our strategy is to promote this state-level action. But I don't want people to think we can turn it on or off. A lot of it is indigenous. The activity reflects real concern at a grass-roots level that the global process and the U.S. federal process are working too slowly."

"We don't need these state and local initiatives to persuade the industry that we have to get out of these compounds," Fay says. "We know that. States and localities would be far better off finding where they use CFCs and putting their own ozone protection programs into place rather than trying to ban the registrations of auto air-conditioning systems or banning individual products. That is not going to affect the total amount of CFC use in this country because we are going to be in a shortage situation governed by the Montreal protocol. All these individual efforts to try to ban a product here or a product there are not going to accomplish anything."

But according to environmentalists who have been involved in state initiatives, the goal of the bills is not just to tighten supplies of CFCs. It is to restrict needless emissions and conserve CFCs for essential uses like servicing existing refrigeration equipment.

It will not be long before the effects of limited supplies of CFCs extend to the consumer.

"I can understand how industries who make products they'd like to sell in nationwide markets are concerned about labeling requirements and restrictions and so forth that have popped up at the state level. The most efficient answer to that, though, is for them to come to Washington and support national control measures. If we had a national auto recycling law, we wouldn't need to have 50 state recycling laws. If we had national labeling requirements, we wouldn't need inconsistent state labeling requirements."

—David Doniger,
National Resources Defense
Council

"We're working with states on banning frivolous uses and on mandatory recycling for auto air-conditioning," FOE's Cook says. She points out that releases of CFC-12 from car and truck air conditioners are currently the largest single source of CFC emissions in the U.S.

Technology for recycling CFC-12 from auto air conditioners is available now, says EPA's Anderson. Earlier this year, EPA and major auto manufacturers announced an agreement on standards of purity for recycled CFC-12 that will allow mechanics to reuse the old refrigerant without voiding the air conditioner warranty.

"I can understand how industries who make products they'd like to sell in nationwide markets are concerned about labeling requirements and restrictions and so forth that have popped up at the state level," Doniger says. "The most efficient answer to that, though, is for them to come to Washington and support national control measures. If we had a national auto recycling law, we wouldn't need to have 50 state recycling laws. If we had national labeling requirements, we wouldn't need inconsistent state labeling requirements."

EPA's Claussen says that the agency has no plans to initiate such national regulations on its own. She would, however, look into it if asked to by the industries affected.

Claussen also asserts that EPA has no plans to restrict the use of HCFCs, although some politicians and environmentalists are calling for controls. CFC producers have been concentrating on developing HCFCs and HFCs as substitutes for the fully halogenated compounds. And the current refrigerant of choice for home air-conditioning in the U.S. is $HCFC-22(CHClF_2)$.

The hydrogen atoms on HCFCs make them susceptible to oxidation in the lower atmosphere. But some fraction reaches the stratosphere where UV radiation can release chlorine atoms that catalyze ozone destruction.

"I think in the end you have to be practical," Claussen says. "It is more important to get out of CFCs by some date certain than to regulate the HCFCs. And you need the HCFCs, for at least some CFC uses, in order to do that. If you use HCFCs wisely and not that much, it is probably okay. But I don't want to specify in a regulation how much is wisely, or what uses. On the other hand, I want to monitor exactly how much is being produced and what it is being used for, on a worldwide basis."

But pressures are mounting for restrictions on the future output of HCFCs. In the international arena, there was limited discussion at the May Helsinki meeting of whether HCFCs should be included in the renegotiations of the Montreal protocol. In the U.S., a draft bill, circulating in the Senate, would limit the time period over which HCFCs could be used. At the extreme, Greenpeace has called for banning all production and new consumption of HCFCs. And both NRDC and FOE hold that future limits on HCFCs must be spelled out now.

"These chemicals are useful because if you use them now you can get rid of the hard CFCs that much sooner," Doniger says. "But we want to make sure we don't have topsy-turvy growth that slows down or even prevents the reduction of atmospheric chlorine levels and contributes to global warming."

Doniger says that before 1986 there was not much development work on HCFCs and HFCs. Until it was clear that restrictions would be placed on the existing CFCs, companies had no incentives to invest in more expensive alternatives. "As we put HCFCs into service we ought to continue the research—both from chemical companies and users—into other ways of getting the job done with less and less of those chemicals and ultimately none at all," he says. "If you create the false impression that HCFCs have an unlimited future, there will be no interest in working on a better answer."

But the idea of a limited future is causing the chemical companies to balk. "We are very disturbed by the regulatory uncertainty," says Allied-Signal's Corcoran. "We plan to produce a full line of substitutes. But when we get to the point where the management committee has to approve plans for large-scale investments—a quarter of a billion dollars over a decade—if these kinds of restrictions go through it will be much harder to justify."

Du Pont's McCain adds: "We have not decided to go forward in the alternatives business. We are making small-scale plants. But if in a few years, when we have to get authorization for world-scale production facilities, we don't anticipate we can make money, we won't do it. Faced with potential regulations like that, why would any reasonable businessperson want to invest in something that would have a short lifetime?"

Doniger suggests that a balanced position in the middle is available. Industry, he argues, should work toward a regulation that would allow companies enough time to recoup their investments and then get out of the business. "At least they'd know that the cloud over those chemicals isn't going to result in the rug being pulled out from under them two, three, or four years down the road," he says.

In the meantime, the uncertainty continues. For the moment it is limited to companies that produce and use CFCs and that are trying to plan for the future. But it will not be long before the effects of limited supplies of CFCs extend to the consumer.

"I don't think people have any idea of the impact this is going to have over the next few years," says Leo E. Manzer, research manager at Du Pont's central research and development department. "It's not going to be until people can't get their air conditioners charged up and have to suffer in the kind of weather we've had in the last few weeks that they'll realize how important CFCs are in all aspects of life." (pp. 10–13)

Pamela S. Zurer, "Producers, Users Grapple with Realities of CFC Phaseout," in Chemical and Engineering News, Vol. 67, No. 30, July 24, 1989, pp. 7–13.

The hard-liners might have succeeded had not Interior Secretary Donald Hodel weighed in with his own solution: Everybody could stay indoors, or wear hats, sunglasses, and sunscreen for protection against increased UV. The ridicule that greeted his proposal spurred passage, by a lopsided majority, of a Senate resolution urging a two-stage phase-out of CFCs and halons.

Can We Repair the Sky?: Effective Elimination of CFCs

In the spring of 1985, representatives of 21 nations met under the auspices of the United Nations Environment Program to consider worldwide restrictions on CFCs. The Soviet Union, Japan, and the European Economic Community argued for a freeze on existing CFC levels only. The U.S., Canada, and Scandinavian countries, however, pressed for a virtual phase-out of CFCs by the year 2000.

The phase-out proposal, a personal initiative of then EPA Administrator Lee Thomas, was actually opposed by hard-liners in the White House. Prompted by industry lobbying, the Departments of Interior and Commerce and the Office of Management and Budget sought to scuttle the phase-out plan.

The hard-liners might have succeeded had not Interior Secretary Donald Hodel weighed in with his own solution: Everyone could stay indoors, or wear hats, sunglasses, and sunscreen for protection against increased UV. Hodel later explained that his only intention had been to offer the President an alternative to regulation. But the ridicule that greeted his proposal spurred passage, by a lopsided majority, of a Senate resolution urging a two-stage phase-out of CFCs and halons.

As a compromise, the U.S. negotiators proposed a 50-percent reduction in CFC production and a freeze on halons. That's essentially the plan later adopted at a 1987 meeting in Montreal. The Montreal Protocol, as the accord is known, calls for a freeze this July at 1986 production levels for the five most widely

CFCs are ubiquitous. You can walk on urethane soles, ride on foam car seats, and sleep on pillows and mattresses all made from CFC-blown foam.

used CFCs. (Three of those, CFC-11, CFC-12, and CFC-113, account for some 90 percent of all CFC production.) The freeze will be followed in four years by a 20 percent reduction, and then a further 30 percent cut in 1998.

A Sudden Call for Speed

The agreements hammered out in Montreal, though, may soon be ancient history. As each new piece of evidence strengthens the CFC-ozone connection, international support for broader and swifter action is gathering steam. Many industry representatives already recognize the need for a total phase-out. DuPont, for one, has announced its intention to end manufacture of all CFCs by the end of the century. And recent news from Europe marked an even more dramatic about-face.

In March [1989], the 12 European Community countries that had opposed the U.S.-sponsored phase-out voted to eliminate all CFC production by the end of the century. Moreover, they also agreed to cut production by 85 percent as soon as possible.

The Job Ahead

Phasing out CFCs won't be easy, though. Besides being highly stable and virtually nontoxic, they're nonflammable, noncorrosive, and conduct heat poorly—all of which makes them work extremely well in many applications. Relatively simple and cheap to manufacture, CFCs are excellent refrigerants as well as outstanding insulators. They also make ideal packaging—from the plastic foam that protects TVs and VCRs in shipping cartons to the pellets around fine china.

They're also ubiquitous. You can walk on urethane soles, ride on foam car seats, and sleep on pillows and mattresses all made from CFC-blown foam. Among numerous other uses, CFC products help sterilize surgical instruments, freeze seafood, and clean the printed circuit boards in computers, CD players, and TVs.

By contrast, halons are used only in fire extinguishers. Even so, they are unlike other chemical extinguishers in that they leave no residue, which makes them excel in such applications as protecting electronic equipment or valuable books and papers. They're also safe to breathe in high concentrations, an advantage for use in aircraft and army tanks.

Proposed replacements for the major CFCs all have certain drawbacks. Many are simply different CFCs with chemical structures that break down readily in the lower atmosphere. That makes them safer for the ozone but often not as effective as the original chemical in the same application. They may be less stable or less durable than the original, or more corrosive, or less efficient as an insulator or cleaner. Also, the substitutes all cost more than the older CFCs.

Despite such drawbacks, the move to replace CFCs is under way, and there are already some signs of progress. Dow Chemical, for example, is ending its use of CFC-11 in making foam packaging. The company is switching to the chemical HCFC-22, which has only one-twentieth the ozone-depleting potential of CFC-11. DuPont is building a plant to manufacture HFC-134a, a refrigerant the firm expects to substitute for CFC-12 in some applications, including car air-conditioners.

Meanwhile, the Mobile Air Conditioning Society and most major U.S. and foreign car makers recently agreed on purity standards for recycled coolant. The agreement removes a major obstacle to recycling—concern by car makers that recycled coolant might damage car air-conditioners and thus void the warranty.

Various alternative technologies are also emerging from both small and giant companies. AT&T and Petroferm, a Florida-based solvent manufacturer, jointly developed a substitute for CFC-113 that's made from orange peels. Thermalux, of Emeryville, Calif., has produced a form of glass sheet made of tiny vacuum cells that is intended to replace CFC-11 insulation in refrigerators. Union Carbide has found a way to manufacture cushioning foams without CFCs for bedding and upholstered furniture.

All of those developments may ease the threat to the ozone layer, but they won't end it. Because of the long lifetime of many CFCs and halons, those produced today will still be depleting ozone decades from now. Minimizing the long-term damage will require action on several fronts.

What Consumers Can Do

It's quite a challenge," says Liz Cook of the Friends of the Earth. "We have to make people aware of the impact of an invisible gas on the invisible ozone layer, which increases an invisible form of radiation." Becoming aware of products that contribute to ozone depletion and what can be done about them is one way consumers can help.

Auto air-conditioning. Ninety million cars and light trucks in this country have air-conditioning. Much of the coolant used by them never cools anyone—it's vented during servicing of the units. Lost coolant from automotive air-conditioners accounts for an estimated 16 percent of ozone destruction. Accordingly, the most significant single step car owners can take will be to insist on recycling when air-conditioners are serviced.

The Mobile Air Conditioning Society says prototype recycling equipment is now being tested and will become available in many shops during the coming months. (The devices, which suck coolant out of the unit, have informally been dubbed "vampire" machines.) Stations that offer recycling will display a sign advertising the fact. Meanwhile, avoid using do-it-yourself recharging cans to replenish coolant. Refilling a leaky air-conditioning system only adds more CFCs to the atmosphere.

Refrigerators. Models with CFC-free coolants and insulation are not yet available. For now, the best consumers can do is to keep their present fridges working until recycling programs for CFC coolants are developed. Cleaning the coils regularly and checking the door seals for damage will help.

Insulation. If you're having a new home built, or adding insulation to your present one, don't use rigid foams unless you know they were made with ozone-safe blowing agents. Alternatives are fiberglass and cellulose. If you use cellulose-fiber insulation, look for a label that indicates the material meets standards of the Cellulose Industry Standards Enforcement Program.

Fire extinguishers. In the past, CU has recommended halon fire extinguishers for home use. We now believe the high ozone-depletion potential of halons outweighs other considerations. Anyone who owns a halon extinguisher should retain it until programs for reclaiming halon have been developed. Dry-chemical extinguishers are adequate for most home uses.

Plastic foam products. Many foam plastics are now made with HCFC-22, which has only five percent as much ozone-depletion potential as CFC-11 and CFC-12. Nevertheless, it's still worthwhile to limit any use of foam cups, plates, and similar products.

Other products. Technicalities in the law have enabled such aerosol products as spray confetti, VCR-head cleaners, film-negative cleaners, and boat horns to escape the 1978 ban on nonessential CFC aerosols. Some of these products are being reformulated without CFCs, so check the label before buying any. (Labeling of CFCs is not mandatory, but many manufacturers do it anyway.)

What Industry Can Do

Companies that make CFCs and halons can read the handwriting on the wall. Top priority will have to be assigned to developing effective CFC alternatives. But industry in general can also lend a hand in various ways. Here are just a few:

CFCs and halons aren't necessarily predestined to cruise the stratosphere. Improved handling of the chemicals can significantly limit emissions to the atmosphere.

As international agreements begin to reduce CFC production, the cutback in supplies of those chemicals is likely to increase their price. CFC manufacturers would reap windfall profits. To encourage those companies to plow the money into developing CFC replacements, Congress should consider enacting a tax on CFC production, with credit for relevant R&D expenses.

Labeling. Companies that make products in which CFCs have been eliminated should call that fact to consumers' attention. Alternative products without CFCs are often available, and the labeling or advertising should let people know.

Car design. Design changes in automobile cooling should be explored, including ways of eliminating CFC coolants altogether. Present car air-conditioners are often powerful enough to cool a small apartment. Smaller units would be practical if, for example, a solar-powered ventilation system limited the heat buildup while the car was parked.

Recovery systems. CFCs and halons aren't necessarily predestined to cruise the stratosphere. Improved handling of the chemicals can significantly limit emissions to the atmosphere. Recovery equipment is readily available for CFC solvents. Similar systems could be adapted to recover other evaporated CFCs. Electronics and metal-cleaning firms should also apply the same approach to another ozone depleter, methyl chloroform. Though not covered by the Montreal Protocol, 200,000 tons of this solvent are used in the U.S. each year.

Aerosol holdovers. Discontinue the use of CFCs in all aerosol products apart from essential medical applications. Miscellaneous products that still use CFCs should be reformulated with other gases.

The Government's Role

Despite the regulatory paralysis of the Reagan years, the Environmental Protection Agency still succeeded in making progress in the battle to save the ozone layer. Stephen Andersen and John Hoffman, who have headed up most of the EPA's ozone work, win praise from environmentalists and industry sources alike.

The EPA needs to continue on that course. In addition to setting a timetable for the total U.S. phase-out of ozone-depleting chemicals, the agency should make international cooperation a top priority. Nearly 70 percent of the world's total of CFCs and halons are now used outside the U.S. Meanwhile, other Government actions should also be explored:

The military. The Department of Defense is a major user of CFCs and halons. Some of that use is the result of military specifications developed over the years to assure uniformity and efficacy in DOD purchasing. The military should review its specifications to facilitate a switch-over to effective replacements.

Regulation. EPA regulation is needed in several areas. The agency, for example, should require labeling of products made with CFCs and halons, recycling of auto air-conditioner coolant, and recovery and recycling of refrigerator coolant. It also should ban do-it-yourself coolant cans.

Trade sanctions. Once alternative solvents are available, Congress should consider legislation halting the import of electronic products produced with CFC solvents. The Japanese have been slow to recognize the need for eliminating CFCs. The prospect of losing the U.S. market could spur some action.

Windfall-profits tax. As international agreements begin to reduce CFC production, the cutback in supplies of those chemicals is likely to increase their price. CFC manufacturers would reap windfall profits. To encourage those companies to plow the money into developing CFC replacements, Congress should consider enacting a tax on CFC production, with credit for relevant R&D expenses.

Such legislative or regulatory proposals are likely to meet stiff resistance. But the stakes are high, for the world at large as well as the U.S. The CFCs manufactured today won't even reach the stratosphere until the mid-1990s. And millions of tons of chlorine are already eating away at the ozone shield. Because of the longevity of CFCs, the amount of ultraviolet radiation reaching the earth's surface may rise for years before tapering off.

No one knows exactly what will happen. Projections based on computer modeling have their limits. One model predicted a 3 percent drop in ozone by the middle of the next century; that has already occurred. No one predicted the emergence of the Antarctic ozone hole, and no one can say precisely how the atmosphere will respond as chlorine levels rise. The only responsible course is to pursue every measure possible. The potential consequences are too serious to do otherwise. (pp. 324–26)

"Can We Repair the Sky?" in Consumer Reports, *Vol. 54, No. 5, May, 1989, pp. 322–26.*

Sources For Further Study

Benedick, Richard Elliot. *Ozone Diplomacy: New Directions in Safeguarding the Planet.* Cambridge, Mass.: Harvard University Press, 1991, 300 p.
    Reviews the diplomatic process that resulted in the Montreal Protocol and discusses the agreement's implications for future international action concerning environmental issues.

Brune, William H. "Ozone Crisis: The Case Against Chlorofluorocarbons." *Weatherwise* 43, No. 3 (June 1990): 136–43.
    Proposes an immediate ban on CFC production and use in industrialized countries while advocating a gradual, less economically disruptive phase-out of the chemicals in developing nations.

Cary, John. "A Red Alert Over the Ozone." *Business Week,* No. 3210 (22 April 1991): 88–9.
    Reports on the conflict between the EPA and certain industries concerning stricter controls on CFC use.

Cogan, Douglas J. "Living in a Glass House." *Environmental Science and Technology* 23, No. 1 (January 1989): 20–2.
    Brief introduction to ozone depletion and global warming.

Connelley, Joyce A. "Solving the Ozone Problem before It's Too Late." *Electronic Business* 17, No. 4 (20 February 1989): 72–3.
    Examines how phasing out CFCs will effect the electronics industry.

Glas, Joseph P. "Protecting the Ozone Layer: A Perspective from Industry." In *Technology and Environment,* edited by Jesse H. Ausubel and Hedy E. Sladovich, pp. 137–55. Washington D.C.: National Academy Press, 1989.
    Overview of ozone depletion that concentrates on the Montreal Protocol and industry's response to its restrictions.

Jones, Robin Russell, and Wigley, Tom, eds. *Ozone Depletion: Health and Environmental Consequences.* New York: Wiley, 1989, 203 p.
    Compilation of essays which address the major issues of ozone depletion.

Kripke, Margaret L. "Depletion of Ozone Layer and Health." *Forum for Applied Research & Public Policy* 5, No. 2 (Summer 1990): 37–42.
    Predicts the potential consequences of increased exposure to ultraviolet radiation, including skin cancer, cataracts, and damage to human immune systems.

Lemonick, Michael D. "Deadly Danger in a Spray Can." *Time* 133, No. 1 (2 January 1989): 42.
    Outlines the effect of CFCs upon atmospheric ozone and the policies instituted to eliminate their use.

Lyman, Francesca. "As the Ozone Thins, the Plot Thickens." *The Amicus Journal* 13, No. 3 (Summer 1991): 20–8, 30.
  Overview of the issues surrounding ozone depletion.

MacKenzie, Debora. "Cheaper Alternatives for CFCs." *New Scientist* 126, No. 1723 (30 June 1990): 39–40.
  Investigates the proposed strategies for the replacement of CFCs in developing countries with the help of western technology.

Makhijani, Arjun, and Bickel, Amanda. "Protecting the Ozone Layer." *Energy Environment Monitor* 6, No. 1 (March 1990): 5–10.
  Reviews the medical and environmental consequences of increased exposure to ultraviolet radiation as a result of ozone depletion and discusses the alternative technologies aimed at reducing CFC use.

Maxwell, J. Barrie, and Barrie, Leonard A. "Atmospheric and Climatic Change in the Arctic and Antarctic." *Ambio* 18, No. 1 (1989): 42–50.
  Emphasizes the adverse effect of climate change in the polar regions upon the entire planet.

McElroy, Michael B., and Salawitch, Ross J. "Changing Composition of the Global Stratosphere." *Science* 243, Vol. 4892 (10 February 1989): 763–70.
  Technical analysis of the chemical reactions that lead to ozone depletion.

Ozone Layer Depletion: Hearing before the Subcommittee on Oversight and Investigations of the Committee on Energy and Commerce, House of Representatives, One Hundred First Congress, first session, May 15, 1989. Washington, D.C.: U.S. G.P.O., 1990, 1079 p.
  Gathers testimony and debate before the U.S. Congress concerning ozone depletion and the regulation of CFCs.

Voyteck, Mary A. "Addressing the Biological Effects of Decreased Ozone on the Antarctic Environment." *Ambio* XIX, No. 2 (April 1990): 52–61.
  Presents data concerning the detrimental effects of decreased ozone on antarctic life and urges further scientific study of this little-understood subject.

11: Pest Control

Humans, Pests, and Pest Control

The definition of "pest" is totally human-oriented. Organisms designated *pests* compete with people for food, fiber, and shelter; transmit pathogens; feed on people; or otherwise threaten human health, comfort, or welfare. It could be said that, previous to the appearance of humans, there were no pests—just millions of different organisms struggling for survival; the arrival of humans and the continuing development of the human life-style have provided the sole basis for labeling an ever-increasing number of these surviving organisms "pests."

A strictly ecological viewpoint would consider every link in the food chain (or each of these differently adapted organisms) as equally important in an ecosystem's assemblage of plants, animals, and interacting physical environment. To such pure ecologists, describing an organism as a negative factor (or a "pest") just because its link in the food chain happens to be at the same spot as or right next to our own would be unthinkable!

But in human-oriented sciences—e.g., economics, medicine, agriculture, silviculture, and park and recreation area management—which aim to insure human survival and enhance our life-style, the role of such competing or consuming organisms, whose appetites or habits might limit our "success," can be considered nothing short of adverse. When, why, how, and to what degree various organisms become pests, however, is a matter of considerable debate in all these sciences.

Organisms that have become "pests" are not limited to any class, phylum, or even kingdom. They are as varied as the habits that make them undesirable. Insects are frequent pests (and it is no wonder, since they make up more than 75% of the world's animal species!) A number of mite, tick, nematode, mollusc, and other invertebrate species have become pests. Vertebrates, including rodents, deer, coyotes, and birds, may become serious pests in some situations. Microorganisms (e.g., bacteria, fungi, protozoa, rickettsiae, viruses, and mycoplasmas), particularly those that are pathogenic to important plants and animals, cause many problems. Weeds—ordinary plants in places where they are not wanted—comprise another category of common pestiferous organisms.

In the human war against pests, our battle strategies and tactics have evolved through the ages, becoming more sophisticated and, for the most part, more effective. Our first methods of pest control were undoubtedly the hand-picking, swatting, and squashing of insects and other small invertebrates. Later we learned how to manipulate the environment so that it became less favorable to pests; examples of these early environmental modifications include flooding or burning fields to destroy weed, insect, and other invertebrate pests, and using scarecrows to keep birds away. The utilization of natural enemies to control pest organisms dates back several thousand years; but it was the rather recent application of such "biological control" methods against the devastating cottony cushion scale insect that truly demonstrated the value of this approach to pest control. In this case, an imported lady beetle saved the California citrus industry from total ruin in the late nineteenth century.

The definition of "pest" is totally human-oriented. Organisms designated *pests* compete with people for food, fiber, and shelter; transmit pathogens; feed on people; or otherwise threaten human health, comfort, or welfare. It could be said that, previous to the appearance of humans, there were no pests—just millions of different organisms struggling for survival; the arrival of humans and the continuing development of the human life-style have provided the sole basis for labeling an ever-increasing number of these surviving organisms "pests."

Environmental contamination and the killing of wildlife were perhaps the greatest tragedies of the widespread overuse of pesticides. Honeybees and fish, birds, and other wild animals were the innocent and often unknown victims of the massive pesticides spraying of agricultural crops and forest and recreation areas.

Materials with pesticidal properties, such as plant-derived chemicals (e.g., pyrethrum) and arsenic and sulfur, were used sporadically and largely ineffectively from the time of the Greek and Roman Empires. More sophisticated use of pesticides evolved in the latter half of the nineteenth century after two copper-based fungicides, Bordeaux mixture and Paris Green, were found to be effective against mildews and other diseases that were threatening the grape industry in France. Both fungicides, especially Paris Green, which contained arsenic in addition to copper, turned out to be useful as insecticides as well and were subsequently used regularly to kill a spectrum of insect pests.

The years preceding World War II saw increasing use of these and other chemical control materials against arthropod pests and plant diseases. However, because of the hazardous nature of these pesticides, their expense, the poor application techniques available, and the ineffectiveness of the materials in many situations, chemical pest control remained a limited technology, and pest management still depended largely on environmental manipulation, sanitary practices, biological control, and, to a certain degree, luck.

But then, the discovery of the insecticidal properties of DDT in the 1940s changed all that. Here was an apparent "miracle" pesticide—cheap, incredibly effective at low dosages, long-lasting, easy to apply, and lethal to an unprecedented spectrum of insect pests. Soon other chlorinated hydrocarbons joined the list of "miracle" insecticides, e.g., lindane, dieldrin, methoxychlor, chlordane, and heptachlor. Another class of highly effective insecticides, the organophosphates, which includes parathion and malathion, was developed in Germany around the same time. The organophosphates were then followed by the carbamates. Modern herbicides, fungicides, rodenticides, and other pest control chemicals quickly followed on the heels of the "miracle" insecticides, and their use has continued to increase.

Initially, control by these chemicals was so effective that some entomologists and pest managers even foresaw the eradication of entire species of pests and in partial seriousness advised young collectors to catch specimens of the doomed species while they could still be found.

But though control by the new pesticides was spectacular, their utilization was often mindless. The grower, government pest-control specialist, commercial applicator, or home gardener simply applied the chemical according to a schedule (often suggested by the pesticide manufacturer). Few stopped to consider the effects of the pesticide on other organisms or even to determine whether the pests were present or in what density.

The post-World War II era produced a whole generation of entomologists, plant pathologists, weed scientists, and pest managers well-trained in the art of proper pesticide application, in choosing the most potent and/or economical material, and in the complexities of spraying equipment. Frequently, however, they were less educated about the biology and ecology of the target pest organism and were often unaware of the natural control factors operating in the treated ecosystem or of the nature and identity of other nontarget organism casualties of their biocidal assault.

However, the DDT "miracle" was indeed too good to be true. Problems did arise. The first hint of modern insecticides' fallibility was the development of resistance in insects exposed to the toxic materials. In other words, some populations that had been frequently doused with particular insecticides developed strains (*resistant strains*) that were able to survive in the presence of even heavy doses of the chemicals—becoming more serious pests than ever before.

The post-World War II pesticide revolution also ushered in a whole new spectrum of previously unknown pests. Suddenly many arthropods, especially spider mites, whose populations had been generally small or moderate, became major pests of crops and other resources. For the most part this sudden leap to prominence was prompted by the insecticides' destruction of natural enemies that had previously held potentially injurious species under restraint. Freed of their natural enemies and tolerant of the pesticides, these organisms survived and multiplied with incredible speed.

Environmental contamination and the killing of wildlife were perhaps the greatest tragedies of the widespread overuse of pesticides. Honeybees and fish, birds, and other animals were the innocent and often unknown victims of the massive pesticides spraying of agricultural crops and forest and recreation areas. Unlike pest insects, many of these organisms had neither the reproductive capacity nor the short generation time required to develop resistance. Reports of death and injury among farmworkers and other human victims imprudently exposed to toxic dosages of pesticides were numerous and sparked the enactment of laws regulating and even prohibiting the use of many of these toxic substances.

Yet many of the negative side effects resulting from the overdependence on pesticides should not have been surprising to twentieth-century scientists and could have been predicted had thoughtful biologists, ecologists, public health specialists, and geneticists been closely involved and on the lookout for possible problems. For instance, the development of insecticide resistance among important agricultural pests had been documented as early as 1912, and warnings about the serious problems that could result from such insecticide resistance had been sounded well before the advent of the synthetic organic insecticides. Such a speedy evolution of tolerance to new environmental stresses is a major reason that many rapidly reproducing invertebrates have been so successful; it is a process that follows well-known laws of natural selection. As for environmental contamination and the killing of wildlife, pollinators, and important natural enemies, these too could have been predicted by biologists, ecologists, toxicologists, and others familiar with the basic concepts of food chains and the biosphere's biogeochemical cycles. Yet somehow these questions (in fact raised by a few scientists) were pushed aside, and most pest managers and pest control researchers of the 1940s and 1950s, mesmerized by the seeming simplicity and efficiency of complete reliance on pesticidal control, forgot the laws of ecology and stumbled into chaos.

Thus, it is of critical importance to remember that pest management is basically an ecological matter. Man wants to secure as much of a given resource as possible with minimum competition from other organisms in the ecosystem. Therefore, effective pest management must begin with an ecological outlook. Artificial controls (e.g., pesticides and cultural practices) must be looked on as tools to be fitted into the environment as unobtrusively and with as little disruption as possible. It is imperative that we consider the effects of the various control actions both on each other and on the rest of the environment, and thus prevent the negation of one pest control factor by another (e.g., biological control by chemical control).

In recent years a new comprehensive approach to pest control has been developing; it is termed *integrated pest management* or *integrated control*. Integrated pest management (IPM) is an ecologically based pest control strategy that relies heavily on natural mortality factors such as natural enemies and weather and seeks out control tactics that disrupt these factors as little as possible. IPM uses pesticides, but only after systematic monitoring of pest populations and natural control factors indicates a need. Ideally, an integrated pest management program considers all available pest control actions, including no action, and evaluates the potential interaction among various control tactics, cultural practices, weather, other pests, and the crop to be protected. Under IPM, natural enemies, cultural practices, resistant crop and livestock varieties, microbial agents, genetic manipulation, messenger chemicals (such as sex attractants), and pesticides become mutually augmentative instead of individually exclusive or even antagonistic—as has been so often the case under pesticide-dominated control.

An integrated pest management program is comprised of six basic elements: (1) people: the system devisers and pest managers; (2) the knowledge and information necessary to devise the system and make sound management decisions; (3) a program for monitoring the numbers and state of the ecosystem elements—e.g., resource, pest, and natural enemies; (4) decision-making levels: the pest densities at which control methods are put into action; (5) IPM

> It is of critical importance to remember that pest management is basically an ecological matter. Man wants to secure as much of a given resource as possible with minimum competition from other organisms in the ecosystem. Therefore, effective pest management must begin with an ecological outlook. Artificial controls (e.g., pesticides and cultural practices) must be looked on as tools to be fitted into the environment as unobtrusively and with as little disruption as possible.

"Resistance to pesticides is no different from resistance to any other means of control. If you have 50 flies in your house, and you catch 45 with a flyswatter but five fast ones get away, they will interbreed to produce a faster fly. Pests interbreed for survival, regardless of what tool you use to control them."

—Homer M. LeBaron,
basic research manager,
agricultural division,
Ciba-Geigy

methods: the techniques used to manipulate pest populations; and (6) agents and materials: the tools of manipulation.

Integrated pest management systems are dynamic, as are the ecosystems in which they are invoked, and usually involve continuous information gathering and evaluation as the resource and its associated physical and biological environment go through their seasonal progressions. Thus, in inspect IPM, control action programs evolve as and if pest problems develop; the preprogrammed rigidity present in conventional pesticide systems, where pest managers spray automatically according to a predetermined schedule, has been eliminated.

The integrated pest manager or adviser is the key to this dynamism. He/she must constantly "read" the situation, evaluate pest populations according to previous experience and knowledge, and initiate actions and choose appropriate materials and agents as conditions dictate. It is imperative that pest managers be aware of the ecological and biological effects of their actions at all times, not only on the target pest organisms, but also on natural enemies and nonpest organisms.

While the need for integrated pest management is now accepted by workers in most areas of pest control, effective and working programs have been implemented for only a dozen or so resources. These are mostly agricultural crops and are largely for the control of insect and mite pests. . . . However, programs involving a spectrum of pest problems for livestock and in urban, forest, and recreation areas are currently being worked out. . . . (pp. 1–7)

Mary Louise Flint and Robert van den Bosch, "Man, Pests, and the Evolution of IPM: An Introduction," in their Introduction to Integrated Pest Management, *Plenum Press, 1981, pp. 1–7.*

Pesticide Development

Each year fewer than 20 pesticides are registered as new weapons in the battle against the insects, diseases and weeds that interfere with crop production. And every year pests build up a resistance to those compounds. To stay one step ahead of the adaptive prey, the pesticide industry is forced to develop new chemicals and techniques nonstop.

Pesticides are big business. Currently, annual pesticide sales in the U.S. are in the range of $5 billion—or 1 billion lb/year of active ingredients—says Earl C. Spurrier, vice-president for state affairs at the National Agricultural Chemicals Assn. The annual world market is nearly $20 billion. There are 1,250 active ingredients being used in 45,000 different formulations, Spurrier adds. More than 500 of those ingredients are used in agriculture, and of those, about 125 are used most extensively.

In general, the major pests will eventually be able to beat whatever method is used to control them. Pesticides have "nothing magic in them," says Homer M. LeBaron, basic research manager of Ciba-Geigy's agricultural division (Greensboro, N.C.). "Resistance to pesticides is no different from resistance to any other means of control," he explains. "If you have 50 flies in your house, and you catch 45 with a flyswatter but five fast ones get away, they will interbreed to produce a faster fly. Pests interbreed for survival, regardless of what tool you use to control them."

Resistance can build up in a matter of one to several years, depending on the pest and the methods used to fight it, says LeBaron. For example, pathogens that cause plant diseases need only a few days to go through a complete cycle of development. If the pathogen has the ability to develop resistance to a fungicide, it may do so in as little as one year, particulary if that chemical is the only means used to control the disease. Insects develop resistance primarily through enhanced metabolism, or breakdown, of a pesticide, says LeBaron. The genetic changes that confer resistance may require 6–20 generations, or typically 3–4 years. Herbicides used to control weeds, which have one-year life cycles, may become ineffective after about six years.

There are exceptions. Even after 20–30 years of fairly continuous use of some pesticides, LeBaron says, resistance doesn't develop. With other pesticides, though, strong resistance has built up after two or three generations.

Usually, such cases of speeded-up resistance development occur when a single pesticide is used continually in large quantities to control a pest. But researchers have come up with a number of ways to avoid or at least delay the development of resistance. They suggest using a combination of chemicals and limiting application to the lowest "rate" possible. And farmers must learn to alternate between chemical classes that kill insects in different ways, says Pamela G. Marrone, an insect biology research group leader in Monsanto's agriculture division. To treat cotton bollworms, for example, pesticide users may want to switch between pyrethroid compounds and organophosphorous compounds, which affect an insect's sodium channels and acetylcholinesterase, respectively. Alternatively, plant breeders can develop disease-resistant crops.

Farmers also can integrate the two methods. With fungicides, LeBaron says, "We suggest the farmer use the crop that is most resistant to the pest, and use the chemical only when the disease is not contained by the plant's natural ability." He notes, however, that "the farmer often depends too much on the pesticide because it is so easy to use and faster in its effectiveness." Farmers also should monitor pest populations, perhaps weekly, says Marrone. That way they need only spray when they see a problem developing, instead of spraying regardless of whether any pests have shown up.

More than 500 pests have developed resistance to pesticides, and that number is increasing, says Marrone. And she adds that insects have become resistant to "all major classes of insecticides."

Mosquitoes and house flies have developed resistance to "virtually everything that has been thrown at them," LeBaron says. They are a particular problem in the Third World, where they carry malaria and other diseases. Late blight on potatoes and blue mold on tobacco are resistant to phenylamide fungicides, and diseases in small grains and fruits are resistant to sterol-synthesis-inhibiting fungicides. As far as herbicides go, LeBaron thinks the most serious problem involves weeds resistant to triazine herbicides. "Fifty-four species of weeds that had been previously susceptible to triazine herbicides are now known to be resistant," he says.

One of the most serious problems in herbicide resistance, and still a fairly new phenomenon, says LeBaron, involves sulfonylurea compounds that have been on the market for only five or six years. The resistant weeds that are springing up take over quickly and are much more fit than triazine-resistant weeds. "These are brand-new herbicides. This is creating tremendous concern in the industry," LeBaron says. "Already Du Pont is withdrawing some and requiring that they be used in combination with other kinds of herbicides."

Industry researchers are especially worried because the weeds also are showing resistance to pesticides that are not related chemically, but that use similar modes of action. They include products Ciba-Geigy is currently developing, LeBaron says, as well as American Cyanamid's imidazolinone herbicides and some Dow products. This cross-resistance will be "an important part of this future problem."

Replacements for these products aren't cheap. A new pesticide costs about $30–40 million. Du Pont says it takes $60 million over 5–7 years to discover, develop, register and market a product. Du Pont, which has 65–70 major crop protection products, has been cranking out 6–8 new products per year in the past few years, says a spokesman for the company's agricultural products business. The company is spending "well beyond $100 million/year in crop

In general, the major pests will eventually be able to beat whatever method is used to control them.

Few individuals who have not been faced with the daunting task of controlling pests on a wide scale can appreciate the value of pesticides. Indeed, to the people who require their use, the synthetic chemicals that comprise the bulk of today's pesticides are seemingly miraculous in their effects on target organisms. Unfortunately, these same chemicals also may have adverse environmental effects, although the probability, frequency, and degree of these effects are highly contentious.

protection research and development," he says. And Du Pont should bring in more than $1 billion worldwide from sales in this market.

On average, Monsanto and Ciba-Geigy register a new pesticide every year or so. But LeBaron warns that the number of compounds available to farmers from all producers is shrinking. "We're going through the reregistration process now. Our own decisions led us to drop several compounds that have been a great help, not because of human exposure or the environment but because of the workload. EPA requires so much research on old, established products that we can't get to it within the time requirements available."

In addition to traditional areas of pesticide research and developing crop plants with genetic resistance to pests, Ciba-Geigy is looking into such new approaches as plant and soil microorganisms, and pathogens that can control insects and plants. One of biotechnology's main efforts is directed at transferring resistance from one crop to another, says LeBaron. The corn rootworm, which chews up corn roots, has no effect on sorghum. So scientists are trying to transfer that resistance to corn. Ultimately, the insects may evolve the ability to break through the resistance mechanism and, may reinfest the crop. The company is also studying "safeners," or antidotes, that can be used, for example, as a protective coat on sorghum seeds. Then a herbicide can be applied without harming the seeds, because the safener enhances the crop's ability to metabolize the herbicide.

Considerable time is spent on studying mechanisms of pesticide action, Marrone says. "You have to understand the mechanism to understand how insects become resistant, and to understand how you might be able to delay resistance."

Monsanto's focus in the insect battle is in the biotechnology area, she adds. While the company markets herbicides, such as Lasso and Roundup, it doesn't market insecticides or fungicides, though Marrone says Monsanto hopes to get into these fields. One biotechnology program involves *Bacillus thuringiensis* (BT), a microorganism that controls insects. Monsanto has taken from BT the gene that codes for production of a protein that kills the insects, and has transferred it into plants such as tomatoes, Marrone says. In July, she organized a working group of 22 companies to look at insects' potential to develop resistance to BT. A similar group has been around for two years that is studying pyrethroid compounds.

Marrone sees positive signs in industry's move to "address the issue of resistance prior to marketing pesticides." Is the fight against resistance a battle that can be won? Never completely, says LeBaron. "There is no way in my lifetime that we will have all pests contained. It will be a constant effort and we must never become complacent. But I am very optimistic that we can keep ahead of the pests."(pp. 73, 75, 77)

Sophie Wilkinson, "Pests Resist, Researchers Fight On," in Chemical Week, *Vol. 149, No. 16, October 19, 1988, pp. 73, 75, 77.*

Pesticide Alternatives to Sustainable Agriculture

Pesticides are used widely in the United States. In 1988 the USDA Economic Research Service expects pesticide use for major agronomic crops in the United States to range from 420 to 464 million pounds of active ingredient. An appreciable segment of American society objects to the prodigious production of these compounds, to their transport on public roadways, and to their widespread application on both private and public lands.

On the other hand, few individuals who have not been faced with the daunting task of controlling pests on a wide scale can appreciate the value of pesticides. Indeed, to the people who require their use, the synthetic chemicals that comprise the bulk of today's pesticides are seemingly miraculous in their effects on target organisms. Unfortunately, these same chemicals also may have adverse environmental effects, although the probability, frequency, and degree of these effects are highly contentious. Because agriculture is the primary recipient of pesticides, the potential adverse effects of these chemicals invoke concern over the ability of agriculture, as it is currently practiced, to sustain itself.

In the paragraphs that follow, I shall discuss what I believe to be five major perceptions concerning pesticides and sustainable agriculture, namely, perceptions about energy consumption for pesticide production; toxicity; environmental risk; costs to farmers, the primary users of pesticides; and social acceptance. Only two of these perceptions will be found to merit attention regarding sustainable agriculture.

Energy Consumption

As a rule of thumb, the production of 1 pound of pesticide requires 1 gallon of oil, about 33,000 kcal of energy. Thus, roughly 13 to 15 million barrels of oil are used annually to produce the pesticides we apply every year to our most important agronomic crops in the United States. Herbicides are the chemical control agents most often applied, accounting for about 85 percent (on a weight basis) of pesticides applied to agronomic crops. (Pesticides include herbicides, fungicides, and insecticides.) Therefore, we may speculate about the amount of energy consumed in manufacturing pesticides in general by looking at herbicides.

Older herbicides, those whose marketing commenced between 1945 to about 1980, typically are applied at rates of 1 to 3 pounds of active ingredient per acre. Chemicals developed roughly within the last decade, however, often are applied at rates of only 1 to 3 ounces per acre, a reduction in application rates of active ingredients of approximately 90 to 95 percent.

Although many older herbicides are still used today at traditional rates, we may speculate that newer chemicals will replace these old stalwarts rapidly in the next decade. If such replacement does occur, as seems likely, then we may anticipate energy use for herbicide production to change accordingly. Assuming that the new herbicides have energy requirements for their synthesis similar to those of their predecessors, future energy consumption for herbicides used in the United States (and, therefore, for pesticides in general) may drop greatly, to 1 to 2 million barrels of oil annually. A single supertanker could ship this amount of oil. Consequently, considerations of pesticide energy consumption probably do not bear on the problem of pesticide use in sustainable agriculture.

Toxicity

Prior to 1972, when Congress passed significant amendments to the Federal Insecticide, Rodenticide, and Fungicide Act of 1947, screening for human, animal, plant, and microbial toxicity of pesticides before they were placed on the market was much less intensive than it is today. Some of these older pesticides were known to be toxic, whereas the toxicities of others were relatively unknown. Examples of three herbicides should provide some insight into the former state of the art of pesticide toxicology.

Paraquat, a broad-spectrum herbicide, causes painful and almost certain death if ingested. It achieved notoriety through accidental poisonings, especially of children, and as the poison-of-choice for some religious sects prone to suicide. Paraquat's once-high stature and large market share have decreased steadily, due in part to its designation by the Environmental Protection Agency as a "restricted-use" herbicide, users' perceptions of its danger, the lack of *good* antidotes, and its replacement by newer, safer, and equally effective products.

Environmental risk is commonly perceived as involving off-site movement of pesticides. After pesticides are applied, off-site transport may occur via two media: through wind-induced movement of pesticide-laden air or soil particles, and by water-mediated transport over soil (runoff) or through soil (percolation). Two of the older herbicides, atrazine and 2,4-D, are now infamous for their ability to move off-site. Atrazine's low but significant solubility in water effectively increases its probability of transport in runoff and percolating water. Eventually this compound may reach surface and underground drinking-water supplies. The second herbicide, or at least some of its formulations, is moved easily even by gentle breezes, potentially damaging many sensitive plants that grow in the wake of its vapor trail.

As a rule of thumb, the production of 1 pound of pesticide requires 1 gallon of oil, about 33,000 kcal of energy. Thus, roughly 13 to 15 million barrels of oil are used annually to produce the pesticides we apply every year to our most important agronomic crops in the United States.

Another herbicide, dinoseb, was recently taken off the market because of new evidence demonstrating its involvement in health and reproductive disorders, particularly in men. Lastly, alachlor, which is the most widely used pesticide in the United States, has been added within the past year to the growing list of "restricted-use" pesticides, because new toxicological research implicated it as a tumor-forming agent in laboratory animals.

Toxicities of all older pesticides are being reevaluated. The cost of these reevaluations is so prohibitive that production of many older chemicals will cease. Only for those with large market shares, like alachlor, will the cost of reevaluation be justified economically. Should the chemicals, or their various formulations, prove unduly toxic during reevaluation, their registrations will be revoked by the EPA.

Because of these new laws, modern pesticide development includes numerous screenings for human, animal, plant, and microbial toxicity. Chemicals found to be toxic at very low levels to nontarget organisms simply are not developed further by modern industry. Consequently, new pesticides are almost inevitably safer than those developed previously. This is not to imply that the long-term environmental effects of all new pesticides will be less than those of older products. Instead the implication, based on our current understanding of acute and chronic exposures to these chemicals, is that the newer pesticides have much higher probabilities of having greater safety margins than older compounds. An example comparing the quantities of new and old chemicals that cause 50 percent death (LD_{50}) in laboratory rats may be useful at this point.

Bromoxynil is an older product whose main use is control of broadleaf weeds in small grain crops. Its LD_{50} for rats is 440 milligrams per kilogram of body weight. A new herbicide called thiameturon, used essentially for the same purpose, has an LD_{50} of greater than 5000 milligrams per kilogram of rat body weight, or a safety margin one order of magnitude greater than that for the older herbicide.

As a consequence of the increased safety associated with new pesticides, toxicity probably will play a small role, if any, with respect to the importance of alternatives to synthetic pesticides for sustainable agriculture.

Environmental Risk

As opposed to toxicity, environmental risk is more commonly perceived as involving off-site movement of pesticides. After pesticides are applied, off-site transport may occur via two media: through wind-induced movement of pesticide-laden air or soil particles, and by water-mediated transport over soil (runoff) or through soil (percolation). Two of the older herbicides, atrazine and 2,4-D, are now infamous for their ability to move off-site. Atrazine's low but significant solubility in water effectively increases its probability of transport in runoff and percolating water. Eventually this compound may reach surface and underground drinking-water supplies. The second herbicide, or at least some of its formulations, is moved easily even by gentle breezes, potentially damaging many sensitive plants that grow in the wake of its vapor trail. Although neither of these chemicals is especially toxic to humans, their off-site movements are nightmares for both industry and agriculture with respect to public relations.

Research and development industries and institutions are cognizant of public opinion. New chemicals are screened for volatility and solubility. Their probabilities of off-site movement can be estimated prior to their release, although not always judiciously, as the recent case of the herbicide known as clomazone indicates.

Persistence, or residual activity, may be a pesticide trait more important to consider than water solubility in regard to off-site movement. For example, atrazine can remain in the soil one year after its application at standard rates. Although persistence can be detrimental to crop rotations, it can be useful with respect to weed control. Whatever the case, residual activity in pesticides also substantially increases probabilities for their off-site transport, especially in wind-blown soil, runoff, and percolating water. Many new herbicides, and almost certainly most of those to be released in the future, have very short residual times in soil, often just a few days to a week. Additionally, these new compounds are most often applied postemergence—that is, after the crop and weeds have emerged from the soil, rather than before, as with most older herbicides. Late application reduces the length of time the compounds are exposed to wind and water. Short residuals and late applications work in concert to lower markedly the probabilities of off-site movement and risk to the environment. For these reasons, I suspect that environmental risk of future synthetic pesticides will provide little impetus for development of pesticide alternatives in sustainable agriculture.

Costs to Farmers

Many of the older herbicides have a variety of inherent dangers associated with their use. However, most of these chemicals are highly cost-effective in terms of weed control and maintenance of crop yields. They are cheap, with applications costing only $2 to $10 per acre. Few comparable bargains exist.

New and future herbicides, which have or will have low toxicities and environmental risks, are as effective for weed control as the older compounds, but they may cost much more to use. Newer herbicides, such as acifluorfen and glyphosate, cost farmers about $15 to $20 per acre to use typically, but up to $20 to $50 per acre for certain spectra of weed species. Fifty dollars represents 10 bushels of soybeans, or one-fourth to one-third of an average soybean farmer's gross economic yield per acre. With commodity prices stagnating or decreasing, such costs are prohibitive.

The chemical industry estimates the cost of discovery, development, and screening a new marketable herbicide to be up to 50 million dollars. Although this phenomenal expense may justify the industry's high charge for new products, high product cost probably will be a factor dictating research, development, and use of pesticide alternatives for a sustainable agriculture.

Social Acceptance of Synthetic Pesticides

Pesticide use and contamination are undeniably emotional issues. Despite the fact that many common household products are more toxic than many pesticides, especially to children, heads of households with such products may be vocal advocates of pesticide-use restrictions. Providing the general public with proper perspectives concerning pesticides and other hazardous products may be a future role of education, as education often is touted as a panacea for many of society's other troubles. With enough money, many argue, proper information and education can correct almost any public problem, from littering to communicable diseases. To be sure, education can influence society's attitudes dramatically: toward cigarette smoking, for example. But education has its limits, especially when emotional issues are involved. At least a half-century of objective science education has not exorcised from American society notions of the supernatural, be they in the form of Californian "channels" or more traditional forms. Indeed, even societies with formalized educational systems in place for millenia still are not able to deal objectively and unemotionally with issues involving their neighbors and/or themselves. I suspect that educational campaigns emphasizing the greatly enhanced safety features of new and future pesticides will do little to mollify the public's stance on pesticides. Consequently, the most important reason to develop pesticide alternatives is the persistent lack of confidence in synthetic chemicals by a discerning society.

In the last decade, steadily increasing interests have been building among scientists and the farming community in developing safer and more cost-effective pest-control systems. Many such systems are in active stages of development. These systems do not necessarily exclude the use of synthetic pesticides but

> Pesticide use and contamination are undeniably emotional issues. Despite the fact that many common household products are more toxic than many pesticides, especially to children, heads of households with such products may be vocal advocates of pesticide-use restrictions.

"Since 1945 pesticide use has increased tenfold, and at the same time crop loss from insects has increased twofold, from about 7 percent to 13 percent."

—David Pimentel,
professor of insect ecology
and agricultural sciences,
Cornell University

use them more judiciously and in smaller amounts than in traditional pest-control programs. These new systems hold great promise for the future. Buyer beware, however. As with every new scientific endeavor arising because of society's emotions and concerns, charlatans exist who propose, or claim to possess, phantom-like solutions to pest control. Charlatans aside, true alternatives to current pest-control practices are within sight. Stimulated by public and fiscal pressures, these systems are being developed through close collaboration among farmers and scientists at public and industrial research laboratories. (pp. 41–3)

Frank Forcella, "Importance of Pesticide Alternatives to Sustainable Agriculture," in National Forum, *Vol. LXVIII, No. 3, Summer, 1988, pp. 41–3.*

Kicking the Pesticide Habit

Entrenched as habit and dignified as tradition, saturation of soil and crops with pesticides has been accepted agricultural practice in the United States for some forty years. Since 1970, the most lethal have generally been replaced by chemicals with less persistence in the environment, but no synthetic pesticide is safe, and many of those banned here are sold abroad and return to us in imported food. Eleven years ago, integrated pest management (IPM) became part of national policy, but it is still regarded with skepticism by most farmers, and has rarely achieved more than rudimentary application. Meanwhile, overall pesticide use has actually gone up, without a corresponding reduction in pest damage.

"Since 1945 pesticide use has increased tenfold, and at the same time crop loss from insects has increased twofold, from about 7 percent to 13 percent," says David Pimentel, professor of insect ecology and agricultural sciences at Cornell University. A preeminent entomologist, Pimentel has served on committees for the National Academy of Sciences, the EPA, the Congressional Office of Technology Assessment, and the National Institutes of Health, and is the author of eleven books and over 300 articles. Why, he asks, "when you're using ten times as much pesticide, are you losing twice as much to insect pests?"

The answer, in part, can be found in government policies. Federal incentives encourage monocultures, which are less resistant to stress than diversified crop systems. Widespread abandonment of crop rotation (planting corn in alternate years with soybeans, wheat, or oats, for example) has helped to make corn growers the most lavish users of insecticides in the United States. In 1945, when farmers universally rotated corn and used no insecticides, crop loss to insects was 3.5 percent; today the loss is 12 percent.

"When you plant corn on corn," explains Pimentel, "you intensify not only the insect problem but also the weed and disease problems," creating a need for more herbicides and fungicides. Federal policy also encourages farmers to grow certain crops in regions where they are more susceptible to pests— white potatoes and cotton in the South, for instance. Pimentel maintains that eliminating price supports would reduce insecticides for some crops by about a third.

Farming practices remain pesticide-oriented. Disposing of infested or diseased crops on a timely basis (sanitation), well-planned weeding and tillage, and proper storage techniques—all integral to full-fledged IPM—are neglected by farmers in favor of pesticides. Many also plant less pest-resistant crops. And with increased aircraft application, most pesticides are poorly targeted (only 0.1 percent of the chemicals applied reach their target). Further, pesticides create the need for more pesticides: insecticides breed insecticide-resistant insects and kill bugs' natural enemies; herbicides and fungicides create resistant weeds and pathogens, and herbicides can increase the susceptibility of crops to insects and diseases.

Another misguided policy emphasizes high "cosmetic standards." Consumers are perceived as demanding flawless-looking fruits and vegetables, to the extent that the FDA has raised standards even for processed foods like applesauce and ketchup, requiring that they include fewer insect residues. Beauty and purity both demand increased use of pesticides, although neither has anything to do with nutritional quality.

Pimentel has just released a study exploring the results of cutting pesticide use by 50 percent, on forty different crops. "Environmental and Economic Impact of Reducing U.S. Agricultural Pesticide Use" . . . is based on exhaustive research by students as a seminar project. The study provides a crop-by-crop, step-by-step illustration. By reducing pesticide use to half its current level, concludes Pimentel, farmers would spend only about $830 million, and food costs would rise 0.5 percent. Farmers now spend $4.1 billion a year on pesticides, and the price of these petroleum-based chemicals is steadily rising.

And the farmers' outlay does not, of course, include pesticides' costs to public health, and natural and agricultural ecosystems. "A conservative estimate suggests that the environmental and social costs of pesticide use in the United States amount to about $1 billion annually," Pimentel states, "and the actual cost is probably double this amount." If the public can be assured that pesticides in their food and environment are greatly reduced, he maintains, they will be willing to pay the slight increase in food cost, and accept a reduction in cosmetic standards. Pimentel was recently invited to Sweden to advise officials there on a new national policy aimed at reducing pesticide use by half within the next four years. Denmark will follow in 1997.

In this country, a vigorous national policy would seem to be the answer as well. But government action has been sporadic. Federal funding for IPM has remained static at $7.5 million for the past eight years; meanwhile stop-gap measures that, taken alone, often look both radical and impractical help make farmers leery of IPM (examples are re-registration and restriction of traditional chemicals and difficult to implement spraying requirements).

Practiced thoroughly, IPM is a sound basis for the reforms Pimentel has in mind. IPM takes all of the factors of the ecosystem, such as weather and natural enemies, into consideration.

There are five basic aspects to IPM: cultural, environmental, physical, biological, and chemical. Cultural control of pests involves soil mix, growing methods, pest-resistant crops, and timing and quantity of watering; environmental control requires temperature and humidity regulation; physical control includes weeding, disposal of diseased or infested plants, and insect traps; biological control demands an awareness of life cycles and the encouragement and/or introduction of natural enemies; and chemical control allows only precisely targeted use of insecticides, fungicides, and herbicides. At each stage, decisions are based on the "economic threshold"—the point at which the cost of potential crop loss without control outweighs the cost of control.

In actual practice, however, IPM is often used to describe programs far less advanced. A farmer is said to be applying IPM if he simply uses pesticides based on his observations of his fields (called scouting) rather than on routine, calendar-based spraying. Testimonials to IPM's success often cite a farmer who scouts for insect behavior and sprays accordingly, saving money on insecticides. The real success of IPM at this point is that it signals a shift in attitude on the part of farmers who now see their crops as part of a natural system. While it is not IPM at its most effective, this is no small achievement, since this change in attitude is crucial to breaking the pesticide syndrome.

"For farmers, working with an ecosystem is an alien concept," says Carol Glenister, who owns and operates IPM Laboratories, Inc., in upstate New York, just outside the small town of Locke. In addition to serving as a consultant, Glenister sells biological controls such as fly parasites, spider mite

Saturation of soil and crops with pesticides has been accepted agricultural practice in the United States for some forty years. Since 1970, the most lethal have generally been replaced by chemicals with less persistence in the environment, but no synthetic pesticide is safe, and many of those banned here are sold abroad and return to us in imported food.

> **"A conservative estimate suggests that the environmental and social costs of pesticide use in the United States amount to about $1 billion annually, and the actual cost is probably double this amount."**
>
> —David Pimentel

predators, and biopesticides, made from natural organisms. Abandoning traditional pesticide practice is risky and frightening, she says. "A lot of things are happening all at once. You're talking about changing the whole farming system. You have to listen to the farmer," she insists. "The farmer is on the firing line." Glenister would like to see large-scale financial and educational support for low-pesticide experiments on portions of crops, so that experience can be gained without risking the whole, because "the hands-on knowledge is not there yet." In her most optimistic moments she predicts an army of IPM consultants out there in the field, listening to farmers while providing expertise. As it stands now, true IPM is practiced only in indoor areas like barns and greenhouses.

With IPM stalled in its initial stages and national policy fragmented, the critical situation has led to polarization: proliferation of organic markets on the one hand and heavy investment in biotechnology on the other.

Food grown organically (with no synthetic fertilizer or pesticides) is in increasing demand; sales totaled $10 million in 1988 alone. According to a recent report from the Center for Science in the Public Interest, sixteen states have passed laws or adopted regulations defining "organic" for labeling purposes.

Organic farmers tend to be young and well-educated, and hold to a philosophy some describe as "spiritual" or "holistic." A favorite resource is *The New Farm*, a magazine written by and for farmers, which monitors agriculture's frontier, where knowledge is put into practice. To its readership of over 100,000, *The New Farm* reports on such topics as insect-tolerant crop varieties, nutrient recycling, crop/weed interactions, and biological pest control, and often documents these with lively case studies. Profiles include that of California farmer turned businessman Paul Bezzerides, who invented the Spyder, a machine that "makes herbicides obsolete," and the Bug Zapper, resembling "two industrial vacuum cleaners," that travels down crop rows sucking up insects. The very names of Bezzeride's machines are indicative of the changing image of environmental sensitivity. As one *New Farm* contributor put it, organic produce now sells in "real retail outlets, not just the hippie coops."

Organic farmers' polar opposites in viewpoint—though equally spurred forward by alarm over pesticides—are the promoters of biotechnology. Genetic engineering has made possible the precise control of mutations, and even man's creation of new life forms. Commercial applications of biotech burgeoned in the 1980s, with big business (among others Union Carbide, Eastman Kodak, Monsanto, and General Foods) making big investments in the potentially lucrative market. Supporters claim enormous agricultural as well as medical benefits and hail the new science as a boon for mankind. Critics call biotechnology "the panacea of the '90s," and predict unforeseen environmental hazards and even catastrophes such as unintended new life forms. Some problems with agricultural applications are already obvious. Herbicide-resistant corn, for example, encourages greater herbicide use. Monsanto plans to market a soybean genetically altered to resist a herbicide it sells. Such package deals may lock farmers into a new kind of pesticide syndrome.

"As far as I can see, herbicide-resistant tomatoes only benefit the pesticide people," says William Liebhardt, director of the Sustainable Agriculture Research and Education Program at the University of California at Davis. Biotechnology investors should not have carte blanche to do whatever they want to the environment, he warns, and compares their claims of a perfect solution to those of early nuclear power advocates. We also have to ask some hard questions about how biotechnology will affect genetic diversity, and "the structure of agriculture"—by possibly centralizing technology and putting "a few companies in control." Biotechnology can be used as a tool to enhance low-input agriculture, Liebhardt says, and it is in this light that it should be evaluated.

While organic food and genetic engineering square off on center stage, another star further dims the prospects of IMP. The new arrival is low-input sustainable agriculture (LISA). Ideally, LISA is an environmentalist's dream.

While IPM deals only with pesticides, LISA encompasses every aspect of the agroecosystem, ranging from fertilizer and irrigation to erosion, and even tractor fuel. It minimizes human input and emphasizes maintaining the resources of the land. The danger is that this dream will overshadow IPM's prosaic but proven success, however limited at this point.

Mary Louise Flint, a colleague of Liebhardt's at Davis and acting director of IPM education and publications for all branches of the University of California, sees LISA as both threat and promise. Flint has edited nine books on IPM, co-authored *Introduction to IPM* with Robert Van der Bosch, and has in press a book on garden pest management. "In politics you have to have a new acronym every few years," she says, calling LISA "the new buzz word in Washington." It could weaken support for IPM, she fears, particularly because IPM often does use pesticides, so the antipesticide forces may be more vocal in their support of LISA.

But Flint is enthusiastically optimistic about IPM in California. State funding for IPM amounts to almost $2 million a year, which includes a competitive grant program awarding $760,000 to forty different projects carried out on commercial farms by university researchers and county-based advisors. One success Flint points to with pride is cotton grown in the San Joaquin Valley. Ten to fifteen years ago, six or seven pesticides were used while today, "it's getting under one per year." Strawberry growers "used to laugh you off the front porch," if you suggested using fewer pesticides, she recalls. Now they are among the multitude of farmers calling her to say they want to market pesticide-free food.

Many states have experienced explosive growth in private pest control advisers (PCAs). Some, like New York's Carol Glenister, are IPM advocates, some are pesticide advocates, and some are truly independent (they don't sell anything except their expertise). PCAs should not be confused with salesmen for the chemical companies, who greatly outnumber the advisers. Both consultants and salesmen constitute a direct route to farmers. Their visits provide a crucial information and support network, and must be recognized as an essential conduit for any coherent change. That the network still consists in large part of chemical salesmen—backed at the top by the powerful National Agricultural Chemical Association lobby in Washington—is a serious obstacle to low-input and IPM. Farmers trust the salesmen, get to know them well, and receive personal service.

"The Monsanto agent is a friend of mine," says Howard Bassett, who has been farming his 115 acres outside Interlaken, New York, for forty-five years. The state extension agent gives good advice "when you can find him," but for "nitty-gritty" details he consults the salesmen because they're always available and can spend more time with him. The winter meetings farmers rely on to catch up on information are most often organized by the chemical companies, he says.

As Bassett indicates, state extension agents are also a resource for farmers. The major federal vehicle for IPM is the Extension Service of the U.S. Department of Agriculture (USDA). Extension's IPM branch as been in full operation since 1978 and administers $7.5 million in annual Smith-Lever funds. An IPM coordinator in each state reports to the program leader in Washington. At least forty-two colleges and universities offer IPM Extension education programs. A 1987 USDA report cites 250,000 clients participating in 150 separate IPM programs incorporating 27 million acres.

Jim Tette is New York's Extension coordinator, based at Cornell University's land grant agricultural school. He says for every 500 farms in New York, there are about ten chemical agents and only one Extension agent. But more and more PCAs are independent, and Tette puts great faith in their potential for providing disinterested IPM advice to farmers. There are now at least a dozen independent consultants in New York, he estimates, while five years ago there were only a couple. He calls them "the plant health doctors of the future."

There are five basic aspects to IPM: cultural, environmental, physical, biological, and chemical. Cultural control of pests involves soil mix, growing methods, pest-resistant crops, and timing and quantity of watering; environmental control requires temperature and humidity regulation; physical control includes weeding, disposal of diseased or infested plants, and insect traps; biological control demands an awareness of life cycles and the encouragement and/or introduction of natural enemies; and chemical control allows only precisely targeted use of insecticides, fungicides, and herbicides.

Integrated pest management (IPM) is still regarded with skepticism by most farmers, and has rarely achieved more than rudimentary application.

Cornell students can qualify for such jobs through various programs, particularly a newly instituted Master of Professional Studies.

New York is one of only eight states (including California) to contribute funding to IPM programs, allocating $900,000 in 1989. There are about thirty ongoing demonstration projects a year, each of which has a "lifetime" of three years. Extension picks up the tab for the first year, the farmers are expected to cost-share the second year, and by the end of the third year the financial responsibility is entirely their's. Most then join a grower's association, like the Pest Management Cooperative, to share the cost of hiring a consultant.

The 1988 annual report for New York's IPM program shows a continuing decrease in pesticide use. Potato growers, for example, used 21 percent less fungicides and 7 percent less insecticides guided by IPM prediction techniques, in some cases planting marigolds to repel pests. Most of the reduction is the result of better understanding of life cycles and recognition that up to a certain point, pests can be tolerated without any economic loss.

Like Mary Louise Flint, Tette is concerned that the"glamor" of LISA has begun to undermine federal support for IPM, just when IPM success has been proven. But he points to a major weakness in IPM as one reason for LISA's appeal: IPM neglects weeds while focusing on insects and pathogens. Weeds are much harder to forecast and monitor, but Tette singles out a dearth of research as the most important factor. "For every thirty or forty scientists working on diseases and bugs," he says, "only five or six are working on weed science." The pesticide ratio has shifted in recent years to heavier use of herbicides; of the one billion pounds of pesticides used in the Untied States, 11 percent now are fungicides, 23 percent insecticides, and 66 percent herbicides. Stepping up research on weeds should therefore be a top priority for IPM, he urges.

According to David McNeal, the National Program Leader for IPM in Washington, a "marriage" between IPM and LISA is both probable and desirable. He says that in addition to herbicides, IPM has neglected synthetic fertilizers, but he believes that IPM's successes, along with its solid "people base" of researchers and agents, can serve as a building block for the broader low-input sustainable concept. We have to look at the whole farming system, he maintains, including economic and social issues as well as environmental factors. (pp. 10–16)

Practicing LISA relies on the assumption that profits come second to environmental safety—a truly revolutionary concept.

Meanwhile, federal policy remains locked into the pesticide syndrome. We have only the faltering steps of IPM to point to on the road to a solution, and IPM seems stalled in its tracks. IPM requires an unfamiliar approach and far more expertise than present practice; scarcity of demonstrated economic success leaves farmers still very skeptical; and the traditional information network in place works against IPM. In addition, IPM has remained largely rudimentary and has neglected to adequately address herbicides and synthetic fertilizers. Ardent LISA fans claim that IPM has been co-opted by the system, and in a sense they are right. We are still eating chemical poisons in more than half our food.

In the end, however, these explanations pale beside the change in attitude that is required by all of us. It is no accident that DDT insecticide and nuclear weapons were invented at the same time, both hailed as technological miracles with untold promises for a better world. There is a kind of generation gap between that quick-fix mentality and recognition of the earth's fragility.

"There's no silver bullet in this whole situation," says Pimentel. "That's where we made the mistake in 1945 and 1950—we took pesticides to be the silver bullet. Humans seem to do that—we want to find THE solution." But the only answer is the ecological approach, which is highly complex, and to achieve that, he says, "we've got a long way to go."

Learning to love dandelions, spiders, and imperfect apples may be the hardest and most urgent task ahead. (p. 17)

Kitty Mattes, "Kicking the Pesticide Habit," in The Amicus Journal, *Vol. 11, No. 4, Fall, 1989, pp. 10–17.*

Pesticides and Ground Water

Agricultural Pesticide Contamination

The nation's farmers have long enjoyed the use of pesticides to control weeds and insects. Revealing research developed over the past decade has, however, countered the long-held belief that all pesticides are biodegradable. The research has clearly shown that some pesticides can leach through earth layers and eventually contaminate ground water. In light of these findings, public outcry concerning ground-water protection from pesticide contamination has been justified and warrants further study and investigation.

Pesticides may contaminate ground water during their manufacture, distribution, storage, application, or disposal. Contamination, though not intentional, may result from accidental spills during any of the above steps of pesticide usage. Both state and federal environmental laws . . . decrease the possibilities for point-source pollutions by providing penalties and demanding cleanup when accidents occur.

The most common use for pesticides is to control insects and weeds on agricultural and forest land, rights of way, and lawns and gardens. After serving their purpose, pesticides may be transported by rainfall runoff and eventually reach ground water by returning to an aquifer through a sinkhole, uncapped well, or natural river recharge of an aquifer. Pesticides may also infiltrate the soil with rainfall or snowmelt. Leaching can occur at the point of application or in the area of recharge. The latter is more costly in terms of greater ground water contamination. The application of chemicals using irrigation systems may result in serious contamination if a backflow of water containing these chemicals occurs. The Nebraska Chemigation Act of 1986 requires backflow safety devices in that state.

Careless spills, involving the disposal of leftover pesticides and their containers, frequently occur at loading and mixing areas, causing contamination. Contamination from land application generally occurs over large areas and results from low concentrations that build up over time. Currently technology is not available for cleanup of contamination that involves a large geographical area. Thus, prevention involves both the regulation of the pesticides and improvement of land management practices.

Contamination Prevention

Contamination of ground water over large geographical areas may be increasing because of changing agricultural practices. The Soil Conservation Service, a federal agency charged with saving the nation's topsoil, has been promoting reduced tillage methods. By leaving 30 to 100 percent of crop residue on the surface, soil erosion is effectively controlled on highly erodable soils. Although reduced tillage diminishes erosion, larger amounts of chemicals are needed to eradicate weeds that conventional tillage methods control. Increased chemical use increases potential contamination. In this lies a contradiction: Should ground water be sacrificed to save topsoil? Further development of current technology could help eliminate or reduce the potential ground water contamination.

> Pesticides may contaminate ground water during their manufacture, distribution, storage, application, or disposal. Contamination, though not intentional, may result from accidental spills during any of the above steps of pesticide usage. Both state and federal environmental laws decrease the possibilities for point-source pollutions by providing penalties and demanding cleanup when accidents occur.

It has been estimated that less than 1 percent of a pesticide application actually performs its functions of controlling insects and weeds. As a result of misapplication, drift, and other transport mechanisms, the remaining 99 percent represents potential ground water contamination.

It has been estimated that less than 1 percent of a pesticide application actually performs its functions of controlling insects and weeds. As a result of misapplication, drift, and other transport mechanisms, the remaining 99 percent represents potential ground water contamination. Efforts are being made to reduce misapplication by the development of an applicator that injects the chemical directly into the water-carrying lines, eliminating the need for tank mixing. Pumps and spray booms that more efficiently and accurately deposit chemicals are also being developed. Further development would be facilitated by small federal grants to university programs. More specifically, because this research would most likely be done by undergraduate honor students, funding for such projects could be reduced if incorporated into the schools' undergraduate honors programs. Pilot projects could test this idea.

Biotechnology also offers alternatives to excessive chemical application. Research in genetic engineering may reveal a new class of insecticides. Insect pathogens including bacteria, fungi, and viruses may be used in the future to control insects. The bacterium Bacillus thuringiensis is already used in some areas to control caterpillars on crops. Plant breeding resulting in new varieties of pest-resistant plants is a possibility for biological pesticides. A March 1986 report states that ". . . use of genetic engineering to transfer genes from resistant wild plants to crop cultivators holds great potential for insect management, but requires very specific knowledge of the biochemical bases of resistance crop to be transferred. In most cases, the requisite knowledge is not yet available." Although EPA's ground water protection efforts are not directly interested in plant genetics, "backdoor" answers like this could reduce agricultural chemical ground water contamination.

Because concern about ground water has surfaced recently, past monitoring has been minimal. Several instances have, however, brought the pesticide problem to light. In 1979, the discovery of DBCP in numerous California Central Valley wells contradicted the belief that soil naturally purified returning ground water. The initial reaction to this discovery was that only large amounts of these chemicals would cause contamination. However, it was determined that the widespread and approved use of this product in agriculture actually caused the contamination. DBCP contamination was then found in four other states.

During that same year another chemical, aldicarb, was found in wells on Long Island, New York, as a result of approved use for control of insects and nematodes on potato fields. Since then, 14 other states have found aldicarb in ground water. The seriousness of this contamination has resulted in the need for a national regulation on aldicarb which will accompany the Agricultural Chemicals in Ground Water Strategy.

The EPA should consider the method that Florida uses to curb aldicarb contamination. After it was declared a restricted chemical in September 1983, followed by a ruling in 1984, aldicarb cannot be applied wiithin 100 ft of a drinking well. In addition, farmers are required to notify the state 30 days in advance, documenting the exact date of application, site, and the licensed applicator. A reduced application rate on pecans and citrus from label directions is also required. The fields must then be posted for 30 days following application.

Later, in 1984, an additional 1000 ft setback from a drinking well established additional protection for highly permeable soils. Aldicarb may be applied within this radius if the farmer can satisfy the state's well-construction requirements. If random inspections after application reveal a violation, the state has three options:

1. revocation of the applicator's license

2. a warning letter to the applicator for unintentional, minor violations

3. a fine of $1000 imposed on the applicator

Vincent Giglio, Director of the Division of Inspection, Florida Department of Agriculture and Consumer Services, indicates that there are few violations and that the regulations are well-respected. A similar program for ground water other than drinking water could be employed to protect remaining ground water.

Detecting Contamination

Models to determine the leaching potential of a chemical have been refined to estimate the amount of potential contamination over a large area. These models attempt to simulate the fate of pesticides as they move through the soil and water. Ranking models assign weighted values to key factors that influence potential for ground water contamination. The EPA has used these models to identify and rank pesticides for their leaching potential. Dynamic fate models simulate the transport and transformation of the pesticides over time. Modeling will continue to be a primary tool for evaluating ground water contamination potential.

Monitoring determines whether or not pesticides are contaminating ground water. Most monitoring has been a response to known contaminants or a suspected problem. Thus, potential threats to ground water are not necessarily monitored. From the limited amount of monitoring data collected (about half of the states conduct some monitoring), 17 pesticides have been detected in 23 states as a result of agricultural practices. The recent rise in pesticide contamination of ground water is more likely due to an increase in the number of studies rather than an actual increase in the problem. Conclusions must be carefully drawn here. Although one state shows contamination and a nearby state does not, the latter state may have only limited monitoring efforts. Identification of ground water contamination does not necessarily mean that a serious problem exists. For example, Pennsylvania has found at least three pesticides in ground water as a result of agricultural practices. When asked about the level of concern about pesticides in ground water, however, Gerald Florentine, Pesticides Operations Coordinator for the Pennsylvania Department of Agriculture, commented that pesticide contamination was not a great concern in that state. The state monitors only in response to a complaint.

In Mississippi, Robert McCarty, Assistant Director of the Division of Plant Industry at Mississippi State University, believes that additional extensive monitoring is not necessary in that state. A preprint of "Monitoring Ground Water for Pesticides in the USA" identifies the need for clearly stating and limiting the objectives of the studies to obtain more uniform monitoring methods. The EPA should consider this need and then enhance funding of general monitoring efforts.

One EPA study noted that "the increased concern about ground water contamination generally, and the recognition of pesticides as a potential contaminant, have led several states to initiate more comprehensive monitoring programs." Nebraska, for example, is studying the extent of contamination from its agricultural practices and Oklahoma is coordinating activities for generating, storing, treating, and disposing of pesticide waste. The study also stated that these efforts are primarily in the planning stage and are focused on the areas most vulnerable to ground water contamination. Some states have begun educational programs designed to inform farmers on the effects that agricultural practices may have on ground water contamination. Several states are currently proposing and enacting legislation that will further protect ground water in general, including consideration of pesticide contamination.

Ground Water Protection Needs

Limited by current monitoring efforts and technology, the extent of ground water contamination caused by pesticides is unknown. A recent EPA report states that " . . . EPA's efforts to develop controls to mitigate ground water contamination by pesticides have been hampered by a lack of basic information." There is a basic need for a national information system concerning

Biotechnology offers alternatives to excessive chemical application. Research in genetic engineering may reveal a new class of insecticides. Insect pathogens including bacteria, fungi, and viruses may be used in the future to control insects.

"The principal criterion for whether pesticides had been detected in the groundwater in a state appears to be whether or not they had looked."

—D. W. Parsons and J. M. Witt, "Pesticides in Groundwater in the United States of America," Oregon State University Extension Service, 1988

pesticides in ground water to estimate contamination based on use, farming practices, and hydrogeologic factors that determine the vulnerability tocontamination. Many ground water managers, as well as officials at all levels of government, would benefit from a shared data system. More field data is needed to help identify affected areas and problem chemicals. Increased understanding is also needed in the area of pesticide behavior in the saturated zone, aquifer mapping, pesticide accumulation, and the health effects of pesticides in ground water. Methods for obtaining site-specific soil hydrogeologic data to enter into models mentioned earlier are needed as are up-to-date and accurate pesticide use data to identify areas of concern. Further model development to access pesticide accumulation in ground water would facilitate the prediction of future contamination. Because exposure to pesticide-contaminated ground water is not well understood, public health may be over-protected. If this is true, EPA's concern about agricultural chemicals in ground water may be too intense. The strategy should address this point by channeling some efforts into assessing the exact health dangers of this type of contamination. (pp. 23–5)

Dennis A. Shields, "Agricultural Chemicals in Ground Water: Suggestions for the Enviromental Protection Agency Strategy," in The Journal of Enviromental Science, *Vol. XXX, No. 3, May-June, 1987, pp. 23–7.*

Pesticides and Human Health

The effects of agricultural chemicals on groundwater are determined by relative rates of percolation and degradation within the soil profile and by several factors controlling these processes, including climate, soil properties, microbial activity and the chemical properties of the pesticide. Groundwater monitoring in the United States has shown that significant amounts of parent pesticide, and some metabolites, are passing through the unsaturated soil zones to groundwater, where they are present at measurable levels.

The increasing evidence of groundwater contamination and the public health and policy implications of such findings are a source of intense debate. Groundwater contamination may occur from normal agricultural use of pesticides (non-point sources) or following mishandling, improper disposal, accidents or spills (point sources.)

The Oregon State University Extension Service recently reported that 33 states had found detectable levels of 67 different pesticides in groundwater. The "Most Severe" candidates for ameliorative action (defined as pesticides found at levels exceeding the Health Advisory in more than one state or in more than four wells) were 1,2-dichloropropane, 1,3-dichloropropene, aldicarb, atrazine, DBCP, dinoseb and EDB.

According to the authors, "the principle criterion for whether pesticides had been detected in the groundwater in a state appears to be whether or not they had looked."

The U.S. Environmental Protection Agency's National Pesticide Survey currently is performing a nationwide sampling of community and domestic drinking water wells to gather a representative sample of pesticide contamination levels in the nation's 51,000 community water wells and more than 13,000 domestic wells. As of Sept. 1, 1989, six of 180 community wells and nine of 115 private wells had been found to contain some level of pesticide residues.

California's well inventory database reports a total of 10,929 wells sampled, with 2,345 found to contain pesticide residues. Hallberg reports that the pesticide compounds most often found in groundwater are mobile and/or volatile soil fumigants and nematocides, used on vegetable or specialty crops, and commonly used herbicides from the humid corn-belt region, with atrazine being found most often. Nearly 60% of private rural drinking water wells and as many as 30% of community wells may contain detectable levels of pesticides.

While low-level contamination of groundwater from non-point sources has been reported nationwide, it appears that much higher levels of contamination may result from point sources, for example, when bulk pesticide mixing/loading facilities contaminate the groundwater of adjacent private wells. Persons using this highly contaminated water often are exposed to pesticides at concentrations equal to or above levels of significant health concern.

Science vs. Values

It is generally understood that pesticides are used to kill pests. In 1962, publication of *Silent Spring* brought an awareness to the public that pesticides were affecting non-target organisms and damaging the natural environment. Food chain effects became public knowledge, resulting in citizen concern that these contaminants could affect human health.

Creation of the U.S. EPA and the strengthening of the Federal Insecticide, Fungicide and Rodenticide Act to control pesticide use, based on environmental impact and human health guidelines, gave credence to public concerns. Regulatory science, in the form of toxicological risk assessment, evolved to fill the scientific data gaps which had previously hampered proper evaluation of the potential toxic effects of pesticides.

Improved animal testing and human epidemiological studies provide increasing evidence that chronic exposure to low levels of pesticide residues is associated with health effects, such as cancer and immunological perturbations.

Almost 20 years after the congressional mandate to fully reassess the 600-plus pesticide active ingredients it regulates, EPA has been unable to complete its prodigious task. Its failure has engendered public consternation and, in some cases, anger.

The mass media regularly report the presence of pesticide residues in food, water, air and human tissue, while researchers and regulators are unable to provide concerned citizens with positive proof that the public is not being harmed by such exposures. It is not surprising then that persons with contaminated drinking water are greatly disturbed and demand that their water be made pure and safe.

But what is "safe" drinking water? For non-carcinogens, a modified Acceptable Daily Intake (ADI) formula, now termed RfD or Reference Dose, is used to calculate an acceptable contaminant concentration for human consumption of drinking water. For carcinogens, scarce human data or, more usually, laboratory animal bioassay data, are inserted into complex mathematical formulas to generate a calculated lifetime cancer risk based on numerous assumptions and extrapolations.

Once either of these "risk assessment" steps is performed and a concentration is calculated, risk managers must decide whether this number is appropriate and implementable. It is the risk managers who establish what is an acceptable contaminant concentration and in many cases their determinations can be very different from those of the risk assessors who generated the original risk numbers.

What this discussion should point out is that mere science will not answer the fundamental question of what is "safe" or "acceptable risk". This is a values question which must be answered on a societal level, with input from all segments of society, including the scientific community. The major reason for the continuing controversy over such topics as contaminant clean-up levels, relative risk, health-based standards and advisories, and de minimis risk, is that only limited progress has been made in defining what types and levels of risk this society will accept to maintain its current lifestyle.

Groundwater monitoring in the United States has shown that significant amounts of parent pesticide, and some metabolites, are passing through the unsaturated soil zones to groundwater, where they are present at measurable levels.

The mass media regularly report the presence of pesticide residues in food, water, air and human tissue, while researchers and regulators are unable to provide concerned citizens with positive proof that the public is not being harmed by such exposures. It is not surprising then that persons with contaminated drinking water are greatly disturbed and demand that their water be made pure and safe.

Since neither Congress nor the courts have provided a uniform, clear and precise definition of acceptable and unacceptable risk levels, executive agencies have inherited the task of defining such boundaries. These agencies, in turn, have looked to their risk assessment scientists for technical answers to values questions, resulting in may cases, in an endless loop of quantitative answers to qualitative questions.

Lacking uniform national standards, regional, state or local consensus-building should be pursued on an issue-by-issue basis. Meanwhile, in the absence of legislative leadership, clarity and continuity, we as scientists must strive to establish consensus on how we will proceed in protecting the environment and human health, while maintaining our institutions and standard of living.

Outstanding Issues

Opposing viewpoints representing competing interests must be carefully considered. Pesticide groundwater contamination issues of the past decade that remain to be addressed include:

● *Are federal drinking water standards suitable as groundwater protection standards?*

MCLs (maximum contaminant levels) are risk management concentrations created by EPA to regulate public drinking water supplies and protect public health. MCLs for carcinogens reflect different risk levels, some set at greater than the 1 in 10,000 lifetime risk level.

Point: Groundwater standards should be designed to uniformly protect the resource based on health effects toxicology data. There should be no benefit/risk considerations used to determine a groundwater standard or any risk management input. MCLs, designed as regulatory concentrations for drinking water supplies, are not suitable for use as groundwater protection standards.

Counterpoint: MCLs provide real world achievable levels of groundwater protection. It is impossible to protect the resource down to levels which, in some cases, are below today's analytical capabilities.

● *Can separate groundwater protection standards and MCLs co-exist?*

Different standards often are set for different uses of a single resource. For example, truck and automobile speed limits may differ on a given highway. Streams also receive different levels of protection and management based on water quality and their ability to provide recreation or other benefits. Non-uniformity in regulating a resource, according to its use, appears to have been accepted by government agencies.

Point: Given different protection missions, it is appropriate to have different standards for public drinking water systems and groundwater resource protection. Regulatory agencies argue for uniformity between drinking water and groundwater protection standards, yet accept differing levels of health protection provided by MCLs. Therefore, they should be able to accept and explain diversity in resource standards.

Counterpoint: Water is water and it should all be clean enough to drink whether in a stream, an aquifer or coming from a tap. Furthermore, it is costly to increase the complexity of rules and regulations governing the variety of water uses. Insufficient staff and limited resources make implementation of and compliance with a multi-faceted water resource protection scheme difficult. To maintain a competitive business climate and to streamline the regulatory process, one set of standards should be developed, particularly at the national level.

● *Are agrichemical bans justified based on risk assessment criteria?*

Point: Such agricultural bans of pesticides are justified, if regulators determine that the pesticide, when normally used, poses an unreasonable risk to human health or the environment. If the public supports such findings, then the chemical should be banned. Human health and environmental protection are more important than preserving the use of a dangerous chemical. If the chemical is consistently found in the groundwater/drinking water at levels equal or above health concern, its use should be banned.

Counterpoint: The benefit/risk process is a valid mechanism to determine whether pesticide usage results in unacceptable environmental degradation or human health risks. Basing a pesticide ban on theoretical risk calculations alone, without considering the inherent benefits of pesticide use, is inappropriate and likely to cause unnecessary economic hardship.

Economic food protection depends on the protection offered by pesticides. Without such chemicals, consumers could face unacceptable food costs and periods of scarcity or unavailability. Unfortunately, pesticide use may result in groundwater contamination. Simply finding a pesticide, its metabolites or formulation materials in groundwater does not mean that it is in any way a threat to public health.

● *Is a "risk-neutral" complex-mixtures-additivity approach appropriate public health policy?*

Contamination of drinking water by more than one substance is common. Drinking water standards or advisories usually are based on the potential toxic effects of a single substance any may not account for the possibility of antagonistic, additive or synergistic effects.

Lacking data on potential interactive effects, regulatory agencies may use an additivity approach. For non-carcinogens, the concentration of each substance found in a water sample is divided by its standard, advisory or other designated concentration and the various ratios are added. If the sum of these ratios is equal to or greater than one, a water use advisory may be issued.

This additivity approach can be termed "risk neutral". Similarly, when no interactive effects toxicology data are available, assuming potentiation or synergism in risk calculations could be termed "risk conservative" and less than additive effects "risk liberal".

Point: When evaluating the potential risks posed by two or more contaminants in drinking water and lacking data to the contrary, a risk neutral approach is inappropriate. The risk conservative approach, a "worst case" analysis technique commonly employed by environmental and health agencies, is proper policy.

Counterpoint: Lacking data that chemicals potentiate each other, a risk neutral policy is more than sufficient given the inherently conservative nature of contaminant risk assessment.

● *Should groundwater sampling focus on "routine monitoring" or "at risk" areas?*

Point: Lacking a clear understanding of the extent of private well contamination in the U.S., regional or national baseline data must be obtained before targeted monitoring should be performed.

Counterpoint: If the goal of monitoring is to protect the most fragile parts of the groundwater resource and those persons at highest risk from exposure to groundwater contaminants, at-risk areas should receive the highest priority sampling, especially in an era of limited funding.

● *Can standard toxicological research better address real world exposures?*

On this particular topic, point-counterpoint arguments are difficult to propose. Relating real world exposures to potential human health impacts is difficult due to databases unsuited to answering such questions. In our opinion, toxicological research could be better targeted toward answering the needs of

In 1962, publication of *Silent Spring* brought an awareness to the public that pesticides were affecting non-target organisms and damaging the natural environment. Food chain effects became public knowledge, resulting in citizen concern that these contaminants could affect human health.

Integrated Pest Management—IPM—is an approach to pest control that relies far less on blanket spraying of chemicals than on a sophisticated understanding of both plants and pests—the mechanics, chemistry, and biology of natural systems.

health and environmental professionals who must answer queries related to the normal household use of contaminated drinking water.

For pesticides, if the regulatory community's primary research goal is to register or re-register these substances, data probably will not be generated to directly answer even the most common questions asked by individuals whose drinking water supply is contaminated by pesticides. Providing communities with pesticide-contaminated water supplies with health advice based more on science than policy could result in a populace more willing to recognize and assume reasonable risks associated with agricultural production.

Conclusion

Reaching consensus on what is acceptable or unacceptable risk, based on a safety standard, may be impossible in the near term. It is clear, however, that lacking such consensus, the debate on issues like those presented above will continue to swirl in a state of public point and counterpoint.

Risk assessment and risk management decisions are based on a process which is itself based on laws and/or values determinations of a law's intent. If we spend major portions of our professional lives attempting to second guess the intent of environmental and health protection laws, the public good that these laws strive to protect may be the ultimate loser in the process. (pp. 11–13)

David A. Belluck and Sally L. Benjamin, ''Pesticides and Human Health: Defining Acceptable and Unacceptable Risk Levels,'' in Journal of Environmental Health, *Vol, 53, No. 1, July-August, 1990, pp. 11–13.*

Integrated Pest Management Systems In Action

It's a beautiful summer day. You go out in your backyard to sit in the shade of your favorite tree. But to your dismay, you discover that caterpillars are gnawing away on leaves that are already partly chewed. What should you do?

> A. Call a tree-care company and tell it to spray the tree with the most potent insecticide it has.
>
> B. Ignore the problem and let nature take its course.
>
> C. Prune the infested limbs, and pull off all the caterpillars by hand.
>
> D. Spray with a biological pesticide like Bt, which will kill caterpillars—and only caterpillars.

If this feels like one of those trick questions that made you dread multiple-choice tests, it's because there is no ''right'' answer. Depending on the circumstances, any one of these four approaches—or some combination of them—might be an appropriate way to tackle pests on lawn trees and shrubs.

Thirty or 40 years ago, the answer would have been immediate and unthinking: ''Spray.'' At that point, pesticides like DDT seemed like miracle cures for pest problems. After all, DDT wiped out malaria in the U.S. almost single-handedly by eradicating the mosquitoes that spread the disease. As we eventually discovered, DDT also quickly worked its way into the food chain, where it damaged the nervous and reproductive systems of animals, including humans.

We understand a lot more now than we used to about the complexity of the natural world and how our attitudes affect it. We've learned that we can't keep pumping tons of chemicals into the environment without dangerous consequences. Our understanding of the dangers of pesticides and the horrible cycle we can get into when a pest builds up resistance to them is pointing the way toward a safer alternative—integrated pest management (IPM).

IPM is an approach to pest control that relies far less on blanket spraying of chemicals than on a sophisticated understanding of both plants and pests—the mechanics, chemistry, and biology of natural systems.

Applying IPM to ornamental landscaping doesn't necessarily preclude spraying. It does require knowing enough about the plant—and the pest—to be able to evaluate all the options for tackling a pest problem. The ultimate prescription to upgrade your tree's health is then based on short- and long-term effectiveness, environmental safety and cost, and integrating the best options into a management program. Pesticides are used only if nothing else works. The goal isn't to obliterate every pest on the tree but to achieve the maximum amount of good with the minimum amount of harm.

Looking at three landscape firms that have adopted IPM in recent years will give you some idea of how it works and what you can expect if you decide to try an IPM approach. The landscape companies featured vary in size from a small, locally known firm to a large, well-known tree-care company.

White Oak Pest Management, Inc. of Manassas, Virginia, is small enough that its staff IPM expert, Ed Milhous, can give every site his personal attention. White Oak, which concentrates on small trees, shrubs, and ground covers, now bases its entire maintenance service on IPM. Milhous lists the elements in White Oak's intensive IPM program: "Good cultural (caretaking) practices, including the use of resistant varieties, proper pruning, fertilization, and mulching.

"Our service is built around the key-plant/key-pest concept," says Milhous. "A study at the University of Maryland several years ago indicated that certain plants in certain situations have a disproportionate share of troubles. For example, one would expect azaleas in the sun to have lacebugs, dogwoods in droughty spots to have borers, almost anything in a parking-lot island to have problems.

"We use the University's pest-appearance timetable to help schedule monitoring, and pay special attention to those red-flag plants and situations."

Milhous says his staff does a lot of pruning, almost always "drop-crotching" (cutting a branch off where it attaches to the tree) instead of shearing. "The interesting thing about pruning this way is that many problems just disappear. We have seen heavy infestations of armored scale on plants when we began thinning them, and when we came back to check for crawlers, there were none left.

"The longer we take care of a site," says Milhous, "the more predators and fewer pests we see. In fact, other than for weeds, we hardly spray anything on landscapes that have been under our care for three years or longer." In the rare instances when White Oak does spray (the company bought only $300 worth of pesticides last year), it uses products that are mostly "soap, oil, Mavrik, and Orthene (low-toxicity pesticides)."

White Oak's clients—and their plants—benefit from White Oak's intensive approach, but that level of care doesn't come cheap.

American Tree Care of South Hampton, New York, is a bit larger than White Oak. When it adopted IPM several years ago, it had to drop about 600 customers serviced under a traditional chemical spray program. It now claims about 400 IPM clients, so this was no small sacrifice in the name of environmental conscience.

The first year it used an IPM approach, American Tree cut pesticide spraying by 73 percent. Now it only sprays "individual plants when absolutely necessary with materials that are least disruptive to the natural environment," says owner John Holmes.

In the short run, using IPM to control the pests on plants in our cities and around our homes will probably continue to be expensive for homeowners and tree firms alike. But those costs will come down. And in the long run IPM will save us all money: It's better for our health, it's better for our environment—and it's better for your tree.

In looking for alternatives to full-strength insecticides to control pests on trees, researchers mixed soaps with smaller amounts of pesticide. They found that soaps not only control pests but can also act as an adhesive, keeping the mixture on the plant longer.

The firm also has been able to steadily decrease the toxicity of the pesticides it must use, thanks to careful monitoring of pest life cycles to identify the most vulnerable stages for chemical intervention. Also, more intensive caretaking practices such as pruning, feeding, and mulching aid in reducing the need for more and stronger pesticides. By American Tree's third season using IPM, more than 90 percent of the materials it was using were relatively non-toxic and the firm was making a profit equal to what it had made using traditional spray methods.

American Tree credits part of its success to its use of an innovative software program. The Arbor Tracking System enables the firm not only to "inventory, monitor, diagnose, make control decisions, and treat client properties," says Holmes, but also to issue reports tracking everything from the species and locations of a client's plants to the treatments a particular plant has received over the years.

Perhaps success stories such as this helped convince Davey Tree Experts early this year to announce plans to introduce new programs that would reduce its use of traditional pesticides up to 80 percent by 1990. Davey, based in Kent, Ohio, provides residential tree and lawn care services nationwide and is one of the biggest in the business.

The firm's announcement followed several years of experimenting with IPM. In several cities around the country, Davey cut down on spraying traditional herbicides and insecticides by about 50 percent while increasing its use of alternative materials and better targeting insects, diseases, and plant disorders.

Once Davey discovered that the IPM approach could kill just as many weeds and insects as cover spraying, the company decided to implement what it calls the "Plant Health Care" approach on a company-wide basis.

In looking for alternatives to full-strength insecticides to control pests on trees, Davey researchers mixed soaps with smaller amounts of pesticide. They found that soaps not only control pests but can also act as an adhesive, keeping the mixture on the plant longer. Company researchers are continuing to test alternative products as potential pesticide substitutes, including mineral, Neem, and citrus oils, and plant-derived pesticides such as Rotenone and Pyrethrum.

Davey researchers are projecting another 25 percent drop in traditional pesticide use in its tree-care activities this year. New application equipment and spraying techniques that reduce drift, as well as more effective plant monitoring by trained field staff, will help Davey achieve this goal.

At the same time that Davey is upgrading its technology, it is training its employees to identify more kinds of plants and plant diseases while educating them in the importance of early detection and surveillance and in how weather patterns affect both plants and pests.

A landscape company the size of Davey Tree Experts, which serves thousands of clients every year, can't provide services on as intensive a level as a small company like White Oak Pest Management. Davey can't afford to hire the number of university-trained entomologists, horticulturists, arborists, and agronomists it would take to staff such an effort—not if it wants to keep its prices at levels customers are willing to pay.

What Davey can and does do is rely on experts on its national research and development staff to come up with ways the company can cut back on spraying and implement features of IPM. The research staff is topnotch and guided by nationally recognized experts such as Dr. Roger Funk. While the techniques they develop are more sophisticated than conventional "cover" spraying, they are basic enough to be mastered by hundreds of Davey employees without their having to get a degree in entomology.

Plant-care firms like Davey Tree Experts, White Oak Pest Management, and American Tree Care are aided in their search for alternatives to traditional pesticides by the growing number of biotechnology companies working to locate and create biological controls that will attack a specific pest.

Biological pesticides are naturally occurring chemicals that can be produced in the laboratory. Although it will be several years before many of these biologically engineered products reach the marketplace, a few are performing well enough in the laboratory to be made available now. Three or four varieties of *Bacillus thuringiensis* or Bt are now commonly used, and about 100 types are being tested.

A new company called Mycogen has developed a product that's ready for the market. Called M-one, it contains *Bacillus thuringiensis variety san diego*—an effective controller of potato-beetle larvae. Products like M-one interrupt the life cycle of the insect rather than poisoning the pest chemically.

It will also be a while before the cost of biological controls makes them affordable for a lot of landscape companies—and certainly before you and I will be able to buy them over the counter. This is another field where research and expanded production will lead us in the right direction. Already, prices are coming down as more and more companies enter the field.

Will integrated pest management take hold throughout the landscape-maintenance industry? To some people it's more a question of when than whether. The science and technology of IPM are advancing every day. If you visualize the process as a 10-rung ladder, we are at the second rung and climbing. Citizens are increasingly opposed to widespread pesticide use. The government is likely to continue to restrict, and in some cases ban, the use of pesticides on landscape plants.

Add to those prospects the experience of companies like American Tree that make a profit using IPM, and adopting integrated pest management begins to seem like good business sense. Add to that the effect on the rest of the industry when a giant like Davey embraces IPM, and it begins to seem inevitable.

In the short run, using IPM to control the pests on plants in our cities and around our homes will probably continue to be expensive for homeowners and tree firms alike. But those costs will come down. And in the long run IPM will save us all money: It's better for our health, it's better for our environment—and it's better for your tree. (pp. 61–4)

Zak Mettger and Gary Moll, "IPM: Best Approach to Pest Control," in American Forests, *Vol. 95, Nos. 1 & 2, January-February, 1989, pp. 61–4.*

> **In the short run, using IPM to control the pests on plants in our cities and around our homes will probably continue to be expensive. But in the long run IPM will save us all money: It's better for our health, it's better for our environment—and it's better for your tree.**

Sources for Further Study

Balling, Steven S. "Managing Pesticides for a Safe Food Supply: An Industry Program." *Association of Food and Drug Officials Journal* 54, No. 2 (April 1990): 19–29.
 Asserts that health risks from agricultural chemicals are less than the public commonly believes, and calls for the food industry to educate the public to this point of view.

Carson, Rachel. *Silent Spring.* Boston: Houghton Mifflin Co., 1962, 368 p.
 Influential and controversial indictment of the widespread use of chemical pesticides, warning of their potentially dangerous effects on birds, animals, and humans. Carson's book is widely considered to have initiated the first controls on indiscriminate pesticide use and research into their effects.

Dennehy, T. J., et. al. "Managing Pest Resistance to Pesticides: A Challenge to New York's Agriculture." *New York Food and Life Sciences* 17, No. 4 (1987): 13–17.
 Examines research into insect resistance to pesticides, with the objective of developing pesticide-use procedures that are compatible with other control strategies used in integrated pest management programs.

Edwards, Clive E. "The Importance of Integration in Sustainable Agricultural Systems." *Agricultural Ecosystems and Environments* 27, Nos. 1–4 (November 1989): 25–35.
 Outlines financial and environmental advantages of integrated agricultural systems over conventional farming practices.

Efron, Edith, *The Apocalyptics: Cancer and the Big Lie—How Environmental Politics Controls What We Know about Cancer.* New York: Simon and Schuster, 1984, 589 p.
 Investigates what is termed "a complex corruption of science and a prolonged deception fo the public" with regard to issues of industrial carcinogens (including pesticides), environmental cancer, and cancer prevention.

Ehart, Orlo R., et. al. "Pesticide Wastes Disposal." *Pollution Technology Review* 148 (1988): 23–34.
 Reviews current pesticide disposal regulations and discusses the need for less burdensome and more feasible solutions to the disposal problem.

Flint, Mary Louise, and Bosch, Robert van den. *Introduction to Integrated Pest Management.* New York: Plenum Press, 1981, 240 p.
 Presents a comprehensive review of the basic principles and methods of Integrated Pest Management (IPM). Chapters are devoted to defining what a pest is; a history of pest control; assessing the economic, social, and environmental costs of different pest management systems; the philosophy of IPM; IPM procedures; case histories of IPM programs; the IMP specialist; and a prediction of the future of IPM systems.

Gosling, Morris. "Extinction to Order." *New Scientist* 121, No. 1654 (4 March 1989): 44–9.
 Account of programs instituted to eradicate the coypu, classified as a vertebrate pest, in Great Britain.

Gotsch, N., and Rieder, P. "Forecasting Future Developments in Crop Protection." *Crop Protection* 9, No. 2 (April 1990): 83–9.
 Surveys new biotechnologies designed to protect crops, including the use of hyperparasites and predators in pest control.

Halstead, Andrew. "The Use and Abuse of Garden Chemicals." *Chemistry and Industry,* No. 22 (21 November 1988): 718–20.
 Discusses common misuse of often-hazardous garden chemicals, including pesticides, and offers safety tips for home gardeners.

Hileman, Bette. "Alternative Agriculture." *Chemical and Engineering News* 68, No. 10 (5 March 1990): 26–40.
 Approaches a definition of "alternative agriculture" and its aims, focusing on different methods of raising livestock. The author also includes discussion of different methods of pest control.

Hoy, Marjorie A. "The Importance of Biological Control in U.S. Agriculture." *Journal of Sustainable Agriculture* 1, No. 1 (1990): 59–79.
 Identifies the most damaging weed and insect pests to crops and outlines the advantages of fighting pests with biological controls instead of chemical pesticides.

Khan, M. A., and Liang, Tung. "Mapping Pesticide Contamination Potential." *Environmental Management* 13, No. 2 (March-April 1989): 233–42.
 Presents a method of screening pesticides for groundwater contamination potential.

Kourik, Robert. "Controlling Pests without Chemical Warfare." *Garbage* II, No. 2 (March-April 1990): 22–8.

Offers Integrated Pest Management (IPM) strategies for controlling and eradicating common household pests, including ants, roaches, mice, flies, and fleas.

Leslie, Ann. "Pest Management for Local Governments." *American City and Country* 106, No. 3 (March 1991): 62, 64.
   Proposes a model pest management program for implementation by local governments.

Marco, Gino L.; Hollingworth, Robert M.; and Durham, William, eds. *Silent Spring Revisited*. Washington, D.C.: American Chemical Society, 1987, 214 p.
   Collection of essays based on a symposium sponsored by the Pesticide Subcommittee of the Committee on Environmental Improvement addressing environmental and health issues concerning pesticides.

Marer, Patrick J. *The Safe and Effective Use of Pesticides*. Edited by Mary Louise Flint. Statewide Integrated Pest Management Project, Division of Agriculture and Natural Resources, Publication 3324. Davis: University of California, 1988, 387 p.
   Manual designed to teach safe and effective ways of using pesticides. The volume includes chapters on pest identification and management, pesticide laws and regulations, hazards associated with pesticide use, protective measures for people and the environment, emergency procedures in case of accident, effective pesticide use, and pesticide application equipment,

Pimentel, David, et. al. "Low-Input Sustainable Agriculture Using Ecological Management Practices." *Agriculture Ecosystems and Environment* 27, Nos. 1–4 (November 1989): 3–24.
   Advocates the development of a complex holistic approach to agriculture that will be productive while protecting the environment. A section entitled "Pests and Their Control" recommends the use of bioenvironmental controls including natural enemies, crop rotation, host plant resistance, sanitation, timed planting, tillage, and crop and genetic diversity instead of reliance on chemical pesticides.

Popkin, Roy. " 'Alternative Farming': A Report." *EPA Journal* 14, No. 3 (April 1988): 28–30.
   Defines alternative farming, surveys some environmental concerns that are leading farmers to institute alternative methods, and outlines some trends in farming practices and consumer demands that encourage alternative methods. Popkin also discusses integrated pest management programs.

Sattaur, Otto. "A New Crop of Pest Controls." *New Scientist* 119, No. 1621 (14 July 1988): 48–51, 54.
   Account of the successful integrated pest management program (IPM) instituted in Peru's Cañete Valley cotton fields in 1956. This program was the first large-scale implementation of IPM anywhere in the world.

Schneider, Keith. "Agriculture is Learning to Fight Nature with Nature." *New York Times* (28 February 1988): 7.
   Gives examples of the growing use of biological and natural pest controls, assesses their effectiveness, and notes some reasons for their adoption.

Shapiro, Michael. "Toxic Substances Policy." In *Public Policies for Environmental Protection*, by Roger C. Dower, et. al., edited by Paul R. Portney, pp. 195–242. Washington, D.C.: Resources for the Future, 1990.
   Defines pesticides, briefly surveys health and environmental concerns regarding pesticide use, and discusses the role of various government agencies in implementing regulations.

Simonian, Lane. "Pesticide Use in Mexico: Decades of Abuse." *The Ecologist* 18, Nos. 2–3 (1988): 82–7.
   Examines the impact of the "Green Revolution"—advanced technologies designed to increase agricultural yields—in Mexico since the 1940s, focusing on the ecological damage and health problems caused by pesticides.

Sweet, Robert D. "Pesticide Regulation and the Vegetable Industry." *New York Food and Life Sciences* 17, No. 4 (1987): 4–6.
    Expressed concern that despite stringent regulations, pesticide use on vegetables is still perceived as dangerous. Sweet calls for public education to stress the benefits of pesticides.

Thomas, Larry. "Pesticides and Endangered Species: New Approaches to Evaluating Impacts." *Endangered Species Technical Bulletin* XIV, Nos. 1–2 (January-February 1989): 1, 7.
    Notes that the use of both herbicides and insecticides contributes to the endangerment of plant and animal species, and surveys attempts to evaluate the impact of pesticides on endangered species.

Torgersen, Torolf R., and Torgerson, Anna S. "Saving Forests the Natural Way." *Pest Control* 96, Nos. 1–2 (January-February 1990): 31–3, 46.
    Includes examples of biological pest controls implemented by the United States Forest Service.

12: Population Growth and Overcrowding

Population Growth, Resource Use, and Environmental Quality

The Debate

Classical and Neoclassical Economists

Over centuries of debate, prevailing opinion over population growth's effects has shifted back and forth with ideology and economic conditions. The classical economists—notably Adam Smith, Thomas Malthus, and David Ricardo—reacted to the arguments of the earlier mercantilist writers of the 16th to 18th centuries. Mercantilists such as Jean Bodin, reflecting the rise of nation-states and vigorous commercial expansion, believed "one should never fear there being too many subjects or too many citizens, seeing there is no wealth or strength but in men."

Malthus and other classical economists, writing at the start of the 19th century when accelerating population and industrial growth were raising demands for food faster than English agriculture could respond, saw real wages falling and food imports rising. They emphasized the limits that scarce farmland imposed on agricultural expansion, arguing that applying ever more labor and other inputs to a fixed land base would inevitably bring diminishing returns, reducing output per worker. The classical economists also stressed the tendency for population to rise with any widespread improvement in living standards, through lower mortality rates and earlier marriage. In their view, this tendency continually depressed real wages toward a subsistence level while rents to landowners grew.

This stress on the inherent limits to the availability of natural resources and consequent diminishing returns to other inputs and rising production costs is still the core of contemporary Malthusian perspectives. These concerns, however, now encompass scarcities not only of agricultural land but also of exhaustible resources such as fossil fuels (oil, coal, and natural gas) and limits on the capacity of global life-support systems to withstand human disruptions.

Most contemporary rebuttals of Malthusian viewpoints repeat objections that were first raised at least 150 years ago. The utopian Condorcet argued in 1795 that scientific advance would offset diminishing returns: "New instruments, machines, and looms can add to man's strength and improve at once the quality and accuracy of man's productions, and can diminish the time and labor that has to be expended on them. . . . A very small amount of ground will be able to produce a great quantity of supplies . . . , more goods will be obtained for a small outlay, the manufacture of articles will be achieved with less wastage of raw materials and will make better use of them." (pp. 221–22)

The views of 20th century neoclassical economists reflect the enormous 19th century expansion of land under cultivation beyond the borders of Europe, the diminished importance of agriculture in modern industrial economies, and a century of rapid technological progress and declining relative prices for resource-based commodities. . . .

> To a certain extent, labor and capital can substitute for materials in the manufacturing process, but no amount of additional kneading and baking will produce more bread from an ever-decreasing supply of wheat.

Estimates of the carrying capacity of the earth relative to human populations range from 7.5 billion people to over 40 billion people.

[Neoclassical economics] emphasizes the adaptability of modern economies through market-induced substitution and innovation. If some resource cost rose, industry would reduce costs by substituting other materials, labor, or capital. Consumers would also reduce purchases of commodities that use the resource intensively in favor of other kinds of goods. If the resource scarcity were local, rising prices would make imports from other regions more attractive and trade patterns would shift. Neoclassical economic models imply that if substitution possibilities remain sufficiently great, income per capita can be sustained with rising population even if the resource is ultimately exhausted.

Technological change has understandably come to the forefront of modern economic thought. There is ample evidence that increasing resource scarcities, signaled by rising relative prices, induce innovators to develop and introduce new production processes. The Industrial Revolution is often portrayed as a series of technological innovations induced by successive resource bottlenecks. (p. 223)

Neoclassical economists also emphasize the ability of markets to adapt to resource scarcities over time. Anticipated future scarcities induce businesses to hold supplies off the market in expectation of higher future prices, and to spend more to discover and develop new supplies. Even though those still unborn exert no direct market influence to preserve resources for their use, anticipation of future demand represent them indirectly by bidding up the asset values of resource stocks.

These insights are valuable in explaining how market economies have dealt effectively with resource constraints. But most contemporary economists acknowledge that there are limits to their applicability. Prices can guide market adjustment processes only if resources can be bought and sold, which presupposes that they can be owned. Many important resources are not privately owned, usually because it is impossible to segregate one person's portion from another's and reserve it for exclusive use. (pp. 223–24)

Unless the community collectively exercises control over the use of such "common property" resources, through legal and regulatory restraints in modern states and by customs or decisions of the leaders in traditional societies, scarcity feeds on itself. Users assume that if they take less of the depleted resource, others will just take more; if they find ways to increase its availability, others will garner the fruits of their efforts. Or, if the resource is vast, like the atmosphere, their small sacrifices to preserve it would have insignificant effects. Even if market processes could be relied on to deal effectively with privately owned resources, the importance of common property resources in our basic life-support systems gives grounds for concern about future scarcities in the face of increasing demands on them.

But market processes are also short-sighted about future private demands. A business that holds resources off the market for future sales ties up capital that could be profitably invested elsewhere, and expects an equivalent rate of return. Even if returns on alternative investment are no more than seven percent per year, one could justify conserving a resource for 100 years if its value were expected to rise more than 800 times over that period.

Natural Science Views

Natural scientists see other limitations of neoclassical analyses of population and resources. Economic models can be misleading if extrapolated too far. For example, typical "long-term" economic growth models imply that with the population growing at a constant rate, output will also reach a rate of equilibrium growth determined by the rates of technological advance and labor force increase.

This conflicts with the scientist's knowledge of equilibrium in finite natural systems. If world population were to grow continuously at the 1987 rate of 1.67 percent per year, then the earth's land area, excluding Antarctica, would be packed solid by 2667. Although Antarctica is chilly, in a pinch it could provide additional standing room—for seven more years. The year 2674 may seem remote, but if we look 686 years back in time we find Marco Polo returned from his journeys to China, the great cathedrals of Notre Dame and Chartres already dedicated, and the era of modern warfare opening in Europe with gunpowder introduced from the East.

Continuing exponential growth of output is, of course, equally impossible. Automobiles, whose numbers are increasing more rapidly than the human population, would occupy all available space much sooner, starting from certain cities where they have already done so.

Scientists also see limits to substitution possibilities. To a certain extent, labor and capital can substitute for materials in the manufacturing process, but no amount of additional kneading and baking will produce more bread from an ever-decreasing supply of wheat. More fundamentally, energy is essential to all life-sustaining processes, which dissipate useful energy. Substituting for the decreased richness or accessibility of mineral ores generally requires more energy per unit of output. Substituting for the decreased availability of agricultural land by raising yields per hectare generally requires more energy per unit of output, in the form of labor, chemical, and machinery inputs. While energy can be used more efficiently in these processes and also in the conversion of energy sources to useful forms, nothing could be substituted for increasingly scarce energy if low-cost, concentrated sources were depleted.

Biologists sometimes apply the concept of carrying capacity to questions of human population pressure. In population biology, carrying capacity is the maximum population of a species that its habitat can sustain. In a density-dependent species, like fruit flies in a bottle, it is the limit to which population will grow. Estimates of the carrying capacity of the earth relative to human populations range from 7.5 billion people to over 40 billion people.

Such an application of the carrying capacity concept is misleading. Many countries that lack agricultural resources, such as Kuwait and Korea, can readily trade for food with nonagricultural exports. Furthermore, the implicit analogy to nonhuman species, which do not approach man's ability to modify both his environment and his way of using it, is faulty. From the beginning, humans have adapted to population pressures. Hunting societies used fire to drive game and to reduce cover, altering the landscape in the process. When prized large mammals became scarcer, these people broadened their diet to include more plentiful food sources. Technological and cultural responses to population growth have been accelerating ever since. Agriculture developed largely in response to population density, from shifting cultivation with long fallow periods to short fallow and crop rotations dependent on organic manuring to intensive monocultures using high-yielding seed varieties, irrigation, chemicals, and energy inputs.

Moreover, social mechanisms that regulate population growth are found in both traditional and modern societies. Outmigration has always been a response to population pressure. Prolonged breastfeeding and sexual taboos restricted births in hunting societies to well under half of the biological potential. Fertility in preindustrial Western Europe was restrained by inheritance laws that delayed marriage. Contemporary societies also resort to contraception and abortion. In societies subject to high mortality rates, mechanisms have evolved to keep fertility high, such as early and universal marriage.

But human adaptations often impinge on local and global ecosystems. A large and growing share of the biosphere's net primary production has been appropriated for human use. Diverting more of the earth's biomass for human use leaves less for the maintenance of the biosphere, destroying other species' habitat, impoverishing ecosystems, and accelerating extinction.

Examples of disturbed natural systems are widespread. Worldwide, the burning of fossil fuels for energy and other processes leading to large emissions of "greenhouse gases" have disrupted the carbon cycle and global heat balance,

A large and grow~~g~~
share of the bi~~ere's~~
net primary ~~priated~~
has been a~~uction~~. Diverting
for huma~~arth's bio-~~
more of~~man use~~
mass f~~for the main-~~
leav~~f the biosphere,~~
ter~~ng other species'~~
~~d,~~ impoverishing
~~s~~tems, and acceler-
~~g~~ extinction.

setting off a process of substantial climate modification and warming. Scientists emphasize that they cannot predict with any certainty what will happen as such critical ecosystems are disturbed and that, by the time the consequences are evident, the changes may be irreversible. The ecological limits being tested are not protected by rising prices, since the threatened resources—biological diversity, climate, and communal woodlands—are mainly in the public domain.

The Population Prospect

Although the debate about population growth and resources is long-standing, recent demographic developments are unprecedented. When Malthus wrote at the end of the 19th century, world population was growing slowly in both absolute and relative terms. World population was about one billion, and it took 130 years to double. The third billion was added in only 30 years, in 1960, the fourth billion was reached 14 years after that, in 1974, and the fifth billion 13 years later, in 1987. The scale of current population growth is unlike anything seen before. More than 85 million people, the size of Mexico, are currently added to the world's population each year.

Also unique is the shift in population growth to the less developed countries. Until the 1930s, population grew more rapidly in the richer countries. High mortality checked growth in the poorer countries; but since World War II, vaccines, antibiotics, insecticides, and improved sanitation and nutrition have markedly reduced their death rates. Birth rates have fallen much more slowly, as marriage ages have gradually risen and contraception use has spread. Since 1950, 85% of the total population increase has been in the Third World.

Dramatic as these changes are, they are overshadowed by the downturn in the world population growth rate in the early 1970s. Annual growth reached two percent in the late 1960s, implying that population would double within 35 years, but the rate then dropped off. Thus a progression of ever-shortening doubling times that began in prehistoric times has finally been reversed. This change does not relieve the pressures of rapid growth—*absolute* annual increments are projected to rise to a peak of about 90 million in the late 1990s—but we can now see the passing flood crest of population growth.

As of 1987, the world's demographic future holds another doubling of population and an increasing divergence between developing countries other than China and the industrial world. Current United Nations medium projections, assuming fairly rapid declines in birth and death rates in developing countries, foresee the global population stabilizing toward the end of the next century at about 10.2 billion people. These projections put an *additional* five billion people in the developing world.

Consequences of Population Expansion

Later marriage and falling fertility, rather than the Malthusian checks—war, famine, and pestilence—have reduced growth rates, even as mortality has fallen. Modernization and rising living standards, not poverty and resource limits, have checked population growth.

Although rapid population growth has strained the capacities of developing economies to provide food, jobs, and municipal investments, living standards have risen in almost all countries. During periods of maximum growth rates, income and food production, school enrollment and literacy, life expectancy, and other quality of life indicators have risen. Population increases may have complicated the task of development but clearly has not precluded some degree of success.

Expanding Cropland

Until World War II, the world's growing population could be fed by simply expanding the amount of farmland. This expansion was not only limited to the New World. Vast new areas were put under the plow in the Soviet Union, southern Asia, and Africa as well as in North and South America. During the first part of the 20th century, pioneers were clearing forests in southern Burma, battling malaria in the shadow of the Himalayas, and pushing cultivation northward into the Sahelian region of Africa.

The expanding farmlands have cut into other important ecosystems—temperate and tropical forests, grasslands, and wetlands. No area is immune to agricultural intensification. Almost a billion hectares of forests and woodlands have been cleared since 1850, about half of the total amount since prehistoric times. Temperate woodlands have suffered the greatest amount of conversion but population growth in the tropical third world has shifted the focus of land conversion. More than 11 million hectares of tropical forest—the size of Pennsylvania—have been cleared every year since 1980. But deforestation statistics might underestimate the actual situation. Even land that has only 10 to 20% of its original woody growth, or has been picked over by loggers is considered forested. A few trees may remain but the rich diversity of other plants and animals is often exterminated or reduced.

In semi-arid regions, tree density is dwindling as the result of foraging and fuelwood collection. The open savannas of the Sahel are rapidly being stripped of their remaining trees; annual fuelwood consumption alone exceeds annual tree growth by about thirty percent. In Niger, twice as many trees are cut down as planted. The United Nations Food and Agriculture Organization (FAO) estimates that about 75% of the two billion fuelwood users gather wood faster than it can grow back, and more than a million people cannot find enough wood to meet their needs.

In the humid tropics, forest conversion has imperiled the principal source of the world's biological diversity. Tropical forests are home to an uncharted wealth of animals and plants with value to agriculture, medicine, and science. The total extinction rate cannot be readily estimated because scientists, who so far have catalogued 1.5 million species, do not even know if another 1.5 million, 15 million, or even 30 million species remain to be classified. (pp. 224–29)

Like tropical rain forests, wetlands are biologically and ecologically productive ecosystems, providing a way of life for fish, crustaceans, amphibians, birds, and small mammals. Vast areas of wetlands, especially in the temperate zones, have been drained over the last 150 years for farming. Between 25 and 50% of the world's wetlands have been lost to date.

The amount of grasslands and pastures has remained relatively stable (when compared to farmland) since the middle of last century. But there has been some notable conversion. Most often the farmer's plow tills the best rangeland. Herders must then move onto less productive soils and wild herds, left with nowhere to go, often perish. Domestic cattle, even under "controlled" grazing, eat away vast areas of vegetative cover and expose the fragile lands to harsh wind and water erosion. Nutrients and organic matter are washed away because the soil can no longer hold water. Only desert remains. More than 60% of the world's rangelands have turned to sand—65 million hectares in Africa alone over the past 50 years.

Cultivation has also moved from the plains and valleys into the mountains. Watersheds, from the foothills of the Andes and the Himalayas to the highlands of Central America and Ethiopia, are stripped of soil that is almost twice as nutrient-rich as the remaining dirt. Productivity losses are particularly noticeable in the tropics and semi-arid regions. On densely populated Java, more than a million hectares of farmland are underproductive due to erosion and this area expands by 200,000 hectares every year. In Guatemala, farm productivity has been reduced by 40% due to erosion. And in Mexico, roughly two-thirds of the land is eroded in one way or another. The FAO estimates that erosion will extract 20% of the potential agricultural productivity by the end of this century.

Erosion also extracts off-site economic and environmental costs. Reservoirs are filling up with silt much faster than anticipated—two to three times faster in

The scale of current population growth is unlike anything seen before. More than 85 million people, the size of Mexico, are currently added to the world's population.

No area is immune to agricultural intensification. Almost a billion hectares of forests and woodlands have been cleared since 1850, about half of the total amount since prehistoric times.

Southeast Asia. The added soils abrade turbines, require additional water treatment, reduce fish populations, alter water routes, and ultimately shorten the lives of power and irrigation projects. Upstream devegetation also increases flooding after the rainy season and reduces dry season flows.

Technology and Increased Yields

Until 30 years ago, cultivating new lands was the principal means of raising agricultural production. Since the early 1960s, the situation has reversed; productivity has out-paced cropland expansion three to six times. Part of this is due to a global squeeze on available land in densely populated areas, such as China and Southeast Asia where there is less than one hectare of cropped land for every five persons. High-yield plant hybrids and inexpensive pesticides and fertilizers were developed in response to the scarcity of arable land.

The new technology and rising food demands also encouraged large irrigation projects. By 1980, one out of every six cultivated hectare was under irrigation and, because of the substantial capital investments, most farming innovations were concentrated on these lands. This technological package—hybrids, chemicals, and irrigation—spurred the "green revolution."

But this productivity has not come without environmental costs. The agricultural intensification over the past 20 years brought with it a panoply of ecological effects due to the widespread use of pesticides and chemical fertilizers. Previously benign insects and weeds have become major pests when their natural enemies were eradicated by chemical poisons. Other species have developed resistance to some pesticides, requiring heavier doses of more potent chemicals to keep them in check.

Pesticides also exert their toxic effects on humans. The World Health Organization estimates that hundreds of thousands of people die each year from acute pesticide poisoning. Chronic pesticide exposure is widespread, either in the air, as runoff into drinking water supplies, and as residue on food. And the risks are uncertain. Many pesticides frequently used in developed countries have not been thoroughly screened for health hazards. And many developing countries, in which the toxic effects of pesticides are exacerbated by malnutrition and disease, still use those that have been banned elsewhere.

Large-scale irrigation can also plague the farmers and rural planners who benefit from the assured water supply. Inadequate drainage, poor operation and maintenance, and excessive water loss during conveyance flood the land with unwanted water and markedly concentrate salts in the root zones. Providing the necessary drainage and efficient water transport can tack on substantial costs to water projects and is frequently deferred or neglected.

In India and Pakistan, for example, water tables have risen to within a few meters of the surface. About 10 million hectares of Indian land are not suitable for farming and salinization affects another 25 million hectares. In Pakistan, more than half of the Indus Basin canal command system, some 12 million hectares, is waterlogged and 40% is saline.

India illustrates the uncertain interplay between population growth, agricultural production, and land use. In this century, the Indian population has more than tripled to almost 800 million in 1987. The agricultural response has been equally dramatic.

In the first half of the century there was a massive expansion of cropland. Farm acreage jumped by more than 25 million hectares or 45% between 1890 and 1970. Other terrestrial ecosystems—forests, woodlands, grasslands, and scrub—were reduced by 30 to 40 percent. But because of the rapid population rise, the amount of agricultural land per person diminished sharply, from 0.39 to 0.23 hectares per person.

Irrigation and cropping intensity offset the relative scarcity of arable land. Irrigated acreage expanded almost nine-fold, from 2.6 million hectares (4.4% of the total arable land) in 1890 to 22.3 million hectares (26% of the total) in 1970.

Cropping intensity rose sharply on the irrigated land. Fallow area fell from 17 to 10% between 1930 and 1970. Almost 160 kilograms of chemical fertilizer were applied to each acre of irrigated land, especially in conjunction with high-yielding seed varieties.

The agricultural drive exerted its effects on the remaining non-farm land. Livestock, which are fed primarily crop residues rather than fodder crops, grew proportionally with the expanding acreage of farmland. But the ratio of livestock to people fell from 98:100 to 59:100 between 1900 and 1972 as pastures disappeared.

The trends in land use had a great impact on the rural poor. Most of the land conversion transformed common property to private ownership. This excluded a great number of poor households from the land on which they depended for livestock grazing, fuelwood, and raw materials for handicrafts.

Although some conversion programs were designed to alleviate rural poverty, most of the new cropland ended up in the hands of better-off households. For rural India, a valuable and accessible resource disappeared.

Future Population Growth and Agriculture

To feed twice as many people throughout the third world with improved diets, agricultural production must increase to about 10 billion tons of grain each year. To achieve this, all of the world's arable land would need to match the productivity of the average Iowan corn farm (7 tons per hectare). The current global average yield is 2.3 tons per hectare and Indian farmers manage barely half of that. These staggering figures raise doubts as to whether agricultural production can keep pace with the demands for food and non-food crops without severe pressures on the ecosystem.

In terms of absolute area, there is room to accommodate about twice the current amount of cropped land. An FAO assessment of 90 developing countries (excluding China) found that less than half of the potential agricultural land is now cultivated. But all of this available land (and water) is far from where the people are. China, India, Java, Egypt, and the Middle East, countries that account for most of the population of the developing countries, do not have an abundance of arable land. Rather, North and South America, Oceania, and parts of Africa, where population is relatively sparse, hold the promise of future expansion. Thus, extending production onto open land implies considerable global trade of manufactured goods for agricultural products by the food-starved countries. Extending cultivation in the tropics, apart from its impacts on forests and grasslands, depends on solving problems of soil fertility, pests, and disease.

Biotechnology could be the catalyst toward greater agricultural productivity. Genetically engineered vaccines and growth hormones are available that raise feed efficiency 25 to 40 percent. Nitrogen-fixing bacteria and plants can reduce dependence on chemical fertilizers and raise crop yields on nitrogen-poor tropical soil. Ultimately, scientists hope to develop plants that extract more energy from the sun and that survive and even flourish in drought, flooding, disease, high salinity, and extreme temperatures. The implications for agricultural yields and the use of marginal lands are enormous. According to the National Research Council on Agriculture, genetic engineering "will likely have an impact on agriculture comparable to that of Mendel's laws in the late 1800s." Such scientific changes make long-run forecasts based on existing agronomic technology highly speculative.

Adaptations to Population Growth

Although innovation is a successful response to scarcity, whether from population growth or resource depletion, the science often loses something in the

The agricultural intensification over the past 20 years brought with it a panoply of ecological effects due to the widespread use of pesticides and chemical fertilizers.

To feed twice as many people throughout the third world with improved diets, agricultural production must increase to about 10 billion tons of grain each year. To achieve this, all of the world's arable land would need to match the productivity of the average Iowan corn farm (7 tons per hectare). The current global average yield is 2.3 tons per hectare and Indian farmers manage barely half of that.

translation. Technology from the more-advanced countries is sometimes irrelevant or inappropriate to developing countries' economies, industrial capabilities, and levels of education.

Just as technology was able to grow with and adapt to population expansion in Europe and the New World, technological innovations must conform to the needs and social systems of developing countries. But it is not clear whether such farmer-initiated innovations can raise yields at the pace required by the exceptionally rapid population growth in sub-Saharan Africa and some other developing countries. European agricultural output grew one to two percent per year. Africa's current demographic growth, ranging up to nearly four percent annually, requires rates at least twice as high. Although communities do adapt to rising agricultural demands through evolution of land tenure arrangements and farming practices, Africa may not be able to keep pace.

Increasing population and demand for food induce farmers to use land and labor more intensively. As fallow periods shorten, more labor is needed to control weeds and provide supplemental soil nutrients. When farming shifts to annual or multiple cropping, green manures and animal wastes are required to maintain fertility. Since these require substantial additional labor and land inputs, eventually chemical fertilizers become economical.

There is a corresponding evolution in land preparation. When land is abundant, the lighter mid-slope soils tend to be cultivated first with hoes and other simple tools. These soils are relatively susceptible to erosion, so labor-intensive construction of bunds, ridges, and terraces often evolves as farming pressures increase. Agricultural demands also push cultivation into the valleys requiring extensive water control. By this stage, the energy requirements justify keeping draft animals and investing in heavy farm equipment.

Stump clearance, land leveling, terracing, drainage, and irrigation require substantial investments of time and labor that are not readily made unless individual property rights ensure that the long-term economic and environmental benefits will accrue to the investor and heirs.

This agricultural escalation involves more than just technological advances to succeed. Local rules governing inheritance, community membership, land tenure, and common property rights need to evolve along with agricultural intensification. Government actions that influence market accessibility and prices also affect agricultural adaptation. Time is required for institutions, customs, and policies to evolve.

Room to Maneuver

Agricultural progress is possible, despite resource limitations. China has raised net agricultural output since 1978 at an average rate of about seven percent per year, largely by putting more land under individual household management and improving farmers' incentives.

In sub-Saharan Africa, Malawi's agricultural output has also increased by more than seven percent annually since 1973, although its rural population density of 59 people per square kilometer is the third highest in Africa and the typical land holding is less than two hectares. Malawi's president, Kamuzu Banda, is also the Minister of Agriculture and has promoted agricultural research, the planting of diversified cash crops, fair market prices, and investments in rural road networks, farmer education, and other extension services.

The key to feeding the next five billion people is managing available resources wisely. Too often, government subsidies promote waste and degrade the resource base at heavy economic and environmental cost.

In most developing countries agricultural prices are kept low to benefit the urban minority. Consumer subsidies discourage more productive use of good agricultural land and spawn large factory farms, which drive the rural poor onto more marginal soils. At the other extreme, the United States, Japan, and Europe community keep agricultural prices artificially high to benefit the rural minority. This induces farmers to overuse chemicals, water and other inputs, producing costly surpluses and degrading rivers and aquifers.

Such policies retard constructive innovation while adding to environmental pressures. Agricultural scientists have developed farming systems for tropical areas that preserve soil fertility by reducing erosion and increasing organic nutrient availability. For example, the International Institute of Tropical Agriculture has developed a system of alley cropping that raises yields 40% by planting maize or cassava between rows of closely pruned leguminous trees, which provide wind protection, water retention, organic mulch, and residual soil nitrogen. Subsidized chemical fertilizers, however, bring down the costs for lost soil fertility and discourage the use of organic nutrients.

Integrated pest management—rotating crops, planting pest-resistant varieties, and carefully timing small chemical applications—is another way to increase yields and reduce dependence on chemical pesticides. This can be beneficial in the tropics, for crops such as rice, where large amounts of chemical pesticides are often prohibitively expensive. But many governments maintain generous pesticide subsidies that reduce farmers' incentives to adopt such programs.

These examples indicate the scope of the potential improvements in natural resource management. Population growth is also a major variable in resource management. In China, Korea, Cuba, and Sri Lanka, two mutually reinforcing strategies have lowered growth rates and stabilized the resource base. First, basic health care and family planning services have been widely accessible. There is little reason for families to limit the number of their children when two out of every five children die before the age of five from easily preventable or curable diseases. Where contraceptive supplies and information have not been broadly distributed, the majority of women who want to prevent or delay further births are not adequately protected.

In a larger sense, economic and social development has changed the conditions that perpetuate high fertility and mortality. Development strategies that expand urban and rural employment opportunities as rapidly as possible provide escapes from poverty and reduce the most severe of all resource wastages—human potential. (pp. 229–35)

Robert Repetto, "Renewable Resources and Population Growth: Past Experience and Future Prospects," in Population and Environment: A Journal of Interdisciplinary Studies, *Vol. 10, No. 4, Summer, 1989, pp. 221–36.*

> **One of the toughest things for a population biologist to reconcile is the contrast between his or her recognition that civilization is in imminent serious jeopardy and the modest level of concern that population issues generate among the public and even among elected officials.**

The Population Explosion

In the early 1930s, when we were born, the world population was just 2 billion; now it is more than two and a half times as large and still growing rapidly. The population of the United States is increasing much more slowly than the world average, but it has more than doubled in only six decades—from 120 million in 1928 to 250 million in 1990. Such a huge population expansion within two or three generations can by itself account for a great many changes in the social and economic institutions of a society. It also is very frightening to those of us who spend our lives trying to keep track of the implications of the population explosion.

One of the toughest things for a population biologist to reconcile is the contrast between his or her recognition that civilization is in imminent serious jeopardy and the modest level of concern that population issues generate among the public and even among elected officials.

Our own species, *Homo sapiens*, evolved a few hundred thousand years ago. Some ten thousand years ago, when agriculture was invented, probably no more than five million people inhabited Earth—fewer than now live in the San Francisco Bay Area.

Much of the reason for this discrepancy lies in the slow development of the problem. People are not scared because they evolved biologically and culturally to respond to short-term "fires" and to tune out long-term "trends" over which they had no control. Only if we do what does not come naturally—if we determinedly focus on what seem to be gradual or nearly imperceptible changes—can the outlines of our predicament be perceived clearly enough to be frightening.

Consider the *very* slow-motion origins of our predicament. It seems reasonable to define humanity as having first appeared some four million years ago in the form of australopithecines, small-brained upright creatures like "Lucy." Of course, we do not know the size of this first human population, but it is likely that there were never more than 125,000 australopithecines at any given time.

Our own species, *Homo sapiens*, evolved a few hundred thousand years ago. Some ten thousand years ago, when agriculture was invented, probably no more than five million people inhabited Earth—fewer than now live in the San Francisco Bay Area. Even at the time of Christ, two thousand years ago, the entire human population was roughly the size of the population of the United States today; by 1650 there were only 500 million people, and in 1850 only a little over a billion. Since there are now well past 5 billion people, the vast majority of the population explosion has taken place in less than a tenth of one percent of the history of *Homo sapiens*.

This is a remarkable change in the abundance of a single species. After an unhurried pace of growth over most of our history, expansion of the population accelerated during the Industrial Revolution and really shot up after 1950. Since mid-century, the human population has been growing at annual rates ranging from about 1.7 to 2.1 percent per year, doubling in forty years or less. Some groups have grown significantly faster; the population of the African nation of Kenya is estimated to be increasing by over 4 percent annually today—a rate that if continued would double the nation's population in only seventeen years. That rate *has* continued for over a decade now, and only recently has shown slight signs of slowing. Meanwhile, other nations, such as those of northern Europe, have grown much more slowly in recent decades.

But even the highest growth rates are still *slow-motion changes compared to events we easily notice and react to.* (pp. 22, 24)

The time it takes a population to double in size is a dramatic way to picture rates of population growth, one that most of us can understand more readily than percentage growth rates. Human populations have often grown in a pattern described as "exponential." Exponential growth occurs in bank accounts when interest is left to accumulate and itself earns interest. Exponential growth occurs in populations because children, the analogue of interest, remain in the population and themselves have children.

A key feature of exponential growth is that it often seems to start slowly and finish fast. A classic example used to illustrate this is the pond weed that doubles each day the amount of pond surface covered and is projected to cover the entire pond in thirty days. The question is, how much of the pond will be covered in twenty-nine days? The answer, of course, is that just half of the pond will be covered in twenty-nine days. The weed will then double once more and cover the entire pond the next day. As this example indicates, exponential growth contains the potential for big surprises.

The limits to human population growth are more difficult to perceive than those restricting the pond weed's growth. Nonetheless, like the pond weed, human populations grow in a pattern that is essentially exponential, so we must be alert to the treacherous properties of that sort of growth. The key point to remember is that *a long history of exponential growth in no way implies a long future of exponential growth.* What begins in slow motion may eventually overwhelm us in a flash.

The last decade or two has seen a slight slackening in the human population growth rate—a slackening that has been prematurely heralded as an "end to the population explosion." The slowdown has been only from a peak annual growth rate of perhaps 2.1 percent in the early 1960s to about 1.8 percent in 1990. To put this change in perspective, the population's doubling time has been extended from thirty-three years to thirty-nine. Indeed, the world population did double in the thirty-seven years from 1950 to 1987. But even if birth rates continue to fall, the world population will continue to expand (assuming that death rates don't rise), although at a slowly slackening rate, for about another century. Demographers think that growth will not end before the population has reached 10 billion or more.

So, even though birth rates have declined somewhat, *Homo sapiens* is a long way from ending its population explosion or avoiding its consequences. In fact, the biggest jump from 5 to 10 billion in well under a century, is still ahead. But this does not mean that growth couldn't be ended sooner, with a much smaller population size, if we—all of the world's nations—made up our minds to do it. The trouble is, many of the world's leaders and perhaps most of the world's people still do not believe that there are compelling reasons to do so. They are even less aware that if humanity fails to act, *nature may end the population explosion for us*—in very unpleasant ways—well before 10 billion is reached. (p. 24)

Global warming, acid rain, depletion of the ozone layer, vulnerability to epidemics, and exhaustion of soils and groundwater are all related to population size. They are also clear and present dangers to the persistence of civilization. Crop failures due to global warming alone might result in the premature deaths of a billion or more people in the next few decades, and the AIDS epidemic could slaughter hundreds of millions. Together these would constitute a harsh "population control" program provided by nature in the face of humanity's refusal to put into place a gentler program of its own.

We should not delude ourselves: the population explosion will come to an end before very long. The only remaining question is whether it will be halted through the humane method of birth control, or by nature wiping out the surplus. We realize that religious and cultural opposition to birth control exists throughout the world; but we believe that people simply do not understand the choice that such opposition implies. Today, anyone opposing birth control is unknowingly voting to have the human population size controlled by a massive increase in early deaths.

Of course, the environmental crisis is not caused just by expanding human numbers. Burgeoning consumption among the rich and increasing dependence on ecologically unsound technologies to supply that consumption also play major parts. This allows some environmentalists to dodge the population issue by emphasizing the problem of malign technologies. And social commentators can avoid commenting on the problem of too many people by focusing on the serious maldistribution of affluence.

But scientists studying humanity's deepening predicament recognize that a major factor contributing to it is rapidly worsening overpopulation. The Club of Earth, a group whose members all belong to both the U.S. National Academy of Sciences and the American Academy of Arts and Sciences, released a statement in September 1988 that said in part:

> Arresting global population growth should be second in importance only to avoiding nuclear war on humanity's agenda. Overpopulation and rapid population growth are intimately connected with most aspects of the current human predicament, including rapid depletion of nonrenewable resources, deterioration of the environment (including rapid climate change), and increasing international tensions.

When three prestigious scientific organizations cosponsored an international scientific forum, "Global Change," in Washington in 1989, there was general agreement among the speakers that population growth was a substantial contributor toward prospective catastrophe. Newspaper coverage was limited, and while the population component was mentioned in the *New York Times*'s

---

We should not delude ourselves: the population explosion will come to an end before very long. The only remaining question is whether it will be halted through the humane method of birth control, or by nature wiping out the surplus.

"Overpopulation and rapid population growth are intimately connected with most aspects of the current human predicament, including rapid depletion of nonrenewable resources, deterioration of the environment (including rapid climate change), and increasing international tensions."

—Club of Earth statement, September 1988

article, the point that population limitation will be essential to resolving the predicament was lost. The coverage of environmental issues in the media has been generally excellent in the last few years, but there is still a long way to go to get adequate coverage of the immediately connected population problem.

Even though the media occasionally give coverage to population issues, some people never get the word. In November 1988, Pope John Paul II reaffirmed the Catholic Church's ban on contraception. The occasion was the twentieth anniversary of Pope Paul's anti-birth-control encyclical, *Humanae Vitae*. (pp. 25–7)

The bishops who assembled to celebrate the anniversary defended the encyclical by announcing that "the world's food resources theoretically could feed 40 billion people." In one sense they were right. It is "theoretically possible" to feed 40 billion people in the same sense that it is theoretically possible for your favorite major-league baseball team to win every single game for fifty straight seasons, or for you to play Russian roulette ten thousand times in a row with five out of six chambers loaded without blowing your brains out.

One might also ask whether feeding 40 billion people is a worthwhile goal for humanity, even if it could be reached. Is any purpose served in turning Earth, in essence, into a gigantic human feedlot? Putting aside the near-certainty that such a miracle could not be sustained, what would happen to the quality of life?

We wish to emphasize that the population problem is in no sense a "Catholic problem." Around the world, Catholic reproductive performance is much the same as that of non-Catholics in similar cultures and with similar economic status. Nevertheless, the *political* position of the Vatican, traceable in no small part to the extreme conservatism of Pope John Paul II, is an important barrier to solving the population problem. Non-Catholics should be very careful not to confuse Catholics or Catholicism with the Vatican—most American Catholics do not. Furthermore, the Church's position on contraception is distressing to many millions of Catholics, who feel it morally imperative to follow their own consciences and disregard the Vatican's teachings on this subject in their personal lives.

Nor is unwillingness to face the severity of the population problem limited to the Vatican. It is built into our genes and our culture. That is one reason many otherwise bright and humane people behave like fools when confronted with demographic issues. Thus, an economist specializing in mail-order marketing can sell the thesis that the human population could increase essentially forever because people are the "ultimate resource," and a journalist can urge more population growth in the United States so that we can have a bigger army! Even some environmentalists are taken in by the frequent assertion that "there is no population problem, only a problem of distribution." The statement is usually made in a context of a plan for conquering hunger, as if food shortage were the only consequence of overpopulation.

But even in that narrow context, the assertion is wrong. Suppose food *were* distributed equally. If everyone in the world ate as Americans do, less than half the *present* world population could be fed on the record harvests of 1985 and 1986. Of course, everyone does not have to eat like Americans. About a third of the world grain harvest—the staples of the human feeding base—is fed to animals to produce eggs, milk, and meat for American-style diets. Would not feeding that grain directly to people solve the problem? If everyone were willing to eat an essentially vegetarian diet, that additional grain would allow perhaps a billion more people to be fed with 1986 production.

Would such radical changes solve the world food problem? Only in the *very* short term. The additional billion people are slated to be with us by the end of the century. Moreover, by the late 1980s, humanity already seemed to be encountering trouble maintaining the production levels of the mid-1980s, let alone keeping up with population growth. The world grain harvest in 1988 was some 10 percent *below* that of 1986. And there is little sign that the rich are about to give up eating animal products.

So there is no reasonable way that the hunger problem can be called "only" one of distribution, even though redistribution of food resources would greatly alleviate hunger today. Unfortunately, an important truth, that maldistribution is a cause of hunger now, has been used as a way to avoid a more important truth—that overpopulation is critical today and may well make the distribution question moot tomorrow.

The food problem, however, attracts little immediate concern among well-fed Americans, who have no reason to be aware of its severity or extent. But other evidence that could make everyone face up to the seriousness of the population dilemma is now all around us, since problems to which over-population and population growth make major contributions are worsening at a rapid rate. They often appear on the evening news, although the population connection is almost never made.

Consider the television pictures of barges loaded with garbage wandering like the Flying Dutchmen across the seas, and news stories about "no room at the dump." They are showing the results of the interaction between too many affluent people and the environmentally destructive technologies that support that affluence. Growing opportunities to swim in a mixture of sewage and medical debris off American beaches can be traced to the same source. Starving people in sub-Saharan Africa are victims of drought, defective agricultural policies, and an overpopulation of both people and domestic animals—with warfare often dealing the final blow. All of the above are symptoms of humanity's massive and growing negative impact on Earth's life-support systems.

The average person, even the average scientist, seldom makes the connection between such seemingly disparate events and the population problem, and thus remains unworried. To a degree, this failure to put the pieces together is due to a taboo against frank discussion of the population crisis in many quarters, a taboo generated partly by pressures from the Catholic hierarchy and partly by other groups who are afraid that dealing with population issues will produce socially damaging results.

Many people on the political left are concerned that focusing on overpopulation will divert attention from crucial problems of social justice (which certainly need to be addressed in *addition* to the population problem). Often those on the political right fear that dealing with overpopulation will encourage abortion (it need not) or that halting growth will severely damage the economy (it could, if not handled properly). And people of varied political persuasions who are unfamiliar with the magnitude of the population problem believe in a variety of farfetched technological fixes—such as colonizing outer space—that they think will allow the need for regulating the size of the human population to be avoided forever.

Even the National Academy of Sciences avoided mentioning controlling human numbers in its advice to President Bush on how to deal with global environmental change. Although academy members who are familiar with the issue are well aware of the critical population component of that change, it was feared that all of the academy's advice would be ignored if recommendations were included about a subject taboo in the Bush administration. That strategy might have been correct, considering Bush's expressed views on abortion and considering the administration's weak appointments in many environmentally sensitive positions.(pp. 27–9)

All of us naturally lean toward the taboo against dealing with population growth. The roots of our aversion to limiting the size of the human population are as deep and pervasive as the roots of human sexual behavior. Through billions of years of evolution, outreproducing other members of your population was the name of the game. It is the very basis of natural selection, the driving force of the evolutionary process. Nonetheless, the taboo must be uprooted and discarded.

> **If everyone in the world ate as Americans do, less than half the *present* world population could be fed on the record harvests of 1985 and 1986.**

Consider the television pictures of barges loaded with garbage wandering like the Flying Dutchmen across the seas, and news stories about "no room at the dump." They are showing the results of the interaction between too many affluent people and the environmentally destructive technologies that support that affluence.

There is no more time to waste. Human inaction has already condemned hundreds of millions more people to premature deaths from hunger and disease. The population connection must be made in the public mind. Action to end the population explosion *humanely* and start a gradual population *decline* must be lowered to slightly below the human death rate as soon as possible. There still may be time to limit the scope of the impending catastrophe, but not *much* time.

Of course, if we do wake up and succeed in controlling population, that will still leave us with all the other thorny problems to solve. Limiting human numbers will not alone end warfare, environmental deterioration, poverty, racism, religious prejudice, or sexism; it will just buy us the opportunity to do so. As the old saying goes, whatever your cause, it is a lost cause without population control.

America and other rich nations have a clear choice today. They can continue to ignore the population problem and their own massive contributions to it. Then they will be trapped in a downward spiral that may well lead to the end of civilization in a few decades. More frequent droughts, more damaged crops and famines, more dying forests, more smog, more international conflicts, more epidemics, more gridlock, more drugs, more crime, will mark our course. It is a route already traveled by too many of our less fortunate fellow human beings.

Or we can change our collective minds and take the measures necessary to lower global birth rates dramatically. People can learn to treat growth as the cancerlike disease it is and move toward a sustainable society. The rich can make helping the poor an urgent goal, instead of seeking more wealth and useless military advantage over one another. Then humanity might have a chance to manage all those other seemingly intractable problems. It is a challenging prospect, but at least it will give our species a shot at creating a decent future for itself. More immediately and concretely, taking action now will give our children and their children the possibility of decent lives. (p. 29)

Paul R. Ehrlich and Anne H. Ehrlich, "The Population Explosion," in The Amicus Journal, *Vol. 12, No. 1, Winter, 1990, pp. 22–9.*

The Ultimate Resource: Population Growth as a Positive

Erroneous belief about population growth has cost dearly. It has directed attention away from the factor that we now know is central in a country's economic development, its economic and political system. Economic reforms away from totalitarianism and central economic planning in poor countries probably would have been faster and more widespread if slow growth was not explained by recourse to population growth. And in rich countries, misdirected attention to population growth and the supposed consequence of natural resource shortage has caused waste through such programs as synthetic fuel promotion and the development of airplanes that would be appropriate for an age of greater scarcity. Our antinatalist foreign policy is dangerous politically because it risks our being labeled racist, as happened when Indira Ghandi was overthrown because of her sterilization program. Furthermore, misplaced belief that population growth slows economic development provides support for inhumane programs of coercion and the denial of personal liberty in one of the most sacred and valued choices a family can make—the number of children that it wishes to bear and raise—in such countries as China, Indonesia, and Vietnam. (pp. 12–13)

Unlike the earlier period of rampaging worry following Earth Day 1970, . . . it is now well-established scientifically that population growth is not the bogey that conventional opinion and the press believe it to be. In the 1980s a revolution occurred in scientific views toward the role of population growth in economic development. By now the economics profession has turned almost completely away from the previous view that population growth is a crucial negative factor in economic development. There is still controversy about whether population growth is even a minor negative factor in some cases, or whether it is beneficial in the long run. But there is no longer any scientific support for the earlier view which was the basis for the U.S. policy and then the policy of other countries.

For a quarter century our "helping" institutions misanalyzed such world development problems as starving children, illiteracy, pollution, supplies of natural resources, and slow growth. The World Bank, the State Department's Aid to International Development (AID), The United Nations Fund for Populations Activities (UNFPA), and the environmental organizations have asserted that the cause is population growth—the population "explosion" or "bomb," the "population plague." But for almost as long as this idea has been the core of U.S. theory about foreign aid, there has been a solid body of statistical evidence that contradicts this conventional wisdom about the effects of population growth—evidence which falsifies the ideas which support U.S. population policy toward less-developed countries.

The "official" turning point came in 1986 with the publication of a report by the National Research Council and the National Academy of Sciences (NRC-NAS), entitled *Population Growth and Economic Development*, which almost completely reversed a 1971 report on the same subject from the same institution. On the specific issue of raw materials that has been the subject of so much alarm, NRC-NAS concluded: "The scarcity of exhaustible resources is at most a minor constraint on economic growth . . . the concern about the impact of rapid population growth on resource exhaustion has often been exaggerated." And the general conclusion goes only as far as "On balance, we reach the qualitative conclusion that slower population growth would be beneficial to economic development for most developing countries . . . " That is, NRC-NAS found forces operating in both positive and negative directions, its conclusion does not apply to all countries, and the size of the effect is not known even where it is believed to be present. This is a major break from the past monolithic characterization of additional people as a major drag upon development across the board. This revolution in thought has not been reported in the press, however, and therefore has had no effect on public thought on the subject.

There now exist perhaps two dozen competent statistical studies covering the few countries for which data are available over the past century, and also of the many countries for which data are available since World War II. The basic method is to gather data on each country's rate of population growth and its rate of economic growth, and then to examine whether—looking at all the data in the sample together—the countries with high population growth rates have economic growth rates lower than average, and countries with low population growth rates have economic growth rates higher than average.

The clear-cut consensus of this body of work is that faster population growth is *not* associated with slower economic growth. On average, countries whose populations grew faster did not grow slower economically. That is, there is no basis in the statistics for the belief that faster population growth causes slower economic growth.

Additional powerful evidence comes from pairs of countries that have the same culture and history, and had much the same standard of living when they split apart after World War II—East and West Germany, North and South Korea, and China and Taiwan. In each case the centrally planned communist country began with less population "pressure," as measured by density per square kilometer, than did the market-directed noncommunist country. And

Unlike the earlier period of rampaging worry following Earth Day 1970, it is now well-established scientifically that population growth is not the bogey that conventional opinion and the press believe it to be.

> **The plain fact is that, given some time to adjust to shortages, the resource base does not remain fixed. People create more resources of all kinds.**

the communist and noncommunist countries in each pair also started with much the same birth rates and population growth rates.

The market-directed economies have performed much better economically than the centrally planned countries. Income per person is higher. Wages have grown faster. Key indicators of infrastructure such as telephones per person show a much higher level of development. And indicators of individual wealth and personal consumption, such as autos and newsprint, show enormous advantages for the market-directed enterprise economies compared to the centrally planned, centrally controlled economies. Furthermore, birth rates fell at least as early and as fast in the market-directed countries as in the centrally planned countries.

These data provide solid evidence that an enterprise system works better than does a planned economy. This powerful explanation of economic development cuts the ground from under population growth as a likely explanation. And under conditions of freedom, population growth poses less of a problem in the short run, and brings many more benefits in the long run, than under conditions of government planning of the economy.

One inevitably wonders: How can the persuasive common sense embodied in the Malthusian theory be wrong? To be sure, in the short run an additional person—baby or immigrant—inevitably means a lower standard of living for everyone; every parent knows that. More consumers mean less of the fixed available stock of goods to be divided among more people. And more workers laboring with the same fixed current stock of capital means that there will be less output per worker. The latter effect, known as "the law of diminishing returns," is the essence of Malthus's theory as he first set it out.

But if the resources with which people work are not fixed over the period being analyzed, then the Malthusian logic of diminishing returns does not apply. And the plain fact is that, given some time to adjust to shortages, the resource base does not remain fixed. People create more resources of all kinds. When horse-powered transportation became a major problem, the railroad and the motor car were developed. When schoolhouses become crowded, we build new schools—more modern and better than the old ones.

As with Man-made Production Capital, So It Is With Natural Resources

When a shortage of elephant tusks for ivory billiard balls threatened in the last century, and a prize was offered for a substitute, celluloid was invented, followed by the rest of our plastics. Englishmen learned to use coal when trees became scarce in the sixteenth century. Satellites and fiber-optics (derived from sand) replace expensive copper for telephone transmission. And the new resources wind up cheaper than the old ones were. Such has been the entire course of civilization.

Extraordinary as it seems, natural-resource scarcity—that is, the cost of raw materials, which is the relevant economic measure of scarcity—has tended to decrease rather than to increase over the entire sweep of history. This trend is at least as reliable as any other trend observed in human history; the prices of all natural resources, measured in the wages necessary to pay for given quantities of them, have been falling as far back as data exist. (pp. 13–14)

The most extraordinary part of the resource-creation process is that temporary or expected shortages—whether due to population growth, income growth, or other causes—tend to leave us even better off than if the shortages had never arisen, because of the continuing benefit of the intellectual and physical capital created to meet the shortage. It has been true in the past, and therefore it is likely to be true in the future, that we not only need to solve our problems, but we need the problems imposed upon us by the growth of population and income.

The idea that scarcity is diminishing is mind-boggling because it defies the common-sense reasoning that when one starts with a fixed stock of resources and uses some up, there is less left. But for all practical purposes there are no resources until we find them, identify their possible uses, and develop ways to obtain and process them. We perform these tasks with increasing skill as technology develops. Hence, scarcity diminishes. (pp. 14–15)

There is, however, one crucial "natural" resource which is becoming more scarce—human beings. Yes, there are more people on earth now than in the past. But if we measure the scarcity of people the same way we measure the scarcity of economic goods—by the market price—then people are indeed becoming more scarce, because the price of labor time has been rising almost everywhere in the world. Agricultural wages in Egypt have soared, for example, and people complain of a labor shortage because of the demand for labor in the Persian Gulf, just a few years after there was said to be a labor surplus in Egypt.

Nor does it make sense to reduce population growth because of the supposedly increasing pollution of our air and water. In fact, our air and water are becoming cleaner rather than dirtier . . . wholly the opposite of conventional belief.

The most important and amazing demographic fact—the greatest human achievement in history, in my view—is the "recent" decrease in the world's death rate. It took *thousands of years* to increase life expectancy at birth from just over twenty years to the high twenties. Then in just the last *two centuries*, life expectancy at birth in the advanced countries jumped from *less than thirty years* to perhaps seventy-five years. What greater event has humanity witnessed?

Then starting well after World War II, life expectancy in the poor countries has leaped upwards by perhaps *fifteen or even twenty years* since the 1950s, caused by advances in agriculture, sanitation, and medicine. Is this not an astounding triumph for humankind? It is this decrease in the death rate that is the cause of their being a larger world population nowadays than in former times.

Let's put it differently. In the 19th century the planet Earth could sustain only one billion people. Ten thousand years ago, only four *million* could keep themselves alive. Now, *five billion* people are living longer and more healthily than ever before, on average. The increase in the world's population represents our victory over death.

One would expect lovers of humanity to jump with joy at this triumph of human mind and organization over the raw forces of nature. Instead, many lament that there are so many people alive to enjoy the gift of life because they worry that population growth creates difficulties for development. And it is this misplaced concern that leads them to approve the inhumane programs of coercion and denial of personal liberty in one of the most precious choices a family can make—the number of children that it wishes to bear and raise. (pp. 15–16)

The most important benefit of population size and growth is the increase it brings to the stock of useful knowledge. Minds matter economically as much as, or more than, hands or mouths. Progress is limited largely by the availability of trained workers. The main fuel to speed the world's progress is the stock of human knowledge. And the ultimate resource is skilled, spirited, hopeful people, exerting their wills and imaginations to provide for themselves and their families, thereby inevitably contributing to the benefit of everyone . . . .

Which should be our vision? The doomsayers of the population control movement offer a vision of limits, decreasing resources, a zero-sum game, conservation, deterioration, fear, and conflict, calling for more governmental intervention in markets and family affairs. Or should our vision be that of those who look optimistically upon people as a resource rather than as a burden—a vision of receding limits, increasing resources and possibilities, a game in which everyone can win, creation, building excitement, and the belief that persons and firms, acting spontaneously in the search of their individual

In the 19th century the planet Earth could sustain only one billion people. Ten thousand years ago, only four *million* could keep themselves alive. Now *five billion* people are living longer and more healthily than ever before, on average. The increase in the world's population represents our victory over death.

The main fuel to speed the world's progress is the stock of human knowledge. And the ultimate resource is skilled, spirited, hopeful people, exerting their wills and imaginations to provide for themselves and their families, thereby inevitably contributing to the benefit of everyone.

welfare, regulated only by rules of a fair game, will produce enough to maintain and increase economic progress and promote liberty.

And what should our mood be? The population restrictionists say we should be sad and worry. I and many others believe that the trends suggest joy and celebration at our newfound capacity to support human life—healthily, and with fast-increasing access to education and opportunity all over the world. I believe that the population restrictionists' hand-wringing view leads to despair and resignation. Our view leads to hope and progress, in the reasonable expectation that the energetic efforts of humankind will prevail in the future, as they have in the past, to increase worldwide our numbers, our health, our wealth, and our opportunities. (p. 16)

Julian L. Simon, "Population Growth is Not Bad for Humanity," in National Forum, *Vol. LXX, No. 1, Winter, 1990, pp. 12–16.*

The Relevancy of Population Growth: Is the Bomb a Dud?

Look around you: The world is a mess. Poisons are seeping into our air and water. Beaches are defiled by oil spills and medical debris. The homeless roam our cities. People are starving in Africa. Global warming threatens to disrupt the world's climate and economy. Tropical rain forests are going up in smoke. The ozone layer is being depleted. The AIDS epidemic is reaching worldwide proportions.

All of these ills, we are informed by Paul and Anne Ehrlich in their book *The Population Explosion,* have a common source: overpopulation. This may come as a surprise to you, but the Ehrlichs are biologists so they understand. They have studied animal populations and seen them explode and then crash from starvation and disease. *Homo sapiens* is no exception, they assert. Unless we act fast, not only to curb population growth but also to shrink our numbers, we face catastrophes including "the total collapse of civilization and the disappearance of the United States as we know it."

The Ehrlichs' sweeping review of the human condition is marred by their often casual treatment of evidence and their penchant for hyperbole and lurid predictions. These will allow the champions of complacency, who claim it is all a false alarm, to score unearned debating points. But the environmental and social ills the Ehrlichs recount are all too real. What is wacky is their diagnosis.

The Ehrlichs provide a handy formula to help us "laypeople" grasp the role of population growth in the environmental crisis. The impact (I) of any human group on the environment is the product of three factors: the number of people (P), their average level of consumption or affluence (A), and the environmental disruptiveness of the technologies (T) used to produce what they consume. So I = PAT. All else equal, twice as many people means twice as much pollution, global warming, homelessness, tropical deforestation, and so on.

The Ehrlichs recognize that there may be some scope for changing the affluence and technology factors, A and T. We can eat less meat and more vegetables. We can wear sweaters and turn down our thermostats. We can donate some of our leisure time to planting trees instead of watching television. They are now writing another book full of such helpful tips.

In *The Population Explosion,* however, the Ehrlichs zero in on what they see as the crucial factor, the P in the PAT equation. If we focus only on A and T, they explain, "the P factor will always get us in the end." And because of the long time-lag between initiating action and achieving population shrinkage, "first priority must be given to achieving *population control.*"

The Ehrlichs define "overpopulation" as any situation in which "the long-term carrying capacity of an area is clearly being degraded by its current human occupants." Whenever humans degrade the environment, the problem is over-population *by definition*.

Under this rather curious assumption, the Ehrlichs concede, "a condition of overpopulation might be corrected with no change in the number of people. For instance, the impact of today's 665 million Africans on their resources and environment theoretically *might* be reduced to the point where the continent would no longer be overpopulated." In practice, however, the Ehrlichs see few "bright spots" on what they, like the white colonialists of bygone days, call "the Dark Continent." Overpopulation, they lecture, "is defined by the animals that occupy the turf, behaving as they naturally behave, not by a hypothetical group that might be substituted for them."

Ehrlichian overpopulation is not just, or even primarily, a matter of human numbers. Its history is long indeed, stretching back at least 10,000 years to the time when our hunter ancestors caused, "or at least abetted," the extinction of woolly rhinoceroses and mammoths, "the first instance we know about in which human populations exploited a resource with such ferocity that it was extinguished." The world's total human population at that time was about five million.

Then humans invented agriculture, and some two thousand years ago, our population had reached 200 million to 300 million, "an unprecedented outbreak of a single animal species." Today we number more than five billion, and the outbreak continues. Tens of millions more people—or "more mouths," as the Ehrlichs refer to people born in Bangladesh and the Philippines—are added every year.

Could population growth have some positive effects? Julian Simon, an economist at the Heritage Foundation, thinks so. In his book *The Ultimate Resource*, Simon argues that more people mean more producers and more technological progress. If one birth in every million produces a genius, a doubling of the population means twice as many geniuses.

The views of Simon and the Ehrlichs are mirror images of each other. Both are anchored in selective logic. For the Ehrlichs, human ills are "population-related" but human achievements are not. For Simon, human numbers multiply the good but not the bad.

Reducing a society's well-being to a multiple of population, one positive and the other negative, both obscure the truth that, within wide bounds, what matters is not so much the number of people, but how they interact with each other and with their environment.

A more balanced view of the "population problem" would start with the recognition that environmental degradation brings benefits to some even as it imposes costs on others. This, of course, is why the beneficiaries make it happen. The winners tend to be rich and disproportionately male, the losers poor and disproportionately female.

Rapid population growth is a symptom of this unequal distribution of wealth and power. For the dispossessed, and for impoverished women in particular, children may not be the "ultimate resource," but they are one of the few resources at their command. At the same time, many women and men who want safe birth control and abortion cannot get it, just as they cannot get adequate food, health care, education, and other basic needs. The need for children and the lack of birth control both contribute to rapid population growth. This in turn can have a negative feedback effect, putting greater stress on environmental resources. But to identify population as the root of the problem is to mistake a symptom for the cause.

> **Reducing a society's well-being to a multiple of population, one positive and the other negative, both obscure the truth that, within bounds, what matters is not so much the number of people, but how they interact with each other and their environment.**

The danger of population reductionism is not only that it diverts attention from more basic causes of environmental degradation and human suffering. More disturbing is that it paves the way for assaults upon individual rights in the name of population control.

Some biologists may find it easy to make the logical leap from animal to human populations, glossing over the capacity for social and technological change which distinguishes us from butterflies and rabbits. But the appeal of population reductionism to many people, including some in the environmental movement, lies more in its political implications. These were spelled out two centuries ago by the Ehrlichs' intellectual forefather, the Reverend Thomas Malthus.

"That the principal and most permanent cause of poverty," Malthus wrote, "has little or no *direct* relation to forms of government, or the unequal division of property; and that, as the rich do not in reality possess the *power* of finding employment and maintenance for the poor, the poor cannot, in the nature of things, possess the *right* to demand them; are important truths flowing from the principle of population."

This is blaming the victim, writ large.

The danger of population reductionism is not only that it diverts attention from more basic causes of environmental degradation and human suffering. More disturbing is that it paves the way for assaults upon individual rights in the name of population control.

In *The Population Bomb*, published in 1968, Paul Ehrlich endorsed compulsory sterilization in India, a step he termed "coercion in a good cause." In *How to Be a Survivor*, published in 1971, he called upon governments to put "criminal sanctions on overbreeding" if gentler means of persuasion fail.

In their latest book, the Ehrlichs are more circumspect. Population control "need not be coercive," they assure us. They urge us to follow their personal example of not giving baby presents for any child past number two, and recommend that stories and films in schools should never depict happy families with more than two children. As Paul Ehrlich did in *The Population Bomb*, they provide sample letters to be sent to politicians, the Pope, and other influential persons.

But their retreat from "coercion in a good cause" seems tactical. "One must always keep in mind," the Ehrlichs caution, "that the price of personal freedom in making child-bearing decisions may be the destruction of the world in which your children or grandchildren live."

Is this really the price of reproductive self-determination? Or might it be the price of continued concentration of economic and political power in the hands of wealthy elites who arrogantly pursue their narrow, short-term interests at the expense of most of humankind and the environment? (pp. 24–5)

As the environmental movement grows in myriad forms around the world, people are searching for new understandings of our problems and their solutions. Ruling elites are divided over their versions of events. Some "conservatives" resolutely maintain that there really is no environmental problem.

Others acknowledge the environmental crisis and espouse population reductionism in an effort at ideological spin control. Neo-Malthusian influence within the U.S. environmental movement is considerable. The executive director of the Sierra Club wrote the foreword to *The Population Bomb*. Friends of the Earth sponsored *How to Be a Survivor*. This spring the Natural Resources Defense Council devoted its journal's cover story to an excerpt from *The Population Explosion*.

The environmental movement contains within it seeds of democratic revolution and of technocratic totalitarianism. The Ehrlichs' population reductionism provides nourishing organic manure for the latter. But what will ultimately flower and bear fruit remains to be seen. The Ehrlichs are right on one point: The stakes are high. (p. 25)

James K. Boyce, "The Bomb Is a Dud," in The Progressive, *Vol. 54, No. 9, September, 1990, pp. 24–5.*

Population and the Environment:
Excuse or Real Concern?

The problems of feeding ever-growing populations" are leading to "tropical forests . . . being cleared at the rate of between 50 and 100 acres per minute," according to the U.S. Agency for International Development (AID), which lobbies for and administers the foreign aid of the United States. At this rate, "today's forests could be cut in half by 2035 and gone entirely by the end of the next century," the agency quotes a curator at the Smithsonian Institution, which is also supported by the federal governement, as saying.

The deforestation crisis is spawning other environmental crises, according to the agency: "The burning of tropical forests pumps nearly 1 billion tons of carbon dioxide into the air each year . . . causing . . . global warming . . . [and] a rise in the sea level . . . because of the melting of glaciers and polar ice caps." Global warming will raise sea levels, so that "most U.S. coastal lowlands . . . would be flooded. . . . The . . . nation of the Maldives would be entirely submerged." Moreover, "deforestation . . . causes soil erosion" which will affect "half of the world's population" and will lead to "desertification and spreading wastelands." And, as if all this were not enough, in these tropical forests which "are home to more than half the world's plants and animals . . . each day as many as 140 species of plants and animals may be disappearing."

Believing that these catastrophes result from trying to feed "ever-growing populations" makes it easier to believe in the wisdom of AID's efforts to control population growth in the countries receiving U.S. foreign aid. Requiring a foreign government to promise (as, for example, in the 1988 contract between AID and Costa Rica) that it will try to reduce its crude birthrate to 28/1000 might seem to be a tad nosy, were it not for the exigencies of the environment. Requiring the government of Costa Rica to provide sex education to its population of school-age children and to achieve a "contraceptive prevalence rate at 70 percent by 1992" might seem a bit officious, did we not know that this is saving the polar ice caps.

In a word, the environment is proving to be the best excuse yet for imposing population control. And just in time, too, since the earlier threats of resource exhaustion and economic stagnation and starvation that were supposed to result from population growth have not materialized. AID is only one of many government-funded agencies that are now gathering at the altar of Mother Earth. Right alongside AID and the Sierra Club, the Audubon Society, Zero Population Growth, and the National Wildlife Federation at the new holy mysteries are, to name a few of the organizers of the typical environmental event, representatives of Planned Parenthood, the Population Reference Bureau, and the World Bank.

However, the promoters of this belief make two errors—their claims about the state of the environment are highly questionable, and their claim that "overpopulation" is the cause of environmental degradation has no basis in fact.

Forests still cover almost a third of the earth's land surface, the same share as in 1950, and there is no statistically verifiable trend in the temperature of the atmosphere or the number of species or the much belabored stratospheric ozone layer, although a multitude of voices insist that cataclysmic changes will soon overcome us. This is not to deny that pollution and traffic jams are not big problems in many places, but this is not global climate change.

One reason it has been so easy to argue that the earth is "overpopulated" is that now, as always, most people live in crowded conditions, not because of lack of space—we actually occupy only about 1 percent of the earth's area—

One reason it has been so easy to argue that the earth is "overpopulated" is that now, as always, most people live in crowded conditions, not because of lack of space—we actually occupy only 1 percent of the earth's area—but because we need to work together, to buy and sell, to give and receive services from one another.

The Chernobyl nuclear accident could not have been prevented by providing more and better condoms to the Russians, in whose vast and empty country levels of pollution are 10 to 100 times as high as in the West.

but because we need to work together, to buy and sell, to give and receive services from one another.

Urbanization is, of course, increasing throughout the world, as rising agricultural productivity has made it possible for a smaller proportion of farmers to feed a growing proportion of city workers. Increasing urbanization makes us feel more crowded at the same time as it discourages the raising of large families. Unlike a farm wife, a city mother cannot raise her children while she works. She has to sacrifice income in order to raise them. It is not surprising, therefore, that in the developed countries, zero or negative population growth is already at hand, while in the less developed world it is approaching at a rate that will bring it about well before the end of the next century, if present trends continue.

Knowing this, the more forthright of the environmentalists frankly admit that they are aiming for a substantial *reduction* in world population. Paul Ehrlich, for example, has called for world population to be reduced to "perhaps" one-fifth its present size. Herman Daly, who works for the World Bank, has called for government licensing to limit births to levels consistent with a stationary or, better yet, declining population. The U.N. Fund for Population Activities gave an award to the Chinese one-child family program that features compulsory abortion. (pp. 23–4)

[The new defenders of nature] misconstrue the relationship between population growth and environmental stress. People in many places in Africa pull up young trees without replanting, not because of overpopulation in that largely empty continent (which has one-fifth the population density of Europe), but because no one owns the trees and therefore no one can expect to benefit in the future from a tree that he plants now. Industrial pollution in Silesia darkened the sky and caused cancer not because of Polish "overpopulation" (there are half as many Poles per square mile in Poland as Germans in western Germany), but because factories could meet their centrally planned output quotas more easily by not using pollution control equipment. (The Chernobyl nuclear accident could not have been prevented by providing more and better condoms to the Russians, in whose vast and empty country levels of pollution are 10 to 100 times as high as in the West. The problem was, in all cases, one of *behavior* in response to *incentives*, not one of numbers.)

Governments that have a sincere interest in protecting the environment can do so whenever they choose to provide the appropriate incentives, regardless of the size or rate of growth of the population. But the environment now serves a number of purposes that have little to do with saving the trees or the air or the whales. There are fortunes to be made in reporting and combating the various crises. Apparently no threat or proposal is too fantastic to generate hundreds of thousands or even millions of dollars in government grants. Above all, no better excuse for denying basic civil rights has ever appeared. If it's a question of the ozone layer, who cares about liberty? (p. 24)

Jacqueline R. Kasun, "A Nation of Davids: Population Control and the Environment," in Chronicles: A Magazine of American Culture, *Vol. 15, No. 10, October, 1991, pp. 23–4.*

Sources For Further Study

Benedick, Richard E. "Population-Environmental Linkages and Sustainable Development." *Populi* 15, No. 3 (September 1988): 14–21.
    Advocates the development of public environmental policies that recognize the integral role that overpopulation plays in environmental degradation.

Brown, Lester R. "Divided by Demography: Analyzing the Demographic Trap." *Current*, No. 301 (March-April 1988): 28–35.
    Analyzes the social and environmental degradation that results when improved public health measures lower the death rates of developing countries but birth rates remain high due to the lack of economic and social incentives that encourage contraceptive use.

———. "Feeding Six Billion." *World Watch* 2, No. 5 (September-October, 1989): 32–40.
    Examines how population growth and environmental degradation have depleted world food supplies and what steps researchers and governments are taking to achieve a balance between food and people.

Donaldson, Peter J. *Nature Against Us: The United States and the World Population Crises, 1965–1980*. Chapel Hill: University of North Carolina, 1990, 207 p.
    Investigates "the origins, implementation, and impact of the American effort—both private and government—to regulate fertility and thus to slow population growth throughout the developing world."

Fornos, Werner. "Population Politics." *Technology Review* 94, No. 2 (February-March 1991): 43–51.
    Outlines the social and environmental consequences of overpopulation and describes the political controversy in the United States concerning funding for family planning programs abroad.

Harrison, Paul. "Too Much Life on Earth?" *New Scientist* 126, No. 1717 (19 May 1990): 28–9.
    Reports on the debate surrounding population growth and its effect on the biosphere.

Hinrichsen, Don. "Critical Links Between Population and Resources." *Populi* 15, No. 1 (1988): 14–25.
    Asserts that population growth should be managed by all nations, not just those with the highest birth rates.

———. "Population Boom Takes Environmental Toll." *World Wildlife Fund News*, No. 65 (May-June 1990): 4–5.
    Presents the possible global consequences of population growth in developing countries and proposes specific measures to address this issue.

Joekes, Susan. "Women's Programmes and the Environment." *Populi* 16, No. 3 (September 1989): 4–12.
    Acknowledges that women are the main users of natural resources in developing nations as the food, fuel, and water suppliers for their households, and asserts that environmental management programs must meet womens' survival needs and provide them with continued motivation to protect their environments.

Keyfitz, Nathan. "The Growing Human Population." *Scientific American* 261, No. 3 (September 1989): 118–26.
    Summarizes recent trends in population growth and the actions that public and private groups are currently taking to alleviate overcrowding before irreparable damage to the earth's ecosystems occurs.

Mellor, John W. "The Intertwining of Environmental Problems and Poverty." *Environment* 30, No. 9 (November 1988): 8–13, 28–30.
    Examines the relationship between poverty and environmental degradation in the developing world.

Philip, Prince, Duke of Edinburgh. "The Human Population Explosion." In his *Down to Earth: Speeches and Writings of His Royal Highness Prince Philip, Duke of Edinburgh, on the Relationship of Man with His Environment*, pp. 117–32. Lexington, Mass: Stephen Greene Press, 1988.
    Essay based on a speech given by the Prince as the president of the British National Appeal for the World Wildlife Fund in which he outlines the threat that increased human population poses for the environment.

"Human Needs and Nature's Balance: Population, Resources, and the Environment." *Population Reference Bureau Report,* October 1987.

　Discussed the possible environmental costs of global achievements in food production, water use, and energy consumption, and the potential for maintaining these resources to sustain future population growth.

"Fertility Around the World Shows Surprises." *Population Today* 18, No. 5 (May 1990): 8–9.

　Presents data originally published in *1990 World Population Data Sheet* concerning the fertility rates of such countries as the U.S., Bangladesh, and China.

Sadik, Nafis. "World Population Continues to Rise." *The Futurist* XXV, No. 2 (March-April 1991): 9–14.

　The executive director of the United Nations Population Fund outlines current world population trends and suggests strategies for curbing population growth rates.

Schmidt, Stanley. "Of Mice and Men." *Outdoor Life,* 187 (April 1991): 48, 52.

　Warns of the dangers of overpopulation and faults environmental organizations, the media, and the United States government for ignoring this issue which arguably contributes to most environmental problems.

Shaw, R. Paul. "Population Growth: Is It Ruining the Environment?" *Populi* 16, No. 2 (June 1989): 20–9.

　Discusses the effects of poverty, industrialization, and overcrowding on the environment and argues against the view that limiting population growth will result in the regeneration of the environment.

Silver, Cheryl Simon, with DeFries, Ruth S. "Humanity: An Agent of Global Environmental Change." In their *One Earth, One Future: Our Changing Global Environment,* pp. 49–60. Washington, D.C.: National Academy Press, 1990.

　Examines how population growth and technological advances have affected the environment.

Simmons, I. G. *Changing the Face of the Earth: Culture, Environment, History.* Oxford: Basil Blackwell, 1989, 487 p.

　Studies the impact of human activity on the earth's biophysical systems.

Toufexis, Anastasia. "Too Many Mouths." *Time* 133, No. 1 (2 January 1989): 48–50.

　Outlines the environmental consequences of overpopulation and calls for the wide availability of birth-control information and devices coupled with the expansion of educational and employment opportunities for women.

van de Kaa, Dirk J. "Six Pillars of a Population Strategy." *Populi* 17, No. 1 (March 1990): 26–31.

　Proposes an international population policy that incorporates six precepts: political commitment at all levels, the development of distinct national policies, community involvement, increasing the outreach of family planning programs, strengthening the role of women, and resource mobilization.

The World Bank. "Making Choices: Population." In *Striking a Balance: The Environmental Challenge of Development,* pp. 39–40. Washington D.C.: The World Bank, 1989.

　States the World Bank's commitment to world population control.

13: Rain Forest Depletion

Playing with Fire: The Destruction of the Amazon

After years of inattention, the whole world has awakened at last to how much is at stake in the Amazon. It has become the front line in the battle to rescue earth's endangered environment from humanity's destructive ways. "Save the rain forest," long a rallying cry for conservationists, is now being heard from politicians, pundits and rock stars. The movement has sparked a confrontation between rich industrial nations, which are fresh converts to the environmental cause, and the poorer nations of the Third World, which view outside interference as an assault on their sovereignty.

Some of the harshest criticism is aimed at Brazil. The largest South American country embraces about half the Amazon basin and, in the eyes of critics, has shown a reckless penchant for squandering resources that matter to all mankind. Government leaders around the world are calling on Brazil to stop the burning. (p. 76)

The vast region of unbroken green that surrounds the Amazon river and its tributaries has been under assault by settlers and developers for 400 years. Time and again, the forest has defied predictions that it was doomed. But now the danger is more real and imminent than ever before as loggers level trees, dams flood vast tracts of land and gold miners poison rivers with mercury. In Peru the forests are being cleared to grow coca for cocaine production. "It's dangerous to say the forest will disappear by a particular year," says Philip Fearnside of Brazil's National Institute for Research in the Amazon, "but unless things change, the forest *will* disappear."

That would be more than a South American disaster. It would be an incalculable catastrophe for the entire planet. Moist tropical forests are distinguished by their canopies of interlocking leaves and branches that shelter creatures below from sun and wind, and by their incredible variety of animal and plant life. If the forests vanish, so will more than 1 million species—a significant part of the earth's biological diversity and genetic heritage. Moreover, the burning of the Amazon could have dramatic effects on global weather patterns—for example, heightening the warming trend that may result from the greenhouse effect. "The Amazon is a library for life sciences, the world's great pharmaceutical laboratory and flywheel of climate," says Thomas Lovejoy of the Smithsonian Institution. "It's a matter of global destiny." (pp. 76–7)

The river and forest system cover 2.7 million sq. mi. (almost 90% of the area of the contiguous U.S.) and stretches into eight countries besides Brazil, including Venezuela to the north, Peru to the west, and Bolivia to the south. . . .

The jungle is so dense and teeming that all the biologists on earth could not fully describe its life forms. A 1982 U.S. National Academy of Sciences report estimated that a typical 4-sq. mi. patch of rain forest may contain 750 species of trees, 125 kinds of mammals, 400 types of birds, 100 of reptiles and 60 amphibians. Each type of tree may support more than 400 insect species. (p. 77)

But the diversity of the Amazon is more than just good material for TV specials. The rain forest is a virtually untapped storehouse of evolutionary

Time and again, the forest has defied predictions that it was doomed. But now the danger is more real and imminent than ever before as loggers level trees, dams flood vast tracts of land and gold miners poison rivers with mercury.

If the forests vanish, so will more than 1 million species—a significant part of the earth's biological diversity and genetic heritage.

achievement that will prove increasingly valuable to mankind as it yields its secrets. . . . [Jungle] chemicals have already led to new treatments for hypertension and some forms of cancer. The lessons encoded in the genes of the Amazon's plants and animals may ultimately hold the key to solving a wide range of problems.

Scientists are concerned that the destruction of the Amazon could lead to climatic chaos. Because of the huge volume of clouds it generates, the Amazon system plays a major role in the way the sun's heat is distributed around the globe. Any disturbance of this process could produce far-reaching, unpredictable effects. Moreover, the Amazon region stores at least 75 billion tons of carbon in its trees, which when burned spew carbon dioxide into the atmosphere. Since the air is already dangerously overburned by carbon dioxide from the cars and factories of industrial nations, the torching of the Amazon could magnify the greenhouse effect—the trapping of heat by atmospheric CO_2. (pp. 77–8)

Many Brazilians still believe the Amazon is indestructible—a green monster so huge and vital that it could not possibly disappear. . . .

Yet the rain forest is deceptively fragile. Left to itself, it is an almost self-sustaining ecosystem that thrives indefinitely. But it does not adapt well to human invasions and resists being turned into farm- or ranchland. Most settlers find that the lush promise of the Amazon is an illusion that vanishes when grasped.

The forest functions like a delicately balanced organism that recycles most of its nutrients and much of its moisture. Wisps of steam float from the top of the endless palette of green as water evaporates off the upper leaves, cooling the trees and they collect the intense sunlight. Air currents over the forest gather this evaporation into clouds, which return the moisture to the system in torrential rains. Dead animals and vegetation decompose quickly, and the resulting nutrients move rapidly from the soil back to growing plants. The forest is such an efficient recycler that virtually no decaying matter seeps into the region's rivers.

But when stripped of its trees, the land becomes inhospitable. Most of the Amazon's soil is nutrient poor and ill-suited to agriculture. The rain forest has an uncanny capacity to flourish in soils that elsewhere would not even support weeds. (p. 78)

If the rain forest disappears, the process will begin at its edges in places such as Acre and Rondônia. While the Amazon forest as a whole generates roughly half of its own moisture, the percentage is much higher in these western states, far from the Atlantic. This means that deforestation is likely to have a more dramatic impact on the climate in the west than in the east. . . . The process of deforestation could become self-perpetuating as heat, drying and wind cause the trees to die on their own.

This does not have to happen. A dramatic drop in Brazil's birth rate promises to reduce future pressures to cut the forests, and experts believe the country could halt much of the deforestation with a few actions. By removing the remaining subsidies and incentives for clearing land, Brazil could both save money and slow the speculation that destroys the forests. Many environmentalists prefer this approach to the enactment of new laws. Brazilians have developed a genius, which they call *jeito,* for getting around laws, and many sound environmental statutes on the books are ignored.

The government could also stop some of the more wasteful projects it is currently planning. Part of the problem in the Amazon has been ill-conceived plans for development that destroy forests and drive the country deeper in debt. (p. 82)

Perhaps the best hope for the forests' survival is the growing recognition that they are more valuable when left standing than when cut. Charles Peters of the Institute of Economic Botany at the New York Botanical Garden recently published the results of a three-year study that calculated the market value of rubber and exotic produce like the Aguaje palm fruit that can be harvested from the Amazonian jungle. The study . . . asserts that over time selling these products could yield more than twice the income of either cattle ranching or lumbering.

But if the burning of the forests goes on much longer, the damage may become irreversible. Long before the great rain forests are destroyed all together, the impact of deforestation on climate could dramatically change the character of the area, lead to mass extinctions of plant and animal species, and leave Brazil's poor to endure even greater misery than they do now. The people of the rest of the world, no less than the Brazilians, need the Amazon as a functioning system, and in the end, this is more important than the issue of who owns the forest. The Amazon may run through South America, but the responsibility for saving the rain forests, as well as the reward for succeeding, belongs to everyone. (p. 83)

Eugene Linden, "Playing with Fire," in Time, *New York, Vol. 134, No. 12, September 18, 1989, pp. 76–83.*

Left to itself, the rain forest is an almost self-sustaining ecosystem that thrives indefinitely. But it does not adapt well to human invasion and resists being turned into farm- or ranchland. Most settlers find that the lush promise of the Amazon is an illusion that vanishes when grasped.

Foreign Aid: The Politics of Tropical Deforestation

The earth's tropical forests are almost all contained within a belt delineated by the Tropics of Cancer and Capricorn. Within this broad zone, the Congo and the Amazon contain the world's largest expanses—green seas of extremely diverse vegetation. The Congo forests are hardly disturbed, since the population there is small. But Amazonia, vast as it is, is already under assault in Brazil. . . .

[In 1987] the United Nations Development Programme (UNDP), the World Bank, the Food and Agriculture Organization of the United Nations (FAO), the Rockefeller Foundation, and the World Resources Institute decided to awaken governments that are bankrupting tropical forests.

They made a list of 56 tropical countries suffering from serious deforestation—28 in Africa, 12 in Asia, and 16 in Central and South America and the Caribbean—and called their first meeting at the Rockefeller Foundation's international conference center at Bellagio in northern Italy.

No political leaders of any importance from the developed or developing countries—except the chairman, Mabubul Haq, Minister of Development and Planning of Pakistan and a distinguished development economist—bothered to come. . . .

The Bellagio group puts the annual rate of permanent tropical deforestation worldwide at about 43,000 square miles and growing. This would be comparable to the disappearance each year of extremely rich and diverse forests about the size of Pennsylvania. Since the start of the 20th century, when the world's economic and demographic cruising speed accelerated greatly, the tropical forests were reduced by half. (p. 21)

Deforestation in the tropics has to be seen in conjunction with the great efforts that many developing countries have made in the past 40 years to improve and expand their agriculture. There have been many successes as a result of this drive, and foreign aid from the rich countries deserves much of the credit.

Agriculture has been the major focus of foreign aid since its inception after World War II, mainly due to American efforts and money. In spite of some

> **In the tropics, even more than in the temperate zones, agriculture requires forests and forestry to sustain it. Without forestry, much of what has been won in tropical agriculture will be lost.**

inevitable failures and a lot of scattershot criticism of foreign aid, aid for agricultural development has been overwhelmingly successful.

Now it is time for the same kind of concerted international effort to be made for tropical forestry. It is especially needed because the penchant for expanding agriculture in the tropics at the expense of forests has begun to work against agriculture in many places.

In the tropics, even more than in the temperate zones, agriculture requires forests and forestry to sustain it. Without forestry, much of what has been won in tropical agriculture will be lost.

One of the ways in which the tropics differ from the temperate zones is that the latter is endowed with generally better soils. The forests of the tropics play a vital role in recycling nutrients to poor soils. Because the tropics are subject to heavy seasonal rains, their forests are also extremely important for erosion protection and as watersheds that store water and prevent floods and drought. (pp. 21–2)

The deforestation policy of Brazil is a classic case of history repeating itself. It is also an example of a kind of warlike mentality regarding forests that is not unusual among agricultural expansionists in the tropics.

Early in the century, Brazil encouraged many poor, landless farmers to settle in the country's northeast. The first result was massive deforestation. Then the migrants were faced with ruined soils, a changed climate, and cycles of droughts and floods. The northeast became one of the poorest, most politically turbulent parts of the country, as it is today.

Brazil is now repeating the same colonization and deforestation policy in the western Amazonian province of Rondonia. . . . The goals are to relieve the poverty and population pressure of the northeast, to favor big ranchers, and to physically occupy a frontier area of the Amazon adjacent to Bolivia.

Eighty percent of the deforestation is being done by cattle ranchers who receive sizable tax breaks for setting up in Rondonia. Without the tax breaks, they would not be there, because the soils are poor. But with the tax advantages, they expect to get rich, and when the soils give out, there is a lot more forest free for the burning.

Behind such government policies—not exclusive to Brazil—are mentalities shaped by psychological, political, and economic factors.

In Brazil there is a love-hate relationship with the forest. The country possesses most of Amazonia, and yet this forest world is too big and too wild to be possessed. The government fears that if it doesn't occupy Rondonia with people and all the authorities that go along with a population of farms and towns, then anybody—Brazilians or foreigners—can take and do what they please there.

The scale on which the forests of Rondonia are being burned has been heavily criticized in Brazil and abroad. (p. 22)

Worldwide reaction to the burning of Rondonia has not stopped Brazil from doing it but has strengthened the position of environmentally responsible Brazilians, including many working for the government.

It has also had a catalytic effect on long-overdue environmental reforms at the World Bank, which is the most important, and in some respects the most progressive, of the international foreign-assistance agencies. Progressive enough, that is, to admit its errors and undertake to reform itself by creating an important department to pass on the environmental merits of all its projects and environmental controls. The World Bank granted Brazil a $250 million loan to build a highway through the Amazon to make the Rondonia project feasible. It made this loan against the strong advice of its own experts and outside consultants who agreed that the project was economically, socially, and ecologically disastrous. Why, then, did it give the loan?

A high Bank official interviewed on the CBS program "60 Minutes" said that had it not done so, Brazil would have gone ahead anyway, so the Bank thought it might have some good influence by becoming a partner.

This point of view provides an insight into the politics of not only the World Bank but foreign-aid agencies in general. Partnerships between development agencies and governments that are receiving assistance are often based on pumping as much money as possible through the agencies' project pipelines, thus benefiting the growth of the agencies as well as the recipient governments.

The same rationale also favors big projects that carry more rank and bigger staffs and budgets than smaller, unglamorous, cheaper projects that may actually be better suited to a particular situation. But when things go wrong with big projects, they go wrong in a big way, especially environmentally.

The examination of the environmental fitness of project proposals is seen by both the recipient governments and the development agencies as something that gums up the works and slows the flow of money.

Historically, the role of forestry and the status of foresters in the development organizations—international ones such as the FAO and national ones such as the United States Agency for International Development (AID)—have been kept small so as not to challenge budget allocations for agricultural projects.

With some exceptions, the foresters in the foreign-aid agencies became accustomed to playing minor roles and seldom fought for larger budgets. They became survivors.

All this may now be changing. In the United States and most of the other industrialized nations, foreign aid remains more or less unpopular. But almost overnight, foreign aid for tropical forestry is receiving much support. . . . Total budget allocations for forestry in the 26 organizations most concerned with development assistance went from $606 million in 1984 to an estimated $1.1 billion in 1988.

This trend shows every sign of continuing. The emphasis within the agencies that finance or manage projects has also moved away from production forestry and is now favoring community forestry, agro-forestry, and projects that both conserve and manage forests as renewable resources.

Agriculture still receives proportionately much more money than forestry in overall foreign-aid budgets—as only makes sense for a basic priority. But forestry is no longer the foreign-aid stepchild that it was. It is entering its Cinderella years. (pp. 22–3)

The international cohesiveness of foresters. . . . is one of their strongest characteristics, and it is beginning to come forth in two important ways. One is the agreement that has been reached on a single Tropical Forestry Action Plan by three important international agencies, the United Nations Development Programme, the World Bank, and the Food and Agriculture Organization of the United Nations.

The other is the willingness with which these and other organizations of different kinds, such as the International Union of Forestry Research Organizations, are cooperating within an international committee made up of representatives from national forest services and bilateral agencies such as USAID and the other national foreign-aid offices.

This committee, headed by George Holmes of the United Kingdom, is giving guidance, especially regarding priorities, to the Tropical Forestry Action Plan and is trying to plug other tropical forestry efforts into that effort.

This development is encouraging in view of the opportunity that more than a billion dollars worth of foreign-aid money affords for wasteful, bureaucratic competition and turf battles. So far, this kind of contention is not taking place.

Partnerships between developing agencies and governments that are receiving assistance are often based on pumping as much money as possible through the agencies' project pipelines, thus benefiting the growth of the agencies as well as the recipient governments.

Agriculture still receives proportionately much more money than forestry in overall foreign-aid budgets—as only makes sense for a basic priority. But forestry is no longer the foreign-aid stepchild that it was. It is entering its Cinderella years.

It is axiomatic in international development that relatively minor amounts of money invested in research, policy analysis, and training of key officials can achieve multibillion-dollar results in fairly short periods of time.

This was one of the keys to success of foreign aid in South Korea, Taiwan, and Singapore. However, as in those lands, it happens only when embraced on the political level within the developing countries themselves.

Dr. Haq, the Pakistani chairman of the first Bellagio meeting, made an important point when he noted the difference in the way politicians look at agriculture and forestry.

"The trouble," he said, "is that presidents and prime ministers do not get easily excited about investments in forests that take 13 to 20 years to mature when they have two to three years in office."

Therefore, it is fundamentally important that these politicians are awakened to the fact that they are bankrupting their countries' forest resources and at the same time ruining the environmental support for agriculture. They should know that this will be seen in the industrialized countries as a waste of foreign aid and as environmentally damaging well beyond their frontiers—in the industrialized countries, on whom they depend in many ways.

There are at least three ways to deliver such messages.

● Publicly, by shedding light on the folly of tropical deforestation policies such as those in Brazil. Matters of global concern ask to be taken up in the press but also by concerned governments of developing and industrialized countries at the United Nations and its agencies.

   The UN organizations are more effective platforms from which to address developing countries than is generally recognized. People in industrialized countries tend not to take the UN organizations seriously, in part because they see them as "Third World territory," which to a certain degree they are. But 75 percent of the world's population is in developing countries.

● The international environmental, biological, and economic importance of tropical forests should be much higher on the regular agendas of diplomatic and political contacts between industrialized and developing countries. The United States should take the lead in this area since its people are environmentally alert.

● All foreign aid going to tropical forestry projects should be made conditional on environmental and economic soundness and should be withdrawn from projects that turn out to be neither.

There is not a great deal of time left in which to conserve one of the world's most valuable resources—a resource that is being prodigiously wasted. (pp. 23–4)

T. M. Pasca, "The Politics of Tropical Deforestation," in American Forests, *Vol. 94, Nos. 11 & 12, November-December, 1988, pp. 21–4.*

The Healing Forest: The Potential Loss of New Medicines

The rate of species extinction is increasing at an alarming pace. The majority of the world's threatened species—both animal and plant—inhabit the tropical forests. These forests cover less than 10% of the earth's surface, but they are believed to contain more than half the world's species. Among the devastating impacts of the current destruction of tropical forests will be the loss of raw materials for future medicines and the loss of the knowledge needed to utilize them. Rain-forest plants are complex chemical storehouses that contain many undiscovered biodynamic compounds with unrealized potential for use in modern medicine. We can gain access to these materials *only* if we study and conserve the species that contain them. (p. 9)

Plants have traditionally served as man's most important weapon against the bacteria that cause disease—in fact, it seems that even the Neanderthals knew and made use of medicinal plants. As early as 2000 B.C., the Chinese were using molds to treat festering ulcers, and the ancient Egyptians are known to have applied moldy bread to open wounds.

It is only relatively recently, however, with the advent of modern technology and synthetic chemistry, that we have been able to reduce our almost total dependence on the plant kingdom as a source of medicines. Nonetheless, we continue to rely on plants to a much greater degree than is commonly realized. Almost half of all prescriptions dispensed in the United States contain substances of natural origin—and more than 50% of these medications contain a plant-derived active ingredient. In 1974 alone, the United States imported $24.4 million worth of medicinal plants.

There are four basic ways in which plants that are used by tribal peoples are valuable for modern medicine. First, plants from the tropics are sometimes used as sources of direct therapeutic agents. The alkaloid D-tubocurarine is extracted from the South American jungle liana *Chondrodendron tomentosum* and is widely used as a muscle relaxant in surgery. Chemists have so far been unable to produce this drug synthetically in a form that has all the attributes of the natural product, and we therefore continue to rely on collection of this plant from the wild. (pp. 10, 12)

The second way in which modern medicine can use tropical plants is as a starting point for the development of more complex semisynthetic compounds. An example of this would be saponin extracts that are chemically altered to produce sapogenins necessary for manufacturing steroidal drugs. Until relatively recently, 95% of all steroids were obtained from extracts of neotropical yams of the genus *Dioscorea*.

Third, tropical plants are also sources of substances that can be used as models for new synthetic compounds. Cocaine from the coca plant, *Erythroxylum coca*, has served as a model for the synthesis of a number of local anesthetics, such as procaine. New and unusual chemical substances found in plants will continue to serve as "blueprints" for novel synthetic substances and will prove to be increasingly important in the future.

Fourth, plants can also be used as taxonomic markers for the discovery of new compounds. From a plant-chemistry standpoint, the plant kingdom has been investigated in a very haphazard manner; some families have been relatively well studied, while others have been almost completely overlooked. For example, many uses have been documented for Liliaceae, and the family is known to be rich in alkaloids. Although little was known of the chemistry of the Orchidaceae, plants of this family were investigated because of its close relationship to the Liliaceae. The research demonstrated that, not only were Orchidaceae rich in alkaloids, but many of these alkaloids were unique and thought to be of extreme interest for the future.

Of the hundreds of thousands of species of living plants, only a fraction have been investigated in the laboratory. This poor understanding of plants is particularly acute in the tropics. The noted Brazilian plant chemist Otto Gottlieb wrote in 1981: "Nothing at all is known about the chemical composition of 99.6% of our flora." It is worth noting that Brazil probably has more species of flowering plants—approximately 55,000—than any other country on earth.

In a region like the Amazon, home to tens of thousands of plant species, how do we begin to decide which plants are of potential use? Randomly screening

> Among the devastating impacts of the current destruction of tropical forests will be the loss of raw materials for future medicines and the loss of the knowledge needed to utilize them.

A single shaman of the Wayana tribe in the northeast Amazon may use more than a hundred different species for medicinal purposes alone. Furthermore, a great many of the remedies *are* effective.

plant materials for new biodynamic compounds has proven to be very expensive. A most cost-effective method to find new and useful plant compounds is the science of ethnobotany.

Ethnobotany is the study of tribal peoples and their utilization of tropical plants. The importance of ethnobotanical inquiry as a cost-effective means of locating new and useful tropical-plant compounds cannot be overemphasized. Most of the secondary plant compounds employed in modern medicine were first "discovered" through ethnobotanical investigation. There are some 119 pure chemical substances extracted from higher plants that are used in medicine throughout the world, and 74% of these compounds have the same or related use as the plants from which they were derived.

The rosy periwinkle (*Catharanthus roseus*) represents a classic example of the importance of plants used by local peoples. This herbaceous plant, native to southeastern Madagascar, is the source of over 75 alkaloids, two of which are used to treat childhood leukemia and Hodgkin's disease with a very high success rate. Annual sales of these alkaloids worldwide in 1980 were estimated to reach $50 million wholesale prior to 100% markup for the retail market, according to International Marketing Statistics. This species was first investigated in the laboratory because of its use by local people as an oral hypoglycemic agent. Thus, we can see that investigation of plants used for medicinal purposes by "unsophisticated" peoples can provide us with new biodynamic compounds that may have very important applications in our own society. (pp. 12–13)

Tropical-forest peoples represent the key to understanding, utilizing, and protecting tropical-plant diversity. The degree to which they understand and are able to sustainably use this diversity is astounding. The Barasana Indians of Amazonian Colombia can identify all of the tree species in their territory without having to refer to the fruit or flowers—a feat that no university-trained botanist is able to accomplish.

Nevertheless, to this day, very few tribes have been subjected to a complete ethnobotanical analysis. In 1981, Robert Goodland of the World Bank wrote, "Indigenous knowledge is essential for the use, identification, and cataloguing to the [tropical] biota. As tribal groups disappear, their knowledge vanishes with them. . . . The preservation of these groups is a significant economic opportunity for the [developing] nation, not a luxury."

Since Amazonian Indians are often the only ones who know both the properties of these plants and how they can best be utilized, their knowledge must be considered an essential component of all efforts to conserve and develop the Amazon. Failure to document this ethnobotanical lore would represent a tremendous economic and scientific loss to mankind.

What can modern medicine learn from the witch doctor? Certainly, much more than one might think. (p. 13)

These medicine men usually have a profound knowledge of tropical plants and the healing properties for which they may be employed. A single shaman of the Wayana tribe in the northeast Amazon, for example, may use more than a hundred different species for medicinal purposes alone. Furthermore, a great many of the remedies *are* effective. Fungal infections of the skin are a common affliction in the humid tropics, and modern medicine can only suppress—not cure—serious cases. On more than one occasion, I have had serious infections successfully treated by shamans using jungle plants.

Unfortunately, however, the oral tradition of these medicine men is not being passed on to the next generation. With the advent of Western medicine in many of these remote areas, the young members of the tribe demonstrate little interest in learning the traditional ethnomedical lore. Of all the shamans with whom I have lived and worked in the northeast Amazon, not a single one had an apprentice. We are, in my opinion, facing a critical situation—unless we act now, thousands and thousands of years of accumulated knowledge about how to use rain-forest plants is going to disappear before the turn of the century.

What can the medical community do to aid both the struggle to conserve tropical forests and the search for new jungle medicines? Certainly, a much more prominent role needs to be played if both of the aforementioned efforts are to prove successful. Many reasons for species conservation have been presented to the general public—aesthetic, ethical, etc.—but the most relevant for the medicinal profession is the utilitarian: that species are of direct benefit to us. The few examples I have mentioned are indicative of the kinds of undiscovered compounds that are undoubtedly out there.

We now know that synthetics are not the only answers to our medical needs. European pharmaceutical firms are showing renewed interest in the potential of the tropical flora, and there is heightened awareness in the United States, as well. The National Cancer Institute recently awarded more than $2.5 million in contracts to the New York Botanical Garden, the Missouri Botanical Garden, and the University of Illinois to collect and test tropical-plant species for anti-tumor activity.

With the moral and financial support of the U.S. medical community, the conservation movement can help protect and utilize tropical species for human welfare.

We must also consider the importance of medicinal plants in the developing countries themselves. The World Health Organization has estimated that 80% of the people in the world rely on traditional medicine for primary health-care needs. In many cases, developing countries simply cannot afford to spend millions of dollars on imported medicines that they could produce or extract from tropical-forest plants.

Several African and Asian nations have begun to encourage traditional medicine as an integral component of their public health-care programs. Indigenous medicines are relatively inexpensive, locally available, and usually readily accepted by the local populace.

The ideal scenario for the future would be the establishment of local pharmaceutical firms in developing countries of the tropics. These firms would create jobs, reduce unemployment, reduce import expenditures, and generate foreign exchange. Beyond the economic advantages, however, such enterprises would encourage documentation of traditional ethnomedical lore and would promote the conservation and sustainable use of the tropical forest. (pp. 13–14)

Mark J. Plotkin, "The Healing Forest," in The Futurist, Vol. XXIV, No. 1, January-February, 1990, pp. 9–14.

Several African and Asian nations have begun to encourage traditional medicine as an integral component of their public health-care programs. Indigenous medicines are relatively inexpensive, locally available, and usually readily accepted by the local populace.

Sustainable Use: The Forest Industry Perspective

In forestry schools throughout the world, including those in tropical countries, students learn that timber should be removed from natural forests in such a way that periodic harvesting can be sustained more or less perpetually. The immense gap between such presumption and reality has never been wider over the great majority of tropical forests.

The consequences may be termed "catastrophic," not only for the forests themselves and industries that depend on wood products, but perhaps more so for the forestry profession due to loss of credibility. It is no wonder that in many tropical countries foresters are held in low esteem, particularly by conservationists who feel that foresters involved in logging practices are accomplices to the forest destruction that affects so many tropical countries.

Few tropical foresters nowadays advocate the clearing of natural forests and replacing them with what appear to be easier-to-manage monocultures.

Conflict over land use is likely to increase in future years. The higher value of timber and other forest products should help to ease the transition toward sustained yield, but such a shift will require drastic changes in official policies for timber concessions. . . .

It may be necessary to offer incentives to compensate groups that take effective steps in this direction.

There will always be a large percentage of tropical forests in which the goal of sustained yield probably will not be attainable. Such forests may be situated on steep slopes and contain species of little interest to the sawmilling industry. Moreover, their intrinsic value for watershed and soil conservation, science, education, tourism, and as a genetic reservoir and home for native people and their culture, will dictate some type of management that implies protection.

Some of these management possibilities involve designation of certain forests as national parks, wildlife reserves, and biosphere reserves. Such units can then be managed for their unique values and other uses, with the possibility of establishing zoned areas for specific management categories, with adjacent buffer zones where some kind of sustainable forestry may be possible.

There is some ongoing promising research in managing natural forests without destroying their essential features. Fewer tropical foresters nowadays advocate the clearing of natural forests and replacing them with what appear to be easier-to-manage monocultures of fast-growing species, as was done in Jari, Brazil. What is more, there is wider recognition that the tropical forest contributes significantly to the economy of local populations, particularly through the so-called "minor products" (a misnomer) including fruits, honey, thatch, hunting, fishing, medicinal products, erosion control, and a variety of scientific, educational, recreational, aesthetic, and even ethical benefits.

Given the complexity of tropical forests, can any generalization be drawn concerning sustainable timber yields there? From the ecological perspective, it may be possible to reason: the more primary (more "virgin") the forest, the more heterogeneous its floristic composition the higher the rainfall and the poorer the soils, the more difficult it will be to reach sustainable timber production. Poor accessibility, rugged topography and scarcity of nearby markets are powerful factors that act against sustainable production.

One corollary of such statements could then be stated: as a general rule, secondary forests or those where one or a few species dominate the stands are more amenable to sustained production, particularly if they grow on better soils and rainfall is not too high.

Nevertheless, in many countries the various types of heterogeneous primary humid forests have often been described as "a rich untapped source of valuable timbers." How true is this?

Because of our incomplete present knowledge, no sweeping statements can be made. Natural regeneration, for instance, is a very complex process when over 100 different species of trees may be found on only one hectare (2½ acres), a common phenomenon in tropical forests. We know that regeneration depends on gaps—natural (as when a tree falls) or man-made. But what kind of opening brings about what result? This is one of many questions that need to be answered.

One additional problem is the lack of accurate tree identification abilities so prevalent among tropical foresters. One must generally depend on often illiterate local forest workers to get even common tree names, with poor prospects of retrieving the Latin equivalent that would make it possible to consult the scientific literature. This difficulty is compounded when it comes to identifying seedlings, which is sometimes essential to devising adequate silvicultural treatments to favor the valuable species. No wonder so many tropical foresters shun the natural forest and prefer to work in plantations of monocultures or in an office! We badly need practical identification manuals for trees and their seedlings.

The key to sustainable production in the different types of tropical forest is clearly an adequate supply of natural regeneration. Several techniques to encourage such regeneration have been described. They range from drastic treatments such as clearcutting—usually in strips, followed by tending of natural regeneration—to less drastic interventions that include maintaining a certain amount of cover ("shelterwood"), and finally very conservative or cautious steps involving creating openings within the forest.

There are also techniques to combine natural regeneration with artificial plantings that enrich the forest with few seedlings of valuable species. Logging practices often create favorable conditions for inducing natural regeneration, but at present very little attention is given in most timber exploitation schemes to taking good care of existing seedlings, saplings, and pole trees of desirable species.

The key to sustainable management, however, is not only to induce the proliferation of seedlings through judicious openings but also to see that an adequate quantity of these seedlings reaches the canopy in successive years. This implies careful tending by eliminating vines and competing trees that have no commercial value. It implies thinking in terms of the next crop. All these operations add to costs, but "creaming" (high-grading) the natural forests must soon come to an end. We may even think of various types of incentives to bring about the necessary transition. (pp. 34–7)

The main problem at present is that there are no incentives to reach sustainable yield, and the "cut-and-get-out" practice is predominant. Moreover, the roads built by lumber companies favor encroachment by farmers. . . .

Until we have better ecological and socio-economic data, it is sage policy to concentrate sustained-yield management efforts on secondary forests and certain types of flooded forests. Manipulating these forests for timber production is likely to be much less conflictive than tinkering with the disappearing primary forests that are so important to science and deserve to be preserved.

Even for primary forests, there are some possibilities. But much research must be done before the best management technique is selected. An ever-growing proportion of tropical foresters believe that for some primary forests, management for sustainable timber production is the best strategy to save them from destruction.

But we desperately need more and better data and, above all, more success stories. (pp. 80–1)

Gerardo Budowski, "Is Sustainable Harvest Possible in the Tropics?" in American Forests, Vol. 94, Nos. 11 & 12, November-December, 1988, pp. 34–7, 79–81.

Logging practices often create favorable conditions for inducing natural regeneration, but at present very little attention is given in most timber exploitation schemes to taking good care of existing seedlings, saplings, and pole trees of desirable species.

Extractive Reserves: Marketing Non-Timber Products

In 1985 an opportunity arose for maintaining tracts of Amazonian forest under sustainable use. Brazil's National Council of Rubber Tappers and the Rural Worker's Union proposed the creation of a set of reserves of a new type, called extractive reserves. The first six are being established in one of the Brazilian states most threatened by deforestation.

Opposition to extractive reserves has taken on a violent character in Acre, where leaders of the rubber tappers' organization live under the threat of death by gunslingers hired by ranchers.

The creation of extractive reserves grants legal protection to forest land traditionally used by rubber tappers, Brazil-nut gatherers, and other extractivists. The term *extrativismo* (extractivism) in Brazil refers to removing nontimber forest products, such as latex, resins, and nuts, without felling the trees. Approximately 30 products are collected for commercial sale. Many more types of forest materials are gathered, for example as food and medicines, for the extractivists' own use.

Extractivists, principally rubber tappers, have been living in the forest and collecting these products since the rubber boom in the late nineteenth century. Brazil counted 68,000 rubber-tapper families in its 1980 census. These families are estimated to occupy 4–7% of the legal Amazon at a typical density of one family per 300–500 ha. Rubber-tapper organizations claim that the number of tappers is much greater than that registered by the census.

The extractive reserves, as proposed, are to be communally run, with the government retaining land ownership in a manner similar to Amerindian reservations.

But the system is not a form of resource collectivization. Although not issued separate deeds, individual families retain their rights to tap in their traditional collecting territories (*colocações*) within the reserves. The land cannot be sold or converted to nonforest uses, although small clearings for subsistence crops are permitted (usually not exceeding 5 ha per family, or approximately 1%–2% of a reserve).

The first two extractive reserves were decreed in Acre by the governor in February 1988. Four more have since been established there. However, opposition to extractive reserves has taken on a violent character in Acre, where leaders of the rubber tappers' organization live under threat of death by gunslingers hired by ranchers. The assassination of rubber tapper leader Francisco (Chico). Mendes Filho on 22 December 1988 brought this violence to world attention.

Provisions for extractive reserves are included in Brazil's new constitution, which took effect 5 October 1988. Additional reserves are currently proposed in Acre, Rondônia, Amazonas, and Amapá. Loans to Brazil that include funds for extractive reserves are under consideration by the Interamerican Development Bank and the World Bank.

The reserve proposal is attractive for several reasons related to social problems. It allows the rubber tappers to continue their livelihood rather than be expelled by deforestation. However, it is unlikely that sufficient land will be set aside as extractive reserves to employ all the tappers. Displaced rubber tappers already swell the ranks of urban slum dwellers in Brazil's Amazonian cities, and they have become refugees to continue their profession in the forests of neighboring countries, such as Bolivia. (p. 387)

Acre and Rondônia, states that are undergoing rapid deforestation, have the greatest proportion of free, or autonomous, rubber tappers and the strongest rubber-tapper organizations, which see a need to defend the forest for the tappers' survival. Most tappers elsewhere are still under the *aviamento*, or debt peonage, system. Whitesell says that support for the reserves can help rubber tappers outside Acre and Rondônia escape from *aviamento*. Rubber tappers under *aviamento* sell their products to, and buy their provisions from, a rubber baron or *seringalista*. The tappers are "held captive" by the ever-increasing debts they owe the *seringalista*.

Unlike almost all other Amazonian developments, the extractive reserve proposal originated at the grass-roots level. Amazonian development projects are usually decreed by government decision makers or come from the private initiative of outside investors. The local origin of the extractive reserve proposal greatly increases the likelihood that the facilities and the system will be maintained as planned. In settlement projects and other developments planned and delivered from outside, the recipients often lapse into complaining rather than organizing as a community to solve problems and maintain the roads, schools, and other facilities.

Economic self-sufficiency is an important goal of the extractivists. Self-sufficiency will require maximizing the variety and value of the products sold, limiting the drain of money to intermediaries, and minimizing the cost of establishing and maintaining the reserves. Although improving living conditions for the extractivists is a motivation of the proposal's originators, the government is unlikely to be persuaded to create extractive reserves primarily to provide health and education facilities to rubber tappers, because larger, more accessible populations also lack minimal services.

Therefore, the first priority for use of any funds received for extractive reserves must be to demarcate quickly as many reserves as possible. Development of infrastructure to improve living conditions in the reserves should come later and be kept as modest and locally supported as possible. The cost to install health centers and schools in remote areas through the government bureaucracy and its contracted construction firms can be astronomical. Expensive facilities might make the extractive reserve system unsuccessful as an economic venture. Requirements of constant government input would be gleefully seized upon by those waiting for the first sign that the extractive system has failed. They would then insist the forest be cut to give rapid profit to outside investors.

Finding effective ways to block the process of forest loss is an obvious priority. The benefits of deforestation are marginal; cattle pasture, the land use that sooner or later takes over almost all deforested land in Brazilian Amazonia, is unsustainable.

Timber management projects and extractive reserves should be promoted as alternatives to deforestation. The forest remaining in the region is ample for both. Where conflicts of interest occur between these options, extractive reserves are preferable.

If the Brazilian government promotes forestry management for timber production, those in power will increase their vested interest in the forester's survival. But forestry management projects, such as an International Timber Organization scheme proposed in Acre, have several disadvantages when compared to extractive reserves:

● Their sustainability is unproven;

● They provide less benefit for the local population;

● They provoke greater disturbance of the forest;

● Their top-down planning and administration reduce the likelihood that they will resist the constantly changing winds of official policies, thereby reducing the chances of a consistent long-term management routine;

● Their management routines are more susceptible to circumvention through corruption (e.g., a major impediment to sustained management schemes in Indonesia);

● Because of reliance on paid guards, they are less likely to resist invasion by migrants and speculators.

In contrast, extractive reserves produce salable goods on a sustainable basis, using known harvesting techniques that have proved themselves over approximately a century of continuous use in these areas and that rely on the people who live in the reserves and whose livelihoods depend directly on the forest's continued existence. Production of economic goods, especially rubber, is the principal argument used by the rubber tappers in justifying their proposal to the government. The value of nonwood products extracted in Acre, Rondônia, and Amazonas totaled US $48 million in 1980, according to official statistics. But this argument may not be strong enough to withstand future pressure to allocate land to other uses. This pressure is expected to mount as the price of tropical hardwood continues to rise and when the flood of migrants to Acre increases after completion of the reconstruction and paving of the BR-364

Extractive reserves produce salable goods on a sustainable basis, using known harvesting techniques that have proved themselves over approximately a century of continuous use in these areas and that relay on the people who live in the reserves and whose livelihoods depend directly on the forest's continued existence.

Amazonia might prove to be less of a pharmaceutical treasure house than some have claimed. But, at the very least, the forest should not be thrown away before there is a systematic evaluation of the compounds it contains.

Highway from Porto Velho (Rondônia) to Rio Branco (Acre) in 1989 (and later from Rio Branco to the Pacific).

The production of nonwood economic goods is less of a justification than it may appear, because Amazonian rubber is highly subsided. Rubber prices in Brazil are approximately three times higher than the international price. Rubber is more cheaply produced on plantations in Southeast Asia than in Amazonia, because Asia does not suffer from South American leaf blight fungus (*Microcyclus ulei*, formerly *Dothidella ulei*). This fungus increases costs and lowers productivity in Amazonian plantations.

Although rubber trees in natural forests suffer only light levels of fungal attack, the long distances that must be walked between forest trees make labor requirements high per ton of rubber collected. Of the Brazilian rubber production, the proportion obtained from plantations is steadily increasing as rubber planting spreads in Brazil's non-Amazonian states.

Brazil produces less than 1% of the world's natural rubber. The country imports approximately half the natural rubber it uses. This fraction is down from a previous reported level of two-thirds. However, as domestic production expands, the rubber subsidy is expected to become more and more onerous to Brazilian consumers. (pp. 387–92)

World Prices for natural rubber have been low for several years, so that even some Asian plantations have become unprofitable. For an increasing number of uses, synthetic rubber, particularly polyisoprene, can substitute for natural rubber.

The cost of synthetics is heavily dependent on petroleum prices. Thus in the long run, oil prices can be expected to increase as global supplies dwindle, thereby improving the relative demand for natural rubber.

The rubber tappers would be wise to make a major effort to diversify the products they extract and sell. This strategy would require collaboration with researchers (such as pharmacologists, chemists, and botanists) to develop new products, especially from medicinal plants. By limiting the products collected and the intensities of harvesting, care must be taken that only sustainable extraction is practiced.

Marketing mechanisms for new products need to be developed if extractivists are ever to enjoy a reasonable standard of living. As the misery of the rubber tappers during the rubber boom shows, when the value of the products accrues to intermediaries, extractivists remain poor, regardless of the amount of wealth they generate. Also, institutional arrangements need to be made to assure that the extractivists receive royalties from the future sale of the products, including synthetic copies and subsequent modifications of plant compounds.

Biological information is a valuable extractive resource, although the monetary value of genetic material and potential pharmaceutical compounds is difficult to assess.

The forest has inspired flights of fancy since the search for the fountain of youth almost 500 years ago, but information on the potential value of the forest as a source of medicinal plants is scanty and largely anecdotal. No one pays indigenous peoples for traditional knowledge that leads to identification of new compounds from nature. Amazonia holds the world's largest store of species. Deforestation destroys both the compounds themselves and the traditional knowledge of the medicinal uses of each plant.

Most drugs now produced synthetically in laboratories were almost invariably obtained originally from living organisms (e.g., the mold that produces penicillin and the willow that produces the active ingredient in aspirin). New drugs continue to be needed because new diseases continue to appear and drug-resistant strains of old diseases are constantly arising. Recently anticancer agents were discovered in the Madagascar periwinkle, a tropical plant containing more than 60 useful alkaloids. Analysis of the periwinkle, whose promise was indicated by its use in folk medicine, revealed a class of compounds whose pharmacological activity could not have been guessed on the basis of existing chemical knowledge.

One drug (vincristine or leurocristine) extracted from the periwinkle has reduced mortality from lymphocytic (child) leukemia from 80% in 1960 to 20% today, and another (vinblastine or vincaleukoblastine) has raised the 10-year survival rate for Hodgkin's disease from 2% to 58%.

Statements submitted by pharmceutical firms to a US congressional committee that assessed impacts of tropical deforestation described the value of forest compounds as models for subsequent industrial synthesis. However, even in the absence of any arrangement for returning some of the profits to the extractivists, activity in exploring tropical plants is limited among large pharmaceutical firms.

The lack of substantial effort by pharmaceutical companies to screen Amazonian plants for new compounds is frequently put forward by governmental agencies as evidence that the forest's potential usefulness is low. The tepid response is better explained by the costs and risks of the search for new compounds. The long process of testing not only makes future returns weigh little when discounted for financial decision making, but it also extends product development beyond the job longevity of most corporate executives. The attraction of a faster payoff favors investments in less substantive activities, such as refining the packaging and advertising of current products. Because drug company executives are guided by their financial balance sheets, these companies are not likely to initiate a screening program with the speed and scale required.

Similarly, some firms are more interested in the Amazonian forest's potential for providing ingredients for soaps and cosmetics. Part of the attraction of cosmetics is the more rapid and inexpensive process of gaining approval for marketing, as compared with drugs, which are encumbered by requirements for extended clinical testing. These nonmedicinal uses, although providing some potential income, lack the important moral appeal that pharmaceutical compounds have in justifying the maintenance of forests.

Amazonia might prove to be less of a pharmaceutical treasure house than some have claimed. But, at the very least, the forest should not be thrown away before there is a systematic evaluation of the compounds it contains. As is the case for many potential uses of the forest, cost-benefit analysis for pharmaceutical screening is inherently unreliable, because it is based on estimating the difference between large and uncertain numbers. Although monetary value is often cited as a principal reason for not destroying the Amazon forest, good reasons would exist for saving it even if the forest were not financially valuable. These reasons would remain important even if its replacement were a miraculous crop that produced sustainable yields of US dollar bills. These reasons include the forest's role in macroecological processes, such as the water cycle and the balance of atmospheric gases that affect global climate.

Some have argued that substantial tracts of natural ecosystems should be preserved just because there is so much about the forest that is not yet understood. Humility should motivate at least some preservation. Such explicitly noneconomic and nonutilitarian arguments for saving tropical forests as those made by Budowski, Ehrenfeld, Jacobs, Janzen, and Poore are usually dismissed in Brazil pejoratively as "poetry" or "very beautiful." But a strong case must be made for saving substantial tracts of forest on the basis of human self-interest in spheres unrelated to direct use of the forest's products.

The question of whether Brazil should allow its Amazonian forest to be destroyed is not related to direct economic costs and benefits. If financial benefit is insufficient, one should not cut down the forest but rather alter the economic equation until conservation becomes profitable.

Finding ways to make sustainable uses profitable and nonsustainable ones unprofitable is essential.

Maintaining the forest should be a given, from which economic mechanisms must follow. The proposed plan for a set of extractive reserves offers an excellent opportunity to act on this precondition in a way that is inexpensive, solves an number of social problems, and, above all, is likely to be effective.

The idea of Lovejoy's study is to create little, big and bigger islands of rain forest, ranging from 1 to 10,000 hectare. Biologists regularly census each tract before and after it is isolated and compare the results with plots of similar size in the unfragmented forest.

Researchers are racing to find ways to make saving the forest economically advantageous. These efforts include identifying new products obtainable from the forest, finding sustainable economic uses for timber trees, demonstrating the feasibility of sustained forest management, and documenting both the environmental costs (including the greenhouse effect) of forest loss and how short-lived are the benefits of most land uses that replace it.

Other actions could include altering the relative prices of sustainable and non-sustainable products to favor the sustainable ones and changing the discount rates used in evaluating forest-use options. High discount rates provide economists with a rationale for disregarding the future costs and benefits, which may be a rational way for investors to decide how to maximize profits, but it is no way for a country to decide how to develop in the best interests of its people.

To point the government's activity in the direction of sustainable forest use will require disposing of traditional economic calculations rather than tinkering with their input parameters. The real reason for maintaining forest is not directly economic.

Maintaining forest should be treated as a constraint on development options that is accepted before cost-benefit or other economic calculations are made. This constraint should have a place similar to that of national security. For example, security considerations have led the Brazilian government to force consumers to pay higher prices to help the country to gain independence in producing such products as computers, automobiles, small aircraft, rubber, and fuel alcohol. Rather than simply selecting the cheaper option for supplying these products, the government has forced the economy to adapt itself to overriding considerations.

The same logic applies to controlling deforestation and favoring sustainable forest use. Maintaining the forest should be a given, from which economic mechanisms must follow. The proposed plan for a set of extractive reserves offers an excellent opportunity to act on this precondition in a way that is inexpensive, solves a number of social problems, and, above, all, is likely to be effective. (pp. 392–93)

Philip M. Fearnside, "Extractive Reserves in Brazilian Amazonia," in BioScience, *Vol. 39, No. 6, June, 1989, pp. 387–93.*

Minimum Critical Size: Fragments for the Future

Talk about topsy-turvy.

The goal of the enterprise is, ultimately, to save the rain forests of the tropics. The biologists are standing in the searing equatorial heat, dark stains on their soggy shirts. Stretching away in nearly every direction is destruction. A war zone. Tree trunks lie in disarray awaiting the torch, a blanket of corpses punctuated by jagged stumps covering gentle slopes and lowlands.

A few miles south, coarse green grass has begun to grow up among the stumps. Small herds of Zebu cattle had stared indifferently with African-mask countenances as the biologists had driven here over a dirt track in rattletrap trucks and four-wheel-drive vehicles. This place is a ranch, a *fazenda*, aborning a little more than 2 degrees south of the Equator and about 50 miles north of the city of Manaus in Brazil—an area that recently had hosted unbroken stretches of one of the most diverse ecosystems on the planet, the Amazon rain forest. Now great patches are being systematically clear-cut.

But the rancher is having labor problems: work has stopped. Rob Bierregaard, a tropical biologist and ornithologist, becomes impatient. He rounds up a chain saw, waggishly affixes to it a decal of the World Wildlife Fund's panda emblem and proceeds to hack away at the tall trees.

That was a few years ago, although fundraisers still cringe at the thought of that decal. Today the biologists—Americans with the World Wildlife Fund (WWF) and Brazilians working for the National Institute for Research on Amazonia (INPA)—are hoping that a lull in Brazil's typically feverish economy will soon end so the ranchers can get back to work yet again, cutting down more rain forest so that, in turn, the single largest conservation-ecology study ever mounted can continue.

Tropical biologists do not normally show delight in the midst of a clear-cut rain forest, much less collude with the clear-cutters. They among all people are too aware of what such a loss means. But this group is taking the long view. Bierregaard purposefully took up his heretical chain saw to help speed the eventual isolation of a patch of forest, one of many that range in size from 1 hectare (about 2.5 acres) to 100 and even 1,000 hectares. It is all part of a study that will help settle some complex questions in ecology and in the process provide a key to preserving at least some of this fast-disappearing resource. No one knows how rapidly tropical rain forests are vanishing but it is generally accepted that we are losing each year enough to cover the state of Minnesota.

The idea for this study popped up fully formed (like an eco-Athena) from the brain of Thomas Lovejoy, then vice president for science of the World Wildlife Fund (and now an Assistant Secretary of the Smithsonian Institution), a few days before Christmas in 1976. Today, well after the fact, it can be seen as a natural confluence of conservation need, scientific question and Brazilian law: an opportunity for a prepared mind. Part of the economic plan for the Brazilian state of Amazonas, of which Manaus is the capital, called for the creation of large cattle ranches in the forest. The law decreed that, in clearing away forest for pastureland, 50 percent of the forest had to be left standing.

The scientific question, briefly stated, had arisen from the ecological study of islands and extinction rates: How big must a tract of rain forest be to maintain its biological integrity?

The conservation need was obvious. (pp. 107–08)

To preserve such places, however, is a practical matter involving politics and, importantly, scientific certainty. Developers tend to ignore arguments from emotion or esthetics. The idea of Lovejoy's study is to create little, big and bigger islands of rain forest, ranging from 1 to 10,000 hectares. Biologists regularly census each tract before and after it is isolated and compare the results with plots of similar size in the unfragmented natural forest. To date, in four connected *fazendas*, there are five 1-hectare isolates, five of 10 hectares and one of 100, with more of each planned, along with two 1,000-hectare plots and one of 10,000. The goal is to watch the islands degrade—to observe which species leave or die out, and in what order—with a view ultimately to discovering the minimum critical sizes reserves must be for given species to survive. The project is now some eight years old and expected to run until 1999. It will continue to produce answers well into the next century, but even now the findings emanating from the *fazendas* are suggestive. (p. 109)

One of the earliest researchers on the project was Judy Rankin de Merona, a University of Michigan botanist now on the INPA staff whose responsibility is nothing less than the trees in the forest. In the Amazon, she explains, "10 hectares will support 300 different tree species. That's 10 times what you find in a typical temperate zone forest." (p. 110)

While Rankin de Merona looks into the tree population, other creatures must also be assayed. This can be done by sampling representative locations: placing traps and nets on specific transects of the island-to-be and making extrapolations from what is caught. Butterflies can be lured into nets with the likes of rotting fruit and favored plants: other insects will wind up in ultraviolet

Once they've dried out a little, the trees are given the torch and fire rages over hundreds of hectares in a matter of hours, filling the sky for miles with a thick, yellow smoke; the Armageddon sun comes and goes, a bruised and wan source of light.

Patterns of life can change swiftly in the tropical rain forest and few effects of isolation were so quickly apparent as what biologists call the "edge effect."

prisons, in tin cans set in the ground or in what are called malaise traps, which work on the principle that some insects fly upward at any sign of danger. Mammals, including 8 kinds of marsupials and 11 rodents, can be snared. Birds fly unwittingly into mist nets, strung up in extensive lines across known or suspected flyways. These are extremely delicate nets that would be suitable for a ghostly brand of volleyball; the birds become entangled and wait with what looks like patience to be released, a complaining mate often hanging around nearby. Those that frequent the canopy at heights of 100 feet or more must simply be counted by observations. (p. 110–11)

Once such censuses are done—and one of the deadlines involves the schedule of the rancher—then the destruction begins. The trees are felled by the Amazon version of migrant workers. It is extremely dangerous work with trees falling at a stupendous rate. Later, once they've dried out a little, the trees are given the torch and fire rages over hundreds of hectares in a matter of hours, filling the sky for miles with a thick, yellow smoke; the Armageddon sun comes and goes, a bruised and wan source of light.

The INPA staff must often participate in the pyrotechnics. Alerted to a burn, project workers head out from Manaus to set their own fires, in this case fire lines to protect the precious isolates, just as firefighters do in our national forests. The complicity is always seen as ironic. (p. 111)

Early on, the scientists began to see specific results. After isolation, for example, a one-hectare plot of forest would soon gain more than twice as many understory birds as it would usually have. With their habitat eliminated, they naturally flocked to the remnant, turning the normal noise of the place into a cacophony of squawks, screeches and chirps. After about six months, there would be a precipitous decline.

In such a habitat, there are what are called behavioral guilds of birds. Some are ground feeders, other specialize in the life around fallen trees. Some eat fruit and some are obligate ant-followers. In the labyrinthine ways of life here, the ant-following birds—woodcreepers, for example—depend entirely on the forays of army ants to flush other insects such as grasshoppers, crickets and cockroaches. In 10-hectare plots the colonies of army ants, which in their periodic movements range over as much as 30 hectares, couldn't survive; deprived of the flushed insects, the birds also vanished. Such plots were also, expectedly, too small for large mammals like peccaries, which went off in search of other territory. After they left, there was no animal around to create wallows that hold water; as a result, three species of frogs that depend on standing water also disappeared.

Yet other creatures (less-obligate ones, it might be said) simply changed habits. When crowded, flycatchers forage on lower levels than normal. A kind of mouse opossum spends its time in the canopy under normal circumstances. But in isolated plots, Jay Malcolm, whose beat is the largely unknown mammal fauna, found that this omnivore migrated to the ground and became more insectivorous.

Patterns of life can change swiftly in the tropical rain forest and few effects of isolation were so quickly apparent as what biologists call the "edge effect." One day, as we picked our way through the tangle of fallen logs toward a ten-hectare plot, Judy Rankin de Merona announced: "There. See that? There's a really good edge." About 200 yards off was the long straight perimeter of the forest fragment. And indeed, even at that distance, one could see the dense tangle of vines and new trees that formed the edge. Closer up, one could see hundreds of little butterflies.

The rain forest is a soggy place. The humidity seems total; within seconds one's shirt becomes a damp rag. It is also dark. High overhead, the canopy screens out most of the sunlight. If a rainstorm comes up, it may be ten minutes before the rainwater finds its way to the ground. Things are very different when a sharp edge is caused by destroying the surrounding forest. Sunlight pours in where it had rarely been glimpsed. The humidity drops. Relatively dry, hot winds blow on trees and soils that had never felt a breeze. Second-growth plants are quick to take advantage. What is surprising is just how far *in* the edge effect occurs. One- and ten-hectare plots, it has been discovered become completely edge in a matter of months.

Tree-fall around the perimeter occurs at rapid rates, mostly because those trees are now exposed to strong winds, but also in part because of the extremely rapid degradation of soil. The soil is already poor; most of the nutrients of the forest are not to be found in rich soils like those in temperate forests, but tied up in the trees themselves. Leaves fall from the trees at a constant rate, then are rapidly decomposed by insects, bacteria and fungal organisms, and reabsorbed into the trees themselves. In the thin, sandy soil of the tropical rain forest, it doesn't take much of a change in such things as soil moisture or temperature to cause life-changing results for the shallow-rooted trees.

One obvious finding from the early years of the project is that in setting aside a forest preserve one has to leave an adequate perimeter as a buffer zone, perhaps hundreds of meters wide, so that the edge effect can take place and still leave a sufficient core of virgin rain forest. (pp. 111–12)

Some things go slowly in the larger tracts. Even after five years there is not a great deal of difference to the naked eye, besides the edge effect, in a 100-hectare plot. Bierregaard wanted to know if a computer could see differences the biologists could not. He fed the INPA computers codes for each of the 45 most frequently netted bird species in different-sized plots, along with data on the numbers of nettings. The computers could always tell if they were "looking" at an isolated plot or a patch of undisturbed forest, and they could always tell how large each isolated plot was.

The biologists have played with corridors as well; one of the principles in laying out reserves is to maintain corridors of usable habitat between them, whenever possible. They had left a corridor running to undisturbed forest when they isolated a 100-hectare plot in 1983. After a year, they found that the obligate ant-following birds were still there, still being trapped in the mist nets. One possibility is that as individual birds died, they were replaced by others from the corridor—a persisting, if changing, population. Another is that the original population disapppeared at once, but others were using the isolated tract, coming and going via the corridor but not living there full time. When biologists cut a narrow strip across the corridor, the ant-followers vanished almost immediately.

Once the Brazilian economy heats up and the ranchers get under way again, they will isolate another 100-hectare plot, this time with no corridor, and then the biologists may find out exactly what is happening with the ant-followers. Meanwhile, the value of corridors is considered proved; without them, "several gears in the ecological machinery are missing," says Bierregaard.

It remains to be seen just what the right size is for a wilderness area of Amazonian rain forest. Even a 10,000-hectare plot probably will not be large enough to maintain a jaguar population. (John Terborgh has guessed that it would take a minimum of 500,000 hectares to maintain a genetically viable jaguar population, given their usual territories and the matter of inbreeding.) But even when the people at INPA discover the actual minimum critical size, it has been said then all they will be able to suggest to governments like that of Brazil is that the minimum be saved. Lovejoy retorts that without knowing the minimum size even governments with the best intentions will be likely to set aside *less* than the minimum.

Contrary to popular understanding in the United States, some Brazilians are bent on saving what they can of the rain forests. About 15 years ago, a man named Paulo Nogueira-Neto was appointed the Brazilian equivalent of the U.S. Secretary of the Interior. A determined conservationist, he began with two assistants and three desks. In his 12 years in office he arranged for Brazil to set aside areas for the preservation of rain forest habitats that are, all in all, almost equal to the land area of Connecticut. He is a major supporter of the project in Manaus.

It remains to be seen just what the right size is for a wilderness area of Amazonian rain forest. Even a 10,000 hectare plot probably will not be large enough to maintain a jaguar population.

"In a sense, the project is helping to create a new generation of conservation-minded scientists in Brazil— clearly a plus."

—Thomas Lovejoy,
Assistant Secretary,
Smithsonian Institution

The optimism arises from other causes as well. Late last year Lovejoy left the World Wildlife Fund to join the Smithsonian, but he has lost none of his passion for the project. It will continue to be the focus of his own research efforts. In Washington earlier this year he listed some of the benefits of the project. It already has provided training for 100 Brazilian students of rain forest ecology, ranging from people who have helped with birdbanding to others who have gone on to get master's degrees from their work there. "In a sense, the project is helping to create a new generation of conservation-minded scientists in Brazil—clearly a plus. We just added up the numbers the other day. I had no idea we were that far along."

All of the isolates are now preserved for the future by presidential decree. The larger areas, long-term data producers, will continue to change for as long as a century and a half. But more important is that they fit data from the project into a wholly new conservation strategy.

"Conservation," says Lovejoy, "has traditionally been a static, defensive affair. The idea has been to put a fence around it and it'll stay that way." Even the smaller plots, those that have degraded quickly and have mostly given way to the edge effect, hold practical value for the future. "But suppose," Lovejoy says, "you've got an area that is only 10 percent of whatever the right size is. That means that in time you'll end up with only 50 percent of the original species diversity. But that gives you decades before the end result happens, before you're down to 50 percent. You've still got plenty of time to get your hands on the surrounding area and regenerate the forest."

Regenerating what Lovejoy himself has called the "most complex ecosystem that we have yet found in the Universe" seems like pie in the sky. But not, he points out, if you look at the entire watershed of the city of Rio de Janeiro. In the 19th century, it was almost wholly denuded of forest, but then encouraged to regenerate. Now it is in a form similar to the original—not as rich and complex, perhaps, but nevertheless a recognizable rain forest. And the project's islands of forests will themselves serve as "seeds" for the eventual recolonization of the *fazendas*. (pp. 114, 116)

It is dangerous to promise too much in such matters, but rarely have gloom and despair produced much by way of progress. "We've been managing the planet for a long time now, mostly by neglect," says Lovejoy. "Now we simply have to learn how to intervene properly and to manage it positively." (p. 116)

Jake Page, "Clear-Cutting the Tropical Rain Forest in a Bold Attempt to Salvage It," in Smithsonian, *Vol. 19, No. 1, April, 1988, pp. 106–12, 114, 116–17.*

Sources For Further Study

Almeda, Frank, and Pringle, Catharine M., eds. *Tropical Rainforests: Diversity and Conservation.* San Francisco: California Academy of Sciences and Pacific Division, American Association for the Advancement of Science, 1988, 306 p.
    Collects papers that were presented by such noted conservationists as Thomas E. Lovejoy and Mark J. Plotkin at a symposium on tropical deforestation in 1985.

Begley, Sharon. "The World's Largest Lab." *Newsweek* CXIII, No. 8 (20 January 1989): 46–7.
    Reports on the race to study the Amazon's biodiversity before it is lost.

Cockburn, Alexander. "Unto Dust." *Interview* XIX, No. 1 (January 1989): 66–9, 87, 91.

Interview with noted agronomist Susanna Hecht in which she discusses the devastation of the Amazon rain forest.

Copulos, Milton R. "The Environment: A North-South Conflict." *Current*, No. 317 (November 1989): 35–9.
Examines the conflict between developed nations and developing countries concerning rain forest conservation.

"Empire of the Chainsaws." *The Economist* 320, No. 7719 (10 August 1991): 36.
Relates the findings of a World Bank report that assesses many of the measures now in place to save the rain forest as inadequate.

Goodland, Robert, ed. *Race to Save the Tropics: Ecology and Economics for a Sustainable Future*. Washington, D.C.: Island Press, 1990, 219 p.
Collects articles that discuss how the principles of ecology can be used to improve conservation efforts and promote economic growth in tropical countries.

Hecht, Susanna, and Cockburn, Alexander. "Defenders of the Amazon." *The Nation* 248, No. 20 (22 May 1989): 695–96, 698–702.
Chronicles the struggles of Brazilian rubber tappers against their government and cattle ranchers to preserve the forests and improve their way of life.

———. *The Fate of the Forest: Developers, Destroyers, and Defenders of the Amazon*. London: Verso, 1989, 266 p.
A "humanist and ecological manifesto" concerning the destruction of the Amazon.

Jackson, James P. "The Edge of Extinction." *American Forests* 94, Nos. 11–12 (November-December 1988): 41–5.
Considers the many endangered species of the rain forests and the efforts underway to preserve them.

Joyce, Stephanie. "Snorting Peru's Rain Forest." *International Wildlife* 20, No. 3 (May-June 1990): 20–3.
Reports on how the demand for cocaine has resulted in massive deforestation as vast tracts of land are given over to the cultivation of coca.

Katzman, Martin T., and Cale, William G., Jr. "Tropical Forest Preservation Using Economic Incentives." *BioScience* 40, No. 11 (December 1990): 827–32.
Frames the problem of deforestation in economic terms and propose a system of conservation easements sponsored by industrialized nations to compensate individual nations for protecting specific habitats.

Landis, Scott. "The Peruvian Experiment." *Wilderness* 53, No. 188 (Spring 1990): 58–60, 62.
Reports on the attempts of scientists and international aid workers to introduce sustainable tropical agriculture to Peru.

Lewis, Scott. *The Rainforest Book*. Los Angeles: Living Planet Press, 1990, 112 p.
An accessible guide to rain forest conservation.

Linden, Eugene. "Good Intentions, Woeful Results." *Time* 137, No. 13 (1 April 1991): 48–9.
Discusses why the Tropical Forestry Action Plan, a conservation program sponsored in part by the World Bank and the United Nations, has in fact contributed to tropical deforestation.

Lora, Mary Elaine. "Gardens of Hope." *American Forests* 96, Nos. 11–12 (November-December 1990): 57–9, 76.
Reports on the attempts of Peruvian Indians to reclaim degraded land through the planting of trees and native crops.

Lugo, Ariel E. "The Future of the Forest." *Environment* 30, No. 7 (September 1988): 16–20, 41–5.
Outlines possible strategies for rehabilitating rain forest ecosystems.

Monastersky, Richard. "The Fall of the Forest." *Science News* 138, No. 3 (21 July 1990): 40–1.
> Presents data from a World Resources Institute report on tropical deforestation in which the estimated rate of destruction is revised upward from 11.3 to 16.4–20.4 million hectares per year.

Morell, Virginia. "A Genetic Storehouse Goes Up in Flames." *International Wildlife* 20, No. 2 (March-April 1990): 6–7.
> Investigates the new partnership between researchers and local people in designing strategies for sustainable use of the Amazon rain forest.

Nelson-Horchler, Joani. "Please Save the Rain Forests!" *Industry Week* 239, No. 12 (18 June 1990): 85–6.
> Discusses the timber industry's growing awareness of the need for rain forest conservation.

Omang, Joanne. "In the Tropics, Still Rolling Back the Rain Forest Primeval." *Smithsonian* 17, No. 12 (March 1987): 56–60, 62, 64–7.
> Reports on the growing threat to Costa Rica's farsighted conservation plan by coffee growers, cattle ranchers, and subsistence farmers.

Parafit, Michael. "Whose Hands Will Shape the Future of the Amazon's Green Mansions?" *Smithsonian* 20, No. 8 (November 1989): 58–68, 70–2, 74.
> Reports on how Brazilian wild rubber tappers and Indians, long regarded as the primary defenders of the rain forest, are losing land to cattle ranches and foreign-owned rubber plantations.

Patterson, Alan. "Debt for Nature Swaps and the Need for Alternatives." *Environment* 32, No. 10 (December 1990): 4–13, 31–2.
> Outlines the benefits and drawbacks of the economic incentive program proposed by Thomas E. Lovejoy and suggests other methods for promoting conservation in tropical countries.

Posey, Darrell A. "Alternatives to Forest Destruction: Lessons from the Mêbêngôkre Indians." *The Ecologist* 19, No. 6 (December 1989): 341–44.
> Argues that modern land use practices in Amazonia are inherently unsustainable, and that in destroying Indian societies the Brazilian government is losing a vital source of information as to how people can live in and enrich, rather than destroy, the rain forest.

Prance, Ghillean. "Fruits of the Rainforest." *New Scientist* 125, No. 1699 (13 January 1990): 42–5.
> Discusses how the marketing of such tropical rain forest-derived products as fruits, nuts, resins, and medicinal plants can aid in preserving the Brazilian rain forest.

Repetto, Robert. "Needed: New Policy Goals." *American Forests* 94, Nos. 11–12 (November-December 1988): 59, 82–6.
> Proposes a means for reforming the approach of governments and aid agencies to tropical forest management and land use, which Repetto argues, has often been misguided.

——— . "Deforestation in the Tropics." *Scientific American* 262, No. 4 (April 1990): 36–42.
> Presents evidence that tropical forestry has not resulted in expected economic development but has been a costly drain of increasingly valuable resources due to poor stewardship by governments and private industry.

Roberts, Leslie. "Ranking the Rain Forests." *Science* 251, No. 5001 (29 March 1991): 1559–560.
> Reports on the Rapid Assessment Program, a research project sponsored by Conservation International that quickly gathers data on threatened tracts of rain forest to determine which areas most deserve protection.

Shiva, Vandana. "Forestry Myths and the World Bank." *The Ecologist* 17, Nos. 4–5 (July-December 1987): 142–49.

Repudiates *Tropical Forests: A Call to Action*, a report by the World Resources Institute that attributes tropical deforestation to the poor of developing countries and promotes commercial forestry as a solution to the problem.

Shukla, J.; Nobre, C.; and Sellers, P. "Amazon Deforestation and Climate Change." *Science* 247, No. 4948 (16 March 1990): 1322-325.
Presents data from a coupled numerical model of the global atmosphere and biosphere used to assess the effects of Amazon deforestation on the regional and global climate.

Smith, Nigel J. H.; Williams, J. T.; and Plucknett, Donald L. "Conserving the Tropical Cornucopia." *Environment* 33, No. 6 (July-August 1991): 7–9, 30–2.
Investigates the possible loss of foods, fuels, spices, and other valuable products as a result of rain forest depletion.

Sun, Marjorie. "How Do You Measure the Lovejoy Effect?" *Science* 247, No. 4947 (9 March 1990): 1174–176.
Profile of Dr. Thomas E. Lovejoy, a noted expert on tropical ecology and assistant secretary at the Smithsonian Institute whose innovative conservation programs have garnered worldwide attention.

Uhl, Christopher, et. al. "Disturbance and Regeneration in Amazonia: Lessons for Sustainable Land-Use." *The Ecologist* 19, No. 6 (November-December 1989): 235–40.
Discusses how rain forests regenerate after such natural disruptions as fires and tree-falls and contends that understanding this process is vital to the restoration of tropical ecosystems following human-induced devastation.

Wade, Alan. "Treasures of the Guatemala Rain Forest." *The New Leader* LXXII, No. 7 (3–17 April 1989): 11–13.
Reports on efforts to develop *La ruta Maya*, a tour of Mayan archeological sites in Mexico and Central America that would help preserve the encompassing rain forest.

Wallace, Joseph. "Rainforest R$_x$." *Sierra* 76, No. 4 (July-August 1991): 36–41.
Describes the efforts of botanists and environmentalists to save the rain forest through the discovery and promotion of indigenous medicinal plants.

Warner, Edward. "Ecotourism: New Hope for Rainforests?" *American Forests* 97, Vols. 3–4 (March-April 1991): 37–44.
Examines the ecological benefits and drawbacks of tourism in rain forests and other ecologically threatened areas.

Whitmore, T. C. *An Introduction to Tropical Rain Forests*. Oxford: Clarendon Press, 1990, 226 p.
Provides a comprehensive introduction to rain forest ecology and conservation.

Worcman, Nira Broner. "Brazil's Thriving Environmental Movement." *Technology Review* 93, No. 7 (October 1991): 42–51.
Investigates the efforts of some Brazilians to preserve the Amazon despite official and economic pressure to continue deforestation.

14:   Recycling

Recycling: What It Is and How It Works

Recycling involves using materials which are at the end of their useful lives as the feedstocks for the manufacture of new products. It is differentiated from reuse by the reprocessing and remanufacture operations.

Within recycling, a further hierarchy can be defined. Primary recycling is the use of recycled products to make the same or similar products. Examples include the use of aluminum cans to make new aluminum cans and glass bottles to make new glass bottles. Because this is at least partially a closed loop process, it can and should be regarded as having a higher value than secondary recycling.

Secondary recycling is the use of recycled materials to make new products with less stringent specifications than the original. This allows for downgrading of the material to suit its possibly diminished properties, and hence is of lower value than primary recycling.

The recovery of chemicals or energy from waste materials . . . is often classified as tertiary or quaternary recycling, respectively.

All recycling systems must have three major components in order to function. First, they must have a consistent and reliable source of recycled material. . . . Second, methods for processing the recovered materials into a form suitable for reuse must be in place. . . . Third, markets must exist for the reprocessed material. It is only when all these components function in an economically viable manner that a recycling system exists.

Collection

Recycling in this writing is differentiated from resource recovery by noting the point at which the separation of materials is made. In resource recovery operations, materials are recovered for reuse from a mixed stream of solid waste. Recycling programs rely on separation of recyclable materials before they are mixed in with the rest of the waste, known as source-separation. The separation may be complex or simple, involving separation into a number of different categories, or only into recyclable versus nonrecyclables.

Source-separation-based recycling programs differ from each other in several respects, most notably in the materials included, whether they provide collection or are drop-off programs, and whether they are voluntary or mandatory in nature. They are all similar in that their success depends on community involvement and in community education to achieve the change in habits needed.

Drop-Off Programs. Drop-off programs rely on the participants to deliver materials for recycling to a centralized location or locations. These locations may be as convenient as a bin in an apartment laundry room, or as inconvenient as a location a number of miles away which is open for only a few hours one day a month. The individuals bringing the items to the collection point may or may

---

Recycling involves using materials which are at the end of their useful lives as the feedstocks for the manufacture of new products. It is differentiated from reuse by the reprocessing and remanufacture operations.

Primary recycling is the use of recycled products to make the same or similar products. Examples include the use of aluminum cans to make new aluminum cans and glass bottles to make new glass bottles.

Secondary recycling is the use of recycled materials to make new products with less stringent specifications than the original.

Barriers to recycling include lack of awareness, indifference, inconvenience, the feeling that an individual's activities have no real impact, and attitudes which look for a "technological fix" rather than lifestyle changes.

not receive monetary compensation for their efforts. The drop-off locations may be manned or unmanned. In many locations these programs are run and staffed by volunteers. Their revenue is derived from the sale of the collected materials.

Many of the most successful drop-off recycling programs in the United States are multimaterial recycling centers which are part of the Beverage Industry Recycling Program (BIRP). These centers were established with assistance from the beverage industries to recycle primarily beverage containers as an alternative to bottle deposit legislation. All of the programs accept both glass bottles and jars and aluminum cans and, in many cases, also handle plastic soft drink bottles, bimetal cans (steel with aluminum ends), and newspaper. Most of the centers are located in the western half of the United States. Some of the states which have BIRP multimaterial recycling centers are Arizona, California, Colorado, Illinois, Kansas, Kentucky, Maryland, Missouri, Nevada, New Mexico, North Carolina, Ohio, Oklahoma, Texas, Washington, and West Virginia. Most of these centers pay consumers for the material brought in for recycling. As an additional incentive for consumer participation, many of the centers are set up as theme parks to make recycling fun. Circus themes are especially popular, with other themes including riverboats, railroads, and mining camps. The emphasis is on making the recycling centers clean, efficient, and family oriented.

Pickup Operations. Recycling programs that provide collection for recyclables also differ significantly from one another. Some programs are run by volunteer groups, while others are run by professionals. Pickup may be weekly, monthly, or intermittently. Newspapers are the material most frequently collected. The first United States curbside collection program for newspaper began twenty years ago in Madison, Wisconsin.

Curbside pickup programs offer collection of recyclables from the curb like regular garbage service. Collection is generally done either once a month or more frequently, and may be at the same time as normal garbage service or at a special time. The collection vehicle may be the same truck used for garbage service, or may be a special vehicle. The cost of collection is usually the largest obstacle in establishing such programs.

Participation/Convenience/Motivation Relationships

A number of studies have been done on ways to improve participation in source-separation for recycling and on the determinants of recycling behavior. It is generally agreed that the more convenient recycling is made for people, the higher participation will be; similarly, the higher the motivation (reward) for participating in recycling, the higher the participation.

Thus the keys to improve participation in recycling are to either make recycling easier, to increase the reward for recycling (or the negative consequences of not recycling), or both.

Deposits on beverage bottles can be thought of as a powerful monetary incentive for engaging in source-separation. The five or ten cents per container is successful in achieving the return of the majority of the containers, usually achieving return rates of 90 percent or more in the United States. The monetary return provided by most of the BIRP centers is considerably lower, on the order of one cent per container, and is not as effective, especially considering that going to the centers is much less convenient for most people than returning empty containers to their local grocery store, as is done in most deposit states.

Drop-off programs have also experimented with other types of awards, such as raffles, contests, and prizes, in efforts to promote participation in recycling. Adequate publicity and education is very important for both drop-off and pickup programs, as is community involvement in the program.

Curbside pickup programs generally have significantly higher participation rates than any drop-off programs other than deposit-based ones. Curbside pickup-based recycling operations have found that participation is increased by offering weekly rather than monthly collection and by having the collection of recyclables on the same day as normal garbage pickup. Researchers have also found that participation is greatly enhanced by providing recycling containers for each household. The containers serve two functions, especially if they are bright and easily visible: they provide convenience in storing separated recyclables and they facilitate peer pressure to reinforce recycling behavior (if your container is not at the curb, all your neighbors will know you are not recycling).

On some other variables, studies have reached differing conclusions. Some investigators report that mandatory programs are more effective than voluntary ones, while others report that mandatory programs can lead to public resentment and poor participation. Requiring little preparation or separation of materials should improve convenience and therefore enhance participation. However, . . . in a study of thirty-nine curbside programs in the United States and Canada found that the more effective programs (in terms of quantity of waste diverted) had residents sort recyclables into a relatively large number of categories. Even the role of incentives has been questioned, with some feeling external incentives such as money may discourage those who would participate based on internal, ecologically-based motivation.

Some curbside programs have gone even further. In a few communities which charge for garbage pickup by the bag, recyclables are picked up free or at a reduced charge, adding a monetary incentive. In others, waste haulers, either individuals or commercial operations, pay lower tipping fees if separated recyclables are included in the load. In communities where recycling is mandated by law, failure to participate in recycling results in either no garbage pickup, or in a fine or other legal action.

It is generally agreed that the more convenient recycling is made for people, the higher participation will be; similarly, the higher the motivation (reward) for participating in recycling, the higher the participation.

Economics

The economic viability of recycling programs is based on the ability of the operation to at least cover its costs. Different types of materials offer different values. Newspaper and aluminum are generally the largest money generators for recycling operations. Glass and plastic are of less value per pound. There is an increasing tendency to provide, in some form at least, a proportion of the avoided cost of disposal as revenue to the recycling operation. In fact, it is claimed that nearly all recyclable materials in municipal solid waste, with the exception of aluminum, are worth more in terms of avoidance of disposal cost than for their actual material value.

Costs of operation of curbside recycling programs in several California communities were in the range $40 per ton, after subtracting return from sales of recovered materials. Since the cost of collection and disposal in these communities was $60 per ton, recycling was $20 per ton cheaper than disposal. A similar investigation for New Jersey put the cost of curbside pickup of recyclables at $50 per ton, compared to disposal costs approaching $100 per ton. In Rhode Island the net economic benefit of curbside pickup of recyclables versus landfilling was calculated at $56 per ton. Other estimates put the net cost of weekly curbside collection at $20–30 per ton, compared to landfilling costs of $40–60 per ton and incineration costs of $90–110 per ton.

Barriers to Recycling

Within the three-tiered recycling structure of collection, processing, and markets, there are several places where barriers to increased use of recycled materials may arise. In a study by the Secondary Resources Development Council in Canada, these barriers have been grouped into five broad categories:

(1) Economic/financial barriers

(2) Barriers related to the general public

(3) Barriers relating to the existing solid waste management system

Confused about what's recyclable and what's not—an increasingly complex question—they often make mistakes. They mix high-grade white paper with the low-grade colored kind, making the whole bunch worthless. They throw ceramic cups in bins of glass, turning it all into trash. They even put toxic and explosive materials into recycling boxes. The resulting contamination of recycled materials—which had an estimated value of $14 billion in the U.S. last year—is a quality-control problem on an unprecedented scale.

(4) Market barriers

(5) Other barriers

Economic/financial barriers include lack of financial incentives, lack of research and development expenditures, and the vertical integration of industries which favors use of company-controlled virgin resources. Also included is the incomplete costing of resources, in which the long-term social and environmental costs of use of virgin resources are not included in prices paid.

Barriers relating to the general public include lack of awareness, indifference, inconvenience, the feeling that an individual's activities have no real impact, and attitudes which look for a "technological fix" rather than lifestyle changes.

The existing solid waste system's barriers include lack of internalization of waste system costs, local laws which either inhibit or fail to aid recycling, and a tendency to pass the buck between jurisdictions.

Market barriers include product design which inhibits recycling, lack of both consistent and reliable supply and demand for material, and procurement practices.

The council concluded that the most significant barrier was the attitude of some governments. Positive trends were also identified, including the growth of pro-recycling lobbies and growth of financial incentives and industrial markets. They also concluded that the general public is much more willing to do the work involved in source-separation than politicians had thought.

[Barriers to buying recycled plastic products include] the reluctance of manufacturers and dealers to admit to recycled content in their products and the lack of a definition of recycled content (e.g., postconsumer only versus other waste materials) as major problems. (pp. 85–91)

Susan E. M. Selke, "Overview of Recycling," in her Packaging and the Environment: Alternatives, Trends and Solutions, *Technomic Publishing Co., Inc., 1990, pp. 85–94.*

Sorting It All Out

Among the raw materials recently supplied to George Wolfson's company were a few imperfections: a bottle of mercury, soiled diapers and a desk-sized representation of the Nativity.

"We call it the drag," says Mr. Wolfson, vice president, marketing, of REI Distributors Inc., which sorts and sells materials collected in municipal recycling programs. "You allow one thing" to be recycled, "and it drags in everything you don't want," including the three wise men in unrecyclable plastic.

As recycling takes off, millions of Americans are, in effect, suddenly learning on the job as front-end sorters in a fast-evolving manufacturing business. Confused about what's recyclable and what's not—an increasingly complex question—they often make mistakes. They mix high-grade white paper with the low-grade colored kind, making the whole bunch worthless. They throw ceramic cups in bins of glass, turning it all into trash. They even put toxic and explosive materials into recycling boxes. The resulting contamination of recycled materials—which had an estimated value of $14 billion in the U.S. last year—is a quality-control problem on an unprecedented scale.

Contamination worries have been one of the main stumbling blocks to the use of recycled material in food packaging and are likely to become a bigger issue as pressures mount to "close the loop," or recycle items into original form.

Plastic, for example, can absorb toxins from oil, pesticides or other hazardous substances consumers might store in them before recycling.

In March [of 1991], Coca-Cola Co. became one of the first food concerns to close the loop when it began testing marketing soda bottles partly made with recycled plastic. To ensure purity, Hoechst Celanese Corp., a unit of Hoechst AG that is recycling the bottles for Coke, intentionally contaminated them with various things before recycling them in tests to make sure they emerged pure. The process breaks down the plastic to basic molecules, which are then repeatedly distilled before being reconstituted into new bottles, says Hoechst.

The difficulties attendant to recycling are a heavy drag on the nascent industry America is counting on to alleviate its trash problem and help preserve its natural resources. Added to these problems is a glut of recyclable materials. Consequently, there are increasing questions about the economic viability of some popular recycling methods.

One method calls for contaminants to be culled by recycling concerns. At Mr. Wolfson's company, workers stand at conveyer belts laboriously plucking out every thing from tennis balls to old binoculars from a moving stream of recyclables. But such screening is costly and troublesome—REI recently was cited for violating trash laws when it accumulated a heap of culled materials next to one of its centers here. Moreover, some contaminants aren't easily extracted and even dangerous.

Glass shards, for example, somehow got mixed in with bales of old U.S. newspapers sent to Korea two years ago, says Ken Choi, a Portland, Ore., paper recycler who shipped the paper. When mill workers cut their hands opening the bales, "we almost had a lawsuit," he adds.

Even more worrisome are used propane tanks from backyard grills that turn up in metal-recycling bins, notes Adam Marks, a manager with Rhode Island's state-run recycling program. The tanks seem empty but contain enough gas to blow up when being mangled during recycling—as one did last year in Rhode Island's main recycling center. "There were no injuries, but it was pretty scary," Mr. Marks says.

Contamination has considerable economic consequences. It cuts proceeds from recycled materials, making it harder for towns to afford recycling. And as more towns recycle, standards are getting stricter on the amount of contamination allowed by buyers of recyclable goods. That makes consumers' recycling chores even harder.

The stricter standards stem partly from the oversupply of various recyclable materials, which have sharply lowered their value, says Jerry Powell, editor of Resource Recycling, a trade journal. "If you've got contamination in something worth $90 a ton," he explains, "you can afford to buff and shine it. But when its worth only $5 a ton clean, you say, 'Keep It.' "

"Six months ago, I could sell [used office] paper that was 95% clean," says Matthew Costello, a Cambridge, Mass., consultant who sets up and oversees corporate recycling programs. "Now paper mills want it to be 98% clean." To ensure purity, employees at his company, Corporate Conservation, often spend their evenings combing clients' recycling bins for contaminants, "One person who tosses in a half-filled coffee cup can turn a whole floor's good intentions to wasted effort," Mr. Costello says.

Contamination is especially nettlesome in plastics recycling. Tossing just a few bottles made of a plastic called PVC into a truckload of bottles made of a plastic called PET can contaminate the lot—PVC fouls the process used to recycle PET.

Few consumers seem aware of these subtleties. When BPI Environmental Inc., a Taunton, Mass., maker of plastic grocery and shopping bags, began recycling the bags about a year ago, the loads it received from stores sometimes contained more contaminants than usable material, says C. Jill Beresford, vice president, marketing. "One retailer even got a dead dog" in its bag recycling

> **Contamination has considerable economic consequences. It cuts proceeds from recycled materials, making it harder for towns to afford recycling. And as more towns recycle, standards are getting stricter on the amount of contamination allowed by buyers of recyclable goods. That makes consumers' recycling chores even harder.**

> **Mandated recycling policies—designed to save landfill space (or trees, or whatever)—actually require for many cities the expenditure of more resources at a time when municipal budgets are already strained. One New Jersey study showed recycling programs sometimes cost cities $200 per ton of materials collected. Even in New Jersey, with the highest landfill disposal costs in the nation, this cost exceeds the amount required to put trash in a landfill. Even low-priced recycling programs, at $40 per ton, cost more than the average landfill fee of $28 per ton.**

box, she says, adding that such problems are one reason recycled plastic for the bags costs more than 10 times as much as virgin plastic.

Contamination lies at the heart of the growing controversy about the right way to recycle. An increasing number of towns—mainly on the East Coast—allow recyclable items to be commingled for collection in a single container; workers later separate them at recycling centers. Other towns use "mixed-waste composting," in which recyclable items are culled from trash after it's collected as usual—with no curbside separation of recyclables.

Commingling speeds up collection and makes recycling easier for citizens. But some environmentalists oppose the new methods because they cause more contamination, which then makes it harder to recycle used products into high-value things. "It's hard enough to market recyclables when they aren't encrusted with garbage," says Lisa Collaton, who follows solid-waste issues at the Environmental Action Foundation in Washington, D.C.

To be sure, contaminated materials, such as glass that isn't clean and separated by color, often can be recycled into products such as "glassphalt" for paving roads. But critics of commingling assert that recycling into such relatively low-value products doesn't do enough to stimulate recycling markets and conserve virgin materials. And officials with companies that process recyclable goods generally say they prefer goods that haven't been mixed with possible contaminants.

The commingling trend and the rapid growth of recycling means the contamination problem probably will get worse before it gets better. But recycling experts say there is reason for optimism. Researchers are developing better technology to screen out contaminants. Manufacturers are beginning to design products for easier recycling. Last year, California even banned the sale of glass beverage containers with ceramic parts, which are hard to screen out during recycling and cause imperfections in recycled glass.

Some cities also are beginning to prod citizens who flout recycling rules. In Newark, N.J., the amount of recycled materials shot up 20% in January from year-earlier amounts after the city issued hundreds of notices of potential fines to people who mixed recyclables with garbage, says Frank Sudol, a city official who monitors the recycling program.

Recycling companies are also using their economic clout to enforce the rules and increasingly grade and pay for recyclables based on contaminant levels. John Van Devender, an Aluminum Co. of America spokesman, says, "We can get very hard-nosed [about contamination] "because our customers can get very hard-nosed" about the quality of aluminum supplied by Alcoa from recycled cans. (pp. B1, B4)

David Stipp, "Consumers Who Can't Sort It Out Turn Recyclable Refuse into Just Plain Trash," in The Wall Street Journal, *May 9, 1991, pp. B1, B4.*

Does Recycling Help or Hurt?

Some 40 states now have recycling laws. A handful have banned specific products, with certain plastics and disposable diapers targeted most often. Others have implemented deposit-refund systems. California is even considering a special "disposal fee" on virtually all products, to be paid at the point of purchase.

The federal government is likely soon to begin drafting new solid-waste regulations. High on the list will be proposals for all states to reach specified recycling levels. At the same time, policies to facilitate disposal will be ignored, or even undermined with regulations restricting the interstate transfer of solid waste.

Yet this regulatory fervor is ill-conceived. Recycling is only a second-order goal. The more basic objective is to pursue the efficient use of all resources.

Strained Budgets

Santa Barbara, Calif., four years of drought have left us scrambling for water. Recycling requirements that might induce consumers to switch to washable cloth diapers from disposable ones would mean more local water consumption—all with the aim of saving on landfill space that, if not abundant, is nonetheless reasonably available.

Mandated recycling policies—designed to save landfill space (or trees, or whatever)—actually require for many cities the expenditure of more resources at a time when municipal budgets are already strained. One New Jersey study showed recycling programs sometimes cost cities $200 per ton of materials collected. Even in New Jersey, with the highest landfill disposal costs in the nation, this cost exceeds the amount required to put trash in a landfill. Even low-priced recycling programs, at $40 per ton, cost more than the average landfill fee of $28 per ton.

Curbside recycling programs put more collection trucks—one set to pick up recyclables, another for the remaining waste—on the road. This means more fuel consumption, which means more air pollution. And some recycling processes produce high volumes of water waste and are energy intensive. In short, what saves landfill space may use more water or fuel.

Recycling does sometimes make sense, of course, and the marketplace stimulates recycling under these conditions. The recycled aluminum can, for example, requires less than 10% of the energy necessary to transform bauxite into aluminum. These savings have given industry an incentive to purchase recycled aluminum, which in turn gives entrepreneurs an incentive to collect used cans.

A few decades ago, soda cans were made of heavy tinplate with soldered lead side seams. As manufacturers looked for ways to cut costs, they engineered lighter-weight cans. The introduction of aluminum cans resulted in a decade-long competition between steel-can and aluminum-can manufacturers to bring the costs of their products down. The three-piece steel can gave way to the two-piece can; the soldered side seams gave way to adhesive bonding.

The aluminum can, too, underwent a series of changes—all the result of competitive processes. In the '60s, squashing a soda can was a sign of virility among teenage boys. It took real muscle to crush a can. Try the same deed today. A middle-aged, out-of-shape man (or woman) can crush the soda can one-handed and then, Godzilla-like, tear it into two pieces.

What happened in the intervening years? New processing techniques reduced the thickness of the can. In the '60s it took 164 pounds of aluminum to make 1,000 cans. It now takes only 35 pounds. Competition resulted in conservation.

Product bans and waste reduction engineered by government central planners interrupt this process and force inefficient production. Maine, for example, recently banned aseptic packages—those little juice boxes—under the excuse that they are nonrecyclable. This ban has forced out of the marketplace a product that emerged from the continuous search by manufacturers for less-costly packaging.

This search for cost reduction has meant decreases in energy usage and waste. Filling aseptic packages requires about half the energy needed to fill glass bottles. Transporting the aseptic package from its manufacturer to the bottling site also dramatically reduces resource use, primarily fuel. For a given beverage

> **Recycling is only a second-order goal. The more basic objective is to pursue the efficient use of all resources.**

Curbside recycling programs put more collection trucks—one set to pick up recyclables, another for the remaining waste—on the road. This means more fuel consumption, which means more air pollution. And some recycling processes produce high volumes of water waste and are energy intensive. In short, what saves landfill space may use more water or fuel.

volume, it takes 15 times as many trucks to transport empty glass bottles as it does aseptic boxes.

Because the end-product is lightweight, small and rectangular, the filled aseptic package can be more efficiently transported as well, using 35% less energy per unit than alternative glass packages. And the aseptic container is the only one in which dairy products can be packaged without requiring refrigeration—again saving energy and reducing the need for CFC-using refrigerants.

Several cities—for example, Portland, Ore., and Newark, N.J.—have essentially banned polystyrene food packages, yet a Franklin Associates comparison of polystyrene packaging and its alternative, paperboard containers, showed that the polystyrene hamburger clamshell uses 30% less energy than paperboard. Its manufacture results in 46% less air pollution, and 42% less water pollution.

Much of the so-called excess packaging condemned by the current environmental movement conserves resources by reducing breakage or spoilage. The United States produces less food waste than anywhere else in the world except parts of Africa, where the threat of starvation means even rotten food is consumed.

Recycling has symbolic appeal—it makes us feel virtuous and frugal. Product bans and waste-reduction mandates seem to put the environment first, efficiency second. But the two—environmental protection and economic efficiency—aren't really competitors. In a market economy, prices contain information about the relative scarcities of resources—all resources, including labor, land, material, capital, and energy. The search for cost-effectiveness thus drives us toward, not away from, environmental conservation.

In the real world, there are, of course, all sorts of impediments to competition. And some "scarce resources"—like air basins—don't figure into the process well, hence the drive for regulatory standards. But the processes of producing, using, and disposing of consumer goods that are now the target of solid-waste regulations have none of the hallmarks of public goods. Competition exists. And regulations are already in place that incorporate the costs of protecting health and safety in disposal.

If there is a problem in this picture, it is that too many local governments have failed to charge anything—or anything like the actual costs—for collecting and disposing of garbage. Cities such as Baltimore, Denver, and Los Angeles do not directly charge households for garbage collection. In fact, a study of more than 200 U.S. cities found that 39% charge no direct fees at all for garbage service, giving consumers little incentive to "conserve" on their waste production. Instituting pricing for collection and disposal will remedy that. Seattle's introduction of per-can charges a few years ago encouraged more than 70% of all residents to recycle and reduce waste.

The Big Picture

Product bans and the mandated use of certain materials not only reduce competition and undermine the drive toward resource conservation and efficiency, they also neglect the big environmental picture. They treat one resource, landfills, as the most important, while failing to consider the whole set of resources that any product uses from its initial production, through its consumption, and then on to its disposal. The result? We get bans of aseptic packages because they are not recyclable, although they conserve other resources, especially energy.

The goal of efficiency doesn't have the same emotional ring as "saving the planet." But this seemingly mundane goal, sought in the context of competition, yields resource conservation. That, not recycling, is the fundamental goal. (pp. 17–18)

Lynn Scarlett, "Will Recycling Help the Environment?" in Consumers' Research Magazine, *Vol. 74, No. 3, March, 1991, pp. 17–18.*

It's Not Easy Being Green: Marketing Strategies and Consumer Confusion

As Kermit the Frog sings, It's not easy being green. Ask any parent facing the great diaper dilemma. Unbeatable for convenience, disposables generate as much guilt as garbage. But it's no longer certain that switching to cloth nappies will do the environment any good. A study by Franklin Associates, a research firm, slams the reusable variety because washing them at home uses up to 9,620 gallons of water per child per year. If you employ a diaper service, the delivery trucks add to your town's air pollution. Says Allen Hershkowitz, a senior scientist at Natural Resources Defense Council, an environmental advocacy group in New York City: "The diaper debate is unresolvable." Hershkowitz, by the way, swaddles his two youngest children in disposables.

So it goes in the chaotic world of environmental marketing: What's green is rarely as simple a choice as black or white.

Manufacturers eager to appear ecologically correct are frantically relabeling, repackaging, and repositioning products, often in the face of fast-changing and inconsistent state laws. Customers, paying more than they used to for garbage collection and anxious to do well by the planet, try to shop smart. Stores that provide shelf space for such products are scrambling to keep pace with the changing definitions of what's green and what isn't. Wal-Mart, the nation's second-largest retailer, is winning kudos from some environmentalists for using special shelf markers to highlight new versions of products or their packaging that are environmentally friendlier. The markers proclaim WAL-MART RECOMMENDS. . . and identify the improvement, such as containers that use less material.

Many consumers are skeptical of manufacturers' labels. Marketing Intelligence Service of Naples, New York, which tracks product launches, says 26% of all new household items last year boasted that they were ozone-friendly, recyclable, biodegradable, compostable, or some other shade of green. At the same time, Environmental Research Associates of Princeton, New Jersey, found that nearly 47% of consumers dismiss environmental claims as "mere gimmickry."

The adventures of makers of trash bags help explain such suspicions and illustrate the hell many manufacturers have lived through while trying to do the right thing. After years of pressure from consumers to make a biodegradable version of its Hefty bags, Mobil did so in June 1989. Each box, decorated with pine tree, sunbeam, and eagle, proclaimed the bags degradable—and so they are if exposed to open air and sunlight. But over 90% of plastic bags are entombed in landfills almost devoid of the oxygen, moisture, and light that are needed to trigger the degradation process.

This was one reason that six months later the Environmental Defense Fund, a national research and advocacy group, called for a boycott of the bags. Minnesota Attorney General Hubert Humphrey III sued Mobil last summer for misleading advertising. By then, Mobil had already removed all environmental claims from Hefty boxes. But the company refuses to pull older boxes from stores. Five other states are suing Mobil, including California and New York.

Mark Green, the aptly named commissioner of consumer affairs in New York City, accuses marketers who peddle degradable bags of perpetrating "green-collar fraud." In March he filed a notice of violation against four distributors of bags—including Webster Industries of Peabody, Massachusetts, which makes the Good Sense line—accusing them of deceptive advertising. Like Mobil, Webster opted for the good-sense solution: Before Green took action, the

---

After years of pressure from consumers to make a biodegradable version of its Hefty bags, Mobil did so in June 1989. Each box, decorated with pine tree, sunbeam, and eagle, proclaimed the bags degradable—and so they are if exposed to open air and sunlight. But over 90% of plastic bags are entombed in landfills almost devoid of the oxygen, moisture, and light that are needed to trigger the degradation process.

Customers who read and heed labels are often victims of their own ignorance. Shoppers told Abt Associates, a Cambridge, Massachusetts, research firm, that among the green products they bought most often were aerosols claiming to contain no ozone-depleting chlorofluorocarbons. Big deal. The government banned CFCs from all but a minuscule number of medicinal aerosols 12 years ago. But spray cans still contain smog-creating propellants like butane and propane and are far from benign.

company dropped the claim that its bags biodegrade. The company's new packages, however, claim the bags are made of recycled materials.

That in itself threatens Webster's nation-wide sales because of the hodgepodge of inconsistent laws of various states. Eleven, for example, regulate environmental claims. Rajeev Bal, the company's president, fears he would have to have two or three different boxes for each of his products. "It's a logistical nightmare," he says. "Our labels would read like essays to comply with all the state requirements.

A bill in the California legislature, meanwhile, would outlaw the word "recyclable" on all labels unless consumers have easy access to a recycling facility. Marketers, who want to crow about recycled content in their packaging would also have to specify the exact percentage salvaged from the waste stream. Most states in the Northeast are pushing for similar laws. Says Jane Hutterly, director of environmental efforts for S. C. Johnson & Son, maker of Johnson Wax: "All the state initiatives are making it uneconomical for marketers to make environmental claims for products and distribute them nationally."

Johnson and some other companies have avoided fuss by largely refraining from flaunting the environmental soundness of what they sell. Says John Lister, head of Lister Butler, a New York City packaging design firm: "As soon as you go out on a limb and say you're doing something, a consumer group attacks the validity of your claim."

Relief could be at hand. A coalition of trade associations representing some 1,000 major corporations, including Scott Paper, Lever Brothers, and Procter & Gamble, has petitioned the Federal Trade Commission for guidance on green labeling. The FTC will soon hold hearings on the matter and says it is anxious to help curb deception. The Environmental Protection Agency, in on the name game as well, is about a year away from issuing definitions on what the terms "recyclable" and "recycled content" really mean. Adds Mary Gade, director of the Illinois EPA: "So many claims are unsubstantiated, misleading, and confusing."

Customers who read and heed labels are often victims of their own ignorance. Shoppers told Abt Associates, a Cambridge, Massachusetts, research firm, that among the green products they bought most often were aerosols claiming to contain no ozone-depleting chlorofluorocarbons. Big deal. The government banned CFCs from all but a minuscule number of medicinal aerosols 12 years ago. But spray cans still contain smog-creating propellants like butane and propane and are far from benign. Lever Brothers and P&G are testing alternatives to gas propellants, as are some other companies.

If you're curious about just how confused consumers are on the environmental score, peek inside a household trash bag. Better yet, leave the dirty work to William Rathje, a University of Arizona archaeologist who studies fresh garbage and landfills. "We find that people's garbage is schizophrenic," he says. "In a single bag you might see a special-order vegetable-based furniture polish and a nasty, nonrecyclable microwaveable dish." Adds John Lister, the packaging consultant: "Consumers have set perceptions. Paper's good; plastic's bad. Chances are neither will get recycled."

In the absence of national guidelines, cities hard hit by solid-waste-disposal costs are finding ways to make residents think twice about what they buy and throw away. In Perkasie, Pennsylvania, near Philadelphia, people have to buy specially marked garbage bags from the city; $1 for a 20-pound bag or $1.75 for a 40-pounder (up from 85 cents and $1.50, respectively last year). The charge cut the tonnage of residential waste nearly in half in 1988, the first year of the program. Residents of High Bridge, New Jersey, pay $200 a year for stickers good for 52 bags of garbage. The cost of a sticker for each additional bag thereafter: $1.65. In ten months the town cut its waste by 24%.

Shoppers and marketers are focusing their attention on packaging, which takes up about a third of the nation's landfills. In some cases the effort is purely a relabeling job to trumpet existing attributes. "Paper from paper, not from trees," reads the new Marcal toilet tissue package. Marcal Paper Mills of Elmwood Park, New Jersey, has made paper products from recycled junk mail, glossy inserts, and the like for 40 years, but until recently was loath to advertise it. "Just two years ago the consumer perception was that 'recycled' meant 'dirty' says Jacquelyn Ottman, a green market consultant in New York City. "Today it's a virtue."

More often a green makeover goes beyond mere repositioning. The watchwords are "smaller," "reusable," "refillable," and, despite the fuzzy definitions, "recycled" and "recyclable." Says Lister: "Marketers are reverting to traditional single-layer packaging like glass and paper. They're throwing out or reexamining decades of progress in industrial design: composites, laminated paper, and plasticized metal."

These materials are generally lighter, easier to ship, and better insulators. Going back to old-fashioned wrapping may be ecologically sounder, but it can cost the consumer more. Manufacturers have to write off previous capital investment and spend more to retool. Not inconceivably, they will pass the bill on to the customer, who will also have to lug extra weight home from the store.

But customers can do better from some changes in packaging. Take P&G's new refill concept for its Downy Fabric softener. "Put a little more in your pocket . . . and a little less in your garbage," goes the ad. Downy fans who finish the softener in the large plastic bottle can buy concentrate in a small milk carton-like container that will fill the old bottle when mixed with water. The refill cuts waste by 75% and is about 40 cents cheaper than the plastic jug. In test markets, the refill won 20% of Downy sales.

Hounded by environmentalists, H. J. Heinz spent $8 million over three years to develop a squeezable ketchup bottle that could be recycled. The old bottle, a composite of layered plastics and adhesives, was not recyclable unless people were prepared to sit down and pick it to pieces. The new one is made of polyethylene terephthalate plastic. Better known as PET, it is used in soda bottles and is one of the few commonly recycled plastics in the U.S.

ConAgra Pet Products of Omaha has started to market its Sergeant's Flea & Tick Spray in dispensers decidedly greener than aerosol cans. At the core is a PET bottle that is pleated, fitted with a valve, and inserted in a rubber sleeve. When the value is compressed, the rubber contracts, providing pressure to produce the spray. Some 50 other companies, including Revlon and Bristol-Myers Squibb, are trying out the gas-free technology, developed by Exxel Container of Somerset, New Jersey.

Lever Brothers, makers of Wisk laundry detergent, has hit upon a winner and a dud. The more promising delivery system, which environmental affairs director Melinda Sweet says is selling well, is Wisk Power Scoop. The highly concentrated powder yields almost the same number of washes as the old 64-ounce plastic bottle but comes in a recycled cardboard box one-third the size.

Wisk selling via a system called bag-in-box is doing less well. A soft plastic sack of liquid detergent is housed in a recyclable corrugated box with a spout on the side. Environmentally responsible, yes. But so cumbersome that even the nation's greenest consumers in the Pacific Northwest have ignored it. "What really hurt the product," says consultant Ottman, "is that Lever charges the same amount for a less convenient package."

The environmentalist of the Nineties is influenced by price and down-to-earth penalties for careless consumption. Jeffrey Hollender runs Seventh Generation, a Colchester, Vermont, mail-order company that last year sold $7.5 million worth of unbleached toilet paper, vegetable-based household cleaners, and unpetroleum jelly for babies' bottoms, among other such products. He says of his customers: "These people are *not* crunchy granola Sixties leftovers. They're surprisingly mainstream." Ottman describes the typical green consumer as a well-educated middle-class mom 30 to 49, the one who generally shops, cooks and takes out the trash.

> **"Just two years ago the consumer perception was that 'recycled' meant 'dirty.' Today it's a virtue."**
>
> —Jacquelyn Ottman, green market consultant, New York City, 1991

Many consumers are skeptical of manufacturers' labels. Marketing Intelligence Service of Naples, New York, which tracks product launches, says 26% of all new household items last year boasted that they were ozone-friendly, recyclable, biodegradable, compostable, or some other shade of green. At the same time, Environmental Research Associates of Princeton, New Jersey, found that nearly 47% of consumers dismiss environmental claims as "mere gimmickry."

So far, there is no evidence that companies make much money from green products. They guard the numbers jealously. But increasingly, even price-conscious shoppers want to know if what they're buying is the earth's friend or enemy. Says Robert Viney, environmental point man at Procter & Gamble: "We know from letters and calls on our 800 lines that this concern is not a fad. It's not going to go away." Adds David Marshall, vice president for marketing and sales at Mobil: "The biggest thing we've learned in this whole environmental issue is that today's answer may not be tomorrow's. Companies have to be quick on their feet." So they do. But it would make the game easier if federal, state, and local authorities agreed on the rules. (pp. 91–2, 96, 100–01)

Jaclyn Fierman, "The Big Muddle in Green Marketing," in Fortune, *Vol. 123, No. 11, June 3, 1991, pp. 91–2, 96, 100–01.*

Recycling Gains Ground

Recycling programs that make good use of all types of solid waste are a welcome adjunct to resource-recovery operations, lowering the cost of burning trash, improving combustion, appeasing environmentalists, protecting water supplies and promoting recycling industries.

"Absolutely, there is a national trend to recycle along with resource recovery," says Allen Hershkowitz, president of the Municipal Recycling Association in Elmsford, N.Y. Cities, townships and counties proceed with numerous schemes to recycle and burn on the drawing boards, but few put these ideas into operation.

Hershkowitz, formerly of the New York-based environmental research group Inform, urges communities to hire recycling specialists, not just lawyers and engineers, when setting up a recycling program. Obtaining good advice is the biggest obstacle in launching a recycling program, he says.

"Sometimes there is an inversion of sound economics, with siting of waste-to-energy plants, before recycling is underway, as in Albany and Westchester County, N.Y., and Boston," Hershkowitz says. One solution is to create a recycling blueprint before the costly system is built, lowering the amount of garbage guaranteed by the community and decreasing the burn plant's volume . . . .

The keys to successful recycling are the market, collection and public relations. Unsteady markets may crash, and a three-or five-year purchasing contract is difficult to come by, recycling coordinators say.

An Albany, N.Y. environmental consultant, Gordon Boyd, says intermediate-processing facilities (IPFs), also called materials-recovery facilities, represent a new trend in garbage-disposal efforts.

Whether publicly or privately owned and operated, these centers take care of sorting, baling, cleaning, shredding, storing and marketing recyclables. Industries buying used materials prefer clean and sorted goods in large, consistent quantities, made possible by IPFs. (p. RR 10)

The biggest disadvantage of IPFs, according to Boyd, is "sometimes having to travel hundreds of miles." Another major IPF pitfall is disposing non-recyclables. Even shredding a junk car leaves 25 percent unusable waste. This is the cost of doing business, Boyd says.

Mixed recyclables can be transferred best directly from curbside to be sorted and upgraded at the processing center. "By pulling out valuables, the volume of waste can be reduced 30 to 60 percent," Boyd says.

The number of processing centers expands to cover large areas or deal with large populations. A new IPF is on-line for New York in Queens, and a $4-million IPF is under construction in Brooklyn.

The more-common collection methods, either curbside or drop-off centers,create logistical problems. "If you can't harvest it, you can't market it," Boyd says.

When implementing collection, "the first hurdle is how to integrate the historical service in your town with what you want to change it to," Boyd says. "If people have taken papers to the church each week, do you want to interfere?" he asks, adding politically strong leaders can develop popular plans that induce cooperation with haulers and the public.

"Source-separation entails work," Boyd says. "I'd rather talk about not mixing. Would you throw your beer bottles into the laundry basket? Mixing makes an unmarketable product." (pp. RR 11–12)

Where source-separation is voluntary, various imaginative schemes lure participation. In Columbus, Ohio, officials conduct a monthly lottery, asking residents to label their curbside recycling bins with their name and address for the drawing.

"A weekly pickup becomes so habitual, residents get used to doing it, so it's nothing special," says [Illinois General Services Director Samuel] Chandler. "You need consistency, a separate day for recycling, always the same day."

Pilot studies are useful sometimes as in Columbus, a city with voluntary recycling and a 2,000-tpd [ton-per-day], refuse-derived fuel facility. Public-works officials provide special collection bins to some homes but not to others, initiate recycling in both low- and high-income areas, place polyurethane refuse bins in alleys, encourage curbside pickup in other parts of the city, and try out automated vs. manual waste collection. With these pilot-study parameters involving 3,000 households, policymakers hope to calculate what works best. . . . (p. RR 12)

Anne Magnuson, "Recycling Gains Ground," in American City & County, *Vol. 103, No. 8, August, 1988, pp. RR10–RR12.*

Recycling programs that make good use of all types of solid waste are a welcome adjunct to resource-recovery operations, lowering the cost of burning trash, improving combustion, appeasing environmentalists, protecting water supplies and promoting recycling industries.

Sources For Further Study

Angulo, Jeffrey, and Linsen, Paul. "Recycling: The Coming Age of Recovery." *2000 & Beyond* (February 1990): 112–15.
  Examines the critical need for more practical methods of recycling trash paper.

Arner, Robert. "Used Oil Recycling: State and Local Collection Programs." *Resource Recycling* 8, No. 2 (May-June 1989): 22–5.
  Notes that low oil prices and high collection costs hamper efforts to install effective programs to recycle used automotive oil from "do-it-yourself" home oil changes. Some state and local collection programs are discussed.

Ballo, Richard. "Plastics Again: Recycling Polystyrene." *Resource Recycling* 8, No. 5 (September 1989): 26–9.
  Discusses the operations of Plastic Again, a joint venture of Genpak Corp. and the Mobil Chemical Co., to recycle polystyrene.

Becker, Charlotte. "Recycling Information Center: A Popular Service." *Resource Recycling* 8, No. 2 (May–June 1989): 28–33.

Traces the development of the Oregon Environmental Council's Recycling Information Center from its inception in 1971 through 1988, focusing on its databases, printed information services, and computerized library.

Bremner, Brian. "Recycling: The Newest Wrinkle in Waste Management's Bag." *Business Week*, No. 3148 (5 March 1990): 48–9.
Surveys recycling programs instituted by the multinational corporation Waste Management Inc. under its Recycle America subsidiary.

Darecy, Susan. "Recycling Resurges as Viable Option to Disposal." *World Wastes* 30, No. 7 (July 1987): 28–32.
Assesses factors contributing to interest in recycling programs.

De Young, Raymond. "Exploring the Difference between Recycler and Non-Recyclers: The Role of Information." *Journal of Environmental Systems* 18, No. 4 (1988–89): 341–51.
Reports on a study intended to establish differences between recyclers and non-recyclers.

Gagliardo, Michael A. "Recycling in the 90s: A Resource Recovery Perspective." *Resource Recycling* 8, No. 8 (December 1989): 20–2.
Calls for the government to mandate recycling goals, industry to develop and expand uses of recycled materials, and consumers to purchase recyclable and recycled goods.

Glenn, Jim. "The State of Garbage in America: Parts I and II." *BioCycle* 31, Nos. 3–4 (March–April 1990): 48–53; 34–41.
Part I includes information regarding the impact of recycling programs on the nation's waste stream. Part II focuses on the passage of recycling legislation in 1989.

———. "Curbside Recycling Reaches 40 Million." *BioCycle* 31, No. 7 (July 1990): 30–7.
Examines a representative sample of curbside recycling programs in the United States, offering an estimate of how much recyclable material is removed from the waste stream through such programs.

Golueke, Clarence G., and Diaz, Luis F. "Quality Control and Waste Management." *BioCycle* 30, No. 7 (July 1989): 65–7.
Insists that quality control—efforts to upgrade the quality of materials reclaimed from the waste stream for reuse—is essential to an effective recycling program and an aid in reducing solid waste.

Gordon, Judith G. *Assessment of the Impact of Resource Recovery on the Environment.* Cincinnati: U.S. Environmental Protection Agency, 1979, 136 p.
Examines the environmental impact of resource recovery from municipal solid waste disposal systems.

Henstock, Michael E. "The Impacts of Materials Substitution on the Recyclability of Automobiles." *Resources Conservation & Recycling* 2, No. 1 (December 1988): 69–85.
Reviews current programs for recovering materials from discarded motor vehicles and considers possible future composition of vehicles and the effects of materials substitution on vehicle recycling.

Hunt, Robert G., and Sellers, Jere D. "A New Look at Recycling Subsidies: Part I." *Resource Recycling* 8, No. 2 (May–June 1989): 32–4.
Examines the areas in recycling systems where government subsidies are most effective.

Huntley, Jery. "Plastics Recycling: Now and For the Twenty-First Century." *Resource Recycling* 8, No. 8 (December 1989): 21–3.
Calls for the establishment of a national infrastructure that would render plastics recycling economically viable and geographically feasible.

Joseph, Lawrence E. "Saving the Earth." *New Choices for the Best Years* 30, No. 4 (April 1990): 48–53.

Commemorates the twentieth anniversary of Earth Day and suggests that individuals practice environmentally beneficial activities, including recycling and "precycling": avoiding single-use products such as foam cups and disposable razors.

Kuniholm, Peter F. "Accurate Estimates for Recycling Capture Rates." *BioCycle* 31, No. 7 (July 1990): 70–3.
Stresses that it is essential when developing a recycling program to correctly predict the quantities of recyclable material that will be collected. A sidebar offers statistical information about community participation in recycling programs in fifteen American cities.

Miller, Chaz. "Glass Recycling: Where We've Been and Where We're Going." *Resource Recycling* 8, No. 8 (December 1989): 23–5.
Examines the goals of the Glass Packaging Institute, which operated recycling programs in 23 states, to promote recyclability through curbside programs and surveys some problems concerning glass recycling.

Mills, Jeffrey H. "Building Design for Recycling in Multi-Unit Structures." *Resource Recycling* 8, No. 1 (March–April 1989): 42–4.
Notes essential design elements for recycling transfer stations in multiple-unit buildings.

Moore, Allen. "Recycling in the 1990s: The Waste Management Industry Perspective." *Resource Recycling* 8, No. 8 (December 1989): 19–21.
Maintains that government intervention will be needed to achieve a significant level of recycling in the United States, including the establishment of federal laws to define national recycling goals, the consolidation of the waste management industry, and changes in consumer buying habits.

Nelson-Horchler, Joani. "Old Packages Never Die . . ." *Industry Week* 238, No. 17 (4 September 1989): 88–90.
Surveys some innovations in package design intended to minimize waste and render packaging more easily recyclable. A sidebar presents information drawn from studies which indicate that consumers express interest in recycling but overwhelmingly chose products packaged in nondegradable and nonrecyclable packaging.

Noll, Kenneth E., et. al. *Recovery, Recycle and Reuse of Industrial Wastes.* Chelsea, Mich.: Lewis Publishers, 1985, 195 p.
Explores the advantages of recovering, recycling, and reusing industrial waste products.

"Scrap: America's Ready Resource." *Phoenix Quarterly* 20, Nos. 1–2 (1988): 25 p.
Identifies scrap as a pervasive and readily available resource that could alleviate environmental and waste disposal problems if effectively exploited. A history of scrap collection and utilization is provided, and modern handling methods of ferrous and nonferrous metals, precious metals, paper, textiles, plastic, and glass through the scrap cycle are described.

"It's Time to Design Our Manufactured Products for Recycling." *Phoenix Quarterly* 21, No. 1 (Winter 1989): 4–7.
Discusses the Design for Recycling program of the Institute for Scrap Recycling Industries, which encourages the elimination of hazardous materials from the production process so that spent products can be recycled safely.

Pollock, Cynthia. "Mining Urban Wastes: The Potential for Recycling." *Worldwatch Paper* 76 (April 1987): 58 p.
Reports on the integration of recycling programs into solid waste management programs worldwide.

Powell, Jerry. "Tire Recycling Bounces Along." *Resource Recycling* 7, No. 3 (July 1988): 22–4.
Examines a scrap tire recycling process in place in Babbitt, Minnesota.

Quigley, Jim. "Recycling Frontiers: Glutted Markets and Spurred Demands." *Resource Recycling* 8, No. 1 (March–April 1989): 46–9.
Explores supply and demand in recycling markets.

Rankin, Sidney. "Plastics Recycling: Time for Industry Action." *Resource Recycling* 7, No. 3 (July 1988): 28–32.
Noting that nondegradable plastics are perceived as a major solid waste disposal problem, Rankin reviews ways to encourage and improve plastics recycling that were offered at a conference sponsored by the Society of Plastics Engineers in March 1988.

Robinson, David. "One Person's Opinion: Recycling in the Inner City." *Resource Recycling* 7, No. 7 (January–February 1989): 40–1.
Outlines a strategy for implementing a successful recycling system in an inner-city minority community.

Selke, Susan E., and Lai, Christopher C. "Recyclability Aspects of Packaging Design." *Resource Recycling* 7, No. 3 (July 1988): 36–41.
Examines recyclability of metal, plastic, glass, paper, and paperboard packaging materials and urges the use of reusable packaging and one-material packaging as well as environmentally responsible package design.

Shea, Cynthia Pollock. "Building a Market for Recyclables." *World Watch* 1, No. 3 (May–June 1988): 12–18.
Examines public and private efforts to market recyclable materials.

Smalberg, Kurt. "Steel Can Recycling: A New Leader in the Steel Recycling Legacy." *Resource Recycling* 8, No. 8 (December 1989): 22–4.
Notes that steel is a readily recyclable resource and examines advantages of steel can recycling.

Stauffer, Roberta F. "Energy Savings from Recycling." *Resource Recycling* 7, No. 7 (January–February 1989): 24–30.
Notes some of the variables that affect calculations of energy savings when secondary rather than virgin materials are used in production of paper, glass, plastics, and aluminum. Barriers to effective utilization of recycled materials are discussed.

Ward, Mark L., Sr. "Recyclers Trying to Tread Right Path in Processing Tires." *Recycling Today* 28, No. 4 (15 April 1990): 82–4.
Surveys problems associated with the disposal of tires, which are banned from many landfills and have limited recycling potential.

Watson, Tom. "Recycling the Landfill: The Mining of Disposal Sites." *Resource Recycling* 7, No. 5 (September–October 1988): 20–3.
Considers landfill mining as a solid waste management technique combining landfilling, recycling, and composting.

———. "Polystyrene Recycling: Big Money, Big Implications." *Resource Recycling* 8, No. 5 (September 1989): 24–8.
Examines plastics producers' investment in recycling programs and notes that environmental activists claim that the reduced use of polystyrene packaging, rather than recycling, would more effectively address problems of solid waste disposal posed by plastics.

Young, Robert F., and Campbell, Edward C. "Recycling May Hold the Solution to Problem of U.S. Trade Deficit." *Recycling Today* 27, No. 2 (February 1989): 144–46.
Suggests that widespread resource recovery in the United States, particularly of paper, paperboard products, and aluminum, could significantly reduce U.S. dependency on imported raw materials and lower the nation's trade balance.

15: Sewage and Wastewater Treatment

Cities and Sewage Treatment

William Golden keeps in shape, which is evident by looking at his trim, muscular frame. Even with a busy schedule, the young, two-term state senator from south Boston nonetheless finds time to jog and exercise. But while running along Wollaston Beach one hot August day in pursuit of fitness, Golden decided something needed to be done to make Boston Harbor healthy again.

Several hours before his run, outgoing tides flowed out to Massachusetts Bay, and when the tide came back in, large amounts of human feces came with it. Now, Golden had seen many unusual things along the beach before, such as children building sand castles out of tampon applicators. But this latest horrifying discovery prompted Golden, then city solicitor for Quincy, to storm into the mayor's office in jogging shorts and shoes and demand action.

"The mayor told me to go into my office later, think about it, and write a memo," he says. "My proposal included establishing a water pollution task force to study the problem, made up of all municipal department heads, city officials and civic associations.

"The whole situation was appalling. Hundreds of children play in the water every day. The task force found out three things—the harbor was far more polluted than we thought, no single individual or agency could clean the harbor alone, and that we were at the wrong end of the political majority. To clean up the harbor, other communities did not want to pay more than they absolutely had to."

After lawsuits and countless political and judicial delays and manueverings, the result of Golden's run along the beach that day in 1982 is a massive, $6.1 billion plan to stop polluting Boston Harbor, the nation's filthiest. By the late 1990s, when New England's largest public works project in history is completed, metropolitan Bostonians will be paying some of the highest utility rates in the nation.

What caused the harbor to become so polluted? The answers—an outdated wastewater treatment system and public apathy—are not uncommon in many American cities and counties today. Even in the wake of mandates set forth by the U.S. Environmental Protection Agency (EPA), there are many glaring examples of archaic, outmoded wastewater plants coughing up and spewing raw, milky sewage that floods clean water supplies through rusting, leaky pipes.

Scenes along America's waterways and beaches are reminiscent of the 1960s, when over-reliance on water-borne disposal methods resulted in quarantined waterfronts and overflowing sewers. Congress responded with the Federal Water Pollution Control Act in 1972, now known as the Clean Water Act. Every municipal wastewater plant in the nation was required to establish secondary treatment by 1977; Congress extended the deadline to July 1, 1988. EPA Administrator Lee Thomas announced recently that 87 percent of all publicly

> "The whole situation was appalling. Hundreds of children play in the water every day. The task force found out three things—the harbor was far more polluted than we thought, no single individual or agency could clean the harbor alone, and that we are at the wrong end of the political majority. To clean up the harbor, other communities did not want to pay more than they absolutely had to."
>
> —William Golden, Massachusetts state senator, on Boston Harbor.

Even in the wake of mandates set forth by the U.S. Environmental Protection Agency (EPA), there are many glaring examples of archaic, outmoded wastewater plants coughing up and spewing raw, milky sewage that floods clean water supplies through rusting, leaky pipes.

owned sewage plants had met those deadlines, adding that 95 percent of U.S. sewage receives secondary treatment.

Ironically, these optimistic statements came in the midst of additional lawsuits and rising public concern about polluted beaches, waterways and oceans.

There are 3,731 large municipal wastewater treatment facilities in the United States. More than 400 cities failed to comply by July 1. While 235 of these municipalities were in final judicial or administrative compliance stages, the federal government filed suits against 35 others. Also, 11,800 smaller facilities that process less than 1 million gallons per day (mgd) were required to meet the deadline; 1,700 failed.

Secondary treatment, which has been around for about 20 years, removes almost 90 percent of the fluid's impurities by adding oxygen and bacteria. Primary treatment merely removes 30 to 40 percent of pollutants, mainly floating debris and suspended solids. So why all this fuss over secondary treatment lately, especially since the technology has been available for so long? What has been the major stumbling block in implementing a process that can only help save water supplies and the environment as well?

"Mainly its high cost," says Bill Simpson, an engineer with Post, Buckley, Schuh & Jernigan's Orlando, Fla., office. "Here in Florida, cities and counties have been forced by regulatory agencies to employ secondary treatment. Most plants just were not designed with secondary capabilities, so many have had to be modified.

"The death knell has sounded for dumping raw sewage and sludge into other bodies of water."

Despite tremendous advances in engineering, the basic premise of wastewater disposal has not changed very much over the past 200 years. But Beth Turner, outgoing president of the Water Pollution Control Federation (WPCF), says there has been enormous progress since the Clean Water Act went into effect.

"Streams and rivers that 20 years ago would have had no chance of life in them now are thriving and viable," she says. "By and large, it is very easy to focus on the bad situations, but for every bad example, there are many good ones."

Since 1972, the federal government has spent $45 billion to build and upgrade wastewater treatment plants. An additional $15 billion has been invested by states and local governments. "What we are seeing now are site-specific problems. We have a much more uniform wastewater treatment system in the nation today, and the major problems remaining are unique to that geographic region," Turner says. "In 1972, sewage treatment problems were generic and common among most areas. Problems today are more specific and glaring."

Boston's two wastewater plants, located on Deer Island and Nut Island, receive an average 500 mgd of sewage from 2.5 million people in 43 bayside cities and towns. But the facilities were outdated almost the day they came on line. Holding tanks on 19-year-old Deer Island can process 343 mgd; on a normal day, it receives 346 mgd. Nut Island, in operation for 35 years, usually overflows by 16 mgd.

Then there is the matter of combined sewer overflows. The city's 108 sewer pipes pour about 9 billion gallons a year into the water. All total, an estimated 500 mgd of sewage flows into Boston Harbor.

The islands are located on the harbor's northern and southern edges. Once processed, the sewage is released into the harbor, where incoming tides wash it back in. So the human excrement Golden was running in had passed through the city's complete wastewater treatment system, just as it was supposed to.

Political problems delayed finding a solution in Boston before now. The Metropolitan District Commission (MDC) was in charge of sewage treatment, as well as other public utility functions. Seeing no other solution, Golden reluctantly filed suit against MDC in December 1982. "As a trial attorney, I know that the last thing you want to do is sue somebody," he says. "We did not want to go to court, and when we did, we were not optimistic. We were one city (Quincy) against 42 other communities."

Golden realized the judicial branch would be the force needed to motivate the state Legislature to remedy the problem. He delayed filing the suit for six months so he could rotate around Superior Court Judge Paul Garrity's schedule. Garrity, with the reputation of an activist judge, delayed ruling on the case for a year, hoping lobbyists could persuade Massachusetts lawmakers to come up with a solution.

While there was speculation around the statehouse of creating an independent water resources authority, nothing of substance ever happened. When he ruled on the case, Garrity prohibited new MDC sewer tie-ins, sending a message that he was willing to stop urban growth because it would pollute the harbor even more.

The Massachusetts attorney general appealed to the state's Supreme Judicial Court, which ruled Garrity had no legal authority to issue such an injunction. But the movement had already begun. The day Garrity's decision was overturned, Michael Deland, EPA's administrator for its Northeast Regional Office, announced the EPA and the U.S. Justice Department would use federal sanctions unless immediate action was taken to save Boston Harbor, an unprecedented move.

So the Massachusetts Water Resources Authority (MWRA) was born, an independent agency now in charge of all water and sewer service. The average rate for a family of four under the MDC was $90 a year. Already, ratepayers have experienced a 54 percent increase. As the MWRA plan to stop polluting the harbor gets into full swing, that same family will pay more than $1,000 annually. Appropriately, MWRA is headquartered in a refurbished, reinforced gray brick warehouse in Boston's Charlestown Navy Yard, next to the legendary Old Ironsides.

This project easily could become the biggest, most comprehensive public works undertaking not only in New England, but in the nation. Two ultramodern treatment plants will be constructed on Deer Island, with a combined capacity of 480 mgd. Piers must be constructed to move equipment to Deer Island; these will be completed by October of next year. Interim sludge facilities will be phased in until December 1991, accounting for 16 percent of the project's cost.

Several million dollars worth of improvements are planned for Deer Island, once used as a quarantine and a prison during colonial times. Construction on an upgraded primary treatment plant is set to begin in January 1991. Secondary treatment accounts for 24 percent of the overall cost. Both plants will be constructed in phases, with the secondary plant completed only a few months before the turn of the century.

The Nut Island treatment facility will close eventually, but since tunnels and other channeling equipment already are in place, wastewater still will be pumped from Nut to Deer through an upgraded tunnel. Once processed, the treated effluent will be pumped eight to 10 miles out to sea, and discharged at an Atlantic outfall through a new tunnel.

The outfall tunnel will be located 400 feet beneath the ocean floor. "We wanted a site to discharge the effluent that would not affect marine life significantly," says Bill Callahan, senior vice president for Camp Dresser & McKee, the engineering firm that provided the facilities planning aspect of the project. "The effluent will be 90 percent pure by the time it reaches the ocean. Deer Island now has five outfalls, and Nut Island has one. Things really get sloshed around out there, and it's no wonder everything eventually washes back in."

Using conventional building techniques, the complete facility would have occupied the entire island. "This is too big of a project for it to become a

Despite tremendous advances in engineering, the basic premise of wastewater disposal has not changed very much over the past 200 years.

"Streams and rivers that 20 years ago would have had no chance of life in them now are thriving and viable. By and large, it is very easy to focus on the bad situations, but for every bad example, there are many good ones."

—Beth Turner,
former president of
the Water Pollution
Control Federation

proto-type," Callahan says. "We wanted to use new but proven technologies." To make room, an oval-shaped hill called a drumlin will be excavated for the new primary facility. The remains of the drumlin will be moved to another portion of the island. Also utilized are unusual stacking techniques for storage basins and clarifiers. The design life of the overall project is through 2020.

Now that the plan is in place and under way, the next big test will be dealing with the public. Golden has seen survey after survey where three out of every four Bostonians had no idea where the sewage went.

"Ian Menzies of the *Boston Globe* and I attended a seminar at the New England Aquarium, and he said 'an intelligent, but barely restrained mob' is needed to motivate people to do something about the harbor," Golden says. "Well, we have an institution with a mandate to run a decent sewer system, we have an official objective provided through a court order, but we still don't have that mob. We have spent 40 or 50 years trashing the harbor, and here we are trying to clean it up in a decade. The cost is going to be very expensive.

"The people out there who are paying for this are full partners. How can they help when they don't know they're polluting the harbor?"

"One of the more important aspects of my job is to educate the public and work with their elected officials," says Paul Levy, who, as MWRA's executive director, is on the firing line. "The next big issue will be siting the new facilities. A couple of cities (near the new facilities) will receive financial compensation for any disruption that may occur as a result, which has never been done around here before."

"In general, there is public support for this effort," says Jaime Hoyte, Boston's secretary for environmental affairs. "Unfortunately, the public doesn't understand the overall cost impact. And they also don't understand their role in polluting the water. But it is their harbor."

Public education is one of the major problems remaining nationwide. "The public knows what it wants," Turner says. "It doesn't want sewage and sludge in its backyard. But paying for treatment is another matter. While there is not a lot of new technological development going on today, there has been so much progress over the last 20 years that the problems today are ones money cannot buy, such as dealing with the public."

Still, this massive undertaking will not clean up Boston Harbor. Dealing with combined sewer overflows may cost an additional $1 billion. "The only thing this project will do is stop further pollution of the harbor, so it can regenerate itself through its own ecological systems," Levy says. "Basically, we have not come a long way since the 1890s, when we were dumping sewage into outgoing ocean tides. The only difference today is that the sewage is purified more. The rudimentary process is still the same."

But the problems resulting from this process are getting bigger. In New York, a project to clean up the Hudson River has been 57 years in the making. The idea of a sewage plant in Manhattan began in 1931, when 39 plants were proposed to handle the city's complete wastewater needs. Nine years later, the city's Public Works Department decided to build a single plant on the Hudson for New York's west side. Once a site had been selected and design work was nearing completion, a series of water-quality upgrades complicated the situation.

About this time, New York hit a financial crunch, and the river got even dirtier. Each day, 150 million gallons of raw sewage found a home in the Hudson. Because of steeper federal regulations and deeper federal cutbacks, the proposed facility went from a primary treatment plant to an advanced preliminary treatment plant to a complete secondary treatment plant today.

But New England is not the only area of the nation swimming in its own sewage. In 1965, President Lyndon Johnson took a personal interest in cleaning up the Potomac River when he signed the Federal Water Quality Act. Johnson vowed to reopen the river for swimming and fishing by 1975. Though the 1975 goal was never met, the $1 billion Blue Plains Advanced Wastewater Treatment Plant recently went on line, pumping 309 mgd of highly treated effluent into the river. The plant soon will be presented with a special recognition award from WPCF.

An ambitious wastewater management plan developed for Sarasota County, Fla., by Dames & Moore, Los Angeles, calls for development of a split-stream water supply enhanced by using recovered sewage. The city is being forced to pay a $500,000 fine for violations of the Clean Water Act.

The new water scheme is a dramatic departure from previous policies in the Florida community. Local water resources are constrained by limited ground-water supplies and seasonal droughts affecting surface water uses. So a lot of water is purchased from neighboring Manatee County.

Plans call for consolidating existing utility lines for centralized wastewater treatment. Sewage will receive a high level of treatment, removing nutrients and viruses, making the water safe for human consumption. Then the effluent will be pumped to the Ringling-MacArthur Reserve, a 33,000-acre tract of wetland.

By recycling the water, the county will increase available river water supplies from eight mgd to more than 20 mgd. This split-stream system will meet a project demand of 36 mgd through 2020. Construction costs range between $200 million and $300 million. "Although this project is one of the first of its kind, it will not be the last," says County Commissioner Mabry Carlton. "It has become mandatory we maximize fresh water use and stop wasting water by discharging into streams, the ocean and deep injection wells."

Pacific coastal waters are no better. Seattle's Elliott Bay is filled with by-products of the electrical industry, such as arsenic and lead. San Francisco Bay is contaminated from heavy metal discharges from shoreside industries. Urban run-off in Los Angeles has almost destroyed life in Santa Monica Bay. Divers off San Diego's Point Loma are exposed to bacterial infection. And there is so much sewage runoff flooding the city from Tijuana, Mexico, that a plan is in the works to build a giant U-shaped, "return-to-sender" pipe to ship it back.

But the answer to the nation's wastewater problems does not lie with secondary treatment alone. Indeed, when effluent flows through a secondary treatment system, sludge is generated, and that has to go somewhere as well. Los Angeles dumps its sludge three miles offshore, while Boston has been disposing of it less than one mile away from the shoreline, in about 35 feet of water. As part of its plan, MWRA has chosen a pelletization process by Enviro-Gro Technologies, Baltimore, to dispose of the by-product. But that has got to go somewhere too, perhaps a landfill.

"Over the next 10 to 20 years, sludge management will be a major area of concern," Simpson says. "Many cities have been dumping into the ocean, whereas municipalities in Florida have been placing it in sanitary landfills."

Sludge management is just one aspect of a confusing and frustrating problem—wastewater management. "It is very easy to focus on gloom and doom," Turner says. "But our progress has been so significant that the key issue today is public acceptance of their role in wastewater management." And the cost of not educating the public today could have effects lasting well into the future.

"Our infrastructure must be in balance," Golden says. "We no longer have the luxury of a sustained imbalance. If we do not do something to save our water, future generations will ask us why." (pp. 40–2, 44, 46, 48)

> "The public knows what it wants. It doesn't want sewage and sludge in its backyard. But paying for treatment is another matter. While there is not a lot of new technological development going on today, there has been so much progress over the last 20 years that the problems today are ones that money cannot buy, such as dealing with the public."
>
> —Beth Turner

Tim Darnell, "Straining to Clean Our Waterways," in American City & County, *Vol. 103, No. 10, October, 1988, pp. 40–2, 44, 46, 48.*

Sometimes called "the urban sea," Long Island Sound sits in the most densely populated region of the United States. Each day 1 billion gallons of treated sewage from plants in New York City and Connecticut flow into the Sound. When rainfall is high and sewers overflow, raw sewage and rain water go in, too.

Long Island Sound: When Sewage Meets the Ocean

The waters of Long Island Sound look clear from this central part of the island where teens fish for small snapper. But looks do not always tell the full pollution story.

At the center of debate over the seriousness of pollution in the Sound are questions about the effect of the heavy supply of nutrients pouring into its western part—and what, if anything, should be done about them.

Their effect on low dissolved oxygen levels in deep water, a conditions known as hypoxia, is the central focus so far in the massive, federally funded Long Island Sound Study (LISS), underway since 1985 and due to be completed [in the fall of 1992].

Sometimes called "the urban sea," Long Island Sound sits in the most densely populated region of the United States. Each day 1 billion gallons of treated sewage from plants in New York City and Connecticut flow into the Sound. When rainfall is high and sewers overflow, raw sewage and rain water go in, too.

Studies Show Problems

Many experts say that the added nitrogen from the treated sewage can damage or kill fish and shellfish in bottom waters or force them to flee to areas where oxygen is more abundant. Hypoxia occurs naturally to some degree in summer as warm surface waters forms a distinct layer over colder bottom water, and oxygen in surface water is prevented from replacing that used by marine life below. Added nutrients can speed up and intensify the oxygen loss by fueling the growth of single cell marine plants in surface waters. When the algae dies and drops to the bottom, it uses scarce oxygen there as it decomposes.

In an interim report issued last year, the LISS, a study overseen by the US Environmental Protection Agency, urges that treatment plant discharges of nitrogen into the Sound be restricted to 1990 levels.

Environmentalists say the recommendation should include a timetable. "We think the process of capping nutrients should be started now so that we aren't continually increasing the amount of nitrogen that goes into the Sound," says Jane Moffat, coordinator of the Long Island Watershed Alliance. It is a coalition of 60 groups that grew out of a series of National Audubon Society hearings on the Sound [in 1990].

"We should at least keep the situation from getting any worse," agrees Jeff Kane, program coordinator of the Citizen's Campaign for the Environment and a member of the LISS Citizen's Advisory Committee. Yet he says the study has spent too much time, money, and energy on hypoxia and not enough on other pollutants such as toxic chemicals and pathogens.

Other recent studies confirm that such problems exist. A national Oceanic and Atmospheric Administration study of coastal waters found chemical contamination declining in many areas but still serious in urban areas such as the Western Sound. A recent natural Resources Defense Council report claims the coastal waters of New York, Connecticut, and New Jersey have the worst bacterial contamination problem in the US, due largely to outdated sewage treatment systems.

LISS officials insist that other pollution problems will be studied before the final report is issued.

Mr. Kane is also critical of what he sees as the study's emphasis on engineering solutions and development of computer models: "Ultimately it's the residents . . . that cause the problems and are going to have to change their lifestyles."

Cities around the Sound are taking steps that may help. Some, including New York City, plan to build holding tanks to store storm water until it can be treated along with regular sewage. Some communities are limiting new sewer hookups. Others are looking at new ways to get nitrogen out of treated sewage.

Some remedies are very costly. Upgrading New York City's sewage plants to tertiary treatment levels, for instance, could cost as much as $6 billion. City officials insist that nitrogen discharge levels from city plants have remained stable for 40 years and question the cost benefit ratio.

"Before you make a multibillion dollar investment, you ought to have a better notion of the return; we need to keep looking constantly for different solutions," says J. R. Schubel, dean and director of the Marine Sciences Research Center at the State University of New York at Stony Brook and a member of the LISS technical advisory committee.

Just last week the research center held a workshop that included talk of other options: tidal locks along the East River to keep sewage effluent from moving directly into the Sound, installation of long pipes so that treated swage is discharged only into distant, deep waters, and the possible use of aerators to recharge the water with oxygen.

Dr. Shubel and William Wise, associate director of the Marine Center, stress that there is nothing inherently wrong with adding nutrients. "Most of the ocean is underfertilized," insists Schubel. Mr. Wise suggests that overfishing may pose more of problem for marine life in the Sound than hypoxia. He says much more needs to be known about how specific dissolve oxygen levels translate into a direct effect on marine life. Also key, he says, is knowing whether low oxygen levels in the Sound are really declining or just holding steady.

Sound Solutions Needed

Environmentalists point to the summer of 1987 when there was a particularly intense bloom of algae and sample trawls of LISS scientists brought up no bottom-level fish in some areas an a high percentage of dead crabs and starfish. Yet Mr. Wise notes that the problem has not resurfaced.

Shubel says that research should never be sued as an excuse to delay needed action, but he adds that the Sound's pollution problems are complex and deserve carefully chosen, long-term solutions. He says that it is important to cap nutrient input from sewage treatment plants in New York and Connecticut, as the interim report of the LISS urges, but also to take action to protect the central and eastern Sound which he says are in "remarkably" good condition. "It's always a lot cheaper and more effective to protect an environment that's still in good shape than to let it go and rehabilitate it."

Lucia Mouat, "Pollution Lurks in 'Urban Sea'," in The Christian Science Monitor, *August 29, 1991, p. 8.*

A national Oceanic and Atmospheric Administration study of coastal waters found chemical contamination declining in many areas but still serious in urban areas such as the Western Sound. A recent natural Resources Defense Council report claims the coastal waters of New York, Connecticut, and New Jersey have the worst bacterial contamination problem in the US, due largely to outdated sewage treatment systems.

Organic Treatment: Wastewater Marshlands

Collins, Mississippi—In the heat of the summer, thousands of people come out to enjoy the Okatoma Creek. The Okatoma is the biggest recreational

Plants are being used as a key element in artificial marshland wastewater treatment systems that take advantage of natural processes to make a significant difference in the purity of wastewater effluent. In most cases, the natural systems work better and are less expensive to build, operate and maintain than mechanical systems replaced.

draw in the county and now, thanks to a new artificial wetlands wastewater treatment system installed upstream in Collins, the county seat, people are swimming and canoeing in cleaner Okatoma water.

San Diego, California—The City of San Diego, forced to import 90 percent of its water, has several projects underway to recycle water. One is an aquaculture system that uses water hyacinths to turn wastewater into a valuable commodity: drinking water.

Monterey, Virginia—This small town, population 300, is installing an innovative wastewater treatment system that uses an underground Imhoff tank (similar to a septic tank) in combination with an artificial marsh planted with cattails and bulrushes. After cycling through the Imhoff tank, the waste will be pumped to the artificial marshland for final treatment. Since the wastewater retains heat while stored underground, the marsh filter is expected to work well even during the extreme cold of winter.

Haughton, Louisiana—Mayor Harold Lee gets a kick showing off the city's new flower garden. That's because the garden isn't in a park downtown; it's a part of the city's wastewater treatment system. Haughton has changed over from an activated sludge treatment plant to an artificial wetlands wastewater treatment system that, with its colorful yellow and orange canna lily blooms, looks like a flower garden for much of the summer.

The cities listed above are just a few of the many in the U.S. that are joining a quiet revolution in wastewater treatment. Plants are being used as a key element in artificial marshland wastewater treatment systems that take advantage of natural processes to make a significant difference in the purity of wastewater effluent. In most cases, the natural systems work better and are less expensive to build, operate and maintain than the mechanical systems replaced.

Cities which have installed artificial wetlands are finding themselves role models for other municipalities. "We've had people from Germany to look at it, and people from 12 to 15 states in the U.S.," says Haughton's Mayor Lee. "They're amazed at how beautiful it is. I think it's the greatest thing that ever came along. The effluent looks like a Rocky Mountain stream. It's just crystal clear. We could get Coors beer down here and show them some water as pure as a Rocky Mountain stream."

This is quite a change for a city that was found in violation of EPA standards in 1985, and ordered to upgrade its sewer system. Improving its activated sludge plant would have cost an estimated $1.2 million, compared to the artificial wetlands system cost of $400,000.

"The activated sludge plant used a tremendous amount of electricity," says Lee. "It also didn't do as good a job. And because of the lower costs, we've been able to reduce our sewer user fee by 25 percent. Anytime you can reduce costs to citizens, that's good politics. The big problem is getting engineers to go along with this type of system. Since it doesn't cost as much, the engineers can't make as much money. So far engineers are not very favorable to them."

Besides discharging cleaner water and pleasing customers by reducing charges, Haughton is actually making some money on the system. "We'll recoup our costs off the plants the first year when we harvest them to sell to other municipalities in the area that are building similar systems," the mayor says. "The plants have to be harvested anyhow because they multiply so fast. And we can sell the plants every year, as long as someone is building a new system."

Collins, Mississippi was also under the gun to improve its wastewater treatment. Officials were notified that because of upgraded Clean Water Act standards, Collins had to have an improved system in place by mid-1988. The city received Environmental Protection Agency funds for a pilot project in artificial wetlands wastewater treatment. The $364,000 grant (85 percent of the project cost) went for a supplementary system which directs the discharge from the city's sewer lagoon into a shallow, open-channel wetlands system planted with southern bulrush and duckweed.

Where there are pilot projects, there can be mistakes due to inexperience, which is what happened in Collins. The contractor initially used plants ordered from a nursery in the northern U.S.; those plants didn't survive in the South. The system was later replanted with native plants appropriate to the region.

"The plants are looking very healthy at this time," says Collins' Mayor V. O. Smith. "EPA is still monitoring the discharge, and it's working just the way expected. The effluent is a lot cleaner. We're very happy with it, and have had people from all over come to look at it."

Research Pioneer

Dr. Bill C. Wolverton, a National Aeronautics and Space Administration (NASA) scientist who has pioneered the use of aquatic plants for wastewater treatment in the U.S., says that the number of communities, industries and homes using artificial wetlands to treat wastewater is multiplying rapidly.

"The artificial marsh concept for treating and recycling wastewater is, in most cases, a viable alternative to conventional mechanical systems," Wolverton says. "Artificial marsh treatment has a number of advantages over conventional mechanical treatment systems: They are less costly to install in most locations. Operational and maintenance costs are lower. Non-technical personnel can operate and maintain the system. There is more flexibility and less susceptibility to shockloading. Less energy is required to operate the systems, especially when gravity flow can be maintained. And, the systems are more reliable."

Wolverton's research has been funded through NASA's Technology Utilization Office, which supports the use of space-developed technology for solving earthly problems such as polluted water. Wolverton has helped develop artificial marsh systems for a number of communities, industries and homes and sees only one major disadvantage to the marsh treatment system: It generally requires more land area than a mechanical plant. But even there, the land required for the marsh could also be used for other purposes. For example, if flowering plants are used in the system, it could be a natural addition to a municipal park.

System Designs

There are numerous designs for artificial marsh treatment systems. Wolverton says that the most effective marshes for treating domestic and industrial wastewaters utilize rock filters.

"Each filter should be designed in accordance with the receiving wastewater stream," he says. "Large rocks should be used in the front portion of marsh filters receiving algae-laden discharged water from sewage lagoons during the summer months to minimize filter clogging. An area of four to five acres of marsh filter is required to treat 1,000,000 gallons of sewage lagoon effluent per day."

Most vegetation in the rock marsh filters must be harvested annually or grazed with animals such as goats as is done in some small towns in Louisiana. However, when bulrush and duckweed are used in open channels, such as in the Collins system, harvesting should not be required for many years, if at all. Harvested plant material can be used for animal feed, compost, or biomass for methane.

Much of the early research into marsh filters has centered on the use of hyacinths, but they're out-of-favor now except in tropical and semi-tropical zones. "We don't recommend water hyacinths anymore because of their potential for spreading into the wild," Wolverton says. "I prefer bulrushes, which aren't a danger for spreading and don't freeze in the winter in northern climates. It is

The City of San Diego, forced to import 90 percent of its water, has several projects underway to recycle water. One is an aquaculture system that uses water hyacinths to turn wastewater into a valuable commodity: drinking water.

It's only been about 10 years since aquatic plants were first introduced as a potential tool in wastewater treatment. Since these systems are still in a state of development, changes and improvements will continue. Technology is evolving quite rapidly.

important when installing these systems to understand plants and use native plants that are compatible with the climate."

Wolverton explains the theory behind marsh filters: "The scientific basis for waste treatment in a vascular aquatic plant system is the cooperative growth of both the plants and the microorganisms associated with the plants. Once microorganisms are established on aquatic plant roots, they form a symbiotic relationship in most cases with the plants. This relationship normally produces a synergistic effect resulting in increased degradation rates and removal of organic chemicals from wastewater surrounding the plant root systems. During microbial degradation of the organics, metabolites are produced which the plants absorb and utilize along with nitrogen, phosphorus, and other minerals as a food source. Microorganisms also use metabolites released through plant roots as a food source. By each using the other's waste products, this allows a reaction to be sustained in favor of rapid removal of organics from wastewater.

"Electric charges associated with aquatic plant root hairs also react with opposite charges on colloidal particles such as suspended solids causing them to adhere to the plant roots where they are removed from the wastewater stream and slowly digested and assimilated by the plants and microorganisms. Aquatic plants have the ability to translocate oxygen from the upper leaf areas into the roots producing an aerobic zone around the roots which is desirable in domestic sewage treatment.

"In industrial wastewaters, aquatic plant roots are also capable of absorbing, concentrating, and in some cases translocating heavy metals and certain radioactive elements, therefore removing them from the water system."

Wolverton believes the integration of aquatic plants with rock filters has produced one of the most promising wastewater treatment technologies since the development of the trickling filter process in 1893.

The marsh filter process is simply a lateral-flow trickling filter containing rooted aquatic plants. "By utilizing long, shallow rock-plant filters with hydraulic retention times of 24 or more hours, mean cell residence times of several hundred days can be maintained within the marsh filter," Wolverton says. "Operational data with small systems have demonstrated the importance of maintaining dissolved oxygen levels within the filter of 1.5 mg/L or greater. This oxygen level is required to achieve odor free, low BOD_5 (10 mg/L) levels in the discharged effluent."

Besides treating discharge from Imhoff tanks, septic tanks and sewer lagoons, marsh filters are also capable of treating wastewater discharged from other systems provided sludge is removed to prevent filter clogging.

Effectiveness In Winter

What about the effectiveness of marsh filters in the winter? Wolverton says the systems are still effective because even though the surface vegetation dies back in cold climates, plant roots don't die "and the bacteria associated with the plant roots does most of the work anyway." Or a system can be used such as the one in Monterey, Virginia, which stores heat from the wastewater to keep surface vegetation from freezing.

Some plants are capable of growing even in cold temperatures. Duckweed, for example, can vegetate at temperatures as low as 1 to 3 degrees Centigrade.

In open channels where there may be problems with mosquitoes, control measures such as use of mosquito fish need to be used. In large systems, disinfection is needed to kill human pathogens. Most small towns use chlorine, although there are new systems on the market that use ultraviolet light. If these prove to be effective, Wolverton says they will have an advantage over chlorine systems which may cause harmful effects to the environment if the excess chlorine is not neutralized before discharge. Ozone systems are also being evaluated for disinfection.

It's only been about 10 years since aquatic plants were first introduced as a potential tool in wastewater treatment. Since these systems are still in a state of development, changes and improvements will continue. Technology is evolving quite rapidly.

"The biological reactions that take place between environmental pollutants, plants and microorganisms are numerous and complex, and to date are not fully understood," Wolverton says. "But there is enough information available to demonstrate that aquatic plants serve more of a function than simply supplying a large surface area for microorganisms as some scientists and engineers have suggested." (pp. 48, 50–1)

Becky Gillette, "Revolution in Wastewater Treatment," in BioCycle, Vol. 29, No. 3, March, 1988, pp. 48, 50–1.

Reusing Wastewater in the U.S.

Historically, the greatest impetus for sewage reuse has been in arid areas where water is scarce and where reuse is a necessity. In other areas, wastewater reuse occurred in an unplanned and often unacknowledged manner, as sewage discharged into rivers became a part of the water supply for communities downstream.

Modern concepts of reuse have been driven by the recognition that clean, potable water is not unlimited, even where rainfall is ample. Today, wastewater is being converted from a liability, whose disposal presents continual problems, to a potential resource. Reuse can solve two problems by affording a practical and environmentally sound manner of sewage disposal while providing a new source of water.

Virtually any wastewater discharge can become a source of reclaimed water. Wastewater from agricultural irrigation, power generation, industry and domestic sources all can be reused with appropriate treatment. Reuse may take place on several different scales, from onsite reuse to regional reclamation and redistribution of treated effluent.

Domestic reuse can be implemented, for example, on a small scale by recycling "gray water" generated by sinks and dishwashers for flushing toilets. Large-scale municipal reuse projects can make reclaimed domestic sewage available for a variety of purposes.

California provides several examples of reusing wastewater. The largest use of reclaimed sewage in California currently, and in the United States as well, is for irrigation. A survey by the California Department of Health Services shows of the almost 72 billion gallons of sewage reclaimed in the state annually, 80 percent is used for irrigation. More than half of the total is used for irrigating fodder, fiber, seed crops, orchards and vineyards. A significant amount also is used for landscape irrigation of golf courses, parks, school grounds, freeway plantings and cemeteries. Industrial uses, recreational and landscape impoundments, and groundwater recharge are other uses.

The Irvine Ranch Water District is one of California's large purveyors of reclaimed water. The district provides reclaimed water for landscape irrigation, as well as for crops such as citrus fruits, avocados, tomatoes, corn, peppers, asparagus and cabbage. Reclamation was a condition of development of the Irvine area, since the region is located in water-short Southern California. Thus, the area has a dual water-distribution system serving potable and reclaimed water for domestic and irrigation uses.

"Artificial marsh treatment has a number of advantages over conventional mechanical treatment systems: They are less costly to install in most locations. Operational and maintenance costs are lower. Non-technical personnel can operate and maintain the system. There is more flexibility and less susceptibility to shock-loading. Less energy is required to operate the systems, especially when gravity flow can be maintained. And, the systems are more reliable."

—Dr. Bill C. Wolverton, NASA

Modern concepts of re-use have been driven by the recognition that clean, potable water is not unlimited, even where rainfall is ample. Today, wastewater is being converted from a liability, whose disposal presents continual problems, to a potential resource. Reuse can solve two problems by affording a practical and environmentally sound manner of sewage disposal while providing a new source of water.

In the San Francisco Bay area, a project for industrial reuse of municipal sewage is being proposed in Contra Costa County. The Central Contra Costa Sanitary District will supply treated effluent to the Contra Costa Water District, which will provide additional treatment before the water is supplied to local industries to be used as cooling water. (p. 34)

In the south Bay area, Gilroy, Calif., operates a small reclamation facility supplying reclaimed sewage to the Santa Clara Valley Water District. However, according to Ed Ferguson, head of the Water Facilities Branch, "Increased stringency of regulations has reduced the market for reclaimed water."

Groundwater replenishment with reclaimed water is practiced east of Los Angeles. Since 1962, about 10 percent of the total annual recharge of the Montebello Forebay groundwater basin has been achieved using reclaimed water. The Whittier Narrows Water Reclamation Plant and San Jose Creek Water Renovation Plant supply treated effluent for groundwater recharge. (pp. 34, 36)

[States other than California] and countries are operating similar reclamation projects, and in some areas, wastewater is being reclaimed for potable use. In Israel, treated sewage is used to recharge a groundwater basin for drinking water.

One barrier to more widespread reuse of domestic sewage is its poor public perception. Studies show the degree of acceptance of reuse is related to the type of use proposed. People generally are in favor of low-order reclamation projects, reusing water for irrigation and industrial purposes. Uses such as swimming and drinking are not viewed as favorably.

Educating the Public

Public education is needed to create a positive response to the reuse concept. A University of California study revealed citizens generally favor reuse practices such as irrigation for golf courses, playgrounds and lawns, but not for drinking water.

Accurate information about proposed uses of reclaimed water is important in gaining public acceptance. Adverse reactions to the concept often are based on the assumption the reclaimed water is to be used for drinking.

"The key to public acceptance is a very broad public relations and education program aimed at all parts of the community—starting with fourth grade," says Joyce Wegner-Gwidt, public-relations manager for the Irvine Ranch Water District. The Irvine program stresses both the need for water conservation and the safeguards built into the system. Highly treated wastewater should be used along with a monitoring program to provide assurances of water quality.

Any public-relations campaign should provide accurate, understandable information about the realities of reuse. Although reclaimed wastewater is well-suited for many uses, it is of a different quality than typical surface water. Comparing reclaimed sewage to the quality of other water sources in California's Sierra Mountains has led Alpine County residents to express disappointment in the current reuse program.

"The expectations of residents were greater than the actual system performance," says Robert Karrasch, sanitarian with Alpine County. This has led to a proposal to discontinue using reclaimed sewage in a recreational reservoir in favor of storing the effluent in a special reservoir before using it to irrigate crops.

The public's concern about reclamation is not unfounded, given the fact wastewater contains disease-bearing bacteria and viruses. Sewage also may contain significant amounts of heavy metals and other toxic substances if industrial wastes are processed at the treatment plant. An understanding of the waste being treated is needed before reclamation is deemed appropriate. Proper treatment then is required before the effluent can be reused safely.

Most bacteria and viruses can be removed by disinfection, such as chlorination. Those organisms not removed by disinfection typically are capable of surviving in the environment for only a very short time. Although there have been cases of disease transmitted by irrigation with wastewater, in all cases, the source of the water was raw, undisinfected sewage. No confirmed reports of disease outbreaks have occurred in California as a result of irrigating with reclaimed sewage.

Contamination with heavy metals as a result of wastewater reuse is only of concern if the waste is generated by certain types of industries. Most municipal treatment plants do not produce effluents with high metal concentrations. Even where metals are present in the sewage, the majority are removed with the solids during the treatment's early phases and are concentrated in the sludge produced by the treatment process.

Protecting the Public

To ensure public health, a system of regulatory constraints has evolved to control the uses and quality of reclaimed wastewater. These regulations vary from state to state, but generally are comparable and are administered by similar agencies. The primary agencies involved in regulating sewage reuse are state and local health departments, state water agencies, state environmental-control agencies and public-utility commissions. These agencies may grant licenses, permits and water rights; establish criteria for the degree of treatment or quality of wastewater for reuse; control where reclaimed water may be used; and establish prices.

In California, several state and regional agencies share authority for regulating wastewater reclamation. The State Water Resources Control Board, Regional Water Quality Control Boards and State Department of Health Services work together to enforce reclamation. The Department of Health Services sets criteria for using reclaimed water, which are enforced by regional boards through reclamation requirements imposed on producers and users of reclaimed water.

The Water Resources Control Board also administers water rights. All reclamation projects must meet the requirements of the California Environmental Quality Act, which calls for an environmental-impact report for any project possibly having environmental effects.

Wastewater reclamation in the United States currently is restricted partially by these regulatory constraints. Stringent treatment requirements for many types of agricultural and landscape irrigation have impaired the ability to produce reclaimed water economically in some areas. The costs of advanced treatment can make the price of reclaimed wastewater too high in comparison to other available water sources.

The level of treatment required for sewage reclamation depends on what the water will be used for. The highest level of treatment is required for spray irrigation of food crops. Irrigation of fodder, fiber and seed crops, and surface irrigation of orchards and vineyards require the lowest level of treatment.

The level of treatment necessary to meet reuse criteria largely determines the cost of reclaimed water. Few existing treatment plants include facilities for advanced treatment, and the incremental cost of adding these facilities is one of the major components of the price of producing reclaimed water. Because production for spray irrigation of food crops requires advanced treatment, this reuse cost could be high. Irrigation of fodder crops, however, would be more economical because additional treatment would not be required.

The cost for a reuse system includes several other components, including facilities for distribution, any other required storage facilities and a water-quality monitoring system. Distribution facilities are necessary since reclaimed water cannot be allocated through existing potable-water systems.

Storage often is necessary to take full advantage of producing reclaimed water year-round. In California, for example, there is little need for irrigation during

Domestic reuse can be implemented on a small scale by recycling "gray water" generated by sinks and dishwashers for flushing toilets. Large-scale municipal reuse projects can make reclaimed domestic sewage available for a variety of purposes.

One barrier to more widespread reuse of domestic sewage is its poor public perception. Studies show the degree of acceptance of reuse is related to the type of use proposed. People generally are in favor of low-order reclamation projects, reusing water for irrigation and industrial purposes. Uses such as swimming and drinking are not viewed as favorable.

the rainy season, when the sewage volume is greatest. Storage of treated effluent produced during the rainy season greatly augments the supply of reclaimed water available during drier times.

Some of the basic costs of producing reclaimed water could be passed on to users as part of the water's price.

Individual users also may want to monitor water quality and provide additional treatment to meet their own requirements. If potable water is to be used with the reclaimed water, new piping may be necessary to provide a dual distribution system on-site. Otherwise, blending of potable and reclaimed water could be performed in a storage tank before distribution.

Using reclaimed water could require some changes in normal operating practices. Larger volumes of water, for example, may have to be used to compensate for the higher salinity of reclaimed irrigation water or for the lower quality water reused in recirculating cooling systems. Landscaped areas may have to be irrigated on a different schedule to minimize potential public health risks associated with contact with sprays, such as irrigating parks and golf courses at night.

On the plus side, water reuse can have substantial economic benefits. Reuse can help fund wastewater facilities, especially when the treatment level required by reclamation is the same as the level for disposal. In water-short areas, reclamation costs may be less than the costs of developing new sources of water or importing water. For irrigation uses, the nutrients in sewage provide a benefit to crops and may allow farmers to reduce fertilizer costs.

Because of these and other benefits, many producers of reclaimed wastewater do not charge users the full cost. Wastewater-treatment agencies can sell their treated effluent at a reduced price because they have been relieved of the disposal costs.

Worldwide population growth makes increased water reuse inevitable. Present water supplies simply cannot meet the ever-increasing water demand. Reusing domestic sewage is just one of the avenues available to ensure an adequate supply of good quality water for the future. As technology advances, new treatments and better monitoring techniques will provide more assurance of safety, resulting in a gradual decrease in legal and regulatory constraints. (pp. 36, 38, 40, 44)

Robin P. Cort, "Reusing Wastewater," in American City & County, *Vol. 102, No. 10, October, 1987, pp. 34, 36, 38, 40, 44.*

Wastewater Reuse in the Third World

The recycling of excreta and wastewater has been practised for many centuries. Particularly in Asia, excreta are important in agriculture, fish farming and aquatic vegetable production. In rural China, for example, excreta are used as a soil conditioner and fertilizer. In the hill areas of Java (Indonesia), excreta are traditionally used to fertilize fish ponds. Some of the excreta collected from household bucket latrines in Indian cities are applied by farmers to nearby fields, a practice presenting a serious health risk. However, safety can be achieved through extended storage of excreta from latrines with two pits or vaults for dry or wet disposal. In Viet Nam, "dry" double-vault latrines were introduced several years ago and are now in widespread use. They are also gaining popularity in Central America. "Wet" double-pit pour-flush latrines are an important component of urban sanitation programmes in India.

The use of wastewater in agriculture and fish farming began with the development of flush toilets and sewerage technology more than a century ago. Wastewater from many European cities was applied to nearby farmland, this being the most economic method of disposal. However, as the amounts of wastewater increased, particularly after the Second World War, the availability of land for this purpose decreased. Furthermore, cheap chemical fertilizers came on to the market. Energy- and machinery-intensive methods of wastewater treatment were developed. Most of the sludge produced in sewage works is still used on the land, but in urban areas this practice has become problematic because too much sludge is produced in relation to the available surfaces. Moreover, some sludges have proved unsuitable for agricultural use due to the presence of heavy metals and persistent organic substances.

It should be noted, however, that in developing countries the geographical, climatic and economic factors determining whether wastewater can be used on the land differ greatly from those in most industrialized countries. In fact, the agricultural use of wastewater is rapidly gaining popularity, particularly in arid and semi-arid regions, for the following reasons:

- scarcity of water for irrigation;

- increased need for domestic water;

- expansion of agricultural production;

- high cost of mineral fertilizers;

- few health risks and little damage to soil if precautions are taken.

Wastewater is used notably in India, Latin America, Tunisia, the USA, and West Asia. Practices vary from the totally uncontrolled extraction of raw sewage from broken sewers to the use of well-treated wastewater in strictly administered schemes with restrictions on the crops to which it may be applied.

An alternative waste management scheme has been developed in Guatemala, based on the decentralized, integrated and neighbourhood-controlled collection and recycling of solid and liquid wastes.

Traditional Practices

In China the custom of storing organic human waste from rural and urban populations and using it in agriculture is still practised despite increased urbanization, industrialization and the use of chemical fertilizers.

Excreta collected in urban areas are transported to rural areas by truck, tractor, cart and boat. In 1981, of the 73 million tonnes of excreta and 73 million tonnes of solid waste produced in large towns, 40 million tonnes were used in agriculture, fish farming and aquatic vegetable production.

It has been estimated that of the 150 million tonnes of faecal waste produced annually by some 800 million people in rural China, 60–70% are recycled. The excreta usage rate amounts to at least 60–70%. Some 1.3 billion tonnes of animal manure were used in 1981. In some places excreta are stored for several weeks before use in order to destroy helminth eggs. Co-composting of human and animal excreta with crop residues is also practised, as is biogas production and the use of biogas slurry on the land. About 1.8 billion tonnes of organic fertilizer are produced annually by these processes. Its nutrient value is estimated to be equivalent to that of 100 million tonnes of inorganic fertilizer.

Most human and animal excreta, and excreta-derived compost, is generally ploughed or harrowed into the soil before crops are sown. . . . The exact rate is worked out with reference to: the quantity of available nutrients, especially nitrogen; the risk of inhibiting germination and growth; and the quantity that it is practicable to deposit on or incorporate into the soil.

In the hill areas of Java many villagers own small fish ponds into which human excreta from overhanging latrines are allowed to fall. Some farmers who

Wastewater is used notable in India, Latin America, Tunisia, the USA, and West Asia. Practices vary from the totally uncontrolled extraction of raw sewage from broken sewers to the use of well-treated wastewater in strictly administered schemes with restrictions on the crops to which it may be applied.

Some farmers who produce fish on a large scale now use commercially produced, pelleted fish feed, but most farmers continue to use excreta as the cheapest and most readily available fertilizer.

produce fish on a large scale now use commercially produced, pelleted fish feed, but most farmers continue to use excreta as the cheapest and most readily available fertilizer.

The world's largest combined wastewater disposal and fish production system is in India. Wastewater and drainage water from East Calcutta are stored and treated in over 40 km^2 of lagoons where fish production has become a highly skilled operation. Some 24 000 people are employed, full- or part-time, in this industry. The output provides 10–20% of the fish requirements of 10 million urban dwellers. The system destroys many pathogens, and there are probably few health risks associated with it. Treated wastewater from the lagoons is used to irrigate 6000 ha of agricultural land, thereby providing a full or partial income for 3000 families. The system is an excellent example of ecologically and socioeconomically sound wastewater management.

Wastewater is widely used on the outskirts of Mexico's urban areas, particularly in the arid and semi-arid zones. Most of the wastewater and storm runoff from Mexico City is used to irrigate the Mezquital Valley, 60 km to the north. The wastewater is not treated but some destruction of pathogens occurs during passage through canals and reservoirs. The main crops are alfalfa, maize, beans, chillies and green tomatoes.

Soil Conditioner/Fertilizer from Double-Vault Latrines

In Guatemala, the Centro de Estudios Mesoamericano sobre Tecnología Apropriada (CEMAT), collaborating with the local population, has developed and introduced a double-vault dry alkaline fertilizer latrine. Each vault has an interior volume of about 400 litres. One vault is used at a time and when it becomes full the contents are left in place until the second is full. Filling takes five to seven months, depending on the number of users. (pp. 46, 50–2)

After defaecation, ash is put into the vault; this raises the pH above 9, helping to destroy pathogenic bacteria and viruses. The faecal material decomposes at ambient temperature in mixed aerobic and anaerobic conditions. After removal, the contents are stored in bags. This fertilizer, highly valued by subsistence farmers, is applied to the land by mulching, ploughing or "sandwiching", depending on the crop. . . . According to the users, the principal benefits derived from the latrines are, in order of priority, the production of organic fertilizer, their convenience, and improved hygiene. To date, some 4000 dry alkaline fertilizer latrines have been constructed in Guatemala under the auspices of governmental and private organizations. (pp. 52–3)

Integrated, Decentralized and Self-managed Collection and Recycling of Wastewater and Refuse

In urban areas of developing countries, adequate services for the disposal of excreta, wastewater and solid waste are often restricted to city centres and high-income localities, where technologies developed in industrialized countries are usually encountered, e.g., sewerage, use of vacuum tankers to empty septic tanks, and mechanized refuse collection. Public authorities very often disregard the waste-disposal needs of low-income areas because here the imported technologies are too sophisticated and costly.

In Latin America, many nongovernmental organizations strive to develop technologically and socioeconomically appropriate solutions to problems of excreta and refuse disposal as opposed to conventional ones. The alternative infrastructures tend to be community-based, i.e., planned, implemented and operated by the users.

The Alameda Norte waste-recycling plant in Guatemala City serves approximately 3000 persons in a low-income neighbourhood. The main fractions of solid waste are collected, following which manual separation of compostable and noncompostable material is necessary. Sieved compost is sold, as are plastic, metal and other fractions. Wastewater is treated in a settling and fermentation tank, where gas is produced. Further treatment in waste stabilization ponds is planned with a view to the removal of pathogenic organisms. The resulting effluent will be used to irrigate nearby fields, and the biogas produced will run the irrigation pumps.

Few operational data are yet available on the new system. It is not possible to say how the users cope with the many technical and managerial tasks. However, this technology represents an ecologically and socially sound alternative to the conventional centralized, government-administered disposal methods that have been developed in industrialized countries over the last century.

Hygiene

In developing countries where several types of enteric disease are prevalent there is a risk to public health from excreta that are not stored for an adequate period or effectively treated in some other way.

Excreta and wastewater must be either stored long enough or treated adequately before use. The longest-surviving pathogens are worm eggs, particularly those of the roundworm *Ascaris*, which may remain viable for many months or even a few years. *Salmonella* may survive for a few months. Time and temperature are the two most important factors determining the duration of survival. (pp. 53–5)

Storage periods of several months to a few years are required at ambient temperatures, but treatment periods can be reduced proportionally to achieve hygienically safe products at higher temperatures. With thermophilic composting, for example, at temperatures of 60–70°C, safety can be achieved within a few weeks.

In tropical countries, the retention of wastewater in stabilization ponds is often the most feasible method of removing pathogens. The wastewater flows through several ponds in three to four weeks. Helminth eggs and protozoan cysts are removed by sedimentation, while bacteria and viruses die. . . .

There is strong epidemiological evidence that the use of untreated/unstored excreta or wastewater can be associated with an actual risk of excess infection from intestinal nematodes, i.e., roundworm (*Ascaris*), whipworm (*Trichuris*) and hookworm (*Ancylostoma, Necator*). The actual risk of excess infection by bacterial and viral diseases appears to be lower than for nematode infections. The epidemiological evidence for this is relatively weak, owing to a paucity of credible epidemiological investigations, but the the assumption is based on sound theoretical considerations of potential risk (typical transmission routes, pathogen die-off, and infective dose).

Agriculture

Human excreta can be used to restore and maintain good soil structure and fertility. They are as good a source of nitrogen, phosphorus and potassium as any other organic fertilizer or composted material. During storage or treatment much nitrogen is lost because of leaching and volatilization, a drawback also affecting other organic fertilizers.

Excreta are valued mainly for their soil-conditioning and humus-building potential. However, their nutrient content ban be used to estimate a family's fertilizing potential, assuming a daily dry-weight excreta production of 110 g/person. A family of five adults can provide sufficient nitrogen and phosphorus to cultivate a rice plot ranging in area from 1600 m^2 to 2000 m^2. For maize, the area would be 20–30% smaller, while for soya beans it would be 25–50% larger.

The evaluation and promotion programme for the dry alkaline fertilizer latrine in Guatemala comprised trials in which crops cultivated without any fertilizer were compared with others receiving organic fertilizer from such latrines and with ones receiving mineral fertilizers. As between organic and mineral fertilizer, the results were inconclusive for green peas, kidney beans, and radishes, but the organic fertilizer led to increased yields over untreated controls. For

Public authorities [in developing countries] very often disregard the waste-disposal needs of low-income areas because here the imported technologies are too sophisticated and costly.

In developing countries where several types of enteric disease are prevalent there is a risk to public health from excreta that are not stored for an adequate period or effectively treated in some way.

other crops the latrine fertilizer did not lead to a significant increase in yields. The application rates for the organic fertilizer were equivalent to 2500–3000 kg/ha/year of the material produced in the latrines.

Fertilizer derived from excreta should be valued more for its humus-forming capacity than for the nutrients it provides. Although excreta-derived products contain nutrients in concentrations comparable to those of other organic manures, it should be borne in mind that organic products cannot compete on a unit weight basis with mineral fertilizers as suppliers of nutrients. Mineral fertilizers, however, have no humus-building capacity. Humus, the organic body of the soil, plays a decisive role in the adsorption, storage and regulation of nutrients and water, as well as influencing the aeration and temperature of the soil. (pp. 55, 58)

Martin Strauss, "Food from Waste," in World Health Forum, *Vol. 11, No. 1, 1990, pp. 46–59.*

Water Reclamation and Waste Treatment: Industry's Efforts

Much of the recent news on industry and clean water focuses on past mistakes: waste dumps and polluted streams. Far too little spotlights what industry has done—and is doing—right.

For many industries, water is a continuing concern, but not because they must find ways to get rid of their waste water—although they must. Many of these manufacturers are big consumers, and must also find adequate water with enough quality to meet their own needs.

A small company may simply plug into a municipal system. A larger manufacturer, such as Lone Star Steel in Texas, can't do that. The mill uses up to 150 million gallons per day.

Other facilities, such as GE Plastics' polycarbonate resin plant in Alabama, can find plenty of groundwater, but has innovative systems for disposing of its own waste.

Meanwhile, water treatment companies, such as Calgon, are turning to the latest in artificial intelligence and expert systems to help other manufacturers keep track of their own process water.

When looking for water, a manufacturer has a number of options: a public water supply, groundwater, or surface water. Each has its pros and cons in terms of supply, price, and quality. Eventually, it becomes a tradeoff, as the following case histories indicate.

Lone Star Steel: Man-made Solutions

The Piney Woods of East Texas is an unlikely place for a steel mill. At least that's what the government thought when it began building just such a mill in the early days of World War II, hoping to decentralize steel production. However, the war ended before the plant could come on line.

Long since in the private sector, Lone Star Steel now processes millions of tons of steel. Its electric arc furnaces feed raw material to its other operations, most notably the specialty tubing and flat roll manufacturing divisions that have dominated the company since sales of its oil country products took a nose dive along with the oil industry.

The sprawling plant lies on the shores of Lone Star Lake, a man-made lake that provides all the cooling and process water necessary for plant operations—100 million to 150 million gallons per day—as well as on-site drinking water for the employees.

G. C. "Cliff" Wright, director of corporate environmental affairs for Lone Star, relates how the 1500–acre lake, along with the plant's drinking water treatment plant, once also supplied potable water for the town of Lone Star for about 30 years. The drinking water treatment plant effluent is still a public drinking water supply approved by the state health department.

Wright oversees the entire Lone Star operation, which involves taking water from the lake, apportioning it to the various operations, including the drinking water plant, collecting waste water, treating it, and sending it back to the lake.

Designed as a self-sufficient mill, Lone Star boasts everything from iron ore mining and ore beneficiation plant, coke plant, blast furnace and open hearth shop, through rolling mills, to the pipe manufacturing and tubing mills. An electrical power generation plant is also part of the scheme. The ore mining, blast furnace, and open hearth shop are shut down now, and the coke plant is on idle hot, but water is still needed for the electric power plant, electric arc furnaces, and the remainder of the mill's rolling and pipe manufacturing processes.

Wright says the design of the environmental control system in the furnaces is the "best available." The water is crucial to the air emission scrubbers to allow air emissions to meet environmental standards. The system is 98% recirculating, with 800 gpm clarified and returned to the system. The sludge is vacuum filtered and the 6 to 10 tons per day is hauled off to an approved site.

Other plant service water that does not beome contaminated, mostly water for cooling furnace walls, is returned to the lake. Water used for quenching, descaling, and in other processes, and which does become contaminated, passes through a series of pits and settling tanks before recycling.

For example, the specialty tubing operation uses a series of pickling, coating, and lubricating treatments, followed by rinses. This places the plant under two sets of guidelines: iron and steel, which covers sulfuric acid pickling, and metal finishing, for zinc phosphate coating.

The rinse water is treated in a series of reaction tanks, where lime is added to bring the pH to between 7 and 9. The water then goes through a clarification and filtration process before it is discharged back into the lake.

Lone Star also collects all surface water, along with the process and non-process water, from the 500-acre complex and runs it through a 50-acre system of ponds that serve as settling basins, complete with oil skimmers. Just as it supplies its own drinking water, the firm also treats and disposes of all its own sewage—about 150,000 gallons per day—in an activated sludge plant.

Lone Star has 15 employees working on its plant utilities program, seven of these involved solely in monitoring and reporting water quality. But the system directly affects all employees, both in their work and personal lives.

Lone Star Lake is certified as "contact recreational" by Texas environmental officials, allowing boating, fishing, and swimming. All Lone Star employees are entitled to bring their families to camp at the Starlite Park on the shores of the lake, and available time is at a premium.

GE Plastics: Kudos from the State

When GE Plastics opened its $325-million Lexan® resin plant in Burkville, AL, in 1987, it was billed as the most advanced such facility in the world and the largest construction project in GE's history.

For many industries, water is a continuing concern, but not because they must find ways to get rid of their waste water—although they must. Many of these manufacturers are big consumers, and must also find adequate water with enough quality to meet their own needs.

When General Electric Plastics opened its $325-million Lexan resin plant in Burkeville, AL, in 1987, it was billed as the most advanced such facility in the world.

As with other manufacturing facilities, the GE plant comes under both EPA and state guidelines. In fact, the state of Alabama recently cited GE for its excellence in waste water treatment.

Bob Smith, general manager of operations, says the facility uses 1.3 million gallons per day of "use-once" water. Three wells on the 6300-acre facility provide the water, which is later discharged into the Alabama river.

As with other manufacturing facilities, the GE plant comes under both EPA and state guidelines. In fact, the state of Alabama recently cited GE for its excellence in waste water treatment.

Six different operations at Burkville feed into the waste water system. Two of the waste streams combine, according to Smith, but the others are kept separate until the operators can monitor such things as pH and suspended solids.

This has several advantages. It allows operators to "blend" waste streams to achieve the best mixture to put into the treatment system. This produces a more consistent waste stream and makes the water treatment more efficient.

It also allows plant supervisors to monitor the different processes, since problems can be highlighted earlier, rather than being detected in a combined waste stream.

Water from each stream goes into a 100,000-gallon holding tank. Contents of each tank are checked for pH, suspended solids, organic materials, and metal contaminants. Blended according to the operator's judgment, the waste goes by gravity feed into a 15,000-gallon mixing chamber and then into a clarifier.

Sludge from the clarifier is tested for contaminants, but is not considered a hazardous waste and is incinerated in a normal incinerator.

After the clarifier, the waste goes into an anthracite filter, is checked once more for pH, and then is discharged into the river.

GE also collects all the rainwater that falls on the plant site. This water is channeled into a 10-million-gallon outdoor storage vessel, which is essentially a pond with a liner, where it is checked for contaminants, treated if necessary, and then discharged.

The rainwater system is designed to handle the maximum daily rainfall in the last 100 years, a total of 8 inches in a 24-hour period.

The Burkville plant also handles its own sewage treatment, something that assists in the other waste treatment. Smith says the organic matter in the sewage aids in other biological treatment.

GE designed the Alabama setup after studying operations at other plants. Engineers tried to copy the best features found elsewhere—or improve on them. It's not an easy system to retrofit to existing plants, Smith says, but it will definitely be studied in new construction.

While GE Plastics won't give production figures for the plant, it says it is doubling its capacity and, therefore, the capacity of its waste treatment system.

Calgon Corp.: Expert System

Waste water, however, isn't the only problem faced by industries. Many operations recirculate cooling water and find they have to closely monitor the quality of this water to ensure the efficient operation of the plant, as well as prevent damage to the system.

In many cases, the determination of proper chemistry is left up to the expertise of an operator, who may or may not be an expert.

Calgon Corp., Pittsburgh, and Texas Instruments recently joined forces to put ears of experience from water treatment experts into a system that will allow even novice operators to keep a recirculating process running at peak efficiency.

Marketed by Calgon as Helmsman®, the system is an on-line, real-time program that uses thousands of rules covering hundreds of possible situations. (pp. 98–101)

The rules allow the system to alert the operator to changes in pre-determined parameters, and to suggest steps to rectify any undesirable conditions.

Richard Herrod, manager of industrial AI applications for Texas Instruments, says the development of Helmsman was a joint two-year effort by the two companies, in which they interviewed numerous experts and captured their knowledge about water treatment. (p. 101)

Other manufacturers—often smaller—are faced with challenges that are just as perplexing, if not as large in volume.

Al Miller, president of Miller Newell Engineering Ltd., Newport, AK, and a vice president of the American Consulting Engineers Council, says he often solves water problems for his clients with solutions that meet their needs and pocketbooks at the same time.

"It's easy to put in the most state-of-the-art equipment, if you've got millions of dollars to spend," says Miller. Yet he admits that many of his clients have to look long and hard at the bottom line.

Some have unique problems. One of his clients, which makes Mexican corn chips, needs quality drinking water for processing its product. That means using the public water supply. However, says Miller, he's studying whether it would be more economical for the company to treat its own potable water.

The chip factory also faces a challenge in disposing of its waste water, since the process introduces salt and grease into the discharge, along with suspended solids. This means screening, separating, and aerating the water to achieve state and federal standards before releasing it into public supplies.

With increased awareness, industry responsibility, and government supervision, we are unlikely to repeat our past mistakes. But water—both supply and disposal—will continue to challenge manufacturers. (pp. 101–02)

Carlton F. Vogt, Jr., "Clean Water: Coming and Going," in Design News, Vol. 45, No. 3, February 13, 1989, pp. 98–102.

With increased awareness, industry responsibility, and government supervision, we are unlikely to repeat our past mistakes. But water—both supply and disposal—will continue to challenge manufacturers.

Sources For Further Study

Angel, Marvin V. "The Deep-Ocean Option for the Disposal of Sewage Sludge." *Environmentalist* 8, No. 1 (1988): 19–26.
Recommends that sewage sludge be discharged into the ocean at a depth of over 4 km, close to the abysmal sea bed, thereby isolating it from humans and causing minimal damage to marine ecosystems.

Brown, Timothy S. "Household Hazardous Waste: The Unresolved Water Quality Dilemma." *Water Pollution Control Federation Journal* 59, No. 3 (March 1987): 120–24.
Relates concerns about the presence and treatment of hazardous chemicals in municipal wastewater.

Burke, William. "Restoring Water Naturally." *Technology Review* 94, No. 1 (January 1991): 16–17.
Discuss the benefits of ecological waste engineering.

Cheremisinoff, Paul N., et. al. "Management of Wastewater Solids." *Pollution Engineering* 21, No. 9 (September 1989): 69–74.
 Relates the various processes by which suspended solids are removed from wastewater and treated.

Crook, James, and Okun, Daniel A. "The Place of Nonpotable Reuse in Water Management." *Water Pollution Control Federation Journal* 59, No. 5 (May 1987): 237–41.
 Outlines the ways in which wastewater can be reused.

Gilges, Kent W. "Waste Problem has a Natural Solution." *Industry Week* 238, No. 21 (6 November 1989): 51–2.
 Describes the increasing use of artificial wetlands for wastewater treatment.

Goldstein, Nora, and Riggle, David. "Healthy Future for Sludge Composting." *BioCycle* 30, No. 17 (December 1989): 28–34.
 Presents the results of a 1989 survey of sludge composting facilities that indicate the growing potential of this waste management option.

Hart, James B., et. al. "Silvicultural Use of Wastewater Sludge." *Journal of Forestry* 86, No. 8 (August 1988): 17–24.
 Advocates applying wastewater sludge to forestland, which, it is argued, is more practical and less hazardous than agricultural use.

Institution of Civil Engineers. *World Water '89: Managing the Future—Learning from the Past*. Proceedings of an International Conference Organized by the Institution of Civil Engineers, 14–16 November 1989. London: Thomas Telford, 1990, 249 p.
 Assesses the achievements of the United Nation's Water and Sanitation Decade of the 1980s, the goal of which was to provide the world's population with safe water and adequate sanitary facilities by 1990, and identifies areas for future improvement.

Waste Collection and Treatment Systems: Tackling the Disposal Problem." *Jubail Development Quarterly* 3, No. 1 (March 1988): 10–11.
 Describes the wastewater treatment system in place in Jubail, Saudi Arabia.

Kellog, Stephen R. "Sludge Management: Changing Times." *Pollution Engineering* 21, No. 12 (November 1989): 50–7.
 Comments on the rapid evolution of wastewater sludge management over the past three decades and discusses emerging trends in treatment.

Knight, Dave. "Nice Work for a Worm." *New Scientist* 123, No. 1672 (8 July 1989): 55–9.
 Considers the role earthworms may play in future waste management methods.

Kourik, Robert. "Greywater for Your Garden." *Garbage* 2, No. 1 (January–February 1990): 41–5.
 Describes how gray water—the wastewater from domestic plumbing—can be used to irrigate gardens and outlines the possible legal implications, installation procedures, and cost.

Kriz, Margaret E. "Effluent, Not Affluent." *National Journal* 21, No. 12 (25 March 1989): 740–42.
 Reports on the complications arising from the federal government's move away from EPA grants to small communities for sewage treatment to state-administered loans.

Lee, Kun M., et. al. "Conversion of Municipal Sludge to Oil." *Water Pollution Control Federation Journal* 59, No. 10 (October 1987): 884–89.
 Evaluates the praticality of converting municipal sludge to oil using water as a solvent.

Liepa, Ingrid. "What to Do with Poo." *Alternatives* 16–17, Nos. 4–1 (March–April 1990): 12–13.
 Discusses alternatives to sewage disposal, including wastewater irrigation, aquaculture uses, and composting.

Lowe, Marcia D. "Down the Tubes." *World Watch* 2, No. 2 (March–April 1989): 22–9.
Discusses the advantages of using human waste as fertilizer.

Mara, Duncan, and Cairncross, Sandy. *Guidelines for the Safe Use of Wastewater and Excreta in Agriculture and Aquaculture: Measures for Public Health Protection.* Geneva: World Health Organization, 1989, 187 p.
Comprehensive guidelines for the safe use of waste products in agriculture and aquaculture. Written for engineers and planners.

Marecos de Monte, H., et. al. "Effects on Soil and Crops of Irrigation with Primary and Secondary Effluents." *Water Science and Technology* 21 (1989): 427–34.
Presents data from a study in which sorghum, maize, and sunflower crops were irrigated over a two-year period with municipal wastewater.

Marinelli, Janet. "After the Flush: The Next Generation." *Garbage* 2, No. 1 (January–February 1990): 24–34.
Proposes artificial marshes as an alternative to conventional sewage treatment plants.

Maye, Peter R. "Urban Water Reuse." *Georgia Operator* 25, No. 4 (Fall 1988): 16–20.
Asserts that urban water reuse must be strictly regulated by the states to protect public health.

Milne, Roger. "Sludge Disposal Becomes a Burning Issue." *New Scientist* 128, No. 1745 (1 December 1990): 35.
Reports on the trend in Great Britain toward incineration as a means for sludge disposal.

Mininni, Giuseppe, and Santori, Mario. "Problems and Perspectives of Sludge Utilization in Agriculture." *Agriculture, Ecosystems and Environment* 18, No. 4 (April 1987): 291–311.
Academic study outlining the benefits of sludge use in agriculture, including the increased availability of nitrogen and phosphorous, while warning of such drawbacks as the presence of pathogens and heavy metals.

Nolte, Joachim. "Pollution Source Analysis of River Water and Sewage Sludge." *Environmental Technology Letters* 9, No. 8 (August 1988): 857–68.
Demonstrates methods by which wastewater pollutants can be traced to their sources.

Oron, Gideon, and Willers, Hans. "Effect of Wastes Quality on Treatment Efficiency with Duckweed." *Water Science and Technology* 21 (1989): 639–45.
Evaluates duckweed pond treatment of various types of wastewater.

Oron, Gideon, and DeMalach, Joel. "Reuse of Domestic Wastewater for Irrigation in Arid Zones: A Case Study." *Water Resources Bulletin* 23, No. 5 (October 1987): 777–83.
Presents data from a study conducted in Israel concerning the use of a desert city's wastewater for irrigation.

Phillips, John D. "An Evaluation of the Factors Determining the Effectiveness of Water Quality Buffer Zones." *Journal of Hydrology* 107 (1989): 133–45.
Evaluates the effectiveness of a proposed buffer zone along shorelines in which runoff pollutants would be diluted before being introduced into the ocean.

Shahalam, Abul Basher M. "Wastewater Effluent vs. Safety in Its Reuse: State-of-the-Art." *The Journal of Environmental Sciences* XXXII, No. 5 (September–October 1989): 35–42.
Presents "a state-of-the-art review of the human health risks associated with the reuse of wastewater effluent."

Short, C. S. "The Bramham Incident, 1980—An Outbreak of Water-Borne Infection." *Institute of Water and Environmental Management* 2, No. 4 (August 1988): 383–91.

Documents how researchers linked the 1980 outbreak of gastroenteritis in rural Great Britain to the contamination of drinking water by sewage and evaluates the altered treatment system now in place.

Trivedy, R. K. "Organic Wastes—Sources, Effects and Treatment." *Indian Journal of Environmental Protection* 8, No. 5 (May 1988): 362–71.
Presents data on sewage and industrial effluents from major Indian cities and selected industries, as well as actual treatment practices and proposed methods.

Wong-Chong, George M. "Wastewater Treatment Plant Management." *Advances in Environmental Technology and Management* 2, (1990): 103–39.
Outlines how managers of wastewater treatment plants can best address the many laws and regulations pertaining to their field.

16:   Soil Quality

Soil Pollution: The Nature and Scope of the Problem

Fifteen years ago [in 1972] the Clear Air Act and Clean Water Act became the foundation of environmental protection in the United States. Unfortunately, by focusing only on air and water, legislators created the impression that once pollutants were out of these media, they would be out of the environment entirely. In fact, although our air and water are now arguably cleaner, our soils and sediments are becoming significantly more polluted.

Pollutants permitted to be discharged under the Clean Air and Clean Water acts may not damage the environment directly via air or water, but they can cause harm after settling and accumulating on soils and the sediments of water basins. Consider acid deposition. Even when the National Ambient Air Quality Standards are not exceeded, coal-burning power plants in the Midwest emit enough sulfur dioxide to acidify soils hundreds of miles away. This can lead to large-scale loss of valued species of forest trees. To protect the soil, we must pass a clean soil act to force us to treat the environment as the complete system that it is.

Regulations pertaining to soils focus primarily on hazardous-waste disposal and cleanup requirements. And these concern only two means of chemical exposure: leaching and volatilization. Leaching occurs when rainwater or snowmelt passes through soils and carries contamination deep into the ground, sometimes to groundwater. Volatilization takes place when a soil contaminant vaporizes into the air.

Yet contaminated soil particles can also pose a hazard when inhaled or ingested. These forms of exposure are rarely considered in risk assessments or in determining acceptable levels of pollutant emissions.

Danger from Dust

The high concentrations of heavy metals in the soils and house dusts near smelters show how health risks can be underestimated. Clean Air Act regulations address lead only in the ambient air. But in these communities, residents' elevated blood-lead levels have been linked to concentrations of lead in the soil. These increased concentrations are the result of ambient air standards too high to account for deposition and accumulation. Elevated blood-lead levels in children can cause developmental problems, while chronic lead poisoning in adults can damage the peripheral nervous system and increase the risk of heart disease.

People inhale and ingest soil in several ways. Every breath takes in numerous suspended dust particles. Chewing on a pen or eating, for example, brings hands to the mouth, transporting dust to the digestive tract. Children, who often eat dirt, are more sensitive than adults to many toxins. Amounts of soil ingested by children vary, but recent estimates suggest that even through normal activities such as playing with toys children generally eat between 0.1 and 10 grams of soil daily.

> **Pollutants permitted to be discharged under the Clear Air and Clean Water acts may not damage the environment directly via air or water, but they can cause harm after settling and accumulating on soils.**

People inhale and ingest soil in several ways. Every breath takes in numerous suspended dust particles. Chewing on a pen or eating, for example, brings hands to the mouth, transporting dust to the digestive tract. Children, who often eat dirt, are more sensitive than adults to many toxins. Amounts of soil ingested by children vary, but recent estimates suggest that even through normal activites such as playing with toys children generally eat between 0.1 and 10 grams of soil daily.

Soil contaminants can also be ingested through food. Some root vegetables may accumulate dioxins, heavy metals, and PCBs from the soil, while leafy vegetables may incorporate contaminants from dust. Grazing animals ingest dust and dirt, and shellfish and bottom-feeding fish concentrate pollutants from sediments when they feed. The toxins can then be transferred to humans. For example, pesticides and heavy metals that are deposited on the sediments of the Great Lakes become concentrated as they are passed along the food chain. Regional authorities therefore recommend that the consumption of salmon and other kinds of sport fish be limited or avoided.

Through ingestion or inhalation, soil contaminants can enter the body directly and move through the bloodstream to the liver and other organs that accumulate toxins. In pregnant women, the rapidly developing cells of the fetus are especially vulnerable to toxins, increasing the posibility of birth defects or developmental problems.

Pollution From Ill Winds

Environmental laws also neglect the fact that contaminated soils and sediments can travel long distances suspended in air or water. Consider how pesticides adhering to soil particles can be blown into the air, traveling great distances before returning to earth dissolved in rain. Potentially toxic pesticides used primarily in the South have turned up in the Great Lakes region, in concentrations that are too high to have come from local farms.

A radical rethinking of how we protect our environment is required. Soils and sediments must be brought into the picture. Consequently, air and water pollution must be lowered to compensate for the soil's ability to accumulate and disperse all kinds of contaminants. Also, reductions of emissions are essential for chemicals such as metals and persistent pesticides that are not readily degraded in the environment.

In addition to emission controls, the prevailing approach to both industrial waste and household garbage must be changed from "Where will we put it?" to "How can we minimize it?" While soils have always been the ultimate dumping ground, a recognition of the environmental harm this is causing may convince our throwaway society that there is no "away."

Revamping Statutes Is Not Enough

Such major changes do not happen easily. A law on the order of the Clean Air Act or Clean Water Act is necessary, since all the laws pertaining to air and water pollution, toxic substances, and hazardous wastes would be affected. The necessary changes could not be brought about—certainly not consistently—in the course of reauthorizing existing environmental statutes. But a clean soil act could adopt the regulatory structure created by our existing environmental laws and incorporate a coordinated effort to protect our nation's soil.

Such a statute would explicitly recognize the hazards that contaminated soils and sediments pose to human health and the environment. The use of soils and sediments for waste disposal would have to be restricted. Regulations concerning emissions into air and water would have to deal with soil deposition and accumulation. In addition, remediation projects directed at contaminated soils and sediments that are outside the scope of existing programs like Superfund are needed. Such projects could range from schoolyards with lead-contaminated by agricultural run-off. Since the scope of these projects demands deliberation, we can at least begin now to change our attitude toward soils and sediments. (pp. 22–3)

David L. Boose, "Needed: A Clean Soil Act," in Technology Review, *Vol. 90, No.7, October, 1987, pp. 22-3.*

Spoiled Soil: Identifying Soil Pollutants and Cleanup Options

North of the Mason-Dixon line, cultivation of the tobacco plant is an anomaly. But in the Connecticut River Valley, tobacco has been grown since the 1640s, and for centuries was one of the main exports of the region. Silvery, weathered drying barns are still a common sight in the New England hills, but there as elsewhere, the small farm is conceding to condominiums, malls, and office parks.

As the farms disappear, tobacco farming is leaving a different kind of legacy to the land—in the soil itself. On the site of a former tobacco farm in Simsbury, Connecticut, where a tract of houses was built in the mid-seventies, scientists have found traces of the banned pesticide ethylene dibromide (EDB), last applied to the field nearly twenty years ago. Their concern that other environmental contaminants also may persist in the soil for decades is now being confirmed, bringing into question the continuing use of chemicals that we are only beginning to understand.

In studying topsoil from the Simsbury field, Joe Pignatello and Charles Frink, soil scientists at the Connecticut Agricultural Experiment Station (CAES), concluded that traces of EDB had secreted themselves in minuscule chambers in the soil, called micropores. A fraction of the compound can find its way into these spaces, and once hidden there, it is out of reach of its degraders, soil microbes and water molecules. Over time, more and more of the EDB residue seeps into the pores, binds tightly to the surface of soil particles, and forms what are called "resistant fractions." The EDB that is less tightly bound will interact with water percolating through the soil. Eventually, the resistant fractions are likely to be degraded, but these interactions are taking place on a much longer time frame than previously believed.

This description of EDB's behavior has added a piece to the complex puzzle of how organic contaminants interact with the environment, and has spurred other environmental scientists to test a range of organic compounds for similar behavior. In the past year, Pignatello has received reports that numerous contaminants besides EDB also can diffuse into soil micropores where they are able to resist extraction. The tendency is almost universal, and the implications are unsettling. "The soil is acting as a reservoir," Pignatello explains, "not only for EDB, but for herbicides, solvents, and PCBs." The ability of these chemicals to contaminate groundwater, topsoil, and stream sediment is greatly prolonged.

According to Pignatello, researchers at CAES first got on the trail of EDB in 1983, when by chance, groundwater in Georgia was discovered to be tainted with the fugitive substance. Authorities in other states where EDB had been used as a fumigant began to test their own water supplies, because studies of EDB's effect on laboratory animals had shown the compound to be a powerful carcinogen.

Following Georgia's lead, Connecticut tested the groundwater in its tobacco region, and discovered that 400 wells in the north-central part of the state were contaminated with EDB at levels higher than deemed safe by Connecticut. The state had set a safety limit, or action level, at one-tenth of a part per billion (ppb). (California, Florida, South Carolina, Washington, Arizona, and Massachusetts, also have discovered unsafe levels of EDB in their groundwater since testing began in 1984. Typically, findings range between 0.05 and 20 ppb, according to Nate Erwin of the Rachel Carson Council, while state "safe" levels range from 0.02 to 0.1 ppb.)

As the farms disappear, tobacco farming is leaving a different kind of legacy to the land—in the soil itself. On the site of a former tobacco farm in Simsbury, Connecticut, where a tract of houses was built in the mid-seventies, scientists have found traces of the banned pesticide ethylene dibromide (EDB), last applied to the field nearly twenty years ago.

Traces of ethylene dibromide (EDB) secrete themselves in minuscule chambers in the soil, called micropores. A fraction of the compound can find its way into these spaces, and once hidden there, it is out of reach of its degraders, soil microbes and water molecules. Over time, more and more of the EDB residue seeps into the pores, binds tightly to the surface of soil particles, and forms what are called "resistant fractions." The EDB that is less tightly bound will interact with water percolating through the soil.

During its career as a legal fumigant, from its registration in 1948 until its ban in 1983, EDB was used in agriculture primarily to fumigate the earth. Several weeks before planting, farmers would pump liquid EDB into the soil to kill off nematodes, a family of worms whose most harmful members bore holes in plant roots, leaving them susceptible to disease. EDB was widely used and valued as a fumigant because of its volatility, which enabled it to spread rapidly and evenly through the airspaces in the soil. This characteristic, as well as its water solubility, low affinity for chemical reactions with soil, and rapid breakdown by soil microbes, led scientists and farmers to believe that it should disperse quickly and disappear without a trace.

Citrus, pineapples, soybeans, cotton, tobacco, and more than thirty other fruit, vegetable, and nut crops were fumigated, as were grain stores and milling equipment. Before its suspension in September 1983, almost 20 million pounds of EDB were pumped into the soil every year.

In animal studies, EDB has been shown to be cancer-causing. It is able to mutate genetic material, reduce sperm count and egg fertility in mammals, and is suspected of causing birth defects. Researchers at the National Cancer Institute reported EDB's potential threat to human health in 1977, and a ban was set in motion that year by the U.S. Environmental Protection Agency (EPA). But during Anne Burford's tenure as EPA head, the ban was stalled. Five years later, EDB, still legal, turned up in cake mixes, cereal, and grain, and an outcry in the media against poor regulations ensued. EPA rapidly executed its ban in the face of public anger and fear.

When EDB appeared in Connecticut groundwater around that time, scientists at CAES obtained support to initiate a study of the fate of the compound once it gets into soil and water. According to Pignatello, "One of our big questions at that time was how to predict EDB's lifetime. There was little information on the ability of bacteria to degrade EDB, on how quickly it would degrade in water, and how it moves through the soil and groundwater."

They began by studying the ability of soil microbes to degrade EDB. They compared soil fumigated one, three, thirteen, and nineteen years previously, with soil to which EDB had been newly added. The freshly added compound was rapidly broken down by microbes—within two days. But the older soil samples taken from the field all held minute quantities of EDB which the microbes were unable to break down, indicating that under natural conditions, the compound's disappearance is not, in fact, complete.

The EDB in the older samples also resisted degradation by water and air, and was much more difficult to extract with accepted laboratory techniques, presenting the researchers with a paradox. Why would EDB persist in soil after three, thirteen, and most surprisingly, nineteen years, when by all accounts it should degrade quickly? And why would it become more difficult to wrest from the soil with the passage of time? Pignatello and Frink extracted what they believe to be all the residues from the field samples, but this required using intensive extraction methods—pummeling the soil in a ball mill, and passing heated solvents through it. When treated roughly, the residual EDB was released in a detectable burst, as though from a popped bubble, leading the researchers to conceive of the micropore model.

Pignatello and Frink were able to delve more deeply into the mechanism of these interactions because their extraction techniques went beyond previous methods. Standard modes of extracting organic compounds from the soil (treatment with solvents but at lower temperatures (Soxhlet), and sonication, or agitation with sound waves) were weak by comparison. The Connecticut scientists extracted an average of 50 percent more using the ball-mill and heated solvents. The purge-and-trap method, advocated by the EPA for extracting contaminants from solids, was even less effective. Using the more thorough techniques, Frink and Pignatello extracted about 90 percent more contaminant.

The Connecticut study suggests that residue analyses are not reliable, says David Pimentel, a professor of entomology at Cornell University and an expert in integrated pest management. "These findings raise a flag. Just because you run an analysis, you may not be able to detect a residue. But if it's there, it probably has an impact. There's no question that we've put a lot of pesticides out there, and they all have problems for the environment."

Other scientists who have adopted the ball-mill and heated solvents also are finding much higher concentrations of contaminants in soil than they would have expected with the older techniques. Pignatello has compiled data from other researchers who are finding environmental poisons able to form residues resistant to degradation and extraction. The list includes parathion, 2,4-D, napthalene, carbon tetrachloride, carbaryl, picloram, and hexachloroethane. "We haven't covered the entire range of contaminants," says Pignatello, "but between our own studies and those being conducted by others, we've learned that this kind of interaction with the soil is very, very common. Any compound that adsorbs to the soil (binds to the surface, but without forming a chemical bond) in any amount has been found to form these very resistant fractions."

Pignatello and his colleagues are now studying soil samples from a field from Windsor, Connecticut, which contains the widely used weed killer, metolachlor, made by Ciba Geigy. They are finding that this herbicide, too, can bind or adsorb tightly to the soil. Extraction experiments show that at 20 to 100 ppb, the soil is rich with the compound. "We pumped water through a sample of contaminated soil for a month, and the metolachlor is still coming out," Pignatello says. Trichlorethylene (TCE) and tetrachlorethylene, frequently found where wastes are dumped, are some of the most common contaminants in the world, he adds. "These substances have many opportunities to come into contact with the soil. And in all the samples we've looked at, they formed slow desorbing (resistant) fractions." While the characteristic seems prevalent, some contaminants are slightly more likely than others to form resistant fractions. So far, characteristics such as molecular structure are providing no clues to explain why.

Once topsoil becomes laced with contaminants, mechanical cleanup is hardly an option. Current methods for decontaminating soil are either exorbitant or impractical, but usually both. "The only sure way to get organic contaminants out of soil," Pignatello explains, "is to dig up the whole field and put it through an oven at 1,500°F, and put what comes out back into the ground." One scoopful of earth, a cubic meter, would cost between $500 and $1,000 to incinerate, he learned at a recent EPA workshop.

Microbiologists are researching the feasibility of decontamination by stimulating the growth of bacteria that preferentially degrade organic compounds, or by creating bacteria that prefer a diet of contaminants and mixing them with soil in the field. "Recently, companies have popped up all over whose single purpose is to come up with these specialized microorganisms, and pilot studies are under way. But a lot of these new companies have already folded, because they can't come up with an effective method at a reasonable price," Pignatello says.

Left to its own devices, EDB that has adsorbed to the soil can be expected to degrade very slowly as it is released back into availability. The speed of natural degradation will vary greatly. Factors such as temperature, degree of bacterial activity, the amount of organic versus mineral matter in the soil, the pH of the soil, and the amount of light reaching the substance all influence the rate at which any pesticide breaks down, says Donald Lisk, a professor of toxicology at Cornell University. "You're going to have many different reactions taking place in the soil, a real mixed bag, and studies done in California may not apply to New York." The degradation of EDB in Connecticut's soil will be largely temperature-dependent, Pignatello says. AT 20°C, the half-life of EDB in water (the time required for half of the original amount to degrade) is four years. At 10°C, the average temperature of the soil in Connecticut, EDB's half-life is twenty years. Wells in the region around Simsbury found to contain EDB at one ppb will therefore take about sixty years to reach the state's "safe" level of

Once topsoil becomes laced with contaminants, mechanical cleanup is hardly an option. Current methods for decontaminating soil are either exorbitant or impractical, but usually both.

In animal studies, EDB has been shown to be cancer-causing. It is able to mutate genetic material, reduce sperm count and egg fertility in mammals, and is suspected of causing birth defects.

one-tenth ppb, Pignatello predicts, and restoration of the soil to its original state could take equally long.

Pignatello and Frink also are studying the persistence of contaminants in groundwater. The scientists monitored the aquifer under the Simsbury tobacco field, and found that the water contained constant levels of EDB over a period of a year and half. Current theories about water contamination suggest that aquifers contain regions of both "mobile" and "immobile" water. Movement of water and other materials by dispersion occurs only in the mobile regions. Immobile water, regions analogous to micropores in the soil, consists of tiny spaces between particles of water and matter in the aquifer. Contaminants such as EDB can enter these spaces (which are too small for water molecules and microorganisms to follow) when the concentration in the mobile water is high, and will be released when the concentration in the mobile region lessens. Thus, concentration of the contaminant in the mobile water will remain constant. The restoration of an aquifer to pristine condition requires measures as dramatic as those necessary to clean up a field. "You'd have to pump all of the water out and detoxify it," explains Lawrie Mott, a scientist at NRDC. "At the same time contaminated water is being pumped out, clean water must be pumped back in, so that contaminants from other regions in the aquifer aren't drawn into the emptied spaces."

The price tags on mechanical cleanup of both soil and water are very high. Although the Superfund list includes both industrial and municipal sites, EPA had declined to invoke Superfund for areas contaminated by pesticide use. Although it seriously considered allocating Superfund monies for five sites in Hawaii where the groundwater is contaminated with EDB and DBCP (a closely related compound known to cause cancer, genetic changes, male sterility, and damage to the kidneys, lungs, and liver), the EPA finally rejected the proposal because it would set an unmanageable precedent, Mott believes. "Pesticide contamination is more and more ubiquitous, and the Superfund resources are not enough to clean up the already designated sites." She predicts that pesticide-contaminated sites will never get Superfund coverage.

For the most part, EPA's strategy has been to leave monitoring and regulation of pesticides in groundwater up to each state government. Recently, it issued a strategy proposal for addressing the growing pesticide problem, in which the problem is called serious, but the proposal reiterates that states have primary responsibility. "Under this proposal, EPA provides no financial resources, technical advice, or legal action to back the states up," says Mott. While fifty pesticides have been found in drinking water in thirty states, only ten states so far have passed legislation that specifically regulates pesticide use. She expects more states to pass such regulations, providing some states' residents with stronger regulation than could pass at the federal level, while pesticide use in other states will be covered by weaker laws. The result: a regulatory patchwork.

[In 1988] EPA undertook a survey of the nation's drinking water, for which it expects to publish the findings sometime in 1990. The scope of the study is limited to areas where agricultural use of pesticides is high, or to regions with vulnerable hydrogeology. The survey is looking at existing wells only, ignoring sites as yet untapped but equally susceptible to contamination.

NRDC is undertaking its own report, to be published early next year that will document the extent of groundwater contamination. It will focus on Iowa and California, where the use of agricultural chemicals is especially high, and will identify agricultural techniques that would reduce contamination in those states. According to Mott, "We intend to show that the real solution to the problem is going to be a change in agricultural methods. The government's protective measures focus on restricting the use of pesticides, forcing farmers to switch to others. Ultimately, we'll come up with more and more contaminants in the groundwater. Shifting from one to another is not the best way to proceed." With integrated pest management, biological control mechanisms, and changed cropping patterns, pesticide use can be cut dramatically, Mott believes.

For now, pesticide use continues to escalate. This year, agricultural chemical use in the United States will reach more than 1.1 billion pounds. As we learn more about pesticides through studies such as Pignatello and Frink's, the balance in the risk-versus-benefit equation seems to tip toward increasing caution. (pp. 3-7)

Beth Hanson, "Spoiled Soil," in The Amicus Journal, *Vol. 11, No. 3, Summer, 1989, pp. 3-7.*

Trapping Toxics in the Trenches

Cleaning up hazardous waste is difficult, but not impossible. Even the most tainted site can, in theory, be restored. But it is fantastically expensive. There are 951 sites on the Environmental Protection Agency's Superfund priority list, and many environmental watchdogs say thousands more sites—abandoned factory dumps, gulleys filled in with toxic garbage, roadsides lined with rotting drums—are yet to be found. The cost could top $300 billion.

Even if the money were available, however, there would still be a problem. In cases where pollutants have tainted large amounts of soil, the only practical way to deal with the mess has been to dig it up and cart it away to a landfill certified to accept hazardous waste. Unfortunately, available landfill sites are rapidly filling up.

But there may be another solution. [In 1988] the EPA conducted its first test of a new hazardous-waste treatment process that may dramatically cut the cost of the nation's cleanup by immobilizing and neutralizing toxic chemicals where they lie. The process, developed by Kansas-based International Waste Technologies, uses an auger to blend contaminated soil with liberal amounts of cement, clay, and neutralizing chemicals. The idea is to break down the toxic compounds as much as possible, lock them inside the clay's tightly packed molecular layers, and freeze the whole mess with the cement.

"The clay molecules build very tight molecular cages around toxics," explains company president Jeffrey Newton. "The bonding strength is very high." Of course, the resulting rockhard soil has few uses. "It's unlikely you would put a housing development on a site treated like this," says Mary Stinson of the EPA, who supervised the test. "And you're not going to use it for farmland. But the process appears to be a good idea."

Until now the only way to deal with toxic-waste spills without carting them away wholesale has been to entrap the toxic materials in a monolithic block of cement. But that doesn't neutralize the offending chemicals. If the cement were broken up, Newton says, the still-active contaminants could leach out. Newton labels such techniques the "kitty litter" approach, because contaminants are absorbed but not immobilized.

The problem Newton had to overcome was that while clay bonds rather easily to inorganic substances, such as heavy metals, it does not do so with organics—and most toxic chemicals, whether they are pesticides, industrial solvents, or petrochemicals, are organic. Clays, composed chiefly of layers of molecules containing aluminum, silicon, and oxygen atoms, are normally highly hydrophilic: they actively attract and absorb water. And the water keeps bonds from forming between the clay and organic compounds. But when additional compounds are mixed with the clay, its normally tightly packed molecular structure opens up, and organic molecules that would otherwise be repelled can bond to it.

A new hazardous-waste treatment process may dramatically cut the cost of the nation's cleanup by immobilizing and neutralizing toxic chemicals where they lie. The process uses an auger to blend contaminated soil with liberal amounts of cement, clay, and neutralizing chemicals. The idea is to break down the toxic compounds as much as possible, lock them inside the clay's tightly packed molecular layers, and freeze the whole mess with the cement.

In cases where pollutants have tainted large amounts of soil, the only practical way to deal with the mess has been to dig it up and cart it away to a landfill certified to accept hazardous waste. Unfortunately, available landfill sites are rapidly filling up.

By varying the concentrations and types of additives, the clay can be made to react with any number of organic compounds. "The chemistry can be tailored to the local pollutants," Newton says. "The clay becomes like flypaper for organic molecules."

The first test of the process took place at a General Electric service shop in Hialeah, Florida, where cancer-causing PCBs (polychlorinated biphenyls) had tainted a 13,000-square-foot area to a depth of up to 18 feet. Enviresponse, an independent testing firm hired by the EPA, took soil samples that contained as much as 5,628 parts per million of PCBs and mixed them with the clay-cement-chemical mixture. After the mixture set, the samples were soaked in water to try to draw out any contaminants that were still loose. There were none.

Next came the real, on-site test, which took place in April [1988]. The machine drilled thirty-six 20-foot-deep, 3-foot-diameter holes into each of two 200-square-foot test plots, churning up every bit of soil and injecting International Waste Technology's immobilizing mixture through the tip of its paddle-bladed auger. The results, based on core samples drawn from the hardened earth, will be presented by the EPA at a conference this month.

Stinson emphasizes that while the technique is promising, it will be useful at only a limited number of sites. "When you can sacrifice the land and make it permanently into a parking lot," she says, "you can use this process." But a variety of technologies will be needed to deal with other situations.

There is no hard data yet on how long the chemicals will stay locked up. "The developer says that the longer it stays, the better it gets," Stinson says. "And most experts agree. But we'll need to study this site for up to five years."

Newton agrees that his process is not suitable for every toxic spill. "If you've got a barrel of gasoline, you should burn it. With liquid organics there are other solutions. But most sites are a mixture of soil and waste." He's confident that there's enough of a potential market to make his business thrive. Others in the field agree, pointing out that there's no real competition on the horizon. The technology may also be used to neutralize new waste as it is created—itself a cleanup headache costing $12 billion to $15 billion a year. (pp. 10, 12)

Andrew C. Revkin, "Trapping Toxics in the Trenches," in Discover, Vol. 9, No. 11, November, 1988, *pp. 10, 12.*

Lessening the Impact of Erosion

The United States Department of Agriculture recently reported, with some pride, that soil erosion on U.S. cropland was reduced by 460 million tons between 1986 and 1987—making for the greatest year-to-year reduction in this country's history and, in all likelihood, the greatest annual reduction ever achieved anywhere. For a country that was suffering excessive soil losses on nearly 40 percent of its cropland, this was welcome news.

Ironically, the program responsible for this dramatic reduction originated not with the USDA, but with a coalition of environmental groups. The legislation behind the breakthrough, the Food Security Act of 1985, provides for the conversion of 40 million acres of highly erodible cropland (11 percent of total U.S. cropland) into grassland and woodland. As the first effective response by a major food-producing country to the heavy loss of topsoil, this initiative offers hope for other countries whose economic security is being slowly undermined by erosion.

Grave though the loss of topsoil may be, it is a quiet crisis, one that is not widely perceived. And unlike earthquakes, volcanic eruptions or other natural disasters, this human-made disaster is unfolding gradually. Often the very practices that cause excessive erosion in the long run, such as continuous row cropping and the plowing of marginal land, lead to short-term production gains that create an illusion of progress and a false sense of security.

Headlines during this decade have focused attention on "a world awash in grain" and on the depressed prices that have resulted. The real story, however, is not the surpluses but the soil losses incurred in producing them. The surpluses are a fleeting phenomenon, but the soil losses will have a lasting effect on land productivity.

On a third of the world's cropland, soil erosion far exceeds the natural rate of newsoil formation of two to five tons per acre per year. At the core of this problem is the world's incessant demand for more food, which is driven by rising affluence and the annual additon of 86 million people. As the demand for food climbs, the world's farmers are beginning, in effect, to mine their soil. What was once a renewable resource is becoming a nonrenewable one.

Extent of the Loss

Three dimensions of the global soil-erosion threat stand out—its scale, its seriousness and the lack of an effective response. Throughout the Third World, population pressures are pushing farmers onto steeply sloping, erodible land or into semi-arid regions where plowed land is vulnerable to wind erosion. (pp. 19-20)

The worldwide loss of soil from cropland, according to a 1984 Worldwatch Institute estimate, was 26 billion tons per year. Assuming an average topsoil depth of seven inches and an average weight of 160 tons per inch per acre, this is equal to the loss of 23 million acres of cropland per year, an area only slightly smaller than the wheat-growing region of Australia, one of the world's leading grain exporters.

Such heavy soil losses are already beginning to affect food production in some countries. In Africa, where land degradation is gaining momentum, per-capita food production has fallen by nearly one-fifth from its historical high in 1967. Allowed to continue, soil erosion could sap the productivity of one-third of the world's cropland, leading eventually to higher food prices and persistent pockets of famine.

The Roots of Erosion

Soil erosion is not a new phenomenon. We study the archeological sites of civilizations that were undermined by soil erosion. The fertile wheat-growing lands that made North Africa the granary of the Roman Empire are now largely desert. And the lowlands of Guatemala that once nourished a thriving Mayan culture of five million people were drained of their fertility by soil erosion.

Twice in this century the United States has faced the economic and environmental ravages of escalating soil losses, first in the Dust Bowl era of the thirties and a second time early in this decade. In both cases, creative policies and decisive action averted disaster. The response to the Dust Bowl crisis came from the federal government, specifically the Department of Agriculture with strong backing from the White House. The response to [the erosion threat of the 1980s] was led by public interest environmental groups.

The Dust Bowl was an environmental crisis with immediate economic and social consequences. It ruined crops, bankrupted farmers, destroyed rural economies and, finally, produced a steady flow of environmental refugees from the southern Great Plains to California.

In the opening pages of *The Grapes of Wrath* John Steinbeck describes the degradation of the land in painful detail:

Grave though the loss of topsoil may be, it is a quiet crisis, one that is not widely perceived. And unlike earthquakes, volcanic eruptions or other natural disasters, this human-made disaster is unfolding gradually. Often the very practices that cause excessive erosion in the long run, such as continuous row cropping and the plowing of marginal land, lead to short-term production gains that create an illusion of progress and a false sense of security.

In the spring of 1935, the Soil Conservation Act was introduced in Congress. Department of Agriculture historian Wayne Rasmussen writes that "on April 2, 1935, Bennett was testifying before the Senate Public Lands Committee. Senators were questioning his data concerning soil erosion, when the sky suddenly became dark with dust from the drought-stricken West. Nothing could have been more convincing." That afternoon when members headed for their cars, they discovered them covered with dust so thick they could write their names in it. On April 27th, the act was passed.

The wind grew stronger. . . . The dust lifted out of the fields and drove great plumes into the air like a sluggish smoke. . . . The corn fought the wind with its weakened leaves until the roots were freed by the prying wind and then each stalk settled wearily sideways toward the earth and pointed the direction of the wind.

The dawn came, but no day. In the grey sky a red sun appeared, a dim red circle that gave a little light like dusk; and as that day advanced, the dust slipped back toward darkness, and the wind cried and whimpered over the fallen corn.

Steinbeck could have been describing conditions in the African Sahel during the famine-ridden eighties.

Contrary to popular belief at the time, the drought years of the thirties were not the cause of the Dust Bowl, they were only the triggering event. The Dust Bowl resulted from the overplowing and continuous cropping that removed too much of the land's protective vegetation.

Some, like soil conservation crusader Hugh Hammond Bennett, had foreseen the disaster. In 1928, he wrote that soil erosion is "a loss to posterity, and there are indications that our increasing population may feel acutely the evil effects of the scourge of the land, now largely unrestrained."

The struggles of Bennett and other agricultural leaders began to pay off during the early thirties. Secretary of Agriculture Henry Wallace and President Franklin Roosevelt both realized that the situation called for a strong response.

In the spring of 1935, the Soil Conservation Act was introduced in Congress. Department of Agriculture historian Wayne Rasmussen writes that "on April 2, 1935, Bennett was testifying before the Senate Public Lands Committee. Senators were questioning his data concerning soil erosion, when the sky suddenly became dark with dust from the drought-stricken West. Nothing could have been more convincing." That afternoon when members headed for their cars, they discovered them covered with dust so thick they could write their names in it. On April 27th, the act was passed.

Even though the country was in the midst of the worst economic crisis in its history, Congress had created the Soil Conservation Service (SCS) and funded the programs needed to secure the nation's topsoil. The SCS actively assisted farmers in adopting soil-conserving farming practices. Throughout the Great Plains, farmers began planting rows of trees for windbreaks, fallowing land, and strip-cropping. These and other government-assisted conservation practices brought the Dust Bowl crisis under control within a few years, restoring the land and economy of the Great Plains.

History Repeats Itself

But even as the dust clouds were disappearing, the seeds of another crisis were being sown. The unprecedented surge in agricultural output in response to soaring world food demand, which marked the fifties and sixties, came not from expanding the cropland area but from the adoption of new agricultural technologies—including hybrid seeds, irrigation and chemical fertilizer—that dramatically raised land productivity.

With these advances, exports of wheat, corn, and soybeans soared. The United States emerged as the world's breadbasket. By 1980, it was exporting nearly 100 million tons of grain each year, enough to feed 500 million people at third world consumption levels.

The advent of cheap chemical fertilizer enabled farmers to dispense with the traditional rotations that included nitrogen-fixing legumes, such as clover, and turn to continuous cropping of corn. But legumes not only fixed nitrogen, they held the soil in place. Land on a test plot in Missouri that was losing three tons of soil per acre in a corn-wheat-clover rotation began losing 10 tons a year when it was planted continuously in wheat and more than 19 tons when planted continuously in corn.

As farmers turned to ever-larger farm equipment, the two-plow tractor gave way to the ten-plow tractor. Huge grain combines, which could cut and thresh 100 acres of wheat or barley a day, required larger fields to be used efficiently. A new generation of farmers too young to remember the lessons of the thirties began eradicating the shelter belts, those long strips of trees planted to break the wind's force.

Then came the doubling of world wheat prices following the Soviet wheat purchase of 1972. Over the next few years, below-normal harvests kept world grain prices up, leading U.S. farmers to plow millions of acres of new land, much of it highly erodible. Secretary of Agriculture Earl Butz urged farmers to plant "from hedgerow to hedgerow" to combat inflation and expand exports to pay the soaring oil-import bill.

During the early seventies, U.S. farmers planted just under 150 million acres of grain per year, but by 1977 they were planting 180 million acres, an increase of more than one-fifth. As production climbed, so did soil erosion. That year, the Department of Agriculture reported the United States was losing topsoil at an annual rate of some three billion tons, losses that may have matched those at the Dust Bowl's peak. But this time, erosion was caused less by wind than by water and was concentrated not in the western plains but in the Corn Belt and the South.

A Strong Coalition Emerges

Information and analysis, rather than photographs of dust-laden clouds, served to catalyze the response to this second soil-erosion crisis. The first signs of trouble emerged in 1977 from the comprehensive body of information on soil erosion collected by the National Resource Inventory.

Five years later an even more detailed inventory confirmed reports of heavy soil losses. Farmers were losing 3.1 billion tons of topsoil per year, exceeding the rate of new soil formation by two billion tons. At that rate, every ton of grain produced meant six tons of soil lost.

Using NRI data, conservation groups alerted the public to the crisis unfolding in rural America. Well-publicized studies by the American Farmland Trust, Rodale Press, Worldwatch Institute and many others detailed the scale of soil loss and how it would affect farm output.

These and other studies showed that the loss of an inch of topsoil typically reduces wheat yields by 0.5 to 2.5 bushels per acre and corn yields by 3 to 6 bushels. For both wheat and corn this translates into a yield decline of 6 percent for every inch of topsoil lost.

The public's concern about the economic effects of topsoil loss converged in the early eighties with its resentment over the soaring cost of farm price-support programs, setting the stage for a new approach to soil conservation. Up until that time, cropland was selected with no regard for its erodibility when idled to balance the supply of farm commodities with their demand.

During the early eighties, however, a coalition of environmental groups and soil conservation professionals set out to implement a new approach. Working together, they helped shape the soil conservation section of the Food Security Act. Norman Berg, a former chief of the Soil Conservation Service, brought his experience to the contest as Washington representative of the Soil Conservation Society of America. Robert Gray of the American Farmland Trust coordinated meetings for the conservation coalition.

Agronomist Kenneth Cook, initially with the American Farmland Trust and later with the Conservation Foundation, and the Audubon Society's veteran agricultural lobbyist, Maureen Kuwano Hinkle, worked as a lobbying team, providing a nucleus around which the other groups coalesced. The Sierra Club made the legislation one of its chief priorities for 1985. Audubon and the Sierra Club, with close to one million members between them, helped mobilize broad political support for the bill.

Although the immediate effects of soil erosion are economic, the ultimate effects are social. When soils are depleted and crops are poorly nourished, people are often undernourished as well. Failure to respond to the erosion threat will lead not only to the degradation of land, but to the degradation of life itself.

The loss of an inch of topsoil typically reduces wheat yields by 0.5 to 2.5 bushels per acre and corn yields by 3 to 6 bushels. For both wheat and corn this translates into a yield decline of 6 percent for every inch of topsoil lost.

This legislation, which would determine the farm programs for the 1986-90 period, contains the most ambitious soil-conservation initiative undertaken by any country. While it retained traditional programs to curb surpluses, the Food Security Act contains three provisions designed to reduce soil erosion.

The first, the Conservation Reserve Program, aims to convert 40 million acres of highly erodible cropland to grass or trees by 1990. In general, only land that is eroding at three times the rate of natural soil formation is eligible. Farmers who agree to convert such land to grass or trees for 10 years receive annual government payments in exchange.

The second provision, designed to control erosion on the remaining 118 million acres of highly erodible land, requires farmers with such land to implement a soil-management program by 1995 or lose all farm program benefits, including price supports, low-interest loans and crop insurance.

The third key soil-conserving element is the "sodbuster" provision. Any farmer plowing highly erodible new land without an approved soil-management program stands to lose subsidies and other farm benefits.

Enthusiastic Reception

Farmers initially were cautious about the Conservation Reserve Program during the earliest of the five sign-up periods in 1986 and 1987, but as they received more information about this novel approach to stabilizing soils, their enthusiasm increased.

The Conservation Reserve is attractive to farmers who worry about the loss of soil from their land but who cannot afford to convert the land to grass or trees on their own. At the end of 1987, farmers had committed 23 million acres, more than half of the 40-million-acre target. More than 90 percent of the land will be planted in grass, the remainder in trees.

The cost of establishing grass cover is estimated at $80 per acre, tree cover at $76 per acre, half of which is defrayed by the Department of Agriculture. These reimbursements are in addition to the annual payments, which averaged just under $50 per acre during the first two years of sign-ups.

If this annual "rental" rate of $50 per acre holds for the entire 40 million acres slated to be retired, the annual cost to the government in 1990 would be $2 billion per year. This, combined with the government's $1.6-billion share of the one-time outlay to establish grass and tree cover ($320 million per year over the five-year retirement period), is only a fraction of the $20-billion-per-year cost of curbing surplus production. The net effect of the Food Security Act is to lower the cost of controlling surplus production while protecting the soils on which the productivity of U.S. agriculture depends.

A study by Norman Berg indicates that soil erosion on the eight million acres signed up in 1986 was reduced from an average of 29 tons per acre to 2 tons for a total savings of over 200 million tons of topsoil per year.

The USDA reported that acreage added to the conservation reserve in 1987 saved 300 million tons of topsoil. Combined with the reduction in 1986, this amounts to more than half a billion tons, close to one-fourth of the excessive soil erosion occurring on U.S. cropland before the program began. Other soil conserving practices adopted in 1987, such as rotations and terracing, saved another 160 million tons of soil, bringing the total reduction to a record level.

When the 40 million acres are planted to grass or trees and the conservation-compliance provisions of the Food Security Act begin to take effect in 1990, excessive soil loss from croplands could be reduced by four-fifths or more. This assumes, of course, that USDA will enforce compliance and that most farmers will choose to comply rather than lose their subsidies.

One of the most obvious benefits of protecting U.S. cropland from erosion, and of converting highly erodible land to less-intensive agricultural uses before it becomes wasteland, is an increase in global food security. For the 100 or so countries that import grain for food and/or feed from the United States, the Food Security Act ensures a steady flow of food from the North American breadbasket.

The U.S. breakthrough in reducing soil erosion is a major step forward, returning the world to a sustainable development path. As a national initiative, it may rank second only to China's halving of its population growth rate over the last decade.

Leading By Example

The conservation provisions of the Food Security Act demonstrate the pivotal role public-policy research institutes and environmental groups can play in raising public awareness and engineering an effective political response to serious environmental threats. Public concern over heavy soil losses culminated in overwhelming support for the new legislation in Congress with members from both sides of the aisle vying to be identified with the legislation.

An analysis of the process of public education and political organization that helped enact these soil-conservation measures may also shed some light on how other countries can mobilize support for sustainable development initiatives that go beyond halting soil erosion, such as preserving tropical rain forests, raising energy efficiency in order to minimize global warming, and putting the brakes on population growth.

With food-production capacity that far exceeds domestic needs, the United States found it relatively painless to convert highly erodible cropland to grass or trees. Lessons learned in the fight to pass the Food Security Act apply to other countries as well. The issue facing all societies is whether they can curb short-run demands to assure a sustainable future.

Third world countries filled with hungry people will be hard pressed to rescue rapidly eroding land by converting it to less-intensive uses, such as growing firewood. The question, however, is not whether the highly erodible cropland eventually will be abandoned; it will be once the topsoil is gone. The real question is whether it can be converted to less-intensive but sustainable uses, such as fodder and firewood production, before it becomes wasteland.

S. A. El-Swaify and E. W. Dangler, soil scientists from the University of Hawaii, have observed that in regions with high population density "farming of marginal hilly lands is a hazardous necessity. Ironically it is also in those very regions where the greatest need exists to protect the rapidly diminishing or degrading soil resources." It is this vicious cycle, set in motion by the growing human demands for food, fodder and fuel, that makes mounting an effective defense particularly difficult.

A successful response to the third world soil erosion menace requires political will and public support. Mobilizing support for adequately funded soil-conservation programs demands extensive public education on the dimensions and consequences of the problem, a task complicated by illiteracy and subsistence-level living in many rural societies. Farmers there can muster little concern about their long-term future when their immediate survival is in question. In India, says resource analyst B. B. Vohra, "An informed public opinion cannot . . . be wished into existence overnight. A great deal of painstaking and patient work will have to be done to wipe out the backlog of ignorance, inertia and complacency."

Government's Business

Although farmers often can carry out the agricultural changes needed to check excessive soil erosion, only governments can afford the sophisticated scientific techniques and equipment for measuring this loss; only they have the means to determine whether a particular field is eroding excessively. Also, farmers can do the work, but may be unable to afford the sophisticated conservation

The worldwide loss of soil from cropland, according to a 1984 Worldwatch Institute estimate, was 26 billion tons per year. Assuming an average topsoil depth of seven inches and an average weight of 160 tons per inch per acre, this is equal to the loss of 23 million acres of cropland per year, an area only slightly smaller than the wheat-growing region of Australia, one of the world's leading grain exporters.

Conservation compliance has considerable potential to enhance the quality and quantity of habitat for fish and other aquatic animals; for waterfowl, game, and nongame birds dependent upon undisturbed grasslands; and for the many species of mammals and raptors that feed on them.

measures that are necessary—terracing, contour farming, strip cropping, cover cropping, rotating crops, fallowing and planting shelter belts. When individual farmers cannot afford to invest in soil conservation or to convert their eroding cropland to less-intensive but sustainable uses, it makes sense for society as a whole to do so.

Where soil erosion is believed to be a serious threat, the first step for governments is to carefully assess the extent of soil loss. Only after such an inventory has been taken can cost-benefit calculations be made and appropriate conservation programs designed. In India, for example, it is estimated that a comprehensive nationwide soil inventory would cost some $30 million—a small price to pay for a guide to intelligent policymaking.

There is no set formula that all countries, industrial and developing, can adopt for saving soil. To succeed, each will need to fashion its own response, one that takes into account its cropping patterns, soil types, climate, social structures and farming traditions.

The nagging question is whether public awareness of the extent of soil erosion and of its social consequences can be raised to the point where effective conservation programs can be mounted. Leadership in this process can come from governments, as it did in the United States in the thirties, or it can come from environmental groups, as it did in the United States during the eighties.

Although the immediate effects of soil erosion are economic, the ultimate effects are social. When soils are depleted and crops are poorly nourished, people are often undernourished as well. Failure to respond to the erosion threat will lead not only to the degradation of land, but to the degradation of life itself. (pp. 21-5, 42)

Lester R. Brown, "Breakthrough on Soil Erosion," in World Watch, *Vol. 1, No. 3, May-June, 1988, pp. 19-25, 42.*

Soil Quality, Conservation, and Wildlife

Conservation compliance, along with its companion provisions in the Food Security Act of 1985, the conservation reserve (CRP), sodbuster, swampbuster, and conservation easements, has considerable potential to enhance the quality and quantity of habitat for fish and other aquatic animals; for waterfowl, game, and nongame birds dependent upon undisturbed grasslands; and for the many species of mammals and raptors that feed on them.

It is likely, however, that compliance itself will have a negligible impact on terrestrial wildlife species compared with the CRP and swampbuster provisions because much of the cropland acreage subject to compliance will continue in row crops or be used for hay production. The primary contribution of compliance to wildlife probably will be in the area of water quality, leading to better habitat for fish and other aquatic species.

Unfortunately, changes in the Soil Conservation Service's policies for implementing compliance may reduce the measure's potential to enhance wildlife habitat. The decision to make alternative conservation systems available to all farmers, with no reference to soil loss tolerances or maximum levels of erosion, could reduce soil-savings opportunities and undermine an important incentive for enrolling farmland in the CRP.

Potential Wildlife Enhancements

A 1985 U.S. Department of Agriculture (USDA) brochure, "Going Wild with Soil and Water Conservation," states that "wildlife can benefit from many cropland conservation practices, especially those for erosion control." Among these practices are conservation tillage, cover and green manure crops, stripcropping, grass waterways, narrow-base bench terraces, field windbreaks, and field borders. Whether such practices significantly benefit wildlife remains a point of debate.

Birds and other terrestrial species. Some research indicates that upland wildlife habitat improves with use of soil-conserving measures. But the positive impacts of soil conservation practices on wildlife are largely secondary and depend upon the vegetative composition of cover, stripcrops, and edge.

If carefully managed, some erosion control practices can enhance wildlife habitat. If farmers are aware of opportunities for improving terrestrial wildlife habitat, there is evidence that many will manage their land for the dual purpose of erosion control and wildlife habitat. An Illinois study of grassed-backslope terraces found 35 species of vertebrates using the terraces; pheasant nesting success was about 20 percent.

Conservation compliance is providing a strong impetus for more farmers to adopt conservation tillage, a range of practices that leave crop residue on the land to protect soil from erosive forces. Preliminary studies show that conservation tillage has the potential for reducing or eliminating bird nest disturbances in small grains and row crops. Research also suggests that no-till corn fields offer more food and cover than conventionally tilled corn fields, leading to a greater diversity of invertebrate species and a more stable population of small mammals.

Although an expansion of conservation tillage probably will benefit farm wildlife, the increased use of herbicides that often accompanies these practices poses some risks. Again, careful management can help wildlife. Chemical contamination can be reduced by injecting pesticides, by splitting applications, by timing preemergent herbicides prior to nesting, or by selecting less toxic chemicals. Farmers who use little or no pesticides are reporting success with such tillage practices as ridge-till. Their experiences deserve attention from those concerned with wildlife and environmental quality.

Overall, changes in land use have a greater impact on habitat quality than do changes in management practices. In Illinois, for example, a 46 percent decline in farmland game harvest was reported at the same time as a 48 percent increase in "cropland adequately treated" to control erosion. The proportion of cropland used for row crops increased almost 80 percent during the 15-year study period. A study of eight grassland bird species in Illinois roughly during the same period showed that bird numbers declined 80 to 95 percent and more.

Compliance, by itself, will result in few land use changes to less intensive agricultural practices, except as it encourages CRP participation. As noted, this incentive has been weakened by allowing alternative conservation systems across the board. In fact, USDA's expressed purpose in weakening the requirements for conservation plans was to avoid forcing farmers to change land use—to more pasture and less row crops.

Fisheries. Fisheries literature on the expected impacts of the conservation provisions is virtually nonexistent. Even generic information relating erosion control practices and water quality is limited. Yet it is in the area of aquatic habitat improvement that compliance probably has the most potential for wildlife.

Conservation compliance should significantly reduce sediment and associated pollutants that run off cropland, thus improving water quality and habitat for fish and other aquatic species. USDA originally estimated that conservation compliance could prevent about 1.2 billion tons of soil from eroding off farmland each year after 1995. Considering the alternative conservation systems, it may be more realistic to expect that the provision will be able to achieve only one-half to three-quarters of the erosion reduction originally predicted. While

If compliance is to fulfill its promise for improving the condition of soil and water resources and offer wildlife habitat benefits, the goal of farmers' conservation plans must ultimately be T, the soil loss tolerance level. Even this goal may have to be revised, based on the scrutiny of the T standard taking place among soil scientists.

It is not in Americans' best interests to continue mining soils until production is severely disrupted and lakes and streams are filled with silt and agricultural runoff. Our farm programs should discourage such abuse, as compliance was designed to do, recognizing that taxpayers should not be underwriting erosive practices.

it is impossible to calculate how much this will reduce the amound of sediment flowing into streams, lakes, potholes, and rivers, it is obvious that the measure will contribute to improvements in aquatic ecosystems.

Nonpoint-source pollution is the nation's most serious, difficult-to-address water quality problem, and agriculture is the largest, single nonpoint contributor. Eroded soil, or sediment, deposited on the bottom of lakes and streams stresses fish. Heavy soil deposits can eliminate aquatic plants that provide cover for fish and habitat for invertebrates that fish eat. Sediment reduces the number of bottom-dwelling organisms. Spawning fish deposit their eggs on the bottom where heavy sediment can smother eggs and newly hatched fry.

Soil particles degrade habitat while suspended in water and after settling out of it. In both cases, sediment harms aquatic life all along the food chain, from microscopic algae to valuable game fish. For example, a study of long-term changes in fish populations in Illinois' streams identified excessive siltation as the principal cause for the disappearance of native fish species. Research on fingernail clams, a widely distributed, important food source for ducks and many fish, shows that these clams respond to muddy water by closing their shells, greatly reducing their ability to filter food from the water flowing by. Siltation and turbidity also have had impacts on many other types of clams once abundant in midwestern waters.

Sediment that blows or washes off land frequently carries nutrients, such as nitrogen and phosphorus, that otherwise are limited to aquatic systems. These nutrients cause one of the most serious water quality problems—eutrophication. This is particularly a problem for lakes. In Lake Erie, for instance, a marked decline in the commercial fishing industry has accompanied eutrophication. Besides carrying nutrients, cropland runoff also carries pesticides and other contaminants into streams and lakes.

Reducing sediment inputs to already damaged streams or lakes may not improve fishing immediately. Many factors are involved, making the link between erosion reductions and fisheries difficult to pinpoint. One must still conclude that policies to reduce erosion have a great potential to improve fish habitat.

A study of Black Creek in Indiana found that erosion control measures had measurable benefits for fish. Terraces or retention basins designed to hold water on the land and direct it through a subsurface drainage system proved quite effective in reducing sediment and phosphorus loads in the waterway. Conservation tillage was somewhat less effective, but still of significant benefit. Grass waterways reduced the sediment and phosphorous entering the stream. Because of their small total area, however, were not as effective as either terraces or conservation tillage in improving water quality.

More research is needed on the aquatic habitat benefits of erosion control practices. Meanwhile, fisheries scientists, the commercial fishing industry, and sport fishing organizations need to take increased interest in agricultural policy as it relates to conservation. Good policies could have big payoffs for fish.

Potential for Erosion Reduction

If compliance is to fulfill its promise for improving the condition of soil and water resources and offer wildlife habitat benefits, the goal of farmers' conservation plans must ultimately be T, the soil loss tolerance level. Even this goal may have to be revised, based on the scrutiny of the T standard taking place among soil scientists.

It is not in Americans' best interests to continue mining soils until production is severely disrupted and lakes and streams are filled with silt and agricultural runoff. Our farm programs should discourage such abuse, as compliance was designed to do, recognizing that taxpayers should not be underwriting erosive practices.

The selective use of alternative conservation systems at some point should be reinstated. Initially these systems were being used for areas where farmers face real hardship meeting erosion control standards. Alternative systems used in this way are probably necessary, and should stand until the plans being developed now are implemented. By then, there is hope that many farmers will have achieved significant erosion reductions. Those whose farming practices still continue to cause excessive erosion should make the final increment of improvement within a reasonable period or expect penalties that may go beyond loss of whatever USDA benefits exist at that time.

Other Conservation Concerns

In the meantime, two other concerns of conservationists must be the related issues of the annual set-aside program and makeup of state and county Agricultural Stabilization and Conservation Service (ASCS) committees, which have considerable power to implement federal agricultural programs at the local level.

The annual set-aside, in a variety of forms, has been used in most years since 1961 to control production of annual commodities. Lenient rules for managing the set-aside acres often leave the land exposed to wind and water erosion and are frequently detrimental to wildlife. Funding levels for this program are high enough to effectively outcompete the CRP and other conservation programs for acres.

A broad framework of rules for managing set-aside acres are made at the federal level, but many details are left to the discretion of state and county ASCS committees. These committees are made up of producers and elected by producers only, though the large amounts of money they dispense come from all taxpayers. In many areas, the ASCS committees have been so concerned about such issues as weed control that they have neglected the "conservation" portion of their charge. Surveys in many states indicate that the concern among committee members for soil and water conservation has been minimal.

This is not surprising, considering that there is no representation on ASCS committees by natural resource professionals or others concerned with the off-farm impacts of agricultural programs. Though some states require the committees to "consult" with resource professionals, there is no obligation to use this information. As concerns for water quality and wildlife impacts of farm programs increase, it is clear that broader voting representation on ASCS committees will be needed to improve management of such programs as the annual set-asides.

The Upshot

Conservation compliance will bring much-needed erosion reductions in many areas, but unless policies are rolled back to the alternative systems compromise as it was being implemented early in 1988, much of the measure's potential may be unrealized. To those who insist that the widespread use of alternative conservation systems is a necessary first step, one must ask what is represented by the preceding 50 years of soil conservation education and effort.

The conservation provisions represent significant improvement in farm policy in relation to natural resources, but the detrimental aspects of some ongoing farm programs still work against conservation. Keeping this in mind, conservationists must look ahead to see where the next gains can come in devising a wise, workable set of agricultural programs that protect soil, water, and wildlife. (pp. 44-6)

Ann Y. Robinson, "Conservation Compliance and Wildlife," in Journal of Soil and Water Conservation, *Vol. 44, No. 1, January-February, 1989, pp. 44-6.*

Nonpoint-source pollution is the nation's most serious, difficult-to-address water quality problem, and agriculture is the largest, single nonpoint contributor.

Sources For Further Study

Barrow, C. J. *Land Degradation: Development and Breakdown of Terrestrial Environments.* Cambridge: Cambridge University Press, 1991, 295 p.

Defines land degradation, explores the scope and principal causes of the problem, and proposes conservation, remedial, and preventative strategies to minimize land degradation.

Berger, John J., ed. *Environmental Restoration: Science and Strategies for Restoring the Earth.* Washington, D.C.: Island Press, 1990, 398 p.
Includes sections devoted to methods of restoring lands that have been depleted through a variety of uses.

Blaikie, Piers, and Brookfield, Harold, et al. *Land Degradation and Society.* London: Methuen, 1987, 296 p.
Examines the social impact of land degradation.

Cairney, T., ed. *Reclaiming Contaminated Land.* Glasgow: Blackie, 1987, 260 p.
Collection of technical studies surveying types of contaminated lands, identifying prevalent contaminants and the hazards they pose, and exploring various reclamation procedures.

Cheng, H. H. "Organic Residues in Soils: Mechanisms of Retention and Extractability." *Internation Journal of Environmental Analytical Chemistry* 39, No. 2 (1990): 165-71.
Discusses using solvent extraction processes to remove pesticides and related organic chemicals from soil and to gain an understanding of the binding mechanisms that cause these substances to adhere in soil.

Czarnecki, Raymond C. "Making Use of Contaminated Soil." *Civil Engineering* 58, No. 12 (December 1988): 72-4.
Suggests that some contaminated soils can be used in the manufacture of hot-mix asphalt.

Czupyrna, G., et al. *In Situ Immobilization of Heavy-Metal-Contaminated Soils.* Park Ridge, N.J.: Noyes Data Corp., 1989, 155 p.
Evaluates a variety of chemical treatments for on-site immobilization of soils contaminated with heavy metals.

Downey, Douglas C., and Elliott, Michael G. "Performance of Selected *In Situ* Soil Decontamination Technologies: An Air Force Perspective." *Environmental Progress* 9, No. 3 (August 1990): 169-73.
Summarizes the results of several field tests using a variety of on-site technologies to treat contaminated soil.

Driver, Jeffrey H.; Konz, James J.; and Whitmyre, Gary K. "Soil Adherence to Human Skin." *Bulletin of Environmental Contamination and Toxicology* 43, No. 6 (December 1989): 814-20.
Considers potential public health risks posed by dermal exposure to soils contaminated with toxic chemicals.

Hadley, Paul W., and Sedman, Richard M. "A Health-Based Approach for Sampling Shallow Soils at Hazardous Waste Sites Using the AAL$_{soil\ contact}$ Criterion." *Environmental Health Perspectives* 84 (March 1990): 203-07.
Proposes several different soil sampling procedures for the efficient evaluation of public health risks from exposure to contaminated soils.

Hoag, Dana, et. al. "Extension's Role in Soil and Water Conservation." *Journal of Soil and Water Conservation* 43, No. 2 (March-April 1988): 126-29.

Examines the growing involvement of the Agricultural Extension Service and other agriculturally-based groups in educational programs regarding soil and water conservation.

Hsieh, Hsin-Neng, and Raghu, Dorairaja. "Site Cleanup with Soil Washing Technology." *Advances in Environmental Technology and Management* 2 (1990): 157-70.
Describes soil-washing or soil-flushing techniques in which soil contaminants are extracted or immobilized via a liquid medium.

Johnson, Paul C.; Kemblowski, Marian W.; and Colthart, James D. "Quantitative Analysis for the Cleanup of Hydrocarbon-Contaminated Soils by In-Situ Soil Venting." *Ground Water* 28, No. 3 (May-June 1990): 413-29.
Examines factors necessary for ensuring efficient soil venting operations, explores advantages and disadvantages of using soil venting as a remediation tool, and develops models to help determine if soil venting will be effective at any given spill site.

Karlen, D. L. "Conservation Tillage Research Needs." *Journal of Soil and Water Conservation* 45, No. 3 (May-June 1990): 365-69.
Surveys current research on conservation tillage and calls for improved understanding and employment of conservation tillage technologies.

Lalo, Julie. "Pennsylvania's Dead Mountain." *American Forests* 94, Nos. 3-4 (March-April 1988): 55, 69.
Reviews an innovative project involving the combined application of sewage sludge and fly ash to a contaminated Superfund site.

Lühr, H. P. "Requirements on the Handling of Chemicals and Wastes Regarding Soil and Groundwater Protection." *Ecotoxicology and Environmental Safety* 13, No. 3 (June 1987): 282-89.
Notes the disastrous effect of discharging hazardous wastes into the environment and calls for stringent guidelines for chemical and waste handling.

Nash, J. Madeleine. "It's Ugly, But It Works." *Time* 135, No. 21 (21 May 1990): 29-30.
Notes that American farmers are intensifying their use of sustainable agricultural techniques in order to reduce erosion and improve soil quality.

Morgan, Philip, and Watkinson, Robert J. "Assessment of the Potential for *In Situ* Biotreatment of Hydrocarbon-Contaminated Soils." *Water Science and Technology* 22, No. 6 (1990): 63-8.
Considers the potential for effective biotreatment of three hydrocarbon-contaminated sites: one contaminated with crude oil, one with lubricating oil, and one with gasoline.

Napier, Ted L., and Camboni, Silvana M. "Attitudes Toward a Proposed Soil Conservation Program." *Journal of Soil and Water Conservation* 43, No. 2 (March-April 1988): 186-91.
Analyzes the opinions expressed by 552 land operators in erosion-prone areas of Ohio regarding a proposed soil conservation program.

Rittmann, B. E., and Johnson, N. M. "Rapid Biological Clean-Up of Soils Contaminated with Lubricating Oil." *Water Science and Technology* 21, Nos. 4-5 (1989): 209-19.
Examines the technology available to speed the biodegradation of lubricating oil in contaminated sites.

Sims, Ronald C. "Soil Remediation Techniques at Uncontrolled Hazardous Waste Sites." *Journal of the Air and Waste Management Association* 40, No. 5 (May 1990): 704-32.
Surveys available soil remediation technologies as well as regulatory and technical issues relating to remediation methods.

Thomas, J. M., and Ward, C. H. "In Situ Biorestoration of Organic Contaminants in the Subsurface." *Environment Science and Technology* 23, No. 7 (July 1989): 760-66.

Evaluates various biorestoration techniques and defines the ultimate goal of biorestoration as being "to convert organic wastes into biomass and harmless byproducts."

Tibke, Gary. "Basic Principles of Wind Erosion Control." *Agriculture Ecosystems and Environment* 22-23 (August 1988): 103-22.
Decribes and assesses conservation practices that can reduce wind erosion.

17:   Solid Waste Management

Tons of Trash: The Garbage Crisis

If you really want to know about garbage, New Jersey's the place. There, in a taste, or perhaps smell, of what's ahead everywhere, the American penchant for throwing away any and everything has at long last come face to face with a shortage of space to throw it. Garbage has literally backed up in the streets, supermarkets have taken to guarding their dumpsters and Goodwill Industries reports that half of the "contributions" to its collection boxes have been garbage—*real* garbage. Some of the more circumspect donors place a few articles of clothing on top of their trash in case anyone's looking. Goodwill's take has ranged from pieces of dry wall and broken liquor bottles to dirty diapers and half of a goat.

New Jersey is also practically alone in doing something about the problem: It enacted the nation's first mandatory-recycling law and launched a massive program of building high-tech garbage-burning plants. But elsewhere complacency reigns, even as a genuine crisis looms: America's dumps are simply filling up, and no new ones are being built. By 1995, half of the existing dumps will be closed. Many do not meet modern environmental standards. They're leaking, contaminating ground water and posing a danger that may surpass that of hazardous waste. In many areas, political paralysis and environmental fears have blocked alternatives to landfills as well, such as recycling and waste-to-energy plants.

Often, the official response is a variation on an old theme: Out of sight, out of mind. Chicago has only four years before its 33 dumps will be full; it has done almost nothing toward finding a solution. Los Angeles's dumps should reach capacity by 1995. Many cities that are already in a crisis have adopted a simple expedient for their trash: They ship it. Some New England towns run trucks 24 hours a day to Pennsylvania and Ohio. Towns on Long Island ship as far west as Michigan. In Miami, county officials even considered sending their trash to Curaçao off the coast of Venezuela.

But it's New York City that produces the ultimate symbol of America's failure to deal with the problem. The city's Fresh Kills landfill on Staten Island already stands 150 feet high. Soon to be the sole recipient of New York's daily load of 27,000 tons of trash, Fresh Kills is expected to reach a peak of 500 feet when it closes in a decade. It can't go any higher because it's in Newark International Airport's flight path.

An American Tradition

From the days of the earliest settlements, Americans have had a special knack for producing trash—and for not really caring where it goes. Historical archaeologists use a foolproof technique to pinpoint the location of windows and doors of colonial houses where nothing but foundations remain: They just look for the heaps of garbage. That carefree attitude, spawned in a country of seemingly boundless space, is finally catching up with us. How did the crisis evolve? Most municipal trash used to be burned in open dumps or low-tech

America's dumps are simply filling up, and no new ones are being built. By 1995, half of the existing dumps will be closed. Many do not meet modern environmental standards. They're leaking, contaminating ground water and posing a danger that may surpass that of hazardous waste. In many areas, political paralysis and environmental fears have blocked alternatives to landfills as well, such as recycling and waste-to-energy plants.

From the days of the earliest settlements, Americans have had a special knack for producing trash—and for not really caring where it goes. Historical archaeologists use a foolproof technique to pinpoint the location of windows and doors of colonial houses where nothing but foundations remain: They just look for the heaps of garbage. That carefree attitude, spawned in a country of seemingly boundless space, is finally catching up with us.

incinerators. Clean-air laws ended that practice in the early 1960s, and "sanitary landfills" were born.

But they weren't sanitary. None of the planners took into account the liquid ooze in the daily loads of rotting food, old paint cans, used oil and household sprays. Supplemented by a soup of solids washed out by rain, the liquids have risen to ground-water-threatening levels. The Meadowlands landfill in New Jersey now stands in 40 feet of toxic liquid leached out from its contents. Fresh Kills leaks 4 million gallons of toxic liquids a day into nearby streams. Ooze from Michigan landfills has caused at least 139 cases of ground-water contamination.

Even though technology is now available to build safer landfills, a political career goes on the line when an officeholder tries to put a new dump—even a high-tech dump—in someone's neighborhood. So it's not surprising that new landfills aren't being built. There are today just half as many landfills as there were eight years ago.

Where officials have persisted, they've set off minor civil wars. "As soon as any kind of waste-management project gets started, a citizens' group rises out of the ground," says Frank Leary, who regularly fought battles as chairman of the Warren County Solid Waste Advisory Board in New Jersey. Bearing names like CRAP (Citizens Reacting Against Pollution), the groups have tended to become increasingly confrontational in opposing planned projects. "Public hearings are now a disgrace," says New Jersey's assistant commissioner of environmental protection, Donald Deieso. "It's bedlam." At one meeting this year, a county official was knocked to the floor and punched by residents angered over a plan to put a waste-transfer station in their town. In Delran, N.J., mothers turned out with baby carriages to block trucks going to a recycling center.

Sanitation officials complain that opponents never present alternatives—their sole aim is to block a dump or incinerator in their neighborhood. "The public can't be expected to feel any sense of urgency about solid-waste disposal when trash is removed from their curbside with predictable regularity," says Sheila Prindiville of the National Solid Wastes Management Association. Adds one state official: "The garbage crisis is unlike any other we've faced. If there's a drought, people cut back on water. But in this crisis, we simply produce more garbage."

That, in fact, seems to be a special American genius. We produce 400,000 tons of trash a day, making us the world's leading discarders. New Yorkers generate almost twice as much trash per person as do Parisians. About one half of the volume of our trash is from packaging alone. And U.S. know-how keeps creating new forms of trash, from the 16 billion disposable diapers a year to mountains of computer printouts. By the year 2000, each American will generate 6 pounds of junk a day—roughly double the 1960 output.

High-Priced Landfills

One thing that's starting to bring the problem home is the soaring cost of disposal. "Rate shock has hit solid waste," says Richard Dewling, New Jersey's environmental-protection commissioner. Until 1978, the town of Summit, N.J., paid $2.60 per ton to dump its garbage at a landfill. Today, the cost is $74 a ton. Some towns in the Northeast pay well over $100 per ton.

Those prices provide potent incentives for innovative approaches to waste disposal—as well as for actions that range from the antisocial to the criminal. The garbage business, an estimated $15 billion-a-year industry, is not "the home of the most enlightened entrepreneurs," says one official. Just as homeowners care little about what happens to their trash once it leaves the curb, so have many localities been content to turn theirs over to private haulers and not ask many questions.

Anthony Noto, the town supervisor of Babylon, N.Y., is one who did ask questions. He hired retired police officers to follow garbage trucks that he suspected were bringing other towns' refuse to Babylon's dump in the middle of the night. One hauler was arrested and convicted. Soon after that, Noto says, "the D.A. calls me and says, 'You need protection.' " Apparently, certain people who were being wiretapped—"the kind who end up in trunks of cars at La Guardia Airport," as Noto puts it—were discussing ways of getting rid of him. "I literally wore a .357 magnum," says Noto. "It was about 2 inches shorter than Dirty Harry's gun. I had to project an image that I was tougher than them. We made the whole industry change in our town."

That's what the Justice Department is trying to do to the garbage business in at least nine states, as its lawyers push grand-jury investigations into bid rigging and price fixing. So far, six persons and 12 firms have been convicted, most for conspiring to keep prices high by dividing customers among themselves. A federal judge in Ohio fined America's two biggest waste haulers, Browning-Ferris Industries and Waste Management, Inc., the maximum $1 million apiece in October after they pleaded guilty to criminal antitrust charges. Last month, Waste Management pleaded no contest to similar charges in Florida. Waste Management also is charged in Los Angeles and is reportedly the object of grand-jury probes in Arizona, California and Tennessee.

Check the Beer Cups

Less dramatic is the corner-cutting battle between landfill operators and garbage haulers. "The opportunity to cheat becomes greater and greater," says Thomas Marturano, director of solid waste at the Meadowlands landfill. "We have 15 guys who do nothing all day but pick through garbage looking for envelopes and letterheads." Haulers found bringing in trash from outside New Jersey are fined and turned away. One hauler was caught with a load of New York Knicks basketball programs and Madison Square Garden beer cups. "It was pretty obvious where it came from."

The other side of the coin is that garbage is finally becoming the valuable commodity that environmentalists bent on recycling have insisted it could be. What were once utopian schemes for saving the environment are now hardheaded business opportunities. As J. Rodney Edwards, a vice president of the American Paper Institute, notes, a $50-per-ton disposal fee is "all the incentive you need for recycling." The real payoff for municipalities and businesses is in cost avoidance: Every ton of garbage that's recycled is a ton they don't have to pay someone to get rid of. "Recycling is not a free operation," says Wayne DeFeo, recycling coordinator of Somerset County, N.J., which recently built a recycling plant. "At best, marketing [of recycled materials] would pay for half of the cost of operation." But the county expects to get a net saving of $10 million over the next five years in reduced landfill disposal fees.

Paper now makes up about 40 percent of American garbage—about 50 million tons a year. Nearly half of that is recycled. About 200 paper mills already rely solely on waste paper.

But the real moneymakers in recycled paper are cardboard boxes, which fetch about $100 per ton, and high-quality paper like computer printouts, which go for $200 a ton. Pulp from high-quality paper has more long fibers and can be remade into high-quality products. Corrugated-cardboard boxes are, in fact, the port of New York's No. 1 volume export—800,000 tons a year. Much of that goes to South Korea and Japan and is recycled into new boxes for—you guessed it—TVs, stereos and VCRs that are shipped to America.

The American Paper Institute estimates that the recycling business has spawned some 2,000 waste-paper dealers and brokers in the U.S., plus 100,000 individual "scavengers," for whom collecting waste paper is the main source of income.

Hard economics is also behind the 25 percent recycling rate of aluminum cans. Because of the large amounts of energy required to turn raw aluminum-oxide ore into aluminum metal, reycling saves 95 percent of the cost of

> Even though technology is now available to build safer landfills, a political career goes on the line when an officeholder tries to put a new dump—even a high-tech dump—in someone's neighborhood. So it's not surprising that new landfills aren't being built.

"The public can't be expected to feel any sense of urgency about solid-waste disposal when trash is removed from their curbside with predictable regularity."

—Sheila Prindiville,
National Solid Wastes
Management Association

manufacturing a new aluminum can. Nationwide, Reynolds has paid $750 million in the past two decades for used cans at 1,500 collection points.

Still, those recycled cans account for only a tenth of a percent of the 140 million tons of trash that Americans throw out each year. And several states with severe disposal problems have decided that the magic of the marketplace alone won't produce the recycling rates needed to alleviate the landfill crisis. For one thing, the economic incentives to recycle rarely reach individuals directly. A penny for an aluminum can or a pound of newspapers is not exactly big bucks. Large markets for plastic and glass are unlikely to develop as long as there's no system for separating such materials from other waste.

Bottle-deposit laws, enacted mainly to prevent litter, are creating the conditions necessary for a recycling market to take off. One Massachusetts firm, New England CRInc., collects plastic soft-drink bottles that have been returned to stores and distributors. So far, it has recycled 3 billion containers.

Oregon, New Jersey and Rhode Island have taken more-drastic steps. New Jersey now orders municipalities to separate recyclable materials from the trash they haul to state-owned landfills. Some require households to put newspapers, glass, grass clippings and other recyclables into separate containers; others have built recycling centers that use a combination of automatic machinery and manual separation, typically employing handicapped persons to, for example, sort different-colored glass that's carried along a conveyer belt. Starting next year, Rhode Island residents must place cans, glass, and plastic bottles into a separate container for curbside pickup. Oregon provides curbside pickup of recyclables.

But even with such help, recycling is not a cure-all. In Japan's disciplined society, a recycling rate no better than 65 percent is achieved. Many Americans clearly dislike the inconvenience of separating their trash, removing metal lids from glass jars, washing out cans and bundling up newspapers. And if a major city such as New York or Los Angeles suddenly began recycling, it could inundate the market, driving prices to disruptively low levels. Projections by Franklin Associates suggest that even by the year 2000, recycling will eliminate at most 20 to 25 percent of the garbage.

Computer-Age Burning

With recycling only a partial answer, many municipalities are again looking to incineration as the other major way to cut the flow of waste into landfills. Technology has improved considerably since the uncontrolled burning of the 1950s. And after some spectacular failures with high-tech incinerators in the early 1970s, the industry appears to be back on its feet. About 70 large incinerators now operate in the United States, 20 more are being built and 100 are planned. High-temperature burning—as hot as 2,800 degrees Fahrenheit—and computer-controlled feeders, which keep the combustion constant even as garbage flow varies, have cut pollution substantially.

Controversy remains over emission of dioxins—a suspected carcinogen—and other hazardous pollutants. Dioxin worries prompted the shutdown of incinerators on Long Island and in Denmark. Recent studies show, however, that modern plants can hold dioxin emissions to negligibly low levels. A thornier problem is disposing of the ash residue. Toxic metals in trash become concentrated during burning. A recent Environmental Defense Fund report found that the average concentration of lead and cadmium in ash exceeds the regulatory limit defining hazardous waste. For now, the Environmental Protection Agency has exempted incinerator ash from the hazardous-waste laws, but pending legislation would change that. Hazardous waste must be disposed of in specially designed, secure—and expensive—landfills.

The new plants turn the heat from combustion into a useful product, either electricity or steam. Sales of those products, combined with escalating dumping fees, have made the plants an attractive investment for private firms.

Baltimore's state-of-the-art waste-to-energy plant—one official calls it "the cathedral of garbage plants"—has been one of the success stories, all the more so since it replaced a disaster of the '70s. The city in those years had built a $16 million plant that relied on a process called pyrolysis: The "baking" of garbage in an oxygen-starved cooker. In theory, that makes for a more efficient conversion to energy. In practice, the plant never operated more than 23 days without shutting down. It couldn't adjust to the ever-changing makeup of incoming garbage. And, says George Hudnet, manager of the city's new RESCO plant, "if they had a problem with the load, they had to go in there with a jackhammer to get it out." When the plant shut down on the inside, trash piled up on the outside, triggering a tide of neighborhood complaints.

Garbage In, Energy Out

Baltimore finally tore the old plant down in 1983. Wheelabrator, a leading builder of the new generation of waste-to-energy plants, put up $63 million of its own capital and obtained $191 million in industrial-revenue bonds to finance the new plant on the same site. Now a steady stream of trucks arrives to dump their loads—in all, about 2,000 tons a day—into a 100-foot-deep indoor pit. Ventilators keep odors from drifting over the neighborhood. A crane dips into the pit to feed the boilers. At the other end, 60 megawatts of electricity and 60 tons per day of scrap metal emerge. A smaller stream of trucks hauls away the ash, which amounts to 5 percent of the volume of the garbage that came in. The city of Baltimore didn't have to put up any capital: It simply promised a steady supply of garbage at an agreed disposal fee—currently $33 per ton.

If all the waste-to-energy facilities now planned in America are actually built, they'll take in about one quarter of the current flow of municipal waste. But, according to the Franklin Associates study, that will just keep up with the expected growth in waste output over the next decade. About 125 million tons per year still will go into landfills. (pp. 58–62)

Stephen Budiansky with Robert F. Black, "Tons and Tons of Trash and No Place to Put It," in U.S. News & World Report, *Vol. 103, No. 24, December 14, 1987, pp. 58–62.*

Producing garbage seems to be a special American genius. We produce 400,000 tons of trash a day, making us the world's leading discarders. New Yorkers generate almost twice as much trash per person as do Parisians. About one half of the volume of our trash is from packaging alone. And U.S. knowhow keeps creating new forms of trash, from the 16 billion disposable diapers a year to mountains of computer printouts.

Taking Out the Garbage: Methods of Waste Disposal

Americans produced 227 million tons of garbage last year [in 1987]. That's nearly 2,000 pounds for every person in this country. It's more per capita than anywhere else in the world, and it's more in toto than even China, which has over four times our population. Garbage is the price of convenience, and increasingly, it's a price we may not be able to afford.

Already, we are running out of ways to get rid of it. Starting in 1990, ocean dumping, [once] a common method on the East Coast, [was] outlawed by federal law. That [forces] the solutions onto the land: incineration, landfills and recycling.

None of these solutions comes cheap, however. Currently, the annual bill for taking out the garbage is at $30 billion, and rising. Household disposal costs have risen in the past five years from an average of $130 a year to more than twice that. And in some areas, like Long Island, New York, the price per family is already well over $300.

Yet at the same time, we are creating garbage at a faster rate. The volume Americans produce has leaped ahead about 10% just since 1980, as more

As the proportion of paper and then rubber and plastics in garbage began to increase, and as rain seeping through mountains of garbage leached acids and heavy metals into the soil, Americans followed the Europeans in moving from landfills to incinerators, which proved to be another kind of environmental hazard, spewing ash and toxic gases into the air. With increased attention paid to air pollution in the 1970s, most communities reluctantly shut their incinerators and turned back to landfills.

Now those landfills are being closed up, too, either for environmental reasons or for sheer lack of space.

working couples have caused a dramatic rise in the amount of packaged and frozen convenience foods consumed and, in turn, the amount of packaging thrown out.

A dreadful summer of closed beaches, hypodermic syringes and medical waste washed up on America's shores seemed to bring the garbage problem into such sharp focus that many now believe the U.S. has developed the necessary consensus to spend money on the problem. Certainly the soaring prices of environmental-company stocks express that belief. But if wishing could make things so, the U.S. would have had pristine streets decades ago.

Current solutions are but a small step in the right direction. California can mandate that McDonald's and other fast-food restaurants eliminate Styrofoam packaging, and everyone can feel good about doing his or her small part for the environment by bringing newspapers and aluminum cans to the local recycler. But two intractable problems remain at the heart of the trash buildup.

The first is that most of us are unwilling to take responsibility for the trash we generate. Not In My Back Yard (NIMBY) has become a national battle cry. "Everybody wants to transfer his problem onto someone else," says David Sussman, vice president for environmental affairs at Ogden-Martin Systems, a Fairfield, N.J.-based builder of waste-to-energy power plants. But, of course, waste is a by-product of living. The Indians who roamed North America before 1492 were no better respecters of the land than the Europeans who followed Columbus to the New World. A visit to any modern Eskimo community in Alaska or Canada, with its heaps of nondegradable trash, should dispel any romantic notions to the contrary. If the noble red man looked better, it was only because his culture existed almost entirely at the organic level. Most of his garbage—food wastes, camp-fire ashes, excrement—returned to the soil in a few years.

When our European ancestors arrived, they changed the nature of the garbage. Glass, pottery and iron, all processed products, were added to the midden, and therein lies the second problem: the disposal of modern waste. The more a product is processed, the more it's worth. But processing makes most things harder to break down at the molecular level. Goods made of processed materials last, unless more energy is applied to return them to their component, preprocessed forms. Thus, a container made of wood and one made of plastic are both organic products, but the wooden container, made from a tree that processed some small part of the sun's energy, might decompose after 30 years, while the highly processed plastic one, which contains many more Btus (British thermal units) per pound, might take 10,000 years to break down to its component parts.

And the problem goes way beyond Styrofoam fast-food packaging. "You can say that people should avoid paper waste by buying more unpackaged fruits and vegetables," says [Johannes Weiss, supervisor of Zurich's Josefstrasse trash-to-energy incinerator]. "But what about the industrial waste in manufacturing refrigerators? Most solutions go back to pushing the problem further up the line, making it somebody else's problem. You pay for it differently, but there is still a cost that has to be borne."

Which means that you either have to have better ways to get rid of the garbage, or you have to work out the economic costs of eliminating it before it comes into being. Since the late 19th century, communities and national economies have overwhelmingly chosen the first path. Starting just after the Civil War, when cities first reached a size where organized sanitation—street-sweeping and garbage pickup—became necessary, landfills were a cost-effective solution, especially since most of the waste was still organic and would quickly rot. In fact, advanced social planners of the day envisioned turning their dumps into parks. Brooklyn's Botanic Garden is the perfect example of a dump converted to garden use. But as the proportion of paper and then rubber and plastics in garbage began to increase, and as rain seeping through mountains of garbage leached acids and heavy metals into the soil, ruining the underlying water table, Americans followed the Europeans in moving from landfills to incinerators. Early incinerators proved to be another kind of environmental hazard, spewing ash and toxic gases into the air. With increased attention paid to air pollution in the 1970s, most communities reluctantly shut their incinerators and turned back to landfills.

Now those landfills are being closed up, too, either for environmental reasons or for sheer lack of space. Almost 3,000 have shut down in the U.S. in the past five years alone. Which is why so-called "mass-burn" plants have become the rage. More than $17 billion has been pumped into the construction of these plants, which convert unsorted garbage to electricity and super-heated steam. (pp. 48, 51–2)

But mass burn is a controversial solution, also. At the center of the debate are two alleged flaws in mass-burn technology: The first is that the plants produce dioxin, a chemical suspected of being a carcinogen that collects in fatty tissues; and the second is that American companies build far larger mass-burn plants than Europeans do, and these plants burn at higher, and therefore more dangerous, temperatures.

According to Zurich's Weiss, the dioxin charge is frivolous. "Dioxins are a by-product of combustion," he says. "The largest single source of atmospheric dioxins is auto emissions." Ogden-Martin's Sussman seconds that. "A well-run waste-to-energy plant emits femtograms of dioxin," he says. For nonscientists, the quantity represents a quadrillionth of a gram, far below even federal Environmental Protection Agency parts-per-billion emission guidelines.

As for the charge that American plants run at higher temperatures, William Sim, president of American Recovery, a joint venture between Potomac Electric & Power Capital Investment and Sorain Cecchini of Rome says, basically, that they are designed to. "The European plants produce mostly district heat and steam," he says, "while we produce electricity, so there are design changes that we make for higher boiler temperatures, things like corrosion resistance. But power companies have been doing that for decades. We're very cautious about design, and we've already been burned by our experiences with nuclear, so we're trying to be more conservative than we perhaps need to be to ensure the safety and reliability of these plants."

Still, it is a fact that American mass-burn plants erected so far have a poor record of emission control, and several plants have been repeatedly shut down due to poor operation. The solution, says Weiss, a mechanical engineer like many of his staff, is education. "Workers must be trained in what they do."

All of the 284 people who collect trash in Zurich are put through a rigorous course in collection procedures, plant operation, maintenance and safety. In West Germany, which incinerates almost three times as much of its trash as the U.S., the training is even tougher: Waste management is taught as an academic subject in technical high schools. That is followed by months of on-the-job training.

And European mass-burn plants have more built-in safeguards. There is a degree of presorting, for example, that is not yet practiced by most American plants. Televisions, old appliances, dead animals, glass, car batteries and bio-wastes are all collected and disposed of separately in most European cities. That keeps the most dangerous and hardest-to-burn items out of the stream of household garbage and paper and avoids the problems that can lead to plant explosions—like the one that killed three workers at the Akron, Ohio, mass-burn plant in 1984. To help the plant maintain an optimal burn, crane operators inside the plants sort through their garbage, using television cameras down in the waste bunker where garbage is dumped by trucks.

Those opposed to both incineration and landfills advocate a heavy push into recycling. States like New Jersey, Pennsylvania and Florida, whose dumps have either been closed by the Environmental Protection Agency or which are running out of room, are pushing hard to eliminate as much trash as possible before it has to be disposed of. In Pennsylvania, Gov. William Casey has

> **Those opposed to both incineration and landfills advocate a heavy push into recycling. States like New Jersey, Pennsylvania and Florida, whose dumps have either been closed by the Environmental Protection Agency or which are running out of room, are pushing hard to eliminate as much trash as possible before it has to be disposed of.**

"When the housewife goes to rinse out her tuna can and peel off the label, so she can dump it into one trash bag and the can into another, she wastes two resources: fresh water and the energy needed to get it hot enough to melt the glue on the label."

—*James Reuter,*
president, Reuter, Inc.

signed into law a bill mandating 30% recycling by 1992. Residents will have to separate their paper, glass, plastics, metal and other wastes at pickup, with stiff fines for anyone who fails to comply. This, too, is wasteful, says James Reuter, president of Reuter, Inc., a Hopkins, Minn., manufacturer of computer equipment and garbage-collection systems: "When the housewife goes to rinse out her tuna can and peel off the label, so she can dump it into one trash bag and the can into another, she wastes two resources: fresh water and the energy needed to get it hot enough to melt the glue on the label." Not to mention the five trash cans she'll need.

Curbside recycling may well make Rubbermaid a hot stock, but most experts think it will prove a more difficult solution than anyone imagines. "Look at something like juice packs," says Weiss. "On the outside they look like paper, but when you open them up you see that there is a layer of metal, which acts as a barrier, and then a layer of plastic. Will you be required to separate the pack into its components? I don't think it makes too much sense." To that you can add disposable diapers, old household appliances, even compound aluminum and steel cans. (pp. 52–4)

[There] are far-reaching economic consequences to [laws that mandate recycling]. For example, the paper industry as a whole uses about 10% recycled paper and 90% virgin pulp. In Japan and Europe, the amount of paper recycled is closer to 40%. If trash paper becomes a cheap feedstock for U.S. mills, the value of companies such as Jefferson Smurfit would rise, because it is heavily into recycled products, but forest products-based paper companies like International Paper, Weyerhaeuser, Great Northern Nekoosa and Georgia-Pacific, much of whose value is in the tree-producing land they own, could fall dramatically.

There is another approach to solving the waste-disposal problem: rethinking production and distribution patterns to eliminate trash before it is produced. The Japanese, whose prosperity ranks with our own, have mastered this technique. Tokyo is able to keep its volume of trash haul to a bit more than half of New York's—4.5 million tons compared with 8 million tons annually—at least in part because Tokyo's truck farms still grow roughly a quarter of all the vegetables consumed in the city. With a steady supply of locally grown fresh vegetables and an intricate distribution system that allows farmers outside Tokyo to move their produce quickly into the city, packaging is lessened. That cuts a huge chunk out of the waste load. In addition, Tokyo has hundreds of small incinerators to burn what cannot be recycled. Altogether, Japan's Ministry of Public Cleansing operates more than 2,000 incinerators nationwide.

To subsidize a system that produces less trash at the outset and gets rid of what remains more efficiently, Japanese housewives pay almost twice as much for their food as their American counterparts. And, ultimately, that may be what it takes. Americans may just have to get used to the idea that a cleaner environment is also a more expensive environment.

After listening to the experts, *Financial World* recommends the following:

- Adopt a uniform national disposal fee on garbage. By leveling the playing field, it will largely eliminate the incentive for shipping garbage across state lines. That forces communities to solve their problems locally. Shipping garbage is already a $1 billion-a-year industry. That money could better go toward solving the problem than making it someone else's.

- Collect an advance disposal tax on every package and hazardous item sold. That cost should accurately reflect either the cost of disposing of the package, or, in the case of hazardous wastes such as lead-acid batteries, the cost of cleaning up their effects on the environment.

- Mandate that the people who operate the plants be qualified not by civil-service seniority, but by expertise and qualification. That goes for people who operate landfills and recycling centers. You can't eliminate "accidents" until people know how to prevent them.

- Make illegal dumping of any kind a major-league crime. Cheap technology already exists to tag waste so that its source can be identified later. Tagging and accurate record keeping, as well as strict enforcement, can eliminate most illegal hazardous-waste dumping.

Garbage is a fact of life, but the U.S. can solve its problems. As Pogo 'Possum put it, "We have met the enemy, and he is us." (p. 56)

Stephen Kindel, "Taking Out the Garbage," in Financial World, *Vol. 157, No. 26, December 13, 1988, pp. 48, 51–2, 54, 56.*

The Problem of Plastics

In 1987, Campbell Soup Company introduced the Souper Combo, a line of frozen soup and sandwiches. Melvin Druin, vice-president for packaging, called it "the perfect combination of old-fashioned good taste and today's convenience. No mess. No fuss. Easy to use. All you have to do is clean your spoon. Everything else just throw away." Unfortunately, the multi-layered plastic-coated packaging does not just disappear when thrown away. Plastics packaging, particularly from convenience products, has become a waste disposal nightmare. *Garbage,* an environmental magazine, gave the Souper Combo an "in the dumpster" award, saying, "It's precisely the kind of product that's created the municipal landfill monster."

Our American society, which is consumption-driven, convenience-oriented, and dominated by advertising and marketing, has never thought of the consequences of convenience. Today's lifestyle has changed the composition of garbage and multiplied waste disposal problems. The average American produces 3.5 pounds of trash a day, nearly 1,300 pounds per year from each one of us according to the U.S. Environmental Protection Agency. We throw away 18 billion disposable diapers, 1.6 billion pens, 247 million tires, 12 billion mail order catalogs, and enough aluminum cans to make about 30 jet airplanes.

Plastics Revolution

In 1960, waste consisted mostly of discarded food, yard clippings, and other organic wastes. Today, packaging predominates in the waste stream. It is estimated that one-third of the trash by weight and 50 percent of the space in the nation's landfills is taken up by cans, boxes, bottles, and wrapping. The packaging market is in the midst of a "plastics revolution." The packaging industry has emerged as the highest growth industry in the nation's economy. Plastics make up the third largest, and fastest growing, segment of the packaging industry. The volume of plastics used in the United States now exceeds that of steel.

The development of plastics has accelerated since World War II, when plastics were first used in hot, humid environments as a substitute for natural materials such as paper, metals, glass, rubber, and wood.

In addition to being a substitute product, plastics are used to create hundreds of new products, especially products designed for one-time use. In 1986, 75 percent of the 45 billion pounds of plastics sold in the United States were used for long-life applications in transportation, health care, and construction. The remaining 25 percent—11.5 billion pounds—were utilized in packaging and other short-life uses. Plastics industry leaders say the ubiquitous nature of plastics is the result of demand from consumers for convenience. The unique properties of plastics—lightweight, flexible, inert, safe, permanent, and economical—are responsible for their value.

> The packaging market is in the midst of a "plastics revolution." The packaging industry has emerged as the highest growth industry in the nation's economy. Plastics make up the third largest, and fastest growing, segment of the packaging industry. The volume of plastics used in the United States now exceeds that of steel.

The growth of plastics products has created a wide range of environmental problems and hazards. Plastics are synthetic polymers that are produced from highly toxic petrochemicals to create long-chain molecules. The U.S. Environmental Protection Agency has reported that five of the six most hazardous chemicals—propylene, phenol, ethylene, polystyrene, and benzene—are used by the plastics industry.

However, environmentalists say that, because plastics are often cheaper to produce than other types of packaging, consumers are in fact not given a choice in materials. And in the competitive marketplace in which manufacturers seek to differentiate their products through packaging, plastics packaging is proliferating and replacing other more environmentally sound choices.

Environmental Impact

The growth of plastics products has created a wide range of environmental problems and hazards. These problems are present at both the front end and back end of the production cycle. At the front end, plastics are synthetic polymers that are produced from highly toxic petrochemicals to create long-chain molecules. The U.S. Environmental Protection Agency has reported that five of the six most hazardous chemicals—propylene, phenol, ethylene, polystyrene, and benzene—are used by the plastics industry. But it is the back end, where plastic products are discarded and become a part of the solid waste stream, that may prove to have the most damaging long-range implications. The consequences of convenience in using plastic packaging are occurring now in overloaded landfills, polluted groundwater, hazardous emissions from incinerators, depletion of the ozone layer, dwindling natural resources, wildlife entanglement, and unsightly plastic litter on land and in the oceans.

Solid Waste Disposal Crisis

There has always been discarded waste, from the time of ancient civilizations. The limited space and dense populations of urbanization, however, have created a solid waste pollution with environmental repercussions that were unknown to earlier agrarian societies. The evolution of urban solid waste management has moved over time from a nuisance to be ignored, to a health problem, to our current organized technological management. Only recently are we facing the fact of an affluent lifestyle in terms of the ultimate solid waste disposal.

Each year in the United States, we produce more than 160 million tons of garbage, which the experts term municipal solid waste (MSW). As long as we continue to consume huge amounts of packaged products and as long as plastics continue to be the primary packaging agent, the municipal waste stream will become more plastics. By the year 2000, the volume of plastics in the waste stream is estimated to approach 30 to 40 percent.

Public officials and environmentalists agree that for social, economic, and environmental reasons something must be done to contain the waste disposal crisis. Plastics packaging has become the symbol of our wasteful lifestyle. Between the fall of 1988 and the fall of 1989, some 350 new laws and ordinances were proposed at various levels of government to ban or strictly curb the use of plastics in packaging. Hamburger fast-food clamshell boxes of polystyrene foam were a particular target. The adverse publicity encouraged plastics producers to begin looking for workable recycling processes and markets.

H. J. Heinz Company announced in *Packaging* magazine that it will introduce a squeezable ketchup bottle made of clear barrier PET resin. According to the company, the new bottle will fit into existing recycling networks for PET soft drink bottles. . . . Heinz sells 400 million bottles of ketchup annually worldwide and this change to environmentally benign packaging places the company in a leadership role for promoting "green" packaging. Consumer awareness also led Campbell Soup Company to convert its Souper Combo packaging from polystyrene to a recycled paper pulp tray and eliminate a package component.

At present, the nation burns 10 percent of its garbage, recycles 10 percent, and buries 80 percent. The federal government is encouraging the reduction of landfill waste to 55 percent and dividing the remainder between recycling and burning. Many environmentalists contend the better solutions are more recycling and composting. They say it is most important to avoid the use of toxic chemicals in the manufacture of consumer goods. Therefore, the plastic industry should be restricted from using toxic lead, cadmium chromium, and mercury in inks, dyes, and packaging materials.

Landfill

Traditionally, landfills were the bottomless pits that kept garbage out of sight and out of mind. Up to the 1960s much of municipal solid waste was disposed of in open dumps. Now sanitary landfills are lined and monitored and regulated. However, declining landfill capacity, environmental risks, and the rising costs have forced communities to look for alternative methods of managing waste.

The environmental impact from landfill disposal occurs when rain water passing through the refuse accumulates various contaminants. This percolate or leachate then enters the underlying groundwater and can seriously degrade the water quality of the aquifer. Widespread groundwater contamination from unlined and poorly sited landfills has led to stricter government regulation. Landfill in popular perception has become synonymous with contamination and the result is the not-in-my-backyard (NIMBY) syndrome. Few new landfills are being sited. According to the U.S. Environmental Protection Agency, more than half the landfills in the United States will reach capacity in eight years. The problem is most acute in the densely populated Northeast. The nation has not run out of landfill space, but in many parts of the country there are no places where new landfill space can be sited without protest.

Incineration

The diminishing number of acceptable landfill sites has led to a resurgence in incineration of solid waste as an alternative disposal method. Although waste reduction and recycling can reduce the solid waste crisis, experts agree that the total waste stream cannot be recycled. Mass burning, a technology used in Europe for decades for energy recovery, has become the top alternative in many communities. The United States is far behind other developed countries in the use of municipal solid waste as a source of energy. Incineration started out badly in the United States in the early 1970s with inadequate technology and poor management. Presently only four to five percent of municipal solid waste is incinerated. However, predictions to the year 2000 indicate a range as high as 25 percent of municipal solid waste will be incinerated. The United States now has 74 waste-to-energy incineration plants.

Incineration Technology

Two types of combustion systems are in the forefront of incineration technology: mass burn and refuse-derived-fuel (RDF). Mass burn incineration involves burning minimally treated municipal solid waste in a thick bed supported by a travelling grate. The furnaces are lined with water-filled tubes that capture combustion heat for conversion to steam or electricity. Refuse-derived-fuel is the combustion portion of waste that has been separated from the noncombustible elements. RDF goes through several size reduction and screening steps to reach its final form—three- to four-inch pellets. The pellets are then co-fired with another fuel, such as coal, or burned alone.

The three components of any combustion process are the waste receiving area and feed system, the combustion system, and the air quality control system. An ash disposal system may be considered a second process. A heat recovery and utilization system, called waste-to-energy (WTE), may be another distinct process.

Any toxic organics remaining after combustion are captured by means of air pollution control devices such as electrostatic precipitators (ESP), fabric filters or baghouses, and scrubbers.

As long as we continue to consume huge amounts of packaged products and as long as plastics continue to be the primary packaging agent, the municipal waste stream will become more plastics. By the year 2000, the volume of plastics in the waste stream is estimated to approach 30 to 40 percent.

Plastic debris constitutes a serious and growing impact on the marine environment. Miles of plastic debris floating on the surface or submerged in the oceans are ingested or entangled by wildlife and marine species. According to an estimate by the Entanglement Network, a coalition of environmental groups, lost or discarded plastic is causing the death of perhaps 2 million sea birds and 100,000 marine mammals every year.

Environmental Hazards

Modern incinerators in Europe and Japan have demonstrated that the technology can be safe and clean when operated properly. There is concern in the United States that improperly operated incinerators will produce harmful emissions. European technology cannot transplant directly to the United States because American garbage contains much more plastics which produce acid gases that add to pollution and corrode plant equipment. This, combined with the memory of older incinerators, has made incineration as a waste disposal method a controversial topic.

There is much public concern about the environmental and human health hazards from emissions, fallout contamination of surrounding areas, and disposal of potentially toxic fly and bottom ash. No issue is more controversial than the emissions of dioxins and furans. These artificial organic compounds—especially polychlorinated dibenzo-dioxins (PCDD) and polychlorinated dibenze-furans (PCDF)—are suspected of causing a wide range of illnesses, from cancer to birth defects. However, these effects are still subject to scientific dispute, and thus far the federal government has not established any standards for incineration emissions or human exposure.

Degradable Plastics

The growing use of plastics and their negative impact on marine environment and solid waste management stimulated and revived the development of plastics that degrade at a relatively rapid rate.

The two mechanisms that are considered for degradable plastics are photodegradation and biodegradation. Photodegradation is the process by which sunlight reduces the molecular weight of polymers so that the plastic article becomes brittle and disintegrates. Biodegradation is the process whereby bacteria, fungi, yeasts, and their enzymes consume the plastic as a food source so that its original form disappears.

Considerable confusion exists in the field about degradable plastics and expectations may be unrealistic. Degradable plastics do not degrade in landfills because in modern sanitary landfill there is no light or microbial action. Degradable plastics as a waste disposal solution render recycling efforts more difficult to propose and implement. Degradable plastics are suited to fill certain unique niches such as yard waste composting, agricultural mulches, and six-pack rings.

Marine Pollution

Plastic debris constitutes a serious and growing impact on the marine environment. Miles of plastic debris floating on the surface or submerged in the oceans are ingested or entangled by wildlife and marine species. According to an estimate by the Entanglement Network, a coalition of environmental groups, lost or discarded plastic is causing the death of perhaps 2 million sea birds and 100,000 marine mammals every year.

No worldwide central data collection source is operating to determine the extent of the plastic debris being dumped from land or at sea or the extent of the impact on marine ecosystems. It is known that many species—seals, sea lions, pelicans, and sea turtles—have become entangled in plastic debris. The most commonly reported plastics found entangling wildlife are nonfilament fishing lines and six-pack rings. Ghost fishing—the ability of lost or discarded fishing nets to continue to entrap—goes on for years after the nets have been lost or discarded, ensnaring valuable commercial fishes.

The federal government is being pressured to assume a more active role in helping to find solutions for the waste disposal crisis and pollution of the marine environment. These issues and the broader concerns for global warming, natural resource conservation, and pollution control are all interconnected with how we as Humankind perceive and treat our world. (pp. 79–82)

JoAnn DeVries, "The Impact of Plastics on the Environment," in Reference Services Review, *Vol. 19, No. 3, Fall, 1991, p. 79–96.*

Medical Waste

In this age of environmental concern, the vast majority of the public was totally unaware of what became of medical waste until it began washing up on a few popular beaches.

Ocean dumping is, of course, a violation of long-established regulations for biomedical waste disposal, but when detected, it focused attention on a problem intensifying in every state. Biomedical waste is increasing in volume, and present facilities for disposal generally are inadequate or unsafe.

Biomedical waste is a class of substances apart from what is designated "hazardous" waste. It includes blood products, body fluids, bile, human tissue, medical cultures, nasal secretions and many of the health care products which come in contact with them, such as rubber gloves, syringes, IV bags, bedding, and bandages. Though medical waste often is described as hospital waste, it also is generated by doctors' and dentists' offices, walk-in clinics, laboratories, mortuaries, veterinary clinics, research facilities, blood banks, nursing homes and local health centers.

Typically, workers at these locations will "red bag" infectious materials, meaning they place them in designated red bags and boxes for special handling and disposal. So-called "sharps," such as needles and glass containers, go into rigid plastic containers so they will not injure handlers or tear the bags in which they are transported.

But the next step should concern the public.

Small generators of biomedical waste may send it along with household garbage to the local sanitary landfill. Large generators, such as hospitals, most often burn it on-site in aged, inefficient incinerators. New York found that none of its 300-plus on-site hospital incinerators could pass muster. There is little reason to assume that other states have better incineration facilities at this time.

Air quality inspections around the nation reveal that few hospital incinerators have the smokestack scrubbers necessary to remove hydrochloric acid and chlorine resulting from burning plastics that make up so much of the volume in hospital waste. Moreover, relatively few attain the recommended 1,800 degrees F for a minimum of two seconds in the final burn chamber.

According to a study by the University of Minnesota School of Public Health, "conventional methods for managing, treating and disposing of biomedical waste are relatively unsophisticated and need updating."

Virtually every community in the country is confronted with the problem of collecting and disposing of biomedical waste safely. Every citizen, at some point in his life, will generate biomedical waste. The waste volume is increasing rapidly due to disposable hospital products such as syringes, plastic IV bags instead of bottles, and paper, rather than fabric, gowns.

The states have begun to address collection and disposal, and a new federal Medical Waste Tracking Act should help refine the methodology. Meanwhile, a great deal of untreated biomedical waste is entering local sanitary landfills which were constructed before liners and leachate collection systems were

Biomedical waste is increasing in volume, and present facilities for disposal generally are inadequate or unsafe.

Biomedical waste is a class of substances apart from what is designated "hazardous" waste. It includes blood products, body fluids, bile, human tissue, medical cultures, nasal secretions and many of the health care products which come in contact with them, such as rubber gloves, syringes, IV bags, bedding, and bandages.

Virtually every community in the country is confronted with the problem of collecting and disposing of biomedical waste safely. Every citizen, at some point in his life, will generate biomedical waste. The waste volume is increasing rapidly due to disposable hospital products such as syringes, plastic IV bags instead of bottles, and paper, rather than fabric, gowns.

required. Many hospitals are using incomplete incineration and releasing air pollutants that would not be allowed from industrial stacks.

A *New York Times* story recently stated that hospital officials are trying to decide whether to install modern incinerators that meet tighter emissions standards, to modify old ones (at estimated costs of up to $250,000 each), or to join other hospitals in building regional incinerators that would be more efficient and perhaps less costly to individual hospitals. These options do not even address what is to be done with the small biomedical waste generators who do not have access to an on-site incinerator.

The only safe alternative to incineration is autoclaving to destroy infectious material. An autoclave is a chamber in which steam is superheated under pressure. While suitable for a doctor's office or surgery, it handles relatively small amounts and does nothing to reduce the volume of waste. Incineration reduces the amount of waste up to 90 percent.

Instead of going further down the costly road of on-site incineration—and all the upgrading of equipment this would entail—authorities should be looking at biomedical incineration on a scale that would be practical to maintain.

Many communities already have private collection and disposal of biomedical waste. For a fee frequently based on pick-up, weight, or other standards, the private collector transports the waste in specially designed vehicles (often refrigerated) to high-volume incineration units. From the collection vehicle, the waste goes directly into an enclosed building where it is conveyed through a series of incineration chambers with temperatures reaching 1,800 F. All along the way, the waste is accounted for and its movement documented.

Given the modern picture of medical care delivery, privatization of biomedical waste has much to offer. Hospitals, most of them tax supported, can be spared the cost of installing and monitoring individual incinerators capable of meeting standards for high temperatures and removal of air pollutants.

Availability of private biomedical waste collection in every community will mean that more small generators will dispose of waste properly instead of allowing it to enter the local landfill along with household waste.

Even though hospitals now account for over 3 million tons of biomedical waste per year, they are handling proportionally less of what is generated. Outpatient surgery clinics, walk-in medical emergency offices in suburban areas, nursing homes, and more treatment of patients in their homes add to the list of small waste generators. Their waste is the most difficult to track for safe disposal, and they have the least access to incineration. Improved incineration plants at area hospitals would not increase their safe options significantly.

As the public and the scientific community become more aware of the biomedical waste disposal issue, states are adopting standards and outlawing some practices. Some are outlawing household biomedical waste channeled to an ordinary landfill. Others are requiring permits for operation of medical incinerators which are inspected periodically for efficiency. Each state sets its own standards for emissions of particulate matter from smokestacks, and if those are stringently enforced, hospitals are going to be found among the most frequent offenders. Higher volumes of plastics in hospital waste often are the cause.

Local officials have a major role to play if their communities are to attain safe biomedical waste disposal. Either they must find the tax revenue to upgrade existing on-site incineration at public medical facilities (including public hospitals, nursing homes and health clinics) or they must encourage private sector incinerators that will pay their own way.

Encouragement will take the form of adequate zoning and public support through the dissemination of accurate information concerning biomedical waste disposal.

Most of the general public is unaware of current incineration practices at local hospitals, even though they may be located among residences. A medical incinerator would be located in an industrial zone. Furthermore, it would be enclosed in a building and none of the waste it receives would be dumped, even temporarily, outdoors. Air quality control standards already in place ensure that no pollutants or contaminants would drift through the air.

Citizens often give emotional reactions to a facility as unglamorous as a medical incinerator, even if located on zoned industrial property. Nevertheless, the public is best served by proper biomedical waste disposal for this generation as well as those to come. They have a responsibility to face up to the necessity—and the real cost—of safe waste disposal.

Their elected officials will demonstrate leadership when they refuse to succumb to the outcry of citizens whose objections are purely emotional rather than based on facts and an understanding of the stringent regulations which protect the health and welfare of the public.

Liane Levetan, "Medical Waste Disposal: A Growing American Crisis," in American City and County, *Vol. 105, No. 5, May, 1990, pp. 68, 70.*

Rubbish! Misperceptions about American Garbage

Newspapers. Telephone books. Soiled diapers. Medicine vials encasing brightly colored pills. Brittle ossuaries of chicken bones and T-bones. Sticky green mountains of yard waste. Half-empty cans of paint and turpentine and motor oil and herbicide. Broken furniture and forsaken toys. Americans produce a lot of garbage, some of it very toxic, and our garbage is not always disposed of in a sensible way. The press in recent years has paid much attention to the filling up (and therefore the closing down) of landfills, to the potential dangers of incinerators, and to the apparent inadequacy of our recycling efforts. The use of the word "crisis" in these contexts has become routine. For all the publicity, however, the precise state of affairs is not known. It may be that the lack of reliable information and the persistence of misinformation constitute the real garbage crisis.

But we have learned some things over the years. My program at the University of Arizona, The Garbage Project, has been looking at landfills and at garbage fresh out of the can since the early 1970s, and it has generated important insights. During the past two years I have visited all parts of the country and spoken with people who think about garbage every day—town planners, politicians, junkyard owners, landfill operators, civil engineers, microbiologists, and captains of industry—as well as many ordinary men and women who help make garbage possible. When seen in perspective, our garbage woes turn out to be serious—indeed, they have been serious for more than a century—but they are not exceptional, and they can be dealt with by disposal methods that are safe and already available. The biggest challenge we will face is to recognize that the conventional wisdom about garbage is often wrong.

To get some perspective on garbage let's review a few fundamentals. For most of the past two and a half million years human beings left their garbage where it fell. Oh, they sometimes tidied up their sleeping and activity areas, but that was about all. This disposal scheme functioned adequately, because hunters and gatherers frequently abandoned their campgrounds to follow game or find new stands of plants. Man faced his first garbage crisis when he became a sedentary animal—when, rather than move himself, he chose to move his garbage. The archaeologist Gordon R. Willey has argued, only partly in fun, that *Homo sapiens* may have been propelled along the path toward civilization by his

The press in recent years has paid much attention to the filling up (and therefore the closing down) of landfills, to the potential dangers of incinerators, and to the apparent inadequacy of our recycling efforts. The use of the word "crisis" in these contexts has become routine. For all the publicity, however, the precise state of affairs is not known. It may be that the lack of reliable information and the persistence of misinformation constitute the real garbage crisis.

While many normal activities come to a halt on weekends and holidays, the production of garbage flows on. Indeed, days of rest tend to create the largest waves of garbage. Christmas is a solid-waste tsunami.

need for a class at the bottom of the social hierarchy that could be assigned the task of dealing with mounting piles of garbage.

This brings us to an important truth about garbage: There are no ways of dealing with it that haven't been known for many thousands of years. These ways are essentially four: dumping it, burning it, converting it into something that can be used again, and minimizing the volume of material goods—future garbage—that is produced in the first place ("source reduction," as it is called). Every civilization of any complexity has used all four methods to varying degrees. (pp. 99–100)

An Unknown Quantity

What most people call garbage, professionals call solid waste. The waste that we're most familiar with, from the households and institutions and small businesses of towns and cities, is "municipal solid waste," or MSW. Professionals talk about what we all throw away as entering the "solid-waste stream," and the figure of speech is apt. Waste flows unceasingly, fed by hundreds of millions of tributaries. While many normal activities come to a halt on weekends and holidays, the production of garbage flows on. Indeed, days of rest tend to create the largest waves of garbage. Christmas is a solid-waste tsunami.

One might think that something for which professionals have a technical term of long standing should also be precisely calibrated in terms of volume. As we shall see, this is not the case with MSW. Nonetheless, there has been a good deal of vivid imagery relating to volume. Katie Kelly, in her book *Garbage* (1973), asserted that the amount of MSW produced in the United States annually would fill five million trucks; these, "placed end to end, would stretch around the world twice." In December of 1987 *Newsday* estimated that a year's worth of America's solid waste would fill the twin towers of 187 World Trade Centers. In 1985 *The Baltimore Sun* claimed that Baltimore generates enough garbage every day to fill Memorial Stadium to a depth of nine feet—a ballpark figure if ever there was one.

Calculating the total annual volume or weight of garbage in the United States is difficult because there is, of course, no way one can actually measure or weigh more than a fraction of what is thrown out. All studies have had to take shortcuts. Not surprisingly, estimates of the size of the U.S. solid-waste stream are quite diverse. Figures are most commonly expressed in pounds discarded per person per day, and the studies that I have seen from the past decade and a half give the following rates: 2.9 pounds per person per day, 3.02 pounds, 4.24, 4.28, 5.0, and 8.0. My own view is that the higher estimates significantly overstate the problem. Garbage Project studies of actual refuse reveal that even three pounds of garbage per person per day may be too high an estimate for many parts of the country, a conclusion that has been corroborated by weight-sorts in many communities. Americans are wasteful, but to some degree we have been conditioned to think of ourselves as more wasteful than we truly are—and certainly as more wasteful than we used to be.

Evidence all around us reinforces such perceptions. Fast-food packaging is ubiquitous and conspicuous. Planned obsolescence is a cliché. Our society is filled with symbolic reminders of waste. What we forget is everything that is no longer there to see. We do not see the 1,200 pounds per year of coal ash that every American generated at home at the turn of the century and that was usually dumped on the poor side of town. We do not see the hundreds of thousands of dead horses that once had to be disposed of by American cities every year. We do not look behind modern packaging and see the food waste that it has prevented, or the garbage that it has saved us from making. (Consider the difference in terms of garbage generation between making orange juice from concentrate and orange juice from scratch; and consider the fact that producers of orange-juice concentrate sell the leftover orange rinds as feed, while households don't.) The average household in Mexico City produces one third more garbage a day than does the average American household. The reason for the relatively favorable U.S. showing is packaging—which is to say, modernity.

No, Americans are not suddenly producing more garbage. Per capita our record is, at *worst*, one of relative stability.

What's in a Landfill?

A sanitary landfill is typically a depression lined with clays, in which each day's deposit of fresh garbage is covered with a layer of dirt or plastic or both. A great deal of mythology has built up around the modern landfill. We have stuffed it with the contents of our imaginations. It is a fact, however, that there is an acute shortage of sanitary landfills for the time being, especially in the northeastern United States. From 1982 to 1987 some 3,000 landfills have been filled up and shut down nationwide. The customary formulation of the problem we face (you will find it in virtually every newspaper or magazine article on the subject) is that 50 percent of the landfills now in use will close down within five years. As it happens, that has always been true—it was true in 1970 and in 1960—because most landfills are designed to be in use for only about ten years. As noted, we are not producing more household garbage per capita (though we are probably producing more garbage overall, there being more and more of us). The problem is that old landfills are not being replaced. Texas, for example, awarded some 250 permits a year for landfills in the mid-seventies but awarded fewer than fifty last year.

The idea persists nevertheless that we are filling up landfills at an exponential rate, and that certain products with a high public profile are disproportionately responsible. I recently ran across articles in two different newspapers from Oregon in which the finger of blame was pointed at disposable diapers; one of them claimed that disposable diapers accounted for a quarter of the contents of local landfills and the other put the figure at "five percent to thirty-two percent." A recent editorial in *The New York Times* singled out fast-food packaging for straining the capacity of the nation's landfills. Fast-food packaging is, perhaps not surprisingly, almost everyone's villain of choice. I have over the years asked many people who have never seen the inside of a landfill to estimate what percentage of the contents consists of fast-food packaging, and the answers I have gotten have ranged from five to 35 percent, with most estimates either 20 or 30 percent.

The physical reality inside a landfill is considerably different from what you might suppose. I spent some time with The Garbage Project's team over the past two years digging into seven landfills: two outside Chicago, two in the San Francisco Bay area, two in Tucson, and one in Phoenix. We exhumed 16,000 pounds of garbage, weighing every item we found and sorting them all into twenty-seven basic categories and then into 162 subgroupings. In those eight tons of garbage and dirt cover there were fewer than sixteen pounds of fast-food packaging; in other words, only about a tenth of one percent of the landfills' contents by weight consisted of fast-food packaging. Less than one percent of the contents by weight was disposable diapers. The entire category of things made from plastic accounted for less than five percent of the landfills' contents by weight, and for only 12 percent by volume. The real culprit in every landfill is plain old paper—non-fast-food paper, and mostly paper that isn't for packaging. Paper accounts for 40 to 50 percent of everything we throw away, both by weight and by volume.

If fast-food packaging is the Emperor's New Clothes of garbage, then a number of categories of paper goods collectively deserve the role of Invisible Man. In all the hand-wringing over the garbage crisis, has a single voice been raised against the proliferation of telephone books? Each two-volume set of Yellow Pages distributed in Phoenix last year—to be thrown out this year—weighed 8.63 pounds, for a total of 6,000 tons of wastepaper. And competitors of the Yellow Pages have appeared virtually everywhere. Dig a trench through a landfill and you will see layers of phone books, like geological strata, or layers of cake. Just as conspicuous as telephone books are newspapers, which make up 10 to 18 percent of the contents of a typical municipal landfill by volume. Even after several years of burial they are usually well preserved. During a recent landfill dig in Phoenix, I found newspapers dating back to 1952 that

> **Americans are wasteful, but to some degree we have been conditioned to think of ourselves as more wasteful than we truly are—and certainly as more wasteful than we used to be.**

Our society is filled with symbolic reminders of waste. What we forget is everything that is no longer there to see. We do not see the 1,200 pounds per year of coal ash that every American generated at home at the turn of the century and that was usually dumped on the poor side of town. We do not see the hundreds of thousands of dead horses that once had to be disposed of by American cities every year. We do not look behind modern packaging and see the food waste that it has prevented, or the garbage that it has saved us from making.

looked so fresh you might read one over breakfast. Deep within landfills, copies of that *New York Times* editorial about fast-food containers will remain legible until well into the next century.

As the foregoing suggests, the notion that much biodegradation occurs inside lined landfills is largely a popular myth. Making discards out of theoretically biodegradable materials, such as paper, or plastic made with cornstarch, is often proposed as a solution to our garbage woes (as things biodegrade, the theory goes, there will be more room for additional refuse). Laboratories can indeed biodegrade newspapers into gray slime in a few weeks or months, if the newspapers are finely ground and placed in ideal conditions. The difficulty, of course, is that newspapers in landfills are not ground up, conditions are far from ideal, and biodegradation does not follow laboratory schedules. Some food and yard debris does degrade, but at a very, very slow rate (by 25 to 50 percent over ten to fifteen years). The remainder of the refuse in landfills seems to retain its original weight, volume, and form. It is, in effect, mummified. This may be a blessing, because if paper did degrade rapidly, the result would be an enormous amount of inks and paint that could leach into groundwater.

The fact that plastic does not biodegrade, which is often cited as one of its great defects, may actually be one of its great virtues. Much of plastic's bad reputation is undeserved. Because plastic bottles take up so much room in our kitchen trash cans, we infer that they take up a lot of room in landfills. In fact by the time garbage has been compressed in garbage trucks (which exert a pressure of up to fifty pounds per square inch on their loads) and buried for a year or two under tons of refuse, anything plastic has been squashed flat. In terms of landfill volume, plastic's share has remained unchanged since 1970. And plastic, being inert, doesn't introduce toxic chemicals into the environment.

A new kind of plastic that is biodegradable may in fact represent a step backward. The definition of "biodegradable" plastic used by most manufacturers focuses on tensile strength. Plastics "totally" degrade when their tensile strength is reduced by 50 percent. At that point—after as long as twenty years—a biodegradable plastic item will have degenerated into many little plastic pieces, but the total volume of plastic will not have changed at all. The degeneration agent used in biodegradable plastic, usually mostly cornstarch, makes up no more than 6 percent of a biodegradable plastic item's total volume; the 94 percent that's left represents more plastic than would be contained in the same item made with nonbiodegradable plastic, because items made with biodegradable plastic have to be thicker to compensate for the weakening effect of the degenerating agent.

The potentially toxic legacy of landfills that may long ago have been covered over by hospitals and golf courses illustrates one of the terrible ironies of enlightened garbage management: an idea that seems sensible and right is often overtaken by changes in society and in the contents of its garbage. The idea of the sanitary landfill was advanced by civil engineers who lived in a simpler age. Industries used very toxic chemicals, yes, but most households lacked the array of pesticides, cleansers, and automotive fluids that one can find today in virtually every American home. Moreover, the landfill movement that matured after the Second World War, though hardly messianic, was led by people who had a vision. They believed that in the disposal of garbage two birds could almost always be killed instead of one.

This is a historically peculiar trait of garbage science in the United States. The safe and efficient disposal of garbage has never been deemed a high enough end in itself by the professionals here. The goal has always been to get rid of garbage and do something else—create energy, make fertilizer, retrieve precious metals. In the case of sanitary landfills, their proponents hoped not only to dispose of mountains of garbage but also to reclaim thousands of acres of otherwise "waste" land and, literally, to give something back to America. The ideal places for landfills, they argued, were the very places that most scientists now believe to be the worst places to put garbage: along rivers or in wetlands.

It is in unlined landfills in places like these that, not surprisingly, the problem of chemical "leachates" has been shown to be a matter of grave concern.

Environmental scientists believe that they now know enough to design and locate safe landfills, even if those landfills must hold a considerable amount of hazardous household waste such as motor oil and pesticides. The State of Delaware seems to be successful at siting such landfills now. But places like Long Island, where the water table is high, should never have another landfill. In the congested northeastern states there may simply be no room for many more landfills, at least not safe ones. Some 1,550 twenty-ton tractor trailers laden with garbage now leave Long Island every week bound for landfills elsewhere. But the country at large still has room aplenty. The State of New York recently commissioned an environmental survey of 42 percent of its domain with the express aim of determining where landfills might be properly located. The survey pinpointed lands that constitute only one percent of the area but nevertheless total 200 square miles.

The obstacles to the sanitary landfill these days are monetary—transporting garbage a few hundred miles by truck may cost more than shipping the same amount to Taiwan—and, perhaps more important, psychological: no one wants a garbage dump in his back yard. But they are not insuperable, and they are not fundamentally geographic. Quite frankly, few nations have the enormous (and enormously safe) landfill capabilities that this one has. Iraj Zandi, an environmental scientist who teaches at the University of Pennsylvania, said to me recently during a discussion about landfills, "Have you ever taken a flight from San Diego to Philadelphia? For three thousand miles you look down out of the plane and there's nothing there!" (pp. 100–03)

Demand-Side Economics

The yards of America's wastepaper and scrap-metal dealers are located near interstates and in warehouse districts, and they contain piles of crushed automobiles, railroad cars filled with cans, and baled newspaper and cardboard stacked several stories high. These are the trading pits of the recycled-materials markets. There is a big split between those who would recycle to make money and those who would recycle to do good. (p. 105)

Recycling by anyone should be encouraged, in my view, but it is important to understand at the outset what kind of recycling works and what kind may end up doing more harm than good.

Newsprint illustrates one potential problem. Only about ten percent of old newspapers go on to be recycled into new newspapers. What newspapers are really good for is making cereal and other boxes (if it's gray on the inside, it's from recycled stock), the insides of automobiles (the average car contains about sixty pounds of recycled newsprint), wallboard, and insulation. All these end uses are near saturation. Scrap dealers are in the precarious position of being able to obtain enough newsprint to supply demand completely but not daring to sell so much that the price of newsprint plummets and puts them out of business. What happens when the market is suddenly flooded with newsprint? Last year the State of New Jersey implemented new legislation requiring every community to separate at curbside, and collect, three categories of recyclables. As a result, in recent months the price of used newspaper in most parts of New Jersey has plummeted from up to $40 a ton to −$25 a ton—in other words, you have to pay to have it taken away. If legislation like this became widespread, without complementary measures to increase demand for recycled-paper products, the effects could be precisely opposite those intended.

The fact is that for the time being, despite the recriminations and breast-beating, we are recycling just about as much paper as the market can bear. As noted, the market for recyclable paper is glutted; expansion is possible only overseas. The demand for recyclable plastic and aluminum has not yet been fully met, but Americans have been doing a pretty good job of returning their plastic bottles and aluminum cans, and the beverage industry, which hates it

> **There are no ways of dealing with garbage that haven't been known for many thousands of years. These ways are essentially four: dumping it, burning it, converting it into something that can be used again, and minimizing the volume of material goods—future garbage—that is produced in the first place ("source reduction," as it is called). Every civilization of any complexity has used all four methods to varying degrees.**

Dig a trench through a landfill and you will see layers of phone books, like geological strata, or layers of cake. Just as conspicuous as telephone books are newspapers, which make up 10 to 18 percent of the contents of a typical municipal landfill by volume. Even after several years of burial they are usually well preserved. During a recent landfill dig in Phoenix, I found newspapers dating back to 1952 that looked so fresh you might read one over breakfast.

when states pass bottle bills, has pre-empted the issue in most places by opening up successful recycling centers.

Suppose there were a lot of room for growth and that the demand for recycled paper, plastic, and aluminum were insatiable. How much garbage would Americans be prepared to recycle? The only factor that could conceivably drive a systematic recycling effort is money. Money is the reason why junk dealers pay attention to some kinds of garbage and not to others, and it is the reason why most people return cans to supermarkets, and newspapers to recycling centers.

I belabor that point because it is so often lost sight of, and because there are studies that seem to suggest—erroneously, I think—that for noble motives alone people would go to considerable lengths to make recycling a basic feature of American life. Barry Commoner, the biologist and environmentalist, recently conducted a study of a hundred households in Easthampton, Long Island, in which participants were asked to separate their garbage into four containers: one for food debris and soiled paper (to be composted into fertilizer), one for clean paper, one for metal cans and glass bottles, and one for all the rest. Commoner found that because the garbage was rationally discarded, a stunning 84 percent of it could be sold or recycled. Only 16 percent had to be deposited in a landfill. Of course, this experiment lasted only a few weeks, and the households surveyed had actively volunteered to take part. Recognizing that his results were perhaps a little skewed, Commoner conducted a survey in Buffalo, New York, and ascertained that a reassuring 78 percent of all respondents said, sure, they'd be willing to separate their garbage into four containers. However, only 26 percent of the respondents said that they thought their neighbors would be willing to do so. This "What would the neighbors do?" question has a special resonance for Garbage Project researchers. We have found over the years, by comparing interview data with actual trash, that the most accurate description of the behavior of any household lies in that household's description of the behavior of a neighboring household.

There have been studies that have claimed that the people most likely to recycle are those with the most money and the most education, but all these studies are based on people's "self-reports." A look through household garbage yields a different picture. From 1973 to 1980 The Garbage Project examined some 9,000 loads of refuse in Tucson from a variety of neighborhoods chosen for their socioeconomic characteristics. We carefully sorted the contents for newspapers, aluminum cans, and glass bottles (evidence that a household is not recycling), and for bottle caps, aluminum pop-tops, and plastic six-pack holders (possible evidence, in the absence of bottles or cans, that a household *is* recycling). A lot of complicated statistical adjustments and cross-referencing had to be done, but in the end we made three discoveries. First, people don't recycle as much as they say they do (but they recycle just about as much as they say their neighbors do). Second, household patterns of recycling vary over time; recycling is not yet a consistent habit. Third, high income and education and even a measure of environmental concern do not predict household recycling rates. The only reliable predictor is the price paid for the commodity at buyback centers. When prices rose for, say, newsprint, the number of newspapers found in local garbage suddenly declined.

If there is a prosperous future for recycling, it probably lies in some sort of alliance between wastepaper and scrap dealers and local governments. Where recycling is concerned, municipalities are good at two things: collecting garbage and passing laws to legislate monetary incentives. Wastepaper and scrap dealers are good at something different: selling garbage. Local programs run by bureaucrats and tied to strict cost-accounting measures need predictable prices. Stability in a commodities market is rare. Secondary-materials dealers thrive on daily, hourly fluctuations. (pp. 106–08)

Life-Style Override

Source reduction is to garbage what preventive medicine is to health: a means of eliminating a problem before it can happen. But the utility of legislated source reduction is in many respects an illusion. For one thing, most consumer industries already have—and have responded to—strong economic incentives to make products as compact and as light as possible, for ease of distribution and to conserve costly resources. In 1970 a typical plastic soda bottle weighed sixty grams; today it weighs forty-eight grams and is more easily crushed. For another, who is to say when packaging is excessive? We have all seen small items in stores—can openers, say—attached to big pieces of cardboard hanging on a display hook. That piece of cardboard looks like excessive packaging, but its purpose is to deter shoplifting. Finally, source-reduction measures don't end up eliminating much garbage; hamburgers, eggs, and VCRs, after all, will still have to be put in *something*.

Most source-reduction plans are focused on a drastic reduction in the use of plastic. And yet in landfills foams and other plastics are dormant. While some environmentalists claim that plastics create dioxins when burned in incinerators, a study by New York State's Department of Energy Conservation cleared the most widely used plastics of blame. The senior staff scientist of the National Audubon Society, Jan Beyea, contends that plastics in landfills are fine so long as they don't end up in the oceans. There plastic threatens marine animals, which can swallow or become enmeshed in it. Beyea's big complaint is against paper, whose production, he believes, creates large volumes of sulfur emissions that contribute to acid rain.

Ultimately, the source-reduction question is one of life-style override. The purists' theory is that industry is forcing plastics and convenience products on an unwilling captive audience. This is nonsense. American consumers, though they may in some spiritual sense lament packaging, as a practical matter depend on the product identification and convenience that modern packaging allows. That's the reason source reduction usually doesn't work.

Our "wasteful" life is a product of affluence; disregard for the environment is not. Indeed, our short-term aesthetic concerns and long-term practical concerns for the environment are luxuries afforded us only by our wealth. In Third World countries, where a job and the next meal are significant worries, the quality of the environment is hardly a big issue in most people's minds. Concern for the environment can be attributed in major part to the conveniences—and the leisure time they afford—that some activists seem to want to eliminate.

None of this makes us unique. For all our newfangled technologies, Americans are not that different from those who inhabited most of the world's other great civilizations. Our social history fits neatly into the broader cycles of rise and decline that other peoples have experienced before us. Most grand civilizations seem to have moved, over time, from efficient scavenging to conspicuous consumption and then back again. It is a common story, usually driven by economic realities. (pp. 108–09)

I am not worried that even if present trends continue, we will be buried in our garbage. To a considerable extent we will keep doing what other civilizations have done: rising *above* our garbage. (One of the great difficulties I have met in excavating landfills is finding municipal sites that have not already been covered by new facilities.)

A rough consensus has emerged among specialists as to how America can at least manage its garbage, if not make it pretty or go away. Safely sited and designed landfills should be employed in the three quarters of the country where there is still room for them. Incinerators with appropriate safety devices and trained workers can be usefully sited anywhere but make the most sense in the Northeast. And states and municipalities need to cut deals with wastepaper and scrap dealers on splitting the money to be made from recycling. This is a minimum. Several additional steps could be taken to reduce the biggest component of garbage: paper. Freight rates could be revised to make the transport of paper for recycling cheaper than the transport of wood for pulp. Also, many things could be done to increase the demand for recycled paper. For example, the federal government, which uses more paper by far than any

> **We need to expand our knowledge base. At present we have more reliable information about Neptune than we do about this country's solid-waste stream.**

The physical reality inside a landfill is considerably different from what you might suppose.

other institution in America, could insist that most federal paperwork be done on recycled paper. Beyond confronting the biggest-ticket item head-on, most garbage specialists would recommend a highly selective attack on a few kinds of plastic: not because plastic doesn't degrade or is ugly or bulky but because recycling certain plastics in household garbage would yield high-grade costly resins for new plastics and make incineration easier on the furnace grates, and perhaps safer. Finally, we need to expand our knowledge base. At present we have more reliable information about Neptune than we do about this country's solid-waste stream.

One way or another, Americans will someday stand as exemplars of responsible garbage management. This could happen in the not too distant future, when time and resources and society's margin of error run out, and a Decadent America learns painfully to reuse and make do with whatever is at hand. (p. 109)

William L. Rathje, "Rubbish!" in The Atlantic Monthly, *Vol. 264, No. 6, December, 1989, pp. 99–106, 108–09.*

Solutions to the Waste Disposal Problem

The most logical solution to the disposal problem is to create less trash. This requires a change in lifestyle habits and manufacturing processes. The convenience of throw-away goods—whether they be fast food containers or appliances that are cheaper to replace than to repair—should be replaced with an ethic towards recycleables. If the public is aware of the dimensions of the garbage disposal problem then they will be more willing to participate in recycling programs.

A policy that fosters returning or recycling beverage containers, either by economic incentives (to the manufacturers and the public) or convenient curbside pick up, is an easy first step. Over half of the aluminum and glass, and one quarter of the iron in the waste stream comes from beer and soft drink containers. Paper is the most abundant component of the waste stream, yet only twenty percent is recycled. It is more expensive for a manufacturer to haul recycled paper to a paper plant for reprocessing than it is to harvest and transport virgin trees to the plant and manufacture a new product. The cost analysis, as well as consumer preference for new paper products, deters recycling. Taxing virgin products or offering tax incentives to use recycled paper may make paper recycling a viable proposition. We need to change our public policy preferences. The United States Forest Service, for example, loses more than a half billion dollars annually in timber sales because building and maintaining logging roads often costs more than receipts from timber sales.

It is very difficult to recycle some products, especially certain types of plastic. In addition, plastics take years or even centuries to biodegrade. Some cities have passed laws banning certain plastic products. Suffolk County in New York, for example, has banned fast food packaging made of polystyrene and polyvinyl chloride. The city of Berkeley, California, concerned that certain constituents of foam packaging may damage the ozone layer, has banned take-out food containers made from chlorofluorocarbons. A ban or tax on certain non-biodegradable plastics, such as grocery store bags and disposable diapers, is being studied by a number of state and local governments. Taxing these items will mean higher prices for consumers. Cheap plastic products that do not reflect their true costs when the cost of disposal is factored into the product should no longer be entitled to a free ride.

When Congress enacted RCRA [the Resource Conservation and Recovery Act] it was aware that the "continuing technological progress and improvement in methods of manufacture, packaging, and marketing of consumer products has resulted in an ever-mounting increase, and in a change in the characteristics, of the mass material discarded by the purchaser of such products. Under RCRA, Congress endeavored to set out a national policy towards the conservation of materials. It offered grants to the states for planning and offered federal assistance in setting up guidelines for solid waste management. While this is the policy on paper, it obviously is not working in practice. The delay in the states submitting—and the EPA [Environmental Protection Agency] approving—management plans needs to be controlled and expedited. This will not occur unless there are sanctions imposed on the states for noncompliance. Part of the lack of action in the area of municipal solid waste disposal may be because the EPA and the states are overburdened in handling hazardous waste disposal and cleanup.

Inertia in dealing with solid waste translates into public distrust of the current system. There is no assurance that the soil, water, and air around a disposal site is safe. Officials cannot respond because of the lack of monitoring and other data. Incineration of waste is unacceptable to many people because of the dangers of uncontrolled air pollution and lack of standards for the disposal of potentially toxic ash residue.

Incineration is a viable alternative, and in some cities the only alternative, but only when tighter regulatory controls are promulgated and enforced. In Europe, for example, incinerator operators are specially trained. In West Germany, in addition to two years' on-site training, there is also instruction on the theories of combustion and emission control. West Germany also has very strict penalties for noncompliance with environmental standards, including a two-year mandatory jail term for operators who knowingly violate certain regulations. Mandatory jail sentences seem a little excessive, but the United States should at least insist upon operator certification to ensure the efficient operation of a facility.

The major public concern about incineration is the toxicity of ash residue. RCRA regulation of hazardous waste under Subtitle C is stringent and onerous. There needs to be an intermediate standard for municipal ash residue. For example, the ash could be monofilled and monitored at suitable prepared sites. In order to prevent future international embarrassment to the nation, there should be federal control over interstate and international transportation of waste. A waste hauler should not be permitted to take off willy nilly with a load of ash residue and circle the globe looking for a disposal site. A long-term disposal strategy should be part of a state's management plan.

Congress was far-sighted in offering funds and technical assistance to state and local officials for solid waste management and planning. Solid waste disposal is an area that cannot be ignored, and an overall state strategy identifies problem areas and presumably forces local officials to deal with the problem. It seems that neither the EPA nor the states have lived up to the spirit of the statute. The EPA laments that there are over 10,000 municipal landfills and that they do not have the manpower to manage such a vast enterprise. States are faced with a political parochial issue for which there is no easy answer.

We need more than a euphoric Alice in Wonderland approach to municipal solid waste disposal. Congress should develop a comprehensive national policy towards waste disposal setting guidelines for state and local officials, as well as providing federal funds to implement these goals and stiff penalties for noncompliance. Such a scheme has worked under the Clean Air Act to alleviate air pollution. Our present approach is to procrastinate. As Sarah Cynthia Sylvia Stout discovered, such an approach produces deleterious results:

> Sarah Cynthia Sylvia Stout
> Would not take the garbage out!
> She'd scour the pots and scrape the pans,
> Candy the yams and spice the hams,

The most logical solution to the disposal problem is to create less trash.

Congress should develop a comprehensive national policy towards waste disposal setting guidelines for state and local officials, as well as providing federal funds to implement these goals and stiff penalties for noncompliance.

And though her daddy would scream and shout,
She simply would not take the garbage out.
And so it piled up to the ceilings:
Coffee grounds, potato peelings,
Brown bananas, rotten peas,
Chunks of sour cottage cheese,
It filled the can, it covered the floor,
It creaked the window and blocked the door
With bacon rinds and chicken bones,
Drippy ends of ice cream cones,
Prune pits, peach pits, orange peel,
Gloppy glumps of cold oatmeal,
Pizza crusts and withered greens,
Soggy beans and tangerines,
Crusts of black burned buttered toast,
Gristly bits of beefy roasts . . .
At last the garbage reached so high
That finally it touched the sky.
And all the neighbors moved away,
And none of her friends would come to play.
And finally Sarah Cynthia Stout said,
"OK, I'll take the garbage out!"
But then, of course, it was too late . . .
The garbage reached across the state,
From New York to the Golden Gate.
And there, in the garbage she did hate,
Poor Sarah met an awful fate,
That I cannot right now relate
Because the hour is much too late.
But children, remember Sarah Stout
And always take the garbage out!
—Shel Silverstein, "Sarah Cynthia Sylvia Stout"
(pp. 231–35)

Denise N. Chancellor, "Municipal Garbage Disposal: A Problem We Cannot Ignore," in Journal of Energy Law and Policy, *Vol. 9, No. 2, 1989, pp. 213–35.*

Waste-Reduction Strategies

Recycling is the rage today, but whatever happened to waste reduction? U.S. Environmental Protection Agency guidelines are aiming for 25-percent recycling and waste reduction by 1992.

"It is a slippery concept," says Carl Woestendiek, waste reduction planner in Seattle. "It's really a conservation program involving shopping practices and reuse strategies."

Waste reduction, also known as source reduction, is an activity that prevents waste by reusing materials, lengthening a product's life, or precycling (changing buyer or consumer habits). For local governments, this means financial incentives or bans, reduction efforts in municipal offices and workplaces, and aggressive public education. Many locations such as Seattle employ a broader definition which includes municipal or backyard composting and redesigning products to lessen toxicity.

Analysts say the best way to complete this task is to "divide and conquer" all the little details which make up a successful program. Ellen Harrison, associate director of the Cornell Waste Management Institute, says each community's solid-waste plan should include a variety of trash-prevention schemes.

"People want a quick and easy path to reduce waste, but there is no quick fix," she says.

Perhaps the most effective, single method is for communities to reduce the sheer volume of waste by charging residents a flat fee for every trash bag. For example, recycling is voluntary in Woodstock, Ill. A 32-gallon bag for the remaining refuse costs $1.83 at curbside with a weight limit of 50 pounds per bag. David Danielson, assistant city manager, says an independent study tallied source reduction at 38 percent.

In some towns, this personal, monetary incentive to reduce trash works best if a mandatory recycling law also is in place. Charging for bags did not lessen the volume of trash noticeably in Ilion, N.Y., until the village mandated the recycling of glass, newsprint and corrugated cardboard. Then the volume of waste fell by one-third, says Debra Greig of the Ilion department of public works. (p. 30)

Beyond charging a fee per bag, municipalities labor toward other waste-reduction practices which take more time and effort. For most communities, reduction starts in municipal offices and private business establishments. Consultant Pam Winthrop Lauer of Apple Valley, Minn., says her favorite way of encouraging waste reduction is to start a program first in government offices and garages. Then the municipality asks business and industry to join the program while advertising the values of reduction and reuse to the community.

"You go through the steps in your own courthouse and then you go one step further, to help others in the community do the same," she says. "Keep the message in peoples' sights constantly, or else it will be forgotten."

Minnesota reduction guidelines, which Lauer helped formulate, suggest a multitude of reuse strategies for business and municipal offices, many of which save money. In addition, the Minnesota Office of Waste Management's reduction checklist recommends offering incentives to employees for thinking of new ideas to reduce waste. (pp. 30, 32)

Some prevention programs, such as the war on packaging, are perhaps best handled by large municipalities or states. According to industry sources, packaging costs for manufacturers climbed from $32 billion in 1980 to $60 billion in 1987. Packaging (one-third of the waste stream) can be reduced by statewide taxing or granting tax credits to manufacturers that cut back on boxes and plastic bubbles.

Denise Lord, director of planning for the Maine Waste Management Agency, says the result of the new law is that more beverages now are available in glass, metal and plastic. (pp. 34, 36)

Another form of waste reduction which is difficult to achieve locally is preventing toxins from entering the waste stream. The Coalition of Northeastern Governors has a source reduction council working on an array of issues including recent legislation to ban lead, cadmium, mercury and hexavalent chromium in packaging. Lead is found in the solder of cans, tin and wine and liquor bottle caps, and cadmium and chromium in ink pigments on labels or other parts of a wrapper or box. A package, according to the law, includes the label, binding, shipping pallet and secondary or tertiary boxes. (p. 36)

Federally, the government has not enacted legislation to foster source reduction. EPA regards itself as an "information exchange," says Paul Kaldjian, source reduction coordinator in EPA's Office of Solid Waste. EPA offers a 44-page booklet, "The Environmental Consumer's Handbook," which summarizes waste reduction and offers a bibliography of EPA sources.

Kaldjian suggests local officials also subscribe to "Reuseable News," a quarterly newsletter put out by EPA's Office of Solid Waste's municipal and industrial solid waste division.

In addition, EPA helps finance packaging and product life assessment (PLAs) studies. Kaldjian says these life-cycle analyses will determine the

Waste reduction, also known as source reduction, is an activity that prevents waste by reusing materials, lengthening a product's life, or precycling (changing buyer or consumer habits).

The waste exchange concept is simple. An intermediary tries to match up waste generators with reclaimers. There are numerous ways this can take place, although most intermediaries can be classified as either information exchanges (often called clearinghouses) or materials exchanges.

environmental impacts of different products or packages not only during disposal but also during the manufacture and use phases. This would include risk calculations for natural resources and energy, emissions during manufacture and disposal characteristics.

"The issue of PLAs is a long way from being resolved," says Susan Mooney of Chicago's EPA office. "Environmental impact assessment is a big, black box, and we don't know what's in it and we don't know its borders. The hope is PLAs would provide a systematic way to compare or look at a product or material."

Mooney says grocery shoppers now notice paper and plastic bags, consider where they come from and their biodegradability. Life-cycle analyses for these bags will calculate the whole gamut of environmental effects. "In the end we'll have all the information laid out," she says.

A long time may be needed before these assessments are of practical, everyday use to the public and localities. But the advantage of PLAs from a waste-reduction point of view is to improve product labeling programs. This would encourage consumer "smart-shopping."

There are numerous proposed laws regarding waste reduction before state legislatures across the nation which would affect local waste-prevention programs. For example, the waste reduction and packaging law ("the wrap act") to be proposed in New York, would require all packaging to be 50-percent recycled and have a statewide recyclability rate of 60 percent.

An exception would be if the package could be refilled a minimum of five times. The sale in disposable wraps of food to be eaten on the premises would be prohibited, says the bill's author, Judith Enck of the New York Public Interest Research Group. There would be a charge of five cents for each paper or plastic bag used in retail transactions.

With legislation in the wings, localities and residents still want a quick and easy path toward waste prevention. But American cities and counties should resist passing the waste-reduction buck back to the state and federal level, Harrison says. She adds that a tendency exists for local governments to wait for higher action and for the federal government to pass it down.

"In the end, consumers have to do this thing," she says. "In fact, educating the public may be the most important aspect of a waste-reduction program." (pp. 36–7)

Anne Magnuson, "What Has Happened to Waste Reduction?" in American City and County, Vol. 106, No. 4, April, 1991, pp. 30, 32, 34, 36–7.

Waste Exchange

Garbage to one person is often gold to another. But if the two parties don't know about each other, the waste won't be used as a resource.

Throughout much of Canada and the U.S., there's a successful solution: the waste exchange service. An idea borrowed in the 1970s from Europe is now a stable part of the recycling infrastructure.

The waste exchange concept is simple. An intermediary tries to match up waste generators with reclaimers. There are numerous ways this can take place, although most intermediaries can be classified as either information exchanges (often called clearinghouses) or materials exchanges.

The Information Exchange

This type of exchange is typically a non-profit organization that receives governmental support to provide its services. The information exchange attempts to facilitate waste recovery by bringing together waste generators and waste users. The principal tool is the catalog—a publication containing confidential listings of wastes that are either available or wanted.

Readers who desire a listed waste or want to reach a waste reclaimer contact the exchange operator, who then relays the letter of interest on to the lister. If all goes well, a business transaction occurs between the parties and waste is exchanged. Our research shows that more than 520,000 waste exchange catalogs were distributed last year by waste exchanges in the U.S. and Canada.

Most information exchanges use a set of standardized categories for waste listings. The 11 categories are:

- acids
- alkalis
- other inorganic chemicals
- solvents
- other organic chemicals
- oils and waxes
- plastics and rubber
- textiles and leather
- wood and paper
- metals and metal sludges
- miscellaneous.

The Materials Exchange

This type of exchange takes a more active approach. Usually a for-profit firm, the materials exchange either acts as a for-free broker, bringing together waste producers and users, or takes possession of wastes for subsequent marketing.

A Mini-Industry

Most of the U.S. and Canada are served by regional information exchanges. (pp. 82–3)

In discussions with program managers, it is obvious that waste exchanges entered the '90s with an eye to new, expanded services. Many exchanges are developing computer databases that can be used by patrons. In particular, this allows those firms that want specific wastes to check periodically by using a computer and modem to see if new listings have been posted.

Some of the computerized databases provide more than listings of materials available or wanted. As an example, the Michigan-based Resource Exchange has developed Envirox, an on-line environmental information management system. Subscribers to the service can use a computer to get information on existing and proposed environmental legislation in selected states, listings of environmental conferences, a director of consultants, etc.

Some information exchanges also undertake special contracts. For instance, the Northeast Industrial Waste Exchange has been hired by the New York State Department of Economic Development to compile a computerized database of recycling processors, brokers and exporters that target post-consumer

Many exchanges are developing computer databases that can be used by patrons. In particular, this allows those firms that want specific wastes to check periodically by using a computer and modem to see if new listings have been posted.

An increasing number of waste exchanges are receiving requests for catalogs and specific wastes from as far away as Germany, Hong Kong, Israel and Taiwan. Changes in the trade relationship between the U.S. and Canada have also led to growing waste exchange activities across the border.

residential and commercial wastes. In addition, the Northeast exchange operates a nonhazardous waste marketing service for businesses in Onondaga County, New York. The project is sponsored by the county's industrial development agency.

An Evaluation

Given their longevity and increasing support, existing exchanges do their job successfully.

A survey of six major information exchanges found that by publishing nearly 2,000 listings of materials available in 1988, some 9,000 requests for information were received. The estimated volume of listed wastes was nearly 9 million tons, with exchange officials estimating that 10 to 30 percent of the listings were representative of the types of wastes commonly transferred for recycling or reuse. Because of the proprietary nature of the exchange system, precise estimates of program effectiveness can not be estimated. (pp. 83–5)

More and more exchanges are expanding their service areas. The best example is the joint operational agreement between the Resource Exchange and the Pacific Materials Exchange. Launched in mid-1989, the tie-up provides combined listings for a geographic area encompassing 26 states and the Pacific Rim countries. Each of the partners maintains its regional focus but eliminates geographic duplication, thus lowering program costs.

The move from operating on a purely regional basis to serving businesses across the nation is accompanied by greater contacts internationally. An increasing number of waste exchanges are receiving requests for catalogs and specific wastes from as far away as Germany, Hong Kong, Israel and Taiwan. Changes in the trade relationship between the U.S. and Canada have also led to growing waste exchange activities across the border.

On the downside for most exchange services, there has never been enough money to provide all the needed services. Although some waste exchanges report economies of scale through the growing use of computers in general and on-line databases in specific, funding problems have killed more than one exchange. About a dozen materials and information exchanges bit the dust in the last decade. But with rising costs of waste management and increasing regulation of waste generators, the simple concept of waste exchange will prove more and more successful. (pp. 85, 106)

Jerry Powell and Meg Lynch, "Successfully Simple: The Waste Exchange," in Resource Recycling, *Vol. IX, No. 4, April, 1990, pp. 82–5, 106.*

Sources For Further Study

Allerton, Hugh G., III. "Hazardous Waste Minimization: Source Reduction Alternatives in the Aerospace Industry." *Journal of Environmental Health* 53, No. 1 (July-August 1990): 28–9.
  Examines hazardous waste minimization, reduction, and disposal programs in the aerospace industry.

Baker, L. E. "Incineration of Hazardous Waste and Air Pollution." *Water and Environmental Management* 2, No. 3 (June 1988): 289–94.
  Examines primary concerns involved in the establishment and maintenance of effective hazardous waste incineration services.

Basta, Nicholas, et. al. "Waste: An Ounce of Prevention . . . " *Chemical Engineering* 95, No. 11 (15 August 1988): 34–7.

Surveys current waste-reduction programs and controversies regarding the practice, including issues of industry compliance and government monitoring and regulations.

Begley, Sharon, and Waldrop, Theresa. "Microbes to the Rescue!" *Newsweek* CXIII, No. 25 (19 June 1989): 56–7.
Discusses the practice of "bioremediation," or using bacteria and fungi to degrade certain kinds of wastes.

Blumberg, Louis, and Gottleib, Robert. *War on Waste: Can America Win Its Battle with Garbage?* Washington, D.C.: Island Press, 1989, 301 p.
Surveys the background, present "state of crisis," and possible future of waste disposal.

Boerner, Deborah. "Paper or Plastic?" *American Forests* 96, Nos. 1-2 (January-February 1990): 21–5, 46.
Examines the ecological impact of the manufacture and eventual disposal of both paper and plastic grocery bags.

Brown, Michael D., and Jarvie, Kirk. "The Future of Waste-to-Energy in the United States." *Solid Waste & Power* 3, No. 3 (1989): 12–22.
Nontechnical explanation of current and possible future waste-to-energy technologies. Brown and Jarvie suggest that the future of waste management lies in integrating various complementary programs including waste-to-energy systems.

Burns, P. "Hazardous Waste Management—The Way Forward." *Water and Environmental Management* 2, No. 3 (June 1988): 285–89.
Considers current hazardous waste disposal practices and speculates about the development of future disposal options.

"Think of It as an Icebox for Toxic Waste." *Business Week,* No. 3187 (21 November 1990): 84.
Outlines a new process, trademarked Cryocell, to contain hazardous waste in landfills by freezing the earth under and around the waste.

Campbell, James E., and Cranwell, Robert M. "Performance Assessment of Radioactive Waste Repositories." *Science* 239, No. 4846 (18 March 1988): 1389–92.
Assesses U.S. Nuclear Regulatory Commission and Environmental Protection Agency regulations for radioactive waste storage facilities and discusses risk factors associated with storing nuclear waste.

Cheremisinoff, Nicholas P., and Cheremisinoff, Paul N. "Special Report: The Plastics Waste Problem." *Pollution Engineering* XXI, No. 8 (August 1989): 58–67.
Contends that plastics disposal has reached crisis proportions and that resolution of this disposal problem is necessary. The authors consider the impact that addressing disposal issues would have on the plastics industry and survey various disposal methods.

Cheremisinoff, Paul N., and Shah, M. K. "Hospital Waste Management." *Pollution Engineering* XXII, No. 4 (April 1990): 60–6.
Defines different types of hospital wastes and assesses hospital waste collection systems, methods of processing and disposal, and regulatory bills that affect hospital waste.

Cheremisinoff, Paul N., ed. *Encyclopedia of Environmental Control Technology, Volume 1: Thermal Treatment of Hazardous Wastes.* Houston: Gulf Publishing Co., 1989, 827 p.
Collects current scholarship regarding thermal treatment of hazardous waste, providing an overview of technology and research activities in the field.

Christensen, Thomas H.; Cossu, Raffaello; and Stegmann, Rainer. *Sanitary Landfilling: Process, Technology and Environmental Impact.* London: Academic Press, 1989, 592 p.

Compilation of international papers on such landfill-related topics as the degradation process, leachate, lining and drainage, and site design.

Clark, Robert B. *Marine Pollution*. Second edition. Oxford: Clarendon Press, 1989, 220 p.
Details the types of waste that reach the sea and analyzes which wastes constitute pollution by causing an undesirable effect.

Conner, Daniel K., and O'Dell, Robert. "The Tightening Net of Marine Plastics Pollution." *Environment* 30, No. 1 (1988): 16–20.
Contends that the long-term health of the marine environment demands greater control of plastics manufacture and disposal.

"The Garbage Crisis: Will We Learn to Handle It before It Buries Us?" *Countryside and Small Stock Journal* 74, No. 1 (January-February 1990): 13–16.
Suggests that widespread adoption of the "homesteader attitude" of self-sufficiency, which includes composting, reusing most household goods, and the avoidance of disposable items, would lead to reduction of the solid waste stream.

Curtis, Denise Brinker. "Waste Treatment: Better Safe than Sorry." *Chemical Engineering* 95, No. 8 (23 May 1988): 131–36.
Discusses ways to select a reputable and qualified waste-treatment and disposal contractor. Curtis includes a checklist for companies to follow when investigating waste-disposal businesses.

Daniel, David E., et. al. "Interaction of Earthen Liner Materials with Industrial Waste Leachate." *Hazardous Waste and Hazardous Materials* 5, No. 2 (Spring 1988): 93–108.
Technical study of the effect of liquid industrial wastes on the compacted clay soil commonly used to line landfills.

Darnell, Tim. "The Politics of Dumping Garbage." *American City and County* 103, No. 5 (May 1988): 38, 42, 44.
Discusses the dynamics of public opposition to siting landfills and garbage dumps.

Denison, Richard A., and Silbergeld, Ellen K. "Risks of Municipal Solid Waste Incineration: An Environmental Perspective." *Risk Analysis* 8, No. 3 (1988): 343–55.
Explores the impact of such control technologies as filters and scrubbers on the nature and amounts of solid residue that incinerators will produce.

Denison, Richard A., and Ruston, John, eds. *Recycling and Incineration: Evaluating the Choices*. Washington, D.C.: Island Press, 1990, 322 p.
Evaluates and compares recycling and incineration as waste management practices.

Dernbach, John C. "Industrial Waste: Saving the Worst for Last?" *Environmental Law Reporter: News and Analysis* XX, No. 7 (July 1990): 10283–294.
Examines provisions for addressing industrial waste in current Resource Conservation and Recovery Act (RCRA) authorization bills and suggests that more should be done to address energy and materials conservation, ensure that health and environmental concerns are addressed at waste management facilities, guarantee prompt and significant results, and establish a genuine state and federal partnership to address these goals.

Derrington, J. A. "Toxic and Radioactive Waste Management." *Journal of Professional Issues in Engineering* 114, No. 4 (October 1988): 463–67.
Describes accepted methods of disposing of both liquid and solid toxic and nontoxic waste, concluding that satisfactory methods exist for the disposal of all forms of toxic and radioactive waste.

Donnelly, John. "Degradable Plastics." *Garbage* (May-June 1990): 42–7.
Examines claims that cornstarch-based plastics are biodegradable.

Dover, Diane. "The Three R's of Trash Disposal: Reduce-Reuse-Recycle." *Countryside and Small Stock Journal* 74, No. 3 (May-June 1990): 16–17.
    Outlines simple procedures that can be implemented by individual households to significantly reduce the volume of trash they produce.

"Rubbish: Burning Question." *The Economist* 307, No. 7552 (28 May 1988): 29–30, 32.
    Surveys the feasibility of incinerating much of the waste from American cities that currently goes into landfills, concluding that incineration is an imperfect solution and new technologies must be sought.

Edworthy, K. J. "Waste Disposal and Groundwater Management." *Water and Environmental Management* 3, No. 2 (April 1989): 109–115.
    Investigates indications that waste-disposal methods must be improved to guard against groundwater contamination.

Fahey, Robert E. "Landfill Lodes." *Natural History* 99 (May 1990): 58–60.
    Examines a program in which the Collier County, Florida, landfill is mined for recyclable materials.

Fee, Rich. "Biodegradable Plastics: Myth or Magic?" *Successful Farming* 88, No. 9 (September 1990): 32–3.
    Briefly surveys the controversies surrounding corn-based degradable plastics, including questions concerning the rate of degradation, the release of pollutants during the degradation process, and the interference of the new product with plastics recycling.

Forbes, C. J., and Chiquelin, W. R. "WIPP Operations: A Quality Waste Handling Environment." *Radioactive Waste Management and the Nuclear Fuel Cycle* 14, Nos. 1-2 (1990): 63–88.
    Analyzes operations at the U.S. Department of Energy's Waste Isolation Pilot Plant (WIPP), which is characterized as a comprehensive waste handling environment emhasizing safety, quality, and the protection of workers, the public, and the environment.

Forester, William S. "Solid Waste: There's a Lot More Coming." *EPA Journal* 14, No. 4 (May 1988): 11–12.
    Outlines some solid waste disposal problems, including increasing amounts of waste and decreasing landfill capacity.

Frizelle, Chris. "A Million Years in the Life of a Waste Site." *New Scientist* 120, No. 1634 (15 October 1988): 44–7.
    Examines the development of computer models that are intended to allow the nuclear industry to design nuclear waste repositories that will remain safe and stable for the million-year period that the waste will remain hazardous.

Gilbert, Susan. "Finding a Place for Hazardous Waste." *High Technology Business* 8, No. 10 (October 1988): 26–30.
    Examines various treatment and disposal alternatives to placing hazardous waste in landfills.

Glenn, Jim, and Riggle, David. "Where Does the Waste Go?" *BioCycle* (April 1989): 34–9.
    Surveys municipal solid waste generation and disposal practices by state.

Gronow, J. R.; Schofield, A. N.; and Jain, R. K., eds. *Land Disposal of Hazardous Waste: Engineering and Environmental Issues.* Chichester, West Sussex: Ellis Horwood, 1988, 311 p.
    Presents the research findings and practical experience of a range of international contributors investigating problems concerning hazardous waste in landfills.

Hager, Mary, et. al. "Dances with Garbage." *Newsweek* CXVII, No. 17 (29 April 1991): 36.
    Discusses the leasing of Native American reservation land for toxic waste dumps.

Haigh, C. P., and Luke, J. A. "Recent Developments in Power Station Waste Management Procedures." *Radioactive Waste Management and the Nuclear Fuel Cycle* 9, Nos. 1-3 (1987): 71–84.
Examines a volume-reduction process for low-level nuclear wastes that must be stored temporarily in the absence of suitable repositories.

Hanson, David J. "Hazardous Waste Management: Planning to Avoid Future Problems." *Chemical and Engineering News* 67, No. 31 (31 July 1989): 9–14, 16–18.
Finds that generators of hazardous wastes, as well as waste-disposal professionals, are increasingly investigating and implementing on-site or source reduction as a component of the waste management process.

Harper, Stephen R., and Pohland, Frederick G. "Landfills: Lessening Environmental Impacts." *Civil Engineering* 58, No. 11 (November 1988): 66–9.
Suggests that the presence of leachate liquids in landfills with leachate recycling systems in place enhances the anaerobic breakdown of garbage, leading to swifter contaminant stabilization.

Hull, David. "Garbage Barge Earth." *American City and County* 103, No. 5 (May 1988): 32–4, 36.
Pronounces solid-waste management one of the most serious problems facing American cities and counties, and outlines some possible solutions.

Husain, T.; Hoda, A.; and Khan, R. "Impact of Sanitary Landfill on Groundwater Quality." *Water, Air, and Soil Pollution* 45, Nos. 3-4 (June 1989): 191–206.
Presents the results of monitoring shallow groundwater quality around two municipal landfill sites in Saudi Arabia.

Johnson, L. F. "Managing Solid Waste Safely." *Nuclear Engineering International* 35, No. 435 (October 1990): 35–8.
Considers some safe and effective radioactive waste management practices.

Klemchuk, Peter P. "Degradable Plastics: A Critical Review." *Polymer Degradation and Stability* 27 (1990): 183–202.
Presents an overview of information about degradable and other kinds of plastics in the municipal waste stream.

Land, Thomas. "Managing Toxic Waste." *The New Leader* LXXII, No. 18 (27 November 1989): 4.
Discusses a treaty between more than fifty countries that regulates the transport and disposal of hazardous waste. The treaty is expected to benefit global public health standards and pollution control.

Lisk, Donald J. "Environmental Implications of Incineration of Municipal Solid Waste and Ash Disposal." *The Science of the Total Environment* 74 (1988): 39–66.
Considers the potentially hazardous effects of particulate and gaseous emissions from waste incineration.

Lowe, Marcia D. "Down the Tubes." *World Watch* 2, No. 2 (March-April 1989): 22–9.
Contending that common disposal methods often allow human excrement to become a source of pollution, Lowe explores the feasibility of processing and using it for fertilizer.

Luoma, Jon R. "Trash Can Realities." *Audubon* (March 1990): 86–97.
Calls for citizen involvement with local landfill or resource recovery facilities, suggesting that greater awareness of waste management problems will encourage individuals to produce less waste.

Mather, J. D. "Groundwater Pollution and the Disposal of Hazardous and Radioactive Wastes." *Water and Environmental Management* 3, No. 1 (February 1989): 31–5.
Asserts that hazardous waste containment sites require long-term monitoring to ensure groundwater safety.

Melosi, Martin V. *Garbage in the Cities: Refuse, Reform, and the Environment, 1880–1980*. College Station, Tex.: Texas A&M University, 1981, 268 p.

Entertaining and informative history of the nature and extent of U.S. urban waste problems.

Moyers, Bill, and the Center for Investigative Reporting. *Global Dumping Ground: The International Traffic in Hazardous Waste.* Washington, D.C.: Seven Locks Press, 1990, 152 p.
    Results of four years of investigation into international commerce involving hazardous waste, documenting violations of disposal restrictions and concluding that much of the world's production of hazardous waste is unnecessary.

Parkinson, Gerald. "Reducing Wastes Can be Cost-Effective." *Chemical Engineering* 97, No. 7 (July 1990): 30–3.
    Credits new waste-minimization laws with encouraging the chemical industry to formulate and implement plans for on-site waste reduction.

Pollock, Stephanie, and Shulman, Seth. "Toxic Responsibility." *The Atlantic* 263, No. 3 (March 1989): 26, 28, 30–1.
    Examines problems and dangers connected with cleanup programs at nuclear and toxic waste storage and disposal facilities owned by the U.S. military.

Raloff, Janet. "Helping Plastics Waste Away." *Science News* 135, No. 18 (6 May 1989): 282–83.
    Surveys research into the manufacture of biodegradable plastics.

———. "EPA's Strategic Revolution." *Science News* 138, No. 18 (3 November 1990): 283–84.
    Assesses the Environmental Protection Agency's "toxics initiative"—a program for controlling those toxic chemicals that most threaten human health and the environment—as well as several other aggressive programs aimed at early identification of potential environmental problems.

Rathje, William L., and Ritenbough, Cheryl K., eds. "Household Refuse Analysis: Theory, Method, and Applications in Social Sciences." *American Behavioral Scientist* 28, No. 1 (1984): 9–160.
    Includes nine scholarly articles exploring various aspects of household refuse analysis.

Rutala, William A.; Odette, Robert L.; and Samsa, Gregory P. "Management of Infectious Waste by US Hospitals." *JAMA* 262, No. 12 (22 September 1989): 1635–40.
    Presents the results of a survey of randomly selected hospitals' infectious waste disposal practices, concluding that most hospitals are generally consistent with Centers for Disease Control guidelines but many employ overly inclusive definitions of infectious waste.

Savage, George M.; Golueke, Clarence G.; and Sharpe, Henry. "Council Studies Contents of Municipal Solid Wastes." *World Wastes* 29, No. 12 (December 1986): 22, 24–5.
    Notes that an analysis of municipal garbage in Washington state found 1,500 hazardous nonregulated substances destined for landfills, and suggest that such sampling is helpful in monitoring quantities, types, concentration levels, and consequences of hazardous wastes entering a municipal waste stream.

Senior, Eric, ed. *Microbiology of Landfill Sites.* Boca Raton: CRC Press, 1990, 220 p.
    Technical analysis of the microbiology and biochemistry of refuse decomposition, essential components of effective landfill management.

Schendel, K., and Kresny, H. S. "The Institutional Process." *Radioactive Waste Management and the Nuclear Fuel Cycle* 14, Nos. 1-2 (1990): 155–68.
    Examines aspects of the "institutional process" of the U.S. Department of Energy's Waste Isolation Pilot Plant, including regulatory considerations, technical programs, and public perception.

Shupe, M. W., et. al. "Status of Activities: Low-Level Radioactive Waste Management." *Radioactive Waste Management and the Nuclear Fuel Cycle* 12, Nos. 1-4 (1989): 257–61.
Discusses low-level waste management activities and issues facing individual states and regions seeking to dispose of such waste.

Silver, E. G., ed. "Waste and Spent Fuel Management." *Nuclear Safety* 31, No. 3 (July-September 1990): 376–86.
Includes reports on administrative, regulatory, and technical activities related to the research, development, and implementation of facilities and technologies for handling radioactive wastes.

Steisel, Norman; Morris, Regina; and Clarke, Marjorie J. "The Impact of the Dioxin Issue on Resource Recovery in the United States." *Waste Management and Research* 5, No. 3 (September 1987): 381–94.
Discusses the issues concerning dioxin and furan emissions from resource recovery plants, including the toxicity of dioxin and furan and steps to reduce these emissions.

Suess, Michael J. *Solid Waste Management: Selected Topics.* Copenhagen: World Health Organization Regional Office for Europe, 1985, 210 p.
Urges international cooperation in addressing solid waste management problems.

Tauscher, Deborah M. "Municipal Waste Incineration: An Issue of Concern." *The Journal of Environmental Sciences* XXXII, No. 2 (March-April 1989): 18–20, 22–3, 25, 66–7.
Notes that public awareness, site location, air quality, and ash disposal are all factors that bear on the issue of municipal waste incineration.

Travis, Curtis C.; Hattemer-Frey, Holly A.; and Silbergeld, Ellen. "Dioxin, Dioxin Everywhere." *Evironmental Science and Technology* 23, No. 9 (1989): 1061–63.
Challenges the perception that dioxin emissions are primarily a problem of municipal solid waste incinerators, and calls for research into other known or suspected dioxin-emitting sources, including motor vehicles, steel and paper mills, hospitals, and sewage sludge incinerators.

Turque, Bill, and McCormick, John. "The Military's Toxic Legacy." *Newsweek* CXVI, No. 6 (6 August 1990): 20–3.
Outlines the enormous problems and costs associated with cleanup of the U.S. military's hazardous waste sites.

Whelan, Tensie, and Schwartz, Anne. "Demonstrating Solutions to the Solid-Waste Crisis." *Audubon* 92, No. 2 (March 1990): 142–43.
Discusses Audubon society member involvement in programs to reduce solid waste.

Wolfe, Douglas A., ed. "Plastics in the Sea: Selected Papers from the Sixth International Ocean Disposal Symposium." *Marine Pollution* 18, No. 6B (1987): 303–65.
Twelve papers selected from the Sixth International Ocean Disposal Symposium to provide a comprehensive overview of the problems related to plastic debris in the oceans and current research topics in the field.

18: Wetlands Preservation

Defining Wetlands: Private Property Owners Dispute Current EPA Regulations

In early August [1991], amidst outcries from professional environmentalists, the Bush Administration moved to lift some of the more onerous property restrictions imposed by its own Environmental Protection Agency. Earlier, on June 12, property rights won another victory. After hours of acrimonious debate, the Senate voted 55 to 44 to tack on a very powerful amendment to a highway funding bill. Called the Private Property Rights Act, the amendment seeks to restore some of the sanctity of private property that has eroded in recent years in the U.S.

If the amendment passes in the House of Representatives as well, it will require the government to be a little less cavalier with its environmental regulations. When the authorities issue rules that damage property values, they must at least consider treating the rules as a "taking" under the Constitution. If a taking there is, the property owner would be compensated—just as he would be if the government took his land outright.

The conflict between private property rights and governmental power goes back a long way—as evidenced by the attention that the founding fathers paid to it. The writers of the Constitution declared in the Fifth Amendment that "private property [shall not] be taken for public use without just compensation."

For the first century this limitation on governmental power was the law, it wasn't the subject of much debate. If the government needed land for a garrison or a prison, it might compel an owner to sell, but the owner got paid. The only issue was how much.

Then, beginning around the turn of the century, battles over land-use controls landed in court. A landowner might be prohibited from putting up a slaughterhouse where he wanted, lest the smells and noise and blood offend neighbors and lessen their property values. Was such a restriction a taking of private property? In most cases, the courts said no. Your right to go into the fat-rendering business or erect a 20-story apartment building clashes with my right to clean air or sunlight. And so a zoning law that decrees where factories or tall buildings can go doesn't amount to a confiscation of private property, even though it might make some property owners poorer. If there was an erosion of property rights, few people objected. The restrictions were sensible and hardly onerous.

So it went in the courts—zoning laws were almost always upheld. But governments can go only so far with their restrictions, and California crossed the line. In a 1987 Supreme Court case, Nollan v. California Coastal Zone Commission, the Court ruled that the state's attempt to condition a building permit on a property owner's granting of access to a public beach was a taking and required compensation. It was a turning point for a court system that had for a long time been much more protective of political liberties than of property

> The conflict between private property rights and governmental power goes back a long way—as evidenced by the attention that the founding fathers paid to it. The writers of the Constitution declared in the Fifth Amendment that "private property [shall not] be taken for public use without just compensation."

With wetlands rules and endangered species protection, the federal government is in the business of land-use control.

rights. The justices said, in effect: If California wants more public beaches, it should buy the land it needs, not just take it.

The ancient controversy has taken a dramatic new turn with the rise of environmentalism in recent years. With wetlands rules and endangered species protection, the federal government is in the business of land-use control. So the old question again arises: When does regulation amount to confiscation? If your waterfront parcel is ecologically precious, can the government simply declare it unbuildable? Or must it appropriate the money to buy you out? If the government wants to preserve a species of owl, can it tell an owner of timberland that he can't touch the trees he owns? Or must it buy him out?

The Senate bill requires federal agencies to assess the regulations a second time before regulating a property to the point of uselessness. There is nothing antienvironmental in the bill. It puts no limits on environmental protection measures. But it does impose a cost. It would simply require the government to compensate property owners for a significant loss they incur from environmental restrictions imposed upon their property.

Consider what happened in 1988 in Riverside County, Calif. The U.S. Fish & Wildlife Service declared the Stephen's kangaroo rat an endangered species. The result: Riverside County and local cities set aside 80,000 acres as wildlife preserves. Where the money would come from was not the Fish & Wildlife Service's problem. As then FWS Field Supervisor Nancy Kaufman told the *Washington Post*, "I'm not required by law to analyze the housing price aspect for the average Californian." If her enforcement helped deprive lower-income people of housing, that was no concern of hers. A local government agency financed the preserves with a fee of $1,950 imposed on every acre developed in the county. Up went the price of housing.

But under the new Private Property Rights Act, bureaucrats like Kaufman will have to consider the cost. The proposed law codifies an executive order issued in 1988 by President Reagan. This order required every federal agency to assess in advance the impact of any regulation or sanction on property values, to determine whether that impact constitutes a taking under law, and to seek to avoid such impacts. The potential for substantial monetary impact was borne out by a series of recent court decisions. In the U.S. Claims Court in 1990 and 1991, Judge Loren Smith awarded $64 million plus interest to property owners injured by such environmental sanctions.

The Senate bill has some professional environmentalists up in arms. If each of their efforts to protect "biodiversity" carries a price tag, the terms of the debate shift in ways they do not like. It will no longer be: Should we protect the spotted owl? It becomes: How much are we willing to spend to protect the spotted owl?

A setback for the environment? Not at all. If the Private Property Rights Act passes the House of Representatives, people will continue to look to the government to protect the environment. However, the bill will serve notice on the extreme environmentalists that Americans are not willing to give them a license to ignore property rights in the guise of protecting biodiversity.

When the final Senate vote was tallied, the environmental groups and their numerous representatives on the staffs of U.S. senators were lined up at the back of the Senate Chamber, visibly stunned at the suddenness and magnitude of their defeat. It was a complete reversal in just nine months of the defeat—by nine votes—of a similar provision.

It was a bitter pill for Senate Majority Leader George Mitchell (D-Me.), who wound up the debate with an impassioned cry that this bill, like Reagan's executive order, sought "to undermine regulatory protection by chilling agency action." But his motion to table the bill was shot down by 17 Democrats who teamed with 38 Republicans to hand environmental extremists the biggest legislative defeat in their history. The fact that 17 Democrats *did* vote for the Private Property Rights Act may demonstrate the rising political backlash against the extremes of the green lobby.

Ironically, this setback had its roots in what had looked like a major victory for the greens. In 1988 presidential candidate George Bush pledged "no net loss in wetlands." But on taking office, Bush faced the consequences of his statement. When the government enlarged the definition of "wetlands," Bush met angry protest from traditional Republican constituencies, farmers, businesses, real estate developers, landowners and local governments.

What caused the backlash was not the statement itself but an act of bureaucratic high-handedness apparently encouraged by Bush's pledge. This took the form of the 1989 *Federal Manual for Identifying and Delineating Jurisdictional Wetlands*, which extended federal jurisdiction over some 100 million additional acres of property, most of it privately owned. What outraged so many people was that most of the newly restricted land had only the remotest connection with water.

Why did the bureaucracy get so out of hand? When President Bush appointed William Reilly to head the Environmental Protection Agency, Bush confirmed the Washington adage that "personnel is policy." He had selected one of the most committed land-use planners in the environmental movement.

No question, there was and is a real need to arrest the long-term trend of draining and filling wetlands, marshes, bogs, swamps and lowlands for conversion to active farming and commercial and residential development. The EPA claims this has destroyed over half of all U.S. wetlands—or more than 100 million acres. But how to protect the wetlands? Reilly gave his answer long ago: As executive director of Laurance Rockefeller's Task Force on Land Use and Urban Growth, he helped write *The Use of Land: A Citizens' Policy Guide to Urban Growth*. It laid out many of the premises for using biological diversity as a rationale for limiting the two bêtes noires of environmentalism: single-family housing expansion and commercial agriculture. It noted that land use could be restricted at no cost to the government, through jurisdictional control.

Reilly's appointment as EPA administrator coincided with the early 1989 release of the new manual, which, in attempting to define "wetlands," extended the reach of the 1972 Clean Water Act. That manual asserted "jurisdiction" (requiring federal permits) well beyond traditional marshes and bogs. It extended it to cover *any* land with "hydric soils" or "hydrophytic vegetation." In plain English, that is land showing evidence of periodic saturation or containing plants, such as cattails, that are characteristic of wetlands. A third criterion defined as "wetland" land where there is even a hint of water down to 18 inches *below* the ground for seven consecutive days of the growing season. Under the August proposal, some of those criteria were softened. Most important, the length of time a wetland must be saturated would be increased to 21 consecutive days of the growing season.

One of the areas hardest hit by the 1989 rules was Maryland's Dorchester County. Previously some 275,000 acres of privately owned land in Maryland had been classified as wetland. With the 1989 manual, the figure topped 1 million acres. This meant that the government suddenly sanctioned 740,000 additional acres against filling or other disturbance, unless specifically permitted by the Army Corps of Engineers, with the EPA and FWS exercising virtual veto power. Under the new proposal, the amount of wetlands would still increase, but by less than the 740,000 acres. The 1989 manual, however, remains the law of the land. The revisions would be unlikely to go into effect before early 1992. The permitting process itself remains a bureaucratic swamp.

This outraged Margaret Ann Reigle, who had retired from her job as vice president of finance at New York's *Daily News*. With her husband, C. Charles Jowaiszas, a retired Columbia Pictures vice president, Peggy Reigle moved to Cambridge, in Dorchester County, to raise flowers and enjoy life. As a retirement investment the couple had bought a 138-acre abandoned farm that they

If the Private Property Rights Act passes the House of Representatives, people will continue to look to the government to protect the environment. However, the bill will serve notice on the extreme environmentalists that Americans are not willing to give them a license to ignore property rights in the guise of protecting biodiversity.

The fact that 17 Democrats *did* vote for the Private Property Rights Act may demonstrate the rising political backlash against the extremes of the green lobby.

planned to subdivide into 10-acre lots. Within months, however, Reigle was out of retirement and at war with the federal government.

Reigle's war started after she heard what the new definitions had done to an elderly neighbor. The neighbor had been informed that under the new rules, her property was classified as nontidal wetlands and therefore could not be developed. The neighbor had been counting on proceeds from land sales to build a new home.

In May 1990 Peggy Reigle wrote an angry letter to President Bush (one of thousands like it received by the White House). When local papers reprinted the letter, Reigle was besieged by calls from others like her, outraged by the new policy. She formed the Fairness to Land Owners Committee; in two weeks it signed up some 2,000 citizens and now boasts a membership of over 6,000 Marylanders and 2,500 from other states. Its credo: "We will not accept the government's taking our land without just compensation." The grass-roots backlash against federal wetlands imperialism was under way. And soon Congress was paying heed.

In January and February Representative John LaFalce (D–N.Y.), chairman of the House Small Business Committee, held hearings. Builders, realtors, national and local officials and developers shared stories about the quagmire of wetlands regulations. The town supervisor of Wheatfield, in Niagara County, N.Y., told LaFalce that if the Corps issued permits based on the 1989 manual, "areas like Niagara County will be deprived of approximately 65% of the remaining developmental property." David Brody, attorney for the Niagara Frontier Builders Association, said the manual's implementation, along with other problems, would result in "a 35% reduction in new home starts in Niagara and Erie counties in 1991." After the hearings LaFalce sent President Bush a letter "to alert [him] to the regulatory travesty currently masquerading as federal wetlands policy."

In Hampton, Va., meanwhile, Thomas Nelson Community College had made a routine request for a Corps check of a proposed 40-acre site for its new sports complex. The result was a finding of "hydric soils" and "wetlands" at the college. Similar findings could, in a cascade of regulatory mayhem, threaten the 38-acre Nelson Farms subdivision, the 800-home, 133-acre Michael's Woods subdivision, the 300-acre Hampton Roads Center office park, and a 600-home Hampton Woods subdivision. As Hampton Mayor James Eason told the local *Daily Press*, "It's very scary. It's conceivable it could halt all development in the city of Hampton."

This quagmire trapped even some of the most obvious candidates for permits, such as Richard Adamski. This retired state trooper from Baltimore had invested $16,500 in a building lot in the midst of a developed residential area in a hamlet in Dorchester County only to be told the 0.7-acre lot was "nontidal wetlands." Although he wanted to fill only an eighth of an acre to build a retirement home, the U.S. Fish & Wildlife Service recommended denial of his application.

Eventually the Corps did issue a permit to fill the sliver of land, but only if "the permittee shall mitigate at a 2:1 ratio for wetlands losses by constructing 0.25 acres of wooded nontidal wetlands." In other words, Adamski had to find someone willing to sell him a permanent "easement" on twice as much land. No takers yet; Adamski remains in limbo. Yet when I walked through the wettest of these mostly wooded "wetlands" last April (the wettest season), my dress shoes emerged pristinely unmuddied.

As the outrage over his high-handed policies mounted, Reilly had to beat a strategic retreat. On Mar. 7 he admitted to the prestigious American Farmland Trust: "We suddenly found ourselves in the center of a maelstrom. Everywhere I traveled I heard a local wetlands horror story—not just from farmers, but from developers and respected political leaders." He suggested that the entire process had gotten out of hand.

But tell that to William Ellen, a successful and respected Virginia marine engineer who is now appealing a prison term and a large fine for having "filled" more than 15 acres of Eastern Shore "nontidal wetlands" when he bulldozed these seemingly dry and forested acres to create large nesting ponds for ducks and geese as well as a management complex.

Ellen was working on a project for Paul Tudor Jones II, the high-flying futures trader who in August 1987 had bought 3,200 acres in Dorchester County, very close to the Blackwater Wildlife Refuge. Jones' idea was to create a combination hunting and conservation preserve as well as a showplace estate. The centerpiece of the project is a 103-acre wildlife sanctuary developed with the assistance of the Maryland Department of Natural Resources. This sanctuary includes ponds, shrub swamps, food plants and grassland plots all designed to attract geese, ducks and other migrating waterfowl.

In May 1990 Jones suddenly pleaded guilty to one misdemeanor related to negligent filling of wetlands, agreeing to pay $1 million to the National Fish & Wildlife Foundation to help the Blackwater Refuge, plus a $1 million fine. The plea allowed Jones to avoid a costly and debilitating trial, and possibly even a jail term and the loss of his trading license. However, no such deal was afforded Bill Ellen, himself a well-known conservationist who, with his wife, runs a rescue/rehab mission for injured wildlife and waterfowl.

How could Ellen be prosecuted for converting land that was so dry water-spraying had to be used as a dust suppressant during bulldozing into large nesting ponds for waterfowl? That question disturbed trial judge Frederic Smalkin at the U.S. District Court in Baltimore, and the answer he got was bizarre.

Prosecution witness Charles Rhodes, one of the EPA's top scientists on wetlands, said that even though the forested "wetlands" had been replaced by new ponds, the ecology was supposedly worse off.

Why? The problem was bird shit. "The sanctuary pond is designed to have a large concentration of waterfowl, and before the restoration plan was implemented, all that fecal material [from the ducks and geese] was geared to be discharged right into the wetlands, whereas now it is actually designed to go through like a treatment system through the wetlands. So that would have been a negative impact, a water quality impact." In other words, the bird droppings, instead of staying in one place, would be spread over a wider area.

To which Judge Smalkin responded incredulously: "Are you saying that there is pollution from ducks, from having waterfowl on a pond, that that pollutes the water?" Incredibly, a jury convicted Ellen on five counts of filling wetlands. But U.S. Attorney Breckinridge Willcox said Ellen's conviction sends "a clear message that environmental criminals will, in fact, go to jail." The prosecution asked the court for a prison term of 27 to 33 months, but Judge Smalkin sentenced Bill Ellen to six months in jail and four months of home detention.

These examples of federal wetlands policy as practiced in the early years of the Bush Administration are a case of a bureaucracy run amok. In fact, there is little law today that provides due-process federal jurisdiction over wetlands. There is only the Food Security Act of 1985, which asserts jurisdiction over those farmlands under federal subsidy programs. But farmers may remove that jurisdiction by taking their land out of the programs.

Otherwise, the wetlands program is very largely a contrivance of federal bureaucrats, sometimes working with friendly courts to expand Section 404 of the Clean Water Act. Yet this act makes no mention of "wetlands" and is designed to regulate only direct dumping into and pollution of the nation's "navigable waters," rivers, harbors, canals, etc.

In a 1975 decision (Natural Resources Defense Council v. Callaway), a Washington, D.C. district judge ruled that federal jurisdiction applied beyond navigable waters to any wetlands that might remotely feed into such rivers and

Previously some 275,000 acres of privately owned land in Maryland had been classified as wetland. With the 1989 *Federal Manual for Identifying and Delineating Jurisdictional Wetlands*, the figure topped 1 million acres. This meant that the government suddenly sanctioned 740,000 additional acres against filling or other disturbance, unless specifically permitted by the Army Corps of Engineers, with the EPA and FWS exercising virtual veto power.

"While the jury was deliberating, they kept sending out to the judge for copies of the 'wetlands law.' When the judge sent them federal regulations, they sent back and asked for the law. When the judge sent them the Clean Water Act, and said this was all the law he had to give them, they [the jury] decided the government had no case because it had no jurisdiction."

—John Arans, American Agriculture Movement defense lawyer

harbors. But even that did not cover "isolated wetlands" with no connection to "navigable waters"—like the puddles in your backyard after a heavy rain. Nevertheless, since 1975, jurisdiction has been expanded entirely by fiat and court interpretation to cover that definition in the EPA manual—water 18 inches down.

The fig leaf for this judicial and executive imperialism is Article 1, Section 8, paragraph 3, of the Constitution, which gives Congress the right "to regulate commerce . . . among the several states." To assert this power on isolated and local wetlands, the EPA and the Army Corps of Engineers engaged in such creative flights of fancy as declaring ducks and geese "interstate waterfowl." This led to what some call the "glancing goose test," which determines that an area is a wetland if an interstate goose pauses to consider it.

In a brutal display of naked power, the EPA and the Department of the Army plunged ahead in December in their "Wetlands Enforcement Initiative," designed to bring 24 high-visibility defendants like Paul Tudor Jones to justice. The Dec. 12, 1990 memorandum asked all regional administrators to produce a "cluster" of new cases to be announced in an April "first 'wave' of publicity . . . to provide an early deterrent to potential violations which might otherwise occur during the 1991 spring and summer construction season."

But on Apr. 19 a high-visibility case blew up in the government's face. James Allen and Mary Ann Moseley, Missouri farmers, had built a perimeter levee to keep their Mississippi Basin farm from flooding. The government declared the area to be wetlands of the United States, sued the Moseleys for violations of the Clean Water Act and sought fines of $25,000 a day for as long as the violation was in effect.

But the Moseleys are members of the American Agriculture Movement, a progressive farm organization that has joined the mainstream farm groups in opposing the extension of the definition of "wetlands" and supporting the Private Property Rights Act. AAM's Fayetteville, Ark. lawyer, John Arens, has a record of beating the government in court—and he did it again.

When Arens was not allowed to bring in his own "expert witnesses," he minced up the government "experts" by demonstrating the capricious nature of the so-called wetlands law. He asked one EPA expert if it were not true that, were he to play baseball on a diamond built on hydric soils and went into the batter's box and scuffed his cleats, and then knocked the resulting dirt off them, back onto the field, he would be in technical violation of the Clean Water Act?

"When he [the so-called expert] was forced to answer yes, I looked at the jury and I knew we were on our way!" Arens said. "But what really convinced the jury the government had no case was when it discovered that the government prosecutors had no law!"

"While the jury was deliberating, they kept sending out to the judge for copies of the 'wetlands law.' When the judge sent them federal regulations, they sent back and asked for the law. When the judge sent them the Clean Water Act, and said this was all the law he had to give them, they [the jury] decided the government had no case because it had no jurisdiction."

More setbacks awaited the power-grabbing bureaucrats. In January 1989 then Assistant U.S. Attorney General Stephen Markman had a memorandum prepared on a big wetlands case the Justice Department was prosecuting. The memorandum demonstrated, with dozens of citations, the flimsiness of the government's wetlands policies, concluding: "The Corps and the EPA appear to have circumvented the Constitution's requirements . . . and the federal district and circuit courts have not corrected them." The courts have apparently been paying attention.

And so the battle has been joined. On the one hand are the wildlife-at-any-price people. On the other, people who think that environmental policy ought not override property rights.

The environmental extremists have made their intentions clear. In 1975 poet Gary Snyder won the Pulitzer Prize for his radical call for an "ultimate democracy [in which] plants and animals are also people." He wrote that they should "be given a place and a voice in the political discussions of the humans. . . . What we must find a way to do . . . is incorporate the other people . . . into the councils of government."

A few years later, in 1980, a leading ecologist, Joseph Petulla, said, "The Marine Mammal Protection Act [and] the Endangered Species Act [embody] the legal idea that a listed nonhuman resident of the U.S. is guaranteed, in a special sense, life and liberty."

Of course, the Constitution says nothing about the rights of trees, snakes, owls and fish. Which may be why, back in 1973, Reilly's task force essentially called for the repeal of the takings clause of the Fifth Amendment: "Many [judicial] precedents are anachronistic now that land is coming to be regarded as a basic natural resource to be protected and conserved. . . . It is time that the U.S. Supreme Court re-examine its precedents that seem to require a balancing of public benefit against land value loss . . . and declare that, when the protection of natural, cultural or aesthetic resources or the assurance of orderly development are involved, a *mere loss in land value is no justification for invalidating the regulation of land use* [italics added]."

"A mere loss in land value . . . " In that "mere" resides a philosophy that questions the values of private property and individual freedom. But after years of having things pretty much their own way, people who think like Reilly are getting a real fight.

Idaho Republican Steve Symms, who leads the fight in the Senate for the protection of property rights, says: "We should adopt a policy of no net loss of private property." Since the federal government already owns some 40% of U.S. land, Symms argues that it ought to be willing to swap some of its 730 million acres in order to obtain privately owned land that is environmentally sensitive. If, say, the National Park Service wants 50,000 acres to provide more protection for Shenandoah National Park, it can ask the Forest Service or Bureau of Land Management to sell to private citizens a like amount to finance the acquisition. Such a policy of no net gain in federal lands was introduced this summer in the House in legislation drafted by Representative Bill Brewster, Democrat from Oklahoma.

Do we really want the federal government owning even more of the country, whether through outright purchase or through limitations on land use? Free-market environmentalists like R. J. Smith of the Cato Institute argue that more government ownership and control would actually harm the environment. He says: "Ecological devastation . . . invariably accompanies too much government ownership of land. You don't have to look just to Eastern Europe for confirmation. You need only examine the condition of most of the Bureau of Land Management inventory of properties, or remember what the Park Service allowed to happen at Yellowstone."

But the zealots won't give up. On Oct. 1 the EPA's regional office in Chicago awarded a grant of $50,000 over three years to the Sierra Club's local "Swamp Squad," which amounts to an unofficial policing of the environment. These vigilantes spy on developers and other land and property owners to report potential wetland violations. The EPA press release quoted Dale Bryson, the regional director of its water division: "This grant will allow them to continue their valuable work in a more vigorous way."

The Senate has served notice that it thinks some of this "valuable work" has already gone too far. By all the evidence, many of the American people would agree. (pp. 104–12)

Warren Brooks, "The Strange Case of the Glancing Geese," in Forbes, *Vol. 148, No. 5, September 2, 1991, pp. 104–12.*

"Ecological devastation . . . invariably accompanies too much government ownership of land. You don't have to look just to Eastern Europe for confirmation. You need only examine the condition of most of the Bureau of Land Management inventory of properties, or remember what the Park Service allowed to happen at Yellowstone."

—R. J. Smith,
Cato Institute

The War over the Wetlands

The shallow depressions that dot the farm fields of North Dakota would hardly fit most peoples' definition of wetlands. The smallest of these glacier-carved features, known as prairie potholes, are under water for only a few weeks in the spring. During periods of low rainfall, they are almost indistinguishable from any other acreage. But when the frozen ground warms in early spring, the depressions swarm with crustaceans and insects that provide migrating waterfowl with essential protein. The smaller potholes also enable breeding pairs of birds to find the privacy they covet.

Yet seasonal wetlands like the prairie potholes and seemingly dry areas like the edges of lakes and rivers and swamps that are actually waterlogged below ground level are also potential moneymakers for farmers, land developers and oil and gas drillers. Because of pressure from such groups, the Bush Administration has a new policy that endangers these fragile lands. Though the President has not technically violated his 1988 campaign pledge of "No net loss of wetlands," the official definition of a wetland is being narrowed. As much as a third of the 38.4 million hectares (95 million acres) of wetlands in the lower 48 states will be considered wetlands no more and thus will be vulnerable to development. Says Jay Hair, president of the National Wildlife Federation: "The new policy represents a death sentence for much of this critical American resource."

The government action clearly reflects the commonsense—and incorrect—notion that wetlands have to be wet. While swamps and marshes are more important, the dryer wetlands have their unique role in the environment. They are natural flood controls, and they also act as filtration systems for water passing through them. Some wetland plants absorb toxic pollutants like heavy metals.

If the Administration is fuzzy about what constitutes a wetland, that is understandable. Before 1989, there was no official definition, and the four agencies that had jurisdiction over wetland development—the Fish and Wildlife Service, the Army Corps of Engineers, the Environmental Protection Agency and the Department of Agriculture—often disagreed. Says the NWF's Douglas Inkley: "Sometimes the Corps would say one thing to a farmer, and a week later the EPA would come out and say something different."

The confusion was so great that the agencies finally got together in 1989 and wrote a manual, spelling out for the first time what a wetland is: any depression where water accumulates for seven consecutive days during the growing season, where certain water-loving plants are found and where the soil is saturated enough with water that anaerobic bacterial activity can take place. Development in such areas was forbidden without a special exemption. And anyone wanting an exemption from the rules had to prove that there was no practical alternative to wetlands destruction.

Now the Administration has proposed a new manual that relaxes the rules. It designates as wetlands areas having 15 consecutive days of inundation during a growing season or 21 days in which the soil is saturated with water up to the surface. Moreover it redefines the growing season to be shorter and reduces the variety of plants that qualify an area as a wetland. The provision requiring proof of no viable alternative to filling in a wetland will apply only to "highly valuable" areas—the top rung on a new classification ladder to be worked out over the next year by a federal panel.

Perhaps the most controversial change is the decision to permit more extensive "mitigation banking," which requires landowners to restore lost wetlands or create new ones in exchange for destroying an existing site. Critics charge that there is no scientific body of evidence to prove that man-made wetlands are a substitute for the real thing.

Still, the outcome could have been worse. EPA chief William Reilly, who was in charge of rewriting the manual, tried to ease the existing guidelines as little as possible. But he had to win the approval of probusiness presidential advisers. The resulting compromise may not please environmentalists, but it may derail a bill moving through Congress that would have been even more damaging to wetlands.

The manual will not become official until after a 60-day period of public comment and a subsequent EPA review, and environmental groups are gearing up to comment loudly. So are those who want to profit from the wetlands. Says Mark Maslyn of the American Farm Bureau Federation: "The new rules bring some common sense back to wetlands policy." But common sense may not be the best guide in a debate that hinges on scientific questions. As with so many other resources, America's marginal wetlands may not be fully appreciated until they are gone.

Michael D. Lemonick, "War Over the Wetlands," in Time, *New York, Vol. 138, No. 8, August 26, 1991, p. 53.*

The government action clearly reflects the commonsense—and incorrect—notion that wetlands have to be wet. While swamps and marshes are more important, the dryer wetlands have their unique role in the environment. They are natural flood controls, and they also act as filtration systems for water passing through them. Some wetlands absorb toxic pollutants like heavy metals.

Vast, Yet Vulnerable: Alaska's Wetlands

For decades, Jim King had a duck's-eye view of America's soggiest state. A pilot-biologist with the U.S. Fish and Wildlife Service until 1983, he spent several weeks each spring slicing through the airspace above Alaskan wetlands.

Working with an observer, King stitched a path over treeless tundra and boreal forest, across river valleys and coastal deltas, counting every duck visible from a height of 100 feet. Across other parts of North America, similar teams took to the air, conducting the annual breeding bird survey used to set bag limits for fall waterfowl hunting seasons. King's survey area—about 80,000 square miles—kept him aloft for hours daily. With forest fires, flooding rivers and fluctuating waterfowl populations, "I never got bored," he says. "It was a marvelous job to be able to fly over all these great wetlands."

His 100-mph census took him over some of the most productive wildlife habitat in the Northern Hemisphere. Places like the Copper River Delta, where the world's entire population of dusky Canada geese nests and tens of millions of western sandpipers, dunlins, and other shorebirds stop every spring to refuel on their northward migration. And waterfowl factories such as the Yukon Flats, where the meandering Yukon River has created tens of thousands of lakes and ponds yielding, in King's words, "a fall flight of two million ducks." Even so, he says, "These are the kind of places the oil companies think we've got too much of."

Oil companies and other Alaska development interests seldom put it that baldly. What they do say is that the state's wetlands have become a threatening quagmire for those who would help Alaska fulfill its economic destiny. Those development boosters, along with many of the state's politicians, are questioning whether rules intended to protect U.S. wetlands—specifically, President Bush's controversial "no net loss" policy—should apply to Alaska. With wetlands covering so much of the state, they argue, such restrictions would leave little room for growth. "If we have to restore an acre for every acre we build on," huffed a recent editorial in *The Fairbanks Daily News-Miner,* "we'll have to go to the Lower 48 to find land to restore."

Alaska is more often celebrated for its mountains and snow than for its marshes and mudflats. Yet our biggest state is also our wettest, with approximately 233 million acres of wetlands. Some 70 percent of all U.S. wetlands are found in Alaska.

[Early in 1990], the Administration drew fire from environmentalists when it signed a watered-down version of a wetlands agreement, which would have been an important first step toward the President's no-net-loss goal. A loophole in the revised document allows developers to sidestep the requirement that they restore or create new wetlands if their projects cause supposed minimal environmental damage. "If this is any sign of what it will take to get a no-net-loss policy out of this Administration," says National Wildlife Federation attorney Jan Goldman-Carter, "then we cannot expect much leadership on this issue."

Alaska is more often celebrated for its mountains and snow than for its marshes and mudflats. Yet our biggest state is also our wettest, with approximately 233 million acres of wetlands. Some 70 percent of all U.S. wetlands are found in Alaska, where muskegs, alder swamps, river deltas, coastal lagoons and tundra support everything from salmon to grizzly bears. Most of all, the state's wetlands are prime habitat for waterfowl and shorebirds.

Alaska sits at the top of bird migration routes that stretch from tundra to tropics. The seasonal traffic in feathered fliers is intense. Jim King recalls that the ducks he banded on the Yukon Flats "showed up all over the place." His canvasbacks were brought down by sportsmen on New York's Finger Lakes and the Chesapeake Bay. His lesser scaup turned up in Mississippi and Louisiana. "We even got bands from the Dominican Republic and Haiti," he says. Fully 11 percent of all ducks harvested in North America summer in Alaska, as do 17 percent of all geese.

But some of Alaska's duck and goose producing wetlands overlie oil fields or surround towns and villages. Development interests worry that protection of wetlands will stymie economic growth. At its heart, the battle over use of such areas involves differing visions of wealth. To conservationists like King, oil industry claims that Alaska has a surplus of wetlands are "like saying that we've got more good health than we need."

Alaska's politicians fired the first round in the wetlands war last fall. In a letter to President Bush, they asked the Administration to delay its heralded "no net loss" policy. During his election campaign, Bush pledged to make wetland protection a priority. Shortly after taking office, he declared—at a Ducks Unlimited symposium—that "no net loss of wetlands" must be a national goal.

But for many of Alaska's economic boosters, such a goal was unfair—a case of penalizing their state for sins committed in the rest of the country. Responding to the landmark agreement between the Environmental Protection Agency and the U.S. Army Corps of Engineers that formally acknowledged the nation's new wetland policy, Alaska Governor Steve Cowper warned of "a grave threat to future oil and gas development."

The *Anchorage Times* warned that "vast regions of this state for all practical purposes would be closed to any kind of development whatsoever." Meanwhile, Alaska's Resource Development Council, a pro-development organization, suggested that Alaska should be exempt from "no net loss" laws until the state had used 5 to 20 percent of its wetlands—a proposal that in effect would grant developers the license to destroy an area of wildlife habitat potentially larger than Georgia.

For many conservationists, the heavy hand of the oil industry was evident behind the anti-wetland protection campaign. As part of their lease agreements for North Slope oil fields, oil companies are required to restore lands that have been filled with gravel for construction of roads, buildings and drill sites. Exemption from that requirement could save the companies perhaps billions of dollars.

"The Alaska oil industry has organized a sort of preemptive strike to get Alaska wetlands excluded from the provisions of the president's no-net-loss policy," says Ann Rothe, a regional representative in the National Wildlife Federation's Alaska Natural Resources Center in Anchorage.

Two oil companies, ARCO and British Petroleum, the major leaseholders on the North Slope, recently funded a report maintaining that Arctic wetlands are understocked with wildlife (or, as the report reads, "North Slope wildlife populations are below the carrying capacities of their habitats"). The report also holds that major losses of tundra ("far beyond any currently foreseeable consequence of petroleum development") would be required to affect bird populations on the oil fields. Thus, according to the report's author, oil-industry consultant Robert Senner, measures to repair wetland damage now "probably wouldn't make any difference at all biologically."

Such conclusions are strenuously opposed by biologists not on the oil industry payroll. In most cases, northern wetlands are believed to be fully stocked with wildlife, even if they host fewer animals than wetlands farther to the south. "It takes more land to support an animal in the north," says Tom Rothe, a biologist for Alaska's Department of Fish and Game.

One observation in the Senner report, which its author says was based on available scientific literature about Arctic wetlands, is that "bird use" of North Slope wetlands "is not greatly affected by the long-term presence of a major oil field." Senner's study, however, failed to cite research conducted by U.S. Fish and Wildlife Service biologist Rosa Meehan.

Meehan's 1986 study on the impact of oilfield development on shorebirds in the Prudhoe Bay area blamed habitat loss (plus "fragmentation" of tundra by roads and other oil facilities) for causing an estimated "18 percent reduction" of six common shorebird species "within the perimeter of the oil field." Meehan's conclusion: overall habitat value of wetlands in oil fields is diminished, even in areas not directly affected by drilling. Responds Senner: "I'm very familiar with her work, and I realize now I probably should have included that stuff in here."

Opponents of protecting Alaska wetlands frequently argue that the state's tundra scarcely behaves like a wetland. Underlain by frozen subsoils, tundra on the North Slope and other parts of the state fails to provide some normal wetland functions, such as replenishing groundwater or controlling floods. The tundra is also surprisingly arid for a wetland, getting only about 8 to 10 inches of rain or snow per year—about as much as some deserts receive in more southerly regions.

But because the tundra's basement never thaws, when spring rolls around the winter precipitation melts with nowhere to sink in, and the tundra becomes soggy. Frozen nine months of the year, the seemingly barren landscape suddenly changes character. "We have 24 hour daylight above the Arctic Circle," says Tom Rothe. "When June hits, things go crazy."

The summer tundra's proliferating plant life pulls in waterfowl and shorebirds by the millions. The North Slope alone hosts an estimated half-million breeding ducks, geese and swans. As many as one million king eider ducks migrate past Point Barrow along Alaska's northern coast, as do countless other birds.

Such Alaskan wetlands function as a "refugium," says Craig Altop, a biologist in the Alaska office of the federal Bureau of Land Management. When pintails, for example, are forced out of Canada's Prairie Provinces and similar areas in the Lower 48 states by farming or drought, "they blow on up to Alaska," says Altop. Over the past few summers, North Slope tundra has sheltered from 300,000 to 400,000 pintails—10 percent of the North American population. Says biologist Rothe, "It serves as a bit of a sanctuary when times are bad."

Times are bad indeed for waterfowl in much of North America. More than a dozen duck species have declined within the past decade alone, mostly from loss of wetland habitat. All the world's cackling Canada geese nest in the pristine, 250,000-square-mile Yukon-Kuskokwim Delta of western Alaska. But those birds (along with Ross' goose and the Aleutian Canada goose) winter only in California's Central Valley, where the 4 million acres of wetlands that greeted early settlers have diminished 96 percent.

Development interests worry that protection of wetlands will stymie [Alaska's] economic growth.

Alaska's Resource Development Council, a pro-development organization, suggested that Alaska should be exempt from "no net loss" laws until the state had used 5 to 20 percent of its wetlands—a proposal that in effect would grant developers the license to destroy an area of wildlife habitat potentially larger than Georgia.

Although Alaska is a long way from the condition of California, conservationists have focused special attention on several of the state's wetlands. Ducks Unlimited, for example, helped the state create ponds for ducks and nesting structures for dusky Canada geese at the Copper River Delta.

Most of Alaska's wetlands are visited by far more birds than people. One exception is the Business Park Wetland in midtown Anchorage, a wee patch of bog amid the streets and buildings that lures a steady stream of picnickers, joggers and city tour buses. Home to 20 pairs of Canada geese and several other bird species, the urban wetland is undeniably productive habitat. Its greater value, though, is symbolic, as a reminder of both the possibilities and limits of life in the Far North.

Alaska's largest city, Anchorage has lost more than half its wetlands. For some time now, a small coalition of citizens has labored to preserve the Business Park bog, which its owner has wanted to develop. Now an agreement has been reached that will allow about 10 acres to be saved—a victory that comes with "a certain bitter-sweetness," says Marideth Sandler, head of the coalition. After all, she notes, it was a 20- or 30-acre wetland when her group began its work.

Campaigning for an urban wetland may seem silly in a state blessed with places like the Copper River Delta. "But most people can't get to the rest of the state," says Sandler. "There aren't roads to the rich waterfowl breeding areas."

Anchorage, goes a local saying, is 15 minutes away from Alaska. As the city grows, saving a smidgeon of the great outdoors becomes all the more meaningful. "It isn't beautiful," Sandler says of the city's wetland. "If you take your eyes off the waterfowl and look up, you see ugly condominiums. But when you get down there, it's really special. It helps people remember why they moved to Alaska." Maybe that remembering will help Alaskans protect the magnificent but still vulnerable wetlands they seldom see. (pp. 18–22)

Michael Lipske, "How Much is Enough?" in National Wildlife, *Vol. 28, No. 4, June–July, 1990, pp. 18–22.*

Wetlands: The Lifeblood of Wildlife

Introduction

This [essay] provides a general overview of the types of wildlife that wetlands—both naturally occurring as well as constructed or man-made—can attract rather than an exhaustive treatment of the subject. Although the literature on wildlife associated with naturally occurring wetlands is considerable, little information is available for wildlife associated with constructed wetlands and even less for wetlands constructed for wastewater treatment.

It includes an introduction to the importance of wetland ecosystems as wildlife habitat, an overview of the types of wildlife associated with naturally occurring wetlands in the United States, and design considerations, issues, and research needs concerning wildlife utilization of constructed wetlands for wastewater treatment. It also examines how constructed wetlands might augment the nation's diminished wetlands inventory and provide additional habitat for wildlife.

Wetlands as Wildlife Habitat

Two points bear mentioning before introducing this section. First, as used in this chapter, the term *wildlife* refers to invertebrate animals as well as vertebrate animals. Wildlife biologists oftentimes exclude "lower" life forms such as mollusks and arthropods from working definitions of wildlife, instead focusing narrowly on "high profile" species such as waterfowl and large carnivores. Although this distinction may at times be useful, because invertebrate animals provide critical links in most wetland food chains, it is essential they be included in any discussion of wetlands wildlife.

Second, wetlands created where none previously existed should be described as "constructed" rather than "artificial." Man-made wetlands—regardless of whether they provide one function or a dozen—are, indeed, real wetlands and not artificial.

Wetlands are described as providing both value and function. Importantly, these terms are not synonymous. *Function* refers to what a wetland does, regardless of interpretation of its worth. For example, a wetland may function by storing 25,000 m^3 of flood water, producing 100 mallard ducks/ha, or retaining 15 tons/ha/yr of sediment. Wetland value, on the other hand, is an interpretation of relative worth of a wetland function and can be high or low. For example, flood storage capacity of a wetland upstream from a town has high value to the town residents, yet the same wetland downstream might have low value to town residents because it affords them no flood protection. Although 15 or more functions have been described for wetlands, those most frequently cited include water quality, flood conveyance, sediment control, barriers to waves and erosion, open space and aesthetic values, and wildlife habitat.

Wildlife habitat, in simplest terms, is the combination of food, water, and cover needed by a species to survive and reproduce. Odum describes habitat as the place in which an organism lives or where one would go to find it, and Weller defines it as the place where an organism finds food, shelter, protection from enemies, and resources for reproduction [E. P. Odum, in his *Fundamentals of Ecology,* 1971 and M. W. Weller, in "Wetland Habitats," in *Wetland Functions and Values: The State of Our Understanding,* edited by P. E. Greeson, J. R. Clark, and J. E. Clark, 1979]. I like to describe wildlife habitat as simply its kitchen, dining room, and bedroom—the requisites for life itself.

Wetlands are among the most vulnerable and most threatened habitats of all our natural heritage. Of the 87 million ha of wetlands existing in the United States when the colonists arrived, less than half, or approximately 44 million ha remain. Wholesale destruction of this natural resource is the result of generations of contempt and ambivalence toward wetlands, due in part to lack of appreciation and understanding of the important ecological and economic benefits they provide. Wetlands were believed wastelands, an impediment to progress, and something better drained, ditched, filled, and developed. Although misguided attitudes toward wetlands have changed somewhat, we continue to lose an estimated 150,000 to 225,000 ha of wetlands each year.

Wetlands represent a very small fraction of our total land area, but they harbor an unusually large percentage of our nation's wildlife. For example, 900 species of wildlife in the United States require wetland habitats at some stage in their life cycle, with an even greater number using wetlands periodically. Representatives from almost all avian groups use wetlands to some extent and one-third of North American bird species rely directly on wetlands for some resource.

Stability is neither common nor desirable in wetland systems. Unlike upland habitats, wetlands are dynamic, transitional, and dependent on natural perturbations. The most visible and significant perturbation is periodic inundation and drying. Changing water depths, either daily, seasonal, or annual, have an overbearing influence on plant species composition, structure, and distribution. Other influences, such as complex zones of water regimes, salt and temperature gradients, and tide and wave action produce wetlands vegetation that is generally stratified, much like forests. These factors combine to create a diversity and wealth of niches that make wetlands important wildlife habitat.

Although 15 or more functions have been described for wetlands, those most frequently cited include water quality, flood conveyance, sediment control, barriers to waves and erosion, open space and aesthetic values, and wildlife habitat.

Wetlands are among the most vulnerable and most threatened habitats of all our natural heritage. Of the 87 million hectares of wetlands existing in the United States when the colonists arrived, less than half, or approximately 44 million ha remain.

Constantly varying environmental conditions of wetlands compel plants to adapt to stress and tolerate ever-changing biophysical conditions to establish, live, and reproduce. Like wetlands plants, animals inhabiting wetlands have evolved adaptations for surviving in these dynamic habitats. One common strategy—exemplified by birds—is mobility that allows daily, seasonal, and annual movement. Another common strategy is to use wetlands for only a part of a life cycle, as do most reptiles and many amphibians. Many wildlife species totally dependent on wetlands have developed mechanisms, such as dormancy, to survive periods of low water or times of no water at all. Several species of upland wildlife—primarily mammals and birds—also use wetland habitats extensively.

Wetlands Wildlife

The following is a brief overview of wildlife types occurring in wetlands. Because the literature is voluminous, this section is a general introduction and not a comprehensive or exhaustive treatment of the topic. Moreover, the information derives from research on natural or restored wetlands rather than from constructed systems. Nonetheless, because natural and constructed wetland habitats have similarities, cautious extension of these data to constructed systems is justified. For organizational purposes, this review is arranged by taxonomic group, beginning with invertebrates and concluding with mammals.

Invertebrates

Invertebrates are critical to energy dynamics and functions of wetlands and the foundation of wetland food chains. Some of the least conspicuous forms have important roles in converting plant energy into animal food chains. Despite this, invertebrates have been largely ignored, and far too little is known, especially regarding invertebrate habitat selection and niche segregation. All freshwater wetlands contain protozoans and 25 species of sponges occur in freshwater wetlands of the United States. Several rare and unique groups of freshwater jellyfish and sponges have been documented, but the more abundant, ubiquitous invertebrates provide the principal source of food that fuels wetland food chains.

Most wetlands macroinvertebrates fall into four groups: annelid worms, mollusks, arthropods, and insects. Annelid worms are most frequently represented by the oligochaetes, which burrow into substrates or adhere to submersed aquatic vegetation. Densities of these worms can be very low—as in acidic bog lakes—or extremely high, as in California fens with 30,000 worms/m^2. Although we now recognize annelids, flatworms, leeches, earthworms, nematodes, and other worms as vital to wetlands food webs, far too little is known about the natural history and role of these animals.

The second category, mollusks, are a dominant group of animals found in wet meadows as well as in deepwater habitats. Mollusks include several genera of snails—both aquatic and terrestrial—clams, and mussels. Mollusks are primarily benthic or associated with aquatic vegetation and may have densities up to 40,000/m^2 (fingernail clams). Mollusks are usually abundant and important food items for many vertebrate species, including ducks, fish, mink, otter, muskrat, raccoons, turtles, and salamanders.

Wetlands are favored habitats for diverse, abundant and oftentimes large arthropods, which are important foods of frogs, fish, toads, turtles, birds, and mammals. Most common are crustaceans—exemplified by crayfish and freshwater shrimp—the most abundant and widespread of all wetland invertebrates. Crayfish are particularly important food items for mink, raccoons, and predaceous fish.

Finally, 11 orders of insects are aquatic or semiaquatic, including such familiar examples as stoneflies, damselflies, dragonflies, mayflies, midges, mosquitoes, aquatic beetles, water striders, and springtails. As with most invertebrates, the larval stage—largely unnoticed by humans—provides the most important conduit of energy in wetlands systems. Insect aquatic larvae commonly occur on edges and surfaces of freshwater wetlands as well as in bottom soils and organic debris, providing abundant food for fish, frogs, ducks, shorebirds, and other invertebrates.

Although information on wetland invertebrates is limited, we recognize their crucial role in wetlands systems. For example, invertebrates are vital links in food chains supporting valuable animals such as songbirds and waterfowl. They not only process living and dead organic matter, channeling it to producer and detrital food chains, but they physically modify wetland habitats, enhancing their value for other wildlife species. Major factors influencing abundance and diversity of wetland invertebrates appear to be wetland size, location relative to other wetlands, wetland setting, substrate, vegetation structure, water regime, water quality, competition, and predation. Significantly, these same factors influence abundance and diversity of poikilotherms, birds, and mammals in wetlands.

Poikilotherms (Cold-Blooded Vertebrates: Amphibians, Reptiles and Fish)

The conglomerate of wetland poikilotherms includes species totally dependent on wetlands, such as fish and amphibians, as well as those species requiring wetlands for only a limited period of their life cycle, such as reptiles.

Amphibians

Two groups of amphibians are endemic to the United States: anurans—the frogs and toads, and urodels—the salamanders. Although certain members of these groups may be largely terrestrial, there are few exceptions in the 190 species of North American amphibians that do not require wetlands for at least a part of their life cycle.

Frogs and toads are so ubiquitous that most every freshwater wetland harbors some species of frog and toad during either the breeding or the nonbreeding season. Some species, such as the leopard frog and the wood frog, are predominantly terrestrial, feeding mainly on upland insects. These species survive dry periods by taking refuge in wet depressions. Similarly, toads and wood frogs are terrestrial except when they move into wetlands during the breeding season.

In the warmer climes of the Southeast, bullfrogs are a dominant life form and a major predator, consuming other frogs as well as small ducklings. The green frog is also very closely tied to the marsh, with almost a third of its diet derived from aquatic organisms.

Salamanders occur at various levels in wetlands, but perhaps the most numerous and widespread species is the tiger salamander, the only salamander occurring in the dry Southwestern United States. The tiger salamander is also best known because of the public attention in spring when hundreds—and sometimes thousands—move across highways from deepwater habitats to shallow water to breed.

Adult salamanders and frogs, as well as millions of egg masses and tadpoles, are important foods for birds such as ibises, egrets, and white pelicans; snakes and fish; small mammals such as otter, mink, and raccoons; and other frogs, toads, and salamanders. Species richness and diversity of frogs and salamanders vary with latitude and annual rainfall. Thus, these animals are abundant and well-represented in southern marshes but much less so in the north and west. For example, a study in Florida found 1600 salamanders and 3800 frogs and toads using a pond less than 30 m wide.

Fish

Diversity of fish species, especially in dense marsh systems, has not been explored in depth, but these systems provide important shelter and food for fish. Major factors influencing a wetland's habitat value for fish include water quality—temperature and dissolved oxygen—water quantity, and cover—substrate and interspersion.

Many wildlife species totally dependent on wetlands have developed mechanisms, such as dormancy, to survive periods of low water or times of no water at all.

Frogs and toads are so ubiquitous that most every freshwater wetland harbors some species of frog and toad during either the breeding or the nonbreeding season.

The freshwater wetlands fishes are dominated by forage species such as killifishes, shiners, mosquito fishes, and sunfishes. In fact, forage minnows account for a high proportion of the fish population as well as the fish biomass of freshwater wetlands. For example, three species comprise more than 75% of the population and more than 85% of the biomass in Florida's Everglades and Big Cypress Swamp. However, not all freshwater wetlands—notably small isolated or seasonally dry potholes and acidic bog lakes and fens—support fish.

Most larger fish species are transients of freshwater marshes, entering only diurnally to feed or seasonally to breed and spawn. Familiar species that move from adjacent lakes into marshes to breed include northern pike, walleye, black bullhead, yellow perch, and bluegill. Freshwater fish and their fry are important food items for wading birds such as storks and herons, amphibians and reptiles, and many aquatic and upland mammals.

Reptiles

Most reptile species in freshwater wetlands employ a reverse strategy to amphibians: they use wetlands for food, cover, and water but seek out drier areas and wetland fringes to reproduce. Three major groups of reptiles occur in freshwater wetlands of the United States: snakes, turtles, and alligators. Of these, turtles are the most diverse and the most common. Familiar representatives include mud and musk turtles, softshell turtles, painted turtles, sliders, cooters, box turtles, and pond turtles. Some, snapping turtles, are omnivorous while others, softshells, are carnivorous or vegetarian. Dependence on water varies dramatically with various species of turtles. Some, snapping turtles and mud turtles, are truly aquatic, emerging from water only to lay their eggs. Others, box and wood turtles, are largely terrestrial, consuming fruit, berries, worms, and insects and entering the water only to hibernate in the muddy substrate.

Snakes are the second major reptile group inhabiting freshwater wetlands. The only snake common in northern marshes is the garter snake, occurring primarily in fringe wetlands and feeding on amphibians, eggs, and small birds. In the south, the cottonmouth moccasin is most frequently mentioned, but it is less important in numbers or biomass than water snakes found in freshwater wetlands throughout the United States. Other snakes common in freshwater wetlands include queen snakes, mud snakes, and swamp snakes. Many snakes are highly dependent on wetlands wildlife, preying heavily on crayfish, fish, salamanders, ducklings, earthworms, slugs, and snails.

The third category, alligators, is a dominant factor in some freshwater wetlands. Alligators from Texas and Oklahoma to North Carolina dig "holes" in the marsh for nesting, reproduction, and refuge in dry periods that provide critical habitat for other wildlife. Their predation on fish, birds, and mammals can be significant and is well documented. So, too, is man's historic predation on the American alligator for food and hide, which decimated populations until the species was listed as endangered. Through research and management, alligator populations have rebounded and now sustain a closely-regulated harvest in several Gulf Coast states.

Birds

Wetland birds are those species deriving any essential part of their existence from wetlands. Freshwater wetlands use by many species of ducks, geese, swans, coot, loons, pelicans, grebes, shorebirds, cranes, and others is well known. These birds come to mind when one mentions wetlands, and they have become "ambassadors" of wetlands. Because these birds are spectacular to observe, relatively easy to find, and have much broader appeal than amphibians or fish, they have historically and currently raised the public consciousness on the importance and plight of our nation's wetlands. One need simply reflect on the artwork, organizations, and revenues that pivot on these birds to understand their substantial roles.

Despite the attention, excitement, and broad constituency that revolves around some wetland birds, another important category is not so commonly associated with wetlands but very much a part of and dependent on these systems. These birds and their use of wetlands is more subtle and indirect than trumpeter swans or sandhill cranes. For example, the blackburnian warbler nests in upland spruce but flies miles to collect bog lichens for nest materials. In fact, representatives from almost all avian groups use wetlands to some extent, and one-third of North American bird species depend directly on wetlands for some resource.

Birds are unique because of their mobility and ability to use disjunct wetlands. Many species are migratory, allowing them to use geographically disparate wetlands—many of which are seasonal—at varying times of the year. Some birds, such as the pied-billed grebe which can hardly walk on land and even builds a floating nest, are intimately tied to wetlands for survival. Others, such as flycatchers, are less dependent, only using the areas periodically for foraging or for nesting. Wetlands provide birds with food (tubers, invertebrates, seeds, and vertebrates); cover (nesting, hiding, and weather protection); and, obviously, water. Wetlands are strong attractors of birds not only because of abundant food resources but also because they provide excellent nesting and feeding sites protected from predators.

Examples of some representative wetlands birds bear mentioning. Waterfowl have been discussed. Loons and diving ducks are typically associated with larger, more sterile lakes, whereas grebes are associated with marshy areas. Of the herons, bitterns are probably most closely associated with freshwater wetlands, building solitary nests in reeds and rushes and feeding on frogs, fish, and small mammals. Herons, egrets, and ibises, on the other hand, nest colonially in wetlands, feeding on frogs, fish, crayfish, and other invertebrates. Occasionally, local colonies of these birds may conflict with humans. Rails are common residents of larger marshes. These rarely seen ground dwellers use the entire marsh, from the driest edges to areas of standing water. In addition to waterfowl, passerines, and shorebirds, freshwater wetlands are also home to many of our nation's raptors, or birds of prey. The more common include marsh hawks, bald eagles, and osprey, all using the abundant prey base—frogs, fish, birds, invertebrates, and small mammals—associated with freshwater wetlands.

Because so many species depend on wetlands, birds are one of our best bellwethers of the health of our wetlands resources. Said differently, as the birds fare, so do the wetlands. That the United States is entering what may be the worst year of waterfowl production on record should remind us all that unabated alteration and outright destruction of our nation's wetlands must no longer be condoned.

Mammals

Unlike many representatives of the above categories of wildlife, very few mammals are marsh specialists clearly adapted to water and hydrophytes and characterized as truly aquatic or wetland-dependent. Nevertheless, many mammals have individuals or populations that are wetland-dependent in certain areas and at certain times of the year. A primary reason wetland-dependent mammals may be underrepresented is that these animals, unlike birds, are nonmigratory and unable to escape and survive seasonal and annual dry periods. Despite fewer numbers of mammalian species associated with wetlands, they are extremely important to the maintenance and functioning of these systems.

Examples of mammalian species that are totally wetland-dependent are nutria, beaver, marsh rice rats, and swamp rabbits. The muskrat is perhaps the most characteristic example of a mammal inhabiting the broadest array of wetland types. Muskrats are distributed widely throughout North America, living in fresh and brackish water covering thousands of hectares as well as small roadside pools. Muskrats are dependent on emergent marsh vegetation, notably cattails, for food and shelter and can "eat out" a marsh if their population is too large. They can, however, shift to upland foods in times of stress.

Because [wetland] birds are spectacular to observe, relatively easy to find, . . . they have historically and currently raised the public consciousness on the importance and plight of our nation's wetlands.

That the United States is entering what may be the worst year of waterfowl production on record should remind us all that unabated alteration and outright destruction of our nation's wetlands must no longer be condoned.

Surprisingly, cutting vegetation for lodging, storage, and nests influences the marsh more than food consumption.

The muskrat house, common in marshes nationwide, can reach 2 m in height and 5 m in diameter. These houses are obviously important to muskrats. They are also important as nesting and loafing areas for birds, living quarters for other animals, and germination sites for semiaquatic plants. Muskrat houses create microhabitats for smaller organisms such as spiders, mites, and insects and aquatic crustaceans, and resting and feeding areas for frogs, toads, turtles, garter snakes, water snakes, birds, mink, and raccoon. Interestingly, the warmth generated by vegetation decomposition in the house provides hospitable microclimates for poikilotherms and enhances early ice melting in northern marshes.

Partially wetland-dependent mammals include mink and raccoon. The meadow mouse is mainly a field dweller but swims well underwater and may live in over-water nests of diving ducks or in muskrat houses. The list of wetlands mammals would not be complete without bog lemmings, cotton mice, wood rats, swamp rabbits, and short-tailed shrews. Most of these species occupy wetlands and regularly use adjoining upland habitats.

Finally, wetlands are used by larger mammalian species such as coyote, fox, bobcat, white-tailed deer and moose that are more or less dependent on wetlands. Moose, for example, browse on rooted aquatic and submerged vegetation in northern bogs during the summer to supply their sodium requirements. Other use of freshwater wetlands by large mammals is seasonal—such as winter protection, shelter, and feeding for white-tailed deer.

Threatened and Endangered Wildlife

In addition to abundant species of wetlands wildlife discussed above, wetlands also provide essential habitat for many threatened and endangered species. Williams and Dodd reported that 16% (5 of 33) of endangered mammals, 31% (22 of 70) of threatened and endangered bird species, 31% (22 of 70) of endangered and threatened reptiles, and 54% (22 of 41) of threatened and endangered fishes are dependent on wetlands or found in freshwater wetland habitats during part of their life cycle [J. D. Williams and C. K. Dodd, in "Importance of Wetlands to Endangered and Threatened Species," in *Wetland Functions and Values: The State of Our Understanding,* edited by P. E. Greeson, J. R. Clark, and J. E. Clark, 1979]. Wetlands obviously play a vital role in the maintenance of biological diversity.

Constructed Wetlands for Wastewater Treatment as Wildlife Habitat: Considerations, Issues, and Research Needs

In certain circumstances, constructed wetlands can be a useful mechanism for treating wastewater—municipal and otherwise. Societal and ecological benefits accruing from this low level technology are extremely exciting. Wetlands constructed for the singular purpose of wastewater treatment can obviously yield benefits beyond simply discharging water that meets local, state, and federal water quality standards. For example, appropriate design and siting in the landscape may contribute to groundwater recharge or help moderate storm surges. From the perspective of a wildlife biologist, one of the most exciting derivatives of constructed wetlands may be their benefits as wildlife habitats. Although wildlife cannot be the primary purpose, proper planning, implementation, and maintenance can enormously enhance the value of constructed wetlands for wildlife. For example, establishing vegetation for wildlife food and cover should be an integral design element. Constructing wetlands that maximize edge, provide transition zones into uplands, and use existing wildlife corridors are examples of important design considerations. Planning should also incorporate control structures, public entry, and training facilities such as boardwalks and viewing platforms to enhance public enjoyment.

However, full benefit realization is dependent on related issues and research needs. First, what, if any, impact might wetlands constructed for wastewater treatment have on the short and long-term viability of wildlife attracted to these areas? Might we be innocently creating another Kesterson or Salton Sea National Wildlife Refuge by drawing animals into potentially hazardous and harmful environments? What might be the lethal and sublethal impacts of contaminants in water, vegetation, and soils on wildlife? Who has legal responsibility for potential impacts, especially in the case of migratory or threatened and endangered species? How can these problems be anticipated, avoided, and remedied? Obviously, we need to initiate long-term research to answer these and other questions on operating systems.

Another important issue is how or whether constructed wetlands for wastewater treatment will be managed. The dynamic fluctuating nature of natural wetlands makes these systems productive and important to wildlife. Can perturbations be included in designs of constructed wetlands, and can these systems be managed so as to replicate natural wetlands without impairing their function and utility for treating wastewater effectively? Managing change in constructed wetlands, as we do in many other wetlands, will significantly influence the wildlife value of these areas.

Public information and education programs should be considered in planning, design, and operating stages. Certainly, public information campaigns and outreach programs will be vital to acceptance and long-term success of this technology and should be a major element of any planning effort. Encouraging public visits to view the processes at work will enhance a project's acceptance, win over valuable allies, and garner broader public support for using constructed wetlands for wastewater treatment.

Part of this effort should develop support from local sportsmen's organizations; environmental groups; naturalist, birdwatching, and wildflower societies; and other associations and individuals interested in wetlands and wildlife. Constructed wetlands may prove to be excellent areas for hunting and birdwatching and other outdoor recreation. For example, a 1988 issue of *Birder's World* [May–June 1988], a national birdwatching tabloid, has a five-page article on California's Arcata Marsh and Wildlife Sanctuary. Entitled "Birding Hot Spots," the story describes the history of the town's wastewater treatment project and over 200 species of birds and thousands of waterfowl and shorebirds using the marsh. User surveys of visitors to the Arcata wetland rank walking and isolation as important values. Widening the support circles to include average citizens will improve acceptance of this important technology.

Constructed Wetlands to Augment Our Nation's Wetlands Base

We have already destroyed more than 50% of our nation's wetlands. Although increased attention may attenuate these losses, clearly it will be years, if not decades, before we will stop and perhaps reverse these losses. Will constructed wetlands for wastewater treatment play a role in augmenting our nation's wetlands inventory?

Because constructed wetlands are small, isolated, and slow to come "on line," it is unrealistic to suggest they will play a significant role in augmenting the nation's overall wetland inventory. Nonetheless, constructed wetlands can be significant in increasing local wetlands and in creating wetland habitats where none previously existed. These activities can have positive benefits for local wildlife populations by enhancing habitat richness in areas lacking wetlands. But perhaps the greatest potential of constructed wetlands for wastewater treatment is that we will not only be gaining wetlands, but doing so using low-impact technology to solve an important environmental problem.

In conclusion, constructed wetlands for wastewater treatment is a shining example of finding creative solutions to tough problems. This approach to a national—indeed an international—issue is bold, exciting, and visionary but not without risk. However, with determination and commitment of time, research, and capital resources, constructed wetlands for wastewater treatment can mature into one of those rare "win-win" situations. We owe it to ourselves, as well as to our children, to ensure that the technology succeeds so that we as well as our wildlife resources may benefit. (pp. 107–17)

From the perspective of a wildlife biologist, one of the most exciting derivatives of constructed wetlands may be their benefits as wildlife habitats. Although wildlife cannot be the primary purpose, proper planning, implementation, and maintenance can enormously enhance the value of constructed wetlands for wildlife.

J. Scott Feierabend, "Wetlands: The Lifeblood of Wildlife," in Constructed Wetlands for Wastewater Treatment: Municipal, Industrial and Agricultural, *edited by Donald A. Hammer, Lewis Publishers, 1989, pp. 107–18.*

Sources For Further Study

Abernethy, Y., and Turner, R. E. "U.S. Forested Wetlands: 1940–1980." *Bio-Science* 37, No. 10 (December 1987): 721–27.
  Evaluates the changes in forested wetland environments based on U.S. Forestry Service field-data surveys from 1940 to 1980.

Barrow, C. J. "The Degradation of Wetlands, Tundra, Uplands and Islands." In his *Land Degradation: Development and Breakdown of Terrestrial Environments*, pp. 117–40. Cambridge: Cambridge University Press, 1991.
  Includes an examination of wetlands degradation in various regions.

Bingham, Gail, et. al., eds. *Issues in Wetlands Protection: Background Papers Prepared for the National Wetlands Policy Forum.* Washington, D.C.: Conservation Foundation, 1990, 230 p.
  Contains several essays that focus on key topics regarding wetland preservation, including current legislation, wetlands programs, mitigation policy, and scientific issues relating to wetland restoration.

Cable, Ted T., et. al. "Simplified Method for Wetland Habitat Assessment." *Environmental Management* 13, No. 2 (March–April 1989): 207–13.
  Ranks eleven tidal wetlands in Delaware by assessing the number of bird species that live in the ecosystem and correlating the figure to overall habitat quality.

Cahan, Vicky. "The Good Earth May Get Even Harder to Till." *Business Week,* Nos. 0007–7135 (4 June 1990): 140, 144.
  Discusses efforts by farmers to overturn strict wetland legislation which prohibits them from farming about eight million acres of fertile land.

"A Better System to Protect Wetlands Is Needed." *Conservation Foundation Letter,* No. 5 (1988): 1–8.
  Documents the findings of the National Wetlands Policy Forum convened by the Conservation Foundation in 1988, which concluded that federal agencies such as the Environmental Protection Agency urgently need to develop a better system for the management and protection of wetlands.

"Protected Lands, Critical Areas, and Wildlife (State of the Environment: A View Toward the Nineties)." *Conservation Foundation Report* (1987): 275–337.
  Maintains that the increase in the total amount of federal lands designated for resource protection and recreational use since 1960 has had a generally positive impact on the protection of wetlands.

Deland, Michael. "Wetlands Protection . . . A Dangerous Opportunity." *Water Connection* 6, No. 1 (Winter 1989): 1–3.
  Contends that the EPA has begun to aggressively pursue the preservation of wetlands and outlines procedures for similar action that can be initiated at the state level.

Ewel, K. C. "The Use of Wetlands for Wastewater Treatment." *Water Quality Bulletin* 13, No. 1 (January 1988): 21–6.
  Supports using wetlands for wastewater treatment, maintaining that nutrient removal, denitrification, and other functions of conventional wastewater treatment plants can be performed by natural wetlands.

Fellman, Bruce. "Watery Nurseries Dry Up and Wither." *International Wildlife* 20, No. 2 (March–April 1990): 12–13.
Asserts that the development of new strategies to make profitable use of wetlands may bring about increased preservation of the natural resource.

Fleischer, Siegfried. "Wetlands—A Nitrogen Sink." *Acid Magazine*, No. 9 (June 1990): 26–8.
Investigates the use of coastal wetlands in Sweden as a natural purification system to reduce nitrogen input into the marine environment.

Fried, Eric. "Why We Need Our Wetlands." *The Conservationist* 34, No. 6 (May–June 1980): 2–4.
Cites various ecological, recreational, and social reasons for preserving wetlands.

Goldstein, John H. "The Impact of Federal Programs and Subsidies on Wetlands." In *Transactions of the Fifty-third North American Wildlife and Natural Resources Conference*, edited by Richard E. McCabe, pp. 436–43. Washington, D.C.: Wildlife Management Institute, 1988.
Summarizes the research findings of a U.S. Department of the Interior study regarding the impact that federal programs and subsidies have had on the conversion, degradation, and conservation of wetlands in the United States.

Graham, Frank, Jr. "Of Broccoli and Marshes." *Audubon* 92, No. 4 (July 1990): 102–06.
Examines President Bush's stand on wetlands protection.

Hammer, Donald A., ed. *Constructed Wetlands for Wastewater Treatment: Municipal, Industrial, and Agricultural*. Chelsea, Mich.: Lewis Publishers, 1989, 831 p.
Contains the proceedings from the First International Conference on Constructed Wetlands for Wastewater Treatment held in Chattanooga, Tennessee on June 13–17, 1988. The volume presents general principles of wetlands ecology, case histories of specific types of constructed wetlands, construction management guidelines for wetlands treatment systems, and recent theoretical and empirical results from operating constructed wetland systems and research facilities.

Henderson, Rick. "The Swamp Thing." *Reason* 22, No. 11 (April 1991): 30–5.
Examines the provisions of government legislation designed to protect wetlands, asserting that "expansive government wetlands policy not only violates the rights of property owners but defies common sense."

Hickman, Clifford A. "Forested-Wetland Trends in the United States: An Economic Perspective." *Forest Ecology & Management* 33–34, Nos. 1–4 (1 June 1990): 227–38.
Notes the benefits of forested wetlands and threats posed by development.

"Turnabout on Wetlands: From Destruction to Preservation and Construction." *Impact* 11, Nos. 1–2 (March–June 1988): 2–18.
Surveys activities of the Tennessee Valley Authority to minimize further destruction of wetlands and to help identify and preserve remaining Tennessee Valley wetlands.

Lambers, C. "Wetlands: The (Im)Possibilities of Law?" *Nature Management & Sustainable Development International Congress, Gronginen, Netherlands* (6–9 December 1988): 372–81.
Asserts that international law and cooperation should be strengthened to protect wetlands since migratory animals and the transportation of pollution across borders make protection and management more difficult.

Levinson, Marc. "Nurseries of Life." *National Wildlife* 22, No. 2 (February–March 1984): 19–21.
Surveys the various kinds of wetlands in the U.S. and explains how they are endangered by land developers.

Lurz, William H. "The Call of the Wild Turns out to Be Costly." *Professional Builder* 54 (November 1989): 22–3.

Examines environmental considerations that now confront builders who plan sites on wetlands for construction.

Mitsch, William J., and Gosselink, James G. *Wetlands*. New York: Van Nostrand Reinhold Co., 1986, 539 p.
Provides a comprehensive analysis of the history and status of wetlands in the United States, the importance of preserving wetland ecosystems, and the increasing need to promote values and incorporate proper management techniques to preserve wetlands.

Nichols, Alan B. "Natural Processes: A Vital Role for Wetlands." *Journal: Water Pollution Control Federation* 60, No. 7 (July 1988): 1214–121.
Explores how the development of artificial wetlands not only enables communities and companies to provide an ecologically sound disposal of sewage waste, but also offers a safe environment for wildlife.

Pezeshki, S. R., et. al. "Flooding and Saltwater Intrusion: Potential Effects on Survival and Productivity of Wetland Forests along the U.S. Gulf Coast." *Forest Ecology & Management* 33–34, Nos. 1–4 (1 June 1990): 287–301.
Contends that as the sea level rises due to global warming, coastal wetland environments will experience inundation and salinity.

Raver, Anne. "Let Us Now Praise Famous Swamps." *The New York Times Magazine* (18 August 1991): 20–3.
Offers a brief survey of issues confronting wetland preservation.

Seltzer, E. Manning, and Steinberg, Robert E. "Wetlands and Private Development." *Columbia Journal of Environmental Law* 12, No. 2 (1987): 159–201.
Surveys various legal proceedings involving private developers and federal agencies determined to prohibit them from building on wetlands. The authors recommend that in the future developers should reevaluate the viability of attempting to build on ecologically sensitive land.

Shabecoff, Philip. "Restoring the Wetlands." *San Jose Mercury News* (9 February 1988): 6C.
Outlines the goals of North American Waterfowl Management Plan, a program established by the governments of Canada and the U.S. and private conservation and wildlife groups to restore the continent's waterfowl populations by the year 2000 to the levels of decades ago.

Skousen, Jeff. "Wetlands Are More Than Two Cattails!" *Green Lands* 19, No. 2 (Spring 1989): 45–7.
Asserts that research on wetlands continues to demonstrate their value in terms of wildlife, water treatment, and flood control and discusses how water permits are granted in West Virginia to protect wetlands.

Strutin, Michele. "Critical Wetlands Added to Everglades." *National Parks* 64, Nos. 3–4 (March–April 1990): 9–10.
Explores the circumstances surrounding a federal bill that will add more than 100,000 acres of wetlands to Everglades National Park.

Tripp, James T. B., and Herz, Michael. "Wetland Preservation and Restoration: Changing Federal Priorities." *Virginia Journal of Natural Resources Law* 7, No. 2 (Spring 1988): 221–75.
Proposes ways in which federal policies can be improved to accomplish the objectives set in the Clean Water Act of 1982 and more efficiently preserve the nation's wetlands.

Van Hees, Willem W. "Boreal Forested Wetlands: What and Where in Alaska." *Forest Ecology & Management* 33–34, Nos. 1–4 (1 June 1990): 425–38.
Details the timber composition of the relatively pristine boreal forested wetlands in Alaska's interior, maintaining that resource utilization has been minimal since human populations are low.

Walter, John. "Environment." *Successful Farming* 88, No. 8 (August 1990): 73.
Briefly examines current governmental regulations regarding wetland preservation, and their impact on farmers.

Williamson, Lonnie. "The Swampbusters." *Outdoor Life* 179, No. 2 (February 1987): 42–3.
Surveys the magnitude of the wetland depletion problem in the U.S. and assesses various programs underway to prevent further degradation of this valuable natural resource.

———— ."Making the Grade." *Outdoor Life* 186 (August 1990): 55–7.
Recounts a meeting with President Bush to discuss recent gains in such environmentally sensitive areas as wetland conservation. Williamson gives Bush a C+ for his current policy, but declares that the President shows potential for improvement.

Wilen, Bill O., and Frayer, Warren E. "Status and Trends of U.S. Wetlands and Deepwater Habitats." *Forest Ecology & Management* 33–34, Nos. 1–4 (1 June 1990): 181–92.
Documents the steady decrease in acres of wetlands and notes that Congress has passed The Emergency Wetlands Resources Act of 1986 which calls for status updates every ten years.

Willwerth, James. "A Swamp Makes Waste to Be Sweet Again." *Time* 133, No. 12 (20 March 1989): 10–16.
Examines how the community of Arcata, California, converted their sewage waste problem into an environmentally friendly artificial wetland through the use of new technology in sewage waste treatment.

Wright, Karen. "Diluvian Tremens." *Scientific American* 261, No. 4 (October 1989): 32–3.
Discusses current measures to deal with wetland preservation, particularly focusing on how the erosion of wetlands is affecting Louisiana.

19: Wildlife Conservation

Protecting Biological Diversity: Reasons and Methods

What is Biological Diversity?

Biological diversity, in the words of scientist Paul R. Ehrlich, "is the tens of millions of distinct species—and the billions of distinct populations—of plants, animals, and microorganisms that share Earth with us."Simply put, it is the variety of species in ecosystems as well as the genetic variability within each species. Maintaining biological diversity involves conserving a wide array of life forms, from obscure plants and insects to well-known species such as polar bears and whales. Efforts to conserve biological diversity (or biodiversity) embrace three types of conservation:

- the protection of individual species;

- the protection of communities of species and the ecosystems of which they are a part, such as tropical forests, wetlands, virgin prairies, and coastal mangroves; and

- the preservation of diverse gene pools within species, or genetic diversity.

In the United States, game species, such as pheasant, trout, and deer, have received the most attention from policy makers. Now, nongame species, such as the California condor, are brought to the public's attention almost daily by television, magazines, newspapers, and mail solicitations. Some—such as the panda, grizzly bear, and various types of whales—generate substantial publicity and aggressive preservation efforts. Other endangered species have garnered little attention. For example, few people have heard of the Tecopa pupfish, Sampson's pearly mussel, or longjaw cisco, all of which have been declared extinct in the last five years.

The survival of a species in the wild depends on a well-functioning ecosystem. By conserving such ecosystems, it is possible not only to protect one particular species, but many other species as well. The members of an ecosystem live together in complex, interlocking ways, such that the fate of one species is closely tied to that of others. Because of this interdependence, ecosystems have a certain amount of resilience. Yet they also react to perturbation with long-term changes, often in complex and unpredictable ways. For example, a human-caused decrease in the population of one species is likely to trigger an increase in another species that uses the same resources, just as the near extirpation of the wolf in the United States may have promoted the ascendancy of the coyote.

The third type of diversity is genetic. Genetic diversity is the variation among the members of a population, all of which are genetically unique. It determines that some roses have red blooms and others yellow, that some types of wheat will be resistant to drought and others not, that some chickens will be best for producing meat and others eggs.

For many conservationists, protecting the biological resources of the earth is a moral imperative requiring no economic or practical justification; the diversity of biological resources represents a natural endowment that human stewards must not squander.

Why Protect the Diversity of Biological Resources?

One of the most compelling arguments for protecting diversity is that so little is known about what exists and what is being lost. There is no consensus on how many species exist in the world, the potential usefulness of most of them, or the rate at which they are disappearing.

For many conservationists, protecting the biological resources of the earth is a moral imperative requiring no economic or practical justification; the diversity of biological resources represents a natural endowment that human stewards must not squander.

Aldo Leopold, who wrote eloquently about the need for a land ethic that appropriately recognizes the value of all life, saw the issue also in a more pragmatic way:

> If the biota, in the course of aeons, has built something we like but do not understand, then who but a fool would discard seemingly useless parts? To keep every cog and wheel is the first precaution of intelligent tinkering. [*A Sand County Almanac.*]

For many policy makers, moral and aesthetic arguments require some bolstering. And there are, to be sure, economic and other pragmatic arguments for protecting species, ecosystems, and genetic diversity.

Agriculture

Biological diversity holds out two important opportunities for agriculture: (*a*) a source of genetic materials for improving strains of crop plants that are under cultivation and (*b*) a source for development of "new" crop species. (pp. 537–39)

Health and Medicine

The diversity of wild plant and animal species also provides enormous potential for both the development and testing of new drugs. By one estimate, some 25 percent of the prescription medicines currently sold in the United States are based on chemicals derived originally from wild plants. Wild species are estimated to be even more important in Europe and especially in developing countries, where many people depend directly on the curative powers of the plants, themselves rather than on derived drugs. (p. 540)

Because the pharmacological properties of only a few species have ever been tested, wild species continue to hold substantial promise for the development of new drugs. Moreover, as one medical researcher has noted, "without naturally occurring active principles, it seems probable that neither the principle nor the activity would otherwise have been discovered. Put yourself in the place of a chemist who would like to develop a remedy for cardiac insufficiency; methods currently available would not lead him to synthesize a digitoxin-like molecule without knowledge of the natural prototype" [*World Conservation Strategy*].

Tourism and Recreation

Places such as parks, reserves, and wildlife refuges, where people go to see wild species and other natural features, contribute enormously to the economy. Recent studies have found that Americans alone spend some $30 billion a year "on wildlife-associated recreation: $16.25 billion fishing; $7.15 billion hunting; and $6.6 billion in nonconsumptive (or nonharvesting) ways such as whale watching, feeding wild birds, and photographing wildflowers." (pp. 540–41)

"Ecosystem Services"

In addition to acting as a haven for all the individual species within it, an ecosystem often provides other benefits that humans take for granted: the biologically mediated recycling of nutrients, purifying of water, flood control, breakdown of pollutants, protection of soil, fixation of solar energy, and other so-called ecosystem services that sustain life. . . .

The costs of protecting ecosystems, and the services they provide, though sometimes significant, are generally not nearly as great as the costs of returning degraded ecosystems to a functional level. (p. 541)

Lack of Information

One of the most compelling arguments for protecting diversity is that so little is known about what exists and what is being lost. There is no consensus on how many species exist in the world, the potential usefulness of most of them, or the rate at which they are disappearing.

The severe limit of existing knowledge is apparent when considering the issue of the number of species that inhabit the planet. In total, about 1.7 million species have been formally named under the system Linnaeus established in 1753. Some 751,000 are insects; about 440,000, plants, including algae and fungi; 47,000, vertebrates; and the rest, invertebrates and microorganisms. Yet millions of species have yet to be identified. As one expert observed: "How many species of organisms are there on Earth? We don't know, not even to the nearest order of magnitude." (pp. 541–44)

The number of extinctions is even less clear. The discovery that species are far more numerous than previously thought suggests that extinctions, too, are far more frequent than estimated earlier. The extinction rate is a matter of some controversy. According to one authority, 15 to 20 percent of the species that inhabited the earth in 1980 are likely to have been lost by the turn of the century. If there are 30 million species, this rate would mean losses of 4.5 to 6 million species. This estimate is vigorously disputed by some, although the fact that great losses will be suffered as tropical forests are cleared seems indisputable. Further, as a recent report by the Office of Technology Assessment concluded,

> global and national data and projections may mask the localized nature of resource degradation, diversity loss, and the consequences of both. Large inaccessible areas of forest, for example, may make the global deforestation rate seem moderate, but destruction of especially diverse forests in local areas . . . proceeds at catastrophic rates [*Technologies to Maintain Biological Diversity*].

Threats

Biological resources today are under tremendous stress. Hunting and harvesting are often assumed to be the main culprits. Ultimately, however, they are probably less important than some other threats—notably, loss of suitable habitat and chemical poisoning of that habitat.

Many organisms are exposed to a variety of human-caused threats. A single species may be hunted for food and clothing, have its habitat reduced by development, and be controlled as a nuisance. Chemical pollution can be another threat in degrading habitat and destroying specific plants and animals.

As a population is decreased in size and fragmented by these processes, there is a greater probability that it will become extinct due to genetic and demographic effects or because of random ecological disasters such as fires and floods. Even an apparently widespread species with many separate, small subpopulations may ultimately become extinct if each subpopulation itself has a high probability of vanishing.

In some instances, one form of human activity may increase risks from another. New development such as houses and roads may not only lead to a species' decline because of habitat loss but also leave the remaining population more vulnerable to hunters. (pp. 544–45)

Harvesting and Killing

Excessive commercial harvesting has caused the virtual elimination of several species of rhinoceroses, seals, and wild cats. And hunting for sport, unless carefully regulated as it usually is in the United States, has been and may continue to be a particular threat to certain larger animals. Even in the United States, however, some wild species' populations have plummeted in part due to overharvesting, including several species of Pacific Flyway geese and, some scientists say, the Alaska king crab.

Biological resources today are under tremendous stress. Hunting and harvesting are often assumed to be the main culprits. Ultimately, however, they are probably less important than some other threats—notably, loss of suitable habitat and chemical poisoning of that habitat.

The problems of habitat destruction, fragmentation, and degradation threaten more resources and may be more difficult to solve than those caused by direct killing and harvesting. Valuable habitats are being destroyed at unprecedented rates around the world.

In many other countries, harvesting is a far more serious problem. There is enormous global trade in smuggled wildlife and wildlife products—from butterflies and parrots to lizard skins and elephant tusks. The annual U.S. share of international trade in live animals, ivory, and skins is valued at a minimum of $4 billion, according to one estimate. Up to one-third of this trade is illegal.

Species may be threatened by nuisance controls, which can be particularly damaging when broad-gauge poisons are used. Heavy pesticide spraying, for instance, can directly or indirectly eliminate a wide range of species, both beneficial and bothersome.

Habitat Destruction

The problems of habitat destruction, fragmentation, and degradation threaten more resources and may be more difficult to solve than those caused by direct killing and harvesting. Valuable habitats are being destroyed at unprecedented rates around the world.

Deforestation is perhaps the single greatest cause of decline in global biological diversity. Loss of diversity is greatest in the tropical forests because the rate of deforestation there is rapid and the communities being destroyed contain many species. An estimated 29,000 to 36,000 square miles are being cleared each year to provide fuel wood, timber for export, and new land for raising crops and livestock.

Some types of nonforest terrestrial habitats have all but disappeared in many parts of the world. (pp. 545–46)

Wetlands and marshes, too, are being extensively destroyed for farmland and urban development. Some 80 percent of the 300,000 to 500,000 acres of wetlands cleared in the United States each year are converted to agricultural uses. (p. 546)

Perhaps the most biologically diverse saltwater communities under severe assault are coral reefs—among the more fragile, complex, species-rich ecosystems on the planet. Reefs are imperiled by fishing with dynamite, commercial collection of corals, and extensive mining for concrete production. Furthermore, relatively small amounts of silt deposited on a coral reef, from a dredging operation or from deforestation and erosion on land, can interfere with the feeding of the coral polyps that build the reef.

The problem of very long-term, if not irreversible, damage affects many natural communities. In forests where large areas have been cleared, natural regeneration may not occur because seed sources may not be available, symbionts (such as nitrogen-fixing bacteria) may have been removed, and soils may have been degraded. This is particularly true in tropical forests, where climax species have large and poorly dispersed seeds, where close interdependence with microorganisms is probably common, and where nutrients are rapidly leached from exposed soils. Reforestation by planting can provide wood and watershed protection, but it will rarely replace the natural forest. Plantations are often of a single species and generally lack most of the forest's original plant and animal inhabitants. (pp. 546–47)

Habitat Degradation

Biological diversity is threatened not only by outright physical destruction of habitat. Many habitats have been seriously polluted and degraded through chemical contamination and the invasion of exotic species. (p. 547)

CHEMICAL CONTAMINATION

[Recent] revelations about contamination of the National Wildlife Refuge System are particularly disturbing, for refuges are places specifically established to protect wild species. The threats to wild plants and animals resulting from chemical contamination have been recognized for decades, however. The pesticide DDT (dichloro-diphenyl-trichloro-ethane) was implicated in the rapid population declines of eagles, falcons, and other raptors. Oil spills may be accompanied by the death of large numbers of seabirds and other aquatic wild species. Contamination with polychlorinated biphenyls (PCBs) is strongly implicated in the decline of Baltic seals, including the grey seal, whose numbers dropped from 20,000 in the 1940s to a few thousand individuals in the early 1980s.

Concern has been growing, sharply and internationally, over acid precipitation and its degradation of habitat. The effects on aquatic life have been particularly damaging. Lakes and streams with increased acidity frequently suffer decreased fish populations. Young fish may be more susceptible to the negative effects of high acidity (including death) and its capacity to mobilize heavy metals. (pp. 547–49)

PROBLEMS RELATED TO EXOTIC SPECIES

The introduction of exotic species into habitats, through planned release or escape, may also endanger native species—by spreading disease, inflicting environmental damage, adversely affecting commercial and recreational use of fish and wildlife, and causing other resource management problems.

A 1980 National Park Service survey of 326 park system units in the United States revealed a total of 210 problems related to exotic species. The full effects of the encroachment of most exotic species are generally complex and difficult to predict, but may be far-reaching.

The Challenges Ahead: Preserving Biological Diversity

To counteract the many threats to biological diversity, decision makers face difficult choices. With limited funds and staff, one could, for example, be forced to choose between committing another million dollars to protect a single hard-pressed species and purchasing a tract of virgin forest threatened with logging to protect several less-publicized species and perhaps others not yet identified.

In all probability, many species, ecosystems, and gene pools will continue to be lost, while others will be saved. The core issues are: What should energies be focused on trying to save? How should those energies be allocated among various strategies, such as setting up reserves, restoring damaged habitat, regulating illegal trade, and so forth, to maximize protection efforts for biological resources? And how should broader constituencies be built for conservation? (pp. 549–50)

Unfortunately, such choices usually must be made despite substantial uncertainty and ignorance. For example, although most warm-blooded vertebrates (birds and mammals) are believed to have been discovered, named, and described, scientists frequently lack the information needed to determine the survival status of these species or to protect them adequately if they are found to be in jeopardy. Information about the values and needs of ecosystems—and threats to them—is often lacking. (p. 550)

Although research is needed to reduce this ignorance, decisions and actions cannot be put off, since to do so might cause the needless loss of biological resources that later could be found to have had substantial value. The need is to act as wisely as possible in the face of uncertainty.

Just as efforts to protect biological resources and counteract the threats they are under have stepped up in recent years, so has understanding of the efficacy of those efforts. New capability to address the problems facing biological resources has come as a result of advances in the field of conservation biology and experience and insights gained in other fields of wildlife management and habitat protection. (pp. 550–51)

Nevertheless, efforts to protect biological diversity are not growing as fast as the threats. The goal of conservation means that protection efforts must be focused on ecosystems and genetic diversity as well as species. It is not enough to answer the traditional question, How many wild species and which species can or should be saved? Other questions also must be addressed: How many

Paying attention simply to individual species—whether in the wild or ex situ—will not by itself sustain and conserve biological diversity. The most cost-efficient, and sometimes only, means of protecting large numbers of species and associated ecological processes is through the conservation of habitat.

The national parks in the western United States are among the areas that have been held longest as public reserves. It is now being discovered that they may not provide all the protection expected of them.

ecosystems of what size should be conserved? How many members of an individual species must be protected for species survival? In using and analyzing conservation strategies, it is important to understand how they apply—to species, ecosystems, and gene pools—what their strengths and limitations are, and how they will need to be advanced and refined in the coming years to adapt to rapidly changing conditions and scientific understanding.

Species Management

Individual species and categories of species have traditionally attracted the most public interest and support among wildlife-related efforts. Management tools have followed from this, having long been directed at animals that the public is most concerned about.

Game species have traditionally received the most attention. Predator control, supplemental feeding, and domestic propagation, in addition to hunting regulations, are techniques that have been used to protect these species. Humans have hunted wolves for centuries, one of the justifications being to eliminate an undesirable predator. Hatcheries and stocking of inland waters have been used to enhance fish populations.

In recent years, attention to species-level efforts, reflecting public interest, has broadened to include endangered and nongame species. (pp. 551–52)

International efforts to protect species have also increased. The Convention on International Trade in Endangered Species and Wild Fauna and Flora (commonly known as CITES), signed by 21 countries in 1973, is a global mechanism to control trade in all rare and threatened species. Since 1975, when the treaty came into force, 95 countries have become parties to CITES, making it the most widely supported of any conservation convention in the world. (Over half of these parties are developing countries, where wild species are sometimes crucial for local industries, food, and tourism.) As a result, trade in wild species has a functioning international regulatory framework and a secretariat to oversee implementation.

Clearly, some species attract more interest than others. The amount of resources devoted to, say, grizzly bears and condors is staggering compared to what is allocated to species of beetles, frogs, and cacti. (p. 552)

Focusing protection strategies on individual species quickly runs into problems. One is that popular attention, and through it political support, can focus only on a limited number of species at one time. These fortunate few tend to be what one observer has called "the charismatic megafauna—big, fierce, or attractive animals." Other species with less charismatic attributes have a more difficult time competing for attention, though they may be just as important.

The focus on a few select, popular species does, however, have an important role to play in galvanizing public interest and support. Condors, grizzly bears, and panthers, important in and of themselves, serve a broader purpose as well: they act as so-called flagship species for attracting attention and resources to protection efforts that might not otherwise be available.

Moreover, measures used for flagship species often provide increased protection for other endangered species and other members of native ecosystems. They key is to ensure that these species are protected while using the support for them to enhance the biological resources they are dependent on and the broader efforts devoted to biological diversity in general.

MULTIPLE TECHNIQUES

Management of the endangered whooping crane is an example of how multiple techniques can be used to increase a species' chances of survival. In an attempt to establish a second population, eggs are being transferred from both the wild flock nesting at Wood Buffalo National Park in Canada and a captive flock in Maryland to sandhill crane nests in Grays Lake National Wildlife Refuge in Idaho. The cranes are also protected during migration by a monitoring network and kept away from areas that may be hazardous due to disease, chemicals, or danger of accidental shooting. Since a major cause of death in migrating whooping cranes is collision with power lines, utility companies have been asked to make the lines visible with bright aircraft marker balls. Whooping crane habitat management includes burning, cutting, or grazing to control vegetation height and increase insect availability. Crops, including corn and chufa, are planted at many refuges, and fresh water is pumped in to decrease the probability of diseases such as botulism and avian cholera.

The success of these management techniques is reflected in population increases. (pp. 552–53)

In some instances, if threats in the wild can be sufficiently reduced, species management techniques may need to be adopted only until a viable population reestablishes itself. But, in other cases, particularly if aggressive management is used as a substitute for habitat acquisition and protection, such management may become a permanent necessity if the species is to survive.

EX SITU CONSERVATION

When efforts to protect a species from the many threats it faces in the wild are not sufficient by themselves, ex situ (that is, off-site) conservation may be considered. (pp. 553–54)

Types of Ex Situ Conservation. Ex situ conservation methods may be separated into two categories. The first group of methods, used to save the peregrine falcon, involves creating situations in which captive populations continue to reproduce normally, even though matings may be controlled. Examples are populations kept in zoos, botanical gardens, game parks, agricultural stations, fish hatcheries, and facilities specially dedicated to raising rare species.

The second ex situ conservation category includes facilities like seed and germ plasm banks, where the goal is to store genetic information in the form of seeds and frozen embryos. In the future, storage of a variety of pure, isolated, or synthesized genetic materials (DNA sequences) could be possible. Collectively, these facilities have been likened to genetic libraries for space-efficient storage of genetic variability.

Zoos, botanical gardens, and other breeding facilities are the traditional ways of conserving organisms out of their environment. Successful captive propagation depends on careful research and the creation of environmental conditions appropriate to the species. With good facilities, planning, knowledge, and luck, mortality may be significantly reduced from what it would be in the wild. Populations of rare plants or animals can be raised and released into suitable habitat. Some of the more successful captive breeding programs have involved golden lion tamarins, Arabian oryxes, peregrine falcons, Przewalski's horse, and European bison.

Even in the recent past, many of the institutions specializing in exhibition paid little attention to the needs of rare species, which often could be replaced from the wild more cheaply and easily than they could be bred. When the animals were bred, genetic records were rarely used, because inbreeding and other genetic problems were not well understood.

This situation is changing. Many institutions have evolved a more sophisticated conservation ethic, necessitated in part by tighter restrictions on trade in rare species. The $35,000 cost of a female bongo antelope is an excellent incentive for developing the facilities needed for producing baby bongos.

Management methods today have become more sophisticated. For years, efforts to maintain viable populations of endangered golden lion tamarins in captivity were unsuccessful; second-generation individuals were unable to raise their offspring. In time, breeders discovered that the problem lay in the common practice of removing juveniles from the family group when their younger siblings were born, under the supposition that their presence might harm the newborns. This isolation prevented the juveniles from learning how

Better management of nonreserved lands in general could substantially benefit many types of biological resources; in a conflict with more profitable uses of the land, however, wild species are likely to lose out.

For a variety of economic, political, and social reasons, the practical opportunities to preserve biological diversity often do not take advantage of the optimum technical solutions.

to care for their own offspring. For this species, as for some others, intensive research has paid off. However, adequate research tends to be the exception rather than the rule.

An increasing number of zoos and botanical gardens have made ex situ conservation of rare species a major goal and have even begun to coordinate management of their collections. Such plans are designed to ensure that frequent interchanges of individuals among zoos, determined by analysis of genetic records, will decrease the probability of inbreeding problems, while maintaining enough separation of populations to avoid catastrophic losses due to disease. In some cases, analyses of captive populations have indicated a need to capture fresh wild stock so that genetic diversity can be added to the captive population. In principle, captive populations could provide the same service to wild populations.

Drawbacks of Ex Situ Conservation. Although ex situ techniques will likely play an increasing role in species conservation, particularly with emergency measures, a number of drawbacks exist. One of the weaknesses inherent in any method of ex situ conservation is that even sizable collections represent only a sampling of individuals and may not include all the important genetic traits. A founding population may not include enough genetic variability for long-term survival. Successive generations may experience genetic deterioration.

For long-term survival, ex situ populations require careful, sustained management based on good research. Continuity of care over the years is vital. A fire, cut in government funding, a power loss, a poor administrator—any of these could cause the loss of irreplaceable specimens. (pp. 554–56)

No matter what measures are taken, it may be difficult or impossible to breed some species in captivity. Moreover, another major issue, raised in the controversy over how to save the California condor, is whether captive populations can be successfully reintroduced into the wild. They may fail to learn the behavior necessary for survival and reproduction in another habitat. It is the long-term selection of genes for survival in captivity and the loss of genes useful for survival in the wild that results in domesticated animals and plants. Also, the natural habitat of some species may change during the time they are being captive-bred; when released, they might be unable to cope with the new environment.

A final limitation on the contributions of ex situ measures is that they can only deal with a limited number of species. There is only so much "captive habitat." (p. 556)

The number of species that can be maintained in zoos, moreover, is always a function of money. The yearly maintenance costs for a family of gorillas, for instance, easily exceed $50,000. Because of limited resources, institutions and, by extension, society face tough decisions about which species and strains to concentrate on.

Habitat Management

Paying attention simply to individual species—whether in the wild or ex situ—will not by itself sustain and conserve biological diversity. The most cost-efficient, and sometimes only, means of protecting large numbers of species and associated ecological processes is through the conservation of habitat: by establishing reserves that encompass ecosystems and natural communities and by fashioning strategies to protect and restore nonreserve habitat.

THE ROLE OF ECOSYSTEM RESERVES

National parks, nature reserves, and other protected areas are the cornerstones of most national strategies to preserve wild plants, animals, and ecological communities. (pp. 556–57)

If suitable habitat is available, reserves can confer important benefits: (*a*) they may provide protection for an entire ecosystem, not just for species of particular interest; (*b*) they are likely to provide recreational, aesthetic, natural resource conservation, and other environmental benefits to the surrounding area; and (*c*) they are likely to be inexpensive to maintain compared to the amount of diversity they protect and, if acquired before other uses contend for the land, relatively inexpensive to create.

In most areas of the world, there are not enough properly located reserves of sufficient size to adequately protect biological diversity. Moreover, the ones already established provide less security to biological resources than most people think, sometimes because of inadequate internal management and often because of encroaching activities on lands outside their boundaries. (p. 557)

The national parks in the western United States are among the areas that have been held longest as public reserves. It is now being discovered that they may not provide all the protection expected of them. To most Americans, these parks represent the essence of wild, primitive America: spectacular scenery, vast tracts of pristine forests, and, in particular, abundant wildlife. They contain a great diversity of plants and animals. For most park visitors, however, the wild species of greatest interest are the native mammals, especially large ones such as bear and elk.

Recent advances in biological understanding have made it clear that such isolated populations of plants and animals, surrounded by spreading human development, are prone to extinction and that large mammals and rare species are at greatest risk. The effect is correlated with area size: the smaller the area to which a group of species is newly restricted, the greater the number of extinctions likely to occur. (pp. 557–60)

In practice, species protection is, at best, only one of the factors determining the size, location, and management of reserves. Commonly, historical accidents and financial opportunity have also been important factors, especially in determining reserve size and location. Instead of a single large reserve that might best meet ecological requirements, a government might create two smaller reserves to please two constituencies. Instead of a reserve in a biologically rich but distant area, officials may choose one close to a national capital for its recreational benefits and political impact. These factors help build important constituencies and are unlikely to disappear in the future.

Designing Reserves. Reserve creation is critical for protecting biological resources, and reserve expansion may be necessary to secure areas already set aside. As more has been learned about how populations respond when they are isolated in reserves, it has become increasingly clear that careful design is crucial for long-term survival of the species reserves are created to protect. Unfortunately, few existing reserves encompass entire ecosystems or include sufficient habitat for all the wild species that originally used the area.

Research is under way to determine how rapidly species are lost from reserves of particular sizes. How much more rapidly will species be lost from small reserves than from larger ones? Will more total species be saved in one large reserve than in two smaller ones having the same area? What kinds of species will be lost most rapidly? Current research is directed toward determining the minimum viable population necessary for long-term survival of selected species and to estimating how large reserves must be to accommodate the plant and animal species indigenous to them. (pp. 560–61)

Setting up reserves is more complicated than just opting for the largest areas possible. Because of environmental catastrophes, such as forest fires and epidemics, several small reserves could offer more safety than a single large one. Thus, if one population of a species were lost, a second might still be safe.

Location also is an important factor in reserve design. It is obviously best to locate reserves where they can protect as many unique or imperiled species as possible. In Brazil, for example, there is an attempt to create reserves in areas in which an especially high degree of speciation appears to have occurred and which continue to be centers of diversity. (p. 561)

"We have a responsibility to life, to defend it everywhere, not only against our own sins, but also against those of others. We are all passengers, together, in the same fragile and glorious world."

—"The Assisi Declarations"

When people live on and use valuable lands, attempts to establish traditional reserves can have serious economic, social, and political drawbacks. Economic needs or development pressures in many desirable reserve areas may be strong. Worldwide, this is leading to more ambitious and complex responses, namely the creation of fewer traditional parks and more reserves that permit multiple uses.

Managing Reserves. The 1980 *State of the Parks* survey undertaken by the National Park Service uncovered diverse pressures on park resources in the United States. The problems reported in the survey varied in scale and magnitude from park to park. Aesthetic degradation was the most frequently reported threat, followed by air pollution, logging and mining, the encroachment of exotic plants and animals, visitor impacts and pollution, and water quantity or quality problems. The source of more than half of the reported pressures was outside park boundaries. No major park was free from outside pressures on its resources. As discussed earlier, there is also severe habitat degradation in U.S. wildlife refuges.

In general, there can be an inverse relationship between size and the amount of management necessary in a reserve—the larger the reserve, the less management required. But maintaining and restoring natural processes even in large reserves, particularly those accommodating people—as visitors or inhabitants—can be difficult. In many instances, there is a disagreement about why a particular resource is under stress or what should be done about it. On one hand, there is a tendency toward natural-process management, where nature is left to manage more of itself. On the other hand, because most areas are no longer pristine, some active management is needed to maintain or restore naturalness. (p. 564)

New Kinds of Reserves. Conflicts in reserve creation and management values are likely to broaden as more reserves begin to incorporate areas where human settlement is part of the landscape to be nurtured. Even if people are not living within a reserved area, future population growth and efforts at economic development may bring human land use literally "up to the fence."

When people live on and use valuable lands, attempts to establish traditional reserves can have serious economic, social, and political drawbacks. Economic needs or development pressures in many desirable reserve areas may be strong. Worldwide, this is leading to more ambitious and complex responses, namely the creation of fewer traditional parks and more reserves that permit multiple uses. (p. 566)

In countries such as Nepal, Panama, and Peru, reserves are being established that include villages within or along their borders. Planning and operating these reserves involve finding economic opportunities for the affected human population that are compatible with the reserve's purposes.

These are dramatic departures from the usual common perception of a national park or refuge. They require an array of management tools, especially where private land is involved. These new types of reserves are not without problems, for the natural resources, including wild species, sometimes suffer in competition with human needs and desires. Yet coordinated land-use arrangements are preferable to the alternative of no protection and the simple loss of more species.

THE IMPORTANCE OF NONRESERVE HABITAT

Techniques, policies, and funds for creating and maintaining reserves, while vital and necessary, fall far short of being adequate measures for preserving biological diversity. More attention must be directed at the larger landscape. There will never be enough room on reserves to support all of the earth's important biological resources. Moreover, some species, such as migratory birds, cannot be easily managed solely through a system of reserves. And the impacts from activities on lands outside reserve boundaries will require increasing attention to the economic forces and institutional processes that foster that development.

Even with active and effective reserve and species management, the habitats used by many species and populations will remain largely outside reserves. If the fate of these species were dependent solely on the establishment of reserves, most would soon be added to lists of the endangered or extinct. Therefore, an important question is: How can nonreserved lands be managed to help protect the biological resources that depend on them? This applies not just to lands adjacent to existing reserves but to the broader landscape as well.

Frequently this will involve management plans that integrate economic and conservation goals. In Peru, for example, the National Agrarian University (Universidad Nacional Agraria-La Molina), supported by World Wildlife Fund, has devised a strategy for sustained-use management of the mangrove ecosystem in that country, where marine resources have been exploited through harvesting and habitat alteration to maximize yields. The strategy is to coordinate the activities of different local agencies and manage the resources so as to perpetuate those biological processes in the estuaries and mangroves that sustain both the ecosystem and the area's economic base. (pp. 567–70)

Habitat degradation on agricultural lands is a major problem because so many acres are involved and because the conversion of land to agricultural use typically renders the area largely inhospitable to wildlife. For example, World Wildlife Fund is supporting a study of the effects of traditional and alternative agricultural practices on migratory birds in Mexico's Yucatan Peninsula. Mayan farmers are being encouraged to use small-scale, intensive farming techniques aimed at increasing their net income *and* reducing forest habitat destruction. If this alternative to extensive slash-and-burn agriculture becomes widely accepted, it could help to slow the decline of the migratory birds dependent on these tropical forest lands. (p. 570)

Of course, farmers can take actions on their own to improve habitat or minimize damage to wild species. Various tactics—such as delaying plowing until spring so that waste grain and other food is available to wild animals during the winter months, retaining wild hedgerows, controlling overgrazing, and keeping livestock out of certain areas during nesting seasons—are available to improve the ability of farmland to sustain wild species. In many cases, these techniques have the added advantages of reducing soil erosion and improving productivity.

Some large industrial landowners have voluntarily undertaken wildlife enhancement efforts. Tenneco Oil, for example, has undertaken a project to maintain a 5,000-acre marsh it owns in Louisiana. The installation and operation of water control structures prevents saltwater intrusion from destroying the marsh, protecting the company's rights to oil and gas resources and preserving valuable wildlife habitat.

Most "nonreserved" federal lands—that is, lands that are not primarily used for maintenance of wild species—are forest and range areas owned by the Forest Service and the Bureau of Land Management (BLM). These lands are managed under multipurpose or "multiple use" mandates. Wildlife and watershed protection needs are considered along with human needs for timber, beef, minerals, and recreation. (p. 571)

The fact that many populations of wild species may overlap several different governmental jurisdictions and private properties poses unique problems. Thus, achievement of habitat preservation goals requires substantial cooperation among various land managers and owners.

Private lands and federally owned forests and rangeland set aside for multiple-use management will become increasingly important for sustaining wild species in the United States. Fortunately, many types of land use are compatible with wildlife needs. For example, careful selective harvesting of trees can provide a sustained economic return, yet leave adequate stocks for reseeding and for animal needs. (pp. 571–72)

Habitat Restoration. Sometimes a natural community may be so damaged by pollution, deforestation, or other factors that it cannot be revived with simple protection or modest management efforts alone. In such cases, intensive efforts may be made to recreate the original community by essentially "replanting it" or by changing environmental conditions so that it can replant itself. In the United States, replacement of several types of saltwater and freshwater marshes destroyed by development and dredging has been mandated by

Some large industrial landowners have voluntarily undertaken wildlife enhancement efforts. Tenneco Oil, for example, has undertaken a project to maintain a 5,000-acre marsh it owns in Louisianna. The installation and operation of water control structures prevents saltwater intrusion from destroying the marsh, protecting the company's rights to oil and gas resources and preserving valuable wildlife habitat.

Conservationists, for their part, must work toward channeling economic development into areas that will not disrupt valuable habitat, and seeing that sound environmental planning is undertaken when development does occur.

environmental laws. With respect to plant species, at least, the restored communities often can be returned to conditions very similar to the original. However, attention is rarely given to restoring small animals, such as insects and mollusks, to these communities.

Restoration efforts range from simple preparation of a site for natural colonization by a native species to a complex effort to plant many species in ways that mimic natural succession. (p. 572)

Clearly there are many opportunities to restore damaged lands for wild species. Restored areas might help conserve rare species by functioning as corridors or buffer zones adjacent to reserves. Such areas can provide habitat for remnant populations threatened by development or introduced from captive breeding facilities.

Better management of nonreserved lands in general could substantially benefit many types of biological resources; in a conflict with more profitable uses of the land, however, wild species are likely to lose out. In the future, governments will have to become even more creative in encouraging compatible land use through regulations and incentives so that wildlife habitat protection is more beneficial to the landowner. Conservationists, for their part, must work toward channeling economic development into areas that will not disrupt valuable habitat, and seeing that sound environmental planning is undertaken when development does occur.

Concluding Thoughts

In this "age of extinction," as Dr. Thomas E. Lovejoy has called it, powerful forces are diminishing the vast biological richness of the earth. Counter-vailing protective forces, although stronger than a generation ago, are only beginning to come to grips with the problem.

Information—about what species exist, where they are concentrated, how and where they are most threatened, how to design and manage reserves—will permit more efficient allocation of the limited resources available for protection. It remains crucial that scientific knowledge continue to be sought and technical solutions continue to be developed.

At present, however, the constituency for protecting biological diversity as such remains thin. Many people who would be sympathetic with the aim are unfamiliar with the term or, if they have run across it, find it unmoving. For a variety of economic, political, and social reasons, the practical opportunities to preserve biological diversity often do not take advantage of the optimum technical solutions. A strategy is needed to bridge science and policy. To fashion that strategy, conservationists must search for allies and must establish priorities among protection approaches.

One element of a strategy to conserve biodiversity is a vision of the richness of life on earth and the moral and ethical arguments associated with this vision. As a declaration at a major interfaith conference on environmental conservation in 1986 stated: "We have a responsibility to life, to defend it everywhere, not only against our own sins, but also against those of others. We are all passengers, together, in the same fragile and glorious world." These arguments can have an increasing impact—much as the wilderness vision has strengthened wildlands protection measures in the United States during the past generation.

Another strategic element should be to increase awareness of the economic benefits of diverse species, ecosystems, and gene pools to agriculture, medicine, and other quantifiable sectors. Until recently, conservationists did not focus much on the broader issues involving integrating conservation and economic goals more effectively to protect wild species. This has begun to change, especially as reserves have faced mounting pressures from the civilizations that surround them, as environmental concerns have become more institutionalized in government programs, and as conservationists have recognized the indisputable links between an area's needs for economic growth and its environmental goals. Much more work, however, needs to be done.

In fashioning their strategies, those committed to preserving biodiversity need to make choices. Effective support for protection will require a broad coalition of people—of politicians, hunters, pharmaceutical firms, development economists, for example—with diverse interests and methods to forestall destruction. Only by establishing priorities can such a coalition hope to ensure that limited resources are employed effectively. Focusing funds in one reserve or one country may mean important needs are not addressed elsewhere; an all-out effort to protect one species may be bought with the extinction of others. This is not welcome news. By exerting leadership and helping to determine the choices, however, one avoids having them imposed by others.

As time goes on and changes occur in human sensitivities, the values that are perceived in biological diversity may also evolve. (pp. 573–74)

Protection of Biological Diversity: The Challenges of a Broadening Perspective," in State of the Environment: A View toward the Nineties, *The Conservation Foundation, 1987, pp. 535–84.*

We need to ask what difference the loss of species makes. If more do become extinct, so what? How much do chickadees contribute to our gross national product anyway?

Extinction and Humanity: What Is the Connection?

Everywhere humans have gone, they have wiped out whole species of birds, mammals, reptiles, fish, and other forms of life. Indeed, we continue to do so on every continent and island we inhabit, except now we act with a technology and a capacity for destruction far greater than that of our forebears. Many of us—scientist and nonscientist alike—find our increased threat to other species alarming. We fear that we have set in motion a wave of extinction that will ultimately undermine the quality, and perhaps even the possibility, of human life.

Not everyone, however, agrees that the risk of mass extinction is real, nor for that matter that it would do us much harm if it in fact occurred. One of the most frequently cited estimates in the debate, for example, is that humans have caused one percent of all bird species to become extinct within the past few centuries. Yet it's easy to imagine that most birds are superfluous as far as human needs are concerned and that we could safely lose, say, ten times more. We might even believe the same of other endangered species, from gray wolves to blue whales—it would be a pity to lose them, but life would go on.

What is the truth of our situation? Is the mass extinction crisis a hysterical fantasy, a real risk for the future, or a proven event that's already well under way? To answer those questions, we need to step back a bit and examine how the numbers bandied about by both sides in the debate are really arrived at. Then we need to know whether the pace of extinctions is rising or falling; we have to compare modern records with evidence dug up from the past. Finally, we need to ask what difference the loss of species makes. If more do become extinct, so what? How much do chickadees contribute to our gross national product anyway?

Birds keep popping up in the estimates for good reason: they are easy to see and identify, and hordes of bird-watchers keep track of them. As a result, we know more about birds than about any other group of animals, and so they provide a measure of the current destruction.

We know that approximately 9,000 species of birds exist today. Since only one or two new species are being discovered each year, we can safely say that virtually all living birds have been identified. According to the International

Fewer than 2 million plant and animal species have been described, but sampling procedures suggest that the actual number of the world's species may be at least 30 million. Most of them live in rain forests that biologists are just beginning to explore.

Council for Bird Preservation (the world's leading agency concerned with the status of birds), 108 species, a little more than one percent of the total, have become extinct in modern times—that is, since 1600, a date that conveniently marks the beginning of scientific classification.

Is this a fair measure of the rate of extinction? The council's list is intentionally conservative: a bird is registered as extinct only after it has been unsuccessfully searched for in all areas where it might conceivably turn up, and after it has not been found for many years. So there is little doubt about the true status of a bird listed as extinct. Can we be equally certain that all those bird species that have not fulfilled the council's rigorous criteria for extinction still exist? For North American and European birds the answer is yes. The presence of hundreds of thousands of fanatic bird-watchers virtually guarantees that no bird on these continents could drift into extinction unnoticed. In many cases researchers have watched a population dwindle to a few individuals and then followed the fate of those last survivors. (pp. 55–6)

But most tropical countries, where the overwhelming majority of species live, have few, if any, bird-watchers. The fate of many tropical birds is unknown, because no one has seen them or specifically looked for them since they were discovered years ago. Many other species were described from single specimens collected by nineteenth-century explorers who gave only vague indications of the site—such as "South America." We know nothing about the songs, behavior, and habitats of such birds, and even the most dedicated bird-watcher would be hard-pressed to identify one of those birds if he glimpsed or heard it.

Many tropical species therefore cannot be classified as either "definitely extinct" or "definitely in existence," but just as "of unknown status." It becomes a matter of chance which of these species happens to attract the attention of some ornithologist, be searched for, and then possibly be listed as extinct. (p. 56)

Fewer than 2 million plant and animal species have been described, but sampling procedures suggest that the actual number of the world's species may be at least 30 million. Most of them live in rain forests that biologists are just beginning to explore; over 1,500 beetle species, for example, have been found in a single species of tree in Panama.

Humans are now bearing down on this vast, unknown majority of species, and here and there we can glimpse the results. When botanist Alwyn Gentry, for example, surveyed an isolated ridge in Ecuador called Centinela, he found 38 new plant species, many of them strikingly beautiful, confined to that one spot. Shortly afterward the ridge was logged, and those plants were exterminated. On Grand Cayman Island in the Caribbean, zoologist Fred Thompson discovered two new species of land snails confined to a forest on a limestone ridge. When that ridge was cleared a few years later for a housing development, the snails disappeared.

The accident of Gentry and Thompson visiting those ridges before rather than after they were cleared means that we have names for the now-extinct species that lived there. But biologists don't first survey most tropical areas that are being developed. Humans must have exterminated plants and animals on innumerable other tropical ridges before anyone had a chance to discover them.

In short, then, published lists of species known to be extinct must be gross underestimates of the actual numbers. There is a systematic tendency to underestimate extinctions even among birds, which we know best. For many other forms of life the unknown species—and unknown extinctions—must far outnumber the known.

So far we have counted only species exterminated in modern times, that is, since 1600. But were there no exterminations before 1600, throughout the preceding several million years of human history? To find out if the slaughter is gaining momentum, we need to follow the swath we have cut through the past.

Until 50,000 years ago, when humans first reached Australia and New Guinea, we were confined to Africa plus the warmer areas of Europe and Asia. We reached Siberia 20,000 years ago, North and South America 11,000 years ago, and most of the world's remote oceanic islands only within the past 4,000 years. Over this same period we were dramatically improving our hunting skills and our tools, and developing the technology of agriculture. Also, while expanding over the globe, we were increasing in numbers, from perhaps a few million 50,000 years ago to half a billion in 1600.

Paleontologists have studied many of the areas humans have reached within the past 50,000 years. In every one, human arrival coincided with massive extinctions. After people arrived in Australia, that continent lost its giant kangaroos and other giant marsupials. Around the time humans reached North America, that continent lost its lions, cheetahs, horses, mammoths, mastodons, giant ground sloths, and several dozen other large mammals. In all, counting by genus, 73 percent of North American large mammals became extinct near the time of human arrival. In South America it was 80 percent, and in Australia 86 percent.

We know that people hunted many of these animals. And in areas where meaty mammals were not abundant, people killed other prey. For example, paleontologists have found remains of recently extinct bird species on almost every oceanic island they have explored. New Zealand lost its giant flightless moas when the Polynesians arrived, and Hawaii lost its flightless geese and dozens of smaller birds. Extrapolation to islands not yet explored by paleontologists suggests that 2,000 bird species—one-fifth of all the birds that existed a few thousand years ago—fell victim to prehistoric exterminations. That doesn't count birds that may have disappeared on the continents.

Ever since researchers became aware of these prehistoric extinctions, they've debated whether people were the cause or just happened to arrive while animals were succumbing to climatic changes. (pp. 56–7)

To me the evidence seems overwhelming that humans played a role in the earlier extinctions also, especially in Australia and the Americas. In each part of the world in question, a wave of extinction swept over the land after the arrival of humans but didn't appear simultaneously in other areas undergoing similar climatic swings. If climatic changes at the end of the most recent ice age finished off America's big beasts, it's curious that those animals, having survived the previous 22 ice ages, chose to drop dead at the end of the twenty-third, just when human hunters sauntered by.

Moreover, it wasn't just in these newly occupied territories that large animals disappeared. In areas long occupied by humans, a new round of extinctions started 20,000 years ago: Eurasia lost its woolly rhinos, mammoths, and giant deer (the "Irish elk"). At the same time, Africa lost its giant buffalo, giant hartebeests, and giant horses. Like their cousins on the other continents, these big beasts may have been done in by prehistoric humans who hunted them with newer, better weapons.

Evidently, our species has a knack for exterminating others, and we're becoming better killers all the time. The key question for our children, though, is whether the crest of the extinction wave has already passed or whether the worst is still to come.

There are a couple of ways to approach this question. One is simply to assume that the number of tomorrow's extinct species will bear close resemblance to the number of today's endangered ones. Among birds an estimated 1,666 species—18 percent of the total—are now either endangered or at imminent risk of extinction. But this figure is an underestimate for the same reason that one percent is too low an estimate for birds we have already driven to extinction. Both numbers are based only on species whose status caught someone's attention, not on a reappraisal of all birds. The real number of species at risk must be higher.

If climatic changes at the end of the most recent ice age finished off America's biggest beasts, it's curious that those animals, having survived the previous 22 ice ages, chose to drop dead at the end of the twenty-third, just when human hunters sauntered by.

It is likely that more than half of all existing species will be extinct or endangered by the middle of the next century. If the estimate of 30 million for the world's total species is correct, then species are now becoming extinct at a rate of 150,000 per year, or 17 per hour.

The alternative approach to prediction is not to look at other species but rather to look at ourselves. Our destruction of others has kept pace with our population and technology, and it is fair to reason that this will continue until our population and technology reach a plateau. But neither shows signs of leveling off. Our population grew from half a billion in 1600 to more than 5 billion now, and it is still growing at close to 2 percent per year. And every day brings new technological advances by which we are changing Earth and its denizens.

If we are to predict the extent of our future devastation, then we must take notice of the mechanisms by which we cause extinction. Of the four leading ones, the first and most direct is over-hunting, or killing animals faster than they can breed. This is chiefly how we have eliminated big animals, from mammoths 10,000 years ago to California grizzly bears this past century. And we are not yet finished. We no longer depend on such animals for meat, but we kill elephants for ivory and rhinos for their horns. At current rates of slaughter, not just elephants and rhinos but most other populations of large African and Southeast Asian mammals will be extinct (outside game parks and zoos) in a decade or two.

The second method of extermination is more indirect but no less effective: introducing species to parts of the world where they didn't previously exist. When such newcomers spread, they frequently kill off native species because the victims have no natural defenses. In the United States, for example, an introduced fungus has almost exterminated the American chestnut tree, just as on oceanic islands around the world, goats and rats have exterminated many native plants and birds. Although we might try to keep from introducing pests to new parts of the world, they will inevitably keep pace with human travel and commerce. (pp. 57–8)

Destruction of habitat is the third path to extinction. Most species live in only one type of habitat: marsh wrens in marshes, pine warblers in pine forests. Many are even more particular, especially in the tropics. Centinela Ridge is an isolated habitat because it just reaches the clouds; before it was cleared, it was a unique "cloud forest" separated by valleys from similar habitats. When we cut such forests, we eliminate the local species almost as certainly as by shooting each individual. When all the forest on Cebu Island in the Philippines was logged, nine of the ten bird species unique to Cebu became extinct, and that last one may not survive.

The worst habitat destruction is still to come. We are just starting in earnest to destroy tropical rain forests. These forests cover only 6 percent of Earth's surface but harbor at least half of its species. Brazil's Atlantic forest and Malaysia's lowland forest are nearly gone, and most forests in Borneo and the Philippines will be logged within the next two decades. By the middle of the next century the only large tracts of tropical rain forest likely to be standing intact will be in parts of Zaire and the Amazon Basin.

Finally, our fourth method of extermination is by means of an inadvertent domino effect. Every species depends on many others, and often in such complex ways that it's impossible to foresee where any one extinction may ultimately lead. (p. 58)

A realistic projection for the future must take all these effects into account, as well as the knowledge that published lists of extinct and endangered species are gross underestimates. It is likely that more than half of all existing species will be extinct or endangered by the middle of the next century. If the estimate of 30 million for the world's total species is correct, then species are now becoming extinct at a rate of 150,000 per year, or 17 per hour.

Of course, there are people who dismiss the significance of these extinctions. So what if a few million beetle species disappear, they ask. We care about our children, not about bugs.

The answer is simply that, like all species, we depend on others for our existence. We need them to produce the oxygen we breathe, absorb the carbon dioxide we exhale, decompose our sewage, provide our food, and maintain the fertility of our soil.

Then couldn't we just preserve those species we need and let others become extinct? Of course not, because the species we need also depend on other species. The ecological chain of dominoes is much too complex for us to have figured out which dominoes we can dispense with. For instance, if you were the president of a timber company trying to figure out which species you could afford to let become extinct, you would have to answer these questions: Which ten tree species produce most of the world's paper pulp? For each of those ten tree species, which are the ten bird species that eat most of its insect pests, the ten insect species that pollinate most of its flowers, and the ten animal species that spread most of its seeds? Which other species do these birds, insects, and animals depend on?

Even without knowing the answers, you might be willing to take a chance. If you were trying to evaluate a project that would bring in millions of dollars but might exterminate a few obscure species, it would certainly be tempting to run the risk. But consider the following analogy. Suppose someone offers you a million bucks in return for the privilege of cutting out two ounces of your valuable flesh. You might figure that two ounces is less than one thousandth of your body weight, so you'll still have plenty left. That's fine if the two ounces come from your spare body fat and if they'll be removed by a skilled surgeon. But what if the deal requires you to let anyone hack two ounces from any conveniently accessible part of your body, the way much of the tropics are now being razed?

Am I saying, then, that our future is hopeless? Not at all. We are the ones who are creating the problem, so it's completely in our power to solve it. There are many realistic ways we can avoid extinctions, such as by preserving natural habitats and limiting human population growth. But we will have to do more than we are doing now.

If, on the other hand, we continue behaving as we have in the past, the devastation will also continue. The only uncertainty is whether we will halt the juggernaut or whether it will halt us. (pp. 58–9)

Jared Diamond, "Playing Dice with Megadeath," in Discover, *Vol. 11, No. 4, April, 1990, pp. 54–9.*

> **We are the ones who are creating the problem, so it's completely in our power to solve it. There are many realistic ways we can avoid extinctions, such as by preserving natural habitats and limiting human population growth. But we will have to do more than we are doing now.**

Forgotten Species: Plant Conservation

"We are living in an era of mass extinction that is primarily due to large-scale habitat destruction caused by human activity," declared Alan Templeton of Washington University. Although biologists have lately come to realize that this diagnosis applies to all corners of the living world, Templeton made the comment at a recent meeting on the conservation issues of rare plants, organized by the Center for Plant Conservation (CPC). "In the growing awareness of habitat destruction and subsequent extinctions, plant conservation biology has been somewhat neglected," says Donald Falk, director of CPC, which is a nonprofit organization based in Jamaica Plain, Massachusetts.

The recent meeting follows closely on the publication by the center of a survey showing that between now and the year 2000 some 680 plant species native to the United States will probably become extinct, a figure more than three times greater than the total for the preceding two centuries.

What is to be done? "The best remedy to prevent extinction is habitat preservation," said Templeton. "Such a strategy not only preserves species that have

"In growing awareness of habitat destruction and subsequent extinctions, plant conservation biology has been somewhat neglected."

—Donald Falk,
director of the Center
for Plant Conservation

been targeted because they are endangered, but it preserves the entire ecological community in which the species lives, which will often include additional endangered species that we are not even aware of."

But Templeton is a realist, and acknowledges that in many cases habitat preservation is not an option, at least not with current trends of urban and agricultural expansion and natural resources exploitation. "In such cases, offsite breeding of cultivated populations is needed either to preserve a species that has gone totally extinct in nature or to provide a backup for habitat preservation efforts."

In the longer term scheme of things, the maintenance of endangered plant species in botanic gardens is viewed as an interim measure. "It is ultimately hoped that cultivated populations can be released back into preserved or restored habitats," noted Templeton. "Hence, the goal of such breeding programs is to preserve the species in captivity until habitat restoration allows its release back into nature."

Habitat restoration is a controversial topic among ecologists, and so too is the means by which endangered species can be collected, maintained, and ultimately released into such habitats. This latter enterprise—the stocking of the conservationists' ark—was the focus of the recent CPC meeting, with population genetics a key issue. Two critical factors emerge in ensuring the proper rescue of endangered plants (and animals too, for that matter). . . .

First is an understanding of the population genetic pattern of the species to be collected. This is important not only in ensuring that a genetically representative sample is preserved but also because the population genetic pattern will determine how collection must be done. Second is the maintenance of the species in cultivation so that its genetic package will not suffer, thus maximizing the chance of survival on reintroduction into a wild habitat.

For many participants at the CPC meeting, the difficulties of maintaining the genetic integrity of cultivated plants emerged as *the* major problem facing plant conservation biologists. Spencer Barrett and Joshua Kohn of the University of Toronto spoke for many when they said: "A major challenge of ex situ conservation will be to ensure that sexually propagated samples of rare plants do not become museum specimens incapable of surviving under natural conditions." This danger arises from a process they describe as "unconscious domestication."

A tenet of Falk's is: "good science is the foundation of good conservation." But, as Eric Menges of the Archbold Biological Station, Florida, noted at the recent meeting, "conservation biology . . . is a crisis-oriented science." As a result, biologists are often forced to act quickly, often with inadequate theoretical models and inadequate data. And for the botanist there is the additional frustration that theoretical and practical attention has focused mainly on animals, making the collection of information on plants yet more crucial. "Our task is to construct the models and collect the data at the same time as we tackle specific conservation projects," says Falk.

For instance, the restoration of a habitat offers opportunities beyond creating an ecological community. "What to a conservationist would look like a restoration project, to a population biologist would look like an empirical test of the demographics and genetics of small populations," says Falk. And the biology of small populations is central to much of conservation science.

It is true that a plant species may be endangered for any one of several different reasons—such as narrow geographic range or narrow habitat specialization—not all of which involve small populations. Nevertheless, small population size is a leading cause of plant rarity, and once in cultivation, small population size becomes a fact of life and of continued survival. Hence the need to understand the demographic and genetic consequences of small populations.

The central issue in demographics is a measure known as minimum viable population (MVP), a subject of intense interest and research on animal species but of hardly any on plants. The MVP gives "an estimate of the minimum population size necessary to have an acceptably low probability of extinction," explained Menges. "MVP analyses for plants will necessarily differ from animal populations, simply because of the differences between plants and animals."

Animal and plant species face the same kinds of uncertainties—stochasticities—that can edge a population to extinction, four in all. First is environmental stochasticity, which refers to "variation in time in the population's operational environment." Small populations are at greatest risk here. Second is natural catastrophe, such as flood, fire, and other major external perturbations, any of which can affect small and large populations alike. Third is demographic stochasticity, "where chance events affect the survival and reproductive success of individuals." Again, small populations are most vulnerable. Last is genetic stochasticity, caused when small populations become genetically depauparate.

"As analyses of minimum viable population size for plant species are developed, they will differ considerably from those of animals," predicted Menges. The reason is that plants possess a range of characteristics that are absent in animals and will influence the population viability in important ways.

The most obvious difference is that plants are sessile organisms whereas the great majority of animal species move about, a difference that makes plant populations more vulnerable to a range of influences. Balancing this to some degree is the great plasticity plants possess in the face of changing environmental conditions. Other differences include the fact that plants often grow clonally, can exist for long periods as dormant underground structures or seeds, and have a tremendous diversity of breeding systems and life histories.

As a result, MVP analyses for plants are certain to be different—and probably more complicated—than those for animals. However these calculations turn out, Menges predicts that "environmental stochasticity and natural catastrophe will be the primary threats to most plant populations."

Biologists have known for some time that the degree of genetic variation within a species can be crucial to its survival. "Loss of variation is thought to reduce the ability of populations to adapt to changing environments and to increase their susceptibility to pest and disease pressures," explained Barrett and Kohn. Indeed, Templeton characterizes loss of variation in a species as a "partial extinction." Genetic variation is the currency of future evolution.

From the conservationist's point of view, maintenance of natural variation in cultivated populations can determine the success or failure of a conservation effort. "Restored environments will undoubtedly differ from the original habitats and communities," observed Templeton. "It is therefore critical that the released populations have sufficient genetic variability to provide adaptive flexibility in an uncertain future."

Most species naturally have a considerable amount of genetic variation, but they may differ in the way in which the variation is distributed among the existing populations. For instance, if the species is essentially a single population, with migration and gene flow occurring over large areas, then each individual's genetic package contains a fairly extensive share of the overall variation. With just a few individuals the great majority of the species' overall variation is represented. In this case, collection for offsite cultivation would be rather straightforward.

When a species is fragmented into rather isolated populations, a different picture emerges. Here, each population may be genetically rather uniform but different from neighboring populations. In which case, the all important genetic variation is distributed between populations, not within them. A collection taken from just one population for the purposes of conservation would therefore be genetically impoverished. "Without a knowledge of how the species' genetic diversity is divided within and between local populations, it is impossible to design a sampling program that will preserve a substantial portion of the species' genetic diversity," stated Templeton.

Between now and the year 2000 some 680 plant species native to the United States will probably become extinct, a figure more than three times greater than the total for the preceding two centuries.

From the conservationist's point of view, maintenance of natural variation in cultivated populations can determine the success or failure of a conservation effort.

When establishing an offsite population, conservationists prefer to be able to collect a genetically representative sample of the species in question, and in numbers sufficient to maintain a viable population. But, as already noted, conservation biology is a crisis science, and sometimes a population will have crashed to pathetic numbers before action is taken: a good example is the California condor. When this happens the conservation biologist is putting into action what sometimes occurs in nature: a founder event, in which a new population is established from a very few individuals. And the danger is the same in each case, that is, the loss of genetic variation.

Templeton described such a case in which he was involved, the Speke's gazelle. Starting with just one male and three females, Templeton and his colleagues managed to establish a large population, with the loss of remarkably little genetic variation. This was achieved by pushing for a very rapid population increase, as suggested by population genetic theory.

The great danger with small breeding populations is genetic drift, in which the loss of some alleles and the fixation of others occurs simply through the roll of the genetic dice. The genetic character of the population may therefore shift rapidly. Another source of problems, of course, is inbreeding, which may yield offspring with low fertility or viability because of the exposure of normally masked deleterious alleles.

Management of artificial breeding programs therefore has to be intense in order to maintain genetic variation. But this intensity can bring with it other dangers, namely the trap of unconscious domestication. "Unfortunately, as long as the breeding populations in captivity are genetically variable, they will have the capacity to adapt to the captive environment," explained Templeton. "Guarding against inadvertent selection for domestication can help, but we simply cannot anticipate or monitor all the ways in which a population can adapt to a captive environment."

Once again, because of the great variety of reproductive systems in plants, the problems faced in artificial breeding programs will overlap with but not be identical to those of animal breeding. In many instances, these differences make plants better candidates for offsite cultivation. But in some cases plants may be more vulnerable, such as when closely related species are destroyed through readily achieved hybridization that usually does not occur in the wild.

In addition to "a critical role for genetic surveys of natural populations in plant conservation," Templeton concludes that "much more effort will generally be required for plants before the breeding program can even be initiated, and the sampling strategies will often have to be more complex." (pp. 32–3)

Roger Lewin "How to Get Plants into the Conservationists' Ark," in Science, *Vol. 244, No. 4900, April 7, 1989, pp. 32–3.*

A Question of Breeding: Genetics and Wildlife Conservation

For hours on end, she tussles with her towel and bats her ball like a furry Pele, taking a break for avid sucks from the bottle proffered by her caretakers at the Henry Doorly Zoo in Omaha, Nebraska. Mary Alice, tipping the scales at 20 pounds last summer, looks and acts like your basic adorable feline. But she is much more, a rare Bengal tiger, of which 200 survive in the wild and 700 live in zoos. And she is a yellow and black symbol of hope that, through sophisticated breeding techniques, she and animals similarly poised to disappear from the planet may be saved.

Mary Alice is the first tiger born through in vitro fertilization. She and two brothers (which did not survive) were born by Caesarean section after sperm from one Bengal male were mixed with eggs from two female Bengals. The embyros were then implanted in a Siberian tiger at the Doorly Zoo. The procedure promises to increase tigers' genetic diversity by facilitating matings between animals separated by vast distances. For wildlife biologists, that goal is as pressing as increasing absolute numbers of endangered species.

Even after dwindling to fewer than a dozen individuals, a species can rebound—but only if the survivors differ enough in the genes they carry to adapt to a changing environment. If they are too inbred—if there have been too-frequent matings between related individuals—then the consequent loss of gene types could threaten survival. According to conservation biologist Thomas Foose of the international Captive Breeding Specialists Group (CBSG) in Minneapolis, a sort of SWAT team for captive breeding, "Within a few decades, between 2,000 and 2,500 terrestrial vertebrates will be in trouble"—in large part because of a loss of genetic diversity.

Although molecular techniques for measuring genetic diversity have so far been applied only to the cheetah, biologists suspect many creatures suffer from inbreeding. Giant pandas isolated by habitat loss on China's mountaintops, northern white rhinos in Zaire and black-footed ferrets of the American West are only a handful of the creatures threatened by a loss of genetic heterogeneity as well as by a decline in numbers.

To stop the genetic hemorrhaging, scientists are doing sophisticated captive breeding and tracking wild populations at risk of inbreeding. They are even beginning to think of the wild as a global zoo in which animals will one day be managed as closely as those in captivity. The reason: As the human population swells, and as people rob habitat from wildlife, there may come a time when creatures able to survive in nature without close management will be the exception rather than the rule. Few conservation groups have been enthusiastic about captive breeding, preferring to emphasize preservation of habitat as a tool for preventing extinctions. But the two strategies are increasingly difficult to separate.

Genes are the cards nature deals. Without a full deck, a species is like a poker player dealt all spades: doing great for now, but unable to adapt to a new game. Although in theory "there is nothing special about a great deal of genetic variation," says population biologist Michael Soule of the University of California, in reality a species without enough variety, the raw material of evolution, may be doomed—even though it may be finely adapted to the present. Consider, for instance, naked mole-rats, the most inbred mammals known. Although they now thrive in colonies similar to those of bees beneath the soils of East Africa, without genetic variation they are highly susceptible to disease or environmental change.

Animals can lose genetic diversity in several ways. With each generation, a stochastic process called genetic drift erases some gene forms from the population. But in most cases of genetic homogeneity, "the animals are not on the brink of extinction for natural reasons," argues Soule. "It is because of humans." Habitat destruction and human settlement can isolate populations, cutting them off from an influx of new genes and eliminating an important mechanism for avoiding inbreeding: dispersal of littermates. When mankind replaces savannah with parking lots, siblings are physically prohibited from finding well-separated territories.

Nowhere is the danger of genetic homogeneity more apparent than in the cheetah. Using biochemical techniques, researchers led by Stephen O'Brien of the National Cancer Institute have found that genetic variation from one wild cheetah to the next hardly exceeds that of inbred lab rats. The cheetahs have only 1 percent to 10 percent of the genetic variability of other felines. (pp. 12–13)

They are susceptible to disease, possibly because in every cheetah studied, the group of genes that controls the immune response is identical. The consequences can be tragic. In 1982 and 1983, nearly half the cheetahs in an Oregon

According to conservation biologist Thomas Foose of the international Captive Breeding Specialists Group in Minneapolis, a sort of SWAT team for captive breeding, "Within a few decades, between 2,000 and 2,500 terrestrial vertebrates will be in trouble"—in large part because of the loss of genetic diversity.

As the human population swells, and as people rob habitat from wildlife, there may come a time when creatures able to survive in nature without close management will be the exception rather than the rule. Few conservation groups have been enthusiastic about captive breeding, preferring to emphasize preservation of habitat as a tool for preventing extinctions. But the two strategies are increasingly difficult to separate.

wildlife park died from feline infectious peritonitis—which rarely kills more than 10 percent of the house cats it infects. The cheetahs simply did not have the genetic bank on which to draw to produce infection-fighting antibodies.

The cheetah's troubles probably date to 10,000 years ago. Scientists theorize that something—climate apocalypse, plague, habitat destruction or hunting—forced the cheetah through a "genetic bottleneck," making inbreeding inevitable. The term connotes an event in which so many individuals die that the few survivors retain only a fraction of the original genetic palette. But it is somewhat of a misnomer: Even small populations can be genetically viable. "Within the limits of what we know, no species is doomed unless it gets down to two or three individuals," says Ulysses Seal, chairman of the CBSG.

Just seven individuals can carry more than 95 percent of the variation. That's why, says Soule, "Even with only a dozen ferrets or condors, we actually have most of the genes"—because these animals have not suffered a genetic bottleneck. But those genes will evaporate into history unless the species expands quickly and unless its individuals mate so as to foster genetic heterogeneity. For some reason, the cheetah did not. Its plight illustrates the threat facing the world's endangered creatures.

"Loss of genetic variation is inevitable in small populations," says zoologist Georgina Mace of the Zoological Society of London. That means almost every species in captivity. Maintaining genetic diversity becomes ever more crucial as zoos not only breed rare species but try to return some animals to their native habitats. If endangered species are to survive after generations in captivity, they must face the future with a full complement of their genes.

In the simplest case, the best route to genetic diversity may be literally to import fresh genes. This past summer, for instance, the Fossil Rim Wildlife Center in Glen Rose, Texas, brought in a male cheetah from Amsterdam. "His arrival is a major victory in the fight to increase the genetic diversity of the species," says Kelley Snodgrass, cheetah curator at Fossil Rim. "With enough small pockets of the animals around the world, we think we can keep their lack of genetic diversity from pushing them into extinction."

Such gene trades are organized under "Species Survival Plans," overseen in North America by the American Association of Zoological Parks and Aquariums but carried out by member zoos. The idea is to determine the best matings to preserve the genetic vitality of the species. SSPs now cover about 60 beasts in North America, from the Arabian oryx and Bali mynah to the spectacled bear and Sumatran tiger—and about 150 worldwide. Each involves anywhere from two zoos to 85 (for tigers), and serves as a sort of family-tree master guide for choosing matings that will most effectively increase a species' genetic diversity.

All captive animals risk losing genetic diversity without genes from the wild. But since capturing rare breeds is decidedly frowned upon, the next best strategy is to dip into the genes in someone else's zoo. Without cooperation among zoos, the world's captive animals would be like creatures isolated on mountaintops, unable to reach each other and doomed to inbreed.

To find the ideal sire and mother, SSP experts scour animals' pedigrees. Then they calculate the degrees of relatedness and decide which should mate. By factoring in life span, age of reproduction, litter size and age distribution in the existing population, curators can also determine how many animals are needed for species survival. Ulysses Seal of CBSG calculates, for instance, that cooperating zoos need 160 breeding adult Siberian tigers plus about 90 younger ones; in contrast, there must be 1,000 black-footed ferrets for a viable population to thrive.

SSPs may also try to equalize family size; if no two animals contribute more than their share of genes to the next generation, diversity is maximized. For the same reason, each male and each female should be given the same chance for breeding success. Often, that means disrupting natural behavior: Although only the alpha male gorilla will mate in the wild, in captivity all the males might be given a chance at fatherhood.

Over time, loss of genetic variation in captivity is inevitable. By the mid-1980s, every Speke's gazelle in American zoos was descended from one of four animals imported in 1969. By 1979, 80 percent of the young were dying before they could reproduce, in part because of inbreeding. In a crash survival program, mammal curator Bruce Read of the St. Louis Zoo and geneticist Alan Templeton of Washington University devised a drastic plan. Short of doing DNA analysis, they had no way of knowing which animals carried certain unwanted recessive genes (a matching of recessive genes is what gave your child blue eyes despite your brown eyes). So the team mated only close relatives in order to bring together pairs of lethal recessive genes; offspring carrying them died and partly eliminated those genes from the population.

Then the team mated least-related animals to maintain as many diverse genes as possible. Today, more than two dozen Speke's gazelles are scattered around four American zoos, and the species, almost extinct in the wild, seems assured of a future. The quality of that future, of course, depends on how one views the desirability of captivity. Some animal enthusiasts say, that if animals can live only in zoos, they would be better off not living at all. The animals themselves have not been polled on the question.

Though conservationists caution against captive breeding as a replacement for saving habitat, many biologists see the two tactics as unavoidably related. "Vertebrates shape their habitat and thus influence other species, and indeed the whole ecosystem," says Seal. Without the "keystone" species (the one that shapes its habitat most strongly), other animals and plants may not make it.

Moreover, there can be political reasons a habitat needs its inhabitant. In Brazil, the government expanded the protected reserves of the golden lion tamarin only after American zoos returned a few dozen of the tiny primates to the area. "We do not want captive breeding to become an excuse not to do something about habitat," says Seal. "But high-profile species often make it easier to expand the resources for that species in the wild."

Says Foose, "Most of the natural world is becoming a mega-zoo; the numbers of so many species are so small and the populations so fragmented that they will suffer the same problems as captive populations." To save them, biologists may have to transplant their zoo techniques to the wild. If researchers identify a small population in which only a few males are breeding, thus reducing genetic diversity, "you can arrange to have new males brought in," says Foose. "This has been done with black rhinos." Giant pandas, too, could benefit from such management. Of the 700 to 1,500 remaining in China, no population numbers more than 75 or so individuals.

High-tech reproduction, on the other hand, won't be used widely for conservation until scientists know more about species' basic reproduction. David Wildt, a National Zoo physiologist, is optimistic about using in vitro fertilization to introduce genes from wild tigers to captive animals. Says Seal, "If you have separated populations of tigers, you can't just drop one in on another group; he'll get killed. So the ability to move genes without moving animals is enormously important."

For all the gloom and doom, scientists say that a population bottleneck is not a death sentence. In the past, small groups of inbred animals have recovered. (pp.13–16)

"Even if there are only a few animals left, there is no such thing as a lost cause," argues population biologist Soule. "There is only the loss of hope and the shortage of funds. With enough hope, financial support and proper management, we can save almost anything." As the creatures of this world teeter on the edge of disappearance, that hope will be severely tested. (p. 16)

Sharon Begley, "A Question of Breeding," in National Wildlife, *Vol. 29, No. 2, February-March, 1991, pp. 12–16.*

"Even if there are only a few animals left, there is no such thing as a lost cause. There is only the loss of hope and the shortage of funds. With enough hope, financial support and proper management, we can save almost anything."

—Michael Soule, University of California

Although 99 countries are party to CITES, trade experts estimate that as much as $1.5 billion of the $5 billion in annual world trade in wildlife is illegal, contravening CITES and/or domestic laws.

International Trade in Endangered Species: Regulating Wildlife Trade

In March 1987, Ecuadoran traders supplied over 25,000 pairs of olive ridley sea-turtle flippers to a private skin-trading enterprise in Mexico. In November 1986, port officials in Europe confiscated a shipment of 19 African rhinoceros horns purposely mislabeled as "spare parts." During 1985, Japan allowed enormous quantities of illegal crocodilian skins to be imported; included were over 50 tons of spectacled caiman hides from Paraguay, a notorious exit point for wildlife smuggled out of neighboring countries.

These are only a few of the blatant violations of CITES, the Convention on International Trade in Endangered Species of Wild Fauna and Flora, revealed in a report on major treaty infractions presented to delegates from CITES-member countries during a meeting to update the treaty and review compliance issues. (p. 13)

Although 99 countries are party to CITES (as of May 1989), trade experts estimate that as much as $1.5 billion of the $5 billion in annual world trade in wildlife is illegal, contravening CITES and/or domestic laws. According to Eugene Lapointe, director of the treaty's Secretariat of permanent staff, enforcement of CITES is "maybe 60 to 65 percent effective worldwide."

CITES is designed to promote conservation of endangered species while allowing commerce in species of wildlife that can withstand the pressures of trade. The convention has three categories of protection. Under its Appendix I, commercial trade in species that are threatened with extinction is generally prohibited. These species may be traded only under special conditions (usually for scientific research or display purposes). Such transactions require both an import permit from CITES authorities in the recipient country and an export permit from authorities in the country of origin (or a reexport permit if a reexporting country is involved).

Appendix I species include all the great apes, rhinos, sea turtles, great whales, the Asian elephant, the giant pitcher plant, and over 600 other animal and plant species facing extinction. (pp. 13–14)

CITES allows *conditional* commercial trade in species that are not yet endangered but merit monitoring. These species are listed on Appendix II and may be traded only with an export permit from their country of origin. Appendix II covers over 2,300 species of animals and more than 24,000 plants. (p. 14)

A third appendix to CITES is intended to help individual countries gain international cooperation in protecting native species. Any country may place a native plant or animal on Appendix III, making the species conditionally tradable. The species may not be traded without either an export permit from its native country (if that country listed it on Appendix III) or a certificate of origin (if it comes from a country that did not list it).

Under CITES, the burden of trade control is placed squarely on member nations. Like most international treaties, CITES has few enforcement provisions, although its administrative body, the CITES Secretariat, is responsible for monitoring its implementation and can bring international pressure to bear on violators by reviewing their infractions and highlighting other compliance problems. Individual countries are responsible for enforcing CITES within their borders. They are expected to police their own ports of entry and exit, report on trade, and punish violators. CITES does not apply to hunting, poaching, or trade that goes on within a country. National laws and enforcement activities are crucial to CITES success and to the conservation of commercially valuable rare and endangered species. (p. 15)

Major Violators

In 1984, Burundi and the United Arab Emirates were singled out for particularly harsh criticism. Both countries are conduits of smuggled rhino horn and elephant ivory traveling from East Africa to black markets of the Middle and Far East. Burundi, a small African nation bordering Kenya and Tanzania, has long been notorious for exporting elephant ivory marked as native, even though the country has no wild elephant population of its own. Tusks are brought in from neighboring countries and given false permits, a practice known as "laundering." This practice disguises the origin of the contraband and enables it to enter international trade channels. Experts believe that, in 1986, some 50,000 elephant tusks were exported via Burundi.

According to the CITES Secretariat, the UAE is "one of the most important havens" for illicit wildlife trade in the world. In May 1986, for example, smugglers flew over 18 tons of illicit elephant ivory from Mogadishu, Somalia, to Abu Dhabi, UAE. Despite the Secretariat's official queries to UAE diplomats, the tusks apparently entered the country without hazard. (pp. 15–16)

At the 1987 CITES convention in Ottawa, Canada, delegates criticized three major wildlife-consuming countries—Japan, France, and Austria—for ineffective import controls. Latin American nations and nongovernmental conservation organizations argued that poor compliance with CITES in these three countries undermines exporting nations' efforts to protect native plants and animals. To promote international cooperation and goodwill, delegates turned down a proposal to censure the three, instead passing a resolution calling for stricter enforcement of import controls in general.

"Japan has the largest illegal wildlife trade in the world," according to Tom Milliken, director of the Tokyo office of TRAFFIC, an international network that tracks wildlife trade around the world. . . . A large part of the problem stems from the government's reluctance to investigate the veracity of export permits, says Milliken. "By failing to look behind CITES permits to ensure that trade is legal, Japan undermines the effectiveness of the treaty. When questioned about the lack of permit investigations, an official in Japan's ministry of trade and industry claimed that it is "the responsibility of the exporting countries" to ensure proper documentation.

Japan also was criticized in Ottawa for massive imports of endangered species that enter the country under the treaty's special exemption provisions. CITES allows parties to claim a "reservation" to the listing of a species and thus continue to trade, although strict permit requirements still apply. Prior to the conference, Japan had reservations on 14 endangered species, including six whale species, three sea turtles, four reptiles, and the Himalayan musk deer. Startled by a report from TRAFFIC (Japan) that documented Japanese imports of over 2 million sea turtles—including thousands of kilograms of illegal shells and skins—in the past 17 years, conservation groups urged Japan to drop key reservations and improve import controls.

Japanese representatives to the conference responded by abolishing reservations on the green sea turtle and the desert monitor lizard, effective immediately, and the musk deer, as of 1989. Conservationists greeted this action with cautious optimism. At the time of the conference, Japan's 1987 imports of musk were proceeding at a rate triple the annual norm. This spurt caused TRAFFIC (Japan) staff to suspect strongly that traders in that country were stockpiling the substance in anticipation of the import ban, an action that could have disastrous implications for the world's remaining musk deer. (Musk—an expensive, aromatic, glandular secretion of the musk deer—is sold in Japan as a purported heart medicine and energizing drug. Most of the products labeled as musk in the United States are scented with synthetic compounds.)

Another market for exotic endangered species, France, was harshly criticized for failing to clamp down on illicit wildlife goods flowing through French Guiana, a French territory that borders the wildlife-rich countries of Brazil and

Until recently, the Bolivian government paid little heed to CITES and "seemed to strongly promote" illegal trade in wildlife taken from other countries. One trade official was even caught selling export permits to an unscrupulous hide trader, for a personal profit of some $100,000.

Although the United States has serious problems controlling illegal wildlife trade—particularly involving live birds and fashion items made from protected snakes and crocodilians—U.S. wildlife trade law is more extensive than that found in most other countries, and enforcement efforts have brought some noteworthy successes.

Suriname. Following a 1986 fact-finding mission to French Guiana, the Secretariat concluded that the territory was "a turntable for illegal trade" in rare parrots, monkeys, caimans, peccaries, small cats, and other protected wildlife taken from neighboring countries. (pp. 16–18)

France also drew fire for its imports of sea turtle products. Conference delegates voted down France's proposal to allow trade in green sea turtles raised on turtle ranches on its islands of Tromelin and Europa in the Indian Ocean. The green sea turtle is on Appendix I, but parties may vote to transfer populations to Appendix II when certain "ranching" criteria are met. The Ottawa action marked the third time since 1979 that CITES parties failed to accept French efforts to trade in sea turtles. In the past, the opposition argued successfully that biological evidence showed that the turtle populations involved did not yet meet treaty criteria for ranching. This time, the French plan was voted down because of the country's poor enforcement record; other nations doubted France's ability to differentiate between legal trade in ranched turtles and illegal trade in wild turtles.

Policies on trade in endangered species raised in captivity, particularly sea turtles and crocodiles, have caused continual, divisive debate among parties for the past decade. While trade in captive-bred animals provides financial incentives to manage breeding colonies for long-term, sustainable harvests—thus providing conservation benefits—it also can harm the species by encouraging demand for animals taken from the wild. The same holds true for artificially propagated plants. CITES parties have set up strict criteria for trading of Appendix I flora and fauna to avoid such problems. These measures can only be successful, however, if traders, enforcement officers, and consumers can differentiate wild (and illegal) animals and plants from those that are captive-bred or artificially propagated.

Several conference participants criticized Austria for allowing an Austrian pharmaceutical firm to import 20 African chimpanzees in 1986 for use in research. Austrian authorities contended that the chimps were imported for medical purposes and thus did not violate CITES prohibitions. The Secretariat and others argued that this import contravened treaty rules by being, in reality, part of a profit-making transaction for the private company.

Among the wildlife-exporting nations identified by the CITES Secretariat as having the most dismal record in regulating exports of protected flora and fauna, Bolivia and Paraguay were most severely criticized. Both countries are perennial targets of criticism for lax enforcement, particularly for acting as entrepôts for caiman skins, rare macaws, and other threatened species smuggled out of Brazil, where wildlife exports are banned. For example, some 40,000 caiman hides are reportedly smuggled out of the Brazilian Pantanal region to Bolivia and Paraguay every month. From there, the hides are tanned and shipped to luxury leather markets in the EEC and Japan.

In Bolivia, a Secretariat report said, the use of forged or stolen permits is widespread, and genuine permits are often given to illegal shipments. The country has no management program to regulate the caiman-skin trade and ensure that local supplies are not wiped out by profit-seeking hunters. Despite domestic measures to ban live wildlife exports and regulate the reptile-skin trade; an embargo among CITES parties on all wildlife imports from the country; and numerous efforts on the part of CITES staff, conservation organizations, the U.S. government, and others to improve trade controls during the 1980s, Bolivia remains one of the weakest links in the CITES system, according to the report. (pp. 18–20)

The Secretariat expressed optimism, however, about a new agreement between the Secretariat and Bolivia's president, Victor Paz Estenssoro, to improve wildlife trade matters. In April 1987, Paz Estenssoro agreed to a two-part program to oversee and regulate the caiman- and peccary-skin industries and to establish a completely new federal system for CITES compliance, including new laws and training programs for enforcement personnel. The first phase of the program is under way, with experts inventorying legal stocks of caiman and peccary skins in preparation for their export. Funds for the second phase are being sought from the U.S. Agency for International Development.

In Paraguay, too, traders regularly export thousands of skins from protected snakes, caimans, small cats, and other wildlife without CITES permits. This is in clear violation of an existing ban on nearly all wildlife exports. A common ruse is to mark such shipments as "cow and sheep skins" or use other false declarations. In one of the most blatant examples, in 1983 traders exported 2,000 reptile skins labeled as American alligator. Traffic in rare parrots, too, is a perpetual problem. (p. 20)

Notably absent from the list of offenders were Belgium and Singapore, two countries once renowned for their role in laundering illegal wildlife from developing countries to the major markets of the world. Although Belgium—with its strong economic ties to the African states of Brunei, Cameroon, and Zaire—long has been a hub of the illicit elephant ivory trade, controls have improved recently. This has been partly the result of Belgium and these African countries participating in a worldwide quota-and-marking system for elephant tusks adopted by CITES parties in 1985 to clamp down on illegal ivory trade. Singapore, which ratified CITES in 1986 in response to international conservation pressure, also is now tightening trade controls. Unfortunately, as one "black hole" closes up, another usually emerges. In Asia, Taiwan has become a large-scale laundering point for scores of rare parrots, South American reptile skins and African elephant tusks.

The United States, the largest consumer of wildlife in the world, was not singled out for trade infractions. Although the United States has serious problems controlling illegal wildlife trade—particularly involving live birds and fashion items made from protected snakes and crocodilians—U.S. wildlife trade law is more extensive than that found in most other countries, and enforcement efforts have brought some noteworthy successes. The Endangered Species Act sets out domestic requirements to implement CITES, and the Lacey Act makes it a crime to import any animal taken in violation of foreign law. The Lacey Act is often cited by wildlife lawyers as an exemplary, much needed measure to uphold other countries' efforts to protect their wildlife. The U.S. Fish and Wildlife Service (FWS), the nation's lead agency in CITES implementation, has used undercover operations to crack down on international smuggling, resulting recently in major "busts" of illicit parrot- and cacti-trading rings along the Mexican border.

It may be only a matter of time, however, before the United States comes in for increased scrutiny from CITES parties. TRAFFIC (U.S.A.), the Washington-based trade-monitoring arm of World Wildlife Fund (WWF), estimates that as much as $300 million worth of illegal wildlife imports enter the United States each year. "United States trade controls haven't improved since the last CITES meeting in 1985," Ginette Hemley, director of TRAFFIC (U.S.A.), told reporters before the Ottawa conference. (pp. 21–3)

Mexico is the major source of rare and endangered species smuggled into the United States, according to Jerome Smith, deputy chief of the FWS Division of Law Enforcement. . . . Because Mexico has never joined CITES, trade monitoring and controls on both sides of the border are particularly complicated.

Bad News/Good News

In a desperate move to curtail the dramatic decline in world rhino populations, CITES parties in Ottawa voted to ban domestic commerce in rhino horn and other rhino products—the first time members have sought to control internal trade in any species. All rhino species are in imminent danger of extinction. Two species have suffered particularly heavy losses to poachers in the past decade. Only 17 northern white rhinos remain in the wild, down from several thousand in the 1960s, and black rhinos have plummeted from 65,000 in 1970 to fewer than 4,000 today. Demand for rhino horn is centered in North Yemen, where ornate daggers with handles made of rhino horn are fashionable, and in traditional Chinese medicinal markets of the Far East, where horn extracts are

Major wildlife-consuming countries— the United States, Japan, and the members of the EEC—must bear the greatest responsibility for upholding CITES and policing international trade in wildlife and wildlife products.

By refusing to purchase rare parrots for pets, elephant ivory carvings, spotted cat fur coats, sea turtle or tortoiseshell jewelry, endangered wild cacti, or any other items made from threatened species, individuals can greatly curb the market for CITES-listed species.

believed to cure all manner of ailments. As WWF staff told Ottawa delegates, "Every effort to shut down the trade in rhino products completely must be made if rhinos are to be saved."

Looking forward to an update on the new African elephant tusk-marking and export-quota system, delegates were stunned to learn that African elephant populations had fallen by 36 percent since 1981 and that more than 100,000 elephants are being killed each year, the majority by poachers. A report issued by the African Elephant and Rhino Specialist Group (AERSG) called for improved controls on the ivory trade, rather than an outright ban on it. This advisory group of the International Union for Conservation of Nature and Natural Resources felt that such a ban would wipe out African countries' incentives to protect their elephant populations. Delegates agreed to follow the AERSG's recommendations and strengthen the system's provisions, rather than adopt a ban, apparently feeling that the system needs more time to prove itself. However, if the battle against ivory smuggling does not have more to show for itself when CITES parties reconvene in 1989, WWF sources predict, serious efforts to outlaw all trade in elephant and elephant products are likely.

The Ottawa conference did contain some good news. Wild herds of Chilean and Peruvian vicuña, which had been near extinction, are recovering, thanks to legal protection and prohibitions on trade in vicuña cloth. Announcing plans to manage vicuña-shearing operations in the Andes, Chile and Peru successfully petitioned to reopen trade in cloth taken from live animals. Observers were quick to laud the balance struck between conservation and trade. As one reporter wrote, "The vicuña decision exemplifies the treaty's philosophy: managing, not prohibiting, trade in wildlife products and striving to create financial incentives for saving species."

What Can Be Done: The Importance of Citizen Action

It is clear from the revelations in Ottawa that individual governments have much to do to improve international compliance with CITES. Tough domestic legislation, including Lacey Act-like measures to enforce other nations' trade laws and stricter penalties for smugglers, is crucial. Governments also need to give enforcement efforts greater attention—beefing up port-inspection capabilities, educating customs officials to the peculiarities of wildlife trade restrictions, providing secure permitting systems, and taking offenders to court. Better communication with the CITES Secretariat and trade authorities in foreign countries would also help bolster the treaty system.

Major wildlife-consuming countries—the United States, Japan, and members of the EEC—must bear the greatest responsibility for upholding CITES and policing international trade in wildlife and wildlife products. Not only are these countries' markets the driving force behind much of the lucrative international wildlife business, but their governments are generally better equipped with the enforcement personnel, communications systems, domestic laws, and other tools needed to control wildlife imports and exports than are governments in wildlife-rich developing countries. In many cases, the consumer countries also have a significant base of popular support for species conservation, which can encourage governments to carry out their CITES mandate.

Unfortunately, many of these consumer countries are not yet upholding wildlife trade controls as uniformly or as stringently as is needed to give species adequate protection. Market forces in these countries continue to encourage unsustainable use of rare or endangered species. Japan's large-scale trade in products from sea turtles, musk deer, and certain crocodilians is one of the most compelling examples.

The general public in countries can be invaluable in stopping illegal wildlife trade. By refusing to purchase rare parrots for pets, elephant ivory carvings, spotted cat fur coats, sea turtle or tortoiseshell jewelry, endangered wild cacti, or any other items made from threatened species, individuals can greatly curb the market for CITES-listed species. (pp. 24–6)

Expression of public concern is also extremely powerful in influencing wildlife industry officials and trade-policy makers at all levels. Citizens interested in helping stop illegal trade in endangered species can write to their national and state representatives urging greater support for wildlife-trade law enforcement programs. Letters to the editors of newspapers and magazines are tremendously useful in promoting illegal trade issues as well. Direct communication with companies that advertise products made from protected species and local stores that carry such products also can make an important difference. (p. 26)

Sarah Fitzgerald, "CITES in Action and Citizen Action," in her International Wildlife Trade: Whose Business is It? *World Wildlife Fund, 1989, pp. 13–26.*

> **Citizens interested in helping stop illegal trade in endangered species can write to their national and state representatives urging greater support for wildlife-trade law enforcement programs.**

Sources For Further Study

Arrandale, Tom. "A New Breed of Zoo." *Sierra* 75, No. 6 (November-December 1990): 26, 28, 30.
  Examines the changing role of zoos in the effort to preserve endangered species.

Bean, Michael J. "The Endangered Species Act: Protecting the Living Resources of the Parks." In *Our Common Lands: Defending the National Parks*, pp. 253–61. Washington, D.C.: Island Press, 1989.
  Examines how the Endangered Species Act of 1973 has affected the operations of the National Park Service and other federal agencies.

Bell, Nancy. "Congress Reviews International Wildlife and Plant Trade." *Bio-Science* 38, No. 9 (October 1988): 600.
  Reports on the debate in the U.S. Congress concerning the country's participation in the Convention on International Trade in Endangered Species of Wild Fauna and Flora (CITES).

Blockstein, David E. "Toward a Federal Plan for Biological Diversity." *Issues in Science and Technology* V, No. 4 (Summer 1989): 63–7.
  Reviews the inconsistent response of the U.S. government to wildlife endangerment and proposes a federal conservation strategy that would comprehensively address concerns over the loss of biological diversity.

Brower, Kenneth. "Losing Paradise." *Wilderness* 53, No. 187 (Winter 1989): 20–31.
  Reports on the mounting loss of Hawaii's endemic species.

Cadieux, Charles L. *Wildlife Extinction*. Washington, D.C.: Stone Wall Press, 1991, 259 p.
  Updates efforts to save endangered species in North America and provides a broad assessment of wildlife conservation throughout the world.

Chandler, William J., et. al., eds. *Audubon Wildlife Report 1988/1989*. San Diego: Academic Press / Harcourt Brace Jovanovich, 1988, 817 p.
  Extensively treats the significant problems, issues, and developments concerning wildlife conservation.

——— . *Audubon Wildlife Report 1989/1990*. San Diego: Academic Press / Harcourt Brace Jovanovich, 1989, 585 p.
  Focuses on federal wildlife conservation policy.

Cohn, Jeffrey P. "Genetics for Wildlife Conservation." *BioScience* 40, No. 3 (March 1990): 167–71.
  Examines the increasing use of DNA analysis in wildlife preservation.

———— . "The New Breeding Ground." *National Parks* 65, Nos. 1–2 (January–February 1991): 21–5.
> Discusses captive-breeding programs for such endangered animals as the black-footed ferret, the red wolf, and the Florida panther.

Culbert, Robert, and Blair, Robert, eds. "Recovery Planning and Endangered Species." *Endangered Species Update* 6, No. 10 (August 1989): 2–8.
> Discusses the major deficiencies in the recovery plans mandated by the Endangered Species Act and proposes means for overcoming them. Prepared by a class at the University of Michigan School of Natural Resources.

DiSilvestro, Roger L. *The Endangered Kingdom: The Struggle to Save America's Wildlife.* New York: Wiley, 1989, 241 p.
> Overview of wildlife conservation in the United States.

Dolnick, Edward. "Panda Paradox." *Discover* 10, No. 9 (September 1989): 70–6.
> Relates the social, political, and biological obstacles facing those who wish to save the panda from extinction.

"Save the Rhino." *The Economist* 311, No. 7600 (29 April 1989): 18.
> Describes the various proposals aimed at saving the rhino, including bounties on poachers and the legal harvesting of the animal's horns.

Falk, Donald L. "Restoration of Endangered Species: A Strategy for Conservation." In *Environmental Restoration: Science and Strategies for Restoring the Earth,* edited by John J. Berger, pp. 328–34. Washington, D.C.: Island Press, 1990.
> Outlines a program for the preservation of endangered species that combines traditional strategies emphasizing acquisition of land and legal protection of wildlife with offsite propagation, research, and reintroduction efforts.

Favre, David S. *International Trade in Endangered Species: A Guide to CITES.* Dordrecht: Marinus Nijhoff Publishers, 1989, 415 p.
> Detailed guide through the complex legal and bureaucratic procedures involving CITES.

Ferson, Scott, and Burgman, Mark A. "The Dangers of Being Few: Demographic Risk Analysis for Rare Species Extinction." *Ecosystem Management: Rare Species and Significant Habitats,* No. 471 (1990): 129–32.
> Technical analysis of a population dynamic model for endangered species that would aid in predicting their viability under certain environmental pressures.

Fitter, Richard. "Why Wildlife Matters." *UNESCO Courier,* No. 2 (February 1988): 18–21.
> Reviews the reasons why biological diversity must be maintained, the factors that lead to species endangerment, and the United Nations strategies now underway to prevent further loss of plants and animals.

Foose, Thomas J. "Erstwild and Megazoo." *Orion* 8, No. 2 (Spring 1989): 60–4.
> Contends that truly wild sanctuaries for wildlife are a bygone dream and that "megazoos," preserves actively managed by humans, are the only habitats left for large animals.

Griffith, Brad, et. al. "Translocation As a Species Conservation Tool: Status and Strategy." *Science* 245, No. 4917 (4 August 1989): 477–80.
> Investigates the efficacy of releasing into the wild endangered animals raised in captivity.

Grumbine, R. Edward. "Viable Populations, Reserve Size, and Federal Lands Management: A Critique." *Conservation Biology* 4, No. 2 (June 1990): 127–35.
> Suggests that biological diversity is inadequately protected in U.S. parks and proposes a landscape-level approach to ecosystem management based on dynamic rather than static models.

Hall, Sam. "Whaling: The Slaughter Continues." *Ecologist* 18, No. 6 (1988): 207–13.

Documents the continuation of commercial whaling by Japan and other countries despite the ban imposed by the International Whaling Commission.

Holing, Dwight. "Plain Dealing." *Sierra* 74, No. 1 (January-February 1989): 143–47.
Describes how cooperation between conservationists, developers, and oil companies resulted in California's Carrizo Plain reserve, the largest wildlife sanctuary of its kind in the state.

Jackson, Peter. "IUCN Special Report: Endangered Species." *IUCN Bulletin* 18, Nos. 1–3 (January-March 1987): SR1–16.
Report on wildlife endangerment by the Species Survival Commission of the International Union for Conservation of Nature and Natural Resources that uses twenty-four threatened species to represent the innumerable plants and animals that face extinction throughout the world.

Jackson, James P. "The Edge of Extinction." *American Forests* 94, Nos. 11–12 (November-December 1988): 41–5.
Describes the attempts of scientists to preserve the biological diversity of the world's rain forests.

Lazell, James, Jr. "Pushy Wildlife." *National Parks* 63, Nos. 9–10 (September-October 1989): 19–25.
Focuses on edificarian species, or animals that adapt easily to human environmental changes, and their detrimental effect on the habitats of other species.

Lewis, Dale, et. al. "Wildlife Conservation Outside Protected Areas—Lessons from an Experiment in Zambia." *Conservation Biology* 4, No. 2 (June 1990): 171–81.
Proposes that partnerships between government authorities and villagers can significantly improve wildlife conservation efforts in developing countries and cites a successful program in Zambia as evidence.

Linden, Eugene. "The Death of Birth." *Time* 133, No. 1 (2 January 1989): 32–5.
Outlines the disastrous effects that could result from the destruction of the Amazon rain forest and its vast numbers of plants and animals.

Lowe, David W., et. al., eds. *The Official World Wildlife Fund Guide to Endangered Species of North America*. 2 Vols. Washington, D.C.: Beacham, 1990.
Exhaustive guide to the threatened plants and animals of North America.

Mann, Charles C. "Extinction: Are Ecologists Crying Wolf?" *Science* 253, No. 5201 (16 August 1991): 736–38.
Presents arguments against the dire predictions of massive extinctions in coming years.

McKenna, Virginia, et. al., eds. *Beyond the Bars: The Zoo Dilemma*. 1987. Reprint. San Barnardino: The Borgo Press, 1990, 208 p.
Addresses the moral implications of keeping wild animals in captivity. Written in cooperation with Zoo Check, a nonprofit trust dedicated to preserving animals' rights and promoting the conservation of wildlife in its natural environment.

Mittermeier, Russell A. "Primate Conservation." *Orion* 8, No. 2 (Spring 1988): 38–44.
Reviews the many threats to wild primates, including habitat loss, hunting, and live capture for research and pet use. Also examines how the World Wildlife Fund and other environmental organizations are attempting to thwart the extinction of these animals.

Mlot, Christine. "Blueprint for Conserving Plant Diversity." *BioScience* 39, No. 6 (June 1989): 364–68.
Examines what mechanisms are in place to maximize genetic diversity among rare and endangered plants.

Oldfield, Sara. "The Tropical Chainsaw Massacre." *New Scientist* 123, No. 1683 (23 September 1989): 54–7.
 Examines how trade in tropical timber products has contributed to the extinction of vast numbers of species.

Perlez, Jane. "Can He Save the Elephants?" *The New York Times Magazine* (7 January 1990): 28–9, 31–3.
 Profiles Richard Leaky, the director of Kenya's Department of Wildlife Services, and his battle to end elephant poaching in that country's national parks.

Peters, Robert L. "Effects of Global Warming on Biological Diversity." In *The Challenge of Global Warming*, edited by Dean Edwin Abrahamson, pp. 82–95. Washington, D.C.: Island Press, 1989.
 Predicts how the greenhouse effect and the radical climate changes it may provoke will effect the distribution and survival of wildlife.

Reid, Walter V., and Miller, Kenton R. *Keeping Options Alive: The Scientific Basis for Conserving Biodiversity*. New York: World Resources Institute, 1990, 128 p.
 Outlines the options available for preserving biological diversity.

Robbins, Jim. "When Species Collide." *National Wildlife* 26, No. 2 (February-March 1988): 21–7.
 Examines the debate surrounding the protected status of the grizzly bear.

Rousch, G. Jon. "The Disintegrating Web: The Causes and Consequences of Extinction." *The Nature Conservancy Magazine* 39, No. 6 (November-December 1989): 4–15.
 Discusses the importance of biodiversity to human survival, the many threats to species, and the steps being taken to preserve biodiversity.

Sachs, Andrea. "A Grisly and Illicit Trade." *Time* 137, No. 14 (8 April 1991): 67–8.
 Investigates the illegal trade of rare animals in China and Southeast Asia.

Schwartz, Anne. "Banking on Seeds to Avert Extinction." *Audubon* 90, No. 1 (January 1988): 22–4, 26–7.
 Focuses on the Berry Botanic Garden in Portland, Oregon, and its rare plant seed bank.

Steinhart, Peter. "Humanity Without Biology." *Audubon* 92, No. 3 (May 1990): 24–7.
 Contends that the rehabilitation of injured and orphaned wildlife rarely helps, and actually may harm, the viability of their species.

Tober, James A. *Wildlife and the Public Interest: Nonprofit Organizations and Federal Wildlife Policy*. New York: Praeger, 1989, 220 p.
 Investigates the public and private agencies that oversee the protection and exploitation of wildlife in the U.S.

20: World Water Supply

The World Water Cycle

Water is our planet's most accomplished traveler. This peripatetic compound traverses the globe, passing through its states of vapor, ice, and liquid, enduring through the ages so that the sweat of your brow today may have once quenched Plato's thirst or coursed through an ancient dinosaur's veins. It is ubiquitous, and the earth's solar and gravity-powered circulation system that moves water amounts to a giant distillation and pumping machine.

The sun's heat evaporates seawater, but most of this returns as precipitation to the ocean surface. Around 9 percent, however, escapes. It is carried over the continents, joining with evaporation from lakes, rivers, and the land itself. This again falls as precipitation, and although a small portion is retained from years up to millennia in lakes, groundwater, and glaciers, most of this moisture again evaporates into the atmosphere.

The greatest part of this exchange eventually flows back to the oceans by means of channels, either on or under the earth's surface. But no matter how long the water is delayed in any of the natural reservoirs, it is ultimately released to enter the cycle again. Although the hydrologic circle is a closed system that neither loses nor gains water, the amount available in any part of it and the rate of movement between its resting places varies over time. Local, short-term changes cause floods and droughts. The larger geologic fluctuations produce deserts and ice ages across entire continents. And throughout it all, the cycle is the source of our fresh-water needs—from the two quarts necessary daily for every human's survival, to the estimated 1,900 gallons per capita per day use in the United States to satisfy primarily the prodigious requirements of industry and agriculture.

Man has withdrawn water from this system for thousands of years. Ancient civilizations in northern Africa, the Middle East, India, Central America, and China constructed large irrigation systems involving lengthy canals and sizable dams and reservoirs. But it is only in our century with its rapid population growth, industrialization, technological advancement, and the subsequent increased water use that we have radically altered the hydrologic cycle. The scale of interference is vast.

Although rivers comprise the smallest reservoir of the water cycle (an estimated 1,200 cubic kilometers), they have a rapid turnover rate, are easily exploited, and have long been our prime resource of water. We also interrupt the water cycle by drawing from the unseen and often apparently limitless supply below the ground. Groundwater, usually biologically pure, and near enough to the surface to be easily accessible, constitutes a much larger reservoir of fresh water than does surface flow, but its replacement rate is extremely slow. Complete turnover of the most active zone averages 330 years. Rivers, however, replenish themselves, on the average, in only eleven days. Such an enormous contrast is especially surprising as groundwater and surface flow are intimately linked. Depending on the relative elevation of the water table and the river surface, rivers "feed" the groundwater reservoir or vice versa.

> **Although the hydrologic circle is a closed system that neither loses nor gains water, the amount available in any part of it and the rate of movement between its resting places varies over time.**

Humans have withdrawn water from the world's hydrologic system for thousands of years. Ancient civilizations in northern Africa, the Middle East, India, Central America, and China constructed large irrigation systems involving lengthy canals and sizable dams and reservoirs. But it is only in our century with its rapid population growth, industrialization, technological advancement, and the subsequent increased water use that we have radically altered the hydrologic cycle. The scale of interference is vast.

Although dams have been used to modify river regimes since antiquity, the widespread construction of massive structures with huge reservoirs is a twentieth-century phenomenon. Prior to 1900, only forty-one dams had been built with reservoirs whose volume exceeded 100 million cubic meters. Total storage behind these was around 14 cubic kilometers. Today, including those under construction, the number of such structures is over 2,250, with an aggregate storage of 5,181 cubic kilometers—a volume that equals 13 percent of the world's average annual river flow.

Some of the dams and their associated reservoirs built over the last two decades are colossal. The Bratsk hydro complex on the Angara River in the USSR, completed in the mid-1960s, has a dam 106 meters high backing up a 169 cubic kilometer reservoir with a surface area of 5,470 square kilometers. The 90-meter Aswan Dam on the Nile, finished in 1970, created a lake of 157 cubic kilometers and 5,120 square kilometers. The Volta Dam in Ghana, built in the 1960s, has a reservoir of 148 cubic kilometers and an area of 8,480 square kilometers—15 percent of the extent of Lake Michigan.

Such man-made meddling with the water cycle has been a mixed blessing. Although it provides power production, flood control, navigation enhancement and recreation, there have also been severe environmental consequences: reduced access to spawning areas for anadromous fishes, flooding of valuable land and the raising of the water table, increased evaporation from the reservoir surface, and filtration. Changes in water temperature, sediment and nutrient levels, dissolved oxygen, current velocities, and bottom conditions commonly lead to changes in aquatic life. Frequently, the result is replacement of more highly valued species by less desirable ones. Below the dam, probably the most adverse consequence is the reduction of spring floods. Spawning of many fish species is dependent on appropriate inundation of flood plains, which is determined by the intensity and duration of these flows.

Fish ladders and other devices have been installed to alleviate the migration problem, but their effectiveness is questionable. Despite these, dams along the Columbia River have decimated the Pacific salmon runs. In the USSR, the Caspian Sea salmon, whitefish, and sturgeon fishery has been severely damaged by the chain of dams along the Volga River, the sea's main tributary and their primary spawning ground.

Large reservoirs, particularly those created in plains areas, often flood valuable land or so raise the water table as to greatly diminish its worth. One of the worst cases has occurred in the Soviet Union along the Volga and its tributary the Kama, where 20,000 hectares have been inundated by twelve large reservoirs. Not only was substantial resettlement required, but 50 percent of the lost land was agriculturally valuable and a sizable portion of the remainder was covered by commercially valuable forests. Raised groundwater levels damaged land for several kilometers around some of these reservoirs, creating swamps, salinizing soils, and killing forests.

Large reservoirs also directly reduce water flow because of increased evaporation and infiltration. The problem is worst in arid regions where evaporation rates are high and water tables deep, which leads to water percolating from the reservoir beds into the surrounding rock strata. In very dry climates, annual net evaporation from large reservoirs (i.e., evaporation from the water surface minus precipitation on it) may equal 1.7 meters. In the Colorado Basin, for example, net evaporation from reservoirs is around 2.6 cubic kilometers annually—14 percent of the estimated average annual virgin flow of around 18 cubic kilometers.

Besides ill effects from damming the natural water flow, the actual withdrawal of fresh water from the cycle has serious consequences for the downstream environment, especially when withdrawals are not returned (at least directly) to the source from which they came. The worst problem is irrigated agriculture, the largest world-wide water supply user, since most of what is removed evaporates, transpires, or infiltrates into the soil. The global irrigated area in the mid-1970s was around 220 million hectares; withdrawals for irrigation had reached 2,500 cubic kilometers annually.

Withdrawal of surface water is especially excessive in the lower Colorado Basin (drainage area below Lees Ferry, Arizona) and the Aral Sea basin in the USSR. The former is one of the driest areas in North America, with precipitation averaging less than five to fifteen inches annually. The main source of water is the Colorado River, which has been intensively developed for irrigation and other water supply uses. Stream flow here averages 8.5 cubic kilometers annually. Fresh water withdrawals in 1975 equaled 12.3 cubic kilometers. In addition 6.2 cubic kilometers were exported, primarily to southern California via the Colorado aqueduct and the All-American Canal, and 1.7 cubic kilometers were lost to reservoir evaporation. Thus, water used plus water lost equaled 14.3 cubic kilometers, 68 percent greater than surface flow. The difference was made up by using groundwater. However, groundwater is being severely overdrafted. (pp. 30–1)

A similar situation exists in the Aral Sea Basin, the most important region of irrigated agriculture in the Soviet Union, with 8 million hectares receiving supplementary water. Surface flow, which averages around 127 cubic kilometers, is much larger than in the lower Colorado. Nevertheless, during several low flow years in the mid-1970s water demand exceeded flow and required significant reservoir drawdown. (p. 31)

Probably the most outstanding example of a man-made problem is the catastrophic drop in the Aral Sea's level. The water surface has fallen seven meters and the area shrunk from 66,000 to 52,000 square kilometers since 1960. A further decline of eight meters could occur by the year 2000. The discharges of the Syrdarya and Amudarya rivers, the sea's only source of inflow, have dropped 43 percent over the past twenty-two years, and are expected to continue decreasing in the future. The water body's shrinkage has been accompanied by rising salinity, a sharp drop in fishery productivity, and the growth of desert in adjacent lands. Soviet scientists and planners are trying to devise measures that would preserve the sea, although at a much smaller than natural size.

An estimated 60 million cubic kilometers of water lie beneath the earth's surface. Although the supply is enormous, the rate of replacement is very slow, averaging 5,000 years for the entire resource, and around three centuries for that part in the active zone of replenishment. Because it traditionally has been a biologically pure source, many communities depend upon it for drinking supplies. Owing to growing water consumption in arid regions, the resource is being overdrafted or "mined", which occurs when removal from aquifers exceeds recharge. The consequences can be severe: rapidly dropping water tables, requiring deeper wells and more electricity for pumping; intrusion of saline water into groundwater reservoirs in coastal areas; and the sudden appearance of sink holes, as has happened in Florida.

Groundwater overdraft problems are particularly bad in the western United States, where surface water supplies are proving inadequate to meet increasing requirements, chiefly for irrigation. (pp. 31–2)

As population, industrialization, agricultural production, and technological capabilities increase, world water withdrawals could double by the end of the century from their mid-1970 level of 3,625 cubic kilometers. Grandiose and costly water resource management projects have recently been completed, are being constructed, or are imminent. The California State Water Project now carries nearly three cubic kilometers a year from the northern part of the state to the south. Although there is considerable opposition, the diversion may be significantly increased, primarily to meet growing irrigation demands. (p. 32)

The economic, social, and environmental implications of [water diversion] projects are numerous and complex. Areas of water export (northern regions) would, on balance, suffer. Southern importing regions would benefit. Initial phases would cause various kinds of local and regional damage, such as reduced flow below the points of diversion, flooding of valuable land, and degraded habitat conditions for fish. Later, much larger transfers could affect

The widespread construction of massive structures with huge reservoirs is a twentieth-century phenomenon. Prior to 1900, only forty-one dams had been built with reservoirs whose volume exceeded 100 million cubic meters. Total storage behind these was around 14 cubic kilometers. Today the number of such structures is over 2,250, with an aggregate storage of 5,181 cubic kilometers—a volume that equals 13 percent of the world's average annual river flow.

**As population, industri-
alization, agricultural
production, and techno-
logical capabilities in-
crease, world
groundwater withdrawals
could double by the end
of the century.**

environmental conditions over extensive areas. The Arctic Ocean ice cover, for example, might even be sufficiently altered to cause a perceptible influence on the Northern Hemisphere's climate.

Man's interference with the hydrologic cycle has already caused serious regional problems. Larger future disruptions are likely to lead to still greater damage over more extensive areas. To mitigate adverse impacts we need a clearer understanding of the hydrologic cycle and its functioning as a complex and dynamic natural system. We must then devise methods (including mathematical simulation models) to forecast accurately the effect of various major interferences in the water cycle. Only then can we expect that these studies will be given appropriate weight in making decisions on when to interfere with the natural movement of water and when to leave it be. (p. 35)

Phillip P. Micklin, "Interrupting the Water Cycle," in Oceans, *Vol. 15, No. 5, September–October, 1982, pp. 30–5.*

Thirsty in a Water-Rich World: Availability of the Resource

The world is not running out of water. Far from it: enough drinkable water comes down from the sky every year to allow each person on Earth several times the amount needed to sustain a moderate standard of living. Instead of diminishing, today's freshwater supply is the same as when civilization first dawned.

Why, then, do water shortages plague the world? The obvious reason is that, while rain may fall on the just and the unjust, it doesn't do so equally, everywhere. And, unlike other vital resources, such as coal, oil and wood, water is usually needed in vast quantities that are too unwieldy to be traded globally. As populations and economies expand, regional water sources become overtaxed. Today, a once-cheap resource is becoming increasingly expensive as people go to greater lengths to obtain it. In some regions, conserving water, instead of transporting it, may be the only solution.

Most water that falls on land makes its way to the sea as "runoff." Nearly two-thirds of this flows rapidly away in floods, often bringing more destruction than benefit. Only a third is a reliable source of water for drinking or for irrigating crops year-round. Most of this "stable flow" of water infiltrates the soil and flows underground, providing a base for rivers and streams.

If global climates remain the same and populations grow as predicted, the amount of this available water per person at the end of the century will have declined by 24 percent. Shortages will be especially acute in many regions where population continues to grow fastest. Supplies per person in Kenya will drop by half, in Nigeria by 42 percent, in Bangladesh and Egypt by a third and in India by a fourth.

There are already wide disparities in how water is used around the globe. In developed countries, with their water-using appliances and sprinkled lawns, households can easily use more than 150 gallons per person per day. In countries such as Kenya, on the other hand, where women may walk several miles to draw water for their families, daily use can be close to the minimum required for survival: two to five quarts per person.

Agriculture accounts for about 70 percent of total use of available water worldwide. As fertile land has become more scarce, irrigation has enabled farmers to get higher yields from existing fields, essentially substituting water for new cropland. Rice farmers using a controllable, year-round source of water, in combination with generous amounts of fertilizer, pesticides and high-yielding seeds, have been able to triple production. In light of such yields, the amount of land irrigated worldwide has tripled since 1950. It now covers an area of more than a million square miles. Roughly a third of today's harvest comes from the 17 percent of the world's cropland that is irrigated. Irrigation thus helps meet the challenge of feeding an ever-growing population.

The problem is that irrigation demands a large share of a region's available water. Typically, more water is transported and applied to fields than the crops require. Even more important, much of it evaporates and cannot be reused. Often less than half of the water withdrawn for irrigation returns to a nearby stream or aquifer.

Industry is the second major water user, accounting for a quarter of worldwide demand. Most developing nations are just embarking on the industrialization path taken by other countries decades ago, and industrial demand in these countries will burgeon.

Residential and other municipal uses of water account for less than a tenth of total use worldwide. But in developing countries, where fresh water is not yet convenient everywhere, such demand will probably increase considerably. The World Health Organization estimates that, as of 1980, 71 percent of the developing world's rural population had to walk to obtain drinking water. The United Nations has set a goal of providing safe water to all by 1990. This would contribute to a doubling of Third World domestic water consumption by the end of the century, although experts doubt that the goal will be met.

Even given those large increases by the year 2000, total needs worldwide are still likely to comprise less than half the stable, renewable supply. Yet experts say that demands in North Africa and the Middle East will require virtually all usable freshwater supplies in those regions. Use in southern and eastern Europe, as well as in central and southern Asia, will also be uncomfortably close to the volume that those regions can safely and reliably tap. Moreover, even if supplies appear more than adequate, no region is immune from the consequences of mismanagement and abuse.

Some of the worst harm is done underground. Vast quantities of the Earth's water move slowly beneath the surface through the pores and fractures of rock layers called aquifers. Some hold water thousands of years old and receive little replenishment from rainfall. Like oil reserves, water in these fossil aquifers is essentially nonrenewable. Pumping more water than is replaced—which geologists call "mining"—supports only a fragile and short-term prosperity at best. Eventually the water becomes too salty to use or too expensive to pump to the surface—or it runs out altogether. If water pumped from an aquifer is not replaced, the land overlying it can sometimes sink, or "subside." In China, portions of the capital city of Beijing have been sinking up to a foot a year since 1950.

In coastal areas, heavy pumping may reduce the amount of groundwater flowing to the ocean, allowing seawater to invade the aquifer. Salt threatens to contaminate the drinking water of many cities and towns along the U.S. Atlantic and Gulf coasts. Israel, Syria and the Arabian Gulf states are also battling the problem. Once it occurs, contamination is difficult, if not impossible, to reverse.

Excessive demands also take a toll on lakes, estuaries and inland seas that are sustained by fresh water from nearby streams. The Soviet Union's Volga River, for example, is the Caspian Sea's major water source. Construction of huge dams on the river and subsequent withdrawals for irrigation have reduced its flow dramatically. The threat to the sea's fisheries—which support 90 percent of the world's sturgeon catch—is so great that officials, anxious to stabilize the Caspian's level, are planning a vast project to transfer water from northern European lakes and rivers to the Volga drainage basin.

If global climates remain the same and populations grow as predicted, the amount of available water per person at the end of the century will have declined by 24 percent.

Vast quantities of the Earth's water move slowly beneath the surface through the pores and fractures of rock layers called aquifers. Some hold water thousands of years old and receive little replenishment from rainfall. Like oil reserves, water in these fossil aquifers is essentially nonrenewable. Pumping more water than is replaced—which geologists call "mining"—supports only a fragile and short-term prosperity at best. Eventually the water becomes too salty to use or too expensive to pump to the surface—or it runs out altogether.

Among the least affordable consequences of wasteful water use is the degradation of valuable cropland from poor irrigation practices. Most farmers, in developing as well as industrial countries, use the "gravity-flow" method of irrigation, which dates back to ancient Egypt and Babylon. These systems distribute water from a well or surface canal through unlined ditches that allow vast quantities of water to seep down beneath the earth. Where drainage is inadequate, the water table gradually rises, eventually entering the crops' root zone and waterlogging the soil. In the Indian state of Madhya Pradesh, a large irrigation project that originally was expected to increase crop production tenfold led to extensive waterlogging and, consequently, a reduction in corn and wheat yields. The local farmers now refer to their fields as "wet deserts."

In dry climates, waterlogging may be accompanied by salinization as water near the surface evaporates and leaves behind a damaging residue of salt. According to some estimates, waterlogging and salinization are sterilizing some 2½ to 4 million acres of fertile soil each year.

Even where drainage is adequate, irrigation water can pick up chemicals from fertilizers and carry them downstream. Pollution can cause shortages as much as overuse does, by spoiling water. Unless pollution is dealt with, it may render as much as a fourth of the world's reliable supply unsafe for use by the year 2000. In the Soviet Union, industrial wastewaters comprise 10 percent of the Volga River's average flow at Volgograd. According to Thane Gustafson, a U.S. specialist on Soviet affairs, "Footdragging by industry on pollution control will make it necessary to use more water for dilution," helping to cause "a greater demand for water at the end of the century than the available supplies can satisfy."

In attempting to augment available water supplies, society has built many dams and diversion projects to store and redirect water to where it is most needed. Many countries are finding, however, that the list of possible dam sites is growing short, and that the economic and environmental costs of such projects are escalating.

As an alternative, engineers are exploring the idea of storing water underground. Excess runoff can be spread over land and allowed to percolate downward, or it can be injected through a well. This converts damaging flood waters into a stable source of supply, while avoiding the large losses from evaporation that surface reservoirs cause. In India, subsurface storage has sparked interest as a way of providing a reliable source of irrigation for the productive soils of the Ganges River basin. According to some estimates, a fully irrigated Ganges plain could grow crops to feed three-quarters of India's population. Soviet scientist M. I. L'vovich has predicted that "the twenty-first century will undoubtedly be the century of underground reservoirs."

Of the less conventional ways to augment a region's fresh water—such as seeding clouds to induce precipitation, towing icebergs and desalting seawater—desalinization appears to hold the greatest near-term potential. With the oceans holding 97 percent of all the water on Earth, desalted seawater seems to offer unlimited fresh water. Yet the large amount of energy required makes the method five to ten times more costly than supplying water in conventional ways.

As affordable options to augment dependable water supplies diminish, we must learn to use existing supplies more efficiently. Using less water to grow grain, make steel, and flush toilets increases the water available for other uses as surely as does building a dam or diverting a river.

Since agriculture claims the bulk of the world's water budget and is by far the largest consumer, saving even a small fraction of this water frees a large amount to meet other needs. Making irrigation just ten percent more efficient worldwide, for example, would save enough water to supply the entire world's household uses.

One way to do this is with drip or trickle irrigation systems, developed in Israel in the 1960s. These extensive networks of perforated pipes supply water and fertilizer directly onto or below the soil. They release water close to the plants' roots, minimizing evaporation and seepage. Such costly systems are now used on a million acres worldwide, mainly for high-value crops in water-short areas.

Farmers using conventional gravity-flow systems can cut their water demands 30 percent by capturing and recycling the water that would otherwise run off the field. Israel has pioneered the development of automated irrigation, in which the timing and amount of water applied to crops is controlled by computers. The computer not only sets the water flow; it also detects leaks, adjusts water application for wind speed and soil moisture and determines the right amount of fertilizer.

In the Third World, where capital is increasingly scarce, better management of existing irrigation systems may hold the best near-term prospect for increasing crop production and conserving water. At a pilot project in Egypt, improved management of irrigation systems is largely credited with boosting rice yields 35 percent. The savings in water alone may often justify such an investment. By some estimates, better irrigation management in Pakistan could annually save a volume of water equal to four times the storage capacity of the nation's huge Tarbela Dam—at one-fourth the cost of developing new water supplies.

Many other options are available to reduce the demand for fresh water. Some areas are finding, for example, that brackish water and treated wastewater can meet many of their needs. In Saudi Arabia, brackish water irrigates salt-tolerant crops such as sugar beets, barley, cotton, spinach and date palms. In some industrial nations, power plants are using saltwater for cooling.

The key to wise use of water lies in adopting policies that promote efficiency rather than discourage it. The prices charged for water often bear little relation to the real cost and quantity of water supplied. Making people pay for more of water's true cost is the best way to achieve that efficiency.

In an era of growing competition for limited water, heightened environmental awareness and scarce capital, new water strategies are needed. Conservation and better management can free a large volume of water—and money—for competing uses. Thus far, we have seen only hints of their potential.

Sandra Postel, "Managing Freshwater Supplies," in State of the World: A Worldwatch Institute Report on Progress Toward a Sustainable Society, *1985, p. 42.*

> **Engineers are exploring the idea of storing water underground. Excess run-off can be spread over land and allowed to percolate downward, or it can be injected through a well. This converts damaging flood waters into a stable source of supply, while avoiding the large losses from evaporation that surface reservoirs cause.**

Threats to the World's Water

Water is the earth's most distinctive constituent. It set the stage for the evolution of life and is an essential ingredient of all life today; it may well be the most precious resource the earth provides to humankind. One might therefore suppose that human beings would be respectful of water, that they would seek to maintain its natural reservoirs and safeguard its purity. Yet people in countries throughout the world have been remarkably shortsighted and negligent in this respect. Indeed, the future of the human species and many others may be compromised unless there is significant improvement in the management of the earth's water resources.

All the fresh water in the world's lakes and creeks, streams and rivers represents less than .01 percent of the earth's total store of water. Fortunately, this freshwater supply is continually replenished by the precipitation of water vapor from the atmosphere as rain or snow. Unfortunately, much of that

Water is the earth's most distinctive constituent. It set the stage for the evolution of life and is an essential ingredient of all life today; it may well be the most precious resource the earth provides to humankind.

precipitation is contaminated on the way down by gases and particles that human activity introduces into the atmosphere.

Fresh water runs off the land and on its way to the ocean becomes laden with particulate and dissolved matter—both natural detritus and the wastes of human society. When the population density in the catchment area is low, waste matter in the water can be degraded by microbes through a process known as natural self-purification. When the self-purifying capacity of the catchment area is exceeded, however, large quantities of these waste substances accumulate in the oceans, where they can harm aquatic life. The water itself evaporates and enters the atmosphere as pure water vapor. Much of it falls back into the ocean; what falls on land is the precious renewable resource on which terrestrial life depends.

The World Resources Institute estimates that 41,000 cubic kilometers of water per year return to the sea from the land, counterbalancing the atmospheric vapor transport from sea to land. Some 27,000 cubic kilometers, however, return to the sea as flood runoff, which cannot be tapped, and another 5,000 cubic kilometers flow into the sea in uninhabited areas. Of the 41,000 cubic kilometers that return to the sea, some amount is retained on land, where it is absorbed by the vegetation, but the precise amount is not known.

This cycle leaves about 9,000 cubic kilometers readily available for human exploitation worldwide. That is a plentiful supply of water, in principle enough to sustain 20 billion people. Yet because both the world's population and usable water are unevenly distributed, the local availability of water varies widely. When evaporation and precipitation balances are worked out for each country, water-poor and water-rich countries can be identified. Iceland, for example, has enough excess precipitation to provide 68,500 cubic meters of water per person per year. The inhabitants of Bahrain, on the other hand, have virtually no access to natural fresh water; they are dependent on the desalinization of seawater. In addition, withdrawal rates per person differ widely from country to country: the average U.S. resident consumes more than 70 times as much water every year as the average resident of Ghana does.

Although the uses to which water is put vary from country to country, agriculture is the main drain on the water supply. Averaged globally, 73 percent of water withdrawn from the earth goes for that purpose. Almost three million square kilometers of land have been irrigated—an area nearly the size of India—and more is being added at the rate of 8 percent a year.

Local water shortages can be solved in two ways. The supply can be increased, either by damming rivers or by consuming capital—by "mining" groundwater. Or known supplies can be conserved, as by increasing the efficiency of irrigation or by relying more on food imports.

In spite of such efforts, there is no doubt that water is becoming increasingly scarce as population, industry and agriculture all expand. Severe shortages occur as demand exceeds supply. Depletion of groundwater is common in, for example, India, China and the U.S. In the Soviet Union the water level of both the Aral sea and Lake Baikal is dropping dramatically as a result of agricultural and industrial growth in those areas. Contentious competition for the water of such international rivers as the Nile, the Jordan, the Ganges and the Brahmaputra is a symptom of the increasing scarcity of water.

Another problem brought on by overirrigation is salinization. As water evaporates or is taken up by plants, salt is left behind in the soil. The rate of deposition exceeds the rate at which the salt can be removed by flowing water, and so a residue accumulates. Currently more than a million hectares every year are subject to salinization; in the U.S. alone more than 20 percent of the irrigated land is thus affected.

Human activity in a river basin can often aggravate flood hazards. Deforestation and excessive logging lead not only to increased soil erosion but also to increased runoff; in addition, navigation canals are sometimes dug, which may exacerbate flooding by increasing the amount of water that reaches the floodplain.

Finally, of course, any human activity that accentuates the greenhouse effect and ensuing climatic change must inevitably influence the global water cycle. A projected sea-level rise of between .5 and 1.5 meters in the next century, for instance, not only would pose a coastal flooding problem but also would lead to salinization of water resources, create new wetlands while destroying existing ones and increase the ratio of salt water to fresh water on the globe. Precipitation could rise by between 7 and 15 percent in the aggregate; the geographic variations are not predictable.

Assuring an adequate supply is not the only water problem facing many countries throughout the world: they need to worry about water quality. In its passage through the hydrological cycle, water is polluted by two kinds of waste. There is traditional organic waste: human and animal excreta and agricultural fibrous waste (the discarded parts—often more than half—of harvested plants). And there is waste generated by a wide range of industrial processes and by the disposal, after a brief or long lifetime, of industry's products.

Although organic waste is fully biodegradable, it nonetheless presents a significant problem—and in some places a massive one. Excessive biodegradation can cause oxygen depletion in lakes and rivers. Human excreta contain some of the most vicious contaminants known, including such pathogenic microorganisms as the waterborne agents of cholera, typhoid fever and dysentery.

Industrial waste can include heavy metals and considerable quantities of synthetic chemicals, such as pesticides. These materials are characterized by toxicity and persistence: they are not readily degraded under natural conditions or in conventional sewage-treatment plants. On the other hand, such industrial materials as concrete, paper, glass, iron and certain plastics are relatively innocuous, because they are inert, biodegradable or at least nontoxic.

Wastes can enter lakes and streams in discharges from such point sources as sewers or drainage pipes or from diffuse sources, as in the case of pesticides and fertilizers in runoff water. Wastes can also be carried to lakes and streams along indirect pathways—for example, when water leaches through contaminated soils and transports the contaminants to a lake or river. Indeed, dumps of toxic chemical waste on land have become a serious source of groundwater and surface-water pollution. The metal drums containing the chemicals are nothing less than time bombs that will go off when they rust through. The incidents at Lekkerkerk in the Netherlands and at Love Canal in the U.S. are indicators of the pollution of this kind going on worldwide in thousands of chemical waste dumps.

Some pollutants enter the water cycle by way of the atmosphere. Probably best known among them is the acid that arises from the emission of nitrogen oxides and sulfur dioxide by industry and motor vehicles. Acid deposition, which can be "dry" (as when the gases make direct contact with soil or vegetation) or "wet" (when the acid is dissolved in rain), is causing acidification of low-alkalinity lakes throughout the industrialized world. The acid precipitation also leaches certain positively charged ions out of the soil, and in some rivers and lakes ions can reach concentrations that kill fish.

In areas of intensive animal farming, ammonia released from manure is partly introduced into the atmosphere and partly converted by soil microbes into soluble nitrates in the soil. Since nitrate has high mobility (it is soluble in water and does not bind to soil particles), it has become one of the main pollutants of groundwater, often reaching concentrations that exceed guidelines established by the World Health Organization.

The wind can also carry pollutants—fly ash from coal-burning plants, for example, or sprayed pesticides. These can be carried great distances, eventually to be deposited on the surfaces of lakes or of rivers.

The future of the human species and many others may be compromised unless there is significant improvement in the management of the earth's water resources.

Water withdrawal rates per person differ widely from country to country: the average U.S. resident consumes more than 70 times as much water every year as the average resident of Ghana does.

Another recently recognized aspect of water pollution is the accumulation of heavy metals, nutrients and toxic chemicals in the bottom mud in deltas and estuaries of highly polluted rivers, such as the Rhine. Because of their high pollution content, sediments that are dredged up cannot be used for such projects as landfills in populated or agricultural areas. Moreover, there is always the danger that natural processes or human activity will trigger chemical reactions that mobilize the pollutants by rendering them soluble, thus allowing them to spread over great distances.

The quality of inland waters depends not only on the amount of waste generated but also on the decontamination measures that have been put into effect. The degree of success in the battle for water quality differs from country to country, but it can be generalized into a conceptual formula proposed by Werner Stumm and his co-workers of the Swiss Federal Institute for Water Resources and Water Pollution Control in Zurich. The formula holds that the contamination load of a river basin depends on the population in the basin, the per capita gross national product, the effectiveness of decontamination and the amount of river discharge.

Most rivers in the industrialized world, where the population and per capita GNP are stable and decontamination procedures tend to be fairly effective, are nonetheless polluted by both traditional and industrial wastes. Yet some stabilization—if not improvement—of pollution levels was reported in the early 1980's. (Methods for treatment of traditional wastes consist mostly of sedimentation and aerobic and anaerobic microbial degradation, which are intensified forms of natural self-purification.) Methods for degrading inorganic pollutants such as metals and toxic chemicals, although improving, have not been as promising.

Where increasing industrial activity in a river basin has been matched by increasing waste treatment, a decent level of water quality can be maintained. Yet the balance between contamination and decontamination is a precarious one. A serious accidental discharge, such as the one that followed a 1986 fire at a Sandoz factory on the Rhine in Switzerland, is enough to wipe out large numbers of aquatic organisms and force drinking-water purification plants to close their intakes downstream from the accident.

In most newly industrializing countries both organic and industrial river pollution are on the increase, since the annual per capita GNP is rising quickly (as is the population, to a lesser extent) and decontamination efforts are often neglected. In these countries industrialization has had higher priority than reduction of pollution. As a consequence, in some regions (East Asia, for example), degradation of water resources is now considered the gravest environmental problem.

In less developed countries, where the population is growing and where waste treatment is practically nonexistent, water pollution by organic wastes is widespread. As a result, millions of people—and children in particular—die each year from water-related diseases that can be prevented by proper sanitation facilities. These countries still suffer from diseases eradicated in the West long ago. Although the United Nations declared the 1980s to be the International Drinking Water Supply and Sanitation Decade and instituted a program to provide safe drinking water and appropriate sanitation for all by 1990, much remains to be done before the program's ambitious goals are met. Some progress has nonetheless been made in several countries, including Mexico, Indonesia and Ghana.

The quality of the water in lakes is comparable to that in rivers. Thousands of lakes, including some large ones, are currently being subjected to acidification or to eutrophication: the process in which large inputs of nutrients, particularly phosphates, lead to the excessive growth of algae. When the overabundant algae die, their microbial degradation consumes most of the dissolved oxygen in the water, vastly reducing the water's capacity to support life. Experience in Europe and North America has shown that the restoration of lakes is possible—at a price—but that the process takes several years. Liming is effective against acidification; flushing out the excess nutrients and restricting the further inflow of nutrients helps to reduce eutrophication.

Although pollution of rivers and lakes is potentially reversible, that is not the case for groundwater. Actually, little is known about the quality of the earth's vast groundwater reserves, except in those instances where particular aquifers are being actively exploited. In Europe and the U.S., where groundwater represents a significant source of fresh water, between 5 and 10 percent of all wells examined are found to have nitrate levels higher than the maximum recommended value of 45 milligrams per liter. Many organic pollutants find their way into groundwater as seepage from waste dumps, leakage from sewers and fuel tanks or as runoff from agricultural land or paved surfaces in proliferating urban and suburban areas.

Because groundwater is cut off from the atmosphere's oxygen supply, its capacity for self-purification is very low: the microbes that normally break down organic pollutants need oxygen to do their job. Prevention of contamination is the only rational approach—particularly for the developing world, where increased reliance on vast groundwater reserves is likely.

The oceans are part of the world's "commons," exploited by many countries and the responsibility of none and therefore all the more difficult to safeguard. More than half of the world's people live on sea-coasts, in river deltas and along estuaries and river mouths, and some 90 percent of the marine fish harvest is caught within 320 kilometers of the shore. Every year some 13 billion tons of silt are dumped into coastal zones at the mouths of rivers. Although most of those sediments would have found their way into the ocean anyway, a growing part of the accumulating silt can be attributed to erosion and deforestation caused by human intervention. Depending on the particular agricultural and industrial activities in the catchment area, a coastal zone can be both fertilized and polluted by the silt and dissolved materials that reach it.

The coastal zone is the site of important physicochemical reactions between saltwater and freshwater flows; it is the zone of highest biological productivity, supporting marine life ranging from plankton to fish, turtles and whales. Aquaculture in the coastal zone now produces some 10 percent of the world's fish harvest. The 240,000 square kilometers of coastal mangrove forest are essential habitats for many economically important fish species during part of their life cycle, and they also provide timber and firewood; reed and cypress swamps are other examples of biologically rich coastal wetlands. Finally, of course, coastal zones support a highly profitable tourist industry and include a growing number of protected areas, such as the Great Barrier Reef Marine Park in Australia.

Aside from river discharges, diffuse runoff, atmospheric transport, waste dumping or burning at sea, offshore mining and shipping accidents are the primary ways that some 20 billion tons of dissolved and suspended matter reach the ocean, where they exert their initial effect on the coastal zone.

Polychlorinated biphenyls (PCB's) and other persistent toxic chemicals, including DDT and heavy-metal compounds, have already spread throughout the world's marine ecosystems, in part through gradual accumulation in the food chain. A ban on the use of DDT and PCB's has been enforced for some 10 years in the industrialized countries and has reduced the concentration of such chemicals in the marine life of North American and European coastal waters. The chemicals are, however, still being used and injected into the marine environment in many tropical regions.

Ocean currents are also vehicles for the transport of trash and pollutants. Examples are the nondegradable plastic bottles, pellets and containers that now commonly litter beaches and the ocean's surface. They cause the death of thousands of birds, fish and marine mammals that mistake them for food or get entangled in them. Less spectacular but possibly more serious are the chemical and biological processes (as yet poorly understood) whereby toxic substances such as radioactive wastes are distributed and accumulated.

Some pollutants enter the water cycle by way of the atmosphere. Probably best known among them is the acid that arises from the emission of nitrogen oxides and sulfur dioxide by industry and motor vehicles. Acid deposition, which can be "dry" (as when the gases make direct contact with soil or vegetation) or "wet" (when the acid is dissolved in rain), is causing acidification of low-alkalinity lakes throughout the industrialized world. The acid precipitation also leaches certain positively charged ions out of the soil, and in some rivers and lakes ions can reach concentrations that kill fish.

About one tenth of 1 percent of the world's total annual oil production—some five million tons a year, or more than one gram per 100 square meters of the ocean's surface—finds its way to the ocean. . . . Although petroleum is almost entirely biodegradable, it takes the microbes that break it down a long time to accomplish the task, because their activity is limited by the low nutrient concentrations in seawater. In the meantime an oil spill's effects are lethal for a variety of plankton, fish larvae and shellfish, as well as for such larger animals as birds and marine mammals.

Excessive sewage discharges from coastal urban areas lead to eutrophication of coastal waters, which can change the composition of plankton populations. The plankton, provided with abundant nutrients in the sewage, may experience rapid population growth, which depletes the supply of available oxygen and so leads to fish kills. Moreover, the presence of pathogenic bacteria in sewage has forced the closing of many kilometers of beaches to swimmers and has led to prohibitions on the harvesting of shellfish, which concentrate the bacteria in their tissues.

About one tenth of 1 percent of the world's total annual oil production—some five million tons a year, or more than one gram per 100 square meters of the ocean's surface—finds its way to the ocean. Large areas of the ocean would be covered with oil accumulated over the past decades were it not for the fact that the oil eventually evaporates or is degraded by bacteria. Although petroleum is almost entirely biodegradable, it takes the microbes that break it down a long time to accomplish the task, because their activity is limited by the low nutrient concentrations in seawater. In the meantime an oil spill's effects are lethal for a variety of plankton, fish larvae and shellfish, as well as for such larger animals as birds and marine mammals.

It is clear that the quality of the water in coastal zones is seriously endangered and that damage to fisheries and marine wildlife is widespread. Regional seas such as the Baltic and the Mediterranean, which have more coastline per square kilometer than the high seas do, suffer more from water pollution. Their poor condition demonstrates what may happen in the future to the larger oceans of the world.

Human activity is clearly responsible for widespread damage to marine ecosystems. What is not firmly established is how quickly toxic substances can accumulate in marine organisms or whether such accumulation is reversible. Nor has it been determined precisely how synthetic chemicals are transported through the oceans and what the likelihood is that toxic substances in bottom sediments will find their way into the human food supply. Yet experience so far dictates utmost caution, the more so because restoration of the oceans is incomparably more difficult than that of lakes and inland seas, if not impossible.

Some management of water resources—of both their quantity and quality—is now widely practiced all over the world, but the results, particularly in quality control, have been inadequate. All signals point to further deterioration in the quality of fresh and marine waters unless aggressive management programs are instituted.

Many of the guiding principles in water management have evolved from past experience and are well known, and yet their application has lagged. Above all, the need for an integrated approach has become apparent. In every river or lake basin, socioeconomic and environmental aspirations must be orchestrated so that human settlements, industry, energy production, agriculture, forests, fisheries and wildlife can coexist. In many cases varied interests are not necessarily in conflict; they can be synergistic. Erosion control, for example, goes hand in hand with reforestation, flood prevention and water conservation.

As integrated approach calls, of course, for closer cooperation at the governmental and intergovernmental level; it goes against the historical allocation of different tasks to different agencies. In many countries water supply and sanitation are handled by separate departments. Departmental budgets are isolated by money-tight walls, making it hard to balance investments made by one department with any resulting gains or savings accrued to another.

Such obstacles are even more formidable in an international setting. A country is unlikely to make significant investments in the decontamination of a river's water if it is other countries, downstream, that are likely to reap the benefits. The less developed countries may actually have a better opportunity to make progress here than the developed ones, where vested interests have entrenched themselves in rigid administrative structures. The United Nations

Environment Program (UNEP), for example, has drawn up an action plan for the Zambezi River based largely on principles of integrated management.

A water-management project should lean toward increasing the efficiency of water consumption rather than toward increasing the supply of water. To increase the supply is often more costly, and in any case it merely postpones a crisis. Indeed, because many countries are already overtaxing their water reserves, increasing efficiency is the only solution in some cases. Irrigation, for example, is terribly inefficient as it is practiced in most countries. Averaged over the world, only about 37 percent of all irrigation water is taken up by agricultural crops; the rest is never absorbed by the plants and can be considered lost. New microirrigation techniques, by which perforated pipes deliver water directly to the plants, provide great opportunities for water conservation, making it possible to expand irrigated fields without building new dams.

The mining of groundwater in order to increase supply should, of course, be avoided at all costs—unless it can be guaranteed that the aquifer from which the water is taken will be replenished. The protection of groundwater quality also deserves special attention. Government officials are more likely to implement pollution-control measures when they (or their constituents) are presented with highly visible signs of pollution, such as rubbish washed onto a beach. Hidden as it is from view, groundwater can therefore become polluted gradually without eliciting an outcry from the public until it is too late to reverse the damage wrought by the pollution.

It has also become apparent that the prevention of pollution, and the restoration of bodies of water that are already polluted, should gradually take precedence over the development of purification technologies. Water-purifying technology is becoming more complex and costly as the number of pollutants in water increases; the money spent on removing contaminants from drinking water would be better spent on preventing the contaminants from entering the water in the first place. The high cost of restoring polluted water bodies also strengthens the appeal of pollution-prevention programs.

For that reason "end of pipe" remedies for industrial water pollution should be replaced by recycling and reuse. Factories designed to minimize water pollution through waste reduction are often more economic than those that construct their own wastewater treatment plants in order to meet environmental standards. Factories that integrate pollution-control techniques are also likely to be more acceptable to an environmentally conscious populace. As Peter Donath of the Ciba-Geigy Corporation, one of the world's largest chemical companies, said at [the 1988] International Rhine Conference, "Only with environmentally sound products and manufacturing processes will the chemical industry be able to maintain social acceptability in the future." As an example of this new trend in chemical engineering, he cited a novel process for the production of naphthalene sulfonic acids that reduces pollution by more than 90 percent.

Pollution of a river or a regional sea is, of course, more easily perceived than the pollution of the oceans, which are much larger; it is not surprising that the UNEP has already established pollution-control programs for 10 regional seas. Although such programs are a good start, they need to be followed up with protection of the oceans in general. A recent step in this direction is an international agreement forbidding the discarding of plastics from ships, which became effective at the beginning of this year. Other existing international conventions regulating marine resources need to be improved by backing them up with better monitoring schemes and enforcement measures.

Parallel with the need for improved water-resources management is the need for more research on the hydrosphere. For example, ecological and toxicologic studies of marine life are badly needed if we are to improve the husbandry of the oceans and gain better understanding of the ecological effects of long-lived pollutants in ocean waters.

Many aspects of the hydrological cycle, including the fluxes between its compartments and the extent of groundwater reserves, are not accurately known.

The mining of groundwater in order to increase supply should be avoided at all costs—unless it can be guaranteed that the aquifer from which the water is taken will be replenished.

Action is needed to ensure that water resources that have escaped human manipulation are protected and that those that have been despoiled are restored to a cleaner state. If no action is taken, it is unlikely that future generations will enjoy an enviable quality of life.

These problems and others are currently being addressed by the International Hydrological Program of the United Nations Educational, Scientific and Cultural Organization. Moreover, major international research programs to study the interactions between climate and the hydrological cycle have recently been launched by the UNEP as well as by the World Health Organization and the nongovernmental International Council of Scientific Unions.

Predicting what is likely to happen if sound principles of water management are not vigorously implemented is all too easy. We have already seen rivers turn into sewers and lakes into cesspools. People die from drinking contaminated water, pollution washes ashore on recreational beaches, fish are poisoned by heavy metals and wildlife habitats are destroyed. A laissez-faire approach to water management will spell more of the same—on a grander scale. One can only hope recognition of that fact will spur governments and people into action. (pp. 80, 82–94)

J. W. Maurits la Rivière, "Threats to the World's Water," in Scientific American, *Vol. 261, No. 3, September, 1989, pp. 80–2, 84, 86, 88–90, 92, 94.*

Water Management Strategies

Heretofore, the United States has been a leader in designing and applying state-of-the-art methods to identify, understand, and deal with an array of water management issues. But yesterday's policies are inadequate for dealing with today's problems, and new, more sophisticated strategies must be employed to meet the challenge of the future. Action is needed now to ensure that water resources that have escaped human manipulation are protected and that those that have been despoiled are restored to a cleaner state. If no action is taken, it is unlikely that future generations will enjoy an enviable quality of life.

During the last 40 years, there have been many attempts to reshape U.S. water policy. In 1961, the Senate Select Committee on Water Resources released a report that led to passage of the Water Resources Research Act of 1964 and the Water Resources Planning Act of 1965. These acts, often thought of as the starting point of a new era in water management, provided a national focus on water-resources research and planning.

The planning act set up the U.S. Water Resources Council; encouraged a comprehensive, coordinated federal attitude toward water-resources management; and served as the foundation for states' efforts to begin or expand water-resources planning. While the planning act initiated a comprehensive assessment of U.S. water resources and options for dealing with water-related problems, the research act established a Federal Office of Water Resources and Technology and a water-resources research institute in each state to address water management issues.

Shortly thereafter, the National Environmental Policy Act of 1969 and the Federal Water Pollution Control Act Amendments of 1972 (better known as the Clean Water Act) profoundly changed the emphasis of federal funding and effort from traditional water-resources development, such as dam and canal construction, to environmental protection and restoration. The acts also increases states' efforts in comprehensive water management and introduced a legal requirement that environmental impacts be addressed in the planning, design, and construction of water projects.

In 1973, the National Water Commission, created by Congress in 1968 to review national water-resources problems, released the landmark report "Water

Policies for the Future," which further emphasized the need for clean water and environmental protection rather than just water supply. The report endorsed a "user pays" principle and supported the elimination of federal subsidies for water-resources projects and programs. President Carter's 1978 water policy initiatives called for improvements in water-resources planning and management, construction of only cost-efficient water projects, increased attention to water conservation, improved cooperation between federal and state agencies, and greater focus on environmental quality. When the Reagan administration took office in 1981, it supported transferring responsibility for many water programs to the states, sought to increase nonfederal cost sharing of water projects, and encouraged full recovery of expenditures for water projects. The Reagan administration also terminated the Water Resources Council, an action that signaled the end, at least for the time being, of the only umbrella water-resources planning effort in the federal government.

Passage of the Water Resources Development Act of 1986 culminated years of effort by the Carter and Reagan administrations to require greater levels of nonfederal cost sharing for water projects and programs. This act increased the likelihood that states would be more discriminating in pursuing water projects and ensured that states would play a greater role in solving their long-term water supply and quality-control needs.

Today, water management policies no longer focus solely on development. Nonstructural measures, such as land-use modifications and regulations, to solve water problems are favored. Society's attitudes about the value and use of water are changing, especially about what constitutes a beneficial use of water resources. Finally, public perception is becoming more solidly embedded in policy-designing processes.

Issues and Answers

Few would deny that progress has been made in water management, but many concerns remain for which new or revamped water management policies are urgently needed. Not all of these issues directly confront the United States, but their spillover effects make them U.S. problems as well. The issues include

- burgeoning populations, especially in Asia and Africa;
- poverty, with more than 1 billion people living under squalid conditions worldwide;
- daily deaths of thousands of children from avoidable water-borne diseases;
- destruction of forests, wetlands, and croplands;
- depletion of natural resources;
- injurious land development and management practices;
- solid waste disposal;
- acid precipitation's effects on lakes, forests, and structures;
- contaminated drinking water (of those residing in developing nations, about two-thirds do not have access to safe drinking water);
- ocean disposal of threatening substances;
- offshore developments, including oil drilling;
- nonpoint-source pollution; and
- natural disasters such as volcanic eruptions, earthquakes, floods, and droughts.

Furthermore, an array of institutional elements that impede the design and implementation of needed water policies must be dealt with. Such elements include obsolete laws and regulations, water allocation policies that breed

Too many U.S. citizens still believe that water should be free and that they should be able to use it in any way they see fit. . . . If U.S. waters are to be managed to meet future needs, the public will have to begin paying for maintenance and accept a "user pays" system instead of increasing federal subsidies.

Water-environment issues should be introduced directly into school curricula for all grades, and more emphasis should be placed on environmental issues in adult, public, and professional educational programs. College curricula should embrace the legal, social, political, technical, and economic dimensions of water-environment issues. Environmental problems cannot be adequately addressed within narrow disciplinary boundaries; the interdependencies of actions and processes must be considered.

wastefulness, subsidies that encourage inefficient operations, lack of funds, and incompetence.

What can be done to address these issues? The options are many. The United States needs a better informed and educated public; modernized institutions; adequate resources; improved planning and forecasting capabilities; unified land and water management policies; united technology and public policy; improved understanding and handling of risk; and the right forums for problem solving. If the people elect informed, dedicated leaders, demand responsible and timely action, and work at overcoming parochialism, there is hope indeed that sufficient good water can be made widely available.

Public Information and Education

Public education is a critical element in shaping the direction of water policy. The better acquainted with environmental issues citizens are, the more likely they are to demand environmentally sound decisions from their elected officials. Members of decisionmaking bodies must become more conversant with the water-environmental agenda, its roots, and its links to other programs of concern.

To educate future officials and the electorate, water-environment issues should be introduced directly into school curricula for all grades, and more emphasis should be placed on environmental issues in adult, public, and professional educational programs. College curricula should embrace the legal, social, political, technical, and economic dimensions of water-environment issues. Environmental problems cannot be adequately addressed within narrow disciplinary boundaries; the interdependencies of actions and processes must be considered.

Education plays an important part in overcoming the "not-in-my-back-yard," or NIMBY, syndrome. Problems associated with water quality, in particular, are compounded by the blocking actions of people who may be in agreement with the need to solve a problem but do not want it solved in their locality. This attitude encourages continued malpractices and delays even incremental improvements.

Progress is being made in teaching citizens to protect the Earth and in bringing about a more environmentally conscious electorate. For example, in 1983, members of the Texas Society of Professional Engineers became convinced that an informed citizenry was a prerequisite to solving the state's water problems. These far-sighted leaders saw the value of incorporating information on water resources in the curricula of elementary and secondary schools. They believed that, through the students, the benefits would extend to their parents as well. Texas now requires that subject matter on water issues be included in targeted school textbooks.

Modernizing Institutions

Institutions affecting water management include special-interest groups, government agencies, statutes, laws, regulations, and social customs. Many of them are relics: Technological development proceeds at a breathtaking pace while institutional reform crawls. Water and environmental management are impeded by an array of institutional constraints, and the institutional reforms that have been implemented to deal with them are few.

Bringing about institutional change can be tedious and painful. Laws, social customs, and the traditions and philosophies of agencies are deeply entrenched and resist modification. Nevertheless, by objectively exploring alternative ways of solving problems and managing systems, by identifying the pros and cons of implementing various options, and by articulating the payoffs that could result from change, reforms can be effected. In some cases, consolidating functions and reallocating agency responsibilities may be required; in others, legislative action may be needed to amend or rescind outdated statutes. But to do so, hard-hitting campaigns to convince legislators of the efficacy of the proposed changes will be required.

The roles of the federal and state water agencies require thorough and continuing analysis. The change in program emphasis from irrigation development to water-resources management, which was announced by the U.S. Bureau of Reclamation in 1987, is consistent with this recommendation. But it is not enough to say that changes will be made; the machinery for making changes must be solidly in place, and the changes must be more than a justification for renewed funding of a well-entrenched bureaucracy. Even stepwise improvements, such as amendments to the Clean Water Act, can be beneficial, and such options should not be overlooked in pursuit of quick, massive reforms.

Improvements in coordination and consistency among governments and agencies are needed. Links between state and local governments are usually weak, and the same may be said of those between state and federal governments. State officials often view water management only from an allocation perspective, while local governments commonly focus on such issues as storm drainage and wastewater treatment. Where regional planning and management overlap those of other jurisdictions, the problems of coordination and consistency are exacerbated. Implementing plans in such a setting is particularly difficult, especially when governmental subunits or agencies are at odds. What is considered best at one regulatory level is not necessarily best at another, and plans should be developed in recognition of these differences. Thus, planners and managers should be sensitive to the impacts their proposals may have on other government agencies.

The problems associated with fragmented authority and lack of coordination are illustrated by the difficulties encountered in sustaining barge traffic on the Mississippi River during the 1988 drought. Requests to the Army Corps of Engineers to release additional flows from the Great Lakes system raised the question of who had the authority to make such a decision because the responsibility for the vast water resources in question was fragmented among 18 federal agencies and several states. There is no coherent federal water policy for allocating water, even under extreme emergency conditions. Furthermore, as of 1989, only about 15 states had completed sound drought management plans.

Since the demise of the U.S. Water Resources Council in 1982, there has been no federal body overseeing water policy and management. This vacuum needs filling. The council, although flawed, provided a forum for a state-federal partnership that no longer exists. The council recognized the special problems associated with protecting natural systems and was creating an ethic of more reasoned and conservative water use. Above all, the council, unlike more parochial agencies, addressed water issues at a nationwide level.

Some type of national council or water board is urgently needed to guide the design of federal water policy; coordinate federal water programs and agencies; assess the status of U.S. waters; forecast future water supply and demand scenarios; facilitate water research; provide guidance and support to state water planning and management programs; and explore the implications of emerging global problems for water quality and supply. While the value of such an institution may be recognized in certain quarters, the turf-protecting attitude of many members of Congress and the administration stands in its way.

Workable regional, international, and global water management institutions also must be designed and put into operation. Cities, counties, states, and even nations often are too limited in jurisdiction to deal appropriately with water-environment issues. More often than not, local water problems have regional, if not global, dimensions and must be dealt with in that context. A broad understanding of the functioning of entire ecosystems must become the basis for unified action. The responding institutions could range from regional authorities with broad powers to international cooperative agreements among nations. The Florida Water Management Districts, the Nebraska Natural

There is no coherent federal water policy for allocating water, even under extreme emergency conditions.

Some type of national council or water board is urgently needed to guide the design of federal water policy; coordinate federal water programs and agencies; assess the status of U.S. waters; forecast future water supply and demand scenarios; facilitate water research; provide guidance and support to state water planning and management programs; and explore the implications of emerging global problems for water quality and supply.

Resource Districts, and the British Water Authorities are examples of effective regional institutions.

Accepting and Paying The Bill

Too many U.S. citizens still believe that water should be free and that they should be able to use it in any way they see fit. This belief has resulted in government subsidies for some water-using sectors and a backlog of decaying infrastructures in others because many water developments raise insufficient revenue to pay for their own maintenance. The belief also has encouraged inefficient water use, generated excessive capital outlays for both water supply and wastewater works, and fostered policies that generate, rather than manage, growth in water use and development. If U.S. waters are to be managed to meet future needs, the public will have to begin paying for maintenance and accept a "user pays" system instead of increasing federal subsidies. Hence, questions concerning the costs of various water management options and who will benefit from implementing them must be raised.

A particularly troublesome issue demanding increased research and analysis is that of quantifying the values of the environmental benefits associated with various water management proposals. Both the costs and benefits of a water project can be high, and they must be made clear to decisionmaking bodies.

Sources of funds for water projects and economic incentives and disincentives must also be considered. With federal funding cutbacks, state and local governments are bearing an increasingly larger share of project costs. The cutbacks could lead to greater efficiencies and more imaginative approaches to water management, but, at the same time, new and innovative financing mechanisms will have to be developed. For instance, payment for water management facilities and services could be made through capital budgeting, user fees, utility fees, taxes, impact fees, and full-cost pricing.

One interesting and unusual financing mechanism has been used by Florida's Save Our Rivers program (SOR), which was initiated in 1981 to protect Florida's natural waterways, wetlands, and drinking water. The program is designed to remove ecologically fragile river-basin lands from private ownership so that they can be managed in a manner that maximizes their utility for water supply while conserving and protecting water resources. SOR is financed with a documentary stamp tax placed on all real-estate transactions in Florida. Fifty cents is collected on each $100 worth of property sold, and five cents goes directly to the Water Management Lands Trust Fund for SOR.

Water management is a case in point for the need to reshape national priorities and reallocate social assets. Additional water management initiatives cannot be funded when there is no new money. Resources must be shifted from areas of excess indulgence to those in need, such as the water environment.

Planning and Forecasting

Water management plans must be proactive, rather than reactive, and designed to guide water-resources policy-making. Traditional planning processes too often fail to come to closure, are weakly linked to implementation processes, lack coordination with the affected public, and do not embrace all dimensions of the issues on which they focus. As a result, water management decisions frequently are passed to regulators and the courts, which rarely have the expertise to prescribe appropriate courses of action.

To assert the proper role of water-resources planning, planners will need to adjust their plan definitions and philosophies and garner support from legislative bodies, implementing agencies, and the public. Because water management is heavily regulated, it is crucial that regulatory requirements be the result of carefully devised policies. A model planning process should

- recognize and address society's goals;
- identify and deal with the important problems and conflicts;

- function effectively within prevailing legal and institutional frameworks;

- accommodate both short- and long-range scenarios;

- generate diverse alternatives;

- take into account the allocation of water for all needs, including those of natural systems;

- embrace public input as a basic part of the planning;

- take a global perspective;

- be flexible and adaptable;

- drive regulatory processes;

- be the basis for policymaking;

- foster coordination among planning partners and consistency among related plans; and

- produce viable recommendations.

Unfortunately, the adoption of such a process has been hampered by the separation of planning and implementing authorities, a pervasive tendency toward turf protection, inadequate and poorly paid planning staffs, shortsighted efforts, lack of objectivity, poor understanding of the planning role, and limited funds. The states, in particular, have been deficient in their ability to sustain comprehensive water-resources planning.

Coordinating Land and Water Use

Land use and water use are inseparable. What people do to land affects the connected water resources. Policies for land and water management should, therefore, be consistent and coordinated. Yet the scientific community in the United States adheres to reductionism and tends to resist holistic approaches. The long-standing tradition of dealing independently with land, water, and air resources has been a major contributor to the degradation of natural and developed areas. Concerns about water, land, plants, animals, fish, and humans are best dealt with collectively.

The inextricability of land and water problems underscores the need for coordinating water-resources planning and management with land-use planning and regulation. This need has long been recognized, but overcoming the institutional barriers to such coordination has been a slow process at best. A large obstacle is local governments' fear of losing their control over land use. Clearly, the key to coordinated land and water management must be found. One promising model is Florida's state planning system, which requires that state, regional, and local government plans for everything from public education to land use be consistent. Florida's system mandates that decisions concerning water resources in local government comprehensive plans conform with broader state and regional water management policies. The system has only been in effect for a few years, but it shows promise of providing a workable land and water planning forum.

Managing Risk

One of the most troublesome issues facing water-use policymakers—and environmental policymakers in general—is risk management. There are problems surrounding the quantification of risk, the perception of risk, and the assessment of acceptable risk by society. Many individuals press for endless regulations as if they could regulate a zero-risk world. Yet these same people accept a variety of risks every day. Some people voluntarily expose themselves to certain risks, such as smoking, while they consider other, nonvoluntary risks, such as exposure to drinking water that may contain trace contaminants, to be unacceptable.

Water policies of the future must take on broad dimensions. Proactive planning must be implemented, with more emphasis on regional planning and management. The days of managing water resources parochially must cease. Water management, coordinated with land management, must be practiced at and among all levels of government. Policymakers and planners must take preventive rather than remedial approaches to solving the mounting problems of the U.S. water environment.

The inextricability of land and water problems underscores the need for coordinating water-resources planning and management with land-use planning and regulation. This need has long been recognized, but overcoming the institutional barriers to such coordination has been a slow process at best.

There is a great need for good risk communication and for education, not only for those who perceive the danger, but also for those who understand the likelihood of the danger. Scientists often are unable to communicate adequately with the public about risk and leave the policymaker to make judgments about risk in an arena of uncertainty and public fear. Where risk and uncertainty are issues, the costs of reducing risk must be clearly articulated, as must be the benefits of accepting various levels of risk, and the public must be included in policy design.

Finally, there must be a move toward developing water quality standards that reflect technological feasibility rather than arcane estimates of potential health hazards. It is better to get on with the best protection that can be provided than to delay action while arguing about contaminant levels and their effects, which cannot always be substantiated. (pp. 12–15, 33)

Providing a Forum

Water policies that maximize efficiency and effectively address citizens' views can only be developed in the proper forums. In some cases, existing city councils, state legislatures, and public-interest committees are adequate. Numerous occasions and issues, however, require nontraditional approaches. In general, two classes of needs are apparent: those related to resolving or avoiding conflicts (garnering consent) and those related to solving problems that transcend normal political or bureaucratic boundaries. Forums for garnering consent are needed to address points of contention, while forums for breaking down traditional boundaries are needed to analyze issues in their proper contexts. Historically, such forums have been extremely rare, but now they are increasingly being designed and applied for planning and management purposes.

Water-resource protection, development, and management must be designed to address potential conflicts and incorporate mechanisms for dealing with them that have a high probability of being accepted by all the people who have a stake in the issue. To deal effectively with conflicting interests, the principal stake-holders must be brought together in an atmosphere that encourages co-operation and an exchange of views. Building consent among the affected parties—whose consent is necessary to formulate an acceptable action—and identifying common ground should be the objective. To get those parties to the table and keep them there until an agreement is reached, the stakes must be high; each party must have a lot to lose and know it, so that leaving the negotiation table is more painful than staying. The key is to establish negotiation, rather than litigation, as the vehicle for resolving conflicts and designing acceptable alternative courses of action.

Such a process led to passage of Arizona's far-reaching Ground Water Management Act of 1980. Representatives of the mining industry, agriculture, and cities were brought together in a forum designed to keep them there until a solution emerged. It was clear that each party could lose a lot by not participating. The result was a state-of-the-art strategy to bring water supply and use into balance.

Analyses of how conflicts have been dealt with in the past—if adequately documented—could be effective instructional vehicles. University and professional curricula related to environmental problem solving would do well to address fully such subjects as consent building, decisionmaking processes, working with the public and governmental bodies, and policy analysis. Furthermore, scientific and engineering expertise must be more effectively introduced into conflict-resolving arenas. Otherwise, the resolutions may be technologically deficient.

System-encompassing forums are needed to address situations where political subdivisions are too small to deal comprehensively with resource management problems and where the facilities or missions of several agencies are involved. For example, "local" water problems are often regional in scale and, when analyzed in that context, yield efficient solutions that otherwise might not be identified.

Such an approach was applied in the Washington, D.C., metropolitan area, where a protocol was devised to manage all elements of the water supply system in concert, irrespective of ownership. The protocol resulted in an ability to improve water supply during periods of drought without building major new supply projects. The savings in costs over more traditional plans was about $250 million. The success in Washington, D.C., demonstrated that such forums can result in substantial gains and special regional reforms.

A similar approach might be successful in the North Platte River basin, where it has been estimated that water shortages might be cut by 50 percent or more if the system were operated to meet demands rather than to conform to prevailing water-rights policies. And studies of the Houston area water supply have shown that coordinated operation of independent facilities could result in increased safe yields of almost 19 percent. (A safe yield is the maximum amount of water that can be continuously diverted from a body of water during a drought.) In such cases, regional organizations like those mentioned earlier could provide expansive forums needed to formulate effective policies.

Unfortunately, the benefits that could be achieved by integrating the management of water resources are underappreciated. In most river basins, there is no single agency or individual who controls all of the components of the water management system. To overcome this problem, joint and coordinated decisionmaking and comprehensive system-wide analyses are required. Institutions responsible for investigating the integrated management of water systems must be designed and funded. The economic and environmental payoffs from establishing objective, system-encompassing forums could be staggering.

Understanding Natural Systems

The U.S. public is becoming increasingly concerned about protecting, enhancing, and restoring natural systems. However, the scientific knowledge needed to improve human understanding of these systems in the balance of nature is limited. Accordingly, there is an urgency associated with elucidating ecological principles.

The economic and social effects of decisions regarding natural systems can be far-reaching. Economic development and environmental protection can be partners, but only if care is exercised in modifying the landscape. Growth management policies that embrace the many dimensions associated with managing natural systems are badly needed.

Expanded research and monitoring programs must be supported. Most studies of environmental water requirements have dealt with flowing streams. Much less has been done to determine the water needs of wetlands, wildlife habitats, freshwater-saltwater interface zones, and other natural systems. There is a similar lack of knowledge for establishing the value of water in natural systems. Wetlands, for example, may not generate the emotional excitement of national parks or wildlife preserves, but their ecological significance is considerably greater, and their protection, enhancement, and use must become a major factor in water management policy.

Finally, there is the question of who will champion the cause of water allocation for natural systems. Consider allocating a water supply among competing agricultural, industrial, municipal, and environmental sectors. In a marketplace setting, the one with the greatest ability to pay will win. How can environmental uses compete in such an arena? In the final analysis, the public, which means the government, must ensure that the necessary monitoring, research, education, funding, and policymaking occur. Only informed governmental intervention will work, but, for such intervention to give full weight to

In most river basins, there is no single agency or individual who controls all of the components of the water management system. To overcome this problem, joint and coordinated decisionmaking and comprehensive system-wide analyses are required. Institutions responsible for investigating the integrated management of water systems must be designed and funded.

The days of managing water resources parochially must cease. Water management, coordinated with land management, must be practiced at and among all levels of government. Policymakers and planners must take preventive rather than remedial approaches to solving the mounting problems of the U.S. water environment.

environmental concerns, federal, state, and local governments must have a strong mandate from the people to safeguard the environment.

Preparing for the Future

In general, progress in dealing with the above issues has been slow or nonexistent. The U.S. government and public have been slow to correlate public education with improvements in decisionmaking and remain deeply entrenched in existing methods and approaches. The public is rarely involved in developing water management plans, which too often become mired in intergovernmental and interagency turf battles. Problem solving is constrained by the nonconformance of political and hydrological boundaries, and the public is unwilling to recognize and pay appropriately for the development and use of water. Most problem-solving forums are overly focused on today's crises, unexcited about dealing with the future, and unprepared to stave off conflicts.

Water policies of the future must take on broad dimensions. Proactive planning must be implemented, with more emphasis on regional planning and management. The days of managing water resources parochially must cease. Water management, coordinated with land management, must be practiced at and among all levels of government. Policymakers and planners must take preventive rather than remedial approaches to solving the mounting problems of the U.S. water environment. (pp. 33–4)

Warren Viesmann, Jr., "A Framework for Reshaping Water Management," in Environment, *Vol. 32, No. 4, May, 1990, pp. 10–15, 33–5.*

Sources For Further Study

Biswas, Asit K. "Water for the Third World." *Foreign Affairs* 60, No. 1 (Fall 1981): 148–66.
> Surveys the problems of supplying adequate clean water to rural areas of developing nations and assesses various ways to address this vital concern.

Born, Stephen, ed. *Redefining National Water Policy: New Roles and Directions.* Bethesda: American Water Resources Association, 1989, 92 p.
> Includes sections on state and national water policies and management. In an introduction the editor outlines previous efforts to establish a national water policy and assesses ways that the establishment of such could aid state water management programs.

Brundtland, Gro Harlem. "To Meet Human Needs." *World Health* (December 1986): 2–3.
> Notes that an available safe water supply is essential to human health. Brundtland, the Prime Minister of Norway and chairperson of the World Commission on Environment and Development, assesses the progress of the International Drinking Water Supply and Sanitation Decade (IDWSSD) at midpoint and determines program priorities for the remainder of the decade.

Colby, Bonnie G. "Enhancing Instream Flow Benefits in an Era of Water Marketing." *Water Resources Research* 26, No. 6 (June 1990): 1113–120.
> Examines current instream flow policies in the western United States and outlines the economic values generated by stream flows.

"Parched." *The Economist* 315, No. 7654 (12–18 May 1990): 9–12, 17.
> Surveys Middle East water supplies, usage, programs, and international disputes.

Falkenmark, Malin. "The Massive Water Scarcity Now Threatening Africa—Why Isn't It Being Addressed?" *Ambio: A Journal of the Human Environment* XVIII, No. 2 (1989): 112–18.
   Asserts that an improved water supply would significantly improve life quality and food security in semiarid areas of Africa and urges increased awareness of the need for developing adequate water supplies.

Frederick, Kenneth D. "Water Resources." In *Natural Resources for the 21st Century*, edited by R. Neil Sampson and Dwight Hair, pp. 143–74. Washington, D.C.: Island Press, 1990.
   Explains the nature of water resources, analyzes water use, availability, and quality, and considers future water needs.

"Five Potential Crises: The Water Shortage." *Futurist* XVIII, No. 2 (April 1984): 11–13.
   Contends that a worldwide water shortage is a reality and warns of the possibility of long-term reduction in the availability of usable water in many areas. The study recommends implementing conservation of existing freshwater supplies and developing new freshwater supply and delivery systems.

"Reassessing Water: Who Will Get How Much, At What Price?" *The Great Lakes Reporter* 6, No. 4 (July–August 1989): 1, 3.
   Notes that consumption of Great Lakes water is projected to increase dramatically, surveys demands on the existing supply, and examines municipal water pricing policies.

Koehn, J. W., and Stanko, G. H., Jr. "Groundwater Monitoring: Accurate Assessment and Reasonable Economy are Achievable." *Environmental Science and Technology* 22, No. 11 (November 1988): 1262–64.
   Describes an efficient and cost-effective way to monitor groundwater quality.

Laugeri, L. "Water for All: Who Pays?" *World Health Forum* 8, No. 4 (1987): 453–60.
   States the need to improve quantities and quality of drinking water supplies in developing nations and examines the question of who should pay for this commodity.

Leopold, Luna B. "Ethos, Equity, and the Water Resource." *Environment* 32, No. 2 (March 1990): 10, 16, 18–20, 37–42.
   Calls for principals of ethos (a set of beliefs that guide decisionmaking) and equity (fairness to all) on the part of agencies making decisions regarding world water resources.

Lund, Jay R. "Evaluation and Scheduling of Water Conservation." *Journal of Water Resources Planning and Management*. 113, No. 5 (September 1987): 696–708.
   Proposes a linear programming method for evaluating and scheduling water conservation measures to defer or avoid the necessity of expanding existing water treatment and storage facilities.

Ohlendorf, Pat. "The World Water Crisis." *Maclean's* 95, No. 50 (13 December 1982): 40–5.
   Charges that burgeoning population growth and the attendant need for more water have precipitated a global water crisis. Ohlendorf outlines water shortage problems in several areas of the world, including both industrialized and undeveloped areas, and surveys some proposals for addressing water supply problems.

Rajagopalan, S. P., and Prasad, N. B. Narasimha. "Subsurface Water in River Beds as Source of Rural Water Supply Schemes." *Journal of Water Resources Planning and Management* 115, No. 2 (March 1989): 186–94.
   Reports on investigations into the feasibility of tapping subsurface water in river beds to supply drinking water in rural regions of Kerala, India.

Rozengurt, Michael A., and Herz, Michael J. "Water, Water Everywhere, But Just So Much to Drink." *Oceans* 14, No. 5 (September–October 1981): 65–7.

Examines the environmental stresses placed on estuaries by growing demands for water from estuarine systems.

Schwarz, Harry E., and Dillard, Lee A. "The Impact on Water Supplies." *Oceanus* 32, No. 2 (Summer 1989): 44–5.
Sidebar to an article about global warming and the greenhouse effect that surveys the impact that prolonged hot spells could have on water demand, quality, and availability.

Smith, William. "Sustainable Use for Water in the 21st Century." *Ambio: A Journal of the Human Environment.* XVIII, No. 5 (1989): 294–95.
Relates the findings of *Water 2020: Sustainable Use for Water in the 21st Century,* a report from the Science Council of Canada on that country's fresh water supply. Toxic rain, groundwater contamination, and climatic change are assessed as emerging water issues that must be addressed.

Suleiman, M. S. "WHO and the Decade." *World Health* (December 1982): 22–5.
Urges that the World Health Organization (WHO) assist member states in formulating and implementing national plans during the International Drinking Water Supply and Sanitation Decade (IDWSSD) of the 1980s.

Tsur, Yacov. "The Stabilization Role of Groundwater When Surface Water Supplies are Uncertain: The Implications for Groundwater Development." *Water Resources Research* 26, No. 5 (May 1990): 811–18.
Investigates the development of groundwater resources and examines the economic benefits of using pumped groundwater in conjunction with surface water for irrigation to mitigate fluctuations in the available surface water supply.

Watters, Gregor. "The Decade at Half-Time." *World Health* (December 1986): 27–9.
Assesses achievements of the International Drinking Water Supply and Sanitation Decade (IDWSSD) after five years and offers strategies for implementing various water quality and supply programs during the second half of the decade.

Whipple, William, Jr. "Strategy for Managing Depleted Aquifers." *Journal of Water Resources Planning and Management.* 113, No. 3 (May 1987): 368–77.
Outlines engineering concepts and legal and institutional constraints that bear on reducing user withdrawals from depleted aquifers.

"Millions in Need." *World Health* (December 1986): 4.
Pronounces drinking water and sanitation programs essential to basic human health and important in eradicating specific diseases in arid developing countries.

Wurbs, Ralph A., and Bergman, Carla E. "Evaluation of Factors Affecting Reservoir Yield Estimates." *Journal of Hydrology* 112, Nos. 3–4 (January 1990): 219–35.
Evaluates factors affecting estimates of water reservoir yields and identifies and discusses key aspects of reservoir yield analysis.

Environmental Viewpoints
Cumulative Index to Topics

Environmental Viewpoints
Subject and Keyword Index

DATE DUE

HIGHSMITH 45-220